Footprint Ireland

Pat Levy and Seán Sheehan
3rd edition

O
Tell me all about
Anna Livia! I want to hear all
About Anna Livia. Well, you know Anna Livia? Yes, of course,
we all know Anna Livia. Tell me all. Tell me now.

James Joyce, *Finnegans Wake*

1 **Donegal** Surf the beaches and experience the seascapes

2 **Galway City** Eat, drink, laugh, then eat and drink some more

3 **The Burren** Ancient limestone hills filled with prehistoric sites, wild flowers, and good music in the pubs

4 **The Hunt Museum, Limerick** An amazing collection of art and artefacts in the south of Ireland. Take in the lovely old cathedral while you're there

5 **Great Blasket Island, Dingle Peninsula** A boat trip to remember and a stirring island trek

6 **The Dingle Way** Wild, wild country, views across the southwest of Ireland; great bars to while away the nights and beaches to cool those aching feet

7 **The Puck Fair Killorglin, Kerry** A weekend of revelry and pagan behaviour

Ireland Highlights

See colour maps at back of book

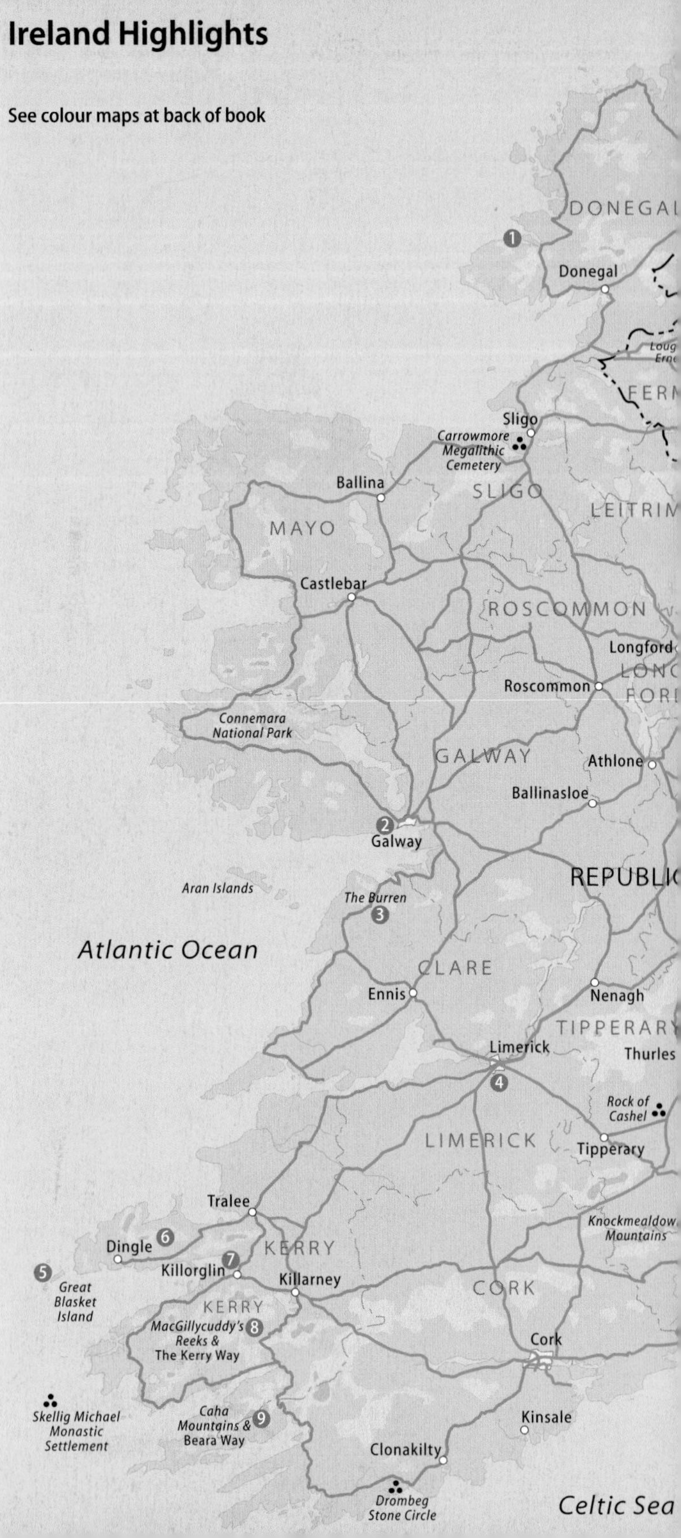

8 Killarney National Park
By-pass the town and head for the countryside of mountains and lakes

9 The Beara Way
An achingly lonely way-marked walk with a desolate beauty of its own

10 Wicklow Hills
Quaint country villages and a long-distance trail to challenge the hardiest walker

11 Dublin
Nightlife, shopping, great food and ancient history

12 Newgrange
Perfectly intact, elaborately inscribed passage graves which pre-date the Pyramids

13 A black taxi tour of west Belfast
Wonder at the resilience of a city that has endured so much

14 The Giant's Causeway and the Antrim coast
A scenic journey and a natural wonder

15 Derry city
The preserved city walls, a lovely old cathedral and an enlightened museum

Contents

Counties Waterford, Tipperary and Limerick

County Cork

County Kerry

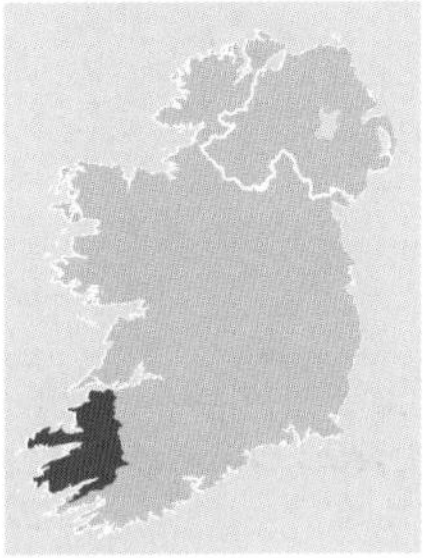

County Clare

Counties Galway and Roscommon

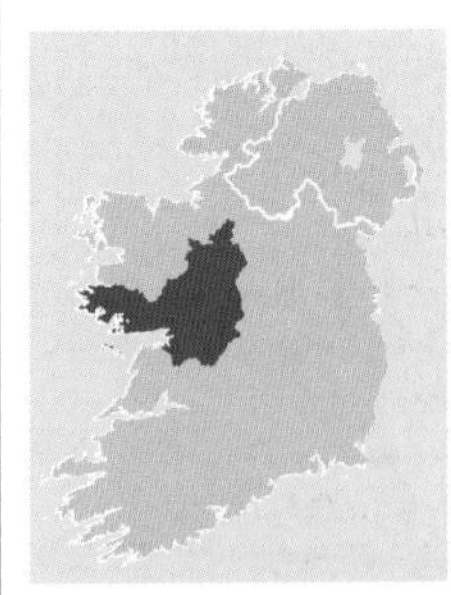

Counties Mayo, Sligo and Leitrim

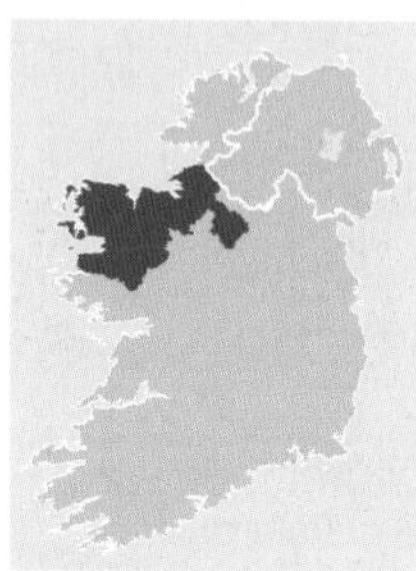

Counties Donegal and Derry

Belfast

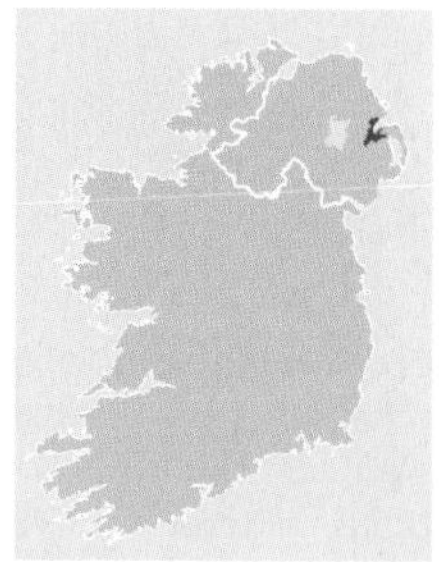

Counties Antrim and Down

Ploughed fields at sunset in County Meath.

Counties Tyrone, Fermanagh, Armagh and Monaghan

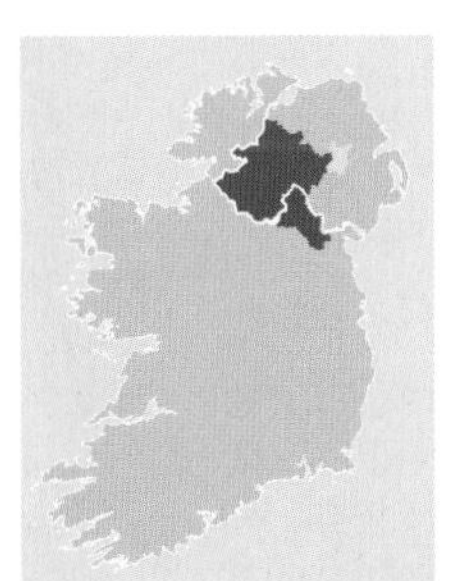

Background

Footnotes

Inside front cover

Tramore Strand
The Horn Head Peninsula in northern Donegal encompasses deserted sandy beaches and jaw-dropping clifftop scenery.

A foot in the door

Ireland is often portrayed as a charming, laboratory time capsule of pre-industrial Europe; its people a beguiling race of quaint and gullible country folk, imbued with a delightful lack of logic and a good line in disingenuous blarney. Once, maybe, it was possible to believe in that image but not any more. Ireland has leapfrogged the 20th century to become a high-tech, on-line, plugged-in kind of place with a complex culture and a lack of industrial baggage that continues to attract people looking for something different. Ireland's tiny cities and larger towns have little of the high-rise anonymity so characteristic of other European centres. They are, instead, cosy, gossipy places where new technology sits comfortably beside farmers' markets and shopping centres. The countryside is changing as well – you're more likely to find a farmer with a mobile glued to his ear bowling along in a four-wheel drive than milking a cow, but, along the western coastline and in Donegal, there are still gloriously empty spaces and scenery that will stir the soul. The living and talking Irish who work there have created a lifestyle that will rub off on most visitors sooner or later. The beaches are inviting – when the sun shines – and there are characterful pubs, arts and crafts, music, dancing and craic for all tastes. Access to adventure sports is easy, with little-known offshore islands to explore, a foreign language to try getting your tongue round, unpolluted rivers to fish and gorgeous land- and seascapes to gawk at in awed silence. Sure, Ireland's idiosyncratic weather is a challenge – you're just as likely to spend a couple of days in wet gear as scantily clad on a beach – but the weather is a metaphor for the country as a whole: a day of rain followed by sunshine, cloudy skies and then a bracing wind, micro-climates where you encounter both the predictable and the unexpected.

Contemporary Ireland

Twenty-first-century Ireland is a booming place, with full employment, a young, well-educated population and a European outlook. Its crime rate is low and its cities are vibrant, cheerful places full of lively pubs and good places to eat. The arts flourish and small theatres and galleries enliven many of the towns. But this new wealth has not arrived without a social and physical price. For centuries, emigration was the only option for thousands of Irish people wanting a decent way of life. Suddenly the tides have turned and for the first time ever Ireland has been faced with labour shortages. Ill-paid workers are recruited from Eastern Europe and the small number of asylum seekers who find their way into the country is magnified by the media into a hostile invasion. From a monoculture that was forced to turn their own children into economic migrants, the small-town Irish have suddenly found themselves in the reverse role of hosts to poorer immigrants. Where other countries have had generations to absorb their minority communities, the tiny Irish population of three or so million souls has suddenly encountered multiculturalism. It is proving a challenge for some, as their own history as the dispossessed in foreign lands, is strangely forgotten.

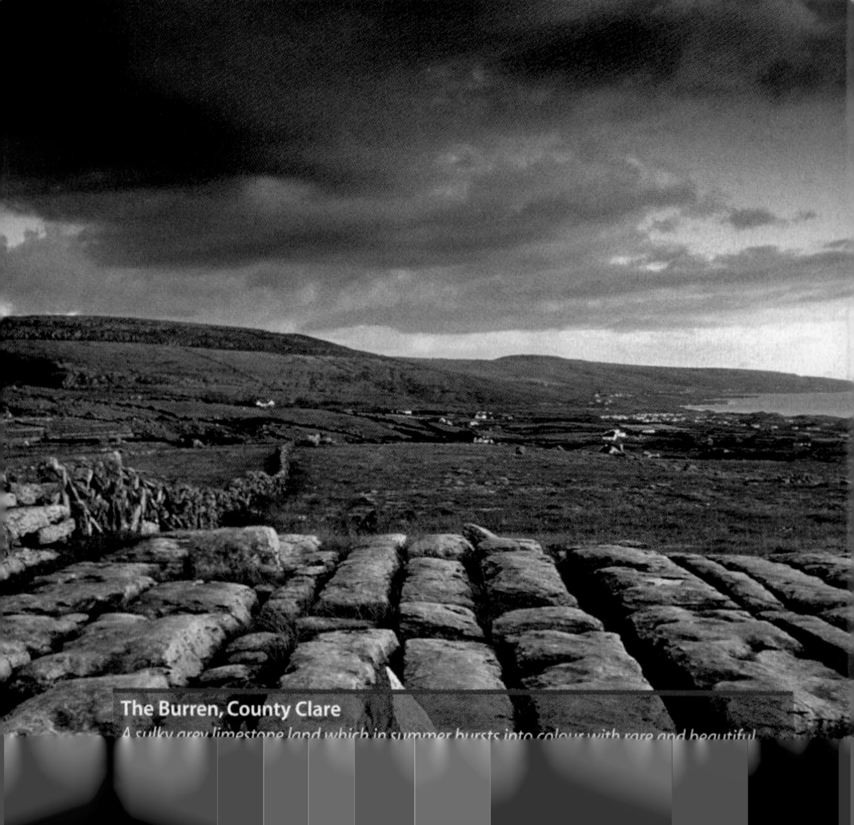

The Burren, County Clare

A sulky grey limestone land which in summer bursts into colour with rare and beautiful

The new-found wealth is reshaping the land – literally. Cars, motorways and by-passes are worshipped like new gods and the east of Ireland is being given a concrete facelift that is out of all proportion for a small island community. Even in the west of Ireland, a huge wave of holiday-home building is beginning to scar the countryside and putting untold stress on the existing infrastructure of roads and services.

Politically, Ireland has been through the wringer too. The two damaged and divided communities of Northern Ireland seem to be finally settling into a state of peaceful co-existence but painful conflicts are still there to be worked through. In the Republic, the last decade or so has seen political brou-ha-has that make the country resemble a banana republic: shocking scandals in business, banking, the police force and the priesthood and never-ending tribunals into corrupt politicians.

So, enjoy the gleaming new roads, the smart hotels and designer restaurants, the new money ringing in the tills and the refreshing confidence that has shaken the chip off the shoulders of past generations but keep an eye open for the cranky old Ireland which still sits in the cracks between the polished surfaces and occasionally leaks out a little.

Hands Across the Divide
The brave and forward-looking city of Derry has led the way in cross-cultural understanding.

1

2

4

5
The súgán
hostel
The Súgán
Hostel

7

8

10

11

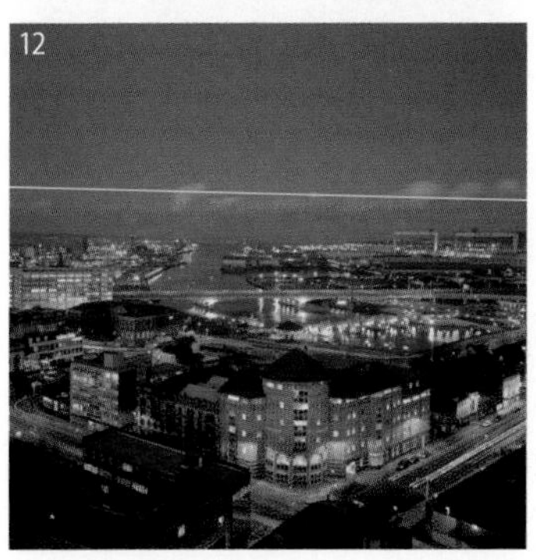

1 *The multicoloured houses of the tiny west Cork village of Eyeries – one of the prettiest parts of Ireland.* ▸▸ *See page 286.*

2 *Trinity College, Dublin. Seat of learning and home to the beautifully illustrated Book of Kells.* ▸▸ *See page 65.*

3 *The smallest and least touristy of the Aran Islands, Inisheer and its surrounding seas can be dangerous in wild weather, as this wreck demonstrates.* ▸▸ *See page 384.*

4 *Enjoying the craic at the ancient Puck Fair in Killorglin. King Puck, the unfortunate wild goat, is released at the day's end.* ▸▸ *See page 303.*

5 *One way to get around the country and meet interesting people is to stay at Ireland's many well-run and cheap hostels.* ▸▸ *See page 300.*

6 *You can still see traditional ploughing at Cooley Fair in County Louth, although modern tractors and mechanical milking machines are the norm across Ireland these days.* ▸▸ *See page 134.*

7 *Dún Aengus, Inishmore, 300 ft above the crashing waves, has withstood the elements for 2,000 years.* ▸▸ *See page 381.*

8 *A delicately-carved medieval high cross, one of Ireland's finest, in the ruins of St Mary's Abbey on holy Devenish Island, County Fermanagh.* ▸▸ *See page 571.*

9 *Come early in the day if you want to see the ancient site of Newgrange at its best.* ▸▸ *See page 130.*

10 *Fishing for monkfish in County Waterford.* ▸▸ *See page 208.*

11 *An isolated folly – what Ireland does best – stands on the cliff edge in Mussenden, County Derry.* ▸▸ *See page 493.*

12 *The city of Belfast with the Queen Elizabeth Bridge and the famous shipyards in the background.* ▸▸ *See page 495.*

A capital place

Dublin is a cracking place. It buzzes with a youthful modernity, best soaked up in a comedy or dance club or by listening to live music in a pub before the vodka-and-Red Bull starts to slur the Dublin wit. Alongside the dot.comers in the sushi bars, the old Dublin is still there – the Georgian architecture, Dublin Castle, Trinity College, the Book of Kells, and Christ Church Cathedral – all steeped in centuries of history. Love it and leave it: the Wicklow countryside is a bus ride away to the south and the east coast has pretty villages and seaside towns. To the north is Newgrange, the most remarkable prehistoric sight in Europe, which can be visited on a day trip or taken in as part of a journey along the coast to the seaside towns of Malahide and Skerries and on to Drogheda.

Go West

A trip to the west of Ireland takes in spectacular landscapes and seascapes, remote islands, Irish-speaking areas, village pubs, castles and fading country houses, traditional music and amazing long-distance walks. It is as well, though, to know what not to do. Driving the Ring of Kerry in July and August is not the best use of a day; Killarney town can seem like a tourist trap; Doolin is seriously overrated; and the fabled Aran island of Inishmor, so loved by Synge, would now have the playwright spinning in his grave. But watch the sun set over the wild flower-bejewelled Clare mountains, wander through the amazing Hunt Collection in Limerick, seek out a quiet backwater in west Cork, take in the buzz of Galway or the wild west of

The Palace Bar, Dublin, where the old city still survives amid the energetic new chaos of Temple Bar.

The ascent of Mount Brandon on the Dingle Peninsula in Kerry was originally a pagan pilgrimage, now appropriated by Christianity. It's a six-hour haul up to the summit.

Mayo and you will experience the best that Ireland's south and west has to offer. The region has excellent walking routes and challenging mountains to scramble up. Travel a mile out of tour bus-infested Killarney and you're alone with nature and a few other discerning souls, or spend a day or two walking the Beara Peninsula and, weather permitting, you will think you are in heaven.

The real hand of Ulster?

This is the first guide since the 1920s that treats Ireland as an island, without tagging on Northern Ireland as if it doesn't somehow fit in the picture. This is not a political statement but a cultural and historical one. Visitors to Donegal who skip Derry or Fermanagh, or vice versa, risk depriving themselves of part of the Ireland experience. Ulster, which included Donegal before its artificial division, offers an engrossing amalgam of landscape and culture. Donegal is so ruggedly beautiful, so visually stunning that we are half tempted to play down its appeal in case too many visitors go there. Its beaches offer windsurfing, adventure sports, horse riding, sea fishing trips and more. The neighbouring city of Derry is a cool place indeed and will pleasantly surprise most visitors. The coastal route that passes the Giant's Causeway and runs down the eastern coast is full of natural beauty and the Mourne Mountains and Armagh are waiting to be discovered by a new generation of visitors. Belfast, too, has much to offer in terms of history, architecture and the telling Black Taxi tours of the city's past trouble spots. Ulster, by whatever name, and it's had a few over the years, offers the discerning traveller a rare old time and some gripping stories to take home.

Mourne Mountains
A patchwork of cultivated fields leads to the blue green mountains of Mourne and the sea beyond.

Essentials

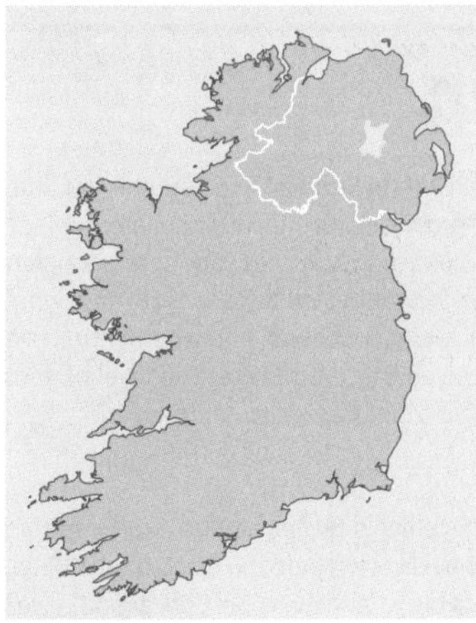

Footprint features

Planning your trip

Ireland is a fairly small country, about 310 miles (500 km) north to south and a little over 186 miles (300 km) west to east, and although it is not difficult to get around (see page 36) there is plenty to see, and some choices have to be made about where not to go, or at least where not to dawdle. Obviously how long you have for your trip, what your mode of transport will be, your interests and inclinations, and whether this is a first-time trip or not will have a bearing on the choices you make. The level of your budget is a factor, but not a critical one, because costs are fairly uniform.

Length of trip

If your stay is from **three to six days** there is little point in tearing around the country, so think about which airport to arrive at. First-time travellers will probably want to see Dublin, and international travellers may have little choice but to land there, but Cork airport is well serviced from London, as is Belfast, and, with an affordable service between London and Derry, the northwest of the country is more accessible than it used to be. With a hired car waiting at Shannon airport, the west coast is half a day's drive away. With a short stay a choice probably has to be made between a city-based vacation or a short rural burst.

For a stay of a **week or more** it is quite feasible to take in Dublin, a few excursions such as Glendalough and Newgrange, and spend some time on the western seaboard visiting the Burren, Kerry or Galway City. With **two weeks or more**, depending on mode of transport, you can pick and choose two, three or more locations and explore them in some depth. There would be time to skip from one end of the country to the other and briefly explore several places in between or, alternatively, focus on just one or two locations and have time for a leisurely walking or cycling trip. With a **month or more** it should be possible to visit most regions in the country that match your interests, and have time to slow down and get to know some places in more depth.

Modes of transport

The 'Getting around' section (page 36) covers the transport options in more detail, but bear in mind that internal flights are limited in choice and usefulness and that the use or non-use of a car or motorbike is likely to be a determining factor in deciding where to go. With vehicular transport the length of stay will be the only major factor limiting your choices, but reliance on public transport will necessitate a fair degree of planning if you wish to get out of the cities and big towns and optimize your time. If you're planning a walking holiday or are focused on other particular activities, such as mountain climbing or windsurfing, public transport is generally adequate, and for walking trips the use of a car can be a hindrance because there is always the need to get back to the vehicle.

Where to go

Scenery and beaches

The obvious destination for visitors interested in getting away from urban life and appreciating wild scenery and beaches is the west coast and County Donegal. From the Inishowen peninsula, just north of Derry, to Roaringwater Bay in West Cork, the coastline follows an almost uninterrupted margin of stunning seascapes and glorious countryside. Patches worth skipping are the stretches between the towns of Donegal and Sligo, between Rossaveal and south of Galway city, and the coastline between Ennis and Tralee; just about everywhere other than those stretches covers the best of Donegal, Mayo, Connemara, the Burren, Clare, and the peninsulas of Kerry and West Cork. This still leaves out some marvellous areas in the rest of the country, chief

Top 10 beaches

Keem, Achill Island, County Mayo (page 424)
Keel, Achill Island, County Mayo (page 424)
Inchydoney Beach, Clonakility, County Cork (page 261)
Dog's Bay, Roundstone, Connemara, County Galway (page 393)
Inishbofin, Inishbofin Island, County Galway (page 394)
Clogherhead, County Louth (page 138)
Portacloy, County Mayo (page 427)
Barley Cove, County Cork (page 274)
Stradbally and Castelgregory, County Waterford (page 212)
Portstewart Strand, County Derry (page 493)

amongst which are the Antrim coastline, the Mourne Mountains in Down, and the Wicklow Mountains south of Dublin. The southern coastline, between Wexford and Cork, is tepid by comparison with the west coast.

Ireland's islands

A favourite for devotees of nature, wildlife and solitude are the offshore islands that pepper Ireland's coasts. The most famous are the **Aran Islands** in County Galway, and although fame has turned the largest of the three islands into a tourist ghetto in July and August, the other two, Inishmaan and Inisheer, are always worth visiting, and the main island of Inishmór is still rewarding in off-season months. **Achill Island** off the west coast of Mayo is reached by a causeway and is large enough to accommodate its popularity, and Mayo also has the lesser known and far smaller **Clare Island**, which is ideal for getting away from it all. The main island of the **Blaskets** in Kerry is glorious in spring and autumn and there is little provision for accommodation or eating here so if you bring a tent you'll have the place more or less to yourself once the last boat has departed. The **Skelligs**, also in Kerry, are justly famous for their bird life, but it is not possible to stay overnight. County Cork has **Dursey Island**, reached by a cable car, off the Beara Peninsula, and there is no accommodation or restaurants. Further south, reached from Baltimore, are **Clear Island** and **Sherkin Island**; both popular in the summer but never overbearingly so. The **Saltee Islands** in County Wexford, like Clear Island, are noted for bird life. The islands of **Rathlin** and **Tory**, off the north coast of Ireland, are easily reached and bask in the glory of not being spoiled by tourism.

Activity trips

Destinations for activity trips vary but **walking** and **cycling** are the most readily available and easy to arrange activities across the length and breadth of the country, though opportunities for a diverse range of sports are well distributed across Ireland. For details of these and other special interests see page 48.

Museums, galleries and stately homes

Museums, galleries and stately homes are dotted around Ireland and the trick is to know which ones to skip. **Dublin** has major museums and galleries which should not be missed, and **Derry**, **Strokestown** in Roscommon, **Enniscorthy** in County Wexford, and **Limerick** all have excellent museums which are worth special journeys, and **Glebe House and Gallery** in County Donegal can probably be added to the 'essential visit' list. As a general rule, beware of places proclaiming themselves to be heritage or interpretation centres. A few are awful and a waste of money, many are just plain mediocre, some are well thought out and genuinely educational. The **Céide Fields Interpretative Centre** in north Mayo, the **Blasket Centre** on the Dingle Peninsula, and the **Cobh Heritage Centre** outside Cork are some of the better ones.

Top 10 places for kids

Dingle Harbour and Fungie the dolphin, Dingle, County Kerry (page 328)
Dingle Oceanworld, Dingle, T066-9152111 (page 328)
Watersports at Portrush, Country Antrim (page 526)
Kerry the Kingdom, 40 English Street, Tralee, County Kerry (page 325)
St Patrick's Trian, Armagh, County Armagh, T3752 1801 (page 578)
Carrick-a-rede Rope Bridge, Antrim, County Antrim, T2073 1159 (page 530)
Aillwee Caves, County Clare, T065-7077036 (page 356)
Downpatrick Steam Railway, Market Street, Downpatrick, County Down, T4461 5779 (page 548)
Boat ride to Sherkin Island and cart ride to the beach, County Cork (page 265)
Dolphinwatch, The Square, Carrigaholt, County Clare, T065-9058156 (page 361)

The stately homes of the Anglo-Irish aristocracy that are open to the public are alluring places but very often a disappointing anti-climax. Mount Stewart House in Down and Westport House in Mayo are notable failures, but **Strokestown House** in Roscommon is absolutely superb and **Castle Coole** in Fermanagh is a wheeze.

Castles and sites of archaeological interest

You'll find castles and sites of archaeological interest everywhere; indeed it is hard to think of a town in Ireland that doesn't have something of interest in its vicinity. **Dublin Castle** in the capital and **Newgrange** in County Meath, the most famous of Ireland's passage graves, within striking distance of Dublin, should not be missed; **Kilkenny Castle** and the **Rock of Cashel** are equally compelling, while **Cork** and **Kerry** are choc-a-bloc with stone circles and other sites of prehistoric interest.

Cultural events

For mainstream cultural events such as theatre and classical music, Dublin has the famous **Abbey**, the **Gaiety**, **Olympia** and **Gate Theatres**, and the Dublin Theatre Festival which takes place in October. Theatres in the cities of **Cork**, **Galway** and **Sligo** usually feature an interesting programme, and **Tralee** is home to the National Folk Theatre. The **National Concert Hall** and events organized by the Royal Dublin Society feature performances of classical music in the capital. Some religious sites are of major cultural interest: these include **Clonmacnois** in County Offaly, **Glendalough** in County Wicklow, **Mellifont Abbey**, and the **High Crosses** at Monasterboice in County Louth.

Partying → *See also 'Festivals', page 46.*

In Ireland socializing and partying are art forms in their own right, with a tendency to be confined within pub culture. Dublin would seem the obvious destination, but there is a hopeless shortage of pubs for the actual population (see box page 43) and this makes them terribly overcrowded. There is also the small problem that licensing laws tend to be enforced in the city centre. For serious boozing and chatting into the early hours of the morning head for small village pubs or just about anywhere off the beaten track. At night and during the summer, some of the off-shore islands like **Clare Island** or **Achill**, **Sherkin** or **Inishbofin**, can have very flexible closing hours.

Festivals are great occasions for partying because licensing hours are sometimes officially extended; the summer festival in **Galway city** is enormously popular with young people, while **Killorglin's Puck Fair** in Kerry attracts an older crowd. There are countless other festivals taking place throughout the summer in most regions of

Ireland, and not all of them are of the partying kind. Visit the **Irish Tourist Board** website for information on festivals and events: www.ireland.travel.ie.

When to go

There is no easy answer to this question. The weather is notoriously changeable and you can have a week of mild, dry days in February or a week of depressing drizzle in August. These are exceptions, however, and extremes of wind, rain or sunshine are rare; the climate is generally mild, thanks to the benign influence of the Gulf Stream. July and August are definitely the busiest months in terms of visitor numbers, so a trip in early spring or late autumn has a lot to recommend it. Dublin is busy throughout the year and accommodation in the capital always needs advance planning.

Some important **festivals** take place at fixed times of the year, so this may be a factor determining when to visit. The Galway Arts Festival takes place in July, and this is a popular time for many summer festivals across the country. Cork's International Jazz Festival takes off in October, as does Wexford's two-week Opera Festival. See page 46 for a list of important dates.

In Northern Ireland the 'marching season' reaches a climax in July and, while this used to be a time to avoid parts of Belfast and towns like Portadown and Kilkeel, the situation looks to improve. If you feel unsure, contact the Northern Ireland tourist board in Belfast and they will advise on the current situation.

Climate

Ireland's climate (a quip with some truth is that Ireland doesn't have a climate, just weather) is equable, with fairly uniform temperatures across the country as a whole: summer temperatures average between 15°C to 20°C while winter temperatures average between 5°C and 10°C. The coldest months are January and February, but temperatures usually stay above 3°C, it rarely snows, and in the southwest heavy frost is unusual. July and August are the warmest months, with exceptional days at this time of the year climbing into the very high 20°Cs. Average rainfall in low-lying areas is between 800 and 1,200 mm, while in mountainous areas it may exceed 2,000 mm. The southeast is the driest part of the country, with less than 750 mm. But pay scant heed to the statistics, because rain is endemic to Ireland and only its unpredictability is certain. Winter on the western seaboard can be exhilarating, to put it mildly, when an Atlantic storm that has been brewing up for thousands of miles across the ocean finally hits land in western Ireland. Hurricane-force storms are not unknown, 15 m-high waves lash the rocks, and power cuts occasionally happen.

Weather forecasts for the Republic are online at www.weather.ie, and for Northern Ireland at www.metoffice.co.uk.

Tour operators

Popular regions of Ireland, such as Killarney, the Burren, the Aran Islands and Connemara, are well served by local tour companies, and from Dublin local tours run to Newgrange, the Wicklow mountains and further afield. **Iarnród Éireann**, the national railway, organizes a variety of guided one-day tours to Connemara, Cork, Kerry, Dingle, the Burren, Leitrim, Wexford, Waterford, Kilkenny, and Antrim and Donegal. For full details contact **Railtours Ireland**, 58 Lower Gardiner St, Dublin 1, T01-8560045.

The following companies offer a variety of tours and holidays, including all or some of your accommodation, activity holidays, city and rural breaks, angling, cycling, golf, walking, car hire, air tickets, river cruising, horse-drawn Romany caravans and self-catering.

Australian tour operators

Adventure World, 73 Walker St, North Sydney, T02-9956 7766, www.adventureworld.com.
Inishfree Travel, T02-9360 3616, fod@dfot.net.au.
STA Travel, T1300-733035, www.statravel.com.au.
Irish Travel T9602-3700, www.irishtravel.com.au.

Irish tour operators

Time Out Tours, T074-73030, www.timeouttours.com. Donegal-based company offering activity, educational and special interest holidays across Ireland. Examples include trips via old-style narrow-gauge railways, Highlands and Islands tour, organic farm stays.

UK tour operators

Aer Lingus Holidays, T0845-9737747, www.aerlingus.com.
Cresta Holidays, Tabley Ct, Victoria St, Altrincham, Cheshire WA14 IEZ, T0870-1610910, www.crestaholidays.co.uk.
Irish Ferries Holidays, Reliance House, Water St, Liverpool, L2 8TP, T0870-5171717, www.irishferries.com.
Leisure Breaks, 33 Dovedale Rd, Liverpool, LI8 5EP, T0151-7345200, www.irelandbreaks.co.uk.
Slattery's, 162 Kentish Town Rd, London, NW5 2AG, T0800-515900, F020-74821604, ireland@slattery.com.
Stena Line Holidays, Charter House, Park St, Ashford, Kent TN24 8EX, T08705-747474, www.stenaline.co.uk.
Swansea Cork Ferries, King's Dock, Swansea, West Glamorgan, Wales, T01792-456116, www.swansea-cork.ie.

USA tour operators

CIE International Tours, T1-800-2486832, www.cietours.com.
Collette Tours, T1-800-3405158.
Destinations Ireland, T1-800-8321848, www.destinations-ireland.com.
Kenny Tours, T1-800-6481492, www.kenny-tours.com.

Finding out more

A great deal of tourist information is available from the tourist boards and their websites. If contacting Fáilte Ireland (The Irish Tourist Board) or the Northern Ireland Tourist Board (NITB), be as specific as possible, because they have far too much literature to send out everything to everybody. The two tourist boards are merged under Tourism Ireland for the purposes of promoting the island of Ireland overseas.

Irish tourist boards

In Ireland

Fáilte Ireland is the official Irish tourist organization. Their main address in Ireland is PO Box 273, Dublin 8, T01-6024000, F01-6024100, user@irishtouristboard.ie, www.ireland.travel.ie.
Northern Ireland Tourist Board, head office at 59 North St, Belfast BT1 1NB, T028-9023 1221, F028-9024 0960, www.discovernorthernireland.com.

Tourist boards outside Ireland

Tourism Ireland, www.tourismireland.com, promotes the Republic and Northern Ireland and their offices are:
Australia: 5th Level, 36 Carrington St, Sydney NSW 2000, T02-9299 6177, info@tourismireland.com.au.
Canada: 2 Bloor St, Suite 1501, Toronto M4W 3E2, T1800-2236470.
France: Office du Tourisme Irlandais, 33 rue de Miromesnil, 75008 Paris, T01-7020 0020, info@irlande-tourisme.fr.
Germany: Irische Fremdenverkehrszentrale, Unter-mainanlage 7, D60329 Frankfurt/Main, T069-6680 0950, info@ irishtouristboard.de.
New Zealand: 6th Floor, 18 Shortland St, private Bag 92136, Auckland 1, T09-9772255.
UK: Nations House, 103 Wigmore St, London WIU IQS, T0800-0399000.
USA: 345 Park Av, New York, NY 10154, T800-2236470, info@shamrock.org.

Websites

Among the most useful are the websites of: **Fáilte Ireland**, **Northern Ireland Tourist Board** and **Tourism Ireland** (see above). Other include:

www.exp.ie, for jobs in Ireland
www.irishfood.com, is a well designed site for Irish cuisine.
www.irlgov.ie, the Republic of Ireland government website, where jobs in Ireland can be found.
www.shopirish.com, a site devoted to Irish goods.
www.usairish.net, US Irish Network site.

Language

English is spoken by everyone in Ireland, and this is the only language you need to know. There are regional accents and if you travel around for any length of time you will begin to appreciate this. There are colloquial and slang expressions peculiar to the English spoken in Ireland, as there are in all cultures that use English, but they are never a barrier to communication and simply add to the pleasure of everyday communication. It often does seem to be the case that the Irish use the English language in a particularly rich and idiosyncratic way and if you keep your ears tuned you will soon collect some creative (and scatological) expressions.

Gaeltacht

Gaeltacht is the name for areas where Irish is still spoken. When Ireland became independent in 1922 the Irish language was still the everyday language of communication in parts of Cork, Kerry, Waterford, Galway, Mayo and Donegal, and it is the more rural parts of these counties that constitute the Gaeltacht. This does not mean English is not understood or spoken as well, but in Gaeltacht areas you will have an opportunity to hear Irish being spoken and used on a daily basis.

The Irish language, and its offshoots of Scottish Gaelic and Manx, is the Irish branch of the Celtic languages that include Welsh, Cornish and Breton. The number of people speaking Irish in Ireland today is somewhere in the region of 80,000 but you are more likely to hear it spoken on **RTE** radio where occasional programmes and daily news bulletins are broadcast in Irish. There is also an Irish-language radio station broadcast from Connemara, **Radio na Gaeltachta**, and a national Irish-language television station, **TG4**.

Some everyday words commonly appear in Irish and it helps to be familiar with them:

'Mná'	*me-naw*	women
'Fir'	*fear*	men
'Gardai'	*gar-dee*	police
'Oifig an Phoist'	*ifig-on-pwist*	post office

See the glossary, page 632, for Irish words that are commonly found in place names. If you want to impress or just show off you can occasionally use fairly common Irish words like 'slán agat' (*slawn-aguth*), meaning goodbye, or 'go raibh maith agat' (*go-rev-moh-aguth*), meaning thank you. 'Fáilte' (*fawl-cha*) means welcome.

Disabled travellers

Improvements continue to be made, but generally speaking Ireland is still lagging behind some countries in its provisions for disabled travellers. However, with advance planning and all the available information at your disposal, a visit can still be an enjoyable experience. Contact both Fáilte Ireland and NITB for their specialist literature, and in the Republic the **National Disability Authority** is well worth contacting for their guides to accommodation, tourist facilities, restaurants and pubs. They also produce a detailed guide to Dublin which contains good general information and advice as well as listings. See also page 60 for more information pertaining to Dublin. **Irish Ferries** and **Stena Line** have discounts for disabled travellers, but it is advisable to check their details *before* booking passage because the date of travel will make a difference.

Contacts

Directions Unlimited, 720 N Bedford Rd, Bedford Hills, NY 10507, USA, T1-800-5355343. Specialize in vacations for disabled travellers.

Disability Action, T028-90929 7880, www.disability.action.org.

Disability Action, 2 Annadale Av, Belfast, www.disabilityaction.org.

Disabled Drivers' Association, Ashwellthorpe, Norwich, NR16 1EX, England, T01508-489449.

Dublin Bus Customer Service, 59 Upper O'Connell St, Dublin 1, T01-8734222. Try their No 3 route through the city with wheelchair access.

Fáilte Ireland, see page 22.

Iarnród Éireann, Travel Centre, Connolly Station, Amiens St, Dublin 1, T01-7032369. Free *Guide for Mobility Impaired Passengers*.

Irish Wheelchair Association, Blackheath Dr, Clontarf, Dublin 3, T01-8338241/8335366.

National Disability Authority, 25 Clyde Rd, Dublin 4, T01-6080400, www.nda.ie.

Northern Ireland Tourist Board (NITB), see page 22.

Restaurants Association of Ireland, 11 Bridge Court, Dublin 8, T01-6779901. Free *Dining in Ireland* booklet identifies wheelchair-accessible restaurants.

Gay and lesbian travellers

Contact information for gay and lesbian travellers is given below, but apart from in the main cities, there is little understanding of gay life, and society is generally blinkered if not intolerant. In rural areas especially, there is widespread ignorance and overt gay behaviour is not advisable. Dublin (see page 122) has gay-friendly accommodation, pubs and clubs.

Contacts

Dublin Lesbian Line, T01-8729911 (Thu, 1900-2100).

Gay Lesbian Youth Northern Ireland (GLYNI), meets every Mon at Cara-friend, Cathedral Building, 64 Donegall St, Belfast, T028-9066 4111, glyni.org.uk.

Gay Switchboard Dublin, Carmichael House, North Great Brunswick St, Dublin 7, T01-8721055 (Sun-Fri, 2000 to 2200, Sat, 1530-1800).

Lesbian Line Belfast, T028-9023 8668 (Thu, 1930-2200).

Student travellers

Some form of identity card confirming your student or youth status is required for any discounts available on travel to and within Ireland, entry charges to museums and sundry other benefits and discounts. Before paying for any form of travel or for any entrance fee or ticket, ask whether a student or youth discount is available. Admission prices quoted in this book are for adults and do not take into account the discounts that are commonly available to students, families and children. The most commonly recognized form of ID is an **International Student Identity Card** (ISIC), available to anyone in full-time education and obtainable from **STA**, www.statravel.com, **Council Travel**, www.statravel.com, or **Travel Cuts**, www.travelcuts.com, offices in your country; in Ireland the card is obtainable through **USIT**, www.usit.ie. Holders of an ISIC card can obtain discount vouchers from Dublin's USIT office, 19-21 Aston Quay, T01-6021600, which cover a variety of shops and places of interest.

Working in the country

Although Ireland's economy is presently tightening its belt and non-skilled work is not as readily available as it was a couple of years ago, employers in Dublin and other cities are still looking for experienced professionals in various fields. Part-time work in restaurants and hotels in the Republic, and the service industry generally, is not difficult to find between April and August. EU citizens can stay and work for as long as they like but non-EU citizens need to register with the local garda as an alien once they have obtained a work visa. Websites worth consulting include **www.gojobsite.ie** and **www.irishjobs.ie**. It is also worth looking at the websites of newspapers to see the kind of employment being advertised: **www.examiner.ie**, **www.ireland.com** and **www.loadza.com**. For information on work visas, contact the Department of Foreign Affairs **www.ir/gov.ie/iveagh** and click on the Travelling to Ireland tab.

Business travellers in the Republic can consult the **Chamber of Commerce of Ireland**, 17 Merrion Sq, Dublin 2, T01-661 2888, www.chambersireland.ie. The Irish Chamber of Commerce in the US has its own website: **www.iccusa.org**. There is also a business information centre in the ILAC Centre, Henry St, Dublin 1, T01-873 3996.

Before you travel

Visas and immigration

Passports

All visitors to either the Republic or Northern Ireland require a valid passport, except British nationals. Holders of UK passports not born in Great Britain or Northern Ireland should bring their passport, and even British nationals should consider bringing theirs because some form of valid ID is required for collecting air tickets booked online, changing travellers' cheques and perhaps also for cases of emergency medical treatment.

Visas

EU nationals can stay in the **Republic** indefinitely without a visa; travellers from the USA, Canada, Australia and New Zealand can stay for three months without a visa, and this can usually be extended by making an application at the local main Garda Síochána (police) station. In Dublin, go to the **Aliens Registration Office**, Harcourt St, T01-4755555. Nationals of other countries should contact the Irish Embassy for details about visa regulations. Further information for the Republic available from the **Department of Foreign Affairs**, Dublin, T01-4780822, www.foreignaffairs.gov.ie.

EU nationals can stay in **Northern Ireland** without a visa; citizens of the USA, Canada, Australia and New Zealand can stay for up to six months without a visa, though evidence of a return ticket and sufficient funds may be required. For an extension of the six month rule write in advance to the **Undersecretary of State**, Home Office, 40 Wellesley Rd, Croydon CR9 2BY, England. Nationals of other countries should contact the British Consular office for details about visa regulations.

Consulates and embassies

Irish

Australia Embassy of Ireland, 20 Arkana St, Yarralumla A.C.T., 2600 Canberra, T02-6273 3022, 612-6273 3201, irishemb@cyberone.com.au

New Zealand 6th Floor, 18 Shortland St,

1001 Auckland, T09-3022867, consul@ireland.co.nz.
United Kingdom 17 Grosvenor Pl, London, SWIX 7HR, T0870-0056725, http://ireland.embassyhomepage.com.
USA (Washington) 2234 Massachusetts Av, N.W. Washington DC 20008-2849, T202-4623939, www.irelandemb.org.
USA (New York) Ireland House, 345 Park Av (17th Fl), New York, NY 10154-0037, T212-3192555, congenny@aol.com.
USA (Boston) Chase Building 535 Boylston St, Boston, MA 02116, T617-2679330, irlcons@aol.com.
USA (Chicago) 400 North Michigan Av, Chicago, IL 60611, T312-3371868, irishconchicago@aol.com.
USA (San Francisco) 100 Pine St, San Francisco, CA 94111, T415-3924214, irishcqsf@earthlink.net.

British
Australia, Commonwealth Av, Yarralumla, Canberra, ACT 2600, T02-6270 6666, www.uk.emb.gov.au.
Ireland, 29 Merrion Rd, Dublin 4. T01-2053700, bembassy@internet-ireland.ie
New Zealand, 44 Hill St, Wellington, T04-9242888, ppa.mailbox@fco.gov.uk.
USA, 3100 Massachusetts Av NW, Washington DC 20008, T202-5886500, www.britainusa.com.

Customs

There are no customs restrictions affecting travel within the EU, and there are no duty free allowances. Pets can be taken freely between Britain, Northern Ireland and the Republic, but strict quarantine regulations are in force for pets from any other part of the world (details from T01-6072000, www.irlgov.ie/daff for the Republic, and T028-7131 9500, www.dardni.gov.uk for Northern Ireland). USA visitors can take home US$800 worth of goods per person www.customs.ustreas.gov/xp/cgov/travel.

Vaccinations

→ *See also the Health section, page 54.*

None are compulsory or even necessary unless arriving from an infected area.

What to take

The two essentials are a state of mind that won't get you down if it rains and wet weather gear for the times when it does rain. Health insurance is advisable for non-EU travellers and a basic first aid kit should include pills for possible hangovers and/or stomach upsets. Walkers should be prepared for blisters and small cuts, and a compass, possibly a mobile phone as well, is advisable for walks in mountainous areas. A sleeping bag and/or a sheet with a pillow cover is a very good idea for stays in hostels. Other useful items include an adapter plug for electrical appliances.

Money

Currency

→ *At the time of writing £1 is worth around 1.5 euros and US$1 is worth about 0.76 euros.*

In the Republic, the euro currency consists of 100 cents. Notes are in 5, 10, 20, 50, 100, 200 and 500; coins are 1, 2, 5, 10, 20 and 50 cents, and 1 and 2 euro.

In Northern Ireland, British Sterling currency is used, with £5, £10, £20, £50 and £100 notes. Coins are £2, £1, 50p, 20p, 10p, 5p, 2p and 1p. However, notes are also issued by Northern Ireland banks and, while these are interchangeable with the standard British notes within Northern Ireland, they are *not* generally accepted in mainland Britain other than through banks.

Until the euro comes into circulation in Northern Ireland (a date still to be decided by Britain), the currencies of the Republic and Northern Ireland are not interchangeable.

Credit cards

Visa and Mastercard credit and debit cards are widely accepted in the Republic and Northern Ireland and, if you have a personal identification number (PIN), cash withdrawals can be made using them from ATMs which are found in all towns. International money systems, like Cirrus and Plus, are linked to ATMs. American Express and Diners' Club cards, especially the latter, are not as readily accepted.

Travellers' cheques → *Travellers' cheques are rarely directly accepted in lieu of cash.*

Using travellers' cheques is the safest way to carry money and all the main brands, Thomas Cook, Visa and American Express, are readily accepted at banks across the whole of Ireland. If travelling between the Republic and Northern Ireland it makes sense to have them issued in sterling, but US dollar cheques are also accepted. Keep a record of the cheque numbers separate from the cheques themselves to facilitate refunds should they get lost or stolen. A commission charge is made when cashing travellers' cheques, this may be avoided by cashing American Express or Thomas Cook cheques at their own offices in Dublin (see page 126) or Belfast (page 522). Eurocheques can also be cashed across Ireland with a Eurocheque card.

Changing money

The best exchange rates are available at banks; the worst are across the counter in hotels. Bureaux de change, found at airports and ferry terminals, city centres and some key tourist areas like Killarney, are useful when banks are closed, but the rate will not be as good. In the Republic banks generally open Monday-Friday 1000-1600, but in many towns they may close between 1230 and 1330. On Thursday banks often stay open until 1700 or sometimes 1900. In Northern Ireland normal banking hours are 0930-1630 (0930-1700 on Thursday), and often also Saturday morning in cities.

Value Added Tax

Visitors from non-EU countries leaving the Republic within two months of a purchase (three months in Northern Ireland) can obtain a refund of the Value Added Tax (VAT) added to the price of most goods. The shop has to be a participant in the Retail Export Scheme, and there will usually be a display at the entrance or on the counter to this effect, but shops have different ways of operating the scheme so enquire before making a purchase. The scheme does not apply to hotel bills and other services.

Money transfers

If the need arises, you can telephone your home bank and arrange for money to be transferred to a local bank in Ireland where you can collect it after showing your passport. Before you leave home, ensure you have the necessary bank details. American Express cardholders can arrange for money to be sent to Ireland; check out the details before you leave home. Western Union arranges money transfers and there is also MoneyGram, T008-008-971 8971 (in the UK), T1-800-543 4080 (in USA) T01-6671577 (Bank of Ireland in Dublin): a quick international money transfer service.

Cost of living

Ireland is not a cheap place to stay or travel in. As a bare minimum, if you stay in hostels and use their facilities to prepare your own lunches and most evening meals, but eat out occasionally at night, and spend about €7 a day on admission charges and/or entertainment, you will need a budget of over €200 a week, and this will exclude any transport costs or other expenses. If you stay in a decent B&B or guesthouse, enjoy a pub lunch and a mid-range evening meal each day, and spend about €15 a day on admission charges and/or entertainment, a budget of at least €500 a week is needed, excluding transport costs and any other expenses. To give you an idea here are some sample prices: pub lunch €8.50; petrol per litre €0.89;

 pint of beer €2.95; Dublin to Galway monthly return bus fare €15.24. And if you are planning to stay in Dublin for any length of time and have much fun, consider taking out a second mortgage.

Getting there

Air

Airports

Flights from Britain, continental Europe and North America arrive at **Dublin**, www.dublinairport.com, **Shannon**, www.shannonairport.com, or **Cork**, www.cork airport.com. Regional airports are in **Kerry**, www.kerryaiport.ie, **Knock** in Mayo, www.west-irl-holidays.ie and **Waterford**. Northern Ireland has **Belfast International**, www.belfastairport.com, **Belfast City** www.belfastcityairport.com and **Derry**, www.cityofderryairport.com.

From Britain

The only consistently available and reasonably priced tickets are the advanced purchase tickets which have various conditions attached to them, the most important being that your return date is fixed and no refunds are available. Such return fares between London and Dublin range from between €75 and €100, between London and Cork from around €115 and between London and Belfast from around €100. In order to secure these prices it is advisable to book as far ahead as possible, especially at peak times like summer, Easter and Christmas. Supply and demand means there are often special offers that represent very good value like two return tickets for the price of one or especially low return fares. But beware: sometimes Ryanair fares can prove more expensive than Aer Lingus fares when demand is high. Online booking is available with both airlines and dates can be changed after booking with Ryanair for €22 for each sector.

Bicycles are normally carried free of charge on Aer Lingus but Ryanair rake in €19 extra each way (same for surf boards). Always check before you purchase a ticket.

Student/Youth fares are always worth asking about, though different airlines have different rules and regulations. An International Student Identity Card (ISIC) is usually required. It is advisable to check through a specialist agency like STA Travel, 86 Old Brompton Rd, London SW7 3LH, T020-7361 6161, who also have offices in a number of other cities across Britain. Another company worth trying is Usit, 52 Grovesnor Gdns, London SW1W OAG, T020-7730 3402, who also have regional offices in cities and at universities in Britain. Usit Now head office: 19 Aston Quay, Dublin 2, T01-6798833, is the Irish youth and student travel organization; other offices are listed in relevant directories.

From Britain to the Republic It takes about an hour to fly between London and Dublin; about 90 minutes to Cork or Shannon. The main destinations in the Republic are Dublin, Cork and Shannon, but it is also possible to fly to Knock, Kerry, Waterford and Galway.

From Britain to Northern Ireland It takes about an hour and a half to fly between London and Belfast, a bit longer to Derry. The airports are Belfast International, Belfast City and City of Derry and while most departures are from London (Heathrow, Stansted and Gatwick), there are also flights from many other cities (see box next page).

Airlines operating between Great Britiain and Ireland

From	To	Airline
Aberdeen	Belfast City, Dublin	Eastern Airways, Ryanair
Birmingham	Belfast Int, Cork, Dublin Shannon, Knock	bmibaby, Aer Arann, Flybe, Aer Lingus, Ryanair, My Travel Lite
Blackpool	Belfast City, Dublin	Ryanair, Flykeen
Bournemouth	Dublin	Ryanair
Bristol	Belfast Int and City, Cork, Dublin	Flybe, Easyjet, Aer Arann, Ryanair British Airways, Ryanair
Cardiff	Belfast City and Int, Cork, Dublin	Air Wales, bmibaby, Ryanair
East Midlands	Belfast Int, Dublin Cork	bmibaby
Edinburgh	Belfast Int, and City, Cork, Dublin, Shannon	Aer Lingus, Ryanair, Aer Arann flybmi, Flybe, British Airways, Easyjet
Exeter	Belfast City, Dublin	Flybe
Glasgow	Belfast City and Int, Derry, Cork, Dublin, Shannon	British Airways, Easyjet, flybmi
Glasgow	Dublin	Ryanair
Guernsey	Belfast City, Dublin	Flybe, British Airways
Isle of Man	Belfast City, Dublin	EuroManx, Flykeen, Aer Arann
Jersey	Belfast City, Dublin	Flybe, Aer Lingus
Leeds Brad.	Belfast City, Dublin Cork	Flybe, flybmi/Ryanair
Liverpool	Belfast Int, Dublin	Easyjet, Ryanair
London City	Belfast City, Dublin	Flybe, Cityjet
London Gatwick	Belfast City and Int, Cork, Dublin, Shannon	Aer Lingus, British Airways, Ryanair
London Heathrow	Belfast City and Int, Cork, Dublin	Aer Lingus, Easyjet, British Airways, Ryanair
London Luton	Belfast Int, Dublin, Galway, Waterford	Easyjet, Ryanair, Aer Arann
London Stansted	Belfast Int, Cork, Dublin, Kerry, Derry, Knock, Shannon	Ryanair
Manchester	Belfast City and Int, Cork, Derry, Dublin, Knock, Shannon, Galway	bmibaby, British Airways, Aer Lingus, Ryanair
Newcastle	Belfast City and Int, Dublin	Flybe, Easyjet, Ryanair
Nottingham	Cork, Dublin, Knock	bmibaby
Plymouth	Cork, Dublin	Air Wales
Southampton	Belfast City, Dublin, Cork	Flybe, Aer Arann
Swansea	Dublin, Cork	Air Wales
Teeside	Dublin, Belfast Int	Ryanair, bmibaby

Specialist travel agents

Claddagh Travel, T0121-2003320, www.claddahtravel.co.uk.
Enjoy Ireland, T01254-692899, www.emjoyireland.net.
Pat Carroll Travel, T020-7625 9669.
Sibbald Travel, T0131-6679172.
Tara Travel, T020-76258601 (London) T0161-2251133 (Manchester), T0121-7022929 (Birmingham), T020-8514 5141 (Essex).

Airline details

Aer Arann, T0800-5872324, www.aerarann.com.
Aer Lingus, T0845-0844444, www.aerlingus.com.
Air Wales, T0870- 7773131, www.airwales.co.uk.
bmibaby, T0870-2642229, www.bmibaby.com.
British Airways, T0870-8509850, www.britishairways.com.
EasyJet, T0870-6000000, www.easyjet.com.
Eastern Airways, T01652-681099, www.easternairways.com.
Eujet, T0870-4141414, www.eujet.com.
EuroManx, T0870-7877879, www.euromanx.com.
Flybe, T08705-676676, www.flybe.com.
flybmi, T0870-6070555, www.flybmi.com.
Flykeen, T0800-0837783, www.flykeen.com.
Ryanair, T0871-2460000, www.ryanair.com.
Thomsonfly, T0870-1900737, www.thomsonfly.com.
My Travel Lite, T08701-564564 www.mytravellite.com.

From Europe

There are numerous direct and indirect flights to Ireland from European cities. The best deals are likely to be found through Ryanair, Aer Lingus, bmibaby and flybmi.

From North America

There are direct Aer Lingus flights to Dublin and Shannon from New York, Boston, Baltimore, Chicago and Los Angeles. Continental Airlines and Delta Airlines also fly to Shannon and Dublin. Flights from the West Coast cost considerably more and it may be cheaper to fly to London and take a flight from there to Ireland. Airlines and some specialist travel agents are listed below and the weekend sections of papers like the *New York Times* and the *San Francisco Chronicle* are worth checking out. Student fares are available through agents like STA Travel in New York and Travel Cuts in Toronto.

There are no direct flights to Ireland from Canada, but Air Canada fly to Dublin, Shannon and Belfast via London from Montréal, Toronto and Vancouver. The cheapest flights from Montréal or Toronto to the Republic entail fixed dates that cannot be changed. As with flights from the US West Coast, it is worth checking out the cost of flying to London and having a separate ticket from there to Ireland.

Airline details

Air Canada, T1888-247 2262, www.aircanada.com
Aer Lingus, T1800-474 7424, www.aerlingus.com
Continental Airlines, T1800-231 0856, www.continental.com
Delta Airlines, T1800-241 4141, www.delta.com
Royal Jordanian Airlines, T1800-223 0470, 212 949-0050, www.rja.com.jo

From Australia and New Zealand

There are no direct flights from Australia or New Zealand, so the usual route is to fly to London and then on to Ireland. Various airlines offer indirect tickets to Ireland this

Airlines operating between USA and Ireland

From	To	Airline
Atlanta	Shannon/Dublin	Delta Airlines
Baltimore	Shannon/Dublin	Aer Lingus
Boston	Shannon/Dublin	Aer Lingus
Chicago	Shannon/Dublin	Aer Lingus, Royal Jordanian
Los Angeles	Shannon/Dublin	Aer Lingus
Newark	Shannon/Dublin	Continental Airlines
New York	Shannon/Dublin	Aer Lingus, Royal Jordanian

way and ones to check out include not only Aer Lingus and British Airways, but also KLM, Singapore Airlines and Malaysia Airlines. The single most important factor determining the price of a ticket is the season and peak times. Between May and August is peak time. Before making a decision check out other major airlines that fly to London, because very often it does not cost a lot to have a London-Dublin ticket added to your main fare.

Airlines and agents offering flights

Aer Lingus, World Aviation Systems, 64 York St, Sydney, T02-9321 9123; 6th Fl, 229 Queen St, Auckland, T09-3794455, www.aerlingus.com.
Air New Zealand, Queen St, Auckland, T09-3662424; 5 Elizabeth St, Sydney, T02-9223 4666, www.airzealand.com.
British Airways, 64 Castlereagh St, Sydney, T02-9258 3300; 154 Queen St, Auckland, T09-3568690.
KLM, Level 6, 5 Elizabeth St, Sydney, T02-9231 6333.
Malaysia Airlines, 16 Spring St, Sydney, T02-9364 3535; 12th Fl, The Swanson Centre, Swanson St, Auckland, T09-3732741.
Qantas, 70 Hunter St, Sydney, T02-9951 4294. Qantas House, 154 Queen St, Auckland, T0800-808767.
STA Travel, 855 George St, Sydney, T1-800-637444.
Singapore Airlines, 17-19 Bridge St, Sydney, T02-9350 0121. Lower Ground Fl, West Plaza Building, Customs & Albert Sts, Auckland, T0800-808909.
Thomas Cook, 175 Pitt St, Sydney, T02-9229 6611; 159 Queen St, Auckland, T09-3793924.
Travellers' Centre, 10 High St, Auckland, T09-3090458 (and branches throughout both countries).
UTAG Travel Agents, 122 Walker St, North Sydney (and branches throughout the country) T02-9956 8399.

Sea

From Britain

The box on page 33 covers the routes and sailing times of passage to Ireland by car and passenger ferries. Car hire in the Republic (see page 38) is more expensive than in Britain or the USA, so if you are planning to use a car a journey by ferry can be worthwhile. Bear in mind, too, that the cost of a ferry fare for a car and passengers may compare favourably with two, three or more individual air fares for the same journey. The Swansea-Cork ferry does not operate over the winter months.

Fares vary depending on the time of year, type of vessel and sometimes the time of sailing. But bear in mind that in the age of low-fares airlines, this is not a cheap way to travel. For example: it will cost two people with a car approximately €500 for a return Swansea-Cork trip, although this could be brought down to around €400 by taking advantage of mid-week travel deals. Also bear in mind extra costs like the price of meals and drinks on board and a possible need for overnight stays in Britain and/or Ireland in order to make unhelpful departure or arrival times. On many of the routes, especially the 10-hour Swansea-Cork ferry, there are extra charges for cabin accommodation, although you can bring a sleeping bag and try to find a quiet corner for a night's sleep. Some companies, like **Irish Ferries**, insist on travel insurance, and unless you can quote an existing policy that covers you (an annual world or Europe travel policy for instance) there will be an extra charge for this as well.

Travelling as a foot passenger on a combined coach/ferry or train/ferry ticket can be good value although obviously it takes far longer than a flight. Holders of ISIC cards should ask about student reductions, whether travelling as a driver or foot passenger, although discounts are not available on all the routes. Cheapest travel of all for a foot passenger is to try and hitch a ride at the ferry terminal, because in a car with fewer than four passengers there would be no extra charge.

There are some big ships sailing to Ireland. The *Stena HSS* is the size of a football pitch, accommodates up to 1,500 passengers and, with four gas turbines producing 100,000 horsepower, belts along with a top speed of over 50 mph. *Ulysses*, an Irish Ferries ship doing the Holyhead-Dublin route, ranks as the world's largest car ferry (over 1,300 cars) and with 12 decks to play with there are plenty of amenities on board.

Ferry operators

Irish Ferries, T08705-171717, www.irishferries.ie.
Norse Merchant Ferries, T0870-6004321, www.norsemerchant.com.
P&O Irish Sea, T0870-2424777, www.poirishsea.com.
Sea Cat, T08705-523523, www.seacat.co.uk.
Stena Line, T08705-707070, www.stenaline.com.
Swansea/Cork Ferries, T01792-456116, T01792- 456116, www.swansea-cork.ie.
Seacat Scotland, T08705-523523, www.seacat.co.uk. Run daily services (2½ hrs; £250 for 2 adults and a car).

From Europe

Irish Ferries, www.irishferries.com, run two routes, from Roscoff and Cherbourg in northern France to Rosslare in Co Wexford. The return fare for both routes with two passengers, a car and a two-berth cabin in the summer months is around €1160. **Brittany Ferries,** www.brittany-ferries.co.uk, run sailings from Roscoff, France, to Cork between April and early October.

Land/sea

Train/ferry

The cost of combined train and ferry tickets depends on the time of year and departure times. Combined train and ferry tickets can be booked through a travel agent or from a mainline railway station. **Stena Line,** T08705-455455, also offer competitive rail/ferry packages, and a return booked in advance for their London-Dublin route can be as low as £32, although the standard economy fare in £74. Travellers under the age of 26 with a Young Person's Railcard can get one-third off standard rail fares. Contact **National Rail Enquiries,** T08457-484950, from outside Britain T207-2785240, www.nationalrail.co.uk. For details of European rail passes that can be used to get to and travel throughout Ireland, see www.raileurope.com.

Ferry crossings and operators between the British mainland and Ireland

From	To	Operator	Approx travel time
Birkenhead	Belfast	Norse Merchant Ferries	8 hrs
Cairnryan	Larne	P&O Irish Sea	Fastcraft, 1hr Superferry, 1¾ hrs
Fishguard	Rosslare	Stena Line	Stena Lynx Fastcraft, 1hr 50mins Superferry, 3½ hrs
Fleetwood	Larne	Stena Line	8 hrs
Holyhead	Dublin port	Irish Ferries	Cruise Ferry, 3¼ hrs Dublin Swift, 109 min
Holyhead	Dublin port	Stena Line	Superferry, 3¼ hrs
Holyhead	Dun Laoghaire	Stena Line	Stena HSS Fastcraft, 99 mins
Isle of Man	Belfast	Sea Cat	2¾ hrs
Isle of Man	Dublin	Sea Cat	2¾ hrs
Liverpool	Dublin	Seacat	4 hrs
Pembroke	Rosslare	Irish Ferries	3¾ hrs
Stanraer	Belfast	Stena Line	HSS Fastcraft , 1¾ hrs Superferry, 3¼ hrs
Swansea	Cork	Swansea Cork Ferries	10 hrs
Troon	Belfast	Sea Cat	2½ hrs
Troon	Larne	P&O Irish Sea	109 mins

Coach/ferry

This is the least expensive but also the slowest method of getting to Ireland. The largest operator of scheduled coach services to Ireland is **Slattery's**, with daily services to Dublin, Galway, Cork, Tralee, Waterford, Limerick and many other towns. Coaches depart from London, Bristol, Birmingham, Reading, Liverpool, Manchester and Leeds.

National Express Eurolines run regular day and night services between London and Dublin, via Birmingham, taking an average of 12 hours, depending on the ferry crossing. Combined tickets from other cities across Britain are available. Tickets using other ferry crossings are also available, as are combined tickets to other parts of Ireland using the **Bus Éireann** network. Enquiries and ticket purchases may be made in person from any National Express station or their agents, or by phone (contact details below). Reductions are available to passengers under 26 and to senior citizens.

Ulsterbus operates a coach/ferry service between London and Belfast via Birmingham, from Birmingham via Manchester, and from Edinburgh via Glasgow using the Stranraer ferry. The return fare from London is around £59 and takes 13 hours; from Edinburgh the coast is from €25 and takes seven hours. Tickets can be purchased through **National Express.**

Bus companies

Bus Éireann, Busaras, Store St, Dublin 1. T01-8366111 (Dublin), www.buseireann.ie.
National Express Eurolines, 52 Grosvenor Gdns, London SW1W OAU, T08705-143219, T08705-808080, www.eurolines.co.uk.
Slattery's, 162 Kentish Town Rd, London NW5 2AG. T0800-515900/020-74851438, ireland@slatterys.com.
Ulster Bus Enquiry Service, Europa Buscentre, Belfast, BT12 5AH, T028-9033 7002.

Touching down

Airport information

The main airports at Dublin, Shannon, Cork and Belfast all have money exchange facilities, car hire desks, taxis and public transport to and from the city. For detailed airport information for Dublin see page 60, for Shannon page 344, for Belfast page 498 and for Cork page 249. For information on the smaller regional airports at Derry, Galway and Waterford see pages 483, 368 and 208 respectively.

Tourist information

Tourist offices

The airports at Dublin, Shannon and Belfast all have tourist information offices which include an accommodation booking service. Local tourist information offices are found in cities and towns all across Ireland and, while they are nearly always staffed by helpful and considerate people, some are better organized and more orientated to the independent traveller than others. In the Republic, most tourist offices are run by the national tourist organisation, called **Fáilte Ireland**, though you will also come across some that have been set up and funded on a local basis, and this includes **Dublin Tourism** as well as village-based offices. Non-Fáilte Ireland offices will not usually arrange to book accommodation for you outside of their local area. The **Northern Ireland Tourist Board (NITB)** runs all the tourist offices in Northern Ireland; you will see the brown signs pointing to them in town centres.

Normal hours for most tourist offices are 0900-1700 Monday-Friday, 0900-1300 on Saturday. In larger towns and major tourist areas, during high season, the opening hours are often extended and they may open all day Saturday and Sunday. But also be prepared to find a tourist office closed on a Saturday, Sunday or a public holiday anywhere and at any time of the year. Outside of the summer months, opening hours can seem idiosyncratic.

Maps and guides → *For guidebooks about Ireland see page 625*

There is no shortage of good quality maps of Ireland. For a single, large-scale road map of the whole country try the *No 405 Michelin* 1:400,000, the *AA 1:350,000* map or the series of Leisure/Culture/Tourist/Touring published by Ireland's **Ordnance Survey**, www.irishmaps.ie. For driving, they also publish a useful *Complete Road Atlas of Ireland* that has all you need. For more detail of a large area your best bet are the four maps that make up the *Ordnance Survey Holiday Maps* series (North, West, East and South), at a scale of 1:250,000. For more detail of a particular area, and essential for walking, it is impossible to beat the *Ordnance Survey Discovery Series* at a scale of 1:50,000 (2.5 in to 1 mile/2 cm to 1 km). **Stanfords,** 12-14 Long Acre, London WC2, T020-7836 1321, can supply all these maps by mail. In the USA, **Rand McNally,** T1-800-3330136, can do the same.

Concessionary cards

A **Heritage Card,** purchased in the Republic for €20, gives unlimited free admission to all the parks, monuments, gardens, inland waterways and cultural institutions under the management of the Office of Public Works (OPW), T01-6472461, www.heritageireland.ie, the national heritage department of the Irish government. The card can be bought at the first site you visit or before your visit. OPW sites are indicated as such in this guide.

In Northern Ireland the **National Trust,** www.nationaltrust.org.uk, is a similar kind

Touching down

Business hours Normal business hours are 0900- 1700, Mon-Fri; shops open 0900-1730 or 1800, Mon-Sat; the large stores in Dublin stay open late on Thu and Fri. In small towns, shops and even businesses may close for an hour over lunchtime and for the whole of one afternoon each week. In popular tourist towns like Killarney shops usually stay open until 2100 in the high season.
Directory enquiries T11811 in the Republic, T118500 in Northern Ireland.
Electricity 230V AC in the Republic and 240V AC in Northern Ireland. Plugs are the three-pin flat sort, and two-pin round wall sockets are also found. British electrical appliances will work everywhere, North American ones will require a transformer and a plug adaptor, and Australian and New Zealand appliances just a plug adaptor.
Emergency services T999 or T112 in the Republic of Ireland; T999 in Northern Ireland.
IDD codes The international direct dialing code (IDD) code for the Republic is 353 and for Northern Ireland is 44.
Official time Ireland is on Greenwich Mean Time (GMT). However, daylight saving time changes mean that clocks are advanced by one hour between mid-March and the end of October.
Weights and measures Confusion reigns because metrication has been adopted but not enforced. Distances are measured in both miles and kilometres; drinks in pubs come in pints, in shops they come in litres; food is weighed and sold in both pounds and kilograms, petrol comes in litres. In this book we have used metric.

of organization but their card costs £28, or £13 if you are under 25. It covers the whole of Britain and Northern Ireland, and does not represent value for money if you are only visiting Northern Ireland.

Local customs and laws

Conduct

By and large the Republic is a laid-back place with a healthy disregard for authority and nit-picking rules. Social customs and etiquette are much the same as the average European, North American or Australasian visitor would expect, although attitudes to gay life need to be taken into account. A dress code in a restaurant is rare indeed and even in the most expensive establishments smart but casual attire is generally acceptable. Acute class divisions certainly exist in Ireland, and in Dublin, Belfast and certain other cities they are very obvious, but in the Republic it can often be more difficult to demarcate social class in terms of behaviour, dress or language than it is in Britain. Northern Ireland is socially very conservative. Racist attitudes, especially as regards black travellers, are common across Ireland as a whole, and the best that can be said is that more often than not it is rooted in plain ignorance rather than deliberate malice. The recent arrival of refugees and migrant workers from eastern Europe has exposed a very ugly strain of virulent racism behind the very discreet charm of the Irish bourgeoisie.

Prohibitions

There is nothing in Ireland that is unusually illegal, with the notable exception of a ban on smoking in places where people are employed – including all pubs and restaurants. Travellers caught importing illegal drugs will be prosecuted according to the law, up to and including imprisonment, but punishments do reflect the nature of the drug in question, see www.oasis.gov.ie. In the Republic, possession of cannabis for personal use carries a fine of €381; for other drugs €1270 or 12 months in jail before a District Court and an unlimited fine and/or prison up to seven years if tried before a judge and jury, and the *garda* (police) can detain anyone for up to seven days without charge on suspicion of a drug offence. The legal age for drinking alcohol is 18, and in city pubs customers may be asked to prove their age. There are strict laws regarding driving while under the influence of alcohol and the traditional tolerance towards drink and driving in rural areas in the Republic is fast disappearing.

Religion

In theory the Republic is overwhelmingly Roman Catholic, but times are changing and in the cities church attendance is not as high as one might expect. In rural areas going to church is a social obligation for the majority of people and should not be mistaken for devotional piety, although that exists in large doses as well. In Northern Ireland religious affiliation is all too often a marker for political and social differences, and visitors are well advised to tread carefully in this area.

Tipping

When it comes to tipping there are no hard and fast rules. Upmarket hotels and restaurants will usually have a service charge (10-15%) added to the bill, but if paying by plastic a space will still be left on the receipt for a tip. As a general rule, a tip of 10% is the norm if you do decide to tip. In bars and even pub restaurants, tipping is not generally necessary or even expected. For porters in hotels or elsewhere think in terms of a 75¢/50p tip for each piece of large luggage; taxi drivers are usually tipped 10% of the fare.

Safety

The general level of personal safety in Ireland is high for both male and female travellers, especially in the countryside, but do not be lulled into a false sense of security. Crimes, minor and major, do occur and common sense should always govern your behaviour. Parts of Dublin are prone to street crime and this includes the city centre. Northern Ireland is remarkably safe for the traveller, both in the cities and in the countryside, and there is no more need to take precautions about personal safety, or where to park your car, than you would anywhere else in Europe. As always, exercise your common sense. Women travellers tend to find Ireland an easier place in which to travel around, alone or in company, than other countries of Europe, and chauvinism is relatively easy to deal with. It is not uncommon to see women hitchhiking alone, but they usually live locally and expect a ride from another local.

Northern Ireland has some of the lowest crime statistics to be found anywhere in Europe and, generally speaking, Belfast is a far safer city for the visitor than Dublin.

If you are a victim of crime in the Republic, you can contact Tourist Victim Support, Garda HQ, Harcourt Sq, Dublin, T01-478 5295, www.touristvictimsupport.ie.

Getting around

Air

Aer Arann, T0818-210210 (Ireland), T0800-5872324 (Britain), www.aerarann.com, flies from Dublin to Cork, Donegal, Galway, Kerry, Knock, and Sligo; from Cork to Belfast; and from Galway city to all three of the Aran Islands.

Rail

Fares and timetables

Trains in the Republic are run by **Iarnród Éireann** (Irish Rail), Travel Centres, 35 Lower Abbey St, Dublin, T1850-366222, www.irishrail.ie, and while there are a number of routes the system is by no means comprehensive and is very much based around routes in and out of Dublin. Many parts of the west and the north are without trains. Sample single fares (and return fares are not much more) from Dublin are €33 to Belfast, €50 to Cork, €52 to Killarney. In the North, T028-9066 6630, www.translink.co.uk, free booklets contain train and bus information for different areas, and are available from stations.

Discounts and passes

Students (see page 28) can obtain discounts and non-students should consider the various train, and train and bus, passes available. A €115.50 **Explorer Rail Pass** allows five days travel out of 15 consecutive days in the Republic and includes DART (page 61); the **Irish Rover** is similar but includes Northern Ireland trains and costs £90. Combined bus and rail passes for the Republic and/or Northern Ireland are also available.

Overseas passes

Rail passes that cover Europe are worth considering if Ireland is part of your itinerary and you are not resident in Europe. A **Eurail Youthpass**, for example, for travellers under 26 costs US$414 for 21 consecutive days. See **Eurail**, www.eurail.com, for details.

Road

Bicycle

The weather notwithstanding, cycling around Ireland is definitely one of the most enjoyable ways to explore Ireland. Cycling allows you to experience the countryside in a way that cannot be compared to seeing it through the window of a car. Country roads, compared to Britain certainly, are less crowded with traffic and the experience can easily become the highlight of any visit to Ireland. An alternative to relying on a bicycle for the whole duration of your trip is to hire one for a few days, or for a week or more; see page 48 for more information.

Bus

Fares and timetables Bus Éireann, T01-8366111/8302222, www.buseireann.ie, operates most of the buses in the Republic, but in some areas, like Donegal, private bus companies are an important supplement and no more expensive. **Ulsterbus** T028-9066 6630, www.translink.co.uk, runs the buses in the North. Bus Éireann offers various deals that improve on the cost of standard single/return tickets: day return tickets (costing little more than single fares), monthly midweek returns (Tuesday-Thursday), student discounts, and family tickets covering a monthly return. A single ticket from Dublin to Cork is €15, an open monthly return is €24, and a student single fare is €10.50. Similar tickets for other journeys from Dublin are €15/€23.50/€11.50 for Ballina, €13/€16/€12 for Galway, €19/€26/€15.50 for Belfast, Bicycles are €10 single, whatever the journey, but space is limited and cannot be taken for granted.

If you are going to be using buses a lot it might be worth buying the inexpensive Bus Éireann national timetable (fare information is not provided). Missing a bus, and they do run on time, can mean a long wait or even an overnight stay. Ulsterbus provides a free booklet detailing the express services between the main towns as well as booklets covering local area bus and train timetables. In the Republic few towns have a bus station as such but the bus stop is normally on the main street and timetables are often shown. Large towns in the North have bus stations near the centre of town.

Discounts and passes Students with an ISIC card receive reductions on bus fares in the Republic and the North. See the bus websites for details. A **Rambler Pass** covers 3/8/15 days' travel out of 8/15/30 consecutive days in the Republic for €68/€152/€226 respectively. The equivalent **Irish Rover** pass covers buses in the Republic and Northern Ireland and costs £44/97/145. Combined bus and rail passes for the Republic and/or Northern Ireland are also available.

Car

Drivers should carry a current licence and non-UK drivers will also need an international driving permit which is readily purchasable through motoring organizations in your country. If you are bringing your own car, bring the registration/ownership documents and check with your insurance company that your policy covers driving in Ireland. If you belong to a motoring organization check with them before you depart because there is usually a reciprocal agreement with the Irish AA in relation to their 24-hour emergency breakdown service.

Driving in the Republic Driving is on the **left** and the national speed limit on main roads is 60 mph/100 kmph, 70 mph/110 kmph on motorways. In towns and built-up areas the normal speed limit is 30 mph/50 kmph but on approach roads to urban areas the speed limit is usually 40 mph/60 kmph. Front and rear seat occupants must wear seat belts, and motorcyclists and their passengers must wear helmets. Unleaded petrol is around 98¢ per litre. Disc parking, purchasable in newsagents and displayed inside your car, applies to an increasing number of towns.

Driving in Northern Ireland Driving is on the left and the national speed limit on motorways/freeways is 70 mph/110 kmph and 60 mph/100 kmph on other main roads. In towns and built-up areas the normal speed limit is 30-40 mph/50-60 kmph, but be guided by posted signs. Front and rear seat occupants must wear seat belts and motorcyclists and their passengers must wear helmets. Unleaded petrol is around 85p per litre.

Car hire Major car hire companies have desks at airports, ferry terminals and cities across Ireland. The best rates are to be found on the internet and/or when booking your flight to Ireland. Tourist areas have their own local car hire companies and these can often be a little cheaper. Quoted rates usually exclude a collision damage waiver and if this is not included the hirer will be responsible for the first €1000 of damage to the car. Car hire to people under the age of 23 is unlikely; over 21 is sometimes possible. Car hire in Northern Ireland follows more or less the same rules as in the Republic but it will cost less. If you are planning to drive between the North and the Republic, starting in either direction, check that this is allowed for under the contract.

Contacts

Argus, T1800-973490 (Britain), www.argusrentals.com.
Avis, www.avis.com. Desk at main airports.
Budget, www.budgetrentcar.com. Desk at main airports.
Dooley Car Rentals, Knocklong Cross, Knocklong, County Limerick, Ireland, T062-53103, wwwdan-dooley.ie. Dan Dooley are a reliable, friendly family business that give you a real Irish welcome. Rates are very competitive and they are the only company operating in Northern Ireland and the Republic that do not charge a cross border driving surcharge nor do they charge road fund tax, saving you an estimated £25 per booking.

Europcar (ISA), T1800-667788 (Republic), T0800-667788 (Northern Ireland or Britain), www.europcar.ie.

Hertz, www.hertz.com. Desk at main airports.
Thrifty, T0800-7830405 (Britain), www.thrifty.ie. Desk at main airports.

Hitchhiking There is always a risk in hitchhiking, whatever your gender, so it can never be recommended as a safe way to travel; this applies to Ireland as it does to anywhere else. Having said that, hitching in the Republic is not uncommon, and you will often see single people and couples outside towns and cities patiently waiting for an obliging driver. It will often take some time, but sooner or later someone usually stops and it can often lead to interesting and informative conversations. Hitching in Northern Ireland is a lot less common, especially for single males, but getting lifts from the Republic into Northern Ireland does not present any special problems.

Sea

Cruising

If holidaying in inland Ireland, cruising the rivers and canals is an option. **Carrick Craft**, T028-3834 4993 (Northern Ireland), www.cruise-ireland.com, specializes in cruising the Shannon and Erne waterways. See also **www.waterwayholidays.com** and **www.waterwaysireland.org** and the box on page 572.

Sleeping

→ *See inside front cover for hotel price codes.*

The choice of accommodation ranges from top-drawer luxury hotels and historic country houses to dormitory beds in hostels or free camping in a farmer's field. In between there are medium-range hotels, one-star hotels, guest houses, farm houses, self-catering accommodation, the ubiquitous bed and breakfast (B&B) in a private home and camping and caravan parks. Prices quoted in this book refer to the price of a double room in high season, so you will often pay less at other times of the year. Single person supplements are common and sometimes exorbitant. Rates for families with children vary depending on the number of children and their ages and the rate is often negotiable. Most rooms in hotels and guest houses, and in a growing number of B&Bs, have tea- and coffee-making facilities. In this guide, email addresses are not given when they can be accessed through the website address provided.

Breakfast is usually included in the price of accommodation, but most hostels charge extra for this. Travellers who are vegetarian, or just diet conscious, often have good reason to feel aggrieved about the inadequate alternatives to the hearty fry-up that is served as the standard breakfast in most establishments. A recent development has been the growth of small hotels charging a flat rate for a room, usually up to three adults or two adults and two children, and not including breakfast. They can be very good value if a cholesterol-laden breakfast is not something you want to feel obliged to eat. Guest houses (but not B&Bs), especially in tourist towns like Kinsale and Dingle, often have interesting breakfast menus that include delights like scrambled egg and smoked salmon.

Always confirm the price of your accommodation when making a reservation and, whenever possible, always try to make a reservation. In Dublin this is essential whatever the time of year, and in popular tourist areas the summer months and holiday weekends can sometimes see most of the reasonably priced accommodation fully booked. This is particularly true at the time of popular festivals (see pages 46 and 117). A surprising amount of accommodation choices, including hotels, close down for varying periods over Christmas.

Online and telephone booking

Gulliverireland, www.goireland.com, is a computer database that includes a booking system for a wide range of accommodation (hotels, B&Bs, farmhouses, guest houses, hostels, self-catering) across the whole of Ireland through call-free numbers. The cost of a booking is €5, and there is also a non-refundable deposit, 10% of the accommodation cost, taken on your credit card; with self-catering accommodation it is also possible to pay by cheque. Telephone reservations can be made Mon-Fri, 0800-2000, and Sat and Sun, 0800-1900. Freephone + 800-6686 6866 (+ denotes the international access code in the country where the call is made), thus within Europe (including Northern Ireland) call T00800-6686 6866, and within the USA T011-800-6686 6866. Within Ireland the final 66 is not used, so call T1800-668668.

Hotels and guesthouses across the whole of Ireland can also be booked online at **www.irelandhotels.com**. Accommodation in Northern Ireland can also be booked online at **www.discovernorthernireland.com**.

Country houses, castles and heritage houses

There is a tempting choice to choose from across Ireland, nearly all of which are in the Republic. Many of the country houses belong to the **Blue Book Group**, T01-6769914, www.irelandsbluebook.com, while **The Hidden Ireland**, T01-6627166, www.hiddenireland.com, is an interesting collection of buildings of character and architectural interest offering accommodation and sometimes meals. Both groups have illustrated brochures, but bear in mind that places pay to be part of the group and their inclusion does not guarantee quality of accommodation.

Hotels and guest houses

Hotels are graded from five-star to one-star, and for €4.45 Fáilte Ireland supplies the **Irish Hotels Federation**'s *Be Our Guest* illustrated guide (T01-4974613, www.irelandhotels.com) to many (but not all) of the hotels and guest houses in the Republic and Northern Ireland registered with them.

Many traditional hotels have touches of character that are sadly missing in a new breed of hotels that are popping up with alarming frequency across Ireland. Often built by business consortiums as a tax avoidance strategy, the latter invariably have a leisure centre and their rooms are like the one Gloria Graham looked into in *The Big Sleep*: "Hey, I like this, early nothing."

Guest houses can provide better value than many hotels because they are invariably family-run, and can often offer a more satisfying degree of pampering. The higher-grade ones will have direct dial telephones in the rooms, a private car park, a lounge and sometimes a bar, and often a more interesting choice for breakfast than many hotels and most B&Bs.

Depending on supply and demand, room rates can be more negotiable than many people realize, and if you can think of a reason for asking for a discount – more than one night's stay, only one night's stay, booking a dinner, commercial traveller's rate, off-season rate, weekend rate, mid-week rate – it is often worth negotiating. You can also find discounted hotel rates through the airline and ferry websites.

B&Bs

If you stay in bed and breakfast places more than just occasionally you will soon discover what a surprising variety of people, decors, gewgaws, and styles of welcome and service lie behind those innocuous B&B boards that pop up everywhere outside farms, houses and bungalows. The most typical is an owner-occupied bungalow with two or three rooms set aside for guests, which are increasingly likely to have their own toilet and shower room. Prices average between €25 and €35 per person sharing, and the less expensive ones are likely to have shared bathroom facilities. Similar prices in sterling apply to the North.

Top 10 hostels

Dublin International Hostel, 61 Mountjoy St, Dublin, T01-8301766 (page 101)
Glendalough Hostel, Glendalough, County Wicklow, T01-8301766 (page 156)
Cashel Holiday Hostel, Cashel, County Tipperary, T052-62330 (page 226)
Aghadoe House, Killarney, County Kerry, T064-31240 (page 299)
The Climbers' Inn, Glencar, on the Kerry Way, T066-9760101 (page 317)
Valentia Island Hostel, Valentia Island, County Kerry, T066-9476141 (page 316)
Ballintaggart Hostel, Dingle, T066-9151454 (page 336)
Old Monastery Hostel, Letterfrack, County Galway, T095-41132, (page 398)
Wild Haven Hostel, Achill Island, County Mayo, T45392 (page 425)
Whitepark Bay Hostel, Ballycastle, County Antrim, T2073 1745 (page 532)

The best B&Bs are professionally run, clean, friendly and helpful. Evening meals are sometimes available, though they tend to be expensive considering the lack of choice and the milieu, while afternoon tea can be a delight if fresh breads and scones are served. The least satisfying B&Bs tend to be those where you are made too conscious of being in someone's home and where it is taken for granted that you want a fried breakfast. B&Bs can be booked through tourist offices on payment of a 10% booking deposit (which is what the tourist board charges the establishment) plus a small fee for a local booking. At the height of the season in popular tourist areas like Dublin, Killarney, Galway, Belfast or Derry this can be well worth the money, because a number of calls may have to be made. There is a **Town and Country Homes,** www.townandcountry.ie, illustrated guide to B&Bs across all of Ireland, sold in tourist offices, which at least allows you to see which ones are modern bungalows and which traditional buildings. There is also an A4-sized, non-illustrated **Accommodation Guide,** T071-9852760, www.taaireland.com, that lists Fáilte Ireland-approved B&Bs, farm houses, historic houses and pubs with accommodation in the Republic. The NITB dispenses free illustrated accommodation guides.

A number of B&Bs choose not to register with Fáilte Ireland and opt instead for the **Family Homes of Ireland** group, Fough West Park, Oughterard, County Galway, T091-552000, www.familyhomes.ie. They tend to be a little less expensive and the group's illustrated booklet (€3.75) is available from their office.

Hostels

Hostels in Ireland fall into three basic categories: independent ones but belonging to a hostel organization, more traditional ones that belong to **Hostelling International (HI)**, (Hostelling International-American Youth Hostels, 733 15th St NW, Suite 840, Washington DC 20005, T1202-7836161, www.hiayh.org; Hostelling International Northern Ireland, 22 Donegall Rd, Belfast BT12 5JN, T028-9031 5435, www.hini.org.uk) though they are still called Youth Hostels despite the fact that people of any age can use them, and truly independent ones that don't belong to any organisation. The traditional hostels have a membership scheme; the independent ones do not. Hostels can represent the best value for money when it comes to accommodation in Ireland. They also provide great opportunities to meet fellow travellers, chat and exchange information in an informal atmosphere.

Independent hostels There are two hostel associations in Ireland which do not require membership. The largest is the **Independent Holiday Hostels (IHH),** 57 Lower

 Gardiner St, Dublin 1, T01-8364700, www.hostels-ireland.com, approved by Fáilte Ireland, and a list and map giving full details of all their 150 member hostels is available from their Dublin office. They operate a book ahead system, and for a nominal fee a bed at the next hostel will be guaranteed. The other association is the **Independent Hostel Owners (IHO)**, Dooey Hostel, Glencolmcille, Co Donegal, T074-9730130, www.hostellingireland.com, the original independent hostel group and still outside Fáilte Ireland's domain, and a map and list of their 130 member hostels is available from their Donegal office. Rooms in IHO hostels can be booked ahead by email through their website.

The overnight fee for a bed, outside Dublin, in high season is around €13 and this gives you a bed in a dormitory, varying in size from two beds to well over a dozen, and use of the hostel's facilities which at their most basic include an equipped kitchen, a common room, usually with a television, hot showers (a very few hostels make a small charge for a shower), and telephone. Some hostels will provide free pick-up from the nearest town or village, some include a free continental breakfast and provide evening meals at reasonable prices and some will have camping space with use of all or some hostel facilities. Better equipped ones have laundry facilities, bicycles for hire and other amenities. It helps to travel with a sleeping sheet or sleeping bag, though some hostels include fresh linen and all will rent you sheets; duvets or blankets are freely provided. There is usually no curfew at independent hostels and you can stay indoors all day if you wish.

Most hostels will also have private rooms, usually for two people (though singles are available in some) or for a family with young children. Outside of Dublin, the price averages about €20 per person and this represents a very viable alternative to B&Bs if you are going to make use of the kitchen and prepare your own meals. At peak times, when some hostels get overcrowded, a private room also minimizes the problem of being kept awake by inebriated hostellers returning early in the morning.

The Backpackers' Press, 2 Rockview Cottages, Matlock Bath, Derbyshire, DE4 3PG, England, T/F01629-580427, publishes annually *The Independent Hostel Guide: Britain & Europe*. This includes descriptions of some 40 hostels in Ireland, nearly all IHH and IHO but some completely independent ones as well, and is available from their England address. Better value is *Ireland – All the Hostels*, Flat 2A, 72 Woodstock Rd, Moseley, Birmingham, B13 9BN, England, which carries details of all the hostels in Ireland, including the totally independent ones, plus short reviews of 200 of what are considered the best hostels.

Traditional hostels Traditional hostels, now under the general umbrella of Hostelling International, are, in the Republic, part of **An Óige**, 61 Mountjoy St, Dublin 7, T01-8304555, www.irelandyha.org, the official Irish Youth Hostel Association, and the equivalent organization in the North is the **Youth Hostel Association of Northern Ireland (YHANI)**, 22 Donegall Rd, Belfast, BT12 5JN, T028-9032 4733. You can become a member for €20 at any of their hostels in Ireland or join through a Youth Hostel/Hostelling International in your own country. Anyone can still usually book a bed for the night, and the rates are usually a pound or more cheaper than the independent hostels. Some hostels have private rooms and some have outstanding locations and/or fine and spacious buildings. A free book-ahead service is available at the hostels, and through their websites, and many provide breakfast, packed lunches and evening meal.

Camping and caravanning

Camping for free is a lot easier in Ireland than many other countries, but you should always take the trouble of finding the landowner and asking permission. If you camp in a field near the farmhouse you should be able to access an outdoor water supply. Some farmers, in touristy areas mainly, may charge a small amount for camping in their fields.

Where to go for a drink – not Dublin!

Unbelievable but true: Dublin is short of pubs. The capital has over 30% of the population but only 10% of its pubs, an anomaly due to an antiquated system that makes it well nigh impossible to open new licensed premises. A 1902 law, strenuously upheld by the Catholic Church and the Licensed Vintners' Association, put the brake on new licenses being created other than under exceptional circumstances. Unfortunately, exceptional circumstances do not include population shifts and the result is that an area like Tallaght in Dublin has the record for the fewest number of pubs per head in the whole of Ireland. In the 1960s, when Tallaght was a village of 400 souls, there were eight pubs; it is now a working class suburb of around 100,000 people and the number of pubs is 10. A tragedy for people living there, but visitors can leave the capital and head for just about anywhere else – where the situation is just a little different...

A number of independent hostels have an area set aside for camping, and usually the charge includes the use of hostel facilities.

Organized camping and caravan parks vary a lot in the level of services they provide, and this is reflected in the rates they charge. Most places will also have different rates for campers on foot, on a motorcycle, in a car or a motor home. **The Irish Caravan and Camping Council** publish an annual illustrated guide, *Caravan & Camping Ireland*, available from PO Box 4443, Dublin 2, F098-28237, www.camping-ireland.ie. This does not include all the camping sites in Ireland, and in tourist areas there are quite a few independent operators. For Northern Ireland, NITB dispenses a free guide to caravan and camping sites.

You won't find the Irish using them, but horse-drawn Romany-style caravans can be hired through tour operators like **Slattery's** or **Enjoy Ireland Holidays** (see page 22).

Eating

Food

Restaurants

→ *See inside front cover for restaurant price codes.*

The much-heralded wave of new Irish cooking does indeed have a lot going for it, and anyone returning to Ireland after an absence of a few years will be in for some gastronomic treats. The best restaurants use local produce to serve up an array of traditional and modern dishes, and when it is done well the results are truly terrific and often good value for money. Sometimes a restaurant tries too hard to be international: Parmesan shavings and goat's cheese on a menu does not guarantee an interesting meal and hotel restaurants sometimes use rich sauces to disguise overcooked food.

Seafood is often the highlight of menus in coastal counties, but do not assume that because a restaurant is near the sea its fish is absolutely fresh. It is not unknown for fresh fish to be landed, hauled up to Dublin and sold through a national wholesaler before being delivered to a restaurant close to where it was first landed. It is always worth asking how fresh the fish is, and more often than not you will receive an honest answer. Locally sourced beef and lamb is another speciality to look out for, and a steak or leg of lamb from Kerry should not disappoint. Vegetarian restaurants

Top 10 pubs

O'Connor's Pub, Fisherstreet, Doolin, County Clare (page 353)
Mansworth's, Midleton St, Cobh, County Cork (page 257)
The Smuggler's Creek, Rossnowlagh, County Donegal (page 458)
Fisherman's Bar, Valentia Island, County Kerry (page 318)
Crown Liquor Saloon, Great Victoria St, Belfast (page 506)
M Hughes, Chancery St, Dublin (page 114)
Henry Downes, 10 Thomas St, Waterford, County Waterford (page 218)
House of McDonnell, Ballycastle, County Antrim (page 533)
Neachtain's, Cross St, Galway (page 376)
Fitzpatricks, Kilcrohane, County Cork (page 275)

Pub hours
In the Republic, pubs are open Mon-Wed 1030-2330; Thu, Fri and Sat 1030-2430; Sun 1030-2300.
In Northern Ireland, pubs are open Mon-Sat 1130-2300; Sun 1230-2200.

are virtually non-existent outside of Dublin and Cork and if you don't eat fish it can be difficult finding a decent evening meal. Most menus include a 'vegetarian dish of the day', but if it turns out to be lasagne then forget it, for in our experience that is one sure sign of a restaurateur's indifference to non-meat cuisine.

County Cork is currently enjoying a well-deserved reputation for some of the best food in the country, and other counties in the west are beginning to catch up. Northern Ireland, though with a growing number of exceptions, can prove too predictable as regards eating out though this is certainly not true of Belfast. Many Irish cities have some excellent restaurants, especially Dublin, but the capital city also has its fair share of trendy and expensive dross. For a combination of value for money and a sense of occasion, excellent meals can be enjoyed in most of the country houses dotted around the country, and most of them welcome non-residents (and vegetarians) as long as a reservation is made in advance.

Restaurants offering Chinese food, and to a lesser extent Indian, are fairly common in the cities and a number of towns but, apart from a few noted places in Dublin, Kilkenny and Belfast, the food is fairly hideous; most offer a take-away service that is slightly better value. Italian restaurants offer good value, and many towns will have places serving pasta and pizza dishes, while the cities have Italian restaurants in their own right. Across the country as a whole, many restaurants close on Mondays.

Pub food

The quality of the food varies enormously, but pubs are nearly always your best bet when looking for an informal and affordable meal at lunch or dinner time. Many pubs serve food from 1200 to 2100 and some will have separate dining areas. The standard price for a pub lunch is around €8 or £7 in the North, and while there is a tendency to rely on the meat/fish with potatoes/chips and vegetables, pubs in tourist areas can be relied on to offer alternatives. Home-made soups may not be filling enough for everyone, but they are often tasty, and salads and open seafood sandwiches are worth considering. Unless you ask for brown, expect tasteless white bread.

Bars in hotels offer comfortable seating most of the time, and competition from pubs ensures that their prices are similar. There is no obligation to consume alcohol as other drinks are also available. Pub food in the North is generally disappointing: the idea of a meal without meat seems quite foreign, and overcooked vegetables and unimaginative presentations are the norm. Champ, potatoes mashed with spring onions, is a tasty speciality in the North, and there are some superb soda breads.

For peat's sake have a whiskey

There are many differences in the distilling process that account for the distinct taste of Irish whiskey as opposed to Scotch whisky (but they don't account for the spelling), and the peaty smokiness of Scotch is often contrasted with the smoothness of Irish. This seems odd to some tipplers who appreciate the spiky aromatics found in some Irish whiskeys and, besides, there is an Irish single malt called Connemara that is sweeter and more peaty than most Scotches. Millar's and Inishowen are blended whiskeys distilled by the same company, and they also turn out an unpeated single malt called Tyrconnell. Bushmills whiskey is distilled in County Antrim (see page 527), while Jameson comes from Midleton near Cork (see page 253). Near-relations of Jameson's are Power's and Paddy, and Tullamore Dew.

Picnic food

When the weather is fine, a picnic lunch is a satisfying and economical way to enjoy a meal, and every town has a supermarket or two, the larger ones with a delicatessen section, and often a good bakery where fresh delicious breads and scones are usually available. Local cheeses are always worth seeking out, and such is their popularity that you will often find them far from their origins. If a town has a river there will usually be bankside benches or somewhere suitable to lay out your food and Northern Ireland is blessed with plenty of designated picnic sites and town parks.

Drink

Ireland is not in the top 10 list of alcohol-consuming countries of the world, but it ranks second, after the Czech Republic, in the list of beer-drinking countries, at 250 pints/142 litres per year per head of the population. (The UK ranks in seventh position at 180 pints/102 litres and the USA is ranked 13th.) **Guinness** is the world-renowned Irish drink, and it is no idle boast to say that the best pint of Guinness is served in Ireland (Dublin to be exact) and if you have tasted draught Guinness in an ordinary pub in Britain this will soon become apparent. Guinness with oysters is a classic lunchtime dish, and on some menus you will see the famous black stuff featured in dishes. There are alternative stouts, and both **Beamish** and **Murphy's** should be sampled; they are not only cheaper, but fine drinks in their own right. A variety of lagers, draught and bottled, is also readily available in all pubs. A pint of beer costs around €4 and unless you ask for "a glass (ie a half pint) of Guinness", or whatever your drink is, a pint will automatically be served.

Irish **whiskeys** taste quite different to Scotch and there are quite a few you can try in order to be convinced. A hot whiskey comes with cloves and lemon and is a heart-warming drink on a cold day. Any spirit served in a pub is a substantially larger measure than its counterpart in Britain or North America.

Wine in pubs is most likely to come in the form of a ¼-bottle and if whole bottles are available there is often not much of a choice. Expect to pay about €12 or £8 for the very cheapest, and usually not very palatable, wine and from around €18 or £12 and upwards for a half-decent bottle.

Non-alcoholic drinks come in the form of a limited choice of bottled beers and outrageously priced soft and fizzy drinks. A cup or pot of tea is available in nearly all pubs and coffee is served with milk.

Major festivals and events

Strokestown Poetry Festival
late Apr/early May,
www.strokestownpoetryprize.com
Listowel Writers' Week
early Jun, www.writersweek.ie
Kilkenny's Cat Laughs Festival
early Jun, www.thecatlaughs.com
Galway Arts Festival
early-mid Jul,
www.galwayartsfestival.com
Galway Races
late Jul, early Sep, early Oct,
www.iol.ie/galway-races
Kilkenny Arts Festival
early Aug, www.kilkennyarts.ie
Puck Fair (Killorglin)
10-12 Aug, www.puckfair.ie
Galway Oyster Festival
late Sep, T091-527282,
www.galwayosyerfest.com
Dublin Theatre Festival
late Sep/early Oct,
www.dublintheatrefestival.com
Kinsale Festival of Fine Food
early Oct, www.kinsale.ie/gfest.htm
Cork Jazz Festival
25-8 Oct, www.corkjazzfestival.com
Wexford Opera Festival
late Oct-early Nov,
www.wexfordopera.com

Entertainment

Ireland is very much a pub-orientated country. There are pubs to suit all tastes, from a quiet drink in surroundings untouched since Edwardian times to theme bars and sports bars. In summer especially, **pubs** mean music and you needn't go a night without listening to someone singing or playing. Festivals are another flourishing activity in Ireland. There are **festivals** (see below) for every imaginable reason from all the sports, to walking, poetry, beauty, music, theatre, film, ploughing, coming home, going away, flowers, fish. Bantry even celebrates small sea creatures with a Mussel Fair.

The cities have good **theatres**, with a strong tradition of local dramatics as well as major theatre companies. Watching a local theatre group doing a Beckett or a John B Keane play can be worth a week of London's West End theatre. The theatres also play host to **music** and **comedy** events with Irish and British big names doing sell out tours.

Variations on the **Riverdance** theme abound in every tourist destination, or you can try out a medieval banquet at one of the castles around Limerick and Clare.

Sports too (see below) are fully catered for, whether it be hang-gliding in west Cork, surfing in Bundoran, deer hunting in Kerry, or golfing practically everywhere. Horse racing is an especially Irish sport and the meetings are generally a source of great fun.

Festivals and events

A *Calendar of Events*, a useful joint publication by Fáilte Ireland and the NITB, has an awesome list of festivals held up and down the country along with dates, contact names and telephone numbers. It also lists the Irish racing calendar. **www.festivals.ireland.ie** has a complete listing and search facility.

Annual public holidays

Republic of Ireland **New Year's Day** 1 January, **St Patrick's Day** 17 March, **Easter Monday** Monday following Easter Sunday, **May Holiday** first Monday in May, **June Holiday** first Monday in June, **August Holiday** first Monday in August, **October Holiday** last Monday in October, **Christmas Day** 25 December, **St. Stephen's Day** 26 December.

Good Friday is not officially a public holiday but is often treated as one. Pubs are closed on Good Friday and Christmas Day.

Northern Ireland **New Year's Day** 1 January, **St Patrick's Day** 17 March, **Good Friday** Friday before Easter Sunday, **Easter Monday** Monday following Easter Sunday, **May Holiday** first Monday in May, **May Holiday** last Monday in May, **July Holiday** 12 July, **August Holiday** last Monday in August, **Christmas Day** 25 December, St. **Stephen's Day** 26 December.

Shopping

What to buy

Visitors from Britain or North America will not find any spectacular shopping bargains in Ireland, but that does not mean there aren't lots of interesting and well priced purchases to be considered. As a general rule, the best buys are in the form of Irish-produced craft and art products like clothing, pottery and jewellery, and tourist areas all have shops filled with a wide choice of possibilities. In these shops you will find everything from tacky leprechaun-shaped telephones to expensive hand-knitted garments, and if you are travelling around Ireland they are a good place to start in order to get some idea of prices, because you will usually come across similar stock in another tourist town.

Aran sweaters, named after the County Galway islands where the women traditionally knitted them, are world famous. If you prefer something less chunky and white, there is a choice of shawls, skirts, blouses, and jackets for both sexes, in a variety of materials from thick tweeds to fine linens.

Irish **pottery** can be exquisitely beautiful, and is available to suit most budgets both in terms of quality and quantity. It mostly takes a practical form in the shape of plates, mugs, bowls, table lamps, clocks and candlesticks, but decorative items, like the Belleek pottery that comes as brooches and little pots of flowers, are also available, and some of the more expensive pottery is best reserved for display anyway. A similar mix of the practical and decorative is found in Irish **crystal**, of which the Waterford variety is famous around the world.

The craft shops that sell pottery often have small but enticing collections of Irish **jewellery** which are often fashioned around Celtic designs; look out also for the distinctive Claddagh rings that originated in Connaught and are composed of a crowned heart nestling between a pair of hands, or jewellery worked in the form of Ogham script. You can often have a necklace made with your own name on it in Ogham.

Irish **memorabilia** takes myriad forms if looking merely for souvenirs or small gifts, including penny whistles with sheet music, shillelagh walking sticks which are traditionally made of blackthorn or oak, carved pieces of Connemara marble and CDs of traditional music ranging from John McCormack to Shane McGowan.

Where to buy

Individual shops worth mentioning are found under the Shopping section for particular towns and cities. Many travellers to Ireland first arrive in Dublin, and if this is where you will also depart from then it makes sense for serious shoppers to conduct a reconnaissance trip around the major shops (see page 117), taking note of the merchandise and their prices, before returning to make purchases after having travelled elsewhere. Some of the best crafts and arts are found in small workshop premises outside of the capital.

For Aran sweaters and other garments, some of the best clothing stores are to be found in the counties of Galway and Donegal, and to a lesser extent Wicklow. The city of Limerick is associated with Irish lace products. Small and large pottery shops are dotted all around Ireland but for real quality head for Kerry, particularly the Dingle Peninsula, and West Cork. The village of Belleek in Fermanagh, easily reached from Donegal, is famous for its bone china. Wexford also has some good pottery shops and in and around Kilkenny there are noted workshops. Outside of Dublin, Kilkenny has a claim to be the single best shopping city in Ireland, and there are quality examples of most crafts and arts as well as jewellery and pottery workshops to the south of the city. For crystal there is the Waterford factory with its comprehensive display of items for sale, but in the city of Waterford itself it is possible to purchase less expensive crystal products and there are other areas in the country that produce their own modest examples of this craft.

Shopping on the internet

A growing number of Irish shopping outlets are adding an internet-based mail order service to their offerings. Among those worth a visit are www.iol.ie/gnorman-photography (a gallery with outlets in Dublin and Kinsale); www.houseofnames.ie (**House of Names**, with heraldic shops in Dublin and Killarney); www.celticrhythm.com (**Soundz of Muzic** in Kenmare); www.heritagecrystal com (**Heritage Crystal** in Waterford); www.moriartys.ie (tourist shop at the Gap of Dunloe in Kerry); and www.kilkennydesign.com (**Kilkenny Design Centre** in Kilkenny).

Sport and activities

Culture and crafts

At Colmcille in County Donegal there are Irish language courses for adults as well as cultural activity holidays with separate week-long programmes in bodhrán and flute playing, Donegal dances, marine painting, archaeology, Celtic pottery, tapestry weaving and some other pursuits. For a brochure write to **Oideas Gael**, Gleann Cholm Cille, Co Dhún na nGall, T074-9730248, oideasgael@iol.ie, oideas-gael.com.

There are various summer schools that can provide a focus for cultural, and especially language and literary interests. For details of the **James Joyce Summer School** that lasts a week and takes place in Dublin each July write to Helen Gallagher, Newman House, St Stephen's Green, Dublin, T01-7068480. For the **Yeats International Summer School** in Sligo each July, another annual week-long event, write to Sheila McCabe, Hawk's Well Theatre, Sligo, T071-42693, F071-42780.

Cycling

There are very few motorways in Ireland so nearly all the roads can be cycled. There is a vast network of quiet country roads and distances between towns and villages are never prohibitively long. Bicycles can brought to Ireland by air or boat, but check with your airline or ferry company for their policy and prices. Within Ireland, north or south, it is possible to carry bicycles on buses, and on nearly all train routes (but not the DART system around Dublin); prices vary, so always check.

Bicycles can be hired on a daily or weekly basis in many towns across Ireland: the daily rate varies around €13; weekly rates are around €55, plus a returnable deposit. The countless independent local operators are listed under the particular town throughout the book. But see also the **Federation of Irish Cyclists**, Dublin, T01-8551522, www.cyclingireland.org; and the **Northern Ireland Cycling Federation**, www.nicycling.homestead.com. **Shannon Development**, Shannon Town Centre, Shannon, County Clare, T061-361555, have useful free leaflets detailing cycling tours in the region. The Northern Ireland Tourist Board issues a very useful *Information Guide to Cycling* with maps for suggested routes, details of bike hire places and operators offering package holidays. Fáilte Ireland have a Cycling Ireland map highlighting the best cycling routes and giving basic details.

Organized cycling holidays are operated by a number of companies who include all or some services like bike hire, airport transfers, luggage storage and transport, booked accommodation, tours for groups or individuals, plus maps and route descriptions. For an idea of prices, **Irish Cycling Safaris** (see below) cost €685 per person per week, €305 for a weekend trip, and cover 7 nights hotel or guest house accommodation, bicycle rental, tour guide and luggage van. **Irish Cycle Hire** (see below) offer a 7-day Dingle Peninsula tour for €830 for two people, including bike, accommodation and packed lunches.

Contacts

Go Ireland in Britain and **Backroads** in the USA (see under Walking below).
Celtic Cycling (specializing in the southeast), Lorum Old Rectory, Bagenalstown, County Carlow, T0503-75282, www.celticcycling.com.
Celtic Trails, 28 Upper Fitzwilliam St, Dublin 2. T01-6619546, www.celtictrails.com.
Classic Adventures, in the USA, T1-800/7778090.
Irish Cycle Hire, T041-6853772, irch@iol.ie.
Irish Cycle Tours, www.irishcycletours.com.
Irish Cycling Safaris, Belfield House, UCD, Dublin 4, T01-2600749, www.cyclingsafaris.com.
Kingfisher Cycle Trail, Tourist Information Centre, Wellington Rd, Enniskillen, County Fermanagh, BT74 7EF, T028-6632 0121.
McCycle Tours, 2 Brookesborough Rd, Maguiresbridge, County Fermanagh, BT94 4LR, T028-6621749.
Raleigh in Ireland, T01-6261333, www.iol.ie/raleigh. Bikes can be reserved in advance €12.70 a day, €50.79 a week.
South East Cycle Tours (specializing in the southeast), 1 Mary St, Enniscorthy, County Wexford, T/F054-33255, seastcyc@iol.ie.
Wrightlines, The Old Mill, Ballydown, Banbridge, County Down, BT32 5JN, T028-4066 2126.

See also: www.irelandrentalbike.com.

Equestrian

The possibilities range from a small farm with horses to hire by the hour to top-notch riding establishments offering post-to-post trail riding, instruction in show jumping, dressage and polocrosse. Contact Fáilte Ireland and the Northern Ireland Tourist Board for literature and information. **Equestrian Holidays Ireland,** www.ehi.ie, issue a booklet with details of riding establishments in Ireland. Other contacts are **The Association of Irish Riding Establishments,** 11 Moore Park, Newbridge, Co Kildare, T045-431584; **The Association of Irish Riding Clubs,** 8 Main St, Bray, Co Wicklow, T01-2860196; **The Irish Pony Club,** Tinnascarty, Freshford, County Kilkenny, T056-82966, www.irishponyclub.ie. The southeast is especially resourceful in this area and a guide to *Equestrian Activity in Ireland's South East* is available from tourist offices in that region.

Fishing

Ireland's reputation as Europe's last unspoilt fishing location is built on its unpolluted waters, a plenitude of fish-bearing rivers, miles of coastline and hundreds of game fishing lakes. There are superb opportunities for game and coarse angling, as well as sea angling. In the **Republic**, salmon and trout fisheries are either privately owned or managed by the state or angling clubs and organizations. Permits are required, the cost of which varies from €7 to €65 per day depending on the location. A state national licence is also required for salmon and sea trout fishing: a 21-day licence costs around €13, a daily licence is €4. These are obtainable at local tackle shops, from the **Western Regional Fisheries Board,** The Weir Lodge, Earl's Island, Galway, T091-563118, or from one of the other regional

Walk this Way

To give some idea of the walking possibilities here are brief details of some of the best Ways.

Wicklow Way Ireland's first long-distance trail is 82 miles (132 km) in length and starts in south Dublin and finishes in Clonegal in the east of County Carlow. The entire Way would take at least 10 days but it is easy to choose a shorter section and variety of terrain is a feature of the Way; longest one-day stage is 14 miles (22 km). Map guides are available (see page 153) and Ordnance Survey Maps Nos 50, 56 and 62 cover the entire route.

Kerry Way Through and around the Iveragh Peninsula and infinitely more enjoyable than driving around the Ring of Kerry. Total length is 134 miles (214 km) and the longest stage is 15 miles (24 km). Some sections are more enjoyable than others (see page 312); map guides are available in Killarney or Kenmare and Ordnance Survey Maps Nos 78, 83, 84 and 85 show the route.

Beara Way Spectacular in places (see page 284) as it weaves its way around the Beara Peninsula in Kerry connecting Kenmare, Glengarriff and Castletownbere, with Dursey Island thrown in for good measure. Total distance is 120 miles (196 km); longest stage is 14 miles (23 km). Ordnance Survey Maps Nos 78, 84 and 85.

Dingle Way Another circular route, this time around the Dingle Peninsula, with the western end of the Way far more fulfilling than the east (see page 332). Total length 95 miles (153 km) and longest stage is 15 miles (24 km). Ordnance Survey Maps Nos 70 and 71.

Sheep's Head Way Starts and ends in Bantry in West Cork with some spectacular views of Bantry Bay and Dunmanus Bay along the way (see page 276). Total length is 55 miles (88 km) and longest stage is 10 miles (16 km). Ordnance Survey Maps Nos 85 and 88, and a local map and guide are available.

Burren Way Only 22 miles (35 km) but covering the jagged terrain of this unique landscape noted for its geological features, archaeological remains, special flora and the magnificent Cliffs of Moher. Longest stage is 12.5 miles (20 km) and Ordnance Survey Maps No 51 covers the route.

Western Way Starts at Oughterard in County Galway, and follows the shore of Lough Corrib and then

boards in Ballyshannon, T072-51435, Ballina, T096-22788, Limerick, T061-55171, Macroom, T026-41222, or Clonmel, T052-23624. Licences are not needed for brown trout, rainbow trout, coarse fishing or sea angling.

In **Northern Ireland** a rod licence is required. For the Foyle area this is obtainable from the **Foyle Fisheries Commission**, 8 Victoria Rd, Derry BT47 2AB, T01504-42100; for other regions from the **Fisheries Conservancy Board**, 1 Mahon Rd, Portadown, Craigavon, County Armagh, T01762-334666. The cost of a licence for outside the Foyle area is £4 for one day, £21.50 for the season. Wherever you fish, a permit is also required, costing £5 for one day or £15 for 8 days, obtainable from the **Department of Agriculture**, Dundonald Hse, Upper Newtownlands Rd, Belfast BT4 3SB, T028-9052 0100.

Fáilte Ireland publish a useful *Angling in Ireland* booklet with practical information about accommodation and charter-boat operators, and separate booklets on sea angling and coarse angling. The regional Fisheries Boards are also worth contacting for information and literature on their areas: **Western Regional Fisheries Board,** The Weir Lodge, Earl's Island, Galway, T091-563118, info@wrfb.ie. **The North-Western Regional** through mountain ranges and down into the narrow valley of Killary Harbour. This leg is 31 miles (50 km) in total. The second leg runs from Killary Harbour across County Mayo to the Ox Mountains near the Sligo border. Superb variety of terrains include the unique boglands of Mayo. Total length of this second leg is 110 miles (177 km) and Ordnance Survey Maps Nos 23, 24, 30, 37 and 38 are required to cover the whole route. Local map guides available.

Grand Canal Way Perfect for the beginner, being flat all the way as it follows the canal; the starting point is reached by bus from Dublin to Lucan or Milltown. Total distance is 71 miles (114 km) and the longest stage is 18 miles(29 km).

Royal Canal Way A walk along the towpath of the Royal Canal from Dublin for 48 miles (77 km), eventually linking up with the River Shannon at Clondra in County Longford. The longest stage is 15.5 miles (25.5 km) and Ordnance Survey Maps Nos 12, 13 and 16 are needed. Information and maps on this Way and the Grand Canal Way from *Waterways Ireland Visitors Centre*, Grand Canal Quay, Dublin 2, T01-6777510, www.waterways.org

Ballyhoura Way A 50-mile (80 km) walk between Limerick Junction, just north of Tipperary town, and St John's Bridge (nearest town is Kanturk in north Cork). The longest stage is 15 miles (24 km) and although parts of the Way are through forestry plantations this is compensated for by the route over Castle Philip and through the Ballyhoura Country Park. Ordnance Survey Maps Nos 65, 66, 73 and 74.

Lough Derg Way Lough Derg is one of the main lakes on the River Shannon, and the best part of the walk is along its eastern shores. Total distance is only 32 miles (52 km) and the longest stage is 11 miles (18 km). Contact *Shannon Development*, Shannon Town Centre, Shannon, County Clare, T061-361555, www.shannonregiontourism.ie, who also have information on other walks in the region.

Ulster Way The total length is around 560 miles (900 km), so choices have to be made. Sections following the north Antrim coast, the Glens of Antrim, and the Mourne Mountains (called the Mourne Trail) are the best, plus the 69-mile (111 km) Donegal section. Advance planning is necessary: The Northern Ireland Tourist Board has information on sections and Paddy Dillon's book (see page 630) should be consulted.

Fisheries Board, Ard na Rí House, Abbey St, Ballina, County Mayo, T096-22788, info@nwrfb.ie. **The Shannon Regional Fisheries Board**, Thomond Weir, Limerick, T061-455171, info@shannon-fishery-board.ie. **Ireland West Tourism**, Áras Fáilte, Galway, T091-563081, dispenses a useful brochure, *The Coarse Angler's Paradise*, covering Counties Galway, Mayo and Roscommon and including practical information on suitable accommodation. *Game Angling Ireland West* is a similar brochure available from the Fishery Boards. **The Great Fishing Houses of Ireland**, PO Box 6375, Dublin 4, www.irelandflyfishing.com, issues a booklet with details of hotels specializing in fishing holidays. These include the Pontoon Bridge Hotel (see page 433) which runs courses for beginners as well as catering for old hands.

Many of the general tour operators, see above, organize specialist fishing packages and in the USA there is also **Fishing International**, T1-800/9504242.

Genealogical research

If you are planning a genealogical fieldtrip, it helps enormously to carry out some preliminary research before reaching Ireland. Try to establish the county and townland from which your ancestors departed plus full names, maiden as well as married ones, and dates of birth, marriage and death. Sources worth exploring in your own country include birth, marriage and death records, immigration and naturalization papers, and ships' passenger lists. For general information and details of local centres within the Republic contact the **Genealogical Office**, 2 Kildare Street, Dublin 2, T01-6030200, www.nli.ie, or the **Office of the Register General**, T01-6354000. For Northern Ireland, contact the **General Register Office**, Oxford House, 49 Chichester Street, Belfast BT1 4HL, T028-9025 2000.

Central records prior to 1922 are held in Dublin, but the Belfast General Register Office will arrange for searches to be made of births, marriages or deaths in Northern Ireland before 1922. The **Public Record Office of Northern Ireland**, 66 Balmoral Avenue, Belfast BT9 6NY, T028-9025 1318, www.proni.nics.gov.uk, does not conduct research but visitors can make their own searches there. In Dublin, records are kept at the **National Library**, T01-6030200, and the National Archives, Bishop St, Dublin 8, T01-4072300.

Birth, death and marriage certificates are available from the Office of the Registrar General, Joyce House, Lombard St East, Dublin 2, T01-6711000.

Fáilte Ireland have a booklet, *Tracing your Ancestors in Ireland*, which is packed with useful contact addresses.

Golf

There are more golf courses per head of population in Ireland than anywhere else in Europe, ranging from lush parkland courses in the east to rugged and challenging links courses on the western coastline. Contact Fáilte Ireland and the Northern Ireland Tourist Board for general literature and information on specialist golfing packages. **Dublin Tourism** publishes *Golfing Around Dublin*, listing all the courses, their services and green fees, **www.golfing-ireland.com**, is worth looking at and **South East Tourism** in Waterford dispenses a useful *Golfers' Guide* with practical information on local golf courses and accommodation. Green fees range enormously: at Hotel Carrigart in County Donegal residents can play for free on a links course, at The K Club in Straffan, County Kildare (designed by Arnold Palmer) residents can expect to pay €105. Average fees are in the €15-30 range.

Walking

Walking is the least expensive and most ecologically sound activity worth pursuing in Ireland, and there are now some 30 waymarked trails covering over 1,492 miles (2,300 km) as well as countless local walking routes in scenic areas. Worth consulting are some of the specialist walking guidebooks that cover the whole country but, unless walking is going to be your sole activity for a fair length of time, they are a less worthwhile investment than some of the smaller books that focus on popular walking areas and which are ideal for one-day walks if staying a while in a particular region (see 'Books', page 625, and on the web www.obrien.ie, for one of the main publishers). Fáilte Ireland (the Irish Tourist Board) sells an inexpensive *Walking Ireland* booklet that describes each of the waymarked Ways and gives contact details for further information, accommodation, travel and maps.

The Northern Ireland Tourist Board hands out a useful booklet detailing 14 walks on the Ulster Way, accompanied with maps and sources of information.

Detailed information about some of the more popular long-distance walks, such as the Kerry Way, the Beara Way, the Dingle Way and the Sheep's Head Way, are included in this book in the relevant section, and shorter details are given of some of the others (see box). To complete all or part of the best waymarked trails all that is really needed are the relevant **Ordnance Survey Discovery Maps** on a scale of 1:50,000 (2.5 in to 1 mile/2 cm to 1 km); they show the routes of the Ways. **EastWest Mapping**, Ballyredmond, Enniscorthy, County Wexford, T/F054-77835, http://homepage.eircom.net/~eastwest, also publishes 1:50,000 scale maps of particular Ways. It is worth checking with the **Ordnance Survey Service,** Phoenix Park, Dublin 8, T01-8025300, www.irishmaps.ie, or **Ordnance Survey of Northern Ireland,** T028-9025 5755, www.osni.gov.uk, to see which is the latest update available and whether the route of the Way is included. Tourist offices in Dublin, Belfast, Cork and Galway, as well as smaller local tourist offices in the relevant areas, also sell mostly inexpensive guides covering a particular Way. Some of these non-OS Way maps are published by **EastWest Mapping,** and they sell a wide range of walking maps as well as their own ones. The Ordnance Survey maps are available in the big bookshops in Dublin, as well as the **Government Publications Sales Office Bookshop,** Sun Alliance House, Molesworth St, Dublin 2, T01-6613111, and are often available in local bookshops and tourist offices around the country. For walks requiring overnight stays it is essential to have accommodation booked in advance.

Organized walking holidays, usually including airport transfers and luggage transport between accommodation stops, are available through various companies, including **Irish Ways,** The Old Rectory, Ballycanew, Gorey, County Wexford, T055-27479, www.irishways.com, and **Go Ireland,** Killorglin, County Kerry, T066-9762094; freephone 0800-371203 (from the UK), 800-7214672 (from the USA), www.govisitireland.com.

For specialist walking holidays in the Burren contact **Burren Walking Holidays,** Carrigann Hotel, Lisdoonvarna, County Clare, T065-7074036. For walks in Connemara, **Connemara Safari,** T095-21071, www.walkingconnemara.com. For walks in Antrim and Donegal, **Walking and Talking Ireland,** T074-9159366, www.walktalkireland.com and www.waltalkdonegal.com. For hikes on the Iveragh Peninsula, including guided trips to Ireland's highest mountain, contact **Wilderness Tours,** Climber's Inn, Glencar, County Kerry, T066-60101, www.climbersinn.com.

Useful websites include Fáilte Ireland's **www.walkingIreland.ie** and **www.walkireland.ie**. In the USA, **Backroads,** T1-800/GO-ACTIVE, 4622848, www.backroads.com, specializes in walking and cycling holidays. For walking holidays in Northern Ireland look at www.walktalkireland.com.

Walking World Ireland is a monthly magazine that carries detailed maps and commentary on walks all over the country; it is available from newsagents or on subscription from 288 Harold's Cross Road, Dublin 6, T01-4923030.

Water sports

Ireland has some magnificent beaches, and while most are safe for **swimming** there are some that can be dangerous. Most of these are mentioned in the text but it is always worth checking, especially if no one else is in the water. **Windsurfing** is growing in popularity, contact the **Irish Windsurfing Association,** www.windsurfing.com.

Surfing beaches in the west of Ireland include Achill Island, Easkey in county Sligo, and Spanish Point and Lahinch in Clare. Further south, there is Castlegregory on the north side of the Dingle Peninsula, Inch on the south side, Caherdaniel on the Iveragh Peninsula and Barley Cove on the Mizen Peninsula. In the southeast, Rosslare Strand in County Wexford, and Dunmore East,

Other activities

Birdwatching	www.birdwatching.ie
Boat cruising	dedibra@ireland.com, www.iwai.ie
Dancing	www.clrg.ie, www.setdancingnews.net
Hang gliding and paragliding	www.ihpa.ie
Mountaineering	www.mountaineering.ie
Orienteering	www.orienteering.ie
Rock climbing	www.climbing.ie

Tramore, Ballinacourty and Dungarvan in County Waterford are all noted for their surfing beaches. In the north, Portrush on the north Antrim coast is the main surfing centre and here, as in most of the other areas (but not Barley Cove), it is possible to hire equipment and garner local information. **The Irish Surfing Association**, based at Tirchonaill St, Donegal, T074-9721053.

For information on **scuba diving** in Ireland contact the **Irish Underwater Council**, 78A Patrick St, Dun Laoghaire, Co Dublin, T01-2844601, www.indigo.ie/scuba-irl. Their website has links to other sites and details of all the diving centres around Ireland are listed. *Subsea*, Ireland's diving magazine, is also online here.

For **sailing**, contact the **Irish Sailing Association (ISA)**, 3 Park Rd, Dun Laoghaire, Dublin, T01-2800239, www.sailing.ie. They provide literature on visitor moorings as well as information on ISA-approved sailing programmes in dinghies, keel boats, catamarans and powerboats. **West Cork Sailing Centre**, Adrigole, Beara, County Cork, T27-60132, www.westcorksailing.com, is a good example of the kind of regional sailing centre available in the west of Ireland, offering courses for children and adults.

For **canoeing** possibilities, contact the **Irish Canoe Union**, T01-4509838, www.irishcanoeunion.com, and/or **Canoe Association of Northern Ireland**, www.cani.org.uk. Canoeing trips are run by **Shannon Adventure Canoeing Holidays**, The Marina, Banagher, Co Offaly, T/F0509-51411, and **Tiglin Adventure Centre**, Ashford, Co Wicklow, T0404-40169.

Water skiing is possible through **Golden Falls Waterski Club**, Knocknacree Rd, Dalkey, Co Dublin, T01-4502122.

Details of short courses in various **crafts** across Ireland, with accommodation sometimes arranged, are available from the **Crafts Council of Ireland**, Castle Yard, Kilkenny, T056-61804, www.ccoi.ie. This is your chance to take up basketry, furniture making, hedge laying, silversmithing, stone work and much else besides.

Health

There are no alarming facts or fears to take into account when travelling within Ireland. The water is safe to drink, no inoculations are required, and there is a generally excellent health service; to cap it all there are no snakes and little danger of sunburn.

What to take

Make sure you are covered for emergency medical treatment in Ireland. Visitors from **EU countries** are entitled to free medical treatment and to facilitate this a new electronic medical card is being introduced in 2005 to replace the old Form E111. British visitors to Ireland can receive emergency treatment and medicines without ever having to show this form, but it is still advisable to bring it because in some circumstances it could make a difference. British visitors to the North require no documents and will receive treatment as they would in Britain. Visitors from **non-EU countries** are charged for all medical treatment except out-patient treatment at accident and emergency units of public hospitals. **Medical insurance** is therefore highly advisable.

Keeping in touch

Communications

Internet

Internet cafés are to be found in all Irish cities and large towns, and in a growing number of small towns and even villages. Most town libraries also have internet facilities open to the public.

Post

Postal services across Ireland are efficient and reliable, with a range of services that include recorded or registered mail. From the Republic, a standard letter or postcard to Britain or Northern Ireland, is 60¢, to other EU countries is 65¢, and to the USA and the rest of the world is 65¢. In Northern Ireland, a letter or postcard to an EU country costs 37p and to anywhere outside the EU is 45p.

Most post offices in the Republic and Northern Ireland are open 0830-1730, Monday-Friday, and 0900-1200 on Saturday. In rural areas and small towns the post office may close for one afternoon during the week, often on a Wednesday. For enquiries in the North T0345-740740.

Telephone

Republic Public payphones are easy to find and come in two versions: coin-operated or cardphone-operated. Phonecards, bought at newsagents and post offices, are more convenient to use, especially for long-distance or international calls.

Making an international call from the Republic Dial 00+country code+area code (without the 0)+number. So, to phone the UK number 0208-123 1234, T00-44-20 8123 1234. To call Northern Ireland, however, T048+ the local number.

Northern Ireland Public payphones, as in the Republic, are either operated with coins or cards (called phonecards). In towns, and rural areas especially, coin-operated payphones are less common than card-operated ones.

Making an international call from Northern Ireland The procedure is the same as in the Republic: Dial 00+country code+area code (without the 0)+number. So, for example, to phone the US number 01-212-1231234, T00-1-212-1231234. The same applies to phoning the Republic, so to reach the Dublin number 01-6024000 you would dial T00-353-1-6024000.

Using mobile phones Digital phones from most of Europe and Australia, but not the US, will work in Ireland but call rates, including incoming ones, are likely to be exorbitant. Check with your supplier before you leave.

Media

Newspapers

Republic The quality daily newspaper is *The Irish Times* and Saturday's edition is the best value for money. Of the other dailies, the *Irish Independent* is lighter in tone while *The Examiner* makes for more parochial reading. The *Star* is a fairly useless tabloid, as is the Irish edition of *The Sun*. All the English daily and Sunday newspapers are readily available and in Dublin city centre, foreign newspapers are also available. Irish Sunday newspapers don't amount to much; the *Sunday World* is sensationalist and the *Sunday Tribune* is probably the best read. Counties produce their own local papers, and Dublin and Cork have evening papers.

Northern Ireland Apart from the British dailies there is the *Irish News*, read mainly by the nationalist community and usually a good read, and the tabloid *News Letter* which presents a staunchly loyalist view of events. The *Belfast Telegraph* is a local interest evening paper. *An Phoblacht* (Republican News) is a Sinn Féin weekly paper.

Magazines

There is a host of Irish-produced magazines catering to special interests and hobbies. The *Phoenix* is a satirical magazine along the lines of Britain's *Private Eye* and there is never any shortage of political and business scandals fuelling its contents. *Magill* is also worth reading when it uncovers a juicy story of yet more political shenanigans. *Hot Press* carries listings of musical gigs and other cultural events and its features on music, politics and much else is often interesting.

Television

RTE (Radio Telefís Éireann) runs 2 national stations in the Republic, RTÉ 1 and RTÉ 2. RTÉ 1 broadcasts the more interesting news programmes and shows of cultural and historical interest. Ocassionally RTÉ 2 has a watchable programme but the usual diet is a mix of chat shows, cheap films and serials. There is also an Irish-language channel (see page 23). Most British channels can be picked up in Ireland through satellite or cable. In Northern Ireland there are the British television channels, and the Republic's channels can also be received. Cable or satellite television is usually found in hotels and guest houses, but too often only the basic package is subscribed to and the film channels are not available.

Radio

In the **Republic** three radio stations are also run by RTÉ: Radio 1, a disappointing mix of news and cultural programmes; 2FM for pop music; and Radio na Gaeltachta, which is an Irish-language station. There is also Lyric FM, a classical music station. Today FM 100-104 provides some competition to RTÉ and is best listened to in the evening. There is also a host of independent local stations. In **Northern Ireland** there is the full gamut of British radio stations and some local stations.

Dublin

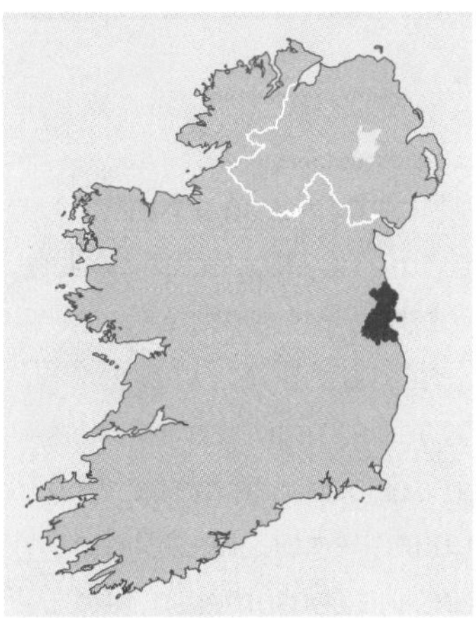

Footprint features

Introduction

Dublin's marriage of modernity and tradition is an unsteady relationship, with neither side quite sure how to accommodate the needs of the other. The statue of the 19th-century nationalist Daniel O'Connell looks across the River Liffey to designer bars, tacky souvenir shops and all night minimarkets, while a gaudy sex shop has its premises opposite the General Post Office, symbolic heart of the unfinished business of the 1916 nationalist uprising. But culture and consumerism find harmony when new wealth is used to celebrate the city's long and creative history, as is the case with the National Gallery's Millennium Wing, the Hugh Lane Gallery's acquisition of the London studio of Francis Bacon, the state-of-the-art centre, the Helix, or the stylish new premises for the Chester Beatty Library.

This new Dublin has at long last regained its status as an economic power in Europe, a role it last experienced in the 18th century. Through the 1970s and 80s Dublin was on the receiving end of EU handouts but nowadays its economy is among the strongest in Europe and it has found a new role as a link between its European partners and the US. Immigration is now the watchword of Dublin: don't be deceived into thinking that the suave city folk ducking and diving through the snarled up traffic are Dubliners born and bred. Many of them are from small Irish towns, villages or farms. They have come to Dublin for employment, or to study, but their childhood was spent in the countryside or in small agricultural towns surrounded by fields and farmland. In this way, traditional patterns of life and thought give a nuance to Dublin's city life. Some Dubliners are even more recent arrivals and from further away than the villages of rural Ireland. In a shockingly brief period monocultural Ireland, and Dublin in particular, has become home to thousands of foreign workers and refugees, not always with harmonious consequences.

★ Don't miss...

1. **Trinity College** Gawk at the brilliantly illuminated Book of Kells, one of the oldest books in the world, page 65.
2. **National Museum of Archaeology and History** Marvel at the hoardes of Bronze Age gold, page 70.
3. **Christ Church Cathedral** Admire the 63 different patterns of medieval floor tiles and the Tomb of Strongbow, page 77.
4. **Phoenix Park** Take a healthy and historical walk around Europe's largest enclosed park, or go to the zoo, page 93.
5. **Prospect Cemetery** Visit the dead famous in Glasnevin, page 94.
6. **Music** Enjoy a night of traditional music at Cobblestone, page 113 or listen to the buskers in Grafton Street, page 63.

Ins and outs → *Phone code: 01. Colour map 4, grid A2/3. Population: 900,000.*

Getting there

Dublin Airport Dublin has one airport, T01-8444900, 12 km north of the city. The airport has money exchange facilities, car hire desks, taxis and public transport to and from the city. In the main arrivals hall is a **Dublin Tourism** counter, open daily from 0800-2200 (2230 in Jul and Aug), which can book accommodation. Next to it is a **CIE** counter with information on buses. There are also left-luggage facilities as well as assorted shops, bars and cafés. A **taxi** from the airport to town should cost around €23.

There is no train service from the airport. **Dublin Bus**, T01-8734222, www.dublinbus.ie, runs two Airlink Express buses: the **No 747** service to and from O'Connell Street, the Central Bus Station and Connolly Rail Station, and the **No 748** service to and from the Central Bus Station, Tara St DART station, Aston Quay and Heuston Rail Station. The fare is €5 single, €8 return; prepaid tickets are available at the CIE information desk; Rambler Tickets (see page 123) are valid on the Airlink service. The No 747 runs every 10-20 minutes, 0545-2330 from the airport (0715-2330 Sun), and 0515-2250 from O'Connell Street (0735-2315 Sun). The No 748 runs about every 30 minutes, 0625-2130 from the airport (0700-2205 Sun), and 0710-2220 from Heuston Station (0750-2250 Sun). Journey time for both routes is about 30-40 minutes.

Local buses **Nos 41** and **41B** travel between the airport and Eden Quay, cost €1.90 but take up to an hour. Their bus stop is outside the airport next to the Airlink Express bus stop. Bus **Nos 16** and **16A** travel between the airport and Aungier Street, via O'Connell Street and Drumcondra Road. Bus **No 58X** is an express service (30-40 minutes) that departs from the airport at 1710, Mon-Fri, to O'Connell Street and Kildare Street. There is also the **No 746** service that runs between the airport and Dun Laoghaire, via Drumcondra Road and Pembroke Street, 0915-2145 Mon-Fri, 0945-2145 on Sat and 1000-1900 on Sun.

Another option is the privately run **Aircoach**, T01-8447118, www.aircoach.ie, that operates every 15 minutes from and to the airport 0530-2330; useful if staying south of the river because, unlike the Airlink Express, it runs to Merrion Square, Pembroke Road, Merrion Road, Simmonscourt Road and Donnybrook Road before returning to the airport via Leeson Street, St Stephen's Green, Dawson Street and O'Connell Street.

Dublin ferry ports Ferries from Britain dock at either **Dublin Port**, Alexandra Road (3 km east of the centre), T01-8722777, or **Dun Laoghaire** (for *Stena Line*), T01-2047700. From Dublin Port, Bus **No 53** meets incoming ferries and takes passengers to the Central Bus Station, €2. From Dun Laoghaire, there are DART trains and buses (see page 124) into the city centre. Some coach companies run their passengers into Dublin from the ferry port.

Getting around → *See Transport, page 123, for more details.*

If you are in Dublin for only a few days the chances are that you will get around mostly on foot (the centre is small enough), with the occasional bus ride to cross from one side of the river to the other. Buses, however, can be very useful for saving time and for reaching some places of interest that are not in the city centre.

Local bus The local buses, fairly frequent and cheap, are run by **Dublin Bus**, T01-8734222, www.dublinbus.ie. Bus stops are painted green, and carry a timetable. You pay the driver on entry and should have the correct fare if you know it; up to three stages costs €0.80, 4-7 stages €1.20, 8-13 stages €1.40, and 14 or more €1.60. Banknotes are not accepted and if you deposit more than the exact fare the driver

See also colour street map of the city at the back of the book.

24 hours in Dublin

To fuel up for the day, try the **full Irish breakfast** (or, if available, Irish smoked salmon and scrambled eggs – particularly good in Ireland). See what's on offer at the **Elephant and Castle**, 18 Temple Bar, T01-6793121, especially their Sunday brunch.

Spend the morning among the museums, wondering at the **gold at the National Museum**, admiring the **Picasso in the National Gallery** and shuddering at the things in alcohol in the **Natural History Museum**. If it's Saturday book yourself on to the amazing tour of the **government buildings**.

For lunch try **Chapter One** (Mondays excepted) for a really classy lunch or wander around Temple Bar and pick a café or a pub (try **Gallagher's Boxty House** for a traditional Irish potato pancake).

In the afternoon it's time for a bird's-eye view of the city. The **Guinness Storehouse** provides the view and a pint of Guinness as well, or try the **Chimney** at Smithfield for another panoramic view. If you want to fit in a spot of shopping, **Kildare Street** and **Nassau Street** have the best Irish crafts while there are more regular stores in Grafton Street.

For dinner go back to Temple Bar and the charms of **Fitzer's** or **Eliza Blue's**. For an ethnic dinner you can't beat **Rajdoot** in Clarendon Street. Afterwards enjoy a drink in **Dohenny & Nesbitt** in Baggot Street or take a walk over to the **Brazen Head**, Dublin's oldest bar where, if you are lucky, there'll be some music on offer.

If all this hasn't exhausted you then your next port of call will probably be Harcourt Street where the clubbers get going around 2300. **Beaujangles** suits the 30-somethings while **POD** and the **Red Box** are the hippest destinations in town.

issues a passenger ticket for the overpayment. Presenting this ticket and your original travel ticket at the O'Connell Street office allows a cash refund.

Bus services stop at around 2330 but **Nitelink** buses run every Thu, Fri and Sat from the city centre to the various suburbs and cost €4.

The Luas It's early days for the new electric tram system which is designed to bring in commuters from the suburbs rather than ferry people about the city. The green line travels from St Stephen's Green southwards to the suburbs while the red line is slightly more useful, travelling from Connolly Street through the shopping streets north of the river and then along the quays to Phoenix Park and Heuston station before heading off to the 'burbs. Tickets are bought at the tram stop just before getting on the tram (a single ticket is valid for only 90 minutes, a return for the whole day). The ticket machines take coins, notes and credit cards. You can buy the various combined season tickets at Luas ticket agents but they may be of little use to visitors. The all-zone combi ticket for bus and Luas is probably the most useful. It is available as a 1-day, 7-day or 30-day ticket. Trams run from 0530 weekday mornings (later at weekends) to 0030 (earlier on Sundays), at 5-15 minute intervals.

Rail Dublin's light railway system, **DART** (Dublin Area Rapid Transit), T01-8363333, www.irishrail.ie, links the coastal suburbs with the city centre and is useful for short hops between the south and north of the city and for transport to some suburban areas where accommodation and the occasional place of interest are located. The system operates between Howth and Malahide to the north and Greystones in County Wicklow to the south. The trains are clean and fast but get very crowded at peak times.

Information

Dublin Tourism Centre, Suffolk St, Jun-Sep Mon-Sat 0900-2030, Sun 1100-1700; Oct-May Mon-Sat 0930-1730. It is a walk-in centre only, as are all Dublin tourist offices. **Dublin Tourism**, Baggot Street Bridge, 0930-1715. There is an **Temple Bar information centre**, 12 East Essex Street, www.visit-templebar.ie, www.temple-bar.ie, which provides information on Temple Bar.

History

Dublin's history has been a turbulent one. Celts gave way to Norsemen, who were driven out by Gaelic-speaking Irishmen, who in turn folded under the assault of the Normans. The English, in one form or another, held the city through many attempts to wrest it back into Irish hands, from the 1798 uprising to the 1916 Easter Rising. Finally Irish again in 1922, the city went into economic decline, from which it has recently been reborn, like a postmodern phoenix, all designer bars and online businesses.

The Vikings The Viking town of Dyfflin, a corruption of the Irish name, *dubh linn*, probably established itself around 917 under Ivar the Boneless. Around 1000 the Vikings built a *thingmote*, a huge earth mound where they held meetings; College Green now stands there.

In 997 coins were being minted and in 1030 a wooden church was erected on the site of what is now Christ Church Cathedral. The settlement had around 5,000 citizens and was the first urban settlement in Ireland. The Vikings gradually intermarried, learned Gaelic and converted to Christianity, and it is probable that the Battle of Clontarf in 1014, generally considered to be the moment when Viking power in Ireland was broken, had Vikings on both sides of the battlefield.

The Normans The Anglo-Norman invasion began in 1169 and Dublin was taken in 1170 by an army led by Richard FitzGilbert de Clare, Earl of Pembroke, better known to posterity as 'Strongbow'. The Vikings still did not leave but shifted to Oxmantown on the north bank of the Liffey. By the 14th century they had become completely assimilated into the Anglo-Norman Gaelic society.

Reformation and restoration In the 16th century the Reformation freed the lands of the religious orders around the city and a wave of building began. Trinity College was built on land formerly owned by a religious order, and other monastic buildings were dismantled for use as building materials.

In the 18th century the first Georgian planned streets were constructed, to the northeast and southeast of the city. Grand public buildings were constructed as well as elaborate townhouses, which expressed the confidence of the Anglo-Irish in their ownership of the city. Dublin became the second city of the British Empire, and each Anglo-Irish family kept a townhouse in one of the Georgian mansions, where they lived during the winter months. The city became the national centre for trade and commerce as well as the seat of government.

Dublin's decline The decline set in after the 1798 uprising: Britain saw Ireland as an unstable colony and passed the Act of Union, dissolving the Irish parliament. The effect on Dublin was enormous. With no parliament sitting, the landowners left for their country estates. Houses stood vacant and industries that had serviced their owners went into decline. Then, 46 years later, the Famine brought thousands of sick and homeless into the city. The great Georgian mansions became tenements.

The decline continued into the 19th century. Half the city's families lived in one-room slums in the old Georgian houses and the infant mortality rate soared. Most of the working classes were employed as casual labourers and experienced long periods of unemployment. By the turn of the century Belfast had replaced Dublin as

The Easter Rising in Dublin

In 1916 a group of Republicans, led by James Connolly, Padraig Pearse, Joseph Mary Plunkett and Thomas McDonagh, seized the GPO and several other sites in Dubin in the vain hope that their stand would prompt other Republicans throughout the country to follow their lead and take up arms in the cause of Irish independence. In Dublin the Post Office was an unofficial focal point for the city and was the first place to be taken by Pearse and Connolly, with a complement of 1,200 supporters. The proclamation of the Irish Republic was read from the front steps of the building. Other contingents took St Stephen's Green and the College of Surgeons, and City Hall which was designated a field hospital.

The life of the city went on around the fighting with many non-combatants suffering. Those in the Post Office resisted for five days before withdrawing their troops. Countess Markievicz who led the taking of the Royal College of Surgeons, not knowing about the surrender, held out for another day at the Royal College of Surgeons, but she too surrendered and, like the other leaders, was sentenced to death, reprieved only for fear of the international outcry sure to follow the execution of a woman. If the city wasn't roused to open rebellion by the sight of the republicans being shelled in the Post Office, both it and the world were outraged at the summary executions that took place afterwards, Connolly strapped to a chair since he was too badly injured to stand and face the firing squad.

the industrial heartland of Ireland and events such as the Great Lockout of 1913 (which started when Dublin employers compelled workers to withdraw from the Transport and General Workers Union or face dismissal, and climaxed with 20,000 workers on strike or locked out of their factories), and the 1916 Easter Rising burdened the city even further.

Modern times The Irish Free State began a series of planned housing developments, creating the suburbs of modern Dublin. Unobtrusively, in the 1990s Dublin began to revive, first with the development of the Temple Bar area, and then as businesses found cheap property and a well educated workforce desperate for employment. Now the Celtic Tiger, as the economic boom in Ireland has been called, has finally put an end to two centuries of decline for Dublin. Today it is near impossible to walk down a city street without seeing planning application notices, and mobile-phone transmitters scar the skylines.

Sights

Grafton Street and around → *Pearse St and Tara St stations.*

With **Trinity College**, the **National Museum** and **National Gallery**, the **Bank of Ireland** and lots more places to see, this is the heart of tourist Dublin where restaurants, gift shops and pubs lie thick on the ground. Most of the big sights are well worth the visit and in between all the tourist stuff and places where Dubliners go about their everyday business are little gems of history, architecture, art and human nature. The

A few minutes away from St Michan's is the **Old Jameson Distillery** ⓘ *Bow St, T01-8072355, daily, 0930-1800 (last tour 1700), €7.95, tours last 45 mins, self-service restaurant, bar and gift shop, bus 67, 67A from Middle Abbey St, 68, 69, 79 from Aston Quay, 90 from Connolly, Luas to Four Courts stop*, now dedicated to the history of whiskey production. A trip to the old Jameson Distillery is by way of a guided tour with an opportunity to ask questions along the way. There is a bar and of course a complimentary tipple at the end of the tour. If you are keen to taste more than one, then hurl yourself forward when the guide looks for four volunteers for the whiskey- tasting session that concludes the tour. This involves comparing the tastes of four Irish whiskeys with a Scotch whisky and a Jim Beam bourbon before staggering away with a certificate to validate your connoisseurship.

The plaza area can hold up to 8,000 people and hosts major civic events.

Outside the Chief O'Neil Hotel is the **Jameson Chimney** ⓘ *T01-8173820, Mon-Sat 1000-1730, Sun 1100-1730 (may be subject to seasonal change), €5, bus 25, 25A, 67, 67A from Middle Abbey St, 68, 69, 79 from Aston Quay, 90 from Connolly and Tara stations, Luas to Four Courts*, 56 m high with a glass-walled lift to take you to the top, from where the city spreads out beneath you. The chimney is the original Jameson Distillery Chimney, built in 1895.

National Museum of Decorative Arts and History

ⓘ *Collins Barracks, Benburb St, T01-6777444, www.museum.ie. Tue-Sat 1000-1700, Sun 1400-1700. Free. Café and bookshop open museum hours. Guided tours. Bus 90 from Aston Quay, 25, 25A, 66, 67 from Middle Abbey St, Luas to Museum stop.*

This is the oldest and largest military barracks in Europe, designed by Thomas Burgh in 1701 to house 5,000 men. It was finally decommissioned in 1969. The barracks now

Smithfield

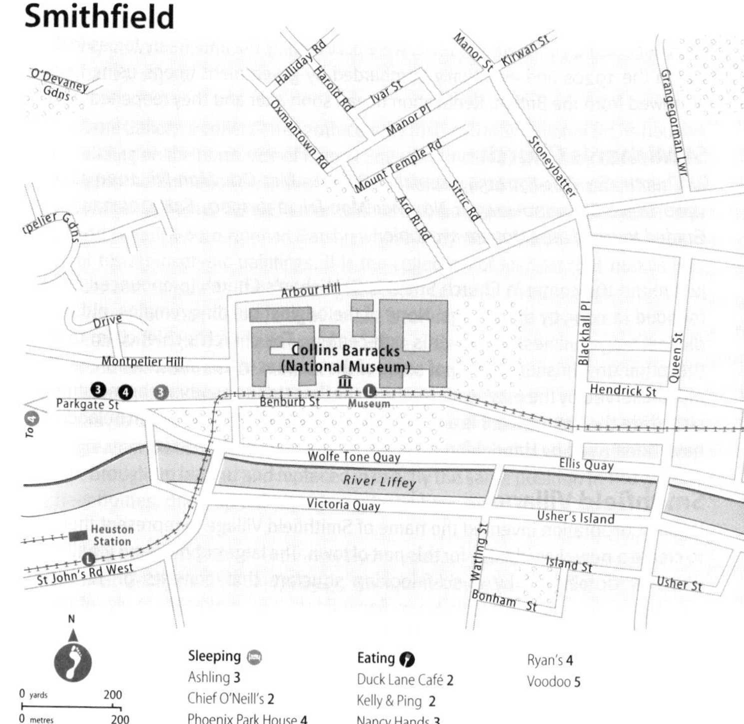

Sleeping
Ashling 3
Chief O'Neill's 2
Phoenix Park House 4

Eating
Duck Lane Café 2
Kelly & Ping 2
Nancy Hands 3
Ryan's 4
Voodoo 5

house the part of the National Museum dedicated to decorative arts, with some intriguing displays such as the curators' favourite pieces, a collection of fascinating rural furniture, displays on disappearing rural crafts, a new costume exhibition and lots more. There are interactive computer displays and some tours with knowledgeable guides. The whole museum is distinguished by the quality of the displays, although it lacks a history of the building itself and the events that have taken place there. But it is early days, and the hope is that that will come in phase two of the museum's development.

Joyce's Dublin

Generally agreed to be the greatest 20th-century novel in the English language, *Ulysses* is set in a single day, 16 June 1904, the day when Joyce first walked out with Nora Barnacle, the woman with whom he shared the rest of his life. The novel traces the wanderings around the city of Leopold Bloom, mirroring the wanderings of Odysseus on his journey home to Ithaca. Stephen Dedalus, Bloom's Telemachus or figurative son, joins him for part of the day. Joyce took the job of getting Bloom's journey technically correct very seriously, consulting timetables, getting relatives and friends to time journeys, check entrance-ways and so on. While many of the shops and pubs he lists have disappeared, several still stand and you can join in the annual fun on **Bloomsday** (details from the James Joyce Centre and see page 117) and spend near enough 24 hours wandering in Bloom's footsteps around the city.

Eccles Street and onwards

No 7 Eccles Street, the home address of Leopold Bloom, no longer exists. It was knocked down in 1980 to make way for an extension to the Mater Hospital, but a plaque marks the spot where Bloom would have lived if he had existed and the real front door is on view in the James Joyce Centre (see page 86).

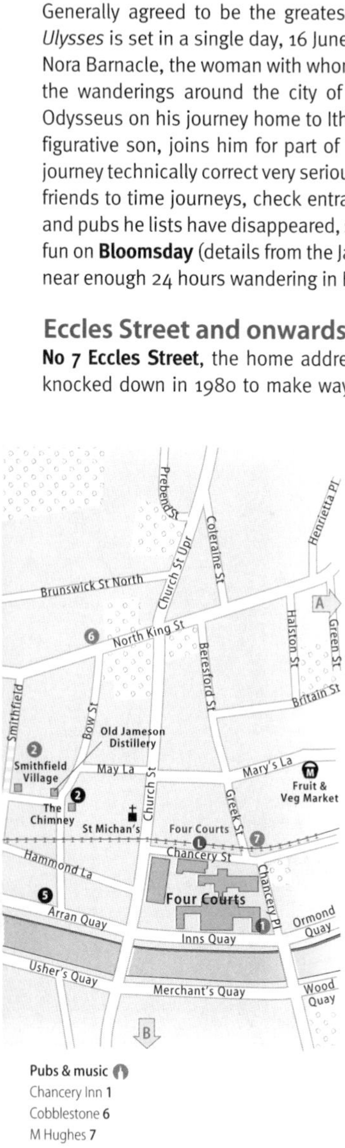

Turning right into Dorset Street, on his way to the butcher's, Bloom pauses at Larry O'Rourke's bar (now the *Snug*) to smell the odour of beer. After returning home and finishing breakfast, Bloom wanders into town down Hardwicke Place, past **St George's Church** (now the Temple Theatre). At the junction of Temple Street and Great Denmark Street you could detour from Bloom's journey to view **Belvedere House** (previously College), where Joyce attended school between 1893 and 1898.

Directly opposite Belvedere House is North Great George's Street, a row of what were very dilapidated Georgian terraces, but now a bijou area once again. At No 35 is the **James Joyce Centre** (see page 86).

Pubs & music
Chancery Inn **1**
Cobblestone **6**
M Hughes **7**

To Leinster Street

Back on the *Ulysses* trail, Bloom heads into town along Gardiner Street. He passes under the railway bridge at the bottom of the street and crosses Butt Bridge, walks along St George's and City Quay and along Lombard Street and Westland Row. In Lombard Street Bloom notices Nichol's Undertakers, which is still there, its appearance barely changed since 1904. In Westland Row he stops at the Post Office, now part of the DART station, and collects a secret letter, which he takes round to the back of the railway arch in Cumberland Street – still much the same as Bloom would have seen it. His next port of call is **St Andrew's Church** in Westland Row, All Hallows in the novel, and watches the sleepy congregation

He travels along Westland Row past **Conway's Pub**, still doing the same trade but now called *Fitzsimon's*, and calls in at **Sweny's Chemist**, still there doing business, with the same shop front and sign 97 years later! Bloom buys lemon soap in the chemist, and it is still sold there: as Bloom says, "Chemists rarely move."

Joyce's Dublin

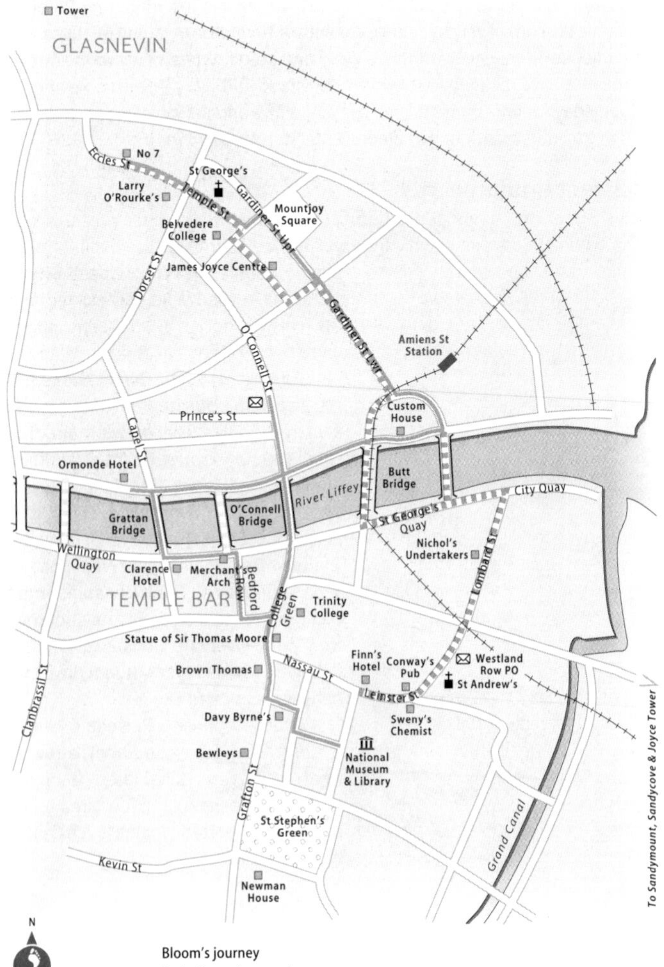

Dublin in film

While Ireland's film industry has always been a bit short of cash, it has been an excellent source of actors, directors and locations. Dublin especially is a seasoned star of the silver screen. Scenes from the original *Italian Job* and the musical *Oliver!* were filmed inside Kilmainham Gaol while Trinity College was used for the making of *Educating Rita*. The back streets were used for the Limerick of *Angela's Ashes* while a piece of Wicklow mountainside stood in for Scotland when they filmed *Braveheart*.

As well as acting as a screen double, the city also stars as itself. The grimier sections of north Dublin went on display both in *My Left Foot*, filmed on location there in 1989, and in Alan Parker's adaptation of Roddy Doyle's novel *The Commitments* which became a worldwide hit the following year. In 1996 various sites around the city were used in *Michael Collins* and in 1998 John Boorman's *The General*, based on the life of a genuine Dublin crook, also used the city as a backdrop. More recent Dublin films include *About Adam* the first Irish film production with a bisexual hero.

Television also loves Dublin, on some days it's difficult to avoid becoming part of the background when they're filming the RTE's *Bachelor's Walk*. The excellent BBC/ RTE production *Rebel Heart*, about the years leading up to Home Rule was partly filmed in Dublin although they used Iveagh Gardens rather than St Stephen's Green to show the fighting around the Shelbourne and the Royal College of Surgeons.

Grafton Street

On O'Connell Bridge he pauses to watch a Guinness Brewery barge go past, buys a bun from a stallholder and throws it to the seabirds over the river. In **College Green** Bloom passes the statue of Thomas Moore, the poet, famous for *The Meeting of the Waters*, and is amused that this man should stand in effigy above a public toilet. He passes down Grafton Street, then as now "gay with housed awnings". **Brown Thomas**, the department store, still in Grafton Street but now on the other side, is noted. Bloom turns into Duke Street and famously pops into **Davy Byrne's**, 'the moral pub', for a Gorgonzola sandwich and a glass of burgundy. Davy Byrne's is still in business and serves the Gorgonzola every 16 June.

National Library to Temple Bar

After this Bloom heads towards the National Library, turning right into Dawson Street. Bloom leaves the library and heads to **Temple Bar** for the second-hand bookshops – he wants to buy his wife a paperback novel to read. He walks along Bedford Row, passes through Merchant's Arch and on to Wellington Quay. By this time it is about half past three. From here he walks along Wellington Quay, past the **Clarence Hotel** and across the river to the **Ormond Hotel** (both still in business). His day continues until well into the early hours of the next morning, when he and Stephen Dedalus return past the Custom House, back up Gardiner Street to Eccles Street.

James Joyce Museum

At Sandycove, 13 km south of centre and set in the **Martello tower** ⓘ *T01-2809265, Feb- Oct Mon-Sat 1000-1300, 1400-1700, Sun and public holidays 1400-1800, €6.25, small bookshop, DART: Sandycove, bus 59 from Dun Laoghaire*, where he lived for a time, is the James Joyce Museum. The collection includes letters and first editions of his books as well as his waistcoat, guitar and piano, photographs and one of the three death masks of Joyce made in January 1945 (the others are in Zurich and Washington DC).

Joyce aficionados might also like to visit the house in Bray where Joyce lived as a toddler (see page 155).

Kilmainham

To the west of the city centre, less than a 10-minute walk from Heuston Station Kilmainham has two major attractions: the Irish Museum of Modern art and the infamous Kilmainham Gaol. Not yet taken up as a desirable residential area Kilmainham still retains a working class mood among its tiny terraced houses and modern housing estates.

Irish Museum of Modern Art

ⓘ *Military Rd, T01-6129900, www.modernart.ie. Tue-Sat 1000-1730, Sun, bank holidays 1200-1730, closed Mon. Free. Guided tours in summer months, garden, coffee shop and bookshop open museum hours. Buses to Heuston station then 10 mins walk: 26 from Wellington Quay, 51, 79 from Aston Quay, 90 from Tara St, Connolly St stations, 123 from O'Connell St, Luas to Heuston.*

The Royal Hospital at Kilmainham, now the Irish Museum of Modern Art, was built between 1680 and 1684 as a retirement home for old soldiers. The design is a rectangle with an interior courtyard and a loggia with open arches on three sides.

The museum organizes a wide-ranging programme of exhibitions and there are always brochures outlining the displays of the moment. The bookshop in the gallery has an excellent collection of books on art and architecture.

Kilmainham Gaol

ⓘ *Inchicore Rd, Dublin 8, T01-4535984, www.heritageireland.ie. Apr-Sep daily 0930-1700; Oct-Mar Mon-Sat 0930-1600, Sun 1000-1700. €5. Visits include a guided tour, last tour is 1 hr before closing. Bus 51B, 78A, and 9 from Aston Quay, Luas Siur Rd.*

Built in 1792, and opened just in time to incarcerate the survivors of the 30,000 rebels who died in the 1798 uprising, this building saw hundreds of men suffer and die for their belief in independence in the uprisings of 1798, 1803, 1848, 1867, 1916 and 1922. Most of the big names in Republican history spent time in here and some of them died here. The last man to walk out was de Valera, at the end of the Civil War in 1923, whereupon the gaol was abandoned as it stood. Forty years later a voluntary group of history buffs decided to restore it, the work was completed by the state and Kilmainham was opened to the public.

Give yourself an hour for the tour and at least half an hour more for the museum.

There is a museum covering the early 20th-century political history of Ireland as well as prison memorabilia where you can wait for a guided tour. It takes you around the dungeons, tiny cells, the chapel where Joseph Plunkett was married three hours before his execution and the grim yard where Connolly, Plunkett and 15 other leaders of the 1916 uprising were executed.

Rathfarnham

Deep in wealthy suburbia Rathfarnham was once a country village and it still has a rural atmosphere. It is home to the school run by Patrick Pearse, the leader of the Easter Rising. Now a museum to his memory, you can also walk in its gardens. Here too is Rathfarnham Castle, a Victorian-looking place but with its origins in the sixteenth century.

The Pearse Museum

ⓘ Grange Rd, T01-4934208. Nov-Jan daily 1000-1600; Feb-Apr daily 1000-1700; May-Aug daily 1000-1730; Sep-Oct daily 1000-1700. Free. Guided tours on request, last admission 45 mins before closing. Self-guided nature trail, Nature Study Centre. Tearoom open in summer and at weekends in Feb-Apr and Oct. Bus 16 from city centre.

Dedicated to the memory of one of the leaders of the Easter Rising, this Georgian mansion in Grange Road, was once St Enda's, the bilingual school that Patrick Pearse and his brother and sister ran along quite radical lines. Displays in the building show Pearse's teaching methods and beliefs. His most famous words are: 'Ireland unfree shall never be at peace'.

Much of the Easter Rising was planned in the basement of the building. Patrick and his brother Willie set off to the GPO with some of their pupils. None of the teachers returned and the students, young as they were, ended up in prison camps. Both Patrick and Willie were executed. The school is also worth a visit for the gardens it is set in. There is a nature centre with information about the park's wildlife and a nature trail which leads to a waterfall.

Look out for the photo of Michael Collins standing on the steps of the school signing Dáil bonds. The block of wood he is leaning on is now in Kilmainham Gaol and is thought to be the execution block of Robert Emmet.

Rathfarnham Castle

ⓘ Rathfarnham Rd, Rathfarnham, T01-4939462. May-Oct daily 0930-1730. €2, last admission 1 hr before closing. Access by guided tour only. Bus 16, 16A from centre.

The 16th-century building was originally a proper castle with battlements and 18 fireplaces, making it the biggest building in the Dublin area. The battlements were removed in the more settled times of the early 18th century. The castle is undergoing renovations and visitors are shown around the works as they progress, getting a different glimpse of structures and alterations at each visit.

★ Phoenix Park

It's easy to put on a good pair of walking shoes and spend a whole day pottering about the sights in the Phoenix Park. The 710 ha make it the largest enclosed public park in Europe and it includes **Dublin Zoo**, a police museum, a visitor centre, an early 17th-century fortified house, monuments to assorted public figures, the homes of the Irish president and American ambassador, several lakes, deer, a thriving wildlife community, a **neolithic cromlech** and the interesting ruins of a **magazine fort**. Dubliners use Phoenix Park for all sorts of activities, from practising their golf swings to flying model aeroplanes, hurling matches and just sitting about in the sunshine. The park lies about 2½ km west of O'Connell Bridge in the city centre and can be reached on foot by walking along the north quays or by bus (see page 124).

Approaching the **Wellington Testimonial**, the sheer scale of the thing is what strikes the eye. It was begun in 1817, and the money for its construction was used up on the first 30 m. Wellington fell from grace at around this time and the monument was not completed. In 1861 work on it began again, with the addition of the bronze plaques celebrating Waterloo, the defeat of the Indian Mutiny and, strangely for someone who opposed Catholic emancipation, civil and religious liberty. But the project was never completed according to the original plan. The lions intended for the statue's feet were never made, and the plinths that had been set out to hold them were taken down.

Dublin zoo

ⓘ *T01-6771425, www.dublinzoo.ie. Mon-Sat 0930-1800, Sun 1030-1800 (closing at dusk daily between Nov and Feb). €12.50, family ticket €40. Daily tours. Bus 10, 10A from O'Connell St, 25/A, 26, 66/A/B, 67, 68, 69, Luas Heuston stop.*

The MGM lion's roar is said to have been recorded from a lion bred in Dublin zoo.

Dublin Zoo, set in 12 ha, is the second oldest zoo in Europe and has a petting zoo and monkey islands. A new extension calls itself the African Plains and serves as home to animals like the rhino, giraffe and hippo.

Glasnevin and Clontarf

Spreading northwards from the city centre, beyond the Royal Canal which marks the outer edges of the city proper, are the twin suburbs of Glasnevin and Clontarf, mainly residential areas, and home to some impressive Edwardian estates full of much sought-after terraced houses. Apart from the bed and breakfast accommodation, visitors are drawn by two major attractions, the **Botanic Gardens** and the **Prospect Cemetery** at Glasnevin. They are close enough to each other to be visited on the same day. For transport information, see page 124.

★ Prospect Cemetery

It's not often you see a cemetery on a list of sightseeing places, but this one is seriously worth a visit for many reasons. First, within its 50 ha are interred the bodies of hundreds of people who have played significant parts in the history, art, literature and religious life of Ireland and beyond, and standing beside their graves gives their stories an immediacy that a dull paragraph in a guidebook never does. Second, it is a stunning piece of social history, written in the architecture and design of the thousands of tombstones, revealing the pretensions, passions, wealth and poverty of the people who are buried there. Whoever said that death doesn't distinguish between rich and poor? Highly recommended is the free tour of the cemetery.

National Botanic Gardens

ⓘ *T01-8374388. Gardens: summer, Mon-Sat 0900-1800, Sun 1000-1800; winter, Mon-Sat 1000-1630, Sun 1100-1630. Free. Glasshouses: summer, Mon-Fri 0900-1715, Sat 0900-1745; winter, daily 1000-1615, closed Christmas Day. Free. Guided tours by arrangement, price €2. Bus 13, 19 from O'Connell St, 134 from Middle Abbey St.*

The gardens, close to the cemetery, comprise 200 ha of plants, both indigenous and exotic. Established in 1795, they are worth the visit just to admire the great 19th-century glasshouses. There are more than 20,000 species here, including several that were developed at Glasnevin. It is one of Glasnevin's collectors that the British Isles has to thank for the stands of pampas grass that grace many a suburban garden. The Botanic Gardens have undergone a massive facelift with the curvilinear range almost completely replaced, a new alpine house and a visitor centre with a good café.

Dun Laoghaire → *Dun Laoghaire Station, 20 mins from Central Dublin.*

If you feel jaded by too much street life you might consider an excursion to the seaside south of the city. Or you may just find yourself in Dun Laoghaire (pronounced Dunleary) waiting for a ferry departure. Nowadays Dun Laoghaire is both an important seaport and a seaside town, with huge Victorian villas lining the seafront and looking out at the great passenger ferries trawling their way in and out of the harbour. The only **tourist office** is a walk-in one, at the ferry terminal, open Mon-Sat 1000-1300, 1400-1800.

History

A fishing village until the middle years of the 18th century, Dun Laoghaire became a major resort and harbour when the two mile-long piers were built between 1817 and 1827. The first car ferry made the journey from Holyhead to Dun Laoghaire in 1966. Thirty years later the harbour got a new lease of life with the opening in 1996 of the new Stena Line ferry terminal. Nowadays the Stena high speed ship swishes in and out and there are warning signs along the shores, telling walkers to keep back for half an hour after the ferry has docked and departed.

National Maritime Museum

ⓘ *T01-2800969. May-Sep daily 1300-1700. €2.* The National Maritime Museum is housed in the Mariner's Church (1837) in Haigh Terrace, Dun Laoghaire. Its interesting collection includes a captured ship's longboat, used for ferrying officers to and from shore, and taken during the aborted French invasion at Bantry in 1796. There are also models of ships and a very large optic which was once the light from the Bailey Lighthouse at Howth.

Dun Laoghaire piers

The two piers, each over a mile long, are grand for a stiff walk. The West Pier, nearest to Dublin, is the least used, while the East Pier is a Sunday constitutional kind of walk with a bandstand, often with some performance going on, a gadget for measuring wind speed, a memorial to a Captain Boyd and, at the end, an unmanned lighthouse. From the end of either pier you can see the shape of Dublin Bay with Killiney at the southern extent and Howth Head to the north.

James Joyce Museum

A very short distance away from the Forty Foot, the James Joyce Museum occupies the **Martello tower** built on a rocky promontory. The first chapter of *Ulysses* is set in this tower, where Joyce lived for a week, and a collection of literary memorabilia and the open roof are the main attractions inside. See page 91 for details.

Howth → *DART trains run from Connolly Station in just over 20 mins.*

Howth, 15 km northeast of Dublin, is a lumpy peninsula that forms the northern part of the lovely horseshoe curve of Dublin Bay and looks south towards Dun Laoghaire. There are **beaches**, starting with the small and stony Balscadden beach which is just past the harbour where the bus arrives. Sutton beach, to the west, is sandy but incredibly shallow. Howth doesn't have that dormitory-town feel of Portmarnock or Malahide, further north of the city, and retains a fishing-village atmosphere.

A pleasant afternoon can be spent walking around the peninsula and across the hill of Howth. From the DART station go directly across the road to a gap in the wall which used to be the entrance to the tram station. Follow the steps and then the footpath uphill and behind some houses to a suburban street, **Grace O'Malley Drive**. Turn right, follow the road a little way, still climbing the hill and then turn right between some houses into a street called **Balkil Park**, and through a fence into the open land of the hill. Head south and uphill across the open land, towards a mobile phone transmitter aerial. From here there are excellent views of the peninsula.

Make your way downhill and west, following a line of white painted stones, to get a view of the golf course and then across heather-covered slopes, but always keeping to pathways, to **Carrickbrack Road**. Turn right and follow the road for a few hundred metres until a sign appears on the seaward side of the road indicating a dangerous cliff edge. Continue along the path towards the cliffs and you will find yourself on the **Howth Head cliff walk**. Follow the cliff round to the left and a two-hour walk brings you back past amazing views of beaches and seabirds to the village, passing on your way footpaths that lead to the summit, from where there are more magnificent views. It was in the area where this cliff walk starts that Erskine Childers landed a shipment of machine guns to help the anti-Treaty party in their struggle against the new Irish Free State. He was captured and executed by his erstwhile friends.

Malahide → *DART trains from Connolly station. See page 126 for Transport information.*

Malahide, Mullach Íde in Gaelic, is a coastal town north of Howth and is pretty much a suburb of the city. It has that feel of a sleeper town which buzzes with activity at rush hours and sleeps quietly in between. The main reason for visiting is the **castle** ⓘ *T01-8462184, Apr-Oct Mon-Sat 1000-1700, Sun and public holidays 1100-1800, Nov-Mar Mon-Fri 1000-1700, Sat, Sun and bank holidays 1400-1700, closed 1245-1400, €6.25, combined ticket with Fry Model Railway available*, set in its own demesne of 506 ha with the Fry Model Railway in the grounds. It's a three-storey fortified house owned for almost 800 years by one family, the Talbots, with a brief interlude during Cromwell's invasion of Ireland. It was bought by Dublin County Council in 1975 and opened to the public. Nothing remains of the original building erected in the 12th century, but a tiny part of one tower (which you don't actually see on the tour) is 14th century. The **Fry Model Railway** ⓘ *T01-8463779, Apr-Sep Mon-Sat, 1000-1300, 1400-1800, Sun and public holidays, 1400-1800, €6.25, suburban rail/ DART northbound to Malahide, 5 min walk*, in an old corn store in the grounds of the castle is usually a hit with children and the **Talbot Botanic Gardens** beside the castle is a great children's playground.

You can hire the Great Hall at Malahide Castle for parties.

Malahide to Portmarnock

There is an exhilarating **walk** along the foreshore from Malahide to the southern end of Portmarnock, full of fresh air and lovely sea views of Howth to the south and Ireland's Eye out to sea. Lots of seabirds pick their way through the shells on the beach; the entire stretch of shore has sandy beaches, although the southern end gets tangled up with Portmarnock Golf Links.

Donabate

ⓘ *Newbridge House, T01-8436534. Apr-Sep Tue-Sat 1000-1700, Sun and public holidays 1400-1800, closed for tours, 1300-1400; Oct to Mar Sat, Sun and public holidays 1400-1700. Organized tours, €6.20 house, €3 farm. Northbound suburban train to Donabate, then 15-min walk.*

One stop on from Malahide on the Dundalk line is Donabate, worth the trip for **Newbridge House**, an 18th-century manor house built by Richard Castle for the Archbishop of Dublin, in 1737, and set in 142 ha of land. The family still live in and own the house and all the original furniture and paintings are still in place. The original plasterwork is by Robert West and the rooms are full of period furniture. The park is maintained in its 18th-century state and includes a walled garden and arboretum. In the courtyard of the house and the outbuildings is a museum of 19th-century farming, complete with pettable animals.

Around Portrane there are excellent beaches and views over Lambay island. Further north is Rogerstown Wildlife Sanctuary, another river estuary full of wading birds.

Skerries

Half an hour by suburban train from the city centre, Skerries makes an excellent out-of-town base for those who prefer the quiet of the countryside to the rush and bustle of the city. Skerries offers pleasant accommodation, good food and a whole slew of places to visit in the surrounding area. The harbour is pretty and there is an abundance of wildlife, including seals.

Tourist information, Skerries Mills Complex, Miller's Lane, Skerries, T01-8495208. Apr-Sep daily, 1030-1730, Oct-Mar daily 1030-1630. Closed 20 Dec-2 Jan. The major attraction in the village itself is the **Skerries Mills Complex** ⓘ *Miller's Lane, T01-8495208, Apr-Sep daily 1030-1800, Oct-Mar daily 1030-1630, closed 20 Dec-2 Jan, €4, café, tourist information point and craft shop*, a heritage centre set in the village park. Visitors can walk around the working water mill and watch it operate as well as see inside the two windmills and inspect the bakery which makes bread from the wholegrain flour ground in the mills. There's a café selling products made at the bakery.

A half-hour walk or brief bus ride out of town brings you to **Ardgillan House and Demesne** ⓘ *Coast Rd, Balbriggan, T01-8492212, house: Apr-Sep Tue-Sun and public holidays 1100-1800 (Jul, Aug, daily), Oct-Mar Tue-Sun and public holidays 1000-1630, closed 23 Dec-2 Jan; park: daily 1000-dusk, e5 includes tour of the building, coffee shops, garden tours Thu 1530*, which has one of the most spectacular views of any country estate in Ireland or Britain. Set on a hillside with panoramic views of the sea all the way north to the Mountains of Mourne this is a castellated 18th-century house.

Sleeping

Grafton Street and around

p63, maps p64 and p66

Grafton Street and around (including Temple Bar) form Dublin's chief accommodation area, with prices either pretty high at the 3-star hotel and upwards end, or low at the few hostels, and with not much in between. Guest houses tend to be quite expensive and there are simply no B&Bs in the area.

Hotels

L Merrion Hotel, Upper Merrion St, T01-6030600, www.merrionhotel.com. The ultimate in understated luxury in the middle of the city. Four converted Georgian houses, one of which was the birthplace of Wellington, plus a new block in the same style surround pretty, formal gardens. Big comfortable rooms, 2 restaurants, a pool and fitness centre plus a fairly astounding collection of artwork scattered around the beautiful Georgian interiors.

L-B Brooks, Drury St, T01-6704000, www.brookshoteldublin.com. Stylish and located in the heart of Dublin, with a restful library and a pleasantly quiet restaurant. Excellent food, very helpful and friendly, sauna, ideal central location. No car park, but a multi-storey one is opposite the hotel and special rates are available.

L-C Camden Court Hotel, Camden St, T01-4759666, www.camdencourthotel.com. Away from the street noise of late night clubbers but close enough to all the sights. Popular bar serves an excellent carvery lunch. Leisure centre with a large pool, jacuzzi and steam room available to guests. Secure car parking. Best value in this price range and area.

A-C Buswell's, Molesworth St, T01-6146500, www.quinnhotels.com. A very central 18th-century townhouse and while the hotel has been extended it still retains all its originality and charm. Secure overnight parking.

A-C Trinity Capital Hotel, Pearse St, T01-6481000, www.capital-hotels.com. Fashionable hotel in a quiet area of the city centre between Trinity College and the river. Outlandish decor and comfortable rooms.

For an explanation of the sleeping and eating price codes used in this guide, see inside the front cover. Other relevant information is found in Essentials pages 39-45.

Complimentary admission to other Capital Hotel clubs.

A-D **Holiday Inn**, 99-107 Pearse St, T01-6703666, www.holidayinndublin citycentre.ie. 10-min walk from the city at the working-class end of Pearse St. Nearly 100 rooms and the benefit of a gym and sauna. The bar has live music at weekends, ranging from jazz to karaoke.

A-D **Mercer Hotel**, Mercer St Lower, T01-4783677, www.mercerhotel.ie. Very central location in a quiet side street off Grafton St. This is a good, new middle-range hotel far enough out of Temple Bar to afford some peace at night but close to shops and city centre sights.

B-D **Harcourt Hotel**, 60 Harcourt St, T01-4783677, www.harcourthotel.ie. Very busy hotel in the heart of the clubbing area. Great if you plan to have a late night out in Harcourt St, but if you want an early night ask for a room at the back. Lots of traditional music, good bar food.

C-D **Jackson Court Hotel**, 29-30 Harcourt St, T01-4758777, info@jackson-court.ie. Big rooms with spacious bathrooms and actual baths, carvery meals in the popular bar, and nightclub free to guests. Right in the centre of the non-Temple Bar nightclub area, so a good place for night owls.

Guest houses

L-D **Baggot Court**, 92 Lower Baggot St, T01-6612819, baggot@indigo.ie. Close to the centre but in quiet area, pleasantly appointed albeit identically pine-furnished bedrooms with bath and shower, small guest lounge area, off-street parking.

B-D **Kilronan Guesthouse**, 70 Adelaide Rd, T01-4755266, www.dublinn.com. An award-winning guest house that can rival most small hotels for its level of service and comfort. Has a private car park.

Hostels

D-E **Ashfield House**, 19-20 D'Olier St, T01-6797734, ashfield@indigo.ie. Multi-bed, single and double rooms, breakfast included, laundry.

E **Avalon House**, 55 Aungier St, T01-4750001, www.avalon-house.ie. Singles and doubles at reasonable rates as well as family rooms and mixed as well as single sex dormitory rooms. Price includes breakfast. Café/restaurant.

Self-catering

D **Trinity College**, Dublin 2, T01-6081177. 16 Jun-3 Oct. Single rooms, some with en suite bathroom. Bar, kitchens, laundry, sports facilities, car park. Breakfast included.

Temple Bar *p75, map p76*

Hotels

L **The Clarence**, 6-8 Wellington Quay, T01-4070800, www.theclarence.ie. There really needs to be a special price category just for the Clarence! Room rates start from €330. Owned by U2, the original wood panelling has been preserved amidst modish embellishments like leather-clad lifts, Egyptian cotton on the kingsize beds, CD player (but no kettle) in the individually designed bedrooms enlivened by rich colours and Irish craftwork. Friendly staff, wearing designer outfits that look vaguely clerical and a bookless lounge called the *Study* with original artwork contribute to the strange mix of the spartan and the sybaritic that characterizes a hotel originally built in 1852.

L-D **Blooms**, 6 Anglesea St, T01-6715622, www.blooms.ie. Centrally located small hotel with 86 well designed rooms. Nightclub doesn't bother guests but would suit clubbers rather than culture vultures.

L-D **Paramount Hotel**, Parliament St and Essex Gate, T01-4179900, www.paramount hotel.ie. In Temple Bar's only quiet street, this recently built labyrinthine place has large comfortable rooms, several of which look out onto an internal courtyard, offering a quiet night amidst the hubbub of the area. Breakfast can get very busy so be prepared to get up before the carousers if you want to eat in peace. Downstairs is the Turk's Head bar for those who want a short stagger back to their bedrooms.

C-D **Jury's Inn Christ Church**, Christ Church Pl, T01-4540000, www.jurysinns.com. Based on a single-room rate for 3 adults, or 2 adults and 2 children, this is reasonable value for fair-sized, comfortable rooms, nice pub with traditional music, secure car park and informal restaurant (breakfast not included in room rate).

Hostels

D-E **Barnacles Temple Bar House**, 19 Temple Lane, T01-6716277, www.barnacles.ie. Nice modern lounge area, big windows, all rooms have en suite bathrooms, good security, left-luggage facility and safes, breakfast included.

D-E **Oliver St John Gogarty's**, 18-21 Anglesea St, T01-6711822, www.gogartys.ie. Lift, safes, luggage storage, internet access, laundry, TV room.

E **Kinlay House**, 2-12 Lord Edward St, T01-6796644, www.kinlayhouse.ie. Dorm beds, singles and doubles, some with en suite bathroom. Breakfast included in the rate, internet access. One of the smartest kitchen and dining areas in any Dublin hostel. Very central, good security, but the usual noise problem at weekends.

The Liberties *p78, map p80*

Hostels

E **The Brewery Hostel**, 22-3 Thomas St, T01-453 8600, www.irish-hostels.com. Good to find a hostel in this part of town and this is open all year with over 50 dorm beds and 5 private doubles. Breakfast included, and a paved area out the back with picnic tables. Staying a night or two in Thomas St can be interesting because this is not tourist Dublin and there are some lively pubs and clubs along here.

E **Four Courts Hostel**, 15-17 Merchant's Quay, T01-6725839, www.fourcourtshostel.com. This is west of the Liberties area itself, directly opposite the Four Courts and close to the Guinness Storehouse. This hostel offers stylish dorms and private rooms. A quiet reading room, a pool table, good kitchens, internet access and lots of tourist information.

O'Connell Street and around
p81, map p82

The O'Connell Street area has a concentration of the more affordable guest houses and hostels, but the central location and the proximity of the bus and a railway station means they tend to fill up the most quickly. **Gardiner Street** is full of guest houses and quite a few hostels are here or in the nearby streets. The top end of O'Connell Street, around Parnell Square, also has some interesting possibilities. Most budgets are allowed for, but this area is rich in mid-range guest houses, hotels and hostels.

Hotels

L **Clarion Hotel Dublin IFSC**, Excise Walk, T01-433 8800, info@clarionhotelifsc.ie. Shiny new hotel overlooking the river and set in the shiny new IFSC area of the city. Riveting industrial riverscapes from the windows, fresh, big, uncluttered rooms with duvets, surprisingly close to the city centre and, with the new docks developments opening up all around it, sandwich bars, restaurants, and clubs nearby. Fitness centre and pool, bar with Asian fusion food, neat breakfast.

L-B **The Gresham**, O'Connell St, T01-8746881, www.gresham-hotels.com. The hotel claims to have the highest ratio of porters to rooms in Ireland. Close to the GPO, it was destroyed by the shelling of the British in 1916 and withstood the Beatles in the 1960s. A scene in Joyce's *The Dead* is set in one of the hotel rooms.

L-B **Morrison**, 15 Ormond Quay, T01-8872400, www.morrisonhotel.ie. Part of the gentrification of north Dublin, this classy building, Ireland's first designer hotel, sits unobtrusively on the bank of the river and vies with *The Clarence* as Dublin's most hip hotel. New-fangled decor, themed in black and white, refreshingly un-Irish. CD players, complimentary tea and coffee on request , mood lighting, quality fabrics and original artwork in the chic, air-conditioned bedrooms. Lots of designer touches about the place waiting to be noticed. Breakfast not included in room rates; brilliant restaurant (see page 107).

L-B **Royal Dublin**, O'Connell St, T01-8733666, www.royaldublin.com. Popular with visitors, this is a friendly well-run hotel at the top end of Parnell St. Gregarious bar alongside the decent Café Royal restaurant (see page 107).

B-C **Academy Hotel**, Findlater Pl, T01-8780666, www.academy-hotel.ie. Modern centrally located comfortable hotel off O'Connell St. Good value. Private car park.

B-D **Castle Hotel**, 2-4 Gardiner Row, T01-8746949, www.castle-hotel.ie. Another lovingly restored Georgian building that offers so much more, at better value, than some of the faceless hotels around town. Car parking available, elegant lounge and comfortable rooms (Michael Collins is said to have used room 201, originally No 23, when sleeping in one of his familiar safe houses during the War of Independence, see page 86).

B-D Hotel St George, 7 Parnell Sq, T01-8745611, hotels@indigo.ie. The bedroom decor may be a little twee but the marble fireplace and original plasterwork in the lounge of this Georgian building help distinguish it. Car park available.

B-D Lynam's Hotel, 63 O'Connell St, T01-8880886, www.lynams-hotel.com. Bang in the centre of O'Connell St, but it's not noisy in the smart, modern bedrooms in 2 Georgian houses once owned by the inventor of the Tilly Lamp. A comfortable lounge on the 1st floor overlooks the main drag.

C-D Jurys Inn Custom House, Custom House Quay, Dublin 1, T01-6075000, www.jurysinns.com. The rooms have a flat rate between €108-140. Rooms at the front offer views of the river and the Wicklow hills in the distance; rooms at the back will be quieter. Breakfast not included in the room rate but there is a self-service cafeteria.

Guest houses

A-E Comfort Inn, Gt Denmark St, T01-8737700, www.comfortinndublin.com. A refurbished, professionally run guest house in a quiet Georgian terrace. Rates are on a room basis for up to 4 people, breakfast not included.

B-E Clifden Guesthouse, 32 Gardiner Pl, T01-8746364, www.clifdenhouse.com. A fair spread of rooms with singles, doubles, triples and family rooms. Rates don't include breakfast but parking is free.

C-D Glen Guesthouse, 84 Lower Gardiner St, T01-8551374, theglen@eircom.net. Small, 12-room guest house, central, reasonable rates, well restored.

C-E Harvey's Guest House, 11 Upper Gardiner St, T01-8748384, www.harveysguesthouse.com. Family-run, 14 bedrooms, free car parking; bus No 41 from the airport stops close by.

D Georgian Court Guesthouse, 77 Lower Gardiner St, T01-8557872, georgiancourt@eircom.net. Secure car parking, showers but no baths, a lounge area with a leather sofa, an airy dining room for above-average breakfast. Triple and family rooms. Popular in summer so advance booking required.

D Othello Guesthouse, 74 Lower Gardiner St, T01-8554271, 8555442, othello1@eircom.net. Some rooms are larger than others but pot luck seems to determine which one you get. A small, boxy conservatory serves as a public guest area. Secure car parking available and all rooms have en suite facilities, with a television and telephone; breakfast included.

D The Townhouse, 47-8 Lower Gardiner St, T01-8788808, gtrotter@indigo.ie. Doubles and triple rooms at competitive prices, some with kitchenette, all have their own bathrooms, tea- and coffee-making facilities, satellite TV. Rates include continental breakfast. The house has a literary heritage which is proudly displayed around the lobby area and which complements the period details which help make this a rather elegant guest house.

E Marian Guesthouse, 21 Upper Gardiner St, T01-8744129. Family-run, standard guest house, B&B prices, fair value, close to Mountjoy Sq and bus No 41 from the airport stops close by. Private car park.

Hostels

A-C Litton Lane, 2-4 Litton Lane, T01-8728389, litton@indigo.ie. Only 3 private rooms in this hostel, breakfast included, laundry.

C-E Abraham House, 82-3 Lower Gardiner St, T01-8550600, stay@abraham-house.ie. Dorm beds and private rooms, though not a lot of comfort. Free car park, launderette, breakfast included in price. Fills up very quickly so book early.

C-E Globetrotters Tourist Hostel, 46-8 Lower Gardiner St, T01-8735893, gtrotter@indigo.ie. One of the most expensive hostels in Dublin if paying for a private room, breakfast included.

D-E Abbey Court, 29 Bachelor's Walk, T01-8780700, info@abbey-court.com. Newish hostel accommodation in central location by O'Connell Bridge. All rooms have en suite bathroom. Barbecue area, TV room, key card access, breakfast included.

D-E Jacob's Inn, 21-8 Talbot Pl, T01-8555660, jacobs@isaacs.ie. Café-style restaurant, internet, free left-luggage facility, TV lounge, safes.

D-E Mount Eccles Court, 42 North Great George St, T01-8730826, www.eccles hostel.com. The Joyce Centre is a few doors down from this fairly new hostel with all the usual facilities. Dorm beds are more reasonably priced than many are during the high season; only 4 private rooms.

E Isaac's Hostel, 2-5 Frenchman's Lane, T01-8556215, hostel@isaacs.ie. Long-established place with deli, cyber café, multi- bed dorms, singles and doubles, safes, free left-luggage facility. No access even to private rooms between 1100 and 1430 but still very popular place, helped by being so close to the bus station.

E Marlborough Hostel, 81-2 Marlborough St, T01-8747629, mail@marlborohostel.com. Good value, relaxed small hostel. Twin rooms particularly reasonable value, TV room, rear garden with BBQ area, security lockers, breakfast included.

F Dublin International Youth Hostel, 61 Mountjoy St, T01-8301766, dublin-international @anoige.ie. *An Óige* (Hostelling International) hostel, multi-bed and a few double rooms, in a renovated old convent. Huge kitchen, secure parking, brilliant dining room in old chapel, TV room, supplement for non-members.

F Goin' My Way, 15 Talbot St, T01-8788484, goinmyway@esatclear.ie. Open between 4 Jan and 22 Dec, vaguely Christian, tiny, ageist hostel, good value twin rooms, breakfast included.

Smithfield *p87, map p88*

Hotels

L-D Ashling Hotel, Parkgate St, T01-6772324, www.ashlinghotel.ie. Close to Heuston Station and the Phoenix Park in the west of the city. Great views of the river and the rising curls of alcoholic steam from the Guinness brewery. Worth considering for any package deals that might be available. Bus stops close by for town. The philosopher Wittgenstein stayed here while writing parts of his Philosophical Investigations in 1948.

A-D Chief O'Neill's Hotel, Smithfield Village, T01-8173838, www.chiefoneills.com. Modern hotel, all frosted green glass and modish lighting, and bedrooms (with CD players, kettles and nifty sinks) that successfully strives to be different. Café/bar downstairs, in the centre of the newly renovated Smithfield Village. Breakfast is extra. If you are fed up with anonymous, all-too-similar hotels, consider staying here.

Guest houses

C-E Phoenix Park House, 38-9 Parkgate St, T01-6772870, www.dublinguesthouse.com. Large family-run place beside Ryan's bar and close to the Phoenix Park. Quiet area of town and close to buses and secure parking.

Ballsbridge and around

Still within walking distance of the centre, but more conveniently reached by bus, Ballsbridge is an expensive residential neighbourhood in the south of the city. Home to some of the plummiest Dublin 4 accents, upmarket cars, tasteful faux Victorian conservatories, and with the densest population of antimacassars, doilies and toilet roll covers in all Ireland, these streets of Edwardian and Victorian houses exude comfortable, middle-class values. In addition to the UK and US embassies is a cluster of quality hotels and guest houses. And even if you're not staying in Ballsbridge, it's worth the effort to go there just for the excellent restaurants.

Hotels

L Four Seasons, Simmonscourt Rd, T01-6654000, www.fourseasons.com/dublin.

Very luxurious hotel, huge public areas, neo-classical decor, attentive staff. Large bedrooms and suites you could live in. Silver service in a grand, roomy restaurant with windows looking out to garden courtyard.

L The Towers, Lansdowne Rd, T01-6670033, towers@jurysdoyle.com. One of Dublin's best hotels. 100 larger than average rooms with a/c, walk-in wardrobe, work area. Hospitality lounge with complimentary cocktails and hot drinks throughout the day, a residents' bar serving until 0130 (0030 on Sun), and all the facilities of the main Jurys Ballsbridge hotel which is reached through a walkway.

L-A School House Hotel, 2-8 Northumberland Rd, T01-6675014, www.schoolhousehotel.com. Beside the canal, this prettily renovated old school offers a high standard of accommodation, a restaurant in a classroom, and lots of history. Small, friendly and closer to town than most Ballsbridge hotels.

A-D Jury's Ballsbridge, Pembroke Rd, T01-6605000, ballsbridgehotel@jurysdoyle.com. Remarkably friendly for such a large hotel, over 300 spacious bedrooms, and well provided for in the food and beverage departments. As well as the top-notch *Raglans* restaurant (see page 108), there is a coffee shop serving meals nearly 24 hrs, and a carvery lunch in the Dubliner pub. Indoor/outdoor pool and gym, free parking, hair and beauty salon, business centre.

A-D The Mespil Hotel, Mespil Rd, T01-6671222, www.leehotels.ie. This quality 3-star hotel is not as far south as Ballsbridge and is easily walkable from the city centre. Bus No 10 from O'Connell St and Kildare St travels close by and the Aircoach is a 5-min walk away outside the *Burlington Hotel* in Upper Leeson St. Free car parking. A modern hotel with a pleasant cosmopolitan feel with a room rate for up to 3 people, excluding breakfast, in generously sized bedrooms.

B-D Lansdowne Hotel, 27 Pembroke Rd, T01-6682522, www.lansdownehotel.ie. Small hotel with 40 bedrooms, a little way out of the centre in a quiet location. Beer garden, good bargain at this price range. Druids Restaurant.

D Bewley's Hotel, Merrion Rd, T01-6681111, www.BewleysHotels.com. Rooms are around €99 for up to 3 adults or a family of 4 and this represents excellent value for smart, spacious and comfortable accommodation, especially in the Ballsbridge area. The red- brick Victorian building has been converted from a convent school and the original entrance way opens into a roomy public area with the quality O'Connells restaurant downstairs (see page 108) and a café. Aircoach stop is right outside.

Guest houses

B-D Aberdeen Lodge, 53-55 Park Av, T01-2838155, www.halpinsprivatehotels.com. Luxurious Edwardian guest house where you are welcomed with tea and biscuits. Elegant lounge, gardens, hotel-standard rooms. Close to Sydney Parade DART station. Hot drinks on call all day. Exemplary breakfast. Good alternative to noisy city hotels.

B-D Merrion Hall, 56 Merrion Rd, T01-6681426, www.halpinsprivatehotels.com. Quiet welcoming place with ample lounge, a library with lots of tourist information, lovely, sunny breakfastroom serving award-winning breakfast, gardens.

B-E Ariel House, 50-54 Lansdowne Rd, T01-6685512, www.ariel-house.com. Listed, red-brick Victorian house, all non-smoking, car park, 3 mins on foot from the Lansdowne Rd DART station. Built in the 1860s, this is a classy guesthouse with a choice of rooms, all with a bath and shower, and 3 with 4-poster beds. Americans, with good reason, adore the decor and antiques.

Self-catering

UCD Village, Belfield, Dublin 4, T01-2697111, www.ucdvillage.com. Early Jun-early Sep. Choice of 3- or 4-bedroomed apartments, 24-hr reception, campus bar, restaurants and coffee shop, nightly or weekly.

Camping and caravanning

D Camac Valley Tourist Caravan and Camping Park, Naas Rd, Clondalkin, Dublin 22, T01-4640644, www.camacvalley.com. 35-min drive from Central Dublin on the N7. 163 pitches and a good range of facilities including a TV lounge, good for those rainy days. Backpackers from around €6 per person, families from €15. No hire caravans. No dogs allowed.

Dun Laoghaire *p94*

L Royal Marine Hotel, Marine Rd, T01-2801911. By far the classiest hotel in Dun Laoghaire, open to the public since 1865, with a grand Victorian staircase and fine views of the incoming boats (supplement for sea views). Elegant restaurant, pretty landscaped garden, some of the rooms are Victorian in style. Closing for a time in 2005 for renovation.

E **Avondale House**, 3 Northumberland Av, T01-2809628. A small and basic B&B on the main shopping street, with shared bathroom facilities.

E **Belgrave Hall**, 34 Belgrave Sq, Monkstown, T01-2842106, www.dublinhostel.com. This hostel is situated between Blackrock and Dun Laoghaire in a rather splendid building. Dorm beds and private rooms. Breakfast included, laundry facility and bikes for hire.

E **Marina House**, 7 Old Dunleary Rd, T01-2841524, www.marinahouse.com. This is Dun Laoghaire's only hostel, with dorm beds and 6 private rooms.

E **Phyllis Brady**, 81 Adelaide Rd, Glenageary, T01-2806781. 3 twin rooms with shared facilities, it only just comes into this price category. Head down Dun Laoghaire's main street in the direction of Sandycove and on Glasthule Rd turn right at the corner with the Eagle House pub. The B&B is up here on the right side.

Skerries *p97*

B **Redbank Guesthouse**, Church St, Skerries, T01-8490439, redbank@eircom.net. Luxurious, friendly place attached to the well-known Red Bank restaurant. Big comfortable rooms, sitting room, courtyard garden. The proprietors regularly arrange golfing, fishing, walking and sailing trips in the area. Amazing breakfast. Try the scrambled eggs and locally smoked salmon.

E **Malting House Inn**, Holmpatrick, Skerries, T01-8491075. Pub accommodation in pretty old stone-built pub close to the Skerries Mills complex. Breakfast not included in the rate.

Eating

Grafton Street and around

p63, maps p64 and p66

While many of Temple Bar's restaurants (see page 105) are fun, fashionable and relatively inexpensive places to enjoy a meal, the area from St Stephen's Green to Merrion Square is where the real money tends to eat. Don't even look at the menus if you are on a tight budget. Reservations are advisable at all times, often essential. Many more moderately priced places can be found in the streets around Grafton St, while South Great George's St and Aungier St have lots of affordable restaurants.

TTT **Browne's Brasserie**, 22 St Stephen's Green, T01-6383939, www.brownes dublin.com. Book well in advance at this well established and busy restaurant. All red plush, white linen, mirrors and chandeliers, it offers modern Irish cooking with lots of inventive sauces. A good place for brown enveloping at lunch time or a romantic dinner in the evening. Excellent value Sun lunch, 1230-1430.

TTT **One Pico**, 5-6 Molesworth Pl, T01-6760300. Close to Stephen's Green, this is a contemporary restaurant with a very modern and innovative menu. Go to this place for the challenging menu but enjoy the sophisticated atmosphere. Bring your gold card.

TTT **Peploe's**, 16 St Stephen's Green, T01-6763144. People seem to love or hate this place. It has been listed among the world's best places to eat by prestigious journals and has a growing band of addicted visitors among Dublin's chattering classes. You can order simple inexpensive dishes in the wine bar or snuggle into the main restaurant set in an old bank vault for an imaginative, well thought out meal in pleasant surroundings. Book well in advance.

TTT **Rubicon**, 6 Merrion Row, T01-6765955. Furiously busy at lunchtime but much quieter and more reflective in the evenings. A muted modern interior with bare floors, two levels with a very welcoming open fire in the basement in winter lends itself to a subtle and sensible fusion menu incorporating Irish cheeses, lots of seafood, and some good options for vegetarians. Small but perfectly formed pre-theatre menu is affordable, 1530-1900, lunch a snip at €15.

TT **Aya**, 48 Clarendon St, T01-6771544. Dublin's only conveyor-belt sushi bar. Different menus for breakfast, lunch and dinner, all authentically Japanese.

Francesca's, Brooks Hotel, 59-62 Drury St, T01-6704455. In the basement of the hotel but is uplifted by soothing background music and a calm, sedate air. Modern Irish food with lots of organic touches Come here for good food and quiet dining.

Fresh, 2nd Floor, Powerscourt Townhouse, South William St, T01-6719669. Dublin now has not just 1 but 3 totally vegetarian restaurants, this place is not only vegetarian but organic to boot. Self service, doing hot dishes and filled rolls and soups. Phone in your order and collect it when you get there.

Juice, T01-4757856, at number 73-78 South Great George's St. A rare commodity in Dublin, a vegetarian restaurant which serves interesting meals in a quiet atmosphere. Inexpensive set lunches and good value early-bird menu. Open late at weekends.

Little Caesar, 5 Chatham House, Balfe St, T01-6718714. A Dublin institution. It has operated out of Balfe St for 15 years, a very long time in the life of a Dublin restaurant and judging by the queues to get in, hasn't lost its touch. It serves pizzas and pastas and some old favourites such as *pollo al freddo* and *bistecca alla griglia*; none of the main course dishes cost more than €20.

Rajdoot, 26-28 Clarendon St, T01-6794274. Much more than an Indian meal. The restaurant is designed to be an evening out in itself, from the elaborate wall hangings and lamps to the unintrusive background Indian fusion music and spacious seating area where you can pick out your meal and discuss your choices with the staff. There is no hassle, no second sitting, calm and deliberate service, from the toasted chickpeas while you wait for your order to the careful coffee service at the end. The dishes are huge, tasty and subtle – no chilli blasts here. Vegetarian Indian food lovers are in seventh heaven – real dishes, not a frozen vegetable in sight. If you eat late you need have no fear of the traditional English lager lout making his appearance after the pubs shut – they are gently moved on.

Salamanca, 1 St Andrew's St, T01-6708628. Offers traditional Spanish tapas from a menu written in Spanish with English explanations. The place is very popular and lends itself to the whole tapas experience; order a couple of dishes and then some more until you're full. 2 or 3 dishes will fill 2 people up for lunch while you can spend longer in the evening, drinking sherry with your dishes and finishing off with a mocha. No reservations and no waiting area so if the place looks full up, try somewhere else (The Havana tapas bar (see page 104) is a possibility and cheaper too.

Chili Club, 1 Anne's Lane, South Anne St, T01-677 3721. A tiny place in a side street off Grafton St. It has been there very long time and seems to know what it is doing. Thai food, slightly moderated to suit the European palate but with a definite reminder of Koh Samui for anyone missing their travelling days. The early-bird menu is tiny but definitely cheap; the regular menu might push your bill up to the next bracket.

Cornucopia, 19 Wicklow St, T01-6777583. A wholefood, vegetarian place a cut above the traditional sandals and dreadlocks image of some wholefood places. Breakfast is served from 0800-1200 and ranges from boxty (a kind of potato pancake) to granola and yoghurt, French toast and vegetarian fry-ups, while lunch and dinner are posted up on blackboards daily. Expect quiche, lots of salads, rice and stews. Scary drinks list includes wheatgrass. Lunch comes into the seriously affordable category. Noticeboard with useful flyers.

Good World Restaurant, 18 South Great George's St, T01-6775373. Opens late and gets lots of its customers when the pubs turn out. During the day it is famous for its dim sum, and the fact that many of its customers are Chinese vouchsafes its authentic cuisine.

Govinda's, at 4 Aungier St, T01-4750309. Does very inexpensive, karmically sound vegetarian food with good lunch specials and breakfasts.

Havana Tapas Bar, 3 Camden Market, T01-4780046. Serves Spanish tapas – little dishes which you can eat while you enjoy the wine and beer. Try the gambas *con aioli* (prawns with garlic mayonnaise) or for a more substantial dish, paella. It also does a takeout service. Open till 2200 weekdays and till late Thu, Fri and Sat.

Hodges Figgis Bookshop, 56-58 Dawson St. Upstairs. Open bookshop hours (0900-1900 daily, 1200-1800 Sun, 0900-2000 Thu). A grand little café where you have lots of choices of filled sandwiches and hot things like quiche. A huge round window lights the place, tables are well spaced, no muzak, and no one hassles you to go away when you've finished your coffee. Buy a book and settle down on a rainy day.

¥ **Mao Café Bar**, 23 Chatham Row, T01-6704899. A modern Asian fusion place with dishes from all over south east Asia. Our favourites are the flaming hot Malay hawker food but there are also Japanese and Thai dishes. Drink it all down with a Mao beer. Good value set dinner menu.

¥ **Messrs Maguire**, in Burgh Quay. A pub with a difference. Besides brewing its own beer (you can get a guided tour of the brewery while you wait for your food), it has an extensive bar menu and restaurant. A lively atmosphere, good food at very reasonable prices and big-screen TVs for sports fans. Traditional music some nights.

¥ **Pizza Stop**, 6-10 Chatham House, Chatham Lane, T01-6798847. Small, crowded furiously busy pizza joint which also does lots of other pretty authentic Italian dishes. Brusque service, no nonsense atmosphere.

¥ **Wagamama**, South King St, T01-4782152, www.wagamama.com. In the basement of the St Stephen's Green Shopping Centre is a Japanese noodle house serving attractive meat and vegetarian noodle dishes plus lots more at very low prices in an unusually clinical atmosphere. Check in Dublin Tourism for a 5% discount voucher.

¥ **Whelan's**, 25 Wexford St. A pub doing an inexpensive carvery lunch or 3 courses.

Temple Bar *p75, map p76*

Temple Bar is a little mecca of eating places, some pretentiously overpriced, others good, basic value for money and some in between, but there's almost no end to the list of eateries in this area. For the money-conscious, check out the early-bird menus that some places do here.

¥¥¥ **Tea Room**, at the Clarence Hotel, 6-8 Wellington Quay, T01-670 7766. Attracts the beau monde. Modern Irish cuisine amidst hushed elegance from 1830 nightly, last order 2245, lunch 1230-1500 and a Sun brunch 1100-1500. Simple table decorations, simple menus and subtle service belie exciting and imaginative dishes

¥¥ **Eliza Blue's**, 23 Wellington Quay, T01-6719114. Mon-Fri 0730-1500, 1700-2300, Sat-Sun 0800-1600, 1700-2300. Smart modern decor, polished wood tables by the riverside, floor-to-ceiling window or by the counter. Modern European cuisine, specializing in, but not limited to, seafood. Vegetarians could get by quite well here. Not your typical Temple bar tourist nosh by any means.

¥¥ **FXB**, 2 Crow St, T01-6711248, www.fxb restaaurants.com. Polished floorboards, painted walls and a menu which guarantees free range meat sourced from the family farm in Offaly. You know you're into serious meat territory when your main course is described by weight! Fish eaters and vegetarians can also get by very nicely here, despite the veg lasagne option. If you like it there's a 2nd branch in Pembroke St. Great early-bird menu daily 1730-1700.

¥¥ **Fan's**, 60 Dame St, T01-6794263. Open daily 0900-2330, offering Cantonese cuisine. Good buffet lunch 1230-1500 and a 3-course early-bird menu 1730-1930 for €12.

¥¥ **Fitzers**, Temple Bar Sq, T01-6790440. Has become a Dublin institution with very different branches around the city. This one is laid back; jazz accompanies the food, which is trendy European in style, and an enormous menu runs to steaks and burgers as well as more sophisticated fare. Open daily 1200-2330.

¥¥ **Gallagher's Boxty House**, 20-21 Temple Bar, T01-6772762. Sells the eponymous filled potato pancakes, plus lots more Irish-sourced things to eat. Vegetarians will do well here. It has a nice old-fashioned country-kitchen feel to it, with newspapers for the clients to read and bookcases with real books in them.

¥¥ **Mermaid Café**, 70 Dame St, T01- 6708236. One of Dublin's better restaurants, has changing menus that show an American influence in the mussel and smoked fish chowder, the New England crab cakes, and the pecan pie with maple ice cream. The wine list is above average. Open daily for lunch and dinner.

¥¥ **Mongolian Barbeque Restaurant**, 7 Anglesea St, T01-6704154. This could be good fun if you like hands-on eating out. Choose whatever you want from a large raw buffet table and watch it being cooked for you, then when you've eaten that go back for a refill. 2 sittings, 1900 and 2100 as well as an early-bird and lunch session.

¥¥ **Monty's of Kathmandu**, 28 Eustace St, T01-6704911. Excellent, inexpensive Nepalese cooking in simple unpretentious surroundings. The 2 floors fill up each and every night and lunchtimes too. 1 menu, 1 set of prices, and still the lunches get bought. They brew their own beer too – a kind of lager made in Ireland and graced with a picture of Lord Shiva on the label. Come early if you want to get a seat or better still make a reservation.

ƚƚ **Nico's**, 53 Dame St, T01-6773062. Ask anyone involved in the food business in Dublin where they like to eat and eventually this place crops up in the conversation. Good traditional Italian food, white cloths, chianti bottles and bustling waiters.

ƚƚ **Oliver St John Gogarty's**, 58/9 Fleet St, T01-6711822. Traditional Irish food in lively, old-fashioned style upstairs above the popular pub. Best starter by a mile is the vast pot of mussels cooked in wine and Baileys sauce, seriously good to peck away at. Main courses are served with colcannon. Low-key Irish music on tape and afterwards go downstairs for the live Irish music. Vegetarians can ask what's on. Reservations necessary and come early. There is a minimum charge of €17.

ƚƚ **Tante Zoe's**,1a Crow St, T01-6794407. This is another place that doesn't get much space in the restaurant reviews in newspapers but has been here forever. Cajun food – blackened chicken, jambalaya, shrimp creole Mississippi mud pie, it's all here and all set in a comfortable spacious dining room. The early-bird menu is a treat – 4 courses for €19.

ƚ **Central Percs**, 10 East Essex St. Does filled baguettes and sandwiches.

ƚ **Freedom Café**, Fleet St. In between the Amnesty posters, free trade chocolate bars, bits of ethnic pottery, calendars and birthday cards is a neat if tightly-spaced little cyber café selling baguettes, ciabata and cakes.

ƚ **Gruel**, 68A Dame St, T01-6707119. Very popular inexpensive restaurant, all bare boards and plain tables inside which serves hearty hot meals such as beef hotpot or pan fried sea trout as well as simpler filled rolls and soups.

ƚ **Luigi Malone's**, Fownes St Lower, T01-6792723. Very popular indeed, an Italian-Irish with a sense of humour, which claims to have food and drink from the 4 corners of the globe. It has a vast menu, comes recommended by lots of Dubliners, and has a fair-priced lunch offer of any main course meal with a glass of wine or beer until 1700. BBQ ribs are a house special and the stone-baked pizzas are popular at lunchtime when the large eating area is filled to capacity.

ƚ **Quays Bar**, Temple Bar Sq. Like most of the other bars in the area does pub grub and they are well worth checking out for their early evening menus.

The Liberties *p78, map p80*

ƚƚ **Brazen Head**, 20 Lower Bridge St, T01-6795186. Famous as Dublin's oldest pub (see page 111), there's a restaurant upstairs with an authentic period feel. A Victorian dresser and piano, low ceiling and decorative stucco complement the interesting menu which combines Californian and modern Irish cuisine, a decent vegetarian choice and hearty helpings. Downstairs they serve carvery lunch and hot specials. Reservations essential.

ƚƚ **The Old Dublin Restaurant**, 91 Francis St, T01-4542028. Is one of the best examples of a rare breed of restaurant which is not easy to pigeonhole. Using 3 rooms of what was a house of tenement apartments until 1981, the restaurant has a relaxed living- room style that has seasoned with age. The food is delightfully influenced by Scandinavian and Russian cuisine and the wine list is impressive. Check out the early evening set dinner 1830-1930.

ƚƚ **O'Shea's Merchant**, 12 Lower Bridge St, T01-679 3797. Old-fashioned pub with huge floor space which gets cleared away later in the evening for set dancing. Lunch specials 1200-1800, lunch upstairs in the restaurant 1130-1430.

O'Connell Street and around *p81, map p82*

The O'Connell St area seems to be woefully lacking when it comes to decent and half-decent places to eat at night but all is not lost. With 1 or 2 noble exceptions, the best restaurants are found in hotels. To the west of O'Connell St, around Liffey St Lower and just across the river from Temple Bar, there is a good choice of cafés for an inexpensive lunch but they close up around 1800.

ƚƚƚ **23 at the Gresham**, Upper O'Connell St, T01-817 6116. This ultra cool interior isn't at all the Gresham style, which is more Titanic just before it sank, but it's getting a good reputation as a place to eat. Austere table settings, black floors and minimalist wall decorations are the backdrop for this simple modern Irish menu. Early evening dinner 1730-1900 is good value, 2 courses for €23.

Chapter One, 18-19 Parnell Sq, below the Dublin Writers' Museum, T01-8732266. Serves the best food north of the Liffey – organic pork, spicy duck, roast venison – and in the basement of an elegant Georgian house to boot. Closed Mon.

Halö, Morrison Hotel, Ormond Quay Lower, T01-8872400. A huge black slab, large mirrors and lamp shades that resemble something the Wright brothers might have flown, form a monumental backdrop to this oh so chic restaurant, where no one over the age of 30 seems to venture. Avant garde menu of imaginative dishes in a dramatic context. This is a place you'll remember long after the taste of the food has worn away.

101 Talbot, 100-102 Talbot St, T01-8745011. Serves modern Irish food with a Mediterranean inflection; prices are reasonable and the reviews posted outside suggest there is good food within. Open 1800-2300 Tue-Sat.

Café Royal, Royal Dublin Hotel, top end of O'Connell St, T01-8733666. Popular, brasserie-style restaurant, usually busy but never frantic, adjoins the hotel bar. Dubliners flock here for meals at a decent price and the assurance of nothing scandalously minimalist appearing on a plate. Hearty main courses are meat-based – steak, Irish lamb with vegetable stew, duck, chicken kiev – plus a couple of fish dishes. The menu, with dependable starters like smoked salmon salad, is available throughout the day.

Grand Central, 10-11 O'Connell St, T01-8728658. A lovely big café bar set in an old bank building and stumbling inside from the tumult of shoppers in O'Connell St is a bit like falling down the rabbit hole to another world. Marble pillars and cool people hanging out just feet away from carrier bag war and bus queues. There's a choice of baguettes and pasta or a collection of tapas at €19 for the equivalent of 2 courses.

Il Vignardo, Hotel Isaacs, Store St, T01-8556215. Mostly pizzas here, in a cellar-like vault (a converted wine warehouse) enlivened, if that's the right word, by florally decorated columns.

Beshoff, No 6 O'Connell St. One of a chain offering very reasonable fish and chips amidst pleasant but scruffy Edwardian decor, and at comfortable prices. Open from late morning to 2100 Mon-Wed, 2300 Thu-Sat. It is named after Ivan Ilylanovich Beshoff, a Russian sailor who fled after mutinying on the battleship *Potemkin* in 1905; he came to Dublin en route to Canada but missed his boat and stayed put.

The Epicurean Food Hall, lives up to its name with a cosmopolitan range of eateries tucked together under one roof. Turkish, Indian, Italian, sushi, taco, crêpe and seafood outlets compete for around €8. Most close by 1830.

Isaac's Deli, 2-5 Frenchman's Lane, is in the same building as the eponymous hostel. On a fine day, the panini, crêpes and open sandwiches.

The Italian Connection, 95 Talbot St, T01-8787125. This is one of the best places for an inexpensive meal, if you can get an empty table in the tiny but pleasant restaurant where pizzas take pride of place on the menu, open 0800-2200.

Soup Dragon, 168 Capel St. A tiny place tucked in close to where the street meets Ormond Quay. Soups, mostly vegetarian but some meat and seafood, come in 3 sizes averaging €8, plus bread and a piece of fruit. Take-away service, and open 0800-1730 Mon-Fri, 1100-1700 on Sat).

Smithfield *p87, map p88*

Kelly and Ping , Smithfield Village, T01-8173840. Mon-Fri 1100-2300, Sat 1700-2300, Sun 1100-1800. In the forecourt beside the Old Jameson distillery this is an Irish- Asian fusion place. Lots of lemongrass and coconut milk but also Malay dishes and some Chinese and Japanese classics. Pleasant enough cocktail bar in deeply decorated black and red with huge painted murals and buddhas.

Duck Lane Café, just by the side of Kelly and Ping. Does a good self-service range of baguettes and Chief O'Neill's Café Bar (see page 101) does a good line in inexpensive filled rolls and coffees.

Nancy Hands, 30 Parkgate St, T01-6770177. An Irish theme pub (yes, in Ireland), but one which does get favourable reviews. Large meat-based salads around €9 are popular and the place won a Pub of the Year award a few years back.

ǂ **Voodoo**, Arran Quay, T01-8736013. A lively club at night and during the day it functions as a regular pub, serving food like goulash, lasagne, pork chops and burgers.

Ballsbridge

ǂǂǂ **Ernie's**, Mulberry Gardens, Donnybrook, T01-2693300. Off the tourist trail but well worth the bus ride. A miniaturist garden with a pear tree is the first distraction and then comes a veritable art gallery of original paintings adorning the dining room (check out John Doherty's Castletownbere and Connemara scenes). Impeccable service without servility and the set dinner menu is a treat. The à la carte menu has an appealing mixture of the traditional and the modern – black sole with lemon butter as well as your Caesar salad served in a wonton basket; early-bird menu would get you great food at very reasonable prices. Bus No 46 from Fleet St or Ballsbridge or No 10 from O'Connell St or Kildare St, ask to be dropped off at *Kieley's Pub* in Donnybrook and take the lane that runs down the side of the fish and chip shop at the end of the row of small shops.

ǂǂǂ **Raglan's**, Jury's Ballsbridge Hotel, Pembroke Rd, T01-6605000. Style and amiability have no trouble mixing in this rather good, comfortingly Irish restaurant. Carpeted, white linen, sedate atmosphere in Edwardian setting. The food is traditional (lamb, Dover sole) with contemporary sauces and an occasional nod to southeast Asia. The reassuringly short menu and generous wine list are testament to the place's quality.

ǂǂǂ **Roly's**, 7 Ballsbridge Terr, T01-6682611. Daily 1200-1445, 1800-2130. Very crowded at all times, Roly's is a Dublin legend, serving reliable Irish favourites tarted up with fashionable accoutrements – chicken stuffed with salmon and Newburg sauce; fish and chips in beer batter with mushy peas, roast cod with black olive mash and pesto dressing. Ring well in advance to secure a table.

ǂǂ **Baan Thai**, 16 Merrion Rd, T01-660 8833. Mon, Tue 1800-2300, Wed-Fri 1230-1430, 1800-2300, Sat 1800-2330. Well-established Thai place serving some authentic Thai dishes in a more familiar European style as appetizers. The interior owes more to Dublin 4 than it does to Koh Samui. Vegetarians might have a little trouble here.

ǂǂ **O'Connells**, Bewley's Hotel, Merrion Rd, T01-6473400. Situated alongside but not managed by the hotel, this is an excellent bistro-style restaurant where diners can view the giant wood oven and see Caesar salads being expertly prepared. Interesting meat dishes and the vegetarian choice puts many restaurants to shame. Open for lunch and dinner, with outdoor tables in the summer, and the main dining area lit by natural light during the day. Choice of main course determines the price of the meal. Inexpensive 2-course early-bird menu. Discerning wine list.

Phoenix Park *p93*

If the weather is good enough to consider a day out at Phoenix Park then it's probably suitable for a picnic lunch. The other option is a pub lunch.

Hole in the Wall, Blackhorse Av, T01-8389491. So named because of the hole broken into the park for soldiers to buy their beer through, in the days when the army was stationed in the park. The pub claims to be the longest in Ireland, and does pub food and live countryish music sessions.

Glasnevin and Clontarf *p94*

ǂǂ **Kinara**, 318 Clontarf Rd, T01-8336759. It's worth the journey to Bull Island just to eat at this north Indian restaurant. Lovely views over the island and thoughtful dishes with careful explanations. Relaxed atmosphere, lots of good service, and vegetarians will have a field day. Dinner nightly, lunch Thu, Fri, Sun. Early-bird 1800-1930.

ǂ **Garden Tea-rooms**, in the Botanic Gardens. An airy self-service restaurant, fine for just a hot drink, light snacks or lunch.

ǂ **The Yacht**, 73 Clontarf Rd, T01-8336364. Serves bar food from 1230-1500 and an evening menu of burgers, steak etc.

Dun Laoghaire and Sandycove *p94*

ǂǂǂ **Brasserie Na Mara**, 1 Harbour Rd, T01-2806767. Close to the DART station and harbour where the innovative, fashionable, mostly seafood menu is good value and where the set dinner should be around €30.

Caviston's, 59 Glasthule Rd, Sandycove, T01-2809120. An excellent small seafood restaurant, offering really fresh fish dishes. This is an exceptionally popular place, only open for lunch (Tue-Sun) and it does three sittings, 1200-1330, 1330-1500 and 1500 till 1700. Lunch will coast about €27.

The Forty Foot, Pavilion Centre, T01-2842982. Amazing views over the harbour from this modern spacious restaurant serving fairly unpretentious modern Irish cuisine. Bar downstairs and lovely terraces for a sunny lunch.

Mao Café Bar, Pavilion centre, T01-2148090. Is a branch of the city centre place, offering good Asian fusion food in a cafeteria-style atmosphere. Health conscious and helpful menu marks low fat, high chilli and nutty dishes. Tables outside and good for a lazy cappuccino or a fun dinner.

Powerscourt Room, in the Royal Marine Hotel. A very popular venue, set in a big old Victorian dining room with huge bay windows looking out to the harbour. Service is pleasant and the atmosphere is relaxed. Fairly traditional menu, but the food is well cooked. Try the hotel's afternoon tea on Sun, a dowager kind of affair in the Victorian drawing room.

Roly @ The Pavilion, 8 The Pavilion, T01-2360286. Another recently built modern room with a luxurious setting and an enterprising very modern Asian/Irish/ Mexican fusion menu. Inexpensive wine list, a la carte menu only.

Howth *p95*

Howth has lots of good pubs, a few very good restaurants and a bustling nightlife.

King Sitric, East Pier, T01-8325235. A well-established fish restaurant with lots of recommendations to its name. The restaurant is on the upper floor of a classy guest house with fine views over the sea so reserve a table with a sea view. Terrific choice of totally fresh fish, from poached turbot to lobster thermidor, as well as meat dishes. Strong wine list, mostly French. Open Mon-Fri for a set lunch around €30, and dinner Mon-Sat.

Aqua, 1 West Pier, T01-8320690. Stunning location with views over Ireland's Eye this former yacht club is now an excellent modern restaurant serving lots of fresh seafood as well as meat dishes. Set menus fall into the mid-range bracket, the à la carte soars higher.

Caffé Caira, 1 East Pier. Serves bags of fish and chips to a long queue of customers. Some seating inside.

Casa Pasta, 12 Harbour Rd, T01- 8393823. Very good value with lots of pasta dishes, but plenty more on offer as well as sea views.

Beshoff's, the exemplary fish and chip shop chain has a takeout place in Harbour Rd and there is also the **Dragon Boat** Chinese takeaway.

Malahide *p96*

Malahide is an expensive sleeper town with lots of restaurants aimed at the well-to-do commuters who live there.

Bon Appetit, 9 St James Terr, T01-8450314. Classy place specializing in seafood and game with a mixture of modern Irish and French.

Cruzzo, Marina Village, T01-8450599. Sitting on a platform right over the waterfront is this purpose built modern Irish restaurant. Live music in the bar area Tue, Fri, Sat, a well proportioned menu with one or two things a vegetarian could be pleased with and rave reviews from those who have eaten there.

Jaipur, St James Terr, T01-8455455. A branch of the restaurant in the city centre. Nice contemporary take on traditional Indian cooking, this place comes recommended by other Indian restaurant owners.

Kingsford Smith Restaurant, White Sands Hotel, Portmarnock, T01-8460420. Sound hotel fare, in a comfortable oak-panelled room. Lots of fish and vegetarian choices.

Skerries *p97*

The Redbank Restaurant, 7 Church St, Skerries, T01-8491005. If it swims in Dublin Bay, it's on the menu in this top-drawer seafood-based restaurant set in an old bank building. The wine cellar is in the bank vault. The chef greets you at the door and you have lots of time to choose your dishes while enjoying the tasty pre-dinner snacks. Dublin Bay prawns are the specialty of the house, served in several different styles, but for a starter you should try the sizzling garlicky shellfish which comes noisily to your table wafting heavenly smells behind it.

Pubs and bars → *See Entertainment, page 112, for music-based pubs and nightlife.*

"Good puzzle would be to cross Dublin without passing a pub," thinks Leopold Bloom as he wanders about the city.

In Dublin there are pubs for every taste, from real Victoriana to fake, from basic 1950s plywood to expensive fantasias, high-tech, early-morning, musical, literary, sporty, the list is endless. The pubs of Dublin are not all wonderful places, the craic inside isn't necessarily better than anywhere else in the world, and drunks are drunks wherever they are but, that said, Dublin has more than its fair share of curious places to drink, eat, people-watch, listen to music, chat to strangers and eavesdrop on other people's lives. Closing time is 2330, Mon-Thu, and 2400 on Fri, Sat and Sun. If a pub has a food licence, drinks can be served until 2430. Pubs with a disco or nightclub stay open until 0230 and can serve drinks until 0130. Quieter pubs tolerate children at least until early evening. Most pubs have finagled some kind of beer garden or outdoor space into their territory in the last year (to combat the no-smoking laws) and if you visit in winter you'll no doubt be blasted with outdoor heating before it takes off into the atmosphere to help with global warming.

Grafton Street and around

p63, maps p64 and p66

If it's a quiet drink you want there are a few of them in this part of the city. Grafton Street has several music-free, if not quiet, pubs.

Bailey, just opposite Davy Byrne's. Another age-old Dublin institution where all kinds of dead celebs once drank. By day it's a busy office workers pub and by night journalists and arty types hang out here snuggled around the braziers on the pavement. Good food at lunchtime.

The Bleeding Horse, 24 Camden St Upper. Has a prime location at a major road junction. Big dark timbers and high ceilings, and all genuinely 19th-century, although a pub has stood here since Cromwell's time.

Davy Byrne's, 21 Duke St. Heaves by day and night. There are remnants of its famous and literary past with sketches by Cecil Ffrench Salkheld, an amazing old mirror, good pub food at lunchtime, but not the Gorgonzola sandwiches that Leopold Bloom ate here in *Ulysses* (except on Bloomsday, see page 117).

Dohenny and Nesbitt, 5 Lower Baggot St, T01-6762945. Pop into Nesbitt's, as locals call it, and admire the gorgeously authentic Victorian interiors, listen to those in the know telling each other loudly what they know and try the really very good pub lunch – baked potato and chilli, pannini, hot beef roll and BLTs all tarted up with lots of good pickles and relishes.

The Hairy Lemon, 42 Lower Stephen St. Said to be named after one of those apocryphal Dublin characters, this one being a dog catcher in the 1950s who was distinguished by a lemon-shaped face and hairy stubble. The pub itself, of the type that Irish theme pubs try to imitate, featured in the film *The Commitments*.

Hogan's, South Great George's St. Where the basement opens 2200 till late, while the bar becomes a quieter place to chat. No cover charge.

The International, 23 Wicklow St. Always has something going on, whether it's the comedy club upstairs, live music or a play. Lovely old interior, quiet in the afternoons.

The Long Hall, 51 South Great George's St, T01-4751590. If you want a traditional Irish pub, this is it.

Temple Bar *p75, map p76*

Front Lounge, 33-34 Parliament St, T01-6704112. Mon, Wed, Sun 1200-2330, Tue 1200-2400, Thu-Fri 1200-0130. The coolest bar in town, all comfy sofas, clever lighting and wine lists.

The Octagon Bar, 6-8 Wellington Quay, T01-6709000. Mon-Sat 100-2300, Sun 1230-2230. The other coolest bar in town, with big comfy sofas and occasional A list celebs. Good cocktails.

The Palace Bar, Fleet St. Where people who live and work in Temple Bar go for a quiet drink. Friendly old pub, totally unattuned to the maelstrom raging in the streets outside.

The Liberties *p78, map p80*

Brazen Head, 20 Lower Bridge St. Dublin's oldest inn, chartered in 1688 but in existence as an inn of one sort or another since the 12th century. The present building was erected in 1754. It's well worth a visit for its moody, low-beamed rooms reeking of history but the live traditional music every night helps keep the place overfull with revellers and space is often at a premium during the summer months. The leaders of the United Irishmen planned their rebellion here and one of them brought a new friend along, one Thomas Reynolds, who promptly informed on them to the government.

O'Connell Street and around *p81, map p82*

Flowing Tide, 9 Abbey St Lower, T01-8744106. Unreconstructed city pub, popular with the locals and workers from the Abbey Theatre across the street. The walls are covered with photos and cartoons of assorted actors.
Parnell Mooney, 72 Parnell St, T01-8731544. Built in 1868 this place retains much of its Victorian atmosphere. You'll see ashen-faced relatives of customers of the Rotunda over the road waiting for the good news of their newly arrived relatives.
Patrick Conway's, 70 Parnell St, T01-873 2687. Mon-Wed, Sun 1000-2330, Thu-Sat 1000-0030. First licensed in 1745, this is the oldest pub on the north side of the river. Like The Parnell Mooney, it is often frequented by newly fledged fathers celebrating their new status in life. Big open-plan bar with lots of space for people-watching and a pleasant hubbub. Legend has it that during the bad old days of public life, brown envelopes changed hands here. Popular with visitors to the Ambassador Theatre.
Toddy Bar, The Gresham, T01-8746881. Mon-Wed, Sun 1000-2330, Thu-Sat 1000-0030. Popular meeting place for Dubliners in suits, comfortable seating and over 60 different brands of whiskey.

Smithfield *p87, map p88*

Chancery Inn, Inns Quay. Interesting old-fashioned pub with good live traditional music nightly.
Nancy Hands, 30-32 Parkgate St, T01-6770177. As utterly constructed as Ryan's, next door, is genuine, this pub has been assembled piece by reclaimed piece from places as diverse as Welsh butcher's shops, Yorkshire churches and Trinity College. Victoriana stuff lies about and hangs everywhere. Food is pretty much the order of the day here but there are some good nooks and crannies if you can't get into Ryan's and, they say, 200 varieties of whisky.
Ryan's, 22 Parkgate St, T01-677 6097. Mon-Wed 1230-2330, Thu-Sat 1230-0030, Sun 1230-2300. This place has authenticity coming out of its ears. It's hard to believe that such a charming old pub wasn't built as a film set for some American movie set in Ireland. In fact it's as genuine as they come.

Dun Laoghaire *p94*

Purty Kitchen, Old Dunleary Rd. Is opposite Dun Laoghaire's only hostel, serves mighty good pub food. Open till midnight daily.
Scott's Café, in George's St Upper, T01-2802657. Has Scott's Pub upstairs where there is live music and a late bar at weekends.
The Noggin Inn, in Sallynoggin, a small village a little way out of Dun Laoghaire up Glenageary Rd, T01-2854602. A pub which regularly has traditional music.

Malahide *p96*

Duffy's Bar and Lounge, Main St, T01-8450735. A staid-looking Victorian pub, but well known for its traditional music sessions on Thu nights after 2100.

Skerries *p97*

There are several pubs offering music of one kind or another in Skerries. **Joe May's**, **Nealon's**, the **Black Raven**, **Coast Inn**, **Fingal's Cave**, and the **Yacht Bar**, a little south of town in Loughshinny, all have music. You could also check out **The Gladstone**, at the Square in Skerries where there is sometimes some good traditional music.

Entertainment

Although most of Dublin's nightlife gravitates towards the area just south of the Liffey, other parts of the city shouldn't be ruled out. Dubliners tend to choose their club and hang out in a restaurant or pub until 2300 or so before making their way to the real night's entertainment. Harcourt St is the centre of clubland. Most clubs serve drinks until 0200 and close at about 0300. Pubs are a major source of entertainment in themselves and many Dublin pubs are great for live music any night of the week. The rock and pop music scene is as vibrant as ever too, with a seemingly inexhaustible supply of fresh young talent raring to be heard and seen. A good variety of classical music seems harder to come by, though. There are several great venues for comedy and performing arts; the best times of year being spring, during the film festival, and in the autumn when there's an important theatre festival.

★ Live music in pubs

Music pours out of most pubs most nights in Dublin but for live music a few places seem to excel. The best bet is to check on noticeboards or the excellent and up to date *The Event Guide*.

Grafton Street and around

p63, maps p64 and p66

The Bruxelles, 7-8 Harry Sq, T01-6775362. Rock music mostly at weekends.
The International, 23 Wicklow St. Has live music of some kind most nights: often jazz, blues or traditional Irish music.
J J Smyth's, 12 Aungier St. Occasional live jazz and blues.
O'Donoghue's, 15 Merrion Row. Famous because The Dubliners played and drank here, there are lots of impromptu music sessions in the unreconstructed and pleasant old pub. A healthy mix of 'real' people and tourists and sometimes some good organized live music.
Café En Seine, 39/40 Dawson St, T01-6774567. Be prepared to be gobsmacked. This place is simply spectacular. Before you settle down for a drink or food just wander round and admire someone's idea of what art deco France might have been like if anyone at the time could have afforded to put this much stuff together. Besides all the things to look at there's live big band music two nights a week and jazz on Sun evenings.
The Spy Bar, Powerscourt House, South William St. Live music on Sun, which might be a good time to discover this very trendy place.
Whelan's, 25 Wexford St, T01-4780766, www.whelansalive.com. Live music nightly and a Sun afternoon session at 1600. When you're at the stone bar, buy a drink for the sawdust man who is always propping up the counter.

Temple Bar *p75, map p76*

At night in summer the heart of Temple Bar turns into a huge street party with people overflowing from the pubs on to the street, with pavement artists, musicians busking, policemen chasing pickpockets. The overall feeling is young and inebriated.
The Auld Dubliner, 17 Anglesea St. Recently spruced up a little, it is one of the area's oldest residents and not too badly tuned into tourists. It has traditional music on Sun mornings and Tue nights and part of its lunchtime menu is coddle.
Bob's, East Essex St. Seriously dedicated to various live music of and drinking. With a happy hour 1600-1930 when cocktails are half-price.
Eamon Doran's, 3A Crown Alley. Live music of various sorts during the evening and turns into an indie/house disco after midnight.
Fitzsimons, Temple Bar. Attracts a lot of tourists due to its sessions of traditional music Mon-Thu, Sat and Sun afternoons and the Ballroom Club in the basement (see page 114).
The Ha'penny Bridge, 42 Wellington Quay. A lively traditional pub with lots of locals and comedy nights.
The Hub, Eustace St. Music for the really wild young ones.
The Temple Bar, 44 Temple Bar. An un-missable red on the outside, and heaving inside at all hours of the day. Live traditional music starts at 1530 from Mon to Thu, from 1300 the rest of the week and a singalong on Sun nights.
Temple Bar Music Centre, T01-6770647, www.tbmc.ie. Innovative music hub which acts as a filming location, musician's hang-out and gig venue.
The Turk's Head, 27-30 Parliament St, T01-679 9701. Overpoweringly decorated bar

Where to buy tickets and useful information sources

For most events you can book by telephone or in person at the box office. The following outlets also sell tickets for various events, especially gigs in clubs. **Big Brother Records**, 4 Crow St, T01-6729355. **Freebird Records**, 1 Eden Quay, T01-8731250. **Road Records**, 16B Fade St, T01-6717340. **Sound Cellar**, 47 Nassau St, T01-6771940. **Ticketmaster**, T01-4569569, www.ticketmaster.ie.

The glossy free **In Dublin** magazine carries daily listings as well as reviews, interviews and features and is available fortnightly from the tourist office. It covers cinema, music, food, books, theatre and visual arts. **The Event Guide**, www.eventguide.ie, is a free fortnightly magazine that carries a broad range of listings, including literary gigs, talks and children's events. Easily the best for information and acerbic commentary, **The Slate** is an irreverent free monthly listings guide aimed at the youth market; especially good on the club scene. Another good free magazine to look out for is **Totally Dublin**, available monthly and aimed at the local market with good listings, restaurant reviews, and other good local articles. These free guides are available in clothes shops, music stores, cafés, internet cafés, universities and cinemas in the city centre, particularly in the Temple Bar area. Also check the **Irish Times** on a Saturday for its reviews and news on the entertainment front. Temple Bar has its own website: **www.temple-bar.ie**.

Other websites worth consulting include: **www.dublinpubscene.com**, for pub listings and events; **http://entertainment.ie**, for cinema, music, clubs, theatre and exhibitions; **www.dublinks.com/entertainment**, club information and current events; **www.eventguide.ie** information on the music scene.

with good bar food and lots of tourists. Live music once or twice a week and a general singalong atmosphere late into the night.

The Liberties *p78, map p80*

Brazen Head, 20 Lower Bridge St, T01-6795186 (see page 106). A famous old Dublin pub with traditional Irish music every night in summer and Wed-Sun in winter.
Molloy's, 13 High St, T01-677 3207. Lots of activities from lesbian night to singer-songwriter competitions and choice of 3 floors.
Mother Redcap's Tavern, 40-48 Back Lane, T01-453 8306. A pub for locals, with live music occasionally and sing songs.
O'Shea's Merchant, 12 Lower Bridge St, T01-6793797. Set dancing nightly as well as live traditional music from 2130 till closing.

O'Connell St and around *p81, map p82*

The Celt, Talbot St. A lively little joint with traditional live music 2000-2100. It can become unbearably crowded, especially on Fri, with a mixture of locals and tourists.
Knightsbridge, Arlington Hotel, Bachelor's Walk, T01-8049100. Tourist Dublin to a tee. If it's ballads, reels and jigs you want, step right in and spare time for the bouts of stiff Irish dancing after 2000 most nights.
Lanigans, Clifden Court Hotel, 11 Eden Quay, T01-8743535. Has free music most nights but there is also a basement venue, T01-9741329, which has Fri night sessions.
Parnell Mooney's, on Parnell St. Comfy seats and a music-rich late- night bar on Wed while next door **Patrick Conways** (see page 111) has various kinds of live music upstairs.

Smithfield *p87, map p88*

The Chancery Inn, 1 Inns Quay, is only a short walk from Temple Bar across the river. Thu night's music and good atmosphere is in a class of its own.
Chief O'Neill's, Smithfield Village, T01-8173838. The bar in Chief O'Neill's Hotel, has some good live music: Sat is traditional, Thu various live bands, Sun Jazz 1230-1500.
Cobblestone, North King St. Musicians turn up each night and this is the place to hear pipes and *sean nos* singing. The pub entertainment is free and while there is also a music place upstairs that charges an entrance fee the word on the street in that the money is better spent extending your stay at the bar.

M Hughes, Chancery St. A lovely pub for an evening's entertainment of traditional Irish music. The sort of place that doesn't feel the need for posters of Yeats and Joyce on the walls to remind you what country you're in.

Larger music venues

Magazines like *In Dublin* and the *Event Guide* provide details of what's on while posters and flyers around Temple Bar are usually up to date. For big names you will need to book in advance, either over the telephone with a credit card or direct from the outlets listed on page 113. Expect to pay from €8 to €30.

The Point, North Wall Quay, T01-8363633. The largest venue for major non-classical concerts in Dublin.

RDS Concert Hall, Royal Dublin Show, Ballsbridge, Dublin 4, T01-6680866. The venue for the annual horse show-jumping competition, but is also used for concerts and special exhibitions. Access for disabled. Bus: Nos 5, 7, 7A and 8 from Burgh Quay or the No 45 bus from Eden Quay.

Vicar St, 58-9 Thomas St, T01-4545533 (information), T0818719390 (credit card bookings) www.vicarstreet.com. Another main venue for non-classical events.

Club scene

Most clubs serve drinks until 0200 and don't close until 0300. Clubs usually charge an entrance fee, which varies from €8-20 according to the day of the week, the gig, or the visiting DJs. They sometimes have a dress code and on student nights ID is usually checked. Most venues host very different events on different nights, from the downright cheesy, with muted TVs in the corners and frayed boozers escaping a hard day at the photocopy machine, to genuine off-the-wall madness, so try to get a handle on what's on before heading off into the night. The listings in the free *Event Guide* or the purchasable *In Dublin* magazine can be of some help. One night draws in hordes of student types attracted by booze promotions promising instant oblivion, while the next night the same club has yuppies waving BMW keyrings in your face. Clubs go in and out of fashion rapidly, and this week's wild spot is next week's bore of the week.

Grafton Street and around

p63, maps p64 and p66

Break for the Border, Lower Stephen St, T01-4780300. Thu-Sun. A bit of a cattle market for young Dubliners, but a good place to drink yourself to oblivion. Popular hits and oldies disco. Over 23s.

Copperface Jacks, Jackson Court Hotel, T01-4758777. Nurses and policemen love this off-the-wall club, but, unlike one postman who used to turn up every weekend, they are not in uniform.

Fireworks, Tara St, T01-6481099, in the old central fire station. Open until 0230 Wed-Sat. Late-night drinking, 3 levels and a dance floor.

Gaiety Theatre, South King St, T01-6771717. Hosts a variety of activities on Fri and Sat from movies to cabaret, live jazz or soul and salsa discos. Lots of floor space and bars. Fri is always salsa night and attracts energetic 30-year-olds.

POD, and **Redbox** 35 Harcourt St, T01-4780225, at the top end of Harcourt St, in what was an old railway station, T01-4780225, www.pod.ie. POD, seriously well designed with rather self-consciously gorgeous clubbers, utilizes 2 stone vaults of the old railway station, and being one of the hippest joints in town can also be one of the most expensive. Celebrities hang out in the VIP bar. Bear in mind that George Wilkinson, who designed the railway station in 1859, also designed lunatic asylums.

Rí Rá, 1 Exchequer St, the basement of The Globe pub, T01-6774835. Young, lively with techno, funky and dance music

Spy/Wax, Powerscourt Centre, South William St, T01-677001. Very sophisticated pair of bar/clubs in Georgian setting with cool rich people eyeing each other up.

Sugar Club, 8 Lower Leeson St, T01-6787188, www.thesugarclub.com. Fri and Sat are music nights at this venue on the site of the old Sugar Company. Cinema screen, soundproofed cocktail lounge.

Temple Bar *p75, map p76*

Ballroom, in the basement of Fitzsimon's pub, Temple Bar, T01-6779387. Not a ballroom, it's a very run-of-the-mill club that has received some poor reviews but, who knows, it could improve.

Club M, Bloom's Hotel, Anglesea St. Open Tue-Sun, T01-6715622. Laser lights, VIP room and busy at weekends.

Eamon Doran's, 3A Crown Alley (see also page 112), T01-6799114. Does assorted DJ-driven sessions nightly. More laid back than some of the more famous clubs, and with affordable prices for admission and alcohol.
The Hub/The Mezz, 23-4 Eustace St, T01-6707655, www.thehubmezz.com. Both club nights and live music these two places have something on from Wed to Sun.
Temple Bar Music Centre, Curved St, T01-6709202, www.tbmc.ie. A mix of vibes that vary nightly. Very functional, techno-looking place.

O'Connell St and around *p81, map p82*

Issac Butt, Store St, opposite the bus station. Gets the weekend going with resident DJs who know their audience.
Spirit, 57 Middle Abbey St, T01-8779999, www.spiritdublin.com. Thu-Sat. Vast newly reconstructed place (HQ as was) off O'Connell St, with strippers and too many customers. Assorted layers of bars, cinema screens, restaurant, dance spaces, yada, yada, yada - all named after spiritual states.

Classical and opera

While Dublin rocks the night away in clubland, classical music is a little less obvious. There are regular concerts in the National Concert Hall, the Hugh Lane Gallery, the Bank of Ireland, the RDS and other venues but they need seeking out from a copy of the *Event Guide* or *In Dublin*. Also check out the two cathedrals, the Irish Museum of Modern Art, the Project Arts Centre and St Stephen's Church. The International Opera Festival takes place in Jun.

Dublin has 2 resident orchestras, the **National Symphony orchestra**, T01- 2083347, and the **RTE Concert orchestra**, T01-2083347, which regularly perform at the national Concert Hall. In addition look out for **Opera Ireland**, T01-208 3347, which performs seasons twice a year at the Gaiety Theatre and the Concorde Ensemble, T091- 522867, a small chamber orchestra which gives regular recitals of contemporary Irish work at the Hugh Lane.

Venues

Bank of Ireland Arts Centre, Foster Pl, T01-6711488, box office open Tue-Fri, 1100-1600, T01-6707555. Free lunchtime concerts during the winter months. Evening shows of classical music and poetry readings.
Gaiety Theatre, South King St, T01-6771717. Box office Mon-Sat 1000-1900. In between the club nights and pantos this pace hosts the Opera Ireland seasons.
Municipal Gallery of Modern Art, Parnell Sq, T01-874 1903. Free concerts Sep-Jun, Sun 1200.
The National Concert Hall, Earlsfort Terr, Dublin 2, T01-4751572, www.nch.ie. Box office open 1000-1900, Mon-Sat. What was the Great Hall of University College Dublin (now shifted to Belfield, southeast of the city centre) is the main venue for classical orchestral performances and what it gains in historical and architectural interest is lost in the less-than-excellent acoustics. Access for disabled. Buses Nos 10, 11, 13, 14, 14A, 15, 15A, 15B, 44, 46A, 47, 47A, 47B, 48A and 86.

Cinema

Dublin's cinemas are centrally located and the largest is the 9-screen complex at the Parnell Centre near the top end of O'Connell St. To escape the blockbusters and Hollywood generally, the Irish Film Centre is a place of refuge although the Screen in D'Olier St is also worth checking out. Daily newspapers carry details of what's on and when, while for reviews look in the *In Dublin* magazine, the *Event Guide*, or Sat *Irish Times*. Dublin's Film Festival comes early in the year (see page 117). Cinema tickets cost at least €10 in the evenings, less before around 1800; student discounts are sometimes available.
Irish Film Centre, 6 Eustace St, T01- 6793477, http://www.fii.ie. Daily membership €1 allows you to buy tickets for yourself and 3 guests. This is the best venue for catching an interesting film and tickets can be booked in advance from 1330 daily. The centre shows a mixture of independent foreign and arty films as well as documentaries and seasons of a particular director's work.
Savoy, O'Connell St, T01-8748487. 5 screens, all the big releases.
Screen, D'Olier St, T01-6725500. 3 screens show a mix of arty and commercial films.
UGC Cinemas, Parnell Centre, Parnell St, T01-8728444. 9 screens, all the big movies.

Comedy clubs

Dublin has several venues for comedy clubs including one 400-seater, purpose-built

Roches, Henry St. Focuses on housewares but has clothing sections too. Competitive prices.

Markets

Moore St is Dublin's famous market, used by one and all for fresh fruit and vegetables and good for listening to Dublin accents, if not actually buying anything.

Music

Waltons, 2-5 North Frederick St, T01-8747805. Branch of the established music business. CDs, cassettes, books on Irish music, harps, bodhráns, accordions, whistles and flutes.

Smithfield *p87, map p88*

Duck Lane, reached from the courtyard outside the Old Jameson Distillery. A large tourist shop where Irish merchandise from clothes to crockery are displayed. It has a section devoted to women's jackets, coats and jerseys from Irish designers, and also sells jewellery, homewares, gifts and crafts. Smaller gift shops attach themselves to the Collins Barracks and the Old Jameson Distillery, while along Upper Ormond Quay, **The Bridge** is an interesting commercial art gallery.

Activities and tours

Dublin can provide the sports-orientated with a full range of things to do and watch, from Ireland's own two field sports – hurling, which dates back about 2,000 years, and Gaelic football, which has a slightly briefer pedigree – to the many golf courses that some might say blight the land. In between there's go-karting, ice skating, windsurfing and even skiing. Horse racing is a national preoccupation and Dublin has plenty to offer there too. The public parks have lots of pitches marked out for hurling, football and rugby, as well as basketball courts, which are free to the public, and tennis courts.

Bowling

Ten-pin bowling is dominated by the Leisureplex group. There are alleys all around the suburbs: among others at Malahide Rd, Coolock, T01-8485722; Tallaght, T01-4599411; Blanchardstown, T01-8223030 and Stillorgan, T01-2881656. **Bowling greens** open to the public are at Moran Park in Dun Laoghaire and Herbert Park in Ballsbridge.

Gaelic football

Gaelic football existed in Ireland as a form of football played with the hands as well as the feet from about the 17th century, but the rules were not formalized until the Gaelic Atheletic Association invented them in 1885. It evolved over the next 20 years to become the game that is so popular in Ireland today. There are 15 players in a team, who play with a ball similar to an English football, but can use their hands to pass it or score goals. The goal resembles that of rugby with a score over the bar being worth less than a score below the bar. You can watch amateur games in the **Phoenix Park** at weekends for free, or check out **Croke Park**, Jones Rd, Drumcondra, T01-8363222, www.gaa.ie.

Greyhound racing

Both courses in Dublin have been recently upgraded to offer a full evening's entertainment with restaurants and bars to supplement the racing and betting.

Harold's Cross Racetrack, 151 Harold's Cross Rd, T01-4971081. Mon Tue, Fri from 2000.

Shelbourne Park Stadium, Lotts Rd, Ringsend, T01-6683502. Wed, Thu, Sat from 2000.

Horse racing

There are 23 race meetings a year at **Leopardstown**, 10 km south of the city centre at Foxrock, T01-2893607, www.leopardstown.com. Admission around €16. This is the most popular race meeting spot with Dubliners and has been since it opened in 1888 in what was then named Leperstown. A special bus service from Dublin (Busáras) is operated on race days, T01-8734222.

Hurling

Europe's oldest field game, hurling is played with a curved ash stick and small hard ball in public parks from Aug-May. Big game watchers could try for the **All Ireland Football and Hurling Finals** in early Sep, at Croke Park, T01-8363222, www.gaa.ie.

Jogging

Dublin's parks are pleasant and safe for jogging.

Rugby

The season is from Aug-May and details of international matches, which take place at **Lansdowne Rd Stadium**, T01-6689300, are available from the Irish Rugby Football Union, T01-6684601. There are 14 domestic rugby clubs, which compete over the course of the season for the Leinster Senior Cup. The **Rugby Six Nations Championship** is held over Feb and Mar, T01-6473800.

Soccer

Increasingly popular in Ireland since the national football team has begun to look more like a major player, football is played professionally by several teams in Dublin, the best being **Shamrock Rovers** at Spawell Leisure Complex, Dublin 6.

Swimming

National Aquatic Centre, Snugborough, Blanchardstown, T01-6464300, www.nac.ie. State-of-the-art water complex with lots of rides, including a water roller coaster, surfing machine etc.

Tennis

The following parks have tennis courts that can be booked by the public:

Albert College Park, Glasnevin, Dublin 9, T01-8373891.

Bushy Park, Terenure, Dublin 6, T01-4900320.

Eamonn Ceannt Park, Crumlin, Dublin 12, T01-4540799.

Herbert Park, Ballsbridge, Dublin 4, T01-6684364.

St Anne's Park, Raheny, Dublin 5, T01-8331859.

Tours

Tours of the city An excellent way to get an insight into the city that tourists often don't have access to is to join one of the many specialist tours doing the rounds of the familiar and not-so-familiar sites of historical and cultural interest. These usually run daily and can be joined at the starting point or booked ahead. Some of the more unusual ones should be booked, since they may not run if there isn't enough interest. They can be booked at the numbers given, or through Dublin Tourism, Suffolk St.

Bus tours **Dublin Bus**, 59 O'Connell St, T01-8734222, www.dublinbus.ie, offers a **Ghost Bus tour** Mon-Fri 2000, Sat Sun, 1900, which visits sites associated with ghost stories. Not suitable for children under age 14. €22. It also offers a **Coast & Castle Tour**, taking in the northern coast and Malahide Castle, €20 and a **South Coast Tour** for the same price.

Guide Friday, Irish City Tours, 33 Bachelor's Walk, T01-8729010, www.irishcitytours.com. Have their own buses, with guides, for a similar kind of service. Their tickets are €12, include discounts for the sights and are also available on the bus or from the tourist offices in Suffolk St and O'Connell St.

Grayline, www.grayline.com, with yellow buses, do a similar tour for €12.

Hop on-Hop off, Dublin Bus, 59 O'Connell St, T01-8734222. Most of the city's major attractions can be reached on the tour and the green and cream open-top buses operate 0930-1630 every 10 mins, and every 30 mins 1700-1830. The €12.50 tickets can be purchased on the bus or from the O'Connell St office. The ticket includes discounts at each of the sights visited. Tickets are valid for 1 day and you can break the tour at any stage and rejoin it when you are ready.

Over the Top Tours, Freefone T1800-424252. Does a 9-hr trip around various ancient sites, picking up outside the tourist office in Suffolk St at 0900, price €26.

Historical walking tours **The 1916 Rebellion Tour**, T01-6762493, 1916@indigo.ie. Good fun, this meets at The International Bar, 2 Wicklow St, at 1130, Tue-Sat and 1230 on Sun, between late Apr and late Sep; in winter, Sat and Sun only. The tour lasts 2 hrs and travels to the relevant sites describing and analysing the events that took place. A free copy of the *Proclamation of the Republic* is included. €8, payable on the day or tickets from Dublin Tourism. Don't forget, too, the free tours of Glasnevin Cemetery every Wed and Fri, see page 94.

Historical Walking Tours of Dublin, T01-8780227, www.historicalinsights.ie. Apr-Sep daily 1100, 1500, and a 1200 tour as well on Sat and Sun; Oct-Apr Fri-Sun 1200. The tours are conducted by history graduates of Trinity College and visit most of the important sites around the old city. They conclude with a look at the current Peace Process. Meeting point is the front gate of Trinity College; €7.62.

Literary tours **Literary/Georgian walk**, T01-4960641. Lasts 2 hrs and costs €9, starts at 1030 on Mon, Wed, Fri and Sat. Check with tourist office or when booking for new start point.

Literary Pub Crawl, T01-6705602, www.dublinpubcrawl.com. Starts upstairs in The Duke pub, 9 Duke St, and crawls its way around pubs associated with Dublin's famous writers. A team of actors perform from their works in situ. 2¼ hrs of Joyce, O'Casey, Behan, Yeats and the occasional drink. Easter to end of Nov, nightly at 1930, and Sun 1200 as well; winter, Thu-Sat 1930, Sun 1200, 1930. €10.

Wilde and Co, Oscar Wilde walks and occasional dramatics, T086-3296304, are at 1100, Tue-Sun, meeting at 1 Merrion Sq. No booking necessary. €25.

Windsurfing

Surfdock Windsurfing, Grand Canal Dockyard, South Docks, Ringsend, T01-6683945. Lessons and equipment for hire.

Gay and lesbian venues

Accommmodation

Inn on the Liffey, 21 Upper Ormond St, T01-6770828; and

Frankie's Guesthouse, 8 Camden Pl, T01-4783087, www.frankiesguesthouse.com, offer city centre gay men only accommodation.

Bars and pubs

The George, South Great George's St, near the junction with Dame St. Dublin's longest-established gay bar. Thu is retro night with a late quiz while Wed includes a drag show and there is a bingo session on Sun at 2000. From Wed-Sat there is an entrance charge (E7-10).

Out on the Liffey, 27 Upper Ormond Quay, T01-8722480. The George is busy, busy, busy so if you want somewhere quieter, more cosy and unassuming, head here for lunch or a peaceful evening atmosphere. Men's night is Sat 2000-0200.

The Front Lounge, 33-34 Parliament St, T01-6704112. A dedicated gay bar with a karaoke night on Tue at 2200 hosted by Miss Panti.

GUBU, 7-8 Capel St, T01-8740710. Very modern with a stark interior and DJs most nights. 'Straight-friendly'.

Clubs

Several clubs have gay and lesbian nights, which tend to vary, so check in the listings.

Strictly Handbag, at Rí Rá, 1 Exchequer St, the basement of the Globe pub, T01-6774835, on Mon nights.

Ham, at the POD, Harcourt St, T01-4780225. Fri nights, E8.

Festivals and events

Mar sees a **St Patrick's Day** drag beauty pageant known as the Alternative Miss Ireland contest while during **Gay Pride** week in **Jun** there is a ceilidh, drag queen contests, theme nights and gay-interest theatre. The highlight of the week is a gay pride parade from O'Connell St to Wood Quay. At the **end of Jul/beginning of Aug** there is a week long **Lesbian and Gay Film festival** hosted by the Irish Film Centre in Temple Bar.

Literature

Gay Community News is a monthly publication which deals with gay issues and which has a good website, www.gcn.ie. **Waterstone's**, the **Winding Stair**, and **Books Upstairs**, 36 College Green, all have gay and lesbian sections.

Other venues

Outhouse, 105 Capel St, T01-8734932. A community centre that provides a meeting place dedicated to gay and lesbian issues.

Saunas

Boilerhouse, 12 Crane Lane, T01-6773130. Sauna and café. Open Mon-Wed, 1300-1700, Thu 1300-0600, Fri 1300-Mon 0530.

The Dock, 21 Upper Ormonde Quay, T01-8724172. Small sauna complex attached to the Inn on the Liffey. Sun-Wed 0900-0400, Thu 0900-0600, Fri, Sat 24 hours. €15, €20 after midnight Fri, Sat. Gay men only.

Transport

Bicycle

Cycling in Dublin has few advantages – traffic is heavy and there are no cycle lanes, parking is difficult since every railing has signs prohibiting bikes and there are few if any actual parking racks. You're also likely to return to your bike and discover that whichever bits of it could be removed have been. There are also no bike hire facilities in the city so you must bring your own.

Bus

Long distance

For excursions outside County Dublin, **Bus Éireann**, Busáras, Store St, T01-8366111/ 8302222, www.buseireann.ie, operates an extensive system of express buses to all parts of Ireland. Express buses go to **Cork** 4 times a day. Journey time including a 30-min stop takes about 4½ hrs. There are hourly buses to **Galway**, 0800-2100, at a journey time of 3½ hrs. Up to 7 daily buses go to **Belfast**, 0800-1945, with a journey time of about 3 hrs.

Express buses also travel daily to **Armagh**, **Athlone**, **Ballina**, **Derry**, **Donegal**, **Killarney**, **Letterkenny**, **Limerick**, **Portrush**, **Portumna**, **Rosslare**, **Shannon**, **Sligo**, **Waterford**, **West Clare**, **Westport** and **Wexford**, and many other towns. Express bus tickets must be bought before you get on the bus. If you intend to do much travelling by bus you might want to consider the Rambler Ticket, which allows you to travel throughout the Bus Éireann network for 3, 8 or 15 days of your choice over a limited period. The 15-day ticket is valid for a month, out of which you may choose any 15 days to make as many journeys as you choose, on local as well as express buses. Buses fill up and there is not much room for baggage inside the bus.

Local

If you plan to get about the city a lot by bus there are several concessionary tickets which will make travel easier and cheaper and which can be bought from some of the bigger newsagents as well as the tourist office in Suffolk Street, and the Dublin Bus Head Office in O'Connell Street, T01- 8720000. Rambler Tickets allow unlimited travel on buses and can be bought for periods of 1 day, 3 consecutive days, 5 consecutive days and 7 consecutive days. There are also prepaid tickets that allow unlimited bus travel and the use of the DART light railway system. These are available for one day, or a week. The weekly prepaid ticket requires a photo ID from Dublin Bus. There is also a monthly ticket. There is also a combined bus and Luas ticket available for 1, 7 or 30 days.

Other discounted tickets include a daily Family Bus Travel Wide ticket which allows unlimited travel on buses and a family pass for bus and DART.

There is a range of **student offers** for which you need an ISIC card and Travelsave stamp (obtainable from Dublin Bus Head Office in O'Connell St).

Grafton Street *p63, maps p64 and p66*

This area is a central point for buses travelling south of the city. **O'Connell St** in the north of the city, and **Busáras**, the central bus station, are reached via O'Connell Bridge. **Heuston Railway Station** is reached by bus No 79 from Aston Quay or the No 90 rail-link bus from Tara St Station. The half-hourly Airport Link bus No 748 also travels close to the area, stopping at **Aston Quay** and **Tara St stations**. For **Kildare St** and **Merrion Sq**: Nos 7, 7A and 8 from Burgh Quay, and Nos 10, 11 and 13 from O'Connell St. For **Fitzwilliam Sq**: Nos 7, 8, 10 and 45 from the city centre. For **St Stephen's Green**: Nos 10, 11, 13, 14, 14A, 15A and 15B.

O'Connell Street and around *p81, map p82*

O'Connell St lies immediately north of the River Liffey and every bus from the **airport**, including the Aircoach service, travels down it, so transport is straightforward. Busáras, the main bus station, is just east of O'Connell St. For **Parnell Sq**: Nos 10, 11, 11A, 11B, 13, 16, 16A, 19, 19A, 22, 22A and 36 all pass Parnell Sq.

Smithfield *p87, map p88*

No 134 from **Middle Abbey St**, Nos 67 and 67A from **Middle Abbey St**. Nos 68, 69 and 79 from **Aston Quay**, and No 90 from **Connolly Station**. Nos 25, 25A, 67 and 67A from **Middle Abbey St**. Nos 68, 69 and 79 from **Aston Quay**, No 90 from **Connolly**, **Tara** and **Heuston stations** all travel to the Smithfield area. All the buses stop at **Merchant's Quay**, on the other side of the river, except the No 90 from **Heuston** which stops at **Arran Quay**. For **Collins Barracks** the **Museumlink shuttle bus** departs regularly from the National Museum in Kildare St and National Gallery in Merrion St.

Ballsbridge
Ballsbridge is less than 10 mins by buses Nos 5, 7, 7A and 8 from **Burgh Quay**, or the No 45 from **Eden Quay**.

Kilmainham *p92*
For the **Irish Museum of Modern Art** Nos 68, 69, 78A and 79 from **Aston Quay**, No 90 from **Heuston**, **Tara St** and **Connolly stations**. For **Kilmainham Gaol**: Nos 51B, 78A and 79 from Aston Quay.

Phoenix Park *p93*
For Phoenix Park and the zoo: No **10** from **O'Connell St** to **Park Gate** on Infirmary Rd; then the park **shuttle bus**. Nos **37** and **38** from **Lower Abbey St** and No 39 from **Middle Abbey St** go to the **Ashtown Gate**, from where it is a 20-min walk to the park.

Glasnevin and Clontarf *p94*
For **Prospect Cemetery**, Nos **40** and **40A**, from **Parnell St**. Nos **16**, **16A**, **41A-C** and **46X** from Drumcondra Rd. From the city centre No **13** from Merrion Sq and O'Connell St, Nos **19** and **19A** from Aungier St and O'Connell St and No **134** from Middle Abbey St.

Dun Laoghaire *p94*
Nos **7**, **7A** and **8** go to **Blackrock** and Dun Laoghaire from **Burgh Quay** in Dublin, via Merrion Sq. No **8** goes on from Dun Laoghaire to **Dalkey**. No **45** goes to Blackrock and on to **Bray** from Eden Quay in Dublin, via Merrion Sq, while the **45A** just runs between **Bray** and Dun Laoghaire.

No **46A** travels to Dun Laoghaire from **Fleet St** in Dublin, via Kildare St. Bus No **59** runs between Dun Laoghaire, **Sandycove** and **Killiney**. No **746** operates between Dun Laoghaire and **Dublin Airport** (see page 60).

Howth *p95*
Nos **31** and **31A** travel to Howth from **Lower Abbey St** via Connolly Station but they take a lot longer than the DART and only go as far as the Summit, outside of the village. The last bus back to **Dublin** leaves Howth at 2400 daily except for Sat when the last one departs at 2245.

Malahide *p96*
For **Malahide**: No **42** from Beresford Pl, near Busáras, the central bus station. No **32A**, a limited service, goes to Malahide via Portmarnock. For **Donabate**: No **33B** from Eden Quay. For **Portmarnock**: Nos **32** and **32B** from Lower Abbey St. Between **Portmarnock** and **Malahide** the No **102** follows the coast road, terminating at **Sutton**. No **230** connects both Portmarnock and Malahide with **Dublin Airport**, more or less every hr.

Skerries *p97*
For Skerries and **Balbriggan** (Skerries Mills and Ardgillan House): No **33** from **Eden Quay** in Central Dublin travels via **Swords**, **Donabate**, **Lusk** and **Rush**. For Ardgillan House, ask for the Ladies' Steps and walk up to the house across the bridge.

Car

While there are car hire places all around the city it is not the most stress-free means of getting around the city centre. During the daytime parking is very limited and movement across the city, even outside the rush hours is slow. Outside of the city driving reverts to something much more like the rest of the island – a much more relaxing experience. Parking is by means of multi-storey car parks, with space availability in each posted up on signboards around the city, or by parking tickets which can be bought from machines on the street. Few hotels have their own car parks but some have allocated spaces in private car parks. To hire a car you must have your driving licence and a credit card.

Useful addresses Automobile Association (AA), 23 Suffolk St, Dublin 2, T01-6779481. Breakdowns, T1800- 677788. **RAC**, breakdowns, T1800-535005. **Alert Towing & Breakdown**, T01-8555220. **Auto Centre**, T01-4901600.

Car hire Access, Dublin Airport, T01-8444848, www.accesscarrentals.com.

Argus, Dublin Airport, T01-8623811, www.argusrentals.com. **Atlas**, Dublin Airport, T01-8444859. **Avis**, Dublin Airport, T01-6057555, www.avis.com. **Budget**, 151 Drumcondra Rd, T01-8379611. **Dooley Car Rentals**, City Centre, T01-6772723 and Dublin Airport, T01-8428864, www.dan-dooley.ie. **Hertz**, 149 Leeson St Upper, T01-6602255. Most of these places also have desks at the Dublin Tourism centre in Suffolk St.

The Luas

Dublin has a shiny new transport system called the Luas, an electric tram network designed to bring in people from the suburbs. There are 2 lines, green and red, the latter heading southwest out of the city from Connolly, along the quays and out to Tallaght and the other south from St Stephen's Green along Harcourt St to Sandyford. The 2 lines do not at the moment link up. Tickets for the Luas can be bought at the tram stop from the automatic machines. A single ticket is valid for 90 mins, a return for the duration of the day on which it is bought. The Luas is probably only useful for trips out to the **Four Courts**, **Smithfield**, **Phoenix Park** and **Heuston**. There is a variety of ticket offers including single day unlimited trips, 7-day unlimited trips and various combinations of bus, Luas and DART travel. Both Luas lines run from 0530-0030 Mon-Fri, 0630-0030 Sat and 0700-2330 Sun and public holidays. Red line trams run about every 10 mins. The green line trams run at various intervals, between 5 and 15 mins apart.

Taxi

There are 24-hr taxi ranks at Aston Quay, College Green, Eden Quay, O'Connell St Upper and Lower, St Stephen's Green and the railway stations. Taxis tend to congregate at these ranks rather than cruise around looking for fares. With licenced taxis flagfall is €2.75 and then the meter goes up by €0.25 per 9th of a mile or 30 secs. There is an additional charge for each extra passenger, for each piece of luggage, for a call out, for travelling on Sun and after 2200. Unlicenced cabs tend to charge a flat fee so you should negotiate a price in advance.

Phone cab companies include: **A to B Taxis**, T01-6772222; **Access** , T01-6683333; **Blue Cab Company**, T01-6677233; **Camden Cabs**, T01-4754000; **Co-op Taxis**, T01-6766666. For complaints or queries contact the **Irish Taxi Federation**, T01-8364166.

Wheelchair-accessible taxis can be booked in advance through **Eurocab/Dublin Black Cab**, T01-8445844, and **National Radio Cabs**, T01-8365555.

For short journeys around **Skerries** the best bet is a cab. **Fingal Cabs**, T01-8492263, and **Abacus Cabs and Minibuses**, T01-8491111 are both based in Skerries.

Train

Long distance

The national rail system, **Iarnród Éireann**, provides the swiftest means of getting out of the city for an excursion. Dublin has 2 intercity railway stations: **Connolly Station**, Amiens St, T01-8363333, www.irishrail.ie, north of the river and on the DART line, serves **Belfast**, **Derry**, **Sligo**, **Roslare**; **Heuston Station**, St John's Rd West, T01-8365421, serves **Cork**, **Galway**, **Westport**, **Tralee**, **Killarney**, **Limerick**, **Wexford** and **Waterford** and places in the south and west. Both these stations have left-luggage offices and bus No **90** runs between the 2 stations. The other city stations are **Tara St** and **Pearse St**.

Suburban rail lines run out westwards and northwards, stopping at suburbs, towns and seaside villages like **Skerries** and **Drogheda**.

Grafton Street *p63, maps p64 and p66*
Pearse St and **Tara St** stations link with **Howth** and places in the north of the city and with **Dun Laoghaire** and **Bray** in the south.

Temple Bar *p75, map p76*
Tara St Station. From the **airport**, take No **748** which travels down O'Connell St and crosses the river before turning into Aston Quay. The bus follows the river west to Heuston Railway Station but get off at Aston Quay and take any street on the left to Temple Bar.

O'Connell Street and around
p81, map p82
Connolly Train Station is within easy walking distance of O'Connell St. There is also a DART station at Connolly.

Dun Laoghaire *p94*
The DART runs at approximately 20-min intervals stopping at **Blackrock**, **Seapoint**, **Salthill**, **Dun Laoghaire**, **Sandycove**, **Glenageary**, **Dalkey** and **Killiney** and **Bray**. The last train out of Tara St is 2321. The last train leaves Bray for Dublin at 2320.

Howth *p95*
DART trains run regularly from **Connolly Station**. Don't get off at Howth Junction, an interchange for trains north to Skerries and Dundalk, but stay on until the train reaches its terminal at Howth. The last train leaves Howth for **Dublin** at 2359 Mon-Sat; a few mins earlier on Sun.

Malahide *p96*
The **DART** runs out as far as Malahide, stopping at **Portmarnock**, although this station is a good way out of the village with no transport into town. A better route into Portmarnock is via Sutton or Malahide and catch the feeder bus No **102**. Beyond Malahide the **suburban rail network** serves **Donabate** (again a good way out of the village), and **Skerries**.

Skerries *p97*
Skerries is 30 mins by **suburban rail**, then a 5-min walk. The last suburban train to Skerries leaves **Connolly** at 2210.

Directory

Cultural centres
Trinity College, College Green, T01-6081000, University College Dublin, Bellfield, T01-2693244. **Goethe Institute**, 62 Fitzwilliam Sq, T01-6611155, www.goethe.de. **Alliance Français**, 1 Kildare St, T01-6761732, www.alliance-francais.ie. **American College**, 2 Merrion Sq, T01-6768939. **Centre of English Studies**, 31 Dame St, T01-674233. **Dublin School of English**, 11 Westmoreland St, T01-6773322. **English Language Institute**, 99 St Stephen's Green, T01-472965. **Gael-linn (Irish)**, 26 Merrion Sq, T01-6767283.

Embassies and consulates
Australia, 6th Flr, Fitzwilliam House, Wilton Terr, T01-6761517. **Britain**, 31 Merrion Rd, Ballsbridge, T01-2053700. **Canada**, 65-8 St Stephen's Green, T01-4781988. **New Zealand Consulate General**, 37 Leeson Pk, T01- 6604233. **South Africa**, 2nd Fl, Alexandra House, Earlsfort Centre, Earlsfort Terr, T01- 6615553. **USA**, 42 Elgin Rd, Ballsbridge, T01-6688777.

Medical facilities
Doctors: For the nearest doctor's surgery enquire at a pharmacy or at your hotel. Expect to pay €40 for a consultation and €15 for each item on a prescription. **Hospitals**: **Adelaide and Meath Hospital**, Tallaght, T01-414 3500. **Beaumont Hospital**, Beaumont Rd, Dublin 9, T01-809 2714. **Mater Misericordia Hospital**, Eccles St, T01-8032000. **Well Woman Clinic**, 73 Lower Leeson St, T01-6610083. The 'morning-after pill' can be prescribed here. **O'Connell's Late-Night Pharmacies**, O'Connell St, T01-8730427. Mon-Sat 0830-2200, Sun 1100-1800.

Telephones
Dublin numbers are all 7 digits and if you are in the city do not need an area code (01 from elsewhere in Ireland, 00 353 1 from abroad). To dial a number outside of the Dublin area you must use the appropriate area code plus the number.

Travel agents
Thomas Cook, 118 Grafton St, T01-6709153.
Maxwell's Travel Ltd, T01-6795700.
GLA Travel Ltd, 64 Abbey St, T01-8731444.
Abbey Travel, 1 Middle Abbey St, T01-8047100.

Useful addresses
For the **Garda (police)**, **fire** or **ambulance** emergency 999 or 112. **Garda stations**: Store St, Dublin 1, T01-8557761. Pearse St, Dublin 2, T01-6778141. Fitzgibbon St, Dublin 1, T01-8363113. **Garda Síochána**, metropolitan HQ, Harcourt Sq, Dublin 2, T01-4755555.

Central North

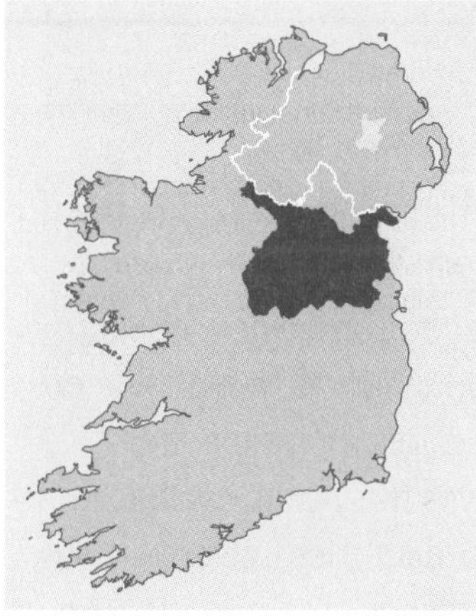

Footprint features

Introduction

This mixed set of counties has little in common other than the dubious distinction of being either places that visitors tend to pass through on their way to somewhere else, or counties with particular attractions, such as Newgrange or the Cooley peninsula. While this elides their separate histories and identities, it also gives the visitor a valuable chance to discover a part of Ireland for themselves without the preconditioned images and clichés of touristland. The main route from Dublin to Donegal passes through the area and along the route there are lots of unspoiled villages such as Virginia in County Cavan where anyone tired of the shillelagh and pishogue syndrome can spend a few days walking or fishing or just enjoying rural Ireland.

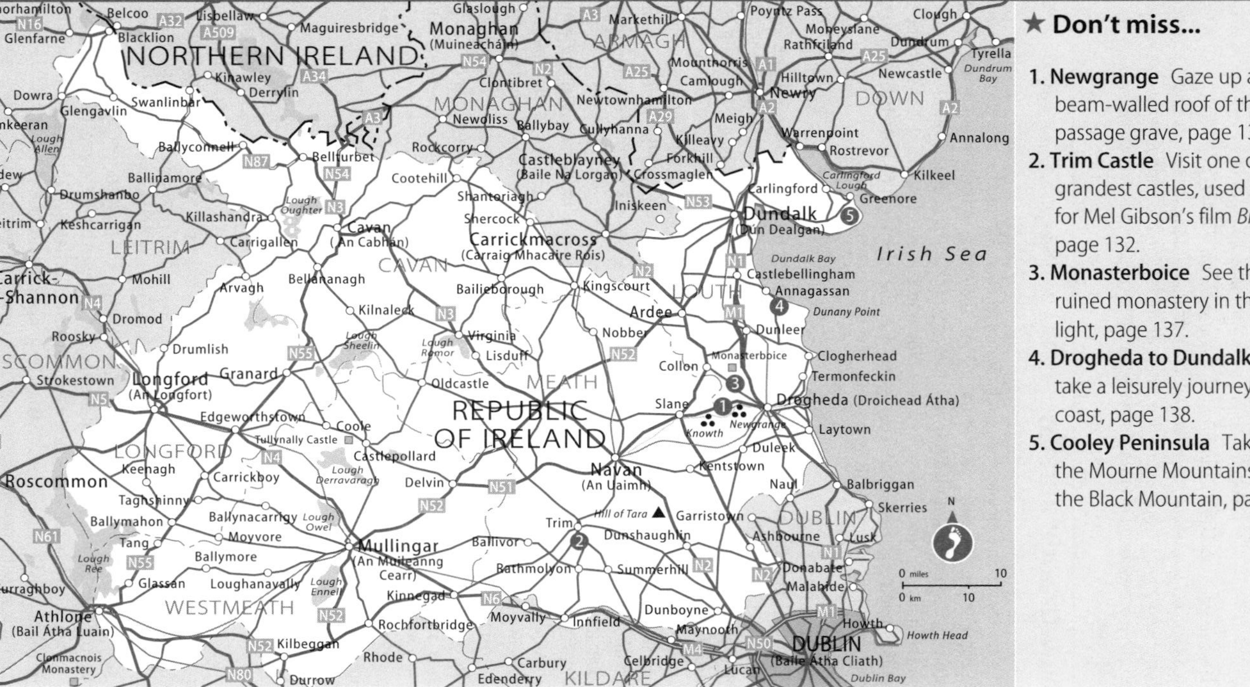

★ Don't miss...

1. **Newgrange** Gaze up at the beam-walled roof of the Newgrange passage grave, page 130.
2. **Trim Castle** Visit one of Ireland's grandest castles, used as a location for Mel Gibson's film *Braveheart*, page 132.
3. **Monasterboice** See this sixth-century ruined monastery in the early morning light, page 137.
4. **Drogheda to Dundalk** If time allows, take a leisurely journey along the coast, page 138.
5. **Cooley Peninsula** Take in the view of the Mourne Mountains with a walk up the Black Mountain, page 140.

County Meath → *www.meathtourism.ie.*

The rich soil of the Boyne valley that first attracted settlers in the Stone Age has now produced a fresh crop of prosperous farmers who manage to make Meath's ancient past infinitely more interesting than anything the contemporary scene has to offer. Newgrange is unmissable and can be managed as a day trip from the capital or an excursion while travelling between Dublin and either Drogheda or Sligo. Both Slane and Trim, with modest but interesting sites in their vicinities, suggest themselves as possible bases for an overnight stay. ▸▸ *For Sleeping, Eating and other listings, see page 134.*

Newgrange and Knowth → *Phone code: 041. Colour map 4, grid A2.*

The valley of the Boyne has a cluster of prehistoric tombs and two of them, Newgrange and Knowth, near to the village of Donore, constitute one of the major Stone Age sites in Europe. Along with the Pyramids and Mycenae, they are variations on the passage grave theme, but any profound cultural connection between these sites is nebulous, to say the least, given that the Boyne tombs have been dated to centuries earlier than those in the Nile valley.

Ins and outs

Getting there Donore is south of the River Boyne on the L21, and the Brú na Bóinne Centre is 1.6 km to the west; signposted from Drogheda, off the N1, and from Slane, off the N2. From Dublin, without your own transport, take either a suburban train or a bus to Drogheda and from there catch the **Bus Éireann**, T01-8734222, service to the Brú na Bóinne Centre. Bus Éireann, departing from the Central Bus Station, and **Irish City Tours**, T01-4011092, departing on Mon, Tue, Fri and Sat from the Tourism Centre in Suffolk St, Dublin, at 1000 (check in before 0940 at Desk 1), run their own tours that cover transport and entrance to Newgrange for €30.

Visits to Newgrange and Knowth begin at the **Brú na Bóinne Visitor Centre** ⓘ *Donore, reached via Drogheda or Slane, T041-9880300/9880305. Jun to mid-Sep daily 0900-1900; May and mid-end of Sep daily 0900-1830; Mar-Apr and Oct daily 0930-1730; Nov-Feb daily 0930-1700. €2.75 for Centre, €5.50 for Centre and Newgrange; €9.75 for Centre, Newgrange and Knowth; €4.25 for Centre and Knowth. OPW site. Guided tours available.* A shuttle bus takes visitors to Newgrange and Knowth for guided tours, and be warned that in summer there are long delays due to the limited number of people allowed to enter Newgrange at any one time. Try to arrive for opening time and still be prepared for a wait.

★ Newgrange

Newgrange (see page 608) has mythological overtones – the home of the Tuatha de Danainn, a subterranean race of supernatural beings dedicated to the goddess Danu – though it was only in 1699 that the central tomb was accidentally discovered. Passage graves are neolithic burial chambers, characterized by a circular mound reached via a straight, long passageway, both lined with stones. At Newgrange, the 19-m passageway from the entrance to the central cavern slopes upwards, so when light shines through it only reaches about half-way. The builders inserted a **roof box** in the roof above the entrance, so that when the sun rises on the shortest day of the year a pencil of light penetrates all the way to the central chamber. This only occurs around the winter solstice, and even then only for a maximum of 17 minutes in the morning: it is not possible for members of the public to experience this on the solstice itself, but the guided tour simulates the effect to give some idea of just how magical a moment this must have been. For the rest of the year, presumably, the massive carved stone that now rests outside blocked up the doorway.

The **geometric motifs** that decorate the interior stones give credence to the idea that Newgrange was far more than just a burial place for some important ruling clan. Lozenge and zigzag designs, and especially the double and triple spiral patterns, have never been interpreted to everyone's satisfaction so your guess is as valid as most, but what remains undisputed is the fineness of the stonecarving chiselled by craftspeople over 5,000 years ago.

Standing in the central chamber the most spectacular sight is **the roof**: it is not regular corbelling, but each stone rests on the twin halves of stones underneath, and the whole construction slopes downwards away from the centre. The effect is dizzyingly angular when viewed from below and, as a feat of engineering that has kept the chamber bone dry for millennia, there is little to match it in the ancient world.

Knowth

Not as well known as Newgrange, Knowth continues to excite the archaeological world. The large central mound, which most unusually has two passage graves back to back, is surrounded by 18 smaller satellite tombs, each with its own grave. The central mound has yielded a number of surprises, the most remarkable being the twin chambers orientated to the east and west. They are built in two different styles and the eastern one, which has a cruciform chamber, is an astonishing 40 m long. A wealth of decorated stones has been found in both chambers, almost as many as previously existed from all other passage graves in Ireland. Unlike Newgrange, the guided tour of Knowth does not bring visitors inside.

Slane

Some 15 km west of Drogheda, the small town of Slane has a certain Georgian charm and the privately-owned **Slane Castle** ⓘ *T041-9884400, www.slanecastle.ie; admission is currently €7*, opens to the public for a fixed period each summer. Opening times vary each year and it is best to phone ahead. It costs nothing to take a walk up the **Hill of Slane**, less than a mile above the village to the north. On a fine day, climbing the steps of the always-open **tower** on the summit that was once part of a Franciscan friary, provides a vantage point for taking in the Boyne valley.

Less than a mile east of the village is the **Francis Ledwidge Museum** ⓘ *T041-9824544, Apr-Sep daily 0900-1300, 1400-1900; Oct-Mar daily, closes 1630, €3*, in the house where a poor peasant family brought up a family of eight children, including the poet Francis Ledwidge (see Books, page 625). A republican and trade unionist, he wrote feelingly in a Keatsian manner and yet went off to fight in France where he died in 1917.

Navan and around → *Phone code: 046. Colour map 4, grid A2.*

An ancient and modern crossroads, Navan town has little to distinguish it, although it suggests itself as a watering hole (see Eating page 134). The tourist office, Ludlow St, T046-9073426, is at hand with local information, and banks, post office and pubs serving food are conveniently located around the shopping centre on Kennedy Street.

Athlumney Castle makes a good destination for an easy stroll out of town: head south over the bridge and follow the signs. A 15th-century four-storeyed tower stands next to a Tudor edifice with its mullioned windows intact. Legend has it that the owner of the place set it alight, rather than see it fall into the hands of the English. Keys to the place can be picked up at the nearby Loreto convent.

Tara

The main attractions around Navan are outside of town on the Dublin road and the chief of these is the hill of Tara, 12 km to the south. What you see is not what you get, although it requires some imagination to empathize with the profound historical and mythological significance of the place: what is basically a mound in a meadow is traditionally regarded as the seat of the high kings of Ireland. Whether any one ruler could have had influence over the whole of Ireland before the ninth century is doubtful, but there is no mistaking the symbolic clout accorded to the notion of a kingship here. The origins and functioning of Tara are lost in the prehistory of late neolithic and Bronze Age times, but so entwined is the place with mythology that what you see today was undoubtedly in some sense the capital of ancient Ireland. A seventh-century history of St Patrick relates how he provocatively lit a bonfire on the hill of Slane and was called to account by the king of Tara (whom he managed to convert in the process). The significance of Tara was also apparent in the 1641 uprising, it played a part in the 1798 insurrection, and in 1843 a million supporters of Daniel O'Connell turned up here to hear him speak. None of this seems to impress the car lobby behind the proposed construction of the M3 motorway, although this is being vigorously resisted by opponents of what is seen as an act of cultural vandalism on behalf of the state.

The **Visitor Centre** ⓘ *Navan, T046-9025903, mid May-mid Sep daily 1000-1800, €2, OPW site*, brings some of this to life with a 20-minute audio-visual show, *Tara, Meeting Place of Heroes*, and a useful guided tour of the site that includes a chance to peer in at a passage grave dated 2000 BC, which yielded a treasure trove of artefacts. There is also the Rath of the Synods, which was vandalized by British Israelites in 1899, putative excavators searching for the biblical Ark of the Covenant. A few days before their visit some Roman coins were buried for them to find by supporters hoping to encourage their belief that Tara was a biblical site, but excavations in the 1950s revealed genuine Roman finds, indicative of trade with the Roman world of the early centuries AD.

Dunsany Castle

ⓘ *T046-9025198. Mid-May to Aug Mon-Sat 0900-1300, and 10 days from 15 Dec. €15.* From Tara it is a short hop to the village of Dunsany and its eponymous castle where the poet Francis Ledwidge found an honourable patron in Lord Dunsany (1878-1957), who introduced the poet's first collection of verse: "I hope that not too many will be attracted to this book on account of the author being a peasant, lest he come to be praised by the how-interesting school." Lord Dunsany later went on to become a most strange writer in his own right. Shot in the face while attempting to help the British in the Easter Rising, he also played a part in supporting another local writer, Mary Lavin. Expensive tours of the house, taking in a noted collection of art and assorted artefacts, are conducted but telephone ahead to reserve a place.

While in the area, it is worth the short journey west of Dunsany to admire **Bective Abbey**, one of the earliest Cistercian abbeys in Ireland. Founded in 1147, precious little remains from that era and most of what you see today, including a fine cloister, was constructed in the 15th century.

★ Trim

Trim wouldn't be Trim without its splendid **castle** ⓘ *T046-9438618, Easter-Oct daily 1000-1700, Nov-Easter Sat-Sun 1000-1600, €3.50 for castle and keep, castle only €1.20, guided tours*, in the centre of town, which waited until 1994 before film people discovered its potential as a set and brought in Mel Gibson to re-enact the Scots' assault on the perfidious English at York for the film *Braveheart*.

The god Lug, the Zeus of the Irish pantheon, is associated with Tara, as are the ancient female fertility figures of Eithne and Medb.

To cover my socialist bones

When in or around Kells, consider a short trip along the R163 before turning off for the village of Crossakeel and its memorial to Jim Connell, author of the socialist anthem *The Red Flag*. Connell was born here in 1852 and wrote the song on a 20-minute train ride from Charing Cross to Lewisham in London in 1889.

His memorial carries his own epitaph:

Oh, grant me an ownerless corner of earth,
Or pick me a hillock of stones,
Or gather the wind-wafted leaves of trees,
To cover my socialist bones.

Construction of the castle was begun by Hugh de Lacy in 1173, who had been sent from England by Henry II to curb the expansionist ambitions of his barons. Strongbow (aka Richard FitzGilbert de Clare, Earl of Pembroke) was a particular worry and to prevent his complete conquest of Leinster, Henry II granted de Lacy the lordship of Meath. With the main tower having walls some 3 m thick, the castle was built to last and a great curtain wall with D-shaped towers was constructed as a secondary line of defence. Pillaged during the Cromwellian wars, it had already fallen into disrepair and was purchased by the State from the Dunsany family in 1993.

On the opposite side of the river to the castle stands **Talbot Castle**, an impressive manor house built by the viceroy of Ireland, Sir John Talbot, in 1415. It was built using part of an earlier Augustinian abbey but all that now remains of this is the **Yellow Steeple**. Also here is the **Sheep Gate**, a surviving remnant of the 14th-century town walls.

A mile-long walk along the Dublin road from Trim Castle, crossing the river once again, brings you to the signposted ruins of **Peter & Paul's Church** and its cemetery. Points of interest are the medieval grave stones and the 16th-century tomb of a couple known as the jealous man and woman; the sword that lies between them giving rise to a story of marital discord! Legend offers a cure for warts for if a pin is left between the man and woman then the wart will disappear as the pin rusts.

For tourist information, call in at the **Trim Visitors' Centre** ⓘ *Castle St, T046-9437227, Mon-Sat 1000-1700, Sun 1200-1730; closed Thu Oct-Mar, €3,* where there is an exhibition on the town's medieval history and a map can be collected to follow a heritage trail around the town.

Kells and around → *Phone code: 046. Colour map 4, grid C1.*

As it is situated on the N3 road between Dublin and Enniskillen, Kells only tends to be visited when travelling that route. Of course, if the famous Book of Kells was actually kept here then life would be very different; as it is, visitors must content themselves with a heritage centre, some fine high crosses and the local memorial to Jim Connell.

Kells Heritage Centre and Tourist Office ⓘ *T046-9247840, May-Sep Mon-Sat 1000-1730, Sun 1400-1800, Oct-Apr Mon-Sat 1000-1700, €4 for the exhibition and audio-visual show,* has an audio-visual presentation and an exhibition on the culture of monastic Ireland; both best saved for a rainy day. The **Church of St Columba**, in the centre of town, is where the monastic settlement stood that received the Book of Kells when it arrived here in 807. Close to the neighbouring round tower there are three **high crosses** as well as the remains of a fourth.

At Oldcastle, 19 km from Kells, **Loughcrew Gardens** ⓘ *Oldcastle, T049-8541356, Apr-Sep daily 1200-1800, Oct to mid-Mar Sat and Sun 1200-1600, mid-Mar to end*

 Mar daily 1200-1600, €5, are on your left just before entering the town. Apart from the intrinsic appeal of these 17th-century gardens, redeveloped in the 19th century, there is a 15-minute walk to the Loughcrew megalithic cairns (the keys are obtainable in return for a €25 deposit).

Sleeping

Slane *p131*
D **Conyngham Arms Hotel**, T041-9884444, www.conynghamarms.com. Fronted with bay trees, this is where Francis Ledwidge supped an occasional pint; it's convenient for bar food and has a restaurant.
E **Boyne View**, T041-9824121. A B&B that avoids being the ubiquitous bungalow, this 2-storey house overlooks the river.
F **Slane Farm Hostel**, Harlinstown, T041-9884985, www.slanefarmhostel.ie, is signposted in the village but offers a free pick-up. Camping space and bikes for hire.

Trim *p132*
E **Crannmor Guesthouse**, Dunderry Rd, T046-9431635, www.crannmor.com. Has 4 bedrooms with en suite bathroom and is a mile out of town.
F **Bridge House Tourist Hostel**, Bridge St, T046-9431848, silvertrans@eircom.net. An IHH place next to the Visitors' Centre, open all year and includes 3 private doubles for €31.75.

Kells and around *p133*
C **Headford Arms Hotel**, T046-9240063, www.headfortarms.com. A run-of-the-mill hotel in the centre of town. With food available daily until 2200 it makes a convenient resting place.
F **Kells Hostel**, T046-9249995, www.kellshostel.com. Part of the Carrick House pub on the Cavan Rd, a 5-min walk from town. Has a few private rooms.

Eating

Slane *p131*
Boyles Tea Rooms, Main St. Scones with cream and jam, pancakes and other home-made goodies.

Navan *p131*
ΨΨ-Ψ **Adam & Eve's**, Ludlow St, T046-9071444, serves delicious steaks and seafood, and vegetarian, and there is an early-bird menu 1700-1900; closed Mon.
Ψ **The Loft**, Trimgate St, T046-9028762. Open every night and with a terrific and good value menu.
Ψ **Ryan's Bar**, Trimgate St. Ideal for lunch.

Trim *p132*
ΨΨ **Franzini O'Briens**, French Lane, next to Bennini's. Modern-style restaurant, better for an evening meal than the others.
Ψ **Bennini's**, French Lane.
Ψ **Brogan's**, High St. Fine for a pub lunch.

Kells and around *p133*
ΨΨ **The Ground Floor Restaurant**, Bective Sq, T046-9249688. Serves as an example of what is becoming rare in Ireland – good food served in pleasant surroundings at prices that can't be complained about. Open nightly, the wide-ranging menu is full of surprises and a 3-course meal could be enjoyed for under €25.

County Louth → *www.louthholidays.com.*

The name of Ireland's smallest county, Louth, doesn't exactly trip lightly off the tongue. But hold on a while, for the two main towns of Drogheda and Dundalk are intrinsically interesting and ideal bases for exploring the surrounding countryside. Drogheda, just north of Dublin, is perfect for taking in the Boyne Valley and Dundalk is at last coming into its own as a jumping-off point for the Cooley Peninsula and the county of Armagh. » *For Sleeping, Eating and other listings, see pages 141-144.*

Drogheda and around

→ *Phone code: 041. Colour map 4, grid A3.*

Wolfe Tone came to Drogheda in 1792 and described it as "a small town enclosing four broad streets, and a collection of miserable cottages within ancient walls". Gaze down on the town from Millmount and you'll see his point. But although it's a scruffy and unpretentious place, Drogheda is in the process of reinventing itself (hopefully it will take a while before Dublin yuppyland and its new money lowers the tone) and there's more than meets the eye to this historic and ancient town. The town was founded by the Vikings, then was a medieval walled town of consequence, ethnically cleansed by Cromwell in the 17th century and ruled solidly thereafter by Protestants through prosperous times over the following two centuries.

Ins and outs

Information Drogheda tourist office, Tredagh House, Mayoralty St, T041-9837070. Open all year, Mon-Sat 0900-1730, and also Sun 1145-1700 in Apr-Nov.

A walking tour

Starting from the tourist office walk along North Quay towards town and cross St Mary's Bridge and either go up Barrack Street or Pitcher Hill steps (next to Ollie's Bar) for the **Millmount Museum** ⓘ *T041-9833097, Mon-Sat 1000-1800, Sun 1430-1730, €3.50,* housed in former barracks built for the British and occupied by anti-Treaty forces in the civil war. Drogheda was fiercely anti-Treaty and some of the artillery used to shell the Four Courts in Dublin was brought up here to shell the rebels. This is a lovely old museum, run by dedicated locals who on a quiet day will find time to explain the arcane iconography of the precious 18th-century guild banners on display. The **Martello Tower** ⓘ *Millmount, Mon-Sat 1000-1800, Sun 1430-1730, €3, but a combined ticket for the museum and tower is €5.50,* with its own military exhibition open to the public. The tower offers a fine view of the town.

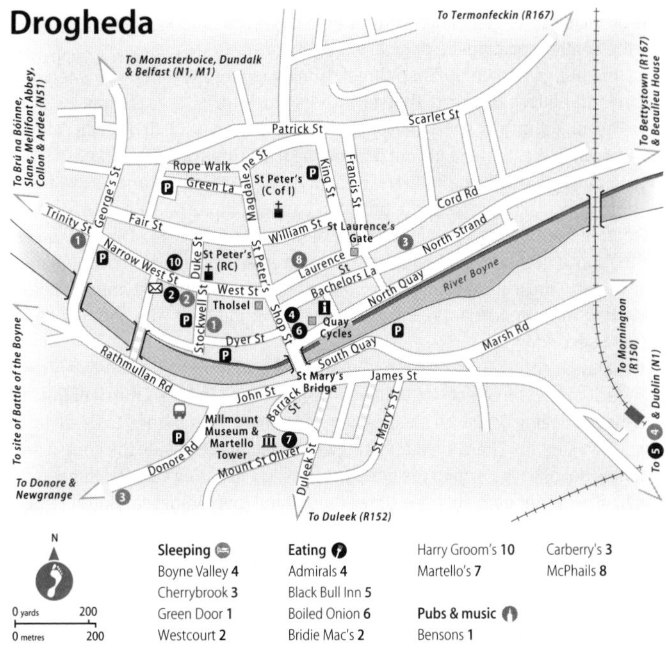

Sleeping
Boyne Valley 4
Cherrybrook 3
Green Door 1
Westcourt 2

Eating
Admirals 4
Black Bull Inn 5
Boiled Onion 6
Bridie Mac's 2
Harry Groom's 10
Martello's 7
Carberry's 3
McPhails 8

Pubs & music
Bensons 1

Was Cromwell an honourable enemy?

The 1640s was a particularly unstable decade in Ireland, beginning with the rising of 1641 and ending with the fall of Drogheda to Cromwell in 1649. Events were complicated by the outbreak of civil war in England, with royalists in Ireland on the defensive and the insurgents organizing themselves into the Confederate Catholics. A ceasefire was established, but this broke down in 1646 and Cromwell arrived in August 1649 with an army of 20,000 men, a navy and heavy artillery. On the 10th September his handwritten ultimatum was delivered to the governor of Drogheda, a royalist town, promising that an "effusion of blood may be prevented" if surrender was swift. There was to be no surrender, Cromwell's army breached a hole in the city's defensive walls and in the ensuing fight around 3,000 people lost their lives. At Millmount, a converted Viking fort, the leaders were cornered and slain and the town's governor, Aston, was seized. Rumour had it that his wooden leg was packed with gold but angry soldiers, finding the leg empty, used it to beat him to death.

However, in his *Cromwell, An Honourable Enemy* (see page 625), Irish historian Tom Reilly argues that there is in fact no primary evidence for the folk tradition of wholesale slaughter at Drogheda. He sees the siege as a military encounter between two English factions struggling for power where there was no more indiscriminate killing than the rules of war allowed for. Is it possible that Cromwell's infamy arose later in accounts of the siege by people who never took part in it?

Back down at the bridge, pause to admire the elegant viaduct to the east that carries the Dublin to Belfast trains (original journey time was 17 hours), a superb example of Victorian engineering, with an Irish-designed 1920s, single-track steel girder in the centre replacing the original wrought iron.

Cross the bridge and go up Shop Street, turning left into West Street, where the Bank of Ireland utilizes the 1770 **Tholsel** with its clock tower that chimes every 15 minutes. The building has style, unlike the Gothic enormity of **St Peter's Roman Catholic Church** in West Street, in your face on the right. The church is famous as the final resting place of **St Oliver Plunkett** – well, of his head at least – and you will also find the door of his cell from Newgate prison in London, where he was held for eight months before being hung, drawn and quartered on 1 July 1681. Oliver Plunkett (1625-1681) was a Catholic Archbishop who was arrested on suspicion of planning a French invasion. The case against him collapsed when witnesses, mostly fellow priests he had managed to antagonize, withdrew, but Plunkett was shipped off to London for a second trial.

By the church corner, turn right into Duke Street and right again into Fair Street, which leads across Peter Street into William Street where **St Peter's Church of Ireland** stands. Citizens fleeing Cromwell and seeking refuge here were burned to death in its former wooden steeple. There are interesting memorial tablets inside the church and though it may not always be open the graveyard has a fascinating cadaver tombstone dated 1520. The father of Swift's one-time student and lover Vanessa, Bartholomew Van Homrigh, who came to Ireland from Amsterdam with William of Orange before the Revolution of 1687, is buried here – Van Homrigh acquired the Freedom of Dublin by 1685, was a member of Dublin Corporation, and then Alderman (1688). Walk down William Street, turn right into Palace Street and go to the end to stand before the 13th-century **St Laurence's Gate**, an impressive reminder of the way most important

Irish towns were walled and protected by barbican gates such as this. Turning right into Laurence Street leads back to Shop Street and the Tholsel.

Around Drogheda

Drogheda makes a great base for visiting Boyne Valley sights such as Newgrange (see page 130). But there are other nearby sights within County Louth which can easily be taken in on day trips from Drogheda by bicycle or car.

Beaulieu House ⓘ *T041-9832265. May-Sep Mon-Fri 1100-1700. House and garden €10; garden only €5.* A couple of miles east of town along North Strand brings you to Beaulieu House on the banks of the Boyne. Constructed between 1660 and 1666, it was one of the first unfortified houses to be built in Ireland and the present residents are direct descendants of the original owner, Henry Tichbourne. The house has a hipped, Dutch-style roof, an interior crammed with interesting art works and a walled garden.

Mellifont Abbey ⓘ *T041-9832265. May-Sep Mon-Fri 1100-1700. House and garden €10; garden only €5.* The first Cistercian abbey in Ireland was founded 8 km north of Drogheda in 1142 at the behest of St Malachy of Armagh as part of his drive to reform the laid-back monastic life of Irish monks. Mellifont, with hundreds of resident monks, came to preside over dozens of other Cistercian abbeys across the country until they were all suppressed by Henry VIII in 1539. The place was converted into a private mansion and gave refuge to Hugh O'Neill, who surrendered here in 1603 after his defeat at Kinsale.

Like the ruins of a Greek temple, there is not a lot to see on the site but with the help of the free ground plan it is possible to trace out the buildings from the excavated foundations. The substantial remains of a 13th-century **lavabo**, an octagonal washing house for the monks, help evoke the architectural elegance that the French brought to monastic design.

It is easy to get misty-eyed imagining pacifist monks tending beehives and chanting in dulcet tones about the place, but history presents a less flattering picture. Irish monks affiliated to Mellifont did not take kindly to spot checks by the order; a monastery in County Limerick, for instance, barred its doors, laid an ambush and attacked the visitors. And it wasn't just the Cistercians who took to fisticuffs; in-fighting by Franciscan friars led to a pitched battle in 1291 with several fatalities.

★ Monasterboice

→ *Colour map 1, grid C5.*

ⓘ *Take the signposted slip road off the N1 at the Monasterboice Inn 10 km north of Drogheda. If travelling by bus between Drogheda and Dundalk, it may be possible to ask to be dropped off by the pub and still use the ticket to resume the journey by hailing down a later bus on the same route.*

Monasterboice is an old Irish monastery founded by St Buite in the sixth century, the kind of place that the Cistercians of Mellifont were designed to eclipse. Nothing remains of the monastery, but there is an elegant round tower and one of the most elaborately decorated high crosses to be seen anywhere in Ireland.

There are two crosses to admire and the best is the first one that you come to on entering the churchyard: **Muiredach's Cross**, dating from the 10th century. It is astonishing to find such priceless art plonked here in a quiet countryside setting. On the east side, there are two animals on the base, with the panel above showing Adam and Eve on the left and Cain and Abel on the right. Above this there are scenes from the life of David, a panel showing Moses striking a rock for water, and then a panel of the Adoration of the Magi. Below the central cross depicting Christ in Majesty there is a graphic scene of St Michael weighing a soul on scales with the devil pulling for all his worth from below. The scene at the very top is hard to decipher. The west side has an inscription at the bottom with cats, then a panel showing the arrest of Christ, a panel

Battle of the Boyne

The Battle of the Boyne in July 1690, the one that loyalists in the North are so intent on celebrating, took place at Oldbridge 5 km upstream from Drogheda. The battle itself, which saw the retreat of the Jacobites, was not as decisive as the later encounter at Aughrim, but its fame developed from the personal presence of both William and James. The Orange Order, celebrating the event from the 1790s onwards and misunderstanding the workings of the 1752 calendar reform, incorrectly dated it as the 12th July when it fact it took place on 1st July. The battle had a wider European significance, the British throne and French hegemony in Europe being at stake.

Getting to the battleground
The site of the battle is signposted off the N51 at Slane/Drogheda, the N1 at Drogheda, the N2 at Slane/ Ashbourne and the M1 at Boyne Bridge. Now an OPW site, there is a display and tours available on request, T041-9884343, www.battleoftheboyne.ie. May-Sep, daily 1000-1800. No admission charge while the site is being developed.

above depicting the doubting Thomas and then a scene with the Apostles. The central cross, showing the Crucifixion, is surmounted by a biblical scene featuring Moses.

The other cross, the **West Cross**, has faded badly, but there is a notice board explaining the content of its panels. The **round tower** is a fine example of its type but is closed to the public. Not-so-ancient tombstones fill the churchyard and one, on the east side of the crumbling old church near Muiredach's Cross, erected by Thomas Cregan to members of his family is, literally, monumental proof of the Irish diaspora.

★ Drogheda to Dundalk

The main N1 road is the speediest way to travel between Drogheda and Dundalk, but apart from accessing Monasterboice along the way the journey is purely functional. An inland route is possible via Collon and Mellifont Abbey and, midway to Dundalk, the rural town of **Ardee** offers itself as a tranquil backwater for anyone with a lazy itinerary wishing to take in this little-visited corner of Ireland. There are a couple of crumbling castles, nature walks in Ardee bog, fishing and other activity possibilities, and a smattering of places to eat and stay. There is no tourist office, but the town library has some local information.

If time allows, take the coastal road via **Baltray**, with its famous golf course, T041-9881530, and refreshments at the nearby The 19th Hole pub. There is also lovely **Termonfeckin** with its old castle (key available from neighbouring bungalow), and fine food (see page 142).

Follow the coastal road north to **Clogherhead** and a superb beach – one of Ireland's least known safe and sandy beaches – that stretches up to Port and looks across to the Sellafield nuclear plant in England. From Port the road travels inland rather scenically to reach the coast again at **Annagassan**, which also has a huge, safe beach, and then it is just a short hop to **Castlebellingham**, where pub and restaurant food and bedrooms await (see page 141).

Dundalk → *Phone code: 042. Colour map 1, grid C5.*

Dundalk, midway between Belfast and Dublin, is a lively, underestimated town, well worth considering as a base for exploring south Armagh and Monaghan. Once tagged as a border town of ill-repute, it is justifiably fed up with tired clichés from the past, and for visitors who appreciate a town unsullied by mass tourism smart Dundalk is a place to see and savour.

Ins and outs

Information Dundalk tourist office, Jocelyn St, 042-T9335484, May-Sep Mon-Sat 0900-1800; Oct-Apr Mon-Fri 0930-1300 and 1400-1730.

Walking tour

This is a short walk that takes in the most interesting buildings but if you have the time collect the free Heritage Trail map from the tourist office and follow the longer self-guided walk it describes.

Starting outside the tourist office, the **County Museum** ⓘ *T042-9327056, Mon-Sat 1030-1730, Sun 1400-1800, €3.80*, is next door in a restored 18th-century warehouse and houses two new floors, one devoted to archaeology and early history and the other to Norman and medieval history.

Walk down Jocelyn Street, past the tourist office, to the road junction; don't turn directly right into Chapel Street but head for Crowe Street, the right fork along Roden Place, pausing before you do so to admire the art nouveau Century Pub on the corner.

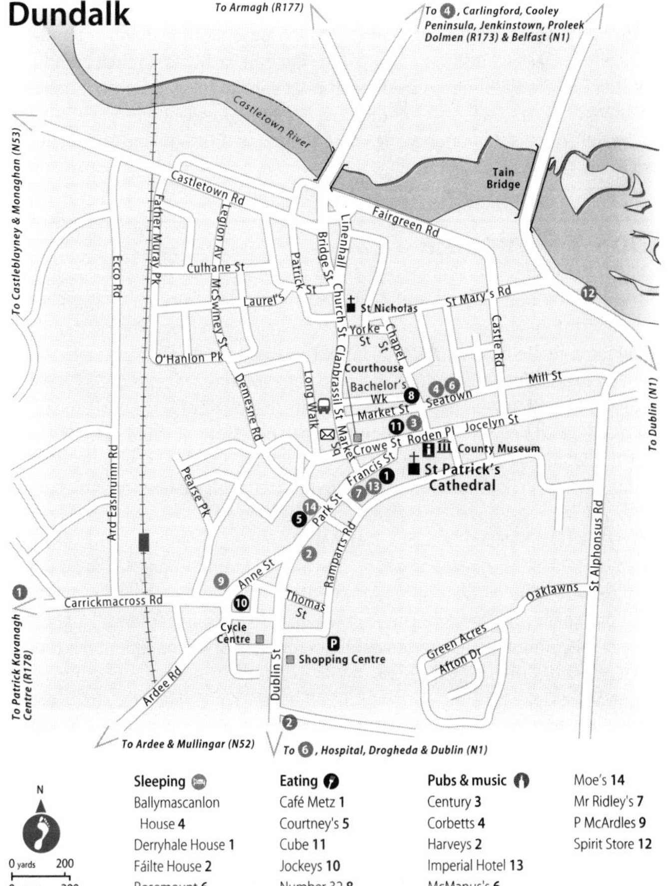

The cattle raid of Cooley

One of the most ancient tales in Europe's oral tradition, the *Táin Bó Cuailnge* (Cattle Raid of Cooley) received a written form in the eighth century. It tells of Medb, Queen of Connaught in the west, and her attempt to steal a great bull from the Ulstermen on the Cooley Peninsula to rival her husband's fine beast. Only the Homeric Cú Chulainn is free of a debilitating curse and able to mount resistance and the saga recounts in fantastic manner his superhuman exploits and the final duel between the two bulls. The best modern translation of this Celtic saga, complete with a map, is by Thomas Kinsella, *The Táin* (1969).

Built to celebrate the beginning of the 20th century, original features of its design are retained externally and inside there are more features, such as the fireplace, to admire over a morning drink. Crowe Street leads past the Greek-style **Courthouse**, one of the finest examples of a 19th-century courthouse in Ireland, on the corner of Market Square. Doric columns cut from white Portland stone, and the granite ashlar blocks of the stern flanking walls of this still-functioning courthouse proclaim a Spartan rather than Athenian sense of justice.

Go up Clanbrassil Street from Market Square, passing the superb example of Victorian commercial architecture at No 70, to where **St Nicholas' Church** stands on the right just past Yorke Street. A mishmash of architectural styles, the churchyard has the grave of Agnes Galt, sister of the poet Robert Burns, who lived just outside town for nearly 20 years. Continue along Yorke Street and turn right into Chapel Street to return to the Century Bar.

★ Cooley Peninsula → *Phone code: 042. Colour map 2, grid B6.*

Nestled between Dundalk Bay and Carlingford Lough (a true fjord), the Cooley Peninsula and the view across to the Mourne Mountains never looks better than on a soft day when a gentle mist shrouds the land. The area's association with a rich vein of Irish mythology then seeps through the landscape evoking the tales of Cú Chulainn who, in just one of his adventures, had to cope with the magic of Morrígan in the triple guise of a red-eared heifer, a she-wolf and a black eel. More down to earth in every sense of the word is Carlingford, a village that retains its medieval heritage to a remarkable degree yet risks mutation into an overpriced, Kinsale-like consumer den.

Walking in the steps of Cú Chulainn

With a copy of Kinsella's translation of *The Táin* and Ordnance Survey sheet 29 in the Discovery Series a day or even an entire holiday could be spent walking the hills between Carlingford and Omeath. The **Táin Way**, a 40-km waymarked walking route, is one possibility (though restricted to asphalt too much of the time) and the tourist office in Carlingford sells *The Táin Way Map Guide* with a 1:50,000 scale map. *Rambles* is a booklet with simple maps that briefly describes nearly a dozen walks that all begin from Carlingford and last from one to six hours. With just the OS map you can devise your own route: start, for example, on the Táin Way, and head off for the **Windy Gap**, Bernas Bo Ulad in the saga, and the setting for a much later love tragedy featuring the death of a Spanish woman who is brought here after being deceived into thinking she has a rich land to inhabit.

Another recommended 12-km walk (OS map essential) is a circular route from Ravensdale up the Black Mountain to Clermont Cairn (1675 ft; 510 m), along the Táin

Trail and through Ravensdale Forest to the R174 road. Between May and August a flower guidebook would be useful.

Medieval Carlingford

What makes Carlingford unique is that this medieval town remained largely unchanged throughout the 1960s and 1970s, when the rest of Ireland was reinventing and repackaging itself for Nostalgia Inc. It still has the feel of an unmolested little corner of Ireland and there are marvellous medieval remains: the **Mint** in Tholsel Street, with its machicolated and carved limestone windows, **King John's Castle** by the lough, and the **Tholsel**, a surviving gate. In the **Holy Trinity Heritage Centre** ⓘ *Churchyard Rd, T042-9373454, Mid-Mar to Sep, daily, 0930-1700*, a mural, video and exhibitions tell the history. The **tourist office**, T042-9337033, is in the middle of the village, open Mon-Sat, 1000-1700, www.carlingford.ie.

Sleeping

Drogheda *p135, map p135*

B **Boyne Valley Hotel**, T041-9837737, www.boyne-valley-hotel.ie. Almost a 30-min walk from town on the Dublin Rd, but if arriving on bus from Dublin ask to be dropped off outside. It is a comfortable country house with tennis courts and leisure centre.

B **Westcourt Hotel**, West St, T041-9830965, www.westcourt.ie. A lively, centre-of-town hotel where Michael Collins and Harry Boland stayed in Sep 1921 (then called the White Horse).

D-E **Boyne Haven House**, on the Dublin Rd near Bettystown, T041-9836700, www.boynehaven.com. This is a top-notch B&B with a breakfast menu to die for.

E **Cherrybrook**, Cherrybrook Dr, off Donore Rd, close to the bus station, T041-9841200.

F **The Green Door**, 47 John St, T041-9834422. Open all year, with dorm beds and private rooms.

Drogheda to Dundalk

B **Bellingham Castle Hotel**, Castlebellingham, T042-9372176, www.bellinghamcastle.com. A refurbished 17th-century castle with characterless modern decor in the rooms.

B **Smarmore Castle**, near to Rolf's Bistro in Ardee, T041-6857167, www.smarmorecastle.com. A rather strange combination of ancient and modern. A (in places) 700-year-old fortified house with an on-site leisure complex and a decent Italian restaurant. But no bar, although they have a wine licence for the restaurant.

E **The Railway Bar**, Main St, Ardee, T041-6853279. Is an attractive, old-style pub offering B&B and with a restaurant at the back serving good food.

Dundalk *p138, map p139*

B **Ballymascanlon House Hotel**, T042-9371124, www.ballymascanlon.com. Out of town on the road to the Cooley Peninsula, this is a grand Victorian edifice modernized with top-class sports facilities but hardly able to forget the past with the impressive Proleek Dolmen from around 3000 BC in its grounds; a good restaurant.

C-D **Derryhale House Hotel**, Carrickmacross Rd, T042-9335471, derryhale@eircom.net. A listed Victorian building within walking distance of town.

D **Rosemount**, Dublin Rd, T042-9335878. Just south of town off the N1, this is generally regarded as one of the best B&B establishments in the area.

E **Fáilte House**, Dublin Rd, T042-9335152. Reliable B&B, on the corner with Long Av.

Carlingford *p141*

A bed in Carlingford needs advance booking in the summer but accommodation is also available at Omeath, which is up the main road.

B **Ghan House**, T042-9373682, www.ghanhouse.com. An 18th-century house with walled grounds, forbiddingly expensive room rates and an excellent restaurant.

For an explanation of the sleeping and eating price codes used in this guide, see inside the front cover. Other relevant information is found in Essentials pages 39-45.

B-C McKevitt's Village Hotel, Market Sq, T042-9373116, www.mckevittshotel.com. A welcoming place but busy in the summer.
C-F Carlingford Adventure Centre & Holiday Hostel, Tholsel St, T042-9373100, info@carlingfordadventure.com. Over 30 dorm beds and a small number of private rooms edging into the **E** price range.
D Beaufort House, Ghan Rd, T042-9373879, www.beauforthouse.net. By the water's edge, this guest house has hotel-standard rooms with views.
E Grove House, Grove Rd, T042-9373494. One of the least expensive B&Bs in town.

Camping

Gyles Quay, 16 km west of Dundalk on the Cooley Peninsula, T042-9376262. A well supplied caravan and mobile home site but has space for 10 tent pitches between Apr and Sep.

Eating

Drogheda *p135, map p135*

ƚƚ Bacchus, out of town at Bettystown, T041-982851. Has been recommended for the quality of its cuisine. Tue-Sat for dinner, Sun lunch. Early bird menu from 1800.
ƚƚ Martello's, Millmount Sq, T041-9834759. Has a spacious upstairs restaurant with window tables overlooking the town. Opens Tue-Sun from 1800. When night falls, from a window table at Martello's, the Dublin to Belfast train chugging across the Victorian viaduct east of town is a stirring sight.
ƚ Admirals, Shop St. Worth trying for a pub lunch.
ƚ The Black Bull Inn, T041-9837139, just outside of town on the road to Dublin. Open all day for a good choice of meals, and a delicatessen for picnic supplies.
ƚ The Boiled Onion, Shop St, T041-9875566. Good for an evening meal.
ƚ Bridie Mac's, Narrow West St. A comfortable alternative for a pub lunch.
ƚ Harry Groom's, Narrow West St. Popular with locals, especially for Sun lunch, serving beef, lamb and the like with chips.
ƚ The Triple House, Termonfeckin (see page 142), 10 mins away by car. See the early bird menu for another good-value meal.

Monasterboice *p137*

ƚƚ Monasterboice Inn, T041-9845284, www.monasterboice-inn.ie. Owned by a controversial ex-minister of defence in a 1970s government. A standard menu of steaks, lamb cutlets and mixed grills, and a somewhat retro selection of prawn cocktails and gammon steaks with pineapple. Also has a children's menu.

Drogheda to Dundalk *p138*

ƚƚƚ Smarmore Castle, Ardee, T041-6859955, www.smarmorecastle.com. Italian restaurant La Cucina "brings classical Italian cuisine to the heart of County Louth".
ƚ Rolf's Bistro, Market St, Ardee. For an evening meal, the Scandinavian chef brings surprises to the menu and there is an early dinner for €15 (closed Mon).
ƚ The Triple House, Termonfeckin, T041-9822616. Fine food at this converted 200-year-old farmhouse.
ƚ Waterside Inn, Termonfeckin. A less expensive option for a pub lunch.

Dundalk *p138, map p139*

ƚƚ Café Metz, Francis St. Trendy, opens for breakfast, €10 lunch, and dinner around €30; drop in for a coffee and check out the menu.
ƚƚ Cube, opposite St Patrick's Cathedral, T042-9329898. Stylishly utilises a Georgian building with original features. Lunch for under €10 if you stay off the seafood, and a choice of evening dishes including a sushi starter; closed Sun and Mon for dinner.
ƚƚ Number Thirty Two, 32 Chapel St, T042-933113. Retro-style, serves substantial lunches and a varied menu with dishes like leek sausages, pork and cider, and decent vegetarian choices. The early dinners 1730-1900 are €15-20 and represent excellent value.
ƚƚ-ƚ Derryhale Hotel, Carrickmacross Rd. Restaurant in this convivial hotel, both the bar food and the restaurant are reasonably priced, and food from the bar menu can also be enjoyed sitting in the period reception area.
ƚ Courtney's, Park St. Pleasant, for light food.
ƚ The Jockeys, 47 Anne St. For a filling carvery.

Carlingford *p141*

Everywhere's a bistro in Carlingford and many of them only open for dinner and are closed on Mon.

Ghan House, T042-9373682, www.ghanhouse.com. Reservations are essential, for its 'set country-house dinner' at around €50 on Fri and Sat only. Also a cookery school which includes accommodation if necessary.
The Oystercatcher Bistro, opposite McKevitt's Hotel, T042-9373922. Keen on seafood, oysters cooked half a dozen different ways, Cooley mountain lamb and vegetarian choices.
Magee's Bistro, Tholsel St, T042-9373751. Has an affordable menu of pizzas and a more formal, restaurant area.
Kingfisher Bistro, in the Heritage Centre. Has interesting starters and vegetarians have more than just a token dish to consider.
Georgina's, a little walk up Castle Hill, T042-9373346. One place that should not be missed, a modest little teashop dishing up superb open and regular sandwiches, perfect cakes such as cream gâteaux or cheesecake, and a takeaway service; open all week but closes at 1800.
O'Hare's Pub, does oysters and Guinness.

Pubs and music

Drogheda *p135, map p135*

Carberry's, on North Strand. Is the town's best known traditional Irish music venue, sessions every Tue night and Sun morning. Other good music venues are **McPhails** in Laurence St and **Bensons** in Trinity St. Check out, too, the **Droichead Arts Centre** in Stockwell St, T041-9833496.

Dundalk *p138, map p139*

Corbetts, Seatown. Try on a Thu.
Fitzpatrick's, Jenkinstown, T042-9376193. If heading out to the Cooley Peninsula this is along the way. Pleasant bar and restaurant.
Harveys, Park St. A big modern pub with sessions every Tue night.
Imperial Hotel, Park St. Has a weekend disco.
The Jockeys, 47 Anne St. Traditional Irish music every Fri.
McManus's, Seatown. Mon and Fri nights music starts at 2100.
Moe's Bar, close to Courtneys, Park St. Popular beer garden and music most nights.
P McArdles, Anne St. A quieter atmosphere, attracts a more purist crowd of performers and audience on 1st and 3rd Thu of each month.
Mr Ridleys, Park St. Weekend disco.
Sextons, on a Tue head out of town for a couple of miles on the Dublin Rd and enjoy traditional music at this pub.
The Spirit Store, by the harbour, T042-9352697. Very atmospheric music venue; trad, jazz, rock, and world beer on draught.
Terrace Bar, in the Ballymascalon Hotel. Music of a non-traditional kind comes alive on Sat night and there is also a live band in the ballroom.

Carlingford *p141*

Lily Finnegan's Pub, at Whitestown, a couple of miles outside Carlingford, on the Dundalk Rd. Go as far as The Cooley Inn, take a right, pass the church and go through the village. If you hit the beach, you've gone too far. Good place for a quiet evening.
P J O'Hares, aka **the Anchor Bar**, T042-9373106. An atmospheric pub, still with the old-style grocery/bar division and traditional music on Thu and jazz on Sun afternoons.

Festivals and events

Drogheda *p135, map p135*

Samba Festival, T041-9833946, www.solo.ie/samba. 2nd week in **Jul**.

Activities and tours

Drogheda *p135, map p135*

Walking tours
Mon-Fri at 1020 and 1420 departing from the tourist office; to book in advance, T041-9845684.

Carlingford *p141*

Adventure sports Carlingford Adventure Centre, T042- 9373100, www.carlingfordadventure.com. Land- and water-based activities bookable.
Táin Adventure Centre, T042-9375385, www.tainvillage.com. Land- and water-based activities bookable.

Sailing Carlingford Yacht Charter & Seaschool, T042-9373878. Courses and yacht chartering.
Dundalk and Carlingford Sailing Club, T042-9373238. Courses and yacht chartering.

Transport

County Louth *p134*
Bike hire Quay Cycles, 11a North Quay, Drogheda, T041-9834526.

Bus Drogheda bus station, T041-9835023, is on Donore Rd south of the river and there are a number of daily connections with **Dublin**, **Dundalk** and **Belfast** as well as services to **Athlone**, **Downpatrick**, **Galway**, **Kells**, **Mullingar**, **Navan**, **Newgrange**, **Newry**, and **Slane**. Dundalk station, Longwalk, T042-9334075, has services to **Armagh**, **Belfast**, **Carlingford**, **Drogheda**, **Dublin**, **Enniskillen**, **Galway**, **Mullingar**, **Newry** and **Sligo**. Bus Éireann runs a service, Mon-Sat, between **Dundalk** and **Newry** via Carlingford 3 times a day.

Taxi **Drogheda Cabs**, T041-9832211, T041-9832211, T041-9837082 and T041-9822666. **Top Rank**, Dundalk, T042-9326555. **Gally Cabs**, Carlingford, T042-9373777.

Train Drogheda train station is east of town and south of the river, off the Dublin Rd, T041-988749. Drogheda is on the Dublin-Belfast line and there are at least 7 trains a day in either direction and 4 on Sun. Dundalk station: Carrick Rd, T042-9335521. Dundalk is also on the Dublin to Belfast line with the same service.

Counties of Longford, Westmeath and Cavan

When visitors dismiss the midlands of Ireland as boring, it is the counties of Longford and Westmeath they usually have in mind. But speak to the anglers who fly in from Britain and head straight for Lanesborough and they wouldn't have it any other way, left alone to pursue their sport with not a tour coach or backpacker in sight. The waterways of Longford – the River Shannon, Lough Ree, the Royal Canal (see page 572) – have boating and other water-based activities that attract families on holidays, but there is precious little else to detain the traveller.

Westmeath is a county of some consequence, benefiting from some of the richest farming land in the country and within commutable distance of Dublin. The main N4 road from the capital to Sligo passes through Mullingar, and while this busy commercial town sums up what is unappealing about Westmeath, other areas of the county are worth exploring: the Fore Valley in the northeast and Athlone, on the N6 road between Galway and Dublin. ▸▸ *For Sleeping, Eating and other listings, see pages 147-148.*

Mullingar and around → *Phone code: 044. Colour map 2, grid B6.*

The county town of Westmeath is not the kind of place to fall in love with but convenient nevertheless for breaking a journey, and a couple of places of interest around town might detain you longer than anticipated. Mullingar's one long street changes its name from Austin Friar Street at the Dublin end to Pearse Street and Oliver Plunkett Street in the centre, and finally to Dominick Street and Patrick Street heading out west to Athlone. The Royal Canal does a perimeter loop around town, and Mount Street heads south to Belvedere House and Kilbeggan from the junction of Pearse and Oliver Plunkett Streets. It's hard to get lost. At some stage you will find yourself gawking at the aesthetically-challenged **Cathedral of Christ the King**, though inside there are some large mosaics by the Russian artist Boris Anrep.

“” Adolphus Cooke served under Wellington before losing his mind to the notion that the family turkey was his grandfather reincarnated... his highly individual tomb makes sense once you realize he was destined to be reincarnated as a bee...

Ins and outs

Getting there **Bus Éireann**'s Dublin to Ballina service goes via Mullingar a few times each day, as does the Dublin to Sligo service. Twice a day, and once on Sunday, the Galway to Newry bus stops in Mullingar and connects the town with Athlone, Navan and Dundalk. Trains from Dublin to Sligo stop in Mullingar, T044-48274, at least four times a day, three on Sunday.

Information **Mullingar tourist office**, Pearse St, Market House, T044-48650, www.westmeathtourism. Open daily 0930-1300 and 1400-1700. **Mullingar Arts Centre**, Mount St, T044-47777, www.mulingarartscentre.com. Local arts information and a regular programme of events.

Around Mullingar

A visit to the **Market House Museum** in Mullingar may have introduced you to the eccentric **Adolphus Cooke** who served under Wellington before losing his mind to the notion that the family turkey was his grandfather reincarnated. When he later sentenced his dog to death for immoral behaviour, the executioner was attacked by his dog; this convinced him of another family connection and the dog was duly pardoned. To find his highly individual tomb, the design of which makes sense once you realise he was destined to be reincarnated as a bee, take the N52 to Delvin for 12 km and, before reaching the village, look for a set of large gates on the left side of the road and park outside. Inside the arched entrance, cross the field to the old churchyard and the beehive grave is easily found.

If staying overnight in the area, a short drive on the N4 to the less frantic village of Multyfarnham is worthwhile: here there are pubs with traditional music, good food and accommodation.

Belvedere House and gardens ⓘ *T044-49060, www.belvedere-house.ie. May-Aug daily 0930-1800; Mar, Apr, Sep daily 1030-1800; Oct-Feb daily 0930-1630. €6.* Belvedere House and Gardens, south of town on the N52 road to Tullamore, are noted for the Jealous Wall, an elaborate folly built by Lord Belvedere to block the sight of a neighbouring house belonging to his younger brother. If you think this was taking sibling rivalry too far, then pity the plight of his poor wife who was incarcerated in the house for 31 years because Lord Belfield suspected another brother of having an affair with her. She died protesting her innocence and the brother was jailed in London for the rest of his life.

Locke's Distillery ⓘ *T0506-32134, www.lockesdistillery.com. Apr-Oct daily 0900-1800; Nov-Mar daily 1000-1600. €4.50. Food served all day, including a take-away service, and drink at the nearby Black Kettle pub.* Further south at Kilbeggan, Locke's Distillery has produced whiskey for 200 years and now dispenses a wee drop to visitors as well.

 Tullynally Castle gardens ⓘ *T044-61159, www.tullynallycastle.com. Jun-Aug daily 1400-1800.* €5. Some 19 km north of Mullingar the R394 leads to Castlepollard, and then the road to Granard and Tullynally Castle Gardens. Owned by the Pakenhams, later the Earls of Longford, since the 17th century, the exterior of this vast Gothic Revival 'castle' (a castellated house really) is not pleasing to the eye and the interior is closed to individual visitors. The woodland gardens, a walled garden and a more recent Chinese garden remain open.

Fore To the east of Tullynally, reached via the R195 from Castlepollard, the village of Fore is the natural starting point for walks into the **Fore Valley**. The village has pubs, but a day out with a picnic from Mullingar is quite feasible. The valley is home to the **Seven Wonders**, a group of early Christian sites associated with St Fechin and illustrated in murals in the Abbey village pub. **St Fechin's Church**, with a Greek cross on the lintel, is easy to find and from here a path leads to the **Anchorite's Cell** (key available from Seven Wonders pub in the village).

Athlone → *Phone code: 090. Colour map 2, grid B5.*

The strong castle of Athlone, commanding a strategically important crossing point of the Shannon, sums up the town's troubled history as a place to be fought over down the centuries. **Athlone Castle and Museum** ⓘ *see tourist office below*, has exhibits on the Shannon's flora and fauna and the life of the great tenor John McCormack, as well as the castle's history. The top floor of the museum is well worth a visit, a little gem of a folk collection which includes a working gramophone that John McCormack travelled with. Ask for a record to be played while sauntering around the miscellany of other exhibits.

Ins and outs

Getting there The bus and train stations, T090-73300, are on the other side of the river to the castle. Athlone is a major transport link and there are buses to just about every main town in Ireland. Trains connect the town with Westport, Galway and Dublin.

Information **Athlone tourist office**, Market Sq, T090-6494630. May-Sep Mon-Sat 1000-1600. €5.

Around Athlone

The road north of Athlone, the N55, heads up the east side of Lough Ree to what numerous brown signs will tell you is **Goldsmith Country**. The poet, playwright and novelist Oliver Goldsmith (1728-1774) was born just north of Glasson in County Longford. The country is pleasantly flat for cyclists, mildly distracting, and the village of Glasson is picturesque enough, but there is not a great deal to see or do other than pass through admiring the countryside.

County Cavan → *Phone code: 049. Colour map 1, grid C3.*

Cavan is most likely to be visited while travelling the main route between Dublin and Donegal. Until the plantations of the early 17th century the land belonged mainly to the native O'Reilly clan and they took their revenge in the 1641 rebellion by releasing their prisoners "turned naked, without respect of age or sex, upon the wild, barren mountains, in the cold age, exposed to all the severity of the winter". Since partition, when Cavan (along with Donegal and Monaghan) was cut adrift from Ulster, life has proceeded fairly uneventfully and this is part of the county's appeal. Everything is low key, there are no major places of interest, and time spent here is best devoted to the wilder west Cavan around Ballyconnell.

Ins and outs

Getting there The Dublin to Donegal service, at least four times a day, three on Sunday, stops at Cavan (and Ballyconnell on request). Ballyconnell can also be reached on a local bus, Mon-Sat, that travels between Cavan and Bawnboy. From Cavan buses connect with Armagh, Athlone, Belfast, Clones, Dundalk, Enniskillen, Galway, Kells, Killybegs, Longford, Monaghan, Portadown and Roscommon.

Information **Cavan tourist office**, Farnham St, T049-4331942. Mon-Fri 0900-1700, Sat 0900-1300, www.cavantourism.com.

Cavan town and around

Cavan developed from a Franciscan friary of 1300 and, although nothing of this now remains, the tourist office has some information on a few places of minor interest, namely the **Lifeforce Mill**, T049-4362722, by the Kennypottle River. A tour begins with the making of soda bread and ends with collecting it hot from the oven. The **Cavan Crystal Centre** ⓘ *Dublin Rd, T049-4331800, just outside town on Dublin Rd*, is also worth a visit.

For an excursion, try the **Killykeen Forest Park**, or the miscellany of folk artefacts at the **Pighouse Folk Museum**, *T049-4337248*.

Virginia

Right on the main route from Dublin to Donegal this village is a regular retreat for Dubliners wanting a quiet weekend. This is drumlin country, low quiet hills with lots of lakes for fishing. The village has some good pubs and a **theatre**, T049-8547074, with regular travelling theatre companies.

West Cavan → *Phone code: 049.*

If you're just speeding through between Dublin and Donegal you will miss the most interesting part of the county, though it is only a short detour off the N3 at Belturbet to access **Ballyconnell** on the R200. The **Cavan Way**, a 26-km waymarked walking trail, connects Blacklion with Dowra and could be completed in a day. Accommodation and food is better in Blacklion, so start from Dowra with the help of Ordnance Survey map No 26 and the Cavan Way Map guide available from the tourist office in Cavan. From Blacklion the Way is mostly by road but it ends up as hill walking.

Sleeping

Mullingar *p144*

B-C Greville Arms Hotel, Pearse St, T044-48563, www.grevillearms.com. A busy and buzzing town centre hotel redeemed by its garden, conservatory and general air of hospitality. The wax effigy of James Joyce in the *Ulysses* bar has its basis in Joyce's two trips to the town as a young man visiting his father, who was employed here for a while.

E An Tintáin, Main St, Multyfarnham, T044-71411, www.antintain.info. Guest house with 6 bedrooms, sitting room, good restaurant (category) and a comfortable bar.

E Hilltop, Delvin Rd, T044-48958, www.hilltopcountryhouse.com. Has 5 comfortable bedrooms with en suite bath.

E Woodville House, Gaybrook, T044-43694, www.woodvillehouse.com. A 19th-century house, 8 km from town on the R400 road to Rochfordbridge, with a restaurant.

Athlone *p146*

A Hodson Bay, on the shore of Lough Ree, 9 km from town, T090-6442000,

For an explanation of the sleeping and eating price codes used in this guide, see inside the front cover. Other relevant information is found in Essentials pages 39-45.

www.hodsonbayhotel.com. A centre for water-based activities on the lough and a good restaurant but not very peaceful.

E **Dun Mhuire House**, Bonavalley, Dublin Rd, T090-6475360. Typical of the countless B&Bs spread out along the approach roads (but at least it's not a bungalow).

F **Lough Ree Lodge**, Dublin Rd, T090-6476738, www.athlonehostel.ie. A functional place that should meet your needs. Plenty of dorm beds, private rooms nudging into the E price range, open mid-May to mid-Sep.

Cavan town and around *p147*

E **Lisnamadra**, Killeshandra Rd, Crossdoney, T049-4337196, lisnamandra@eircom.net. Pleasant accommodation on a dairy farm 7 km southwest of Cavan. Why stay in town?

Virginia *p147*

B **The Park Hotel**, T049-8546100, www.bichotels.com. The best place to stay and to eat. Set in vast parklands where you can walk for hours without ever leaving the hotel grounds.

West Cavan *p147*

L **Slieve Russell Hotel**, Ballyconnel, T049-9526444, www.quinnhotels.com. All the facilities expected of 4-star accommodation, plus a 18-hole golf course; worth popping in for the range of food options.

E **Hi Way Inn**, Dowra, T071-9643025. Another B&B handy for those walking the Cavan Way.

E **Macnean House and Bistro**, Main St, Blacklion, T071-9853022. B&B on the Cavan Way and serving an excellent early dinner for €30.

F **Sandville House Hostel**, 3 km west of Ballyconnell (telephone for a pick-up), T049-9526297, sandville@eircom.net. This makes a comfortable base if walking or cycling through the local countryside. Bikes are available, there are 2 private rooms and camping is also possible.

Eating

Mullingar *p144*

There is no problem finding places to eat in Mullingar, with a host of busy cafés, restaurants and pubs all in the town centre.

TT-T **Austin Friar Hotel**, Austin Friars St. Good.

TT **Crookedwood House**, Crookedwood, T044-72165, www.crookedwoodhouse.com. For something on a grander scale head for the late 18th-century rectory here. Accommodation in the **B** category) a few miles north on the R394 road. Dinner menu.

T **The Fat Cats Brasserie**, Market Sq. More old-fashioned than the name suggests, is worth considering during the day.

T **Gallery 29 Café**, 29 Oliver Plunkett St. For light meals.

T **Greville Arms**. Good pub food.

T **Ilia**, 28 Oliver Plunkett St. Mullingar is the capital of a beef county where vegetarianism is seen as some kind of disease, but non-meat eaters will survive here, for lunch at least.

Athlone *p146*

TT **Left Bank Bistro**, Fry Pl. Arty place with good food.

TT **The Olive Grove**, Bridge St. Good food.

TT **Restaurant Le Château**, St Peter's Port, the Docks, T090-6494517. An old church on the banks of the river down from the castle. A romantic, candle-lit atmosphere at night though open daily from 1230 and an early bird menu 1730-1845 for around €25.

Sean's Bar, Main St, close to the tourist office. Claiming with some authority to be the oldest in the land (all owners since the year 900 are recorded), it does have some character, and a beer garden overlooking the Shannon.

Cavan town and around *p147*

TTT **Oak Room Restaurant**, at the Cavan Crystal Centre, T049-4360099. Serves colourful, quality food at night. Bootom of this price category.

TT **Annalee Restaurant**, Hotel Kilmore, Dublin Rd, T049-4332288. For something more memorable this restaurant has a reputation for dishing up local fish and game, open for lunch and dinner, closed Mon.

TT-T **The Side Door**, Drumalee Cross, T049-4331819, less than half a mile from Cavan town. A funky kind of place, dinner and Sun lunch, with good, tasty food.

Activities and tours

Athlone *p146*

Tours M.V. Ross, T090-6472892. Does a 90-min cruise on the Shannon for €9, daily, departing from the Jolly Mariner Marina.

Viking tours, St Mary's Pl, T090-6473383, www.vikingtoursireland.com. A replica Viking boat departs daily in the summer, from the Strand in front of the Fishing Tackle Shop, for Clonmacnois (€10) or into Lough Ree (€15)

Counties Wicklow and Wexford

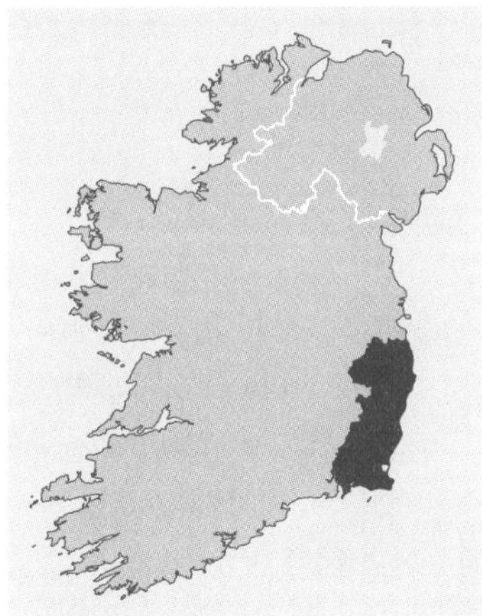

Footprint features

Introduction

County Wicklow's sobriquet, 'The Garden of Ireland', gives some hint of the beauty that singles out this part of the country. The northern border of Wicklow is only 19 km from Dublin's city centre, which is astonishing to reflect on when walking alone in the heather-coloured Wicklow Mountains. As well as the grandeur of the mountains the county boasts stately homes, archaeological and historical sites, superb beaches and some of the best food in the whole of Ireland. The county divides neatly into three areas: the north including the picturesque village of Enniskerry and the seaside town of Bray; Glendalough and West Wicklow including Blessington; and south of Glendalough with the county town of Wicklow, nearby Arklow and the Vale of Avoca, better known to couch potatoes as Ballykissangel.

Dubbed the 'sunny southeast' because of slightly higher average temperatures and lower rainfall than the rest of Ireland, County Wexford, and especially the towns of Wexford and Enniscorthy, have strong historical connections with the 1798 rebellion. The south Wexford coast is most attractively represented by the fishing village of Kilmore Quay and the Hook peninsula, while the east coast has long stretches of sandy beach.

★ Don't miss...

1. **Wicklow Gardens Festival** Enjoy the gardens throughout the county, page 152.
2. **Glendalough** Monastic sites and walks, page 158.
3. **1798** Visit the 1798 Centre in Enniscorthy, the opposite of history dumbed down, page 170.
4. **Wexford Opera Festival** Check out the fringe events and rare opera, page 174.
5. **Wexford Coastal Path** Walk from Courtown Harbour on the east coast to Carnsore Point, page 175.

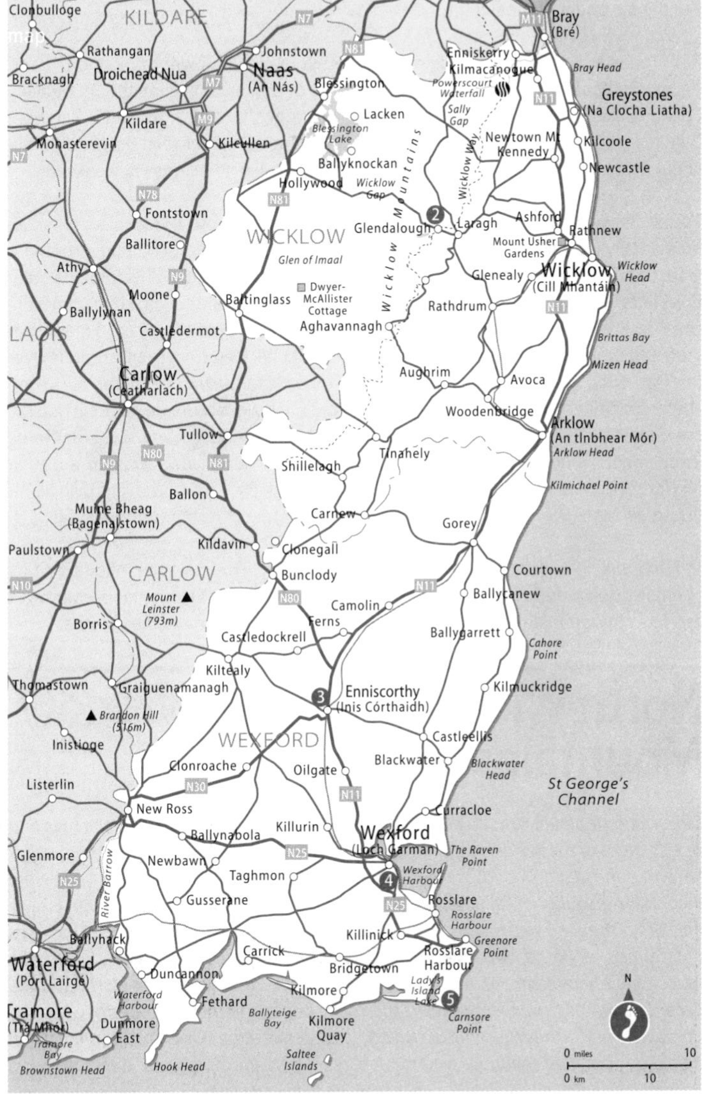

County Wicklow → www.wicklow.ie.

Ins and outs

Getting there and around

Bus The county of Wicklow is just a short bus ride away from Ireland's capital city. Daily Dublin buses serve Bray, Enniskerry and Blessington: details are shown in the Transport sections for these towns (see pages 157, 162 and 167). Provincial buses serve Arklow, Avoca, Laragh, Jack White's Cross (for Brittas Bay), Rathdrum, Wicklow and Woodenbridge. There is a useful **Saint Kevin's** daily bus service to Glendalough; see details under Glendalough.

Rail The main Dublin-Wexford line runs through Bray, Wicklow town, Rathdrum and Arklow. **Railtours,**T01-8560045, www.railtours.ie, offer a tour that departs from Dublin's Connolly station by train to Wicklow town, then a bus to Avoca. The DART line from Dublin goes as far south as Bray and Greystones. Trains run between Bray and Dublin about every 15 minutes during weekdays and up to every 30 minutes at weekends.

Tours Between mid-April and October **Bus Éireann**, T01-8366111, www.buseireann.ie, runs a daily tour from Dublin to Glendalough and Powerscourt, departing at 1030 for €30. During the winter, the tour operates on Wednesday, Friday and Saturday. **Dublin Bus Tours** T01-8734222, www.dublinbus.ie, run a half-day South Coast tour, down the coast to Greystones, returning inland via Enniskerry and Avoca for €20, departing at 1100 and 1400. Private companies running tours into Wicklow from Dublin include **Over the Top Tours,** T1800-424252 (reservations), T01-8386128, www.overthetoptours.com. Their whole-day tours, taking in Glendalough but not Powerscourt, depart from outside the Dublin tourist offices in O'Connell St and Suffolk St, costing €24. **DayTours Unplugged,** T1800-609606, T01-8340941, www.discoverwicklow.com, run a similar trip for €28. So too do **Wild Wicklow Tours,** T01-4753313, www.discoverdublin.ie, for the same price. See also the walking tours over the page, for county information.

★ **Festivals** The **Wicklow Gardens Festival,** May-July, T0404-20070, allows visitors to enjoy the wonderful variety of gardens that the country has to offer and while most are open throughout the three months some only open for one of the months.

North Wicklow and the Wicklow Mountains

Discerning Dubliners know well how blessed they are by having the granite hills and purple glens of the Wicklow Mountains almost in their backyard. The R115 road, better known as the Military Road, makes its way through Glencree and the Sally Gap before meandering south to Glendalough and it can be joined at Glencree from Enniskerry and Bray. The road was made by the British in the years after the 1798 rebellion, in a determined effort to wipe out the remaining insurgents who were using the inaccessible mountains as their base. A suggested tour of the area starts with the seaside town of Bray before taking the road west to the postcard-pretty village of Enniskerry and – the reason for the village's existence – the Powerscourt Estate. From Enniskerry the road continues west to Glencree, where the Military Road can be picked

up. Rather than stay on this road all the way south to Laragh, it is worth heading off to Roundwood at the Sally Gap and then going on to Laragh and Glendalough from there. The scenery between the Sally Gap and Roundwood is quite spectacular and the village of Roundwood itself makes a pleasant place to stop for a meal and a rest.
▸▸ *For Sleeping, Eating and other listings, see pages 156-157.*

The Wicklow Way

There are many well laid out and exciting walks in the Wicklow Mountains. The best way to see the mountains is by walking the five days of the Wicklow Way, Ireland's first and oldest waymarked walking route, 131 km. It is well signposted and you are unlikely to travel as much as a day without meeting anyone.

The Wicklow Way
DUBLIN
Marlay Park
Two Rock Mountain
Bray
Enniskerry
Glencullen
Knockree
Kippure (752m)
Djouce (724m)
Roundwood
Mullaghcleevaun (847m)
Tonelagee (816m)
Scarr
Glendalough
Laragh
Mullacor (664m)
Glenmalure
Rathdrum
Lugnaquilla (924m)
Croaghanmoira (662m)
Aghavannagh
Shielstown Hill
Aughrim
Moyne
Garrymore (432m)
Croghan (605m)
Tinahely
Stookeen Hill (419m)
Shillelagh
Clonegall
N
0 miles 3
0 km 3

Mapping and information **EastWest Mapping** (see page 52) produces a strip map and booklet about accommodation along the Way, which you could just about get by with, but ideally you should bring with you the Ordnance Survey Discovery Series maps Nos 50, 56 and 62. You must have good walking boots, wet weather gear, food for each day you intend to walk, and, as a minimum of safety equipment, a whistle, compass and first aid kit.

Day 1: Wicklow to Knockree (21 km)
Day 1 begins in **Marlay Park** ⓘ *open 1000, bus No 47B from city centre*, to the south of the Dublin. It quickly leaves suburbia behind as you head up Kilmashogue Lane to Kilmashogue Wood. As you make your way upwards, views open up of the coast and the city that have been left behind. Crossing **Two Rock Mountain**, high up at about 450 m you come to the R116 and **Glencullen**. Out of the village and on to open moorland again you come eventually to **Knockree**. There you can break for the evening and perhaps make a trip into Enniskerry for dinner and provisions.

Day 2: Knockree to Glendalough (29 km) Day 2 is a lovely walk along a river and then past the waterfall at **Powerscourt**; you are truly among the Wicklow Mountains, with the Sugarloaf behind you and Maulin stretching beautifully up to the north. Go down to the Dargle River and then along the shoulder of Djouce Mountain to **Lough Tay**. The day

Walking in Wicklow

If you can only afford one day on the Wicklow Way the best is Day 2, from Knockree to Glendalough past the Powerscourt Waterfall, but do not walk it if it is misty.

An alternative to the Wicklow Way comes by way of a useful *Wicklow Walking Guide* booklet available in tourist offices. It contains details and useful maps for a number of short walks in the county.

For organized walks consider a tour operator such as Footfalls Walking Holidays, T0404-45152, www.walkinghikingireland.com. They conduct group walking tours of from 10-15 km each day, with luggage, food, accommodation and transport organized as part of the package. Self-guided tours are also available for independent walkers.

For another company organizing walking trips and self-guided tours see www.dirtybootstreks.com.

could end at **Roundwood**, which is a little way off the track. There are a few B&Bs there (see page 156). Alternatively, you can walk on to **Glendalough** (see page 158), an excellent place to rest for a day or so and explore the walks in the area.

Day 3: Glendalough to Aghavannagh (29 km) Day 3 passes through **Glenmalure**, with glorious views of the valley since the forestry has been felled, passing Lugnaquilla, which is the highest point in the Wicklow Mountains. Crossing Slieve Maan, Carrickashane, you arrive at a tarmac road at **Iron Bridge**, from where you can easily find your way to the village of **Aghavannagh**.

Day 4: Aghavannagh to Tinahely (22 km) Day 4 is less demanding but still passes through some beautiful scenery. Climbing up **Shielstown Hill** and down again by a curious route, keep an eye out for waymarkers along this stretch of the Way. Following a minor road for a time you cross a valley and begin to climb Garryhoe Mountain with views all around of the Wicklow Hills. You cross another mountain, **Coolafunsgoge**, around its lower slopes and catch sight of the next stop – **Tinahely**, which has shops.

Day 5: Tinahely to Clonegal (29 km) Day 5 involves quite a lot of road walking but it will be deserted most of the way. The highlight of the walk is **Urelands Hill**, where there are wonderful views of Mount Leinster.

Enniskerry → *Phone code: 01. Colour map 4, grid B3.*

The pretty, busy little village owes its existence to the Powerscourt Family who had the nearby estate and the village was laid out during the 18th century, when they were lords of all they surveyed. Besides a few cafés and pubs (see page 157) and one of the first Gothic Revival Catholic Churches in Ireland (1843, Patrick Byrne), its chief claim to fame is as a stepping-off point for walks in the area, and of course the nearby Powerscourt Gardens.

Powerscourt gardens and waterfall

ⓘ *Powerscourt Estate, Enniskerry, T01-2046000, www.powerscourt.ie. Gardens and house open all year, daily 0930-1730, but check winter opening times as they are subject to alteration; waterfall: summer daily 0930-1900, winter daily 1030-dusk. €8. There is a free leaflet available with routes for a 1-hr walk and a 40-min stroll around the various points of interest in the garden.*

The Powerscourt estate lies just 19 km south of Dublin, in the foothills of the Wicklow Mountains. It is a huge estate – the approach road to the house is nearly 2 km long and it has the magnificent backdrop of the two Sugarloaf mountains. It also has the imposing presence of Powerscourt House, designed, like Russborough House on the other side of the mountains, by Richard Castle in the first half of the 18th century.

The house is open to the public but don't expect a restored period house because only the ballroom and a garden room are on show; other parts of the building house the visitor centre and its amenities. The house burnt down in 1974 and photographs of its former glory can be seen as part of the exhibition.

The **formal gardens** are the major highlight of any visit, if only to admire how the natural landscape helps moderate the ostentatiousness of the landscaping. The gardens were laid out in the 18th century but substantially modified in the 19th century. Accounts of the **Italian garden** often tell the story of how it was designed by Daniel Robertson while he was being wheeled around in a barrow with a bottle of sherry to stimulate the flow of his imagination; it then took 12 years for over 100 labourers to transform his visions into reality. The **Japanese gardens** attract a lot of attention but numerous manifestations of European high art have also been imported into the landscape: the entrance gate comes from a Bavarian cathedral, classical statutory and urns copied from Versailles are dotted around and there is a fountain imitating that in the Piazza Barberini in Rome.

There is a signposted 6-km walk through the estate to the lovely **Powerscourt Waterfall**. It's a great opportunity to admire the landscape and wonder at the sheer size of this estate and the Anglo-Irish ebullience that led to its creation.

Bray → *Phone code: 01. Colour map 4, grid A3 and B2.*

Once a genteel Victorian resort and now a rather humdrum dormitory town of 28,000 souls that stirs to life in the summer when hordes of Dubliners and their families come and fill up the boarding houses, play on the stony beach and in the amusement arcades, and pack the pubs at night. On the plus side, there is plenty of accommodation, a mile-long promenade, an excellent little town brochure that the tourist office dispenses and a delightful cliff walk, and the town could be considered as a place to stay for a day or two as a base for exploring parts of County Wicklow.

In 1887 James Joyce came to live at **1 Martello Terrace** with his family, when he was six, and remained there until 1891. The dining room of this house was the setting for the acrimonious Christmas dinner scene in *A Portrait of the Artist as a Young Man*. Martello Terrace is at the north end of the esplanade, easily reached by walking to the end of Strand Road or down Seapoint Road from the **tourist office** ⓘ *Old Court House, Main St, T01-2866796, Jun-Sep Mon-Fri 0900-1700, Sat 1000-1500, Oct-Apr Mon-Fri 0930-1630, Sat 1000-1600, closed 1300-1400 throughout the year*. The tourist office also houses a **heritage centre** focusing on local history and personalities. A big attraction in Bray is the **National Sea-Life Centre** ⓘ *T01-2866939, www.sealife.ie, Easter-Sep daily 1000-1700, weekends only the rest of the year*, a hi-tech aquarium on the seafront.

The pub on the corner, the Harbour Bar, marks the site where two United Irishmen were executed in 1798 for their part in the uprising.

For an **architectural tour** of the town and its fine examples of Georgian and Victorian dwellings, get the tourist office's booklet and set off to explore some of the streets and buildings it describes. An excellent 8-km **cliff walk** threads its way from the south end of the promenade to Greystones and you could return on the No 84 or 184 bus or by the DART. It is easy to find a well-worn path at the south end of the esplanade, near the beginning of the cliff walk, that brings you up to Bray Hill with its

"They halted, looking towards the blunt cape of Bray Head that lay on the water like the snout of a sleeping whale." Ulysses, *James Joyce*

 cracking views, as far as Wales on a fair day. This is an easier walk, taking from 30 minutes to an hour.

Just south of town, **Kilruddery House and Gardens** ⓘ *near the roundabout on the Greystones road, T01-2863405, www.killruddery.com, gardens open Apr weekends, May-Sep daily 1300-1700, house May, Jun and Sep daily 1300-1700, €6 for house and garden, €4 garden only*, has the largest surviving French-style garden in the country, dating back to the 1680s, with twin canals and a lovely avenue of lime trees.

Kilmacanogue

The **Avoca Handweavers** ⓘ *daily, bus No 145 runs between Bray's DART station and Kilmacanogue*, have one of their large craft stores open daily in Kilmacanogue, just a few kilometres south of Bray, and there is also a terrace restaurant that serves excellent food. The store has its own **gardens**, created by a member of the Jameson whiskey family in the 1870s, which contain the only mature specimen of the rare Weeping Monterey Cypress in the world.

National Garden Exhibition Centre

ⓘ *T01-2819890, Mon-Sat 1000-1800, Sun 1300-1800, €3, Bray Bus Tours, T01-2828602, run a return trip on Tue at 1430 and Thu at 1000 for €6.30.*

Garden-lovers may wish to make another 7 km journey south to the National Garden Exhibition Centre, Kilquade. Stay on the N11 as far as Kilpedder and take the signposted left turning for Kilquade. There are 16 different gardens on 1.2 ha with names like the 'Seaside Garden', the 'Herb Knot', the 'Geometric Garden', 'Acid Garden', and 'Pythagoras at Play'. A timbered pavilion houses a horticultural shop.

Sleeping

The Wicklow Way *p153, map p153*

D **Glendalough Hostel**, Glendalough, T0404-45342. See page 161.

D **Knockree Hostel**, Lacken House, Knockree, T01-2864036. Advance booking also essential at this *An Óige* hostel.

E **Woodside**, Roundwood, T01-2818195. Rooms with and without en suite bathrooms in this B&B.

F **Ballincar House**, Roundwood, T01-2818168, ballinacor@eircom.net. B&B, shared bathroom, for €25 per person sharing.

Enniskerry *p154*

D **Coillte**, 4 Enniskerry Demesne, Enniskerry, T01-2766614, smyt@eircom.net. About 5-min walk from the village, en suite bathrooms, but pricey.

D **Knockree Hostel**, Lacken House, Knockree, T01-2864036. *An Óige* hostel, 7 km southwest of Enniskerry and on the Wicklow Way, and reachable by a private bus, T01- 2862547, in the summer from Bray DART station.

D **Powerscourt Arms Hotel**, Enniskerry, T01-2828903. Conveniently located in the centre of the village, with 12 bedrooms.

E **Corner House**, Enniskerry, T01-2860149. In the village, 3 bedrooms sharing bathrooms.

Camping

Roundwood Caravan and Camping Park, Roundwood, T01-2818163, www.dublinwicklowcamping.com. Opens late Apr until late Sep.

Bray *p155*

B-D **Esplanade**, Esplanade, T01-2862056, www.esplanadehotel.com. Victorian-era hotel on the seafront with reasonable restaurant and leisure facilities.

C **Westbourne Hotel**, Quinsboro Rd, T01-2862362. Minutes from the beach, a bar with live music many nights in the summer.

E **Rosslyn House**, Killarney Rd, T01-2860993. Open from Mar-Oct. En suite bathrooms. Close to everything in town.

For an explanation of the sleeping and eating price codes used in this guide, see inside the front cover. Other relevant information is found in Essentials pages 39-45.

Eating

Enniskerry *p154*
There are a number of little cafés and restaurants serving food in Enniskerry.
ΨΨ-Ψ **Powerscourt Arms Hotel**, has a restaurant and pub food.
Ψ **Glenwood Inn**, serves pub food.
Ψ **Poppies**, on the village square. Offers snacks and light meals around €7.
Ψ **Powerscourt Terrace Café**, T01-2046070, at Powerscourt House. Run by the same family that cooks the food at Avoca Handweavers and it is equally satisfying. Open daily until 1700, outdoor seats on the terrace.

Bray *p155*
ΨΨ **Avoca Handweavers**, self-service restaurant, produces above-average food that is well worth considering. Interesting soups and meals with a taste.
ΨΨ **The Hungry Monk**, south of Bray, in Greystones, T01-2875759. Can be relied on for good food, including vegetarian, from its seasonal menus; superb choice of wines.
ΨΨ **Tower Bistro**, Strand Rd, T01-2868000. Try this place for an elegant evening out.
ΨΨ **Vino Pasta**, Church Rd. Bistro-style with generous plates of pasta and pizza.
Ψ **The Porterhouse**, between the DART station and the Esplanade hotel. Typical of joint on the seafront, lunch is around €8 and nachos and baguettes with steak or chicken are popular at night.

Pubs and bars

Bray *p155*
A list of pubs and their musical nights is on the wall in the tourist office.
Clancy's Bar, Quinsborough Rd, the road linking Main St with the esplanade. Offers refuge from families with noisy children. Dark wood, comfortable alcoves, and Sun night sessions of traditional folk music.
Katie Gallagher's, by the DART station. Has set dancing on Mon nights.

Transport

North Wicklow *p154*
Bus From **Dublin**, No **44** goes to **Enniskerry** from Hawkins St. No **45** runs from Corn Exchange Pl to **Bray** regularly throughout the day 0630-2300, travelling past Merrion Sq and Ballsbridge but not Dun Laoghaire. The **45A** travels between Bray and **Dun Laoghaire**, also daily. No **84** bus also runs between **Dublin** and **Bray**, Mon-Fri. St Kevin's Bus Service, T01-2818119, runs between **Dublin** and **Glendalough**, via the town hall in Bray. It is also possible to get off Bus Éireann's, T01-8366111, **Rosslare Harbour** to **Dublin** service at Bray. Bray bus No **85** goes to **Enniskerry** and **Alpine** Coaches, T01-2862547, runs a summer service from **Bray** DART station to **Powerscourt** and **Glencree**.

Train DART electric trains, T01-8366222, run from **Howth** to **Bray** via Dublin city centre every 15 mins on weekdays and up to every 30 mins at weekends.

Bicycle Bray Cycle Centre, The Boulevard, Quinsborough Rd, Bray, T01-2863357.

West Wicklow

This area of Wicklow takes in the extremely scenic Glendalough and the equally pretty area to the west including Blessington, where there is some excellent walking, the grand Russborough House, a Palladian mansion which, due to a quirk of history, has quite an exceptional collection of art, and Baltinglass Abbey, a 12th-century ruin. The road there from Glendalough is a delightful one, rolling across the Wicklow Mountains and through the Wicklow Gap down to Holywood on the N81. At Donard to the south there is a turning for the sombre Glen of Imaal. Lugnaquilla (926 m), the highest mountain in County Wicklow, is nearby. ▸▸ *For Sleeping, Eating and other listings, see pages 161-162.*

★ Glendalough → *Phone code: 0404. Colour map 4, grid B3.*

Glendalough has become enormously popular in recent years and if you arrive on a busy day in summer and only visit the monastic sites, then the natural magic that attracted St Kevin and his cohorts may escape you. Up to 1,000 people can turn up on one day and both the car parks may be full. At any time, the flavour of the place is best enjoyed by heading off for a walk in the area around the Upper Lakes.

There is a **tourist information** office at the Glendalough Visitor Centre, T0404-45325, and there's also a smaller office, near the Upper Lake, T0404-45425.

History In the sixth century an early Christian monk, St Cóemgen (Kevin), a member of the ruling clan of Leinster, established a monastery (at the time he was living in a tree) in a valley setting beside two lakes (*Glean dá Loch*, glen of the two lakes) and the wisdom of his choice is still apparent in the stark beauty of the place. Perhaps the picturesque setting helped attract the growing number of pilgrims and devotees who came after St Kevin, causing new monastic buildings to spring up as Glendalough's reputation as a place of learning spread across Europe in the Dark Ages. Monastic life was not finally extinguished until the early 17th century, having survived several Viking raids and, later, sacking by the English in 1398.

Glendalough Visitor Centre ⓘ *T0404-45325. Mid-Mar to Oct daily 0930-1800, mid-Oct to mid-Mar daily 0930-1700. €2.75. OPW site.* This is the logical place to begin a tour of the sites. There is an important cluster of buildings nearby at the Lower Lake, and from there you can take the 20-minute walk westwards along the designated green road to the sites around the Upper Lake. Guided tours of the site leave every half-hour and take an hour and there is a 17-minute audio-visual presentation on Irish monasticism. It is not necessary to purchase entry to the Centre in order to walk around the sites.

Walking

ⓘ *Between May and Aug, on Tue at 1100 and 1400, there is a guided nature walk from the Upper Lake Information Office.*

The information centres at the Lower and Upper Lakes hand out a booklet, *Exploring Glendalough* (€1.90), with details of two short nature trails and a longer 8-km route in

Glendalough

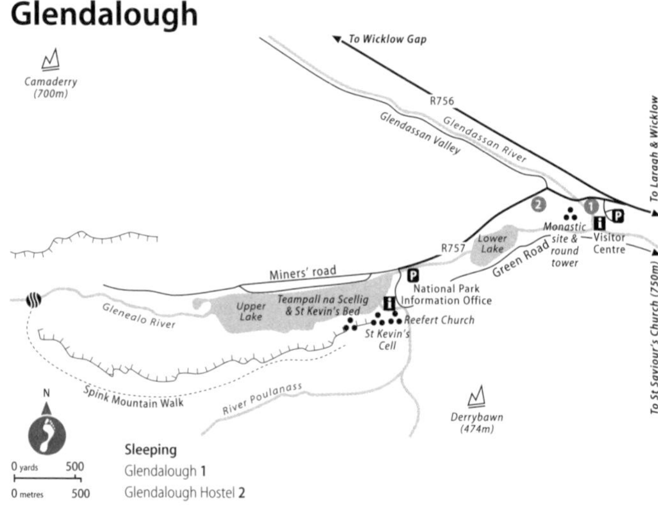

Wicklow's Hollywood

The pulse of Ireland's film world is felt amongst the small towns and countryside of County Wicklow, including a village named Hollywood which was converted for Neil Jordan's memorable film *Michael Collins*. Remember the scene where Collins dashes with glee into his local West Cork pub? *Dancing at Lughnasa* also used the village and its two pubs, as did the film *Rebel Heart*. Before reaching the village, a small road runs off to the right, the R758, along the eastern shore of Blessington Lake to Lacken. Scenes from *Dancing at Lughnasa*, *Braveheart* and *Widow's Peak* were filmed here.

There are plenty more links with films in Wicklow. At the Powerscourt waterfall, scenes from John Boorman's *Excalibur* were shot. One of Boorman's more recent films, *The General*, the tale of a noted Dublin gangster, also has an amusing scene on a mountain road, the Sally Gap, when the *garda* run out of petrol. The General drove back to Dublin, but stay on the road south to Laragh before turning left for the road through Wicklow Gap to Hollywood.

Angela's Ashes, *Far And Away* and *The Commitments* have also all used locations in the county and maps and brochures are available from the tourist office in Wickow town.

the Upper Lake area. A half-hour stroll along the north side of the Upper Lake, parallel to the road, is pleasant enough and it leads to old zinc and lead mines. A more vigorous excursion would be to walk along the south side of the Upper Lake and this could be continued to complete a circuit of the entire lake. It takes about six hours to complete the 17-km circuit and it would be advisable to use a local walking guide, such as David Herman's *Hill Walkers' Wicklow* (€4.76). This also includes a shorter and easier four-hour circuit of Spink Mountain to the south of the Upper Lake.

Lower Lake monastic sites The 10th-century **Round Tower**, with its doorway characteristically placed some 3 m above the ground, is not easy to miss. The nearest ruin to the Visitor Centre is the **cathedral**, begun perhaps as early as the ninth century but added to in the 11th-12th centuries, and with an ornamental east window worthy of appreciation. There are fine examples of 18th-century tombstones around the place. To the south, the **Priest's House** dates originally from the 12th century but a lot of what you see today was restored in 1875-80. The name derives from the practice of burying priests here. The most interesting site is **St Kevin's Church** or **Kitchen**, a fine two-storey oratory that may date back to St Kevin's own times although the belfry is 11th century and the sacristy at the other end was added later. The other main site involves walking eastwards to the other side of the Visitor Centre, but because the 12th-century **St Saviour's** has the finest examples of Irish Romanesque decoration in Glendalough it is worth the detour.

Upper Lake monastic sites As you approach the Upper Lake along the green road, **Reefert church** is over to the left and overlooking the lake. It is a straightforward Romanesque structure of the 11th century and while in fairly good condition it cannot match St Saviour's for decorative details. There are steps from the churchyard leading to the Pollanass Waterfall and further to the west are the remains of **St Kevin's Cell**, a small beehive hut associated with the saint. **St Kevin's Bed**, further to the west and above the line of the water, is a cave on a rocky ledge where, legend has it, the holy Kevin dealt with the unwelcome solicitations of a young woman by hurling her into the lake below. Still further west are the very scant remains of **Teampull na Scellig** ('the church of the rock'), thought to be the earliest site in the valley.

Dwyer and McAlister

Michael Dwyer (1771-1826), the 'Chief', was the leader of a guerrilla band that roamed the Wicklow Mountains in the aftermath of the 1798 insurrection. In the winter of 1799 he and his band took refuge in a cottage at Derrynamuck where they were surrounded and vastly outnumbered by English soldiers. One of the group, Sam McAlister, drew the fire of the English by running from the cottage, and his death allowed Dwyer to escape and flee barefoot in the snow pursued by a pack of hounds. On this occasion he escaped but finally surrendered at the end of 1803 and was transported to Australia where he spent some time on Norfolk Island and then Van Diemen's Land, both prison islands, before, ironically, ending up as High Constable of Liverpool, Australia in 1815. He was shortly afterwards sacked for drunkenness and became the owner of an inn.

In Derrynamuck, the cottage itself was later destroyed by fire but was finally restored in 1946 and renovated in 1992.

ⓘ *Mid-Jun to mid-Sep, 1400-1800, €5, to reach the cottage take the road from Knockanarrigan to Rathdangan in the Glen of Imaal and it is on the right about a mile from Knockanarrigan.*

Russborough House (Blessington) → *Phone code: 045. Colour map 4, grid B2.*

ⓘ *T045-865239. May-Sep daily 1030-1730; Apr (from Easter) and Oct Sun and public holidays 1030-1730. €6 for 45-min tour of main rooms and paintings. 30 km from Dublin on the N81, 3 km south of Blessington on the N81. The tourist office in Blessington, T045-865850, is open Jun-Aug Mon-Sat 1000-1800.*

A particularly fine expression of Anglo-Irish confidence from the first half of the 18th century, Russborough was in fact only one of a flush of extravagantly elegant houses built around that time. Like Westport House and Powerscourt, it was designed by Richard Castle who was brought to Ireland for just this kind of job. He worked on Russborough House with Francis Blindon, an architect from the west of Ireland. They almost went over the top with the immensely horizontal exterior; it stretches out on both sides from the main granite-built house with colonnades, walls, pillars and pavilions that finally terminate with kitchen and stable quarters. This is the Palladian style at its grandest and paler imitations are dotted around the Irish countryside.

The interior is noted for the plasterwork by the famed Lafranchini brothers.

The art collection of Russborough owes its richness to the profits of South African diamond mines. The owner who purchased the house in 1952 inherited the prized paintings of his uncle Sir Alfred Beit, co-founder with Cecil Rhodes of the De Beer Diamond Mining Company. The collection includes Gainsborough, Goya, Rubens, Velázquez and others, and while some may be on loan to the National Gallery of Ireland, at any one time there is always a remarkable set of paintings on show. The house also has its fair share of fine furniture, tapestries, porcelain, silver and bronzes, every example of which is tirelessly itemised on the compulsory tour.

Baltinglass Abbey → *Phone code: 0508. Colour map 4, grid B2.*

ⓘ *24 hrs.Free.* Glendalough and the area around Blessington are the most frequently visited parts of west Wicklow, but the N81 continues south through to County Carlow and on the Wicklow side of the border lies the small town of Baltinglass. Its abbey is to the north of town on the east bank of the River Slaney. It was founded in 1148 by Diarmit Mac Murchadha, the king of Leinster, for the Cistercians, and functioned as a

House of heists

The selection of paintings at Russborough House was especially rich when Rose Dugdale burgled 16 of them for the IRA in 1974, all of which were subsequently recovered undamaged.

But there was no political motive to the 1986 larceny in which 18 paintings were stolen, from loot which has still not been fully recovered. The mastermind behind this robbery was Martin Cahill, a Dublin criminal known as 'The General', the anti-hero of John Boorman's film, see page 159.

In 2001 there was yet another robbery, where two paintings worth nearly €4 million were taken. It is thought that the house was cased by two men who visited as tourists and joined one of the guided tours. The robbery itself was in broad daylight, the thieves arriving at the front door in a jeep and driving off three minutes later with the paintings.

working abbey until the middle of the 16th century. Only fragments of the church and parts of the cloister have survived, but points of interest include the Romanesque doorways, the sedilla in the presbytery and details of the decorative stonework. The neo-Gothic bell tower belongs to the early 19th century, as does the granite mausoleum of local landed gentry.

Sleeping

Glendalough *p158, map p158*

B Glendalough Hotel, T0404-45135, www.glendaloughhotel.com. Just beyond the Lower Lake car park, the only hotel in the vicinity and called the Royal Hotel when Yeats stayed there in 1932.

D Glendalough River House, Derrybawn, T0404-45577. An old restored stone house, bedrooms (with en suite bathrooms) overlooking the river. A walking trail leads past the house to Glendalough.

D Wicklow Way Hostel, Laragh, T0404-43545/45364. Next to Lynham's Inn. Completely independent hostel, which also has private rooms.

E Derrymore House, T0404-45493, patkelleher@eircom.net. A relaxing B&B overlooking the Lower Lake, with a pleasant garden and lovely home-made bread on the breakfast table.

E Valeview, T0404-45292, valeviewhouse@eircom.net. Comfortable rooms at a B&B that fully justifies its name.

F Glendalough Hostel, T0404-45342, glendaloughyh@ireland.com. *An Óige* hostel in a terrific location, being only a few hundred metres from the Lower Lake sites. Renovated to a high standard, the private rooms are a good way of minimizing the occasionally hectic atmosphere; bike hire and internet access.

Blessington *p160*

L Rathsallagh House, Dunlavin, T045-403112, www.rathsallagh.com. Converted stables from the late 18th century provide the setting for a comfortable and friendly country house which has been recommended for the quality of the food served. Just the place to stay if Russborough House has inflamed an itch for aristocratic country living.

B Downshire House Hotel, T045-865199, www.downshirehouse.com. On the main street in Blessington, comfortable, well-run and above-average food.

D Beechwood House, Manor Kilbride, T045-4582802, www.beechwoodhouse.ie. A pleasant house in the countryside where a vegetarian breakfast is part of the considerate service.

For an explanation of the sleeping and eating price codes used in this guide, see inside the front cover. Other relevant information is found in Essentials pages 39-45.

E **The Heathers**, Poulaphouca, Ballymore Eustace, T045-864554, www.celticretreat.com. A bungalow next to Poulaphouca Lakes, reached by the 65 bus from Blessington, evening meal an option.

F **Baltyboys Hostel**, Baltyboys, T045-867266. *An Óige* hostel in a converted old school house overlooking water.

Eating

Glendalough *p158, map p158*

ΨΨ-Ψ **Glendalough Hotel**, is the most convenient place for a meal after visiting the monastic sites. The evening menu is not cutting-edge cuisine and the ubiquitous vegetarian lasagne may make an appearance. The lunch menu has main courses like lamb stew and fried plaice and also offers open and toasted sandwiches; an identical menu serves for bar food.

Ψ **Lynham's Inn**, at the main junction in the village of Laragh. A comfortable low-ceilinged hostelry with a bar food menu and specials on a blackboard. Tables and beer garden outside in summer, and in winter a warm inviting fire.

Ψ **Wicklow Heather**, around the corner from Lynham's Inn, on the road to Glendalough, T0404-45157. Has fairly standard meals of fish, chicken and meat for around €15.

Blessington *p160*

ΨΨΨ **Rathsallagh House**, Dunlavin, T045-403112. For an evening dining experience, this restaurant can be relied on for traditional hearty fare in Irish classical style.

Ψ **Courtyard Restaurant**, T045-865850. Has affordable meals like hake with mustard cream.

Ψ **O'Connors**, Main St. Recommended for its home-cooked pub lunches.

Activities and tours

Blessington *p160*

Blessington Lakes Adventure Centre, T045-865092, www.blessingtonsports.com. A few hundred metres south of Blessington on the shores of the Blessington Lakes. Land- and water-based activities, including windsurfing and lake tours on the *MV Blessington*.

Transport

West Wicklow *p157*

Bus See Ins and outs, page 152 for details of bus tours from Dublin. St Kevin's Bus Service, T01-2818119, daily via **Bray** to **Glendalough** (outside the College of Surgeons) off St Stephen's Green in Dublin, 1130 and 1800. Bus Éireann's **Dublin** to **Waterford** and Dublin to **Rosslare Harbour** services stop in Blessington and Baltinglass. The suburban No 65 bus service from **Dublin** runs to **Blessington**.

Bicycle Hillcrest Hire, Main St, Blessington, T045-865066. Bike hire.

South Wicklow

If your trip so far has taken you around the beauties of Glendalough and Blessington, and the glorious views over Loughs Tay and Dan on the Wicklow Way, then a couple more days' travel will introduce you to equally pretty views and perhaps your first sighting of a small Irish market town. The Vale of Avoca, especially seen out of season when the tour bus syndrome subsides, has a still kind of beauty; while modest and engaging Wicklow town is small, with narrow winding streets and traditional ornamental shopfronts that lend the place some character. Further south is Arklow, another ancient and very popular seaside town with a long history and some pretty sights. Throw in some gardens and Brittas Bay and you have a couple of days pleasant sightseeing. ▸▸ *For Sleeping, Eating and other listings, see pages 165-167.*

Wicklow Town → *Phone code: 0404. Colour map 4, grid B3.*

A settlement of sorts here goes back to AD400, and after the Vikings arrived in the 10th century the town's Norse name, Vikinglough, gradually gave way to Wicklow. Its

Irish name is *Cill Mhantáin* (the church of St Mantan). Wicklow saw most of the action during the 15th and 16th centuries when the English lords were at the mercy of the O'Byrnes, the local clan who raided the place regularly, demanding rents and finally razing the castle in 1580. Soon after, the town became part of the Pale, a safe area dominated by the English gentry who settled all around here in their great houses. The 1798 rebellion passed the little town by although there were several trials of rebels, one of whom, Billy Byrne, possibly a descendant of the O'Byrnes who caused so much trouble in the 16th century, was the son of a wealthy Catholic family and led the south and central bands of the Wicklow rebels until he was caught and executed at Gallow's Hill in the town. A monument in the town stands in his memory.

The **tourist office** is on Fitzwilliam Square, T0404-69117. Open Jun-Sep Mon-Sat 0900-1800; Oct-May Mon-Fri 0900-1800.

Gaol ⓘ *Kilmantin Hill, at the southern end of town, beside the courthouse, T0404-61599, www.wicklow.ie/gaol. Mid-Mar to Oct daily 1000-1800. €6.50. Regular tours every 10 mins.* Wicklow's historic gaol, built in 1702, held insurgents from 1798 and other political prisoners awaiting transportation in the years that followed. Exhibitions on three floors focus on the terrible prison conditions that people endured, the 1798 Uprising, the tragedy of the Famine years and the trauma of transportation that carried some 50,000 Irish people to Australia. The gaol also houses a genealogy centre, a shop and a café, but the best reason for a visit lies with the gaoler who summons you inside and scares the life out of you.

Mount Usher Gardens ⓘ *Ashford, T0404-40116, www.mount-usher-gardens.com. Open early Mar-end of Oct daily 1030-1800. €6.50. Tea room and craft shops but no picnics allowed, off the N11 road, 7 km from Wicklow Town.* Mount Usher is regarded as an exemplary garden of the romantic Robinsonian type, with cascades, suspension bridges, and trees and shrubs introduced from many parts of the world. It dates back to 1860 and is laid out along the River Vartry in a style of natural, relaxed informality. In spring the meadows are bursting with flowering bulbs and the autumn colours are sublime.

Beaches Brittas Bay ⓘ *Bus Éireann's No 2 service from Dublin to Jack White's Cross, then a walk of about 2 km*, is one of the best beaches on the east coast of Ireland and especially popular with daytripping Dubliners. The Blue Flag beach is midway between Wicklow town and Arklow and stretches for over 3 km with lovely powdery sand and sand dunes where botanists search for plants. **Silver Strand** is nearer town and also has a car park, but it is far smaller and lacks the grandeur and appeal of Brittas Bay.

Wicklow Town and cliff walk This walk begins outside Wicklow's gaol, from where you go down to Main Street and pass the monument to Billy Byrne. Continue along Main Street and past the post office until you reach another monument, the **Halpin Memorial**. Captain Robert Halpin sailed Brunel's steamship *The Great Eastern* to America, laying the first transatlantic cable from Valentia to Newfoundland. He was born in the town and also died nearby, from a septic toe that was not properly treated.

Turn up Church Street and take the first turning on the right, which leads towards the river. Do not go as far as the bridge but turn to the right and walk along South Quay by the side of the River Vartry. South Quay leads to the shore where the bare ruins of **Black Castle** stand. It was built in the 12th century by the Norman Fitzgeralds who were granted the land around Wicklow by Strongbow (Richard fitz Gilbert, ex-Earl of Pembroke who fought for Diarmit Mac Murchadha in his efforts to regain the kingship of Leinster around 1170). The castle was destroyed by local clans in 1301. With the ruins behind you, walk along Travilahawk Strand for a cliff walk of 3 km to Wicklow Head's three lighthouses.

Clovers rare in Ireland, brought from Scandinavia by 12th-century Vikings, are said still to grow along the river.

The Parnell Split

Born in 1852 at Avondale to an Irish-American mother, Anna Parnell learned radical politics at an early age. In the US the family supported the anti-slavery and women's rights movements and in 1881 Parnell was asked by Michael Davitt to return to Ireland, the family home, to organize the Land League while its former leader was serving time in Kilmainham Gaol. The Land League was a disparate group ranging from the very radical who were prepared to use any tactics they could, to the conservatives, who were willing to use parliamentary politics to get what they wanted. The Land League embraced a range of demands, from the appropriation of the land by the people to the more modest demands of fair rents and security of tenure.

Parnell travelled widely across the country, encouraging people to refuse to pay rent to the landlords, organizing meetings, distributing the Land League newspaper, arranging shelter for dispossessed tenants, but above all encouraging women to join the front line in the resistance against evictions. The right wing of the Land League, most notably her brother Charles Stewart Parnell who was negotiating a deal on a watered-down form of land reform, grew alarmed. The now time-honoured epithets emerged in the press – "harpy", "harridan", "fanatic" – and eventually Anna's Ladies Land League was dismantled by Charles Stewart Parnell himself, who cut off their funds. Anna Parnell left Ireland and never spoke to her brother again. She drowned in 1911.

Vale of Avoca → *Phone code: 0402. Colour map 4, grid B3.*

The Vale of Avoca is one of those places highlighted on maps as a 'scenic route' and in recent years it has been rendered even more popular thanks to the previously nondescript little village of Avoca being chosen as the location for the *Ballykissangel* television series. The scenic highlight is the **Meeting of the Waters**, where the confluence of the rivers Avonbeg and Avonmore form the River Avoca, immortalized by Thomas Moore in a poem and now marked by a pub, The Meetings.

Avoca Village The village of Avoca is reached by a narrow bridge from the main road and the place everyone heads for is the pub, in the hope of nosing themselves into the background of a *Ballykissangel* scene. Another attraction is **Avoca Handweavers,** located in the oldest working mill in Ireland and offering guided tours to see weavers at work. The shop is open daily and has an excellent range of crafts and clothing, and the café is worth visiting in its own right.

Avondale House and forest park ⓘ *Rathdrum, T0404-46111. Mid-Mar to Oct daily 1100-1800. House: €4; park in grounds: €5.50 (but not staffed outside of summer months). Bus Éireann's 133 service stops 1.6 km from the house.* Charles Stewart Parnell, one of the great Irish nationalist leaders of the 19th century, was born into a Protestant landlord family in Avondale. The house, although it was built in 1777 and designed most likely by James Wyatt, has an interior restored to a mid-Victorian setting. There is also the obligatory video about the life and times of Parnell, one that fails to make any mention of the Catholic Church's role in his downfall. The adjoining forest park has nature trails from an easy 1.75 km stroll to a 5-km riverside walk that requires sensible footwear. There are also picnic tables at the coffee shop.

Arklow Busy traffic on the N11 Dublin to Wexford road, which now bypasses the town's main street, was coming close to destroying the appeal of this once-famous port. During the 1798 uprising a bloody battle for control of the town saw hundreds of rebels mowed down by the superior guns and artillery of the English. There is a small **maritime museum** ⓘ *St Mary's Rd, daily 1000-1300 and 1400-1700, €3*, that traces the eventful history of the town and its port. There is a seasonal **tourist office**, T0402-32484, next to the Catholic church.

Clogga Beach is about 7 km south of town and is safe for swimming.

Sleeping

Wicklow Town *p162*

L **Tinakilly Country House & Restaurant**, Rathnew, T0404-69274, www.tinakilly.ie. An impressive Victorian mansion built for Captain Halpin (see page 163) and now a comfortable hotel with modern extensions sympathetic to the character of the place. Nautical artefacts and Halpin memorabilia, large bedrooms, an excellent restaurant and good service. Dickens and Tennyson stayed here.

C-D **Ballyknocken House**, Ashford, T0404-44627, www.ballyknocken.com. A superb guest house with some fine rooms with brass bedheads and claw feet baths, and a pretty good restaurant.

E **Bridge Tavern**, Bridge St, T0404-67718. Captain Halpin was born here but it is a pub now.

E **Thalassa**, Dunbar Park, T0404-67135. A Greek-inspired B&B, 10 mins on foot from town.

F **Wicklow Bay Hostel**, Marine House, The Murrough, T0404-69213, www.wicklowbayhostel.com. Recommended for its friendliness and spaciousness. Open from Apr-early Dec and there are 2 private rooms.

Camping

Avonmore Riverside Caravan and Camping Park, Rathdrum, T0404-46080.

Vale of Avoca *p164*

B **BrookLodge Hotel**, T0402-36444, www.brooklodge.com. A short, signposted, way from Aughrim lies this modern new hotel complex with a relaxed country house atmosphere. There is a micro distillery, a pub, an exceptional restaurant and a luxury spa.

D **Vale View Hotel**, Avoca, T0402-35236, valeview@indigo.ie. Terrific views from the bedrooms of the only hotel in Avoca. Bar and restaurant food.

E **Ballykilty House**, Coolgreaney, T0402-37111. A dairy and sheep farm, 1.6 km from the village of Coolgreney. A peaceful location, and a tennis court on the grounds.

E **Vale View**, Coolgreaney Rd, Arklow, T0402-32622. A large Edwardian house with panoramic views from the rooftop sun lounge.

F **The Old Presbytery**, The Fairgreen, Rathdrum, T0402-46930, theoldpres@eircom.net. Cleverly designed modern hostel. 6 private rooms and over 50 dorm beds. Bicycles for hire and open all year.

Camping

River Valley Caravan & Camping Park, Redcross Village, on the R754, T0402-41647. Open from mid-Mar to late Sep.

Eating

Wicklow Town *p162*

TTT **Tinakilly House**, Rathnew, T0404-69274. For an evening meal of distinction this place is worth a visit to experience sophisticated country-house cooking in the hotel's dining room. Wicklow lamb on the menu is a clear favourite but the seafood, like monkfish with goat's cheese, is equally satisfying. A 4-course dinner is around €55.

TT **Bakery Café & Restaurant**, Church St, around the corner from the tourist office. Undoubtedly the best place in Wicklow town for a meal. There is an early-bird menu for around €25 and a bistro menu with 2 courses for around €30.

TT **Hunter's Hotel**, inland, on the Rathnew to Greystones road, T0404-40106. The restaurant can be recommended for the

For an explanation of the sleeping and eating price codes used in this guide, see inside the front cover. Other relevant information is found in Essentials pages 39-45.

quality of the food, and a pre-dinner drink in the garden that overlooks the River Vartry makes the perfect start to an evening's fine dining. Expect to pay around €40.

¥ **Ernie's**, The Square. One of the pubs doing food, serves delicious crab specials.

¥ **Grand Hotel**, Abbey St, T0404-67337. Offers carvery lunches.

Vale of Avoca *p164*

¥¥¥-¥¥ **The Strawberry Tree Restaurant**, Brook Lodge Hotel, T0402-36444. Has a most unusual decor that is likely to provoke mixed reactions but the food is a resounding success. Organic produce is the order of the day and the menu is meticulous in this respect. Well worth the journey.

¥¥-¥ **Kitty's of Arklow**, Main St, Arklow. Retro-style, pub and restaurant where vegetarians can also find something worth eating.

¥¥-¥ **The Woodenbridge Hotel**, a little south of Avoca, on the main road and virtually impossible to miss, T0402-35146. A very old coaching inn, such a stupendous establishment it almost obliges one to stop (as did Eamon de Valera, Michael Collins and others in their time). Bar food all day and a restaurant.

¥ **Avoca Handweavers**, Avoca, T0402-35105. Wholesome affordable food, open daily until 1700.

¥ **The Avoca Inn**, Avoca. Decor won't be winning any prizes but the bridge-side location is enviable and the downstairs restaurant, with fairly standard food, overlooks the river.

¥ **Christy's**, 38 Main St, Arklow, T0402-32145. A smart pub that serves an interesting variety of dishes, from fish and chips to Mexican beef wrap.

¥ **Joanne's**, Main St, Arklow. Runs a bakery as well as a restaurant. Consider taking a picnic down by the river where there are benches. From the car park opposite Joanne's there is direct access to the river.

¥ **Murphy's**, Main St, Arklow. Pub is popular with shoppers for its restaurant's large menu of standard dishes, including steaks.

¥ **The Ostán Beag**, Main St, Arklow, T0402-33044. A faded-looking hotel with an old-fashioned bar and a wide range of food, including lunch specials listed on a pavement blackboard.

For a quick bite to eat, there is a fish and chip shop opposite the *Avoca Inn*.

Pubs and music

Wicklow Town *p162*

The Bay View Hotel, has music Thu-Mon.

Bridge Tavern, has music of some kind every night.

O'Connor's, pub has thoroughly enjoyable sessions music, especially on Thu nights.

Vale of Avoca *p164*

The Brook House, Arklow. Music Thu- Sun.

Christie's, Arklow. Has live entertainment in its garden during the summer.

Fitzgerald's, Avoca, T0402-35108. The film pilgrim's shrine, impossible to miss as you enter the village across the bridge.

The Mary B, Arklow. Has some enjoyable informal music sessions.

The Meetings, T0402-35226. A pub and restaurant on the Vale of Avoca road, has an open-air ceilidh every Sun afternoon between Apr and Oct and entertainment of one sort or another most days of the weeks in summer.

The Nineteen Arches, Arklow. Worth checking out to see what musical entertainment might be on.

Shopping

Vale of Avoca *p164*

Arklow Pottery, at the seaward end of South Quay, T0402-39442. Established in 1934 and now specializes in earthenware dinnerware. Guided factory tours in summer Mon-Fri.

Avoca Handweavers, a far more interesting proposition.

Country market, in the Masonic Hall, Arklow.

Fitzgerald's Crafts, Avoca. Sells *Ballykissangel* souvenirs and general gifts.

Noritake Arklow Pottery, South Quay, Arklow, T0402-31101. Opens its factory shop daily.

Wicklow Vale Pottery, The Old School House, Tinahask, Arklow, T0402-39442. Has showrooms and tea room and a range of crystal and Avoca Blue and Wicklow Vale ceramics. Open daily. On Sat, 1030-1200.

Activities and tours

Wicklow Town *p162*

Adventure centre

Tiglin Adventure Centre, at the Devil's Glen near Ashford, T0404-40169. Specializes in weekend and weekly courses in orienteering, caving, hang gliding, rock climbing and various water sports.

Fishing

National Disabled Angling Facility, Aughrim, T0402-36552. 2-ha lake stocked with game fish. Equipment for hire. Open all year; summer 0800-2000 (to 2200 Jul and Aug).

Horse riding

Ballinteskin Farm, near Wicklow Town, T0404-69441. **Bel Air Riding School**, Ashford, T0404-40109. **Broom Lodge Stables**, Nun's Cross, Ashford, T0404-40404. **Devil's Glen Equestrian Centre**, Ashford, T0404-40637.

Transport

South Wicklow *p162*

Bus Bus Éireann, T0902-73300. Service No 133, **Dublin** to **Arklow**, calls at Wicklow 9 times daily in each direction, stopping outside the Grand Hotel (via Avoca, The Meetings and Woodenbridge). The **Dublin** to **Rosslare Harbour** service stops outside the Grand Hotel in Wicklow at 0830 and 0930. From Rosslare to Dublin there is a drop-off service only at Wicklow. Of the 9 daily buses from Dublin, only 2 stop at Avoca and Arklow. On Sun, only the 1400 departure from Dublin goes on to Avoca and Arklow.

Train Trains running between **Dublin** and **Rosslare Harbour** stop in **Wicklow Town**, T0404-67329, **Rathdrum**, T0402-46426, and **Arklow**, T0402-32519.

County Wexford

Wexford and around

The compact little town of Wexford, with a fair range of accommodation and some first-rate, reasonably-priced restaurants, is an obvious base for a tour of the county. Its closeness to Rosslare and the ferry routes makes it a busy place in the summer months but its soul has not been lost to tourism, helped by the fact that there are no major attractions within the town itself. Satirist Jonathan Swift liked Wexford, advising Stella in 1711 to pay a visit: "Go and drink your waters and make yourself well; and pray walk there." Sound advice. ▸▸ *For Sleeping, Eating and other listings, see pages 171-175.*

Ins and outs

Getting there and around See the Rosslare section (page 175) for details of the ferry routes from Britain and France to Rosslare Harbour 20 km south of Wexford. The bus and train stations are together and link Wexford with Rosslare Harbour, Dublin, and other cities. The town is small enough to walk around, but this also means parking space is limited: a parking-disc system operates. ▸▸ *See Transport, page 174, for further details.*

Information **Wexford tourist office**, opposite Crescent Quay, T053-23111. Open Apr-Jun and Sep-Oct Mon-Sat 0900-1800; Jul and Aug Mon-Sat 0900-1800 and Sun 1100-1700; Nov-Mar Mon-Fri 0930-1300 and 1400-1730.

Wexford Town → *Phone code: 053. Colour map 4, C2.*

Wexford was a Viking settlement until Diarmit Mac Murchadha and his Anglo-Norman chums took over in 1169. The Normans built an encircling wall in the 12th century and the town was safe until 1649 when Cromwell (who stayed where *Penny's* department store on North Main Street now stands) left his usual visiting card in the form of a mass slaughter and the destruction of the churches. In the momentous 1798 rising, Wexford was held by the rebels and a commemorative stone was laid in the town on the 200th anniversary of the event. Lady Wilde, poet and mother of Oscar, was born in a rectory in Main Street in 1826. A large historical map in the George Street entrance of White's hotel conveys a good impression of the old walled town and sites of historical interest.

Sights In the centre of the town where a number of streets meet, the **Bull Ring** was where bull-baiting took place, but the square also marks the place where Cromwell's massacre occurred. It was the obvious place to erect the Lone Pikeman statue to the insurgents of the 1798 rebellion, and in 1998 a tree was also planted here to commemorate the revolutionary event. A stone laid on the pavement behind it is inscribed with the words of the United Irishmen catechism, about the tree of liberty growing in the United States (the American War of Independence), blooming in France (the French Revolution) but falling in Ireland (in 1798).

The **West Gate** is a restored city gate from around 1300 and the best-preserved sections of the original **city walls** can be seen nearby. Also nearby is the 12th-century **Selskar Abbey** ⓘ *T053-46506, summer only Mon-Fri 0900-1700, €4,* but what you see today is what remained after Cromwell's troops paid a visit in 1649. There is a heritage centre of sorts, with an audio-visual film at scheduled times on the town's history, which is best saved for a rainy day.

On Main Street is **St Iberius church** ⓘ *daily 1000-1600*, an elegant 1775 church with a 19th-century façade, offering a guided tour around the interior; a donation is appreciated but by no means obligatory.

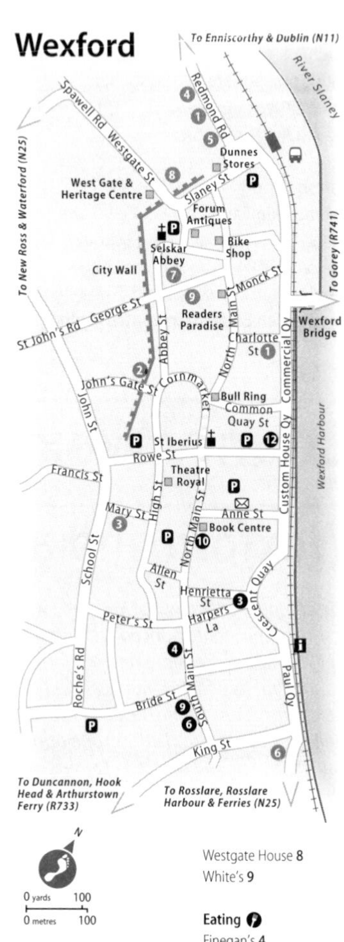

Sleeping
Auburn House 1
Blue Door 7
John's Gate St House 2
Kirwan House 3
McMenamin's Townhouse 4
Mount Auburn 5
Talbot 6
Westgate House 8
White's 9

Eating
Finegan's 4
Forde's 3
Gusto 6
La Riva 3
Premier 9
Robertino's 10
Wren's Nest 12

Pubs & music
Centenary Stores 1

Around Wexford

Irish National Heritage Park ⓘ *T053-20911, www.inhp.icom, daily 0930-1830, €8, restaurant open throughout the day, located at Ferrycarrig, 5 km from Wexford town just off the N11 road.* Ambitious to say the

Radical mother to a radical son

Born in Wexford town, Jane Elgee (1826-1896) was a champion for the romantic nationalists of the Young Ireland movement before she met and married William Wilde in 1851 and settled in what was to become the famous address of 1 Merrion Square, Dublin (see page 69). She became Lady Wilde after her husband was knighted, but this did little to dilute her strong republican sentiments and she continued to write nationalist pamphlets. Oscar Wilde was influenced by this political atmosphere and he went on to build and develop libertarian ideas that were probably first suggested by his mother. Lady Wilde shared with her husband a keen interest in folklore and after his death she moved to London where she published his collections of folktales and legends of the Irish countryside. She was fully behind her son's decision to face trial rather than flee the country, but by this time she herself had little money and managed on very little until her death in 1896, four years before the demise of Oscar himself.

least, this historical theme park sets out to encapsulate nearly 9,000 years in the country's development: starting with the earliest prehistoric settlements and finishing with the arrival of the Normans in the 12th century. Models of dolmens and other modes of burial, stone monasteries, a High Cross, and *raths* are just some of the displays making up a series of 14 replicated sites dotted around the park. There is, of course, the inevitable audio-visual show, and for young visitors or anyone with little or no acquaintance with pre-Norman Ireland the Park's guided tours do offer a bird's-eye view of what can be sought out for real in the rest of the country.

North Sloblands ⓘ *Wexford Wildfowl Reserve, North Slob, T053-23129. 20 Easter to end of Sep daily 0900-1800; Oct to Easter daily 1000-1700. Free. Reached from the R741 Gorey Rd; leave Wexford over the River Slaney bridge and after 2.9 km turn right, beside Grannal's Mazda garage, into Ardcavan Lane.* Not the most endearing of names but the white-fronted geese are not bothered because they arrive in their thousands every year from Greenland and stay for the winter. There are hides for bird watching, and a visitors' centre with exhibitions on the various birds that can be spotted here. See the box on page 177 for details of other bird-watching locations in Wexford.

Rosslare Strand Not to be confused with Rosslare Harbour, Rosslare is 8 km north of the ferry port and 15 km south of Wexford town. It is worth visiting for its long, safe, sandy beach, with a lifeguard, and opportunities for water sports.

Rosslare Harbour Two major ferry companies, *Irish Ferries* and *Stena Line*, operate out of Rosslare Harbour and so for many visitors this is their first or last port of call in Ireland. This is all Rosslare Harbour amounts to and there is no reason to stay any longer than it takes to board or disembark from one of the ferries. Depending on the weather, especially in the winter months, there can, however, be delays to the sailing schedules and sometimes an overnight stay may be necessary. If you are delayed for a long time at Rosslare harbour, there is a small sandy beach within walking distance.

Enniscorthy → *Phone code: 054. Colour map 4, grid C2.*

The town of Enniscorthy is worth visiting for its 1798 connections, but there is little else to recommend about the place. The **tourist office** is in the 1798 Visitor Centre.

Oliver Cromwell before the town of Wexford

For the Commander-in-Chief within the town of Wexford:

Before Wexford, 3rd October 1649

Sir, Having brought the army belonging to the Parliament of England before this place, to reduce it to obedience, to the end effusion of blood may be prevented and the town and country about it preserved from ruin, I thought fit to summon you to deliver the same to me, in the use of the State of England. By this offer, I hope it will clearly appear where the guilt will lie, if innocent persons should come to suffer with the nocent. I expect your speedy answer; and rest, Sir,

Your Servant, O Cromwell.

Cromwell's Roundhead army took Wexford with force and 1,500 defenders were killed in the assault. The market place, now called the Bull Ring, is where a great deal of the killing took place.

★ **1798 Visitor Centre** ⓘ *T054-37596. Mon-Fri 0930-1800, Sat-Sun 1100-1800. €6.* This is the highlight of any visit to Enniscorthy and should not be missed; a brilliant example of a visitor centre that achieves the opposite of dumbing down, and which places the 1798 rebellion within both its Irish context and the larger European and American dimensions that gave such it such force and meaning. Allow at least an hour to immerse yourself in the revolutionary mood of late 18th-century Europe, listening to the debate between Edmund Burke and Thomas Paine, and visiting the Chess Room, which graphically depicts the struggle of the times. The Wexford Room focuses on the events in the county itself, a 15-minute film brings to life on a multi-screen the showdown at Vinegar Hill, and the aftermath of the event is chronicled in a look at the growth of democracy in Ireland. The shop includes a good selection of books on 1798.

County Museum and Vinegar Hill ⓘ *T054-35926. Mar-Sep daily 1000-1800, shorter hours in the winter. €4.* Somewhat eclipsed by the 1798 Visitor Centre, and operating in a quite different mode, the County Museum is also worth a visit for its material relating to the 1916 Easter Rising. The setting is a grand one, a Norman castle that dates back to the 13th century.

It was at Vinegar Hill that the rebels encamped in June 1798 to await developments in the tumultuous aftermath of the initial uprising. On the 21st June General Lake, with 400 coaches of ammunition and 20 pieces of artillery, stormed the hill with 10,000 men. However, reinforcements under General Needham arrived too late to complete the encirclement of Vinegar Hill and through a gap, known thereafter as Needham's Gap, the majority of the 20,000 insurgents managed to escape southwards to Wexford, leaving behind 500 dead and many injured. There are great views of the surrounding countryside from the top of the hill, which is reached from town by crossing the bridge, taking the first right turn after Treacy's Hotel and following the signs. The sight is 10 minutes away from town in a car.

Gorey, Courtown Harbour and east coast beaches → *Phone code: 055.*

The R742 road follows the coast for most of the way from Courtown Harbour, near Gorey in the north of the county, south to Wexford town. Courtown and Curracloe have Blue Flag beaches and it was at Curracloe that scenes from Spielberg's *Saving Private Ryan* were filmed. The beach at Courtown is the most commercially developed and

At Vinegar Hill, in the memorable words of Seamus Heaney (Requiem for the Croppies), the rebels faced the English "shaking scythes at cannon".

1798 and County Wexford

One of the four main centres of action during the insurrection of 1798 (see page 594) was County Wexford. On 27 May the rebels attacked the yeomanry at Oulart, before moving on to capture Enniscorthy. Within three days Wexford town was taken and for the next three weeks it remained the revolutionary capital of the insurgents. Unfortunately, after the failure to take New Ross and Arklow early in June, the rebels chose to encamp on Vinegar Hill and await a showdown with the English military. This decision was not unanimous, but calls for rural guerrilla tactics were not heeded and the decisive encounter duly took place on 21 June. The Irish survivors were lucky to escape and on the following day Wexford itself was reclaimed by the English.

Some controversy surrounds the Wexford uprising because in the southeast, where there was a relatively large Protestant presence, a vein of sectarianism manifested itself in acts like the burning to death of 200 Protestants in a barn at Scullabogue and mass executions by the rebels in Wexford town. Notwithstanding this, recent research has confirmed that the Wexford uprising was a remarkably revolutionary act that involved some 20,000 men and women, many of whom were quite aware of the political significance of what they were attempting to achieve.

the best choice of accommodation is here (see page 173). The Wexford Coastal Path (see page 175) runs close to the coastline for most of the way between Courtown and Wexford. There is a **tourist office** in Main Street, Gorey, T055-34699. Open Jun-Sep Mon-Fri 1000-1800.

New Ross → *Phone code: 051. Colour map 4, grid C2.*

Given its prominent position by the River Barrow and on the N25 road between Wexford and Cork, the town of New Ross is frequently passed through by travellers but quickly dismissed for not looking sufficiently glamorous or twee. But there are fine views of the river from the top of the steep and narrow streets, which have their own unreconstructed character, and the ruins of the 13th-century **Church of St Mary** contain some interesting medieval tombs. The failure of the insurgents to capture New Ross in the 1798 uprising was decisive in halting the march of the revolutionaries and thousands died in the battle for the town. The **tourist office** is on The Quay, T051-421857. Open mid-Jun to Aug Mon-Sat 1000-1800.

Places of interest nearby include the **John F Kennedy Arboretum** ⓘ *T051-388171, May-Aug daily 1000-2000; Apr and Sep daily 1000-1830; Oct-Mar daily 1000-1700, €2.75, OPW site, 12 km south of New Ross on the R733*; the US president's grandfather was born in nearby Dunganstown. Time could also be spent in News Ross visiting a reconstructed 19th-century Famine ship, the **Dunbrody** ⓘ *T051-425239, www.dunbrody.com, Apr-Sep daily 0900-1800; Oct-Mar 1000-1700, €6.50*, with a database of all Irish immigration from 1845 to 1880.

Sleeping

Wexford *p167, map p168*

B **Talbot Hotel**, Trinity St, T053-22566, www.talbothotel.ie. Sociable hotel, good restaurant, and a leisure centre with pool, gym and sauna. The hotel dates back to 1905 and, although modernized, the rooms could be bigger.

B **White's Hotel**, George St, T053-22311, www.whiteshotel.ie. Far older than the Talbot, there was an inn on this site in the

1790s, but rebuilding may endanger its character.

B-C **Ferrycarrig Hotel**, T053-20999, www.griffingroup.ie. A gem of a place off the NII by Ferrycarrig bridge just outside Wexford. All the rooms have serene views of the river, the restaurant is top drawer as are the gym and health club facilities.

D **Auburn House**, 2 Auburn Terr, T053-23605, www.obriensauburnhouse.com. A late Victorian dwelling, now a smart guest house with large bedrooms, some with river views.

D **The Blue Door**, 18 George St, T053-21047, www.thebluedoorwexford.com. An elegant B&B in a Georgian townhouse opposite White's hotel.

D **McMenamin's Townhouse**, Auburn Terr, T053-46442. This B&B has been recommended as a good place to stay if passing through the town and the breakfasts are a treat.

D **Mount Auburn**, Auburn Terr, Redmond Rd, T053-24609. B&B, next to Auburn House, en suite bathrooms and car park.

E **John's Gate Street House**, John's Gate St, T053-41124. This B&B has 6 bedrooms in a Georgian house in the centre of town.

E **Westgate House**, Westgate, T053-22167. A guest house, close to Selskar Abbey, furnished in period style befitting a house that was a 19th-century hotel, and with its own car park.

F **Kirwan House**, 3 Mary St, T053-21208, kirwanhostel@eircom.net. Hostel open all year with over 30 beds and 2 private rooms. Breakfast included and bike hire available.

Around Wexford *p168*

B-C **Kelly's Resort Hotel**, Rosslare, T053-32114, www.kellys.ie. This is the best place to stay round here, and can accommodate children without having them take over the place. Immaculate bedrooms, good restaurant, and delightful gardens. All sorts of special interest packages, from gardening to art to feng shui.

C-E **Ferryport House**, Rosslare Harbour, T053-33933, www.ferryporthouse.com. Less than 500 m from the harbour, a very smart guest house with good facilities.

E **Carragh Lodge**, Station Rd, Rosslare Harbour, T053-33492. B&B just off the N25.

E **Clover Lawn**, Kilrane, T053-33413. It is possible to get an early breakfast at this B&B, if catching an early ferry.

E **Kilrane House**, Kilrane, T053-33135. B&B less than 5 mins from the harbour, with a pub and restaurant opposite.

F **Rosslare Harbour Hostel**, T053-33399, rosslareyh@oceanfree.net. *An Óige* hostel on the hill overlooking the ferry port. There is one private double, the other beds are in 4- and 6-bed rooms. From the harbour, up the hill and left (right, coming from Wexford) by the church with the 10-m cross, then right at the supermarket into the car park, the hostel is over the green. If on foot, turn right at the top of the hill and immediate right after Hotel Rosslare.

Camping

St Margaret's Beach Caravan & Camping Park, Our Lady's Island, 9 km from Rosslare Harbour, T053-31169, stmarg@indigo.ie. Open Easter-late Oct. Follow the signs for Lady's Island/Carne south from Tagoat.

Enniscorthy *p169*

B-C **Riverside Park Hotel**, The Promenade, T054-37800, www.riversideparkhotel.com. A short walk from the town centre and overlooking the River Slaney but hardly merging with the landscape. Two bars and a restaurant, dreadful modern decor.

D **Salville House**, Salville, T054-35252. A most satisfying B&B if you want a good dinner (bring your own wine) served in the house around a communal table, and an above-average breakfast the next morning.

E **Don Carr House**, Bohreen Hill, T054-33458. The least expensive B&B in town with 4 bedrooms (with en suite bath). Open all year.

E **Lemongrove House**, Blackstoops, T054-36115. A large B&B house with 5 rooms. Less than 2 km north of town at the roundabout on the Dublin/Rosslare N11 road.

F **Platform 1**, T054-37766. Close to the railway station, has a range of hostel accommodation and free internet access.

For an explanation of the sleeping and eating price codes used in this guide, see inside the front cover. Other relevant information is found in Essentials pages 39-45.

Courtown Harbour and east coast beaches *p170*

B **Bayview Hotel**, Courtown Harbour, T055-25307, www.bayview.ie. Overlooks the marina. Squash and tennis centre for guests.

E **Harbour House Guesthouse**, Courtown Harbour, T055-25117. A residents' lounge, garden, just 3 mins away from the beach.

New Ross *p171*

C-D **Creacon Lodge Hotel**, Creacon, T051-421897, www.creaconlodge.com. A comfortable place outside of town, with pleasant garden, restaurant and bar.

E **Riversdale House House**, Lower William St, T051-422515. Comfortable lodgings in an oversized house.

F **MacMurrough Farm Hostel**, T051-421383, www.macmurrough.com. A few km northeast of town, off the N30, signposted from the Statoil petrol station. A working farm where produce is available for sale in season. One private room.

Eating

Wexford *p167, map p168*

TTT **Boathouse Bistro**, at the Ferrycarrig Hotel, T053-20999. Reserve a riverside table and choose from a catholic menu that includes ostrich and Indian-accented monkfish alongside more conventional dishes. Prices are equally satisfying and just tip the bottom end of this price category.

TT **The Book Centre**, North Main St. Serves coffee.

TT **Forde's Restaurant**, Crescent Quay, T053-22816. Overlooking the harbour from the 1st floor of an old building and recommended for an evening meal. The carefully-prepared, seasonal food is delicious, including vegetarian dishes, and the early-bird menu is especially good value. Mon-Fri and Sun lunch.

TT **Gusto**, South Main St. Little café serving similar food to Into the Blue (below) but slightly lower prices.

TT **Into the Blue**, 80 South Main St. Fine for a quick meal in the €7-10 range. There are Tahi fish cakes, paninis, melts, wraps and baguettes. At nights, Wed-Sat, an Indian chef prepares tasty Indian meals for around €25 and there is also a take-away service.

TT **Premier**, South Main St, next door to Gusto. A take-away fish and chip joint.

TT **La Riva**, Henrietta St, T053-24330. Just around the corner from Forde's, and equally worthy of a visit. Most of the food is organic and there are creative touches that will refresh the jaded food lover.

TT **Robertino's**, 19 North Main St. Has a bit of everything on the menu: pizza, pasta, burgers, steak, fish.

TT **Wren's Nest**, near the quayside. A lovely old bar doing sandwiches, salads and takeaways.

T **Finegans**, bottom end of South Main St. A cocktail bar and bistro with daily specials.

Around Wexford *p168*

None of the B&Bs does an evening meal so if you are staying overnight there is little choice but to eat in one of the hotels. The average price for a dinner is €23.

TT **Kelly's Resort Hotel**, Rosslare. Has an excellent bistro and the formal dining room is especially recommended. Live music and dancing afterwards in the Ivy Room.

T **Portholes Bar**, in the Hotel Rosslare. The best bet for bar food and serves complete meals in comfortable surroundings.

Enniscorthy *p169*

TT **Riverside Park Hotel**, has a spacious dining area for standard lunch meals the hotel's Moorings restaurant, T054-37800, is worth considering and for an evening meal. Or tuck into tex-mex at the hotel's other restaurant, The Alamo.

T **Antique Tavern**, at the end of Slaney St that runs down to the river from near the monument in the centre of town. For a light meal this is a small and snug place. Some hot meals are available plus sandwiches, toasted or plain, with a large choice of fillings. Along Rafter St, the main street that runs down to the central monument, there are a number of small restaurants and cafés.

T **Cozy Kitchen**, serves inexpensive meals.

Courtown Harbour and east coast beaches *p170*

TTT **Marlfield House**, a mile outside Gorey on the R742 Courtown Rd, T055-21124. If you are after a special, dare we say romantic, dining experience, the restaurant here should not disappoint. The dinner menu hovers close to €60 and Sun lunch is about €40.

Bayview Hotel, Courtown Harbour. A reliable place for food.

Pooles Porterhouse, in Gorey's main street. A welcoming pub where good bar food is available until 2100 and, from 1900, a more elaborate dinner menu.

New Ross *p171*

Galley Cruising Restaurants, T051-421723. Operate from New Ross between Apr and Oct, cruise the River Barrow and include either lunch for €20, afternoon tea for €10 or an evening trip with dinner for €38. In New Ross itself the pubs are the best bet for a meal. **John V** has been recommended.

Pubs and music

Wexford *p167, map p168*

Centenary Stores, Charlotte St. Worth a visit on Sun morning for its traditional music, though every night is fairly lively.

Trinity Bar, in the Talbot. Music at weekends, attracting an older set of customers.

The Wren's Nest, Custom House Quay. Has traditional music on Wed nights in winter.

Festivals and events

Wexford *p167, map p168*

Annual Wexford Opera Festival in **late Oct/ early Nov**. Internationally renowned for the opportunity it presents to see full stagings of lesser-known works, supported by a catholic programme of concerts, recitals and lectures. A healthy fringe programme of drama, art exhibitions, special tours and assorted events is now a regular part of the occasion. Book as early as possible for the 3 main operas. Contact: Theatre Royal, High St, T053-22144, www.wexfordopera.com. The theatre also plays host to visiting drama groups.

Wexford Arts Centre, Cornmarket, T053-23764, is open all year and with regular exhibitions.

Enniscorthy *p169*

Late Jun and early Jul sees the Strawberry Fair, 3 days of music and craic, T056-21688, and in **early Sep** there is the Blackstairs Blues Festival, T054-33747.

Shopping

Wexford *p167, map p168*

Barker's, 36 North Main St. Has an array of glass and crystal gifts plus pottery.

The Book Centre, North Main St. A good bookshop for Irish-related literature.

Forum Antiques, close to Selskar Abbey. Has a good selection of second-hand books as well as prints and bric-à-brac.

Readers Paradise, North Main St. Has lots of second-hand books.

Enniscorthy *p169*

Local potteries, dating back to the 17th century, can be visited and their produce purchased.

Carleys Bridge Potteries, Carleys Bridge, on the road to New Ross, T054-33512.

Kiltrea Bridge Pottery, northwest of town and reached by taking the signposted right turn off the R890 road, T054-35107.

Activities and tours

Wexford *p167, map p168*

Fishing

Murphy's Tackle Shop, 92 North Main St, T053-24717. Licences and permits obtainable.

Horse racing

Wexford Racecourse, Battyville, Newtown, T053-421681. Admission €10.

Enniscorthy *p169*

Greyhound racing

T054-33172, Mon and Thu at 2000, €7.

Guided walks

T054-36800. May-Sep. Depart from town at 1030 and 1430. €3.50.

Transport

Wexford and around *p167*

Bicycle Kennys for Bikes, Enniscorthy, Slaney St, T054-33255. Bike hire.

Bus Bus Éireann, T053-33114/33162, arrive and depart from outside the bus station in Wexford. Up to 6 buses a day run from **Dublin** to **Rosslare Harbour** via **Bray**, **Wicklow**, **Enniscorthy** and **Wexford**. There

is also a service from Rosslare Harbour to **Tralee**, via **Wexford**, **Waterford**, **Cork** and **Killarney**. Other buses connect Wexford with **Limerick**, **Kilmore Quay**, **Fethard-on-Sea** and other parts of the county. In the summer 1 bus a day runs from Rosslare Harbour to **Galway** via **Cahir**, **Limerick** and **Ennis**. In **Enniscorthy** on Wed only there is a bus to and from **New Ross** and on Wed and Fri there is a service to and from **Wexford**.

Car hire Cars can be hired from a desk in the terminal at Rosslare Harbour, including Budget, T053-33318.

Ferry Irish Ferries, Rosslare Harbour, T053-33158, sails daily to and from **Pembroke** and **Cherbourg**. Stena Line, T053-33115, sails daily to and from **Fishguard** (3½-hr voyage).

Taxi Wexford Taxi Service, T053-46666; Whitty Cabs, Wexford, T053-22221.

Train Up to 3 trains a day stop at Wexford railway station, T053-22522, on the **Dublin** to **Rosslare Harbour** route. Trains also run daily from Wexford to **Wicklow** and **Enniscorthy** (station T054-33488).
The railway station at **Rosslare Harbour**, T053-33114, now has the grand name of Rosslare Europort and trains depart at 0720 (0852 on Sun), 1445 and 1825 for **Dublin**, via **Wexford**, **Wicklow** and **Bray**. There is also a Mon-Sat service from the harbour to **Waterford**, which connects with a service to **Limerick**.

South Wexford Coast

Most travellers head north from the entry point of Rosslare Harbour to Wexford before going north again to Dublin or west to Waterford; and on leaving Ireland there is the same tendency to speed by on one's way to the ferry port. But the south coast of Wexford, and the Hook Head Peninsula in particular, has its modest charms and with the help of the 7-minute ferry journey across Waterford Harbour, you can enjoy a leisurely meandering journey between Rosslare Harbour and Waterford. ▸▸ *For Sleeping, Eating and other listings, see pages 177-178.*

Kilmore Quay → *Phone code: 053. Colour map 4, grid C2.*

This fishing-cum-tourist village, the departure point for trips to the Saltee Islands, see box page 177, has thatched cottages, a craft shop, sandy beach, a marina, and probably too many visitors in summer months for its own good. Early to middle July is especially busy, when a **Seafood Festival** brings the place alive (see page 178).

★ The Wexford Coastal Path

The Wexford Coastal Path is a signposted long-distance walk of 200 km, starting at Courtown Harbour near Gorey on the east coast and making its way south to Carnsore Point. It then heads west to follow the south Wexford coast as far as Kilmore Quay, passing lagoons and fine views of the Saltee Islands. The Way then diverts inland to pass around Bannow Bay via Wellington Bridge and subsequently goes south again around Hook Head and up the east side to end at Ballyhack.

Mapping and information Ordnance Survey maps, Nos 62, 69, 76, 77 and 82 are needed to cover the whole Way but shorter sections may be enjoyed along the south Wexford coast. Further information from T053-42211, and Wexford County Council also publishes a guide to the Way.

Hook Head Peninsula → *Phone code: 051. Colour map 4, grid C2.*

Even if the peninsula weren't steeped in history this would still be the most interesting part of the south Wexford coast to visit. Accommodation is dotted around

the place and the area is small enough to make everywhere conveniently close. The roads are straight and flat, ideal for a cycling trip out of Waterford using the ferry from Passage East. For picnic food and general supplies, including a post office and a seasonal tourist information post, head for **Wellington Bridge** at the top of Bannow Bay on the northeast side of the peninsula.

It was in **Bannow Bay** in May 1169 that a force of mercenaries landed and met up with Diarmit Mac Murchadha (see page 163) before their combined forces captured Wexford. This brought Strongbow and then Henry II to Ireland, thus setting the stage for 800 years of conquest. In the 17th century when Oliver Cromwell was playing his part in that sorry drama, he noted that Waterford would be taken by "Hook or by Crooke", signifying the two places where an assault could be launched: the Hook peninsula or Crooke on the other side in county Waterford.

Tintern Abbey ⓘ *Near the village of Saltmills, off the R734 road, T051-562650. Mid-Jun to Sep daily 1000-1800; Oct daily 1000- 1700. €2. OPW site.* An austere but impressive and well-preserved Cistercian abbey founded around 1200 and named after the famous Tintern Abbey in Wales, from where its first monks came. The founder, William the Earl Marshall, on a particularly rough voyage over to Ireland is said to have promised God he would found a church if he survived the journey (anyone who has made a stormy passage in winter will find this quite believable). Occupied as a private home from the 16th century until the 1960s, the nave, chancel, chapel, cloister and a tower remain.

Ballyhack Castle ⓘ *in Ballyhack village, T051-389468. Jun-Sep daily 1000-1800; Oct-May Fri-Wed 1100-1700. €2. OPW site.* Strategically located on a slope overlooking Waterford estuary, this substantial tower house was built around the middle of the 15th century. Very little is definitely known about its history, and although the official line is that it was probably built by the Knights Hospitallers of St John this is just speculation based on the fact that the Knights Templar did have a presence at this inlet in the estuary. On another tack, the castle is a roosting site for a colony of Whiskered bats.

Dunbrody Abbey ⓘ *T051-388603. May to mid-Sep daily 1000-1800. €2, admission to hedge maze and castle is €4.* The second of two Cistercian abbeys on the peninsula, Dunbrody was founded in the late 12th century by an uncle of Strongbow. It has the distinction of being one of the longest Cistercian churches in Ireland (59 m) and the east window is architecturally the most interesting part to have survived the centuries. The adjoining Visitor Centre has a small museum, the ruins of an old castle, a hedge maze, and a craft gallery.

South Wexford Coast

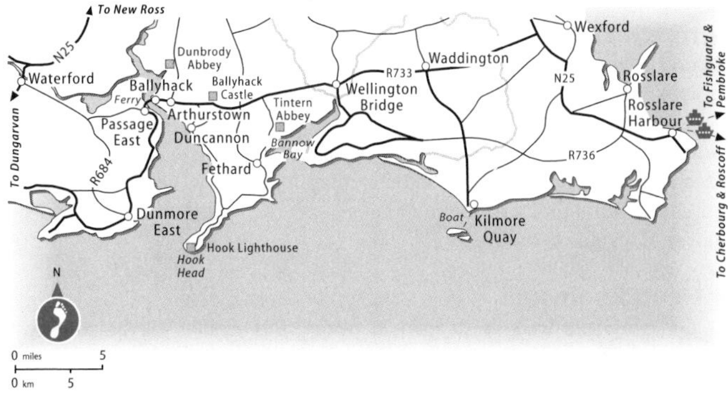

Birdwatching and the Saltee islands

Apart from the North Sloblands (see page 169) there are other local places suitable for birdwatching. Viewing from the shore of Our Lady's Island, nesting terns can be seen in the summer alongside teals, redshanks and godwits. In nearby Tacumshin Lake waterfowl are present in the winter. Brent geese and herons can be seen at Fethard and at nearby Bannow Bay waterfowl also arrive in the winter. Hook Head is always a good place to visit with binoculars and migrant landbirds are the speciality here, but take care clambering over the rocks because there are unmarked blowholes and a danger of freak waves. The last of the now extinct great auks to be found alive in the British Isles was brought past Hook Head in 1834 by local fisherman – so you're unlikely to spot any more of them.

The real draw for anyone with an ornithological interest are the uninhabited Saltee Islands. From late spring to early summer the rocks are alive with puffins, kittiwakes, gannets, razorbills, shearwaters and other sea birds. Boat trips can be arranged in Kilmore Quay, and Declan Bates, T053-29684, is one of the more established operators, dropping visitors off on the island around 1030 and returning for them at 1600. The evening boat trips around the islands run by Dick Hayes, T053-29704 also provide birdwatching opportunities.

Hook Head lighthouse ⓘ *T051-397055, www.thehook- wexford.com. Mar-Oct daily 0930-1730. €4.75.* The story goes that this is Europe's oldest lighthouse, monks having lit a beacon here from the fifth century onwards, and that marauding Vikings never visited their customary ransacking on the place because of this. A more permanent lighthouse structure was built by the Normans in the late 12th century and the circular keep that is still visible dates back to this time.

If tempted to wander over the rocks take note of the sign warning of freak waves.

Sleeping

Kilmore Quay *p175*

C-F Pier House, T053-29703, scubabreaks@eircom.net. Opens all year with 5 private rooms, no dorm beds, and bike hire.

D Hotel Saltees, T053-29601. The only hotel in the village is a characterless-looking place although the restaurant is fine.

D Quay House, T053-29988, www.quayhouseguesthouse.com. A neat and tidy guest house that just enters this price category, attracting divers and fishing folk because of its storage and freezing facilities.

Hook Head Peninsula *p175*

L Dunbrody Country House Hotel and Restaurant, Arthurstown, T051-389600, www.dunbrodyhouse.com. A Georgian manor set in 200 acres of parkland, which boasts an award-winning restaurant. On the R733 and close to the Ballyhack ferry. Large bedrooms with pacific views and lavish breakfasts.

D Glendine Country House, Arthurstown, T051-389258, www.glendinehouse.com. A substantial 1830s building, offering comfortable and hospitable service and pleasant views across the estuary.

D Marsh Mere Lodge, Arthurstown, T051-389186. Pink-coloured guest house at the Ballyhack end of town, with 4 rooms.

E Arthur's Rest, Arthurstown, T051-389192. The large yellow-coloured house just past the ferry is a B&B.

F Coastguard Station, Arthurstown, T051-389411, anoige@iol.ie. *An Óige* hostel, ½ km from the ferry, open from Jun-Sep, with about 30 beds and including 2 double rooms.

Camping

Fethard Caravan and Camping Park, Fethard, T051-397123/397230. At the north end of the village.
Ocean Island Caravan and Camping Park, Fethard, T051-397148. Within walking distance of the sea.

Eating

Kilmore Quay *p175*
ΨΨ **Coningbeg Seafood Restaurant**, in the Hotel Saltees. Has fresh fish, as you would expect.
ΨΨ **The Silver Fox Seafood Restaurant**, T053-29888. Open for lunch and dinner, serves mostly seafood and dull vegetarian choices.
Ψ **Kehoe's Pub**, T053-29830. With a dedicated maritime theme, a beer garden to the rear and an affordable bar menu of seafood and meat dishes. Very popular.

Hook Head Peninsula *p175*
There are bars in Fethard serving the usual run of bar food.
ΨΨΨ **The Harvest Room**, Dunbrody Country House, T051-389600. Offers an evening's dining in elegant surroundings for around €50.
ΨΨ-Ψ **Templer's Inn**, T051-397162, on the road from Duncannon to Hook Head, at the junction for Templetown. A large pub with outdoor tables, serving bar food as well as having a seafood restaurant.

Pubs and music

Hook Head Peninsula *p175*
Fethard is the best place for evening entertainment, in pubs like **Molloy's**. **Droopy's Inn**, very popular, often has music, and local fisherman frequent the place. **Neville's**, more a place to go for a quiet drink and a chat.

Festivals and events

Kilmore Quay *p175*
Seafood Festival in **early to middle Jul**. Food tastings, music and dance.

Hook Head Peninsula *p175*
A noteworthy music festival, the **Phil Murphy Weekend**, T051-561159, www.philmurphyweekend.com, takes place in **late Jul** each year in the village of Carrig, 5 km from Wellington Bridge.

Activities and tours

Kilmore Quay *p175*
Fishing and diving
Kilmore Quay has a few places catering to fishing and diving enthusiasts.
Kilmore Quay Angling and Diving Centre, T053-29988.
Dick Hayes, T053-29704. Runs deep-sea angling trips and scenic boat trips around the Saltee Islands, departing at 1730, depending on demand but usually there is a trip every other day in the summer.
Paul Bates, T053-29831, www.wexfordboatcharters.com.

Transport

South Wexford Coast *p175, map p176*
Bus Bus Éireann, T01-8366111, runs a shuttle bus from **Wexford** 3 times a day. And there's a service between **Waterford** (T051-879000) and **Wexford**, which on Mon and Thu only travels via **Duncannon**, **Templetown** and **Fethard**. Buses depart Waterford at 0945 and Wexford at 1450.

Ferry The Passage East Car Ferry, T051-382480, www.passageferry.com, runs a service between **Ballyhack** in county Wexford and **Passage East** in County Waterford. The service is an all-year one (except 25 and 26 Dec) between 0700 (0930 on Sun) and 2200 (2000 between Oct and end of Mar). No reservations, just turn up and wait a few minutes for the 5-min crossing. €7/€10 for cars single/return; €1.50/2 for pedestrians single/return; €2/€3 for cyclists single/return.

For an explanation of the sleeping and eating price codes used in this guide, see inside the front cover. Other relevant information is found in Essentials pages 39-45.

Central South

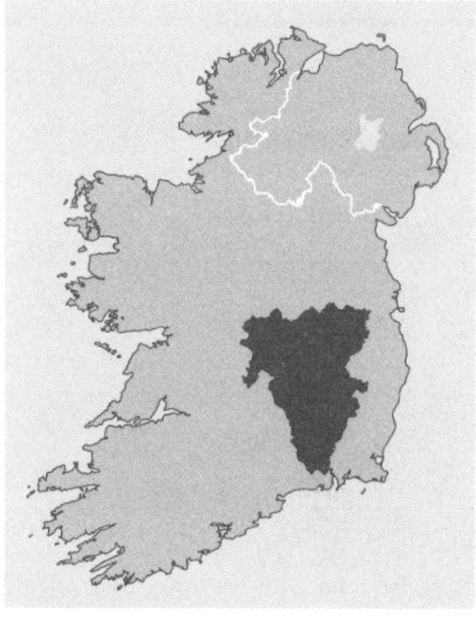

Footprint features

Introduction

The city of Kilkenny, with its medieval history and flavour, has excellent transport links which make it an obvious destination as a base for exploring the lush and picturesque countryside to the south. Cycling is an ideal way to discover the quaint villages that lie dotted along the Nore and Barrow Valleys, and for walkers the undemanding South Leinster Way winds its way gently through the county.

Carlow is one of Ireland's more modest counties, covering a small area of land surrounding the rivers Barrow and Slaney. Laois (pronounced 'Leash') is another of Ireland's lesser-known counties, one of those places that travellers can pass through without ever registering the fact. A dull kind of prosperity characterises its towns, but the Slieve Bloom Mountains open up unspoilt Irish countryside.

County Kildare is close enough to the capital to turn parts of it into commuter land, but this also makes it handy for excursions out of Dublin. The north of County Offaly is marked by bogland, the northwest by the twisting River Shannon and the south by the rising hills of the Slieve Bloom range. Though visitors find this region relatively flat, it holds much of interest to those who appreciate places off the well-trodden tourist tracks.

★ Don't miss...

1. **St Canice's Cathedral, Kilkenny** Visit the second largest cathedral in Ireland and its miscellany of tombstones and effigies, page 184.
2. **Souvenirs** The Irish craft items for sale in the Kilkenny Design Centre, page 192 and/or the village of Bennettsbridge, page 187.
3. **Kilfane Church** Come face to face with a 14th-century Norman knight, page 187.
4. **Jerpoint Abbey** Impressive 12th-century Cistercian abbey just outside Thomastown, page 187.
5. **Tynan's Bridge House pub** A rare opportunity for solace and a quiet drink away from the crowds in Kilkenny, page 192.

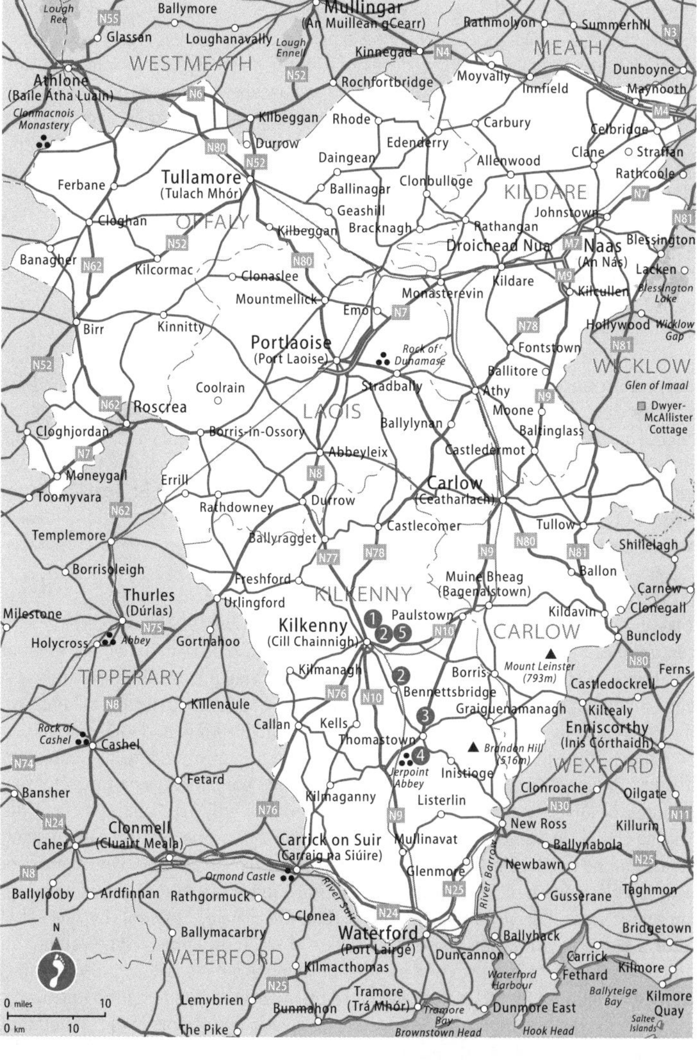

County Kilkenny

County Kilkenny can boast rich farming land and picturesque river valleys formed by the Rivers Barrow, Nore and Suir; qualities that attracted the Anglo-Normans and helped make the county the base for the Butler lordship in the 13th century. Nowadays, the geography and history combine to make the county a major area of interest and alongside the old stone walls and medieval remains there are some first-rate restaurants and interesting places to stay. ▸▸ *For Sleeping, Eating and other listings, see pages 189-193.*

Kilkenny → *Phone code: 056. Colour map 4, grid B1.*

Most of Ireland's more interesting cities are found close to the sea, a pattern first established by the Vikings, but Kilkenny is a rich exception to the rule and we have the Normans to thank for this. The town developed in importance under their influence, and the medieval legacy of their era is one of the chief delights of a visit to a humming city that integrates tasteful shops and restaurants into time-hallowed streets and preserves a tangible sense of olde-Ireland. The downside to the town's cunning blend of the medieval and the cosmopolitan is that Kilkenny features on countless coach tours – in summer, make sure you book your accommodation well in advance.

Ins and outs

Getting there The bus and train stations are together. There are direct bus links to Dublin, Cork and Waterford and trains to Dublin (2 hrs away) and Waterford. ▸▸ *See Transport, page 193, for further details.*

Getting around Kilkenny is a small and compact town and the medieval attractions and the castle are within walking distance of the centre. Bicycles and cars can be hired. You can get parking discs for the city centre from newsagents and other shops.

Information **Kilkenny tourist office**, Shee Alms House, Rose Inn St, T056-7751500, www.southeastireland.com. Open Apr-Jun and Sep Mon-Sat 0900-1800; Jul-Aug Mon-Sat 0900-1800; Oct-Mar Mon-Sat 0900-1700.

History

Kilkenny's known history goes back to early Christian times but it was in the 13th century that the place grew to prominence under the Marshall family, the earls of Pembroke and lords of Leinster. William Marshall married the daughter of Strongbow and spent a lot of time in Ireland consolidating his position and putting Kilkenny on the political map. Wealth to some came from trading in wool, and Kilkenny had its own Anglo-Norman parliament that at times made the town the effective capital of Ireland. The most famous legislation arising from its parliament were the notorious Statutes of Kilkenny of 1366, aimed at reversing the growing Gaelicization of the English colony. In the 16th and 17th centuries Kilkenny was the political capital of the great Ormond family, also known as the Butlers because an ancestor who came over with the Normans became chief butler to Prince John. After the rising of 1641, an important gathering of Catholic interests took place here, attended by the Papal Nuncio Rinuccini, known as the Confederation of Kilkenny. Papal power wanted the full restoration of Catholicism and excommunicated any party willing to do business with Cromwell. The Protector himself turned up in 1650 and battered the town walls for five days, but although economic power passed to Protestants in the last quarter

of the 17th century the town never quite lost its Catholic flavour. Kilkenny prospered through to the 19th century, with an important road link to both Dublin and Cork, and never lost its cultural influence within the country as a whole. In the last quarter of the 20th century this cultural significance reasserted itself and Kilkenny has emerged as a provincial centre for the arts and, in particular, for the promotion of native crafts.

Sights

Kilkenny Castle ⓘ *T056-7721450. Jun-Sep daily 1000-1900; Apr and May daily 1030-1700; Oct-Mar Tue-Sun 1030-1245 and 1400-1700. Compulsory 1-hr guided tour. €5. OPW site.* The original castle was built in 1192 by William Marshall, Strongbow's son-in-law, but the strategic site commanding the river suggests that a

Kilkenny

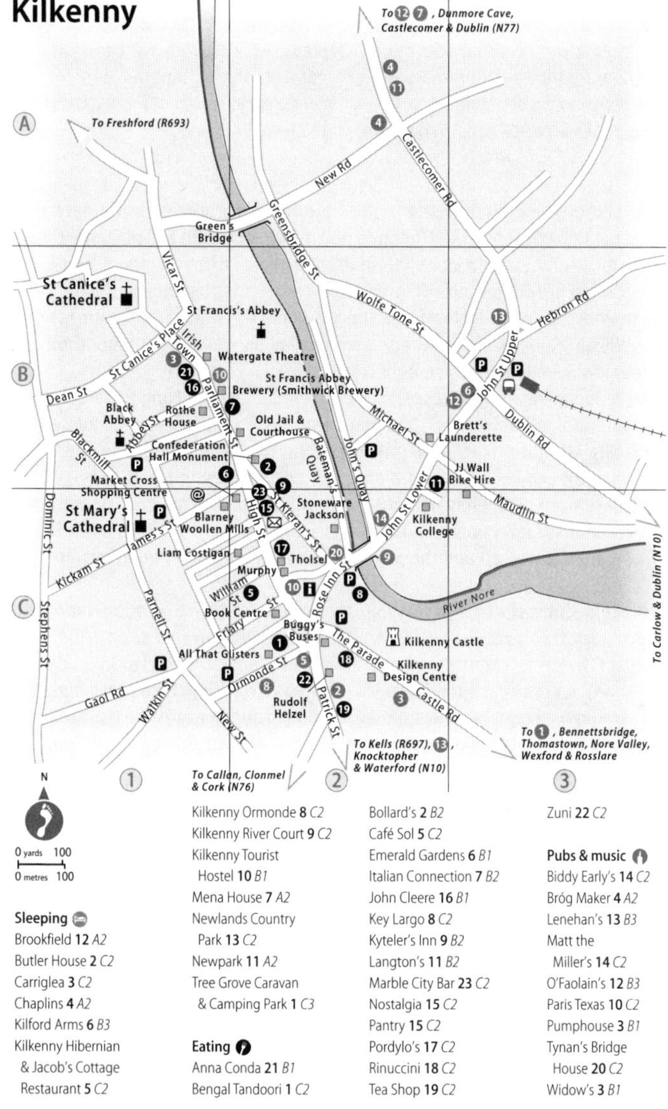

Sleeping
Brookfield **12** *A2*
Butler House **2** *C2*
Carriglea **3** *C2*
Chaplins **4** *A2*
Kilford Arms **6** *B3*
Kilkenny Hibernian & Jacob's Cottage Restaurant **5** *C2*
Kilkenny Ormonde **8** *C2*
Kilkenny River Court **9** *C2*
Kilkenny Tourist Hostel **10** *B1*
Mena House **7** *A2*
Newlands Country Park **13** *C2*
Newpark **11** *A2*
Tree Grove Caravan & Camping Park **1** *C3*

Eating
Anna Conda **21** *B1*
Bengal Tandoori **1** *C2*
Bollard's **2** *B2*
Café Sol **5** *C2*
Emerald Gardens **6** *B1*
Italian Connection **7** *B2*
John Cleere **16** *B1*
Key Largo **8** *C2*
Kyteler's Inn **9** *B2*
Langton's **11** *B2*
Marble City Bar **23** *C2*
Nostalgia **15** *C2*
Pantry **15** *C2*
Pordylo's **17** *C2*
Rinuccini **18** *C2*
Tea Shop **19** *C2*
Zuni **22** *C2*

Pubs & music
Biddy Early's **14** *C2*
Bróg Maker **4** *A2*
Lenehan's **13** *B3*
Matt the Miller's **14** *C2*
O'Faolain's **12** *B3*
Paris Texas **10** *C2*
Pumphouse **3** *B1*
Tynan's Bridge House **20** *C2*
Widow's **3** *B1*

The Statutes of Kilkenny

Terms like 'apartheid' and 'ethnic cleansing' were not around in the 14th century, but clauses in the Statutes of Kilkenny seem to have been directed along those lines. Anglo-Normans residing in the colony of Ireland were required to use only the English language and to have recourse only to English law in settling disputes. Marriage to the native Irish was forbidden in an attempt to preserve the racial purity of the colonizers and non-martial games of Gaelic provenance were also punishable activities. In order to prepare for the military quashing of any outbreaks of native Irish rebellion, the sale of horses or armour to the Irish was outlawed and regular reviews of the colonial forces were instituted. Many of these clauses had been promulgated before but the Statutes were a systematic attempt to reinforce colonial rule and preserve the ruling class from infiltration by the resurgent Irish. They were broadly enforced throughout the 15th century and were not repealed until the early 17th century.

defensive site of some kind existed before the Normans arrived. In the late 14th century ownership passed to the Ormonds and in 1967 the 24th Earl of Ormond sold the castle to the State for a nominal sum, after most of the contents had been auctioned. While the outer walls of the castle are original, substantial rebuilding and renovation work took place in the 1820s and 30s under the supervision of the London architect William Robertson. So what is seen today as you are led around on the guided tour is very much a 19th-century creation.

Much of the guided tour focuses, naturally enough, on the **Long Picture Gallery** on the first floor. The wooden hammer-beam roof is profusely decorated in Pre-Raphaelite style, a project undertaken by John Hungerford Pollen in 1861, and while the array of exotic beasts and birds is undeniably a surprise, the images are fading and what can be seen is not artistically brilliant by any means. The walls are lined with countless family portraits. There's an exhibition in the basement (the Butler Gallery) of contemporary art and the original kitchen is now a very good restaurant.

★ **St Canice's Cathedral** ⓘ *T056-7764971. Easter-Oct Mon-Sat 0900-1300 and 1400- 1800, Sun 1400-1800; Oct-Easter Mon-Sat 1000-1300 and 1400-1600, Sun 1400-1600. €3, €2 to climb the round tower.* The largest medieval cathedral in Ireland after St Patrick's in Dublin was built in the 12th and 13th centuries, but suffered enormous damage after the usual bout of vandalism by Cromwell's army. The English took the roof off, stole the bells and the valuable glass, and left only the hinges on the doors "that Hogs might come, and root, and Dogs gnaw the bones of the dead". Restoration work means that none of this is now obvious and the architectural form of this Early Gothic church remains sufficiently unaltered to make it the finest example of its kind outside Dublin. The actual site has an ecclesiastical history that goes as far back as perhaps the sixth century, and this itself suggests that the ground may have a pre-Christian significance. At the end of the 17th century, philosopher George Berkeley and satirist Jonathan Swift were educated in a school that once stood in the cathedral grounds.

The round tower that abuts the south apse is accessible and offers good views from the top, but forego the experience if you are given to claustrophobia or vertigo.

Do not be put off by the symmetrical dullness of the exterior; the inside of St Canice's Cathedral is a rich pot-pourri of funeral monuments and effigies. Check out the tombstone near the stall that sells postcards and the like: its 10-line epitaph

records the death of Mary Stoughton, who died in childbirth in 1631. There is no end to the fine carved effigies accompanying the tombs of more illustrious folk and while most of them are 16th-century, there are a couple dating back to the 13th century. The naturalistic style of the effigies of Margaret and Piers Butler in the south transept makes a dramatic contrast with the inept renderings of various Apostles liberally dotted around, but this is all part of the wonderful variety of sculptures in the church.

Rothe House ⓘ *Parliament St, T056-7722893. Jul and Aug daily 0930-1800; Jan-Jun and Sep-Nov Mon-Sat 1030-1700, Sun 1500-1700; Nov-Feb Mon-Sat 1300-1700. €3.* This stone-built Tudor merchant's house is a superb survivor of Kilkenny's prosperous era. The Rothes came to Ireland from Yorkshire in the 14th century and by the late 16th century they were sufficiently wealthy to have built this substantial house in the centre of the town. It is made up of three buildings linked by courtyards and small rooms and the Kilkenny Archaeological Society, which now owns the place, has used the rooms to display a collection of costumes and assorted artefacts. These are laboriously described in a 20-minute video, which is worth missing, but the building itself has been cleverly restored and has some fine features. The stonework is original and the Irish oak roof on the second floor has been sensitively rebuilt using the medieval methods. Features worth admiring include the octagonal chimneys, the mullioned windows, and the original escutcheon next to the restored oriel window that rests on the original corbel. The reception area, entered through an original arcade and where 400 years ago the merchant owner laid out his wares for prospective buyers, has a collection of books about Ireland for sale.

Other historical sights **Black Abbey**, Abbey Street, is a Dominican church, founded in 1225 by William Marshall and dissolved in 1543. It earns the name because the Dominicans were called the Black Friars. Cromwell's army vandalized the place and it remained a ruin until it was again used as a church in the 18th century. Some of the original windows that date back to the 14th century are worth admiring.

The Tholsel, High Street, was built in 1761 by an amateur architect and perhaps this helps account for its aesthetic appeal. A *tholsel*, or *tolsel* or *tolzey* court, is an ancient name for a tollbooth or guildhall and here in Kilkenny it continues – uniquely – to fulfil its historical function as it is now the local office for the collection of rates. It has a projecting arcade and an octagonal clock tower, built on the spot where the unfortunate Petronella was executed as a witch in 1324. A little further up the High Street, just past the Tholsel, is a narrow medieval alley called the **Butter Slip** where nowadays, instead of butter, you can buy sushi rolls in a modern little restaurant.

Continuing back up the High Street, which turns into Parliament Street, there is a **monument** marking the location of the Confederation Parliament of 1641 and just past this, opposite Rothe House, the **courthouse and former prison** is where insurgents from the 1798 rebellion were executed. The only way to see some of the cells is by joining Tynan's walking tour of the town (see page 192).

Shee Alms House, home to the tourist office in Rose Inn Street, dates back to the late 16th century, when it was built as an alms house by local bigwig Sir Richard Shee.

St Francis Abbey Brewery ⓘ *T056-7721014. Late Jun-Aug Mon-Fri. A limited number of tickets available from 0900. Free admission to a video of the brewing process at 1500, and yes, there is a free drink (but no guided tour).* Now part of the Guinness empire and producing Smithwicks, Budweiser and Kilkenny Irish beer for home and export, the fact that the brewery occupies the site of a Franciscan monastery founded by William Marshall in 1232 has little to do with the enormous popularity of a visit here.

Alice Kyteler and Petronella – the witches of Kilkenny

Ireland largely escaped the great witch hunts of the 16th and 17th centuries, but around the 1320s Alice Kyteler and her maid Petronella de Midia got a foretaste of what was to come elsewhere. Alice was of Flemish descent and the first of her four husbands was a member of the influential Outlawe family. She was accused by a witch-obsessed English bishop of having sex with a demon spirit named Robin FitzArt and sacrificing cockerels to the devil. Family members of her subsequent husbands, who saw a chance to weaken the power of the Outlawes, accused her of sorcery in order to favour her first son. She was put on trial and, though she managed to escape to England, her unfortunate maid was put to death.

Around Kilkenny

Historically, the city and the county of Kilkenny prospered because of the gently flowing rivers and their pasture-rich valleys. Today, you could enjoy a day or two exploring this elegant countryside outside the city. The River Nore, which flows through Kilkenny city, is particularly attractive as it winds its tree-lined way through hill and vale in the south, while to the east the lush valley of the River Barrow competes for attention.

From Kilkenny you could travel (by car or bike) south on the R700 following the River Nore to Bennettsbridge and Thomastown, and then pick up the N10 at Knocktopher after visiting Jerpoint Abbey. Then make a short detour to visit medieval Kells on the return journey to Kilkenny.

Kells → *Phone code: 056. Colour map 4, grid C1.*

This little village nestles on the banks of a Nore tributary and is only 12 km south of Kilkenny. Not to be confused with its more famous namesake in County Meath, Kells is a showcase for the beauty of the Nore valley. Its lovely stone bridge and ancient watermill are a treat to behold on a summer's day and close by are some of the most captivating monastic ruins you are likely to come across in Ireland.

Kells Priory ⓘ *Free.* The priory was founded in 1193 by Augustinians brought over from Cornwall but what you see today dates mostly from the 14th and 15th centuries. The survival of the church, and especially the complete wall with towers enclosing a 2-ha site, creates a more tangible sense of what a medieval settlement was like than most other ruins of this period in the country (including, ironically, Kells in Meath). To the south of the church are remains of what were the priory's domestic buildings.

Kilree Round Tower and High Cross The ruins of another monastic site lie just over a mile south of Kells and the way is signposted from Kells Priory. The church is in ruins although there is a well-preserved 17th-century tomb in the chancel, but what dominates the site is a 29-m high round tower, minus its top. In a field just to the west there stands a faded High Cross that is thought to date back to the ninth century. It is hard to make out any of the original pictorial representations, although various geometric patterns can be traced, and on the east face you can see a stag-hunting scene with a chariot. The story that the cross commemorates Niall Caille, a king of Ireland who drowned while trying to save a squire, is apparently a piece of blarney.

“” At one time Kilfane church was used as a school and naughty scholars were chastised by being forced to kiss the forbidding lips of the conquering Norman...

★ Bennettsbridge → *Phone code: 056. Colour map 4, grid C1.*

The main attraction in the village of Bennettsbridge is two of the country's finest pottery workshops. **Stoneware Jackson Pottery** ⓘ *T056-7727175, Mon-Sat 1000-1800*, is just north of the village and the workshop can be viewed from a relaxing garden setting before you are tempted to make a purchase in the showroom. There is also a modest selection of seconds on sale.

Nicholas Mosse Pottery ⓘ *T056-7727505, www.nicholasmosse.com, Mon-Sat 0900-1800; Sun 1130-1700*, is based around an old mill by the river and water from the Nore is used to generate the electricity for firing the pots, which are brightly coloured earthenware with traditional, floral-style motifs. Seconds are for sale.

Other craftshops in Bennettsbridge include **Keith Mosse Craftsmen in Wood** ⓘ *T056-7727860, www.keithmosse.com*, and a candle-making workshop.

Thomastown → *Phone code: 056. Colour map 4, grid C1.*

Although on the busy Dublin to Waterford N9 road, Thomastown is worth considering as a place to rest for a drink or meal either before or after visiting Jerpoint Abbey and nearby Kilfane. In town there are fragmentary ruins of the wall that enclosed this medieval settlement and the uninteresting ruins of a 13th-century church with only the north aisle and parts of the foundation still to be seen.

★ **Jerpoint Abbey** ⓘ *2.5 km southwest of Thomastown on the N9, T056-7724623. Jun- 13 Sep daily 0930-1800; 14 Sep-Oct daily 1000-1700; Mar-May daily 1000-1700; Nov daily 1000-1800. €2.75. OPW site. Guided tours available.* This impressive Cistercian abbey, one of the best monastic ruins in the country, was founded between 1163 and 1165. After the Dissolution of the Monasteries in 1540 it was leased to the earls of Ormond. The church retains Romanesque features, although the arches in the aisles are recognizably Gothic, and there are some excellently preserved sculptured tombs. These include a bishop who died in 1202 and two knights from the late 13th century. There is also a harper and his wife, one of only two civilian effigies from the 16th century remaining in Ireland. The real highlight, however, is the cloister that dates from the 15th century, delightful in its lively array of sculptured knights, saints and other figures.

★ **Kilfane** A small village just north of Thomastown on the N9 road, Kilfane is signposted to the right just before the Long Man pub. It is noteworthy for its ruined 14th-century **church**. Inside you will be surprised by the imposing, larger-than-life effigy of a medieval knight. With his legs crossed, wearing a fine suit of chain mail, spurs and accompanied by his trusty shield, this is Thomas de Cantwell, who died some time around 1320. History is suddenly brought to life by this animated Norman conqueror who displays in his figure and accoutrements the daunting new forces that came from across the water to subdue the native Irish. At one time the church was used as a school and the story goes that naughty scholars were chastised by being forced to kiss the forbidding lips of this conquering Norman.

Further along the road that leads to Kilfane church, less than 3 km from Thomastown, **Kilfane Glen and Waterfall** ⓘ *T056-24558, May-late Sep Sun 1400-1800; Jul and Aug daily 1100-1800, €5, tea-shop*, is a woodland garden dating

from the late 18th century. There are paths to stroll along, a hermit's grotto, a waterfall and one of those little villas with an affectation of rusticity known as a *cottage ornée*. These diversions add to the charms of the planted woods – perfect for a picnic on a good day.

Inistioge → *Phone code: 056. Colour map 4, grid C1.*

This quaint little village, pronounced 'Inisteeg', is on the west bank of the Nore and the agreeable 18th-century, 10-arched bridge adds considerably to its charms. The photogenic quality is further enhanced by an ancient-looking church and neat lime trees in a village square from which spidery lanes radiate. Such an evocation of the past makes it unsurprising that a number of films have used the location, including *Widow's Peak* in 1993. Inistioge derives its name from the Tighes, whose family seat was a grand 18th-century house that was burned down during the civil war in 1922. The Tighes left for England when the War of Independence broke out and later the Black and Tans used it as a local headquarters. What was the Tighe demesne, Woodstock Park, is now the state-owned **Woodstock Gardens** ⓘ *T056-7752699, open to the public all year round*. There are various walking trails and picnic areas.

Mount Brandon stands 519 m high and lies to the northeast of Inistioge and a road leads through the mountain to the village of Graiguenamanagh.

Graiguenamanagh → *Phone code: 059. Colour map 4, grid C2.*

The small town of Graiguenamanagh ('the granary of the monks'), is attractively situated on the banks of the River Barrow, and has another of those pleasing 18th-century arched bridges. The attraction of Graiguenamanagh, apart from the beauty of the location and pleasant walks along the riverside using the South Leinster waymarked route (see below), is the Cistercian abbey in the town.

Duiske Abbey, founded in 1207 by William Marshall, was well preserved enough after a restoration project in the 1970s for parts of it to be still in use today. Inside there is a fine doorway from the early 13th century thought to be one of the best examples of its type to have survived the Dissolution of the Monasteries. Equally eye-catching is an effigy of a knight from the same period and nearby a glass panel reveals some authentic 13th-century fleur-de-lys tiling. Outside the church there are two high crosses and the nearby **Abbey Centre** houses a modest exhibition.

The South Leinster Way

The total length of this long-distance waymarked walk is 100 km, starting at Kildavin on the slopes of Mount Leinster in County Carlow and finishing at Carrick-on-Suir in County Tipperary. It takes four to five days to complete and the first day's walk ends in Borris on the border between Carlow and Kilkenny. The second day is a very manageable 13 km, mostly following a towpath alongside the River Barrow as far as Graiguenamanagh. The distance on the third day is similar and skirts Brandon Hill before reaching the lovely village of Inistioge. The fourth day (20 km), follows the river and uses forest roads before ending in the village of Mullinavat in southern Kilkenny. The last day's walking crosses into Tipperary over farmland and, in places, roads.

Mapping and information **EastWest Mapping** produce the *South Leinster Way Map Guide* and **Ordnance Survey** maps Nos 68, 75 and 76 are needed to cover the whole walk. Maps and information are available from the tourist office in Carlow (see page 193), Kilkenny (see page 182) or from EastWest Mapping (see page 52).

North of Kilkenny → *Colour map 4, grid B1.*

Castlecomer is the main town in the north of the county, but there's not much to see and most visitors content themselves with a trip to Dunmore Cave, only a few kilometres north of Kilkenny. Castlecomer rose to local prominence after the

discovery of anthracite in the 17th century and in the 1798 uprising (see page 594) the town was captured by insurgents led by Father John Murphy. All that remains of the Anglo-Norman castle that gave the town its name is a mound.

Dunmore Cave ⓘ *Ballyfoyle, 10 km from Kilkenny, signposted off the N78, T056-67726. Mid-Jun to mid-Sep daily 0930-1830; mid-Mar to mid-Jun and mid-Sep to Oct daily 1000-1700; Nov to mid-Mar Sat-Sun 1000-1630. €2.75. OPW site. Buggy's Coaches, T056-4441264, run 4 buses a day, Mon-Sat, from Kilkenny, €3 each way.* This site consists of limestone caverns and impressive calcite formations. There is an exhibition centre and a compulsory guided tour that lasts about 45 minutes. Geology aside, there is a reference in Irish sources to a Viking massacre here in 928 and excavations in the 1970s did reveal the skeletons of nearly 50 women and children.

Sleeping

Kilkenny *p182, map p183*

Kilkenny is close enough to Dublin to attract weekenders and some B&Bs, guest houses and hotels in the centre have a habit of jacking up room rates to milk the demand.

L-C Kilkenny Hibernian, 33 Patrick St, T056-7771888, www.thehibernian.com. A 19th-century bank building converted into a spacious boutique hotel retaining original features, old paintings and an award-winning, comfortable bar and restaurant.

L-C Kilkenny Ormonde, Ormonde St, T056-7723900, www.kilkennyormonde.com. The glitzy modernism of the Kilkenny Ormonde, with coaches regularly disgorging large groups outside its doors, hardly complements the city's heritage appeal but it does have restaurants, bars, large rooms and a leisure centre.

L-C Newpark Hotel, Castlecomer Rd, T056-7760500, ww.newparkhotel.com. Just outside town, a smart modern hotel with a refreshing decor as well as a lively bistro.

L-D Kilkenny River Court Hotel, The Bridge, John St, T056-7723388, www.kilrivercourt.com. Tucked away beside the river in a private courtyard, with all the mod cons and views of the castle.

A-D Kilford Arms, John St, T056-7761018, www.kilfordarms.ie. A pub guest house about 50 m from the station. Traditional Irish restaurant, a night club and 3 bars.

B-C Butler House, Patrick St, T056-7765707, www.butler.ie. Easily the best place to stay in Kilkenny, a Georgian residence restored in the early 1970s in a kind of art deco style featuring light colours and natural fabrics which blend remarkably well with the original features of the house. There is a lovely walled garden. Breakfast is served in the Kilkenny Design Centre.

E Carriglea, Archers Av, Castle Rd, T056-7761629. A family home up past the castle in a residential cul-de-sac offering B&B.

There is a string of family homes offering B&B along **Castlecomer Rd**, past the Newpark hotel and just about within walking distance of town. They include:

E Chaplins, T056-7752236, chaplins@eircom.net;

E Brookfield, T056-7765629, trants@esatclear.ie;

E Mena House, T056-7765362, www.menahousekilkennybandb.com.

E Newlands Country House, Seven Houses, Danesfort, T056-7729111, extremeovenclean@iol.ie. B&B in a very modern house, 7 km outside town just off the N10. Plush decor, canopied beds and room facilities to rival most hotels. A place to feel pampered in, and good classical French cuisine in the attached restaurant.

F Foulksrath Castle, Jenkinstown, T056-7767674. *An Óige* hostel 13 km south of Kilkenny on the N76 road but Buggy's Coaches, T056-4441264, run a Mon-Sat bus service from outside the castle (last bus 1730) that will stop nearby at Conahy Cross. The hostel building is superb, a 16th-century tower house with medieval features, spiral

For an explanation of the sleeping and eating price codes used in this guide, see inside the front cover. Other relevant information is found in Essentials pages 39-45.

staircase and stupendous dining room with fireplaces big enough for bunk beds. No private rooms.

F **Kilkenny Tourist Hostel**, 35 Parliament St, T056-7763541, kilkennyhostel@eircom.net. Open all year, with over 60 beds, including 2 private rooms at €38.

Camping

The Tree Grove Caravan and Camping Park, Danville House, T056-7770302, treecc@iol.ie. Good facilities and well regarded, about 2 km from the city on the New Ross Rd (R700). Open all year.

Bennettsbridge *p187*

Nore Valley Caravan and Camping Park, coming from Kilkenny turn right just before the bridge in Bennettsbridge, T056-7727229. Award-winning campsite, open Mar-Oct.

Thomastown *p187*

L-A **Mount Juliet Conrad**, Thomastown, T056-7773000, www.conradhotelst.com. Mega-expensive hotel and self-styled 'sporting estate' beside the river, with rooms in the 18th-century house or adjoining lodges. Golfing, fishing, shooting, archery, tennis and an equestrian centre available.

D **Abbey House**, Jerpoint Abbey, T056-7724166, www.abbeyhousejerpoint.com. A delightful period house directly opposite the abbey, with a spacious lounge and a patio by the river, offering B&B. Closed at Christmas.

E **Carrickmourne House**, New Ross Rd, T056-7724124. B&B but no evening meals.

Inistioge *p188*

D **Cullintra House**, The Rower, T051-77423614. An old farmhouse at the foot of Mount Brandon where dinner (around €25) is announced with a bell at 2100.

E **Ashville**, Kilmacshane, on the Kilkenny to Rosslare road, T056-7758460. B&B but no evening meals. Open Mar-Oct.

Graiguenamanagh *p188*

D **Waterside**, The Quay, T059-9724246, www.watersideguesthouse.com. All rooms, ones at the top are bigger, overlook the river in this highly picturesque building. Weekend and short break packages worth considering.

Eating

Kilkenny *p182, map p183*

TTT **Jacob's Cottage**, 1 Ormonde St, T056- 7791220, www.jacobscottage.com. The restaurant is attached to the Hibernian Hotel. It's a bistro-ish sort of place, with mood lighting, lots of artwork on the walls and an intimate atmosphere. Imaginative modern Irish food, a bit meat-orientated, but the vegetarian option is always good. Not the typical hotel restaurant.

TTT **Pordylo's**, Butter Slip Lane, T056-7770660. As popular as Zuni and with food that is every bit as good. Starters like oak-salmon blinis and a good choice of chicken, steak, duck, fish, pasta and vegetarian dishes all set in a beautifully restored medieval building. Useful early-bird offers bring this place into the mid-range category.

TTT **Zuni**, 26 Patrick St, T056-7723999, www.zuni.ie. A trendy, currently popular restaurant serving modern Irish cuisine. The dining room is a minimalist, contemporary kind of a place.

TT **Bengal Tandoori**, Pudding Lane (behind the Book Centre), T056-7764722. If it's Indian food you're after you could visit this place where dishes are inexpensive and lunch comes in at €10-12.

TT **The Emerald Gardens**, High St, T056-7761812. Chinese food, as good as it gets in Ireland. A sophisticated eatery with a takeaway service. Try the *yuk sung* for starters, followed by monkfish with crabmeat and sweetcorn sauce or Thai beef curry.

TT **Langton's**, 69 John St, T056-7765133, www.langtons.ie. A popular restaurant with a large menu offering any 2 courses for €25, 3 courses for €28. On entering you may be flummoxed by the greenery amidst the dark cavernous interior and mullioned windows.

TT **The Marble City Bar**, T056-7761143. A recently modernized old pub, now a cool café bar which does value for money Asian fusion food in a stylish atmosphere until 2030 daily.

TT **Ristorante Rinuccini**, The Parade, T056-7761575, www.rinuccini.com. A very decent 3-course meal makes Rinuccini good value, and explains why it is packed out with visitors and locals and why a reservation is necessary. Tasty tortellini alla gorgonzola or spaghetti

with lobster and truffle. Unashamedly Italian wine list. Good early-bird offers.

¥ **Anna Conda**, Parliament St, T056-777165. An old pub with tables for diners and an above-average choice of bar food.

¥ **Bollard's**, where Kiernan St meets Parliament St, T056-7721353. A pub and restaurant serving snacks, lunches and evening meals.

¥ **Café Sol**, William St, T056-7764987. Open 1000-2100, later on Fri and Sat, closed Sun. Pannini during the day and Mediterranean-influenced modern Irish cuisine by night.

¥ **Italian Connection**, 38 Parliament St, T056-7764225. Another pasta and pizza place, cosier than Key Largo, and with fish and curries on the menu as well. Open daily 1200-2300.

¥ **Key Largo**, Canal Sq, T056-7723922. Facing the river, just up from the tourist office. A tiny restaurant serving an odd mixture of Mexican and Italian. The dinner menu includes fish and meat dishes and fajitas for around €16 and there are a few outdoor tables. OK for lunch too, with vegetarian possibilities. Early-bird menu 1500-1800 of 2 courses for €10.

¥ **Kilkenny Castle**. A delightful setting and you don't have to have a ticket to the castle in order to eat here.

¥ **Kilkenny Design Centre**, The Parade. Self-service café inside, has good food but can become too full.

¥ **Kyteler's Inn**, Kiernan St, T056-7721064. Where Alice Kyteler (see page 186) lived and although the food is not bewitching the place is very popular with locals.

¥ **Nostalgia**, next door to Pantry. A tea shop open until 1800 on Thu and 2100 on Fri.

¥ **Pantry**, St Kieran's St, opposite Dunnes supermarket. Serves its own breads and cakes and quick lunches. Has outdoor tables.

A picnic by the river is always a possibility and there are some benches on Bateman's Quay and, on the other side, eastwards past Kilkenny River Court hotel. Take-away hot drinks are available from a sandwich bar next to the riverside Key Largo restaurant. The following should provide for your needs: ¥ **Gourmet Store**, High St; and ¥ **Shortis Wong**, 74 John St.

Thomastown *p187*

¥¥-¥ **Hudsons**, Station Rd, T056-7793900. A warm and welcoming restaurant where you can experience what is now well-established modern Irish cuisine.

¥ **Carrolls**, Logan St, T056-7724273. Worth a visit because as well as serving doorstep sandwiches and Irish stew there is a beer garden and sessions of traditional music.

¥ **Long Man of Kilfane**, outside town, on the N9 Dublin road, T056-7724774. Has a large bar area serving food until 2200.

¥ **The Watergarden**, on your left as you come into the village from Bennettsbridge. Fine for coffee and snacks.

Inistioge *p188*

¥¥ **The Motte**, Plas Newydd Lodge, T056-7758655. A culinary adventure, flowers on the table, intimate lighting and superb food. Dinner only, closed Mon and Tue, dinner menu around €35.

¥ **The School House Café**, by the river. Serves snacks and standard light meals in summer.

Graiguenamanagh *p188*

¥¥ **Waterside**, T059-7724246. A restaurant in a restored 19th-century corn store overlooking the river. An evening meal here is around €30.

¥ **Anchor**, Main St, T059-7924207 (with B&B in the **E** range). Basic pub food.

Pubs and music

Kilkenny *p182, map p183*

Kilkenny's bustle can rush you off your feet but Tynan's by the river or The Hibernian in town are places of welcome repose.

Anna Conda, Parliament St. Has a beer garden and regular sessions of traditional music that attract older folk.

Biddy Early's, John St, T056-7722689. For cocktails and Djs.

Bollard's (see above), has traditional music every Tue from 2130.

The Bróg Maker, further out on Castlecomer Rd, T056-7752900. Has an olde worlde atmosphere and a regular programme of music as well as a restaurant.

John Cleere a couple of doors down from Anna Conda, T056-7762573. Has music as well as a tiny theatre. Bursting to the seams with a mixed crowd when something is on.

The Hibernian, Patrick St. Even better than Tynan's Bridge House, a modern bar with seats that compel you to order another round and peruse the menu of good food.

Langton's, John St, T056-7765133. A very lively pub indeed with DJs and live music.

Lenehan's, Castlecomer Rd. An old-style pub with Victorian decor, offers quiet repose.
Matt the Millar, bottom of John St. Attracts a younger crowd.
O'Faolain's, in John St Upper. Has live traditional music on Mon, Tue and Wed.
Paris Texas, High St, T056-7761822. Live traditional music on Wed and regular live music Sun.
The Pumphouse, Parliament St, T056-7763924. Popular with students.
★ **Tynan's Bridge House**, at St John's Bridge. Antiquarian and wonderfully civilized, a sheer delight, the kind of place that Irish theme pubs try so dismally to imitate.
The Widow's, Parliament St, T056-7752520. Has music on Sun mornings.

Entertainment

Kilkenny *p182, map p183*
The *Kilkenny People* is a weekly local newspaper that carries details of what's on and where. There is also a free booklet available in the tourist office called *WhazOn*.
Watergate Theatre, Parliament St, T056-7761674, www.watergatekilkenny.com. Has regular programmes of theatre, dance and music.

Festivals and events

Kilkenny *p182, map p183*
Jun The Cats Laugh Festival, 50 John St, Kilkenny, T056-7751254. Features comedy and theatre and is very popular.
Aug Kilkenny Arts Festival, 92 High St, Kilkenny, T056-7763663, www.kilkennyarts.ie. The big event of the year, this is a multi-arts event with all kinds of music, sculpture, painting, literature, film and theatre. A very popular festival, tickets sell out quickly for many of the events.
Oct The Kilkenny Racing Festival, T056-7726225. At Gowran Park (see below).
Kilkenny Celtic Festival, Shee Alms House, T056-7721122, usually a long weekend in early Oct explores the links between the various Celtic communities of Europe and includes a craft fair, street entertainment, storytelling, concerts and more.

Shopping

Kilkenny *p182, map p183*

Crafts

★ **The Kilkenny Design Centre**, The Parade, opposite the castle. A comprehensive range of Irish craft goods for sale: ceramics, clothing, crystal, linens and assorted gifts. Open daily 0900-1800, except Jan-Mar, when it closes on Sun and national holidays. This area was Kilkenny Castle's stables and a number of studio showrooms under the aegis of the Crafts Council of Ireland occupy the grounds. There is also a number of upmarket studio workshops in the Nore valley (tourist board has a brochure with a map highlighting 6 of them) as well as small display cases exhibiting some of their products.
Rudolf Heltzel, 10 Patrick St, T056-7721497. Specializes in contemporary jewellery.
All that Glisters, Ormonde St, T056-7756111. Sells gemstones, marble and stone carvings and very pretty jewellery.
Liam Costigan, Collier's Lane, T056-7762408. Gold, silver and platinum jewellery.
Kilkenny Crystal shop next to the tourist office.
Murphy, 85 High St. More traditional pieces.

Activities and tours

Kilkenny *p182, map p183*
Birdwatching T056-7762130, birdwatchkilkenny@aircom.net. (Pat Durkin). Local outings on 1st Sun of each month. Meet at Castle Park, 1000.

Outdoor **Countryside Leisure Activity Centre**, Bonnettsrath. 2 km outside Kilkenny. Quad biking, archery, clay pigeon shooting.

Racing **Greyhounds**: **James Park**, Freshford Rd, T056-7721214. Wed and Fri, 2000. Reached from the R693 road out of town.
Horses: **Gowran Park Racecourse**, Gowran just east of town, T056-7726225. Racing festival in early Oct. Admission around €11.

Tours **Coach**: T056-7751500. Open-top coach tour of city, May-Sep, daily 1030, 1130, 1230, 1400, 1500, 1600, 1700. Departs from Castle Gates area, €9. **Walking**: **Tynan Tours**, T087-2651745, www.tynantours.com. Apr-Oct, Mon-Sat up to 3 tours a day; winter,

Tue-Sat 3 a day. 45 mins long, covering all the main sights except the castle, begins from the tourist office. €6.

Transport

County Kilkenny *p182*

Bus Bus Éireann, T056-7764933, operates from Kilkenny railway station but also stops in Patrick St outside the useful little tea shop. Daily buses to **Dublin**, **Cork** and **Waterford**; and the Waterford to **Longford** via **Athlone** bus stops in Kilkenny and Thomastown. On Thu there is a local bus to and from **New Ross** and **Bennettsbridge**. Buggy's Coaches, T056-4441264, run buses Mon-Sat from The Parade to the *An Óige* hostel at **Jenkinstown**, **Ballyragget**, **Dunmore Cave** and **Castlecomer**. **Dublin** to **Waterford** buses, five a day, stop in **Thomastown**. On Thu only the local 374 **New Ross** to **Kilkenny** service travels via **Inistioge**, **Thomastown** and **Bennettsbridge**.

Car hire Michael Lyng, Hebron Rd, T056-7770700; Barry Pender Motors, Dublin Rd, T056-7765777.

Taxi Kevin Barry, T056-7763017/ 088-574343. Mick Howe, T056-7765874/ 088-574141. David Nagle, T056-7763300/ 088-586060. Mike O'Brien, T056-7761333/ 088-586085.

Train **Kilkenny** station, T056-7722024, is at the top end of John St. Daily trains to **Dublin** and **Waterford** (via **Thomastown**).

County Carlow

County Carlow, positioned between the River Barrow and the Blackstairs Mountains, would be the smallest county in Ireland were it not for Louth. Not surprisingly, the town of Carlow gets most of the attention and it justifies a visit because it is a welcoming little metropolis with a good choice of places to stay, eat and drink. ▸▸ *For Sleeping, Eating and other listings, see page 194.*

Carlow and around → *Phone code: 059. Colour map 4, grid B1/2.*

Carlow town is too easily dismissed as a one-street wonder, but the main drag, besides having plenty of affordable places to eat, boasts a buzzing nightlife with lots of pubs offering live music. The town has a long history, being for centuries an Anglo-Norman base perched at the dangerous interface between Gaelic Ireland and the Pale, and it's regrettable there is so little to see beyond the crumbling remains of Carlow Castle in Castle Street.

There might have been a little more to see here had it not been for the crazy Dr Middleton who inadvertently blew up most of the **castle** in 1814 in order to make the rooms larger. Far more interesting to look at, and well worth seeking out, is the **courthouse** at the top end of Dublin Street. Most of Ireland's most impressive courthouses were built just before and after the 1798 insurrection – hardly a coincidence – and the Greek style of architecture was very popular. Perhaps ancient Athens conjured up a suitable image of the rule of law because this courthouse, designed by William Morrison in 1830, is an unashamed copy of the Parthenon.

For unchallenging walking Carlow's **The Barrow Way** follows the towpath of the River Barrow and the full distance of 113 km would take less than a week. The Way breaks downs into a number of stages, from 3 to 19 kms, covered by OS Discovery Maps Nos 16 and 19, and EastWest Mapping (see page 52) publishes a dedicated map.

The well-resourced **tourist office** is on College St, T059-9131554, www.carlowtourism.com. Jun-Aug Mon-Sat 1000-1800; Sep-May Mon-Fri 0900-1700. Their free county guide is an excellent source of local information.

Browneshill dolmen ⓘ *Beside a car park, just 3 km from town on the R726 road to Hacketstown.* Weighing in at 100 tons as the heavyweight champion of Europe, the

 capstone of this dolmen is now stuck in the earth at one end while resting on three stones at the other. As the construction dates back to around 2500BC, the individual who occasioned this feat of engineering and toil is now completely lost to time.

Carlow Brewing Company ⓘ *near the train station, T059-9134356, www.carlowbrewing.com. May-Sep Mon-Fri 1000-1200 and 1600-1700. €3.50.* The brewery produces three beers – O'Hara's, a stout, Curim, a wheat beer, and Mollings, a red ale – and they are all well worth tasting during the guided tour.

Sleeping

Carlow *p193*

D **Barrowville Town House**, Kilkenny Rd, T059-9143324, www.barrowvillehouse.com. Within walking distance of town, this above-average guest house serves a good breakfast from a conservatory overlooking gardens.

D **Borlum House**, Kilkenny Rd, T059-9141747. Ivy-clad old coaching inn set amidst secluded gardens.

E-F **Otterholt Riverside Lodge**, Kilkenny Rd, T059-9130404. Open all year, a hostel with lots of beds and a few private rooms that push the room rates into the higher price category. Camping is also possible.

F **Verona Hostel**, Pembroke St, T059-9131700/31846. Also open all year. 10 beds including 2 private rooms.

Eating

Carlow *p193*

‡‡‡ **The Beams Restaurant**, 59 Dublin St, T059-9131824. You will quickly realize where this place gets its name from once inside the door. The decidedly French-Irish menu should not disappoint. Expect to pay around €40 for dinner. Closed Sun and Mon.

‡ **Brook's Café Bar**, in the arcade in Tullow St. Has a very modern themed interior and lots of Californian options.

‡ **Buzz's**, 7 Tullow St, T059-9143307. Serves food and alcohol on cast iron tables on wooden floors and lives up to its name.

‡ **Reddy's**, 67 Tullow St, T059-9142224, across the road from Plough Bar. Provides meals.

‡ **Scragg's Alley**, Tullow St. Good bar food.

Pubs and music

Carlow *p193*

Carlow has a booming nightlife with lots of trendy places opening up and music everywhere.

The Carlovian, Tullow St. For traditional music on a Thu night.

Teach Dolmain, in the same street.

Transport

County Carlow *p193*

Bus Bus Éireann (nearest office, T051-879000) has daily services to **Dublin**, **Kilkenny** and **Waterford**.

Taxi Carlow Cabs T059-9140000.

Train **Station** at Railway Rd, T059-9131633. A 5-min walk from the town centre. Carlow is on the **Dublin** to **Waterford** line. Trains to both 6 times a day, 4 on Sun.

County Laois

The only county in Ireland that does not border a county that touches the sea, in the 16th century Laois was decisively conquered by the English and plantations by the colonisers swiftly followed, hence its original name, Queen's County. The towns of Abbeyleix and Mountmellick, each with a population of under 3,000, are especially pretty places, little visited by travellers busily speeding through to somewhere else, that offer rewards to those who take the time to linger and explore. ▸▸ *For Sleeping, Eating and other listings, see pages 196-197.*

Around Portlaoise → *Phone code: 0502. Colour map 2, grid C6.*

Travellers always used to pass through Portlaoise ('Portleash'), because it is on the major Dublin to south and southwest of Ireland route, and dutifully take note of the town's maximum security prison and its Ulster-style concrete observation posts at the east end of the main road. With a modern bypass, even that dubious claim to fame will pass unnoticed, but at least the town should benefit from a decline in heavy traffic. The **tourist office** is in the centre, T0502-21178. Open May-Sep Mon-Sat 1000-1800.

Rock of Dunamase ⓘ *Open access. 5 km east of Portlaoise on the N80 to Stradbally.* The Rock of Dunamase is the best reason for lingering around Portlaoise, for although not much remains of the castle that once stood there, the site is extraordinarily well situated and on a fine day there are superb views of the surrounding countryside from the top of the mound. An Iron Age fort predates the castle, which was built some time around the end of the 12th century and changed hands between Irish and English lords more than once before Cromwellian forces took it apart in 1650. It was briefly restored but little now remains of what must have been a spectacularly-sited fortress.

Stradbally As home to a Guinness Brewery steam locomotive of 1895, Stradbally, on the N80 road west of the Rock of Dunamase, will be of interest steam trainspotters. Trains run to Dublin half a dozen times each year. Its **Steam Museum and Narrow Gauge Railway** ⓘ *T0502-25154, Easter-Oct, Mon-Fri 1100-1300 and 1400-1600, €2,* has a collection of traction engines.

Mountmellick Mountmellick, 10 km north of Portlaoise, was founded by Quakers in the 17th century and a number of Georgian houses remain from its heyday in the late 18th century, when the famed Mountmellick linen was exported by canal to Dublin and beyond. There is a small **heritage centre** ⓘ *T0502-24525, on the Portlaoise road, just outside of town.*

Emo Court ⓘ *Mountmellick, T0502-26573. Mid-Jun to mid-Sep Tue-Sun 1200-1830. Guided tours. €2.75. Free admission to Garden. OPW site. 2.5 km from Emo, 13 km from Portlaoise, and signposted off the Kildare to Portlaoise N7 road.* An impressive example of neo-classical architecture, Emo Court was designed in 1790 by James Gandon for the first earl of Portarlington but not completed until 1874. It was run as a novitiate by the Jesuits until the 1960s and is now open to the public. Combine a visit with a walk through the extensive grounds.

Coolrain About 12 km west of Portlaoise this picturesque little village is nestled in the foot of the Slieve Bloom Mountains and bicycles can be hired from The Thatched Village Inn, T0502-35277, which will also suggest routes and provide maps for trips in the local uncrowded roads.

The Slieve Bloom Way

This energetic two-day walk covers 51 km of sweeping views of the Slieve Bloom Mountains as the Way travels through moors, valleys and forests. However, it is a path that requires planning because of the limited public transport in the area and the need to book accommodation in advance. For a one-day excursion covering part of the Way, consider parking on the R422 between Mountmellick and Clonaslee and heading off for a day's exhilarating walk with a picnic.

Mapping and information **Ordnance Survey** map No 54 in the Discovery series covers the Way, and **EastWest Mapping** (see page 52) publishes *The Slieve Bloom Way Map Guide* using the same 1:50,000 scale. There is also a booklet published by

the local council, *Slieve Bloom Environment Park*, available from the tourist office in Portlaoise. See also page 625 for walking guides that cover the Way.

Abbeyleix and around → *Phone code: 0502. Colour map 4, grid B1.*

Abbeyleix, about 16 km south of Portlaoise, has an interesting story to tell. It grew up around a 12th-century Cistercian abbey, but 600 years later the local landlord, Viscount de Vesci, relocated the village to its present site and planned the layout that is such an attractive a part of the modern town. The country house of de Vesci, **Abbeyleix House**, outside of town on the Rathdowney road, was built by James Wyatt and remodelled in the Victorian age, but it remains closed to the public apart from the occasional opening of the gardens. Worth admiring is the architecture of the town's **Bank of Ireland**, replete with mullioned windows, classical columns, a corner oriel and a copper-domed tower, all built at the beginning of the 20th century. **Morrissey's** ⓘ *Main St, Abbeyleix, T0502-31233*, half-pub and half-shop is well known to discerning travellers on the Cork-Dublin run who value a place to rest and relax without being forced to listen to the blather of radio phone-ins or crass music. It's been in the same family since 1775, and with ancient shelves packed with old biscuit tins and a pot belly stove there is little to suggest that much has changed since. The perfect place for a quiet pint or a cup of Morrissey's own special brand tea.

Heritage House ⓘ *Off Main St, T0502-31653. Mar-Oct Mon-Sat 1000-1800, Sun 1300-1800; Nov-Feb shorter hours. €3.* This was one of the two schools that de Vesci built, and its interesting and well presented displays are worth a look. Worth considering as a place to stop for its coffee shop, tourist information and craft shop.

Heywood House ⓘ *7 km southeast of Abbeyleix off the R432 road to Ballinakill, T087-66752, 056-21450. Open daylight hours. Tours can be arranged by telephoning in advance. Free.* Heywood House, thought to have been landscaped by Gertrude Jekyll, has a noted garden designed by Edwin Lutyens, now well restored and open to the public. The house itself was destroyed by fire in 1960 and nothing of it remains. Picturesquely-framed views of inland Ireland can be seen through the oeil-de-boeuf windows in Lutyens' sunken terrace.

Sleeping

Portlaoise *p195*

B **Heritage Hotel**, Main St, Portlaoise, T0502-78588, www.heritagehotel.com. With architectural style reflecting the prosperity of contemporary Ireland, and amenities to match: 3 bars, 2 restaurants and a spa.

C **Ivyleigh House**, Portlaoise, T0502-22081, www.ivyleigh.com. A Georgian house, carefully restored, with comfortable bedrooms, 2 sitting rooms and glorious alternatives to the Irish fry-up for breakfast.

F **Traditional Farm Hostel**, Farren House, Ballacolla, Portlaoise, T0502-34032. Open all year, private rooms and dorms, bicycle hire and space for camping. A couple of km from Durrow on the R434.

The Thatched Village Inn, Coolrain, T0502-35126. Self-catering accommodation in a restored cottage next to the Inn. The pub serves meals throughout the day. Also sessions of set dancing and traditional music.

Abbeyleix and around *p196*

C **Castle Arms Hotel**, The Square, Durrow, T0502-36117. Conventional, family-run hotel with 14 bedrooms. One of the few places to stay in Durrow.

D **Preston House**, Main St, Abbeyleix, T0502-31432. Has 4 large bedrooms handsomely furnished with antiques, and makes canny use of the available space to incorporate modern facilities.

For an explanation of the sleeping and eating price codes used in this guide, see inside the front cover. Other relevant information is found in Essentials pages 39-45.

Eating

Portlaoise *p195*
¶¶ **Kingfisher Restaurant**, Main St, T0502-62500. Makes for an interesting mix: Punjabi food in a former bank building.
¶ **The Kitchen and Foodhall**, Hynds Sq, T0502-62061. Serves delicious home-cooked food, including decent vegetarian choices, for lunches and dinner Mon-Sat. Wine from the shop can be selected for your meal.
¶ **Thatched Village Inn**, see Sleeping.

Abbeyleix and around *p196*
¶¶ **Preston House**, Main St, Abbeyleix. Well worth checking out this creeper-covered restaurant. Tasty scones and home-made preserves in the morning, while the lunch menu includes appetizing chowder with brown bread and delicious vegetarian dishes. The early-bird dinner (Thu-Sat) is good value.
In Durrow the choice is disappointing, try:
¶ **Castle Arms**, standard hotel food;
¶ **Copper Kettle**, The Square, modest, but more interesting choices.

Transport

County Laois *p195*
Bus Buses from most parts of the country pass through Portlaoise, especially routes between **Dublin** and the south and southwest of the country, T01-836611. Bus Éireann's **Dublin** to **Cork** service stops in **Abbeyleix** 3 times a day, twice on Sun.

Train Services to and from **Dublin** and **Cork**, **Limerick**, **Tralee** and **Tipperary** stop in Portlaoise, T0502-21303,

County Kildare

County Kildare has a venerable and ancient history, St Brigid having established a monastery here in the fifth century. It was claimed by the English by the end of the 13th century and served as a defensive barrier between Dublin and the barbarian Irish who threatened the Pale. Today, it is a rich county where property values are sky-high and the discreet charms of the bourgeoisie not so discreetly on show. It is also the centre of Ireland's bloodstock industry and home to the famed Curragh racecourse.
»» *For Sleeping, Eating and other listings, see pages 200-201.*

Maynooth and around → *Phone code: 01. Colour map 4 grid A2.*

Head due west from Dublin's city centre for about 19 km – though it will seem a lot longer if you get caught in rush-hour traffic – and a mixed landscape of rolling countryside and suburban dwellings awaits you. This is modern Ireland, depressingly modern at times, and the key sights can be comfortably taken in on a day trip.

Castletown House ⓘ *Celbridge, 20 km from the centre of Dublin on the R403, T01-6288252. Easter-Sep Mon-Fri 1000-1800, Sat-Sun 1300-1800; Oct Mon-Fri 1000-1700, Sun 1300-1700; Nov Sun 1300-1700. Guided tours. €3.50. OPW site. Bus No 67/67A from Middle Abbey St and No 66X.* Ease of access from Dublin increases the appeal of a visit to Ireland's largest and architecturally most important country house. Castletown House was built around 1722 for William Conolly, the Speaker of the Irish House of Commons. He spared no expense in employing the Italian architect Alessandro Galilei, although the work was completed by Edward Lovett Pearce, an Irish Italophile architect and others. It is the finest expression of the Palladian style to be found in the country and this can first be appreciated by simply standing outside and admiring the symmetry of the façade. The philosopher Bishop Berkeley was more aware of the type of stone that went into its building, "fine wrought stone, harder and better coloured than the [English] Portland" stone, and like other Ascendancy figures rejoiced at what he saw as an expression of Irish culture.

Conolly died before the house was finished, but his wife lived for another 23 years and in 1740 she commissioned the building of a monumental **folly** in the grounds as a way of providing relief to the local poor. Before she died in 1752, she had a tent put up on the lawn so that she could admire her home for the last time. She died childless and the house ended up with Conolly's grand-nephew whose wife, the English Lady Louisa, daughter of the Duke of Richmond, was responsible for much of the interior decoration. Some of her ideas, like the Pompeii-style decorations on the walls, can be seen in the most distinctive room, the Long Gallery on the first floor. She also created the Print Room, the last surviving example of its kind in Ireland.

Straffan Only 5 km southwest of Celbridge, the village of Straffan has a **Steam Museum** ⓘ *T01-6273155, www.steam-museum.ie, Jun-Aug Tue-Sun 1400-1800, Easter-May and Sep Sun 1430-1730, €4, café*, with working steam engines and a small exhibition about the impact of steam power. The best time to visit is over the holiday weekend at the very beginning of August when an annual Steam Rally brings together a big display of steam engines and working models and an opportunity to ride on the longest established steam-powered narrow gauge railway in Ireland.

Also in Straffan, next to the Steam Museum, is **Lodge Park Walled Garden** ⓘ *Jun-Jul Tue-Fri and Sun 1400-1800; Aug Tue-Fri 1430-1730, €4*, part of a late 18th-century house. Close by is the **Straffan Butterfly Farm** ⓘ *Jun-Aug daily 1200-1730, €4.50*, with its array of colourful butterflies and scary-looking insects and spiders.

Maynooth A famous place to the Irish, the town is home to the country's leading seminary for the training of priests. **Maynooth College** was founded in 1795, at a time when the government wanted the support of moderate Catholics, and Augustus Pugin was commissioned to design the college; building began in 1847. Architecturally, it is not a particularly interesting example of Victorian Gothic and there is little here to engage your attention. University colleges are now based here and they account for the majority of students; young men actually studying for the priesthood are an endangered species. At the college entrance stand the ruins of **Maynooth Castle**, a stronghold of the Norman Fitzgerald family, the Earls of Kildare. It was treacherously taken in 1535 after a rebellion by its owner, 'Silken Thomas', the son of the ninth Earl of Kildare, against the English, and abandoned some time around 1656.

Larchill Arcadian Gardens ⓘ *Kilcock, west of Maynooth on the N4, T01-6287354. May-Sep daily 1200-1800. €4.12. Bus No 66 from Middle Abbey St, Dublin.* These are more interesting than Maynooth, and only 6.5 km away. Here is claimed to be the only surviving example in Ireland or England of the mid-18th century *ferme ornée*. A circular walk links 10 follies, with gazebos and a tiny island with a Greek-style temple.

Kildare Town and around → *Phone code: 045. Colour map 4, grid B2.*

Try to avoid a drive between Kildare Town and Dublin during the morning or evening rush hours. There is a motorway, the M7, for a stretch of the way, but traffic snarls are still very common. Another tip is not to bother stopping at Naas (pronounced 'nace'), which has little to recommend it, unlike the pretty and prosperous little town of Kildare. This town is forever associated with the legendary St Brigid, who by the middle of the seventh century already had a church and shrine dedicated to her here; by the ninth century she was the major saint in Ireland. She remains a very popular figure and St Brigid's Cross, easily crafted from reeds, is commonly found in souvenir shops.

Christopher Paris, the constable of Maynooth Castle in 1535, was bribed into betraying it with a promise of leniency but, nevertheless, was executed afterwards. 'The pardon of Maynooth' became an ironic term for such breaches of trust.

Canals – Royal and Grand

Linking Dublin with the River Shannon through 44 locks, and with a branch that heads south to Waterford, the Grand Canal was built between 1756 and 1804 and stayed in operation until 1960. It is now managed by the Office of Public Works (OPW) whose **Waterways Visitor Centre** in Dublin provides information on its history. Boats are available in Vicarstown, a few km northwest of Athy, T0502-25189, 25544. OPW manages the Royal Canal as well, which also links Dublin with the River Shannon and which is in the process of being cleaned up. Its towpaths are being restored for walkers at the same time.

Now that the Shannon to Erne Waterway is running (see page 572), it is possible to travel from Belturbet in Fermanagh to Dublin. For information on both canals, www.waterwaysireland.com.

The Protestant Cathedral of St Brigid ⓘ *May-Sep Mon-Sat 1000-1300 and 1400-1700, Sun 1400-1700. €2.54.* The cathedral dates back to 1243. It was largely destroyed in the 17th century but rebuilt around 1875, following the original cruciform structure with a dose of Victorian romanticism thrown in for good measure. The adjoining **round tower** has an elaborate, Romanesque doorway and battlements added during the 19th-century rebuilding work on the cathedral.

The Curragh ⓘ *south of Kildare town, T045-521617. Mid-Feb to mid-Nov daily 0930-1800, E8.50 joint ticket with Japanese Garden.* Some 2,000 ha of land, dedicated to dozens of studs and a famous racecourse, constitute the Curragh. The word itself means 'racecourse' though the origins of the area's association with horses is lost in time. It may have something to do with its being flat and fertile or perhaps to do with soil which builds strong bones in horses. Organized horse racing has been taking place here from at least the 18th century, and in the 19th century the British established a training camp here, which developed into a permanent military base. You cannot just wander around the private studs but the government-owned **National Stud** is open to the public, includes a museum as well as tours of the stables and is within walking distance of Kildare town.

Japanese Gardens ⓘ *See the Curragh.* It seems an unlikely mix but the eccentric Colonel William Hall Walker, who established what is now the National Stud in 1900, also had an area of bog drained and brought in two Japanese gardeners to landscape the place. The resulting Gardens offer an odd philosophical/garden tour based around various stages of male life from birth to the hereafter.

South Kildare → *Phone code: 059. Colour map 4, grid B2.*

Ballitore The Quaker origins of Ballitore are remembered in the **Ballitore Quaker Museum** ⓘ *in the centre of the village, free,* and the walled Quaker cemetery is also worth a visit. The most famous product of a Quaker education in Ireland is the political thinker Edmund Burke (1729-1797), who attended the village school.

Moone South of Ballitore, on the N9, this village would hardly merit attention were it not for the **Moone High Cross** ⓘ *shop: T059-8624164, Mon-Fri, 1000-1630*, on the site of an Early Christian monastery just to the west of the village. The highly attractive High Cross shows Daniel, the sacrifice of Isaac, Adam and Eve, and the Crucifixion on the east side, the Apostles on the west side, various miracles on the south and two saints breaking bread in the desert on the north side. A few miles south, the **Irish Pewter Mill** has a casting room open to the public and a factory shop.

Athy The town of Athy (pronounced 'a-thigh'), west of Ballitore, has the potential to make itself far more interesting as the **heritage centre** ⓘ *T059-8633075, Mar-Oct Mon-Fri 1000-1700, Sat 1200-1600, Sun 1400-1700, shorter hours in winter, €3*, in the 18th-century town hall highlights major historical events such as the 1798 uprising and the explorer Ernest Shackleton. For local **walks** see box above.

Castledermot (*Phone code: 0503*) South of Ballitore, on the N9, is Castledermot, where there is a surprisingly large amount to see. As you come into town down Main Street there are reminders of an ecclesiastical past that goes back to a monastery founded by St Dermot and raided by the Vikings in 841. What stands today is a remarkable Romanesque doorway, a round tower and two fine granite crosses. Nearby **Kilkea Castle** (see 'Sleeping' below) ⓘ *a caretaker lives next door and will open the gates on request*, though originally built in 1180, has been substantially modified and restored between the 17th and 20th centuries. At the southern end of town stand the remains of a Franciscan friary founded in the early 14th century and suppressed in 1541.

Sleeping

Maynooth and around *p197*

L **Moyglare Manor**, Maynooth, T01-6286351, www.moyglaremanor.ie. The nearest country house to Dublin airport, this is the place to make your first (or last) stop in Ireland a memorable one. Antiques, portraits and gilt-framed mirrors everywhere, rooms with 4-poster beds and a fine restaurant.

E **Lotus Lodge**, Ladychapel, Maynooth, T01-6286027. Over 4 km from the college, this is one of the better-value B&Bs in this well-heeled part of the country. There's a Holistic Healing Centre attached.

Kildare Town and around *p198*

B **Martinstown House**, The Curragh, T045-441269, www.martinstown.com. Part of a large farm, B&B is not exactly at giveaway prices, but this is a recommended, welcoming house.

E **Singleton**,1 Dara Park, Station Rd, Kildare Town, T045-521964. Three comfortable bedrooms in an immaculate B&B.

South Kildare *p199*

LL **Kilkea Castle**, Castledermot, T059-45156, www.kilkeacastle.ie. The oldest inhabited castle in Ireland, this hotel has installed an indoor pool and gym and an 18-hole golf course.

B **The Rath House**, Moone, T059-24133. L-shaped bungalow with 4 bedrooms, including a single.

B **Woodcourte House**, Moone, T059-24167. B&B in a large country house and with the option of an evening meal for €20.

Eating

Maynooth and around *p197*

ΨΨΨ **The Byerley Turk**, T01-6017200, in the Kildare Hotel and Country Club in Straffan. Specializes in French cuisine and does it with classical panache: crisp white linen tablecloths and enough fine china, crystal and silver around your table to make you feel rich enough to afford one of the racehorses painted and framed on the walls. Dinner is a throwaway €70.

ΨΨΨ **The Castle Restaurant**, Barberstown Castle hotel, Straffan, T01-6288157. Wins hands down for character and atmosphere. Dining tables occupy whitewashed rooms in a basement setting with low lighting and the food includes sumptuous seafood and satisfying vegetarian dishes. Lunch is around €25 and dinner €45.

ΨΨ **Glenroyal Hotel**, Maynooth. Has a decent carvery and a bar serving food. Pubs in Maynooth offer the usual pub food.

ΨΨ **Moyglare Manor Restaurant**, Maynooth, T01-6286351. Enjoy pre-dinner drinks in an antique-laden room with a turf fire while perusing a non-nonsense, refreshingly direct menu. A 4-course dinner is around €46, live piano music in the background and a mostly French wine list.

Kildare Town and around *p198*

ΨΨ **Silken Thomas**, T045-521264. A popular pub with decent food and a restaurant that opens for lunch and dinner every day.

South Kildare *p199*

ΨΨΨ **D'Lacy's Restaurant**, T059-45156. Dinner in Kilkea Castle's restaurant is a grand affair

and worth making a reservation for. Dinner is around €40 and diners can enjoy splendid views from the dining room and excellent food using local produce and fresh vegetables from the hotel's garden. The roast of the day rarely disappoints and there is a terrace for drinks before or after meals.

Tonlegee House and Restaurant, Athy, T059-31473. A fine restaurant for anyone wishing to tuck into local Kildare lamb. Quail and wild mushroom pie with Madeira sauce is a house speciality.

Activities and tours

Kildare Town and around *p198*

Race meetings at the Curragh Big flat races include the 2,000 and 1,000 Guineas towards the end of May, the Irish Derby and the Pretty Polly Stakes towards the end of June, the Irish Oaks in early July, the Moyglare Stud Stakes in early September, the Irish St Leger and the Aga Khan Studs National Stakes in mid-September. Bord Fáilte issues more information and their annual Calendar of Events booklet includes a racing calendar. For big meetings at the Curragh, T045-441205, there are often special bus and train services running to and from Dublin; T01-8302222/8366111 for transport details, www.irish-national-stud.ie.

Transport

County Kildare *p197*

Bus Bus No **67/67A** from Middle Abbey St, and No **66X**, connect Maynooth and **Dublin**. Many of the **Bus Éireann**, T01-8366111, services to **Galway** and **Sligo** also make a stop in Maynooth. Services on the **Dublin-Kilkenny-Clonmel-Cork** route stop in **Athy**, and Bus No **130** between Dublin and Kilkenny also stops daily in Athy as well as **Moone** and **Castledermot**. There are numerous services to **Kildare** from Dublin.

Train Suburban and main line trains from **Dublin** stop at **Maynooth** station, T01-6285509. **Kildare**, T045-421224, is on the main route from **Dublin** to the west and southwest, so there are good connections with **Ballina**, **Westport**, **Galway**, **Ennis**, **Tralee**, **Cork** and **Waterford**.

County Offaly

Separated from County Laois by the Slieve Bloom Mountains, County Offaly is distinguished by flat areas of bogland and a rich heritage that includes, in Clonmacnois, one of the most important ecclesiastical sites in early Irish history. Conquered by the English in the middle of the 16th century, the southwest of the county was granted to the Parsons family of Norfolk in 1620 who established themselves at Parsonstown (Birr), a town well worth a visit and an overnight stay.

For Sleeping, Eating and other listings, see pages 203-204.

Clonmacnois → *Phone code: 090. Colour map 2, grid C5.*

Between the seventh and 12th centuries Clonmacnois was the largest and most important monastic centre in Ireland, developing around the nexus where the River Shannon meets the Eiscir Riada, a 'running ridge' formed at the end of the Ice Age and a legendary boundary dividing Ireland. Founded by St Ciarán in the mid-sixth century, the monastery attracted scholars from all over Europe as well as artists working with stone and metal, and such was its fame that high kings of Ireland were buried here. It also attracted marauders and between the ninth and 12th centuries was plundered some 35 times by Vikings and natives alike. The size and prosperity of Clonmacnois may be gathered from the fact that over 100 houses were destroyed when the Anglo-Normans attacked in 1179. When English forces from Athlone robbed the monastery of everything in 1552 the life of the centre was finally brought to an end.

 Visitors' Centre ⓘ *Shannonbridge, south of Clonmacnois, 21 km from Athlone and Ballinasloe, signposted from the N62 and the R357, T090-9674195. Mid-May to mid-Sep daily 0900-1900; mid-Mar to mid-May and mid-Sep-Oct daily 1000-1800; Nov to mid-Mar daily 1000-1700. €5. OPW site. There is also a separate tourist information office, T090-9674134.*

Architectural sights There are three impressive **High Crosses**, which have been moved inside the Visitors' Centre for safe-keeping, including one that is very unusual due to its probable representation of a non-biblical scene. The **cathedral**, which is not as impressive a building as the name might suggest, was originally built in the early 10th century but sections have been added over the centuries. The other buildings dotted around are the remains of eight churches from the 10th to the 13th centuries but again with additions, some as recent as the 17th century. One of them, the Nun's Church, is to the east of the main centre and well worth seeking out for its Romanesque doorway and chancel arch. Of the two **round towers**, one, O'Rourkes, is named after a high king of Connaught and the other, overlooking the river, is next to one of the eight churches, Teampall (church) Finghin.

Clonmacnois and West Offaly Railway ⓘ *Shannonbridge, on the R357 Tullamore Rd, T090-9674114, www.bnm.ie. Apr-Oct daily 1000-1700. Trains leave every hour, on the hour, but try to see the video first. €5.50.* The Clonmacnois and West Offaly Railway runs on a narrow gauge line which trundles a 8-km circular route around the Blackwater Bog. The journey is a surreal one, the forbidding towers of Bord na Móna's (Irish Peat Development Board) peat-fuelled power station reminding you that the bog is being exploited to extinction while Bord na Móna run the tour and show a useful video on the flora and fauna that will one day disappear.

Banagher → *Phone code: 0509. Colour map 2, grid C5.*

Banagher, where Charlotte Brontë spent her honeymoon, is the epicentre of Offaly's new-found identity as a leisure centre for the Midlands and the first place to visit is the **tourist office**, in Crank House, Main St, T0509-51458, Mar-Oct Mon-Fri 0930-2000, Sat-Sun 0930-1700, which has information on various local places of interest.

Birr → *Phone code: 0509. Colour map 2, grid C5. www.elyocarroll.com for county information.*

If you are thinking of basing yourself in Offaly for a day or two then the pretty, Georgian town of Birr, or Kinnitty a couple of miles to the west, compete favourably with Banagher as the place to stay overnight. The Birr **tourist office**, Market Sq, T0509-25015, May-Sep 0930-1700, dispenses a useful town trail leaflet that details some of the interesting buildings.

Birr Castle Demesne ⓘ *T0509-20336, www.birrcastle.com. Demense and Science Centre: Mid-Mar to Oct 0900-1800; Nov to mid-Mar 1000-1600. €8. Guided tours, plants and flowers for sale.* The Parsons family in Birr climbed the social ladder in the 18th century, became earls of Rosse and settled into Birr Castle, where they still live. The house is not open to the public but Birr Castle Demesne is, a superb 18th-century park with a lake, river, waterfalls, box hedges that have to be seen to be believed, and an astonishing collection of 2,000 species of rare trees and shrubs. Also here is the **Great Telescope**, built in 1845 as the largest in the world (which it remained for 75 years), and fully operational once again. (The 6-ft-diameter reflector, removed during the Troubles, is in London's Science Museum.) The telescope, which in its time made many important astronomical observations, is the most dramatic achievement of a remarkable family of Irish scientists. Their story is told in the adjoining Science Centre.

Leap Castle ⓘ *T0509-31115. Open on request. €6.* Outside Birr, on the road between Kinnitty and Roscrea, a little way past Clareen, are the spooky remains of Leap Castle. It was widely believed to be the most haunted house in Ireland, if not the whole of Europe, with a renowned 'smelly ghost' manifesting itself to the senses. The house was destroyed by Republican ghostbusters in 1922, but some say the smell still lingers. It is slowly being rebuilt.

Tullamore → *Phone code: 0506. Colour map 2, grid C6.*

The Victorian-style town of Tullamore on the Grand Canal has three worthy attractions, two in the town and one a few miles to the north. The **tourist office**, is on Bury Quay, T0506-52617. Open May-Sep Mon-Sat 0900-1800, Sun 1200-1700; Oct-Apr Mon-Sat 1000-1700, Sun 1200-1700.

Tullamore Dew Heritage Centre ⓘ *Bury Quay, T0506-25015, www.tullamore-dew.org. May-Sep Mon-Sat 0900-1800, Sun 1200-1700; Oct-Apr Mon-Sat 1000-1700, Sun 1200-1700. €5.* Tullamore is famous for whiskey, and though it is no longer distilled here the Tullamore Dew Heritage Centre tells its history and looks at the impact of the Grand Canal on the development of the town. The Centre is in an 1897 warehouse on the banks of the Grand Canal and you can try on clothes from the 1850s and see bees making honey for the Irish Mist liqueur. The customary courtesy tipple rounds off a visit.

Charleville Forest Castle ⓘ *Charleville Rd, south of town on the road to Limerick, signposted for Birr, T0506-21279. Under refurbishment at the time of going to press but you are free to visit the grounds.* The Bury family founded Tullamore in 1750 and their family home was Charleville Forest Castle, a superb Gothic-Georgian pile with everything you might expect: turrets, spires, ivy on the walls, dark trees. In 1875 William Morris was commissioned to decorate the interiors but his socialist sympathies led him to show more interest in the plight of the rural Irish and he never publicized this work of his for the super-rich. Most of his contributions, including wallpapers, have disappeared but there is some painted decoration and a frieze in the dining room.

Durrow Abbey Durrow Abbey, founded in the sixth century and birthplace of the famous illustrated gospel, the *Book of Durrow*, now in Trinity College Library, Dublin (see page 65), is long gone but a Georgian mansion and a deserted church stand near the site. The house was burnt down in 1922 but the owners rebuilt it, "a rare example of a house improved as a result of its destruction in the Troubles" says Jeremy Williams in his excellent *Architecture in Ireland* (see page 625). Recently purchased by the OPW, there are plans to preserve the 10th-century high cross and old burial slabs by the church.

Sleeping

Clonmacnois *p201*

E Kajon House, Creevagh, 1.6 km from Clonmacnoise on the road to Shannonbridge, T090-74191, www.kajonhouse.cjb.net. B&B with the option of an evening meal.

Banagher *p202*

D Brosna Lodge Hotel, Main St, T0509-51350, www.brosnalodge.com. Good restaurant and bar in this family-owned hotel. Close to the river.

F Crank House Hostel, Main St, T0509-51798. Open all year. 40 beds and 2 private rooms. Not as zany as the name suggests; beds, bathrooms and kitchen are all tip-top.

Birr *p202*

L Kinnitty Castle, Kinnitty, T0509-37318, www.kinnittycastle.com. Gothic pile on a 8,000-ha estate on the slopes of the Slieve Bloom hills. Stuffed with antiques and the multi-million-pound refurbishment does justice to the huge bedrooms.

E Ardmore House, Kinnitty, T0509-37009, www.kinnitty.net. Traditional home comforts and a knowledgeable host as regards local

walks in the Slieve Bloom mountains.
E **Maltings Guesthouse**, Castle St, T0509-21345. Good value rooms in an old malt storage building with a riverside location close to Birr Castle.
E **Spinners Townhouse**, Castle St, T0509-21673. Another interesting place to stay, with a choice of rooms and a relaxing courtyard.

Tullamore *p203*
C-D **Moorhill Country House**, Clara Rd, T0506-21395, www.moorhill.ie. Victorian retreat set amidst chestnut trees and manicured lawns.
D **Annaharvey House**, on the R420 to Portalington, T0506-43544, www.annaharvey farm.ie. Rooms in a restored grain barn, with exposed beams and open fires creating a rustic atmosphere. Equestrian options.
D **Sea Dew Guesthouse**, Clonminch Rd, T/F52054, www.seadewguesthouse.com. Large, purpose-built edifice within walking distance of town centre. Benefits from a conservatory breakfast room.
E **Ivy Lodge**, Daingean Rd, T41151. A mile from the town centre. Really does justify its name.

Eating

Clonmacnois (Shannonbridge) *p201*
¶ **The Old Fort**, T0509-9674973. Really is an old fort, serves a decent meal from 1700 Wed-Sat.
The Village Tavern cannot be beaten for a quiet drink and a bit of atmosphere and there is often music here at night.

Banagher *p202*
There is a coffee shop in Crank House, Main St, and a couple of pubs in the town centre worth checking out for their pub fare.
¶¶ **The Snipes Restaurant**, Brosna Lodge Hotel. A tad more expensive and perhaps a little more interesting.
¶¶ **The Vine House**, T0509-51463. Close to the river this place has seafood and meat dishes at lunchtime and evenings.
J.J. Hough, Main St, T51893. A charming vine-blanketed old pub with legendary status as a venue for traditional music. There is nearly always something happening here in summer, and at weekends in winter.

Birr *p202*
¶¶¶ **Kinnitty Castle**. Gourmet food, with dinner every evening and lunch also on a Sun. Open to non-residents.
¶ **Spinners Bistro**, T0509-21673. Organic food and enlightened vegetarian dishes.
¶¶ **The Stables Townhouse Restaurant**, Oxmantown Mall, T0509-20263. Has bare brick walls and serves filling meals at lunchtime and at night.
¶¶ **Thatch Bar**, just outside Birr at Crinkle, T0509-20682. Worth the journey for the imaginative and occasionally exotic pub food and restaurant fare.
The Chestnut, Green St. Makes for a relaxing port of call for a coffee or pint.

Tullamore *p203*
¶¶ **Anatolia**, Harbour St, T0506-23669. The best place for lunch (but not on Sat) or dinner (not Fri or Sat). A mixture of European and Turkish.
¶ **The Bridge House**, Bridge St, T0506-21704. Pub/restaurant serving familiar dishes all day.

Transport

County Offaly *p201*
Bike hire Buckley Cycles, Tullamore, T0506-52240.

Boat hire Silverline Cruises, The Marina, Banagher T0509-51112, www.silverline crusies.com, rent self-drive cruisers on the River Shannon.

Bus Bus Éireann's, T01-8366111, **Dublin** to **Birr** service stops daily in **Banagher** and also connects the town with **Tullamore**. The **Cork** to **Athlone** service and the Athlone to **Tralee** services also make daily stops in Birr. Kearns Coaches, T0509-20124, run daily services between **Portumna** in Galway, **Birr**, **Tullamore** and **Dublin**. There is no bus service to **Clonmacnois** but **taxis** run from **Athlone** in the summer and will wait about an hour for around €45; enquire at the Athlone tourist office, T0902-94630. A better deal is the bus most Sundays from Athlone by Paddy Kavanagh, T090-6474839/ 087-2407706, for €25. It departs around 1100 from St Peter's Church near the tourist office but telephone to confirm; a trip can be fun.

Train **Dublin** to **Galway** trains stop at Tullamore station, T0506-21431, throughout the day.

Counties Waterford, Tipperary and Limerick

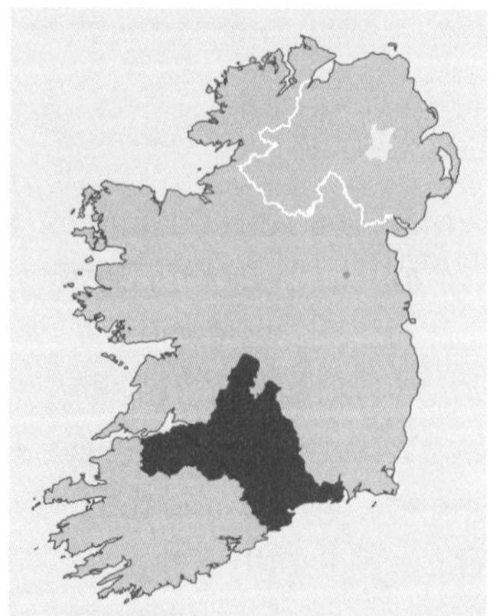

Footprint features

Introduction

Waterford's coastline stretches for more than 80 km, but it is only 44 km from the north of the county to the south. Despite these modest dimensions there is enormous variety in the cultural and physical landscape: wood-clad hills and sheltered inlets in the east, sandy beaches and resorts along the coast, a tiny Irish-speaking area around Ring to the west, and the Comeragh/Monavullagh Mountains in the north of the county, where historic river valleys frame castles and great houses bear testimony to the English invasions of the past.

Tipperary, Ireland's largest inland county, has some of the best farming land in the country in the aptly named Golden Vale that stretches westwards to Limerick. Most people who visit, though, are drawn instead to the historic towns of Cashel and Clonmel.

County Limerick has diverse attractions: the unbelievably cute Adare so beloved of gawking tour groups; Lough Gur, a major Stone Age site in Europe; and Limerick city booming with new money and home to the amazing Hunt Collection and the beautiful old Church of Ireland cathedral.

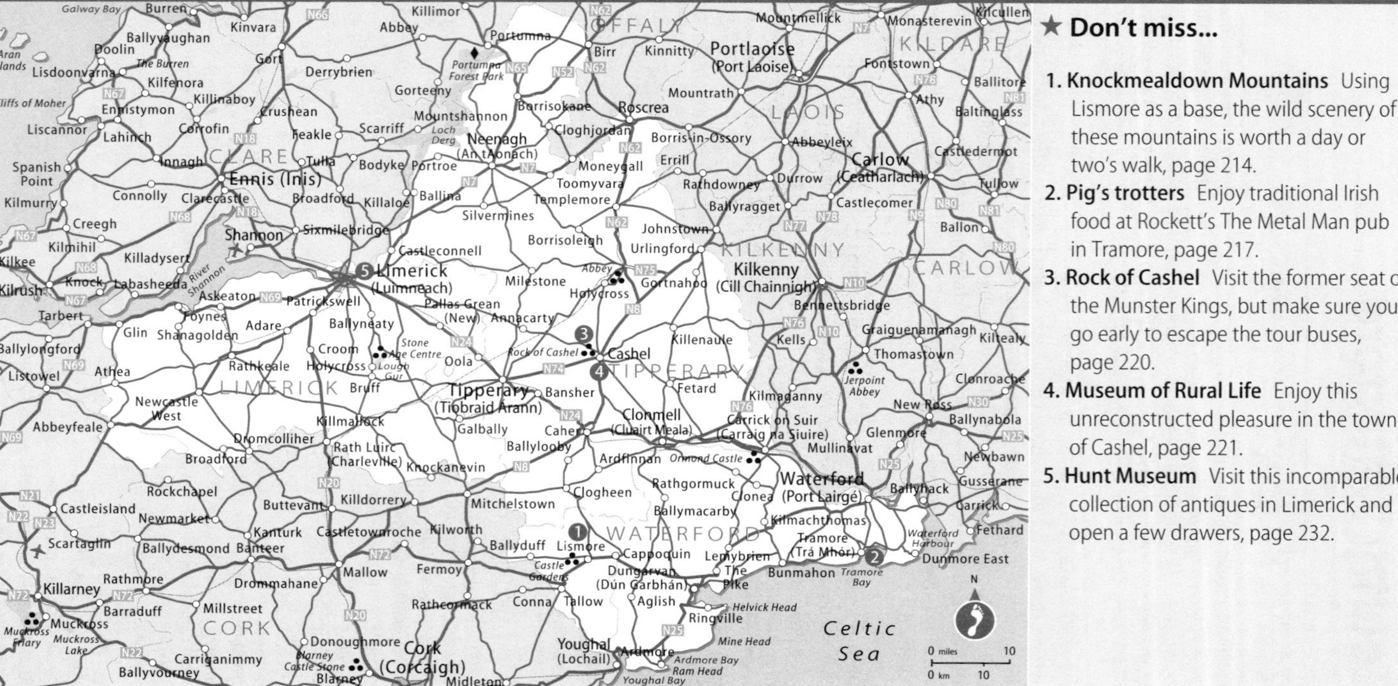

★ Don't miss...

1. **Knockmealdown Mountains** Using Lismore as a base, the wild scenery of these mountains is worth a day or two's walk, page 214.
2. **Pig's trotters** Enjoy traditional Irish food at Rockett's The Metal Man pub in Tramore, page 217.
3. **Rock of Cashel** Visit the former seat of the Munster Kings, but make sure you go early to escape the tour buses, page 220.
4. **Museum of Rural Life** Enjoy this unreconstructed pleasure in the town of Cashel, page 221.
5. **Hunt Museum** Visit this incomparable collection of antiques in Limerick and open a few drawers, page 232.

County Waterford → www.waterfordtourism.org.

Waterford → *Phone code: 051. Colour map 4, grid C1.*

Waterford oozes a sense of the ancient, with modern shops squeezed into the narrow spaces of the medieval town centre, and no end of fine old buildings to admire. With good facilities, it warrants a short stay before you head off to the varied attractions south and west of the city. A drawback is the lack of budget accommodation. ›› *For Sleeping, Eating and other listings, see pages 215-219.*

Ins and outs

Getting there Waterford has an airport (**Aer Arann** flights to Luton), train and bus links, and easy access to the ferry ports of Rosslare and Cork. A seven-minute car ferry across Waterford harbour saves time travelling between Waterford and County Wexford. From Rosslare it takes about 45 minutes to drive to Ballyhack, where the ferry hops over to Passage East in Waterford. Dublin is 2½ hours away from Waterford, Cork about an hour. ›› *See Transport, page 219, for further details.*

Getting around The city centre is small and compact, and though the Waterford glass factory is on the outskirts of town there are bikes and taxis for hire.

Information Waterford Tourist Office, The Quay, T051-875823. May-Sep Mon-Fri 0900-1800, Sat 1000-1800; Oct-Apr Mon-Sat 0900-1700. Also at Waterford Crystal, T051-358397. Apr-Oct daily, 0830-1800; Nov-Mar daily 0900-1700.

History

The town's history begins with the Vikings who established a settlement in the early 10th century close to where Reginald's Tower now stands. Vadrafjord, as they named it, prospered undisturbed until the King of Leinster, Diarmit Mac Murchadha, called upon his Welsh Anglo-Norman allies to help him take the town. Led by Strongbow, Waterford fell in 1170 and the significance of this Norman-Irish alliance was cemented by Strongbow's marriage to MacMurrough's daughter. Henry II arrived the following year to claim the town for himself, putting his Welsh barons in their place, and then this English power was further reinforced by King John, who turned up in 1210. Between them, John and Henry had firmly established the city of Waterford as a Norman town; it became the unofficial capital of Ireland and flourished as a European port well into the 16th and 17th centuries.

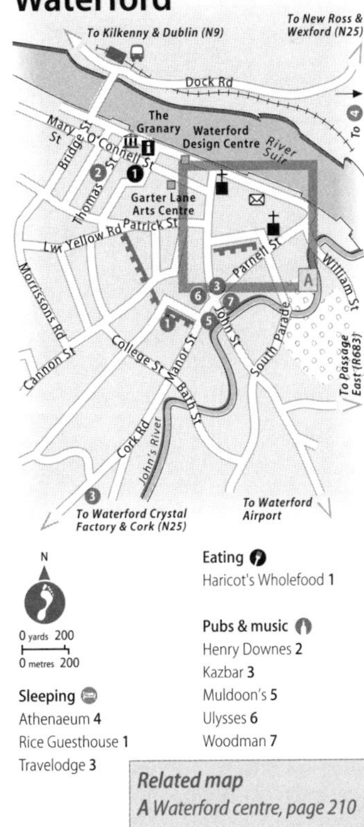

Related map
A Waterford centre, page 210

The Newfoundland Connection

It was around 1650 that fishermen from southeast Ireland first began crossing the Atlantic on a regular seasonal basis to take advantage of the lucrative fishing grounds off the coast of Newfoundland. This seasonal migration continued throughout the 18th century, and from around 1800 families from Waterford and its hinterland began to settle on a permanent basis in that part of North America. By 1830 an estimated 30,000 people, the vast majority from the county of Waterford, had emigrated and begun to make their cultural presence felt. Linguistic studies have shown that, until very recently at least, echoes of this unique wave of Irish immigration could literally be heard in the language of the communities where they settled.

Cromwell failed to take the city in 1649, but it fell to his son-in-law General Ireton the following year. Although this led to a Protestant elite, Catholic interests were not erased, and between 1750 and 1850 Catholic merchants rose to prominence as food exporters. Religious sectarianism seems not to have blighted the city and this helps explain why Waterford was one of the few places that did not register a victory for Sinn Féin in the historic 1918 general election.

Sights

Waterford Treasures at The Granary ⓘ *The Granary, The Quay, T051-304500, www.waterford-treasures.com. Apr-Sep daily 0900-1800; Oct-Mar Mon-Fri 1000-1700, Sat and Sun 1100-1700. €6. Multi-lingual handsets for self-guided tours and regular guided tours at 1030 and 1500. A City Pass ticket for €8.90 saves a few euros if visiting The Granary, Waterford Crystal and Reginald's Tower.* This is a kosher museum, bringing to life the 1,000-year history of the city with exhibits that include, on the third floor, an 11th-century pestle, a 12th-century ring mould for manufacturing finger rings for the merchants and a 12th-century gaming board for the Viking game of *hnefataf*. The second floor covers Cromwell, the 19th century and Waterford crystal. There are also exhibits and information on T F Meagher (see box, page 211).

A 1-hr walking tour covers the main sites and meets daily, Mar-Oct, at the Granary/Tourist Office at 1145 and 1345, T051-873711. €5.

Reginald's Tower ⓘ *Parade Quay, T051-304220. Jun-Sep daily 1000-1800; Easter-May daily 1000-1800; Oct daily 1000-1700; Nov-Easter Wed-Sun 1000-1700. €2. OPW site.* Possibly the oldest civic building in Ireland, this late 12th- early 13th-century pepper-pot tower built by the Normans stands on the site of a Viking tower that was built in the early 11th century. The upper floors date from the 15th century. Despite the busy flow of city traffic past it, the tower remains as solid and unyielding as it did in 1495 when it was subjected to the first artillery siege in Ireland. It now houses a collection of artefacts and material relating to the history of the city.

The Mall and the City Walls The Mall, a broad street built in the 18th century, contains a number of fine buildings, and pride of place goes to the 1783 **City Hall**, built as a meeting hall for merchants and reflecting their self-confidence in its stately proportions. Continue into Parnell Street, and a little way past the junction with John Street the road meets remnants of the **medieval city walls** and their towers. Turn right to follow a well-preserved section of the line of the wall that formed the western side of the old city.

 Churches The Waterford designer John Roberts was responsible for both the Protestant and Catholic cathedrals here, but they are quite different in their style and mood. The Protestant **Christ Church Cathedral** ⓘ *Bailey's New St, T051-858958, Easter-Oct, Mon-Sat 1000-1700; Sun 1130-1700, €3*, rebuilt in the 1770s, has the cool reticence of Georgian architecture, and the removal of furnishings in the 19th century created a sense of space that allows one to appreciate its elegant proportions. Look for the fine stucco ceiling and the gory *memento mori*: a tomb of a 15th-century mayor. A 45-minute audio-visual show relates the cathedral's history.

The Catholic 1793 **Holy Trinity Cathedral** ⓘ *Barronstrand St, free*, modified in the 19th century, is by contrast a monument to ornateness, with a multitude of Corinthian columns, opulent Waterford glass chandeliers and a carved oak pulpit. Though the tourist literature describes the place as "warm, luscious and Mediterranean", this may not be everyone's response.

St Patrick's, a small but interesting Catholic church off Great George's Street, was built in the mid-18th century with funds from Irish merchants in Spain and remains substantially unaltered. Revisionist historians would pounce on the fact that it remained in use throughout Penal times.

Municipal Art Gallery ⓘ *Greyfriars, T051-860856. Wed-Fri 1000-1700, Sat and Sun 1100-1600. Free.* The gallery mounts temporary art exhibitions, including some prize-winning Irish artists from the council's collection of over 300 paintings.

Waterford crystal ⓘ *T051-332500. The Visitor Centre is 3 km out of town on the N25 to Cork. Factory tours Mar-Oct daily 0830-1615 (last tour); Nov-Dec daily 0900-1700,*

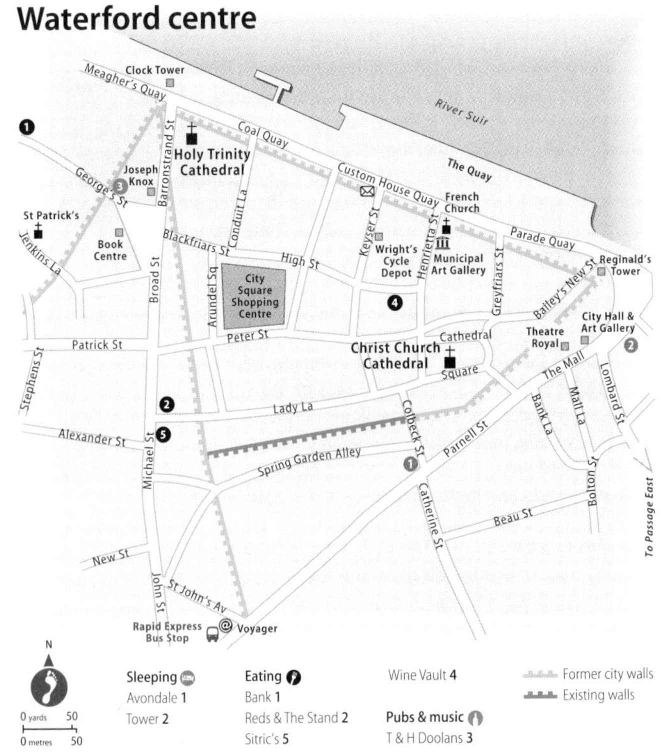

Meagher of the Sword

Thomas Francis Meagher (1823-1867) was born in what is now the Granville Hotel in Waterford. He became a member of the Young Ireland movement, a romantic nationalist group of the 1840s, and his disagreement with the more cautious approach of Daniel O'Connell earned him the epithet 'Meagher of the Sword'. He was transported to Tasmania for his involvement in the abortive 1848 rebellion but managed to escape in 1852 to New York where he became a journalist. During the American Civil War he commanded the pro-Union Irish Brigade in Fort Sumter and Fredricksburg. He became a temporary governor of Montana territory in 1866 but died the following year after falling overboard from a Missouri paddle steamer. Meagher is credited with having chosen the Irish national flag.

Jan-Feb Mon-Fri 0900-1515. €7.50, tickets available from the tourist office, free admission to the shop, daily 0830-1800 (slightly shorter hrs in winter). The city's most famous export is its crystal, dating back to 1783 when George and William Penrose opened their first glassmaking factory. The mix of silica sand, potash and litharge (a form of lead) is transformed into a glowing ball of molten crystal before being fashioned by craftsmen and then cut and engraved into intricate patterns. Tours of the factory are popular and there is also an audio-visual presentation, a restaurant, and a gallery with a comprehensive display of items for sale.

Waterford coast

The Waterford coast has a number of sandy beaches, and is perfect for watersports and exhilarating coastal walks. There are good bus connections to Waterford city in the summer season, but a bicycle is the best way to reach and explore lesser-known spots. Both Dunmore East and Tramore are possible day trips from Waterford. ▸▸ *For Sleeping, Eating and other listings, see pages 215-219.*

Dunmore East → *Phone code: 051. Colour map 4, grid C1.*

Dunmore East is not as picturesque as the tourist literature suggests. Thatched cottages and a winding main street give the appearance of a quaint old-fashioned village but this is a fairly affluent area and the big old houses that were built for British merchants are now owned by well-heeled Irish families, the herring boats of the 1960s replaced by ocean-going yachts. There are two **beaches**: one is in the village itself while Counsellor's Strand, a Blue Flag beach, is near the golf course and has a car park above it. The large colony of seabirds nesting in the cliffs are kittiwakes.

Tramore → *Phone code: 051. Colour map 4, grid C1.*

Tramore deserves its name (*Trá Mhór* meaning 'big strand') and the 5-km beach has turned the place into one of Ireland's most popular holiday resorts. This inevitably means amusement arcades, fast-food joints and family-orientated attractions, but there is also the signposted 8-km **Doneraile Walk**, which starts at the tourist office, Turbey Road, T051-381572, as well as opportunities for water sports.

Tramore to Dungarvan → *It is 41 km between Tramore and Dungarvan.*

The R675 stays inland west of Tramore before dropping down to the village of **Annestown**, where the beach is popular with surfers and is safe for swimming. A short

Women of Dungarvan

Two stories about Dungarvan bear testimony to the seductiveness of its womenfolk. In 1649 Cromwell was about to wreak his usual bout of wanton violence on the place when his eye was drawn to a woman apparently drinking his good health at the town walls. Charmed and disarmed, he desisted. Given Cromwell's penchant for slaughtering the Irish this seems remarkable, but there is another story that lends credence to the allure of the town's females. Before a bridge was built over the River Colligan there was a crossing point where the water was shallow and it was known as 'Dungarvan's Prospects' because men couldn't resist ogling when local women raised their skirts to negotiate the crossing.

way before Bunmahon, **Waterford Woodcraft** ⓘ *T051-396110*, sells items sculptured from Irish timbers and stays open until 2100. **Bunmahon** has its own Blue Flag beach, which can be reached on foot from the village though it also has its own car park.

The beach at **Stradbally** is sandy and suitable for families. The village also has a Protestant church with an interesting old churchyard which includes an early 17th-century tombstone with an incised skull and crossbones.

Clonea Strand is a Blue Flag beach that fits snugly into the coastline and further west there is another surfing beach at **Ballinacourty**.

Dungarvan → *Phone code: 058. Colour map 3, grid B6.*

The origins of the town go back to Anglo-Norman times, but it was in the early 19th century that the Duke of Devonshire established the grid design of streets around the generous space of Grattan Square. The town is a humdrum kind of place but it suggests itself as a possible base for trips to the Comeragh mountains, the Irish-speaking Ring Peninsula or the Ardmore beaches. The well-resourced and helpful **tourist office** at The Courthouse, Meagher St, T058-41741, dispenses a town map and inexpensive local walks sheets, with trails lasting from 45 minutes to three hours. Open May-Sep Mon-Sat 1000-1800; Oct-Apr Mon-Fri 1000-1700. There is a small museum of local history: **Dungarvan Museum** ⓘ *Augustine St, T058-45960, Jun-Aug Sat 1000-1645. Free.*

An Rinn (Ring) → *Phone code: 058.*

An Rinn, 12 km south of Dungarvan, is a little oasis of Gaelic culture and famous for its language school. Follow the Cork road out of Dungarvan, and take the signposted left turning on to the R674. Shortly afterwards there is another left turning, signposted for An Cuinigear, that leads to a sand and shingle beach and a 5-km finger of land that stretches into Dungarvan Bay. It makes for a pleasant stroll and there are bird-spotting opportunities along the way. Back on the R674, the road leads to Ceann Heilbhic (Helvic Head) and along the way there is a sign for **Criostal na Rinne** ⓘ *T058-46174, www.criostal.com*, a workshop producing and selling crystal giftware.

Ardmore → *Phone code: 024. Colour map 3, grid B6.*

A popular seaside resort with four very lovely beaches to choose from, Ardmore is surprisingly picturesque and with a history to boot which claims that St Declan established the first Christian settlement in Ireland here. The **tourist office**, at the seafront car park, T024-94444, May-Sep Mon-Fri 1100-1600, has a free leaflet describing an undemanding 4-km circular **cliff walk** that begins just beyond the Cliff House Hotel and close by St Declan's Well.

Built on the site of the saint's original monastery, **St Declan's Cathedral** dates back to 1203, with parts of the walls and the east gable dating from the 14th century. The chancel, however, is formed from parts of an older church, probably from the ninth century. It is the west gable, however, that you should look out for – it carries Romanesque sculptures depicting biblical scenes that, though badly eroded in places, can still be discerned. Try to make out Michael the Archangel weighing souls, Adam and Eve, the Judgement of Solomon and the Adoration of the Magi.

Two Ogham stones have been placed inside the church, one of which carries the longest known Ogham inscription in Ireland. The 12th-century **tower**, just under 29.5 m, is in good condition. There is a small oratory said to contain the grave of the saint.

St Declan's Way This is a 94-km walk that is based upon an ancient pilgrim's route that connected the churches of Ardmore and Cashel. The tourist office in Ardmore sells a map guide covering the route in a series of strip maps, and while the Ordnance Survey 1:50,000 maps (the same scale as the strip map guide) would be a very useful addition, you would need four of them – Nos 66, 74, 81 and 82 – to cover the whole Way. Generally speaking, the walk is not especially difficult and the only part that is critically dependent on good weather is the way through the Bearna Cloch an Bhuidéal pass in the Knockmealdown mountains.

Lismore and around

→ *Phone code: 058. Colour map 3, grid B6.*

Perhaps it was Lismore's charming location, on the River Blackwater with the Knockmealdown Mountains as a backdrop, that appealed to St Carthage in 636 when he chose the place for a monastic school. It developed into a major European seat of learning and despite being attacked by Vikings on a number of occasions it retained its importance until falling into decline towards the end of the 12th century after the arrival of the English. The rest of the town was laid out in the early 19th century and the tourist office (see Heritage Centre, page 214) dispenses a walking guide leaflet witha tour of the main streets and places of interest (also guided tours for €3.50), chief amongst which is St Carthage's Cathedral. The long-distance St Declan's Way (see above) passes close to Lismore. ⏩ *For Sleeping, Eating and other listings, see pages 216-219.*

Lismore Castle and gardens ⓘ *T058-54424, www.lismorecastle.com. Gardens: 14 Apr-Sep daily 1345-1645. €5.* Henry II visited Lismore in 1171 to meet with the chiefs of Munster and chose a site for a castle overlooking the river, but it was left to Prince John to start building it in 1185. At the end of the 16th century the castle passed to Walter Raleigh, but he sold it to Richard Boyle, first Earl of Cork, who went on to become the richest man in Ireland. It was Richard Boyle who set about landscaping the countryside around Lismore in the style of an English estate. In 1753 the castle passed to the fourth Duke of Devonshire, though it was the sixth Duke in the 19th century who hired Joseph Paxton to fashion the imposing and dramatic edifice that now towers over the river, incorporating into the structure parts of the earlier castle and monastic remains. During this rebuilding work a 13th-century crozier was found hidden in the walls and this famous Lismore Crozier can now be seen on display in the National Museum in Dublin. Also hidden, presumably during the Reformation years, was a 15th-century book recounting the lives of saints, along with an Irish translation of Marco Polo's travels.

Lismore Castle remains the private property of the Devonshires and is not open to the public. Hoi polloi can enter the **gardens**, however, and there are fine views of the castle from here as well as from the Ballyduff road. The lower level, planted with peat from the Knockmealdown Mountains, is rich with rhododendrons and magnolias – and modern sculptures including a work by Antony Gormley – while the formal upper level still has an Elizabethan layout.

The sceptical chemist

Robert Boyle (1627-1691), the son of the first Earl of Cork, was born in Lismore castle and educated at Eton. He returned to Ireland in 1652 for a couple of years but lived most of his life in England. He is famous for formulating the principle that the pressure of a gas varies with its volume at a constant temperature – Boyle's Law. Although a deeply religious man, he played an important part in debunking pseudo- scientific, scholastic explanations for the physical world. His best-known work in this respect is *The Sceptical Chymist*, published in 1661.

Lismore Heritage Centre ⓘ *T058-54975. Heritage centre and adjoining tourist office open all year, daily 0930-1800, but closed on Sun between Nov and the end of Feb.* In the old courthouse, along with the **tourist office**, the Lismore Heritage Centre offers an introduction to the history of the town through a multimedia presentation in the guise of Brother Declan, a follower of St Carthage.

Cappoquin

This small town, to the west of Lismore, is a renowned centre for both coarse and game angling and **Tight Lines Tackle Shop** ⓘ *Main St, T058-54152*, is the place to visit for information and tackle. But fishing aside, the countryside around Cappoquin is delightful and at the town the River Blackwater makes an audacious 90-degree turn to the south for its descent into Youghal Bay. In the centre of town, an 18th-century Georgian mansion was built on the site of an old castle that commanded the river at this point. **Cappoquin House and gardens** ⓘ *T058-54004, Apr-Jul Mon-Sat 0900-1300, €3.50*, offer a superb view of the Blackwater. The gardens are mostly informal and boast a magnificent rhododendron arboretum, with some interesting architectural plants dotted around the place.

Glenshelane Forest Tourist Park ⓘ *T058-52132.* Close to Cappoquin is the Glenshelane Forest Tourist Park. There are 12 km of riverside walks. Accommodation is in three-bedroomed self-catering log cabins, and camping is also possible. The recommended walk is the one that brings you close to **Mount Melleray** ⓘ *T058-54404*, a Cistercian abbey about 6 km north of Cappoquin. The Cistercian order was finished off in Ireland during the Reformation but was re-established in 1832 when a dozen or so monks came here and developed a community that numbered around 140 in the 1950s. Numbers are once again in serious decline, but visitors who wish to visit the abbey for peaceful contemplation can stay in the **guest house** on the grounds.

★ Walking the Knockmealdowns → *See also Activities and tours page 219.*

Lismore is an excellent base for a one- or two-day walk across the wild and amazing scenery of the Knockmealdown Mountains. The route is fairly simple since it forms part of the waymarked **Blackwater Way** but to get to the walk from Lismore, you need transport for about 12 km to the **Vee Gap** (there is no public transport but ask at your accommodation about a taxi there or consider hitching). The Vee Gap is a beauty spot on the R668 road to Clogheen and you could begin in Clogheen and follow the Blackwater Way from there to the Vee Gap. Once there, you are in the middle of the Knockmealdowns, the Blackwater Way stretching off to the west over Knockolugga, through some very rugged land with glorious views of the surrounding countryside. To the east the waymarked route, through forest at quite a low level, is less interesting.

At the Vee there is a **Bianconi hut**, used in the last century for changing horses for the big carriages that once travelled across the mountain road (see page 224). From

Chatterbook

In the course of some interior decoration on the castle in 1814, a box of 15th-century manuscripts secretly recessed behind a wall came to light. Known as the *Book of Lismore*, the texts contain both sacred and secular tales including one about three sinners who retreat into a vow of silence. After the first year one of them comments on the wisdom of their deed; after the second year another voices his agreement; after the third year the last one complains that he is sick and tired of their chatter and contemplates a return to the world.

here you will see paths and waymarkers threading the way uphill to the west. The route is quite challenging to begin with, as it makes its way over rocky tumbled stones, but it then meets a forestry road for a while before climbing above the young trees. As you climb **Knockolugga** the path is merely a series of markers and sheep tracks, so choose a clear day or you could lose your way uphill. At the top spend a little time just taking in where you are and what you can see: on a windy, sunny day it is truly exhilarating.

A wide tumbled road takes you west and downhill past some strange objects – an abandoned car nowhere near where it could possibly have been driven to, pieces of corrugated iron roofing which must have been carried by the winds since there are no buildings for miles around. At the bottom of the hill you travel briefly along a tiny road and then head off west again up **Crow Hill**, with wide, worn footpaths that bring you down eventually to farmland and minor roads to **Carran Hill. Araglin** is a couple of miles to the south.

At Carran Hill there is a B&B (see page 217) or walk on to the road junction known as **Mountain Barracks** from where the you could be picked up if staying at the walker-friendly B&B at Creamery View (see page 217). The next day, the walk to Fermoy (B&B T025-31704) is very manageable.

Mapping and information It's about 15 km from the Vee Gap to Araglin, while to Mountain Barracks is a much stiffer 35 km. Even though the walk is well provided with waymarkers, it would be useful to have the OS Discovery series map 74 or the Blackwater Way Map Guide published by EastWest Mapping (see page 52).

Sleeping

Waterford *p208, maps p208 and p210*

A-B **Tower Hotel**, The Mall, T051-875801, www.towerhotelwaterford.com. Elegant and European, a smartly-styled hotel with good food options and 20 m swimming pool.

A-D **Athenaeum Hotel**, Ferrybank, T051-833999, info@athenauemhousehotel.com. Good *feng shui* across the river in a hotel built around the shell of a fine Georgian dwelling and merging classicism with contemporary colours and clean, cool lines.

D **Avondale**, 2 Parnell St, T051-852267, www.staywithus.net. Quality B&B in the centre of the city where there is no supplement for singles.

D-E **Rice Guesthouse**, centrally located, modern guest house with a bar on the ground level.

E **Travelodge**, on the N25 road to Cork, T1800-709709, www.travelodge.ie. A motel with rooms sleeping up to 3 adults and 1 child. Lots of other B&Bs along the Cork Rd.

Dunmore East *p211*

B-C **Haven Hotel**, Harbour Rd, T051-383150, www.thehavenhotel.com. Built as a family home for a shipping magnate, this family-friendly hotel has a decent restaurant and attracts holidaymakers.

E Carraig Liath, Harbour Rd, T051-383273. A large house in the centre of the village and overlooking the harbour, with 4 rooms. Open Apr-Oct.

E Church Villa, T051-383390, churchvilla@eircom.net. A comfortable Victorian townhouse, close to the Protestant church, and open all year.

Tramore *p211*

B-D O'Shea's, T051-381246, www.osheas-hotel.com. Sociable hotel, bar and restaurant with nightly entertainment in the summer.

C Majestic Hotel, T051-381761, www.majestic-hotel.ie. Popular with Irish holiday-makers. Guests have use of a nearby leisure centre.

E Cliff House, Cliff Rd, T051-381497, www.cliffhouse.ie. B&Bs line Cliff Rd and this is one of the better ones.

Camping

Fitzmaurice's Caravan Park, T051-381968. Has only a few pitches for tents.

Newtown Cove Caravan and Camping Park, T051-381121. Open early Apr to early Oct. Take the R675 coast road to Dungarvan and take the left turn opposite the golf course 1 km from the town. Superior to Fitzmaurice's.

Tramore to Dungarvan *p211*

B-C Clonea Strand Hotel, Clonea, T058-45555, www.clonea.com. Virtually on the sandy beach 6.5 km east of Dungarvan. It has the usual leisure centre facilities and the distinction of being Ireland's only hotel to boast a tenpin bowling complex.

C Annestown House, Annestown, T051-396160. Overlooking the sea and boasts a billiard room. Evening meals available.

E Park House, Stradbally, T051-293185. Has 4 rooms, most of which share bathroom facilities.

Dungarvan *p212*

C-D Powersfield House, T058-45594, www.powersfield.com. The most comfortable accommodation in the area, on the R672 just outside of town.

E Rose Bank House, Coast Rd, T058-41561, www.rosebankhouse.com. Nearly 2 km outside town on the R675 Clonea road, this pleasant little B&B has a varied breakfast menu – the soda bread is delicious – and large gardens.

F Dungarvan Holiday Hostel, Youghal Rd, T058-44340, www.dungarvanhostel.com. Opposite the police station; dorms and private rooms, occasional coach-party groups.

Camping

Bayview Caravan and Camping Park, Coast Rd, Ballinacourty, T058-45345. Open Easter-Sep but only space for about 6 tents.

Casey's Caravan and Camping Park, Clonea, T058-41919. Far larger and open May to early Sep, and has direct access to the beach. No pre-booking from Jul-15 Aug.

Ardmore *p212*

D Round Tower Hotel, T024-94494, rth@tinet.ie. Only 10 bedrooms but with a bar and reasonably priced restaurant.

E Byron Lodge, T024-94157. A fine Georgian house at the end of town, overlooking the beach. Open Apr-Oct.

E Newtown Farm Guesthouse, Grange, T024-94143, www.newtownfarm.com. A guest house on a working farm some 6.5 km from Ardmore on the N25, with sea views, well-provided rooms, lounge, tennis court and good food.

F Ardmore Beach Hostel, Main St, T024- 94501. Has over 20 beds and some private rooms.

Lismore and around *p213*

L-B Richmond House, Cappoquin, T058-54278, www.richmondhouse.net. An 18th-century country house full of charm offering accommodation and a very fine restaurant open to non-residents.

C Ballyrafter House Hotel, T058-54002. Built in the 1880s as part of the Devonshire estate, the hotel offers fine country-house accommodation, and game fishing enthusiasts are particularly well catered for. The atmosphere is genuinely laid back, there's nothing pretentious in the air of this welcoming house.

For an explanation of the sleeping and eating price codes used in this guide, see inside the front cover. Other relevant information is found in Essentials pages 39-45.

C-D Lismore Hotel, T058-54555. Built as a lodge for the Devonshires, this lovely old house in the centre of town has big, old-fashioned rooms.
E Barnahoun Farm, T058-50007, Carran Hill. Offers B&B in roooms with en suite bath and will provide packed lunches for the next day's walk. Accommodation also available at **Buggy's Glencairn Inn** (see Eating below).
E Beechcroft, Deerpark Rd, Lismore, T058-54273. A bungalow on the outskirts of town and also offers self-catering accommodation.
F Mrs Norah Fennessy, Creamery View, near Araglin, T058-50077. A welcoming B&B, with one double and one single not en suite, that will pick up walkers from Mountain Barracks and provide a good value evening meal.

Eating

Waterford *p208, maps p208 and p210*
TTT-TT Reds, 45 Michael St, T051-820022. Good steak and fish dishes above The Stand pub (which also does food).
TTT-TT Zaks, Athenaeum Hotel, Ferrybank, T051-833999. Requires transport from town but makes for a genteel evening out.
T The Bank, 30 O'Connell St, T051-872170. Closes at 1800, good value salads, panini, bagels, wraps.
T Haricots Wholefood Restaurant, 11 O'Connell St, T051-841299. Is showing its age but lots of cakes and meals like spinach and mushroom pancake with salad for €9.50.
T Sitric's, 41 Michael St. Good coffees, gourmet burgers and all-day breakfast. Closed Sun.
T The Wine Vault, High St, T051-853444. Fine for lunch or dinner and a good value early-bird menu from 1730.

Dunmore East *p211*
TT-T The Ship, T051-383141. A bar and restaurant overlooking the harbour, the best place for a seafood meal.
T Power's. The locals' local and definitely worth a visit.
T The Strand Inn, T051-383174. Has a picturesque spot by the water's edge and there are a few outdoor tables.

Tramore *p211*
The hotels all serve bar food and have their own restaurants.
TT Coast Restaurant, T051-393646, on Upper Branch Rd. For a posher night out.
T Rockett's The Metal Man, T051-381496. Worth seeking out at the west side of the beach. Has been serving crubeens (pig's trotters) for well over 50 years; or try the bacon ribs with colcannon at this gem of a sociable pub. From €10 per person. Closed Mon.

Dungarvan *p212*
If spending time in west Waterford, pick up the free food guide from the tourist office.
TTT Powersfield House (see above) has a restaurant Thu-Sat evenings. A reservation is advisable in the summer.
TT The Tannery, 10 Quay St, T058-45420. Undoubtedly the most interesting place to eat, with delicious salads, innovative fish dishes, good value lunches and an early dinner around €25.

An Rinn (Ring)
T The Marine Bar and Restaurant, Pulla, T058-46520. A traditional Irish pub with Irish music every night in the summer. Bar food served daily.

Ardmore *p212*
There are a couple of tourist-friendly restaurants and pubs along Main St serving standard meals.
TT White Horses Restaurant, on the main street, T024-94040. Consider this for something more interesting, fine for snacks and lunches during the day while at night the menu offers imaginative dishes that include above-average vegetarian choices.

Lismore and around *p213*
TTT Ballyrafter House Hotel, T058-54002. The restaurant here has a menu that changes nightly. Fresh salmon from the Blackwater is one of the specialities. Sun lunch is very popular.
TTT Richmond House, Cappoquin, T058-54278. Traditional country-house cooking with touches of more adventurous cuisine and pukka vegetarian options.
TT Buggy's Glencairn Inn, Glencairn, T058-56232, www.lismore.com. A couple of miles outside Lismore and has acquired a reputation for mighty good food. The bar itself is tiny and space is at a premium in the

dining room too, so booking is essential. Open 1930-2100 but not on Mon or Tue outside of summer.

🍴🍴 **Lismore Hotel**, T058-54555. Dinner is recommended here and the hotel bar also does good food.

🍴 **Eamonn's Place**. A pub serving generous portions of dishes like lamb's liver and bacon casserole and lovely puddings.

Pubs and music

Waterford *p208, maps p208 and p210*
Pick up a copy of *Whazon?* from the tourist office for the current music and entertainment scene. www.whazon.com.

T&H Doolans, George's St, T051-841504. Is justly famous for its traditional Irish music sessions, and proud of the fact that Sinéad O'Connor began her career here.

Henry Downes, 10 Thomas St. Worth squirrelling out, it has been in the same family since the late 18th century, and the proprietors blend their own whiskey, Downes No 9.

John St has a number of pubs popular with the young, including: **Muldoon's**, T051-873693, with live music. Best of all are **The Kazbar**, T051-843729, **Ulysses** and **The Woodman**.

Dungarvan *p212*
Anchor, down by the quay.

Bean a'Leanna, worth checking out at the weekends.

Marine Bar, recommended for Irish music, Thu-Mon in summer and Sat and Mon Oct-Apr.

Lismore *p213*
O'Brien's, Main St, T058-54816. A delightful, quiet place for a pint.

Entertainment

Waterford *p208, maps p208 and p210*
Garter Lane Arts Centre, 22a O'Connell St, T051-855038, www.garterlanewaterford.com. Has a rich programme of music, theatre, film, exhibitions, workshops and talks.

Festivals and events

Waterford *p208, maps p208 and p210*
Spraoi, www.spraoi.com, is a street festival at the **end of Jul**. From around **late Sep until early Oct** there is the Waterford International Festival of Light Opera. Contact Theatre Royal, The Mall, T051-874422, www.waterfordfestival.com.

Dungarvan *p212*
The **Féile na nDéise** is a traditional music festival that enlivens the town over the bank holiday weekend, early in **May**. The sessions of live music are spread around the various pubs and for further information contact the tourist office.

Shopping

Waterford *p208, maps p208 and p210*
City Square Shopping Centre, modern and is packed with consumer outlets, 2 department stores and fast food places.

The Granary/Tourist office, has a shop area selling gifts, jewellery, and the useful *Discover Waterford* by Eamon McEneaney (O'Brien Press).

Joseph Knox, 3 Barronstrand St, T051-875307. Centrally located and stocks Waterford crystal, Donegal china, Belleek pottery and the like.

Activities and tours

Dunmore East *p211*
Dunmore East Adventure Centre, T051-383783. Offers water- and land-based sports and summer camps for children aged 10-17 in Jun-Aug.

Angling Very popular and daily or weekly charters can be arranged.

Sea Angling Charters, Pelorus, Fairybush, Dunmore East, T051-383397.

South East Charters, Dunmore East, T051-389242.

Tramore *p211*
Family attractions **Splashworld**, T051-390176. For water-based fun.

For an explanation of the sleeping and eating price codes used in this guide, see inside the front cover. Other relevant information is found in Essentials pages 39-45.

Horse racing **Waterford and Tramore Racecourse**, at Tramore, T051-421861. Has occasional fixtures in Jan, Mar and Nov, but the main 4-day event is in mid-Aug.

Surfing **Tramore Surf Club**, at the end of the promenade, T051-386022. Has facilities for watersports and surfing lessons.

Knockmealdown Mountains
Mountain Craft, T058-47509, mountaincraft @hotmail.com. For organized walks.

Transport

Waterford County *p208*
Airport Waterford Airport, Killowen, T051-875589, 7 km south of the city, with flights to **Luton** (see page 29).

Bus Bus Éireann, The Quay, Waterford T051-879000, has express services to **Dublin**, **Wexford**, **Rosslare**, **Galway**, **Cork**, **Killarney**, **Tralee**, **Clonmel**, **Enniscorthy** and **Athlone**. Rapid Express Buses, Parnell Ct, Parnell St, Waterford, T051-872149, is a private bus company running several buses daily between Waterford, **Dublin** and **Dublin Airport**. Suirway, T051-382209 (24-hr talking timetable T051-382422), is another private company operating from Waterford to **Dunmore East** and **Passage East**.

The **Rosslare Harbour** to **Tralee** bus goes via **Waterford**, **Dungarvan** and **Cork**.

There are also plenty of buses running daily from **Tramore** to **Waterford** and on Wed and Fri a **Dungarvan** to **Waterford** service stops at Tramore. The **Dublin** to **Dungarvan** service also makes a stop.

A service connects **Dungarvan** with **Cappoquin**, **Lismore**, **Waterford**, **Kilkenny** and **Dublin**. The **Waterford-Ring-Ardmore** bus stops in **Dunvargan** as well and another bus goes along the coast road between **Dungarvan** and **Waterford**. The Waterford to **Mallow** stops at **Dungarvan** (and **Lismore**) and there is also a service between **Clonmel** and **Dungarvan**.

From **Ardmore** there are daily buses to and from **Cork**, via **Youghal** and **Midleton**, and a **Waterford** to Ardmore service, via **Dungarvan** and **Ring**, that does not operate on Sun.

From **Lismore** there is a daily service to **Dublin** via **Waterford**. On Fri and Sun there is a service from **Lismore** to **Waterford** and **Cork** via **Dungarvan** and **Cappoquin**. There is also a daily local bus to **Dungarvan**.

Ferry The Passage East Car Ferry, T051-382480, www.passageferry.com. Provides a useful shortcut between Waterford and **Wexford** by crossing the harbour between Passage East and **Ballyhack** in County Wexford. A continuous service, with first sailing at 0700 (0930 Sun) all year and last sailing at 2000 Oct-Mar; 2200 Apr-Sep. €5.08 single, €7.62 return.

Taxi Rapid Cabs, Waterford, T051-858585.

Train Waterford station, T051-873401, 873402 (24-hr talking timetable T051-876243) serves **Dublin** via **Kilkenny**, **Rosslare** via **Wexford** and **Limerick** via **Carrick-on-Suir**.

Directory

Waterford *p208, maps p208 and p210*
Language schools English Language Centre, 31 Johns Hill, T051-877288, welc@iol.ie. Runs language courses for adult and young learners; individuals and groups. Waterford Language Learning, 9 Leoville, Dunmore Rd, T051-872227. **Medical services** Doctor: Dr Keogh & Partners, 0900-1700, T855411, emergency T051-580935. Hospital: Waterford Regional Hospital, Dunmore Rd, T051-873321.

County Tipperary

Cashel and around → *Phone code: 062. Colour map 3, grid A6.*

The ecclesiastical remains on the stupendous Rock of Cashel consist of a round tower, a 12th-century chapel, a 13th-century cathedral and 15th-century residential buildings. The Rock is conveniently located just off the main Dublin to Cork road, making the market town of Cashel a major stopping-off point for travellers. Tourist information available from the tourist office T062-61333. » *For Sleeping, Eating and other listings, see pages 226-228.*

★ Rock of Cashel

ⓘ *The Rock of Cashel (including Cormac's Chapel), T062-61437. Mid-Mar to early Jun daily 0900-1730; early Jun to mid-Sep daily 0900-1900; mid-Sep to mid Oct daily 0930-1730; mid-Oct to mid Mar daily 0900-1630. €5. OPW site. Guided tours every hour on the half hour in summer (worth joining) and scheduled times for an audio-visual show.*

The Rock, a limestone outcrop that rises 61 m above the plain like the Acropolis of Athens, was the seat of Munster kings from the fourth to the early 12th century, and in 978 Brian Bóruma (Brian Ború) was crowned here. In 1101 the Rock was given to the Church, and Cormac's Chapel was consecrated in 1134 under the auspices of the king and Bishop Cormac McCarthy. The cathedral was built in the following century, on the site of an earlier one, but in 1495 it was set alight by the Earl of Kildare because, as he later humorously explained to the understandably irate Henry VII, he thought the archbishop was inside. The cathedral was plundered in 1647, and its lead roof was removed some time in the 18th century: a consequence of the fact that the archbishop of the time was said to be too lazy to climb the rock and so he took little interest in preserving the building.

The Rock of Cashel is extremely popular with coach tours, and during summer months it is advisable to arrive early in the morning to avoid the crowds; don't say you weren't warned.

Hall of the Vicars Choral This 15th-century building is now the entrance to the Rock and home to the useful video that recounts the history of the site. There is a small museum, the chief exhibit of which is the famed **St Patrick's Cross**. It originally stood outside, where there is now a replica, and tradition states that the cross's plinth was the coronation stone for the inauguration of Irish kings, including Brian Ború.

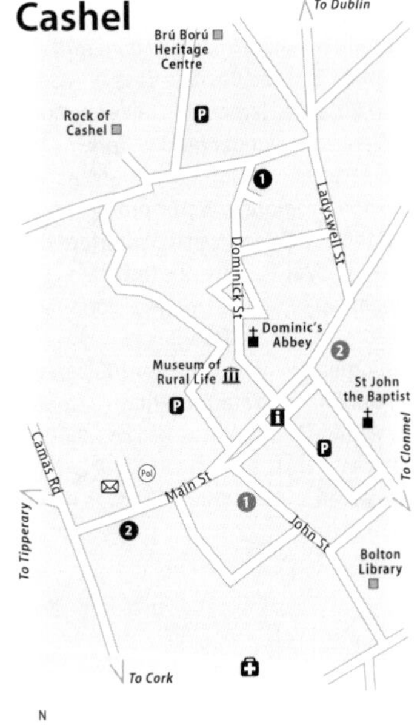

Cormac's Chapel Cormac's Chapel, standing immediately to the south of the cathedral, is the earliest and most elegant Romanesque church in Ireland. Its remarkable steep stone roof, unusual twin square towers instead of transepts, and carved arcading are all noted features of its exterior. Above the north door, which was the main entrance before the cathedral got in the way, there is a lively sculpture of a lion being shot at with a bow and arrow by a helmeted figure that looks like a centaur.

The ribbed, barrel-vaulted nave is wonderfully small, and recent restoration work on the chancel roof has revealed some of the frescos that once were probably a feature of the whole ceiling (Cromwell's troops are said to have whitewashed over them), lending glorious colour to what is now a dark interior. There are many fine sculptures over the archway that leads to the east chancel, and there is also a superb **sarcophagus** that dates back to around the 12th century and is said to be the tomb of King Cormac. Its sophisticated decorative design of interlacing beasts is Ireland's best example of the Urnes style, chiefly recognizable by the intertwining of broad and narrower animals, which came to the country from Scandinavia at the end of the 11th century. Like the design of the square towers, which are thought to hail from Germany, this is another example of how remarkably open to European art Ireland was at this time.

Cathedral What you see today is the shell of a cathedral that was first built in the 13th century but which was restored more than once since. The west side has the addition of a small castle, built as a secure residence for the archbishop early in the 15th century, the main hall of which was spread over the top of the nave; the corbels are still visible. It was also in the 15th century that the central tower of the cathedral was raised to its present position of dominance. The tower reduces the length of the nave, so that the choir is actually longer, and the main attractions inside the church are the high-set lancet windows, classic examples of 13th-century style, and a multitude of memorial tombs. The adjoining round tower is the earliest surviving structure on the Rock and was part of the early Christian enclosure.

Brú Ború ('Palace of Brian Ború') Heritage Centre ⓘ *T062-61122, www.comhaltas.com. Tue-Fri 0900-1930; Sun and Mon 1000-1700.* This centre, with some very naff sculptures outside, stands at the foot of the Rock adjoining the car park. The centre offers a 15-minute audio-visual presentation on cultural history, a restaurant and gift shop. A theatrical show of music and dance takes place here at 2100, costing €15 and with the option of dinner at 1900 for €25.

> ! *If short of time, skip the Brú Ború centre and come here instead.*

★ **Museum of Rural Life** ⓘ *Dominic St, T062-62525. Daily 0930-1930. €3.50.* This is a brilliant museum and more engaging than many of the heritage centres created off the back of government subsidies. To say it is a collection of house fronts, shops, farming implements and memorabilia from the 18th-20th centuries fails to do justice to the sense of history that it evokes. Information on all of the exhibits in half a dozen European languages.

Bolton library ⓘ *T062-61944. Mar-Oct Tue-Sun 0930 (1230 on Sun) -1730; Oct-Feb Mon-Fri 0930-1730. €4.* A specialist museum for connoisseurs of the printed word: the library has manuscripts and maps, some of which date back to the earliest days of printing. Check out the smallest book in the world (a photographic reduction), the ultra-tiny New Testament from the 1860s and two pages from a Caxton's Chaucer.

Tipperary town → *Phone code: 062.*

Is it just nostalgia that makes Tipperary a name that still evokes something imagined about a past Ireland? The town that actually carries the resonant name is a dreary, workaday kind of place that will disappoint visitors seeking something more than the prosaic. A statue to Charles Kickham (1828-1882), Fenian and author of *Knocknagow* (who came from the county, not the town) is proudly ensconced in Main Street. The father of the American playwright Eugene O'Neill came from a farm just outside town. For information on anything that might be happening in the town, call into the **tourist centre** which is on Mitchell St, the road that goes off Main St by the AIB and Bank of Ireland. ⓘ *T062-80520, www.tipperary-excel.com. Daily 0900-1800.*

Cahir → *Phone code: 052.*

Cahir Castle ⓘ *Castle St, T052-41011. Mid-Mar to mid-Jun daily 0930-1730; mid-Jun to mid-Sep daily 0900-1900; mid-Sep to mid-Oct daily 0930-1730; mid-Oct to mid-Mar 0930-1630. €2.75. OPW site.*

Traffic-choked Cahir (pronounced 'care') is home to a massive castle, originally built in 1142 by Conor O'Brien, which later came into the possession of the Anglo-Norman Butler family in 1375. It was the Butlers who built most of what you can see today. After a 10-day siege in 1599, during the Elizabethan Wars, they lost it to the Earl of Essex but it stayed in the Butler family only to be again attacked by English artillery in 1647; the castle was then surrendered to the Parliamentary commander, Lord Inchiquin. Three years later it was surrendered again, this time without a shot being fired, after Cromwell had delivered a terse statement that grimly concluded: "if I be necessitated to bend my cannon upon you, you must expect the extremity usual in such cases"; message understood.

There is an exhibition on the 1599 siege (by the Earl of Essex) of the castle, display panels on Irish castles and on women in Tudor Ireland; all good stuff for a rainy afternoon. You'll get most out of a visit by joining one of the guided tours, available on request and there is a 17-minute video, a portcullis to admire and walls to walk along.

The tourist office is in the car park next to Cahir Castle. T052-41453. Open Apr-Oct Mon-Sat 1000-1800.

Swiss Cottage ⓘ *Kilcommon, T052-41144. Mid-Apr to mid-Oct daily 1000-1800; mid-Mar to mid-Apr and mid-Oct to Nov Tue-Sun 1000-1300 and 1400-1630. €2.75. OPW site. To drive there, take the R670, the road to Ardfinnan, from by the side of the Cahir House Hotel in town.* From the car park at the side of Cahir Castle there is a 2-km path running alongside the river and under horse chestnut trees that leads to Swiss Cottage, a delightful *cottage ornée* built in the early 19th century by Richard Butler but designed by the Regency architect John Nash. An Alpine look is discernible from the outside, hence the nickname it acquired some decades after it was built, but the interior is unique. The elegant spiral staircase is worth admiring and the Dufour wallpaper in the salon that displays the Bosphorus was one of the first commercially produced Parisian wallpapers.

Clonmel → *Phone code: 052. Colour map 3, grid B6.*

The lively town of Clonmel has at least two claims to fame: it is the birthplace of both Laurence Sterne (1713-1768), a novelist whose hilarious style predates post-modernism by a couple of centuries, and author of freewheeling *Tristram Shandy*; and of the Bianconi system of public transport. Another noted resident was the novelist Anthony Trollope, who left his homeland to set up house here in 1848 (the epitome of the style that Sterne so delightfully subverted). The many fine old buildings dotted around Clonmel are a chief attraction of the town and the tourist office, in Sarsfield St, opposite the Clonmel Arms Hotel, T052-22960, www.clonmel.ie, is open all year Mon-Fri 0930-1300 and 1400-1700. It dispenses a Heritage Trail booklet with a useful map.

▸▸ *For Sleeping, Eating and other listings, see pages 227-228.*

A buildings tour

If nothing else, find time to stand before the **Main Guard** ⓘ *at the eastern end of O'Connell Street. Open mid-Mar to end of Oct daily 0930-1800. €2. OPW site.* It is one of the oldest public buildings in Ireland, was built in the 1670s as a courthouse, and recently restored to give some idea of its imposing structure. It was not here, however, that the leaders of the Young Ireland movement were prosecuted for their part in the abject failure of the 1848 rising; by that time the County Courthouse in Nelson Street (see below) had been standing for nearly 50 years. To get there from the Main Guard continue eastwards along Mitchell Street and turn right into Nelson Street after passing Dowd's Lane (and a statue to the '98 rebellion, erected in 1904). It was at the County Courthouse that Thomas Francis Meagher and others were sentenced to transportation to Australia (see box on page 211).

Retrace your steps back up Nelson Street to Parnell Street and **Hearn's Hotel**, where Bianconi started his cart transport system in 1815. Return to the Main Guard and walk down to the western end of O'Connell Street where, facing the Main Guard from this end of the street, is the **West Gate**. It was built in 1831 on the site of an original gate in the medieval walls that once enclosed the town. The Tudor style was being popularly imitated at the time and this shows in the inclusion of machicolated battlements, hardly a necessary feature of town planning in the 1830s, even in Ireland. On the other (west) side of West Gate lies **Irishtown**. This is a name commonly found in towns to designate the living area for the indigenous, non-Anglo-Normans who could work, but not live, inside the town walls. From the West Gate, walk north up Wolf Tone Street, passing **White Memorial Theatre** that was built in the Greek Revival style in 1843 as a Wesleyan Methodist chapel. Continue up to **St Mary's Church**, dating back to 1204 but largely rebuilt in the 19th century and boasting a superb, 25 m ziggurat belltower that was built up on the foundations of an earlier tower. The only remaining section of the **town walls** can be seen nearby, restored and renovated 20 years ago.

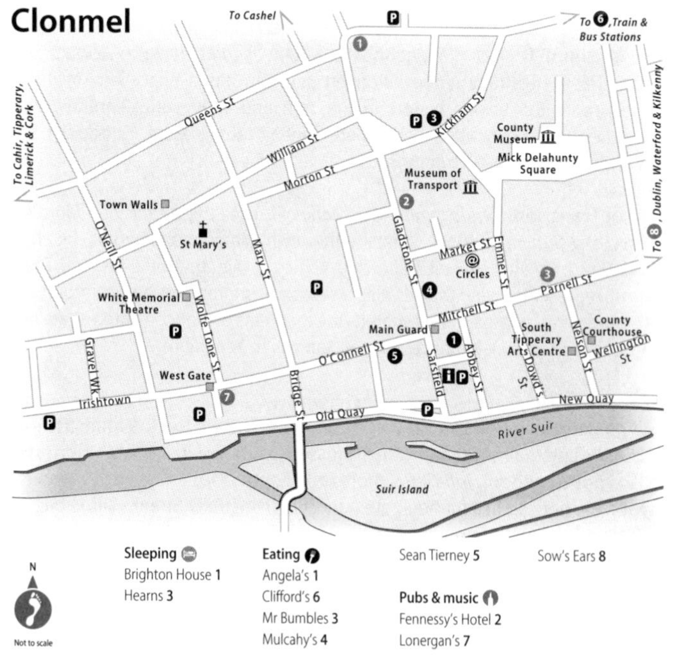

Finn McCools and Massey Dawsons

Charles Bianconi (1786-1875) came to Ireland from Lombardy in 1802 at the age of 16 as a pedlar of prints. He was sent to Ireland to avoid a scandal over his friendship with a local girl who was betrothed to a nobleman. His travels across the country convinced him of the need for a low-cost system of public transport, and in 1815 he started the first service between Clonmel and Cahir using one horse to pull a two-wheeled car with passengers, mail and small freight. Success was instant and, taking advantage of low prices for horses and cars following the end of the long war against Napoleon, he was soon able to upgrade the quality of the service. Stage coaches continued to make long-haul trips out of Dublin and other large cities, but Bianconi's open-topped cars were ideal for inexpensive and shorter journeys between small towns. By the 1840s Bians, as they came to be known, were operating across 3,000 miles of road every day and the largest coaches, called *Finn McCools* and *Massey Dawsons*, could carry up to 20 passengers. For countless thousands of ordinary people, Bians opened up the Irish countryside and made travel affordable in a way that was undreamt of before the Italian began his first service from outside what is now *Hearn's Hotel* on Parnell Street in Clonmel.

County Courthouse ⓘ *Nelson St, T052-22960. Jul-Aug Fri-Sat 2100. €12.* Song, dance and theatre come together at the County Courthouse when some of the county's more famous trials are recreated where they originally took place. Each show includes a presentation of Tipperary's history, and a light snack and local cider feature in the festivities.

Museums

County Museum ⓘ *Mick Delahunty Sq, T052-25399. Tue-Sat 1000-1300, 1400-1700.* This delightfully unreconstructed museum has a miscellany of items relating mostly to the town's history in the 19th and early 20th centuries, and occasional temporary exhibitions of a more sophisticated nature. Check out the anti-de Valera election poster from 1932.

Museum of Transport ⓘ *Richmond Mill, Market Pl, T052-29727. Jun-Aug Mon-Sat 1000-1800, and Sun 1430-1800.* Opposite the town's large supermarket, this has exhibits dating from the earliest motorized vehicles. Jaguar, Mercedes and Rolls Royce are all represented, and there is also a section on motorbikes and memorabilia such as period petrol pumps. Unfortunately, the few items of Bianconi interest are not on show because of a lack of space, but you can ask to see them.

Carrick-on-Suir → *Phone code: 051. Colour map 4, grid C1.*

As towns go Carrick-on-Suir is a dull, workaday kind of place but the attractions of Ormond Castle and the neighbouring high crosses justify a visit. There's a **Heritage centre** ⓘ *T051-640200, Jun-Sep Mon-Sat 1000-1700; Oct-May Mon-Fri 1000-1700, €4,* housed in a former Protestant church off Main Street. This is part of the **tourist office** and contains a collection of photographs, artefacts and documents relating to local history.

Ormond Castle ⓘ *Castle Park, off Castle St, T051-640787. Mid-Jun to early Sep daily 1000-1800. €2.75. OPW site. €2.50, access by guided tour only.* The fact that Ireland was far from being a settled country in the 1560s, when this castle was built, makes this imposing Elizabethan mansion all the more remarkable. Its tranquillity, reflected in the steady repetition of mullioned windows, would not be out of place in Shakespeare's England, but this was a turbulent Ireland at a troubled time. The first castle was built at the beginning of the 14th century, and then in the mid-15th century a larger fortified enclosure was built on this side of the River Suir. A century later Thomas, Earl of Ormond, added a mansion and further sophisticated improvements were to follow. The original motive for the Earl's substantial tarting up of the place was an expected visit by Queen Elizabeth I, and portraits of her are decorated in stucco around the Long Gallery, part of a highly elaborate use of decorative plasterwork. This is the highlight of the castle's interior and the guided tour draws attention to it.

Ahenny high crosses About 5 km north of Carrick-on-Suir, signposted off the R697 road to Windgap, there are two highly decorated and unusual high crosses. Instead of the usual pictorial panels, the main body of each cross is covered with geometric, reticulated patterns of spirals. There are human figures found along the base: on their north sides there is a strange scene of travelling figures, but easier to interpret is the other side that shows Christ and the apostles. The Ahenny crosses make an interesting contrast with those at Monasterboice (see page 137), representing what is probably an earlier and abstract kind of Celtic aesthetic before a more didactic strain of Christianity was imposed on it. By this reasoning, the Ahenny crosses are dated a century earlier than the ninth-century crosses at Monasterboice.

Tipperary Crystal and Blarney Woollen Mills ⓘ *T051-641188. Free guided tours are available mid-Mar to Sep Mon-Thu 0900-1630, Fri 0900-1530.* Waterford crystal may have a more successful marketing history, but there are alternatives and one of them is Tipperary crystal, housed close to the River Suir at Ballynoran on the N24 road between Carrick and Clonmel.

North Tipperary

Attractions in the north of the county are a scattered mix and it is very much a case of catching places of interest as one is travelling through to somewhere else, partly because there is no town or area that can be singled out and recommended as a base for a longer stay and partly because the countryside is very boring, unless you enjoy looking at large farms, their crops and their cattle. Holy Cross Abbey is a good example because while the abbey is definitely worth seeing there is not much to detain you in the nearby town of Thurles 6 km to the north. » *For Sleeping and Eating, see pages 227-228.*

Holy Cross Abbey

ⓘ *On the R660, signposted from Thurles and Cashel.* Benefiting from a new roof some 30 years ago, the Cistercian abbey of Holy Cross exhibits itself proudly as both one of the most accomplished 15th-century churches in the country and a functioning place of parish worship. The foundations go back to the 12th century though most of what stands today was built around 1440-1470, almost certainly a reflection of the increasing popularity of the place with pilgrims, thanks to the abbey's claim to hold a sacred relic from Calvary (hence the abbey's name). In medieval Ireland, Holy Cross surpassed all other places of pilgrimage and the relic was still there when O'Donnell and O'Neill stopped over on their way to Kinsale in 1601, but it hardly brought them much luck. Medieval pilgrims visiting the abbey donated alms for the upkeep of the shrine, and this accumulated

There is a visitor information centre within the abbey complex, a shop selling crafts, and snacks are available as well as drinks.

 wealth was used to finance the costly 15th-century rebuilding programme that used the best craftsmen available.

Aesthetically, the most successful part of this rebuilding programme is the chancel with its delicate ribbed vaulting and an exquisite window on the east side. Here you will also find a superb sedilia, stone seats for the priests, with graceful arches, delicate foliage patterns and finely sculpted with the royal arms of England and the escutcheon of the Earls of Ormond. The transept to the north, left of the nave, is noteworthy because the west wall carries a rare example of medieval wall painting in Ireland. The fresco shows a hunting scene, with the helpless deer seeking refuge on its knees behind a tree. The three original colours are reasonably well preserved.

Roscrea → *Phone code: 0505. Colour map 2, grid C6.*

Roscrea is the most pleasant town in the north of the county, marred unfortunately by having the Dublin to Limerick main road running not just through the town but also right by the side of the remains of the 12th-century **St Crónán's Church**, and a truncated round tower on the other side of the busy road. It is said that the British reduced the tower's height in 1798 after a gun shot at the castle was thought to have been fired from it. **Roscrea Heritage Centre** ⓘ *T0505-21850, mid-Mar to Oct daily 1000-1800; Nov-Dec Fri-Sun 0930-1630, €3.50, guided tours available, OPW site,* consists of a castle and the early 17th-century Damer House. The castle – made up of a gate tower, curtain walls and two corner towers – dates from the late 13th century while Damer House is a fair example of a prototype Palladian architecture. Despite being used as a military barracks at one stage, Damer House retains its original staircase gloriously intact and provides space for temporary exhibitions.

Sleeping

Cashel *p220, map p220*

A **Cashel Palace Hotel**, Main St, T052-62707, www.cashel-palace.ie. Built in 1730 as an archbishop's palace and a distinctive hotel since 1962, with its own walled gardens and a private walk to the Rock. The entrance hall has its original wood panelling and grand staircase and the basement bar displays the names of famous guests, from the sublime to the ridiculous (Robert Mitchum, Charles Bronson, George Best...).

D **Bailey's of Cashel**, Main St, T052-61937, www.baileys-ireland.com. A fondly restored period piece, pre-Georgian, with parking area, restaurant. Some rooms have Rock views.

E **Georgesland**, T052-62788, www.georgesland.net. B&B in a large modern bungalow 1 km outside town, on the Dualla Rd. Has a good reputation.

E **Thornbrook House**, Dualla/Kilkenny Rd, T052-62388, www.thornbrookhouse.com. A ponderosa-style bungalow with some rooms shared bathroom facilities.

F **Cashel Holiday Hostel**, John St, T052-62330, www.cashelhostel.com. A happy place with an airy kitchen. Well-informed about local walks (ask for Karen). B&B is also available through this hostel.

F **O'Brien's Holiday Lodge**, St Patrick's Rock, Dundrum Rd, T052-61003, obriensholidayhostel@eircom.net. A short walk from the town centre, just far enough away to escape the traffic noise. A converted stone stable with excellent views of the Rock. Lots of private rooms. Camping also possible.

Cahir *p222*

B-C **Cahir House Hotel**, The Square, T052-43000, www.cahirhousehotel@eircom.net. This fine Georgian building in the centre of town, home to Lord Cahir's family until 1961, is a very comfortable place to stay and enjoys a pleasant old-fashioned atmosphere.

E **Carrigeen Castle**, Cork Rd, T052-41370, carrigeencastle@yahoo.com. Quite a remarkable sight and one of Ireland's more unusual B&Bs. 1 km outside town.

For an explanation of the sleeping and eating price codes used in this guide, see inside the front cover. Other relevant information is found in Essentials pages 39-45.

E **Silver Acre**, Clonmel Rd, T052-41737. A bungalow in a cul-de-sac offering B&B that has been well spoken of.

F **Lisakyle Hostel**, Church St, T052-41963. Opposite The Craft Granary, on your right, if entering town from Cashel. Dorm beds, 2 private rooms and camping space.

Clonmel *p222, map p223*

D **Brighton House**, Brighton Pl, T052-23665, brighton@iol.ie. A Georgian, family-run guest house not far from the town centre.

D **Hearn's Hotel**, Parnell St, T052-21611. Has changed a bit since Bianconi's days in the 19th century but history clings on to the place and its very lively pub remains a popular meeting place.

E **Kilmaneen Farmhouse**, T052-36231, www.kilmaneen.com. It's a tranquil spot with local walks and dinner available.

Clonmel can be a noisy place. To escape the urban buzz, head out of town on the R665 road to Ardfinnan and follow the Newcastle road from there.

Carrick-on-Suir *p224*

E **The Grand Inn**, 11 km from Carrick on the N76 Clonmel to Kilkenny road, T051-647035. A former coach house inn with antiques to testify to its venerable past.

Roscrea *p226*

D **Grant's Hotel**, Castle St, T0505-23300, www.grantshotel.com. For a meal or an overnight stay, centrally located and serves a carvery lunch and evening meals in its bar. The hotel's restaurant, The Lemon Tree, is for a more formal meal.

Eating

Cashel *p220, map p220*

TTT **The Bishop's Buttery**, Cashel Palace Hotel. Dishes come to your table, appropriately enough, on ecclesiastical-style silver plates. The restaurant has a cellar-like setting enlivened by light colours and, over weekends, the subdued piano playing of popular Irish parlour music. Afternoon tea in the Cashel Palace is a grand affair,

TTT **Ches Hans**, Dominick St, T052-61177. An ex-Wesleyan chapel with a dinner-only, very French menu. Starters like tiger prawns and avocado salad and main courses that include grilled lobster. Closed Sun and Mon. Early-bird menu 1800-1930. 2 courses for €22 or 3 courses for €29.

TT-T **Café Hans**, Dominick St. Conjures up delicious salad lunches, except on Sun and Mon when it's closed.

TT-T **Dowling's**, at the bottom of Main St heading towards Cork, T052-62130. A lovely unreconstructed pub serving homely food and good coffees.

Fehan, next to the tourist office. Is fine for a pub lunch. For picnics, plonk yourself on the Rock and watch the tour buses come and go.

Cahir *p222*

TTT-T **Cahir House Hotel**, the first port of call for food in the town, from a sociable repast in the bar area to the locally-sourced meat dishes in the calm Butler's Pantry restaurant; good value throughout and comfy.

TT **Gannon's**, Pearce St. Has a local reputation and an early-bird, meat-orientated, menu for €25.

T **Galileo Café**, next to The Craft Granary. Good for a light meal.

Or enjoy a picnic by the side of the river walk to Swiss Cottage; there are benches, once you get past the golf course, overlooking the Suir.

Clonmel *p222, map p223*

TT-T **Angela's**, in Abbey St. Has specials posted on a blackboard, lunches like chicken with Thai curry, gourmet sandwiches, some non- meat choices from this popular self-service restaurant that closes at 1730.

TT **Mr Bumbles**, Kickham St, T052-29188. A terrific all-purpose restaurant in the centre of town, open daily. Everything from tea and cakes to slabs of steak and Tipperary lamb, and some interesting starters and desserts. Expect to pay at least €35 for a good dinner, around €12 for something off the lunch menu.

TT **Clifford's**, T052-70677, opposite the railway station on Thomas St. Mixes Irish ingredients with French-style sauces and comes highly recommended for lunch or dinner.

T **Mulcahy's**, on Gladstone St. A pub with restaurant seating and a menu that ranges from pannini to steaks; popular with locals.

T **Sean Tierney**, O'Connell St. A truly vast menu; bar food and restaurant, roomy.

Carrick-on-Suir *p224*

Ó Ceallacháin, the pub opposite the post office. Does soup, salads, potato wedges, roast of the day, home-made burgers, steak and curries (including a vegetarian one) – all at affordable prices.

Cheese Etc, on Bridge St. For picnic supplies.

Pubs and music

Cashel *p220, map p220*

Daverns and **Cantwells**, both on Main St, have traditional music during the week and **Robbie's** has sessions on Sun afternoon.

Cahir *p222*

W.H.Irwin, in the Square. Has traditional music on Thu nights and the bar in the Cahir House Hotel has ballad/modern music from Wed to Fri in the summer.

Clonmel *p222, map p223*

There are a few pubs with music. Try **Lonergan's** on O'Connell St or the **Sow's Ears** or **Fennessy's Hotel**. **Sean Tierney** is worth looking into. It has more exhibits than many a small museum.

Festivals and events

Clonmel *p222, map p223*

South Tipperary Arts Centre, Nelson St, T052-27877. Well worth checking out to see what's on because there is a lively arts scene in south Tipperary and art exhibitions, drama, literature readings, and a writers' festival in **Oct** all take place here.

Shopping

Cahir *p222*

The Craft Granary, can be reached from the castle by crossing the road and following the river a short distance. Sells woodwork, glass, textiles and the like.

Activities and tours

Cashel *p220, map p220*

Larkspur Park, The Green, T052-61626. Provides golf, tennis, badminton and snooker.

Morelli, Canopy St, T052-61151. Dispenses angling information and tackle.

Cahir *p222*

Cuileoga, in the Square, T087-9769309. For angling information and accessories.

Clonmel *p222, map p223*

The internet café in Market St has an adjoining snooker hall.

Swimming pool, Borstal Sq, T052-21972. Also a sauna and gym.

Transport

County Tipperary *p220*

Bike Both hostels in Cashel rent bikes. **OK Sports**, New St, Carrick-on-Suir, T051-640626.

Bus Bus Éireann runs 6 buses a day between **Dublin** and **Cork** via **Cashel** and **Cahir**. In the summer months 4 extra buses run daily between **Cashel** and **Cahir**, and there is also a daily service between **Cork** and **Athlone** that stops at Cashel. Contact **Rafferty's Travel**, 102 Main St, T052-62121, for schedules. **Bernard Kavanagh**, T056-31189, runs a Mon-Fri service between **Dublin** and **Cashel** and another private bus company called **Kavanaghs**, T052-51563, runs a Mon-Fri service between **Clonmel** and **Thurles** via Cashel.

Cahir also has services to and from **Clonmel**, **Carrick-on-Suir** and **Kilkenny**. The **Galway** to **Rosslare Harbour** service also stops in Cahir and connects with **Ennis**, **Limerick**, **Clonmel**, **Carrick-on-Suir**, **Waterford** and **Wexford**.

Clonmel has services to **Cork**, **Dublin**, **Waterford**, **Limerick** and **Kilkenny**.

From **Carrick-on-Suir** there are 3 buses a day to **Dublin** and **Cork** and a service to **Kilkenny**. 4 buses a day also stop on the **Galway** - **Limerick** - **Waterford** - **Rosslare Harbour** route. Local buses go to **Waterford**, **Clonmel** and **Cahir**.

Train A service between **Cork** and **Rosslare Europort** stops twice, Mon-Sat, in **Cahir**, T052-41578. **Clonmel** has a **Dublin** service and is also on the **Rosslare Harbour-Cork** railway line. Once a day, Mon-Sat, and twice daily in the summer, it is possible to travel by train from **Carrick-On-Suir**, T051-40044, to **Waterford** and **Rosslare Europort** and to **Limerick**.

County Limerick

Limerick → *Phone code: 061. Colour map 3, grid A3.*

If you ever wondered what Irish people do when they're not being engagingly disingenuous, playing traditional music or writing some major work of literature, you should spend some time in Limerick city. It's a busy working town with bus queues, crowds of kids coming out of school and bickering and fighting for the bus, loud country music in naff theme pubs, steak houses, hideous out-of-town three-star hotels with highly priced restaurants full of wedding parties, and muzak-driven shopping malls. What is great is that you can disappear into this heaving mass of people getting on with their lives and enjoy the unrenovated Georgian buildings, sit in the park and be glad you're not at work, wander round the Hunt Museum opening the drawers to find the small wonders inside, and visit John's Castle. In a country that is becoming filled to the brim with heritage, Limerick has a down-to-earth quality to it which can be refreshing after time spent in a more touristy spot. » *For Sleeping, Eating and other listings, see pages 234-236.*

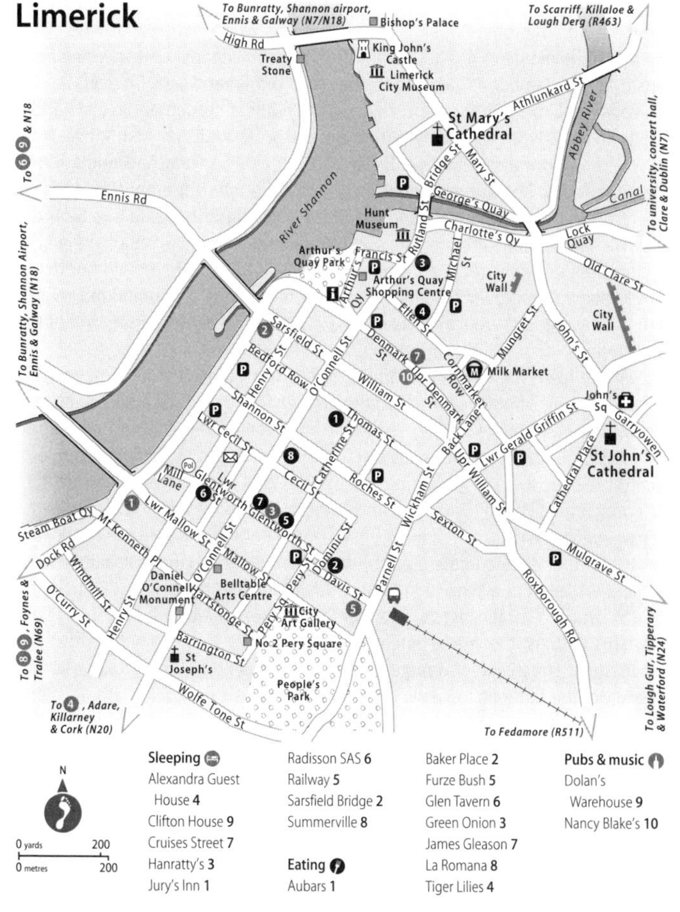

Ins and outs

Getting there Shannon Airport is approximately a 35-min drive away. It has both international and internal flights to Britain, continental Europe and the US, Dublin and Belfast. The bus and train stations are in Parnell Street and have services to most cities and nearby towns. » *See Transport, page 236, for further details.*

Getting around Limerick city centre is a compact area and there is no need to use local buses. Taxis can be found outside the bus and train stations, and off O'Connell Street along Cecil Street and Thomas Street. Driving around the city can be confusing because of the plethora of one-way streets. For parking it is best to follow signs for the tourist office as the Arthur's Quay multi-storey car park is opposite. In summer, though, there is a free car park by the side of the castle.

Information **Limerick tourist office**, Arthur's Quay, T061-317522. Jul-Aug Mon-Fri 0900-1800, Sat-Sun 0930-1730; May, Jun, Sep and Oct Mon-Fri 0930-1730, Sat 0930-1730 (closed 1300-1400); Jan-Apr and Nov-Dec Mon-Fri 0930-1730 (closed 1300-1400), Sat 0930-1300.

History

The very word 'Limerick' conjures up wars, treaties, betrayals, suffering, starvation. Even its most famous writer, Frank McCourt, wrote the most depressing account of the place in his autobiography, *Angela's Ashes*. But it is worth noting that when they came to make the movie of the book, they didn't film in Limerick: there weren't any locations that looked poor enough, so they went to Dublin and Cork instead.

The very first Limerick men were Vikings. They built a settlement in the middle of the river in 922. From here they raided far and wide until the Irish kings, King Mahon of Thomond and his brother Brian Ború, decided they'd had enough and took them on in 967. The armies met at Solohead in County Tipperary and Mahon's troop went on to Limerick and sacked the place. The island became Inis Sibhton, the capital of the O'Briens for 200 years until the Anglo-Norman invasion, when the walled city came under Norman control and Gaelic families were moved out to the area now known as Irishtown. From the 12th-17th century the town remained loyal to the English crown and flourished (there were 15 parish churches by the turn of the 17th century).

In 1642 the town was taken by Catholic forces but suffered little damage. Nine years later Cromwell's troops came through and took the town back again, but it was in 1691 that the real trouble started. As the Jacobite forces lost ground in the north they fell back to Limerick and a great 12-month siege began. A Williamite force of 22,000 attacked the town, but a daring raid behind the Orange lines led by Jacobite military commander Patrick Sarsfield, and the brave defence of the breach in the walls, drove William back. The following year a second attempt was made to take the city, and this time the Jacobites surrendered. The Treaty of Limerick allowed the Jacobite leaders, almost all the ruling native Irish families, to leave for France and promised to protect Catholic rights. Two months later, ironically, a huge French fleet sailed into the estuary, too late to defend the Jacobites.

The Treaty of Limerick led to huge Protestant dismay: they wanted redress and punishment for the Catholic forces and within a few years they got it. Catholic rights were discounted, and by 1695 the Penal Laws gradually wore away at Catholic property, leading to great resentment.

The town recovered from the siege and kept on growing till it had outgrown the city walls and a new area was developed – Newtown Pery, named after the developer – where most of the town's Georgian buildings stand today. After the Act of Union and due to lack of investment, the 19th century saw a period of decline for Limerick that continued well into the 20th century. Nowadays, Limerick is enjoying relative

...it is worth noting that when they came to make the movie of *Angela's Ashes,* they didn't film in Limerick: there weren't any locations that looked poor enough, so they went to Dublin and Cork instead...

prosperity and this goes a long way to explaining the annoyance felt at the way the city is portrayed in *Angela's Ashes*.

English Town

This is the ancient part of the city whose early origins can be seen in the curve of the streets. Not actually in English Town but across the river opposite the cathedral is the treaty stone which Sarsfield is said to have rested the treaty on as he signed it in 1691.

King John's Castle ⓘ *T061-360788. May-Sep daily 0930-1800; Mar, Apr and Oct daily 0930-1700; Jan-Feb and Nov-Dec daily 1000-1630. €6.50.* The castle, which dominates the town, was built in 1210, an Anglo-Norman bastion. Now called King John's Castle it is best viewed from across the river since a daft-looking conservatory has been built over where its east wall once stood. It is five sided, one of them reaching down to the river. The original entrance is at the north side with two round towers and a portcullis between them. In the 18th century a military barracks was built inside the castle and in 1935 a block of council houses went up inside. Conversion to a tourist destination has recovered the basic structure as well as exposing some much earlier buildings below the castle, which can be seen inside.

The castle is great to walk around and the views from the ramparts are literally terrific. The interpretative element isn't too bad – the audio-visual show is a bit high on pathos and the dummies inside the towers are suffering a little from the damp – but the information panels are good. The courtyard has a nice smell of peat and is full of little tents with people demonstrating ancient crafts. You can also watch the ongoing excavations although it's not immediately obvious what is happening.

Limerick City Museum ⓘ *Nicholas St. Tue-Sat 1000-1300 1415-1700. Free.* The museum is next to the castle. It is full of the usual bits and pieces that cities collect over the years, including a 10-shilling note issued by the Limerick Soviet (more of a general strike against British security measures) in April 1919. There is a lot of information on the Lough Gur site (see page 232), as well as some artefacts, so if you intend to visit, this might be a good introduction.

St Mary's Cathedral ⓘ *T061-310293. May-Nov Mon-Sat 0930-1630; Dec-May Sat 0930-1300. Visitors are asked for a donation towards the upkeep of the cathedral.* The cathedral is in a constant state of repair, but even partly dismantled it's a wonderful old building. It is the oldest building in Limerick, built in the late 12th century, although only the west doorway, the nave and parts of the transepts and aisles are original. Most of the chapels are from the 15th century. The main attraction in the cathedral is the misericords, 15th-century carved oak seats that allowed their user to rest while appearing to be standing. They are carved with mythological figures and are labelled for the person who was to occupy them. In the Lady Chapel (dating back to 1997!) the reredos (the ornamental screen behind the altar) was carved in 1907 by Michael Pearse, whose two sons took part in the Easter Rising. In the Chapel of the Holy Spirit, the

 Leper's Squint (which was the original nave of the church) was where people suffering from leprosy could be given communion without infecting the righteous.

Irish Town

This is the place where the Normans sent the native Irish when they adopted the walled city for their own. It developed as an important trading centre and it was given its own set of walls, some of which remain near to **St John's Catholic Cathedral** (1856-1861), not so old as the Church of Ireland one but still quite beautiful and, unlike other Catholic cathedrals in Ireland, without that sense of not quite knowing what it should look like. It was built in the style of Pugin by a London architect, Hardwick, who used light very effectively to create the sense of spirituality that so many modern cathedrals lack. Outside is a statue of Sarsfield.

★ **Hunt Museum** ⓘ *Rutland St, T061-312833, www.huntmuseum.com. Mon-Sat 1000-1700, Sun 1400-1700, €6.50, shop, restaurant.* This has to be the main place of interest in Irish Town: its front is on the river side and is best viewed from the opposite bank. Built by a Sardinian, Davis Duckart, in 1765, it is Palladian with a three-bay pilaster frontispiece creating a sense of grandeur when approached from the river. Inside is the **Hunt Collection**, the most fascinating collection of artefacts of its kind in Ireland. It is only part of the private collection of the Hunts, antique dealers who ducked and dived around Europe until the Second World War, when they found themselves interned in England since Mrs Hunt was German. They offered, and were allowed, to leave for Ireland, which they made their home, first in Howth and then Limerick. They bought and sold antiques from all and sundry, and there were a lot of things going cheap in the 1930s and 40s, and out of the profits built up this amazing collection. In Ireland they took part in the Lough Gur excavations and eventually people just started to bring them things they had turned up while ploughing. In Howth they kept all their antiques lying about the place and there is a photo in the museum of the kitchen with a Picasso hanging next to the stove. It would be fruitless here to point out the most interesting items since the whole place is a wonder. Wander about opening the drawers, but give yourself lots of time and don't miss the Jack Yates paintings.

Pery Square

Built in beautiful Georgian straight lines, these old buildings, like many of those in Dublin, survived because there was no money to redevelop the area in the 1960s. The men who planned this part of the city had great expectations of Limerick's potential and this can be seen in Pery Square, which was to be 49 houses built as a tontine, the last of the original builders to survive to inherit the lot. Only six were built, Pery Square as you see it now, but they are an excellent example of Georgian architecture at its most confident, built in 1839 and symmetrically patterned, the two end houses having gable entrances. **Number 2** ⓘ *T061-314130, Mon-Fri, 1000-1630, €6,* has been restored to form an Ashes Exhibition, based on *Angela's Ashes*.

City Art Gallery ⓘ *Pery Sq, T061-310633. Mon-Fri 1000-1800 (1900 on Thu); Sat 1000-1700, Sun 1400-1700. Free.* Opposite the terrace in Pery Square is the People's Park, originally to have been the private park in the middle of the square but made into a public park in 1874. The gallery-cum-library is at its corner; it was paid for by Andrew Carnegie and built in 1906 in an uneven mixture of Celtic Revival and Arts and Crafts styles. Inside there are paintings by Irish artists from the 18th century to the present, with Jack Yeats and Sean Keatingwell represented. It also hosts temporary exhibitions.

Lough Gur → *Colour map 3, grid A5.*

ⓘ *T061-360788. May-Sep daily 1000-1800. Car parking. Sites (24-hr access) are free but there is a €4.50 entry charge for the interpretive centre. South of Limerick on N24*

Ringforts

Ringforts are the most numerous ancient monument found in Ireland. There are some 45,000 of them, dating from the early Christian period around 600-900, but their distribution is unevenly spread. Donegal, Kildare and Dublin have the lowest density; Roscommon, Sligo and Limerick the highest. One likely explanation is that they were built as a defence against cattle raids and where an area couldn't support many farming communities they were not necessary. Excavations reveal them to be the homesteads of single farming families, although where one ringfort is found there are usually more in the vicinity. Ringforts were first mapped in the mid-19th century, but since then thousands – nearly 40%, it has been estimated – have been destroyed, especially in recent decades, by EU farming subsidies which have encouraged the creation of large fields. Afforestation programmes in upland areas are contributing to this process.

Our knowledge of ringfort culture is supported by contemporary sources, which reveal a hierarchical society based around territorial units, known as tuath, each with a population of around 3,000. At the head of each tuath was a king and filling the next rank down were lords, aire, of varying status. The lowest grade of non-nobles were the bóaire, independent farmers who leased land and paid for it in the form of cattle. There is good reason to believe that the different sizes of ringforts reflected these social and economic ranks.

and then the Kilmallock road, look for sign to Lough Gur. Enquire in advance about walking tours.

One of the most productive and informative Neolithic sites in Europe, Lough Gur doesn't have the grandeur of Newgrange but it is an atmospheric place none the less, and anyone prepared to scramble about a bit and use their imagination can get a good sense of the life of this place 4,000 or more years ago. The lough is shaped like a large horseshoe, and scattered all around it are ringforts, burial chambers, houses, stone circles and middens. You can stop at the interpretative centre and have a look at Grange stone circle or spend the whole day with a map looking for sites. The best compromise is perhaps a walk around the lough, looking at the big sites.

The first site of importance (and the most impressive remains) as you approach the lough from Limerick is the huge **Grange Stone Circle**. It consists of 113 contiguous orthostats, which basically means a lot of big stones. They are bedded into a perfect circle with other stones pegging them into the ground. In the centre, the post hole that men used thousands of years ago to draw the circle with a piece of string was found when the site was excavated. Soil is drawn up around the outside of the stones. An entrance passageway lined with more stones is at the northeast of the circle.

One kilometre further along the road after the stone circle take the left turn marked Lough Gur, then past a 15th-century church ruin to find a wedge tomb. Another 2 km brings you to the car park and interpretative centre which is, for once, a useful addition to the site. From the interpretative centre the next place to head for is **Knockadoon** where there are an enormous number of barely visible remains, including a circular dwelling, and a rectangular stone-age house.

Adare → *Phone code: 061. Colour map 3, grid A3.*

To the south of Limerick Adare was created in the 19th century by the third Earl of Dunraven to house his tenants prettily. Pretty is about the right word too – it's a row of quaint thatched cottages, only a couple of which are actually lived in by anyone. The rest are kitsch antique shops and restaurants catering to the busloads of tourists who are brought in here to be separated from their money. Add on a **heritage centre**, and a manor house converted into an extremely exclusive hotel that you have to pay to get into, and you have a perfect recipe for a naff day out. What is good about the village is the **Augustinian Priory** at the edge on the road to Limerick. It was built in 1325 and is Ireland's most unaltered intact church of that date. It still functions as the Church of Ireland parish church. There is also Ireland's only **Trinitarian Abbey** in the main street, founded in 1230, greatly enlarged in the 19th century and now the Catholic parish church. Surrounded by the golf course is the 15th-century **Franciscan Friary** and an early 13th-century castle, which has been in ruins since the end of the 14th century. It's nice to look at but you can't explore because it's bricked up with warning notices around it. If you don't want to brave the flying golf balls you can just look from the bridge with the tour groups. There is **tourist information** in the heritage centre, Main Street, T061-396666. Daily, 0900-1800 €5.

Sleeping

Limerick City *p229, map p229*
Limerick is a busy commercial centre and en route to most tourist destinations in the south, a fact that is reflected in its accommodation options. Readily accessible for Shannon, there is a raft of hotels and guest houses on the N18 Ennis Rd out of town, taking up great swathes of parking and garden space and some of them are within walking distance of town. There are also good hotels right in the centre and some B&Bs but only one hostel.

C **Radisson SAS**, Ennis Rd, T061-326666, www.radisson.com. Easily the best hotel on the Ennis Rd: classy, spacious, and distinguished by attractive, blarney-free, design features.

D **Hanratty's Hotel**, T061-410999. Close to centre of town with a nightclub, restaurant and bar.

D **Jury's Inn**, Lower Mallow St, T061-207000, www.bookajurysinn.com. On the banks of the river, centrally located, and with a flat room rate of €75 this is good value. Comfortable accommodation if you avoid the rooms facing the main road.

D **Sarsfield Bridge**, T061-317179, www.tsbh.ie. Also by a bridge over the Shannon, some rooms have views of the castle, and a close second to Jury's Inn as a good value place to stay in the centre.

D-E **Cruises Street**, Denmark St, T061-315320. One of the most centrally located, non-hotel, places to stay. En suite bathrooms.

D-E **Railway Hotel**, Parnell St, T061-423653, www.railwayhotel.ie. Opposite the railway station, this is another busy city hotel and not the quietest place to stay but fine if you want to be in the centre.

E **Alexandra Guest House**, 5-6O'Connell Av, T061-318472, info@alexandra@iol.ie. Comfortable rooms and good amenities, at the bottom end of O'Connell St but close to the railway and bus stations.

E **Clifton House**, Ennis Rd, T061-451166, cliftonhouse@eircom.net. A 15-min walk from the centre, this large guest house has 16 rooms and lots of facilities, set in landscaped gardens.

E-F **Summerville** , Courtback Av, South Circular Rd, T061-302500, manager.summerville@mic.ul.ie. Student-room accommodation, mostly double rooms, from early Jun to early Sep.

Adare *p233*

D-E **Carrabawn House**, Killarney Rd, T061-396067, www.carrabawnhouseadare.com. Quality accommodation and pleasant environment for a lot less than the mega-expensive hotels in the village.

E **Elm Housel**, Mondellihy, T061-396306. A short walk north of the village, with 4 comfortable bedrooms.

E **Riversdale**, Station Rd, T061-396751. There are a few B&Bs to choose from on Station Rd but this is one of the best. Open Apr-Nov.

For an explanation of the sleeping and eating price codes used in this guide, see inside the front cover. Other relevant information is found in Essentials pages 39-45.

Eating

Limerick City *p229, map p229*

Too many restaurants in Limerick serve predictable choices such as steak or chicken and veg and the occasional cheeky sauce.

€€ **Aubars**, 50 Thomas St, T061-317799, www.aubars.com. Pub food or more formal meals in a restaurant setting.

€€ **Furze Bush**, 12 Glentworth St, T061-411733. A place worth trying for lunch, it is small but quaintly decorated, and does appealing appetizers, as well as main dishes that include vegetarian meals.

€€ **Porters**, at the Radisson SAS. Is out of town but offers a fresh approach with cool service and a smart meal amidst maple wood, steel and glass.

€€ **Tiger Lilies**, 9 Ellen St, T061-317484. Utilizes an old warehouse to good effect and the seafood and vegetarian dishes should not disappoint. Open for lunch every day except Sun and dinner Tue-Sat.

€ **Green Onion**, Rutland St, T061-400710. Close to the Hunt Museum and makes for an interesting place to eat at any time of the day, whether a light lunch or a more substantial meal.

€ **La Romana**, O'Connell St. Opens at 1700, closed Mon. Pasta and pizza dishes. An early dinner menu, 1700-1845, for under €20.

€ **Baker Place**, in Dominick St. A nicely renovated old pub with a good lunch menu and dinner options.

€ **Glen Tavern**, in Lower Glentworth St. Does food from 1200-1500 in a cheery olde worlde sort of pub.

€ **James Gleason**, aka **The White House** on the corner of Glentworth and O'Connell Sts. The most gloriously unreconstructed Victorian pub for many a mile. Has a limited bar food menu but great atmosphere.

Adare *p233*

€€€ **Maigue**, restaurant in the **Dunraven Arms**, has a good reputation and serves local dishes with a contemporary twist.

€€€ **The Mustard Seed**, in nearby Ballingarry, T069-68508. Has an enormous reputation and very stylish food. The garden is the nicest part of the place. Book well in advance and order a table for later in the evening: if you book for 1900 you may feel the service is a little hurried.

€€€ **Wild Geese**, T061-396451. Is in one of the thatched cottages and also has a high reputation. French cuisine, each course at a set price with supplements for expensive items, classic desserts.

€ If it's a light meal you're after, try the café in the visitor centre **Lena's Bar**, or **Sean Collins**, in the main street.

Pubs and music

Limerick City *p229, map p229*

Pick up a free issue of the *Limerick Event Guide* from the tourist office for current musical happenings. The bar in Hanratty's Hotel has traditional music at weekends and the **Glen Tavern** gets musical on Wed, Thu and Sun nights.

Dolan's Warehouse, T061-314483, www.dolanspub.com. Upstairs from the pub has seriously interesting modern Irish bands Thu-Sat at varying prices for tickets depending on the fame or quality of the performer.

Nancy Blake's, Upper Denmark St. Another place worth checking out.

Entertainment

Limerick City *p229, map p229*

Theatre and cinema

Belltable Arts Centre, 69 O'Connell St, T061-319709. Often has performances by travelling theatre companies, traditional music performances, dance shows as well as a gallery and a film club.

Millennium Theatre, T061-322322, www.lit.ie/theatre. Also has a regular programme of stage events.

University Concert Hall, T061-331549, www.uch.ie. Hosts concerts of classical music and other stage events.

Festivals and events

Limerick City *p229, map p229*

In **Feb** is the Kate O'Brien Literary Weekend, T061-415799 for information, which involves readings, lectures, musical evenings all centred around the work of this important novelist. **Mar** (on the Sun closest to St Patrick's Day) sees the **Limerick International Band Festival**, where there are competitions for drill and dance band recitals, T061-410777 for information. The **Limerick Film Festival** also takes place in **Mar**, focussing on Irish films and film-makers: T061-202986 (Fiona Fennell) for details. **May** sees **Paddy Music** , on the May bank holiday, with concerts, street music and lots of events in the pubs.

Shopping

Limerick City *p229, map p229*
Limerick has all the usual gamut of department stores as well as Arthur's Quay shopping mall with lots of little boutique-type places to browse around.

Books **Celtic Bookshop**, Rutland St. Focuses on books of Irish interest and also has some nice maps and craft items. They will search for out-of-print books.

Clothes **Carraig Donn**, in O'Connell Mall. Does some fashionable things with Aran jumpers.
Irish Handcrafts, Patrick St and Arthur's Quay. Sells expensive but lovely handknitted and handwoven jumpers, tweeds, linens and mohair.

Gifts **Davern & Bell**, 22 Thomas St. Sells interesting examples of contemporary Irish craft and design.

Markets On Sat there is an arts and crafts market from 1100 to 1600 at the Milk Market on the corner of Ellen St and Wickham St.

Activities and tours

Limerick City *p229, map p229*
Bowling **Funworld**, Ennis Rd, T061-325088.

Greyhound racing Market's Field, T061-417808. Meetings Mon, Thu, Sat 2000.

Snooker **Victoria Club Leisure Centre**, Hartsong St, T061-418822.

Walking tours It had to happen: *Angela's Ashes* tours, daily, 1100 and 1430 from the tourist office, lasting 2 hrs for €10.

Transport

Limerick City *p229, map p229*
Air Shannon Airport, T061-471444, in County Clare is 24 km from Limerick and has international flights to **Europe**, the **US** and **Britain** as well as internal flights to **Dublin**, and **Belfast** (see page 36).

Bike hire The Bike Shop, O'Connell Av, T061-315900; **Emerald Alpine**, 1 Patrick St, T061-416983, www.irelandrentalbike.com; **Mahons Cycleworld**, 25 Roches St, T061-415202. The last two places have a delivery and collection service for Shannon Airport.

Bus There is a free phone for bus information in the tourist office, otherwise T061-313333, 0900-1930. The bus station is in Parnell St, next to the train station, and there are buses to most parts of the country: **Athlone**, **Armagh** (Fri only), **Ballina**, **Belfast**, **Castlebar**, **Clonmel**, **Cork**, **Derry**, **Dublin**, **Ennis**, **Galway**, **Killarney**, **Omagh**, **Roscommon**, **Sligo**, **Tralee** and **Waterford**. There is also a bus to **London**, via **Dublin**.

The **Shannon Airport-Limerick** bus service takes 45 mins, €4.70. 0630-2315 (0710-2315 on Sun).

There are 5 buses a day between **Dublin**, **Limerick** and **Killarney**, a summer-only service from **Limerick** to **Liskard** via **Adare**, and 1 daily service connecting **Limerick** and **Ballingarry** via **Adare**.

Car hire Dooley Car Rentals, Shannon Airport, T061-471098/471819; **Budget Rent-a-Car**, T061-471361/471098.

Train Limerick station in Parnell St, T061-315555, has services to **Dublin**, **Rosslare**, **Cahir**, **Tipperary**, **Cork**. From Limerick Junction, southeast of Limerick, more connections are possible.

Taxi Along Thomas St and Bedford Row, off O'Connell St. A taxi to/from the airport is €25 at least: T061-313131 for a fixed-rate taxi.

County Cork

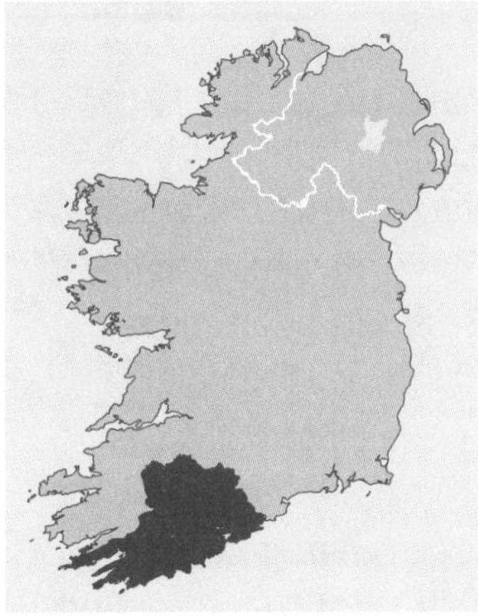

Footprint features

Introduction

Cork city and the coastal route through west Cork remain highly popular with visitors, but the county's magic is that it rarely feels overcrowded. Easy accessibility by air and sea makes the city a contender with Dublin as a first point of arrival in Ireland, especially if you want to head off for a rural idyll in one of the most beautiful corners of the country. The city itself is a tiny, scrambling little gem. A mixture of tourists, workers and 'culchies' – country folk up for a day trip – Cork, European Capital of Culture in 2005, has all the benefits of a small country town with all those of a booming city – theatres, art galleries, good restaurants and more.

From Cork city it is a short hop to Kinsale, Ireland's self-proclaimed food capital, before meandering along the southwest coast, where the landscape plays second fiddle to the mesmerizing seascapes and where reminders of the Anglo-Irish legacy are dotted between the history-laden small towns that keep their dignity and character in spite of tourism.

None of this quite prepares the unsuspecting traveller for the three narrow peninsulas that jut out into the Atlantic, justifying the description by one addicted visitor as a "geographic narcotic" where "it is hopeless to resist the pressure of non-pressure". The pleasures of west Cork are no longer a secret, but little has been spoilt by tourism.

★ Don't miss...

1. **Crawford Art Gallery** Appreciate Irish art and check out the great café, Cork city, page 245.
2. **Blarney** Visit Blarney castle and the famous stone and afterwards enjoy the great pub grub at Blair's Inn, Cloghroe, pages 250 and 256.
3. **Youghal** Search for the Viking boat in ancient St Mary's church, page 254.
4. **Coastal route** Explore the coast between Timoleague and Clonakilty, page 260. Seabirds, seascapes and seaside villages.
5. **Clear Island** A tiny, wild, Gaelic-speaking island with amazing seabirds, a fun ferry ride and scraps of beaches to hunt out, page 265.
6. **Mizen Peninsula** Surfing, swimming at Barley Cove, sandcastles, walks and a whole peninsula to explore, page 274.
7. **Beara Way** The wildest walk in Ireland with ancient standing stones, views to take your breath away and tiny villages with music and craic, page 284.

Ins and outs

Getting around

Driving around the county of Cork is easy – the roads are good, as long as you don't expect expressways, petrol stations are plentiful, and the nearest thing to a traffic jam is when a few cars wait for a farmer to guide his cows along a stretch of road. Out of the city, parking is not generally a problem although some of the towns (Bantry in particular) have limited space at the height of summer.

All year **Bus Éireann**, Cork, T021-4508188, runs daily services between Cork, Bantry and Glengarriff, and between Cork, Clonakilty, Rosscarbery, Skibbereen, Ballydehob, Schull and Goleen. There are also services between Cork, Cork airport and Kinsale and a Mon-Fri service between Skibbereen and Baltimore. A Sat-only bus runs between Macroom and Kilcrohane via Bantry.

Between 24 May and 19 Sep, Bus Éireann also runs a daily service between Cork, Clonakilty, Owenahincha, Rosscarbery, Leap, Skibbereen, Bantry and Glengarriff, with the bus continuing on to Kenmare, Killarney and Tralee. There is also a daily service between Schull, Ballydehob, Skibbereen, Bantry and Glengarriff and a Mon-Sat bus between Skibbereen and Baltimore. The all-year service between Cork and Glengarriff continues in the summer to Castletownbere.

Information For general tourist information on County Cork, www.cork-guide.ie.

Cork → *Phone code: 021. Colour map 3, grid B5.*

Mildly cosmopolitan and yet engagingly Irish, Cork is pleasantly spread out amongst the hills that rise up on both sides of the Lee Valley where the river meanders its way to the open water of Cork harbour. While it is not a conventionally beautiful place, its urban identity is worn lightly and its feel is distinctively different from that of Dublin. The city centre is actually a small island between two channels of the river and the plethora of bridges can be disorientating. Though Cork is a major port, there is little maritime activity in the city centre and the river is usually free of traffic. At night the pubs fuel a mood of ebullience that can occasionally become rowdy, and the usual inner city rules apply. Cork is an easy city to like and if the traffic could be taken out it would reclaim its homely beauty. It makes a good base for day trips to nearby sights including the famous Blarney Castle and the historical towns of Cobh and Youghal.
⏩ *For Sleeping, Eating and other listings, see pages 245-250.*

Ins and outs

Getting there Cork city has an international airport (8 km south of city), ferry connections to Britain and France, and railway and bus stations with good links to other towns and cities across Ireland. There is also a ferry service across Cork harbour that can save time if you wish to avoid the city altogether. Main roads to Cork city include the N8 from Dublin, the N25 from Waterford, the N20 from Limerick, the N22 from Killarney and the N71 from West Cork. From the airport a half-hourly bus service takes you into the city where the bus station is in Parnell Place near Merchant's Quay. Taxis from the airport, usually metered, cost about €15. The rail station is a 20-minute walk from the centre but a frequent bus service brings passengers into the bus station and St Patrick Street, and taxis are abundant (€3.80). ⏩ *For more information, see Transport, page 249.*

Getting around City buses go out from St Patrick Street to all areas of the city. There is a taxi rank in the centre of St Patrick Street and another beside the bus station.

Walking on water – St Patrick Street

Cork city's main thoroughfare curves in the way that it does because it was built over a tributary of the River Lee, and up until the beginning of the 19th century small boats made their way up and down the waterway. At the junction of Tuckey Street and Grand Parade you can still see a bollard where boats moored, and in St Patrick Street itself, outside the Château Bar not far up from Waterstone's, the tall steps bear witness to the days when boats moored beneath them. When the Black and Tans set the city aflame at the end of 1920, it was only the north side of the street that was burnt down and if you walk along this side – between Waterstone's and Eason's – you can look across to the other side and spot some of the original 18th-century bow windows.

Most of the city's interesting sights are walkable, but the No 8 bus route is useful for the hostels and sights at the west of the city. Traffic can get a bit snarled up at peak hours and parking is restricted but there are several big multi-storey car parks.

Information Tourist office, Grand Parade, T021-4273251. Sep-Jun Mon-Sat 0930-1730; Jul-Aug Mon-Sat 0900-1900, Sun 0900-1500. **Usit Now** (student travel), 10 Market Parade, St Patrick Street.

History

The Gaelic for Cork, *Corcaigh*, meaning marshy, evokes the city's origins in broad marshland formed by two channels of the River Lee. St Finbarr founded a monastic settlement here, some two centuries before marauding Vikings arrived in the ninth century. The Danes eventually established a permanent trading post and, after the Anglo-Norman invasion in the 1170s, this evolved into a walled city under Norman control. It wasn't until after a successful five-day siege by the armies of William of Orange at the end of the 17th century that the walls were torn down. By 1800 Cork was a prosperous city built upon trade, increasingly with the English, who valued the city's harbour both for its imperial navy and for shipping home the county's agricultural produce, especially butter. Shandon, to the north of the city centre, was the hub of commercial life at this time and the city's harbour became Europe's major transatlantic port, with ships calling in for provisions and butter being exported to Australia and South America. In the aftermath of Easter 1916, Cork began to develop a reputation for political opposition to Britain and in 1920 the mayor, Thomas MacCurtain, was murdered by the British who also burnt down the city centre. Today, Cork is a thriving city with light industry providing much of the employment.

Sights

St Finbarr's Cathedral ⓘ *Bishop St. Mon-Sat 1000-1700. €2.50 donation suggested.* Not necessarily an essential place to visit, this is the site traditionally associated with the birth of the city. In the seventh century St Finbarr came here from his hermitage in Gougane Barra and founded a monastery on the site of the present late 19th-century cathedral. The interior is as richly embellished as the splendour of the exterior suggests it will be, and no doubt the wealthy merchants who paid for its construction were pleased with the way the English architect, William Burges, combined his love of medievalism with a conspicuous display of Protestant affluence. Highlights include the statuary of the ornate west door, the 1930s roof of the sanctuary, and a memorial stone near the pulpit to Elizabeth Aldworthy, the only woman ever initiated into the Masons.

 form of writing. To the east of the library it is worth seeking out the resplendent, Celtic-inspired interior of the Honan Chapel. Built in 1916, the eye-catching mosaic floor is matched for beauty by the Harry Clarke stained glass windows.

A city tour

This lengthy stroll, starting outside the tourist office, goes across the city, past many of the places of interest. There is too much to see in one day, so either curtail your walking and sightseeing drastically or consider it as two one-day walks.

Day 1 From outside the tourist office turn to the right and look for the first entrance to the **English Market** on the right, before the cinema but after the junction with Oliver Plunkett Street. Pass straight through this interesting arcade of shops, noting On the Pig's Back, a shop selling excellent breads and cheeses, and exit on the other side past the fountain on to the pedestrianized Princes Street. Turn left and walk up to the main thoroughfare of **St Patrick Street**. Cross to the other side and take the first left down Carey's Lane. This area around **Paul Street** has a number of restaurants and shops well worth checking out. Turn right into Emmet Place, passing the **Crawford Art Gallery** on the left; the gallery's café is a smart place for mid-morning tea and cakes. Carry on to the river, cross the bridge and turn to the left into John Redmond Street to the **Shandon sites**.

From the Shandon sites head east along Upper John Street to Coburg Street and straight across to **MacCurtain Street**. A formerly shabby thoroughfare leading to the train station and roads to Dublin and the southeast, MacCurtain Street is gradually sprucing itself up. The ex-temperance Metropole Hotel has been refurbished, but the exterior still evokes a bygone age while, opposite, Isaacs Hostel has a good restaurant and there are also some interesting small shops (see 'Shopping' on page 249).

Day 2 After passing the Metropole on MacCurtain Street, take the second turning on the right, Brian Ború Street, and cross the bridge of the same name that leads to the bus station. This route carries on down until you reach the south branch of the river and cross Clontarf Bridge to Albert Quay. Turn right and pass the stately **City Hall**, the last large-scale edifice to be built in Ireland in the classical style. The original building was burnt down by the British in 1920, but it was reopened in 1936 by de Valera, and in 1963 when President John F Kennedy spoke from its steps, the largest crowd ever to be seen in Cork filled every space hereabouts. Continue along the riverside on Union Quay and when this turns into George's Quay notice the 18th-century houses and their very high roofs. On the other side of the river the distinctive exterior of the neo-Gothic Holy Trinity Church, designed by GR Pain in 1832, is difficult to miss. Cross over to this side by the next bridge, Parliament Bridge, which leads up to **South Mall**, characterized by solicitors' offices and other commercial premises. Turn to the left and walk to the end of the street where the baroque Maid of Erin monument commemorates nationalist heroes of the past. From the nearby footbridge there is a fine view of **St Finbarr's Cathedral**. Stay on the monument side, opposite the tourist office, and walk up Grand Parade. Before reaching the junction opposite the cinema look for the entrance gate to the **Bishop Lucey Park** on the left; inside the gate there is a fragment of the medieval city walls. Walk through the park and exit in the right corner that comes out by the side of an old church, now the Cork Archive Centre; attached to it is the **Triskel Arts Centre**, which has a small café. Turn right and go up to join Washington Street, where a left turn will eventually lead on to Western Road. After passing Jury's Hotel on the left it is a short way to the main entrance of **University College**, while across the street there is a short road that leads to **Mardyke Walk**, a 2-km avenue that was laid out in the early 18th century. Walk along here past a cricket ground and into Fitzgerald Park and the **Cork Public Museum**. Bus No 8 on Western Road brings you back to the city centre.

Museums and art galleries

Cork Public Museum ⓘ *T021-4270679. Mon-Fri 1100-1300, 1415-1700 (1800 in summer), Sun 1500-1700. Free weekdays, €1.50 Sun. Bus No 8 from city centre.* The museum, in a Georgian building in Fitzgerald Park opposite University College, is good on Cork's eventful role in the war for independence; the unstylish archaeological displays on the first floor are less appealing. The adjoining green is a quiet retreat for a picnic and, unlike the Bishop Lucey Park on Grand Parade, is rarely crowded.

Cork City Gaol ⓘ *Sunday's Well Rd, T021-4305022. Mar-Oct daily 0930-1800. Nov-Feb daily 1000-1700. Last admission 1 hr before closing. €6. From the city centre either take a taxi or bus No 8 as far as University College and then walk through Fitzgerald Park, over the delightful suspension footbridge and up the hill to the right before turning left into Convent Avenue. From here a sign points the way.* The city gaol, remarkably well preserved in its essentials, functioned from the 1820s for just under a century. A guided tour by tape comes with the admission charge, followed by a melodramatic audio-visual display. Also housed in the prison is a radio museum.

★ **Crawford Art Gallery** ⓘ *Emmet Pl, T021-4273377. Mon-Sat 1000-1700. Free.* Even if time sis short, spare some for a visit to Ireland's most important art gallery outside of Dublin. The building served as the city's Custom House in the 18th century. Jack B Yeats, Sean Keating, Harry Clarke, William Gerard Barry and Edith Somerville are some of those represented, as well as work by contemporary artists working in Cork. British artists include George Romney, Frank Bramley and Jacob Epstein and there is a gallery dedicated to temporary exhibitions.

Check out the scary photograph of footballer Roy Keane who hails from the city.

Sleeping

Cork city *p240, map p242*
There is a reasonable spread of accommodation, covering most budgets, but in Jul and Aug you should have a room booked in advance or leave it to the tourist office to find somewhere for you. Along Glanmire Rd heading out east of town near the railway station there is a string of similarly-priced B&Bs (see **E** category, below), and the main cluster of hostels is at the bus station end of town.

L Hayfield Manor, Perrott Av, College Rd, T021-4845900, www.hayfieldmanor.ie. An elegant little boutique hotel built in the mature gardens of a Victorian house on the western outskirts of the city. A walled courtyard is an excellent spot for afternoon tea, there is a small leisure centre, a good bar and an award-winning restaurant.

L-A Gresham Metropole, MacCurtain St, T021-4508122, www.gresham-hotels.com. This was once the largest temperance hotel in Ireland. Refurbishment has retained some feel for the past and the rooms are comfortably large. Leisure centre includes a pool. Streetside rooms can be noisy at weekends so ask for a river view. Bar and restaurant.

A Jury's Hotel, Lancaster Quay (though the address is often given as Western Rd), T021-4276622, www.jurysdoyle.com. Cork's best-known hotel. Set alongside the river the hotel offers large, airy rooms, a pool, restaurant and a popular bar serving lunchtime food.

A-D Hotel Isaac's, 48 MacCurtain St, T021-4500011, www.isaacs.ie. Free car parking nearby. City centre hotel with a courtyard garden and a restaurant.

B-C Lotamore House, Tivoli, T021-4822344, lotamore@iol.ie. Just off the dual carriageway to the Dublin/Waterford roundabout. Georgian guest house set in very agreeable grounds and with a period feel but no bar or restaurant.

B-DAmbassador Hotel, Military Hill, T021-4551996, www.ambassadorhotel.ie. A former military hospital, built in the 1870s, with big

For an explanation of the sleeping and eating price codes used in this guide, see inside the front cover. Other relevant information is found in Essentials pages 39-45.

airy rooms, amazing views over the city and a roomy comfortable atmosphere. Sauna, gym, jacuzzi, bar and restaurant.

B-D Victoria Hotel, St Patrick St (entered from Cook St), T021-4278788, www.victoriahotel.com. Joyce once stayed here, as recounted in *A Portrait of the Artist as a Young Man*. No car park, better value outside of summer.

C-D Great Southern Hotel, Cork Airport, T021-4947500, www.gsh.ie. Worth checking out for special rates which can reduce the price of a room considerably.

D-E Jury's Inn Cork, Anderson's Quay, T021-4276444, www.jurysdoyle.com. Reasonable value for money with a room rate rather than price per person, this hotel offers modern comfortable accommodation. Restaurant.

E-F Forte Travelodge, Blackash, Kinsale Rd roundabout, South Ring Rd, Blackash, T021-4310722, www.travelodge.ie. Room rate charged, handy for the airport and for families, but special offers may make the *Great Southern* better value. Little Chef restaurant next door. Breakfast extra.

The following guest houses are all large 3-storey Victorian houses alongside one another on **Western Rd** between Jury's Hotel and the entrance to University College Cork. They all have hotel standard room facilities and are within walking distance of the centre.

A-E Redclyffe Guest House, Western Rd, T021-4273220, www.redclyffe.com. Stands out with its red brick colour and there is car parking at the front and rear.

C-D Garnish House, Western Rd, T021-4275111, www.garnish.ie. Has 24-hr reception and above-average breakfast menu.

C-D Killarney Guesthouse, T021-4270290, www.killarneyguesthouse.com. Large and comfortable guest house opposite University College Cork, car park to the rear. Closed for 4 days over Christmas.

D-E Antoine House, T021-4273494, www.antoinehouse.ie. Private car park at the rear and open all year.

Less expensive accommodation tends to be clustered along **Lower Glanmire Rd**, heading east out of town and close to the railway station. They do not have car parks and to avoid having to pay for parking on the street, even where this is possible, cars need to be left up the hill behind Glenmire Rd.

D Number Forty Eight, 48 Lower Glanmire Rd, T021-4505790. B&B next to the station.

E 55 Wilton Gardens, off Wilton Rd, T021-4541705. B&B at the western end of Cork. Can be reached by bus No 8 and No 5 from the city centre.

E Aaran House, 49 Lower Glenmire Rd, T021-4551501, aarankev@hotmail.com.

E Kent House, 47 Lower Glanmire Rd, T021-4504260, kenthouse47@hotmail.com. B&B with some rooms with en suite bathrooms.

E Lisadell House, Western Rd, T021-4546172, matt@indigo.ie. B&B at the western end of Cork. Take bus No 8 from the city centre.

E Oakland, 51, Lower Glanmire Rd, T021-4500578. B&B.

Other B&Bs in the same price range are found a little way outside Cork in the **Douglas** area and reached by bus No 7 from the city centre. Douglas has its own shops and restaurants and is convenient for the airport or ferry port.

E Coolfadda House, Douglas Rd, T021-4363489, near St Finbarr's Hospital.

E River View, Douglas, T021-4893762, edwardsc@eircom.net.ie. In Douglas village near Barry's Pub.

E-F Cork International Youth Hostel, 1&2 Redclyff, Western Rd, T021-4543289, www.irelandyha.org/anoige/cork3.html. A smart *An Óige* establishment with 2-bed rooms in the **E** category.

F Aaran House Tourist Hostel, Lower Glanmire Rd, T021-4551566, www.aaranhouse.com. Directly opposite the railway station and not to be confused with the B&B of the same name on the other side of the street. Includes 3 private doubles for €30, open all year, bikes for hire.

F Brú, 57 MacCurtain St, T021-4559667, www.bruhostel.com. New place aimed at the upmarket backpacker, mostly dorm beds in 6- and 4-bed rooms, some mixed, all with en suite facilities. Triple/family rooms, no doubles. Bar and internet café, big kitchen.

F Campus House, 3 Woodland View, Western Rd, T021-4343531. All dormitory accommodation.

F Cork City Independent Hostel, 100 Lower Glanmire Rd, T021-4509089. A short way past the railway station, on the opposite side of the road. There are 25 beds and these include 7 private rooms.

F **Isaac's**, 48 MacCurtain St, T021-4508388. Nearest hostel to town, dormitories only, money exchange and email facility.

F **Kelly's**, 25 Summerhill South, T021-4315612, www.kellyshostel.com. IHO hostel, a little way south of the centre, 2 private rooms, bike hire.

F **Kinlay House**, Bob and Joan Walk, Shandon, T021-4508966, www.kinlayhouse.ie. Lots of private rooms, laundry facilities, meals available, light breakfast included, bike hire.

F **Sheila's of Cork**, 4 Belgrave Pl, Wellington Rd, T021-4505562, www.sheilashostel.ie. Provides meals, laundry facilities, private and family rooms, sauna, money exchange and bicycle hire. Parking on site.

Camping

Bienvenue Ferry Caravan and Camping Park, T021-4312711. Opposite the airport, this is handy if heading out to West Cork.

Cork City Caravan and Camping Park, Togher Rd, T021-4961866. This is the nearest to the centre, reached by the No 14 bus.

Self-catering

Castlewhite Apartments, University College, T021-4902793. Rents apartments between mid-Jun and mid-Sep.

Dean's Hall, Crosses Green, T021-4312623, www.deanshall.com. 3 and 5 bedroom apartments from €130-190 a night or €630-680 a week, Jun-Sep only.

Isaac's Apartments, MacCurtain St, T021-4500011. 2- and 3-bedroomed apartments.

Eating

Cork city *p240, map p242*

The narrow lanes between St Patrick St and Paul St are home to quite a few reasonably priced restaurants, varying in quality but usually worth a visit for a quick lunch or a look at their dinner menus. Better restaurants are found at the Western Rd and MacCurtain St ends of town. The price ranges below refer to dinner only; lunch is usually around €10 wherever you go. For picnic provisions, visit the English Market (see page 244).

YYY **The Manor Room**, Hayfield Manor Hotel. The classiest place to eat in Cork these days, where excellent quality food is served in a spacious formal dining room looking out on to the hotel's walled garden. 5 courses will set you back €65.

YY **Amicus**, French Church St, T021- 4276455. Value-for-money meals means Amicus is rarely empty and there are separate breakfast, lunch and dinner menus. Lots of vegetarian choices and evening dishes range from a Thai-style curry to steaks and salmon. Tables in the pedestrianized walkway offer al fresco lunches.

YY **Fenn's Quay**, 5 Sheares St. Has a 2- course early dinner menu at €20.

YY **Greene's Restaurant**, 48 MacCurtain St, in Hotel Isaacs, T021-4552279. A little more expensive than (although not related to) Isaac's restaurant below. It is worth comparing their menus.

YY **Isaac's Restaurant**, 48 MacCurtain St, T021-4503805. Remains very popular due to dependably good food – prawns and chilli, Thai chicken curry for example – at reasonable prices.

YY **Lafayette's**, Hotel Imperial, South Mall. Eat here if an Art Nouveau setting seems more appealing.

YY **Paradiso**, Lancaster Quay opposite Jury's hotel, T021-4277939. Cork's quality vegetarian restaurant.

YY **Probys Bistro**, Probys Quay, T021-4316531. Across from St Finbarr's Cathedral, smart and modern and serves dishes like monkfish with coconut and chilli sauce. Tasty choice of daily specials, an early dinner menu for €22 on weeknights, and good service.

YY **Scott's**, Oliver Plunket St. Big and noisy with pub food during the day and an evening menu of simple burger-type meals.

YY **Seasons Restaurant**, Ambassador Hotel. Has an interesting menu including venison and a turn of the century feel to it with high ceilings, lots of space and a quiet mood.

YY **Table 8**, 8/9 Carey's Lane, T021-4270725. Offers an inexpensive lunch and good dinner options well within the moderate range.

Y **Crawford Gallery Café**, Emmett Pl, T021-4274415. Stylish layout, more expensive than Quay Co-op (below).

Y **Dan Lowrey's Tavern**, MacCurtain St (see Pubs below). Pub food in a characterful setting.

Y **Fellini's**, 4 Carey's Lane, T021-4276083. Good for coffee, snacks and meals, open daily until 1900.

Gino's, 7 Winthrop St. Close to Scuzi's (below), offering pizzas and a vast range of ice cream in a very busy atmosphere.
Indian Palace, 31 Princes St. Has an affordable lunch in arty surroundings; main dishes for dinner are under €15.
The Long Valley, at the top of Winthrop St. Dispenses doorstep-sized sandwiches.
Quay Co-op, Sullivan's Quay, T021-4317026. Serves vegetarian dishes, including breakfast, in a roomy but spartan setting.
Scuzi's, Winthrop Ave. A frighteningly popular café in a quiet alleyway, serving a vast menu of burgers, pizza and much more till 2300. Be prepared to queue.

Pubs and music

Cork city *p240, map p242*
Cork city has a lively music scene and most of the pubs mentioned below have notice boards carrying flyers that advertise what is coming up. The tourist board also dispenses a free listings magazine and events may also be checked out at www.whazon.com.
An Bodhran, Oliver Plunkett St. Traditional music on Mon night.
An Spáilpín Fánach, South Main St, T021-4277949. A wonderfully old-looking establishment, with regular musical evenings.
Dan Lowrey's Tavern, 13 MacCurtain St. Has no music but beautiful old furnishings and a sense of character.
Lobby Bar, Union Quay, T021-4311113, www.lobby.ie. Free musical sessions downstairs Mon-Wed and Fri at 2130. About €7 for regular appearances by Irish and international singers and groups.
Old Oak, 113 Oliver Plunkett St, T021-4276165, www.oldoakbars.com. Has a nondescript exterior but plenty of *craic* inside and traditional music once a week.
Reardon's, Washington St. A cavernous place, with live music on Wed and Fri.
The Thirsty Scholar, Lancaster Quay, T021-4276209. Opposite Jury's Hotel, a studenty sort of place but has live traditional music 2 nights a week.

Entertainment

Cork city *p240, map p242*
Cork Booking Office, facing Washington St near the tourist office, T021-4543210, handles tickets for most theatres and other entertainment events.

To find out what's on at the moment and what is coming up within the week, check out the flyers on the noticeboards, windows and doorways of the following places: for theatre, film, dance and other cultural events check the **Triskel Arts Centre** and the **Granary Theatre**. For live music, concerts and gigs in general the pubs in Washington Street and Union Quay will have all the latest information.

Cinema
Capital Cineplex, Grand Parade, T021-4278777, www.filminfo.net.
Kino, Washington St, T021-4271571. The other main cinema. More art house.

Comedy
City Limits, Coburg St, T021-4501206, www.thecomedyclub.ie. Has live comedy at The Comedy Club on Fri and Sat nights.

Theatre
Cork Opera House, Emmet Pl, T021-4270022. Hosts plays, musicals and concerts, rarely operas, and tends to be conservative in its choice of productions.
The Everyman Palace, MacCurtain St, T021-4501673, www.everymanpalace.com. Often has Irish drama on its programme.
Triskel Arts Centre, Tobin St, T021-4272022. Tucked behind Washington St, usually worth checking out for visiting theatre groups.
UCC Granary Theatre, Dyke Parade, T021-4904275. On the one-way road coming into Cork from the west, parallel to Western Rd, and is run by University College Cork.

Festivals and events

Cork city *p240, map p242*
14-19th Mar Celt Fest, including a St Patrick's Day parade in the city centre. **Late Apr/early May** Cork International Choral Festival, T021-4847271, Mary Hartness, www.corkchoral.ie. Events taking place in the City Hall, cathedrals, churches and arts centres. **Late Jun** Cork Midsummer Festival. Music, theatre, literature and visual arts. **Jul** The weekend around the 10th launches **Seisiún Cois Cuan** in Cobh, featuring sessions of traditional ballads, folk

and Celtic rock. **Early Oct** Cork International Film Festival, T021-4271711, www.corkfilmfest.org. World-renowned film festival. **Late Oct** Cork Jazz Festival, T021-4278979. www.corkjazzfestival.com. The Metropole Hotel hosts many events. **Nov** Cork Arts Festival, T021-4326567. Expect something worthwhile given that Seamus Heaney and dance troupes from Africa have graced previous events.

Shopping

Cork city *p240, map p242*
St Patrick St may be the main street but most of the shops there are disappointingly familiar. More rewarding is the nearby pedestrianized area around Paul St and Emmet Pl.

For straightforward purchases of consumer items and clothes there are 2 department stores on St Patrick St – **Roche's** and **Brown Thomas** – while the modern **Merchant's Quay** shopping centre near St Patrick's Bridge has a supermarket and decent clothes shops.

MacCurtain St has an appealingly eclectic range of shops, including:
Cork Butter Market, in Shandon. Very old, it is now a craft centre with shops, most of which close on Sat afternoon and Sun, selling Irish crystal, Celtic-inspired jewellery and stained glass.
The Living Tradition, at No 40. Specializes in Irish music.

Antiques There are a couple of antique shops appropriately located on Fenn's Quay. This street was laid out in the 1720s and 2 antique shops now occupy part of a row of the old houses which were recently reconstructed, preserving the original internal panelling and staircases.

Bookshops Cork has a good number of bookshops, all boasting a generous stock on subjects relating to Irish literature, history and the like.
Waterstone's and **Eason's** are both on St Patrick St while **Connolly's**, on Paul St, deals in second-hand books, mostly 19th- and 20th-century literature.
Mercier Press, have a shop in nearby French Church St.
Vibes & Scribes, Bridge St. Just over St Patrick's Bridge before reaching MacCurtain St. Has a large selection of discounted books on Ireland and most other subjects, and a café upstairs.

Camping and walking equipment
Tent & Leisure, York St, T021-500702. Visible from the corner on McCurtain St.
The Tent Shop, 7 Parnell Pl, T021-278833.

Fishing gear and tackle Murray & Co, St Patrick St, T021-272842.

Activities and tours

Cork city *p240, map p242*
Greyhound racing Curraheen Park, T1850-525575, www.igb.ie. Has racing every Wed, Thu and Sat at 2000.

Tour operators USIT, 10-11 Market Pde, T021-4270900.
Easytours, T021-4362484, www.easytourscork.com.

Tours Literary Walking Tour, T021-4291649, noreenmurphysheehan@ eircom.net. Meets outside the tourist office in Grand Pde l at 1900 on Tue and Thu, Jun to Aug, €7.

Transport

Cork city *p240, map p242*
Air Cork Airport: T1800-626747/ 021-4313131, for flight information T021-4327100. Direct flights to **Amsterdam**, **Belfast**, **Dublin**, **Edinburgh**, **Exeter**, **Glasgow**, **Jersey**, **Leeds**, **London Heathrow**, **Stansted** and **Gatwick**, **Manchester**, **Milan**, **Newcastle**, **Paris**, **Portsmouth**, **Rennes** and **Southampton**. More direct flights to European cities are being added. **Aer Lingus**, Academy St, T021-4327155; Cork Airport, T4327100. There is a scheduled bus service between the airport and the city bus station in Parnell Pl.

Bike hire Rothar, 55 Barrack St, T021-4313133.

Bus Bus station: Parnell Pl (opposite Merchant's Quay), T021-4508188. Regular services to all parts of Ireland including: **Dublin** (4½ hrs), **Killarney** (2 hrs), **Bantry** (2¼ hrs) and **Wexford** (3¾ hrs).

Car Cars can be hired at Cork Airport or the Cork tourist office. Apart from the car park at **Merchant's Quay** shopping centre and one next to the tourist office, hourly parking vouchers are needed for the limited street space. They're available from newsagents.

Car hire Familiar names have desks at the airport, including: **Avis**, T021-4281111; **Dooley Car Rental**, Cork Airport, T021-4321099; **Europcar**, T021-4917300; **Budget**, T021- 4314000; **National**, T021-4320755. Better rates available outside the airport: **Grandons**, T021-4866217; **Malone**, T021-4506744; **Top Car**, T021-4343366. **Budget** have a desk in the tourist office.

Ferry Ferry terminal: Ringaskiddy, about 16 km southeast of the city. **Brittany Ferries**, 42 Grand Parade, T021-4277801; at the terminal, T021-4277801. Provides a service to **Roscoff** between Mar and Oct. **Irish Ferries**, 9 Patrick's Bridge, T021-4551995. Handles routes to **Le Havre**, **Cherbourg** and **Roscoff**. **Swansea Cork Ferries**, 52 South Mall, T021-4271166; ferry terminal, T021-4378036. Services to the UK; closed between early Jan and early Mar.

Taxi Taxis are often parked in the middle of St Patrick St at the bridge end, while 24-hr companies are based in MacCurtain St. T021-4272222, T021-4508777.

Train Kent railway station: T021-4504777. Tickets and information also from **The Travel Centre**, 65 St Patrick St, T021-4504888. Services to **Dublin** and other cities. A local service to **Cobh** also stops at **Fota Wildlife Park**.

Around Cork

There are a number of places of interest that can be easily reached by bus, car or bicycle from Cork. You could combine Blarney with the Royal Gunpowder Mills at Ballincollig for an interesting day out. Another day out, by car or train, could take in the Fota Wildlife Park and the historic town of Cobh to the east of the city. Either of these places could also be visited as part of a longer excursion taking in the distillery at Midleton and the historical sights at seaside Youghal, although there is a fair bit to see in both Cobh and Youghal and an overnight stay in either town is worth considering. ▸▸ *For Sleeping, Eating and other listings, see pages 255-257.*

★ Blarney → *Phone code: 021. Colour map 3, grid B4.*

The neat green that defines Blarney village (*An Bhlarna*), having been laid out by General Sir James Jeffreys in the early 18th century, is very un-Irish. The MacCarthys' blarney had run dry and they had left in the Flight of the Earls after the defeat at the Battle of the Boyne. Everything is compactly together around the village green, including a small tourist information office, in the old woollen mill buildings, T021-4381624, the bus stop, a large *Blarney Woollen Mills* store that opens daily, pubs and restaurants.

Getting there Follow the N22 to Killarney (ignore the less interesting road signposted for Blarney that keeps on the north side of the River Lee), signposted as a right turn off the Western Road that heads out to West Cork. The road to Blarney (the R579) crosses the Lee after a long, straight stretch of road, and there is another right turn on to the R617 before the village and castle are reached. Buses 224 and 234 run to Blarney Mon-Fri, from the Parnell Place bus station in Cork.

★ **Blarney Castle** ⓘ *T021-4385252. Weekdays Jun-Aug Mon-Sat 0900-1900, May, Sep 0900-1830, Oct-Apr 0900-sundown, Sun 0930-1730, €7.* Tradition has it that the garrulous Cormac MacCarthy, the Gaelic lord of Blarney, was so successful at inventing excuses for not complying with the demands of the English that Queen Elizabeth I dismissed his blather as so much blarney. Kissing the **stone** of his

15th-century castle in order to gain the gift of the gab is itself a mighty piece of blarney played out on a daily basis to countless visitors, but this is all part of the fun and as long as you turn up early enough to miss the queues an enjoyable time can be had. It does help to have a head for heights and care should be taken with children because, although only the one machicolated tower survives, the stairs are steep and accidents have occurred.

Fota House and Wildlife Park

ⓘ Wildlife park: T021-4812678. 17 Mar-30 Oct Mon-Sat 1000-1800, last admission 1700, Sun 1100-1800; winter Mon-Sat 1000-1630, Sun 1100-1630, last admission 1530. €9.50. Wildlife train: €2. Car park fee. House: T021-4815543 daily 1000-1800. €5. From Cork take the N25 to Rosslare and take the signposted road to Cobh. The park is signposted off this road, or take the Cork to Cobh train, which stops at the park.

More than an open-air zoo, Fota was successfully established with the intention of breeding endangered animals. Situated 16 km outside Cork, its 70 acres of open land will appeal to families especially, given the roaming cheetahs, giraffes, kangaroos, monkeys, oryxes, ostriches and penguins. Children will enjoy a visit to the café where a troop of lemurs descend for freebies. You can walk around at will or take one of the small trains that regularly chug around the park. The house, an 18th-century hunting lodge, owned in the 19th century by local nobs the Smith Barry family, is still undergoing renovations but the lower rooms are open to the public. The original decorated ceilings and other interior decorations have been restored but the best of it is the butler's servery, game room and kitchens. The 18th century arboretum has been added to over the years and is well worth a wander round.

Cobh → *Colour map 3, grid B5.*

Pronounced 'cove', and named Queenstown between 1849 (when Queen Victoria dropped by) and 1922, the picturesque town houses rising up the slope of a hill were the last sight of Ireland for the millions of emigrants who left here for America in the 19th and 20th centuries. The scene is graphically described in an 1842 travel book: "Mothers hung upon the necks of their athletic sons; young girls clung to elder sisters; fathers – old white-headed men – fell on their knees, with arms uplifted to heaven, imploring the protecting care of the Almighty on their departing children."

The offshore Spike Island was a holding prison for political offenders prior to their enforced departure for Botany Bay.

Cork city & around

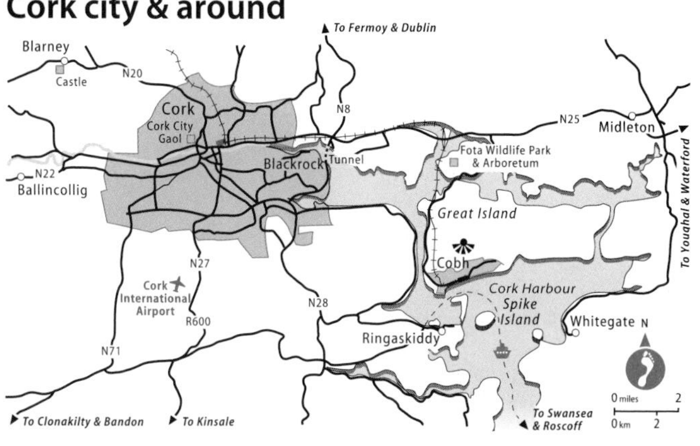

Cobh itself is on an island, Great Island, though it is easy to forget this when one looks out from the town's promenade. To add to the town's unfortunate associations, the *Titanic* paid its last call here in 1912, and three years later the *Lusitania* was torpedoed not far away by a German submarine, an event that brought the US into the First World War. Hundreds of the drowned passengers are buried in an old graveyard to the north of town.

Today, Cobh is a bustling little place with a lively holiday air that attracts as many Irish tourists as overseas ones, and a hugely ugly church that dominates the skyline. Back in 1720 the **Royal Cork Yacht Club**, possibly the oldest yacht club in the world, established a home here. The building they commissioned for their headquarters in 1854, in the very centre of the town, now houses temporary art exhibitions and a well run **tourist office**, T021-4813301, summer Mon-Fri 0930-1730, Sat-Sun 1300-1700; winter Mon-Fri 0930-1730. They publish a *Titanic Trail* guide, €7.50, and can provide details of cruise liners about to arrive in the harbour.

Heritage centre ⓘ *T021-4813591, www.cobhheritage.com. Mar-Dec Mon-Sat 1000-1800, €4.* The town's heritage centre, **Cobh, The Queenstown Story**, in the old railway station, is devoted to the town's poignant associations and there are interesting displays covering the tragedy of mass emigration and the disasters at sea.

Cobh Museum ⓘ *Scot's Church, High Rd, T021-4814240. Apr-Oct, Mon-Sat 1100-1300, 1400-1730, Sun 1500-1800. €1. 50.* There is also a small museum in a defunct Presbyterian church, on the right side as you walk into town from the railway station. The exhibits relate to local, especially maritime, history. Passenger lists and other files are available for research into family history.

A town walk From opposite the museum, walk up Spy Hill to enjoy a fine view of the harbour. The nearest island is Haulbowline Island, while Spike Island is closer to the mouth of the harbour. If you carry on up Bishop's Road, a right turn at the top provides a startling view of just how steeply the houses stand on the hillside. From here it is a short walk across to **St Colman's Cathedral**, designed by EW Pugin and GC Ashlin. Building began in the 1860s but wasn't completed until 1915. If arriving in Cobh by

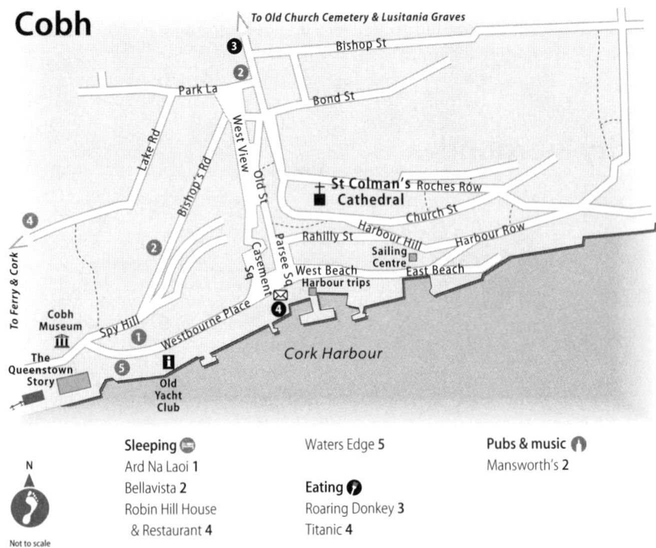

ferry, the commanding presence of the church is hard to miss and the granite and limestone exterior is equally impressive when close up. The spire boasts the country's biggest carillon, with 47 bells covering a range of four octaves, the largest bell weighing in at 3,440 kg.

Midleton → *Colour map 3, grid B5.*

You will find Ireland's chief distillery in Midleton, 24 km east of Cork. When a new distillery was opened here, the original 19th-century works were preserved and opened to the public as the **Old Midleton Distillery,** ⓘ *T021-4613594, guided tours, Mar-Oct daily 1000-1700, last tour at 1400; Nov-Feb, tours at 1130, 1430, 1600, €7.95, there is a frequent Bus Éireann service between Cork and Middleton.* The conducted tour starts with a film show, but the interesting part is the walkabout that takes you through the whole process, from the yard where local farmers arrived with their barley through to the massive machinery, including a powerful waterwheel and a steam engine, and the obligatory free taster in the bar. Further drinks can be purchased and there are some vintage whiskeys for sale. There is also a café serving light meals, but for something more substantial try the pub lunches at the Victorian-style O'Donovans, 58 Main Street.

Youghal → *Phone code: 024. Colour map 3, grid B6.*

Pronounced 'yawl' (from *Eochaill* a 'yew wood'), the town is at the mouth of the Blackwater and was founded in the 13th century by Anglo-Normans, probably on the site of an earlier Danish settlement. During the Elizabethan age the town and surrounding land became the property of Sir Walter Raleigh and during his years as mayor he is credited with having smoked the first pipe of tobacco in Ireland in 1588. In 1602 Raleigh sold out to Richard Boyle, later the Earl of Cork, and he spent far longer in residence here than Raleigh ever did. Nowadays, it is the summer season that attracts most visitors and the Blue Flag beach makes Youghal popular with Irish families, while the places of interest within the town justify at least a half day's visit. The **tourist office** is near Market Square at the harbour side of town, T024-20170. Apr-Sep Mon-Sun 1000-1730; Jul-Aug longer hours; Oct-Mar Mon-Fri 1000-1730. Walking tours from Jun-Aug Mon-Sat 1100, €4.45.

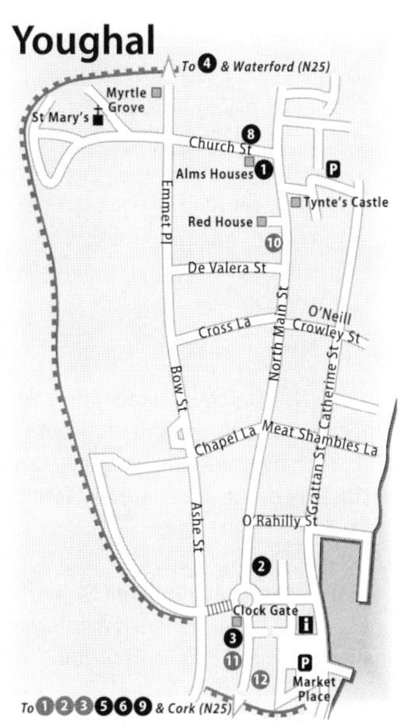

Sleeping
Avonmore House 1
Ballymakeigh House 2
Evergreen House 3

Nook 1
Perfect Blend 2
Red Store 8
Tides 9
Tower 3

Eating
Aherne's Seafood 4
Browne's 5
Clancy's 6

Pubs & music
Imperial Hotel 10
JD's 11
Usual Place 12

Not to scale

A walking tour A good place to begin a walking tour is outside the **Clock Gate,** the quaint but striking structure that divides the town's long thoroughfare into South and North Main Streets. A gate of the original 13th-century town walls stood on this spot, but in the late 18th century the present structure was built as a gaol and the story goes that political prisoners were tortured here and publicly hanged from the windows. Make your way up North Main Street for about 450 m, passing on your left the post office

Michael Collins' last day

At 0600 in a bedroom in the Imperial Hotel in Cork City, Michael Collins unknowingly arose to meet his last day. He had planned a tour around West Cork, dangerous to a degree because this was militant Republican territory and anti-Treaty men were active in the area. He arrived in Macroom at 0730 outside what is now the Castle Hotel and collected a local driver from the hotel before setting off for Bandon. The road to Bandon was blocked in places and taking side roads led at one stage to uncertainty over what direction to take (still a hazard in this area). A local man outside a pub helped them but they were not to know he was a Republican scout who recognized Collins and alerted anti-Treaty men, secretly meeting in the area. They guessed correctly that Collins would return along the same road because they knew the main Bandon to Cork road was impassable because of anti-Treaty sabotage.

Collins and his armed escort made a quick stop in Bandon then headed off for Clonakility, where they stopped at O'Donovan's Hotel before leaving for Rosscarbery and then Skibbereen. They stopped in Skibbereen at the Eldon Hotel until about 1630.

The return journey to Bandon was taken via Sam's Cross in order to visit the ruins of Collins' family home burnt out by Major A E Percival (who years later would blunder into surrendering Singapore to the Japanese). He had a drink in the Five Alls pub before setting off for Bandon and what is now the Munster Arms Hotel. A final photograph (now hanging in the lobby of the hotel) was taken of Collins as he sat in his car for the journey back to Cork. On the way back, in the area of Béal na mBláth, Collins and his convoy were ambushed and the Commander-in-Chief of the Army of the Provisional Government was shot dead. Each year, on the anniversary of his death, 22 August 1922, a commemorative service takes place at the stone memorial at the site of the ambush.

To reach the site of the ambush from Bandon, take the road to Macroom and follow the signs to Béal na mBláth. His family home at Sam's Cross may also be visited (see page 261).

and then the **Red House** on the same side of the road. This Dutch-inspired house was built in the early 18th century and a few doors up there is a different and older type of architecture, a set of restored **Alms Houses** built in 1610 by Richard Boyle a few years after Raleigh sold his land to him. On the opposite side of the street stands **Tynte's Castle**, a 15th-century structure.

★ **St Mary's Church** ⓘ *T024-91014, donation requested.* The Protestant St Mary's Collegiate Church is the real highlight of the town, reached by turning left a little way further up North Main Street. The church, originally built in the early 11th century and restored in the 1850s, has had a chequered history; some of the Victorian excess, such as the plastering that covered the stone walls, has now been removed. Check out the flamboyant tomb of Richard Boyle and his family. Designed by a London sculptor and brought over to Youghal, this is one of the best 17th-century tombs in Ireland. Boyle's two wives are either side of him, the reclining figure at the top is his mother-in-law, and his children are below.

The explanation of the 'leper's squint', at the entrance to the north transept is worth reading and the north-facing wall of this transept, which is thought to date from the original 11th-century church built by Christianized Vikings, carries an etching of a Viking boat inscribed on a lower stone. Interesting old tombstones may also be found outside in the churchyard and there is a stepped path that leads upto a handsome stretch of the medieval town wall.

Myrtle Grove Next to the church gates is a rare example of a 16th-century unfortified house. The home of Walter Raleigh, it is said that under a yew tree in the garden, Edmund Spenser read parts of his *Faerie Queene* to him; story far more probable than another old wives' tale that Raleigh also planted the first potatoes from the New World here. It is not possible to visit the house, but by peeping over the church wall, on the right after passing through the church gate, you can see the Elizabethan chimneys.

Fox's Lane Folk Museum ⓘ *Summer Tue-Sat 1000-1300 and 1400-1800. €3.* At the other end of town, in North Cross Lane near the tourist office, Fox's Lane Folk Museum is filled with an miscellany of domestic artefacts from the late 19th century to the 1950s: moustache cups, hat irons, sausage makers and so on.

Macroom → *Phone code: 026. Colour map 3, grid B4.*

From Cork the N22 road can be taken direct to Killarney by car or bus, missing out West Cork entirely. Macroom could serve as a base for forays into West Cork or the Killarney area itself.

Bandon and Dunmanway → *Phone code: 023. Colour map 3, grid C3/4.*

The above route will also take you from Cork to Bantry via Gougane Barra (see page 277), but a more direct, though far less scenic, route to Bantry is by way of the N71 to Bandon and then the R586 through Dunmanway. Bandon was once a famous old Protestant town ("even the pigs are Protestant" goes the old saying). Someone painted on the walls of 17th-century Brandon "Jew, Turk or atheist may enter here, but not a papist." A reply appeared afterwards "whoever wrote this wrote it well, for the same is written in the gates of Hell." It was also a military barracks during the War of Independence that came under fire from rebels and was the scene of an attempted assassination on Major Percival (see page 254) as described in Tom Barry's *Guerrilla Days in Ireland*. The **West Cork Heritage Centre** ⓘ *North Main St, T023-44193*, in an old church, explains just how important the potato once was to Irish life.

North Cork

North Cork is heaven to fishing folk who flock here annually to cast on the River Blackwater, and **Fermoy** has a fishing shop, **Brian Toomey Sports** ⓘ *18 McCurtain St, T025-31101*, which can advise and sell tackle. However, finding an edible meal in Fermoy is not an easy task. Try the creperie, La Bigoudenne, T025-32832, 28 McCurtain St, which opens every evening except Monday.

The prosperous market town of **Mallow** has a far better choice of places to stay and eat and is another major base for anglers.

Sleeping

Cobh *p251, map p252*
Accommodation needs booking in advance during the regatta in the middle of Aug.
B-D Water's Edge Hotel, next to the Heritage Centre, T021-4815566, www.watersedgehotel.ie. Attractive hotel, 2-night packages, no public bar, sea views.
D Robin Hill House, Lake Rd, T021-4811395, www.robinhillhouse.com. An old rectory with 6 delightfully modern, uncluttered bedrooms (ask for one overlooking the harbour) and a superb restaurant. Easily the smartest place in town.
E Ard Na Laoi, 15 Westbourne Pl, T021-4812742. B&B with fine views of the harbour.
E Bellavista, Bishop's Rd, T021-4812450. This B&B is a good example of Cobh's Victorian houses.

Youghal *p253, map p253*
D **Ballymakeigh House**, at Killeagh 9.5 km west of Youghal, T024-95184, www.ballymaeighhouse.com. Part of a working farm. Has won plaudits for its accommodation and above-average breakfasts.
E **Avonmore House**, South Abbey, T024-92617, avonmoreyoughal@eircom.net. A centrally located B&B; if coming from Cork, just before the road splits into a one-way system.
F **Evergreen House**, The Strand, T024-92877, www.evergreenireland.com. A hostel with dorm beds and private rooms.

Camping
Clonvilla, Clonpriest, T024-98288. Only 10 pitches available for tents.

Macroom *p255*
B-C **Castle Hotel**, Main St, T026-41074, www.castlehotel.ie. Has a decent restaurant, a pool and gym.
D **Victoria Hotel**, Main St, T026-41082. Where William Penn once stayed. A friendly place with affordable bar food and a modest restaurant.

Bandon and Dunmanway *p255*
D **Munster Arms Hotel**, Oliver Plunkett St, T023-41562, www.munsterarmshotel.com. The best place to stay or stop for a meal (see The 'Michael Collins' last day' page 254).
F **Shiplake Mountain Hostel**, T023-45750, www.shiplakemountainhostel.com. A converted 19th-century farmhouse with wood-burning stove, dorm beds and 4 private rooms for €25 to €36 each, depending on the time of year. There is space for camping, bikes can be hired and meals can be arranged.

North Cork *p255*
L-A **Assolas Country House**, to the west of Mallow at Kanturk, T029-50015, www.assolas.com. A gracious country house (dinner for residents only) with elegant rooms, blazing log fires and an admirable policy statement: "We do not apply a service charge and gratuities are not expected."

Eating

Blarney *p250*
Most of the hotels in Blarney are all reliable sources for competitively priced lunches in their bars and all have more expensive restaurants. However, like everywhere in Blarney at the height of summer, it only takes the disgorging of one mammoth coach to suddenly overwhelm a place.
ΨΨ **Blair's Inn**, Cloghroe, a little way out of the village, about 10 mins by car from Blarney on the R579, T021-4381470. A far better option is this well-established pub. Run by owner-managers it has two cosy dining rooms filled with bric-à-brac, a pretty riverside garden and big airy bar. Bar menu until 2130 daily, and also a restaurant open for lunch and dinner serving excellent seafood and much more. Food is served 1230-1530 and from 1830 and there is also traditional music on Sun nights; also on Mon in the summer.

Cobh *p251, map p252*
ΨΨΨ **Robin Hill Restaurant**, Lake Rd, T021-4811395. Dinner here is one of Cobh's finest eating experiences. Starters like gravadlax from wild salmon or avocado and boilie cheese, main courses of meat and fresh fish and a serious wine list. Reserve a harbour-view table if possible.
ΨΨΨ-ΨΨ **Titanic Restaurant**, T021- 4855200. In the centre of town, characterful, interesting food in a restaurant done out like the Palm Court in the Titanic. Dinner nightly except Mon. The Deane Room has a more exotic menu including salmon cooked in tequila. Book a table in advance, Wed-Sat only.
ΨΨ **Jacob's Ladder**, in the Water's Edge hotel. An interesting option at lunchtime with some good lunch specials.
Ψ **Titanic Bar**, with authentic *Titanic* memorabilia around the place, is the most popular place to eat in town and it has outdoor seats over the harbour. The menu covers a range of good modern pub food.

Youghal *p253, map p253*
ΨΨΨ **Aherne's Seafood Restaurant**, T024-92424. At the Waterford end of town, has a bar serving seafood pizza, chowder and open sandwiches.
ΨΨ **Browne's Restaurant**, T024-91373. Hearty Irish cooking, from breakfast to dinner.
ΨΨ **The Red Store**, 150/151 North Main St, T024-90144. Very moderately priced lunches and early evening meals until 1930 Mon-Sat.
ΨΨ **Tides**, Upper Strand, T024-93127. Offers some classy food to compare with *Aherne's*.

Several pubs are worth investigating for their food possibilities at lunch time:
¶ **Clancy's**, Strand Building, T024-20042.
¶ **The Nook**, Main St.
¶ **Quays Bar**, T024-91566.

North Cork *p255*
¶ **The Vintage**, O'Brien St, Kanturk, T029-50549. A traditional pub with food for travellers passing through.

Pubs and music

Cobh *p251, map p252*
The best of the many pubs with music are close to one another:
Mansworth's, Midleton St, T021- 811965, dates back to the late 19th century;
Roaring Donkey, Oreleia Terr, T021- 811739.
Titanic , has open air music on the quayside from Thu to Sun, with traditional Irish on Thu and jazz or rock on Fri.

Youghal *p253, map p253*
Browne's Restaurant, traditional Irish music on Thu.
The Nook, Main St. Has traditional Irish music on Wed nights.
In summer lots more bars offer musical entertainment – try:
Imperial Hotel, T024-92435, music at weekends;
JD's, T024-93011, music at weekends all year;
The Red Store, regular music sessions all year in the bar;
The Usual Place, T024-91617.
In summer, if you have a hankering for **Riverdance** there is a twice weekly show on Tue, Wed in the Town Hall called **Dancing Through the Ages**. Starts at 2000, tickets at the door.

Activities and tours

Cobh *p251, map p252*
Sailing International Sailing, East Beach, T021-4811237, www.sailcork.com. Dinghy and cruiser sailing courses.

Tours Guided Titanic Trail walks through town, 1100 (1100, 1400, 1600 in summer) from the Commodore Hotel, T021-4813878, €7.50. An hour-long harbour tour departs from the pier at 1200, 1400, 1500; 1600 daily Jun-Sep, T021-4811485, €5.50.

Transport

Around Cork *p251*
Bus Bus Éireann's **Cork-Youghal-Ardmore** service, No 260, runs daily with 6 express buses taking 90 mins. The first bus leaves Cork at 0840 and the last bus departs from Youghal at 2225. The main Expressway bus, No 40, travelling a number of times daily between **Tralee** and **Rosslare** stops at **Youghal** and also connects the town with **Killarney**, **Macroom**, **Ballincollig**, **Cork**, **Dungarvan**, **Waterford** and **Wexford**.

Ferry T021-4811485. Daily service 0700-2415. €4.50 return, €3 single, €1.50 foot passenger.

Train A regular service (no bicycles carried) to and from **Cork**.

Directory

Cobh *p251, map p252*
Genealogy For family research contact the Cobh Heritage Centre, T021-4813591; cobhher@indigo.ie, or **Cobh Museum**, T021-4814240, www.cobhmuseum.com.

Kinsale to Baltimore

West Cork begins in picture-perfect Kinsale with its annual stage-managed brouhaha of the culinary kind, an impressive collection of craft shops and crowds of visitors. From these sophisticated heights this route takes you through quiet villages with their own peculiar charms: the Protestant church in Timoleague, the pretty coastal route from Clonakilty to Skibbereen, Rosscarbery with its nearby ruins and stone circle, Glandore, the oldest holiday resort in Cork, and Castletownshend where Somerville and Ross lived out their days. Offshore islands include Cape Clear and Sherkin, and busy little market

The Maid of Erin statue at the tourist office end of town is a tribute to those who struggled for Irish independence. Tom Barry, leader of the famous Flying Column guerrilla force during the War of Independence, comments in his autobiography *Guerrilla Days in Ireland* that Skibbereen was never a safe town for the rebels because of the forelock-tugging mentality of its townsfolk.

Great Famine Exhibition and Lough Hyne Interpretative Centre ⓘ *Upper Bridge St, T028-40900. Mid-May to mid Sep, daily, 1000-1800; mid-Mar to mid-May and mid-Sep to end of Oct, Tue-Sat. €3.* An audio-visual show lasting 15 minutes covers Lough Hyne, and the Famine exhibition amounts to a few display boards, touch screens and an original soup pot. Worth a visit, perhaps, on a rainy day.

Lough Hyne → *Colour map 3, grid C3.*

Signposted off the road to Baltimore, Lough Hyne was once a freshwater lake that sank below sea level, became flooded with sea water and is now a tidal seawater lake with Mediterranean marine life. This is a pretty walk through pleasant woodland to the top of **Knockomagh**, beside Lough Hyne. There are great views on the route up the hill, taking about half an hour, and an amazing panorama at the top. From the car park beside Lough Hyne go back to the Skibbereen road and turn left. Walk about 500 m to where a boreen branches off to the left. Opposite is a track going up into the woods: follow this until it comes to a ruin and bear sharp left in front of it. From here your path to the top is quite clear.

The trees you are walking through are an interesting mixture. This is largely an oak wood, possibly even an aboriginal one; the ancestors of these oak trees may have stood here just after the ice sheets departed. In the 18th century, beech trees were planted and the children of those trees are still very much alive today. Below the canopy of the oak and beech, holly, honeysuckle and ivy thrive. On the forest floor are great stands of wood rush while in spring more woodland plants make use of the period before the oak and beech leaves emerge to flower: bluebells, wood sorrel, and primroses. All summer long herb Robert with its pungent perfume flowers in the shade.

The forest is protected as a nature reserve and as you continue up the well-made stepped path look out for Irish yew trees, another aboriginal plant, and spindleberry trees, a low deciduous shrub rather than a tree, with inconspicuous flowers in May but glorious coral pink berries in autumn.

The view at the top of the hill is breathtaking. Before you lies a whole stretch of West Cork's coastline laid out like an Ordnance Survey map. Immediately below is the lough and it is possible to see the nature of its unusual geography. It lies below the sea level beyond and is almost blocked at its seaward end by a wall of rock allowing only a small channel of water out of the lough. As fresh water feeds into the lough from feeder streams, the water flows out of the creek. But at high tide the sea level rises above the level of the water flowing out, and suddenly the water turns and starts to flow back into the lough raising its level considerably. As a result, it is a salt-water lough, and because it is only exposed to the open sea for part of the day its water is much warmer than the open ocean. Consequently, a very unusual ecosystem has evolved here with plants and animals more like those of the Mediterranean than northern Europe.

It is possible also to see how over the millennia the sea has risen and flooded the once-dry land valleys of this area. Out to sea is Cape Clear Island (see below), once part of the mainland chains of mountains thrown up 300 million years ago by massive tectonic movements originating in southern Europe. Return to the road, going left past the ruin and down through modern conifer plantations.

Baltimore → *Phone code: 028. Colour map 3, grid C3.*

Situated 13 km down the River Ilen from Skibbereen, Baltimore's resident population of around 200 souls swells to an almost unmanageable number of visitors in the summer as the harbour area overfills with people flocking to Cork's two most popular off-shore islands. But Baltimore is nothing if not laid back and welcomes all and sundry, even in winter when the Mediterranean-style harbour, where the guest houses, restaurants and pubs rub shoulders, is transformed into a wild and windy shelter from fierce Atlantic winds. There is **tourist information** at the Islands Crafts and Information Centre, at the pier, T028-20347, open from May-Sep.

In 1631 an Algerian raiding party sailed into Baltimore and kidnapped 100 people for the white slave trade. Apparently some of their descendants can still be traced in Algeria through their family names. Before the 17th century, the land and islands around Baltimore were in the hands of the O'Driscoll family, who collected dues from Spanish and French boats fishing for mackerel and pilchards and using the safe harbour, and the ruined castle in the village harks back to that era. In the 18th century a profitable small industry developed along this part of the coast sending salted mackerel to the US, and as late as the early 20th century some 16 trains were leaving Baltimore every month packed with fish. Today, it is boats that are leaving on a daily basis, ferrying passengers to and from Cape Clear and Sherkin Island. The first lighthouse on the rock here was swept away by gales in 1865 but replaced in 1906.

Sherkin Island → *Phone code: 028.*

ⓘ *Boats leave from Baltimore, T028-20218, www.baltimore-ireland.com, regularly from Jun-Sep, 0900-2030 (around €8 return). There is also a service from Schull, T028-28138.* Sherkin Island, 5 km by 2 km has safe sandy beaches by day (with a tractor, T028-20218, waiting at the pier to tow you to them in the morning and back again in the evening) and opportunities for quiet walks spotting birds and flowers, while at night the island's two pubs are alive with sociable buzz and mercifully within staggering distance of the harbour for the last boat back to Baltimore. The island's sandy beaches are all safe for swimming.

★ Cape Clear Island → *Phone code: 028. Colour map 3, grid C3. www.oilean-chleire.ie.*

It takes 45 minutes to reach this, Ireland's southernmost island, from Baltimore with the boat weaving its way out of the harbour on the same route as the Algerian pirates of 1631. Unlike Sherkin, there are no sandy beaches but for exhilarating country walks, inspiring seascapes, birdwatching and heather-clad hillsides Cape Clear Island, 5 km by 2 km, is a very accessible and enjoyable destination. There is a small **Heritage Centre** ⓘ *open daily in summer from 1400 to 1730,* focusing on the island's history and culture. Before your visit, try to collect the useful map brochure from the tourist office in Baltimore or from the small tourist information post at the harbour when you arrive. About one-third of the 931 different plants in Ireland can be found on the island, so a flower identification book may be helpful. Guided walks, either ecological, T028-39193, or historical, Chuck Kruger, T028-39157, can be arranged.

Cape Clear International Storytelling Festival 1st weekend in Sep, T028-39116.

Sherkin Island

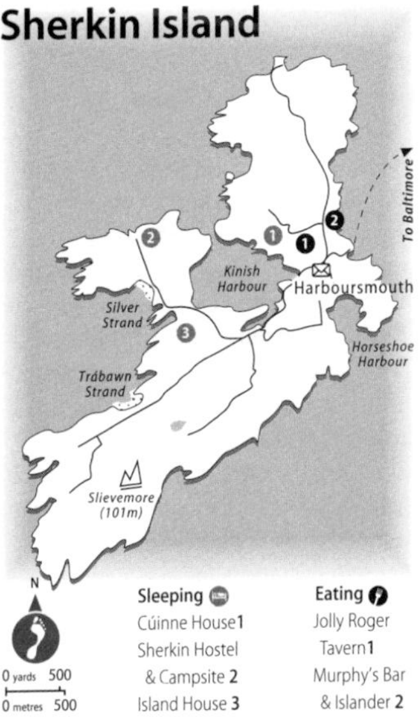

Sleeping
Cúinne House 1
Sherkin Hostel & Campsite 2
Island House 3

Eating
Jolly Roger Tavern 1
Murphy's Bar & Islander 2

Birdwatching on Cape Clear Island

In the summer months thousands of manx shearwaters (a large bird, black on top and white underneath), kittiwakes and fulmars sweep past the southern end of the island on their way to fishing grounds south of Ireland from their rocky abodes off the Kerry coast to the north. In the evening they return along the same route and it is a spectacular sight at any time of the day. Ornithologists should write in advance to the Bird Observatory, Cape Clear Island, Co Cork, T028-39181, for information on organized trips and accommodation. However, all interested visitors arriving on the island are welcome to call in at the Observatory, the white two-storey building near the harbour, or just head off for Blananarragaun at the southwest tip of the island. To get to Blananarragaun follow the path from the harbour up to the café and uphill to the shop. Turn right here, signposted for the camping site, carry on to the end of the road and keep going to the end of the spur of land. Also look out for guillemots (black plumage with a large white area that makes them look like black and white ducks in the water), which breed on the island.

A country walk After disembarking, turn left at the end of the pier and head up the path to the café and pub and continue uphill to the shop. Turn left here and follow the road to the hostel, but just before reaching it turn left and follow the road that passes a lane to the post office. Continue past the windmills on your right and turn right at the T-junction to head out to the eastern edge of the island. Alternatively, turn left and head back to the pier, passing the Heritage Centre on the way.

Sleeping

Kinsale *p258, maps p259 and next page*
L-B Old Bank House, Pearse St, T021-4774075, www.oldbankhousekinsale.com. The fact that this was an old bank explains its prime location in the centre of town. It's a now tasteful guest house with antiques and the original 200-year old walls exposed in the sitting room and breakfast room.
L-C Trident, World's End, T021-4772301, www.tridenthotel.com. More relaxing than the exterior suggests, and with a variety of packages worth enquiring about.
A Old Presbytery, Cork St, T021-4772027, www.oldpres.com. This guest house has a reputation as one of the best B&Bs in town and 2-bedroomed, self-catering suites can also be booked for a minimum of 2 nights.
A Perryville House, Pearse St, T021-4772731, www.perryvillehouse.com. Has a lovely wrought-iron exterior and plush bedrooms; almost too grand for this part of the country.
B Blue Haven, Pearse St, T021-4772209, www.bluehavenkinsale.com. This very central hotel has elegantly decorated rooms named after French-Irish wine families. Lots of mod cons including flat screen TVs and beautiful bathrooms.
B Harbour Lodge, out at Scilly T021-4772376, www.harbourlodge.com. Makes the perfect place to escape the hustle and bustle of town, with sea-facing rooms with kingsize beds and a huge conservatory.
D Kieran's Folkhouse Inn, Guardwell, T021-4772382, folkhse@indigo.ie. B&B and an evening meal in the seafood bistro downstairs available as a package.
E Amarach, The Glen, T021-4774633. Townhouse B&B with 3 rooms with en suite bathrooms; closed in winter.
E Captain's Quarters, Dennis Quay, T021-4774549, www.captains-kinsale.com. Away from the traffic but very central. Rooms are

For an explanation of the sleeping and eating price codes used in this guide, see inside the front cover. Other relevant information is found in Essentials pages 39-45.

refreshingly uncluttered and the maritime theme is inoffensive.
E **Kyalami**, 16 Lower O'Connell St, T021-4772074. One of the town's less expensive B&Bs.
E **Pier House**, Pier Rd, T021-4774475 www.pierhousekinsale.com. A smart, centrally located and relatively quiet B&B.
E **Rock View**, The Glen, T021-4773162. B&B with car park behind the house.
F **Dempsey's**, Eastern Rd, T021-4772124. Next to a garage, this is a fairly basic hostel with dorm beds, and private rooms. Handy if coming from Cork as the bus will stop outside.

Kinsale to Clonakilty *p260*
D **Courtmacsherry Hotel**, T023-46198, www.courtmacsherryhotel.com. Has a pleasing air of gentility and offers a refreshing escape from money-spinning Kinsale. The house lost its pitched roof in the War of Independence, was burnt by the IRA, but there is still an enticing Anglo-Irish nuance to the place. Self-catering accommodation also available.

Kinsale centre

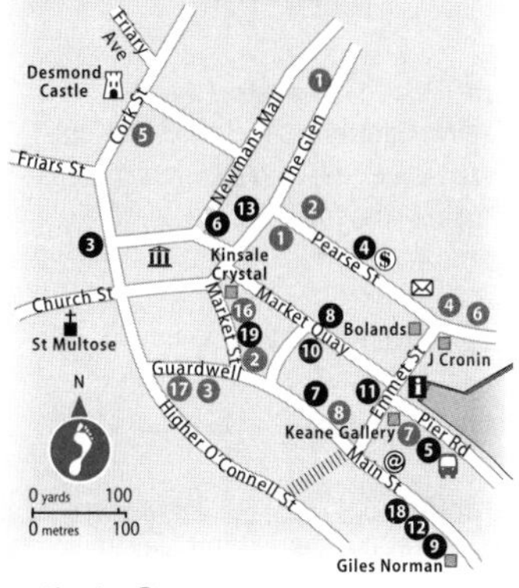

Sleeping
Amarach **1**
Blue Haven & Café Blue **2**
Kieran's Folkhouse Inn **3**
Old Bank House **4**
Old Presbytery **5**
Perryville House **6**
Pier House **7**
Rock View **8**

Eating
Crackpots **3**
Dino's **5**
Gina's Café **11**
Greyhound **6**
Hoby's **7**
Jean Marc's Chow House **4**
Jim Edwards **8**
Little Skillet **9**
Max's Wine Bar **12**
Patsy's Corner **13**
Pearl Palace **10**
Taste of India **19**
Vintage **18**

Pubs & music
1601 **1**
An Seanachai **2**
Shanakee **16**
Tap Tavern **17**

Clonakilty *p260, map p260*
C-D **O'Donovan's Hotel**, Pearse St, T023-33250, www.odonovanshotel.com. Has been in the same family for 5 generations.
E **Chez Nous**, T023-34582, leesean@iolfree.ie. Out on the R600 road to Timoleague; reasonable room rates at the bottom end of this price category, but too far to walk from town.
E **The Glendine**, Tawnies Upper, T023-34824, www.glendine.com. At the top end of this price range, a 10-min walk from town.
E **The Well**, T023-35249, Berder@gofree.indigo.ie. On the R600 to Timoleague. Reasonable rates at the bottom end of this category, but quite a walk from town.
E **Wytchwood**, off Emmet Sq, T023-33525, wytchost@iol.ie. A pleasant townhouse in a quiet location.
F **Old Brewery Hostel**, T023-33525, wytchost@iol.ie. Directly opposite the Wytchwood, and run by the same owners, with 8 dorm beds and 3 double rooms.

Campsite
Desert House, Coast Rd, T023-33331. Open Easter, then May to end Sep, within walking distance of town, overlooks the muddy end of Clonakilty Bay and is signposted from the roundabout at the eastern end of town.

Clonakilty to Skibbereen (coastal route) *p261*
A-C **Celtic Ross Hotel**, N71 at Rosscarbery, T023-48722, www.celticrosshotel.com. Startling looking but modern and comfortable, has another surprise inside in the form of an unusual bogwood sculpture.
B-C **Castle Guesthouse**, Castletownshend, T028-36100. The castellated seat of the Townshend family (it is said that George Bernard Shaw's mother-in-law changed her name from Townsend to Townshend hoping that society would assume she was related), B&B and self-catering apartments.
C **Marine Hotel**, Glandore, T028-33366. Comfortable place to stay for a night or two.
D **Bow Hall**, Castletownshend, T028-36114. 3 rooms, a lovely garden and dinner for around €32 at a communal table.
E **Ardagh House**, Union Hall, T028-33571, www.ardaghhouse.com. B&B and restaurant, facing the water in this village west of Glandore. Open for food all day: steaks, seafood and sandwiches, outdoor tables.

F Curraheen Lodge, Rosscarbery, T023-48498. A useful hostel with 8 beds, 1 private room and camping space.
F Maria's Schoolhouse, Union Hall, T028-33002. An old National School converted to a hostel with dorm beds, family rooms and private rooms with en suite bath available.

Camping
G The Meadow, 2 km outside of Glandore on the road to Rosscarbery, T028-33280, the_meadow@oceanfree.net. A very attractive, quiet camping park set in wooded gardens.

Skibbereen *p263*
C-D Eldon Hotel, Bridge St, T028-22000, www.eldon-hotel.com. Comfortable old hotel in the middle of town with small rooms and a miscellany of prints, pictures and photographs that includes one of Michael Collins leaving the hotel on his last day (see page 254).
E Bridge House, Bridge St, T028-21273. A 19th-century house, across the road from the Eldon, which offers B&B in a veritable shrine to Victoriana.
E Riverview House, Newbridge, T028-21516. A farmhouse within walking distance of town. Some rooms have their own bathrooms.
F Russagh Mill Hostel & Adventure Centre, T028-22451, info@russaghmillhostel.com. On the Castletownshend road 2 km from town with dorm beds and private rooms. The owner has climbed Everest, and various hyper-activities such as rock climbing may be available through the hostel.

Baltimore *p264*
B Casey's of Baltimore, T028-20197, www.baltimore-ireland.com/caseys. A family-run hotel. More than half the generously sized rooms, all with kingsize beds, benefit from lovely views over the bay.
C-E Baltimore Bay Guest House, T028-20600, www.youenjacob.com. 5 of its 9 rooms overlook the harbour but all share a modern, clean style with touches of old furniture alongside contemporary wall hangings.
E Slipway, T028-20134, www.theslipway.com. In the village but just far enough from the centre to escape the hustle and bustle, this B&B has some style and character but only 4 rooms so book ahead.
E The Stone House, Lifeboat Rd, T028-20511, www.aquaventures.ie. Has views of the bay, a homely atmosphere and home-made bread every morning.
E-F Rolf's Holidays, T028-20289, www.rolfsholidays.com. To say there are dorm beds, double (some with en suite bathrooms) and triple rooms makes this place seem just like another hostel. Far from it – this is a superb place to stay, away from the noisy village and with a superb restaurant and café. Real value for money.

Sherkin Island *p265, map p265*
E Cúinne House, T028-20384. If you decide to stay overnight, B&B and an evening meal for €10-16 is available, with ocean views from the bedrooms and evening meals an option.

Other places offering B&B are:
E Horseshoe Cottage, T028-20598, www.sherkinisland.ie, including self-catering cottages;
E Island House, T028-20314;
E Sherkin Hostel and Campsite, T028-20572, basic; and
E Windhoek, T028-20275, windhoeksherkin.com.

Cape Clear Island *p265*
E Ard Na Gaoithe, T028-39160. B&B, open all year, rates are €28-60 for single/doubles.
E Cluain Mara, T028-39153, www.capeclearisland.com. B&B, open all year, with rates of €28-60 for single/doubles.
F Cape Clear Island Hostel, an *An Oige* hostel, T028-39198. ("Your last Irish stop before the South Pole".) Open Jun-Oct.

Camping
Cuas an Uisce, T028-39119. There is a basic campsite here.

Eating

Kinsale *p258, maps p259 and p267*
The plethora of restaurants is a distinguishing feature of Kinsale and, though cynics say that the town's gourmet scene has more to do with selling Kinsale as a 'product' than with good food at competitive prices, there is certainly a generous choice of dishes to consider, from black pudding poached in pink champagne

and Thai fish cakes to home-made burgers and chips. The best deals for 3-course meals under €25 come in the form of early-bird menus and other set dinners.

ΨΨΨ **Blue Haven**, Pearse St, T021-4772209. Has modern Irish cuisine, and it is worth trying to reserve a table by the garden with its waterfall. The excellent wine list is based around Irish families who established vineyards around the world, especially in France, between the 17th and early 19th centuries.

ΨΨΨ **Jim Edwards**, T021-4772541. Can be relied on for meat and fish dishes and starters such as kidneys spiked with madeira and garlic.

ΨΨΨ **Man Friday's**, out at Scilly, T021-4772260. Maintains standards while packing in diners for oysters, steaks and seafood and has the added advantage of being open all year round.

ΨΨΨ **Toddies**, Eastern Rd, T021-4777769. Serves French/Irish cuisine, has good views of the sea, specializes in fish but can offer the carnivore and herbivore a good run for their money. Good value Sun lunch.

ΨΨΨ **Vintage**, Main St, T021-4772502. Serves classical dishes with innovative touches in a comfortable atmosphere. Lots of seafood, a surprise 5-course menu and a cosy little snug for pre-dinner drinks.

ΨΨ **Crackpots**, T021-4772847. Has a 3-course dinner for €20, between 1830 and 1930, eating from pottery hand-made by the proprietor.

ΨΨ **Hoby's**, T021-4772200. Has a set dinner which brings it into this category and rather more expensive à la carte.

ΨΨ **Jean Marc's Chow House**, Pearse St, next to the AIB bank, T021-4777117. Offers a lovely Asian fusion menu with a well-chosen wine list to complement the dishes. Closed Tue in winter.

ΨΨ **The Little Skillet**, Pearse St, T021-4774202. Has a cosy, home-cooking atmosphere. Open Mar-Nov from 1800.

Ψ **Blue Haven**, Pearse St. One of the reliably best places of all for a decent meal at lunch or dinnertime is the bar food at the Fish Market Tavern.

Ψ **Café Blue**, Pearse St. Does a nice line in sandwiches, filled panini and designer coffees.

Ψ **Dino's**, Pier Rd. Serves traditional fish and chips.

Ψ **Gina's Café**, Short Quay. Tiny and with a few tables out on the street. Lots of sandwiches, filled panini and a tempting dessert menu.

Ψ **The Greyhound**, usefully situated in a pedestrianized area near the museum. Has outdoor tables and pub food in the €5-10 range: home-made burgers, baked potatoes, salmon platter, sandwiches.

Ψ **Max's Wine Bar**, Main St, T021-4772443. Has an affordable early-bird menu; otherwise a meal here comes under the mid-range bracket. Some vegetarian choices.

Ψ **Patsy's Corner**, Church St. A tiny tea shop, chairs outside, doing sandwiches and snacks.

Ψ **Pearl Palace**, Short Quay, T021-4777877. Offers all the usual Chinese dishes plus satay, Szechuan dishes and will even deliver to your hotel.

Ψ **The Spaniard**, out at Scilly. Worth the journey for top drawer pub grub and traditional Irish music many nights of the week.

Ψ **Taste of India**, Main St. For those who enjoy a taste of the orient this has an enormous menu of inexpensive fairly authentic dishes (great for vegetarians).

Kinsale to Clonakilty *p260*

ΨΨΨ **Cork Tree**, Courtmacsherry Hotel. Has a 4-course meal for €38 with choices from a menu of fresh, local seafood and beef.

ΨΨΨ **Travara Lodge**, Courtmacsherry, T023-46493. On the waterfront, conjures up innovative dishes with a French twist, Fri-Tue, in a set dinner for €40.

ΨΨ **Dillon's**, Mill St, Timoleague. Open daily in summer with a creative international menu.

Ψ **Gráine's**, Timoleague. Has an affordable menu of meals like shepherd's pie and vegetarian pizza.

At Courtmachsherry, on a fine day, consider a picnic at the wooden tables that look out across the estuary from the side of the road approaching the village. There is pub food at Ψ **The Lifeboat Inn** or Ψ **Pier House Bar**, both on the waterfront.

Clonakilty *p260, map p260*

Nearly all the eating places are on the long main street that changes its name a few times. The tourist office dispenses a useful food and entertainment guide.

¥¥ **Malt House Granary Restaurant**, Ashe St, T023-34355. Serves modern Irish food in a modern Irish setting. Lovely breads, black pudding of course, and reasonable prices.
¥¥ **O'Keefe's**, in the Emmet Hotel facing the square. Serves meals at the top end of this price bracket.
¥ **An Súgán Pub**, 41 Wolfe Tone St, T023-33498. At the east end, serves local seafood though the specials advertised in the window may be better value.
¥ **Macehiter's Restaurant**, T023-34863, opposite O'Donovan's Hotel. Has a predictable menu of dishes at affordable prices; closed Sun.
¥ **Shama**, T023-36945. Across the road from O'Donovan's. Indian food.

Clonakilty to Skibbereen (coastal route) *p261*

¥¥ **Celtic Ross Hotel**, Rosscarbery. Pub grub available at the bar, looks like an Irish theme pub. Nearby holiday homes draw the Irish to Rosscarbery, and the bar is busier at night than one might imagine.
¥¥ **Mary Ann's**, Castletownshend. An olde-worlde pub serving bar food throughout the day, while dinner can be enjoyed in the upstairs restaurant or in the vine-covered room for around €35.
¥¥ **O'Callaghan Walshe**, Rosscarbery, T028-48125. A seafood restaurant in the town square, has atmosphere – stone walls, glass floats hanging around – and fresh food at the expensive end of this price bracket. Closed Mon, 1830-2100.
¥¥-¥ **Ardagh House**, Union Hall, T028-33571. Has a restaurant open for food all day: steaks, seafood and open sandwiches, nothing special, but outdoor tables.
¥ **Casey's**, Union Hall. Strong on seafood.
¥ **Glandore Inn**, Glandore, T028-33468. You will see it as you come into the village.
¥ **Hayes' Bar**, The Square, Glandore, T028-33214. A favourite stopping place with many travellers. Outdoor tables, wholesome sandwiches and an enticing wine list. Food 1200-1800 Jun and Aug.
¥ **Marine Hotel**, in Glandore as you come into the village.
¥ **Pilgrim's Rest**, Rosscarbery town square, T028-31796. Less expensive fare, open until 2000 weeknights but 1800 on Mon.

Skibbereen *p263*

¥¥ **Kalbo's Bistro**, 48 North Rd, T028-21515. Lunch could be salmon and shrimp with pesto, pasta and garlic bread for around €8; main courses in the evening around €18.
¥¥ **Ty Ar Mor**, 48 Bridge St, T028-22100. A seafood restaurant, with a minor nautical theme to the decor and an appealing menu that features dishes like monkfish and cognac, wild salmon and John Dory, plus a couple of meat items. Opens daily at 1830, 1 of the 2 dinner menus puts prices into the expensive category. Upstairs is a wine bar serving Thai food.
¥ **Annie May's**, a few doors down from the Eldon Hotel, T028-22930. Has lunch and evening menus to choose from.
¥ **Church Restaurant**, Bridge St. More appealing than Annie May's. Upstairs you can sit closer to the stained-glass windows than the worshippers ever could in this old Protestant church. Light meals like a melon and grape salad or crab and vegetable spring roll for around €8, steak or hearty, home-made hamburger for €20.

Baltimore *p*

¥¥ **Café Art**, T028-20289. Part of *Rolf's Holidays*, is indeed an arty place, lots of outdoor tables a mile or so from the harbour up a country road. Main dishes from €12.
¥¥ **Casey's Restaurant**, at Casey's Hotel. Has tables worth securing by the window to watch the evening descend over the ruins of a water-edge, 14th-century church. The daily specials and set menus are reasonably priced.
¥¥ **Chez Youen**, T028-20136. Specializes in locally caught fresh fish brought to your white-linen tablecloth in a cosy restaurant with art work by Dali, Sokolov and James Dixon around the walls. Duck and game also available on the dinner menus for €35 to €55; and a *tarte tatin* that just might be the best in the world.
¥¥ **The Custom House**, T028-20200. Has a plain but elegant style and fresh seafood is a choice on the 2 set meals of €25 and €35; closed Mon and Tue (and Wed except for Jul-Aug), 1st week of Jun and Oct-Apr.
¥ **La Jolie Brise**, T028-20600. Has great value pizzas, using fresh dough, from around €7-11, including a delicious one using goat's cheese, to a more expensive rich creamy smoked salmon version. 2 people

could share one for lunch, the house wine is superb, and food is available 0830-2300.

Sherkin Island *p265, map p265*
Abbey Stores Shop, also the post office, food can be obtained here.
Jolly Roger Tavern, T028-20379, across the road from *Murphy's*. Also does food and encourages musicians to play so there is often some live music.
Murphy's Bar, T028-20116. Also a B&B, does bar food all day as well as serving meals in its Islander Restaurant.

Cape Clear Island *p265*
There are a couple of pubs on the island. There is also a chip van by the harbour serving food, but a stopover in Skibbereen for picnic food is a good idea if you are staying for the whole day.
Ciarán Danny Mike's, T028-39153. Has a restaurant in the evening.
Cotters, T028-39102. Serves food.

Pubs and music

Kinsale *p258, maps p259 and p267*
Throughout the summer, most of the pubs in Kinsale are packed with groups of revellers intent on having a good time, occasionally enlivened even more by weekend merry-makers from Cork. Old-time favourites include:
1601, Pearse St;
An Seanachai, has live music or a DJ every night;
The Blue Haven, bar has music at weekends;
The Mad Monk, Main St, very lively at night;
Shanakee, near *1601*;
Tap Tavern, near St Multose Church; quiet pubs in town are difficult to find but this is a local pub where conversation is more important than loud music; though it has traditional music on Thu nights.

Clonakilty *p260, map p260*
Along the main thoroughfare, pubs like:
An Súgán;
An Teach Beag, down the lane by the side of O'Donovan's, whitewashed and tin-roofed, has traditional music;
De Barra's, Pearse St, www.debarra.ie;
O'Donovan's Hotel, nearby, can be relied on for lively musical sessions most nights in the summer;
The Venue, next door to *An Teach Beag*, glossy-looking place with jazz and blues bands. Details of other musical pubs available from the tourist office's entertainment guide.

Clonakilty to Skibbereen (coastal route) *p261*
MacCarthy's, Castletownshend. A fine old traditional pub where camera-toting visitors are tempted to take shots for the album back home.

Skibbereen *p263*
Annie May's, Bridge St, T028-22930. Also worth checking out for its weekend sessions which attract locals as well as visitors.
Baby Hannah's, 42 Bridge St, T028-22783. With sawdust on the floor of one bar, is the favourite venue for music on Thu and Sat nights.
Corner Bar, 37 Bridge St, T028-21522. Has sessions of traditional music on Mon and Sat.
West Cork Arts Centre, North St, T028-22090. Has temporary art exhibitions and the noticeboard at the entrance is a good source of information on current cultural events taking place in the area.

Baltimore *p*
Algiers Inn, T028-20145. With occasional sessions of music and a beer garden.
Bushe's Bar, on the other side of McCarthy's. Does not have music but is equally popular; at quiet times the display of nautical memorabilia can be appreciated.
Casey's, T028-20197. By the road coming into the village, has regular musical sessions.
McCarthy's, T028-20159. Has music most nights and attracts well known bands; see the programme in the window.

Sherkin Island *p265, map p265*
See the Eating above.

Cape Clear Island *p265*
See the Eating above.

Festivals and events

Clonakilty *p260, map p260*
The weekend-long **Clonakilty Festival**, at the end of **Aug**, is a musically rumbustious affair with bands playing in many of the bars. (See also page 262)

Shopping

Kinsale *p258, maps p259 and p267*
Arts and crafts There are 2 shops – facing each other opposite the post office – stocked with souvenirs and Irish crafts: **J Cronin**, a beautifully designed place made to look like an old fashioned hardware store, and **Bolands**.
Giles Norman Photography Gallery, www.gilesnorman.com. A large place stacked with evocative black and white images of Irish life from around €80.
Yello Gallery, www.yellogallery.net. Has artwork from around €100.
Small craft shops can be found in the pedestrianized area past the Greyhound pub near the museum.
Keane Gallery, Pier Rd. Has strange carvings.
Kent Gallery, Quayside. Has paintings, prints and sculptures by its resident artist.
Kinsale Crystal, Market St. Offers an alternative to Waterford glass.
Linda's Antiques, for antiques, with lots of antique jewellery.

Activities and tours

Kinsale *p258, maps p259 and p267*
Deep sea angling T087-2142999 and T021-4774946.
The Hire Shop, 18 Main St. Tackle hire.

Drum workshop and yoga T086-1028983, drumchum2001@yahoo.co.uk. Under the expert guidance of master drum builder Jon Barlow, you can make your own beautiful African djembe drum and have drumming tuition at workshops, either in conjunction with the Kinsale Arts week (27Jun-16 Jul) or throughout the rest of the summer. Susan Allen also holds daily yoga classes. The workshop costs €450, which includes all materials necessary to make the drum. Camping on site is available for €7.50 per day.

Golf **Old Head Golf Links**, T021-4778444. 18 holes.

Horse riding **Balinadee Stables**, T021-4778152. 10 mins from town off the road to Bandon. Pony-trekking available.

Sailing T021-4770738, www.oysterhaven.com.

Tours **Cruises**: T021-4773188. 1-hr cruise of harbour and River Bandon. 1100-1700. €9.
Ghost tour: T021-4772240. Starts outside *Tap Tavern* in Guardwell, Mon, Wed and Fri at 2100. €9.
Walking tour: T021-4772873. Starts outside tourist office at 1115, daily, €6.

Skibbereen
Fishing **Fallons**, North St, T028-22246. Gear and information on salmon and sea trout fishing on the River Ilen.

Baltimore *p*
Diving **Aquaventures**, T028-20511, www.aquaventures.ie. Serves beginners and experienced divers and has been recommended by a reader.

Sailing **Baltimore Sailing Club**, T028-20426, www.baltimoresailingclub.com.
Sea angling and shark fishing, T028-22689, and T086-8240642, info@wreckfish.com, and T028-20549.

Transport

Kinsale to Baltimore *p258*
Bike hire The Hire Shop, 18 Main St, Kinsale, T021-4774884. Mountain bikes children's bikes, tandems available. Also **Mylie Murphy's**, Pearse St. **MTM Cycles**, 33 Ashe St, Clonakilty, T023-33584. **Roycroft's**, Ilen St, Skibbereen, T028-21235.

Bus Bus Éireann runs a number of daily buses, No **249**, throughout the year (and extra ones in summer) between **Cork** and **Garretstown** that stop at **Cork Airport**, **Kinsale** and **Ballinspittle**. The 1st bus departs Cork at 0645; last one from Kinsale at 2220 (1945 on Sat). Timetables are posted in the window of the tourist office and the bus stop is across the road on Pier Rd.

Ferry As well as buses (see page 240) there is a boat service between **Baltimore** and **Schull**, Jun to mid-Sep, T028-39153. Departures from Baltimore at 1030 and 1400, and from Schull at 1130 and 1500; bicycles are carried free.

Boats regularly leave from Baltimore for **Sherkin Island**, T028-20218, Jun-Sep, 0900-2030 (around €8 return). There is also a service from Schull, T028-28138.

From Baltimore, T028-39159, www.capeclearferry.info. €11.50 return, ferries to **Cape Clear Island** depart up to 4 times a day in the summer and at a reduced service other times of the year. Another company, T028-39153, departs from Baltimore to Cape Clear via Schull, mid-Jun to mid-Sep, at 1030, 1400 and 1915 and returns at 0900, 1215 and 1815, taking 90 mins. From **Schull**, T028-28278, the **Karycraft** departs for Cape Clear Island daily in Jun, Jul and Aug at 1030, 1430 and 1630, returning at 1130, 1530 and 1730. Single fare is €7.00, return €12. In Sep there is 1 departure at 1430, returning at 1730.

Taxi Kinsale Cabs, T021-4772642; or try T021-4773600. **Skibbereen**, T028-21258 and 086-8346396.

Around Ballydehob and Bantry

From Skibbereen the N71 main road continues west, turning northwards just before the small town of Ballydehob to head towards Bantry. The R592 road leads west from Ballydehob to Schull and out to Goleen near the end of the Mizen Peninsula. This bulky peninsula lacks the splendid isolation of the Beara further to the north or the quiet beauty of the Sheep's Head, but it strives to assert its own identity once you travel west beyond Goleen and the open Atlantic beckons. From near Goleen you can take a smaller road back along the north side of the Peninsula to the village of Durrus, from where the Sheep's Head Peninsula or Bantry can be reached. The Sheep's Head offers little in terms of beaches or places to visit but it has an unspoiled prettiness while Bantry, set in the heart of the stunning Bantry Bay is a town on the make with its overly grand town square and its stylish new cinema and garda station. The curve of Bantry Bay leads you to the scenic village of Glengarriff from where you can visit Garinish Island. ▸▸ *For Sleeping, Eating and other listings, see pages 278-281.*

Ballydehob and the Mizen Peninsula

Ballydehob → *Phone code: 028. Colour map 3, grid C3.*

At the head of an inlet of Roaringwater Bay, Ballydehob was the market village for islanders from the Bay until it declined after the islands gradually depopulated in the 1930s. Tourism has revived its spirits, and when in the 1980s a small number of well known writers bought up holiday homes in the area, Ballydehob became a small retreat for the London chattering classes. In the summer there is still a middle-class bohemian touch to the place, but in winter Ballydehob drifts back to being a sleepy Irish village. When entering the town from Skibbereen, look out on the left for the disused 12-arched tramway bridge.

There is a café (see page 279), a bookshop and a craft shop along the main street. The otherwise featureless Irish Whip bar, at the Schull end of town, has a faded display on the Ballydehob wrestling champion, Dan O'Mahony, who invented the wrestling throw known as the Irish whip, and to whom a commemorative statue now stands in the village.

Schull → *Phone code: 028. Colour map 3, grid C3.*

Lying beneath the slopes of Mount Gabriel, with aircraft tracking dishes on the summit, Schull bursts into life every summer with Irish and non-Irish visitors. Good restaurants, a decent bookshop, pubs with music, and boats to Sherkin, Cape Clear Island, Fastnet lighthouse and Baltimore all draw in the crowds. The busiest time of

History is a funny old thing

In December 1796 Wolfe Tone (see page 594), arrived in Bantry Bay as part of a French invasion force of 50 ships, some 15,000 soldiers and a military band whose instructions were to teach the Irish the revolutionary '*Marseillaise*'. The aim was to drive the British out of Ireland, but it was not to be. The weather was against them: fewer than a score of ships reached Bantry Bay and after six days struggling with winter gales they reluctantly returned to France. Richard White, the local English landlord, alerted the authorities when he heard the French had arrived and was later rewarded with a peerage. In 1801 he was made Viscount Bantry and became the first Earl of Bantry in 1816.

The irony is that **Bantry House**, still in the same family, now enjoys a nice little earner from an exhibition devoted to the failed invasion.

all is during **Calves Week**, at the beginning of August, when various sailing events take place. It is possible to get a ferry to Cape Clear Island from Schull, see page 281.

★ Mizen Head, Barley Cove, Goleen and Crookhaven

→ *Phone code: 027.*

After passing the brightly painted villages of Ballydehob and Schull, well known retreats for well heeled North Europeans, the social and physical landscape changes as you approach Goleen. The local TD once memorably described his constituency as in danger of becoming a land of "briars, bullocks and bachelors", and indeed the land does become barren, small farms struggle to cope with the centralizing farming policies of the EU and young people are not always keen to grow up as farmers and farmers' wives. Outside winter you will be struck by the flora and fauna, there's teeming birdlife off Mizen Head, wild thyme growing by the roadside and hills turning yellow and purple with autumn gorse and heather.

The most unforgettable sight on this peninsula is the view of the crazy rock formations from the small bridge that takes one out to the **Mizen Vision** ① *T027-35115*, the Mizen Head signal station, at the end of the peninsula. The entrance charge of €4.50 that you have to pay to cross the bridge is unfortunate because a visit to the signal station may prove disappointing. To make matters worse, what used to be a spectacular clifftop walk from here to **Three Castles Head** has been closed off. Notwithstanding, a visit to the 13th-century **O'Mahoney castle** near the edge of sheer cliffs at Three Castles Head is recommended. To get there from the car park at the Barleycove Beach Hotel (see page 278) turn right on leaving the car park, then left at the first T-junction and right at the next junction where a sign points left to the Ocean View B&B. Follow the road to the end where a gate leads up to a farmhouse; the castle is a 10-minute walk beyond. Do not be deterred by the sign at the farm entrance which gives access to the castle; the owners were dismayed at coaches disgorging groups who trooped across their land. Individual visitors are entitled to visit the castle.

The sandy expanse of surfable **Barley Cove** comes as a terrific surprise near the end of the Mizen Peninsula and, although there can be a dangerous undercurrent in places, lifeguards are on duty in the summer and flags indicate where it is safe to swim. If you leave Goleen by heading straight out of the village, instead of turning right for Mizen Head, you will see **Crookhaven** on your left. Once an important harbour, Crookhaven is still patronized by sailing folk and there are a couple of undistinguished pubs serving food (see page 280).

Bantry and around → *Phone code: 027. Colour map 3, grid C3.*

"God gave us Bantry Bay and we gave it to Gulf Oil"; So said the wise folk who objected to the oil company building a major oil depot on the island of Whiddy. In 1979, after a fire broke out at the depot and 51 people died, Gulf Oil departed and left behind the statue to St Brendan the Navigator as their gift. The sweeping entry into Bantry from the Cork road, with Whiddy visible across the harbour, suggests something rather special, but there is surprisingly little of interest in the town itself. What was a vast town square, Wolfe Tone Square, has been turned into a concrete garden and parking space is consequently at a premium. The town is at its best on the first Friday of each month when the traditional market fair still takes place. The main attraction is a visit to Bantry House while the town itself is a useful base for organizing visits to the peninsulas. The **tourist office** is on Wolfe Tone Sq, T027-50229. Its hours vary but it is generally open from Mar-Oct Mon-Sat 0900-1800; Jul-Aug Mon-Sat 0900-1900, Sun 1000-1800.

Bantry House ⓘ *T027-50047. 17 Mar-end Oct daily 1000-1800. House, French Armada Exhibition and garden €10; garden and exhibition only €5.* In the 1820s and 1830s Viscount Berehaven, later the second Earl of Bantry, went on a European Grand Tour, periodically sending back art and artefacts to his family home in Bantry. Visitors walk over them – literally – when entering the porch tiled with panels taken from Pompeii. The rooms are an eclectic blend of the functional and the exotic: tapestries, fireplaces and Spanish chandeliers alongside items such as a 16th-century mosque lamp and a Tibetan water ewer. The interior architecture is remarkably successful, especially the dramatic entrance to the library, and all part of a mastery of style that allows the building and the bow-fronted garden to complement their location. The backdrop is provided by Bantry Bay, with the Caha Mountains of the Beara Peninsula overlooking Whiddy Island. Inside the house there are tantalizing views from the drawing rooms but the baroque dining room cannot match the airy and graceful library.

Around Bantry

Sheep's Head Peninsula is a modest strip of green beauty washed by the wide water of Bantry Bay to the north and the more placid Dunmanus Bay to the south. If coming from Goleen on the Mizen peninsula, take a left turn at the Toormore junction and enjoy the scenic coastal road along the north side of the Mizen peninsula to the village of **Durrus** at the head of Dunmanus Bay. A loop road runs west from here to the small village of **Kilcrohane** (stop in the friendly Fitzpatrick's pub, at the start of the

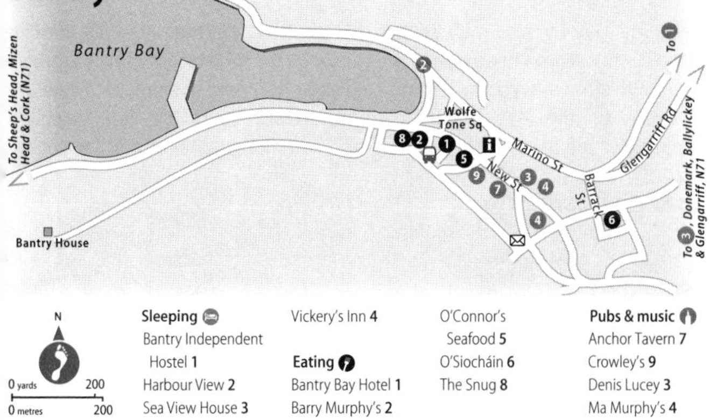

 Goat's Path in Kilcrohane) on the Sheep's Head and then north up the Goat's Path to head back to Bantry along the north side of this peninsula. The best reason for coming to the Sheep's Head peninsula is to walk the **Sheep's Head Way**, whole sections of which are spectacular.

The Sheep's Head Way → *Phone code: 027.*

The Sheep's Head Way is a four-day, 88-km walk which begins along the mountain spine that dominates the centre of the peninsula, and then continues out to the western extremity. The final day of the walk, from Durrus, is less exciting and can be skipped but the first three days are memorable. Arrange accommodation in Bantry before setting off.

Mapping and information The Ordnance Survey map No 88 in the 1:50,000 series covers most of the Way, which is plotted on the map. To cover the whole Way you would also need map 85 for short stretches near Bantry, but it would be possible to get by just using the waymarked signs along the route. There is also the locally produced *Guide to the Sheep's Head Way*, which has its own 1:50,000 map and a booklet that describes the route and gives some local history. These maps are available at the tourist office in Bantry (see page 275). The Bantry Independent Hostel (see page 279) also has information on the Way.

Day one This is a 28-km walk along the central spine of the peninsula to Kilcrohane just below Seefin Mountain. The walk begins in Bantry but some time would be saved by staying west of town on the Way at Dromcloc House, at Cappanaloha (see page 279).

From the car park of Bantry House follow the waymarkers that direct you around the grounds and past the West Lodge Hotel. The way crosses the main road to Cork and heads off down a minor road lined with wild iris and meadowsweet. A little further on is a turn to the left and then the Way leaves the tarmac and starts to climb. After a time, the fields are left behind again and its route goes along some pleasant country roads before striding out on to the central mountain ridge, where the views over Bantry Bay to the north and Dunmanus to the south are amazing. From Seefin, head down to Kilcrohane Village for accommodation (see page 279).

Day two This circular 33-km walk starts at Kilcrohane village and goes to the western end of the peninsula. From the village, retrace your steps to the top of the Goat's Path and follow the signs. At one stage, the route follows the cliff edge then heads inland to Tooreen, where it meets the road back to Kilcrohane. The way is uphill past the ruins of a signal tower before it descends to the shore and follows a lowland route through farms and then along a road back to Kilcrohane.

Day three The day's 20-km walk follows the seashore and then the hills through Ahakista to Durrus. As you head east of the village on the road to Durrus, the markers send you down a boreen, past a few bungalows to the shore and a lake. There are usually swans on the lake which breed here every year. The area is called Farranamanagh, "the fields of the monks", and it is thought that one of the sets of

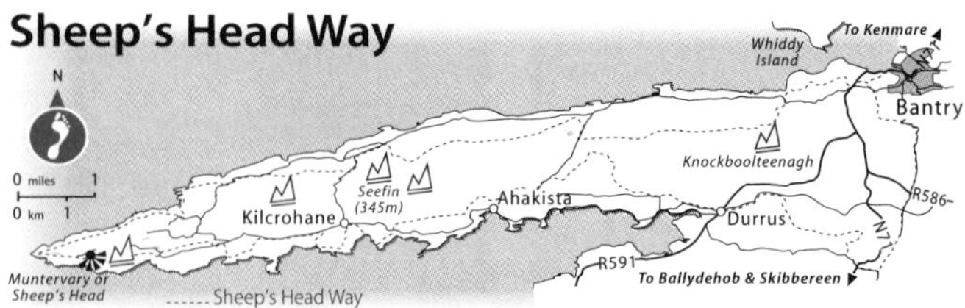

Fastnet Lighthouse

Standing at the top of the Goat's Path on the Sheep's Head peninsula the blinking light that periodically sweeps the night sky emanates from the automated lighthouse on Fastnet Rock. The first cast-iron lighthouse built in 1854, replaced by a granite one in 1906, was the last bit of Ireland that thousands of hapless emigrants glimpsed on their journey from Cobh to the New World. Depending on weather conditions, trips to Fastnet, Karycraft, T028-28278, departs from Schull on Tuesday and Thursday at 1900 in July, Tuesday, Wednesday and Thursday in August, and there is usually a weekly 1900 departure in June and September; €13 return. Pay at the pier.

ruins above the lake is an ancient bardic school where it said that a medieval king of Spain sent his son to study, only to have him drown on the journey there. From the lake the route follows an abandoned road to Ahakista, an apology for a village with two bars but a very pretty garden to peer into and some deciduous woodland. En route, the trail passes a tumbledown stone circle discovered only a few years ago. The old road heads across farmland and uses old roads and boreens.

Day four This is a 20-km walk through minor roads and forestry and doesn't come up to the standard of the first three days. A lift back to Bantry might be in order here. The Way leaves Durrus going east and where the road forks at the east end of the village takes the right fork, past a few shops and then some bungalows and, finally, along the minor road through fields. After a couple of km it turns right on to another minor road through fields. It enters forestry and then joins another road, which meets the N71. The route then goes uphill and along a series of minor roads, descending through Vaughn's Pass to rejoin the outward leg of the route in Bantry.

Gougane Barra → *Colour map 3, grid B3.*

Some time around the seventh century, St Finbarr established a hermitage on a tiny island in a beautiful lake, the source of the River Lee, in a glacial valley surrounded by hills and trees. The church that stands today on its ruin is of little interest, but the scene retains its natural charm and on a fine day is worth a visit. Gougane Barra is signposted off the main Bantry to Macroom road.

Sean O'Faolain set a short story, *The Silence of the Valley* in the Gougane Barra hotel, but the more infamous literary association comes from a local tailor and his wife whose memories of local folklore were recorded by an Irish writer and published as *The Tailor and Ansty* (short for Anastais, his wife) in 1942. The following year the book was banned by the Censorship Board as indecent, but anyone reading it today will be hard put to find what offended them. The ban was revoked in 1964, but not before the poor tailor and his wife had suffered so much local hostility that police protection was necessary. (When the tailor was dying his police guard was cycling to his house with a bottle of whiskey for him.) The tailor and his wife are buried in the graveyard by the lake opposite Finbarr's Island.

Glengarriff → *Phone code: 027. Colour map 3, grid C3.*

Visit Glengarriff when the sun is out and it is easy to concur with Thackeray's rhetorical conclusion after his 1842 visit that tourists need not bother travelling to the Rhine and Switzerland when places like this exist. But come here on a wet day and the place seems depressingly dank, the tourist shops seem tackier than ever and in winter the place literally closes down.

The **tourist office** is on the right, after the Eccles Hotel, coming into Glengarriff from Bantry. Open from end of May to Sep Mon-Sat 0930-1730, but closed between 1300-1400.

There are a few attractions: an island, a noted hotel, and walks along the shore line. **Garinish Island** ⓘ *T027-63040, Mar-Oct, daily 0930-1830 (shorter hours in winter), €3.50, OPW site, boats depart regularly from Mar-Oct, T027-63116, from the pier opposite the Eccles Hotel for €10 return, a second ferry, T027-63333, operates for the same price from the Blue Pool, beside the public toilets*, has a beautiful Italian garden, Illnacullin, designed by Harold Peto, and using sub-tropical plants that only thrive in this corner of Ireland warmed by the Gulf Stream. Look for a larch tree in an ancient Roman pot and a rare and beautiful hanging tree from Tasmania.

The boats to Garinish include a viewing of seals on the rocks, but you can see them for free by walking along the shoreline, in the direction of town, from where the boats depart. A free leaflet outlining different walks around Glengarriff is available from the tourist office.

The **Eccles Hotel** exudes charm with its wrought-iron balconies and period lobby. Enjoy a drink or meal, inside or out, but watch out for the coach parties that can destroy the atmosphere.

Glengarriff Bamboo Park ⓘ *T027-63570, Apr-Oct, daily, 0900-1900, €5*, is not yet a mature garden, so the bamboo, tree ferns and palms may disappoint some, but there are some interesting plants, like the *trachycarpus takil* from India.

Glengarriff Nature Reserve ⓘ *24 hrs, free, 1 km past the village on the road to Kenmare*, is a pretty park which encompasses an ancient oak forest. There is an undemanding, short walk uphill to Lady Bantry's Lookout with amazing views over the Beara peninsula.

Sleeping

Ballydehob *p273*

E **The Old Crossing**, Shanavagh, T028-37148, c21@familyhomes.ie. A former railway-crossing cottage within walking distance of the village.

F **Twelve Arch Hostel**, Palm grove, Church Rd, T028-37232, www.12archhostel.com. Has 30 beds and 3 private rooms; a camping area and bikes for hire.

Part of the northern half of the Beara Peninsula is in County Kerry. The accommodation in that part which is useful for the Beara Way walk is listed in this chapter although Derrynane Gardens, also on Beara, is covered in the next chapter, see page 316.

Schull *p273*

C **Grove House**, Colla Rd, T028-28067, www.grovehouseschull.com. Once accommodated the likes of George Bernard Shaw and Edith Somerville; 5 bedrooms individually decorated, with lots of quaint and quirky features.

C-D **Corthna Lodge Country House**, Schull, T028-28517, www.corthna-lodge.net. A short distance west of the village, enjoys views of Roaringwater Bay from its hill-top position. Internet access, pretty gardens, putting green, gym.

E **Adele's**, Adele's Bakery, T028-28459, www.adelesrestaurant.com. Has 4 rooms, sharing bathroom facilities, on the top floor.

E **Glencairn**, Ardmanagh Dr, T028-28007, c86@familyhomes.ie. An archetypal bungalow B&B; 3-mins walk from town.

F **Schull Backpacker's Lodge**, Colla Rd, T028-28681, www.schullbackpackers.com. Dormitory beds, double and single rooms, (1 double room with en suite bath), limited camping space, and bikes for hire. At the Goleen end of town, and looks quite different inside from what the woody exterior might suggest.

Mizen Head, Barley Cove and Crookhaven *p274*

B **Barleycove Beach Hotel**, T027-35234. Sits at one end of the long beach at Barleycove and does a roaring food trade.

D-E **Fortview House**, Gurtyowen, Toormore, on the Durrus to Goleen R591 road, T027-35324, fortviewhousegoleen@eircom.net. Guests have recommended this B&B for the quality of the breakfast and moderately priced evening meal. A self-catering house is also available.

Camping

Barleycove Holiday Park, Crookhaven, T027-35302. Accepts campers, if they like the look of you, but you could follow the example of others and camp for free at the Crookhaven end of the beach.

Bantry and around *p275, map p275*

B **Sea View House Hotel**, Ballylickey, T027-50073, www.seaviewhousehotel.com. The best place to stay, a couple of miles out of Bantry on the road to Glengarriff. A 19th- century building with attractive rooms, a library of good books to read and an excellent restaurant.

E **Atlantic Shore**, on the road out to Glengarriff, T027-51310, divebantry@aol.com. One of the very best B&Bs. Has been recommended for comfort and friendliness.

E **Vickery's Inn**, New St, T027-50006, www.vickerys.ie. Right in the centre of town, has a sense of history and charges around €80 for a double room.

F **Bantry Independent Hostel**, Bishop Lucey Pl, T027-51050, bantryhostel@eircom.net. Dorm beds and doubles in a quiet location at the top of a hill, signposted from the town square.

F **Harbour View**, Harbour View, T027-51140. Centrally located close to the town square and there are private rooms available.

F **Par Four**, out of town at Donemark, on the Bantry-Glengarriff road, T027-50205, www.par4bantry.com. A free pick-up service is offered by this hostel. Open all year, bike hire and has 3 private rooms.

Sheep's Head Peninsula *p276, map p276*

E **Avoca House**, Durrus, T028-61511. A friendly B&B. 4 rooms with en suite bathroom.

E **Reenmore Farmhouse**, west of Durrus at Ahakista, on the road to Kilcrohane, T027-67051. 6 rooms, 4 with en suite bathroom.

Sheep's Head Way

E **Bay View Inn**, Kilcrohane, T027-67981.

E **Souterrain House**, Paddock, Kilcrohane, T027-67967, kathleengaff@hotmail.com. Secluded house in the village of Kilcrohane in quiet lane running down to the sea.

F **Carbery View Hostel**, Kilcrohane, T027-67035. Basic, no private rooms but camping space is available.

F **Dromcloc House**, Cappanaloha, T027-50030. Open from Mar-Nov. To begin with a head start, stay the night before before your 1st day's walking.

Gougane Barra *p277*

D **Gougane Barra**, Gougane Barra, T026-47069. Solitary hotel, comfortably old-fashioned, open Apr-end Oct. Bar food is available and evening dinner around €32. Sun lunch is popular too. Ask for a table overlooking the lake.

Glengarriff *p277*

A-D **Eccles Hotel**, T027-63003, www.eccleshotel.com. Ancient lineage and the rooms have been modernized without losing all their old charm. Beware of the hotel's disco nights.

D **Casey's**, T027-63010. Right in the middle of the village, a comfortably old-fashioned kind of place.

E **Island View House**, T027-63081, www.islandviewhouse.net. Near to the Eccles, this B&B has only doubles for €45.

F **Cottage Bar Hostel**, T027-63226. Has 12 beds, 4 private rooms; bikes for hire.

F **Murphy's Village Hostel**, T027-63555. Has over 30 beds and 5 private rooms.

F **O'Mahony's Hostel**, coming in from Bantry, it is just past the Eccles hotel and on your right, T027-63033. Keeps to the spirit of independent hostelling and belongs to no hostel organization. Dorm beds and private doubles and is open for most of the year at very affordable rates.

Camping

Dowlings Caravan and Camping Park, Castletownbere Rd, T027-63154.

Eating

Ballydehob *p273*

Annie's Restaurant, on main street, T028- 37292. Has pricey dishes like roast

For an explanation of the sleeping and eating price codes used in this guide, see inside the front cover. Other relevant information is found in Essentials pages 39-45.

duck with port and orange from 1900, closed Sun and Mon. Collect your menu and pop across the street to Levis' pub for a pre-dinner drink. They'll call you when the food is ready. Set dinner around €40.

ꝩ **Clara**, in the centre of the village. Serves toasted pitta bread with various fillings and open crab sandwiches.

ꝩ **Hudson's Wholefoods**, near the Texaco garage. Has a vegetarian café doing cakes, pizzas, samosas and lunch specials.

Schull *p273*

ꝩꝩ **La Coquille**, Main St, T028-28642. A long established place serving classic French dishes – lots of red meats – but the best has to be the locally caught fish daily specials. Open 7 days in summer from 1930; out of season, tends to be only weekends only.

ꝩ **Adéle's**, Main St, T028-28459. A deservedly popular coffee shop doing light meals. Squeeze in here for hand-made bread, ciabatta with Gubbeen cheese and oh-so-delicious cakes and biscuits.

ꝩ **Bunratty Inn**. Serves a vast touristy menu in its restaurant and beer garden. The mussels are particularly tasty but when busy the food is churned out like a factory production line and the quality suffers.

ꝩ **The Courtyard**, Main St. Pub selling a good variety of local cheeses and fresh bread; ideal for a picnic.

ꝩ **Hackett's Bar**, old-style, bar food available.

ꝩ **The Waterside Inn**, bar food is also available here.

Mizen Head, Barley Cove, Goleen and Crookhaven *p274*

ꝩ **The Green Kettle**, Main St, Goleen, T027-35033. There is a pricy restaurant in Goleen But, this might be your best bet with a day menu of affordable sandwiches and seafood and a mid-range evening menu featuring local steak, a fish platter, chicken and lasagne. Open from late Jul to mid-Sep.

ꝩ **O'Sullivans**, Crookhaven, T027-35319. Pub right at the water's edge, serving home-made soups, chowder and open sandwiches till 2000. Gets very busy in height of summer.

Bantry *p275, map p275*

The 2 best places for an evening meal in the vicinity of Bantry are out of town, along the road to Glengarriff.

ꝩꝩꝩ **Larchwood House Restaurant**, Pearson's Bridge, Bantry, T027-66181. Take the road out of Bantry to Glengarriff and look for the sign pointing right after a couple of miles. Intelligently cooked Irish dishes and good value, around €40 per person, considering the quantity and quality.

ꝩꝩ **O'Siocháin**. An affordable "Irish breakfast served all day" kind of place, open until 2200.

ꝩꝩ-ꝩ **O'Connor's Seafood Restaurant**, The Square, T027-50221. Makes a speciality out of mussels; dinner dishes are creative but open for lunch too. Bar food, variations on the sandwich theme and a set menu are available 1215-1700.

ꝩꝩ-ꝩ **Vickery's Inn**, opposite the supermarket. Serves lunch and dinner in the attractive context of what was the lounge of this old hotel.

ꝩ **Sea View House Restaurant**, T027-50073. A spacious dining room, a bar, and first-rate traditional Irish food; Sun lunch is especially popular.

ꝩ Pubs like **Barry Murphy's** and **The Snug**, and the **Bantry Bay Hotel**, all around the town square, serve affordable bar food.

Sheep's Head Peninsula *p276, map p276*

ꝩꝩꝩ **Blair's Cove House**, T027-61127. For that special meal to write home about, consider this place. Dinner in a Georgian country house that is outside Durrus on the R591, just on the Mizen peninsula. mid-Mar to Oct, closed on Sun, and Mon in Jul and Aug.

ꝩꝩꝩ **Three Gables**, T027-61534. Further along the R591 and open all year. This lovely restaurant practises the art of slow food and dinner is a leisurely 3-hr affair. Bougainvillaea flourishes near the entrance, there are sea views and home-cooking using fresh local produce with a tincture of Italian to the cuisine.

ꝩ **Ivo's**, Durrus. Pub food.

ꝩ **Post office**, Kilcrohane. Tea, cakes and bites can be enjoyed in this olde-world post office.

Glengarriff *p277*

There are lots of cafés and bars in the village though little of any distinction.

ꝩꝩ **Casey's Hotel**, in the village, T027- 63010. Does bar food all day while dinner works out at about €30.

ꝩꝩ **Garinish Restaurant**, T027-63003. Within hotel, has a superb old dining room; reserve a table by the window for sea views.

Eccles. Busy bar serves food 1100-2100.

Pubs and music

Schull *p273*
Many of the pubs along Main St have musical evenings. Check to see what is on at **The Courtyard** pub or **Arundel's Bar**.
TJ Newman's, up the hill from the harbour is a lovely old-fashioned pub for a quiet drink and a chat with locals.

Bantry and around *p275, map p275*
Anchor Tavern, New St. Worth a visit for its crazy decor alone.
Crowley's, by the town square in Bantry, T027-50900. Can usually be relied on for live music throughout the summer.
Denis Lucey, opposite the supermarket. Drop in to get away from the tourists.
Ma Murphy's, for a quiet, old-fashioned pint.

Glengarriff *p277*
Blue Loo, music nightly, has occasional blues or jazz sessions.
Johnny Barry's, music nightly.
The Hawthorn, **Harington's**, and **Casey's** also have music, though like the others they can get crowded.
Dowling's Camping Park, on the road to Castletownbere. Consider a short trip out to the public bar, for entertaining, traditional Irish music sessions nightly.

Festivals and events

A Mussel Fair enlivens Bantry in **early May** and in **late Jun-early Jul** a combined week-long West Cork Literary festival and West Cork Chamber Music festival is held, T027-52788, www.westcorkmusic.ie. See also page 262.

Entertainment

Bantry and around *p275, map p275*
Cinemax, The Quay, T027-55777. Has 3 screens and occasionally shows non-blockbusters.

Shopping

Schull *p273*
Books Fuschia Books, has a wide range of second-hand books on Irish subjects from paperbacks to first editions.

Clothes Irish Knitwear, Main St.

Gifts Celtic Crafts, Main St. Sells gifts such as jewellery and pottery.
The Courtyard, Main St. Pub which has a craft shop attached, selling pottery, jewellery and hand-knitted garments.

Glengarriff *p277*
Lots of shops selling cute stuffed animals and quirky 'oirish' teatowels.
Quills, large shop, has a good range of ethnic jewellery, chunky outfits and Aran knitwear.

Transport

Around Ballydehob and Bantry *p273*
Bantry Rural Transport, 5 Main St, T52727, www.brt.ie (scheduled minibus routes to local villages).

Bike hire Kramer's, Glengarriff Rd, Bantry, T027-50278. Jem Creations, round the corner from *O'Shea's* supermarket, Glengarriff, T027-63113.

Bus Bus Éireann buses stop near Barry Murphy's pub in **Bantry** and there are regular daily services to **Cork**, **Glengarriff** and **Castletownbere**. A weekly bus makes the trip from **Kilcrohane** to Bantry and back on Tue, 1130 in Kilcrohane, 1530 in Bantry (outside the Bantry Bay Hotel).

Ferry Boats from **Schull** to **Cape Clear Island**, T028-39153, depart at 1130 and 1500, and for **Baltimore** at 1730, mid-Jun to mid-Sep. Another boat, the Karycraft, T028-28278, departs for Cape Clear Island at 1030, 1430 and 1630 in Jun, Jul, Aug with a single daily trip in Sep. Return trip, with commentary and music is €12. Karycraft also does regular trips to the **Fastnet Lighthouse**, see page 277.

Beara Peninsula → *www.bearatourism.com.*

Without exaggeration, the Beara Peninsula can be described as one of the bleakest and stoniest corners of Ireland yet despite this – or because of it – the land possesses a haunting beauty that finds expression whatever the season. Stretching for 48 km and accessible from Glengarriff or Kenmare, the Peninsula is unspoiled and boasts a long-distance walk, The Beara Way, the ideal way to experience the beauty of the landscape. Hungry Hill is the highest point, at 685 m – easily climbed until the last gruelling stage to the summit that helps make this a whole day's climbing – and 7 km off Adrigole a sign points a route to the top.

The Healy Pass is a spectacular stretch of road that cuts across the backbone of the Caha Mountains and links the south side of the peninsula with the county of Kerry at its 330-m summit. » *For Sleeping, Eating and other listings, see pages 287-288.*

Castletownbere → *Phone code: 027. Colour map 3, grid C2.*

The largest white-fishing port in the country is the largest town (officially named Castletown Bearhaven) on the peninsula and the departure point for a short ferry ride to Bere Island. There is a seasonal **tourist information** office in the grounds of St Peter's Church, T027-70054, www.bearatourism.com, Easter and Jun-Sep Mon-Fri 1000-1700, a good supermarket, and a choice of restaurants and pubs. Between around the 25 Jul and 8 Aug some of the events in the Beara Arts and Allihies Theatre Festival take place in Castletownbere. (Arts events information: T027-70765.)

Puxley Mansion and Dunboy Castle The ruins of both these sites are close to one another though they have nothing in common. Puxley Mansion was the 19th-century home of the family whose wealth came from copper mines further west (see page 284). Commissioned in 1866, it was burnt down by the IRA in 1921 but the ghostly

Beara Peninsula & Beara Way

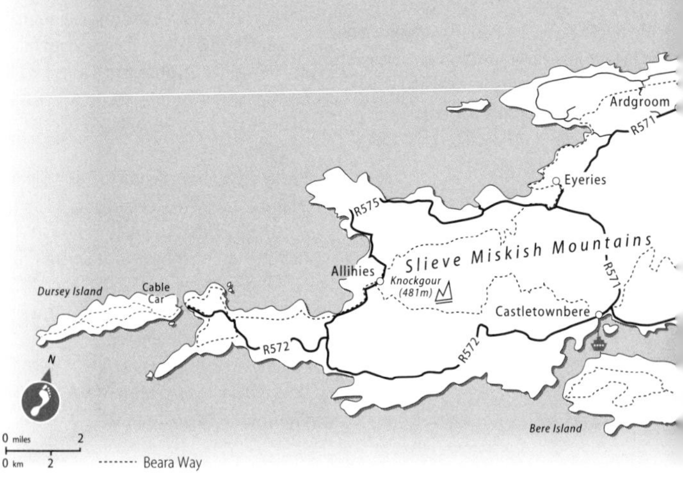

shell of this gothic extravaganza is still very impressive. It was built by Henry Puxley, supposedly as a gesture for his wife who was becoming ill through constant pregnancies, but she died giving birth before being able to live here. Puxley then left for England and never returned. The interior ambitiously imitated a Gothic cathedral with vaulting arches and arcades, and the remains that can be seen are sufficient to give some idea of just how outlandish and colonial Puxley Mansion aspired to be.

Walk on to the end of the land belonging to Puxley Mansion where the very meagre but historically highly significant ruins of Dunboy Castle lie crumbling away. It was here in 1602 that O'Sullivan Beare mounted the last great act of tragic defiance at the English after the defeat of the mighty O'Neill at Kinsale. O'Sullivan refused to accept the authority of the Crown and dug in his forces at Dunboy under MacGeoghegan. The English came across from the Sheep's Head Peninsula under George Carew and captured the castle before MacGeoghegan, knowing the end was nigh, tried to blow everything and everyone up. The Irish were slaughtered and O'Sullivan Beare set off for Ulster in winter time with a thousand followers; only a handful survived and O'Sullivan fled to Spain.

Bere Island The best reason for visiting Bere Island would be to walk around it as part of the Beara Way (see below). Ferries, T027-75009, www.bereislandferries.com, depart from the slipway opposite the SuperValu supermarket daily, seven a day, from 0800 (1230 Sun), with the last boat returning from the island at 2000 (1830 Sun). Another ferry company, Murphy's, T027-75014, www.murphysferry.com, operates from Pontoon, a couple of km east of Castletownbere on the main road. Ferries are also daily from 0730 (0915 on Sun) until 2000, Jun-Aug. A Mon-Fri service operates the rest of the year.

Allihies → *Phone code: 027. Colour map 3, grid C2.*

Situated in the far west of the peninsula, with no public transport, this small village of brightly painted houses overlooks Ballydonegan Bay and a white quartz strand,

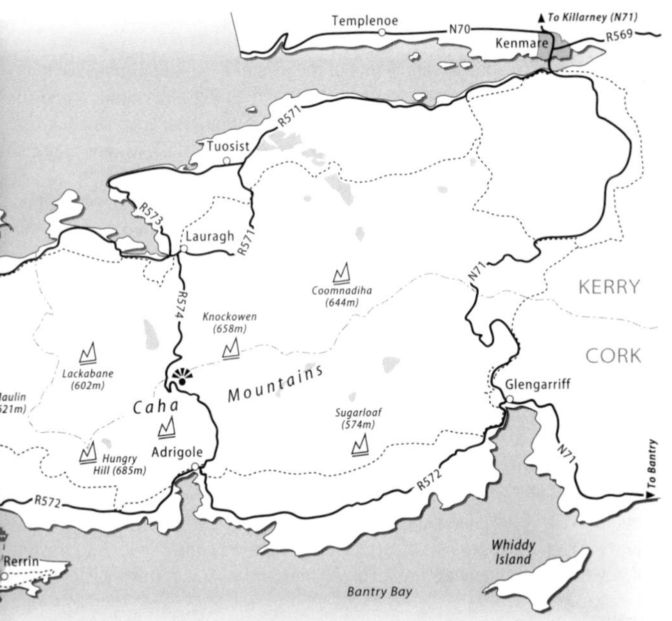

 safe for swimming, that lends considerably to the astonishing beauty of the locality. There is a small, seasonal **tourist information** post in the village and between around the 25 Jul to 8 Aug some of the events in the **Beara Arts and Allihies Theatre Festival** take place here.

Allihies copper mines The unhappy story of the copper mines begins in the early 19th century, when the Anglo-Irish Puxley family opened the first mine. At one time well over a thousand people were employed here, including a whole community of Cornish miners brought in for their specialist skills. These English workers were boycotted by the locals who felt their chances of employment were threatened, and the ships that carried away the ore to Swansea brought in essential supplies for the Cornish families. The mines finally closed in 1930, but only after producing tremendous wealth for the Puxleys, as the ruins of Puxley Mansion (see page 282) make clear.

To walk around the mines, leave Allihies at the top, northern, end, go right at the first fork and look for a dump area on the left of the road. This is the entrance to the mines, and a pathway leads up past the ruins and the chimney stack of one of the pumping stations. The mineshafts are fenced in, but be careful and stick to the path.

Dursey Island → *Phone code: 027.*

ⓘ *Cable car, T027-73017. Mon-Sat 0930-1030, 1430-1630 and 1900-1930 (return to mainland only), Sun 0900-1000, 1300-1400, 1600-1630, 1900-1930 (Jun, Jul, Aug only and only return to mainland), get there 30 mins before closing, €4 return.*

At the end of the peninsula a cable car awaits to carry you over to Dursey Island. The cable car, which has operated since 1969, was designed to carry six people or one person and a cow across the 220-m Dursey Sound. Only a few people still live on the island and the only road ends in a pathway that continues out to a signal tower on the highest point. Tracks also lead out to Dursey Head where the stark beauty of the three rocks off the tip of the island – the Bull, the Cow and the Calf – can be admired. Folk legend has it that the Bull was where one of the original invaders of Ireland, the so-called Milesians, wrecked a boat and was buried. The rock became one of the entrances to the isles of enchantment in the Gaelic afterlife.

The opportunity to spot birdlife is one of the joys of a walk on Dursey. Gannets and choughs are common, as are skuas and terns in spring and autumn, and the island is home to a huge colony of fulmars. Windswept migrants, such as albatross, are also occasionally seen. Dolphins, harbour porpoises and minke whales may also be spotted close to the shore.

The island's history is well told in *Discover Dursey* by Penelope Durrell, and the book is available in the supermarket in Castletownbere and a few other places. It tells the story of Dursey from the time of the Vikings, through the 1602 massacre by the English and up to modern times.

★ The Beara Way → *Phone code: 027.*

This is a well established 197-km walk around what is certainly the wildest countryside in Ireland with coastal views, two island walks, a cable-car ride, old mineworkings, and a sandy beach. It takes upwards of nine days, depending on how much you choose to do, and most of it is well worth the effort, though the last two days are probably better completed on a bicycle. The Way begins in Glengarriff in County Cork, travels westwards to Allihies at the end of the peninsula via Castletownbere and Bere Island and then returns along the northern shore, entering County Kerry but ending back in Glengarriff. If you have only one or two days the tour given for day five (a circular walk based on Allihies and taking in Dursey Island) has the best views.

Mapping and information The best maps to use are 84 and 85 in the Ordnance Survey (OS) 1:50,000 series and there is also a OS Beara Way mapbook, by Michael Fewer, that describes the Way with 1:25,000 maps. The maps and information about accommodation should be available at the tourist offices in Glengarriff, T027-63201 and Castletownbere, T027-70054. See also the bibliography on page 629 for specialist walking guides to Ireland.

Day one (Glengarriff to Adrigole) This is a 16.8-km walk through wild, open land. The walk begins in Glengarriff and heads west on the main road to Castletownbere. Beyond two caravan parks the route turns to the right along a narrow, easily missed boreen, signposted to the Magannagan Walk. At the end of the boreen the route crosses a gate and heads across sheep territory with the stark hillside of Shrone Hill to the right and open land to the left. It meets forestry and skirts its edge, heading uphill towards the next stage of the walk, a narrow valley between Sugarloaf Mountain and Gowlbeg Hill. If you look back at this stage, you will see views over Bantry Bay. The walk passes the steep and forbidding sides of Sugarloaf Mountain to the sound of the nearby waterfall and climbs to meet an old road that runs parallel with the coast and the main road far below. The whole route to Adrigole is a series of panoramas over first Bantry Bay and then Adrigole Bay. The route follows the old road where occasional stone bridges testify to a period when this was the main road to Glengarriff. Descending through a sheep pen, the route joins a tarmac road through still more wild countryside, littered with standing stones, mass rocks and other signs of ancient habitation. The road gradually descends into Adrigole where there are several B&Bs, a hostel, pub and a grocery store where you can get supplies for the next day.

Day two (Adrigole to Castletownbere) This is 21.7 km of challenging but manageable and very satisfying walking. From Adrigole head west along the main road: here the new route diverges from that marked on the OS map, following the metalled road instead of heading uphill at Reen bridge (the footpath had grown too wet and dangerous). About 10 km out of Adrigole the route turns very steeply uphill for just over 1 km to meet an old turf road way up at 250 m on a spur of Hungry Hill. From here the route curves around the flanks of Hungry Hill with its stark, blasted hillsides looming above. It continues along this line, joining and leaving old turf roads and climbing the flanks of Maulin Mountain at about 300 m until it joins an old road down to Castletownbere where food and accommodation are available.

Day three (Bere Island) Boats from Castletownbere (see page 283) travel at regular intervals daily to the island where you will experience a pretty walk, mostly around the island's roads but with one outstanding stretch over the island's highest point. The total distance is 21 km.

From the pier, follow the road until it meets a T-junction where you should turn left. This road has very little traffic on it and meanders around the northern shore of the island with pleasant views of Castletownbere and Hungry Hill. It climbs over the ridge at the centre of the island, passing a Martello tower on the left. At Rerrin, the island's main village, there are some shops and cafés. Here you take a left fork at Rerrin harbour and approach the eastern end of the island past an army training ground and increasingly rugged land where wild flowers fill the roadsides and the fields are full of iris and gorse. The road ends at a locked gate and the route returns to Rerrin by a gravelled road. At the southern shore of the island you have views of the Sheep's Head Peninsula and Bantry Bay. The coast is littered with the remains of the island's days as a British naval base. Returning to Rerrin you retrace your steps for a while over the saddle between the island's two hills and then your next route is clear as you can see a path snaking its way up to the island's highest point, Knockanallig. It is a glorious walk up a clear path through well-nibbled grass with amazing views behind. At the top you can rest for a time by a tumbled signal tower and take in the glory of the coastline and open sea. The route returns through sometimes boggy land along the southern cliffs to meet the lighthouse and then return to the pier via an excellent old military road.

Day four (Castletownbere to Allihies) This is 13.6 km of hillwalking with views of both shores of the peninsula, numerous megalithic sites and a pretty stroll through lanes into Allihies. Leaving Castletownbere and heading west on the main road, the route quickly heads right along a minor road, past a very well preserved stone circle. Further on it heads uphill along an old turf road, and then heads west across the bog with fine views back to Castletownbere. It joins a barely tarmacked road which it follows for a few kilometres (diverting again from the OS map which takes off northwards along the lower slopes of Slieve Miskish, a nicer route but sadly no longer possible) and then climbs quite rapidly up a spur of Knockgur Mountain for fine views to the north of the peninsula. Descending through forestry it follows tarmac for a while and then climbs steeply through more woodland to find a long pleasant green road, which eventually meets a narrow boreen. This descends through ever prettier country lanes into Allihies where there is accommodation and a lovely beach.

Day five (Allihies and back via Dursey Island) This is a lot of walking – over 32 km – and an occasional bit of hitchhiking might be an idea. The first few miles are on the main road to Castletownbere, which can be quite busy in summer. Then the route heads rapidly uphill, first over a boreen and then open, heather-covered moorland with the most glorious views of the whole of the southwest opening up behind you all the way to the Iveragh and beyond. The path crosses the northern coastline high up and descends to meet the road to Dursey Island. It then goes out to Crow Head across more wild moors and descends to meet the cable car. You must be here before 1045 because the cable car stops operating at 1100, before working again in the afternoon. The cable car ride is good fun, if you like swinging in a small box over a chasm, and the trip around Dursey Island is quite excellent, passing the island's village and heading out to the westernmost point where the sea views defy description. Back on the mainland you might want to ignore the rest of the Way around the northern shores of Garinish Bay, although it is quite pleasant, and head back to Allihies.

Day six (Allihies to Ardgroom) This is about 24 km along old roads, open moor and the shores of Coulagh Bay. The Way heads out of Allihies on the roads built when the copper mines were working. It passes the old office building, now converted to a home, several mineshafts surrounded by wired and a still-standing pumping station which kept the seawater out of the mines. Heading uphill on a wide track it crosses a little spur of Knockoura and follows a tarmac road along the flanks of the mountain. At Coulagh it meets the main road for a time and then arrives at Eyeries. From here the route follows the shores of Coulagh Bay before heading over moorland and then steeply downhill into Ardgroom.

Day seven (Ardgroom to Tuosist) This is 19 km, chiefly along boreens but with two good hill walks. From Ardgroom, turn left at the Holly Bar, where the road starts to climb for a time and before it meets the main road again. After 3 km it leaves the road and heads over wild moorland to Lauragh. Another spell on a minor road brings you to Tuosist where there is accommodation, or detour south of Lauragh for the splendidly isolated *An Óige* Glanmore Lake hostel (see page 288).

Day eight (Tuosist to Kenmare) The distance to Kenmare is 18 km. Rejoining the waymarked walk, the Way crosses the flanks of Knocknagarrane Mountain and meets a track passing between the two loughs Inchiquin and Cloonee. The track peters out and the Way continues eastwards overland through a high saddle between two unnamed hills. There are fine views of the loughs behind you as you descend to meet a minor road beside a stone circle near Lough Dromoghty. This road meets another minor road where the Way turns left to Kenmare following more minor roads. At this junction it is possible instead to go to the right and follow another minor road through wild rocky territory, where you might expect an ambush at any moment, back down to Glengarriff and end the walk there.

Day nine (Kenmare to Glengarriff) There is a choice of walks here, both around 24 km along minor roads but through very wild and beautiful scenery. The first route retraces the steps of day eight to the shores of Lough Dromoghty. There it keeps on past the lough and heads towards Kenmare on the walk outlined in day eight's first route. The other route leaves Kenmare and turns left along long minor road through the valley of the Sheen River. The best point is the crossing between the Esk and Barraboy Mountains at 369 m before descending through a wood to the N71 back to Glengarriff.

Sleeping

Castletownbere *p282*
E **Harbour Lodge Hostel**, North Rd, T027-71043, bearalodge@eircom.net. 1 double private room, 2 family rooms and several singles, although it generally caters for group bookings so check availability.
E **Island View**, signposted off main street, T027-70415. Has good views over the harbour.
E **Sea Breeze**, Derrymihan, T027-70508, seabreeze@eircom.net. A couple of mins on foot from the town centre, follow the Beara Way signs.

Bere Island *p283*
E-F **Lawrence Cove Lodge**, Rerrin, T027-75988, www.lawrencecovelodge.com. A comfortable, upmarket hostel, mins from the ferry terminal, with dorm beds, family rooms, doubles, and the option of a cooked breakfast.
F **The Admiral's House Hostel**, Rerrin, T027-75213, www.bereislandhostel.com. Offers upmarket hostel accommodation and B&B. Twin, family and dorm rooms, self-catering, breakfast available.

Allihies *p283*
C-F **Village Hostel**, T027-73107, allihieshostel@eircom.net. Has some 50 beds and 10 private rooms. Bike hire, laundry, open Apr-Oct.
E **Sea View House**, T027-73004, www.seaviewallihies.com. In the village with doubles/singles (with en suite bath) but no evening meals.
F **Allihies Hostel**, Cahermeelabo, T027-73014, mailbox@anoige.ie. *An Óige* hostel, 2 km from the village. Open Jun-Sep.
F **Veronica's**, T027-73072. Does B&B (no en suite facilities), as well as food (see below).

Dursey Island *p284*
E-F **Skellig View**, T027-73129, skelligviewhouse@eircom.net. B&B close by the cable car station. Has rooms with shared bathroom facilities, and evening meals.
E-F **Windy Point House**, T027-73017, www.windypointhouse@eircom.net. There is no accommodation on the island, but this is within walking distance of the cable car station. Evening meals available for guests.

The Beara Way *p284*
E **Inches House**, Eyeries, T027-74494, www.eyeries.com. A B&B which also has self-catering cottages, does evening meals and will collect you from and return you to the walking route. One of Eyeries' pubs, **Causkey's**, T027-74161, has soup and sandwiches and music at weekends.
E **The Lake House**, Tuosist, T027-84205.
E **Ocean View**, Adrigole, T027-60069.
E **Sea Villa**, Ardgroom, T027-74369, seavilla1@eircom.net. Quite good accommodation with TV in rooms and a decent breakfast menu.
Ardgroom has a pub and restaurant, the **Village Inn**, T027-74067.

For an explanation of the sleeping and eating price codes used in this guide, see inside the front cover. Other relevant information is found in Essentials pages 39-45.

E-F Beachmount, Adrigole, T027-60075.
F Glanmore Lake, close to Lauragh, 6 km to the south on the road to Glanmore Lake. *An Óige* hostel using an old schoolhouse at the foot of the Healy Pass.
F Hungry Hill Lodge, Adrigole, T027-60228, www.hungryhilllodge.com. Best value, has dorm beds and private double rooms, including 1 with en suite bath for €50. It also has a camping area, laundry and bike hire.

Eating

Castletownbere *p282*
MacCarthy's, the Square, T027-70014. For seafood chowder and crab sandwiches.
O'Donoghue's, the Square, T027-70007. Bar and garage, also offers bar food all day and several of the town's many other pubs do something at lunchtime.

Bere Island *p283*
Kitty's Café, Rerrin, T027-75996. Serves lunch and evening meals.
Look Out Bistro, at the pier, T027-75999. Does things with chips from 0930-2130.

Allihies *p283*
Lighthouse Bar, opposite the playground, T027-73937. Pub grub.
O'Neill's, T027-73008. Touristy pub food and à la carte meals.
Oak Bar, next door to O'Neill's. Pub grub.
Veronica's, at the Castletownbere end of the village. Does tea and sandwiches and a very nice line in baked goodies.

Dursey Island *p284*
Windy Point House, T027-73017. Close to the cable car station. Functions as a café (closing at 1800), and serves light meals.

Pubs and music

Allihies *p283*
Lighthouse Bar, has music (Wed and Sun nights) and attracts a young set.
Oak Bar, has good sessions of traditional music on Sun and Thu nights.
O'Neill's, next door to Oak Bar. Has music on Wed nights.
O'Sullivan's, has a comfortably quiet atmosphere, which is sometimes enlivened by impromptu singing

Activities and tours

Castletownbere *p282*
Cycling There is a waymarked cycling route around the peninsula largely using the main roads but that shouldn't be a problem. Route maps available from the tourist office.

Diving **Beara Diving**, the Square, T027-71682, www.beardiving.com. PADI registered, company offering instruction and dives.

Fishing **Boat Angling and scenic Cruises**, John Angles, T027-74494. 31-ft offshore angling boat available complete with fishing gear, pick up from Cork or Kerry. €45 per day per person, minimum price €175.
Obsession, Adrian, T027-7093, www.westcorkangling.net. Fishing and scenic trips.

Horse riding **Dunboy Riding Stables**, Dunboy Castle, T087-2267492, www.dunboyridingstables.com.

Sailing **West Cork Sailing and Powerboating Centre**, The Boat House, Adrigole, T027-60132, www.westcorksailing.com. Kayaks, canoes, dinghies, powerboats, skippered sail boats.

Transport

Beara Peninsula *p282*
Bus Harrington's, T027-74003, on Mon, Tue, Wed, Fri and Sat run a minibus, departing at 0800, from **Castletownbere** for **Cork** city, passing through **Glengarriff** and **Bantry**. The bus departs from outside the Bus Éireann station in Cork on the same days at 1800. On Sun, departure time from Castletownbere is 1650, from Cork at 1930. Another company, O'Donoghue's, T027- 70007, departs from the town square at 0730, Thu only. Between late Jun and end of Aug there is a **Bus Éireann** service between **Killarney** and **Castletownbere**. All year there is a **Cork** to **Castletownbere** service via **Skibbereen** and **Glengariff**. There is no Bus Éireann service or private company serving **Allihies**.

Taxi A taxi to **Allihies** from **Castletownbere**, T027-70116, costs around €18 but it's well worth trying to hitch a lift.

County Kerry

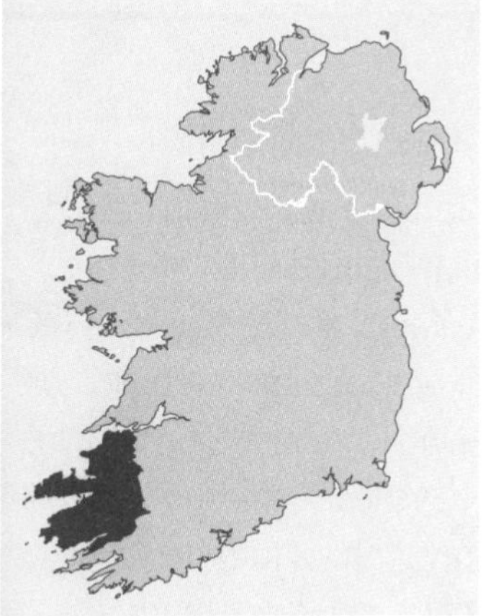

Footprint features

Introduction

Superlatives attach to Kerry: the highest mountain in Ireland, Carrauntuohill; the most spectacular island, Skellig Michael; two of the grandest long-distance walks; and the Gallarus Oratory, one of the country's most precious ancient buildings. Kerry is also home to Killarney, Ireland's premier tourist town, and the Ring of Kerry is the most travelled scenic route in Ireland. Kerry's enormous popularity with visitors, however, need not deter you, because although masses of tourists crowd into the main towns and cars clog the coastal roads, it is very easy to escape the crowds.

There are four main towns, three of them on the coast: Kenmare in the south, Dingle on the famed Peninsula of the same name and Tralee at the northern head of it. Kerry's more rugged beauty is to be found on the Iveragh Peninsula, though to appreciate its wildness it is well nigh essential that you make detours off the main Ring of Kerry road. Only then can you appreciate the brooding mountains and dark valleys, the glorious long-distance walks across the dazzlingly scenic peninsulas and the semi-deserted islands. Then there are the grand old houses and gardens such as Derrynane. Add this to the tourist kitsch of fake thatched cottages, hordes of camera-toting tour bus riders and olde-worlde village pubs, and Kerry becomes a series of wild contradictions.

★ Don't miss...

1. **Puck Fair** Pay homage to the King of the Fair, page 303.
2. **Skellig Michael** Spot the birdlife on a boat trip to the monastic dwellings, page 308.
3. **Kerry Way** Exhaust yourself by walking from Waterville to Cahersiveen, page 312.
4. **Spa luxury** Enjoy the magic of a spa holiday at Aghadoe Heights, page 298 or at the Park in Kenmare, page 317.
5. **Seafood** Enjoy the best at the Point Bar, where the ferry leaves for Valentia Island, page 318.
6. **Dingle Way** Explore the cliffs at Clogher for their multitude of fossils, on day five of the Dingle Way and enjoy a meal and a bed at An Bóthar after walking from Dunquin, page 332.

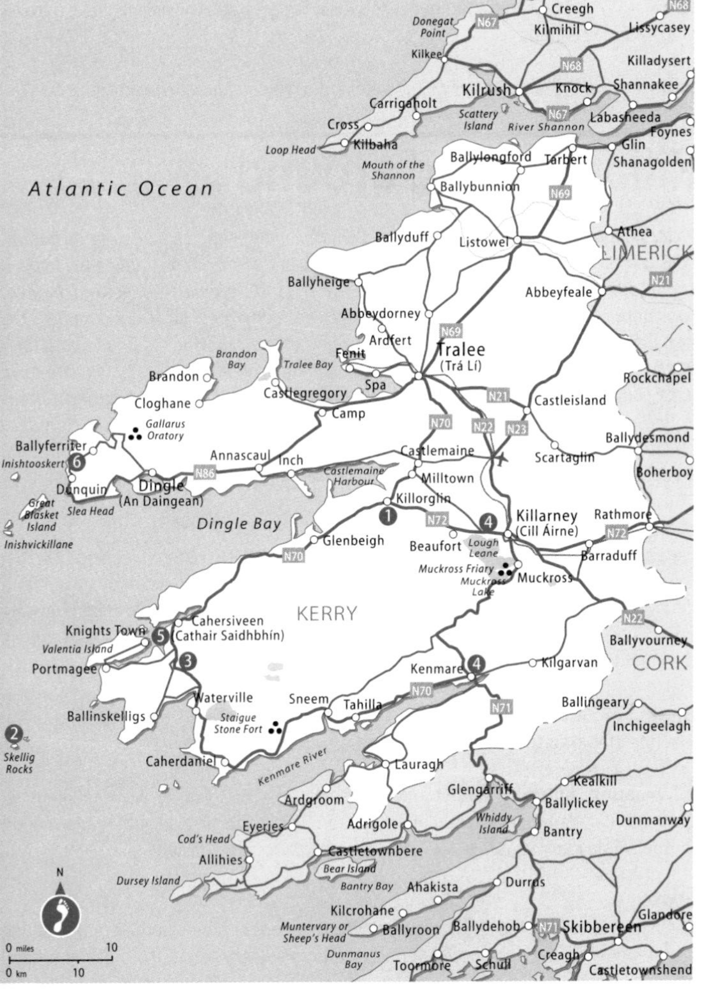

Ins and outs

Getting there

Kerry Airport, T066-9764644, is about 15 km north of Killarney at Farranfore, off the N22. **Aer Arann** flies to Dublin and **Ryanair** flies to London's Stansted airport daily, Manchester three times a week and Frankfurt daily. Farranfore has a train link with both Killarney and Tralee. There are railway stations at Killarney, T064-31067, and Tralee, T066-7123566, connecting with Dublin, Cork and other towns. All the main towns are served by **Bus Éireann** and details are given under each section.

Getting around

In the summer months both the Iveragh and Dingle Peninsulas, unlike the Beara, are reasonably well served by buses. There is also a twice daily summer-only service between Killarney and Castletownbere via Kenmare, Lauragh and Ardgroom (outside summer a Friday-only service covers Ardgroom to Kenmare). Cars can be hired at the airport, where companies like **Dooley Car Rental**, T087-6776068, **Hertz**, T066-9764733, www.hertz@kerry.ie, and **Avis**, T064 3554, www.avis.ie, have outlets, or in Killarney (see page 302).

Information Try websites www.travelireland.org/kerry and www.kerrygems.ie.

Killarney and around → *Colour map 3, grid B3.*

Victorian tourists were the first to come to Killarney; they waxed lyrical over the natural beauty of its lakes and, with well over a century to build up and consolidate the hype, it should come as no surprise to learn that this is Ireland's premier tourist town. Indeed, considering the sheer multitude of visitors who come and go every summer, the ordinary citizens of the town deserve a prize for the way in which they go about their business seemingly oblivious to the tourist tumult around them. Ironically, the town itself is of very minor interest, and as all the attractions lie outside Killarney there is little good reason to stay here for long. But while you are here there are countless restaurants, shops and pubs with music all dedicated to providing creature comforts.
⏩ *For Sleeping, Eating and other listings, see pages 298-302.*

Ins and outs

Getting there See Getting there, above. **Bus Éireann**'s No 286 service departs daily from the airport to Killarney at 1218 and then every two hours until 2218; from Killarney at 0615 (Mon only), 0900, 1000 and every two hours until 1800; journey time 20 minutes. A taxi costs about €20. A shuttle bus, **Corcoran's**, T064-36666, meets the Frankfurt flight only, €10 return.

Getting around Most of the sights in Killarney are accessible on foot or, if you can take the embarrassment, there are horse-drawn jaunting cars.

Information Killarney tourist office, Beech Rd, T064-31633, www.corkkerry.ie. Open all year, daily at the height of the season. This is the place to gather information for the whole Kerry region. ⏩ *See Transport, page 302, for further details.*

History

English landlords in the 18th century developed copper mines in the area, smelting the metal using the rich supply of oak wood, and when word spread of the natural beauty of the surrounding mountains and lakes, early tourists arrived in Bianconi cars (see page 224). Later in the 19th century the introduction of a railway line transformed the tourist scene and Queen Victoria's visit in 1861 really put the place on the map. Before the English arrived there were two chief Gaelic clans, the McCarthys and the O'Donoghues, and while the O'Donoghues' territory was confiscated by Cromwell, the McCarthys managed to hold on to land, some of which passed by inheritance to the Herbert family, the people responsible for Muckross House and creating the estate.

Sights

Muckross House, gardens and traditional farms ① *T064-31440. House: mid-Mar to Oct 0900-1800 (1900 in Jul and Aug); Nov to mid-Mar, 0900-1730. €5.50. Farm: Jun-Sep 1000-1800 (shorter hours in other months). OPW site. Joint ticket for house and farms, €8.25; gardens: 24 hrs, free.* Some 6 km south on the N71 road and with a scheduled bus service from the town centre, the Muckross House complex is a major attraction. The house itself is a fine Victorian mansion (see page 296) replete with the gentry's elegant rooms full of period furniture, while the servants' working quarters in the basement now house various craft workshops. The gardens boast an attractive water garden, a rock garden and more rhododendrons than you may care to see. The traditional farms, brought to life with real animals, pay tourist homage to Eamon de Valera's idyll of rural life in the 1930s, though surely he would have disapproved of the splendid decadence of the 'vintage coach' that shuttles visitors around. Near the house there are maps showing a number of local walks; the most popular route, also suitable for bicycles, heads around the north side of Middle Lake towards the Meeting of the Waters where the Upper Lake – the most beautiful of the three lakes – comes into view.

Muckross Friary ① *Mid-Jun to early Sep 1000-1700. Free.* The remarkably well-preserved Muckross Friary dates back to 1440, although General Ludlow arrived in 1652 and trashed the place after expelling the friars. The solid square tower is the most distinctive feature though the cloisters, surrounding an ancient yew tree, and a vaulted quadrangle are also in good condition.

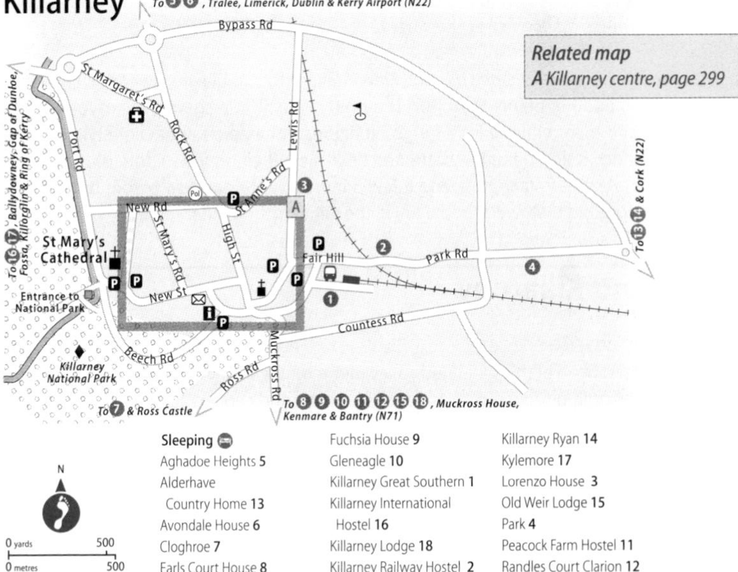

St Mary's Cathedral The finest example of A W N Pugin's work in Ireland was begun in 1842 and restored in the 1970s. Opinions of the exterior range from celebration of its mastery of Early English Gothic to denigration of its repressive presence, but the interior is a minor masterpiece of Irish-inspired architecture. Despite some terrible gaffes in the restoration of the cathedral, Pugin's inspiring vision of an Irish medieval cathedral endures in the delicate use of lancet and rose windows set against the solid interior buttresses. During the Famine, building work on the church was still in progress, and it was used as a shelter for the distressed; the large tree on the lawn marks a mass famine grave.

Ross Castle ⓘ *T064-35851. Jun-Aug 0900-1830 (shorter hours at other times). €5. OPW site.* The 15th-century Ross Castle, just outside town off the N71 road to Kenmare, has gone down in popular history as one of the last strongholds in Ireland to hold out valiantly against Cromwellian forces. In 1652 General Ludlow received its surrender from Muskerry after bringing ships up to Killarney by land and river, thus fulfilling a prophecy that the castle "could not be taken until a ship should swim upon the lake". The truth is that Muskerry, knowing full well that defeat was imminent, had already decided to surrender and the appearance of the boats provided a suitable excuse. The castle has now been completely restored, perhaps a little too clinically, but the lakeside location has its charms – Shelley briefly lived nearby in 1813 – and boats can be hired to row out to Inisfallen Island.

Inisfallen Island ⓘ *€10 per person.* The 21-acre island is about a 2 km from the shore. Nothing remains of the seventh-century monastery founded by St Fenian the Leper, although the ruins of a 12th-century oratory with a fine Romanesque doorway can be appreciated. You will have to travel to the Bodleian Library in Oxford to see the famed *Annals of Inishfallen*, a chronicle of Irish history from the 11th to the 13th centuries, completed on Inisfallen by monks. Rowing boats can be hired from near Ross Castle.

Museum of Irish Transport ⓘ *T064-32638. Apr-Oct 1000-1800; Jul-Aug 1000-2000. €5.* A worthwhile place to visit on a wet day, the museum has a varied display of veteran, vintage and classic vehicles of the road. My favourite is the 1910 Wolseley that belonged to the Gore Booth family in Sligo and carried Yeats around with Countess Markievicz at the wheel.

St Mary's Church ⓘ *Open all year. Free.* Built in 1870, replacing an earlier church of 1812 (and another before that), this is a pretty, musty little church, full of Anglo-Irish names and memorials to long forgotten figures. It has pre-Raphaelite-style stained glass windows and beautiful patterned floor tiles. Right in the middle of the tourist frenzy it is a great place to spend a few minutes' contemplation before buying that sweater/printed teatowel/cuddly toy in the gift shops outside.

Around Killarney

Gap of Dunloe

Arrive at the head of this glaciated valley mid-morning in July or August and the scene resembles rush hour in a city, as coaches, buses and cars jostle for space, let alone the importuning jarveys and camera-toting crowds around Kate Kearney's Cottage. The Gap of Dunloe, however, is some 12 km in length and, since many visitors walk or pony ride only a couple of miles, it is not difficult to leave the crowds behind, either on foot or on a bicycle. A whole-day tour – bookable from any tour company in Killarney (see page 292) or on the spot outside Kate

Take the road out of town towards Killorglin and a short way after the village of Fossa the Gap is signposted on the left. No public transport.

Rhododendrons: the death of the woodlands

As you drive around the peninsulas of the southwest, especially in May, you will notice the beauty of the deep purple flowering rhododendron with its dark evergreen leaves. The plants make an excellent windbreak and, being evergreen, keep the gardens looking alive in winter. There are many different species of rhododendron but the only one to have naturalized here is the purple variety, *Rhododendron ponticum*. It can grow to over six metres, loves the acid soil of Kerry and West Cork and produces about 5,000 seeds in each flower head. It was introduced some time in the 18th century from its native habitat around the Black Sea, and it became very popular with the local landlords who planted it as cover for game birds to give their winter sporting activities an extra edge.

What they did not plan for was the ferocity with which the plant colonized the area. Its evergreen leaves, so good for pheasants and windbreaks, are wide and permanent and quickly cover all the ground available. Where they grow in open land this is no problem to other wildlife, except that after several years' growth they form a dense thicket, which needs cutting back, but in Kerry's native woodlands the plant is a disaster. It takes the niche of holly in the oak and beech woods, resulting in a loss of all the wildlife that depends on those trees. Worse still, it provides a permanent shade on the forest floor, wiping out woodland flowers such as wood sorrel, bluebells, rush, primroses and the many other ground layer plants as well as the insects that depend on them. Worst of all, it prevents the germination of seedling deciduous trees, such as beech and oak, which make the woodlands of Killarney so special. Unchecked it would wipe out the oak forests in a few generations, leaving great tracts of purple flowering woodland with little animal or plant diversity within it. Around Muckross, Torc Mountain, Tomies Woods and Glengarriff eradication programmes are taking place and although the pest is unlikely to be eradicated completely, for the moment it is under control.

Kearney's Cottage – involves riding through the Gap in a pony trap and lunching at Lord Brandon's Cottage before returning to Killarney by boat.

The name of **Kate Kearney's Cottage** ⓘ *T064-44146*, may conjure up an image of a cute, stone-washed, thatched dwelling with a big black kettle on a turf fire, and it probably was when Charlotte Brontë passed this way on her honeymoon, but it is now a hectically busy bar, restaurant, souvenir and gift store where the staff deserve a medal for their patience. Nearby, **Moriarty's** ⓘ *T064-44144*, is a clothing and craft shop with a range of Aran handknits, sports jackets, cashmeres, linens, jewellery, Waterford crystal and Belleek china.

Walks and cycling around Killarney

Killarney may be a busy town, but it is very easy to find beautiful and quite empty countryside in the immediate area. *Mac Publications* in Killarney produces a small pamphlet, available from the tourist office, showing maps of several walks and cycle rides in the area. It includes two excellent expeditions to the east of the lakes, one at Tomies Wood and one along the Gap of Dunloe. The monthly free *Where Killarney* also has walk suggestions with maps.

 Tomies Wood The Tomies Wood walk can be reached by taking the first signposted road to the Gap of Dunloe, just after passing Fossa, a few miles out of town, on the N72. Go down here to a bridge over the road at the River Laune: a left turn 500 m past here, signposted to Lough Leane, brings you to another left turn after a further 500 m where it is possible to park. From here a circular walk of about 6.5 km is possible. Through the gate the walk passes through a farm and enters forestry. The path forks and makes a circuit of the hillside far up above Lough Leane with wonderful views over the water. The forestry is not overbearing, with a great deal of larch and spruce, and much of the walk is over bare rock with the underlying old red sandstone very conspicuous. The walk passes O'Sullivan's Cascade, down by the lakeside and a short detour off the path. Look out for red deer, which are very common in the woods.

Gap of Dunloe The Gap of Dunloe is a much more strenuous walk and makes a much better cycle ride. The journey through the Gap is 9.5 km and, although a steady climb, it is full of reasons to stop and admire the view. At the top of the Gap you are in the Black Valley and a left turn brings you to the Black Valley Hostel (see page 317). From here the route takes you to Lord Brandon's Cottage and a spell over quite rough ground, cycling along the shores of the Upper Lake, following the route of the Kerry Way.

The path finally meets the main N71 road at Derricunnihy and where a left turn takes you back into Killarney (but this is not suitable for walkers). The first part of the route also makes a pleasant walk but both cyclists and walkers should be prepared for a very busy scene at the start of the gap where tour buses, tourist and jarveys jostle for places. The crowds soon fall away once you begin the journey into the Gap.

Muckross

There are a number of walks around Muckross demesne, following the shores of Muckross Lake and around the house and gardens. One walk begins at the first entrance to the park where the jaunting car drivers wait. The walk goes along the main drive and then cuts over to the lake following its shores. This is a particularly interesting walk since it crosses intercut sections of limestone and sandstone rock where the flora change radically from one section to another. The walk goes around the shores of the lake finishing back at the gate you entered by.

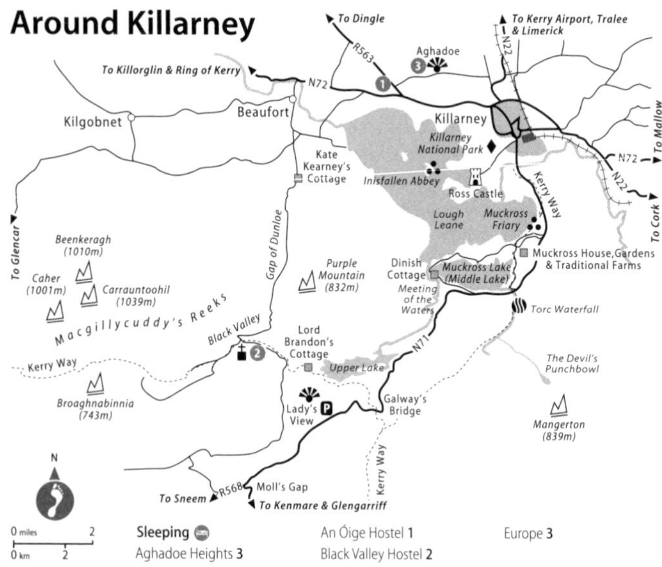

History of the Muckross Demesne

The Muckross Estate belonged to the McCarthy clan, whose leader was known as McCarthy Mór, until the 18th century, despite various attempts at confiscation. It finally passed to a family called Herbert in 1770 and they had Muckross House built between 1840 and 1843. In the process they overspent on their budget and in 1899 the house and estate were sold to Lord Ardilaun, a member of the famous Guinness family. In 1910 the whole property was bought by an American, WB Bourne, as a wedding gift for his daughter, whose family later donated all 11,000 acres of it to the Irish nation.

Other walks that have been laid out in the demesne with markers and a description of the sights are **Arthur Young's Nature Trail**, which makes a loop around the little Doo Lough, and the **Mossy Woods Nature Trail** which is close by Muckross House. The house has leaflets describing both walks. Cyclists are welcome in the demesne and there are any number of possible cycle routes around the grounds.

The Cloghreen Pool is another short, circular walk, taking about an hour. Its entrance is on the left a few hundred metres beyond the entrance to Muckross along the road to Kenmare. A left turn at the sign for Mangerton brings you to a signposted nature trail, complete with guide ropes for the visually impaired. The walk follows the shores of the Cloghreen Pool, an old mill pond with a strange blue colour due to the large amounts of limestone dissolved in the water. The area around the pool has been planted at various times with beech, alder, and pine, but the oak, holly and willow occur naturally. This is a good place to notice the devastating effects of the rhododendron that grows invasively here and has to be culled regularly. Its evergreen nature prevents seedlings of native trees from germinating and threatens the life of all the woods around Killarney.

Ross Castle To the southwest of Killarney is Ross Castle, and a pleasant 8-km walk around the castle and the shores of the lower lake starts in town at the Cathedral. From the cathedral the walk goes into Ross Road, then goes to Ross Island and passes Ross Castle. A circuit can be made of the island, taking in the viewing point at Governor's Rock. Another path goes north along the shores of the lake making a loop back to Ross Road. The walk is through woodland with views of the lake and Innisfallen Island. There are several possible routes for this walk, another taking you over the Deenagh River and back to your starting point via Knockreer House. This route is also suitable for cycling.

Crohane Mountain Travelling on the Kenmare Road out of Killarney (N71) a quite strenuous walk is possible to the summit of Crohane Mountain (656 m). About 3 km out of the town centre a left turn is signposted to Lough Guitane. Just after this a right turn sets off up the mountain, at first a wide tarmac road but gradually giving way to green road and then open hillside. The goal of the walk is the hilltop and, while there is no path, a route to the top is quite clear. The return journey is about 6.5 km and takes about four hours to complete. A clear day is essential for this walk.

Cycling to Tralee Take the N22 out of town and take the road on the left at Cleeny for a more interesting route that avoids the traffic of the N22. A stiff cycle in places.

Sleeping

Killarney *p292, maps p293, 296 and 299*
There is a good range of accommodation in and around Killarney. However, throughout July and August there is a long queue every morning at the accommodation desk in the Killarney tourist office. Hotels and guest houses, and especially B&Bs and hostels, can all be oversubscribed and without an advance booking you may end up being forced into a higher accommodation bracket than you anticipated. Hotels are uniformly expensive and rooms under €90 are as rare as leprechauns. Guest houses usually offer the comfort of a small hotel, but for good value consider also the private rooms in the hostels, charging around €40. Some of the hostels have their transport waiting outside the bus and train station and if you don't have a bed booked it may be worth arranging something on the spot. A vast number of B&Bs, nearly all those registered with the Bord Fáilte, charge a standard rate of around €56 for a double and €38 for a single so you may as well take pot luck with the tourist office. Very few are located within the town and a number close over the winter, so be sure to check. The less expensive B&Bs mostly belong to the Family Homes of Ireland group (see page 41).

L **Hotel Europe**, out of town at Fossa, T064- 31900, www.killarneyhotels.ieiol.ie/khl. Has one of the most scenic locations of Killarney's many hotels, the lakeside rooms have balconies to boot, and the 25-m pool is complemented by a seaweed bath for the hyper health-conscious.

L **Killarney Park**, town centre, T064-35555, www.killarneyparkhotel.ie. Next to the cinema complex, this is a modern 4-star hotel with bourgeois charm and a good restaurant.

L-A **Aghadoe Heights Hotel**, a few miles out of town at Aghadoe, T064-31766, www.aghadoeheights.com. Hillside hotel with an incongruously brutalist exterior but beautifully designed inside with lovely rooms with amazing views and big balconies. Includes pool and leisure centre and a vast complicated spa where you can have everything done including crystals therapy.

L-A **Killarney Avenue Hotel**, Kenmare Pl, T064-32522, www.odonoghue-ring-hotels.com. Centrally located, conspicuous exterior and swanky lobby, olde-Irish restaurant and Irish theme pub.

L-B **Randles Court Clarion Hotel**, Muckross Rd, T064-35333, www.randlescourt.com. Good-sized rooms built in 1906, with some period features retained and within walking distance of town.

L-C **Gleneagle Hotel**, Muckross Rd, T064-36000, www.gleneaglehotel.com. A short way out of town, this hotel is geared up for fun-loving families who want leisure facilities and late-night musical entertainment.

L-D **International Best Western Hotel**, Kenmare Pl, T064-31816, www.killarney-inter.com. Often busy with coach parties, a comfortable and conveniently located hotel opposite the cinema complex.

A-C **Arbutus**, College St, T064-31037, www.arbutuskillarney.com. A friendly family-run hotel in the heart of town, but not the quietest location.

A-C **Killarney Great Southern**, T064-31262, www.gsh.ie. Centrally located, recently refurbished hotel, dating from 1854, this is the place to stay for old-fashioned style plus modern amenities such as a heated pool. The neo-Georgian exterior hides a lush extravagance of style and a sumptuous foyer, which, along with the stately dining room and its Greek columns, makes a visit here worthwhile.

B-D **Killarney Ryan Hotel**, Cork Rd, T064-31555, www.choicehotelsireland.ie. 2 km out of town, ideal for families with its crèche, a young teenagers' club and kids' menus.

C-D **Earls Court House**, Woodlawn Junction, T064-34009, www.killarney-earlscourt.ie. Decorated entirely in 19th-century antique furnishings, with individually-styled bedrooms some of which have balconies looking out on countryside. This is a top-drawer guest house.

C-D **Fuschia House**, Muckross Rd, T064-33743, www.fuchsiahguestouse.com. In this guest house, tea and cakes are served on arrival; good breakfast, utility room with

For an explanation of the sleeping and eating price codes used in this guide, see inside the front cover. Other relevant information is found in Essentials pages 39-45.

fridge and kettle, and the firm beds are a treat in the 10 large bedrooms.

C-D Killarney Lodge, Countess Rd, T064-36499, killarneylodge.net. Superior, large guest house set in modern walled gardens.

C-D Old Weir Lodge, Muckross Rd, T064-35593, www.oldweirlodge.com. Modern, Tudor-style guest house, short walk from town, huge gardens, good facilities.

D-E Linden House New Rd, T064-31379. Hotel in a reasonably quiet part of town, restaurant and 3-night packages.

E Alderhave Country Home, Ballycasheen, Cork Rd, T064-31982, www.alderhaven.com. At Whitebridge off the Cork Rd. Big secluded gardens. Has a good reputation.

E Avondale House, Tralee Rd, T064-35579, www.avondale-house.com. This B&B is 5 mins by car from the centre, open all year.

E Lorenzo House , Lewis Rd, T064-31869, lorenzokillarney@eircom.net. B&B in town with own parking space.

E-F Killarney Railway Hostel, T064-35299, www.railwayhostel.com. Opposite the railway station, well equipped and lots of private rooms.

F Cloghroe, 14 Scrahan Ct, T064-34818, www.geocities.com/cloghroebandb. Small B&B, good prices within walking distance of town centre near Ross Castle.

F Fossa Holiday Hostel, Fossa, T064-31497, wwwcamping-holidaysireland.com. Out of town, no private rooms but worth considering if everywhere else is full.

F Killarney International Hostel, Aghadoe House, T064-31240, anoige@killarney.iol.ie. This *An Óige* hostel is a superb old mansion, 5 km west of town on the road to Killorglin. Free transport from train and bus stations; private rooms, bike hire.

F Kylemore, Ballydowney, T064-31771 kylemorehousekillarney@eircom.net. B&B in a family home on N72 ring of Kerry road.

F Neptune's, off New St, T064-35255, neptune@eircom.net. Smart hostel, possibly the best organized one in town but only 5 private rooms.

F Park, Park Rd, T064-32119. Hostel with 50 beds and 2 private rooms and an admirable policy of charging the same rate per person. Open Apr-Oct.

F Peacock Farm Hostel, Gortdromakery, Muckross, T064-33557. There is a twice-daily

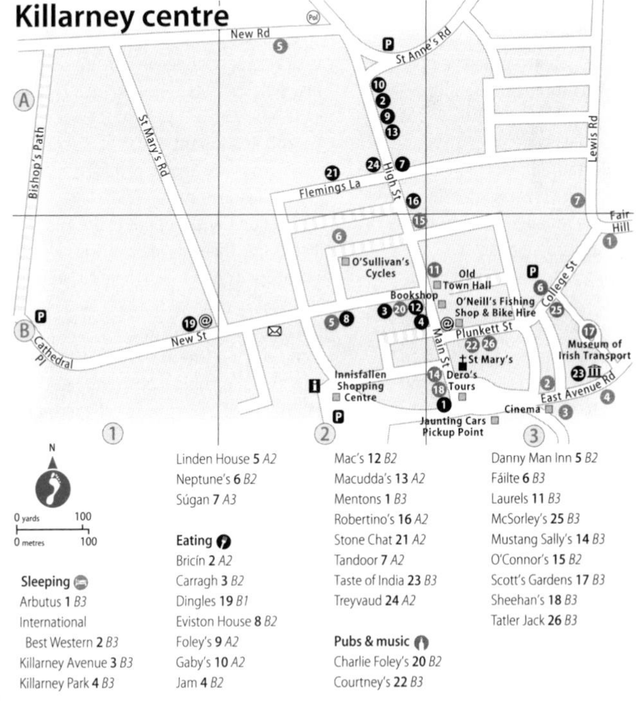

pick-up service but it helps to have your own transport; take Lough Guitane Rd, 1st left after Muckross Hse coming from Killarney.

F **Súgan**, Lewis Rd, T064-33104, info@killarneysuganhostel.com. Good location in town, 2 private rooms, a little hip and a little squashed.

Self-catering

Accommodation Killarney, 52 High St, T064-31787. Handles quality townhouses and plush 3-bedroomed suites.

Camping

There are a few 4-star sites near town:

Fleming's White Bridge Caravan and Camping Park, T064-31590, www.killarneycamping.com. Just off the N22 Cork road.

Fossa Caravan and Camping Park, Fossa, T064-31497, www.camping-holidaysireland.com. On the road to Killorglin.

Killarney Flesk Caravan and Camping Park, Muckross Rd, T31704, killarneylakes@eircom.nettinet.ie.

Killarney Railway Hostel, camping possible.

Eating

Killarney *p292, maps p293, 296 and 299*

TTT **Chequers**, Randles Court Hotel. An Italian-style restaurant worth considering.

TTT **Dingles Restaurant**, New St, T064-31079. Closes on Sun and between Nov and Mar and serves only dinner.

TTT **Foley's Restaurant**, High St, T064- 31217. Fairly typical of the town's expensive seafood and steakhouse restaurants, open all year around for lunch and dinner.

TTT **Frederick's**, Aghadoe Heights Hotel, T064-31766. For a special treat, white cloths, silver service, great views and very traditional, very classy food. Starters such as smoked salmon served in the traditional way and mains which include lobster, roast beef and rack of Kerry lamb. The set menu works out at €60 plus but for ambience and well cooked food and good service it's worth it.

TTT **Gaby's**, High St, T064-32519. Has a reputation as the best seafood restaurant in town and prices to match; open for dinner except on Sun and for lunch Tue-Sat. Apart from the fresh seafood like lobster, they also serve steaks and Kerry lamb, and the salmon pâté starter is a house speciality.

TT **Bricín**, High St, T064-34902, www.bricin.com. Has been around for a while and is still a reliable place for a decent innovative lunch or dinner. Speciality is *boxty*, a traditional Irish dish. Good value early-bird set menu and several vegetarian options. Closed Sun.

TT **Menton's**, Killarney Plaza Hotel, T064-21150, www.mentons.com. A gem of a place, with delicious modern Irish cuisine, a sandwich menu till 1800 which would fill you up for an early dinner, an early-bird menu 1800-2000 for around €23 as well as an à la carte evening menu until 2100. All set in a stylish, cool bar with seats that look like they are covered in wookie fur and frightening lampshades.

TT **Peppers**, Great Southern hotel, T064-31262. Offers modern Irish cuisine – scallops and prawns with couscous, monkfish and asparagus, veal with lemon-scented spinach – in a room that successfully blends period details with self-conscious modern art on the walls. Some dishes could push your bill into the expensive category.

TT **Robertino's**, High St, T064-34966. Has arty Italian decor and serves lunches of pizza, pasta and open sandwiches and an early-bird set dinner.

TT **Treyvaud**, 62 High St, T064-33062. A busy, casual kind of place serving Austro-Swiss-style food. Its early-bird menu is the regular one with a 10% discount.

T **Caragh Restaurant**, 3 New St. Adept at catering to a busy crowd of hungry diners at lunch and dinnertime.

T **Innisfallen Centre**, opposite the tourist office. Inside there are inexpensive cafés suitable for a quick meal. There's a large supermarket, ideal for stocking up on picnic meals and other provisions.

T **Jam**, High St, T064-31441. A good bakery and coffee shop doing food until 1800.

T **Mac's**, Main St. Does good caff food and ice cream.

T **Macudda's**, High St. A good place for an inexpensive early-bird dinner, where if you hang around after your meal you can listen to live music of one sort or another.

T **Stone Chat**, Flemings Lane off High St, T064-34295. Excellent café meals.

T **Tandoor**, 17 High St. Has some good inexpensive set menus but isn't particularly vegetarian-friendly.

Taste of India, down the lane opposite the cinema and Killarney Park hotel, T064-37770. A balti and tandoori restaurant, also with a take-out menu, open 1700 until midnight at least.

Pubs and music

Killarney *p292, maps p293, 296 and 299*
At the height of the season it seems as if every pub in the town has music of one sort or another. The hugely popular and undeniably touristy **Laurels**, Main St, T064-31149, and **Scott's Gardens**, College St, T064-31060, are both in the centre of town and, while not to everyone's taste or musical ear, they can be good fun. Many of the hotels within town and out along the road to Kenmare have musical entertainment.
Arbutus Hotel, College St. Has traditional music every night.
Charlie Foley's, New St, T064-33920. Might seem sophisticated by comparison.
Courtney's, Plunkett St. The best pub for young people.
Danny Man Inn, Eviston House Hotel, New St, T064-31640. Has music every night from 2100, but coach parties can take over.
Hotel Europe, goes for Wed and Fri nights and confines itself to piano music on Sat and Sun.
Fáilte, College St. The bar in this hotel has traditional music on weeknights and a disco on Fri, Sat and Sun.
Gleneagle Hotel, Muckross Rd, T064-36000. Discos amd live music for all ages every night of the week.
Great Southern Hotel. Live piano music in the lobby at night.
Hannigan's, International Hotel. Has Irish music every night except Sun.
Kate Kearney's Cottage, at the Gap of Dunloe. Traditional music on Wed, Fri and Sun nights.
Lake Hotel, has traditional music on Mon, Wed and Sat.
McSorley's Pub, College St, T064-37278. Traditional music.
O'Connor's, High St. Has regular sessions of traditional music.
Tatler Jack, Plunkett St, T064-32361. Regularly has traditional music.
Mustang Sally's, Main St. A music bar with food and music nightly.
Sheehan's, next door to Mustang Sally's. Has traditional music and set dancing nightly.

Shopping

Killarney *p292, maps p293, 296 and 299*
Shops stay open until 2200 in the summer.

Arts and crafts The town is choc-a-bloc with craft shops.
Aran Sweater Market and Museum, College St. With rather more emphasis on the market than the museum aspect.
Blarney Woollen Mills, 10 Main St. Has 2 floors devoted to Irish crafts – especially pottery and crystal – and Aran knitwear, open daily until 2300.
Bricin Craft shop, High St.
Carraig Don, Main St.
Christie's, Main St.
The Crystal and Linen Shop, High St.
House of Names, Kenmare Pl. Quality heraldic products for Irish and other European names.
Killarney Linen and Lace, Plunkett St.
Memories, High St.
Moriarty's, T064-4414, www.moriartys.ie. At the Gap of Dunloe, vast, with every Irish handicraft known to man plus some other stuff. Look in the tourist office before you go for a 10% discount voucher or just ask for the discount.
O'Shea's, Main St.

Books **The Killarney Bookshop**, 32 Main St, T064-34108, www.killarneybookshop.ie.

Activities and tours

Fishing **O'Neill's**, 6 Plunkett St, T064-31970. Tackle, permits and information. River Flesk gets spring salmon and peel (grilse), River Laune has salmon and trout while Barfinnihy Lake is stocked with trout. Permits required for rivers and Barfinnihy Lake but not for Killarney lakes.

Horse riding **Killarney Riding Stables**, Ballydowney, 1.6 km west of Killarney off R562 road to Killorglin, T064-31686, www.killarney-reeks-trail.com. Trips from 1 hr to 6 days.
Muckross Riding Stables, Mangerton Rd, T064-32238. 1-3 hr rides.

Tours **Coach tours**: **Dero's**, Main St, T064-31251. Offers the standard Ring of Kerry coach tour and a Gap of Dunloe tour, both departing at 1030.

O'Connors, the pub in High St, T064-30200. Offers similar tours.
O'Donoghue Brothers, Old Weir Lodge Guesthouse, Muckross Rd, T064-31068, www.killarneydaytour.com. Trips through the Gap of Dunloe by coach, jaunting car/ horse and boat.
Jaunting cars: Gather on East Avenue Rd opposite the cineplex, opposite the entrance to Muckross House and around Kate Kearney's Cottage at the Gap of Dunloe.
Lake tours: Lake cruises on Lough Leane with a commentary on the local ecology and history. The boat departs from Ross Castle and there is a shuttle service from the Destination Killarney information kiosk, Scott's Gardens Hotel, T064-32638. Sailings at 1100, 1230, 1430, 1600 and 1700, subject to the weather.
Killarney Watercoach Cruises, T064-31068 (also bookable through Dero's; see coach tours, or the tourist office). Sail from Ross Castle on the *Lily of Killarney* at 1030, 1200, 1345, 1515 and 1630 and with a commentary covering the folklore and history of the lakes.
Walking: **Kerry Outdoor Adventures**, T087-9724740, www.kerryoutdoors.com. Offers half-day or full-day guided hill walks, rock climbing, canoeing and kayaking.
Walking Tours, T064-33471, 087-6394362, www.killarnetguidedwalks.com. Daily from Shell petrol station in Lower New St, opposite the cathedral, 1100 for a 2-hr stroll around the National Park. €7.

Transport

Killarney *p292, maps p293, 296 and 299*
Bike hire O'Sullivan's Cycles, Bishop's Lane off New St, also at the car park opposite the tourist office and in Brewery Lane, T064-31282. O'Neill Cycle Store, 6 Plunkett St, T064-31970.

Bus Bus Éireann, T01-8366111.
Bus links to all the main cities, and **Kerry Airport**, from the bus station, T064-30011 (T064-34777 outside office hours), alongside the train station. Between Jun and Sep a twice-daily Ring of Kerry bus service runs around the Peninsula on the N70, with the option to stop off and complete travel by a later bus or the next day. All year, there is a regular bus service from Killarney to **Waterville** via **Cahirsiveen**, and to **Dingle** via **Tralee**.

Car hire Budget Rent a Car, International Hotel, Kenmare Pl, T064-34341. Hertz, Plunkett St, T064-34126, also have an office at the airport. Randle's Car Hire, Muckross Rd, T064-31237. A local firm; better rates. Parking can be a problem in Jul and Aug. Use one of the pay and display car parks.

Taxi Killarney Taxi service, T087-2694646, Killarney Hackneys, T064-37752, Killarney Cabs, T064-37444.

Train Iarnród Éireann T01-8366222. The station, T064-31067, is centrally located, with routes to **Dublin** and other main cities.

Ring of Kerry

The Ring of Kerry is a 180-km road route around the Iveragh Peninsula and throughout the summer months it becomes periodically clogged with traffic as a line of vehicles follows in the wake of a slow-moving coach, caravan or car. The mornings are particularly gruesome because this is when massive tour coaches trundle around, but at any time of the day it is difficult to understand the point of setting out to complete the circuit in one or even two days. At times, though, the Ring of Kerry is unavoidable simply because it reaches the far west of the Peninsula, where some of the most interesting sites in Kerry are to be found. ▸▸ *For Sleeping, Eating and other listings, see pages 315-321.*

Ins and outs

Getting around The best way to see and enjoy the Iveragh Peninsula is by walking part or all of the Kerry Way, a long-distance walk that is described in its relevant sections, beginning on page 312. It takes well over a week to complete but with the

★ Puck Fair

The oldest festival still being celebrated in Ireland, Puck Fair has an unmistakable pagan heritage that dates back to the Celtic celebration of the god Lug and the beginning of the harvest. The Gaelic word for August is *Lughnasa*, the festival of Lug, and Puck Fair takes place around the middle of the month, from 10-12th in Killorglin. The bacchanalian celebrations begin on Gathering Day when a white male goat is escorted into the market square, lifted on to a makeshift three-tiered platform and crowned with garlands as the King of the Fair. The goat remains perched there, 12 m above the street, to preside over the alcohol-fuelled revelry that occupies the next couple of days. All the pubs have a special licence to extend their opening hours and the influx of visitors, musicians and assorted entertainers ensures a heady atmosphere. On the evening of 12 August, Scattering Day, the goat is ceremoniously brought down from its perch and led away. Further details at www.puckfair.ie, or from Killarney or Killorglin tourist offices.

help of the summer-only Bus Éireann service it is quite feasible to walk parts of the Way and return by bus to one's base. Another alternative to driving is to cycle and, while the Ring of Kerry itself is best avoided whenever possible – the roads are narrow and impatient drivers pose a threat to life and limb – there is a little-used route across the middle of the Peninsula from Killorglin to Waterville via the Ballaghisheen Pass that is worth taking (see page 309). And to the west of Waterville and Cahersiveen there is a looped route along minor roads, called the Skellig Ring, that accesses Valentia and the Skelligs.

All year around, a bus runs Monday-Saturday between Killarney and Waterville via Killorglin, Glenbeigh and Cahersiveen. In summer buses depart Killarney at 0830, 0950, 1345 and 1500 (outside of summer, only one bus departing at 1500, Monday-Friday). The return journey from Waterville to Killarney is covered by one bus only departing at 0730; but a second bus departs from Cahersiveen at 1215 in summer only. Summer only, a Sneem-Kenmare-Killarney-Tralee service operates daily. For full details, contact Tralee bus station, T066-712 3566, or Killarney T064-30011. ▸▸ *See Transport, page 321, for further details.*

Killorglin → *Phone code: 066. Colour map 3, grid B2.*

The inland 21-km stretch west of Killarney along the R582 is fairly unremarkable until reaching the small messy-looking market town of Killorglin above the River Laune. During the time of the annual Puck Fair a visit is highly recommended (see box), but at other times of the year, apart from the angling, there is little to do or see. A short distance north of the town, at **Ballykissane Pier**, a monument commemorates the death of the revolutionary nationalists whose car plunged into the sea in 1916 on their way to meet Roger Casement near Tralee (see page 325). The odd-shaped building, close to the roundabout where the road heads out to Glenbeigh is a **tourist information office**, T066-9761451, open Apr-Oct daily 0930-1900.

Glenbeigh → *Phone code: 066. Colour map 3, grid B2.*

In Smith's 1786 *History of Kerry* the author recalls how he "accidentally arrived at a little house in a very obscure part of the parish [of Glenbeigh] where I saw poor lads reading Homer, their master having been a mendicant scholar at an English Grammar School at Tralee". Modern visitors are unlikely to hear any ancient Greek, but the small seaside resort of Glenbeigh, 10 km west of Killorglin, is still a surprisingly pleasant place to stay (see page 315). Before entering the town from the direction of Killorglin it is difficult to miss the large Red Fox pub and adjacent **Kerry Bog Village Museum** ⓘ *To66-9769184, open all year until 1830, €4*, by the side of the main road, but they are hardly worth a special trip. The pub food is so-so, with regular musical evenings at weekends, but coach groups make regular stops here. There is no **tourist office**, but local information is available at Brennan's craft shop, To66-9768252, or the post office, To66-9768201, both on Main Street.

Rossbeigh Strand

Glenbeigh itself has a lively pub scene; but on a fine day the real attraction lies outside the village where 5 km of uninterrupted beach make up Rossbeigh Strand, a spit of land pointing out into Dingle Bay with sand on either side and no shelving. The area is safe for swimming, challenging for surfers, ideal for horse riding, and there is a pub nearby. To reach the beach area, bear right at the Y-junction at the Cahersiveen end of town.

If you spend time in the Glenbeigh area it is worth having a copy of map 78 in the Ordnance Survey Discovery Series.

Local walk The Kerry Way passes through Glenbeigh and a recommended local walk can be enjoyed by following the Way west up through Glenbeigh Woods, at the Cahersiveen end of town. The Way makes it way up to high ground from where there is a dramatic view of Rossbeigh Strand and the Dingle Peninsula to the north. With a bicycle or car an excursion can be made to the southwest and the glen of the River Behy along any of the minor roads that branch off south of the

Ring of Kerry & Kerry Way

N70 west of Glenbeigh. These minor roads peter out in a glorious Kerry landscape where three loughs are surrounded by an amphitheatre of forbidding mountains.

Cahersiveen → *Phone code: 066. Colour map 3, grid B1.*

Both the location and the easy-going character of the place make Cahersiveen (also spelt Caherciveen or Cahirciveen) worth considering as a base for a short stay on the Iveragh Peninsula (see page 315). The town itself is agreeably unprepossessing, accommodating visitors with a sufficient number of amenities while providing convenient access to Valencia Island, as well as some enjoyable local walks. Cahersiveen is also on the Kerry Way, Glenbeigh can be easily reached in a day and Waterville is an invigorating 8-hour walk away. From either town, public transport could return you to Cahersiveen. The **tourist office** is on Church St, T066-9472589. May-Sep Mon-Sat 0915-1300, 1415-1730.

The Barracks ⓘ *T066-9472777. May-Sep Mon-Fri 1000-1630, Sat 1100-1630, Sun 1300-1700, Oct-Apr same hours Mon-Fri but closed 1300-1400. €4.* The fearsome, white-painted building that now houses a heritage centre is an unexpected sight. It was built by the British in the 1870s as a Royal Irish Constabulary barracks in response to the Fenian uprising of 1867, which it was feared might lead to a future attack on the new telegraph cable station on Valentia. Is it just pure local blarney or did the British really mix up two sets of building plans and construct in Kerry an edifice intended for the northwest frontier of India? When you see the Barracks you may well wonder.

Local walks The Kerry countryside around Cahersiveen lets you enjoy a lazy day's walk to a beach and a hill-top picnic and take in along the way excellent examples of **stone forts**. If you are planning to spend more than a day or two in the area then Ordnance Survey Map 83 is ideal. A popular walk takes you across the River Valentia, then taking the first turn to the left leads you past the **Cahergal stone fort**. Just before the fort there is a road on the left that heads south to the remains of **Ballycarberry Castle**. To continue, return to the road that leads to the fort and just after it turn to the right along a road that passes **Leacanabuaile**, another stone fort, before going to Kimego Wood via a small beach at Cooncrome harbour.

Heading out along the main road towards Glenbeigh brings you to the birthplace of Daniel O'Connell. Today it is just an ivy-clad ruin, but just opposite it there is the landscaped **O'Connell Memorial Park** and a bust of the man who led the highly successful campaign for the right of Catholics to sit in the British parliament.

Valentia Island → *Phone code: 066. Colour map 3, grid B1.*

In a mad rush simply to 'do' the Ring of Kerry travellers often skip Valentia Island and thereby pass up an ideal opportunity to slow down the pace and explore at leisure one of the modest gems of the area.

Ins and outs There is a land bridge from Portmagee and a passenger and car ferry that operates a shuttle service from Apr-Sep Mon-Sat 0730-2230, T066-9476141, from Reenard just west of Cahersiveen. €5 single for a car, €1.50 for pedestrian, €2 cyclist. ▸▸ *See Transport, page 321, for further details.*

History Even though the land bridge was only completed in 1971 Valentia had a distinguished role in the history of communication. Late-night listeners of the BBC will be familiar with the name of Valentia because the island was the former site of an important meteorological station (now moved to Cahersiveen). It was also the point for the first transatlantic cable station (see box, page 307), and a railway line was built so that travellers from Europe could make their way here for the shortest possible transatlantic sea crossing. The transatlantic sea link never happened and the railway closed down in the 1950s, but go back a hundred years to when the first transatlantic cable was being laid, and Valentia was the Silicon Valley and Cape Canaveral of Victorian Britain. Today, the appeal of a visit to Valentia is simply its off-the-beaten-track location, the remains and reminders of its past history and the opportunity to linger aimlessly in a sub-tropical corner of Kerry. The effect of the Gulf Stream ensures frost-free temperatures all year round and plants that would perish in other parts of Ireland manage to thrive. The Irish poet Aubrey de Vere (1814-1902) advised his friend Tennyson to visit Valentia (which he did) and listen to the sound of the waves, assuring him that those at Beachy Head in England would pale into insignificance. In 1992 the fossilised footprints of a 360-million year old marine tetrapod were discovered in some rocks near the shore at the north east tip of the island. They are signposted from Knightstown. Judging from the size of the prints the creature was a kind of newt about 1 metre long. It lived long before the dinosaurs and was probably one of the first creatures to evolve from whatever was swimming about in the sea in those days. The prints are among the oldest ever discovered in the world.

The Skellig Experience ⓘ *T066-9476306. Mar-Oct from 1000-1700, later in the summer months. €4.40. The centre organizes a daily trip to the Skelligs, weather permitting, summer only, 1500, €21 adults. Ring on the morning to see if weather conditions suit.* This interpretative centre is on the left side immediately after reaching Valentia from Portmagee. Exhibits deal with the lives of the monks and the story of the lighthouse that was built on Skelligs in 1826 and operated until 1986, manned by a team of three who were relieved by helicopter from Castletownbere. A 15-minute

Subterranean blues

The first attempt to lay a cable under the Atlantic Ocean took place in 1857 but ended in failure. A small fleet of ships set off slowly from Valentia lowering cables as they went, but after only 450 km the cable snapped and the enterprise was put on hold. The following year, a second attempt was made, this time using an American ship leaving Halifax and laying cable on its route east while a British ship did the same west from Valentia. The two boats met successfully in the middle and the first transatlantic radio link between the new and old worlds was made. The underwater cable was to snap more than once in those pioneering days but a permanent station was established on the island and Morse code was transmitted at the rate of 17 words a minute.

The cable operators on Valentia were a highly paid, non-Irish elite with their own cricket pitch and tennis courts, but one or two locals were also employed and one cable message did slip out to the US in 1916 with news of the Easter Rising. New technology, ironically developed on Valentia, saw the demise of the cable station and it finally closed down in 1965.

audio-visual show focuses on the Skellig Michael monastery and there is also a section on the wildlife, very useful for brushing up on bird identification before actually visiting the Skelligs. Also useful is the shop with books on local history and wildlife and a café serving snacks and light meals.

Slate quarry ⓘ *Open 24 hrs. Signposted at the T-junction when approaching Knightstown from the west.* Another ambitious Victorian enterprise that focused on Valentia was a slate quarry that opened in 1816 and operated until 1911, employing up to 400 men at its height. Huge sheets of slate 4 m long were lifted out of the mine and cut to size on site by a steam-powered saw, the remains of which can be seen at the mouth of the quarry. Valentia slate, possessing what experts call a good cleavage, could be easily split into thin slabs of exceptional length; it was highly valued and used to grace the roofs of noted London buildings (like the Houses of Parliament) as well as being exported to South America (see San Salvador railway station, El Salvador). Work has recently begun again at the quarry but there is little to see save the vast piles of broken slate lying about, which admittedly do help create a strong sense of place.

Heritage centre ⓘ *T066-9476353. Apr-Sep Mon-Sat 1100-1700. €3. On the right-hand side of the road just outside Knightstown on the road to the slate quarry.* The ex-National School setting for this little museum suits the educational content of what was the schoolroom, now devoted to the history of the cable station. There are also sections on local craft industries. Interesting any time and a godsend on a wet afternoon.

Glanleam House subtropical gardens ⓘ *T066-9476176. May-Oct daily 1100-1700. €4.50.* Despite strong winter winds, which occasionally wreak havoc on the gardens, the balmy influence of the Gulf Stream makes Valentia a subtropical greenhouse when it comes to cultivating plants that would not survive outside the southwest of the country. Glanleam House was the seat of the local 19th-century bigwigs, the Knights of Kerry, and its collection of exotic plants in the 192-acre gardens can still be seen. The garden is a pretty place, full of amazing tree ferns, exotic trees and some lovely walks, perfect if you enjoy pottering about in ancient gardens.

★ The Skelligs

"Whoever has not stood in the graveyard on the summit of that cliff among the beehive dwellings and their beehive oratory does not know Ireland through and through." Hyperbole indeed from George Bernard Shaw, but it is difficult not to agree with him. When a sea mist swirls above the Skelligs they seem to float on the ocean like eerie volcanoes in an imaginary scene from Celtic mythology. The only problem with this magic is that so many people are now heeding Shaw's advice that attempts are being made to limit the number of visitors who can stand on the 44 acres of **Skellig Michael**, the largest of a group of three rocky islets that make up the Skelligs. Also called Great Skellig, with its twin peaks 217 m and 198 m rising above the Atlantic, this is the only one of the rocks that can be landed on and, while a visit here is justifiably the main point of the boat trip, the journey there and back also affords a priceless opportunity to view and admire the birds that inhabit these rocky outposts of Europe. There is a bewildering number of operators running boat trips to the Skelligs but their prices are consistent and it is more a matter of choosing one that departs from somewhere you find convenient. Departure time is usually mid-morning and journey time is 45 minutes. See Transport, page 321.

Take care! Bring sensible footwear and be extremely careful with children or elderly folk when disembarking and making your way to the monastic buildings.

The monastery Skellig Michael is home to some of the few surviving examples of domestic monastic buildings in the early Christian era. After disembarking, visitors follow a path, created in the days when a lighthouse was operating on Skellig Michael, along the southeast cliffs to a series of enclosures perched on steep terraces. The monastic settlement, dedicated to St Michael, the saint of high places, is made up of six beehive cells, and two oratories. The guides will explain their characteristic features, but the sense of wonder comes from being here and wondering why – and in the winter months how – anyone even thought of living here. The dry masonry structures are truly remarkable, not least because they have survived for so long in such an exposed location.

Birdlife It helps to have some basic ornithological knowledge, and a visit to the Skellig Heritage Centre on Valentia will help in this respect (see page 306), but it is usually easy to recognize the **yellow-headed gannet** because of its size – a wing span of around 1.8 m – the elegant angle of its wings in flight and its dramatic vertical dive into the water. Some 20,000 pairs inhabit Little Skellig and these may be seen at close quarters if your boat goes near to the rock for a view of basking seals, which are also a common sight. The **guillemot**, seen and heard particularly around the landing stage area, is a seabird with a black tip to its wings. They spend the winter out at sea but come to Skellig Michael to breed between March and August. The **razorbill** is similar to but smaller than the guillemot and is sometimes recognized by its habit of flying in line in small flocks. Both these birds nest in crevices and ledges of the cliff face. Up until around the first week of August it is difficult to avoid seeing the **puffin**, unmistakable with to its multicoloured beak, dutifully standing at the head of its burrowed nest and occasionally waddling away with as much dignity as it can muster.

Waterville → *Phone code: 066. Colour map 3, grid B1.*

Another landmark town on the Ring of Kerry, Waterville is pleasantly low-key and consists of the usual range of pubs, hotels and restaurants; like Cahersiveen to the

"Moving about the coasts of Kerry afterwards, I understood what a symbol Skellig Michael must have been to those who were neither monks nor clergy, seeing it on the horizon, a single or a double peak, but always blue, always or often, with its nimbus of white cloud, its trailing coif of holiness." Geoffrey Grigson (1905-1985), 'Country Writings'.

Hermits and hedonists on the Skelligs

The desert sands of Egypt provide an unlikely backdrop to the Skelligs, but it was here that the Coptic Church based itself as a splinter group in the sixth century, practising a strict monastic tradition. In the seventh century a group of eremetical Irish monks first established a settlement on Skellig Michael and their anchorite community remained there until the 12th century. They survived a Viking raid in 823 but eventually moved to Ballinskelligs on the mainland.

Although Pope Gregory decreed a 10-day change in the calendar in 1582, it was never applied in the Skelligs and out of this developed the scurrilous *Skellig Lists*. They arose from the tradition of marrying just before Lent, during which no marriage could take place, and the riling of those who remained eligible but unwed. The lists paired off in comic verse suitable bachelors and spinsters. In fact the Skelligs, where Lent had still not started, became popular for late marriages and occasionally infamous all-night drinking binges.

north it suggests itself as a base (see Sleeping, page 316) for exploring the western end of the Peninsula. From Waterville there is also the very useful cross-peninsula road to Killarney via the Ballaghisheen Pass which accesses the frequently ignored interior and also allows one to escape the traffic on the main N70 road. There is little of note in the town itself, but all the attractions of the Iveragh Peninsula are conveniently accessible. In addition, Waterville does have an attractive beach, which is safe for swimming, and at times it is possible to spot a porpoise or dolphin close to shore and terns may often be seen doing their acrobatic searches for a meal in the water. There are shopping possibilities at the **Waterville Craft Market**, T066-9474212, five minutes' walk from town. The **tourist office**, T066-9474646, is open Jun-Sep Mon-Sat 0900-1800, but closed between 1300 and 1400.

Ballinskelligs and the Skellig Ring → *Phone code: 066. Colour map 3, grid B1.*

The Skellig Ring is the name given to a scenic route that links Waterville and Cahersiveen via Ballinskelligs and Portmagee. Characterized by narrow roads and unmarked junctions it is ideal for cycling, and with map No 83 in the Ordnance Survey Discovery series one could explore the landscape as well as fitting in a trip to the Skelligs from Ballinskelligs. There is no public transport, however.

From Waterville take the main road to Cahersiveen and after 5 km take the left turn signposted the Skellig Ring (R567). After 2.8 km from the beginning of this Skellig Ring road there is an unmarked road going south down to a lovely little inlet of **Ballinskelligs Bay**; a perfect spot for anyone wishing to enjoy Kerry in complete isolation. Back on the R567 road, carry on for another 3.2 km and turn left at the T-junction. This road, the R566, leads to Ballinskelligs, passing the Sigerson Arms pub and reaching an unmarked crossroads. The left turn goes down to a lovely expanse of sandy beach overlooking Ballinskelligs Bay and the sea-worn ruins of **Ballinskelligs Abbey**, where the monks from Skellig Michael are said to have moved to when they left their rocky sea-girt abode. The ruins at the western end of the beach are those of a **McCarthy castle**. Straight ahead at the crossroads leads to the departure point for boats to the Skelligs while a right turn passes the *An Óige* hostel (see page 316) before slowly weaving its way to Portmagee and a route back (on the R565) to the main N70 road south of Cahersiveen. After passing the *An Óige* hostel the first left turn takes you along a bumpy road out to **Bolus Head**, passing the pre-Famine village of **Kildreelig**.

Cycle ride An exhilarating cycle, or a drive if you must, from Cahersiveen to Killarney via Ballaghasheen is a journey of 64 km, with the option of an overnight stay at Glencar. Leave Cahersiveen on the road to Kells and after almost 3 km turn right on the 17-km road to Lissatinnig Bridge. At the bridge, the spectacular route through the Pass rises to about 300 m. Turn left at the Bealalaw Bridge junction, where the route meets the Kerry Way, which shortly bends to the right for Glencar and the Climbers' Inn (see page 317). From Glencar, travel for 6 km, passing Lake Acoose, ignoring the turn-offs for Glenbeigh and then Killorglin and follow the signs for Killarney and Beaufort.

Caherdaniel to Sneem → *Phone code: 066.*

Along the southwest coast of the Iveragh Peninsula, between the small towns of Caherdaniel and Sneem, there are two major attractions – Derrynane House and Staigue Fort – as well as a fine stretch of beach. Two local diving schools complement the cultural attractions, while the very touristy town of Sneem only serves to highlight the relative worth of towns like Cahersiveen that manage to avoid selling out completely to the summer tourist trade.

Derrynane House and Park ⓘ *T066-9475113. May-Sep Mon-Sat 0900-1800, Sun, 1100-1900; Apr and Oct Tue-Sun 1300-1700; Nov-Mar Sat and Sun, 1300-1700. €2.75. OPW site. Guided tours available. Signposted on the N70 at Caherdaniel.* Derrynane House is the ancestral home of **Daniel O'Connell**, who earned his place on the old Irish £20 banknote as one of the most important figures in 19th-century Irish history. It was built in 1702 and Daniel O'Connell, the adopted heir of a childless uncle who had inherited the house, took up residence in 1825 and made substantial alterations. The O'Connell family lived in Derrynane until 1958, but the house had begun to decay long before that and what you see today are largely the restored parts that O'Connell himself built. Some of his original furniture is still in place and there are various portraits of him, the most outlandish being an allegorical painting of the hero as Hercules breaking the chains of slavery. His library contains various gifts presented to him as well as personal items such as his duelling pistols, and many of the knick-knacks around the House are highly ornate and artistic but typically Victorian in their ugliness.

The 300-acre grounds are now part of the **Derrynane National Park** and contain pleasant gardens exhibiting many of the delicate sub-tropical plants that flourish in this corner of Ireland. (The monstrous-looking things that grow near the water as you approach the house are gunnera.) From the house a path leads south to an excellent beach with an ogham stone and sand dunes; at low tide it is possible to walk out to **Abbey Island**, which has a footpath around it offering splendid views of the coastline and the Skelligs.

Staigue Fort ⓘ *Easter to end Sep, daily, 24 hrs. Honesty box requesting €1. West of Caherdaniel, before Castlecove, and signposted up a narrow road off the N70.* Staigue Fort is a superb stone ringfort, one of the finest to be seen anywhere in Ireland, complete with a finely constructed system of stairways that lead up to the 4-m thick ramparts. Its walls stand up to 5.5 m high and while its age is uncertain it is likely to have been constructed in the Iron Age, roughly contemporary with the fortress of Dún Aengus on the Aran Island of Inishmore. Considering that Staigue Fort is around 2,000 years old, the intact state of its dry-stone walls is literally a monumental testimony to the skill of its builders and designers.

Sneem → *Phone code: 064. Colour map 3, grid B2.*

This figure-of-eight town, joined in its centre by a picturesque little bridge, is pronounced 'shneem' (Gaelic *snaidhm*, meaning 'knot', describing the twisting course of the river that bisects the village). Tourist literature describes it as "a cornucopia of colour" and the small houses painted brightly and cheerfully sugges

The Great Liberator

Daniel O'Connell (1775-1847) was born just outside Cahersiveen, the nephew and future heir of a Catholic landowner. As a barrister he rose to fame for his opposition to legislation preventing Catholics from sitting in Parliament or from holding other senior positions. The demand for Catholic Emancipation became a highly successful mass movement and O'Connell's skill as an organizer and orator played no small part in the eventual success of the campaign, O'Connell himself becoming the first Irish Catholic to sit in the British House of Commons. He went on to campaign for the repeal of the Act of Union, although he was not a separatist and envisaged Ireland as a self-governing unit within Britain. The repeal movement reached a crisis in 1843 when a series of huge open-air demonstrations led to the British government banning such a 'monster meeting' due to be held at Clontarf. O'Connell backed down and a week later he was arrested. Although released soon after, the whole experience seems to have weakened him and he died in 1847 worn out by a lifetime of struggle. He remained a potent figurehead for moderate nationalists and when the foundation stone for his statue was laid in what is now O'Connell Street in Dublin half a million people attended, making it the largest single political event in the history of Ireland in the 19th century.

an organized and determined effort to woo the visitors into thinking that this is what a quaint Irish village should look like. An unusual attraction is the **Sculpture Park**, which consists of a strange series of sculptures from assorted exotic locations in Asia and elsewhere. The park includes a 1983 monument to an Irish president, Cearbhaill Ó Dálaigh (1974-1976), who has been completely forgotten about by most people, but whom Sneem remembers because he retired here. See page 316 for what choice there is in the way of accommodation.

★ Kenmare → *Phone code: 064. Colour map 3, grid B3.*

This market town, along with Killarney and Sneem, completes Iveragh's tourist triumvirate. It used to be a sedate alternative to Killarney's summer mayhem, but in terms of restaurants and hullabaloo Kenmare is fast catching up. Given its location, however, it is difficult to avoid Kenmare and the amenities are useful, especially if en route to or from the Beara Peninsula or the Kerry Way. The town was founded by Sir William Petty in 1670 and laid out in the late 18th century by the first Marquess of Lansdowne. **Fair day** on is 15 August, when farmers trade cattle and horses in hard cash and a slap of the palm, and a general air of roguery enlivens the place. The **tourist office** is on the right as one enters the town from the Sneem direction, T064-41233. Open mid-Jun to late Sep Mon-Sat 0915-1900. Rest of the year Mon-Sat 0915-1730.

Kenmare Heritage Centre ⓘ *T064-41491, mid-Jun- Oct, Mon-Sat, 0900-1800.* The Heritage Centre displays a great deal of information on the history of the town and has separate sections on the town's association with lacemaking through the Kenmare Poor Clare Convent and with the radical nun, Margaret Anna Cusack (1829-1899) who, because of her politics, was forced to leave Kenmare. The British politician, Margaret Thatcher, is descended from an O'Sullivan family who emigrated from Kenmare in 1811 to work in London as a washerwoman.

Glen Inchaquin Park ⓘ *Daily. €4. 12 km from Kenmare on the road to Castletownbere and then signposted on the left.* The official full title for this park is the

Glen Inchaquin Waterfall Amenity Area and there is a free leaflet available from the tourist office that includes a map. There is a set walk that takes you past the waterfall, streams, a bathing spot, lakes and woodland and the whole place is very suitable for families or anyone wanting a gentle stroll. Bring a picnic or make do with the shop selling hot drinks and home-baked snacks.

Stone circle ⓘ *In the summer there may be an admission charge.* Kenmare's stone circle, easily reached from the tourist office along Market Street, is one of the largest in Ireland. There are 15 stones making up the circle and in the centre is a fine dolmen.

Derreen garden ⓘ *Apr-Oct 1100-1800. €5. Tea room and picnic area. At Lauragh, 24 km west of Kenmare on the R571 road.* Derreen is a woodland garden planted by the fifth Marquess of Lansdowne in the 1870s. Visitors can collect a useful little map that describes and identifies some of the numbered plants, and there is plenty to see. The 42-m giant conifers here today were introduced from North America, and the exotic tree ferns came from New Zealand. One tree, the 18-m high *Cryptomeria Japonica Elegans* with a girth of 3 m, grows directly across the path in the rock garden and requires an artificial support. The Caha Mountains and Kilmakilloge Harbour, which afford such stunning views from Derreen Garden, help shelter and protect the grounds and facilitate the healthy array of plants and trees that are rarely found outside of the southwest.

★ The Kerry Way

This is nine or 10 days of glorious walking around some of the most beautiful scenery in Ireland. The walk is well established and several organizations will be glad to plan your entire trip, including luggage transfer and pickups where the route meets roads into towns. However, it is perfectly possible to do the trip without this and at your

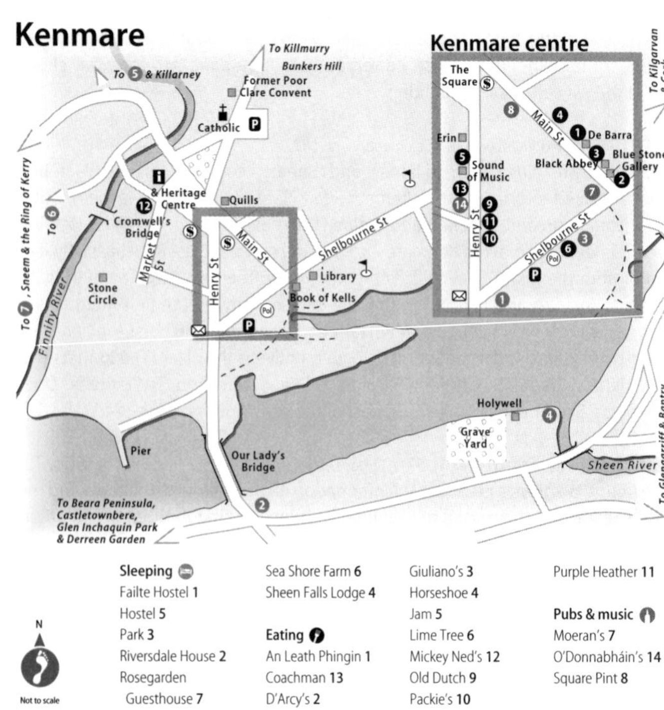

leisure, taking days off to enjoy the villages and make side trips to places such as Valentia and the Skelligs. Drivers can plan the walks in sections, basing themselves at Glenbeigh, Killarney or Waterville, doing one or two days and then moving on. The first three days of the Kerry Way are worth considering as a walking excursion from Killarney with a return by bus after spending the third night in Glenbeigh. With your own transport, the beginning of the first day could be shortened by leaving your car at the Torc Waterfall car park.

The walk is about 215 km and consists of the following sections:
Day 1: Killarney to the Black Valley (22 km)
Day 2: Black Valley to Glencar (20 km)
Day 3: Glencar to Glenbeigh (13 km)
Day 4: Glenbeigh to Cahersiveen (28 km)
Day 5: Cahirsiveen to Waterville (30 km)
Day 6a: Waterville to Caherdaniel (28 km)
Day 7: Caherdaniel to Sneem (19 km)
Day 8: Sneem to Kenmare (30 km)
Day 9: Kenmare to Killarney (24 km)

Mapping and information The first six days are the best for views and terrain while Day 8, Sneem to Kenmare, is seriously not worth doing as it involves walking over 6 km on the main Ring of Kerry Road, a very dangerous activity. The Kerry Way is generally well signposted but the Ordnance Survey (OS) Discovery Series maps sheets 78, 83 and 84 are essential. Cork-Kerry Tourism produces a strip map of the walk which is less useful but likely to be more up-to-date and could be used in conjunction with the OS maps.

Day 1: Killarney to the Black Valley ⓘ *22 km; 7 hrs; total ascent 375 m.* The walk starts just outside the town centre of Killarney at the River Flesk, passes by Muckross Friary and Muckross House (see page 293) and emerges from the park at the foot of the Torc waterfall. Above the waterfall the route heads off along the Old Kenmare Road, quite boggy in places, across deer country with Mangerton Mountain looming ahead and McGillycuddy's Reeks in the distance. Passing a deserted church, the route crosses the Killarney to Kenmare road and heads downhill, following the course of the Derricunnihy River and then the Upper Lake. At a little landing stage and café, the route meets a minor road and follows it to the Black Valley Hostel, which is quite small and should be booked well in advance if you intend to stay there, or close by there is also Hillcrest Farmhouse B&B; they are the only accommodation options at this stage (see page 317).

Day 2: Black Valley to Glencar ⓘ *20 km; 8 hrs; total ascent 500 m.* This is the most stunning day's walk between Killarney and Glenbeigh. It passes through the Black Valley and even on a sunny day you can see why the place has earned the name. The walk climbs gradually up through rugged jagged peaks, leaving all idea of roads and civilization behind. It meets an old butter road and descends into a farmyard and valley and then climbs again over a pass on a spur of Curraghmore Mountain, finally meeting Lough Acoose and a road to Glencar. There are several B&Bs and guest houses around Glencar, including the walker-friendly Climbers' Inn (see page 317).

Day 3: Glencar to Glenbeigh ⓘ *17.5 km; 6 hrs; total ascent 300 m.* This day's walk goes through the Caragh River valley, along some road and forestry roads and culminates in a scenic climb up Seefin Mountain. From here there is a choice of routes skirting Seefin to the east and west, both equally beautiful and both descending into Glenbeigh. For accommodation in Glenbeigh, see page 315.

Climbing Carrauntuohill

Carrauntuohill, at 1,039 m, is Ireland's highest peak and reaching the top requires organization, lots of stamina, and a full awareness of the dangers involved on some of the routes to the top. The challenging Howling Ridge ascent claimed another fatality in December 2001 and since 1966 there have been10 deaths on the mountain. The following route is relatively safe and requires no special skills.

Ordnance Survey Map 78 covers the area and the common starting point is signposted off the road that connects the Gap of Dunloe with Glencar.

The signposted road ends near a farmhouse, with parking space and a coffee machine. Be sure to let someone know where you are going and/or leave a note on your vehicle. The walk has a terrific start, up between Lough Gooragh and Lough Callee, but pace yourself because the ascent of the steep Devil's Ladder requires stamina. From the top, it is about 300 m to the summit and, after celebrating, descend by the same route and take especial care coming back down the Devil's Ladder.

Day 4: Glenbeigh to Cahersiveen ⓘ *28 km; 9 hrs; total ascent 650 m.* This day and the next day's walk could be shortened by 6.5 km by staying at Foilmore rather than going on into Cahersiveen. The first section of the route heads southwest out of Glenbeigh and follows the coast, first ascending Glenbeigh Hill with spectacular views of the coastline. There is a short spell along roads and then another climb up Drung Hill and more wonderful views. There follows a turn inland to Foilmore and then a descent into Cahirsiveen. For accommodation, see page 315.

Day 5: Cahersiveen to Waterville ⓘ *30 km; 8 hrs minimum; total ascent 730 m.* This distance includes the spur from Cahersiveen back to the main route at Foilmore and another at the end of the day into Waterville. Foilmore to Waterville is 24 km. The day's walk climbs on to high ground and for much of the first half of it you are climbing and descending hills with 360° scenery. The walk eventually descends into Mastergeehy, a small village with a tiny post office selling very basic supplies, and then follows an old mass path up Coomaduff Hill and along another series of ridges with fine views into Waterville. On Coomaduff Hill the Way divides, one route going on to Caherdaniel and the other into Waterville. You should take the Waterville route as the final ridge walk to Waterville is well worth the effort. For accommodation in Waterville, see page 316.

Day 6: Waterville to Caherdaniel ⓘ *28 km; total ascent 535 m.* This distance includes walking back to Coomaduff Hill from Waterville and then, at the end of the day's walk, heading away from the main route towards Caherdaniel. It is an excellent walk despite the length and detour, and if you wanted to make the route shorter you might try hitching from Waterville to Dromod, making the walk to Caherdaniel about 21 km.

After rejoining the Way at Coomaduff Hill the route skirts the north side of Lough Currane, crosses some rough land where markers are not clear and follows a boreen for a while close to the eastern shore of Lough Currane. The Way then turns east along another minor road past Lough Isnagahiny. Just beyond an old school the route leaves the minor road and sets off southwards climbing Mount Eagle, crossing to the right of the summit at Windy Gap. The route down is a wide green road, easy to walk until it meets another branch of the Kerry Way travelling from Caherdaniel to Sneem. Your route is westwards to Caherdaniel and a signpost points the way along quite marshy ground but with some excellent views down into Derrynane Bay and the Kenmare River. For accommodation in Caherdaniel, see page 316.

Day 7: Caherdaniel to Sneem ⓘ *26 km; 7 hrs; total ascent 400 m.* For most of the day the route follows the Old Kenmare Road in its modern incarnations of green road, boggy pasture and minor tarmac road. The walk is pleasant enough but has no spectacular sections like the previous day's walk. There are views south over the Kenmare River for most of the day until you reach Sneem. For accommocation, see page 316.

Day 8: Sneem to Kenmare ⓘ *21 km; 7 hrs; total ascent 350 m.* Unless the route is altered to take out the long treks along busy roads, it might be best to catch a bus from Sneem to Kenmare and avoid this section of the walk. It is a fairly pleasant walk as far as Templenoe, but the following long stretch on the Ring of Kerry road is not worth walking. At Reen the Way leaves the main Ring of Kerry road and heads uphill over Gortamullin Hill and then down into Kenmare. For accommodation, see page 317.

Day 9: Kenmare to Killarney ⓘ *24 km; 8 hrs; total ascent 600 m.* A thoroughly pleasant walk still following old roads, which starts along minor roads and then continues through a saddle high up between Knockanaguish and Peakeen mountains with fine views over Killarney's lakes. Descending, the route follows the Derrycunnihy River, finally meeting up with the Kerry Way out of Killarney.

Sleeping

Killorglin *p303*

L-B Caragh Lodge, Caragh, T066-9769115, www.caraghlodge.com. A laid back atmosphere prevails in this elegant Victorian country house on the shores of Lake Caragh a few miles outside Killorglin. Award- winning garden, pretty sitting rooms and an excellent dinner menu.

A-C Carrig House, Caragh Lake, T066-9769100, www.carrighouse.com. A hearty welcome awaits you at this period house with huge fireplaces, lots of little nooks and crannies, books to read, interesting garden with some rare plants, and a restaurant.

D Bianconi, Lower Bridge Rd, T066-9761146, www.bianconi.ie. Family-run guest house, with access to Caragh Lake.

E-F Riverside House, T066-9761184, riversidehouseb&b@eircom.net. B&B with rooms, some with en suite bathroom, overlooking the river.

F Laune Valley Farm Hostel, Banshagh, T066-9761488, launevalleyfarm@hotmail.com. Just under 2 km north of town on the N70 and has 5 private rooms.

Glenbeigh *p303*

B-C Towers Hotel, T066-9768212, towershotel@eircom.net. Comfortable, old hotel with palm trees, a cosy bar and good restaurant.

Camping

Glenross Caravan and Camping Park, T066-9768451. Next to the Glenbeigh Hotel at the Killarney end of town.

Cahersiveen *p305*

D Cahersiveen Park, T066-9472543. The only hotel in town, at the Valentia end. Perfectly adequate and has a pleasant bar and decent restaurant.

E Castleview, T066-9472252, mickomahony@eircom.net. At the Valentia end of town with 1 room with bathroom en suite and 2 rooms sharing facilities.

E Iveragh Heights, Carhan Rd, T066-9472545, www.insightwedmarking.com. Handy if walking into town on the Kerry Way.

E O'Shea's, Church St, T066-9472402, osheasbnb@eircom.net. A central B&B in a large townhouse next to the post office; open all year.

F Sive Hostel, T066-9472717, sivehostel@oceanfree.net. Sociable place in the centre of town, open all year, includes 2 private rooms.

Camping

Mannix Point Camping and Caravan Park, T066-9472806, www.campinginkerry.com. A 10-min walk from town. Has a good reputation.

For an explanation of the sleeping and eating price codes used in this guide, see inside the front cover. Other relevant information is found in Essentials pages 39-45.

Valentia Island *p306*

D-E Moorings Guesthouse, Portmagee, T066-9477108, www.moorings.ie. Superior guest house overlooking the port with modern, comfortable rooms. The telescope in the guests' lounge adds a nice touch.
E Ms Christina Murphy, the Waterfront, Portmagee, T066-9477208. Close to where all the good places to eat are, in the village.
E-F Glenreen Heights, Knightstown Rd, T066-9476241, glenreen@eircom.net. On the road to Chapeltown, lovely sea views.
F The Ring Lyne Hostel, Chapeltown, T066-9476103, seanosullivan@hotmail.com. Lots of facilities, including private rooms, B&B and bike hire.
F Royal Pier Bar and Hostel, Knightstown, T066-9476144, www.royalpiervalentia.com. Overlooking the harbour, private rooms, dorms, camping space, and B&B. Despite its very faded elegance this is a lively place, good for meeting people (and big enough to while away a wet afternoon in the bar).
F Valentia Island Hostel, Knightstown, T066-9476154, www.irelandyha.org/anoige/kerry6.html. *An Óige* hostel that uses the old coastguard cottages. It's a nice idea, with a tangible sense of history about the place, but the creature comforts are at a premium. Open May-Sep, closes 1000-1700.

Waterville *p308*

A-B Butler Arms Hotel, T066-9474144, www.butlerarms.com. Facing the sea, this hotel has a wonderful air of faded elegance (though some bedrooms are in a new wing) as if reluctant to forget the era when star guests like Charlie Chaplin and Virginia Woolf came here to stay; deals available when staying more than 1 night. Good restaurant.
E Bay View Hotel , T066-9474122, www.bayviewwaterville.com. In town centre, comfortable rooms some have sea views.
E Lakelands Farm Guesthouse, Lake Rd, T066-9474303, www.lakelandshouse.com. Out of town, lakeshore location, good for fishing enthusiasts, jacuzzi.
E-F Bru Na Dromoda, T066-9474782, maistirgaoithe@eircom.net. A hostel with dorm beds and 1 private room. It is signposted at the grotto on exiting the Waterville to Cahersiveen road and later 3 km up the road at St Finian's Church. From here it is 8 km along the road; so you need transport.

Ballinskelligs and Skellig Ring *p309*

E-F Rascals The Old School House, Barry's Cross, T066-9479340, www.rascalstheoldschoolhouse.com. Family-run home, close to the beach. Evening meal is also available.
F Ballinskelligs Hostel, T066-9479229, mailbox@anoige.ie. *An Óige* hostel, 1 private double. Bring your own food for lunch.

Caherdaniel to Sneem *p310*

B Derrynane Hotel, T066-9475136, www.derrynane.com. Facilities include an outdoor pool, steam room, sauna, gym and tennis courts. Walking weekends are organized regularly.
C Iskeroon, Bunavalla, T066-9475119, www.iskeroon.com. Not your usual B&B, distinguished by both location, at the bottom of a steep hill by the side of a pebbly beach, and individuality of style. To find it, turn left off the N70 at the Scarriff Inn, signposted to Bunavalla Pier, and just keep turning left.
Regular B&Bs in Caherdaniel include:
E Harbour View, Farraniaragh, T066-9475292. As the name suggests, rooms have views of Derrynane harbour and the sea. On the Kerry Way walking route.
E The Olde Forge, T066-9475140. Family-run B&B with access to the sea.
F Carrigbeg Country Hostel, T066-9475229. A short distance to the west of Caherdaniel, this hostel includes 1 private room and laundry facilities.
F Kerry Way Hostel, Derrynane Beg, T066-9475148, kerrywayhostel@ireland.com. Has 2 private rooms.
F The Traveller's Rest, T066-9475175. A small hostel in Caherdaniel with 8 beds and 2 private rooms.

Camping

Wave Crest Caravan Park, T066-9475188. Overlooking Kenmare Bay, 2 km from town in the direction of Sneem. Accepts tents.

Sneem *p310*

L Parknasilla, T066-7145122, www.gshotels.com. Top-notch accommodation in a massive Victorian mansion set in acres of semi-tropical gardens. A luxury hotel, crammed with original artwork and quiet places to relax.
E Old Convent House, Pier Rd, T066-7145181, www.oldconventhouse.com.

Old stone-built house in private grounds, Kerry Way walkers are welcome.

E-F Bank House, North Sq, T066-7145226. B&B in the centre of town, the green house with window boxes galore.

Kenmare *p311, map p312*

Two of the country's most exclusive 5-star hotels are in Kenmare, as well as a number of regular 3-star places, but there are also many B&Bs, all charging around €45 for doubles/singles.

L Park Hotel, T064-41200, www.parkkenmare.com. For sheer aristocratic class it is hard to beat this place, where each room is furnished with wonderful antique furniture. The Great Southern and Western Railway Company built the Park Hotel in 1897 for the idle rich from England who spent a night here, after reaching Kenmare by train, before being taken by horse and carriage to the sister hotel at Parknasilla (see page 316). The most recent addition to the hotel is the gorgeous spa, a beautiful piece of design and it makes you feel good too.

L Sheen Falls Lodge, T064-41600, www.sheenfallslodge.ie. Equally classy hotel, all rooms have views of the bay or the Falls and, like the Park, boasts a top-notch restaurant.

B-D Riversdale House Hotel, T064-41299, www.kenmare.com/riversdale. Just over the double-arched bridge at the Glengarriff end of town. Ask for a room with a view of the estuary and hills to take full advantage of the hotel's riverside location.

C-D Sea Shore Farm, T064-41270, seashore@eeircom.net. Well nigh perfect: peaceful, homely and friendly, with spacious rooms, a pleasant walk through the fields down to the shore and terrific views of the Caha Mountains. Look for the sign, past the Esso station on the left side of the road out of town to Killarney.

D Rosegarden Guesthouse, Gortamullen, T064-42288, www.euroka.com/rosegarden. A smart, meticulously run guest house just outside town on the Ring of Kerry road. The Dutch owners provide exemplary service, and there is a decent restaurant.

F Failte Hostel, Shelbourne St, T064-42333, www.neidin.net. Has over 30 beds and 2 private rooms.

F Hostel, no telephone but the 5th bungalow on the left, after the petrol station on the right side of the main road from town to Killarney. Nora Burke welcomes hostellers and campers; a small charge for showers and the tumble dryer.

Camping

Ring of Kerry Caravan and Camping Park, Reen, T064-41648. 5 km west of town on the road to Sneem.

The Kerry Way *p312*

D Hillcrest Farmhouse, Black Valley, T064-34702. B&B, close to the Black Valley hostel, which does evening meals and luggage transfer and has a drying room – essential if you hit bad weather.

F Black Valley Hostel, Black Valley, T064-34712, mailbox@anoige.com. *An Óige* hostel. Quite small and should be booked well in advance. It opens at 1700, has a small shop next door and good cooking facilities, but gets crowded and noisy; no private rooms.

F The Climbers' Inn, Glencar, T066-9760101, climbers@iol.ie. Hostel accommodation and B&B at this walker-orientated inn established in 1875 as the first of its kind in Ireland. Kitchen, drying rooms, pub food and restaurant, information about other walks in the area; closed Nov-Mar. In the same area are several B&Bs and guest houses.

Eating

Killorglin *p303*

TTT Caragh Lodge, T066-9769115. Fresh seafood, Kerry lamb, home-grown vegetables and home baking make up an excellent menu in the graceful restaurant overlooking the lake. A reservation for dinner is fairly essential for non-residents.

TTT Carrig House, Caragh Lake, T066-9769100. Offers a choice of rooms for pre-dinner drinks and a congenial atmosphere in a relaxed restaurant serving locally sourced food.

TTT Bianconi, Lower Bridge St, T066-9761146. Has bar food all day and, in the restaurant from 1830-2030, seafood and pasta dishes around €20 for a main course.

TTT Nick's Restaurant, Lower Bridge St, T066-9761219. The steak, lamb and seafood has some oomph, and should not disappoint; dinner is €41, more for lobster.

TT Murrays, in the Square, T066-9790812. A steak and seafood place where 3 courses will cost around €36.

Glenbeigh *p303*

If you do not plan to picnic for the day, the pubs offer the best bet at lunchtime.

¥¥ **Towers Hotel Restaurant**, T066-9768212. At night this place offers good food and an elegant setting. There is a separate bar for cocktails and the warm dark colours of the decor provide a suitable backdrop for a lazy meal. Starters include oysters in a Guinness sauce, while lamb, veal, duck and steaks make up the main courses alongside fish freshly caught in Dingle Bay. The early-bird menu is good value while the bar does pub food until 2130.

Cahersiveen *p305*

¥¥ **An Bonnan Bui**, Main St, T066-9473161. Steaks and seafood till 2130 plus live music.

¥¥ **Daniel O'Connell**, O'Connell St, T066-9472054. An old stone built bar doing bar food during the day and restaurant fare in the evening.

¥¥ **QC's**, 3 Main St, T066-9472244, www.qcbar.com. Has some style – original old fireplace, stone walls, oak bar counter – and tasty chargrills are a speciality. Lots of Spanish wines.

¥ **Frank's Corner**, opposite the post office. Has meals of the 'with chips' variety for under €13.

¥ **Fertha Bar**, some pubs like this one serves reasonably priced standard pub food.

Relish, Church St, T066-9473499. For a picnic lunch, this bakery and delicatessen does lovely home-baked breads and fillings.

Valentia Island *p306*

Portmagee

¥¥ **Moorings**, has a very popular small restaurant for evening meals and Sun lunch, serving seafood dishes like chowder and poached salmon, and steaks as well. Daily list of specials is worth a try.

¥¥-¥ **Fisherman's Bar**, T066-9477103. Has outside tables when the weather is not inclement: the bar menu includes a tasty chowder and appetising crab claws for starters or snacks, and meals of seafood and Irish stew.

¥ **Bridge Bar**, belonging to the Moorings restaurant and guest house, does pub food during the day.

Knightstown

¥ **Fuchsia Restaurant**, T066-9476051. Good for lunch.

¥ **Lighthouse Café**, T066-9476304. Recommended for its outstanding views and charming decor – if you can find it open. Strange opening hours: ring in advance because it's a bit of a trek to get to.

¥ **Royal Pier**. Serves lunch.

Chapeltown

¥ **Ring Lyne Bar**, T066-9476103. Serves food all day along the lines of seafood specials, steaks and Irish stew.

★ Reenard Point

¥ **The Point Bar**, T066-9472165. The ferry runs continuously, so linger here as long as you like. It's been here since the middle of the 19th century and now serves delicious seafood, salads and sandwiches as well as hot meals. All the fish is taken ashore from trawlers docking a stone throw's away from your table.

Waterville *p308*

¥ **Shéilin Seafood Restaurant**, T066-9474231. At the Butler Arms end of town, bistro-style, recommended for its affordable and well prepared meals. Specials are on the blackboard outside and between 1800 and 1930 there is an affordable set dinner; also open for lunch.

¥ **Smuggler's Inn**, T066-9474330. Has tables with sea views, lots of locally caught seafood and a vegetarian menu.

Ballinskelligs and Skellig Ring *p309*

¥ **Siopa Chill Rialaig**, on the R566, before reaching Ballinskelligs from Waterville, T066-9479277. Displaying and selling some beautiful Irish crafts, has a café doing homemade soups and sandwiches. Jul-Aug 1000-1900 daily, rest of year 1100-1700.

Caherdaniel to Sneem *p310*

There are a couple of places to eat in Caherdaniel but nowhere to write home about. The café in Derrynane House is not bad and the adjoining beach suggests itself for a picnic.

¥¥ **Derrynane Hotel**. Restaurant inside serves a decent dinner. Book ahead.

🍴🍴-🍴 **The Blind Piper**, T066-9475126. Opens between May and Sep, for affordable lunches and dinners in a traditional-style restaurant with exposed beams and stone walls. Seafood and local lamb are the specialities; closed Mon.

🍴🍴-🍴 **Scarriff Inn**, T066-9475132. Out on the main road but this place can be overrun with coach parties.

🍴🍴-🍴 **The Stepping Stone**, T066-9475444. A short walk from the harbour and open nightly for dinner only, is a tiny place serving modern-style, affordable dishes like duck with roast pear.

Sneem *p310*

🍴🍴 **Sacré Coeur**, T066-7145186. A well-established restaurant at the other end of town, also open for lunch and dinner.

🍴🍴-🍴 **Blue Bull**, South Sq, T066-7145382. A pub that serves food for lunch and dinner. Seafood a speciality as well as traditional Irish fare like bacon and cabbage and Irish stew.

🍴🍴-🍴 **Pygmalion**, Great Southern Hotel, T066-7145122. The place to go for a special night out, and it is worth arriving early enough to enjoy a stroll around the gardens and woods.

🍴🍴-🍴 **Riverain Restaurant**, North Sq, T066-7145245. Does light snacks as well as lunch and candle-lit dinner.

🍴 **Village Kitchen**, near to the *Riverain*. Serves decent home-cooked food.

Kenmare *p311, map p312*

Kenmare claims to be the only town in Ireland with more restaurants than pubs – at the last count there were 44 places to eat.

🍴🍴🍴 **La Cascade**, Sheen Falls Lodge, T064-41600. On 2 levels; reserve a window table for views of the Falls. Set dinner features scallops with foie gras and oyster cream, there is a vegetarian menu, impeccable service, and vast wine list. Open dinner only.

🍴🍴🍴 **The Lime Tree**, 15 Shelbourne St, T064-41225. Named after the 100-year-old lime tree in its garden. The restaurant stretches over 2 floors and it is obvious from the atmosphere that many of the customers are regulars. Munch on the excellent breads and tapenade as you make your choices from traditional and modern dishes. Vegetarians have some good choices, the wine list is carefully designed and there are some excellent desserts. Apr-Nov dinner only, and reservations are essential.

🍴🍴🍴 **Packie's**, Henry St, T064-41508. Has been around for some time and earned a reputation for good seafood and Mediterranean-style dishes.

🍴🍴🍴 **Park**, T064-41200. Style is everything here and it comes in the form of a grand, high-ceilinged dining room with huge bay windows looking across water, tables with crisp white linen serviced by a bevy of attendants, the best modern Irish cuisine, and a wine list of 600 wines. Open for dinner only.

🍴🍴 **Oscar's**, at the Sheen Falls. Opens nightly for bistro-style dining and a good choice of seafood, meat and pasta dishes.

🍴🍴 **An Leath Phingin**, 35 Main St, T064-41559. Italian-style, has been recommended for its home-made pasta dishes. Again, dinner only and closed Tue and Wed.

🍴🍴 **The Coachman**, has an inexpensive but unadventurous dinner menu for €20 and very affordable lunch specials.

🍴🍴 **D'Arcy's**, Main St, T064-41589. One of a sprinkling of restaurants in this street, has pretty table settings, an international menu and opens only for dinner at 1800. Ring in advance in winter for opening times.

🍴🍴 **Giuliano's**, Main St, T064-41952. At the top of the street, specializes in Italian pasta and pizza, good for vegetarians; lunch and dinner, daily, between Mar and Nov.

🍴🍴 **The Horseshoe**, 3 Main St, T064-41553. A relaxed pub doing bar food with a restaurant to the rear that serves nourishing chowders and burgers and evening meals of steaks and other standard but well-cooked homely dishes.

🍴🍴 **Jam**, Henry St. Café popular with locals.

🍴🍴 **Mickey Ned's**, the Square, T064-40200. Owned by ex-footballer Mickey Ned O'Sullivan, is a grand place for thoughtful pub food with lots of fresh ingredients.

🍴🍴 **Old Dutch Restaurant**, T064-41449. Where the Dutch chef has crab claws for starters, steak, lamb, duck and some fish for main courses.

🍴🍴 **The Purple Heather**, Henry St, T064-41016. Try this place for economically priced daytime meals, soups, seafood salads and omelettes etc.

On a wet afternoon, consider afternoon tea at the **Sheen Falls Lodge**: home-made brown sandwiches, fruitcake, frangipani tartlets and lashings of tea.

Pubs and music

Killorglin *p303*
The Fishery, The Bridge, T066-9761670. Has traditional music some nights.
O'Grady's, Upper Bridge St. Favours a slow pint and a long chat.

Glenbeigh *p303*
Ross Inn, T066-978533. At the beach, has traditional sessions and in summer music and dance sessions.
Sweeney's, only opens in the summer and is usually packed.
Towers Hotel, bar which is usually packed that attracts a younger crowd and has live music of some kind or another in summer on Sun, Tue and Wed.
Village Pub, has music most nights.

Cahersiveen *p305*
Anchor Bar, Main St, T066-9472049. Ancient-looking, with fishing tackle sold alongside pints, is always worth a visit.
Craineen's, T066-9472168. Has traditional music at weekends.
Mike Murt's, near to Shebeen Bar. A real old farmer's pub with some character and a hardware section.
Shebeen Bar, T066-9472361. At the Glenbeigh end. Has Irish dancing on some nights.

Waterville *p308*
Perhaps it is a legacy from the Victorian and Edwardian times when genteel folk came to Waterville, but the music scene here is comparatively subdued.
Fisherman's Bar, in the Butler Arms hotel. Has no music but it is a comfortable place to relax and have a chat.
Lobster Bar. Has a variety of non-traditional music some evenings during the week.

Ballinskelligs and Skellig Ring *p309*
Ballinskelligs Inn, T066-9479106. Has live music most nights. Telephone to make sure.

Sneem *p310*
Blue Bull, usually has music some nights.
Fisherman's Knot, usually has music.
O'Shea's, North Sq. Bar that is also worth checking out to see what might be playing.
Sneem House, seek out for a quiet drink by the river and its bar at the back of the shop. Also has outside tables.

Kenmare *p311, map p312*
Crowley's, Henry St. Try this before the Square Pint (below).
Moeran's Pub, one of the oldest buildings in town, as well as serving food has some lively evenings of music and song.
O'Donnabháin's. Try this place instead of Square Pint, looks authentic despite the wooden beams going in different directions.
Square Pint, near the tourist office. Usually packed with revellers but lacks any identity of its own.

Festivals and events

Cahersiveen *p305*
Cahersiveen's **Celtic Festival of Music and the Arts** takes place at the beginning of **Aug**.

Shopping

Cahersiveen *p305*
Biggs, Old Rd, T066-9472580. An antique shop worth poking around in while **Feirini Crafts** has lots of locally made stuff that you won't see in Killarney.
Gallery One, Main St. Has work by local artists and craftspeople.
Wilhelmina and Pieter Koning out of the village at Teeraha, T066-9472469, pkoning@eircom.net. This is their workshop, with sculptures, paintings and designs in felt.
Ruth Summer, in the village. Studio displaying her paintings and murals.
Regine Bartsch, west Main St T066-9472403. Another showroom.

Kenmare *p311, map p312*
For its size, Kenmare is reasonably well endowed with shops catering to visitors' credit cards. There is a good second-hand bookshop at 3 Bridge St, near the tourist office, and a regular bookshop on Shelbourne St.
Quills. Largish store in the very centre of town, open daily until 2200, sells designer handknits, woollen and cashmere garments and assorted merchandise.
On Henry St there are a couple of antique shops and other stores dedicated to arts, crafts and souvenirs, including:

Erin, strong on Aran garments;
Sound of Music, with a range of bodhrans, tin whistles, flutes, Irish music and dance videos.
On Main St:
De Barra, a small but enticing Irish jewellery shop;
Black Abbey, has some lovely pieces of craftwork;
Blue Stone Gallery, next door, has more in the same vein;
Lime Tree, upstairs is an art gallery which is open while the restaurant is and has some excellent work by local artists.

Activities and tours

Cahersiveen *p305*
Fishing Hugh Maguire, T066-9472049, for deep-sea angling.

Guided walks James A Casey, T066-9473186, jamescasey111@yahoo.com. Daily 2-hr guided walk to historical sites in the area, Jun-Sep, 1100.

Yacht charter 10degrees west, T066-9472244, www. Yachtcharterkerry.com.

Valentia Island *p306*
Diving Des Lavelle, T066-9476124. Well established.
Dive Centre, T066-9476204.

Fishing Michael O'Sullivan, Royal Pier, T066-9476144. Deep-sea fishing.

Waterville *p308*
Fishing Waterville has long been famous as an angling centre.
Tadhg O'Sullivan's T066-9474433. Shop dispensing information and retailing tackle.

Caherdaniel to Sneem *p310*
Diving Activity Ireland, Caherdaniel, T066-9475277, www.activity-Ireland.com. Handles scuba diving for experienced divers as well as complete beginners and also organizes sea angling and boat trips. Land-based activities too.

Kenmare *p311, map p312*
Boat Seafari, T064-83171. Departs regularly from the Pier for a 2-hr, 15-km cruise of Kenmare Bay (€16) with an ecological emphasis. Colonies of grey seals and sea otters are usually spotted and occasionally minke and killer whales are seen chasing shoals of mackerel. There is also a sunset cruise featuring a barbecue and live Irish music. To reach the pier walk out of town towards Killarney and turn right just before the double-arched bridge. This is a pleasant destination in its own right, especially when the tide is in and the Kerry Mountains look down on the graceful flow of the river.

Transport

Ring of Kerry *p302*
Bike hire O'Shea's, Killorglin, T066-9761919. Near the bridge at the Killarney end of town. **Casey's Cycles**, at the Valentia end of town, Cahersiveen, T066-9472474.

Bus See bus information on page 302. In the summer, buses for **Killarney** depart from Cahersiveen at 0800 and 1215.

Ferry There is a continuous ferry service from Reenard Point, 5 km west of **Cahirsiveen**, to **Knightstown** on Valentia Island (see page 306). From **Ballinskelligs**: Joe Roddy, T066-9474268, www.skellig trips.com. From **Portmagee**: Brendan Casey, T066-9472437, www.skelligislands.com; Michael O'Sullivan, T066-9474255. From **Valentia**: Des Lavelle, T066-9476124, http://indigo.ie/~lavelles, picks up at Valentia, Renard and Portmagee.

Taxi McCarty's, Killorglin, T066-9472249.

Dingle Peninsula

Stretching for 48 glorious kilometres from the town of Tralee, the Dingle Peninsula is characterized geographically by high central ridges running up to Mount Brandon at 952 m and the scenery as a whole, etched by the glaciers of the last Ice Age, reveals itself in an epiphany of natural beauty that is stunning and unforgettable. Less rugged and wild than the Beara or the Iveragh, there is a distinct quality to the light and the colours that on a fine day transforms Dingle into Ireland's most magical peninsula. Nowadays more and more visitors are being drawn here and in July and August it is advisable to have accommodation booked in advance; come here outside of the high season and you will feel especially privileged to be here. ▸▸ For Sleeping, Eating and other listings, see pages 335-340.

Ins and outs

Getting there There are two approaches to the Peninsula: coming from the south on the N22 or the N70 it is possible to branch off at Farranfore or Castlemaine and head directly west to the town of Dingle along the road that skirts the south coast. Coming from the east or the north you first reach Tralee at the head of the Peninsula's north coast, before heading west to the village of Camp. From here one road continues along the north coast before descending to Dingle via the phenomenal Connor Pass, while another road heads southwest across the Peninsula to Annascaul where the south coast road is picked up.

Getting around Anyone spending much time on the Dingle Peninsula, especially if planning to cycle or walk, should consider purchasing the Ordnance Survey Map No 70 in the Discovery series. There are so many minor roads, and so few main ones – on top of that there's the practice of signposting places in Irish (see box page 323) to contend with – that it is easy to get confused. All year, **Bus Éireann** run up to five buses, Mon-Sat, between Dingle and Tralee via Annascaul and Camp. There is also a summer Mon-Sat service between Dingle and Dunquin, via Ventry, Slea Head and Ballyferriter (Mon, Thu only outside of summer). A bus also connects Dingle with Ballydavid on Tue and Thu. There are also four buses a day (more in summer)

Dingle Peninsula & Dingle Way

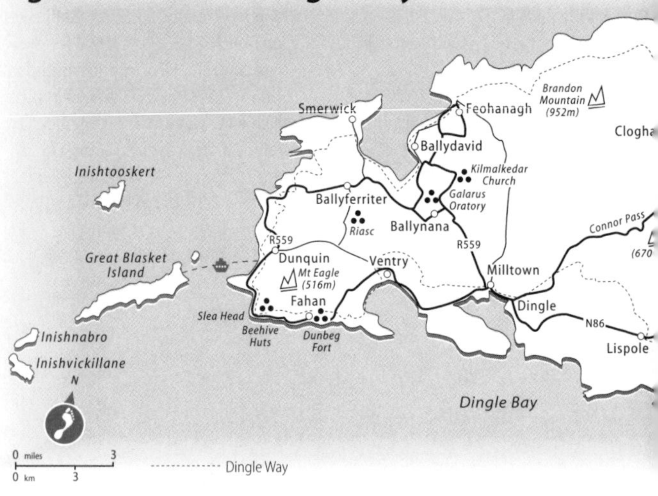

Gaelic place names on the Dingle Peninsula

Annascaul	*Abhainn an Scáil*	Cloghane	*An Clochán*
Ballydavid	*Baile na nGall*	Dingle	*An Daingean*
Ballyferriter	*Baile an Fheirtéaraigh*	Dunquin	*Dún Chaoin*
Blasket Islands	*Na Blascaodaí*	Inch	*Inse*
Brandon	*Bréanainn*	Lispole	*Lios Póil*
Brandon Creek	*Cuas a Bhodaigh*	Ventry	*Paróiste Fionn Trá*

between Killarney and Dingle via Tralee. A summer-only service departs from Dingle at 1530 for Killarney, via Annascaul, and Inch, and passing the *An Óige* hostel at Aghadoe before reaching Killarney. For full details, contact Tralee bus station, T066-712 3566, or Killarney T064-30011. » *See also Transport, page 340, for further details.*

History

Ancient constructs litter the Peninsula – megalithic tombs, cup and circle stones, oratories, beehive huts, high crosses – testimony perhaps to the sense of awe that the landscape inspired in the region's earliest inhabitants. Later groups of visitors – Norsemen in the 10th century, Anglo-Normans in the 13th century followed by traders from Spain – may have felt the same, but the Dingle Peninsula also bears the scars of England's colonialism. People around Ballyferriter still recount the story of the Dún an Óir massacre (near Smerwick, see page 331) and how workmen collecting stones at a nearby beach once refused to go on working when they discovered that this was the infamous "beach of the heads": the heads of those massacred, cut off by English troops, washed up on shore and were buried by local people.

Tralee → *Phone code: 066. Colour map 3, grid B2.*

Not the cutest of Irish towns, the county capital is metamorphosing into a thriving centre of local employment that seasonally tunes into the tourist market whilst otherwise busying itself with the new-found wealth of 21st-century Ireland. Tralee makes a useful base for a day or two (see Sleeping, page 335) before heading west and there are a few attractions to while away the time while planning an itinerary or

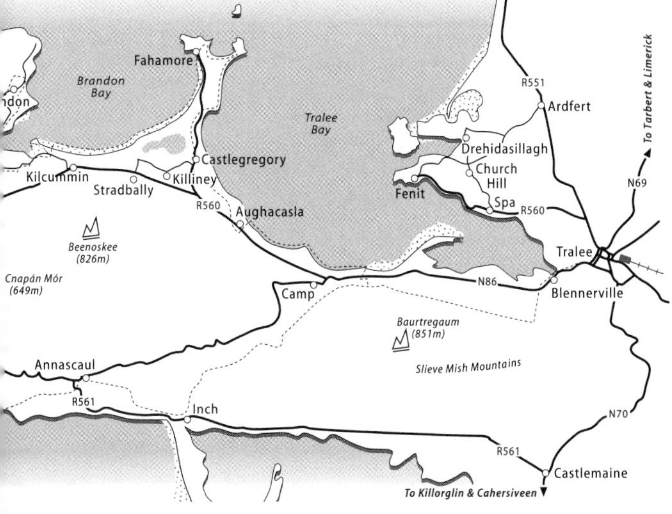

The secret of the Rose

The annual week-long Rose of Tralee festival at the end of August begins with street bands welcoming the would-be Roses – woman of Irish descent from every corner of the world – in traditional style, in which they were led through the streets with an escort of riders bearing burning sods of turf. While tickets are sold out well in advance there is plenty of other entertainment around town – street theatre, extensions to licencing hours, concerts and fireworks. The actual contest to choose the Rose takes up two nights, with not a bikini in sight, for the women compete by way of interviews followed by a display of some expertise, from an Irish jig to a belly dance. The stage event, although a little too long, is laudably low-octane and while the winner is not hurled into an international limelight all the contestants enjoy a week-long freebie and publicans laugh all the way to the bank. The secret of the festival's success is hard to fathom, but it is undeniably becoming increasingly popular. *T066-7121322, www.roseoftralee.ie.*

plotting a route along the Dingle Way, a superb long-distance walk around the Peninsula that provides an ideal introduction to Dingle's charms (see page 332).

The **tourist office** is in Ashe Memorial Hall, Denny St, T066-7121288. Open Jul/Aug Mon-Sat 0900-1900, Sun 0900-1800, Apr, May, Jun and Sep Mon-Sat 0900-1800, Nov-Mar Mon-Fri 0900-1300, 1400-1700. The Rose of Tralee festival office is also here, T066-7121322 and there is a café and craft shop on the premises. The WALK-IN-formation Centre, T066-7128733, stocks OS maps and walking guide books, useful if planning or considering the Dingle Way or other walks in the region.

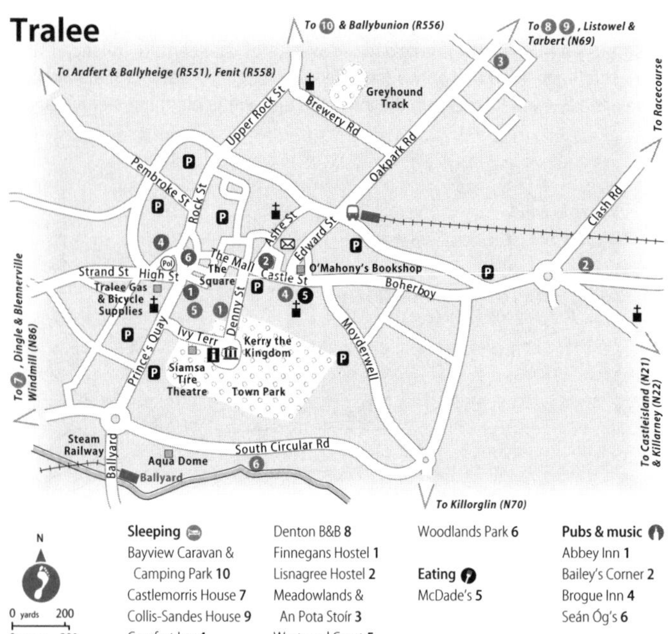

Sir Roger Casement

Casement was a British diplomat, born in 1864 in Sandycove (County Dublin), who first became famous for his denunciations of the exploitation of native workers in the Congo and South America. He was knighted in 1911, but ill-health caused his early retirement, and he settled in Ireland in 1912. His commitment to the cause of Irish nationalism led him to Germany in 1914. The government there agreed to send a shipload of arms, but this was far less than he had anticipated and he returned to Ireland in 1916 in order to try and postpone the planned rising. A German submarine brought him into Tralee Bay, but he was arrested after landing on Banna Strand. Put on trial for treason and sentenced to death, he attracted a lot of support and there were many appeals on his behalf. To discredit him, the government released extracts from his 'Black Diaries' that revealed his homosexuality. He was hanged in London in August 1916. In 1965 his body was returned to Ireland for a state funeral.

Kerry the Kingdom ⓘ *Jun-Aug daily 0930-1730, Sep-Dec Tue-Sat 0930-1700, Apr-May Tue-Sat 0930-1730. €8.* The history of Kerry is told through an audio-visual display, a museum and a reconstructed set of medieval Tralee. The museum is dense with information, though the admission charge is a bit steep.

Blennerville windmill ⓘ *T066-7129999. Apr-Oct daily 1000-1800. €4.* The largest working mill in the British Isles is the centrepiece of this visitor attraction just outside of town on the N86 road to Dingle. The exhibition focuses on the history of 19th-century Blennerville, an emigrant port from where thousands departed for the long and painful journey to America. A guided tour of the windmill is included in the price.

Steam railway ⓘ *T066-7121064. Early May to early Sep daily 1100-1700; closed on certain days in Jun and Jul. €4.* The first 3 km of the narrow-gauge Tralee and Dingle Steam Railway, which ran from 1891 to 1953, has been restored and every hour a train chugs from Ballyard Station in town to the Blennerville Windmill. The journey lasts 20 minutes and makes for a pleasant journey to the windmill (plus a 10 percent discount on the windmill admission) and railway memorabilia is sold on the train.

North of Tralee

Apart from the sights mentioned below, the flat rolling farmland of North Kerry has little to detain the traveller and if you're heading on to Clare, stay on the N69 and cross the Shannon by way of the very regular car ferry from Tarbert.

Listowel On the way to Tarbert, the small town of Listowel is worth noting because of its literary fame as the home of the playwright, John B Keane, who until his death in 2003 ran **John B Keane's** pub ⓘ *37 William St*, an authentic Irish bar. There is a seasonal **tourist office** in St John's Church, T068-22590, and if you plan a visit to the annual Listowel **Writers' Week** in May it is advisable to have accommodation booked in advance. Details of the festival are available from PO Box 147, Listowel, Kerry, T068-21074, writersweek@eircom.net. Throughout the year, something is usually on at **St John's Theatre and Arts Centre** ⓘ *The Square, T068-22566, and information is available at www.listowel.com.*

Ardfert Cathedral ⓘ *On the R551 Tralee to Ballyheigue road at Ardfert, T068-7134711. May-late Sep daily 1000-1800. €2. OPW site. Guided tour available.*

Nuala Ní Dhomhnaill

So many figures from the famed Irish literary tradition, or at least the version marketed by Bord Fáilte, are dead white males that it comes as a refreshing change to know that the Dingle area nurtured the poet Nuala Ní Dhomhnaill. She was born in England in 1952, but her Irish parents sent her back to the Gaeltacht Dingle Peninsula at the age of five. Her first collection of poetry arrived in 1981, announcing a new voice able to blend Irish mythology and folklore with an acute political and social awareness. Marrying feminism with the Gaelic tradition, her work has been translated by Seamus Heaney and other contemporary poets (see page 629). Translations of her work include *Selected Poems* (1986), *Pharaoh's Daughter* (1990), *The Astrakhan Cloak* (1992) and *The Water Horse* (1999).

Depending on your interests and time, it could well be worth skipping the attractions in Tralee and journeying 8 km to the northwest to visit the cathedral in Ardfert. St Brendan founded a monastery here in the sixth century, but what you see today is a medieval cathedral with a superb Romanesque doorway on the west side, and a dramatic triple-lancet window typical of the Gothic style that had been introduced to Ireland by the Cistercians. The 13th-century east window, framed by two ecclesiastical effigies, is also worthy of attention. On the site there are also two other smaller 15th-century churches.

Banna Strand The 8-km stretch of safe and sandy beach at Banna is popular with Irish families, and camping and caravan sites are dotted along the coast up to and including Ballyheigue. On the beach there are panoramic views over Tralee Bay, and Banna Strand has a particular significance in Irish history because it was here that Roger Casement landed and was arrested in 1916 (see page 325). To reach the memorial look for a sign pointing to the left as you approach the beach; from here it is a 10-minute walk past the caravans.

Crag Cave ⓘ *On the N21 road at the Limerick end of Castleisland, T066-7141244, www.cragcave.com. Mid-Mar to Nov daily 1000-1800 (1830 in Jul and Aug). €7.* This limestone cave, discovered by accident in 1983, and now open to the public by way of a guided tour. As caves go this one is quite impressive and the lighting system underground is used to good effect to highlight some of the more dramatic formations. Above ground there is a restaurant and a souvenir minimarket.

Inch and Annascaul → *Phone code: 066. Colour map 3, grid B2.*

Coming from Killarney and the south the route west from Castlemaine follows the coast to Dingle, and the two main villages along the way are Inch and Annascaul. There are places to stay (see page 335), but finding somewhere for a meal is not so straightforward, and this should be borne in mind. See page 332 for the other route out to Dingle via Camp and Castlegregory.

Inch The main attraction at Inch is the gorgeous 6-km beach that provided a location for the filming of *The Playboy of the Western World*. The strand and the two opposite on the Iveragh Peninsula – Rossbeigh and Cromane – are gradually building up, and one day Castlemaine Bay will be enclosed. The beach is vast and you can walk a mile out to sea at low tide and the water is only about an inch deep, which is one explanation for the village's name. Ringed plovers and turnstones, distinctively small black and white birds with white legs, are non-breeding visitors to the beach where they are seen turning stones and weeds with their bills searching for food.

Annascaul In the one-street village of Annascaul visitors often wonder why a pub should be named the South Pole Inn. A villager, Tom Crean, accompanied Scott and Shackleton to the South Pole and he set up this pub afterwards. There is a small **tourist office** in the main street, T066-9157419. When facing **Annascaul Lake**, you are standing at the bottom of a glacier-carved valley, the lough itself having been carved out by the base of the glacier. The scree slopes on the other side have been broken off the top of the sandstone mountain by centuries of weathering. The green road leading away from the lough leads up to the valley following the course of the River Garrivagh, and it is a pleasant stroll in dry weather. Even though the lake is signposted, it is not much visited, and you can usually have the place to yourself. About 6 km from Inch on the road to Dingle you will reach a T-junction: take the right turn for Annascaul and after 1.2 km the road for Annascaul turns to the right, while the left turn is signposted for Annascaul Lake.

Dingle → *Phone code: 066. Colour map 3, grid B1.*

The small town of Dingle, with barely half a dozen streets, has changed almost beyond recognition in the last few years, tourism being the catalyst. Such is the growing popularity of a visit to the Peninsula, that Dingle has been forced to build car parks and introduce one-way systems to cope with the traffic. Out of season, the town reclaims its identity as a market town and fishing port, but in July and August it becomes the main base for visits to the sights and sites west of Dingle. There are places to stay west of town but because this end of the Peninsula is small enough to make most places accessible as day excursions, Dingle heaves with people and vehicles in the summer months. The **tourist office** is on Strand St, close to the pier and bus stop, T066-9151188. Open all year, Mon-Sat 0915-1730; until 1900 in Jul and Aug and until 1800 in Jun and Sep.

Dingle

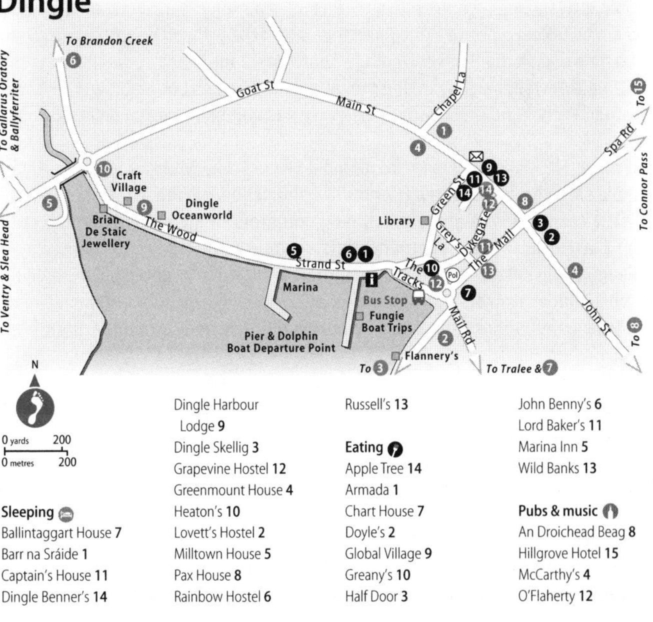

Sleeping
Ballintaggart House **7**
Barr na Sráide **1**
Captain's House **11**
Dingle Benner's **14**
Dingle Harbour Lodge **9**
Dingle Skellig **3**
Grapevine Hostel **12**
Greenmount House **4**
Heaton's **10**
Lovett's Hostel **2**
Milltown House **5**
Pax House **8**
Rainbow Hostel **6**
Russell's **13**

Eating
Apple Tree **14**
Armada **1**
Chart House **7**
Doyle's **2**
Global Village **9**
Greany's **10**
Half Door **3**
John Benny's **6**
Lord Baker's **11**
Marina Inn **5**
Wild Banks **13**

Pubs & music
An Droichead Beag **8**
Hillgrove Hotel **15**
McCarthy's **4**
O'Flaherty **12**

History The Irish form of Dingle, *An Daingean* (fortress), suggests its early involvement in defensive wars, although it has a long history of friendly trade with Spain, and Spanish blood is noticeable in the dark hair and eyes of the inhabitants. In Green Street just past the library there are plaques, still visible, which were set above some of the doors to indicate that Spanish families lived within and, walking up this street from the pier, part of the original town wall can be seen in the old wall on the left.

Fungie the dolphin When a bottlenose dolphin first appeared in the harbour in 1983 the chirpy little chap flirted and frolicked and made a lot of friends with the humans who doggie-paddled in the water hoping for a meaningful relationship. Over 21 years later and he is still there (or have the locals replaced him with an inflatable version?) and he surely deserves an award from Fáilte Ireland for promoting tourism. Weather permitting, boats depart between 0800 and 1000 from the pier, T066-9152626, and the €12 charge is returned in the unlikely event of his non-appearance. There is also an early morning boat for people who want to swim with him and a wet suit can be hired from **Flannery's**, T066-9151967. It is also possible to get reasonably close to where he usually appears without leaving dry land. Take the road out of town towards Tralee and the right turn about a 1.6 km after the Esso garage. It is a narrow lane with gateposts but no gate and there is a small parking area at the bottom; from here it is a short walk in the direction of the old tower.

Dingle Oceanworld ⓘ *T066-9152111, www.dingle-oceanworld.ie. Jul-Aug daily 1000-2000; May, Jun and Sep daily 1000-1800; Oct-Apr daily 1000-1700. €7.50.* This Fungie-inspired aquarium is a cut above the average and presents a good opportunity to view at close quarters the local sealife, from cuttlefish to small sharks, including examples of most of the fish that appear on restaurant menus in Ireland. Children will enjoy the touch pool and there is also a café and a shop.

Dingle to Dunquin → *Phone code: 066.*

Along the coast between Dingle and Dunquin (*Dún Chaoin*) there are a number of ancient beehive huts and forts (signposted along the road). Following the Dingle Way to Dunquin is a fascinating and enjoyable walk (see page 332) and you could skip the first few km by taking a bus to Ventry and then begin the walk on Ventry beach. There would be time to visit the Blasket Heritage Centre at Dunquin before catching the bus back to Dingle or walk back by taking the inland road across Coumaleagua Hill. With fine weather, there is no better way of enjoying this corner of the Dingle Peninsula.

Ins and outs The R559 road is the route most visitors take when heading west from Dingle, passing through Ventry (*Fionn Trá*) and following the coast around the majestically scenic Slea Head before turning north for Dunquin, the departure point for Great Blasket Island. An alternative and swifter route to Dunquin is by way of Coumaleagua Hill; take the signposted turning on the right, about 1 km after the Ventry post office. Walkers will need a copy of Map 70 in the Ordnance Survey Discovery series. Bus 1555 runs a service between Dingle and Dunquin.

Dunbeg Fort ⓘ *T066-9159070. €2. Signposted, about 6.5 km west of Ventry.* This is a particularly well-preserved eighth- or ninth-century promontory fort with two souterrains, underground tunnels used for storing food or perhaps as an escape route in times of trouble, and the remains of a dwelling which can be discerned inside four earthen defensive rings, but the clifftop location is its most impressive aspect.

Beehive huts ⓘ *€2. Signposted, between Dún Beg Fort and Slea Head.* Above the road and stretching for some distance is a group of ancient stone huts, known as the **Fahan group**. Very little is known about them for sure, though a plausible explanation for their existence is that they represent a late pagan or early Christian settlement that stretched out along some long-lost highway, with Eagle Mountain rearing up behind as a natural defence. The fact that they have survived for so long is eloquent testimony to the masonry skills of whoever built them.

Slea Head Slea Head, where the coastal road turns north towards Dunquin, offers spectacular views, and vehicles accumulate here. The Iveragh Peninsula and the Skelligs can be seen to the south, while to the west the Blasket Islands impose themselves on the view. To escape the crowds carry on for a short distance and descend to **Coumeenoole Strand**, a tiny beach with fine white sand. On a hot day it is tempting to go for a swim, but bear in mind that Robert Mitchum almost drowned in the strong undertow here while filming a scene from *Ryan's Daughter*.

Kruger's ⓘ *T066-9156127. Just off the R559 at Dunquin on a road that leads down to the departure point for the Great Blasket Island.* The fame of this pub derives from the eponymous Kruger Kavanagh (Kruger was his nickname). Amongst other achievements, he served in the US army in the First World War, became a bodyguard to Eamon de Valera and a Hollywood agent. The pub itself – "the most westerly pub in Europe" – is remarkably unprepossessing, but anywhere that Robert Mitchum drank regularly has got to be worth a visit. The black and white photographs adorning the walls are fascinating and the pub also hosts sessions of Irish set dancing. Film buffs should enquire here for directions to the remains of the partly fibreglass schoolhouse that was built for *Ryan's Daughter*.

Blasket Heritage Centre ⓘ *T066-9156444. Easter-Jun, and Sep-Oct daily 1000-1800; Jul and Aug daily 1000-1900. €3.50. OPW site.* The exterior of this heritage centre at Dunquin makes some people feel the architect and planning authority should be sacked from their jobs – it is unquestionably a blot on the landscape – but the interior is a masterpiece, and a visit here should not be missed, preferably before making a trip out to the island itself. The 20-minute audio-visual presentation, with archive material of interviews with Blasket islanders, is excellent, and there is also a wealth of material and photographs, including an amusing photograph that accompanies an islander's quote: "I looked west at the edge of the sky where America should be..." from Maurice O'Sullivan's *Twenty Years a-Growing*. Scholars came to the Great Blasket and encouraged the islanders, to whom storytelling and poetry was a part of everyday life, to write down their stories and record their memories. Their books are all on sale in the Centre and the Dingle bookshops and there is some consensus that O'Sullivan's book is one of the more enjoyable texts.

Great Blasket Island → *Colour map 3, grid B1.*

ⓘ *Boats to the island: T066-9156422, 9154864, www.blasketisland.com. Boats sail from Dunquin pier from 0930 onwards, weather permitting, €20 return.*

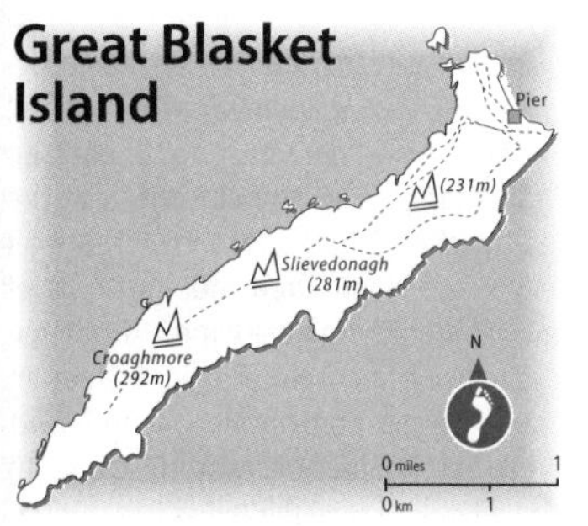

This whale-shaped and marooned-looking island is the largest of a group of islands off the coast near Dunquin. A trip across Blasket Sound to view the remains of the island's village and to walk to its western end is a highlight of any visit to Kerry. It also has one of the best beaches anywhere in the county, *An Trágh Bhán*, outstanding for its cleanliness and the sheltered location, which makes it safe for swimming.

An anarchist society – with a king!

Life on the Blasket Islands consisted of a self-sufficient community of farming families who lived peacefully without a government, a priesthood or a police force. But at some time or other the notion of a monarchy crept in and the islanders took up the practice of electing a notional king from amongst themselves.

The earliest records document families living on the island around 1700, and they were very healthy indeed, only falling sick if they left to go to the mainland. In 1821 there were 128 islanders, rising to 153 before the Famine, which seems not to have been as catastrophic as elsewhere, probably because their diet was not so dependent on the potato. Fishing had always been an important source of food, supplemented by rabbits, seabirds and their eggs.

The difficulty of landing on the island – readily apparent even today – helped preserve their independent way of life, and stories have been told of how the women bombarded landing bailiffs with rocks from the cliffs above as they tried to get ashore. In the early 20th century a school was established, along with a post office in the 1930s, but by 1953 there were only 22 inhabitants. The death in 1952 of a young man simply because the weather prevented him reaching hospital in time, helped the government decide the following year to offer mainland homes to the remaining islanders.

The island is now uninhabited, though in summer there is a small café, hostel, T066-9154864, and a craft shop. Boats, departing from Dunquin every half-hour, can only make the crossing in fine weather.

Inishvickillane and Tearaght Islands

These two islands also belong to the Blasket group and, though neither can be visited by the public, they still have a remarkable presence for anyone walking west on the Great Blasket. Inishvickillane is the one furthest to the southwest; it is partly visible from the mainland, but a clear view of it opens up from the western end of Great Blasket. The whole island was purchased by Charles Haughey, a one-time Taoiseach of Ireland who 'forgot' being given a huge sum of money (€279,000) by a businessman in 1972, and he still occasionally visits his island by helicopter. The smaller island to the north of Inishvickillane is Inishnabro.

Tearaght Island is the small, craggy, westernmost island to the northwest of Great Blasket, distinguished from Inishtooskert, which is closer to Great Blasket, by its lighthouse on the southern side. Tearaght supports large colonies of storm petrels and Manx shearwaters.

Ballyferriter → *Phone code: 066. Colour map 3, grid B1.*

The road from Dunquin continues on to Ballyferriter (*Baile an Fheirtearaigh*), a small village well worth considering as an alternative accommodation base to Dingle (see page 336). The serene beauty of the surrounding landscape, the closeness of the Gallarus Oratory and other sites, plus the nearby lovely Wine Strand beach are all good reasons to linger in the area. The beach, a few hundred metres north of Ballyferriter, is safe for swimming and is usually sheltered from the wind. The village is named after Pierce Ferriter (c.1600-53), a love poet and soldier whose Norman ancestors settled on the Dingle Peninsula, and whose participation in the 1641 rebellion led to his hanging in Killarney. JM Synge, the playwright, came to Ballyferriter in 1905 to polish up his Irish.

Ballyferriter Museum ⓘ *T066-9156333. Easter and Jun-Sep daily 1000-1700. €3.* A modest little museum devoted to local history and culture and covering topics like the Ogham alphabet, cross slabs and promontory forts.

Dún An Óir Fort ⓘ *Going west from Ballyferriter, after 1 km turn right at the brown sign pointing to Smerwick harbour, at the Y-junction bear right and right again at the T-junction; after 300 m the fort is signposted left on a poorly surfaced road.* In 1580, in support of the Desmond rebellion, a party of Italians and Spaniards landed in the bay just north of Ballyferriter and established themselves in a fort that had been built earlier by Irish rebels. While waiting for reinforcements they were besieged by the English under Lord Grey. After three days the fort surrendered and some 700 soldiers and a score or so of Irish were cold-bloodedly and systematically butchered by groups of executioners. Edmund Spenser, the English poet who wrote *The Faerie Queene*, was secretary to Grey at the time and was almost certainly present at the massacre. Grey was later recalled to England, but Spenser, who stayed on in Ireland, remained a hearty supporter of the methods used to suppress the rebellion. The stone sculpture near the remains of the fort commemorates those who died. The beauty of the location is rendered melancholy by the haunting memory of what occurred here.

Ancient and medieval sites

Riasc ⓘ *24 hrs. Free.* The first of these sites, Riasc, is just east of Ballyferriter on the road to Ballydavid and it is also the least engrossing, so if time is limited this is the one to skip. Excavations of the Riasc monastic site in the 1950s revealed that the ruins were built over an earlier site dating back to AD 400. The main attraction for visitors is a pillar stone inscribed with a cross and curling patterns typical of La Tène art; though this is an early Christian site, and La Tène decoration is mainly pre-Christian Celtic.

Gallarus Oratory ⓘ *No admission charge to this OPW site, so feel free to ignore the nearby heritage centre which charges €4 for the predictable 15-min audio-visual presentation. Signposted on the R599 road going east from Ballyferriter. Coming from Dingle, cross the bridge for the road west to Ventry and Dunquin and take the first right for 5 km before bearing left at the Y-junction for the Oratory and Ballyferriter.* Of all the sites on the Dingle Peninsula, the Gallarus Oratory is the one you must not miss. Probably built between the ninth and 12th centuries as a place of prayer for monks, this beautifully crafted little hut has stood intact without the aid of mortar for maybe 12 centuries. The seamless dry stone wall turns into a roof, and it is impossible to tell where the wall ends or the roof begins. The building method, known as corbelling, has each stone supporting another above it, which juts in beyond the perpendicular of the wall. Each stone also slopes slightly downwards, so rain is kept out of the building by running off.

Kilmalkedar Church ⓘ *From Ballyferriter: take the R559 road eastward at Murreagh (heading south back to Dingle); the church is on the left side of the road about 1.5 km east of Murreagh. Coming from Dingle: cross the bridge for the road west to Ventry and Dunquin and take the first right for 5 km before bearing right at the Y-junction for Kilmalkedar Church.* This Romanesque church is thought to date from the 12th century and seems to represent a transitional stage in architecture between the corbelling of the Gallarus Oratory and a tiled roof, as part of the roof that remains is similar in style to the oratory. An interesting feature of the church is the design over the doorway: the tympanum has a head on one side and an imaginary animal on the other. The remains of other monastic buildings are in the vicinity including **Brendan's House**, a two-storey medieval building, and there is an Ogham stone in the church graveyard. The road between the church and Brendan's House is the beginning of the Pilgrim's Way, the traditional route to the summit of Mount Brandon.

Cloghane and Mount Brandon

Cloghane might make a pleasant alternative to staying at *An Bóthar* in Brandon Creek. It is a good base for the many walks around Mount Brandon and Brandon Ridge.

Climbing Mount Brandon It takes about six hours to climb Mount Brandon (952 m) and the place to start from is outside the local information office in Cloghane, T066-7138277/7138137. Mount Brandon has been appropriated by Christianity, but the pilgrim trail known as the saint's road, which goes from Cloghane to Faha, at the foot of the mountain, has pagan Celtic origins. Anyway, after reaching the grotto at Faha there is a walking trail marked by red and white poles that leads you gently on your journey. Gradually, after passing a series of small lakes, the route becomes rockier and after crossing a river it starts to zig-zag in a steep ascent. The views at the top should provide ample compensation for the sore muscles that might make themselves felt the next day.

Camp, Castlegregory and the Connor Pass → *Colour map 3, grid B3.*

As you travel to the Dingle Peninsula from Tralee, the road heads west to the village of Camp – which is strung out along the road and characterized only by a couple of pubs – where a fork in the road leads either southwest to Annascaul or straight on along the northern coast of the Peninsula to Cloghane and the Connor Pass. Before reaching Cloghane, a right turn off the road leads to the Castlegregory Peninsula and the village of Castlegregory (*Caisleán Ghriare*) itself. The village offers little else other than a place to stay and eat (see page 337), but the Peninsula and its beaches attract holiday-makers and there are a number of caravan and camping sites. Far better to stay on the road to Cloghane where Fermoyle Beach is a lovely stretch of sand, safe for swimming and safe for cars, which can be driven onto it.

The Connor Pass connects Cloghane with Dingle and at 456 m offers spectacular views of both Mount Brandon and Dingle to the south. The car park at the summit is clogged with cars during the summer months.

★ The Dingle Way

The Kerry Way is scenically stunning and the Beara Way is wild and empty, but the Dingle Way has touches of both and the largest variety of walks and the most fun things to do when not walking. From miles of empty sandy beaches to fossil-clad cliffs to long mountainside paths and a stiff climb up Mount Brandon this Way has so much to offer it seems a waste that anyone should leave the area not having walked for at least a couple of days.

To complete the Dingle Way requires about seven or eight days:
Day 1: Tralee to Camp (19 km)
Day 2: Camp to Annascaul (17 km)
Day 3: Annascaul to Dingle (22 km)
Day 4: Dingle to Dunquin (22 km)
Day 5: Dunquin to Ballydavid (24 km)
Day 6: Ballydavid to Cloghane (22 km)
Day 7: Cloghane to Castlegregory (22 km)
Day 8: Castlegregory to Tralee (22 km)

Mapping The Dingle Way is covered by the Ordnance Survey Discovery series sheets 70 and 71 and these are essential for the walks. Cork-Kerry Tourism produces a strip map for the Dingle Way, which is not essential but could be used in conjunction with the OS maps.

Natterjack toads

Visitors flock daily to Dingle to catch sight of one socially maladjusted dolphin (dolphins are naturally gregarious creatures living in large communities), when Kerry's real zoological treat lies croaking very loudly on the north side of the Peninsula near Castlegregory. The natterjack is Ireland's only toad, looking like a frog but darker and with a yellow stripe along its spine. If you lurk around Lough Gill at night with a torch you should be able to see one during the mating season (April-June). Their blaring croaks attract females, but the male will launch itself on the first fellow natterjack spotted until a female catch has been confirmed and mating can proceed. The male is possessive, and determined to prevent anyone else from mating with his betrothed, and the poor female remains encumbered by the male clutching her around the abdomen until she is ready to spawn. This encourages her to spawn as soon as she can, up to 4,000 eggs at a time.

Day 1: Tralee to Camp ⓘ *19 km; 6 hrs; total ascent 125 m*. The walk begins on a road but does have the advantage of bringing you along the canal to Blennerville Windmill. Otherwise, catch a bus about 3 km out of town to where the route leaves the main road and heads uphill. Be careful here, as the waymarker is skilfully disguised. The left turn off the main road is followed by a sharp right almost immediately. The route quickly finds the open hillside and rolls gaily along past boulder fields, over streams, by ancient waterworks, with the beauty of the hills to the left and the panoramic scene of the coastline below you. It's an added bonus to be able to look down at the traffic below resembling little Dinky toys scuttling about. The route follows the ditch between the fields and the upland pasture. Camp, the day's destination, is strung out along about 5 km of road, so if you are booking accommodation in advance – for example at Daly's Bar or the Railway Tavern (see page 337) – ask where it is exactly, because there are several places where you can leave the route.

Day 2: Camp to Annascaul ⓘ *17 km; 6 hrs; total ascent 450 m*. The walk is largely along tarmac but the scenery more than makes up for the sore feet. The route crosses the Peninsula, travelling through a low central valley inhabited only by sheep. Emerging on the southern coast it brings stunning views of the beach and sand dunes at Inch. Turning back inland, the route goes uphill and crosses Ardroe and Maum, a saddle between two mountains. From here there are excellent views down into Annascaul Glen. At Annascaul, besides two hostels, there are some B&Bs, which include Four Winds and Anchor House (see page 335).

Day 3: Annascaul to Dingle ⓘ *22 km; 7 hrs; total ascent 400 m*. Another day largely on tarmac but with some good views, lots of antiquities to poke around in and a brilliant storm beach with huge boulders. Leaving Annascaul, the route travels via a minor road to the coast. For most of the day the route keeps close to, and high above, the southern coast, passing by the ruins of Minard castle, destroyed by Cromwell's armies, and an interesting old graveyard at Aglish where bodies are interred in stone mausoleums rather than buried in the ground. See page 335 for accommodation in Dingle.

Day 4: Dingle to Dunquin ⓘ *22 km; 7 hrs; total ascent 350 m*. (**NB** This section of the Way is being altered slightly to avoid the bit of road walking. Check at the tourist office for the most recent routes, the OS map may be out of date.) After the long, rather dull section of the walk on tarmac to Ventry the route takes off with a glorious walk around

St Brendan and Brandon Creek

Legend has it that St Brendan set out from Brandon Creek on the first transatlantic crossing in the sixth century. Brendan was born in 484, and as a young man travelled around Ireland, founding a monastery at Ardfert and building an oratory on Mount Brandon. His wanderlust went into a higher gear when he heard about a wonderful island far to the west of Ireland, and taking 14 monks with him, he set out in a curragh to find the place. An early port of call was an island that turned out to be the back of a whale but after seven years – with stops at what might have been Greenland, Iceland and Newfoundland – he finally reached America. He returned safely to Ireland and died in 578. Improbable as this voyage sounds, Tim Severin showed in 1976 that it could be done. With a group of friends he built a similar boat and reached Newfoundland after a 13-month, 3,000-mile journey.

Coming from Dingle, cross the bridge for the road west to Ventry and Dunquin and take the first right that heads north to Murreagh (*An Mhuiríoch*). Just before Murreagh turn right for the village of An Bóthar Bui, carry on north to Dooneen Pier and follow the road until it ends at Brandon Creek (*Cuas an Bhodaigh*).

Ventry Harbour and then a cliff walk around the coast, with Mount Eagle looming to the landward across a landscape littered with clochâns and other ancient remains. The views are amazing along the last section and more than make up for the little bit of walking that is necessary along the main road. For accommodation see page 336.

This day's walk could be accomplished as a day trip from Dingle by catching the afternoon bus (1555, Jul and Aug only; 1825 Mon and Thu only, all year) from Dunquin back to Dingle. Alternatively, with your own transport you could park at Ventry and have time to reach Dunquin and then walk back to Ventry by taking the short inland road across Coumaleagua Hill.

Day 5: Dunquin to Ballydavid ⓘ *24 km; 8 hrs; total ascent 200 m.* A long wonderful day's walk around Slea Head, first climbing the lower slopes of Croaghmartin and then dropping down to Clogher Beach where there are huge (and dangerous) waves and ancient fossils of ferns and shelled creatures in the rocks at the northern end of the beach. Beyond Clogher the route travels for a time along tarmac roads to Smerwick Harbour, where it follows the line of the shore as far as Ballydavid. From there, another spell on tarmac along a desolate windswept road brings you to Brandon Creek where there are some B&Bs. The best place to stay, the An Bóthar pub, is very comfortable and has live music most nights in summer (see page 337).

Day 6: Ballydavid to Cloghane ⓘ *22 km; 8 hrs; total ascent 750 m.* Of the many amazing walks that this Peninsula has to offer, this has to be the best. The walk starts with a long, challenging hike up to a saddle of Mount Brandon with the most stunning views behind, growing more panoramic the higher you climb. Over the saddle the descent is rapid and the path runs past more spectacular views, to the north this time. On a fine day the coastline around Sauce Creek looks as if it has been painted. The Way carries on through a country park on wide stony tracks and then through Brandon village before following the coast to Cloghane. For accommodation here see page 337.

Day 7: Cloghane to Castlegregory ⓘ *22 km; 6 hrs.* After a few miles of tarmac the route meets the beach and for the rest of the day you follow the coastline around Fahamore and into the village of Castlegregory. The beach is usually quite empty, occasional anglers fish for plaice in the surf. The beach is wide and firm and makes a great walk, even at high tide when there is always some sand still exposed. It passes Stradbally with it church ruins and the wildlife sanctuary at Lough Gill. There are more ruins at Kilshannig at the end of the Peninsula. Castlegregory has B&Bs as well as a hostel, see page 337.

Day 8: Castlegregory to Tralee ⓘ *22 km, 6 hrs; total ascent 275 m.* After walking along the shoreline, the route meets the main road and then the outward leg of Day 1, which you follow in reverse back to Tralee. The first part of the walk is well worth the effort and the hill walk back to Tralee is just as pretty as it was on the way out but, if you don't like backtracking, the Annascaul to Tralee bus can be hailed. There is a daily bus from Dingle, and two buses from Castlegregory to Tralee on Fridays only. Check in Castlegregory for times.

Sleeping

Tralee *p323, map p324*

L-C **Meadowlands**, Oakpark, T066-7180444, www.meadowlands-hotel.com. Modern hotel, out on the road to Listowel, with stylish and well equipped rooms, and an above-average restaurant.

A-C **Comfort Inn**, Castle St, T066-7121877, www.choicehotelsireland.ie. Modern, comfortable and conveniently in the very centre of town. Nightclub on premises.

D **Castlemorris House**, Ballymullen, T066-7180060, castlemorris@eircom.net. A lovely house on the outskirts of the city where guests are greeted with afternoon tea, and an evening meal can be booked in advance. Take the N21 to Dingle and turn right at the T-junction after 1 km.

E **Denton B&B**, Listowel Rd, Oakpark, T066-7127637. Near the Meadowlands hotel on the N69, bathrooms en suite. Open all year.

E **Westward Court**, Mary St, T066-7180081, westward@iol.ie. Double/single rooms with a continental breakfast for up to €51, or a bed in a 4-bed/6-bed room for €17 per person. Launderette, security lockers, TV lounge.

F **Collis-Sandes House**, Oakpark, T066-7128658, colsands@indigo.ie. A lovely old Anglo-Irish house, with the full range of hostel amenities. Will pick up from train or bus station, though a walkable journey out along Oakpark Rd (N69), on the left after a Shell garage.

F **Finnegan's Hostel**, Denny St, T066-7127610, www.finneganshostel.com. Limited facilities, some private rooms and an atmospheric restaurant in the basement.

F **Lisnagree Hostel**, Ballinorig Rd, off the N21 road, T066-7127133. Has private rooms but otherwise is fairly basic.

Camping

The Bayview Caravan and Camping Park, Killeen, T066-7126140. 1.5 km out of Tralee on the R558 road to Ballybunion.

Woodlands Park, South Circular Rd, Tralee, T066-7121235. A modern camping and caravan park.

North of Tralee *p325*

C **Allo's Bar & Bistro**, Listowel, 41 Church St, T068-22880. Has decent accommodation

D **Listowel Arms Hotel**, T068-21500. A decent place to stay.

Inch and Annascaul *p326*

F **Fuchsia Lodge**, Annascaul, T066-9157150, fuchsia@eircom.net. Has all the amenities, including bike hire, and it is a friendly and comfortable place to stay for a night or two; open all year and private rooms available.

E **Anchor House**, T066-9157382, www.walkingbootstours.com. Small place with babysitting service, en suite bathrooms, closed Dec-Mar.

E **Four Winds**, T066-9157168. Cheaper place with child reductions and only 4 rooms, not all with en suite facilities.

Dingle *p327, map p327*

There are quite a few B&Bs in and around Dingle, but most have only a few beds and

For an explanation of the sleeping and eating price codes used in this guide, see inside the front cover. Other relevant information is found in Essentials pages 39-45.

fill up quickly. Join the queue at the tourist office or try to book up before arriving.

L-B Dingle Benner's Hotel, Main St, T066-9151412, www.dinglebenners.com. This comfortable Victorian-style place offers high quality accommodation, a good restaurant during the summer months, pretty gardens and a popular lounge bar.

L-C Dingle Skellig Hotel, T066-9151144, www.dingleskellig.com. Sea views from this 1960s hotel, with leisure centre, megaspa and child-friendly attitude.

B-C Milltown House, T066-9151372, milltownhousedingle.com. A superior guest house serving an above-average breakfast and providing fine views of the harbour from the garden; reached by crossing the bridge heading for Ventry and turning left immediately. Robert Mitchum stayed here in the 1960s when filming *Ryan's Daughter*.

C-D Greenmount House, Gortonora, T066-9151414, www.greenmount-house.com. Includes some rooms with their own fridge and balcony, the conservatory overlooks the harbour, a residents' room, terrific breakfasts.

C-D Heaton's, The Wood, T066-9152288, heatons@iol.ie. Just far enough from the centre to avoid the noise, this top-notch guest house has spacious non-smoking rooms, modern facilities and a breakfast that includes drambuie-topped porridge.

C-D Pax House, Upper St John St, T066-9151518, paxhouse@iol.ie. Really friendly and relaxing guest house with views of the water from the balcony where you can linger over a drink as the sun goes down. A superb breakfast menu with homemade breads, jam and marmalade and healthy alternatives to the heart-stopping Irish fry. Good value.

D Captain's House, The Mall, T066-9151079, captigh@eircom.net. A picturesque setting by a running stream and with a delightfully higgledy-piggledy interior makes this one of the most enjoyable guest houses in town.

D-E Barr na Sráide, Upper Main St, T066-9151331, barrnasraide@eircom.net. Comfortable rooms above a pub.

E Ballintaggart House, a 20-min walk out of town on the Tralee road, Racecourse Rd, T066-9151454. One of the better hostels in Ireland, with private rooms, a restaurant and shop, laundry, bike and wet-suit hire, pony trekking, riding lessons and lovely cobbled courtyard adjoining the self-catering kitchen.

E Dingle Harbour Lodge, The Wood, T066-9151577, www.dingleharbourlodge.com. Upmarket place where all private rooms have TV, coffee making facilities and phone. Communal kitchens, doubles and family rooms.

E Russell's, The Mall, T066-9151747, maryr@iol.ie. A detached house with 6 bedrooms with en suite bathrooms.

F Grapevine Hostel, Dykegate, T066-9151434. A smallish house with 24 beds. No private rooms, but convivial atmosphere.

F Lovett's Hostel, An Cuilin (Cooleen Rd), T066-9151903. On the road opposite the Esso garage, entering town from Tralee. 12 beds in a friendly family house, sheets included in rate, 2 private doubles.

F Rainbow Hostel, Milltown, T066-9151044. Hip place a short way out of town, with private rooms and camping space.

Camping

Ballintaggart House Caravan and Camping Site, T066-915145. 2-star, next to the hostel outside of town on the Tralee road.

Dingle to Dunquin *p328*

E An Portán, T066-9156212. At the junction on the main road where you turn off for Kruger's. 14 rooms all have en suite bathrooms in this well organized place. Evening meals in the restaurant.

E Kruger's, Dunquin, T066-9156127. This famous pub has 7 beds charging €20-30 per person but they are not worth writing home about and bathroom facilities are shared.

E Slea Head Farm, Coumeenoole, T066-9156120, www.sleaheadfarm.com. Farmhouse charging around €64 for en suite rooms and €60 sharing a bathroom.

F Dún Chaoin, T066-9156145/9156121. *An Óige* hostel on the main road near Kruger's and enjoying a wonderful view of the sea.

Ballyferriter *p330*

C-D Ceann Sibeal Hotel, T066-9156433. Newly built in the village of Ballyferriter and offers shiny new rooms and amazing views.

C-D Tigh An Phoist Hostel, T066-9155109. Hostel outside of Ballyferriter, on the road to Ballydavid. Nearly 30 beds and 4 private rooms, and bicycles for hire.

D Black Cat Hostel, in the village, T066-9156286. Has camping space with use of hostel facilities but no private rooms.

E Tigh an t Saorsaigh, in the village, T066-9156344. Does B&B as well as providing bar food and music every night in summer.
F Tigh Uí Mhurchú, in the village opposite the post office, T066-9156224. A pub which also does good bar food and B&B.

Self-catering

Wine Strand Holiday Cottages, T066-325125. Consists of modern self-catering cottages. Ideal for a long stay on the Peninsula.

Cloghane and Mount Brandon *p332*,

E Abhain Mhor, T066-7138211. A local B&B that caters for walkers, has details of walks in the area.
E O'Connor's, T066-7138113. A pub and B&B, open Mar-Oct. Pub food and evening meals for guests are available, has details of walks in the area.
F Mount Brandon Hostel, T066-7138299, www.mountbrandonhostel. A hostel with dormitory rooms and some family rooms (with en suite facilities). Price includes breakfast and bed linen. Laundry, bike hire.

Camp, Castlegregory and the Connor Pass *p332*

C-D Crutch's Hillville House Hotel, T066-7138118, macshome@iol.ie. Tucked away off the main road and conveniently close to Fermoyle Beach, this hotel has good-sized bedrooms with 4-poster beds, sea views and a laid back atmosphere.
E The Fuschia House, West Main St, Castlegregory, T066-7139508. Stone-fronted B&B with a reputation for good food at the breakfast table; dinner for under €20 can be arranged.
E Strand View House, Connor Pass Rd, Kilcummin, T066-7138131, strandview@eircom.net. Quality B&B, hard to miss on the main road, overlooking the bay.
F Connor Pass Hostel, Stradbally, T066-7139179. On the main road, a very basic hostel with 3 private rooms.

Camping

Green Acres Caravan Park, Castlegregory, T066-7139158. Accepts campers.
Sandybay Caravan Park, Castlegregory, T066-7139338. Accepts campers.

The Dingle Way *p332*

E An Bóthar, Brandon Creek, about 1 km inland, T066-9155342. Pub and restaurant, also offering accommodation. Caters to walkers and can organize packed lunches and walks in the area.
E Daly's Bar, Camp, T066-7130125. In the village. Rooms with en suite bathroom.
E The Railway Tavern, Camp, T066-7130188. On the main road to Tralee a little out of the village. Has rooms with en suite bathroom.

Eating

Tralee *p323, map p324*

₮₮₮ An Pota Stoír, Meadowlands Hotel, T066-7180444. A cheerfully informal restaurant with a Mediterranean-style character. Go for the locally caught seafood: oysters, lobster, turbot, John Dory and sole feature regularly. The à la carte dinner is around €40 plus. A good wine list and the usual wicked desserts.
₮₮ McDades, Castle St. A pub and restaurant, recommended for anyone wishing to get away from the usual fish and meat dishes. The interesting menu includes delicious potato skins for a starter, fajitas and pasta dishes.

North of Tralee *p325*

₮ Allo's Bar and Bistro, 41 Church St, Listowel, T068-22880. Reasonable food.
₮ Listowel Arms Hotel. Food is reasonable.

Dingle *p327, map p327*

₮₮₮ Doyle's, John St, T066-9151174. Under new management but keeping the old name. Continues to attract American tourists who have heard of the original legendary seafood restaurant. Traditional Irish inn decor, with tables too close together. Dinner only, closed Sun.
₮₮₮ The Half Door, John St, T066-9151600. Tuck into the seafood platter as either a starter or main course. Closed Sun.
₮₮₮ Lord Baker's, Main St, T066-9151277. An old pub and restaurant that only comes into the expensive bracket when dining at night. Seafood is always the main draw, of course, but plenty of meat-based alternatives. Sun lunch always requires a reservation.
₮₮ Chart House, The Mall, T066-9152255, www.charthousedingle.com. Local ingredients, lots of seafood but not

exclusively so, vegetarian options. Modern Irish. Highly recommended.

₸₸ **The Armada**, Strand St, T066-9151505. Opens 1800-2100, closed Mon, and has a decent 4-course dinner menu of traditional Irish meat dishes and local seafood.

₸₸ **The Global Village**, Main St, T066-9152325. Deserves its name with a menu featuring Thai curries, stir-fried Chinese, German bratwurst sausage, Indian tikka masala, Italian pasta, and UK fish and chips. It's small but perfectly formed with interesting artwork for sale on the walls and a sense of privacy. Set 3 course dinner €21. Open for lunch and dinner.

₸₸ **Wild Banks**, Main St, T066-9152888, www.thewildbanks.com. Modern Irish in this small place with a menu which includes lots of seafood but has meat and vegetarian alternatives. Early dinner menu from 1800-2000 brings this into the mid-range category but the Dover Sole can rack up the cost.

₸ **The Apple Tree**, Orchard Lane, T066-9150804. A tiny place, nicely decorated, great cappuccinos and some homely lunch grub. Lots of baked goods for dessert. Popular with locals.

₸ **Greany's**, Holy Ground, T066-9150924. Deservedly busy because of the location, the prices and the quality of the food. Go late in the evening for a quieter atmosphere.

₸ **John Benny's**, pub opposite the pier, best bet for cheap food.

₸ **Marina Inn**, opposite the pier, the best bet for cheap eats.

Dingle to Dunquin *p328*

₸₸ **An Portán**, T066-9156212. Just up the road from Kruger's, has a modern Irish menu of fish and meat dishes in Gaelic, subtitled in English, but only opens for dinner between 1900 and 2200; expect to pay around €32 for a meal. They also provide the lunches that are available at the self-service restaurant in the Great Blasket Centre.

₸₸ **The Stone House**, Slea Head, T066-9159970. Comes highly recommended by lots of locals. You'd never miss it – it's entirely built of stone, roof and all. Open for lunch and dinner which will set you back about €30, not bad at all, considering how far away it is, and lunch is around €10.

₸ **Dunquin Pottery and Café**, serves soups, savouries and home-baked goodies.

₸ **Kruger's**, Dunquin. Bar food available.

₸ **The Skipper**, at Ventry, west of Dingle on the Slea Head route, T066-9159900. Offers a rare deal in Ireland – good food at quite affordable prices. Genuine French-style cuisine for lunch and dinner, and an early-bird dinner 1800-1930.

₸ **Tig Slea Head**, Slea Head. Has 2 floors of lovely things made mostly in Ireland, photos of Ryan's Daughter as well as a very nice café.

Ballyferriter *p330*

₸₸ **Ceann Sibeal**. Has a restaurant doing pretty dependable if unadventurous food nightly in summer and Thu-Sun in winter for very reasonable prices. Mains are around €19. Its bar offers bar food till 2000 as well as lots of traditional music.

₸ **Ballyferriter Museum**. The café, open daily 1000-1700, serves affordable hot meals like pork and chicken pie.

₸ **Tigh Uí Mhurchú**, pub opposite the post office. A quiet place, serving lunch and dinner meals, and prices are reasonable.

Cloghane and Mount Brandon *p332*

₸ **O'Connor's**, does pub food.

₸ **Tigh Tomsi**, next door to Mount Brandon Hostel. A pub owned by the same people with car food and live music in summer. There is a small shop opposite.

Camp, Castlegregory and the Connor Pass *p332*

Camp

₸₸-₸ **Ashes Restaurant and Bar**, Camp. Serves the best food, from either the pub food or the dinner menu.

₸ **The Junction Bar**, Camp. Serves light snacks throughout the day and there is a pool room and dart board for rainy afternoons.

₸ **The Railway Tavern**, Camp, T066-7130188. May have music sessions on Sun evenings.

Castlegregory

₸ **O'Riordan's Café**, T066-7139379. Has more to offer than the name suggests. As well as tasty home-cooked snacks and light meals there is an enlightened menu that offers non-meat eaters something other than lasagne made from frozen vegetables, as well as local seafood, Kerry lamb and beef in Guinness. Open daily Jun-Sep 1200-2100.

Ned Natterjack's, West End, T066-7139491. A family-friendly pub with garden seating that serves good food throughout the day and live music on a Saturday night.
Ferriter's Loft, T066-7139494. A pub serving steaks, seafood and burgers and evening sessions of traditional music.

Pubs and music

Tralee *p323, map p324*
There is no shortage of pubs and many of them have live music during the summer.
The Abbey Inn, Bridge St. Has music every night of the week until late.
Bailey's Corner, Ashe St. You could also look here where there is lots of local live music.
Brogue Inn, Kirby's. Can usually be relied on for an entertaining night out.
Seán Óg's, Bridge St. Cavernous, has music every night except Wed and Sat.

Dingle *p327, map p327*
An Droichead Beag, Main St, T066-9151723. Has nightly sessions of traditional music and is popular with tourists.
John Benny's, Harbourside, next to the Armada. Music every night in the summer.
Hillgrove Hotel. A popular night club here on Mon, Wed, Fri, Sat and Sun nights that attracts young revellers. There is a cover charge. Traditional Irish dancing session attracting people of all ages on Thu nights.
McCarthy's Bar, Upper Main St, T066-9151205. Has regular sessions of music.
O'Flaherty, The Mall, T066-9151983. The kind of authentic pub that Irish theme pubs (and you will find one or two of them even in Ireland) use as a model: flagstoned floor, high ceiling, music sessions.

Entertainment

Tralee *p323, map p324*
Theatre National Folk Theatre of Ireland, founded in 1974 to present theatrical entertainment based around Irish folklore music and dance. Summer season shows usually start at 2030, and advance booking is recommended in Jul and Aug.
Síamsa Tíre, Town Park, T066-7123055, www.siamsatire.com.

Festivals and events

Tralee *p323, map p324*
Samhlaíocht Chiarraí, Main St, T066-7129934. Contact for details of the Tralee Easter Arts Festival. For details of **Rose of** Tralee festival (**end Aug**), see page 324.

Shopping

Dingle *p327, map p327*
Antiques Antique Corner, Main St. Lace, jewellery and small antique pieces.
Fadó Antiques, Main St. Has a selection of curios, prints, clocks, and jewellery.
Simple Pleasures, The Mall, T066-9151224. Full of antiques, paintings and more.

Books An Liteártha, Dykegate St. A terrific selection of books on most aspects of Irish history and culture.
Léigh Linn, the Dingle Bookshop, Green St. Worth a browse.

Fashion Banshee, Green St. Designer knit-wear, handmade Irish lace and jewellery.
Lisbeth Mulcahy, Green St. Perhaps the classiest shop in Dingle, specializing in quality fashion accessories, like scarves made from Irish linen, cotton, wool, alpaca and silk.

Gifts An Gailearai Beag, 18 Main St, T066-9152976, www.gailearaibeag.com. The showcase for the craftspeople of the Dingle Peninsula. Some very pretty things on offer.
Brian de Staic, across the road from Dick Mack's Yard. A good selection of handmade Celtic-inspired jewellery on which names can be engraved in the Ogham script.
The Craft Village, The Wood. A short way west of the pier, has a cluster of arts and crafts shops.
Dick Mack's Yard, Green St. A small shop selling Celtic-inspired jewellery.
Dingle Crystal, Green St, T066-9151550. Sells the work of glassblower Sean Daly, full of Celtic designs. Hand signed and dated, very pretty.
John Weldon's, Green St, T066-9152522. Has more Celtic handmade jewellery.

Music The Dingle Record Store, in the Green St Arcade. CDs and bodhrans.

Dingle to Dunquin *p328,*
Louis Mulcahy Pottery, on main road past Dunquin, T066-9156229. Two floors devoted to ceramics, ranging from egg cups to enormous garden sculptures. The designs are very attractive and distinctive and overseas delivery is regularly arranged for large items. You can watch the pieces being made and even try your hand on the wheel.

Activities and tours

Tralee *p323, map p324*
Racing Greyhound Stadium, Oakview, T066-7180008. A grandstand restaurant and a bar. The first race starts at 1950 every Tue, Fri and Sat. Pre-booking is required.

Swimming Aqua Dome, T066-7128899. A fun waterworld with slides and raging rapids open daily 1000-2200.

Tours Jackie Power Tours, 2 Lower Rock St, T066-7129444, jackiepowertours@eircom.net. Coach tours of the Ring of Kerry and Dingle Peninsula and Killarney.

Dingle *p327, map p327*
Diving Dingle Marina Diving Centre, The Marina, T066-9152422, info@divedingle.com.

Fishing Nicholas O'Connor, Angler's Rest, Ventry, T066-9159947.

Golf Ceann Sibéal Golf Club, Ballyoughterach, Ballyferriter, T066-9156255.

Horse riding Ballintaggart House, T066-9151454.
Dingle Horse Riding, Ballinaboula, T066-9152018.
Horseriding and Trekking Centre, Mountain View, Ventry, T066-9159723.

Sailing Dingle Sailing Club, The Marina, T066-9151984.

Tours Boat: **Dingle Boatmen's Association**, The Pier, T066-9151163.
Dingle Marine Eco Tours, The Pier, T066-2858802. 2-hr trips cover archaeology, geology, history, birdlife, sealife and local folklore. Tours go either east or west along the southern part of the Peninsula.
Coach: **Moran's Tours**, T066-9151155. 2-hr trip departing from the Pier daily at 1000 and 1400 and taking in most of the major sites on the Peninsula; €12.70.
Walking: **Sciuird Archaeological Tours**, T066-9151606. Daily 2½-hr tours departing at 1030 and 1400. Pick-up arranged on booking. Tour numbers are kept below 10 so booking is advisable. €15.

Windsurfing Focus Windsurfing, T066-7139411, jamieknox@tinet.ie. Based at Castlegregory beach, hires gear and conducts training sessions for children.

Transport

Tralee *p323, map p324*
Air Kerry Airport, Farranfore, 16 km southeast of Tralee, T066-9764644.

Bike hire Dunworth Cycles, Tralee, 97 Rock St, T066-7120666. **Tralee Gas & Bicycle Supplies**, Strand St, Tralee, T066-7122018. **Paddy Rent-a-Bike**, Dingle, T066-9152311. Rents bikes. **Foxy John's**, Main St, Dingle, T066-9151316. Offers the Raleigh Rent-a-Bike scheme. **Tadgh Ó Coileáin**, Holyground, Dingle, T066-9151606.

Bus Bus Éireann, T066-7123566. Buses provide tours of the Peninsula, **Cliffs of Moher** and **West Cork** in the summer months. All year, buses connect **Tralee** with **Killarney**, **Dublin**, **Cork**, **Rosslare** and other main cities. There is a regular bus service between **Tralee** and Dingle, 4 times Mon- Sat, 3 on Sun, and timetables are available from the tourist office. All year around, on Mon and Thu, 3 buses run daily between Dingle and **Dunquin**, and on Tue and Fri 3 buses between Dingle and **Ballydavid**.

Car hire Duggan's Garage, Ashe St, Tralee, T066-7121124. Will also deliver to the airport.

Taxi Taxi rank, Mall St, Tralee, T066-7123159.

Train Tralee station: T066-7123522/7126555. Daily service to **Dublin** and connections to other towns around the country like **Cork** and **Ennis** from **Limerick Junction** and the west of Ireland from **Portarlington**.

County Clare

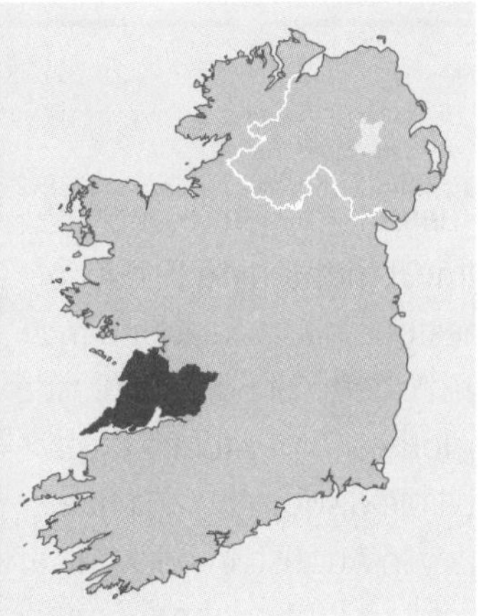

Footprint features

Introduction

From the sublime to the absurd, Clare has much to offer the visitor. Sublime is the majestic, almost frightening beauty of the Burren, with its sulky grey limestone hills and abundance of wild flowers; absurd is the tourist ghetto of Bunratty Castle with students dressed up in daft clothes to pay for next year's college, and coachloads of the gullible disgorging at a rate that almost comes close to Killarney in August. In between are ancient tower houses lurking in fields, mighty dolmens and ringforts, medieval church ruins, the terrifying Cliffs of Moher, a hippy musical centre at Doolin, the seasoned tourist villages of Lisdoonvarna and Ballyvaughan, and the long caravan-dotted western coast from Lahinch, where the Atlantic surf crashes ashore to Loop Head.

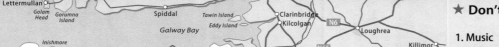

★ Don't miss...

1. **Music** Investigate the sounds emanating from pubs, particularly in Ennis and Doolin, pages 349 and 359. In the summer, there is usually something on every night of the week.
2. **The Burren** Walk in the barrren limestone (karst) scenery, page 350, and take a tour to see some giant bear prints in Aillwee Cave, page 356.
3. **Máire Rua's house** Admire Leamanagh Castle on the road from Ennis to Ballyvaughan, home of one of Ireland's most infamous serial husband killers, page 352.
4. **The love of your life** Find love at the matchmaking festival in Lisdoonvarna in September, or simply indulge in some ballroom dancing, page 353.
5. **Ballinalacken Castle Hotel** Eat chocolate pudding and take in the skyscapes, page 357.
6. **Dolphins** You can spot them on boats trips from Carrigaholt or Kilrush, page 361.

Ins and outs → *Tune in to 96.4 for Clare FM.*

Getting there

Shannon Airport, in eastern Clare, 27 km from Ennis, is a major entry point for many travellers. It's a transatlantic airport with direct flights from a number of US cities, some of which continue on to Dublin. There are also direct flights to London and other cities in England and the rest of Europe. During the summer there is an extensive charter programme from many European destinations. Most visitors will move on to Limerick, 24 km away, from where there are connections by bus and rail to other parts of Ireland but Ennis and the rest of County Clare are an equally good route to take from Shannon. There are frequent **Bus Éireann**, T061-474311, www.buseireann.ie, services from the airport to Ennis, Bunratty and Limerick and also services from Shannon to Galway and Dublin. **Citylink**, T091-564163, www.citylink.ie, run four buses a day between Shannon and Galway. There is internet access, a café and a restaurant at the airport as well as a **tourist information** desk, T061-471664, which will make bookings. Opening hours match arrival times. For **flight information**, T061-712000. A taxi, T061-471538, from Shannon to Limerick or Ennis will cost over €30.

Getting around

There are **buses** to and from Ennis several times a day from Shannon Airport, Galway, Dublin, Cork and Limerick. **Trains** link Ennis with Limerick, from where there are connections to Cork, Waterford and Dublin. If you are travelling between Clare and Kerry there is the Killimer-Tarbert **ferry**, a useful way of saving a long drive round the coast to Limerick (see page 349). **Car hire** is available at the airport from **Avis** *T061-471094*; **Budget** *T061-471361*; **Dooley Car Rentals** *T061-471098/471819*; **Hertz** *T061-471369*; **Johnson & Perrot** *T061-471094*; **Murrays** *T061-701200*; **National** *T061-472633*.

Ennis and around

→ *Phone code: 065. Colour map 3, grid A4.*

Bursting at the seams, the multitude of small shops that make up the main streets of Ennis is testimony to the frenzy of merchant activity that attached itself to the evolution of Clare's main market town from the 11th century onwards. The geometry of the narrow streets and the tiny lanes leading off of them evoke a bygone age, not least because of the air of out-of-dateness that lingers over the town. But it's a pleasant little town with an amazing amount of really good traditional music in the summer months and a few places to keep you busy. Better still, use Ennis as a base for visiting east Clare before moving on to the real highlight of the county – The Burren. ▸▸ *For Sleeping, Eating and other listings, see pages 347-349.*

Ins and outs

Getting there and around **Bus Éireann** runs limited summer services to towns in west and north Clare. From Lisdoonvarna a connection can be made with the Galway to Tralee bus which goes via the Killimer-Tarbert ferry. Ennis itself is small enough to easily walk around. ▸▸ *See Transport, page 349, for further details.*

Information **Ennis tourist office**, Arthur's Row, T065-6828366. Open Jul-Sep daily 0930-1750; Apr-Jun and Oct-Dec Mon-Sat 0930-1730; Jan-Mar Mon-Fri 0930-1730.

Sights

Ennis is a compact little town bisected by the River Fergus. It has expanded south of the original heart of the city, around the **Friary** ⓘ *Abbey St, T065-6829100. Apr-May daily 1000-1700; Jun-mid Sep daily 1000-1800; mid-Sep to Oct daily 1000-1700. €1.50. OPW. Guided tours available on request.* Established in the 13th century by the O'Briens, kings of Thomond, the Friary now stands in a state of beautiful ruin. What you see is largely 14th-century, although the east window with its fine thin mullions between the lancet windows dates back to the original building. In the 14th century there was a large school here with 600 pupils and about 350 friars. The west end of the church is probably 15th century. On the southwest face of the tower is a carving of St Francis showing his stigmata. Inside the tower is a carving of the Virgin and Child and at the east end of the south wall is the ornately-carved McMahon tomb, which depicts a bishop giving benediction, and scenes of the arrest and crucifixion of Christ, all dating to around 1475. On the east side is the figure of a woman, thought to be More Ni Brien, the woman who founded the tomb. The Friary was the last school of Catholic study to survive the Reformation. Franciscans came and went through the 17th century as the buildings gradually decayed and the school dissolved.

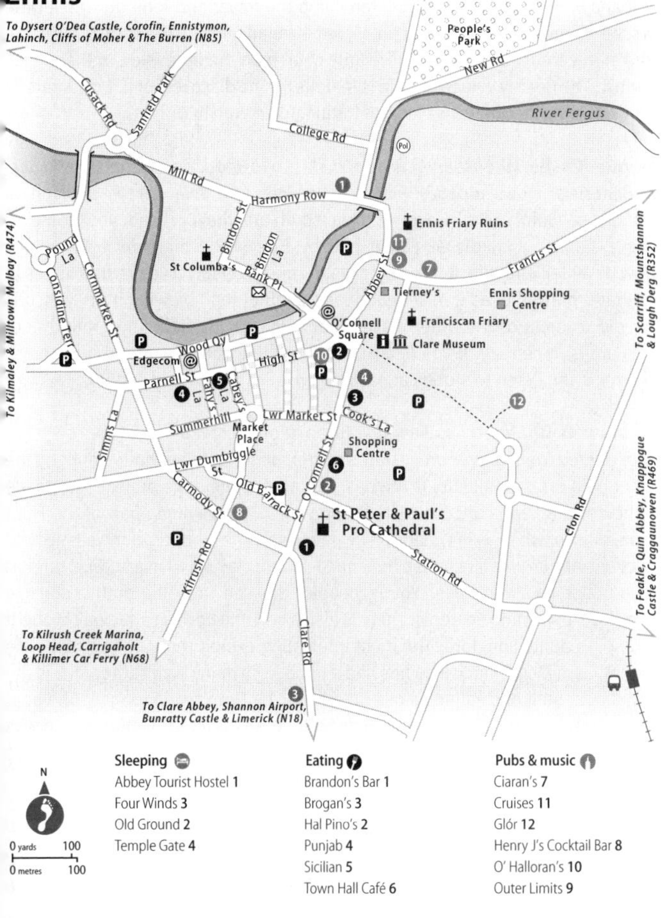

The *Riches of Clare* exhibition at the **Clare Museum** ⓘ *Arthur's Row, T065-6823382, Jun-Sep daily 0930-1830; Apr-May and Oct Mon-Sat 0930-1300 and 1400-1730; Nov-Mar Mon-Fri same hours as Apr-May, no admission at the moment but this may change*, adjoins the tourist office. The display ranges from stone axes and a 16th-century sheela-na-gig to Clare-born JP Hooland's invention of the submarine.

Around Ennis → *Phone code: 061.*

Using Ennis as a base there are several sites of interest to the north and south of the town. The N18 south to Limerick is worth avoiding if you are cycling the suggested route east to Quin and Craggaunowen, and Knappogue avoids the worst of it, although if you want to see Bunratty, part of it is unavoidable. Dysert O'Dea to the north can be done in a day from Ennis or taken in en route to the Burren.

Quin Abbey ⓘ *Jun-Sep daily. Free. From near Ennis train and bus station, take the R469 road.* A building of some kind has stood on this site since the 13th century when a church here was burned and replaced with a De Clare castle, part of the towers of which still survive. In 1236 the castle was sacked by warring Irish clans and replaced by another church, the restored version of which you see before you. If you think about it, quite a lot of murdering must have taken place on this site over the centuries; perhaps the Franciscans brought a bit of peace to the place. The ruins are very beautiful and well preserved and you can climb the tower and look down over the cloisters, which are some of the best preserved in Ireland. Inside the church are some 15th- and 16th-century tombstones. The little church on the other side of the river is 13th-century. The nearby village of Quin is famous for the discovery of a huge hoard of gold, some of which found its way to the National Museum in Dublin.

Knappogue Castle ⓘ *Castle: May-Sep daily 0930-1700, last admission 1645. €5.95. Banquets: T061-360788, €48.50, Apr-late Oct daily 1830, booking is essential.* From Quin Abbey travel 3.2 km south on the L31 and you come to Knappogue Castle, a medieval castle pile by Sean McNamara in 1467, which somehow never fell into ruin. It has a long history and probably owes its intactness to the fact that Cromwell used it as a headquarters rather than blowing it up, which is what he did to most of the other places that could be fortified. The ground floor additions are 19th-century. If you like that sort of thing you can attend a medieval banquet there and listen to stories about women in Irish myth and history.

Craggaunowen ⓘ *Mid-Apr to Sep daily 1000-1800. Last admission 1700. €7.50. Tea shop, guided tours, picnic area.* This, another medieval tower house built by the family that built Bunratty Castle, is the basis for another heritage project. The castle itself is home to a series of 16th-century European woodcarvings, part of the Hunt Collection, most of which is in Limerick (see page 232). The grounds of the castle hold reproductions of a *crannog* (a house built on to an artificial island in a lake), a ringfort and an outdoor cooking place. Young people, dressed in Celtic outfits practise making objects using ancient tools. There is also a genuine Iron Age roadway brought from a bog in County Longford. The most interesting exhibit there, in a glasshouse designed by Liam McCormack who has had a hand in so many Irish cathedrals, is the *Brendan*, a boat built and sailed across the Atlantic by Tim Severin in 1976. The boat is based on descriptions of the kind used by St Brendan to cross the Atlantic and was successfully sailed in an effort to prove that St Brendan's journey was possible (see page 334). Its hull is made from tanned oxhides stretched over an ash frame.

Bunratty Castle ⓘ *T061-360788. Open Jan-Mar and Nov-Dec daily 0930-1730; Apr-May and Sep daily 0900-1730; Jun-Aug daily 0900-1800, last entry 1715. Last entry to castle 1600 rest of year. Closed Good Fri and 24-26 Dec. €10. Banquets, al* *year, daily 1730 and 2045, €49.95. Booking essential.* From Cratloe you can head back towards Ennis on the N18 to get to Bunratty Castle. This is the leprechaun-and-shillelagh version of the Ulster American Folk Park in Northern Ireland, which is surprising since the castle is quite genuine and so are several of the buildings in the Folk Park. The castle was built in 1460 (1425 in some versions of the story) by the MacNamaras and later came into the possession of the O'Briens who held it until 1712. During the English Civil War and Cromwell's invasion of Ireland it was held by the republican forces. What you see is the keep, the main building of the castle, which would have been well inside a curtain wall. Some time after 1712 the keep fell into ruins, which were then bought by Lord Gort in 1954 and restored. Very little of the renovations are invention or guesswork and the furnishing inside is quite genuine. The same goes for the village street and different styles of houses and their contents in the park, yet somehow it all has an air of Disneyland about it. Perhaps it's the gift shop, or the girls in period dress. Anyway, ignore the tour bus groups, dodge the group photos, squeeze through the crowd buying totally unrelated tea towels and have a good look round the old houses. They are a fascinating insight into a bygone, but still almost tangible, age.

North to the Burren

Dysert O'Dea ⓘ *T065-6837401. Open 1st May-30th Sep daily 1000-1800. €4.* Travelling north of Ennis on the R476 brings you to Dysert O'Dea, on the way to Corofin. This is a whole collection of ancient remains, the most interesting being the 1487 **O'Dea Castle**, which now houses an archaeology centre. Cromwell's forces ruined the castle in 1651, but it was renovated in 1986 and has won a number of awards for its exhibitions on archaeology.

The actual dysert or **anchorite church** was founded some time in the eighth century by St Tola, after whom it was first named. What you see is a Romanesque ruin that has been reassembled, incorrectly in places. Particularly beautiful is the doorway with carved geometric patterns and a series of carved heads, human and animal. In the northwest of the site are the remains of a round tower built as a defence for the church property some time around the turn of the last millennium. The church and tower suffered the same fate as the castle in 1651. There is also a 12th-century high cross depicting the crucifixion and a bishop, and with geometric patterns and human and animal figures decorating the sides. The archaeology centre has a suggested walk around these sights and several other historic places in the area.

Clare Heritage Centre ⓘ *Heritage centre: T065-6837955, http://clare.irish-roots.net. May-Oct daily 0930-1730. €4. Research centre: Mon-Fri 0900-1730; May-Sep daily 0900-1730.* This heritage centre is in the village of **Corofin**, about 12 km northwest of Ennis, on the southern fringe of the Burren. Inside are exhibitions on the Famine, emigration and living conditions in the 19th century as well as a room focusing on the 1798 uprising. It's a pleasant little place: no high-tech audio-visuals but lots of source materials. In the same building is a genealogical research centre where people with roots in Clare can search out their ancestors.

Sleeping

Ennis *p344, map p345*

L-A Woodstock Hotel, Shanaway Rd, T065-6846600, www.woodstock-hotel.com.
A 4-star hotel (out of town and requiring transport) majoring in restful neo-classical elegance and smooth efficiency, and with the benefit of a good value restaurant.

A-C Old Ground Hotel, O'Connell St, T065-6828127, www.flynnhotels.com.
In the centre of Ennis, this old hotel has been receiving travellers since the 18th century and modern improvements have not diminished its graceful appeal.

B-D Temple Gate Hotel, The Square, T065-6823300, www.templegatehotel.com. A quality 3-star hotel in the heart of the city, built on the site of a former convent. Professional and friendly.

C Newpark House, Tulla Rd, T065-6821233, newparkhouse.ennis@eircom.net. A working farm about 2 km from the town centre with 6 interesting and individual bedrooms and the option of a communal dinner to which you can bring your own wine.

D Magowna House Hotel, Inch, Kilmaley, T065-6839009, www.magowna.com. A small hotel set in large grounds, 6.4 km west of Ennis. Bar, restaurant, drying facilities for walkers. Good value

D-E Fountain Court, Lahinch Rd, T065-6829845, www.fountain-court.com. A 5-min drive from the town centre, this is a spruce guest house with kingsize beds, power showers and a good choice of breakfast.

E Four Winds, Limerick Rd, T065-6829831. One of the few B&Bs within walking distance of the town centre.

E Glencar Guesthouse, Galway Rd, T065-6822348, www.glencar.ennis.ie. This 12-bedroomed house is fine for a short stay and, with the Auburn Lodge Hotel next door, food, drink and music is a short walk away.

E Moyville, Lahinch Rd, T065-6828278, moyville.ennis@ircom.net. Dormer bungalow B&B with 4 rooms. Open Apr-Oct.

F Abbey Tourist Hostel, Harmony Row, T065-6822620, www.abbeytouristhostel.com. Has a great location overlooking the river and single and double rooms, breakfast included, camping space and bike hire.

Around Ennis *p346*

E Ashgrove House, Bunratty, T061-369332, www.ashgrovehouse.com. One of the quieter B&Bs close to the castle.

North to the Burren (Corofin) *p347*

B&Bs line the road to Kilfenora and they include farmhouse accommodation.

C Clifden House, Corofin, T065-6837692, www.clifdenhouse-countyclare.com. An overnight stay at Clifden House has been recommended by a traveller praising the individuality of this mid-18th-century house. There are 4 bedrooms, and an optional dinner is served communally at 2000 (€35).

E Lakefield Lodge, Corofin, T065-6837675, mcleary.ennis@eircom.net. A B&B that has also been recommended, mid-Mar to mid-Nov, for a comfortable stay.

E Fergus View, T065-6837606, www.fergusview.com. Family home with smallish bedrooms but lovely breakfasts and a helpful host.

Eating

Ennis *p344, map p345*

There are a few restaurants in town with an attitude so your nights here should be filled with good things to eat.

ΨΨ **Hal Pino's**, High St, T065-6840011. Popular with locals for its unchallenging but tasty dinners and a good value early-bird meal.

ΨΨ **Town Hall Café**, O'Connell St, T065-6828127. Is indeed the old town hall but it lacks the character you might expect and the original artwork provides the only distraction while enjoying lunch; a seafood or steak dinner is less than €30.

ΨΨ-Ψ **Cruises Pub and Restaurant**, Abbey St, T065-6841800. Beside the Queen's Hotel. Serves interestingly cooked fish and meat in a traditional Irish style.

ΨΨ-Ψ **JM's Bistro**, Temple Gate Hotel. To escape the busyness of the town's streets and the fiddly-diddlyness of pub music, a calm meal can be enjoyed here.

Ψ **Brandon's Bar**, O'Connell St, T065-6828133. Not too dissimilar to Brogan's.

Ψ **Brogan's**, O'Connell St, T065-6829859. Has a menu of chicken curry, Irish stew, and fish, in pleasant environment.

Ψ **Punjab**, across the road from Sicilian, T065-6844655. Indian food with take away.

Ψ **Sicilian**, Parnell St, T065-6843873. Cheerful decor and affordable pizza and pasta dishes.

Around Ennis *p346*

ΨΨ **Muses Restaurant**, Bunratty, T061-364082, www.musesrestaurant.com. A short walk from the village green and, though unprepossessing outside, the food is above average and vegetarians are accorded some respect. Dinner only, closed Sun-Mon, around €30 for an early dinner, 1800-1930.

For an explanation of the sleeping and eating price codes used in this guide, see inside the front cover. Other relevant information is found in Essentials pages 39-45.

₸₸-₸ **Durty Nelly's**, Bunratty, T061-364861, www.durtynellys.ie. A famous old pub with 2 restaurants to suit different budgets, and bar food. Manages to retain some dignity amidst the tourist clamour; live music some nights.

North to the Burren (Corofin) *p347*
₸₸ **Bofey Quin's**, Main St, Corofin. Has 1 huge menu served in the bar and in the seafood restaurant.
₸₸ **Le Catelinias**, Market St, T065-6837425. French-style nosh, the early dinner is delicious and good value at around €23.
₸ **Corofin Arms**, Main St, Corofin. Serves food until 1900 and often traditional music can be enjoyed here.

Pubs, clubs and music

★ **Ennis** *p344, map p345*
This is where Ennis shines as a place to visit. Most pubs and the hotels have some kind of live music, usually traditional Irish.
Ciarán's, 1 Francis St, T065-6840181. A good bet for the sound of fiddles and accordions.
Cruises, has live traditional music most nights all year round.
Other pubs with at least one night of Irish music are listed below. Sessions start late so if you can't find any music on, take a cruise around town and listen, or just wait where you are.
Cois na hAbhna, just outside town on the Galway Rd, T065-6822347. There are mid-week ceilidh dancing sessions.
Glór, Friar's Walk, T065-6843103, www.glor.ie. Cultural centre with an ambitious programme of traditional music concerts and other events.
O'Halloran's, High St, next door to Hal Pino's.
Preacher's, Temple Gate Hotel, T065-6823300.
Try the following for country and western music or tribute bands:
Brannagan's, **Darcy's Corner**, Upper O'Connell St; **Porter Stall**, Market St and **Henry J's Cocktail Bar**, Upper Market St.

Clubs
The Sanctuary and **Outer Limits** are in the Queen's Hotel. **The Boardwalk**, at Brandon's in O'Connell St. All also worth a look.

Festivals and events

Ennis *p344, map p345*
Among the many festivals and events that take place in Ennis each year, worth looking out for is the **Fleadh Nua**, T065-6828366, a traditional music festival usually held around the last week in **May**. There is another, less well known traditional music festival around the middle of **Nov**, T065-6828366.

Transport

Ennis *p344, map p345*
Bike hire Tierney Cycles, 17 Abbey St, T065-6829433.

Bus Bus Éireann station is by the train station in Station Rd, T065-6824177. First bus to **Shannon Airport** leaves at 0835 and they continue to depart regularly until 2305. Daily buses also to **Adare**, **Athlone** via **Galway**, **Ballina**, **Belfast**, **Castlebar**, **Cork**, **Derry**, **Donegal**, **Dublin**, **Galway**, **Killarney**, **Limerick**, **Tralee** and **Waterford**. A daily bus for **London**, via **Rosslare** and **Dublin**, departs Ennis at 1520.

Car hire TMT Rentals, 70 O'Connell St, T065-6824212. **Car parks**: in Abbey St, Parnell St, Temple gate and The Friary.

Ferry The Killimer-Tarbert ferry leaves daily from **Killimer**, every hour on the hr, 0700-2100 (0900 Sun) Apr-Sep; Oct-Mar, 0700-1900 (1000 Sun). From **Tarbert**, every hour on the ½ hr, Apr-Sep, 0730-2130 (0930 Sun); Oct-Mar, 0730-1930 (1030 Sun) T9053124, www.shannonferries.com. Crossing about 20 mins. €14-22 per vehicle single/return, €4-6 for foot passengers.

Taxi Ennis Cabs, freephone T1800-6842222. **Burren Taxis**, T065-6823456.

Train Trains to **Dublin** and other main cities from Ennis Railway Station, Station Rd, T065-6840444.

The Burren

→ *Phone code: 065. Colour map 2, grid C3.*

Leaving Corofin and heading north you enter the Burren (Boireann – 'a rocky place'), a strange – at times unearthly – looking landscape where it is difficult to imagine anyone could ever have eked out a living amongst the bare limestone rock. But eke they did from earliest times, as the hundreds of prehistoric sites in the area demonstrate. The 160 square kilometres of it is a little paradise for geologists, archaeologists, botanists and people with flashy cameras. It's also a great place for the inexpert traveller, with miles and miles of walking, brilliant views and some cute little villages where there is music, good food and good company. ▸▸ *For Sleeping, Eating and other listings, see pages 357-360.*

Ins and outs

Getting there and around From Ennis the best route into the Burren is via Corofin. From there a good way to proceed is towards Lisdoonvarna: it serves as a useful base and the journey is shockingly beautiful. If you are using public transport, buses (some of which are summer-only routes) travel from Limerick to Ennis and then through Inagh, Ennistymon, Lahinch, Liscannor, the Cliffs of Moher to Lisdoonvarna and then on to Doolin, so this might make a better route around the Burren. Bus Éireann's Galway-Tralee daily services travel via Ballyvaughan, Lisdoonvarna and Lahinch. If you are heading straight to the Burren from outside Clare there are buses from Galway

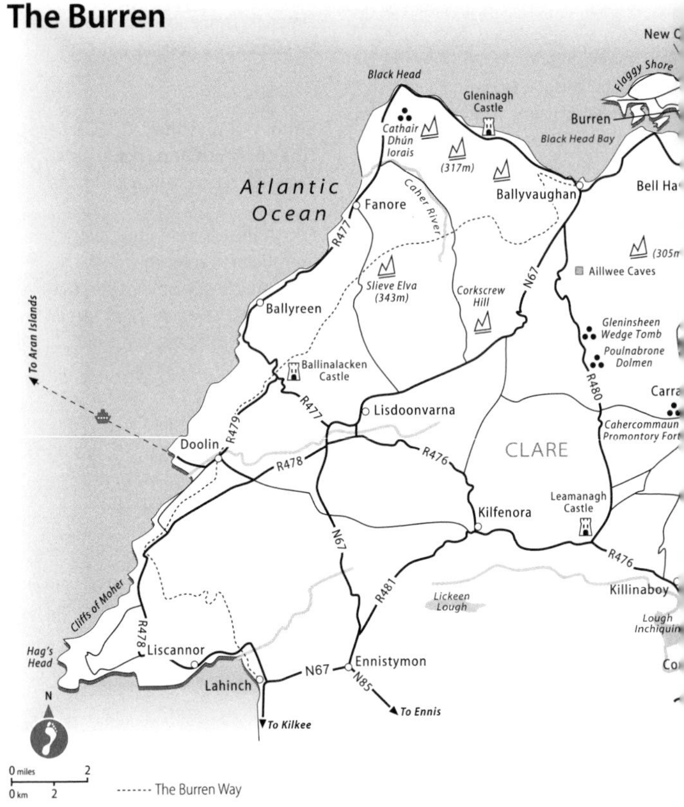

into various villages in the Burren, one of which connects with Tralee via the Killimer-Tarbert ferry. ▸▸ *See Transport, page 360, for further details.*

History

Since limestone is very high in nutrients, plants flourished here, and after the last Ice Age these hills would have been covered in hazel scrub, pine and yew trees. Later, oak, ash and elm replaced them. It wasn't erosion that removed the trees but humans, arriving around 5,000 years ago and clearing the tops of the hills for farms, defence and places of worship. The earliest signs of human presence are the huge dolmens dating back to 3000 BC. Later graves are smaller, the wedge tombs of around 1500 BC. By the Iron Age ringforts were being built, still on the tops of the hills, lived in by important men and surrounded by defensive stone walls. There are around 500 of these on the Burren. The 12th century gave us the church ruins and high crosses such as the one at Dysert O'Dea (see page 347). The 15th century saw the building of fortified houses such as Leamanagh Castle. Towns such as Lisdoonvarna or Doolin arrived much later, in the 18th century. At that time the Burren was crowded with wood cabins thatched with mud. These were later replaced by stone buildings most of which are on the lower slopes, near to old butter roads or routes into the villages. The 19th century, with famine and emigration, saw a vast reduction in the population of the Burren. As you walk around the hillsides, which are now bare of grazing animals, you can see in the cracks of the limestone blackthorn and hazel scrub building up again, creating a new forest until farming becomes viable again.

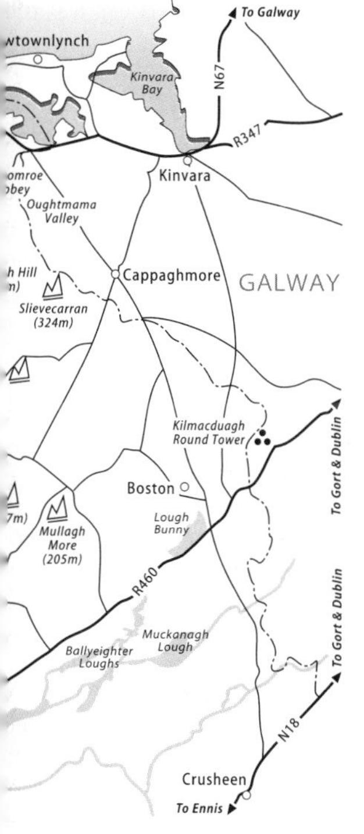

Geology

This area was the bed of a great sea 350 million years ago, its waters filled with tiny, shelled creatures and coral which, as they died, sank to the bottom. Aeons later mud and shale was dumped on top of the layer of shell, crushing it and forming limestone rock. Then the great upheaval that made the Swiss Alps and shook Ireland like a great rug into the huge folds of west Cork and Kerry threw up these lower hills. The erosion that rounded the tops of the Kerry mountains and removed the limestone from their tops removed the shale from the Burren, leaving great sheets of almost horizontal limestone bare to the elements. But limestone is highly soluble and the rain and ice filled cracks in the stone wearing them away and widening them so that what you see today looks like huge pieces of crazy paving with deep fissures. The Ice Ages further rounded and eroded the hills and left great lumps of granite rock abandoned as the meltwaters departed. You can see these huge incongruous boulders as you walk around the hills. Below the surface, cave systems were created by the water, which formed underground streams where it met harder, less soluble rock. In places caves

★ Máire Rua

Some women are destined to get a bad press and Máire Rua is one of them. Máire O'Brien, neé Neylan from Ballynagowan was the wife of Conor O'Brien, the owner of Leamanagh Castle. Legend has it that she often accompanied her husband in his attacks on English settlers in the area. In 1651 Conor met Cromwell's forces in battle and was mortally wounded. Seeing his prostrate form being carried home Maire is said to have called out, "We need no dead men here!" She nursed him all night until he died then, in an attempt to secure her son's inheritance (she would have been driven out of her house otherwise), promptly rode into Limerick and offered herself to any one of General Ireton's Cromwellian forces who would marry her. Her offer was taken up by one John Cooper, who lived to regret it, when she bumped him off (along with 24 other unfortunate husbands). Other legends of her unladylike ways include hanging her servants out of windows, and she died the death she deserved: entombed alive in a hollow tree.

The house was occupied by Cromwell's troops until 1660. When her son Donal reclaimed the house he found it ruined. He became the MP for Clare and served in that position for 20 years, to be followed centuries later by de Valera and Daniel O'Connell, who also held the job.

collapsed, forming deep depressions in the rock above, called *turloughs*, which can fil with water when it rains and the land below becomes soaked.

Corofin to Lisdoonvarna → *Phone code: 065. Colour map 2, grid C3.*

Continuing on the road to Lisdoonvarna brings you first to **Killinaboy Church**, a ruine 16th-century church up on the left-hand side of the road in a field. Not much to look a but worth the stop for the **Sheela-na-gig** over the south doorway. Next stop i **Leamanagh Castle,** rudely bursting out of a field beside the road to Ballyvaughan. Th eastern side is a 14th-century fortified tower with a stone vault on the roof with gu emplacements. The rest of the building was a house added in the 1640s and lived i by various people, among them **Máire Rua**, one of Ireland's very wicked women. Th castle is not accessible but there is a good view from the road.

Kilfenora → *Phone code: 065. Colour map 2, grid C3.*

This is a major part of the tour bus route around Clare. The **Cathedral** is probably on of the smallest you'll ever see, and it is still used for worship. The church was founde by St Fachtnan in the sixth century, replaced by a stone building, which was burne down in 1055 by an unfriendly O'Brien, rebuilt, destroyed in an accidental fire in 110 rebuilt again and made into a bishopric in 1152, an event that you can see pictured o the Doorty High Cross (west of the church; the 12th-century equivalent of the Polaroi snap). It was never a popular place with bishops; Dr Richard Betts, offered the job b Charles I, said he had no wish to become bishop of the poorest see in Ireland.

The current building is a 13th-century site restructured in the 19th century. Th chancel (the east end of the church where the altar was sited) has some badly carve 13th- and 14th-century bishops on it but the north wall has a quite beautiful sedilia (seat set into the wall) with delicate stone traceries on the three-arched design Around the church and in a field to the west are the famous stone crosses.

Beside the church is the **Burren Centre** ⓘ *T065-7088030, www.theburrencentre.ie* Mar-Jun and Sep-Oct daily 1000-1700; Jun-Aug daily 0930-1800. €5.50. It ha information about the Burren, audio-visual displays and lots of people milling about.

★ Lisdoonvarna → *Phone code: 065. Colour map 2, grid C3.*

From Kilfenora a road leads to Lisdoonvarna, home of that catchy song by Christy Moore and the even more famous matchmakers. Until quite recently families would bring their daughters here in September, after the hay was in, to meet gentlemen or, better still , farmers. Nowadays the matchmaking festival is a good excuse for a party, with the various pubs in town and around, each putting on events such as ballroom dancing, ceilidhs and live music. The month-long festival has a host of regular visitors, who come every year to see friends. Midweek the party is good fun, at weekends it gets inevitably more inebriated and loud.

The town is a quiet and pleasant holiday destination for the rest of the year, another good place to consider as a base for your walks around the Burren, and the Carrigann Hotel (see page 357) organizes walking holidays and also has self-guided walks all over the Burren for its guests.

Spa Wells ⓘ *T065-7074023. Jun-Sep 1000-1800.* Lisdoonvarna's chief place of interest is the Spa Wells, Ireland's oldest and only working spa where the waters are drunk and bathed in. The water contains sulphur, iron, magnesium and iodine and the spa offers a sulphur bath, massage, wax treatments aromatherapy and reflexology. Rates start from around €20 for a massage or sulphur bath but aromatherapy treatment costs more.

Burren Smokehouse ⓘ *Doolin Rd, T065-7074432, www.burrensmokehouse.ie. Daily 0900-1900.* Also in town is the Burren Smokehouse, where you can learn all about the traditional way of smoking salmon, try a bit and perhaps buy some. There is a shop and a pub, the Roadside Tavern, where you can try locally smoked trout, salmon, mackerel and eel.

West of Lisdoonvarna

To the southwest of Lisdoonvarna is the little, overcooked village of Doolin, famous for its traditional music; the frighteningly high Cliffs of Moher and, beyond them, Liscannor, quieter but with pleasant pubs and a good hostel; Lahinch, on the very outskirts of the Burren, a popular family resort; and Ennistymon, quietly mouldering inland but with some good music pubs and a stunning waterfall. Part of the Burren Way follows the coast a little way inland, coming close to the cliffs at Doolin and following them closely round to Hag's Head.

★ Doolin → *Phone code: 065. Colour map 2, grid C3. www.doolin-tourism.com.*

This is a long, drawn-out strip of a village, one that you couldn't imagine could be a mecca for anyone. But every summer it heaves with budget travellers and musicians from as far away as Canada, Australia, Sweden, Germany (not Ireland, note) and you're more likely to hear a foreign language here than English. The draw is its reputation as a centre for traditional music but what you are likely to hear – chord sequences repeated ad nauseam – is not always what you might hope for. However, when it's good, it's very, very good. The north end of the village is called Doolin, while the next block of houses, pubs and the post office is called Roadford and the southern end of the village is known as Fisherstreet. Here are a couple of the hostels and O'Connor's Pub, see pages 357 and 358.

Cliffs of Moher

From Lisdoonvarna the cliffs are signposted on the R478. They're impossible to miss – a gigantic car and coach park (free to enter, €3 to leave) marks the spot. Pass beyond the visitor centre, which explains that these are cliffs, leave behind the tour

Cornelius O'Brien

One of Ireland's many eccentric landlords, Cornelius O'Brien, a lesser scion of the O'Brien clan, was MP for Clare from the 1830s until he died in 1857. He helped select Daniel O'Connell for the job before he took it over and supported the repeal of the Act of Union. In the 1847 election he came close to a duel with the agent of his opponent. Lord Palmerston said about him: "He was the best Irish MP we ever had. He didn't open his mouth in 20 years." He was never an absentee landlord and history tells that he considerably improved conditions for his tenants. There were no evictions on his land during the Famine or at any other time. The only blot on his copybook appears to be the fact that the contributions by grateful tenants towards the column erected to his memory in the cemetery above St Brigid's Well in Liscannor were actually written into their tenancy agreements!

groups who walk to the edge and take a photo and follow the path a little way to the south. The cliffs face due west and the best time to go is at sunset on a clear day. In front of you are the Aran islands, and beyond to the north are the hills of Connemara. A little to the north of the visitors' centre is the **O'Brien Tower** built by Cornelius O'Brien, who also built the wall along the edge of the cliffs. The cliffs soar for 8 km all the way south to Hag's Head, and the **Burren Way** footpath follows them. You can join the waymarked route, which isn't signposted from the car park, at the O'Brien tower.

Liscannor → *Phone code: 065. Colour map 2, grid C3.*

Prettier and quieter than Doolin and not so towny as Lahinch further down the coast, Liscannor might make a good place to stop for the night (see page 357). It has two sights to visit, one very old and the other very new, and was also the birthplace of John Philip Holland, a Fenian who invented the submarine in order to sink British warships.

On the road into Liscannor from the Cliffs of Moher is **St Brigid's Well**, noticeable by the enormous great pillar erected by tenants to Cornelius O'Brien at his suggestion. O'Brien improved the well, which is one of the most revered holy wells in Ireland, dedicated to the sixth-century Kildare nun. The grotto is filled with pictures and discarded crutches of the sick who have been healed here. The Aran Islanders traditionally came here to worship in October, but in modern times it is July when the crowds arrive to seek healing and attend services. It is almost certain that the site is pre-Christian in origin, adapted by the Christian missionaries to suit their own needs and adopted into the Christian religion.

Continuing on into Liscannor you pass the ruins of **Birchfield House**, O'Brien's pile on the left, and then arrive at Liscannor's newest contribution to the culture of Ireland – **Liscannor Stone** ⓘ *summer only, daily*, a heritage centre-cum-shop with displays about the area's wavy-patterned slate, which you can see all over Ireland as street paving, stone cladding on houses and even roof tiles. At the western end of the village is a sandy beach.

Lahinch → *Phone code: 065. Colour map 2, grid C3.*

A typical Irish seaside town, Lahinch is full of places to eat and stay (see pages 358 and 359), some good music pubs, a mile-long beach with crashing breakers (see surfing, page 360) and **Seaworld** ⓘ *T065-7081900, www.lahinchseaworld.com; Aquarium €5, pool and jacuzzi €5*, a leisure centre and aquarium with a swimming pool, and sharks plus other sea creatures. The **tourist office**, *Lahinch Fáilte* is in The Dell, T065-7082082, www.lahinchfailte.com. Summer, daily 0900-2200; winter, daily 0900-1700.

Ennistymon → *Phone code: 065. Colour map 2, grid C3.*

To complete this circuit of the area west of Lisdoonvarna, head east out of Lahinch to Ennistymon, a backwater on the tourist trail, which probably looks very much like it did in 1950 or thereabouts. The chief point of interest here is waterfall known as the **Cascades**, especially if it has been raining. It is signposted in the village through a laneway beside the Archway Bar. The town has a couple of interesting old shops whose window displays can't have been changed in years, and some decent pubs (see pages 359 and 359).

North and east of Lisdoonvarna

The area around Ballyvaughan is really the most beautiful part of the Burren, with its dashing coastline and cornucopia of wild flowers. To the west the coast road skirts around to Fanore, a little strip of a village, and to the east is Carron where there are a couple of interesting places to visit. There are lots of good walks in the area, including a section of the Burren Way. The route from Lisdoonvarna to Ballyvaughan passes through Corkscrew Hill, a Famine relief road which twists its way down to the village through some outstanding views of Galway Bay.

Ballyvaughan and around → *Colour map 2, grid C3.*

Ballyvaughan is a tourist-centred village where one of the first holiday villages in Ireland was built. Basically a group of houses, post office, mobile bank and hotel built around a T-junction, it isn't as busy as Lisdoonvarna or Doolin but might make a pleasant night's stay with its quiet pubs and a couple of good places to eat (see page 358).

The **Burren Exposure Centre** ⓘ *T065-707727, Mar-May daily 1000-1700; Jun-Sep daily 1000-1800, €5, on N67 300 m outside Ballyvaughan on route to Galway*, is east of the village on the coast road, and is a good idea for a rainy day or as an introduction to the Burren early on in your visit. It uses giant screens with videos and slide shows to explain the history and mythology and flora of the Burren as well as the nature of the rocks themselves. There is a good restaurant with amazing sea views and a shop selling knitwear and crafts.

A little way beyond the Burren Exposure is **Bishop's Quarter Beach**, a sandy beach with dunes and excellent for swimming. At Bell Harbour are the ruins of **Corcomroe Abbey** ⓘ *1 km inland*, founded by the O'Briens in the late 12th century. Cistercians ran this place, probably well into the 17th century. In a county where Romanesque carvings are ten a penny, these are well worth the visit with carved heads, opium poppies, and lilies of the valley.

The little peninsula along this stretch of coast is called Finavarra. Here is **Mount Vernon Lodge**, one-time home to Lady Gregory and temporary home to such luminaries as Yeats. West of the little village of New Quay is the **Flaggy Shore**, a place where the Burren limestone flags go right down to the sea.

Abbey Hill walk Beyond Bell Harbour is a fascinating and undemanding walk around Abbey Hill, especially if you are interested in wild flowers. At Bell Harbour, instead of turning left for Burren take the right turn, which brings you out to the road from Corofin to Galway. Around 4 km along this road look for a green road on the left as you pass Abbey Hill (also on your left). Park the car here and head along the green road to a gate into a field. The green road continues around Abbey Hill but your walk takes you higher and around the brow of the hill to the south. The glory of this walk are the wild flowers in this field though it is difficult to walk without crushing orchids or burnett roses underfoot. At the top of the hill there are excellent views of Corcomroe Abbey and the green valley that gave it its original name Sancta Maria de Petra Fertili – Saint Mary of the Fertile Rock. Following the contour of the hill round to the west there are stunning views over the long inlet from Ballyvaughan Bay and Bell Harbour, with a Martello tower visible way over to the west at Finavarra Point. Due west at the other side of Poulnaclough Bay is the site of a battle fought in 1267 where Conor O'Brien, whose tomb can be seen in the abbey, died. Follow the contour of the hill around until you can see the green road again below you.

★ **Aillwee Cave** ⓘ *T065-7077036, www.aillweecave.ie. Mar-Oct daily 1000-1730. Admission by tour only, €7.50. Visit early morning before the tour groups build up.* On the road to Lisdoonvarna is the much-hyped Aillwee Cave, another good rainy-day activity. The cave system is typical of the caves that run throughout the Burren, usually where the limestone rock meets the shale or sandstone at the border between the two areas. The huge cave was discovered in 1944 and is about 600 m long with side caves, a waterfall, and stalactite and stalagmite formations. There are also the remains of bear pits where the claw marks of giant brown bears which once inhabited the caves can still be seen. Outside the caves is a nature walk and you can also scramble up the hill above the cave to look at the views over Galway Bay. In the entrance there are cheese-making demonstrations of the local Burren Gold cheese.

Gleninsheen wedge tombs A little way south of the cave on the N480 are the Gleninsheen wedge tombs, a series of tombs constructed of slabs in a box formation, facing west and tapering to the east. They are Bronze Age burial places and nearby, indicated on the *Rambler's Guide & Map, Ballyvaughan*, is the spot where in the 1930s a small boy found a gold gorget, or neck collar, one of the most beautiful and undamaged in existence and now in the National Museum.

Poulnabrone Portal Dolmen Continuing along the N480 brings you to the 5000-year-old Poulnabrone Portal Dolmen, swathed all summer long in tour buses but beautiful nonetheless. It rears up out of the bare limestone, not quite vertical, aspiring to something. When excavated it revealed urns containing the cremated remains of 16 late-Stone Age people, and some polished flint implements.

Burren Perfumery ⓘ *T065-7089102, www.burren-perfumery.com. Jan-May and Oct-Dec daily 0900-1700; Jun-Sep daily 0900-1700; Dec-Feb, phone in advance. Free. From Ballyvaughan take the first left after the Poulnabrone Dolmen, and at Carron turn right at the church and then left to find the perfumery.* East of the N480, just beyond the dolmen along a minor road, is Carron, a tiny village worth visiting for the Burren Perfumery, which has audio-visual displays on the making of perfume, a shop, and you can walk around the still and extracting machinery to watch the process in action.

Ballyvaughan to Fanore

Heading west is a scenic drive through Gleninagh and Fanore around the **Gleninagh Mountains**. About 6 km west of Ballyvaughan is **Gleninagh Castle**, a 16th-century edifice built by the O'Loughlans and inhabited by them until the 1840s. Continuing on, the road hugs close to the coast. Just before a pier a green road sets off around the mountain and makes for a pleasant walk. You can climb anywhere here to the stone ringfort at the top of the hill and on a clear day see what an excellent defensive position it made for a fortified farmhouse. The hillside may be covered in a botanist's daydream of wild flowers, depending on the month. Continuing round **Black Head** to Fanore brings you to a strung-out little village of a few houses, a shop and a pub. There is a good sandy beach with dunes where it is fairly safe to swim (there's a lifeguard there for part of the year) and the Atlantic breakers are often good for surfing.

Sleeping

Kilfenora *p352*
E **Carraig Liath**, on the R476 just outside of town, T065-7088075. This is a pleasant place that does an evening meal on request.
E **Ms Murphy**, Main St, T065-7088040, lika@eircom.net. Affordable B&B.
F **Boghill Centre Hostel**, signposted off the road between Kilfenora and Lisdoonvarna, T065-7074644, www.boghill.com. A terrific hostel, with dorm beds, singles, double en suite rooms, optional breakfast and veggie evening meals. Also runs 'creative energy weeks'.

Lisdoonvarna *p353*
Lisdoonvarna has an inordinate number of hotels, but for all of the places listed here it is a good idea to book in advance if you intend to come in Sep.
B-C **Ballinalacken Castle Hotel**, Ballyvaughan Rd (R477), T065-7074025, www.ballinalacken castle.com. The views are stupendous and the rooms quaintly old-fashioned and huge. Lovely big library, Victorian lobby with a Connemara marble fireplace, stunning views from the dining room of the Cliffs of Moher.
B-C **Sheedy's Restaurant and Country Inn**, T065-7074026, www.sheedys.com. Small but very popular and stylish place with a lobby that wouldn't be out of place in a London warehouse conversion. Minimalist decor downstairs but the rooms are more traditionally furnished.
C **Carrigann Hotel**, Doolin Rd, T065- 7074036, www.gateway-to-the-burren.com. A modern, busy hotel, which caters to an interesting crowd of sporty types and walkers as well as the passing trade. Organizes walking weekends and can arrange individual excursions as well as self-guided walks. Drying rooms are a blessing in this rainy country.
C-E **Kincora House**, T065-7074300, www.kin cora-hotel.com. A small guest house in the centre of town, with popular pub attached.
E **Hilltop**, Doolin Rd, T065-7074134. B&B within walking distance of village. 1 family room, 3 doubles (with en suite bathroom).
E **St Jude's**, on the N67 Doolin Rd, T065-7074108. Bungalow B&B with 4 rooms.

Doolin *p353*
Doolin gets very crowded in the summer, book your accommodation well in advance.
B-D **Aran View House Hotel and Restaurant**, Coast Rd, north end of the village, T065-7074061, www.aranview.com. Comfortable and friendly small hotel in a Georgian house. One of the best places in Doolin to bed down for a night or so.
E **Churchfield**, Fisherstreet, T065-707429, churchfield@eircom.net. B&B with 6 rooms, close to pubs and buses stop outside.
E **Cullinan's Restaurant and Guesthouse**, T065-7074183, www.cullinansdoolin.com. In the village centre, small, comfortable and reasonably-priced place with a good restaurant.
E **Toomullin House**, T065-7074723, www.toomullin.com. This B&B is 1 min walk from the pubs and handy for the Aran ferry.
F **Aille River Hostel**, Roadford, T065-70744260, ailleriver@esatclear.ie. Converted old farmhouse between Roadford and Fisherstreet. Scenic location beside an old stone bridge. Some private double rooms in this friendly hostel with bike hire.
F **Flanagan's Village Hostel**, T065-7074564. Open all year, mostly dorm beds available.
F **Paddy's Doolin Hostel**, Fisherstreet, T065-7074006, www.doolinhostel.com. Very modern, nearly a hundred beds.
F **Rainbow Hostel**, Roadford, T065-7074415, www.rainbowhostel.com. Small hostel in a typical cottage of the area. Very laid back, some double rooms, turf fires, bike hire.

Camping
Nagle's, T065-7074458. By the harbour, €6 per tent plus €3 per person. Apr-Sep.
O'Connor's, T065-7074314. Similar prices and opening times and the option of farmhouse B&B. Best of all, camp at the Aille River Hostel and enjoy the hostel facilities.

Liscannor *p354*
C-D **Logue's Liscannor Hotel**, T065-7081186, www.liscannorbayhotel.com. Excellent views across the bay from some of its rooms and altogether a very comfortable place to stay.

For an explanation of the sleeping and eating price codes used in this guide, see inside the front cover. Other relevant information is found in Essentials pages 39-45.

E **Seahaven**, just out of the village on the way to Lahinch, T065-7081385, seahaven@eircom.net. A big house with 6 rooms, open Jan-Nov with good sea views.
F **Village Hostel**, T065-7081385, liscanorvillage hostel@eircom.net. Open Apr-Oct, has private rooms at reasonable rates, well run, camping.

Lahinch *p354*

A **Moy House**, Main St, T065-7082800, www.moyhouse.com. Stirring sea views from this visually distinctive, luxury-style, country house.
D **Dough Mor Lodge**, T065-7082063, www.doughmorlodge.com. Partly stone-fronted guest house with 6 en suite rooms.
F **Lahinch Hostel**, Church St, T065-7081040, www.visitlahinch.com. Modern hostel with family and double rooms. Downstairs is a very popular restaurant.

North and east of Lisdoonvarna *p355*

There are lots of B&Bs all around the coast east of Ballyvaughan and all of them can get booked up in summer, so book in advance.
A-B **Gregan's Castle Hotel**, Corkscrew Hill, T065-707705, www.gregans.ie. Lovely old country house with lots of room to relax and imagine you are the landed gentry. Big library, lounge, bar. Country house-style bedrooms, no TV, excellent restaurant.
C-D **Clare's Rock Hostel**, Carron, T065-7089129, www.claresrock.com. Dormitory and family rooms in an old stone building, bike hire. Open late May-Sep.
C-D **Hyland's Hotel**, Ballyvaughan, T065-7077037, www.hylandsburren.com. Attractive, old-fashioned hotel run by the same family for generations.
D **Rusheen Lodge**, Corkscrew Hill Rd, Ballyvaughan, T065-7077092, www.rusheen lodge.com. Very pleasant and welcoming guest house. Good bedrooms, great breakfast.

Eating

Kilfenora *p352*

ᛘ **Vaughan's**. Serves a fair range of meals.

Lisdoonvarna *p353*

ᛘᛘᛘ **Ballinalacken Castle Hotel**, has a restaurant that is a rare treat of a place. Nouvelle Irish, without the pretentious vocabulary, and the best dark-and-white chocolate mousse cake on the planet. Eat while admiring the stunning skyscapes of the Cliffs of Moher and the Atlantic. Ask for a window table when making a reservation, or get there early.
ᛘᛘᛘ-ᛘᛘ **Sheedy's Restaurant**. The most fun place to eat in Lisdoonvarna. Excellent balance between stylish Nouvelle Irish cooking and adequate portions. Good wine list and service.
ᛘᛘ-ᛘ **Royal Spa** and **Rathbaun** are opposite each other in the main street. Both with a fairly wide and conventional menu of fish and meat dishes for around the same price.
ᛘ **Dolmen Inn**, in centre. Less expensive fare, quick meals with main courses around €12. Open till 2130.

Doolin *p353*

ᛘᛘ-ᛘ **Cullinan's**, T065-7074183, www.cullinans doolin.com. Specializes in Irish and continental-style seafood using locally caught fish, but also has meat and vegetarian dishes. Closed Wed and an early dinner for around €25.
ᛘ **Bruach na hAille**, Roadford, T065-7074120. Serves seafood and vegetarian dishes in an elegant old house. Open 1000-2100.
ᛘ **Doolin Café**, Roadford. Has vegetarian food.
ᛘ **Flagship Restaurant**, Ballyvoe, T065-7074688. Good food, open Easter-Sep, 1000-1800, for morning coffee, lunch, tea and home-cooked delights. Even better, being part of the Doolin Craft Gallery, there is an excellent collection of art and craft work for sale.
ᛘ **McGann's**, Roadford. Does typical pub food at good prices – Irish stew, garlic mussels, baked salmon, at around €10 for a main course. Food is served till 2130 in a dark, candle-lit interior.
ᛘ **O'Connor's**, Fisherstreet, T065-7074168. Good for pub food.

Liscannor *p354*

The village's pubs all do good pub food with extensive menus, dominated by seafood.
Café, at Liscannor Stone. Conjures up home-made light meals and preserves to take away.
Captain's Deck, T065-7081666. Is at the west end of the village next to the hostel and serves food 1000-2200.
Joseph McHugh, next door to Vaughan's. A totally unreconstructed pub with a grocery section and all. It serves some food and has music on Tue nights.
ᛘᛘ **Vaughan's Anchor Inn**. Has an attached restaurant serving lots of seafood at around €14 for a main course and does pub food

and B&B as well, although since it also has music during the summer this might be a noisy experience.

Lahinch *p354*

₮₮ **Barrtrá**, just outside Lahinch on the way to Milltown Malbay, T065-7081280. Set in a pleasant garden overlooking Liscannor Bay. It is a modern seafood restaurant, focusing on locally available sources but including oddities such as rollmops, duck, and several good vegetarian options. It has an exemplary early evening set menu 1700-1830, around €20. Later than that dinner will work out around €35. Closed Mon except Jul and Aug.

₮₮-₮ **Kenny's**, Main St. A very touristy place, which closes for the winter but has music as well as a good seafood menu in summer.

₮₮-₮ **Village Inn**, Main St. Has a similar menu to Kenny's and does music.

₮ **Bay View Restaurant**, below the Lahinch Hostel. Serves basic dishes with main courses at lunch time around €12.

Ennistymon *p355*

₮ **Byrne's Restaurant**, T065-7071080. Good value meals, especially if you appreciate fresh seafood.

North and east of Lisdoonvarna *p355*

₮₮₮ **Gregan's Castle Hotel**. The grandest place to eat but you should book in advance. Lovely views from the windows, especially at dusk as the Burren hills turn a dull Mars red. Food is well cooked, and comes stacked in little mountains. 5 courses are around €50, any 2 around €40.

₮₮-₮ **Monk's**, just beside the pier on the Fanore Rd at Ballyvaughan, T065-7077059. A pub and restaurant, with a big seafood menu. Very popular, but pricey.

₮₮-₮ **Trí na Chéile Restaurant**, Ballyvaughan, T065-7077103. A newish restaurant in the village, and the appealing food is competitively priced.

₮ **Aillwee Cave**. The café here is not half bad. Try Burren Gold cheese with baked potatoes.

₮ **An Fear Gorta**, by the harbour in Ballyvaughan. Serves superb teas and smoked salmon open sandwiches in the garden, conservatory or dining room. Open Jun-Sep 1100-1730, closed Sun.

₮ **Whitethorn Restaurant**, at the Burren Exposure. Worth trying.

Pubs and music

Kilfenora *p352*

Linane's. Traditional music nights in summer.

Nagle's. Music at weekends all year.

Vaughan's, T065-7088004. Traditional music and set dancing in the barn on Thu and Sun.

Lisdoonvarna *p353*

Most pubs will have some music some nights, so look around town for notices.

Kincora Bar, Doolin Rd. Has music at weekends in summer.

Meg Maguire's, Main St. Music in summer.

Roadside Tavern. Music mostly in summer.

Royal Spa. The bar has a good local reputation.

Doolin *p353*

Considering the number of people in Doolin in the summer it is surprising that they all fit into the 3 pubs. During the summer expect live music every night of the week.

Aranview House Hotel, try the bar inside if you need a rest from the noise and musical mayhem.

McDermott's. Used to be the place where the locals went to get away from the tourists, but now no different from the rest.

McGann's, Roadford end. Just as packed as O'Connor's.

O'Connor's, Fisherstreet. The most renowned of the pubs.

Lahinch *p354*

All the pubs in town offer some nights of music in summer.

The 19th, Main St. One of the best, with music every night in summer and Sat in winter.

Galvin's, at the top of Main St. Music Mon, Wed, Fri and Sat in summer.

O'Looney's. Aptly named, with pub food and music Mon, Wed and Fri.

Ennistymon *p355*

Daly's Pub, Main St. Live music most nights.

North of Lisdoonvarna *p355*

Greene's, Ballyvaughan. Often has a traditional music night.

Monk's and **O'Brien's**, Ballyvaughan. Have traditional music in the summer.

Ólólainn, near the harbour, Ballyvaughan. Check this place out for a quiet drink.

Activities and tours

Lahinch *p354*
Surfing Surf boards for rent on the beach, T065-7081543, www.lahinchsurfshop.com.

North of Lisdoonvarna *p355*
Horse riding **Burren Riding Centre**, Fanore, T065-7076140.

Kayaking **River Ocean Kayak**, 2 Muckinish West, T065-7077043, www.riverocean.com. Sea kayaking trips in Galway Bay.

Transport

The Burren *p353, map p350*
Bike hire **Burke's**, The Square, Lisdoonvarna, T065-7074022. Some of the hostels in Doolin have bikes for hire. **Monk's Bar**, Ballyvaughan, T065-7077059.

Bus Daily buses from Doolin, T065-6824177, to **Ennis**. Also to **Galway**, **Tralee** and **Cork**. The **Limerick** to **Doolin** bus passes through **Lahinch**, T061-313333, 3 times a day in summer, and twice on Sun. So too does the **Cork-Galway** service. Enquire at tourist offices for bus times outside summer.

Ferry From **Doolin**, between Apr and Sep, there are regular ferries to the **Aran islands** with Doolin Ferries, T065-7074455, www.doolinferries.com. In the summer, ferries run up to 7 times a day to **Inisheer** and 3 a day to **Inishmór** and **Inishmaan**. It is possible to get singles and travel on to **Galway** from the islands. Return fares around €28, journey times are between 30 and 50 mins, and departure times run from 1000 to 1830 between Jun and Aug. There are fewer ferries at other months and on Sur

West Clare

The west coast of Clare from Lahinch down through the seaside towns of Miltowr Malbay, Quilty, Kilkee and Loop Head is a pleasant day's drive. Kilkee is an Irish holida destination, while Kilrush offers a heritage centre, trips to Scattery Island, and dolphins in the estuary of the Shannon. » *For Sleeping, Eating and other listings, see pages 361-363.*

Lahinch to Kilkee

Miltown Malbay Through fairly uneventful countryside, the road south from Lahinch finds its way along the coast to Miltown Malbay, a Victorian resort close to **Spanish Point** which is an excellent sandy beach with good surfing when the surf's up. Legend tells that in 1588 sailors from the shipwrecked Spanish Armada swam ashore here to be arrested on the orders of Richard Bingham, the governor of Connaught, and late executed. From Miltown Malbay the road continues past occasional caravan sites to **Quilty** where there is another sandy beach. The next town along the route is **Doonbeg**, a tiny village with a white sandy beach and dunes beyond. Another Armada ship ran aground here in 1588, and its survivors were also carted away to execution.

Kilkee, Loop Head and Carrigaholt

A seaside resort since Victorian times, **Kilkee** is bucket-and-spade and amusement arcade territory. The beach here explains the popularity of the place – long, golden and sheltered, with beautiful cliffs at its western end. At the same end of the beach are 'pollock holes', so called because pollock lurk about in them, as do lots of othe interesting varieties of marine life. There is also a golf club, some excellent walks along the cliffs, and **Waterworld** ⓘ *T065-9056855, Jun 1200-2000, Jul, Aug 0930-2200*, a leisure centre with water slides, a wave machine and kiddies' pools.

Loop Head makes an interesting drive or an exciting cycle or walk. The coastline is full of sea stacks and birdlife and a coastal path follows the cliffs all 24 km down to Loop Head. At **Intrinsic Bay**, named for the emigrant ship that sank here in 1836, is a sea stack with a medieval oratory. In the church in **Kilbaha** is the **Little Ark** dating back to penal times when Catholics were prohibited from saying mass on land: this moveable altar was carried down to the shore and mass said there. The church stained glass window portrays such a mass.

★ **Carrigaholt** has some nice pubs, a tiny beach and **Dolphinwatch** ⓘ *The Square, T065-9058156, www.dolphinwatch.ie, Apr-Oct weather permitting, bookings begin at 0800 on day of trip, 2-hr trips, €18, look for information about individual trips/ weather on the pier*, which does trips out into the estuary to see one of only five known groups of bottlenose dolphins in the waters of Europe. There are about 120 of them and trippers are rarely disappointed, often spotting nursery groups of young dolphins. There is an information centre and booking office in the village with audio-visual displays about the dolphins, and of course t-shirts. The **tourist office** is on O'Connell St. Open Jun-Sep Mon-Sat 1000-1800.

Carrigaholt also has a 15th-century, five-storey tower house very strategically placed overlooking the Shannon. Over the doorway is a murder hole, placed there so that heavy objects could be dropped onto unsuspecting invading heads. The trick didn't work, though, in 1598 when Daniel O'Brien took the castle from the MacMahons. The O'Briens held it till Cromwell turned up in 1651 and got it back for a while at the Restoration. But William of Orange reallocated it in 1691 to the Earl of Albemarle, who sold it to the Burton family. They managed to hold on to it until the late 19th century.

★ Kilrush and Scattery Island → *Phone code: 065. Colour map 3, grid A3.*

On first inspection there does not seem much reason to linger in Kilrush. The old gaol is now a *Supervalu* supermarket and the new self-flushing toilets are a treat, but is that it? Fortunately, there's more. At the mouth of the creek is the **marina**, www.kilrushcreekmarina.com. Then there's the renovated **walled gardens** of the landlord family, the Vandeleurs ⓘ *T065-9051760. €3. Open 1000-1800 in summer (1600 in winter)*. The town also has a **Heritage Centre** ⓘ *The Square, T065-9051596, Jun-Aug Mon-Fri 1000-1800, Sat-Sun 1200- 1600, €3*, telling the story of Kilrush in landlord times. The **tourist office** is in the Town Hall, Market Square, T065-9051577, www.kilrush.ie. Open Jun-Aug Mon-Sat 1000-1300, 1400-1800. **Dolphin-spotting** ⓘ *T065-9051327, Apr-Oct, €16*, trips depart from the marina three times a day subject to the weather.

A car ferry operates between Killimer, 8 km from Kilrush, and Tarbert in County Kerry. See page 349 for details.

Scattery Island ⓘ *Interpretive centre: Merchant's Quay, T065-9052114, mid-Jun to mid-Sep daily 1000-1830, last admission 30 mins before closing. Free. Scattery Island Ferries, Kilrush Marina Building, T065-9051237. Phone for times because trips are subject to demand and the weather. €12, journey time 20 mins.* The best reason to come to Kilrush is to make the trip to Scattery Island, inhabited until quite recently and worth visiting for the remains of the monastic settlement that was established there in the sixth century by St Senan, who first fought a monster called Cata on the island. There is a 36.5-m high tower, and the remains of the cathedral and several other churches. The settlements were attacked by Vikings, who settled there for a time before Brian Ború took the island back. Then the churches were desecrated by an Englishman called William Hoel in 1179. The site became a place of pilgrimage and sailors sailed new boats sunwards round it and collected pebbles from the beach for luck. On the island is an interpretive centre that tells its story.

Sleeping

Kilkee, Loop Head and Carrigahalt *p360*
Kilkee makes a down-to-earth alternative if you've got tired of the ethnic rusticity of the rest of Clare, while Miltown Malbay and Carrigaholt are quieter and a good base if you want to do some walking in the area. Most of the B&Bs in Miltown Malbay charge standard rates of around €30 per person sharing.

B-C Bellbridge House Hotel, Spanish Point, Miltown Malbay, T065-7084038, www.bellbridgehotelclare.com. Close to the golf course and beach. Open all year.
C-D Halpin's Townhouse Hotel, Erin St, Kilkee, T065-9056032, www.halpinsprivate hotels.com. Very central, small renovated townhouse hotel and restaurant. Open fires, old-fashioned bar.
C-E San Antone, Drummin, Miltown Malbay, T065-7084511. B&B 3 km out of town, quiet location, good views.
D-E Kilkee Bay Hotel, Kilkee, T065-9060060, www.kilkee-bay.com. On the road to Kilrush, this huge complex of hotel and apartments is geared to long-stay family groups. Restaurant, nightclub, bar, creche, tennis court.
D-E Strand Guest House, Kilkee, T065-9056177, www.clareguesthouse.com. On the seafront, seafood restaurant.
E Berry Lodge, Annagh, Miltown Malbay, T065-7087022. At the top end of this price category, 5 rooms and a good restaurant.
E Kilkee Hostel, O'Curry St, Kilkee, T065-9056209, kilkeehostel@eircom.net. Well run but no double rooms, just dormitory or family rooms. Café. Bike hire.
E Purtill's, O'Curry St, Kilkee, T065-9056771. B&B in nicely restored townhouse in the main street. Bar and restaurant, traditional music in summer.
E Anvil Farm, a couple of km past Cross, Loop Head Peninsula, T065-9058016, www.anvilfarm.com. This friendly B&B, with the option of dinner, is worth considering.

Camping

Green Acres, Doonaha, Kilkee, T065-9057011. Small place with space for 5 tents, signposted off the N67 Kilkee to Kilrush road.

Kilrush and Slattery Island *p361*

There are no hotels or guest houses in Kilrush. Accommodation is either in B&Bs (around €30 per person sharing) or in the hostel.
E Bruach na Coille, Killimer Rd, T065-9052250, www.clarkekilrush.com. B&B 1 km out of town on the N67 road to Killimer. Set in pretty gardens opposite those of the Vandeleurs.
E Crotty's, Market Sq, T065-9052470. Central B&B and above a pub with live music in summer and rooms share bathrooms.
E Fortfield Farm, Donail, T065-9051457, fortfield@eircom.net. B&B about 4 km outside town on the road to Killimer. Children might enjoy staying here and adults will appreciate the tea and scones on arrival.
E Kilrush Creek Lodge, Kilrush Marina, T065-9052595. Used to be a hostel but now B&B. Rooms overlook the marina or the estuary.
F Katie O'Connor's, Frances St, T065-9051133, www.westclare.com. A pleasant hostel with some character, a choice of rooms and bike hire.

Eating

Kilkee, Loop Head and Carrigahalt *p360*

Long Dock, Carrigaholt, T065-9058106. A pub/restaurant where you can eat locally-caught seafood and listen to good music.
Old Bistro and **Pantry**, both in O'Curry St. Serve palatable meals and the big hotels all have reliable restaurants.

Kilrush and Slattery Island *p361*

Crotty's has a good reputation.
Haven Arms and **Kelly's**, both in Henry St. Do good food.

Pubs and music

Kilkee, Loop Head and Carrigahalt *p360*

Clancy's, Miltown Malbay. Outside of the festival this is the place to find good music.
Myles Creek, O'Curry St, Kilkee, T065-9056670. Regular sessions of traditional music.
O'Mara's, O'Curry St, Kilkee, T065-9056286. Regular sessions of traditional music.
Ocean View Bar, Doonbeg, between Miltown Malbay and Kilkee.
West Clare Jazz School, based in Kilbaha, T065-9058229 for details. Cross and Carrigaholt. Annual summer school in Jun, classes in Kilbaha and free performances in the bars in those 3 villages.
Willy Clancy Summer School, Miltown Malbay. In the 1st week or so of July, everyone in traditional music turns up here.

Kilrush and Slattery Island *p361*

Crotty's, T065-9052470. Good music sessions midweek and Sat in summer.
The Haven Arms, Henry St. Has music every Thu and Fri. Mid-Aug sees a festival celebrating Mrs Crotty, the one-time owner of Crotty's bar who was a renowned concertina player.

Activities and tours

Kilkee, Loop Head and Carrigahalt *p360*
Kilkee Diving and Watersports Centre, Harbour, T065-9056707.
Ponytrekking Centre, Tarmon West, 3 km outside Kilkee, T065-9060071.

Kilrush and Slattery Island *p361, map p*
Kilrush Creek Adventure Centre, Kilrush Marina, T065-9052855. Sailing, kayaking, canoeing, windsurfing.

Lough Derg and around

The area in the east of County Clare around Lough Derg is green pastureland set in a landscape of mountain and lake. The major town is Killaloe with its ancient cathedral, said to be the home of Brian Ború, the old Irish king. The East Clare Way, a signposted walking route, crosses the area, boats can be hired and there are lots of riding centres and golf courses. This is an area for activity holidays rather than a touring holiday.
For Sleeping, Eating and other listings, see page 364.

Killaloe → *Phone code: 061. Colour map 3, grid A5.*

Killaloe and Ballina in County Tipperary are joined by a beautiful old arched bridge over the river Shannon. The main point of interest here is **St Flannan's Cathedral**, named after an abbot who led the monastery that stood here before the cathedral. The building you now see is late 12th century, built by an O'Brien, and it encloses the doorway of an earlier church in its southwest corner. Inside is one of the only stones in existence to have both Ogham and runic writing on it – probably erected by the man whose name it bears: Thorgrim – asking for prayer. The cross once stood at Kilfenora but was moved here in 1821. Beside the cathedral is **St Flannan's Oratory**, also 12th- century, and with a stone roof. In the grounds of the Catholic church in Killaloe is **St Molua's church**, which is older than both of these buildings. It stood originally on Friar's Island in the Shannon estuary but was moved here in 1929 when the island was flooded in the Shannon hydroelectric scheme. The **tourist office** is next to the bridge, T061-376866, May to mid-Sep 1000-1800. Next door, is the **Heritage Centre** €3, with material on local history.

Long-distance walks

Starting off in Killaloe the **East Clare Way** covers 180 km of very untouristy east Clare, travelling through Broadford, O'Callaghan's Mills, Tulla, Feakle, Flagmount, Whitegate, Mountshannon, and Ogonnelloe. Half of the journey is along tarmac road, albeit very quiet tarmac. The best of it is the section between Tulla and Mountshannon: three days' walking through open land, forestry and some road walking. There is accommodation at Mountshannon, Feakle and Tulla.

The **Lough Derg Way** passes through Killaloe on its route from Limerick and follows the eastern shore of Lough Derg to Dromineer in County Tipperary. This is a finer walk than the other, keeping close to the shores of the lake for most of its route but accommodation is a little harder to come by. For more information about the walk you can pick up the *Lough Derg Way Information Sheet* at Ennis Tourist office (see page 344) or the Clare section of the walk is mapped out on the Ordnance Survey Discovery series sheets 65 and 58.

North to Mountshannon and Holy Island

Heading northwards along the shores of Lough Derg brings you to **Tuamgraney** where the **10th-century church** is now another heritage centre. It is the oldest Irish church still used for services and is said to have been repaired in 1000 by Brian Ború himself. Continuing north you come to **Mountshannon**, a quiet little town popular with fishing enthusiasts but where you can get a ferry to **Holy Island** (*Inis Cealtra*) ⓘ *T061-921351, May-Sep, €6*. A monastery was founded here by St Caiman in the seventh century, but was burned down by Vikings in 836 and again in 922. The Abbot of the monastery around 1000 was the brother of Brian Ború, who is said to have built one of the churches on the island. A church remained here into the 16th century but by the 17th this had become a place of pilgrimage rather than a working church. There are around 10 sites of interest on the island, including three churches, all predating the 13th century: a round tower, a tiny tomb known as the 'anchorite's cell', and the holy well that makes this place the centre for pilgrims.

Sleeping

Lough Derg and around *p363*
In Killaloe there is a variety of accommodation, which can be supplemented by walking over the bridge into Ballina, and accommodation is also available along the lough at Mountshannon.

B-C Kincora Hall Hotel, Killaloe, T061-376665, www.kincorahall.com. Just outside Killaloe, with its own marina, grand old fireplaces, but small enough to make you welcome.

B-C Lakeside Hotel and Leisure Centre, Killaloe, T061-376122, www.lakeside-killaloe.com. Lots of facilities including a pool, water slide, jacuzzi and snooker room. Overlooks Lough Derg.

E Carramore Lodge, Killaloe, T061-376704, www.carramorelodge.net. B&B in the village itself with big gardens and pleasant views over the river.

E Whitethorn Lodge, T061-375257. Large modern house within walking distance of amenities; 1 double, 1 single and 1 family room; Mar-Nov.

Camping

Lakeside Caravan and Camping Park, Mountshannon, T061-927225. On the shores of the lough with lots of facilities, mobile homes to hire, boat hire, café, bike hire, pony riding and much more.

Lough Derg Holiday Park, Scarrif Rd, Killaloe, T061-3786329. A big place with lots of facilities – including takeaway and shop, games room, laundry – but with prices to match. There are mobile homes to hire.

Eating

Lough Derg and around *p363*

Cherry Tree, Ballina, T061-375688. The most attractive proposition for dining, at the river-side. Quality food, including vegetarian around €40, open every night except Mon from 1800.

Cois na Abhna, main street. Has music.

Mountshannon Hotel, Mountshannon. The eponymous hotel does good basic food with dinner menu around €25.

Anchor Inn, does pub food and has music on Wed in summer.

Bridge, does pub food.

Molly's Bar and Restaurant, on the Ballina side of the river, T061-376632. Food and music.

Activities and tours

Lough Derg and around *p363, map p*

Fishing **TJ O'Brien**, Main St, Ballina/Killaloe, T061-376009. Tackle for game, sea, sport and coarse fishing.

Horse riding **Carrowbaun Farm Trekking Centre**, Killaloe, T061-376754.

East Clare Equestrian Centre, Tuamgraney, T061-921157.

Walking **East Clare Walking Club**, ECDA, Feakle, T061-924303. Organize regular walks every other Sun.

Watersports **Thomas Bottcher**, Mountshannon, T061-927225. Sailing, canoeing, windsurfing.

Boat hire: **PJ Mason**, Broadford, T061-473194. Boat hire on Doon Lake.

Whelan's, Church St, Killaloe, T061-376159. 5.7 m lake boats with outboard motors.

Counties Galway and Roscommon

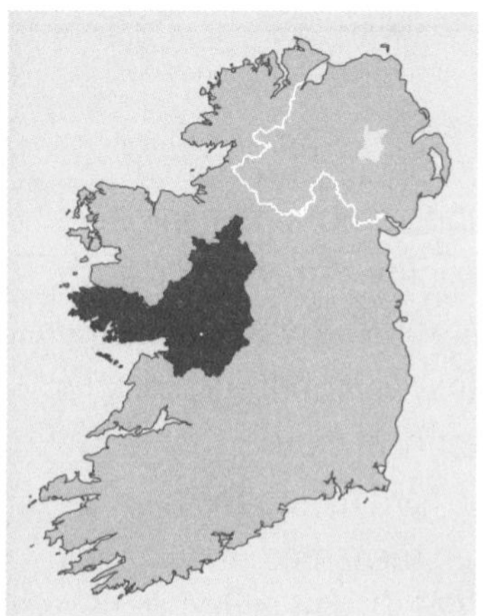

Footprint features

Introduction

Galway is a large county, but Lough Corrib splits it into two quite different regions. For the majority of travellers it is the land to the west, Connemara, that stirs the imagination. Here, a wilderness of bog and mountains rivals Cork and Kerry for splendid scenery and the wild beauty of nature. East Galway is dull by comparison, and it may be hard to find the time to include anywhere in the east when the famed Aran Islands and the exuberantly lively city of Galway are added on to an itinerary that includes Connemara.

The inland county of Roscommon is Irish country life without the tourist trimmings: there are no spectacular sights but a relaxed pace of life and, as ever, history lurks in unexpected places. Few visitors make it their holiday destination, but anyone passing through should definitely take some time to visit Strokestown, Roscommon Town and Boyle.

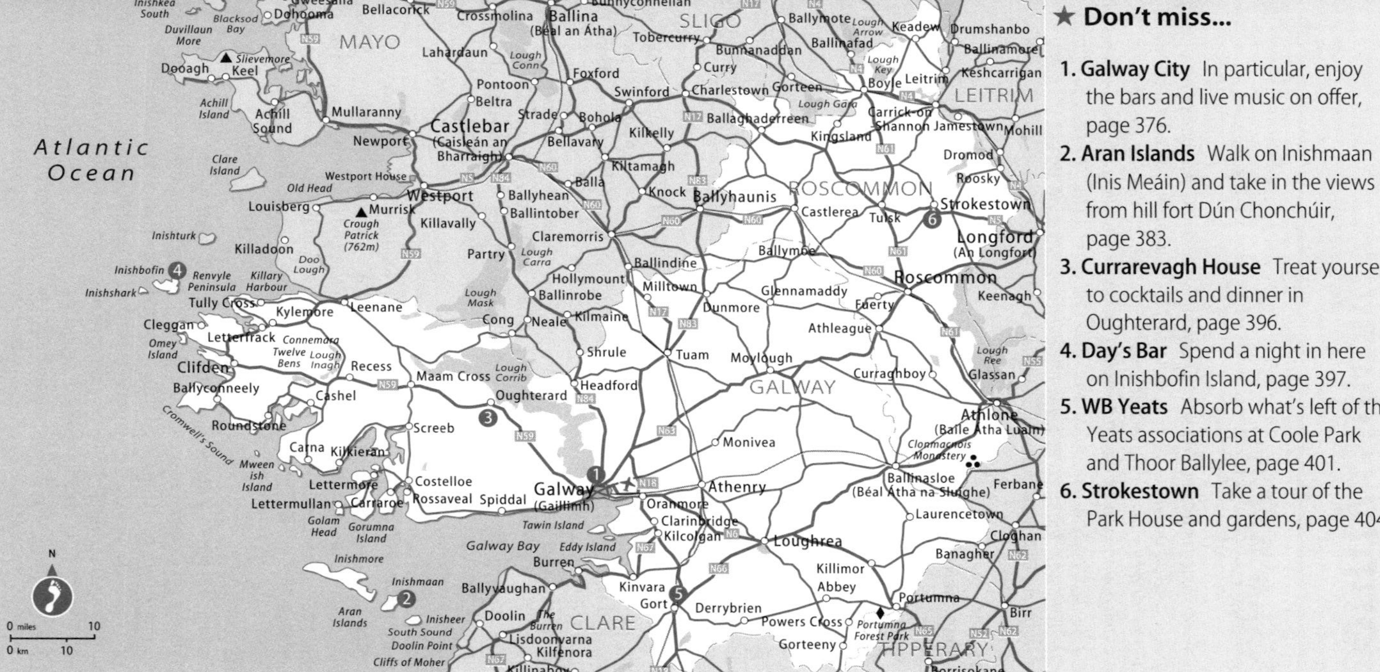

★ Don't miss...

1. **Galway City** In particular, enjoy the bars and live music on offer, page 376.
2. **Aran Islands** Walk on Inishmaan (Inis Meáin) and take in the views from hill fort Dún Chonchúir, page 383.
3. **Currarevagh House** Treat yourself to cocktails and dinner in Oughterard, page 396.
4. **Day's Bar** Spend a night in here on Inishbofin Island, page 397.
5. **WB Yeats** Absorb what's left of the Yeats associations at Coole Park and Thoor Ballylee, page 401.
6. **Strokestown** Take a tour of the Park House and gardens, page 404

County Galway

Galway City

→ *Phone code: 091 Colour map 2, grid C3*

If any one place in Ireland can sum up what the country is all about it has to be this ancient, prosperous and culturally dynamic little city. Easily walked from one end to another in half an hour, it is a tourist paradise of culture, shopping, friendliness, good accommodation, and even better eating. In summer the whole city centre teems with people out having fun, bars and restaurants spill out on to the streets, and with major festivals in July, August and September there is rarely no excuse for some craic.
▸▸ *For Sleeping, Eating and other listings, see pages 374-379.*

Ins and outs

Getting there **Galway airport**, T091-755569, is 10 km east of the city at Carnmore. There are at least two, and up to five, daily **Aer Arann** flights to and from Dublin for around €40 each way. The airline also connects Galway with London, Edinburgh, Manchester and Lorient in France for around €50 each way. A taxi from the airport to the centre costs around €12. Galway city's bus station services main towns throughout Ireland and there are some private companies also running useful routes: to Dublin and Dublin Airport, Belmullet, Newport and Westport; see the Inishbofin Island section page 400 for services between Galway city and Cleggan. From the railway station in Galway city, T091-561444, daily trains serve Dublin, stopping at Athlone for connections to other parts of the country. ▸▸ *See Transport, page 379, for further details.*

Getting around Galway's city centre is tiny. The bulk of the city is on the northwest side of the River Corrib. On the southwest side of the river is the ancient settlement of the Claddagh, which is mostly redeveloped with boring bungalows. From Eyre Square, your arrival point in the city if you have come here on the bus or by train, most places are easily walkable. Taxi ranks are in Eyre Square and by the railway station. Buses leave Eyre Square for Salthill every 20 minutes, but the distance can be walked easily. Parking discs, available from the tourist office and newspaper shops, are required for street parking throughout the city. Designated car parks are dotted around and clearly marked. ▸▸ *See Transport, page 379, for further details.*

Information **Ireland West Tourism** (the main tourist office for the county) is on Forster St, T091-537700, www.irelandwest.ie. Main office open Jun-Sep daily 0900-1745; Oct and Apr-May Mon-Sat 0900-1745; Jan-Mar and Dec Mon-Fri 0900-1745, Sat 0900-1245. They dispense a free *Galway Tourist Guide*. There is another office in Salthill, at the junction of Seapoint Promenade and Upper Salthill Road.

History

The *Annals of the Four Masters*, a 17th-century compilation history of Ireland (see box on page 455) records the presence of a fort at the mouth of the River Corrib in 1124. This would have been the crossing place for traders and travellers moving from Dublin to the west, the route to the north being blocked by Lough Corrib. In 1232 Richard de Burgh, a powerful Anglo-Norman baron, took the area from the dominant Gaelic clan, the O'Flahertys. By 1247 there was a walled town of about 35 acres here. In the 15th century, the town was given a royal charter and control of the parish church of St Nicholas (built in 1320), enhancing Galway's power. For 150 years the townsmen grew wealthy on trade with Spain and France, and even with the Caribbean: animal pelts

Lynch law

The Lynches were an important Galway family, 84 of whom became mayors of the city between the 15th and 17th centuries. One of them is said to have given the English language the word 'lynch'.

In 1493, James Lynch Fitz Stephens' son Walter and his girlfriend Ann were at a dance with their Spanish friend Gomez who, being a polite sort of chap, was very attentive to Ann. Walter became fiercely jealous and secretly followed Gomez home and murdered him. When the body was found Walter's hat and knife were beside it. Walter, an otherwise saintly young man, was accused of the murder and confessed, whereupon his father James Lynch Fitz Stephens dragged him to the town jail. Walter was such a nice young man that the whole town begged James for mercy on his son and even the hangman refused to do the dirty deed. James, in a fury of righteousness and finding his way to the scaffold blocked by angry townspeople, threw his son out of the window, first tying him by the neck to a stake inside the room.

and fish in exchange for wine and fine cloth. The evidence of the wealth is still there in the fine old stone buildings and the many tower houses of the surrounding country.

But the 17th-century English wars brought an end to Galway's prosperity. The cityfolk supported the losing side in both the English civil war – suffering the attacks of Cromwell's troops as a result – and the war between James II and William of Orange, surrendering to William's forces in 1691. After that things declined for about 200 years. There was a brief economic boom in Victorian times and then things began to look up again around the 1960s when government funds were put into developing the west of Ireland. Now Galway booms with a vengeance, consumer amenities and new developments are spreading like an epidemic and on the city outskirts roundabouts and superstores are popping up like mushrooms.

Sights

Eyre Square Newly renovated Eyre Square, with Kennedy Park in the middle, remains a kind of dumping ground for memorabilia that doesn't fit in too well anywhere else. The **Browne Doorway** was in the way of some redevelopment and got moved here – it's a piece of a 17th-century building consisting of a bay window and the eponymous doorway with the date and coat of arms carved into it. Two statues adorn the park: one of **Padraic Ó'Conaire** (1882-1928), a local author whose grim tales have little contemporary appeal to consumer-fuelled Galway – the statue is a replica, the original is in the new City Museum – and another of **Liam Mellows** (1892-1922), a republican and socialist who fought in the 1916 Easter Rising and later in the civil war on the side of the anti-Treaty party. He was executed in 1922 as a reprisal against the murder of two Daíl deputies. When this area of the square was being excavated in 1955, human remains were found, giving credence to the idea that this spot was the town's place of execution, where the bodies of those hanged would have been thrown down and buried beneath the gallows.

In summer the square is often a venue for concerts and other events.

There is also a **plaque** in the square dedicated to John F Kennedy, who addressed the people of Galway from this spot in 1963, after which the park was renamed in his honour. There are also two ancient iron cannons, formerly the property of the Connaught Rangers (see page 372), in the square, while the fountain erected in 1984 to commemorate Galway's 500 years as a town is in the shape of a Galway Hooker, the traditional sailing ship of the area.

Galway city

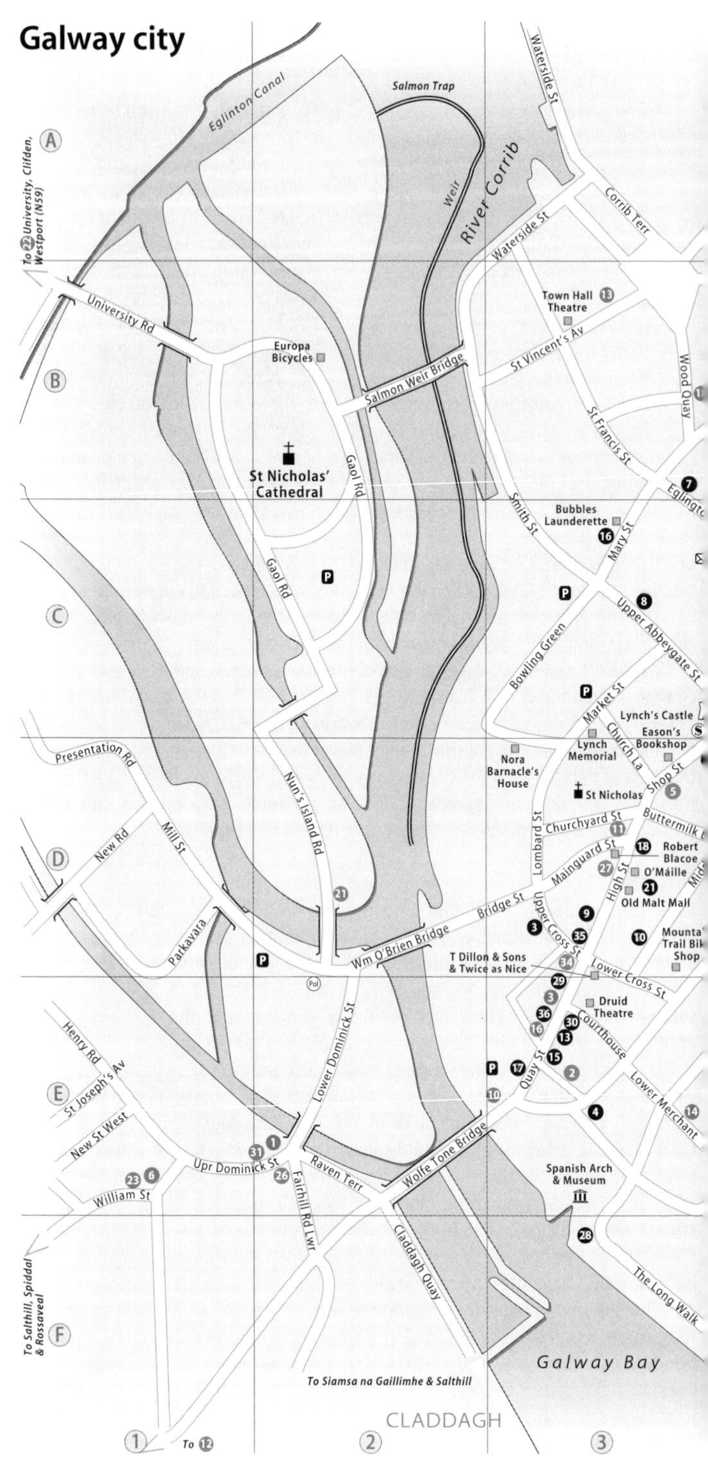
Salmon Trap
Eglinton Canal
River Corrib
Weir
Waterside St
Corrib Terr
Town Hall Theatre
St Vincent's Av
Wood Quay
University Rd
Europa Bicycles
Salmon Weir Bridge
St Francis St
St Nicholas' Cathedral
Gaol Rd
Smith St
Bubbles Launderette
Mary St
Eglinton
Upper Abbeygate St
Bowling Green
Market St
Lynch's Castle
Eason's Bookshop
Church La
Lynch Memorial
Nora Barnacle's House
St Nicholas
Shop St
Presentation Rd
Nun's Island Rd
Churchyard St
Buttermilk La
Lombard St
Mainguard St
Robert Blacoe
O'Máille
High St
Old Malt Mall
New Rd
Mill St
Bridge St
Upper Cross St
Mountain Trail Bike Shop
Parkavara
Wm O'Brien Bridge
T Dillon & Sons & Twice as Nice
Lower Cross St
Druid Theatre
Courthouse
Lower Dominick St
Henry Rd
St Joseph's Av
Quay St
Lower Merchant
New St West
Wolfe Tone Bridge
Upr Dominick St
Raven Terr
Fairhill Rd Lwr
Spanish Arch & Museum
William St
Claddagh Quay
The Long Walk
Galway Bay
To Siamsa na Gaillimhe & Salthill
CLADDAGH
To 22 University, Clifden, Westport (N59)
To Salthill, Spiddal & Rossaveal
To 12
A
B
C
D
E
F
1
2
3

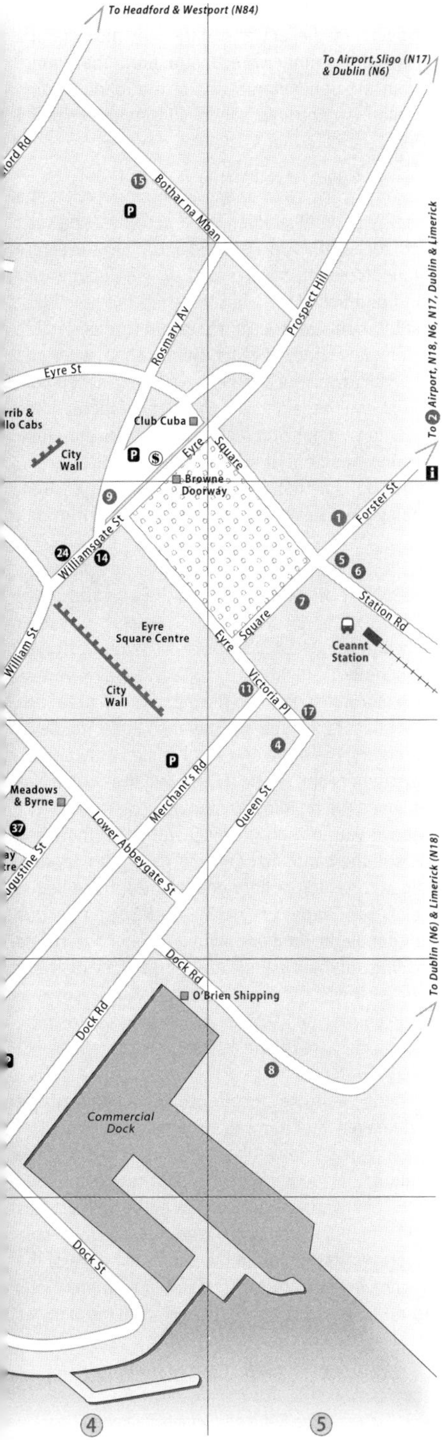

To Headford & Westport (N84)
To Airport, Sligo (N17) & Dublin (N6)
Bothar na Mban
Rosmary Av
Prospect Hill
To 2 Airport, N18, N6, N17, Dublin & Limerick
Eyre St
Club Cuba
City Wall
Eyre Square
Browne Doorway
Forster St
Williamsgate St
Station Rd
Eyre Square Centre
William St
Ceannt Station
City Wall
Victoria Pl
Merchant's Rd
Queen St
Meadows & Byrne
Lower Abbeygate St
To Dublin (N6) & Limerick (N18)
Dock Rd
O'Brien Shipping
Dock Rd
Commercial Dock
Dock St
4
5

N
0 yards 100
0 metres 100

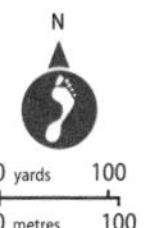

Sleeping

Arch View Hostel **1** *E2*
Ardawn House **2** *B5*
Ardilaun House & Camilaun Room Restaurant **12** *F1*
Barnacles Quay St House **3** *E3*
Brennans Yard **14** *E3*
Celtic Tourist Hostel **4** *D5*
Eyre Square **5** *C5*
Galway Hostel **6** *C5*
Great Southern **7** *C5*
Harbour & Krusoe's Restaurant **8** *E5*
Imperial **9** *C4*
Jury's Galway Inn **10** *E3*
Kinlay House **11** *C5*
Salmon Weir Hostel **13** *B3*
Sleepzone **15** *A4*
Spanish Arch **16** *E3*
St Martin's **21** *D2*
Victoria **17** *C5*
Villa Nova **22** *A1*
Woodquay Hostel **18** *B3*

Eating

Busker Browne's **3** *D3*
Conlon's **7** *B3*
Couch Potatoes **8** *C3*
Da Tang Noodle House **10** *D3*
Elle's **12** *D4*
Fat Freddie's **13** *E3*
Front Door **35** *D3*
GBC Coffee Shop **14** *C4*
Gemelles **15** *E3*
Home Plate **16** *C3*
KC Blakes **17** *E3*
King's Head **18** *D3*
Kirby's **3** *D3*
Kumar's **4** *E3*
Malt House **21** *D3*
Maxwell McNamara's **24** *C4*
Nimmo's **28** *F3*
Pierre's **29** *E3*
Quays **30** *E3*
River God Café **9** *D3*
Tomás O'Riada **35** *D3*
Trattoria **36** *E3*
Tulsi **37** *D4*

Pubs & music

An Púcán **1** *C5*
Bazaar **2** *E3*
Blue Note **6** *E1*
Massimo **23** *E1*
Monroe's **26** *E2*
Murphy's **27** *D3*
Róisín Dubh **31** *E2*
Taafe's **5** *D3*
Tigh Cioli *D3* **11**
Tigh Neachtain **34** *D3*

At the southwest corner of the square is the **Eyre Square Centre** in whose basement can be seen part of the original medieval walls of the city, although it's difficult to distinguish ancient remains from modern reconstruction. The square undeniably is a busy sort of place, but the pedestrianization of the roads leading down to the harbour has shifted the balance of the town a little away from here to the cafés and shops of Quay Street.

Lynch's Castle ⓘ *Open during banking hours, 1000-1600, Mon-Sat. Free.* On the corner of Abbeygate Street and Shop Street the Allied Irish Bank occupies what was once Lynch's Castle, a building thought to date back to 1320 and occupying the centre of the medieval city. It is a single, four-storey block decorated on the outside with gargoyles. The original building would probably have been thatched but much of it burned down in 1473 and was rebuilt by 1503. Cromwell's troops did it considerable damage and it sank into mediocrity for a few hundred years. Before 1820, when the street to the west was rebuilt, the building was much larger, extending westwards. Inside the lobby of the bank are a number of panels telling the story of the building and its owners, as well as a 17th-century bridal fireplace, common to this area, celebrating the marriage of members of two important local families, the Blakes and the ffrenches. It does not belong in this building but was brought here in 1927 from another nearby building which was being remodelled. The entrance doors to the bank were constructed in 1933.

St Nicholas of Myra ⓘ *Shop St. Apr-Sep Mon-Sat 0900-1745, Sun 1300-1700; Oct-Mar Mon-Sat 1000-1600, Sun 1300-1700. €3 donation is requested.* Further south, along Shop Street, is the pretty little church of St Nicholas of Myra, which has been the city's church since the 14th century. St Nicholas is the man we all revere as Santa Claus, the fourth-century bishop of Myra in Lycia and the patron saint of sailors. The nave, chancel and transepts were built at this time and it is the largest medieval parish church in Ireland. In the 16th century, the north and south aisles were added, as well as the chapel of the Blessed Sacrament and the belfry. In 1652, the church was desecrated by Cromwell's forces who used the building as stables.

From the entrance, the room above you in the porchway was once the living quarters of the sexton. In front of you is the **baptismal font**, perhaps 16th century, carved with a figure of a dog, a fleur-de-lys and a three-leafed clover. In front of the Chapel of the Blessed Sacrament are **banners of the Connaught Rangers**, whose cannons decorate Eyre Square and who mutinied in India in support of the Irish War of Independence in 1920. In the north aisle are some ancient gravestones, some of which carry the trade symbols of the men buried beneath them including a goldsmith, a stonemason and a wool merchant. In this area there is also a mass grave with several hundred skeletons.

Legend has it that Christopher Columbus worshipped here in 1477.

In the **Chapel of Christ** is a 13th-century tomb of a crusader, the oldest tomb in the church. Under the **Lynch window**, damaged by Cromwell's forces, is the tomb of Stephen Lynch with the figures of two angels. Some of the original paintwork of the tomb can still be made out. Further along the south transept is another Lynch tomb, with the figure of Christ displaying the five wounds, also damaged by 17th-century soldiers. Here too is the tomb of the infamous James Lynch who hung his own son, Walter. Of especial interest is the apprentice's column in the southeast nave of the church, bearing particularly fancy carvings and thought to be the apprentice's masterpiece (ie the work he had to do to pass his apprenticeship). All around the

The most notable descendant of the Lynches, one of the great tribes who once ruled the area, is Che Guevara. His grandmother's family, on her father's side, was a direct descendant of a Patrick Lynch who left Galway in the 1740s and settled in Buenos Aires.

The Claddagh

When the Anglo-Normans began the development of Galway City, the native population settled to the south in the area known as Claddagh or beach. Like other Gaelic settlements all over Ireland it had its own laws and a ruler. Long after other Gaelic areas assimilated and learned English the Claddagh survived, a little pocket of Gaelic Ireland right up to the early 20th century, with its own customs, dress, and economy. The little township of thatched cottages was demolished in 1937 when the area was needed for modern housing and the Gaelic-speaking residents dispersed. The only thing that remains now is the name, which has been given to a style of ring common to Connaught: the Claddagh ring. This shows a pair of hands, the symbol of friendship, holding a heart, the symbol of love, with a crown, a symbol, to some at least, of loyalty.

church are stone fragments found during various renovations and set into the walls of the church to preserve them.

Outside the church in the wall of the churchyard is the **Lynch Memorial**, a completely modern collection of fragments all said to be connected with James Lynch.

Other sights At No 8 Bowling Green is the erstwhile **home of Nora Barnacle** ⓘ *T091-564743, late May-Aug Tue-Fri, some Sats 1000-1700 (closes for lunch), €2.50, €1.50*, now dedicated to the memory of the woman who captured James Joyce's heart. Joyce visited the house in 1909 and 1912 and wrote his best short story *The Dead*, based on the story of the young man, Michael Bodkin, who died after making his way in the rain to sing to Nora.

In Flood Street is the **Spanish Arch**, one of the remaining sections of the city walls of Galway. It is thought that this was a place where ships could unload their goods in the town's harbour. Its age or function is not really known nor is the origin of its name. Behind the arch, the walls of the city and the ditch that lay outside it can be seen.

Close by is the new **City Museum**, still being built at the time of writing but due to open soon. The old museum's collection of trivia and flotsam representing the hundreds of years of the city's existence was all cluttered together rather haphazardly but expect a more flashy and impressive display in the new place. Enquire at the tourist office for hours of opening and admission rates.

Beyond the Wolfe Tone Bridge is the **Claddagh**, one-time independent state with its own king, laws, language and dress code and later a fishing village where the Galway Hookers were built and used. It once had a population of about 8,000 Irish speakers living in tiny thatched cottages (see box).

Over to the northwest of town is **St Nicholas' Cathedral**, dedicated in 1965. In an epiphany of 1960s bad taste, it is built of limestone blocks with copper streaks from the roof cutting crazy patterns down its walls and an excess of Connemara marble inside. The size of the interior makes it feel more like a hypermarket rather than inspiring any sense of the spiritual.

Salthill West of the city, Salthill is a rapidly developing seaside resort. It has a leisure centre, some interesting nightlife and a pebbly beach. After September, when the schools reopen, Salthill is a perfect place for lovers of deserted seaside towns. In summer there's not much to keep you there except lots of family entertainment such as **Leisureland** ⓘ *The Promenade, T091-521455, Mon-Fri 0930-1400, 2000-2200; Sat 1400-1715; Sun 1100-1800, €4*, with several pools and rides, **Atlantaquaria** ⓘ *T091-585100, daily 1000-1800*, with big tanks full of fish and a touchy-feely pool, and **Seapoint** ⓘ *Seapoint Promenade, T091-521716, daily, 1000-0100, variable rates,* with a casino, video games snooker and daily bingo. The promenade is the longest in Ireland and at the western end is Blackrock diving area, once a men-only swimming spot. When you get to the end of the promenade, kick the wall – it's a tradition.

Sleeping

Galway city *p368, map p370*
The city abounds with hotels, both in the city and on the feeder roads into town, good inexpensive hostels, and lots of B&Bs. There are very few B&Bs or guest houses within the city centre: most are in suburbs or Salthill. B&Bs tend to average around €35 per person sharing a double room. If you turn up in the city with no accommodation try the Ireland West Tourism Office (see page 368), but there can be long delays at the peak of the season. During festival time, in Jul, Aug and Sep, accommodation becomes very scarce. Book well in advance. Galway is crowded with hostels, most of which attract a very young crowd who tend to be noisy: don't expect a quiet, restful time during the summer months.

Galway centre

L-B **Great Southern Hotel**, Eyre Sq, T091-564041, www.gshotels.com. Rates vary according to season and week night; some good special offers. Spacious rooms, award-winning restaurant, roof-top pool.

L-B **Harbour Hotel**, The Harbour, T091-569466 www.harbour.com. Modern, stylish hotel, car park, quiet location, good views, lots of comfort and a decent restaurant.

A-D **Brennans Yard**, Lower Merchant Rd, T091-568166, www.brennansyardhotel.com. A smart, no-nonsense hotel in the heart of the city and worth staying at if a good room rate is available.

A-D **Hotel Spanish Arch**, Quay St, T091-569600, www.spanisharchhotel.ie. Boutique hotel with individually decorated rooms, nice Victorian bar, and bits of 16th-century walls.

A-D **Victoria Hotel**, Victoria Pl, T091-567433, www.byrne-hotels-ireland.com. In a quiet part of the city centre, big spacious rooms individually furnished, pleasant guest areas.

B-D **Eyre Square Hotel**, Forster St, T091-569633, www.byrne-hotels-ireland.com. All the facilities, centrally located, lively pub.

B-D **Imperial Hotel**, Eyre Sq, T091-563033, imperialhtl@hotmail.com. Very centrally located, restaurant popular with locals.

C-D **Ardawn House**, College Rd, T091-568833, ardawn@iol.ie. Big roomy guest house close to town and right next door to the greyhound track so fans can watch from their bedroom windows! Luxury breakfast, comfortable sitting room, good tourist advice and fresh tea, coffee and cakes served all day.

C-E **Jury's Galway Inn**, Quay St, T091-566444, www.bookajurysinn.com. Charging per room, not per person, this has to be the best value hotel in town for more than 2 people sharing. Pleasant and close to river.

E **St Martin's**, 2 Nun's Island Rd, T091-568286. Comfortable, riverside and close-to-town location but very popular because of this and booking is often essential.

E **Villa Nova**, 40 Newcastle Rd, T091-524849. Guest house west of city centre off the road leading to the university.

E-F **Barnacles Quay Street House**, 10 Quay St, T091-568644, www.barnacles.ie. 6 private rooms, family rooms, a laundry and breakfast included. Near the harbour.

E-F **Celtic Tourist Hostel**, Queen St, Victoria Pl, T087-2255919. Some private rooms, meals available and bike hire.

E-F **Kinlay House**, Merchant's Rd, T091-565244, www.kinlayhouse.ie. Just off Eyre Sq, with private rooms. Washrooms and toilets are not gender specific. Price includes continental breakfast.

E-F **Sleepzone**, Bothar na Mban Wood Quay, T091-566999, www.sleepzone.ie. Very central, purpose-built hostel and internet café. Dorm beds, doubles, singles, breakfast included.

F **Arch View Hostel**, 1 Upper Dominick St, T091-586661. No private rooms.

F **The Galway Hostel**, Eyre Sq, T091-566959, www.galwayhostel.com. An elegant old stone building, has several private double rooms. 24 hrs, breakfast included, internet access.

For an explanation of the sleeping and eating price codes used in this guide, see inside the front cover. Other relevant information is found in Essentials pages 39-45.

F The Salmon Weir Hostel, St Vincent's Av, T091-561133, www.salmonweirhostel.com. Has private doubles, family rooms. In the northwest of the city.
F Woodquay Hostel, Woodquay, T091-562618, www.woodquayhostel.ie. Fairly central, one of the tidier hostels in the city, but dorm beds only and no private rooms.

Salthill

L-B Ardilaun House Hotel, Taylor's Hill, T091-521433, www.ardilaunhousehotel.ie. Galway can be intense but this hotel offers refuge, comfort and quality service. Tucked away, on the city side of Salthill, it has a grand leisure centre, an air of grace and old- fashioned Irish hospitality. Smart, individually furnished rooms.
B-D Anno Santo Hotel, Threadneedle Rd, T091-523011, www.annosantosalthill.com. Small, family-run, on main bus route into city. Away from the sea front.
D-E Knockrea Guest House, 55 Lower Salthill, T091-520145, www.knockrea.com. On bus route, 300 m from seafront, walkable distance from city. Friendly. Car park.
E Devondell, 47 Devon park, Lower Salthill, T091-528306, www.devondellcom. Hovering at the top of this price range, tucked away in Salthill and unprepossessing on the outside, this is a fine B&B with special breakfasts.

Furbo

LL-L Connemara Coast Hotel, Furbo, T091-592108. This smart new hotel is 10 mins by car from Galway on the coast road west of Salthill. Stirring views over Galway Bay and a small library.

Camping

There are several campsites to the east and west of Galway along the coast. The best is: **Ballyloughane Caravan and Camping Park**, Ballyloughane Beach, Renmore, T091-755338, galwcamp@iol.ie.

Eating

Galway city *p368, map p370*

TTT You need to push the boat out on the à la carte menus to end up with a bill in the expensive price category here. Even the best restaurants have meals in the mid-range.
TT **Camilaun Room**, Ardilaun House Hotel. One of the most gratifying restaurants in Galway. The menu has few surprises but the traditional-style meals are a treat in the white-tableclothed-and-chandeliered dining room.
TT **Gemelles**, 23 Quay St, T091-568821. Has a tempting menu of fajitas plus chicken and pasta and grills and a 3-course meal will be around €30.
TT **K.C. Blake's**, at the bottom of Quay St, T091-561826. A fashionable-looking place with lots of beech and steel. Has a creative menu that runs to pizzas, pasta and fajitas as well as crab claws and tiger prawns. The dinner menu is around €30 but sticking with seafood would push the price into the higher price category.
TT **Kirby's**, attached to Busker Browne's in Cross St, T091-569404. Visually pleasing, with Munch-like oil paintings on the walls and an extensive menu with fish and vegetarian choices. Open for lunch and dinner daily.
TT **Krusoe's**, in the Harbour Hotel. Independently-run restaurant serving modern Irish cuisine in chic surroundings.
TT **The Malt House**, Old Malt Shopping Mall, T091-563993, www.malt-house.com. Its stone walls are ancient and it is the right size for comfort. A small, traditional Irish menu, extensive wine list and reasonable prices ensure a great meal. There is an early evening menu for around €20 while a dinner menu is €35, closed Sun.
TT **Nimmo's**, in Long Walk, Spanish Arch, T091-561114. Minimalist menu but the dishes, nouvelle Irish, are a surprise when they reach you. No booking. Wine bar downstairs has less expensive food.
TT **Quays**, Quay St, T091-568347. Restaurant at the back of the pub with the same name, has a menu of Irish dishes all individually priced around €20.
TT **Trattoria**, 12 Quay St, T091-563910. A pasta and pizza place. Open daily. Very Italian, dimly lit, lots of Chianti bottles. Dinner could work out at around €30.
TT **Tulsi**, 3 Buttermarket Walk, Middle St, T091-564831. An Indian restaurant with lots of vegetable dishes, enough for a vegetarian to have a banquet.
T **Da Roberta**, 169 Upper Sathill, T091-585808. West of the river, a little Italian-style place where the food is excellent but you have to fight the crowds to find a table.
T **River God Café**, above the Bunch of Grapes pub in High St, T091-565811. Worth checking

out for lunchtime or evening meals. Delights on the menu include Brazilian blackened chicken in a mango and lime sauce and main courses are between €10 and €18. The dinner menu is good value and vegetarians have lots of choices.

Conlon's Fish Restaurant, Eglinton St. Does take-aways and sit-down meals that include lobster, oysters and local mussels as well as tasty fish and chips.

Couch Potatoes, Abbeygate St Lower. A very busy place nicely decorated, with potatoes dominating the menu from filled baked potatoes to potato pizza. A good, value-for-money place with lots of vegetarian choices.

Home Plate, Mary St. Open 1200-2000 for sandwiches, salads, pasta and vegetarian all under €10.

Elle's, 12 Shop St. Café serves soups and sandwiches, filled potatoes and pittas and a nice array of desserts, open until 1830, Mon-Sat, 1800 Sun.

Fat Freddie's, Shop St. Pizzas, quesilladas and more. Not a lot of room inside but put in your order and retire to the pub next door and they'll give you a shout when it's ready.

The Front Door, café connected to *Tomás O'Riada*. You can order the food in any part of the bars or eat in the café itself. Slightly more choices than the typical bar food menu with good vegetarian options and sandwiches. Food finishes about 1600.

GBC Coffeeshop, Williamsgate St. Homely, does lunchtime food under €10 and has a restaurant upstairs, from 1600, with conventional fish and chicken dishes around €15.

King's Head, at the junction of Shop St and High St. A vast, recently themed old pub, which seems to go on for ever, with some good pub food that ceases by early evening.

Maxwell McNamara's, opposite GBC Coffeeshop. Big and busy doing snacks and sandwiches, with a menu full of fish, steak and chicken options as well as a tiny box describing what vegetarians can have.

Tomás O'Riada, Quay St. Another genuinely old pub that has been themed and now forms a warren of little bars.

Da Tang Noodle House, Middle St, T091-561443. If you have a sudden hankering after Asian cuisine try their authentic noodle-based Chinese food with vegetarian options. Dishes are around €15, open for lunch Mon-Sat and for dinner 7 nights a week.

Busker Browne's, Cross St. Pub, serving soups and more substantial choices till 2000, daily in summer

Donagh's Seafood, at the bottom of Quay St. Does excellent fish and chips every day 1200-2400.

Fish restaurant, T091-565001. Open for lunch and dinner.

Kumar's, across the road from Jury's Inn. Has been around a long time and does meat and non-meat thalis for under €10 between 1600 and 1900.

Pierre's, opposite The Quays pub, T091-566066. Open 7 days from 1800 until 2300 in summer, offers a French-style dinner menu for around €25.

Pubs and music

★ Galway city *p368, map p370*

Town centre

In summer there is music all around – in the street and in almost every pub – just wander down the street and follow the noise. *Blitz* (www.blitz.ie) and *Xposed* are two free guides listing what's on in town.

An Púcán, Forster St, just off Eyre Sq. Traditional Irish music.

Bazaar, Spanish Arch, T091-534496. A Moroccan-themed bar, live music and DJs.

Busker Browne's, Upper Cross St. There is live music here most nights.

The King's Head, High St. Has music every night and jazz on Sun mornings.

Quays, Quay St. Has traditional music every night in summer and, with a cover charge, live bands upstairs, Wed-Sun.

Red Square Eyre Sq, T091-569633. Live pop/rock music.

Taafe's, next door to the King's Head. A more traditional bar with traditional music 1700-2100 most nights and Sun lunchtime.

Tigh Cioli, Mainguard St or Churchyard. Has regular traditional music sessions.

Tigh Neachtain, at the junction of Quay St, Cross St and High St. The most famous of the Galway pubs with little booths to sit in, turf fires in the winter and traditional music most nights.

West of the river

Blue Note, William St West. Features largely DJ-driven sounds with live music in between.

Massimo, next door to Blue Note, T091-582239. A designer bar with lots of open spaces and big sofas, noisy when live music attracts crowds and a cover charge but out of season a place for a quiet drink by a turf fire and unusual food like the full Irish breakfast on a pizza!
Monroe's, Dominick St, T091-587419. Hosts a variety of musical activities including set dancing on Tue night.
The Róisín Dubh, Upper Dominick St, T091-586540. Has traditional/rock/folk/ballads music and gigs with admission charges.
Scruffy Duffy's, Upper Salthill, T091-582233. On the other side of the river, has live music or DJs every night in summer.

A quiet drink

Bars to look out for if you enjoy genuine, unreconstructed spit and sawdust, or just calm in the eye of the Galway hurricane.
The Bal, in Salthill. Offers a quiet pint in the midst of bingo, karaoke, drum and bass and British stag parties.
Murphy's, High St. Run by the same family for 3 generations and with special reductions on beer for pensioners.

Entertainment

Galway city *p368, map p370*

Clubs

Boo Radley's, Forster St, T091-569633. Inside the Victoria hotel, a very young and studenty crowd and flexible DJs who adapt their style to the audience.
Central Park, Upper Abbeygate St, T091-565974. Hugely popular and admission is around €10 at weekends. Seriously charts and pop music and young 20-somethings in attendance.
ClubCuba, Eyre Sq, T091-569633, www.cuba.ie. Has 3 levels of bars and dancing areas and varying door charges. Latin nights, comedy nights, soul music, swing and lots of live bands.
GPO, Eglinton St, T091-563073. Still going strong and doors open at 2300 for a variety of sounds and admission charges. Sounds of the 80s, hip hop, and dance celebrated by 20-somethings.
Halo, just up the road from Central Park, T091-565974. Older, chilled-out and more alternative types might like to try this place.
The Warwick, in Salthill, T091-521244. In the Warwick Hotel, is the place to be on weekend nights – if you like chart sounds.

Theatre and cultural centres

An Taibhdhearc na Gaillimhe, Middle St, T091-562024. An Irish-language theatre, look out for notices of events, especially in *List Galway* and on the noticeboards in the *Galway Arts Centre*.
Druid Theatre, Chapel Lane, T091-568617. Puts on the works of Irish playwrights, often in Irish.
Town Hall Theatre, Courthouse Sq, T091-569777, www.townhalltheatregalway.com. Presents more established material and travelling theatre groups.

Festivals and events

Galway city *p368, map p370*
Salthill has an **air display** in early **Jul** with aeronautical displays and live music, www.salthillairshow.com, but there are 3 big festivals that are special to Galway city. The **Galway Races**, T091-753870, www.galwayraces.com, are in the last week in **Jul** and the racing takes place in Ballybrit track, 2 km outside the city on the road to the airport. The race track can accommodate 30,000 people, and usually does, and restaurants, bars and hotels stay open 24 hrs a day for the duration. Book early. There is another 2-day event in **Sep** and again in late **Oct**. The 22-year-old **Arts Festival**, T091- 566577, www.galwayartsfestival.ie, in the middle of **Jul**, is the country's biggest and best cultural bash with theatre companies from all over the world and customary 24-hr opening for everything. Music, art exhibitions, and lots more. Book even earlier, especially for the events. The week before this sees the **Galway Film Fleadh**, T091- 751655, www.galway fleadh.com. The last week in **Sep** sees the **Oyster Festival**, T091- 522066, info@galway oysterfest.com; lots of free oysters and Guinness, street concerts, general craic and of course licence extensions. The highlight of the event is the oyster opening competition.

Shopping

Galway city *p368, map p370*
Antiques **Tempo Antiques**, Cross St. Good for antique aficionados, full of lovely things.

Twice as Nice, 5 Quay St. For connoisseurs of old clothes, sells vintage clothing and jewellery. There is also an **antiques market** on level 1 of Eyre Sq shopping centre.

Art galleries **Galway Arts Centre**, Lower Dominick St, T091-65886, www.galwayartscentre.ie. Exhibits local and national artists' work.
Kenny Gallery, Middle St, a few doors up from Da Tang Noodles. Sells local artists' work.

Books Galway has a healthy number of bookshops as you would expect in a university city.
Easons, 33 Shop St. Has lots of local interest stuff including maps and guides as well as international newspapers.
Kenny's, High St. Seems to go on forever, with the largest stock of second-hand books in Ireland and lots of rare and wonderful tomes such as first editions of Seamus Heaney, Beckett, Yeats and many others. The same company have a bookstore on Merchant's Rd, with out-of-print books where you can spend many hours.

Clothes Jumper and woollens shops abound. There are so many gorgeous places it is impossible to list them all. Just start at the top of Eyre Sq and work your way down to Quay St.
Ó'Máille, High St. Has the full range of chunky sweaters, tweeds, and jackets. It is open daily in summer.
Tribes, William St. Another gorgeous place.

Crafts As well as the locally made clothes, there are a number of places selling little wooden and ceramic things around Eyre Sq and Quay St.
Galway Irish Crystal, Heritage centre, Merlin Park, Dublin Rd, T091-757311, www.galwaycrystal.ie. A place which is part shop and part visitor centre, does factory tours then sells you stuff from the shop.
Kelly's, High St. Good craft shop.
Meadows and Byrne, Castle St. More of a designer furniture and household goods place but has some attractive and functional pottery.

Jewellery A good purchase is, of course, a Claddagh design in a piece of jewellery.
Claddagh Jewellers, in the Eyre Sq centre. With lots more of the same.
T Dillon and Sons, on the corner of Quay St and Cross St. Start off here, they have a little museum (1000-1700) at the back of the shop dedicated to the history of the Claddagh design (see page 373), lots of rings, brooches and necklaces to choose from, and a very famous clientele. Using their prices as a starting point, you could compare prices with any of the other jewellers in town who also sell the Claddagh designs.
Richard Quinn, Dominick St. With more still.
Robert Blacoe, Shop St. Does other interesting Irish/Galway designs.

Activities and tours

Galway city *p368, map p370*
Fishing **Feeney's Sports**, 19-23 High St, T091-568794, www.freeneys.com. Can arrange guides on Lough Corrib, and sea angling trips from July onwards.
Western Region Fisheries Board, T091-563118. Provides information. For the last few years sea trout have been a protected species in this area. The Corrib System allows trout and salmon fishing, and the season opens on Lough Corrib in Feb. A boatman can be hired for around €65 per day.

Horse riding **Feeney's Equestrian Centre**, Toonabrockey, Bushypark, T091-526553. Organizes trekking and hacking around Galway, beach rides, hourly rates, unaccompanied children welcome.
Rockmount Riding Centre, Claregalway, 8 km from the city on main Galway to Sligo road, T091-798147. Indoor arena, trekking and hacking, lessons.
Rusheen Riding Centre, Salthill, T091-521285. Beach riding, trekking, lessons.

Tours Several tour companies have offices in the tourist office in Galway.
Bus Éireann, T091-562000. Runs daily tours to Connemara and Kylemore and to Burren and the Cliffs of Moher. Both €22.
Lally Tours, T091-553555, www.lallytours.com. Do tours of Connemara, the Burren and Cliffs of Moher, and open-top bus tours of the city departing from Eyre Sq every hour from 1030.
O'Neachtain, T091-553188. Runs identical tours from mid-May to late Sep.

Boat trips **Corrib Tours**, Furbo Hill, Furbo, T091-592447, www.corribprincess.ie. Run 1½-hr cruises daily cruises on Lough Corrib from Woodquay, Galway.

Transport

Galway city *p368, map p370*

Bike hire Bikes can be hired from some of the hostels as well as **Europa Bicycles**, Hunter's Building, Earl's Island, T091-563355. Mountain bikes can be hired from **Mountain Trail Bike Shop**, Cornstore, Middle St, T091-569888.

Bus Ceannt Bus Station, T091-562000, is next to the railway station, off Eyre Sq and behind the Great Southern Hotel. There are 15 buses a day to **Dublin**, 12 to **Cork**, as well as frequent buses to other cities in the Republic and the North. Several private companies also operate out of Galway. **Citylink**, T091-564163, (book online) www.citylink.ie, run numerous daily buses to **Dublin** and **Dublin Airport**, departing from outside the tourist office, and 4 buses a day to Shannon airport. **Bus Nestor**, T091-797144, busnestor@eircom.net, provides a similar service. **Michael Nee Buses**, T095- 34682, run between Galway and **Clifden**, via **Letterfrack**, linking up with the boat service to **Inishbofin**.

Car hire Windsor Rent-A-Car, Monivea Rd, Ballybrit, on the way to airport, T091-770707.

Taxi Galway Taxis, 7 Mainguard St, T091-561111, 24-hr service; **Corrib and Apollo**, Eyre St, to the north of Eyre Sq, T091-564444. There is a taxi rank by the railway station.

Train T091-561444. Trains for **Athlone**, **Tullamore**, **Portarlington**, **Kildare**, **Newbridge** and **Dublin** leave Galway 6 times a day (4 on Sun). Connections can be made at Kildare for towns in the south.

Aran Islands

→ *Phone code: 099. Colour map 2, grid C2.*

Three small islands lying 45 km southwest of Galway across the mouth of Galway Bay – Inishmore, Inishmaan, and Inisheer – plus another three very small uninhabited islands make up the famous Aran Islands that continue to act as a magnet for travellers in search of the 'real' Ireland. The course of history helped preserve the islanders' traditional way of life, but beginning in the early decades of the 20th century, writers and film makers celebrated the pre-industrial culture of the Aran Islands and turned the spotlight on them. The rest is history, of a very different kind, and in 1998 the authorities even talked of a 'tourist tax' to help cover the cost incurred by the annual invasion of visitors arriving by boats and planes from the mainland. The tax has not materialized but it gives you some idea of the numbers of people visiting the islands.

The good news is that two of the Aran Islands have not been destroyed by fame; the bad news is that Inishmore, at least in July and August, is best avoided. The two smaller islands, especially Inisheer, are rarely inundated with visitors and in many respects they retain much of the charm that first drew artists to Inishmore. However, the largest island is home to major archaeological sites and the tourist infrastructure has its advantages in terms of creature comforts. ▸▸ *For Sleeping, Eating and other listings, see pages 385-387.*

Ins and outs

Getting there **Aer Arann**, T091-593034, www.aerarann.ie, flies to all three islands, using eight-seater Islander aircraft, from **Connemara Regional Airport** at Inverin, off the main coastal road 28 km west of Galway. With flights every hour in peak months, the return fare is €44.50 and the connecting bus from the tourist office in Galway and Salthill costs €5 but takes longer to reach the airport from the city than the 10-minute actual flying time.

Island Ferries, T091-568903, www.aranislandferries.com, travel to all three islands from Rossaveal, 37 km west of Galway. In July and August there are up to six boats a day to Inishmore. Boats to the other two islands depart at 1030 and 1830 daily

(1730 Nov-Mar). The return fare is €19 and, if travelling from Galway, another €5 for the bus to Rossaveal that leaves from the office at Foster's Court beside the tourist office, 90 minutes before departure. Tickets may also be bought at the **Island Ferries** office at Rossaveal, T091-572050.

Doolin Ferries ⓘ *T065-74455*, run a service from Doolin to Inisheer (takes one hour and return fare is €25) and Inishmore (two hours, return fare €32), between Easter and Sep, and the journey takes about half an hour.

Boat services between the two smaller islands are operated by Island Ferries departing Inishmaan for Inisheer, daily at 11-15 and 1845, and returning 0830 and 1630. Single/return fare is €6-10.

Getting around Only Inishmore is large enough to justify an alternative to walking and upon disembarkation a fleet of bicycles are waiting to be hired. Vans (around €10 per person) are now increasingly common on the island for set tours of the main sites and pony traps with a driver may also be hired for around €15 per person.

Ecology

Geologically, the islands are a continuation of the limestone karsts that are so prominent a feature of the nearby Burren in County Clare. Countless generations of Aran Islanders spent winter months collecting sand and seaweed with which to layer the thin surfaces of bare limestone rock. Although no longer practised, this method produced a soil capable of being planted by farmers and many of the small fields you see today, with their rows of potatoes and vegetables, were built up from bare rock in this way. It is difficult not to notice the characteristic arrangement of 'lazy-beds' in the fields (the practice of using the soil dug for a trench as a bed to build up the adjoining ridge in which potatoes were planted) which minimizes the risk of waterlogging. Equally characteristic are the numberless, small, dry-stone walls that fence off one little field from another and create a maze-like filigree around the islands.

Well over 400 varieties of wildflower testify to the rich flora, seals are not too difficult to spot when they swim into shallow coves – Port Chorrúch is one of their haunts (see page 383) – and the occasional dolphin may be seen offshore. A bird book will be just as useful as a guide to wildflowers, with the increasingly uncommon chough seen around the coast and cuckoos galore heard in May.

History

The pre-historic stone forts found on the islands are testimony to an occupation by Iron Age and possibly late Bronze Age people, though next to nothing is known about their history. The first records of island life relate to the lives of early Christian saints like St Enda, who in around the sixth century founded a monastery that attracted like-minded ascetics from across Europe. In the Middle Ages the islands were fought over by the rival clans of the O'Flahertys and the O'Briens, but the squabbling of Gaelic chiefs was eclipsed by the English, who first took control in 1587. In the following century Cromwell established a garrison on the islands but, as the west of Ireland gradually lost its importance to the colonial power, the Aran islanders were left to themselves.

The outside world rediscovered the islands when their archaeological sites and the remarkable preservation of their Gaelic culture attracted notice. The playwright JM Synge made visits to listen to the Irish language and collect stories, and in 1932 the documentary film-maker Robert Flaherty made his now famously contrived film *Man of Aran*. In the last two decades of the 20th century, tourism has played a pivotal role not only in regenerating the islands' economy but also in their mythologization as the heartbeat of Celtic culture.

Local culture

Take with you JM Synge's *The Aran Islands* (1907), though you're unlikely to encounter the fellow passengers he shared passage with: "a couple of men going out with young pigs tied loosely in sacking, three or four young girls who sat in the cabin with their heads completely twisted in their shawls, and a builder, on his way to repair the pier at Kilronan". WB Yeats urged Synge to head for the Aran Islands, and one result of Synge's sojourn was this book which proved to be extremely influential in highlighting the islanders' traditional culture. Synge preferred Inishmaan because of the Irish spoken there but nowadays you will hear Gaelic spoken on all three islands and students of Irish arrive annually to practise the language. Flaherty's documentary made famous the islanders' involvement in fishing, and the traditional canvas-covered curragh is still used as a boat. Gone are the heel-less rawhide shoes that were so well adapted to clambering over rock but there is no shortage of the hand-knitted white sweaters with various patterns that the islands have given their name to. The novelist Liam O'Flaherty (1896-1984), who in 1921 ran up the red flag over the Rotunda in Dublin and occupied it for three days as "Chairman of the Council of the Unemployed", was born on Inishmore. A contemporary writer, Tim Robinson, has found inspiration on the Aran Islands and, while his *The Aran Islands: A Map & Guide* can be recommended, some may find his *Stones of Aran* books a bit heavy. Two anthologies of essays are worth dipping into: *The Book of Aran*, brought out by Tír Eolas, a local publisher, and available in Galway bookshops, and *An Aran Reader*, edited by Breandán & Ruairí Ó hEithir (Lilliput Press, Dublin).

Inishmore (Inis Mór)

Ins and outs

Getting around The largest of the three islands, Inishmore is about 14 km long and over 4 km at its widest. Boats arrive at Kilronan (Cill Rónáin), the main village, and from there the island's chief road travels both west to Kilmurvey, close to the major archaeological site and an alternative base for accommodation, and east to Killeany where St Enda's monastery once stood.

Tours of the island in a van will get you around the main sites quickly but they have little else to recommend them. Hiring a bike and cycling the Inis Mór Way is a lot more fun.

Information **Tourist office**, Kilronan, on the road up from the harbour, past the American Bar, T099-61263. Open Easter to mid-Sep 1000-1845; Nov-Mar 1000-1600,

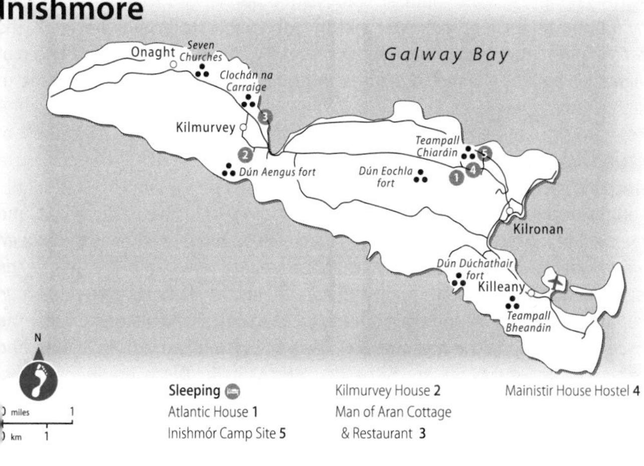

 Mar-May 1000-1700. **Ionad Árann** (Aran Heritage Centre), Kilronan, T099-61355 www.visitaranislands.com. Open Apr-Oct, 1000-1900. €3.50. Combined entrance and film €5.50. Introduces the history, geology and lifestyle of the islanders. The *Man of Aran* film is shown at 1200, 1345 and 1500.

Stone forts

Dún Aengus (or Dún Aonghasa) is the most spectacular site on Inishmore, not least because of its location on the edge of a 91-m cliff. Islanders tell stories of the days when men used to climb down these cliffs to collect bird eggs. This stone fort, one of the finest examples of Iron Age building in Europe and approximately 2,000 years old, is made up of three concentric enclosures, each with walls of dry masonry. The middle wall is defended by a remarkable *chevaux-de-frise* – vertical, jagged, sharp stones set at various angles to entrap an enemy force – while the main, innermost fort is 45 m in diameter, with walls nearly 4 m thick. The parapet and stairways of the inner walls were put in place when restoration work of questionable authority was carried out in 1881, but supporting evidence for this feature comes from the stone fort at Staigue in Cork. Be careful – extremely so with children – when approaching the edge because it is a sheer drop and the erosion that cut off the missing wall of the fort continues to eat away the land.

There are a number of other stone forts and prehistoric sites dotted around, and a copy of Tim Robinson's map is essential for anyone wishing to locate and really explore them. One of the more important is **Dún Eoghanachta**, an impressive circular fort northwest of Kilronan and best reached by taking the main road west of Kilronan (then look for the sign pointing south). There is also **Dún Eochla** inland, less than halfway from Kilronan and Dún Aengus. However, for another dramatically situated fort it is worth seeking out **Dún Dúchathair**, to the south of Kilronan and surrounded by cliffs on three sides.

Monastic sights

Continuing along the road west of Kilronan brings one to **Clochán na Carraige** on the north side of the road. This 8-m dry stone *clochán*, with the corbelled roof characteristic of early Christian buildings, is very well preserved. Travelling a little further west along the road accesses the **Seven Churches**, though you will only find two actual churches plus the ruins of monastic houses, assorted portions of cross-slabs and fragments of high crosses. One stone is inscribed with *VII Romans*, a fact that has given rise to various interpretations, including the unlikely one that Christian Romans are buried here. It is more probable that the graves are of pilgrims who made a journey to Rome.

An interesting ecclesiastical site is **Teampall Chiaráin** (Church of St Kieran) reached by taking the road south at Mainistir, complete with a high cross in the churchyard and an ancient holy well that probably marks a pagan site that early Christians expropriated. Just to the south of Killeany, **Teampall Bheanáin** (Church of St Benignus) is built on the rock orientated north to south and dates back to around the sixth century.

The Inis Mór Way

Mapping and information To enjoy walking or cycling on the island it is essential to get off the main road, and the 34-km Inis Mór Way is fairly well signposted. The drawback is that too much of the Way uses surfaced roads that are hard on your feet but compensation comes in the form of the sweeping views with the sea nearly always in view, enough stone-walled fields to last a lifetime and numerous opportunities to wander off and poke around archaeological and historical sites. The least expensive guide is the *Inis Mór Way* leaflet (€2), which includes a map and some brief descriptions. Ordnance Survey map No 51 in the Discovery series covers the island, and there is also Tim Robinson's map (see page 381) as well as specialist walking guides that cover the Way (see page 629).

The Way begins at **Kilronan** and heads north past the shingle and sand **Trá na bhFrancach** (Frenchman's Beach) before turning west and staying fairly close to the coastline, passing **Port Chorrúch** and meeting the white, sandy beach at **Port Mhuirbhigh** where the width of the islands shrinks to less than 1 km. On the other side of the beach, the Way heads uphill and inland, close by **Clochán na Carraige**, **Dún Eoghanachta** and the **Seven Churches**. It descends to the coast once more and then inland to a T-junction near the western end of the island. From here the Way returns inland again and eventually rejoins the outward route as far as Port Mhuirbhigh, where there is a spur to **Dún Aengus**, before heading southwards to the village of **Gort na bPéist**, where Liam O'Flaherty (see page 381) was born. It continues eastwards to **Dún Dúchathair** before heading north back to Kilronan.

★ Inishmaan (Inis Meáin) → *Colour map 2, grid C2.*

Inishmaan is the second largest of the Aran Islands, with a population of less than 200 as compared to the 800 or so who live in Inishmore. Figures like Synge and Pearse came here because of its reputation as the least culturally spoilt of the three islands and even today, probably because it attracts fewer visitors, this still holds true.

Ins and outs

Getting there and around Boats land at **An Córa** on the east side of the island and the main route leads across the island with *boreens* leading off to the north and south. The airstrip is in the northeast of the island. The island is only about 5 km long by about 3 km wide, and with little high ground it is not difficult to explore on foot.

Information The **Inis Meáin Island Co-operative**, in the middle of the island just north of the post office, T099-73010, is the place to make enquiries.

The Inis Meáin Way

By walking the undemanding 8-km Inis Meáin Way from An Córa, mostly along surfaced roads and quiet boreens, it is still possible to experience the appeal of an island that drew Synge back for five summers in succession at the turn of the 19th century.

From the pier keep the rocky shore on your left and head inland to the remains of **Cill Cheannanach**, a small oratory that dates from the eighth or ninth century, and what was the island graveyard until 1940. Follow the boreen uphill to **Dún na Fearbhaí**, a stone fort from around the same time, which provides good views of Connemara and Clare on a clear day. The Way continues westwards to the village of **Baile an Mhothair** and the island's only pub before passing the island's church, with its startling stained-glass windows by Harry Clarke. On the other side of the boreen, the ruined **Synge's Cottage** comes into view; the playwright spent his summers here between 1898 and 1902 and his *Riders to the Sea* is set on the island.

You will have already noticed the commanding presence of **Dún Chonchúir**, the island's most impressive

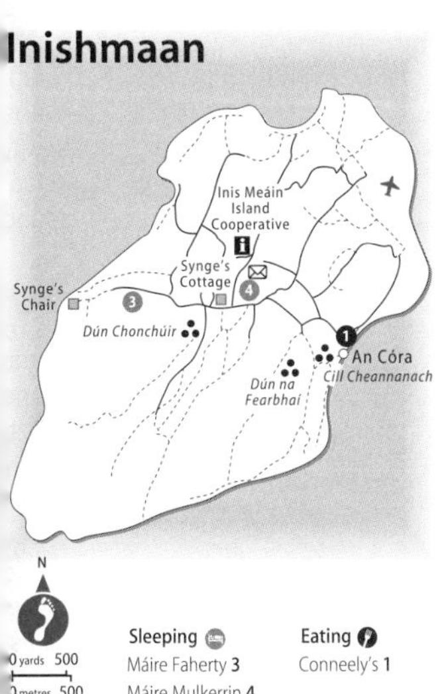

sight, but now it comes clearly into view. Oval in shape and with an outer bailey, this theatrically situated stone fort has walls 5.5 m high and 5 m wide in places. This is almost the highest point on Inis Meáin and the views on a fine day are stunning: from the peak of Mount Brandon on the Dingle Peninsula away to the south with the fantastic patches of surrounding tiny fields etched and defined by their stone walls. The Way continues, uphill along a road for a while and then across bare rock, to the western coastline and **Synge's Chair**. This dry-stone shelter was built by Synge because he liked to come here on a daily basis to contemplate the view and compose his thoughts.

Dún Chonchúir, the most eye-catching hill fort anywhere in Ireland, can be enjoyed in relative peace while hordes of visitors are tramping across Inishmore.

The Way then returns eastwards, a little to the north and at a lower level. It gradually turns into a tarmac road and turns to the left along a road, before the Way then turns right for the route back to the pier. Just before the Way turns to the right, a boreen on the left leads down to the beach, **Trácht Each**.

Inisheer (Inis Óirr) → *Colour map 2, grid C2.*

The smallest of the Aran Islands, with a population of around 300, is 9 km off the coast of Clare and receives a steady flow of travellers from Doolin as well as from Galway. The absence of any major archaeological attractions or other sights, however, helps ensure that the place is rarely overcrowded.

Ins and outs

Getting there and around The pier where boats arrive is on the north side of the island and the airstrip is to the east. The best way to explore this small island is on foot.

Tourist information Available from a small post near where the boats arrive. Open Jun-Sep 1000-1900. Also available from the **Inis Óirr Island Co-operative**, T099-75008.

O'Brien's Castle

Dominating the harbour side of the island, O'Brien's Castle (Caisleán Uí Bhriain) was built by the O'Briens at the very end of the 14th century in the centre of an ancient stone ringfort, **Dún Formna**, and on a clear day there are panoramic views from the walls. Close by stand the ruins of a signal tower from the days when the British feared an invasion by Napoleonic forces.

Churches

On the beach stands – or rather, sinks – **Church of St Keevaun (Teampall Chaoimháin)**, a little 11th-century church with a graveyard that was still being used even when sand had begun to submerge the church. To the west of the pier Cill Ghobnait is a small church dating from around the ninth century and dedicated to the female St Ghobnait.

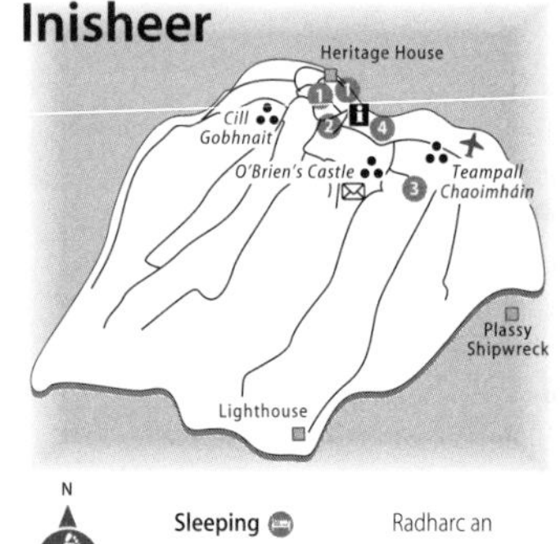

Heritage House

ⓘ *T099-75021. Jul and Aug daily 1400-1600. €1.* At the West Village, this is a stone-built thatched cottage with a collection of old photographs of life on the island, a craft shop and a tea room.

The Inis Óirr Way

Mapping and information As on Inishmaan, the best way to visit these sights and at the same time enjoy the strange and desolate beauty of the landscape is to follow the waymarked Inis Óirr Way. The 10.5 km that make up the Inis Óirr Way is well marked with waysigns but contents itself with tracing a route around the northern part of the island and sticking to surfaced roads, when you are just itching to break out across the tiny fields and explore parts of the limestone landscape for yourself. With a copy of map No 51 in the Ordnance Survey Discovery series this is very feasible indeed.

The Way starts from the pier where you disembark and heads east along the road, with the beach, **An Trá**, on your left. It then turns inland, passing **Teampall Chaoimháin** and the airstrip, before heading southwards to circle its way around **An Loch Mór** (the Big Lake). The wrecked ship that you see was the *Plassy*, driven aground and tossed onto the rocks in 1960. The Way heads north up the west side of the lake, with high walls (3 m) to either side, to the tiny village of **Formna**. It then turns south for a brief while before going west, with **O'Brien's Castle** close by to the north. Turning south again, the route passes the signal tower, and makes its way delightfully alongside stone walls that stretch maze-like in every direction.

When the Way meets the shore on the western side of the island, it turns northwards and follows the coast. You meet the remains of **Cill Ghobnait** before moving inland a little, passing one of the island's pubs and returning to the pier.

A walk to the lighthouse The road that leads to O'Brien's Castle continues on in the direction of a lighthouse at a southern tip of the island. It makes for an enjoyable walk and along the way there are superb views across to the Cliffs of Moher on the Clare coastline to the east. The road peters out at the shore a little way to the west of the lighthouse but it is easy to make your way across the slabs of limestone to the black-and-white strips of the 19th-century lighthouse. It was built in 1857 and though abandoned after being automated in 1978, the sturdily built and photogenic stone cottages built for the lighthousemen remain alongside the cylindrical tower. Either return via the same road or scramble past the lighthouse a little way to the east and find the road that heads north, parallel to the one you travelled south along. With a good map it is more enjoyable to leave the road, shortly after passing through a gate, and head down to the eastern shore to find a grassy path that heads inland for a little while to a junction where a right turn touches the shoreline again – the *Plassy* shipwreck is clearly visible – before heading northwards past the lake to meet the road near the airstrip.

Sleeping

Inishmore *p381, map p381*
There is one hotel and a range of other accommodation. The average B&B rate is €30+ per person and while there is a lot to choose from, it is advisable to have somewhere booked before arrival. The Kilronan, Mainistir and Aharla hostels are open all year.

B-D Aran Islands Hotel, Kilronan, T099-61104, www.aranislands.hotel.com. Open all year, except over Christmas, it proffers the expected creature comforts.

D Kilmurvey House, near Dún Aengus, T099-61218, www.kilmurveyhouse.com. Close to a safe beach. Evening meals available.

E Ard Einne, to the west of Kilronan, T099-61126, www.ardeinne.com. This guest house, with restaurant, enjoys sweeping views of the mainland coast and Galway Bay. Closed Dec and Jan.

E Atlantic House, Mainistir, T099-61185, maseoighe@hotmail.com. At the bottom end of this price category and rooms sharing bathroom facilities are € 25 per person.

E Man of Aran Cottage, Kilmurvey Bay, T099-61301, www.manofarancottage.com. This B&B, where part of the famous film was shot, charges a little above the average rate, open Mar-Oct.

F Aharla Hostel, Kilronan, T099-61305. Near the pier but still a pleasant location. No private rooms.
F Kilronan Hostel, Kilronan, T099-61255, kilronanhostel@ireland.com. Being in Kilronan, near to the pier and above a pub combine to make it both convenient and noisy (though bedrooms are reasonably soundproofed). No private rooms. Bike hire.
F Mainistir House Hostel, Kilronan, T099-61169, www.mainistirhousearan.com. Walking distance from the pier. Has 60 beds including a family room, doubles, twin and small dorms. Breakfast included. Bike hire.
F Ti Eithne, Kilronan, T099-61303. A short walk away from the harbour. 3 bedrooms, sharing facilities, open Jun-Oct.
G Killeany Lodge Pilgrim Hostel, to the southeast of Kilronan, T099-61393, www.ashlinglodge.com. A relatively quiet spot, with 3 private rooms and camping.

Camping
Inishmór Camp Site, at Mainistir, T099-61185. Near the beach. Very basic.
Killeany Lodge Hostel, campsite attached to this hostel has the use of its kitchen and showers.

Inishmaan *p383, map p383*
E An Dún, T099-73047. B&B and restaurant in the centre of the island. Comfortable bedrooms with en suite bathrooms and a mini-spa/sauna.
E Máire Faherty, Ard Alainn, at the end of the road that leads to Dún Chonchúir, T099-73027. B&B open from the end of Apr-Sep.
E Máire Mulkerrin, T099-73016. Welcoming B&B in the middle of the island, near the pub.
E Creig Mór, about 500 m from the pier, T099-73012. Has been recommended as a good B&B for a comfortable night's stay on the island. Evening meal can be arranged. Open Mar-Nov.
E Ostan Inis Meain, T099-73020. Very small place, 10 rooms, with sea views, sound food and lots of music.

Self-catering
For the 'get away from it all' self-catering option contact **Pádraig o Fatharta** at the pub, T099-73047, or **Nora Concannon**, T099-55893.

Inisheer *p384, map p384*
E Ard Mhuire, T099-75005, unamcdonagh@hotmail.com. The first house on the right as you walk up from the ferry can't be accused of cashing in on tourism for visitors have been accommodated here since the 1930s. Tea and scones on arrival and a hearty evening meal is an attractive option. Flat rate per person of €25/30 for en suite/sharing facilities.
E Inisheer Hotel, near the pier, T099-75020. A comfy little hotel with a bar and restaurant.
E Radharc An Chláir, within walking distance of the pier, near O'Brien's Castle, T099-75019. Open all year. There are rooms with and without their own bathrooms and doubles/singles are from €35 to €60. Evening meals available.
F Bru Radharc Na Mara Hostel, T099-75024, maire.searraigh@oceanfree.net. Close to the pier, has nearly 40 beds and 2 private rooms. Bikes for hire and a pub next door.

Camping
Inisheer Camp Site, T099-75008. Functions May-Sep. Situated by the beach.

Eating

Inishmore *p381, map p381*
In summer be sure to make a reservation for an evening meal if not eating in the Kilronan pubs that serve food.
Dún Aonghasa and Aran Fisherman, a short way west of the pier on the road to Killeany. Specializes in seafood but there is a choice of meat, pasta and pizza and dishes range from €8 to €20.
Joe Watty's Bar, comes recommended if you want a sociable night of eating and drinking.
Mainistir House Hostel, offers a sociable evening meal at 2000 for €15, self-described as a "vaguely vegetarian buffet", with diners welcome to bring their own drinks. Good food, good value and, if you're lucky, good company.
Man of Aran Cottage, Kilmurvey Bay, T099-61301. Opens for lunch and dinner, good food can also be enjoyed outside in the garden (where the vegetables you eat are grown).

Inishmaan *p383, map p383*
There are limited opportunities for eating out on Inishmaan, especially outside the

For an explanation of the sleeping and eating price codes used in this guide, see inside the front cover. Other relevant information is found in Essentials pages 39-45.

summer months, and you might want to bring a picnic for lunch.

The island's only pub, T099-73003, serves light meals in the summer until around 1900 but most of the B&Bs will provide an evening meal if you arrange this in advance.

An Dun, T099-73068, near the junction where you turn left for Dún Chonchúir. Opens in the summer for dinner. Great food, especially the fresh fish and local lamb, a reservation is fairly essential.

Connely's/Tig Congaile, T099-73085. 5 mins from the harbour, serves lovely scones and coffee as well as good meals from mid-morning to 2100. The views are just what you would hope for.

Inisheer *p384, map p384*

Inisheer Hotel, the restaurant here is open for lunch and dinner.

Mermaid's Cottage, Castle Village, 5 mins from the hotel and up a hill, T099-75062. Serves organic food, using the traditional method of fertilizing with seaweed, for lunch and dinner between Easter and Oct. Bring your own wine and enjoy a superb dinner.

Rory Conneely/Tigh Ruaírí, less than 5 mins from the pier. Pub food served daily.

Pubs and music

Inishmore *p381, map p381*

Nearly all the pubs on the islands have some form of entertainment at night during the summer months.

American Bar, in Kilronan. A popular place that caters to every type of visitor. Here you'll rub shoulders with an amazing mix of people – from salty fisherman to clueless tourists – enlivened by occasional outbursts of song.

Ragus, Halla Ronain, T099-572525. A traditional Irish dance and music show lasting an hour. Shows are twice daily. €14.

Tigh Fitz, Killeany. Involves a journey if not staying in this part of the island but the musical sessions can be fun.

Inisheer *p384, map p384*

Rory Conneely/Tigh Ruaírí, traditional music sessions at this pub.

Tígh Ned, 200 m from the pier, pub which has sessions of traditional music.

Shopping

Inishmore *p381, map p381*

Inishmore is *the* place to purchase a genuine hand-knitted Aran sweater and there are a few places selling them.

An Teach Ceoil, near to Carraig Donn. Crammed with CDs of traditional Irish music.

Carraig Donn, Kilronan. Has a selection of hand-made sweaters as well as factory knitwear, tweed and wax jackets.

Directory

Inishmore *p381, map p381*

Banks There are no ATMs on the island. Bank of Ireland in Kilronan. Jun-Aug, Wed-Thu; Sep-May, Wed. Bureaux de change: money can be changed at the post office, or the Carraig Donn shop. **Bike hire** Burke Bike Hire, T099-61402, and other outlets around the pier, and from some of the hostels. **Post office** Past the tourist office on the road up from the harbour.

Inishmaan *p383, map p383*

Bank Bank of Ireland, operates on the 2nd Tue of each month.

Inisheer *p384, map p384*

Banks Bank of Ireland, operates on the 4th Tue of each month. Bureau de change at the Inisheer Hotel.

Connemara and Lough Corrib

Connemara is the land to the northwest of Galway – a geographical region and a mythologized one – framed by the sea on three sides. It is famous for its desolate landscape of bogs and mountains and extensive veins of green marble, which were traded in Neolithic times certainly as far away as Lough Gur in Limerick and possibly to the Boyne Valley as well. In Connemara geology, landscape and shifting weather patterns (one way of saying it rains a lot) translate into a singular and inspiring natural beauty: mist-covered mountains, transitory gradations of light and colour, craggy glens and poetic contours of land and sea. Lough Corrib, to the east is the largest lake in the Republic and stretches for some 48 km from Galway city to the border with Mayo. Inchagoill, the largest of the 300 or so islands studded across its surface, is worth visiting for its unique Latin inscription on an obelisk and the photogenic remains of early Christian places of worship. Ask an angler about Lough Corrib, however, and Pavlovian glee will accompany any thought of the mayfly dapping season in early summer – it brings in anglers from all over Europe and beyond, lured by the chance of catching brown trout and salmon. ▸▸ *For Sleeping, Eating and other listings, see pages 396-400.*

Ins and outs

Getting there There is a daily non-stop bus service between Galway and Clifden and, between the end of June and the end of August, a daily service that also stops at Oughterard, Cashel, Roundstone and other smaller towns. The early morning bus on this route continues on from Clifden to Letterfrack, Kylemore, Leenane and Westport. Check with the bus station in Galway, T091-562000, for the schedule.

If you are travelling by car or bike, there is a choice of routes west from Galway: the N59 road through the middle of Connemara via Oughterard and straight on to Clifden, or the R336 road that follows the coast via Spiddal, Rossaveal (departure

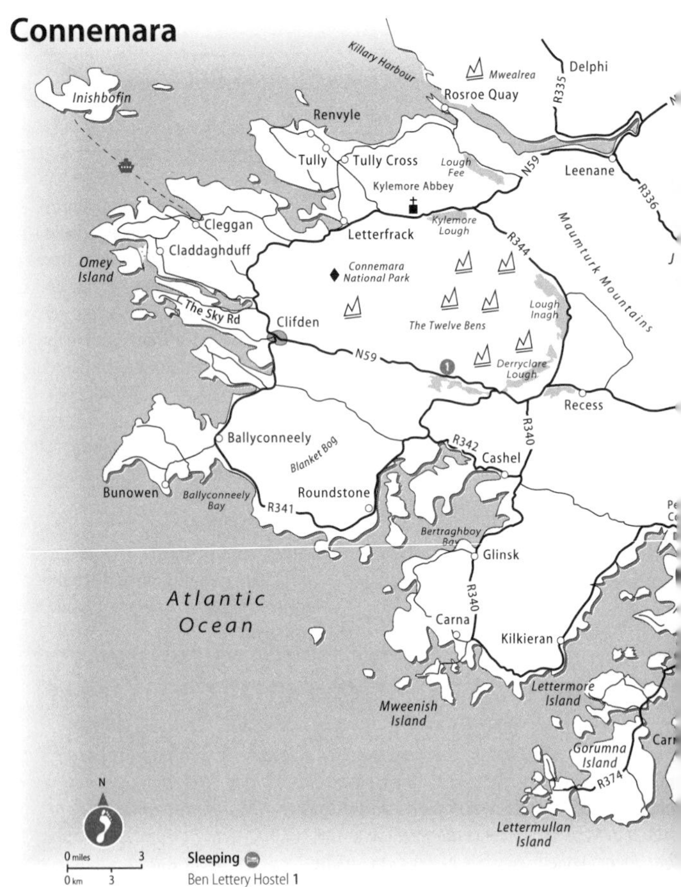

point for the Aran Islands) and north to Maam Cross where it meets the N59. A mountain road cuts a scenic route through a hill pass and a beautifully brooding landscape to link Oughterard with Rossaveal. ▸▸ *See Transport, page 400, for further details.*

Getting around Organized coach tours from Galway are available. **Lally Coaches**, T091-562905, www.lallytours.com, has a day-long tour that takes in most of the main sights. **O'Neachtain**, T091-553188, www.wombat.ie/pages/oneachtain-tours, runs a similar tour. Cruise boats operate between Oughterard and Cong on either side of Lough Corrib, and a cruise is also available from Galway with **Corrib Tours**, T091-592447.

Angling information **Thomas Tuck**, at the Clifden end of Main St in Oughterard, T091-552335, sells tackle and licences. Some of the hotels advise and facilitate angling guests.

Geology

Central Connemara is dominated by the Twelve Bens (see page 391) and the Maumturk mountains, with their peaks of quartzite, while the lowland to the west is more schist and gneiss. The southern part of Connemara, covered by the Spiddal to Clifden section (see page 392), has a different geographic complexion. The land is equally boggy but low-lying and characterized by small lakes of assorted shapes, a heavily indented coastline with tiny islands, and granite rock that imparts a geology different from the central and northern areas. This is also where you are most likely to hear Gaelic being spoken.

Prehistory

At one time Connemara was a byword for cultural backwardness, and even prehistoric communities were thought to have shunned its terrain. However, in the last 20 years a wealth of Neolithic and Bronze Age sites have been discovered, complementing the rediscovery of Connemara as a place of escape from the metropolitan world.

Oughterard

➔ *Phone code: 091. Colour map 2, grid B3.*

The village of Oughterard, where the main Galway to Clifden road crosses the little Owenriff river, is renowned as an angling centre, but it also serves as a comfortable introduction to the wilder Connemara that lies west of here. There is a good choice of accommodation and places to eat, a castle and a mine worth visiting and the chance of an excursion to Inchagoill Island. The *Fáilte Ireland*-affiliated **tourist office** is on Main St, T091-552808, in the centre of village. It also acts as an agents for Corrib Ferries, air or boat passage to the Aran Islands and the boat to Inishbofin. Open all year, daily, 0930-1730. Internet access.

Aughnanure Castle ⓘ *T091-552214. Mid-Jun to Sep daily 0930-1830. €2.75. OPW site. 3 km east of Oughterard, off the main N59 road.* A trip to Aughnanure Castle, a well-preserved tower house built on an island of rock, is well worth the short detour off the N59 road. This is one of the best examples of how Gaelic chiefs lived in the pre-Plantation era. There is little to see inside, but this is an ideal opportunity to view the elemental architecture of a fortified home. The castle is basically a tower house built in the 16th century as a stronghold for the O'Flaherty clan, and its excellent state of preservation is what singles it out. The approach along a footpath by the River Dimneen and across a natural bridge is picturesque, but this sturdy structure was not built for the fine view. Bartizans are still in place half-way up the walls and on all sides there are superb examples of machicolated galleries (galleries with openings between the corbels for dropping stones on to attackers).

To the south stand the remains of the east wall of a banqueting hall, which is said to have contained a trap door for dropping unwanted guests into the subterranean river that flows under the hall. The elaborately carved decorations on the windows of the remaining wall are worthy of appreciation, although the watch tower in the southeast corner is more eye-catching.

Glengowla Mines ⓘ *T091-552360. Mar-Nov daily 0930-1830. €7.50. Outside Oughterard and signposted off the main N59 road to Maam Cross.* The mines date back to the 19th century and have now been opened by the family who live on the land above them. A 25-minute guided tour takes you through the mineral-studded chambers with their lead, pyrite and veins of calcite and quartz, and there is a small exhibition area above ground which includes some minerals for sale.

Inchagoill Island

ⓘ *Corrib Ferries, T091-552808/552170. Daily sailings between Oughterard and Cong, which stops off at Inchagoill for 30 mins. Tickets are €15, obtainable from the tourist office, and departures are at 1100, 1445 and 1700 between May and Oct.*
Inchagoill is the largest of the islands in Lough Corrib and the most intriguing of its ancient remains is the **Lia Luguaedon Mac Menueh** ('stone of Luguaedon, son of Menueh') burial stone. Less than 75 cm high, it is possibly the oldest Latin inscription of Christian origin in Europe (apart from the catacombs). It stands near the **Church of the Saints** (Teampall na Naoimh), a worthy example of Irish Romanesque from the ninth or 10th century, while the **Church of St Patrick** (Teampall Phádraig) is another small oratory of lesser architectural interest on the island.

The Owenriff Way

This is a gentle 45-minute riverside stroll westwards out of Oughterard as far as the bridge next to the Catholic church. Cross the bridge and turn immediately to the right to walk along the footpath that follows the river downstream. Continue for about 400 m to a green metal bridge and walk out along the road – the Glan road – taking the first right turn signposted to the *Camillaun & Corrib Country* B&Bs. After about 200 m cross the river at the footbridge and after another 100 m walk onto Camp Street and take the first turning on the left (the Owenriff Way is signposted on the corner behind greenery) to return to the riverside. Carry on downstream, past the sheds and across a stile. The path leads onto the Pier Road where a right turn brings you back to the village.

"Westward ho! Let us rise with the sun and be off to the land of the West". William Wilde, father of Oscar, warmed to the west of Ireland as the spiritual home of Gaelic culture in his 'Lough Corrib: its shores and Islands'. (1867)

Walking in the West

Oughterard, the self-proclaimed "gateway to Connemara", is indeed a good place to plan and organize a walking trip in the 'real' Connemara that lies just a short distance to the west. The tourist office has a good selection of maps, guides and information.

Mapping and information The tourist office sells a map and guide to the Western Way for €8.25, but many walkers prefer the similarly priced *Mountains of Connemara* booklet by Joss Lynam that comes complete with a 1:50,000 map.

The **Western Way**, which begins outside of Oughterard and amounts to over 217 km on its journey across Connemara and Mayo, is the main long-distance walk, and while the whole Way could take not far short of two weeks to complete, most people choose a one-, two- or three-day section. With the help of the **Bus Éireann** timetable it would be possible, for example, to leave one's transport at Oughterard and walk for three days to Leenane before catching a bus back to base. Public transport will help with a two-day walk to Kylemore or even a one-day walk to Maam Cross.

Oughterard to Clifden

Shortly after leaving Oughterard on the N59 the landscape opens up and the appeal of Connemara begins to make itself felt. Lakes and mountains majestically proclaim themselves, and as the bogland spreads out on either side of the road, mounds of turf set out to dry become a common site. The junction at **Maam Cross** is overshadowed by a huge tourist complex (www.peacockeshotel.com) which includes a craft and souvenir shop, a hotel and a 60-foot viewing tower. Impossible to miss, the bar and restaurant are a useful watering hole but the place as a whole is a bit of an eyesore.

From Oughterard the N59 road carries on due west all the way to Clifden but there are several alternative routes you might consider. At the Maam Cross junction, the R336 road heads north to Leenane, skipping out west Connemara altogether and accessing Mayo. The R336 road also heads south to Screeb where a turning westwards takes the R340 through south Connemara hugging the coast nearly all the way to Clifden (and briefly rejoining the N59 west of Recess). Then again, you could to stay on the N59 until shortly after Recess before heading north on the very scenic R344 road through the Lough Inagh Valley. You could also do this as a roundabout route to Clifden via Letterfrack.

Recess Recess is just a couple of houses, a bar and a shop on the N59 between Maam Cross and Clifden but the area around here is interesting and a couple of diversions suggest themselves. **Ballynahinch Castle** is now a hotel (see page 396), but it was once the home of Humanity Dick (1754-1834), a member of the Martin family who acquired a fearsome reputation for his defence of animal rights. He is reputed to have fought duels on behalf of animals and imprisoned miscreants on his estate in the old tower by the lake for mistreating animals. Humanity Dick also played a pivotal role in establishing the RSPCA. It's expensive to stay here but a passing visit to the public bar at the hotel is a great way to savour the mood of a fine Victorian mansion that was once reputed to have the longest drive of any country house in the land.

Some 5 km west of the Ben Lettery hostel, close to Clifden itself, stands **Connemara Heritage and History Centre** ⓘ *T095-21246, www.connemaraheritage.com, Apr-Oct daily 1000-1800, €6, B&B accommodation is also available (see Dan O'Hara's Farmhouse page 397)*, complete with ersatz dolmen, crannog, 19th-century thatched farmhouse, ringfort, coach park and audio-visual show.

Twelve Bens and Inagh Valley West of Recess the scenery becomes breathtaking as the Twelve Bens mountain range comes into view. Legend has it that St Patrick came to the Twelve Bens but turned back on the assumption that no sane Christian would want to live there. Look for the turning for the R344 road north to Letterfrack and consider this route around to Clifden through the Inagh Valley. This wide valley has stirring views of the forbidding Twelve Bens to the west/left and the Maumturks to the east/right. About 2 km on the road there is the Lough Inagh Lodge (see page 396) and a few hundreds yards past the hotel there is a forestry track that leads to a bridge over the strait dividing Lough Inagh from Lough Derryclare. This is the starting point for a demanding climb to the summits of Derryclare and Bencorr, which should not be undertaken without the Ordnance Survey map No 37 and a specialist walking guide (see page 629).

Spiddal to Clifden

The alternative route through Connemara from Galway is by way of the R336 coastal road that follows the northern coastline of Galway Bay through Spiddal to Ballynahown. Here, the road turns north for Maam Cross where it meets the N59 but take instead the R340 that branches off to the west at Screeb before you reach Maam Cross. The R340 stays close to the coast for most of the way around Kilkieran Bay and then Bertraghboy Bay. At Cashel, the R340 heads north to join the N59 but, again, you can branch off westwards by taking the R341 and approach Clifden from the south.

The Screeb to Clifden route is definitely for travellers who find journeying at least as interesting as the actual destination. Conventional places of interest are few and far between, but there are numerous small roads that weave their way into coastal crevices, and interesting opportunities to encounter a delightful spot while in the process of getting lost. Sommerville and Ross travelled through here in the 1890s equipped with a spirit-lamp, Bovril and a revolver, and noted in *Through Connemara in a Governers-cart* (1893) how "every road we have seen in Connemara makes for water like an otter and finds it with seeming ease, sometimes even succeeding in getting into it". At Costello, the headquarters of Radio na Gaeltachta, a road heads south to **Carraroe** from where there are exciting views of the Aran Islands as well as splendid coral and shell beaches which are rarely crowded. At **Carna** there is an easy walk out to **Mweenish Island** and sandy beaches.

Pearse's Cottage ⓘ *T091-574292, €1.50, mid-Jun to mid-Sep, daily and mid to end Sep, Sat-Sun 1000-1800; open over Easter weekend, Sat-Mon 1000-1700, OPW site*, where Padraig Pearse (executed in 1916 for his role in the Easter Rising) spent summers and used the cottage as a summer school for the students of his bilingual St Enda's School in Dublin, may prove disappointing because there is precious little inside. But a path runs past the front door and down to a bench by a lake where one imagines Pearse enjoyed the view.

Roundstone → *Phone code: 095. Colour map 2, grid B2.*

The village of Roundstone, quaint and quietly popular, is worth considering as a place to stop over for a night. One of the attractions is a climb to the summit of **Mount Errisbeg** (298 m), because it only takes a couple of hours and the going is not difficult. Take the path that goes along the side of O'Dowd's pub and turns into a track up the mountain. From the top there are remarkable views of bog land, mountain peaks and coastline: the essence of Connemara.

Workshops Another attraction is the cluster of art and craft workshops that are open to the public, including the much-visited **Roundstone Musical Instruments**. Tin whistles, harps and flutes are all here, though pride of place goes to the *bodhrán*, the goatskin hand-held drum without which no group of traditional Irish musicians is complete. There is also the **Music Shop** ⓘ *T095-35875, www.Bodhran.com, workshop: Mar-Oct daily 0900-1900*, in the centre of Clifden.

Beaches

Some of the most wonderful beaches in Ireland are to be found around Roundstone and if the climate were more friendly to the tourist industry it would not be difficult to imagine Club Med-type developments mushrooming here. To reach the beaches stay on the road west to Ballyconneely and turn south for **Gurteen Bay** and **Dog's Bay**; the incredible whiteness of the sand is produced by millions of microscopic foraminiferous seashells. It is only another 12 km to **Ballyconneely** where there is another splendid beach and the ruins of Bunowen Castle.

Clifden → *Phone code: 095. Colour map 2, grid B2.*

Its size and location – the largest town west of Galway – makes Clifden the capital of Connemara. The town, laid out by a 19th-century English landlord, is characterized by its geometry, broad streets and the twin spires of 19th-century churches, with the Twelve Bens providing a dramatic backdrop. Travellers' attitudes to Clifden vary and some feel that its forced birth into tourism – the shops and restaurants have all sprung up comparatively recently – has left it strangely bereft of an identity; others revel in its creature comforts, especially welcome after a day or two spent walking in the surrounding countryside. The **tourist office** is on Galway Rd, T095-21163. Open mid-Apr to Sep.

Museum There is little to see in the town itself and the **Station House Museum**, sited in what was the engine shed of the Clifden railway station, is of limited interest. There is an exhibition on the Connemara pony alongside assorted memorabilia.

Walks and cycle rides around Clifden

Maps Maps No 37 and 44 in the Ordnance Survey Discovery Series cover these walks and makes the journeying a lot more interesting. The views are magnificent on the **Sky Road**, heading directly west out of town and around a small peninsula. It is fine for cycling and could be an enjoyable easy walk depending on the amount of cars – do everyone a favour and avoid driving along this road. The total distance is about 13 km; take a picnic because there are no pubs or restaurants until the Sky Road meets up with the main N59.

You can enjoy an undemanding 1½-hour walk along an **old bog road** if you leave your car at the Ardagh Hotel on the Ballyconneely road and walk south for a short distance, until the road crosses Ballinaboy Bridge. Take the left fork there, signposted for Cashel and Recess, and keep the Ballinaboy River on your left after crossing it by another bridge. Turn round after reaching the next small bridge, Beaghcauneen Bridge, and on the way back turn left about 500 m before Ballinaboy Bridge, signposted for Lough Fadda. Walking south to Lough Fadda, passing the much smaller Lough Enask on the way, adds less than an hour to the walk.

In 1919 the first aeroplane to cross the Atlantic, a Vickers Vimy, landed to the south of Clifden and John Alcock and Arthur Whitten Brown stepped on to land for the first time in over 16 hours. To reach the **Alcock and Brown monument**, walk or cycle to the Ballinaboy Bridge on the Ballyconneely road, as for the old bog road walk (see above), but then bear to the right, staying on the R341 for 500 m until you reach a crossroads. Take the left turn, signposted for the landing site, and walk south, passing a small lake and heading for the white monument when it comes into view. This stretch of road follows the line of a narrow-gauge railway and it also passes the place where Marconi operated the first transatlantic wireless, now marked by a plaque.

Retrace your steps from the monument or continue westwards on the green road, passing a lake and then a quarry on your left, until you get to a small road. You will then pass the larger Lake Emlanabehy before rejoining the R341; after that you will have to walk back to Clifden along the main road. The entire walk takes about 1½ hours.

The **Omey Island** walk starts from the village of Claddaghduff, which is 13 km northwest of Clifden near Cleggan, and easily reached by car or bicycle by heading out on the N59 to Letterfrack and then taking the signposted road to the left. You get to the island by following the markers across the sand from the beach at Claddaghduff, but you should avoid high tide; you can check the times at the pub in Claddaghduff.

Cleggan → Phone code: 095.

This small fishing village, 16 km northwest of Clifden, is primarily of interest for visitors heading for the island of Inishbofin. Boats also depart from here for the island of Inishturk in County Mayo (see page 416). The **Cleggan Riding Centre**, T095-44746, provides riding lessons and treks along the beach, to Omey Island. The Sky Road will take you to the tiny village of Claddaghaduff and when the tide is out it is easy to walk over to Omey Island where there are good beaches.

Inishbofin Island → *Phone code: 095. Colour map 2, grid B1.*

Inishbofin can be as whimsical as its name suggests: a magical silence during the day and gregarious pub life at night. This little island – only 6 km long by less than 3 km wide – is easily reached from Cleggan (you can do it as a day's excursion or stay the night). Inishbofin has not been spoiled by tourism – yet – because the majority of the few hundred inhabitants do not depend on the highly seasonal flow of visitors to sustain their way of life. Come here for fresh-air walks and a sense of calm and enjoy the feeling that not everywhere in the west of Ireland is being packaged and marketed by *Fáilte Ireland*.

Getting there Inishbofin is 10 km west of Cleggan from where it takes about 40 minutes to reach the island. **Island Discovery**, T095-45819/45894, is the mail boat that departs from Cleggan every day of the year for €15 return. There is also **Inishbofin Ferries**, T095-45903, but their service operates in the summer only, Apr-Oct. **Michael Nee Buses**, T095-46832, run buses from the Courthouse in Clifden for €10/13 single/return that connect with the Island Discovery departures.

There is no official **tourist office**, but try either hotel for general tourist information and there is a small **heritage centre** near Day's Hotel, open summer, daily 1200-1700, €2.50.

History St Colman came to Inishbofin from Iona in the seventh century to found a monastery after quarrelling with Rome over a new calendar that changed the date of Easter. Nothing remains of his original settlement, but the ruins of a 13th-century church are supposedly standing on the original site. Grace O'Malley, the pirate queen, used Inishbofin, and the ruins of the castle that can be seen when approaching the harbour date from the 16th century when she was alive. Cromwell captured the castle in 1652 and fortified it for the purpose of incarcerating prisoners. A variation on the haunting theme of Cromwell's perfidy, the story goes that he chained a bishop to a large rock in the harbour and left him there until the tide came in and drowned him. Ted Hughes and Sylvia Plath came to Insihboffin, shortly before they split up, as guests of the poet Richard Murphy (see Books, page 629) who was the first to take tourists out to the island.

Island walk/cycle Head west (left) after disembarking at the harbour and follow the road as it turns into a green road and passes, after about 20 minutes of walking, a sparkling little sandy beach. Carry on westwards until the green road fades away and then head for the most westerly point, clearly visible and quite safe to reach on foot or cycling because the ground is flat and there are no cliffs. Sheep, rabbits, seabirds and the occasional seal may be your only company on a quiet day. On reaching the western extremity walk over to the northern side of the island and pick up the path near the metal cross and head back as far as the lake and then south to rejoin the road you started on.

The road going eastwards from the harbour passes the church ruins and accesses a second beach. By following the road around to the north side you'll find a third beach.

From Clifden to Leenane → *Phone code: 095. Colour map 2, grid B2.*

Letterfrack Not so much a town as a roadside collection made up of shops, pubs and assorted houses on the N59 between Clifden and Leenane, Letterfrack lends itself to use as a possible base for a day or two because Connemara National Park and Kylemore Abbey are close by. Cleggan lies to the west and there is an interesting coastal region to the north.

Connemara National Park ⓘ *T095-41054. Mid-Mar to Oct, daily 1000-1730. Grounds open all year round, guided nature walks (2-3 hrs) in Jul and Aug on Mon, Wed and Fri mornings. €2.75. There are outdoor and indoor picnic tables and a café.* Managed by the OPW, much of the Park area once formed part of the Kylemore Abbey estate but the expanses of bog, heath and mountains are now open to the public. At the Visitors' Centre there is a 15-minute audio-visual presentation every half hour and guide books and maps are for sale. The 1.4-km **Sruffaunboy Nature Trail** is an undemanding self-guided stroll, and a useful inexpensive booklet is available that points out ecological features along the way, including Connemara ponies, 'lazy bed' cultivation ridges, bogland flora and fauna and types of Connemara rock. For serious walkers, some of the Twelve Bens are within the Park.

Kylemore Abbey and gardens ⓘ *T095-41146. Mar-Oct daily 0900-1730. €7. Self-service restaurant.* Built as a gift for his wife in the 1860s by Mitchell Henry, an English industrial magnate and MP who was charmed by Connemara, the appeal of Kylemore Abbey is inseparable from its location. The buildings are stepped on terraces overlooking the lake and there are two buildings to admire: the neo-Gothic castle built as a family home and a small chapel a short distance away. Benedictine nuns acquired Kylemore in 1920 and it is now run as a private boarding school for girls. This means that many of the rooms are off-limits to visitors and, combined with the fact that a fire destroyed many of the interiors anyway, the result is that there is not really that much to see inside. The chapel, designed by James Fuller in 1868, is an imitation of an English 14th-century church and the stone vaulting has recently been restored to its former glory. Kylemore Abbey gardens have recently been restored and opened to the public; the late Victorian walled garden was an integral part of Henry's plan to transform the wilderness of Connemara into a country estate. Alas, it was not to be. His wife's health was seriously impaired by the winter climate, Henry himself became bankrupt trying to maintain Kylemore and he died a few years after being forced to sell the property.

Some of the better self-service food in Ireland, including black-eye bean casserole for vegetarians, is available at Kylemore Abbey. Look out for the wholesome homemade jams too.

Renvyle Peninsula and around → *Phone code: 095. Colour map 2, grid 2B.*

Another literary corner of Ireland (though not one of the better-known ones) Renvyle's fame is thanks to Oliver St John Gogarty (1878-1957), who had a home here and invited Yeats, Shaw and others to share his "faery land of Connemara at the extreme end of Europe, [where] the incongruous flowed together at last, and the sweet and bitter blended". The good news is that life is not quite so terminal around Renvyle and there are a number of modest diversions.

At **Lettergesh**, a couple of km east from Tully Cross, there is a lovely little beach and another one, the spectacular white-sand **Glassillaun Beach**, is just past here. From the small golfing green at Renvyle House, you can go for a pleasant walk beyond the lake and along the pebbly beach to the ruins of an old O'Flaherty Castle.

Maritime Museum and Seatrips ⓘ *Museum: T095-43473. May-Sep daily 1000-1800, Oct-Apr daily 1000-1700, closed for 3 weeks over Christmas. €5. Signposted on the road from Letterfrack to Tully. Picnic area and café. €15 (cruise), €45 (fun fishing), sailings at 1000 (fishing), 1230, 1430, 1400, and 1800 (fishing).*

Ocean and Country Museum is an aquarium and maritime museum, scenically located on Derryinver Bay, and devoted to Connemara's marine life. It offers a useful introduction to the ecological richness of the area. Under the same management, four sailings a day cruise around Ballinakill Harbour, Letterfrack, Derryinver and Fahy bays and there is a good chance of seeing a few sociable dolphins and porpoises, perhaps a basking seal or two and certainly plenty of seabirds.

Leenane and Killary Harbour → *Phone code: 095. Colour map 2, grid B2.*

Whether coming from Clifden to the southwest or from Mayo in the north the approach into Leenane along Killary Harbour is unforgettably beautiful. Regarded as Ireland's only fjord, it is sublime or sinister, depending on the play of light. The philosopher Wittgenstein (1889-1951) found it inspiring, living for six months in 1948 near the mouth of the harbour at Rosroe while working on *Philosophical Investigations*. The house where he lived is now the Killary Harbour Hostel, and facing the hostel on the north side of the harbour is Mount Mweelrea (819 m). **NB** If travelling north into Mayo from Leenane be sure to take the R335 road via Delphi and not the main N59, especially if travelling by bicycle. The R335 route offers up a landscape of such serenity and melancholy that is hard to find anything to compare with it in the whole of Ireland. Praise indeed.

Leenane is picturesquely situated at the head of the harbour and such is the grandeur of the scene that many travellers feel compelled to make a stop. The village makes the most of the fact that scenes from John B Keane's *The Field* were filmed here, and an enjoyable walk leads to the **Asaleagh Waterfall** where the church scene was filmed. At **Leenane Cultural Centre**, the focus of interest is on the local wool industry and several breeds of sheep are, as it were, open to the public. Visitors can mingle with the flock and its collie dog in order to identify the different breeds. The **Wool Museum** ⓘ *T095-42323, Apr-Oct, daily 1000-1900, €4, café*, demonstrates the arts of carding, spinning and weaving and a 13-minute video covers the woollen industry and local places of interest.

Cruises on Killary depart from Nancy's point, 2 km west of Leenane on the N59, four times a day, 1030, 1230, 1430 and 1630, between Apr and Sep. There is also a 1900 dinner cruise on Fri and Sat during Jul and Aug. The regular 90-minute cruise costs €17.

Sleeping

Oughterard *p389*

A-B Currarevagh House, T091-552312, www.currarevagh.com. Built as a wedding present in 1840, this guest house has a tranquil location on the shore of Lough Corrib and a 2-night stay here should prove very relaxing. Old-fashioned in the best sense of the word, and with an air of dignity: Irish hospitality with comforting rituals. No televisions, afternoon tea at 1600, dinner announced promptly at 2000 by the ring of a gong and, rather more worryingly, a tiger skin over the stairway.

C-F Canrawer House, Station Rd, just before the church at the Clifden end of town, T091-552388, www.oughterardhostel.com. While it only has 1 private room, the overall standard is very high in this purpose-built, spacious hostel with stone tile floors and smart bedrooms. Bikes for hire.

D Corrib Wave Guest House, Portacarron, T091-552147, www.corribwave.com. A guest house with warm hospitality and a pleasing waterside location that guarantees serenity, plus reliable home-cooked evening meals. Fishing folk are particularly well taken care of.

E Waterfall Lodge, T091-552168, www.waterfalllodge.net. Pleasant waterside location and a choice of breakfasts.

Oughterard to Clifden *p391*

L Ballynahinch Castle Hotel, Recess, T095-31006, www.ballynahinch-castle.com. Set in

For an explanation of the sleeping and eating price codes used in this guide, see inside the front cover. Other relevant information is found in Essentials pages 39-45.

woods on the banks of the river of the same name this place, popular with fishers, is very comfortable and relaxed, with all the qualities of a swanky hotel. Worth dropping by for the bar food and a look round.

L-A Lough Inagh Lodge, T095-34706, www.loughinaghlodgehotel.ie. Makes a suitable place to stop for a rest while admiring the natural spectacle all around you. Some 4-poster beds, and a down-to-earth bar where anglers compare catches.

L-B Cashel House Hotel, Cashel, T095-31001, www.cashel-house-hotel.com. A hotel set in some of the most beautiful gardens in Ireland. Private beach, and award-winning breakfast. If you don't stay here come just to wander round the gardens (open Tue-Sat, 1400-1630) and maybe tuck into the afternoon tea service. Bar food at lunchtime and a five-course dinner at night.

F Ben Lettery, Recess, T095-51136, benlettery@eircom.net. Comfortable, and convenient to reach with the Galway-Clifden bus service passing right by, with one room of 4 beds and others of 6, 8 and 12 beds. A perfect base for walking and cycling.

Roundstone *p392*

C-D Eldons, T095-35933, www.connemara.net. Views of the harbour and Twelve Bens. Most rooms at around €40 per person sharing but there are also more expensive ones.

C-D Roundstone House, T095-35864, www.irishcountryhotels.com. Small, family-run hotel.

D The Angler's Return, Toombeola, 6.5 km outside Roundstone and overlooking the Ballynahinch River, T095-31091. Pretty, rambling gardens and lots of fishing nearby. Ideal for anyone seeking peace and quiet.

E St Joseph's, T095-35865. A friendly B&B with 6 rooms with en suite bathrooms.

Camping

Gurteen Beach Caravan and Camping Park, just west of town near the beach, T095-35882.

Clifden *p393*

There are a number of hotels in Clifden, but for what you pay a more satisfying level of personal service can be enjoyed in some of the town's guest houses. There is also a range of B&Bs – while most are aesthetically-challenged bungalows some at least have locations that provide superb views – and 2 hostels. The minimum price for doubles/singles in B&Bs is €60-40.

A Abbeyglen Castle, Sky Rd, T095-21201, www.abbeyglen.ie. Built in 1832 and looking just like you might imagine a castle hotel to look, this is a wonderfully laidback place with an elegant drawing room and views over Clifden and the sea.

B Ardagh Hotel and Restaurant, nearly 3 km outside town on the road to Ballyconneely, T095-21384, www.ardaghhotel.com. A more relaxing hotel than those in the town. Some of the rooms have enchanting views of Ardbear Bay, and the hotel has a first-rate restaurant.

B The Quay House, Beach Rd, T095-21369, www.thequayhouse.com. Prettily located by the harbour, this guest house, the oldest building in Clifden, dates back to 1820 when it was a harbourmaster's residence, and breakfast is a leisurely affair in the conservatory. There are also self-catering studio rooms for rent.

B **Station House Hotel**, in town, on the left when approaching on the Galway road, T095-21699, www.stationhousehotel.com. A modern, 3-star hotel with a leisure centre and pool and contemporary-style bedrooms.

C Sunnybank House, Church Hill, T095-21437, www.sunnybankhouse.com. This guest house enjoys fine views from a garden setting and has a heated outdoor pool, sauna and tennis court.

E Ardmore House, Sky Rd, T095-21221, www.ardmore-house.com. B&B 5 km out from town, in a location that provides superb views.

E Dan O'Hara's Farmhouse, Lettershea, 8 km from town on the N59 Galway Rd, T095-21246. A B&B that is also a working farm. The rooms are smart and well equipped.

F Brookside Hostel, Fairgreen, T095-21812 brooksidehostel@eircom.net. Includes just 1 private room.

F Clifden Town Hostel, Market St, T095-21076, www.clifdentownhostel.com. Has private rooms, a rather smart sitting room and an air of elegance.

Cleggan *p394*

A Harbour House, T095-44702. B&B available here.

Inishbofin *p394*

A-C Day's Hotel, east from the harbour, T095-45809, www.dayshotel.ie. Open from Jan-Oct, a convivial place, now rebuilt and poshed up with a leisure centre offering seaweed baths etc.

D **Doonmore Hotel**, T095-45804, www.doonmorehotel.com. As with Day's, a 10-min eastwards walk from the harbour. Accurately describes itself as unpretentious but friendly and comfortable. Closed Oct-Easter.

E **Hy Brazil**, T095-45817. Open from Easter to end of Oct. Named after an enchanted island (*Tír na nÓg*) that appears every seven years and is supposedly visible from islands off the west coast, this much more down-to- earth non-smoking B&B is reached by walking west/left from the pier until the sign points inland.

F-G **Inishbofin Island Hostel**, T095-45855, www.inishbofin-hostel.ie. Open from Apr-Sep. Has nearly 40 beds, including 4 private rooms. Camping is also possible.

Clifden to Leenane *p395*

A **Rosleague Manor**, Letterfrack, T095-41101, www.rosleague.com. A Georgian country house overlooking Ballinakill Bay set in 30 acres of landscaped gardens and complete with a billiard table and a tennis court.

F **Letterfrack Hostel**, T095-41222, www.letterfracklodge.com. Similar facilities but only open Jun-Sep.

F **Old Monastery Hostel**, T095-41132, oldmon@indigo.ie. A solid 19th-century house with some character, this is one of Ireland's better hostels and not least because it blends in perfectly with the appeal of Connemara. It has been a favourite with travellers for some years now and with good reason. The room rates, whether sharing (€16) or in a private room (€18-22 per person), include a tasty, non-fried breakfast and an evening meal is available at a very reasonable rate. Open all year. Camping is also possible and bikes can be hired.

Renvyle Peninsula and around *p395*

L-D **Renvyle House**, T095-43511, www.renvyle.com. This is Gogarty's original house, where Yeats sat for his first portrait by Augustus John and where he held a séance in the belief that the place was haunted, and which was burned down in the Civil War but rebuilt. It's a country mansion with log fires, fishing, golf, pool, croquet. Also organizes a variety of special interest weekends.

E **Olde Castle House**, Renvyle, T095-43460. Near to the castle ruins, with a movie history – the house was in the film *Purple Taxi*.

F **Diamond's Bar**, Tully, T095-43486, castlehouse@eircom.net. Modernized pub in the village of Tully. Sea views and dinner.

Camping

Connemara Caravan and Camping Park at Gowlaun near Lettergesh, T095-43406. Open May-Sep.

Renvyle Beach Caravan and Camping Park, just west of Tully, T095-43462. Smaller and has fewer facilities but enjoys a glorious view of Mweelrea, the highest peak in Mayo.

Leenane and Killary Harbour *p396*

C **Killary Lodge**, by the harbour, T095-42276, www.killary.com. Evening meals available and lots of information and ideas for activities in the vicinity.

D **Portfinn Lodge**, Leenane, T095-42265, www.portfinn.com. Comfortable, purpose-built rooms.

E **Glen Valley House**, Glencroff, T095-42269 gvhouse@yahoo.com. Working farmhouse on the route of the Western Way walking route. Connemara ponies to pet.

E **Killary House**, short distance outside town, T095-42254. Pretty house with lovely views.

F **Killary Harbour**, T095-43417. *An Óige* hostel 5 km off the road at Salrock Cross which is passed by Galway-Renvyle buses. Terrific location but bring all you need because there are no shops or pubs.

Eating

Oughterard *p389*

Both the **Boat Inn** and the **Lake Hotel** in the village centre do bar food throughout the day and have restaurants.

Bridge Restaurant, at the lower end of town, T091-557124. Offers food from breakfast-time to late but closed Sun.

Keogh's, a bar/restaurant/craft shop/delicatessen and supermarket: something for everyone.

"Nothing left but a charred oak beam quenched in the well beneath the house. And ten tall square towers, chimneys, stand here on Europe's extreme edge". Gogarty's description of his ruined Renvyle House.

O Fatharta's, Main St, T091-552692.)pen 1800-2200. Has a pretty exterior while he quiet, plain inside is still a pleasant place or a casual meal.

The Yew Tree, Main St, T091-866986. he only bakery in town and good for picnic are as well as a sit-down repast.

oundstone *p392*

Beola Restaurant, Main St, T095-35871. eafood is a big draw here, offers lunches for round €8-20 and main courses for dinner round €20-30.

O'Dowd's, Main St, T095-35809. Has bar ood and a busy seafood restaurant that is ery good. Open for lunch and dinner.

rt and craft workshops. If shopping here, here is a pleasant little teashop.

lifden *p393*

here is no shortage of restaurants here, ut the quality varies in high season.

Ardagh Hotel and Restaurant, allyconneely Rd, T095-21384. Dinner is round €46 but worth splashing out for the uality cuisine and therapeutic view of rdbear Bay.

Signal Restaurant, Clifden Station louse, T095-22946. Opens for dinner Wed-un and tempts the hungry with Connemara nountain lamb and beef on the dinner nenu for around €40.

Fogerty's, Market St, T095-21427.)ffers lobster and a dinner menu.

Mitchell's Restaurant, Market St, T095-1867. Worthy of attention, open from 1000 ntil 2200 and serving a variety of meals and nacks, from sandwiches to local oysters. arly dinner, 1700-1830, for under €25.

Vaughan's, Market St. Has lunch specials and vening dishes like Irish stew for around €12.

Cullen's Bistro, Market St, T095-21983. cosy little restaurant serving dishes from ish stew to interesting salads and ome-made pies and cakes.

Two Dog Café, Church Hill, off the town quare. Head here for home-made cakes or a ortilla wrap and a decent coffee.

leggan *p394*

Pier Bar at the harbour. Pink-coloured pub erving food which has a reputation far eyond the borders of County Galway.

Oliver's Bar, food available here.

Inishbofin *p394*

Both hotels have small restaurants serving lunch, and evening meals for around €25.

Day's Bar, has good pub food. Fresh seafood, as one would hope, is the order of the day.

Clifden to Leenane *p395*

Rosleague Manor, Letterfrack, T095-41101. Welcomes non-residents if a booking is made in advance for its €45 dinner.

Pangur Bán, Letterfrack, T095-41243. A cottage restaurant serving traditional and modern food.

Connemara National Park, the café at the visitor's centre here with its picnic tables (indoors and out) is worth considering.

Kylemore Abbey, economically priced meals are served at the self-service restaurant inside, though the place gets crowded. There is a good food shop in Letterfrack near the main junction.

Renvyle Peninsula and around *p395*

Renvyle House, T095-43511. Convivial dinner is €30 (book ahead in summer).

Renvyle Inn, T095-43954. Pub food throughout the day, it also has a restaurant with fairly unexciting main courses.

Diamond's Bar, Tully. Has pub food throughout the day and is a better bet for cheap food.

Leenane and Killary Harbour *p396*

Portfinn Lodge Restaurant, Leenane, T095- 42265. Hits the jackpot twice with magnificent views over Killary harbour and superb fresh seafood on the menu. Meat dishes, like local lamb, are also available, but the lobster, prawn and turbot are hard to beat. Closed from Nov-Apr.

Leenane Cultural Centre, for a casual meal that doesn't involve visiting a pub this has a café with a decent range of meals and snacks and wines.

In the Leenane itself there is a healthy smattering of cafés and pubs offering food.

Blackberry Café. Seafood, stews, chowder and the like. Open 1200-2100.

Gaynor's Bar. Milks *The Field* theme.

Pubs and music

Clifden *p393*

EJ Kings. Pub serving up pop and rock.

Foyle's Hotel, Main St, T095-21801. Bar at the back has authentic sessions of local music and singing on a Thu night.
Lowry's, Market St. Traditional music.
Mannion's Bar, Market St. Enjoyable evenings of traditional music.

Cleggan *p394*
Joyce's Bar. Music nightly.

Inishbofin *p394*
Day's Bar. Music on Wed to Sun nights.
Doonmore Hotel. Traditional music in the bar on Wed and Sat nights.

Festivals and events

Clifden *p393*
Towards the end of **Sep** the **Clifden Community Arts Week**, T095-21164/21295, takes off with a packed week of musical and theatrical events, lectures, walks, book events, storytelling and more. The **Connemara Walking Festival**, T095-21379, is usually a 4-day event, organized by the Connemara Walking Centre, with walks varying in difficulty. One takes place at the end of **May** and another one at the end of **Sep** to overlap with the Arts Week.

Shopping

Oughterard *p389*
Fuschia Craft, in the centre of the village. Open daily until 2200 in the summer. Galway crystal, porcelain from Donegal, Claddagh rings, tweeds, designer knitwear, prints, bodhrans, jewellery…and a bureau de change.
Galway Woollen Market, at the Clifden end of the village. Has the usual range of garments, souvenirs and gifts.

Clifden to Leenane *p395*
Avoca Handweavers, outside Letterfrack on the road to Clifden, T095-41058. One of the better craft shops in Connemara with a large collection of clothes and crafts plus a bookshop and a café.
Kylemore Craft Shop, at Kylemore Abbey. Run by the Benedictine nuns and has a selection of Irish knitwear and accessories as well as pottery, which is thrown and glazed on the premises, china, crystal and jewellery. The shop can be freely visited without having to view the abbey.

Activities and tours

Oughterard *p389*
Fishing Keogh's, The Square, T091-552583. **Tuck's**, Main St, T091-552335.

Renvyle peninsula and around *p395*
Diving **Scubadive West**, Renvyle, T095-43922, www.scubadivewest.com. Conducts courses for beginners, rents equipment and also offers accommodation.

Transport

Connemara *p387, map p388*
Bike hire Mannion's, Bridge St, T095-21160.

Bus Bus Éireann, T091-562000, connects Clifden with the outside world and there is also a useful private company, **Nee Buses**, T095-34682, that runs daily buses throughout the year between Clifden and **Galway** for €10/13 single/return. Buses depart Clifden at 0915 and 1515, with another one at 1900 on Fri-Sat. They also run 2 buses a day in the summer, 3 a week in winter, between Clifden and **Cleggan**, and a daily summer service to **Kylemore Abbey** and **Letterfack** from Clifden.

South and east Galway

South and east of Galway city is some quiet countryside scattered with lots of ancient sites from the monastic buildings of Kilmacduagh and the ruins of the cathedral at Clonfert to the Norman tower at Thor Ballyle. The two seaside towns of Kinvara and Clarinbridge, both as yet untrammelled by mass tourism, offer some interest and, in the case of Kinvara, also some worthwhile places to eat. *» For Sleeping, Eating and other listings, see page 403.*

Lady Gregory

Lady Gregory (1852-1932) first met Yeats in 1893 and he first stayed at her home, Coole Park, four years later. It was during this visit that they dreamed up the idea of a national theatre. Lady Gregory wrote her own plays as well as editing and publishing various books on Gaelic culture. Her collections of Irish legends and myth were praised by Yeats as "the chief part of Ireland's gift to the imagination of the world." There is an **Annual Autumn Gathering** at Coole Park, always the last weekend in September, with lectures, plays and local excursions to places associated with her. Contact Sheila O'Donnellan, Kingston Rd, Taylor's Hill, Galway, T091-521836. At Kiltartan Cross, 3 km north of Gort on the N128, **Kiltartan Gregory Museum** ⓘ *T091-631069, 632346, 1 Jun-31 Aug daily 1000-1800, 1 Sep-31 May Sun 1300-1700*, contains memorabilia and manuscripts associated with Lady Gregory and the Irish Literary Revival.

★ Coole Park → *Phone code: 091.*

ⓘ *T091-631804. Park open all year, visitor centre: Apr-May daily 1000-1700, Jun-Aug daily 1000-1800. Guided tours in Sep. €2.75. OPW site. 5 km north of Gort.*

In *Coole Park, 1929* Yeats imagined a time:

When all those rooms and passages are gone,
When nettles wave upon a shapeless mound
And saplings root among the broken stone.

The rooms have indeed gone but saplings have a problem because the house where Lady Gregory lived and where Yeats spent summers writing poetry was demolished for no good reason in 1941 and the site cemented over. Frank O'Connor sardonically commented, "sold by Mr de Valera's Government to a Galway builder for £500 and torn down for scrap. Merely as a literary museum its value to the nation was almost incalculable; one feels they should have held out for at least £600." Coole Park is now a nature reserve with an audio-visual show and self-guided trails, the €2 guide booklet is good value and points out details such the signatures on the **Autograph Tree**, a beech tree on which Lady Gregory invited her literary guests (Shaw, Synge, Yeats, O'Casey and others) to carve their initials.

Just north of Coole Park, before the turn-off for Thoor Ballylee, the small **Kiltartan Gregory Museum** (see box, page 401) is at the junction known as Kiltartan Cross that was made famous in Yeats' poem *An Irish Airman Foresees his Death*.

★ Thoor Ballylee

ⓘ *T091-563081. May-Sep daily 1000-1800. €5. OPW site. About 3 km off the N18 Galway to Limerick road.* Thoor Ballylee, a Norman tower purchased by the poet in 1916 for £35, is the other Yeats attraction in the area. The poet called his tower "a powerful emblem" and some of his best poems were written with the place in mind. An audio-visual presentation tells the story and the riverside location is still idyllic.

Kilmacduagh

Near Gort (see page 403), Kilmacduagh has an almost embarrassing richness of ecclesiastical ruins that owe their existence to a monastery founded here in the seventh century. The best preserved building is a slightly leaning but very elegant 35-m round tower, while the roofless cathedral dates mostly from the 15th century though the blocked-up doorway on its west side is possibly 10th-century. The ruins of two small churches, St John's and O'Heyne's, lie to the north and O'Heyne's is worth a visit for its decorated chancel pillars and carved windows. The less interesting ruins of St Mary's Church are on the east side of the cathedral.

Kinvara → *Phone code: 091. Colour map 2, grid C4.*

The natural prettiness of this coastal village on the main route between Galway and the Burren invites a stop, not least because of the surprising number of good places to eat. So far, its charm has not been diluted by its popularity and as a village that has the potential to become another Kinsale, it is well worth visiting before it does so.

Dunguaire Castle ⓘ *Mid-Apr to Sep daily 0930-1700. €4.75.* This 16th-century castle, perched on a promontory, has been well restored and the contents of each floor are devoted to a different period in its history. It was once owned by Oliver St John Gogarty but the last proprietor has also left her mark and one of the rooms is decorated in the style that the owner employed when living here in the 1960s.

A medieval-style **banquet** ⓘ *T061-360788, Apr-Oct daily 1730 and 2045, €47*, at Dunguaire Castle kicks off nightly with harp music, salted bread and mead, and chicken eaten with a dagger, followed by about an hour of singing and story-telling from assorted sources in Irish culture. Coach parties can make up the bulk of the audience but it is all good fun and individuals are welcomed.

Clarinbridge → *Colour map 2, grid C4.*

Clarinbridge is on the main N18 road, 16 km south of Galway City, and apart from the second weekend in September there is little reason to make a stop other than for a shopping trip (see page 403). When the **Oyster Festival** ⓘ *T091-76359*, arrives, however, the place is bursting with visitors and celebrities from all over the world.

Ballinasloe → *Phone code: 090. Colour map 2, grid C5.*

On the main N6 Dublin to Galway road, Ballinasloe and its surrounding places of interest may not be worth a special journey from Galway or Connemara unless you are particularly fascinated by Irish history for the area is important as the site of the Battle of Aughrim. **Tourist information** 6 km southwest of Ballinasloe on the N6.

The Battle of Aughrim Interpretative Centre ⓘ *T090-9673939. May to mid-Sep Tue-Sat 1000-1800 (closed 1300-1400), Sun 1400-1600. €4.* In 1691 Aughrim was the site of the final battle, of momentous significance for European history, between the Protestant William of Orange and the Catholic James II. The Jacobite army was under General St Ruth and his reluctance to work with Sarsfield, his second-in-command, was one factor in their defeat by the numerically inferior Williamite army. The Centre has models and displays, and explains the European dimension to the battle.

Clonfert Cathedral Also nearby, 15 km southeast of Ballinasloe at Clonfert, this 12th-century cathedral, remarkable for its exemplary Irish Romanesque doorway, is both baroque and Celtic in its love of ornamentation. Well worth seeing.

Portumna → *Phone code: 090. Colour map 2, grid C5.*

The attraction of a visit to this small market town is **Portumna Castle and Gardens** ⓘ *T090-9741658, Apr-Oct daily 1000-1800, €2*, a semi-fortified house built in the early 17th century and the best example of Irish Jacobean architecture in the country. Restoration work is ongoing but the ground floor and the highly formal garden is open and there is an exhibition giving the background story. There is a seasonal **tourist office**, in town T090-42131.

Sleeping

Kinvara *p402*
C-D **Merriman Inn**, Main St, T091-638222, www.merrimanhotel.com. A comfortable, modern and relaxed hotel, close to the Castle, with a huge thatched roof.
D **Johnston's Independent Hostel**, T091-637164. Next door to the Merriman Inn, this hostel has 24 beds but no private rooms.
E **Burren View Farm**, Doorus, T091-637142. B&B with a pleasant, away-from-it-all location, pretty views, safe beach nearby, and some rooms with en suite facilities.
F **An Óige Doorus House**, 6 km northwest of Kinvara, signposted off the road to Ballyvaughan, T091-637512, doorushouse.kinvara.com. A hostel with literary associations: Yeats and Lady Gregory first discussed setting up a national theatre here. "On the sea-coast at Duras, a few miles from Coole, an old French Count, Florimond de Basterot, lived for certain months in every year. Lady Gregory and I talked over my project of an Irish Theatre, looking out upon the lawn of his house, watching a large flock of ducks." WB Yeats. No private rooms.

Ballinasloe *p402*
E **Beechwood**, T090-9642691, slatteryfamily@eircom.net. A friendly family townhouse. Open Mar-Oct.
E **Hynes Hostel**, T090-9673734. Very close to the Aughrim Interpretative Centre, and has 2 private rooms. Bike hire, open all year and an adjoining bar.

Portumna *p402*
B **Shannon Oaks Hotel and Country Club**, T090-9741777, www.shannonoaks.ie. A very modern hotel, by the shore of Lough Derg, with a gym, swimming pool and a comfortable bar serving food, as well as a restaurant.

Eating

Gort (near Kilmacduagh) *p401*
In gaunt-looking Gort there is the usual run of pubs serving food.
¥ **The Blackthorn**, Crowe St, T091-632127, on the left coming in from Coole Park. A comfortable bar with tables for eating and a more formal restaurant area upstairs. Vegetarians could eat here. Lunch is around €9, evening dinner €13-20, and there is live music on a Sat night.

Kinvara *p402*
¥¥-¥ **Pier Head**, bar and restaurant, off the road at the harbourside, has good pub food as well as steaks, and seafood.
¥ **Café on the Quay**. Brightly painted, it is worth getting the single window table overlooking the harbour. Open all day.
¥ **Keogh's**, Main St, T091-637145. Serves good modern Irish dishes using local seafood, and there are outdoor tables. Open 1000-2200.
On a fine day, enjoy a picnic on the grass near the castle.

Clarinbridge *p402*
¥¥-¥ **Paddy Burke's Inn**, in the village, T091-796226. A pub of character and while most famous for its seafood, its bar food menu includes steaks and curries. Check out its visitors' book.
¥¥-¥ **Moran's**, a little further south near Kilcolgan, T091-796113. Another pub (and restaurant) closely associated with the festival.

Pubs and music

Kinvara *p402*
Tully's, T091-637146. You can't beat this for somewhere genuinely old and flavoursome with its stone floor, attached grocery store and traditional music on assorted days.
Winkles. Pub with regular sessions of traditional music.

Shopping

Clarinbridge *p402*
Clarinbridge Antiques, T091-796522, or **Clarinbridge Crystal & Fashion Shop**, T091-796178.

For an explanation of the sleeping and eating price codes used in this guide, see inside the front cover. Other relevant information is found in Essentials pages 39-45.

County Roscommon

Strokestown → *Phone code: 071. Colour map 2, grid B5.*

Strokestown is a quaint little 18th-century place laid out in the usual cruciform design by a planter Maurice Mahon, his big house at one end of the village and the church at the other so every Sun he could drive through his domain with his people watching admiringly. It has blossomed each year since 1999 with its tremendously powerful poetry festival (see box next page) and is home to one of the best museums in Ireland.

★ **Strokestown Park House** ⓘ *Strokestown Park House, Garden, and Famine Museum: Strokestown, T071-9633013, www.strokestownpark.ie. Mid-Mar to Oct daily 1100-1730. House €6, museum €6, walled garden €6, house and museum €9; house and garden or museum and garden €9.50; house, museum and garden €13.50*. Of all the big houses of the Anglo-Irish open to the public, Strokestown Park House must rate as one of the most enjoyable and educational. Its history goes back to the 17th century, when an ancestor of Maurice's, Nicholas Mahon, was granted a vast estate of nearly 12,141 ha as a reward for being on the winning side in the civil war. The house is largely 18th-century, designed by the prolific Richard Castle, while much of the contents are 19th-century. The house stayed in the same family until 1981, and its interior was never denuded like so many other places, so there is a wealth of furnishings to admire. The most infamous owner was Denis Mahon who, at the time of the Famine, would ship off his evicted tenants to America in overcrowded and unsafe ships, suitably dubbed 'coffin ships'. He got his comeuppance in 1847 from an assassin's bullet.

Tours of the house are well worth it, because there is so much to see and take in, the dining and living rooms, library and schoolroom. The kitchen also is a must-see; its out-of-reach gallery designed for the mistress to drop down messages without having to converse with the servants is an eye-opener. Along the same lines, and like many Anglo-Irish houses, there was a brick tunnel running between the kitchen and the yard so that the beastly menials were not encountered in person.

The carefully restored 9.9-ha **walled garden** is another attraction. The highlight for many visitors is the herbaceous border, which is listed in the *Guinness Book of Records* as the longest in the Britain and Ireland.

A visit to the **Famine Museum** complements the glimpse into the Anglo-Irish lifestyle afforded by Strokestown Park House. While the lady of the manor was dropping down her menus to the kitchen the peasants were dying of starvation in their homes and in the fields. Much of the material in the museum consists of primary source material from the House but the portrayal of famine extends to the contemporary world and the exhibition as a whole, an exemplary showcase of how history could be presented, puts to shame many of the lacklustre heritage centres around Ireland that claim to offer an insight into past and present times.

West of Strokestown

Tulsk About 10 km west of Strokestown on the N5 there is a cluster of standing stones and other ancient sites but to make sense of their material and mystical significance you need to visit the **Cruachan Aí Visitor Centre** ⓘ *T071-9639268, May-Sep daily 0900-1700, Oct-Apr Mon-Sat 0900-1700. €4.95.*

Douglas Hyde Interpretive Centre ⓘ *T094-9870016. May-Sep Tue-Fri 1400- 1700, Sat and Sun 1400-1800. Free (donation requested).* On the N5 at Frenchpark this centre commemorates the academic who was hugely influential in Irish cultural revival at the turn of the 19th century as well as being a collaborator with Yeats and Lady Gregory on various theatrical productions. The Centre is in an old church, where Hyde is buried.

Strokestown Poetry Festival

ⓘ *Entry forms and details: T071-9633759, www.strokestownpoetryprize.com.*

If you've spent any time at all in Ireland you'll know that every tiny village with an eye on their profit margins has a festival – in honour of ancient rituals, music, returning emigrants, fishing, sailing, even vegetables and molluscs. In 1999, casting about for their own reason for a festival, Strokestown came up with a little gem – poetry. If you have ever spent the long winter months in Ireland you'll know that if you wait long enough in any little bar someone, usually after several pints, will remember a piece of poetry. Not Yeats or Heaney but some inelegant, rumpty-tumpty piece of wickedness written years ago about a local old soak or womanizer or some scandal. Those moments make the rain and the afternoon darkness and the terrible roads and the inability to ever get someone in to fix the plumbing/ electricity/TV totally worthwhile. The Strokestown festival has grown so much that even the big names submit poems to the competition for the Strokestown Poetry Prize. Its three days in early May are accompanied by walks, music, drinking, Gaelic speakers and, best of all, older people who remember some of the satirical local poetry which is probably not written down anywhere. The festival gets top marks for good craic, economic success and preserving a vital aspect of Irish culture. Anyone can submit a poem of up to 70 lines.

Clonalis House ⓘ *T094-9620014. Jun to mid-Sep Mon-Sat 1100-1700. €5.50.* Just west of Castlereagh, reached from Strokestown via Tulsk though the usual route by the N60 Castlebar to Roscommon road, is Clonalis House. The house is the ancestral home of the O'Conor clan, the only chiefdom to be recognized by the Anglo-Normans as Celtic kings, and the present building is an Italianate mansion built in 1878. It was the first of its kind to be built of concrete in Ireland. The archives contain documents, some written on calf skin, that go back over 60 generations, including a copy of the last Brehon Law judgement and a 16th-century prayerbook. Also here is the harp of Turlough O'Carolan (see page 616), Sheraton and Louis XV furniture, portraits and assorted jumble.

Roscommon Town → *Phone code: 090. Colour map 2, grid B5.*

Taking its name from Felim O'Connor, the saint who founded a monastery here in 1253, Roscommon is the essence of the Irish county town with an intact market square, the old town jail (now a mall) and several old ruins to explore. The **County Museum** ⓘ *Harrison Hall, Market Sq, mid-Jun to mid-Aug daily 1000- 1730, free,* is good place to start exploring. It's one of those wonderful unreconstructed museums where you will always find something unexpectedly absorbing (our favourite here is the sheela-na-gig). The same building houses the **tourist office**, T090-6626342, May-Sep, daily 1000-1800.

Roscommon Castle ⓘ *open access, free.* The substantial remains of Roscommon Castle, on the road out to Boyle, are worth admiring. Built as a Norman castle in 1269, it passed through many hands and was captured by the O'Conors more than once. The mullioned windows that look so out of place were added in the late 16th century.

Dominican Priory ⓘ *Open 24 hrs. Free.* At the other end of town, off Circular Road, are the ruins of a Dominican Priory founded in 1253 and deserving a visit for the effigy of its founder, Felim O'Conor. It stands upon a later 15th-century tomb in the north wall and surrounding the figure are eight mail-clad gallowglasses with angels above them.

The Great Famine

After the introduction of the potato to Irish agriculture in the late 16th century it became the staple crop of the mass of Irish peasantry who lived almost entirely off potatoes and buttermilk, a diet just capable of sustaining life. Over the centuries there were periodic spells of crop failure caused by the fungal disease *phytophthora infestans*. Before the 1840s these had caused deaths and emigration, but only on a local scale. Starting in 1845 the crop failure was national and lasted until 1849 in varying degrees. In 1846 only a quarter of the national yield was produced and in 1848 the yield was only two-thirds of what was needed.

To the Irish peasantry this was disaster on a national scale. Potatoes had provided iron and vitamins and suddenly the loss of these made thousands of people susceptible to disease. People flocked to the cities and towns in desperation, hoping for relief from the Poor Houses, which became impossibly overcrowded. Typhus and cholera spread like wildfire and the young and the old were particularly vulnerable. Recent research suggests that over one million people died, while untold hundreds of thousands escaped to the coffin ships. Many of them, already weakened by starvation and disease, died on the journey. The country's population declined by one-fifth and the trauma of the Famine was so haunting and searing that a collective act of denial set in, which is only now in the process of being acknowledged.

Often thought of as a purely natural disaster, it is difficult for many English people to understand why a term like 'genocide' is sometimes levelled at their country, or why Tony Blair felt he had to apologize on behalf of Britain in 1997. The Famine was not genocide in the way that the Holocaust was, and historians disagree about the level of responsibility that can be laid at Britain's door, but there are certain facts about Britain's handling of the disaster which must be recognized. The concept of laissez-faire economics, which dictated that any tampering with market forces, such as subsidising the starving Irish, would destroy the economy, was a large part of the problem. In the first year of the Famine, Peel's Tory government imported Indian meal to Ireland to be sold as replacement for the lost crop, but no one could afford to buy it. While this and the following Whig government introduced public work schemes in exchange for food (generally making the situation worse because the work was so hard and the food so poor), neither interfered with the export, from Ireland, of grain which might have fed people. In 1847, two years into the famine, soup kitchens were finally introduced but they lasted only six months and workhouses alone were expected to support the starving, which they were hopelessly unable to do.

The same economic beliefs saw the potato failure as an opportunity to reorganize the Irish economy by removing thousands of tiny smallholders and creating larger, more efficient farms. Absentee landlords took the opportunity to evict tenants who could not pay their rents, and knocked down their houses to prevent reoccupation. Although some landlords bankrupted themselves keeping their tenants alive, others paid their fares on the emigrant ships to be rid of them: the majority of English landlords saw this as an opportunity to offload unwanted people.

Ultimately, responsibility for the deaths of so many people surely rests on the shoulders of the colonial power that created the subsistence economy in the first place.

Boyle → *Phone code: 071. Colour map 1, grid C1 and map 2, grid A5.*

A tranquil little country town, quite at peace with its slow pace of life, Boyle is worth a visit for its beautiful ruined abbey, interesting interpretive centre and a giant dolmen just outside the town.

Boyle Abbey ⓘ *in Boyle, off the N4 Dublin to Sligo Rd, T071-9662604. Apr-Oct daily 1000-1800. €2. Guided tours. OPW site.* The abbey was founded in the 12th century by Cistercian monks settling here from the great abbey at Mellifont in County Louth, itself a scion of the abbey at Clairvaux in France. The ruins are well kept and it is possible to get some idea of the details of the monks' lives as you wander round the remains. During the period in which the monastery was built, the then-dominant Romanesque style of architecture was giving way to Gothic, hence the different arches on either side. If the ruins are closed you can ask at Abbey House (see page 408) for the key.

King House ⓘ *T071-9663242. Apr-Sep daily 1000-1800, Apr and Oct, Sat and Sun 1000-1800. €4.* This building, which now houses the **tourist office**, T071-9662145, May to mid-Sep Mon-Fri 1000-1700, was lived in by the local landed gentry, the Kings, who built it around 1730 and then moved on 45 years later to the even bigger Rockingham estate, now the Lough Key Forest Park. Serious social climbers, the Kings did everything they could to force their way into the ruling classes, including putting down any local opposition to English rule, for which they were given the land that King's House now stands on. By 1768 the head of the family had obtained an earlship. By the time of the Famine they were absentee landlords, having crawled their way up the social ladder by forcing the Irish off the land and into coffin ships to America. After their complete departure from Boyle in 1775, the house became a garrison for the Connaught (or Connacht) Rangers (see page 372). The interpretive centre is a very hands-on place with lots of activities, including a set of building blocks that, when correctly assembled, make a vaulted ceiling of the type that can be admired for real in the house. There are displays on the Rangers, the construction and renovation of the house, the King family and early Connacht as well as some local art.

Frybrook House ⓘ *T071-9663513. May to mid-Oct daily 1000-1800. €4.* Back in the middle of town beside the river is Frybrook House, built in 1750 and more modest in conception than King House. It was built by Henry Fry, an English Quaker, brought over by the Kings, the local landlords, who wanted to establish a weaving community in the town. It changed hands in 1986 and has been massively renovated although it retains its original Georgian plasterwork and an Adam fireplace. It is furnished with items from the same period and has some good paintings.

Lough Key Forest Park ⓘ *T071-62363. Open 24 hrs. €4. Car parking, access via the N4, east of Boyle.* Less than 3 km east of Boyle, a part of the Kings' Rockingham Estate is now a picturesque forest park with nature walks, boat hire, a camping park, and the ruins of an old castle on a small island. Rockingham House is gone but the tunnels that the servants used, so as not to disturb the equanimity of their masters, can be seen near the lake. If you hire a boat go to Trinity Island where WB Yeats had plans to set up a mystical-political cult.

Sleeping

Strokestown *p404*
E **Woodlawn**, Drummullin, 7 km outside Strokestown, T071-9635111. A B&B with 3 bedrooms sharing bathroom facilities at €50-30 for a double/single room.

Roscommon Town *p405*
B-C **Abbey Hotel**, Galway Rd, T090-6626240, www.abbeyhotel.ie. Ask for a room in the old wing to savour the feeling of staying in an 18th-century manor house.

C-D Glessons, Market Sq, T090-6626954, www.gleesonstownhouse.com. A fine 19th-century manse with excellent guest house accommodation.
D O'Garas Royal Hotel, Castle St, T090-6626317. In the centre of town and buzzing with local social life.
D Regans, Market Sq, T090-6625339, www.regansbar.com. Guest house that also has 2 self-catering apartments.
E Hillcrest House, Racecourse Rd, T090-6625201. Modern country house with pretty gardens.

Boyle *p407*
D Royal Hotel, Bridge St, T071-9662016. In the centre of town and next to the river, this small, 250-year-old, owner-run hotel has a very popular restaurant.
E Abbey House, next door to the ruins of the abbey, T071-9662385. A Victorian house with 6 rooms offering B&B; most rooms have their own bathroom. Nice gardens.
E Avonlea, Dublin Rd, T071-9662538. Opposite the Forest Park Hotel is this modern house B&B within walking distance of the Lough Key Forest Park.

Camping
Lough Key Caravan and Camping Park, T071-9662212. Open May-29 Aug.

Eating

Strokestown *p404*
Strokestown Park House, has a restaurant, keeping the same hours as the House (see page 404, and serving tuna salads, tandoori chicken, home-made jam tarts and trifles. There are lots of pubs in town for bar food.

Roscommon Town *p405*
Abbey Hotel, the restaurant here is open for lunch and dinner.
Glessons, Market Sq, next to the tourist office. The best place for a meal, light or substantial, indoors or outdoors, its coffee shop opens from 0800.
Regans, next door to *Glessons*.

Boyle *p407*
An Craoibhín, near the clocktower. Good pub food.
Royal Hotel. The coffee shop here is very popular with locals. Closes at 1800 and then the hotel's Chinese restaurant opens.
Stone House Café, Bridge St. Fine for lunch and has a pretty riverside location.

Pubs and music

Boyle *p407*
Kate Lavin's, St Patrick St. Has regular sessions of traditional music. This pub first opened its door to customers in 1889 and shut them for 20 years before reopening around its centenary. Mercifully, very little has changed and the pub exudes authenticity.
Moylburg Inn, in the Crescent by the clocktower. Has live music.
O'Dowd's Railway Bar, further out of town. A lively place for a drink and good music.

Transport

County Roscommon *p404*
Bus **Strokestown** can be reached by bus on the **Dublin** to **Ballina** service, which runs 3 times a day (2½ hrs from Strokestown). The **Ballina** to **Athlone** bus also stops once a day and there is a daily service between **Sligo** and **Athlone** that stops in **Strokestown**, **Roscommon Town** and **Boyle**.

From **Roscommon Town**, T071-9160066, the **Dublin** to **Westport** bus passes through 3 times a day, Mon-Sat, and once on Sun. The **Belfast** to **Galway** bus stops daily and the **Athlone** to **Sligo** bus stops twice daily and once on Sun.

The **Sligo** to **Dublin** service, stops in **Boyle** 3 times a day.

Train The **Dublin** to **Westport** train service, T071-6626201, stops in **Roscommon Town** 3 times a day and takes 2 hrs to reach the capital and 1½ hrs to reach Westport. Trains on the **Sligo** to **Dublin** line stop in **Boyle**, T071-9162027, 3 times a day in each direction. Journey time to Dublin is 3 hrs and to Sligo is 40 mins.

Counties Mayo, Sligo and Leitrim

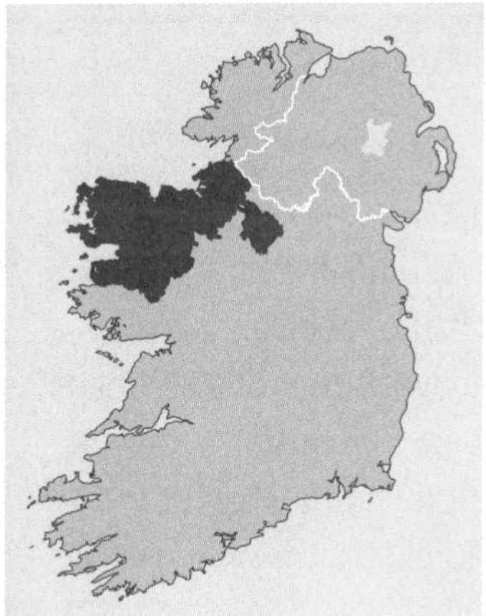

Footprint features

Introduction

There may come a time when Mayo is as successfully marketed as places like Killarney but until then, the county blissfully remains a connoisseur's corner of Ireland. Inland Mayo, characterized by limestone lowlands, is dull compared to the splendour that lies to the west. The bustling town of Westport plays the tourist tune but retains its dignity, while further westwards the easily accessible islands of Achill and Clare offer superb scenery in an unspoilt setting. North and northwest Mayo is a rarely visited, desolate paradise of lonely bogland, calm mountains and haunting beauty, in utter contrast to the village of Cong in the south where the John Wayne connection has been milked for all it is worth. But Cong is easily forgiven in a county that offers more in the way of isolation and remote beauty than anywhere else in Ireland. County Mayo is also one of Europe's top angling destinations with four great lakes – Conn, Cullins, Carra and Mask – all famous for their wild brown trout.

It is hard to travel very far around Sligo and Leitrim without noticing the name Yeats cropping up here and there. But even if you aren't a lover of WB Yeats' poetry or Jack Yeats' art, there is much to admire in the countryside of Sligo and Leitrim, from the surreal protrusion of Benbulbin to the long scenic coastline and the quiet tranquillity of Lough Gill. In the south of Leitrim are gentler, rolling hills, and the developing tourist route of the Shannon to Erne waterway. There are some fine ancient sites to visit, one of which, Carrowmore, holds the only known evidence of a settled Palaeolithic culture anywhere in Europe, and the more modern settlement of Sligo with its pubs, fast food chains, malls and cybercafés.

★ Don't miss...

1. **Croagh Patrick** Climb the site of St Patrick's banishment of snakes from the island and take in the views of Clew Bay, page 413.
2. **Doo Lough Valley** Cycle between Louisburg and Leenane, page 414.
3. **Achill Island** On a fine day here the light casts an aesthetic spell over the land, page 422.
4. **Portacloy** Seek solitude on the remote beach, page 427.
5. **Kilcommon Lodge** Get away from it all at this hostel in Pollatomish, page 429.
6. **Yeats brothers** Admire Jack's collection at the Niland Gallery in Sligo, page 436; and recite some of WB's lines while looking out over the Lake Isle of Innisfree, page 442.
7. **Inishmurray** Enjoy a boat trip out to the deserted island and its monastic ruins, page 439.
8. **Messing about on the river** Consider a canal boat journey up the Shannon all the way to Enniskillen, page 447.

County Mayo

Westport and around

➔ *Phone code: 098. Colour map 2, grid B2 and B3.*

The southwest of County Mayo offers the busy town of Westport, its smaller neighbour Newport, Croagh Patrick with its strenuous footpath to its summit, a long distance walk and a stunning Atlantic coast drive. Westport may ring the tourist bell but it remains a town of some elegance. It acts as a magnet for young folk who fill the many pubs from early evening onwards, whilst also attracting a well heeled set of travellers drawn by the location, the good hotels and restaurants and the air of Georgian refinement that comes from a town designed by James Wyatt in 1780. Not to be forgotten is Cong, to the southeast with its associations with the movie The Quiet Man.

›› *For Sleeping, Eating and other listings, see pages 418-422.*

Ins and outs

Getting there Knock Airport is about 40 km from Westport and has scheduled flights to Dublin and the UK and charter flights to parts of Europe. **Iarnrod Éireann** operates several trains daily between Dublin and Westport. **Bus Éireann** connects Westport with most other large towns in Ireland and a number of the smaller towns in Mayo.

Getting around Westport is a fairly compact town and has no bus service of its own. Places of interest are on the outskirts of town but within walking distance of the centre. Bicycles can be hired in town. ›› *See Transport, page 421, for further details.*

Information Tourist office, James St, T098-25711, www.visitmayo.com. Open all year round.

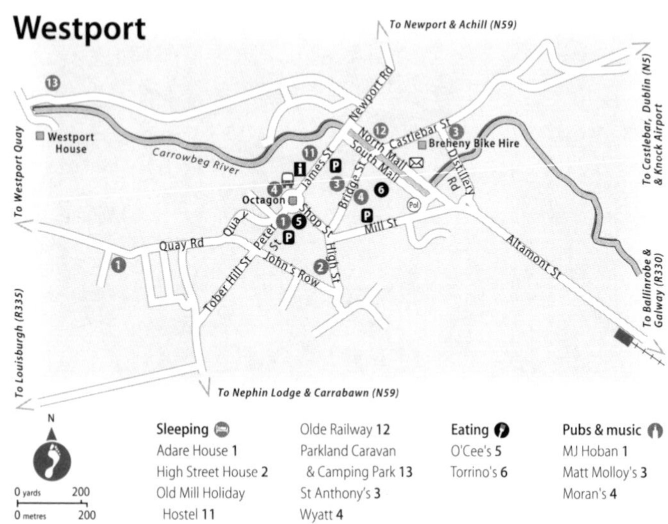

Maud Gonne

Maud Gonne was born in Surrey in 1866 into an army family which moved to Ireland the following year. She never went to school, so avoiding its gender indoctrination, and gave up an upper-class life of hunt balls and dinner parties for revolutionary politics. She went to Paris to campaign for Irish nationalism, where she had two children by a lover, returning to Ireland where she married John MacBride, a disastrous decision in view of his alcoholism, but divorced him after the birth of their son.

William Butler Yeats and Gonne formed a deep friendship, but the poet was driven mad with unreciprocated love, though whether they ever had sex (and even then only once) remains uncertain. Some of Yeats' greatest poetry had its inspiration in their relationship, and when he complained she comforted him with the fact that "you are making beautiful poetry out of what you call your unhappiness and you are happy in that." Their friendship haunted Yeats throughout his life, and 20 years after meeting her he could still feel blessed for having known her, even though "While up from my heart's root/So great a sweetness flows/ I shake from head to foot."

Sights

Westport House ⓘ *T098-25430, wwwwestporthouse.ie. Jun-Sep daily 1100-1700. €10. Take Quay Rd out of town towards Louisburg and the entry is on the right.* Built in 1730 and superbly designed by the master of Irish country-house building, Richard Castle, Westport House is still in the hands of the Browne family. Highlights include Chinese hand-painted wallpaper in one of the bedrooms, a painting attributed to Rubens and doors of Caribbean mahogany (from the family's estates in the West Indies), but whether a visit is worth the hefty admission price is dubious. However, there is a host of other activities designed to attract families, from a model railway and hill slide to a children's zoo, pedaloes and boating.

Clew Bay Heritage Centre ⓘ *Westport Quay, T098-26852, www.museumsofmayo.com. Jun-Sep Mon-Fri 1000-1700, Apr-May and Oct-Nov Mon-Fri 1000-1400, Jul-Aug Sun 1500-1700. €3. Turn right off Quay Rd after passing the turn-off for Westport House.* Crammed with local historical documents and artefacts and with none of the usual gimmicky presentations that pass for substance in heritage centres, this collection is most interesting when showing the role of Westport in the land and nationalist struggles of the 19th and early 20th centuries. **John MacBride** (1865-1916), a revolutionary who was executed for his part in the 1916 rebellion and who was married to **Maud Gonne** (see box above), came from Westport (a bust of him is opposite St Mary's church on the South Mall), and the museum has the gift of a spinning wheel that Mayo people gave Maud Gonne in recognition of her leadership.

Around Westport

★ Croagh Patrick → *Phone code: 098. Colour map 2, grid B2.*

The pyramidal Croagh Patrick (762 m), home to St Patrick in 441CE for a period of 40 days, and the site for his miraculous banishment of snakes (there are no snakes in Ireland), is Ireland's most popular mountain. It is not particularly difficult to climb and there is a well-trodden path to the top, but the scree-laden slope that leads to the summit is steep and when there is a wind about some climbers are reduced to

The Pagan Way

The annual Reek Sunday, the last Sunday in July, sees more than 30,000 devout Catholics setting off to climb Croagh Patrick, many of them unaware they are following in the footsteps of pagan pilgrims. As far back as 3000 BC, people climbed to the summit to mark Lughnasa (the festival of Lug, a god whose name occurs throughout the Celtic world), a pagan celebration of autumn; St Patrick's association with the mountain probably reflects his victory over paganism. The night before they ascend Croagh Patrick, the most devout of modern pilgrims begin their journey by walking 35 km from Ballintubber Abbey along an ancient pilgrim trail, then they attend one of the 15 masses celebrated on the mountain's summit from 0800. Archaeological research shows that a massive rampart enclosed the summit long before the foundations of an oratory were laid some time between 430 and 890. Glass beads excavated near part of the rampart date to the third century BC.

crawling up on their hands and knees. Forget the tradition of climbing Croagh Patrick in bare feet, use suitable footwear and consider bringing a staff-like stick for the final ascent. Allow two hours to reach the top and one for the descent.

The trail begins at the side of Campbell's pub in Murrisk to the west of Westport on the road to Louisburg. There is a car park alongside the **National Famine Monument** ⓘ *Mar 17-Oct daily 1000-1600 (1900 in Jul and Aug)*, a sculptured coffin- ship with skeleton bodies by John Behan, that was unveiled in 1997 on the 150th anniversary of the Famine. It's a 5-minute walk from here to the **Croagh Patrick Information Centre** ⓘ *Murrisk, T098-64114, www.croagh-patrick.com*, which has a self-service restaurant, gifts and books for sale, as well as raingear, walking sticks and shower facilities.

Louisburg → *Colour map 2, grid B2*

Possibly the most laid-back town in Ireland owes its name to Louisburg in Nova Scotia, Canada, where an uncle of the first Marquess of Sligo was part of a besieging force in 1758. Despite its proximity to Westport, Louisburg is contentedly indifferent to tourism although there is the interesting **Granuaile Visitor Centre** ⓘ *T098-25711, Jun to mid-Sep Mon-Sat 1100-1700, €3.50, coming from Westport, turn right at the main junction in town and the centre is a short way down on the left*, dedicated to the 'pirate queen' Grace O'Malley.

There are two local beaches, **Silver Strand** and Old Head, which are gloriously sandy, safe for swimming and suitable for surfing. Bicycles can be hired from Stauntons, the chemist shop on the corner of the crossroads in the centre of town. There is also a splendidly isolated beach at **Killadoon** on the coast southwest of Louisburg, reached by either a dodgy coastal road from town or by turning off the R335 road at Cregganbaun. From the beach there are great views of Inishturk.

★ Doo Lough Valley

The best way to travel between Connemara and Mayo is via the Doo Lough valley on the R335 road, because this part of Mayo is stunningly beautiful and rarely explored. The road skirts the shore of Doo Lough itself, which is sandwiched between the Mweelrea Mountains that overlook Killary harbour to the south, and the wild Sheeffry Hills to the east. The effect of light on the landscape – the massive mountain sides and the fast-flowing silvery stream – changes constantly with the elements. The long-distance walk, the **Western Way**, works its way up from Leenane in Galway to the south side of Croagh Patrick before turning east towards Westport.

Granuaile – pirate queen and feminist icon

Grace O'Malley (c1530-c1603), 'Granuaile' being a corruption of her Gaelic name Gráinne Ni Mháille, was the daughter of a Connacht chief who achieved fame in her own lifetime as a fiercely independent woman. In 1577 her piratical activities led the Lord Deputy of Ireland to mark her down as "a notorious woman in all the coasts of Ireland". She married twice, first Donal O'Flaherty and then Richard 'Iron Dick' Burke, with whom she had an agreement that either party could dissolve the relationship after one year (which she duly did, see page 416). She maintained her own maritime power base from Clare Island and cunningly appeased the English without sacrificing her own independence. In 1593 she came to London with other Connacht chiefs to complain about the heavy-handedness of English rule. Insisting upon regal status as an Irish queen, she petitioned Queen Elizabeth (in Latin, as she had little English and Elizabeth no Irish) for her own lands.

Along the R335 by Doo Lough there is a monument by the side of the road to the hundreds of victims who, during the Famine, set out from Louisburg in winter to walk through the valley to their landlord to beg for assistance. It was a wasted journey and on the return leg of the journey some 400 died from hypothermia and lack of food.

Clare Island → *Colour map 2, grid B2.*

At the mouth of Clew Bay, Clare Island now has a population of about 150, but in pre-Famine days it was over 1,500. The remains of a 15th-century castle, from where Grace O'Malley set off on her piratical excursions, are close to the harbour and further to the west is a 13th-century Cistercian abbey where, legend has it, she is buried. On a fine day, a visit to Clare Island is highly recommended because the place is blessed with an absence of heritage centres, there are superb walks to be enjoyed in all directions and the beach is safe for swimming. Bring your own food or rely on pub grub.

Getting there **Clare Island Ferries,** T098-28288, www.clareislandferry.com (with an office in Westport tourist office and operating throughout the year) and **O'Malleys Ferries,** T098-25045, May-Sep, both run services from Roonagh Quay, 8 km west of Louisburg; €15 return. Check their schedule, but the first boat from Roonagh usually leaves at 1100 and the last one back is at 1900-1930; bicycles carried for free.

Walking

Mapping and information The highest point, **Mount Knockmore,** is a manageable 461 m and for a longer day's exploration of the island map No 30 in the *Ordnance Survey* Discovery series would be useful but not essential. The Bay View hotel (see page 419) has a simple but useful little walking guide with sketches that outlines five walks on the island, lasting from one to over five hours.

If you are staying overnight, a whole day's walk could begin by walking from your accommodation to the disused **lighthouse** at the most northerly point of the island and then setting off across hillocks along the north side en route to **Mount Knockmore.** You will cross several small hills and, although there are high cliffs with sheer drops, by keeping on the safe side of the sheep fencing there is no danger. There is a trigonometry point at the summit and from here it is simply a matter of heading down to the signal tower near the sea at the western end of the island, zig-zagging at times to avoid an inlet. From the tower at the western end a path leads across to the road on the south side of the island, which returns to the harbour. To complete this circuit of Clare Island takes about six hours.

On a day trip, there would be plenty of time for a walk out to the west end of the island by following the road along the southern side of the island from the pier. This road (which you come back along if completing a circuit of the island) passes the abbey where Grace O'Malley is buried, and the O'Malley plaque is clearly visible on the left side after entering the church.

Inishturk Island → *Colour map 2, grid B2.*

Inishturk is smaller than Clare Island and lies to the south, 11 km off the coast. It is one of Ireland's least visited destinations, which is a little surprising because it makes a delightful getaway, offering modest accommodation (see page 419), a pub, restaurant, post office, two sandy beaches, and undemanding walks with terrific seascapes. To the east of Inishturk the tiny **Caher Island** has some strange pre-Christian stones and while there is no scheduled boat service, it is easy to arrange a boat trip from Inishturk, just ask around the harbour.

Getting there Between May and Sep, the **Caher Star** ferry, T098-45541, departs daily from Roonagh at 1100 and 1830, returning at 0930 and 1730, €25 return. On Tue and Thu, there is a mail boat departing from Cleggan at 1100. Bikes are carried free.

Newport and around → *Colour map 2, grid B2.*

Near the northeast corner of Clew Bay, and 12 km north of Westport, the small town of Newport is often just hurried through on the way to Achill Island. There is a **tourist information office** at the western end of Main Street, T098-41822, open Jun-Sep, and they sell inexpensive sheets detailing walks around **Rockfleet Castle** and **Lough Furnace**, which are useful if used with the OS Discovery Series map.

Town walk This walk begins by turning left after leaving the tourist office and heading up to the corner to view the colourful **mural** depicting the trial and public execution of a rebel priest, Father Manus Sweeney, for his part in the 1798 rebellion. Facing the mural, turn left and walk up the hill to **St Patrick's church** where the stained glass east window of the Last Judgement was designed by Harry Clarke and painted under his supervision in 1900, the year he died. From the church, go down the steps and turn right for access to the **Old Viaduct**. Walk across the red sandstone viaduct, built as a railway bridge in 1892 and functioning up until 1937, and down the embankment on the other side. Cross back over the River Black Oak by the road bridge and up Main Street to the tourist office.

Burrishoole Abbey The ruins of this late 15th-century Dominican abbey include the central tower, the vault supported by Romanesque arches and some of the windows. It is hardly worth a special trip, but if travelling on the N59 Newport to Achill road it is signposted on the left less than 1.5 km outside Newport.

Rockfleet Castle ⓘ *Signposted on the N59, after passing the turn-off for Burrishoole Abbey. The Newport tourist office has a sheet describing a 2-hr walk.* Also known as Carrigahowley Castle, Rockfleet has an undisputed association with Grace O'Malley because it was a Burke stronghold before her second marriage to Richard Burke. The story goes that she dissolved this marriage (see box page 415) by having

Wayne's world

John Wayne devotees who flock to Cong will tell you that *The Quiet Man* is better than *Gone with the Wind*. Here there is an annual John Wayne lookalike contest and plans are apace to find a Maureen O'Hara double. The irony is that the film was always expected to flop and was only bankrolled on the understanding that the entire cast shot a western afterwards to recoup the anticipated losses. The film now seems to finance half the village and the story goes that the five-star Ashford Castle Hotel had to stop playing the video in the evenings because no one came to dinner until it had finished. Apart from the eponymous hostel and the coffee shop there is the Quiet Man Heritage Cottage and The Quiet Man Festival in June, with a midsummer ball. Dress code for men is cap, breeches and waistcoat and for women it's bonnets and pretty pinafores. T098-46155.

the castle gates shut in his face and in 1553, after he died, this became her main residence. In a sheltered inlet of Clew Bay that gave safe anchorage to ships, the castle was an ideal base for a seafarer and she beat off an English attack here in 1574.

The Western Way

The Western Way long distance walk starts in County Galway and crosses into Mayo just north of Leenane. Skirting the shoulder of Croagh Patrick, it continues north through Westport and Newport and up to the north coast before swinging eastwards to reach Ballina via Ballycastle and Killala. The ideal way to experience North Mayo would be to take four days and walk the Western Way from Newport to Ballina. A problem with the first day's 33-km walk, from Newport to Bellacorick, is a lack of accommodation in the village of Bellacorick. Unless a pick-up could be arranged there, the only alternatives are either an extra 8-km walk to Bangor, or to catch the Bus Éireann 446 service from Ballina to Bangor that passes through Bellacorick at 1855. The day's journey could be reduced by starting from the *An Óige* hostel (see page 419) which is 8 km north of Newport. The second day's walk, from Bellacorick to Ballycastle, is another 33 km but the next day's journey, from Ballycastle to Killala, is a more manageable 23 km. The last day's walk is a mere 15 km to Ballina, and while it is interesting, the surface is tarmac nearly all the way.

Mularany and the Curraun Peninsula → *Colour map 2, grid B2.*

The village of Mulrany is on the N59 road west of Newport, where the R319 heads west to Achill and the main road continues north to Bangor. There is a garage, and a good-sized supermarket if stocking up on provisions for Achill.

From Mullaranny the R319 follows the route of a disused railway line to Achill Sound, where a bridge connects the Corraun Peninsula with Achill Island. A more leisurely route, signposted the **Atlantic Drive**, goes around the southern end of the Peninsula and on fine days offers tremendous views. Food is available en route at the **George Pub**, T098-45228, where B&B accommodation is also available.

Cong → *Phone code: 094. Colour map 2, grid B3.*

The Cong phenomenon, a tourist extravaganza that is a bit of an anomaly in Mayo, shares with Knock a doggedly fixed identity, this time in the form of John Wayne, who came here in 1951 to star with Maureen O'Hara in John Ford's *The Quiet Man*. The event has not been forgotten and movie fans should buy the excellent *Complete Tour Guide to The Quiet Man Locations* from the tourist office before heading off for the day hunting down all the links to the film that the area still has to offer. My favourite is the sweet shop, used in the film as The Pat Cohan Bar (the one that the horse automatically pulls up outside), owned by a man who was an extra in the movie.

Hollywood apart, Cong would still be worth visiting for Cong Abbey and the archaeological remains in the vicinity, and the **tourist office** (Abbey Street, T098-9546542, open Apr-Oct daily 1000-1800) sells a useful archaeological guide. There is a series of nearby caves but more interesting is the **Ballymacgibbon Cairn** at Cross and the nearby stone circles at **Moytura**.

Quiet Man Heritage Cottage ⓘ *Circular Rd, T094-9546089. Daily 1000-1800. €3.75.* Is this an exercise in ironic post-modernism? It's a replica of a Hollywood set of an Irish cottage interior but located in a real Irish cottage interior, with items such as a copy of Wayne's jacket made by the person who made the original, and an infinite number of video copies of the film for sale; a video about the film is shown upstairs. The blurred line between film and reality is thankfully brought into focus with the cottage's modest exhibition on local archaeology and history.

Cong Abbey ⓘ *24 hrs, free, in the centre of Cong village, opposite the tourist office.* In the ultra-secular grounds of Ashford Castle (see page 419), this Augustinian abbey was rebuilt in the very early 13th century, though the site has religious associations going back another 500 years and, like the neighbouring island monastery of Inchagoill (see page 390), probably usurped a place of Celtic worship. Not too much of the church itself remains but the most outstanding feature – the Romanesque doorway on the north wall, which was actually inserted later – is notable for its sculptured capitals, which represent the last flowering of Romanesque architecture in Ireland. The adjoining Chapter House also has fine windows and decorated stonework.

Sleeping

Westport *p412, maps p412 and 420*
Beware the Reek Weekend at the end of July when pilgrims climb Croagh Patrick (see box page 414). Accommodation is hard to find.
B-C Atlantic Coast Hotel, The Quay, T098-29000, www.atlanticcoasthotel.com. Once an old mill by the quayside, now a modern, 4-star hotel with a pool, gym and spa plus clinical efficiency. Off-season breaks are worth considering.
B-D Wyatt Hotel, The Octagon, T098-25027, www.wyatthotel.com. A 'lively contemporary ambience' is what the brochure says and it seems to suit this comfortable and modern-style hotel.
C-D The Olde Railway Hotel, The Mall, T098-25166, www.theolderailwayhotel.com. Built in 1780 as a coaching inn for guests of Lord Sligo – William Thackeray stayed here – a Victorian charm still characterizes Westport's most genuinely elegant hotel.
D St Anthony's, Distillery Rd, T098-28887, www.st-anthonys.com. At the bottom end of this price range, 5 rooms with en suite bathroom in an attractive house close to the town centre.

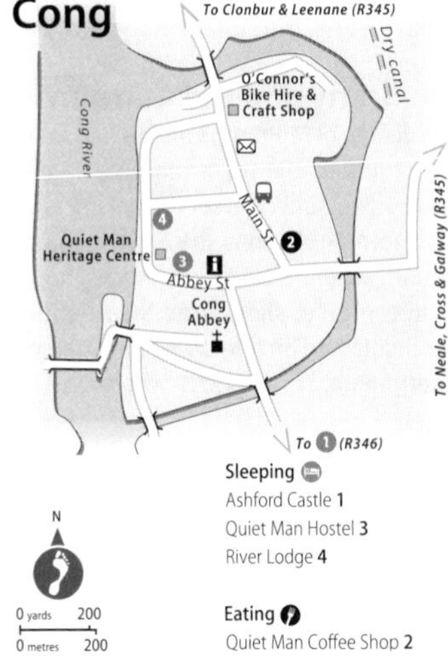

E Adare House, Quay Rd, T098-26102, adarehouse@eircom.net. Firm mattresses and fine views from this B&B just outside the centre.
E Cedar Lodge, Kings Hill, Newport Rd, T098-25417. Within walking distance of town, 4 bedrooms with en suite bathroom.
E High Street House, High St, T098-25813, www.highstreethouse.net. A little townhouse with murals in the doorway, close to the centre but in a quiet location.
E Old Mill Holiday Hostel, Barrack Yard, off James St, T098-27045, www.oldmill-hostel.com. Open all year except Christmas, next to the tourist office and now the only hostel in town.

Camping

Parkland Caravan and Camping Park, T098-27766, in the grounds of Westport House. This place is outrageously expensive.

Around Westport (Louisburg) *p413*

Accommodation can be arranged through the Westport tourist office.
E Carramore House, Carramore, T098-66397, just outside of town.
E Springfield House, Westport Rd, T098-66289.

Camping

Old Head Forest Caravan and Camping Park, Louisburg, T098-66021. Not as expensive as Parkland so worth considering.

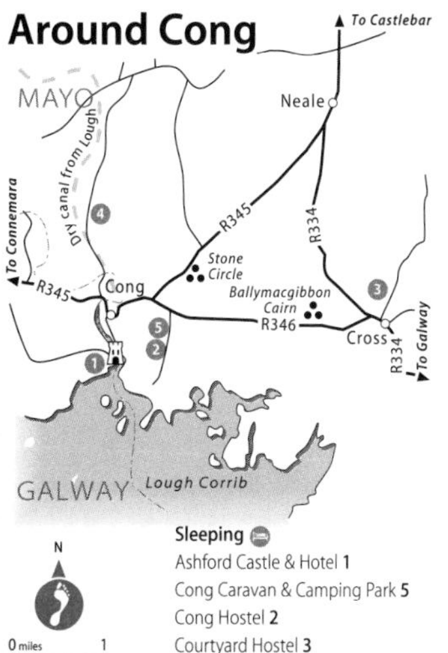

Clare Island *p415*

E Bay View Hotel T098-26307. The only hotel on the island, a short walk from the pier, with pub food available at the bar.
E Cos Abhainn, T098-26216. About 4 km from the harbour, rooms with their own bathroom facilities, evening meal available and a pick-up from the harbour if you phone in advance.
E Sea Breeze, T098-26746. This B&B is only 300 m from the harbour and is signposted. A double is under €70, a single €35 and there is the option of an evening meal.

Inishturk Island *p416*

B Ocean View House, T098-45520. Has rooms with bathrooms and an evening meal can be arranged.
E Teach Abhainn, T098-45510. Has a lovely quiet location, about 3 km from the main harbour, with terrific views and dinner can be arranged. The accordion-playing owner has been known to enliven an evening with live music.

Newport and around *p416*

L Newport House, T098-41222, www.newporthouse.ie. Well-heeled anglers enjoy the period feel of this country house and the fine food.
E Debille House, Main St, T098-41145. This Georgian building does B&B in summer.
F Traenlaur Lodge, Lough Feeagh, T098-41358. This *An Óige* hostel is a few km north of Newport and taxi transport, T087-2202123, costs €7.

Cong *p417, maps p418 and opposite*

L Ashford Castle, about 1.5 km south of the village, T094-9546003, www.ashford.ie. With a rack rate reaching over €500 for the best rooms, this is a lovely place to stay if someone else is footing the bill. If you want to view the garden, a fee of €5 is required.
D-E Lydon's Lodge, Circular Rd, near Ashford Castle, T094-9546053. Comfortable rooms away from the village hub.
E Dolmen House, Drumsheel, T094-9546466. B&B in a large modern bungalow just north of Cong, with a sauna.
E River Lodge, T094-9546057. A typical B&B around Cong, which means it is often booked up in summer.

F Cong Hostel, Lisloughrey, Quay Rd, T094-9546089, www.quietman-cong.com. Next to the camping site, off the R346 road to Galway and about 1.5 km out of Cong. Private rooms and dorm beds in a friendly hostel. Bike hire too.

F Courtyard Hostel, Garracloon Lodge, Dowagh Estate, Cross, T094-9546203. Out beyond Cong Hostel and belongs to an interesting organic farm, which oddly includes its own golf course. Has a couple of private rooms and bike hire.

F Quiet Man Hostel, Abbey St, Cong, T094-9546089, www.quietman-cong.com. In the village itself, has some private rooms.

Camping

Cong Caravan and Camping Park, Lisloughrey, Quay Rd, Cong, T094-9546089. Only 40 pitches for tents and caravans.

Cong Hostel, Cross, T094-9546089. Camping is also possible here.

Eating

Westport *p412, maps p412 and 420*

In town

ΨΨ **The Lemon Peel**, The Octagon. The dinner menu from 1800 to 1900 is under €25. Recommended.

ΨΨ **The Olde Railway Hotel Restaurant**, The Mall, T098-25166. A good dinner for around €35 in a conservatory dining room, and the Victorian-style bar area is also worth considering for a more informal meal in comfortable surroundings.

Ψ **O'Cees**, Shop St. Fine for just something to snaffle while waiting for a bus at the Octagon.

Ψ **Torrino's**, Market Lane off Bridge St, T098-28338. Has been recommended for its Italian-style offerings of pizza and pasta dishes around €15.

Quay Rd

Out near the entrance to Westport House there are a number of expensive and mid-range restaurants specializing in local seafood and mostly open only for dinner; reservations are usually necessary.

ΨΨΨ **Ardmore House Restaurant**, Ardmore Rd, which meets Quay Rd a little further down, T098-25994. Opens in the summer months at 1800 for a grand dinner, around €40, with views of Clew Bay. Seafood is the strength of this restaurant and there is a terrific choice of starters.

ΨΨΨ-ΨΨ **Quay Cottage Restaurant**, Quay Rd, T098-26412. Overlooking the harbour, dinner amidst nautical gewgaws; check the daily specials for fresh fish.

ΨΨ **The Asgard**, Quay Rd, T098-25319. Serves open smoked salmon sandwiches for €10, an evening bar menu with dishes like Irish stew and chicken kiev, and a restaurant for more formal meals.

ΨΨ-Ψ **Sheebeen Pub**, Quay Rd, past the Ardmore Rd turning. Serves a more informal and less expensive lunch or dinner.

ΨΨ-Ψ **The Towers**, Quay Rd, T098-26534, on the other side of the road to Asgard. Food options are very similar but the roadside garden tables have views of Croagh Patrick.

Around Westport (Louisburg) *p413*

JJ's Bar & Weir Restaurant, Chapel St, T098-66140. Serves delicious local seafood and steaks in the bar, daily, until 2100 and in the restaurant, Thu-Sat and Sun lunch.

River Café, Bridge St. Home-made food, open from 1000-1700 for well crafted salads, smoked salmon and fresh bread.

Clare Island *p415*

It is best to bring a picnic but food is available at the Bay View Hotel.

Inishturk Island *p416*

The Community Club, a picnic meal is a good idea but this place functions as the village pub and also does light food like sandwiches.

Westport Quay

Clew Bay Heritage Centre
Carrowbeg River
Quay Rd
Ardmore Rd
To Westport House
To Westport

Sleeping
Atlantic Coast **2**

Eating
Ardmore House **1**
Asgard **2**
Quay Cottage **3**
Sheebeen Pub **4**
Towers **5**

Newport and around *p416*
¥¥¥ **Newport House**, dinner is a cool €55 in this country house dining room with high ceilings and windows to match. A 5-course dinner menu is on offer, whose strong point is locally caught fish cooked in a modern Irish style, complemented by home-grown vegetables.
¥ **Kelly's Kitchen**, Main St. Opens daily 1000-2100 for home-cooked food.
¥ **The Village Bakery**, below Debille House. Food available here.

Cong *p417, maps p418 and p419*
¥ **Lydons**, pub food is available.
¥ **Quiet Man Coffee Shop**, Main St, T094-9546059. Fine for a hearty snack or scones.

Pubs and music

Westport *p412, maps p412 and 420*
The bars out along Quay St have live music, especially at weekends.
M.J. Hoban, at the Octagon. A popular bar with regular musical entertainment.
Matt Molloy's, Bridge St. The town's most famous pub, owned by the eponymous musician from the Chieftains who hails from Westport. It is also one of the most frequented, however, and finding the elbow space to lift a pint can be difficult.
P McCarthy's, Quay St. Recommended.
Moran's, across the road from Matt Molloy's, has a small grocery store at the front and a tiny bar to the rear, and is patronized by locals seeking to escape the better known pubs.
The Sheebeen, Quay Rd. Recommended.

Festivals and events

Westport *p412*
The Westport Arts Festival, T098-24684, generally takes place in **mid-Sep** for 1 week but the dates can vary from one year to the next. There is usually a caravan in Shop St with programmes and ticket sales.

Shopping

Westport *p412*
Westport has a good number of shops worth dipping into for gifts, clothes and outdoor gear and there is a second-hand bookshop opposite the tourist office. On Quay Rd, near the harbour, once-dilapidated warehouses have been restored to house shops.
Carraig Donn, Bridge St. Has a wide range of crafts plus their own knitwear.

Activities and tours

Westport *p412*
Horse riding **Carrowholly Stables**, T098-27057. Guided scenic and coastal treks.

Tours **Adventure Centre**, T098-64806. Covers canoeing, windsurfing, sailing, rock climbing, abseiling and hill walking.
Coagh Patrick Walking Tours, T098-26090, www.walkingguideireland.com. Day trips as well as longer treks with accommodation and transport arranged.
Gerry Greensmyth, T098-26090. Guided walking tours, including Croagh Patrick.
Island Otterwatch, T098-41048. Walking trips to spot otters.

Cong *p417*
Lough Corrib Cruises, T094-9546029. Run a daily sailing between Ashford Castle and Oughterard with a stop-off and guided tour of the ruins on the island of Inchagoill (see page 390). Tickets from the tourist office, T094-9546029/9546542.

Transport

Westport and around *p412*
Air Knock International Airport, T1850-672222 (T94-9367222 outside the Republic), www.knockairport.com. Has connections with **Dublin** on Aer Arann, **London Stansted** with Ryanair, and **Manchester** with British Airways. In the summer there are chartered flights from **Germany** with Lufthansa, from **Zurich** with Crossair and from **Amsterdam** with Transavia.

Bike hire Breheny's, Castlebar St, Westport, T098-25020. Sean Sammon, James St, Westport, T098-25471. A day's cycling in the Cong area, with the local archaeological guide, is recommended and bikes can be hired from some of the hostels and from O'Connor's, Main St, Cong, T094-9546008.

Bus Scheduled daily services from Westport run to **Achill**, **Ballina**, **Belfast**, **Cork**, **Galway**,

Limerick and **Sligo**, and there are 4 buses a day to **Dublin**. Walsh Coaches, T098-35165, run a weekend service to **Galway**.

A summer-only, daily **Galway** to **Clifden** service stops at **Cong** in the morning for Galway and in the evening for Clifden.

Car hire Dooley Car Rental, Knock Airport, T062-53103. National, Knock Airport T094-67252.

Taxi All in Westport: Christy Cawley, T098-28282; Conor Dever, T098-27220; Dever, T098-27220/087-413722. Brenda McGing, T098-26319.

Train Westport train station is on Altamount Rd, T098-25253, and within walking distance of town. There are daily services to **Castlebar**, **Athlone** and **Dublin** with connections to the south and north.

Achill Island

→ *Phone code: 098. Colour map 2, grid A1, A2 and B2.*

Ireland's largest island has a population of 1,800 people, and its five Blue Flag beaches give some indication of just how singularly unspoilt it remains. "The naturalist, the antiquary, the artist, the poet, will find much in Achill that harmonizes with their tastes", is as true today as when a visitor made this remark in 1884. When first-time visitors to Achill hit a spell of bad weather they leave wondering what was so special about the place, but when there is blue in the sky and the light weaves its magic on the landscape a stay on Achill is a memorable experience. The German writer, Heinrich Böll (1917-1985), certainly found it so while living at Dugort in the 1950s. His house is now used as a retreat for writers, as specified in his will, and his Irish Journal (1957) would make suitable reading while on Achill. ▸▸ *For Sleeping, Eating and other listings, see pages 424-426.*

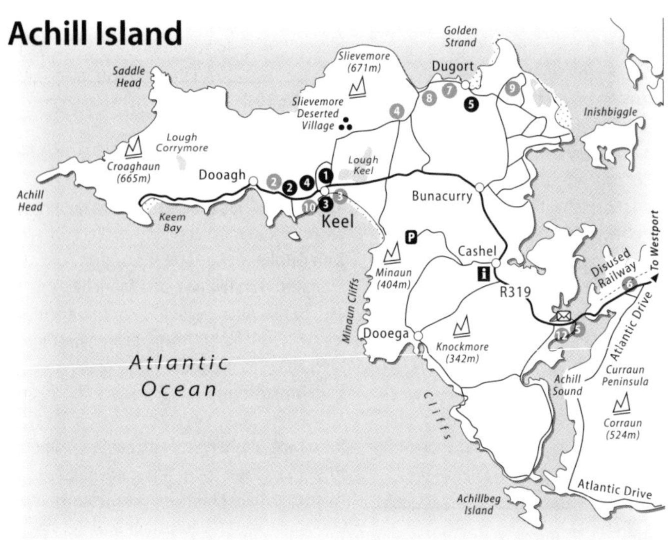

Sleeping
Achill Head **1**
Groigin Mor **2**
Keel Sandybanks Caravan & Camping Park **3**
McDowell's **4**
Ostán Oileán Acla **5**
Railway Hostel **6**
Rich View Hostel **10**
Seal Caves Caravan & Camping Park **7**
Strand **8**
Valley House Hostel **9**
Wild Haven Hostel **12**

Eating
Anchor & Mastersons Pub **5**
Beehive **4**
Calvey's **1**
Chalet Seafood **2**
Village Inn **3**

The Colony

In 1831 Edward Nangle, a young Church of Ireland minister, came to Achill and established the Achill Mission soon afterwards. Learning and using the Irish language, they leased 130 acres of land and established a school and a church on the southeast slopes of Slievemore. The Colony, as the Achill Mission became known, proved highly successful, and a printing press turned out regular publications, to the chagrin of the local Catholic authorities whose previous indifference to the islanders now proved an embarrassment. In the 1840s the Mission had its own hotel and various enterprises, which were able to survive the years of the Famine. By the 1850s, by which time the Mission owned about two-thirds of the island, the Catholic hierarchy fought back by strengthening its presence on Achill and taking an interest in the welfare of its parishioners. A National School was established in 1852 and its success saw the eventual closure of the Mission schools. Emigration in the 1880s, combined with financial difficulties for the Mission, saw a gradual decline in its influence, and it was wound up in 1886.

The now-closed Slievemore Hotel, the original Mission Hotel, stands in the middle of the Mission complex of buildings. The Mission church, a stone's throw from the hotel, has a photograph of the remarkable Edward Nangle. He died in 1883 and his recorded last words were, "Achill may well be called the Happy Valley. In spite of all our trials, I know of no place like it."

Ins and outs

Getting there Achill is separated from the mainland by a channel of sea, Achill Sound, but the Michael Davitt Bridge spans the water at a narrow point, so there is no need for a ferry service. The nearest large town on the mainland is Westport, and from here and Ballina buses run to the island. ▸▸ *See Transport, page 426, for further details.*

Getting around A bicycle is the ideal way to get around the island, and if based near Dooagh or Dugort many places can be reached on foot. The main road crosses the island from Achill Sound to Keem Bay. Also starting at Achill Sound a loop road runs south through Dooega, and at Bunacurry a northern loop accesses Dugort and Slievemore and returns to the main road at Keel.

Information **Achill Tourism**, Cashel, T098-47353. Open all year around, and in Jul and Aug there is also a tourist office at Cashel, T098-45384. Information available on the web at www.visitachill.com and www.achilltourism.com.

Geography

At 22 km long and 19 km wide but with an indented coastline of some 129 km, Achill is Ireland's largest island. The western side is dominated by Mount Slievemore (671 m) and Mount Croaghaun (665 m), and the northwest face of Croaghaun has been eroded to form some of the highest sea cliffs anywhere in Europe. Much of the island is heathland and bog, and the scarcity of good farming land goes some way to explaining the poignant history of emigration from Achill. But there is land, and archaeological evidence shows that people have been living here since about 4000BC.

History

A period in the 19th century when proselytizing Protestants chose Achill for a mission, is a well documented piece of recent history that shares some intriguing similarities with a much more recent controversy. From the mid-1990s onwards coaches were bringing 15,000 pilgrims a year to visit the House of Prayer, a disused convent bought by Christina Gallagher following a vision she had received telling her to open a place of worship surrounded by water. Many people claimed to have experienced or witnessed miracles here, and Christina Gallagher was being invested with too saintly and supernatural an aura to suit the church hierarchy. At one stage the closure of the House of Prayer was tearfully announced by Gallagher but this proved to be premature and the place is still there.

Beaches

Even on a fine day it is possible to have one of Achill's beaches all to yourself. The largest, stretching for 4 km at **Keel**, is safe for swimming apart from one stretch, indicated by a notice, where a riptide occurs. On the north side at **Dugort** there are more sandy beaches, with fine views over Blacksod Bay to north Mayo; the beaches are safe but **Golden Strand** has one section marked as dangerous. The most spectacular-looking beach is at **Keem Bay**, when it is first seen from the road above at a height of 182 m.

Slievemore Deserted Village

The deserted village of Slievemore consists of about 75 houses, built in the 1820s of unmortared stone and mostly parallel to one another with south-facing gables, east-facing doorways and a window to the northeast. Research suggests that the origins of the village lay in the early medieval period, AD 500-1200. In the 19th century, cattle were tethered to the southern end of the houses and tethering rings can still be seen in the walls. Poor management by the landlords, who later sold their land to the Mission, and the effects of the Famine saw villagers move south to Dooagh. It is possible that the Mission ownership of the land in 1851 accelerated the process of abandonment. Up until the 1940s the houses were used as 'booley' dwellings, summer residences for cattle grazers, but they are now in ruins.

Mount Slievemore

This is one of the most easily managed and enjoyable climbs on the island; it takes about 1 hour to reach the summit from the Deserted Village car park. Head first for the white stone that is clearly visible on the slope up behind the ruins and from there head for the ridge and along it eastwards to the summit. There are magnificent views of Blacksod Bay and the Mullet. Descend by the same route.

Mount Croaghaun

Almost as high as Slievemore but a decidedly more difficult climb and best undertaken with the help of *Ordnance Survey* map No. 30. From Keem Bay take the turning on the main road that heads north to Corrymore Lough and begin the climb from there. Precipitous cliffs drop down to the sea from close to the summit, so only climb when the sky is clear and likely to remain so for the rest of the day. Allow five hours for the return journey.

Sleeping

Achill Island *p422, map p422*
The main accommodation centres are Keel and Dooagh in the south and Dugort in the north of the island.

B Joyce's Marian Villa, Keel, T098-43134. B&B overlooking the beach, open Easter-Nov.

C-D Óstán Oileán Acla, Achill Sound, T098-45138, www.achillislandhotel.com.

At the island's gateway, perhaps it is too close to the mainland to provide that island experience.
D Achill Head, Keel, T098-43108, www.achillhead.com. Close to the beach, pub food in the bar and sociable evenings.
D Gray's Guesthouse, Dugort, T098-43244. Preferable in many respects to the island's hotels, especially if you don't want late nights, this is an engagingly cool place that invites relaxation, and has a croquet lawn to boot.
D McDowell's, Slievemore Rd, Dugort, T098-43148. A pretty, cottage-like exterior to a small 10-room hotel at the foot of Slievemore.
D Strand Hotel, Dugort, T098-43241. Within spitting distance of a Blue Flag beach.
E Groigin Mor, Pollagh, Keel, T098-43385. B&B in a small house, not a bungalow, on the main road between Keel and Dooagh. No evening meals available.
F Railway Hostel, Achill Sound, T098-45787. On the mainland just before the Michael Davitt Bridge and looking rather drab, this is nevertheless a roomy hostel with 2 kitchens, 1 private room, open all year and a pub across the road.
F Rich View Hostel, Newtown, Keel, T098-43462. Comfortable, open all year with 10 dorm beds and 3 private rooms.
F Valley House Hostel, The Valley, Dugort, T098-47334, www.valley-house.com. A tad dearer than the other hostels, this is a fine, spacious old residence converted into a hostel and with its own bar. Camping space.
F Wild Haven Hostel, Achill Sound, T098-45392. The first hostel on the island itself, just over the bridge. Enhanced by a comfortable old-fashioned living room and a conservatory for meals. Open all year and has private rooms.

Camping

Keel Sandybanks Caravan and Camping Park, Keel, T094-32054, 098-43211. On the beach.
Railway Hostel, camping possible.
Seal Caves Caravan Park, Dugort, T098-43262. Open Apr-Sep and accepts tents.
Valley House Hostel, possible to camp here.

Self catering

Achill Island Holiday Homes, Keel, T098-43259.
There are various individual houses and cottages for rent:
The Green, Keel, T098-43246.
The Links, Keel, T098-45200, www.achillcottages.com.
Minaun Cliff Cottages, T098-43341.

Eating

Achill Island *p422, map p422*
Most places to eat are in or close to Keel.
ƚƚ **Calvey's**, Keel, T098-43158. One of the easiest places to find, next to the police station on the main road by a junction. Lunch menu 1200-1730 with dishes such as salmon and chips as well as salads and sandwiches. A candlelight dinner features starters such as crab claws or oysters and main dishes such as lamb or baked cod with Pernod. Dishes are around €10-20.
ƚƚ **Gray's Guest House**, Dugort. Always worth dropping into for coffee or afternoon tea, and a wonderfully old-fashioned dinner menu – around €26 for residents – is available to non-residents for €6 more if booked in advance.
ƚƚ-ƚ **Anchor Restaurant**, outside Keel, T098-47216, at Mastersons pub at Dugort. A surf 'n' turf kind of place.
ƚƚ-ƚ **Chalet Seafood Restaurant**, Keel, T098-43157. Seafood has been recommended, and has an attached gift shop selling knitwear and pottery.
ƚ **Beehive**, Keel, T098-43134. A pleasing restaurant and craft shop, using local produce to serve up quality home-made soups, chowder, breads and cakes. Has outdoor tables overlooking the beach.
ƚ **McDowell's**, on the road there from Keel. Meals are available here.
ƚ **Village Inn**, Keel. Does bar food.

Pubs and music

Achill Island *p422, map p422*
Hotels are always a good bet on Achill for late-night drinking.

Achill Head, Keel. Hotel has live entertainment and nearly all the pubs in the vicinity will have some form of music.
Masterson's, Golden Strand. This pub is worth checking out for live music.
Patten's Lounge Bar, Achill Sound, T098-45172. Has music during the holiday season.
Valley House, the bar at this hostel is a good place to meet fellow hostellers.

Festivals and events

Achill Island *p422, map p422*
The **Achill Archaeological Field School** takes place between **late Jun and late-Aug** at the Folklife Centre, Dooagh. Details available from T McDonald, T098-43414. Provisional, but probable, an **Irish Dancing Festival** in mid-Aug, details from D Cafferkey, T098-45073.

Shopping

Achill Island *p422, map p422*
Achill Island Pottery, Keel.
Beehive Craft and Coffee Shop, Keel. Has pottery, knitwear, jewellery etc.
Chalet Craft Shop, Keel.
Shell Craft Shop, Keel. A selection of semi-precious stones such as amethyst, agate and onyx, as well as shell jewellery and other shell crafts.
Western Light Art Gallery, Keel, T098-43325.

Activities and tours

Achill Island *p422, map p422*
Diving **Achill Island Scuba Dive Centre**, T087-2349884, www.achilldivecentre.com. Based at Purteen Harbour at Keel.

Outdoor **Achill Outdoor Education Centre**, T098-47253, www.achilloutdoor.com.
Tomás Mac Lochláinn, T098-45085. Walks, surfing, rock climbing and kayaking.

Fishing **Tony Burke**, Cashel, T098-47257. Departs daily from Purten Harbour at Keel.
Lady Clare, Dooega East, T098-45743. Sea angling and boat trips.

Transport

Achill Island *p422, map p422*
Bike hire O'Malley's Supermarket, Keel, T098-43125.

Bus A Bus Éireann service, T096-71800, runs daily between **Dooagh** and **Westport**, via **Keel**, **Dugort** and **Cashel** on the island and **Newport** on the mainland, taking 2 hrs. The first bus departs Westport at 1500 (2205 on Sun), earliest departure from Dooagh is at 0825 (1600 on Sun).

Taxi M.T. Taxi, T098-45491.

Directory

Achill Island *p422, map p422*
Banks No bank on the island; travelling banks visit. **Bank of Ireland**, T087-2375138. Visits on Mon, Tue and Thu. **AIB Bank**, T098-25466, visits on Mon and Wed. **Bureaux de change**: Beehive Craft & Coffee Shop at Keel. **Medical services** Achill Sound Health Centre, T098-45231. **Achill Pharmacy**, Achill Sound, T098-45248. **Post office** The main post office is in Keel at **O'Malley's Supermarket**, T098-43125, and money can also be changed here. There is also a post office at Dooagh, T098-43107. **Useful addresses** Car breakdown service at Teddy McNulty, T098-45347/45867.

Northwest and north Mayo

The desolate northwest of Mayo is as far off the tourist trail as one can get in Ireland. Here there are only two towns of any size – Bangor Erris (usually just called Bangor) and Belmullet – and everything in between is bogland, heather, bare hills and the occasional farmhouse or weather-beaten bungalow. Travel here for wildlife, walking, fishing, angling – you won't feel crowded whatever you do. The biggest town in the north of Mayo is Ballina, while further to the north, on the coast, is historic Killala.
▸▸ *For Sleeping, Eating and other listings, see pages 429-431.*

Belmullet and the Mullet Peninsula

→ *Phone code: 097. Colour map 2, grid A2.*

One of the least populated corners of Europe, the Mullet peninsula has its own charms, although you won't be thinking this if you arrive on a wet day. At its best it offers splendid wild beauty of an unconventional kind, and in mythology it was the final resting place of the four Children of Lir. Under a spell, they spent their last 300 years here as swans until they heard the bell of a monk, a disciple of St Patrick, who was searching for them. The monk cared for them but when a local chief wanted the swans as a present for his wife they were turned back into humans. But Irish mythology has a hard edge, for when the swans returned to human form they were 900 years old and quickly withered away and died.

Belmullet was founded in the early 19th century by an English landlord, and little has happened since to change the basic layout of the place. There is precious little to see, but travellers pass through on their way south to the Mullet Peninsula on the R313. The road goes to **Blacksod Point** at the southern tip of the Peninsula and passes two good beaches at **Elly Bay** and then **Mullaghroe**. Blacksod Point looks out to where, in 1588, the *La Rata Santa Maria Encoronada*, the flagship of the Spanish Armada, was stranded. The Spanish commander, Don Alfonso de Leyva, was rescued but later lost his life off County Antrim.

There are a number of promontory forts in the area and the one worth seeing is at **Doonamo**, reached by taking a road northwest from Belmullet. Dating back to the Iron Age, it is strategically positioned for defensive purposes and inside it stands a ringfort. Off the west coast of the peninsula lie the islands of **Inishglora**, **Inishkea North** and **Inishkea South**. The Inishkea Islands, where inscribed pillar-stones of uncertain provenance stand, can be visited by boat (see Activities and tours page 431).

There is a seasonal, Easter-Sep, **tourist office** on the left side of the R313 as one enters Belmullet, T097-81500, www.visitbelmullet.com, Mon-Fri, 0930-1630.

★ Portacloy and Benwee Head → *Colour map 2, grid A2.*

If you like the beach all to yourself then take the turning for Portacloy off the R314 road between Belmullet and Ballycastle. After a journey of 13 km across an incredibly flat landscape populated mostly by sheep, you reach a delightful beach, hemmed in by cliffs, at the northwest extremity of Ireland. There are no shops or pubs so bring everything you need. To the west of Portacloy, at Benwee Head, towering cliffs look out to a group of rockstacks standing some 90 m high. From the quayside at the west end of the beach, you can head off up the hills and walk towards Benwee Head; stay clear of the cliff edges at all times as Benwee Head has cliffs of metamorphic schist that drop a sheer 250 m into the sea.

Bangor Erris and the Bangor Trail

The Bangor Trail is a long-distance walk between Newport and Bangor, but for the first few miles north of Newport it shares a route with the Western Way. A short way beyond the *An Óige* Traenlaur Lodge hostel, T098-41358 (see page 419), which is 8 km north of Newport, it turns northwestwards towards Bangor and leaves the Western Way behind. Maps and a guidebook, *County Mayo: The Bangor Trail* by McDermott and Chapman, are available in Westport or Ballina.

Ballina and around → *Phone code 096. Colour map 2, grid A3.*

For many visitors the major attractions in Ballina is the **River Moy** itself, rich in salmon and trout, which passes through the town, and the river's bridges are regularly used by anglers. The town originally developed on the east side of the river, close to where the Victorian cathedral of St Muredach now stands, but from the 18th century onwards it was the west side that developed into the modest commercial centre you see today. The **tourist office** on Cathedral Road, on the east side of the river,

T096-70848, has a good range of information, including where to fish and obtain permits. Open Apr-Sep Mon-Sat 1000-1300, 1400-1745. **Belleek Forest**, about 2 km from the town centre, and about 1.5 km southwest of town, past the railway station, is a popular place for walks. There is the neolithic Dolmen of the Four Maols, associated with a legend of four foster-brothers of the early Christian era who murdered their master and were buried here after being executed.

There are two abbeys near Ballina, both reached by taking the R314 north to Killala, and while not especially spectacular they are worth a visit if travelling that way.

Rosserk Abbey ⓘ *24 hrs. Free. After 6 km on the R314 north of Ballina take the signposted road to the right, left at the next junction and then a right at the next signpost.* The 15th century was a good time for ecclesiastical architecture, not least because of the Franciscans who proceeded to build some of their finest friaries around Ireland: Rosserk Abbey is a particularly good example of what they achieved. Highlights include a double piscina, which is rare due to the inscribed relief of a round tower, and very well preserved windows and substantial remains of the domestic wing.

Moyne Abbey ⓘ *24 hrs. Free. Continue for about 3 km on the R314 after the turn-off for Rosserk until the abbey comes into view on the right near a farm.* This is also a Franciscan abbey, contemporary with Rosserk, though apart from the cloisters it is not as well preserved. An adjoining tower with stairs still stands; however, it is none too easy for the untrained eye to make out the various domestic buildings that surround the church. The English governor of Connaught burned the abbey down in 1590 but the friars remained living there until the end of the 18th century.

Enniscoe Gardens ⓘ *Castlehill. Apr-Sep daily 1400-1800. €6 garden, €6 heritage centre. 4 km from Crosssmolina on the R315.* The original garden of Enniscoe House, an 18th-century country house, is gone but it has been sensitively restored and there is an adjoining little heritage centre housing domestic artefacts. Also home to the **Mayo North Family Heritage Centre** ⓘ *www.mayo.irish-roots.net.*

Killala and the north coast → *Phone code: 096. Colour map 2, grid A3.*

On 22nd August 1798, three French frigates dropped anchor at Kilcummin Strand in Killala Bay and put this quiet corner of North Mayo on the map. General Humbert had over 1,000 men and when they charged the 80 yeomanry outside of Killala with fixed bayonets the English forces quickly surrendered. Killala became the first place in Ireland to be occupied by French revolutionary soldiers, and peasants armed with pikes soon joined them.

Although Killala also boasts a Church of Ireland cathedral with a fine steeple, and a wonky round tower, it is the merging of the insurrectionary United Irishmen movement with Napoleon's revolutionary army that gives this area its powerful sense of history. To reach the beach at **Kilcummin**, 6 km west of town, take the R314 road north and take the signposted turning right. Along the road there is a stirring monument depicting a French soldier in solidarity with an Irish peasant. The **tourist office** on Ballina Road just before entering town, T096-32166, sells a short *Historical Guide to Killala and District*, €2, that covers the rich history of the area: "a miniature of the history of our land" indeed.

Ballycastle and Céide Fields → *Phone code: 096. Colour map 1, grid A5.*

Céide Fields ⓘ *T096-43325. Mid-Mar to May daily 1000-1700, Jun-Sep daily 1000-1800, Oct-Nov daily 1000-1700. €3.50. OPW site. 8 km west of Ballycastle on the R314, look for a pyramidal roof innocuously situated on the bare bog.* The small town of Ballycastle on the north coast would be a fairly forgettable place on the road between Killala and Belmullet were it not for the nearby phenomenon of Céide (pronounced 'cage-a') Fields, the largest known neolithic farm settlement in the world. A schoolteacher in the area had long suspected there was something worth exploring under the blanket bog but it was not until his son became an archaeologist that it was properly examination. The result was astonishing, for sealed under the layers of bog was a sophisticated 5,000-year old network of stone-walled fields. Picks and shovels and resinous pine chips have been found, suggesting the existence of early copper mining, but no signs of defensive walls: the pioneering farmers who worked these fields had little to fear from their neighbours because they didn't have any.

On a fine day, if coming from Killala, take the R314 to Ballycastle and then the signposted turning to the right for Kilcummin and Lackan Bay. The beach here is sandy and safe, and further along the road there are superb views at Downpatrick Head.

The story of Céide Fields is told at the Visitor Centre in a 20-minute audio-visual show, one of the best to be seen anywhere in Ireland, that sets the geological and historical context. Guided tours take visitors around the site and, because the place is not immediately dramatic, a lot depends on getting a knowledgeable and helpful guide who can interpret the scene for you. The centre has a restaurant, or you can have a picnic outside overlooking a spectacular vista of sea and land.

Sleeping

Belmullet and Mullet Peninsula *p427*

E Chez Nous, Church Rd, Belmullet, T097-82167. 4 rooms with en suite facilities in comfortable house.

E Drom Caoin, Belmullet, T097-81195, www.belmullet-accommodation.com. B&B within walking distance of town, views of the sea, choice of breakfast and vegetarians well catered for, bathrooms en suite. Also has a couple of self catering apartments.

E Sea Rod Inn, Doohoma, T097-86767, www.thesearodinn.ie. Before Belmullet, reached by heading south from Gweesalia which is signposted off the R313 road between Bangor and Belmullet. This guest house is open all year and, out of season, what a place to escape from the world!

F-G Kilcommon Lodge, Pollatomish, T097-84621, kilcommonlodge@eircom.net. Open all year, this wonderful hostel has a lot to recommend it. The location is superb with wild walks and beaches nearby, 2 pubs in the village and, though there is a kitchen, a 4-course dinner is available for €12.

Ballina and around *p427*

A-B Enniscoe House, Castlehill, near Crossmolina, T096-31112, www.enniscoe.com. Handsome Georgian house on the shore of Lough Conn, which has been in the same family since the 1660s. Good food and the hint of a Sommerville and Ross setting.

B Downhill Hotel, Sligo Rd, Ballina, T096-21033, www.downhillhotel.ie. Its leisure centre, with pool, saunas, squash court, gym, all-weather tennis courts and snooker table, is an inducement to stay here. A short way outside of town on the N59.

C-D Downhill Inn, Sligo Rd, Ballina, T096-73444, www.downhillinn.com. Sister-hotel to the Downhill, with 2- and 3-night deals.

E Errigal, Killala Rd, Ballina, T096-22563, treacycoaches@eircom.net. This B&B is handy if heading north on the R314.

E Green Hill, Cathedral Close, Ballina, T096-22767. Quiet B&B near the cathedral.

Camping

Belleek Caravan and Camping Park, north of town off the R314 road to Killala, T096-71533, lenahan@indigo.ie. Nearly 60 pitches of which 20 are for tents. Mid-Mar to mid-Oct.

Killala and the north coast *p428*

E Avondale House, Pier Rd, Killala, T096-32229. Has 4 rooms with shared facilities.

E Beach View House, Ross, T096-32023; and **E Chez Nous**, Ross, T096-32056. Both are reached by taking the road out to Ballycastle from Killala and turning right at the sign pointing to Ross Strand.

For an explanation of the sleeping and eating price codes used in this guide, see inside the front cover. Other relevant information is found in Essentials pages 39-45.

Ballycastle and Céide Fields *p428*

A-B Stella Maris Hotel, Ballycastle, T096-43322, www.stellamaris.com. Overlooking Bunatrahir Bay and Downpatrick Head, a former coast guard station has been converted into a boutique hotel. Great sea views, and a restaurant.

E Céide House, Main St, Ballycastle, T096-43105. This pub does B&B but it might not be the quietest place to stay.

E The Hawthorns, Belderrig, T096-43148. B&B in a village on the road 6 km west of Ceide Fields. Open all year and dinner is €17.

E The Yellow Rose, Belderrig, T096-43125. Open all year. The house overlooks the sea, serves dinner and the excavated remains of a smaller Stone Age farm site are nearby.

E Suantrai, outside Ballycastle, on the road to Downpatrick Head, T096-43040. Mr and Mrs Chambers do B&B here from mid-Jun to mid-Aug, but no meals are available. A double room, en suite, is €50, a single is €35, and there is 1 family room.

Eating

Belmullet and Mullet Peninsula *p427*

Lavelle's Bar, Main St, Belmullet. Has a coffee shop and serves seafood, plus a large-screen TV and a pool table.

Western Strands, Belmullet. Hotel serving pub grub all day and a seafood dinner from 1900 to 2100.

In **Bangor** the food scene is even more dismal but there is a pub, opposite the Hillcrest House B&B, T097-83494, on Main St that serves pub food throughout the day.

Ballina and around *p427*

Crockets on the Quay, turn left at the first set of traffic lights on the Sligo Rd, Ballina. Has interesting dishes for vegetarians and carnivores.

The Broken Jug, O'Rahilly St, next to the post office, Ballina, T096-72379. Does pub food nightly until 2100, plus an affordable carvery lunch, and evening meals in its Gallery restaurant.

Gaughan's, Ballina. Serves crab salads, home-cooked quiche, salads and roasts in a laid-back, homely pub atmosphere from mid-morning to closing time.

Killala and the north coast *p428*

Golden Acres, Market St, Killala. Pub serving home-cooked food, and the food at the unprepossessing-looking Anchor Bar includes tasty open crab sandwiches.

The following pubs all serve food:

Spinning Wheel, George St, Killala;

Tower Bar, Market St, Killala;

The Village Inn, Church St, Killala.

B&Bs tend to do dinner for around €18.

Ballycastle and Céide Fields *p428*

Doonferry House, an odd, red-coloured pub outside of town on the road to Céide Fields, serves meals in a restaurant setting, as well as bar food.

Céide Fields Visitor Centre, has a decent tearoom serving quick meals.

Céide House, Ballycastle. Has a restaurant serving café-style meals from 0900 to 2100.

Mary's Bakery, a stone-built house at the other end of the street to Céide House. Does scones, salads and soups and more tempting dishes like wild Atlantic salmon with mayonnaise and soda bread. The evening menu always features a vegetarian dish, alongside a fish and meat choice.

Pubs and music

Ballina and around *p427*

There is the usual plethora of pubs in Ballina, and during the summer months many of them are alive with the sound of traditional Irish music.

Brogan's, Garden St. Recommended.

The Broken Jug, O'Rahilly St. Has its own nightclub, which attracts a young crowd.

Murphy Brothers, Clare St. Recommended.

Killala and the north coast *p428*

Golden Acres, Killala. A good bet for live music between Wed and Sun nights.

Ballycastle and Céide Fields *p428*

Céide House, has sessions of traditional music at weekends.

Katie Mac's, pub next door to Céide House. More of the same.

Polke's, opposite Mary's Bakery. A traditiona grocery and pub combined, a place to sit and while away some time.

Festivals and events

Ballina and around *p427*
The Ballina Street Festival, T096-70905, takes place before **mid-Jul** and lasts for a week. The highlight is National Heritage Day when shop fronts take on a Victorian character, proprietors dress accordingly, and music and theatre enliven the atmosphere.

Shopping

Ballina and around *p427*
Keohane's, Tone St. Complements the tourist office in its stock of maps and guides.

Activities and tours

Belmullet and Mullet Peninsula *p427*
Boat trips Boat trips to the small islands of **Inishkea** North and South through Josephine Geraghty, T097-85741. The trips are on demand and cost €5 for a return trip that gives you a few hours on the islands.
Fishing Possible on Cross Lake, stocked by the fishery board and suitable for boat and shore angling. Boat hire and permits available from **George Geraghty**, Belmullet, T097-81492. In Bangor, day permits for local fishing are available in the **West End Bar**. Boat hire for angling is available through **Vincent Sweeney**, T097-85774.

Transport

Northwest and north Mayo *p426*
Bus A bus service, Mon-Sat, departs from **Ballina**, T096-71800, for **Belmullet**, via **Bangor**, and continues south to **Blacksod Point**, at 1810, and 2145 on a Fri. A daily 1300 departure from **Ballina** terminates at **Belmullet**. McNulty Coaches, Chapel St, Belmullet, T097-81086, www.mcnultys coaches.com, run a daily service to and from **Castlebar**, and a weekend service to **Limerick** via **Westport**, **Galway** and **Ennis**. Corduff, T097-88880, T098-35165 (Westport), www.corduﬀtravel.ie, runs a Fri bus between **Galway** and **Belmullet** via **Castlebar** and **Westport**, returning to Galway on Sun.

From **Ballina** there are daily buses to **Achill**, **Athlone**, **Ballycastle** (not on Sun), **Belmullet**, **Castlebar**, **Cork**, **Crossmolina**, **Derry**, **Donegal**, **Dublin**, **Enniskillen**, **Foxford**, **Galway**, **Killala** (not on Sun), **Letterkenny**, **Limerick**, **Louisburg** (not on Sun), **Pontoon**, **Sligo** and **Westport**. Treacy's, T096-70968, runs a private bus service to **Sligo**.

There's a Mon-Sat service between **Ballina** and **Ballycastle** via **Killala**. First bus leaves Ballina at 0725, then 1000 on a Fri, 1615 Mon-Fri and an 1800 bus on Sat only. Corduff runs a Fri bus from **Galway** to **Rossport** via **Ballina** and **Killala**, returning to Galway on Sun.

Train The **Dublin** to **Westport** train service stops at **Ballina** 3 times a day, and connections to most other parts of the rail network are made at **Athlone**.

Castlebar and around

→ *Colour map 2, grid B3.*

With a population approaching 8,000, Castlebar is a thriving and commercially successfully town, and while there may seem to be a distinct lack of charm about the place, it makes a suitable base for excursions north to Pontoon and Lough Conn, primarily of interest to fishing folk; east to Turlough, Strade and Foxford where there is a round tower, museums and shopping opportunities; or south to Ballintober Abbey, one of the most evocative old churches in Ireland. To the southeast there is also Knock, putative site of visions, apparitions and miracles but also home to an interesting folk museum. ▸▸ *For Sleeping, Eating and other listings, see pages 433-435.*

Information There's a **tourist office** on Linenhall St in Castlebar, T094-9026727. Open mid-Apr to early Sep Mon-Sat 0930-1300, 1400-1730.

Wanted – dead or alive?

Castlebar is the birthplace of notable characters such as Louis Brennan, inventor of the monorail and the torpedo; Margaret Burke Sheridan, the soprano; and Charles Haughey, the former Taoiseach infamous for his financial shenanigans. But the most notorious individual associated with Castlebar is Richard John Bingham Lucan (1934-?), the alleged murderer of his nanny in London in 1974, and Ireland's best-known absentee landlord. A coroner's jury charged him with the murder, the nanny being apparently mistaken for his estranged wife. Some tenants around Castlebar still pay rents to the Lucan estate, which is now officially in the hands of his son, and around the corner from the tourist office there is a Lucan Street. The town park, known as the Mall, was once the cricket pitch of the Lucan family and it now contains a monument to the 1798 rising. In 1999 Lord Lucan was officially pronounced dead, but a body has never been found.

Ballintober Abbey

ⓘ T094-9030934. Daily 0900-2400. Free to enter abbey, though donations welcomed, €4 for the Celtic Furrow. Take the N84 south from Castlebar: signposted (for Ballintubber) on the left after 13 km.

A monastery was founded at Ballintober in 1216, though parts of the church were rebuilt after a fire in the late 13th century. Pilgrims stopped here at a guest house on their way to climb Croagh Patrick (see page 413). Sensitive restoration work has done wonders for the church, which, notwithstanding the aesthetically doubtful Stations of the Cross outside, manages to evoke a sense of ancient spirituality fairly unique for Irish churches. The cold grey limestone interior is startlingly non-Roman Catholic in its lack of adornment. The Early Gothic details in the transepts and nave are interesting and the west door, ascribed by experts to both the 13th and 15th centuries, was removed from the church in the 19th century and only returned in 1964. The nave itself is mostly 19th century. The nearby **Celtic Furow** exhibition traces Celtic festivals.

Knock → *Colour map 2, grid B4.*

Knock's claim to fame goes back to 1879, when two local women claimed to have seen Mary, Joseph and St John appear at the south end of the church, and 13 other people confirmed the apparition. The place quickly became a place of pilgrimage, fuelled by alleged miraculous cures and the blessing of official Church investigations. Thousands turn up every day, and in the summer there is an amazing number of stalls selling religious bric-à-brac. The **Knock Folk Museum** *ⓘ T094-9088100, May-Oct daily 1000-1800, €4, south of the church in the centre of the village, from Castlebar take the N60 south to Claremorris and turn left on to the N17 for Knock*, is surprisingly interesting, with graphic details of the apparition (and photographs of the crutches donated by cured pilgrims) and well presented displays on local farming life.

National Museum of Country Life

ⓘ T094-9031755, www.museum.ie. Tue-Sat 1000-1700, Sun 1400-1700. Free. From Castlebar take the N5 road for Swinford and turn off for Turlough after 3 miles.

Turlough Park, 8 km east of Castlebar, is home to the National Museum of Ireland's folklife collection. Turlough House, built in 1865, has been restored to grace along with the thousands of artefacts in the collection. The range is enormous, covering fishing, agriculture, clothing, furniture, crafts, transport and leisure.

Turlough round tower

ⓘ *24 hrs. Free. A short distance past the National Museum of Country Life, on the other side of the road.*

This is a well-preserved round tower, perhaps a little stouter and shorter (21 m) than most, built between the 10th and 12th centuries next to a church founded by St Patrick. The ruined church that stands here today is 18th-century, though it incorporates a 16th-century mullioned window.

Michael Davitt Memorial Museum

ⓘ *Strade, 16 km northeast of Castlebar, T094-9031022. Daily 1000-1800. €4. Take the N5 road to Dublin and turn left on to the N58 to Strade.*

Michael Davitt (1846-1906) was a founding member of the Irish National Land League in 1879 (in Daly's hotel in Castlebar), but his socialist ideas for land reform later brought him into conflict with Parnell. Davitt, himself the son of an evicted tenant farmer from Strade, was jailed for his Fenian activities in the 1870s and his *Leaves from a Prison Diary* (1885) is still worth reading. This small museum has material relating to his life and times.

Foxford Woollen Mills Visitor Centre

ⓘ *Swinford Rd, Foxford, T094-9356756. Mon-Sat 1000-1800, Sun 1400-1800. €5.*

If visiting the Michael Davitt Museum in Strade it is only a few miles further along the N58 to Foxford and the Foxford Woollen Mills Visitor Centre. The original woollen mill was founded in 1892 by a nun, and today Foxford is a big producer of quality tweed, rugs and blankets. Tours last 35 minutes and as well as the Centre's excellent shop, which sells a wide range of woollen products, there is a jewellery workshop and a woodcraft shop. There is also a self-service restaurant.

The **Foxford Way** is a long-distance walk that extends the Western Way south through the Ox Mountains, from Foxford to Strade and around Lough Cullin. The total distance is 86 km and it starts on the road outside the Woollen Mills Visitor Centre. For a short 45-minute walk follow the signs as they lead you away from the River Moy until meeting a surfaced road where the Foxford Way sign points left but a right turn returns to Foxford along the road. Mayo County Council publish a guide, *The Foxford Way (Bealach Béal Easa)*, available from the Castlebar tourist office, and *Ordnance Survey* Maps Nos 24 and 31 are required in the 1:50,000 Discovery series.

Pontoon and Lough Conn → *Colour map 2, grid A3.*

Life in Pontoon, a premier angling centre not only for Mayo but the whole of Ireland, revolves around two hotels on the narrow strip that divides Lough Conn and Lough Cullin. Pontoon's reputation has taken some flack in recent years because of a decline in the quality of the water due to pollution, and the effects this has had on the fish. But Lough Conn stretches for some 14 km, has an estimated stock of half a million brown trout and also enjoys runs of spring salmon and grilse, so all is not lost. One of the hotels runs a School of Fly Fishing (see Activities and tours, page 434).

Sleeping

Castlebar and around *p431*

B-C Pontoon Bridge Hotel, Pontoon, T094-9256120, www.pontoonbridge.com. On the narrow peninsula between Lough Conn and Lough Cullin. Runs courses for anglers, cooking enthusiasts or budding landscape painters.

B-C TF Royal Hotel & Theatre, Old Westport Rd, Castlebar, T094-9023111, www.tfroyalhotel.com. A friendly and comfortable hotel with smart bedrooms and cosy restaurant.

C Healy's, Pontoon, T094-9256443, www.healyspontoon.com. Close to the Pontoon Bridge Hotel and offering more modest accommodation but an appealing proposition for a couple of days of relaxation.

C **Imperial Hotel**, The Mall, Castlebar, T094-9021961, www.imperialhotelcatslebar.com. A Georgian coaching inn, Daly's still has the wonderfully old-fashioned dining room where the Anglo-Irish got fat until Michael Davitt hired the place for the founding of the National Land League in 1879.

C **Knock House Hotel**, Ballyhaunis Rd, Knock, T094-9388088, www.knockhousehotel.com. Large modern hotel.

E **Kenny's Guesthouse**, Lucan St, Castlebar, T094-9023091, kennys@castlebar.ie. All rooms have en suite bathrooms and there's a residents' lounge.

F **Gannon's**, Providence Rd, Foxford, T094-9256101. Hostel open all year, with a dozen beds and 3 private rooms.

Camping

Camp Carrowkeel, Ballyvary, Castlebar, T094-31264. Open from Easter to end of Sep.

Carra Caravan and Camping Park, Belcarra, Castlebar, T094-32054. Open early Jun-26 Sep.

Knock Caravan and Camping Park, Claremorris Rd, Knock, T094-88100. Open Mar to end of Oct.

Eating

Castlebar and around *p431*

Pontoon Bridge Hotel, Pontoon, T094-9256688. A good place for a meal.

Café Rua, Castlebar, T094-9023376. Around the corner from the tourist office in New Antrim St, great for home-made food at lunch or early evening time, closed Mon.

Foxford Woollen Mills Visitor Centre, if visiting Foxford or Strade this place has a pleasant restaurant serving cheap meals until closing time at 1800.

The Tamarind Seed, TF Royal Hotel, Castlebar, T094-9023111. A cosy and colourful restaurant offering a choice of steaks, and vegetarians can tuck into a hearty stroganoff flambéed in brandy.

Pubs and music

Castlebar and around *p431*

Healy's Hotel, Pontoon. The bar here is a pleasant place to while away some time and there is a beer garden for those odd days when the sun shines.

Johnny McHale's pub, opposite the *Welcome Inn* at the Pontoon end of Castlebar. Serves a good pint in a congenial environment.

Festivals and events

Castlebar and around *p431*

The **4 Days' Walks** takes place in Castlebar in **late Jun/early Jul**, T094-9024102, www.castlebar4dayswalks.com. A varied program of events take place at the **Royal Theatre**, www.royaltheatre, and at the **Linenhall Arts Centre** at the tourist office, T094-9023733, www.thelinenhall.com.

Activities and tours

Castlebar and around *p431*

Courses **Pontoon Bridge Hotel** (see 'Sleeping' above) runs 4-day courses for the **School of Cooking**, and 2- and 4-day non-residential courses between Apr and Oct for the **School of Landscape Painting**.

Fishing **Game Angling Ireland West**, Spencer St, Castlebar, T094-9025006. Dispenses a free brochure on game angling in the west of Ireland as well as stocking all the necessary gear.

Northwestern Regional Fisheries Board, Ardnaree House, Abbey St, Ballina, T096-22788, nwrfb@iol.ie. General information, guides and maps available.

School of Fly Fishing, Pontoon Bridge Hotel, T094-9256120, www.pontoonbridge.com. Runs 1- and 2-day courses for complete novices or those with some experience.

Horse riding **Turlough Equitation Centre**, T094-9026646.

Transport

Castlebar and around *p431*

Bike hire Bike World, New Antrim St, T094-9025220.

Bus Bus Éireann, T096-71800, has an express service between **Castlebar** and

For an explanation of the sleeping and eating price codes used in this guide, see inside the front cover. Other relevant information is found in Essentials pages 39-45.

Dublin as well as services to **Ballina**, **Cork**, **Derry**, **Shannon** and **Sligo**. There is a bus on Fri to Pontoon that departs at 0900, otherwise it is 1215 and 1630 Mon-Sat, and 1705 on Sun. Buses arrive and depart from **Flannelly's** pub in Market St, Castlebar.

Car hire Casey Auto Rental, Castlebar, T094-9021411.

Train The **Dublin** to **Westport** train stops at Castlebar, T094-9021222; the station is outside of town on the N84 Ballinrobe road.

County Sligo

Sligo → *Phone code: 071. Colour map 1, grid B1.*

A rewarding mixture of Irish boom town and rural market town, Sligo is growing by the minute but still has that laid-back Irish charm that you came here looking for. It's just small enough to make walking to sights and places to eat comfortable, but still has the amenities of the county town – leisure centres, a cinema, loads of good places to eat, internet cafés, three festivals and lots of good lively music and other entertainment. Stop here for a few days before moving on into the north and experience your last taste of so-laid-back-it's-horizontal life. ▸▸ *For Sleeping, Eating and other listings, see pages 442-446.*

Ins and outs

Getting there Sligo Airport is at Strandhill, 8 km west of town. It has twice daily flights to Dublin from where connections can be made to other airports. Car hire is available at the airport and there are taxis. Trains connect Sligo with Boyle, Carrick-on-Shannon, Dublin and Mullingar three times a day, but your best bet is **Bus Éireann**, which connects the town with Derry, Donegal, Dublin and Galway. The bus and train stations are in Lord Edward Street. ▸▸ *See Transport, page 435, for further details.*

Getting around Car hire and taxis are available in town, as are bikes for hire. The easiest and most pleasant way around town is on foot.

Information The **tourist office** is on Temple St, T071-9161201. Open Jul-Aug Mon-Sat 0900-2000, Sun 1000-1400, Sep-Jun Mon-Fri 0900-1700.

Sights

It's worth taking in Sligo's sights by walking around the town. Begin at the biggest building in town, the **Cathedral of the Immaculate Conception**, designed by George Goldie and consecrated in 1874. Built to hold the masses, it can seat 4,000 people, despite its relatively small size. It is built in a Germanic Romanesque style and has huge stained glass windows by the French stained glass artist Lobin. No sign of the Celtic revival here. From the Cathedral continue along John Street to the other cathedral, **St John's**, designed in 1730 by Richard Castle, the man who created so much of Georgian Dublin. The cathedral was seriously altered in the early 19th century. The church contains a memorial to Susan Yeats (née Pollixfen) the mother of the famous Yeats brothers, as well as the tomb of Sir Roger Jones (d. 1637), the first governor of Sligo.

Continuing on along John Street, turn right into to Market Street and the High Street, you come to the **Friary**. This is a 1973 building, which partly replaces a Victorian Gothic creation, retaining the apse of the older building. Turn left into Old

Opposite the courthouse in Sligo are the solicitors' offices whose windows still bear the unfortunate name of Argue & Phibbs.

Market Street and Teeling Street and head towards the river. You pass the beautifully renovated Gormenghast-like **Courthouse**, still in use. It is built (in 1878) in sections, the octagonal tower with dormer windows and a chimney stack popping up through it. The entranceway is a great gabled arcade with twin towers at either side. On a working day it is possible to go into the public gallery and view the courtrooms themselves, as well as the top-lit entrance hall.

Past the courthouse, turn right into Abbey Street, where you can view the remains of **Sligo Abbey** ⓘ *Abbey St, T071-9146406, mid-Jun to mid-Sep daily 0930-1830, €2*, a 13th-century Dominican Friary, established by Maurice Fitzgerald, the Baron of Offaly. In 1416 it was rebuilt after an accidental fire two years earlier. In the 1641 rebellion the whole town came under attack and the Friary was burned again, deliberately this time. The ruins are elegant with an intact 15th-century east window and carvings of various figures in the iconography of Christianity on a tomb of 1506: you can see St Katherine's wheel, St Peter's keys and the shield and sword of St Michael.

From the abbey go along Kennedy Parade, named after the President, and cross the river Garavogue at Bridge Street to Stephen Street, where a right turn brings you to the **Model Arts Centre and Niland Gallery** ⓘ *The Mall, T071-9141405, free*, housed in the 1859 Model School, designed by James Owen for the Board of Works. It was a non-denominational school and was the best chance of an education anyone in Sligo had during the 19th century. It now houses the Niland Arts Collection, put together by Nora Niland a former Sligo county librarian. The collection is a reputable one including works by Evie Hone who was a pioneer of abstract painting in Ireland and who later became famous (after she became a nun) for her work in stained glass. Also

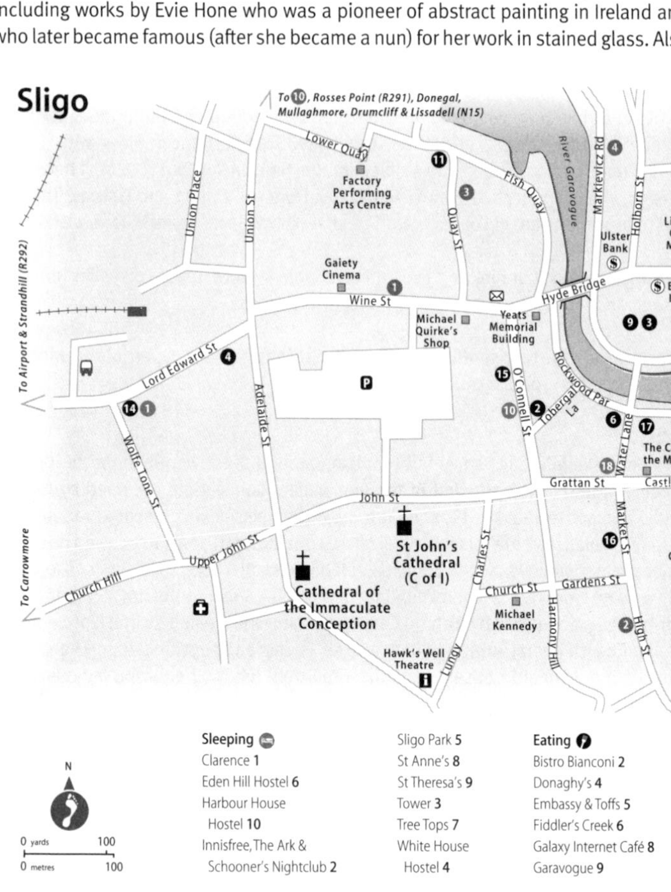

on permanent display are paintings by Jack Yeats including *The Funeral of Harry Boland*, *The Island Funeral* and *Communicating with Prisoners* and a portrait of Yeats by George Russell. There are also works by Paul Henry, Estella Solomons, Linda Howards and John Yeats. Look out for a pencil drawing by Whistler showing an Irish shop owner serving customers. The galleries are beautifully lit by low-lying windows and have some fascinating temporary exhibitions by local and international artists.

Back along Stephen Street towards the river you come to the **County Museum** ⓘ *Stephen St, T071-9142712, Mon-Sat Jun-Sep 1030-1230, 1430-1630, free*, in an old Congregational Chapel of 1851. The museum has lots of old pictures of Sligo, objects belonging to WB Yeats, including his Nobel medal, and other artefacts discovered in and around the town over the years.

From the museum cross Douglas Hyde Bridge – pausing as you do to reflect on the fact that Jack Yeats once claimed to have learned his craft of painting by looking over this bridge into the waters of the Garavogue River – to find the **Yeats Memorial Building** ⓘ *T071-9142693, winter Mon-Fri 1000-1700, summer Mon-Sat 1000-1630, €4*. Another version of the story has it that he learned his craft by spitting over the bridge into the Garavogue – doesn't sound quite so arty though. The Yeats Memorial Building has an exhibition relating the lives of all the Yeats family to Sligo and hosts the annual Yeats Summer School. Its art gallery hosts travelling art exhibitions. It was originally built by the Belfast Banking Company, became the Royal Bank of Ireland in 1899 and was designed by Vincent Craig, the brother of Lord Craigavon, prime minister of Northern Ireland. The building was donated to the Yeats society in 1973. The exhibition includes photographs of the *Le macha*, the Irish navy corvette whose first official job was to bring Yeats' body back to Ireland via Galway. The old safe from the bank is still in place and the downstairs exhibit includes a 10-minute video about the Yeats family.

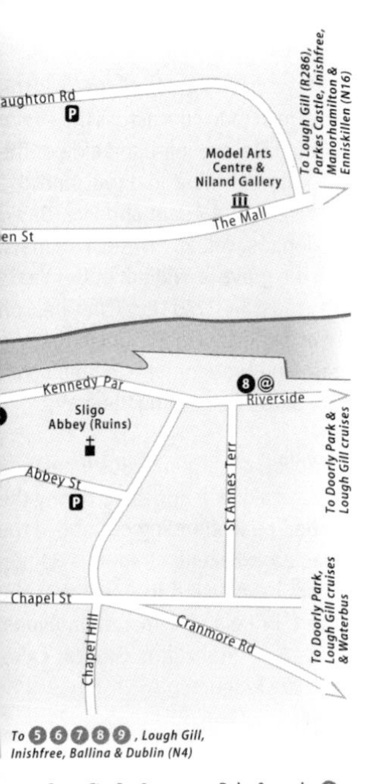

Gurns City Bar 3
Harp Tavern 11
Loft 14
McGarrigle's 15
Montmartre 16
Pepper Alley 17

Pubs & music
Fureys 7
Hargadan's 10
MJ Carr's 1
Shoot the Crows 18

Around Sligo

Drumcliff to Mullaghmore

Getting around Drumcliff, Grange and Cliffony, all the places along the N15, are well served by **buses** since they are on the Sligo to Donegal route, with about 10 buses a day in summer in either direction. A day trip by public transport is feasible, with the last bus back to Sligo passing through Cliffony some time after 1800. **Boat** Inishmurray is accessible by boat from Murraghmore (Rodney Lomax, T071-9166124) or Rosses Point (Tommy McCallion, T071-9142391). There is no landing stage on the island and any poor weather will prevent boats going out.

Rosses Point Immediately north of Sligo town is Rosses Point, where the north shore of Sligo Bay juts out into the sea. It's a seriously quaint little seaside resort with a long sandy beach. Jack Yeats painted it, his brother wrote about

Family Yeats

Sligo is forever associated with the Yeats family; not only the really famous ones, Jack and William, but also the sisters, Susan and Elizabeth, the father, portrait artist John, and the mother Susan Pollexfen. The connection with Sligo is through the Pollexfen family who owned a small shipping company in the town. John, a trained lawyer turned portrait painter, spent little time in Sligo, but the family lived in a kind of genteel poverty for most of their lives and the children often spent months at a time in Sligo with their grandparents. Jack grew up to become a writer and painter, and many of his best paintings are based around the life that he knew as a child. William wrote a great deal and many of his poems are also about the Sligo of his childhood; he and Jack also spent periods of their adult lives there. The sisters became leading members of the Arts and Crafts movement in Ireland. John ended his years in New York, Jack lived to a ripe old age in Dublin, a successful painter, while William became an occultist and admirer of Fascism.

it, and in 1257 Maurice Fitzgerald, the man who gave us Sligo Friary, was cut down here in hand- to-hand battle with Godfrey O'Donnell, the chieftain of another local clan. The reason for the battle no longer matters to the golfers, who now carry irons rather than swords around the ancient battlefield. A bus from Sligo travels to Rosses Point six times a day.

Drumcliff From Rosses Point you can follow the northern coast road back towards the N15 and on to Drumcliff, where WB Yeats is buried. The main road cuts across the site of a sixth-century monastic settlement founded by St Colmcille, the left-hand side of the road revealing the remains of a round tower, struck by lightning in 1396, and the right-hand side a 10th-century high cross bearing the figures of Adam and Eve, David and Goliath, Daniel in the lions' den and the Crucifixion, as well as mythical animals. Beside the high cross is the Protestant graveyard with the **grave of William Butler Yeats** and his wife George, with his famous epitaph "Cast a cold eye/On life, on death/Horseman, pass by". Yeats died in 1939 and was buried in France, but in 1948, in accordance with his wishes, his remains were dug up and brought here. A small craft shop and tea house, T071-9144956, offers a pleasant stop after visiting the grave.

Benbulbin To the east rears Benbulbin, a massive dollop of carboniferous limestone that popped up in relatively recent times, geologically speaking. It appeared during the last ice age as a nunatak: an inland, cliffed, flat-topped peak standing out above the ice. David Marshall in *Best Walks in Ireland* describes an excellent, strenuous 8.5-km walk from close by Drumcliff. Wildflower spotters will be pleased to know that the mountain is a niche for some arctic alpine plants rare in Ireland – mountain avens, mountain sorrel and purple saxifrage. About 5 km east of Drumcliff is **Glencar Lake**, good for fishing and a walk to the waterfall that feeds the lough.

Lissadell House ⓘ *T071-9163150. Easter and May-Sep, Tue-Sun 1100-1800. €6. Tour lasts 40 mins. N15 to Drumcliff, turn west following signs to Carney and Lissadell.* Famous for being rhymed with 'gazelle' by Yeats and as the home of the Gore Booth women (see box next page), Lissadell House is open to the public for part of the summer. The house is an essay in early Victorian austerity, its straight lines undecorated as if to strengthen it in its exposure to Atlantic gales. It is a single block, the usual outhouses are all shoved down into the basement and a tunnel leads to the

Constance Markievicz

Lissadell's most famous scion is of course Constance Gore Booth, later Countess Markievicz, a revolutionary condemned to death after the Easter Rising and the first woman elected to the British Parliament. She never took her seat, although she went to the House of Commons after her release to have a look at her name on a coat hook. She was nominated the Minister for Labour in the first, illegal, Irish Dáil and became the first woman cabinet minister in Europe, albeit one on the run from the British. In the civil war she found herself on the anti-Treaty side. She was elected to the Dáil again in 1927 but would not take her seat. A staunch socialist, she spent her large fortune helping the poor, bringing turf into Dublin in her car for her constituents' fires. She died, aged 59, having lost most of her possessions in various government searches of her house, and her body lay in the Rotunda Hospital, mourned by thousands, having been refused a state funeral by the Free State government.

In 1913, in the great lockout strike, she had manned soup kitchens; in the Easter Rising she commanded the rebels at St Stephen's Green; she fought in the civil war; worked in St Ultan's children's hospital in the great TB epidemics of the 1920s; and spent all her money training young men and women in the republican cause. Yet she is remembered chiefly as the friend of a man whose ideals came dangerously close to Fascism towards the end of his life, and as the subject of one of his lesser poems.

stable blocks. Inside is a family house, full of paraphernalia. It was sold recently by the Gore Booth family, to whose ancestors the people of Sligo owe much: the house was mortgaged to feed the tenants during the Famine and the next generation gladly entered into selling the land to the tenants. Visit is by guided tour and it's well worth the detour. It's also worth driving on to the end of the peninsula to **Raghly**, where there are views of the bay and coastline.

★ **North to Mullaghmore** From Drumcliff the N15 heads on towards Cliffony where a left turn brings you to **Streedagh Point**: a stretch of sandy beach, with caves at the far end. North of Cliffony is the **Creevykeel Court Cairn**, probably dating back to 2500BC, standing on high ground overlooking the sea. It is called a court tomb because of the open courtyard made from stones at its entrance, perhaps used for worship or for mourners. Inside, the tomb itself tapers down and narrows towards the rear and is divided into two chambers; other chambers have been added at a later stage. Four cremation burials were discovered when the tomb was opened in 1935, as well as neolithic pottery. These types of tomb are largely centred around Sligo and Mayo and this one is considered the best.

As the road approaches Mullaghmore, **Classiebawn Castle** appears, built in 1875 for the Hon. Cowper Temple, son of Lord Palmerston, whose family owned a large estate here. The austere baronial castle is built from local sandstone with a square tower and conical turret. The estate eventually passed into the hands of Countess Mountbatten, whose husband was murdered by the IRA in 1979 while boating from Mullaghmore harbour.

Mullaghmore is a quiet little fishing village, with another long sandy beach, and is great for fishing enthusiasts. The area also has lots of stables and both this beach and Streedagh are good for riding.

Difficult to get to, but well worth it, is **Inishmurray**, an uninhabited island 6.5 km off the coast. Its last inhabitants sailed away in 1948, leaving behind a monastic site that had been in use since its foundation by St Molaise in the sixth century, despite being sacked by Vikings in the eighth century. The monastic settlement is enclosed by thick dry stone walls: much of this was reconstructed in the late 19th century, but the rooms built into the wall are probably original. Inside, the enclosure is divided into three areas, one containing what has come to be known as the men's church, where the later islanders buried their male dead, and a much older, smaller church known as Teach Molaise. In here are the famous 'cursing stones', *bullauns*, with smooth stones fitting into their depressions. Originally prayer stones, they came to be used for cursing one's enemies by turning them anticlockwise. In another section of the enclosure is a corbelled, roofed *clochain* used by the islanders as a schoolroom but probably originally an oratory. The island contains many more remains, including inscribed stones around the island marking the Stations of the Cross, as well as another church known as the women's church, where the women were laid to rest. North of the enclosure is a sweathouse.

West of Sligo

The little chink of land to the south and west of Sligo is home to the seaside town of **Strandhill**, with 4 km of sand dunes, and waves good enough to bring surfers from all over Ireland. Behind the village, Mount Knocknaree dominates the skyline with the cairn of Queen Maeve at its summit and the Carrowmore megalithic complex on its western slopes. Coney Island can be reached on foot at low tide, there is a golf course, riding centre and good fishing. While you are in Salthill you might want to try out the **Celtic Seaweed Baths**, T071-68686, www.celticseaweedbaths.com, where you pay for the privilege of sitting in a tub of hot seawater and seaweed for its many apparently therapeutic qualities.

Maeve's tomb

ⓘ *24 hrs, free, from Strandhill follow the R292, southern coastal road, till you see the car park opposite the Sligo Riding Centre.*

Miosgán Meadbha sits on the summit of Mount Knocknaree, a steep one-hour walk from the car park. At 10 m high and 55 m in diameter, it is visible from the surrounding countryside. The cairn has never been opened but is thought to cover a passage tomb built perhaps 5,000 years ago. There are lots of other sites around the cairn, with huge north and south markers, and little huts that may have been lived in during construction by the men who built the cairn: when these were excavated, lots of building implements were found. The connection with Maeve, the Iron Age queen of Connaught, is traditional, rather than based on fact.

Carrowmore megalithic cemetery

ⓘ *T071-9161534. Easter-Sep daily 1000-1800. €2. Audio-visual presentation, guided tours, toilets.*

Continuing on towards Sligo on the R292 brings you to this enormous site full of standing stones, stone circles and dolmens. It was in use for a long time, its oldest constructions dating back to the fifth century BC, making it older than Newgrange (see page 608), and all the tombs were reused many times. There were once 84 monuments here, but quarrying and land use cleared a great number of them. Thirty monuments are now contained here in a preserved OPW site, excavated each summer by a Swedish team of archaeologists. There is an interpretive centre and you can watch the archaeologists at work.

In 1999 the Swedes identified the oldest tomb in Western Europe here, 7,400 years old.

South and southwest of Sligo

Aughris

Aughris is a tiny fishing village, almost but not quite unspoiled by tourism, and worth a visit for its sandy beach, good bar (see page 445) and, if you're into that type of thing, the promontory fort at Aughris Head. Just before Aughris, the road passes a tiny place called **Skreen**, where the present 14th-century church building has a much longer history, dating back to its foundation by St Adaman in 704. The graveyard contains box tombs, including a beautifully carved 19th-century tomb, and east of the church is a holy well.

The coast → *Colour map 2, grid A3/4.*

Surfers will want to go to **Easky**, 8 km northwest of Dromore, where assorted surfing championships are held. There is also a 15th-century castle. A little further along the coast is **Inishcrone**, with an excellent Blue Flag beach 4.8 km long, which is also popular with surfers, caravan parks in the sand dunes, a golf course, and **Kilcullen's Seaweed Baths** ⓘ *T096-36238, Apr-Sep daily 1000-2200; Oct-Mar Mon-Fri 1200-2000, Sat-Sun 1000-2000, €17 per bath*, a beautiful Edwardian bath house where you can experience a steam bath followed by a high iodine salt water, seaweed bath in the original 1912 equipment.

Collooney → *Colour map 2, grid A4.*

If instead of taking the N59 west you head south, the first port of call is Collooney, nondescript except for the **Teeling Monument**, which commemorates the Battle of Carricknaget in 1798 and Bartholemew Teeling's part in it. He was in the French invading force that landed at Killala and was marching to join the United Irishmen in Ballinamuck in County Longford. They had met and defeated English forces that day at Tobercurry, and were met in battle again by 600 English troops strategically holding a hill on their route: Teeling single-handedly shot the gunner in the English force. The French then moved on to Ballinamuck, where they were defeated and Teeling, being an Irishman, was executed. The other claim to fame of Collooney is **Markree Castle**, where you can stay if you can afford it: a 17th-century pile with Victorian additions.

Tobercurry → *Colour map 2, grid A4.*

Pressing on southwards on the N17 brings you to Tobercurry, a working market town, which, as its advertising says, is probably as close as you'll come to the real Ireland. Its traditional Irish music scene is strong and in summer there is the **South Sligo Summer School** ⓘ *contact Rita Flannery, T071-9185010, www.sssschool.org*, in the second week in July, when traditional Irish music students come from all over Ireland and the world to study under the masters. For the unmusical, there is lots of craic to be had with ceilidh dancing, concerts each night and spontaneous outpourings of talent in all the pubs. If you plan to go you might want to book accommodation in advance.

Lough Gill → *Colour map 1, grid C1.*

There are lots of good things to do around Lough Gill, the laziest of them being to take the 50-minute cruise on the **Wild Rose Waterbus** ⓘ *T071-9164266*, from beside the sports complex at Doorly Park. The tour goes to Parke's Castle in County Leitrim,

"I will arise now, and go to Innisfree, And a small cabin build there, of clay and wattles made; Nine bean rows will I have there, a hive for the honeybee, And live alone in the bee-loud glade" WB Yeats, 'The Lake Isle of Innisfree'.

 passing the Isle of **Innisfree** – immortalized in a poem by Yeats – pauses at Parke's Castle for an hour, and then makes its way back along the northern shore of the lough.

If you are cycling or driving, the best thing to do is go clockwise round the lough, following its northern shore. Take the N16 out of town until you meet the R286. Turn right and right again following the signs for Hazlewood. It's a 30-mile (48-km drive), the first stop on the drive being Hazlewood Forest Park Sculpture Trail, which is a park set on the shores of the lake full of carved wooden figures. Continuing on round the lough the next stop is the Deerpark Court Tomb, on a limestone ridge overlooking the lough. It is signposted from the R286, just after the road divides and you take the Lough Gill Loop sign. The site is a 10-minute walk to the top of the ridge. **Parke's Castle** ⓘ *Fivemile Bourne, T071-9164149, Mar-end Oct daily 1000-1800, €2.75, guided tours available, audio-visual show, exhibition, coffee shop*, County Leitrim, is the next stop on the trip round the lough, back on the R286. It is almost entirely a reconstruction of the original 17th-century building, which in turn was a reconstruction from the stones of an earlier castle. The original owner was hanged at Tyburn for sheltering a survivor from a wrecked Spanish armada vessel. It is now home to a heritage centre.

Creevelea Abbey ⓘ *Dromahair village, 24 hrs, free*, is well worth a stop on the circuit of the lough, on the R288 now. It has to be unluckiest of all the early friaries in Ireland: it was the last to be built in 1508, was accidentally burned in 1536, and before it could be fully repaired was sacked by 1590, when Bingham, the Governor of Connaught, turned it into a stables. After his departure the friars were allowed back in, but then, at the end of his Irish campaign in 1650, Cromwell turned up and it was ruined once more. Still, it's a very picturesque ruin, with two well-preserved windows and some good carvings. There are lots of outbuildings and it is possible to get a sense of the life that went on here within refectories, dormitories, the kitchen and other less easily identified buildings.

Re-entering County Sligo the road (the R287) rises and stays some distance from the lough until you see a sign for the **Isle of Innisfree**. The road then takes you down to the shore where you can gaze at the island and wonder that one person with a few words can change a place so much. There's a second opportunity to look at the lake in more touristy surroundings from **Dooney's Rock**, where the tour buses tend to congregate, just to make the place as much like Yeats' poem *The Lake Isle of Inisfree* as possible. From Dooney's Rock it is a short stretch back to Sligo.

Sleeping

Sligo town *p435, map p436*

There are a number of hotels in town, and most of the B&Bs are strung out along Pearse Rd, easily accessible by car and even walkable. There are several hostels in town, all of them getting very full at the peak of summer and around the Yeats festival so book in advance.

A-B **Sligo Park Hotel**, Pearse Rd, T071-9160291, www.leehotels.ie. Big, busy hotel, 1.5 km outside town with all the facilities you could want – pool, jacuzzi, fitness centre, nice big restaurant, music, open fires, big sofas, pub food. Rooms are spacious and those on the ground floor open into a little courtyard. Checking-in time is 1500. At the very top end of this price range.

B-C **Tower Hotel**, Quay St, T071-9144000, www.towerhotelsligo.com. Built beside the town hall and mirroring it architecturally, this is a small, quiet hotel, with modern, well laid out rooms, and lots of comfort.

C **Innisfree Hotel**, High St, T071-9142014, innisfreehotelsligo@eircom.net. Busy small hotel catering to commercial and tourist trades. Nightclub and music in the bar at weekends.

C-D **Clarence Hotel**, Wine St, T071-9142211, clarencehotel@eircom.net. A small hotel in a beautiful old stone building. Music 4 nights a week and busy lunchtime bar trade.

E **Renate House**, Upper John St, T071-9162014. A bit cheaper than the other B&Bs further out of town, and very central. En suite and shared bathrooms.

E **St Anne's**, Pearse Rd, T071-9143188. This B&B is next door to St Theresa's, but slightly larger with an outdoor pool.

E St Theresa's, Pearse Rd, T071-9162230. Small B&B with 3 rooms with en suite bath.
E Tree Tops, Cleveragh Rd, off Pearse Rd, T071-9160160, www.sligoband-b.com. Close to town, this B&B has pretty rooms, lovely garden. Lots of tourist advice and an amazing art collection on the walls.
F Eden Hill Hostel, Marymount, Pearse Rd, T071-9143204, edenhillhostel@eircom.net. About 1.5 km out of town but well signposted. It is open all year, has family and double rooms.
F Harbour House Hostel, Finisklin Rd, T071-9171547, harbourhouse@eircom.net. Has double rooms. It's a good walk out of town but very new and well run.
F White House Hostel Markievicz Rd, T071-9145160. Dorm beds only, some family rooms in this very basic place.

Drumcliff to Mullaghmore *p437*
Mullaghmore is a good place to stop if you intend to spend more than a day in this area.
B-E Beach Hotel and Leisure Club, The Harbour, Mullaghmore, T071-9166171, www.beachhotelmullaghmore.com. Very well-endowed hotel looking out over the harbour, with a swimming pool, sauna and gym. Definitely a family holiday sort of place with a crèche in the summer. Restaurant. Nightly entertainment in the summer. Murder mystery weekends.
C Pier Head Hotel, Mullaghmore, T071-9166171, www.pierheadhotel.com. Smaller hotel, but with equally panoramic views. Restaurant. Nightly entertainment in the summer.
E Mount Edward Lodge, Ballinfull, T071-9163263, mounted wardlodge@ircom.net. B&B in lovely setting, with Benbulbin looming up behind. Child reductions.
F Karuna Flame Hostel, Celtic Farm, Derry Rd, near Grange, T071-9163337. Includes 1 double room for €25. Bikes for hire. Non-smoking but unsuitable for children under 12.

Rosses Point *p437*
A-D Yeats Country Hotel, Rosses Point, T071-9177211, www.yeatscountryhotel.com. This is *the* place to stay, it has everything you could want from swimming pool to concessions at the nearby golf club and is a cheery, family-orientated sort of place with a supervised crèche in the high season.
There are B&Bs strung out all along the road to Rosses Point and there is a campsite: **Greenlands Caravan and Camping Park** at Hughes Bridge, T071-9177113. 2 people and a small tent costs €22.

West of Sligo *p440*
C Ocean View, Strandhill, T071-9168115, www.ovhotel.com. The only hotel in town, small and comfortable, with a respected restaurant.
E Knocknaree House, Shore Rd, Strandhill, T071-9168313, connollyma@eircom.net. A B&B close to the beach. 25% reduction for children.
E Mardell, Seafront, Strandhill, T071-9168295, mardell@oceanfree.net. Small B&B with good views, very central.
E Shalom, Seafront, Strandhill, T071-9168314. Attractive modern B&B by the sea.
F Strandhill Lodge and Hostel, Strandhill, T071-9168313, www.strandhill accommodation.com. Hostel that has mostly doubles.

South and southwest of Sligo *p441*
L Cromleach Lodge, Castlebaldwin, T071-9165155, info@cromleach.com. On the banks of Lough Arrow, accessed via Riverstown after Collooney. Modern with panoramic views over surrounding countryside, for those who like to get away from it all. It draws more people to its nouvelle Irish restaurant (see 'Eating') than to its accommodation. Closed Nov-Jan.
A Coopershill House, T071-9165108, ohara@coopershill.com. Signposted off the N4 halfway between Sligo and Boyle, is an utterly authentic and very graceful Georgian house where a couple of days will comfortably slide by in understated luxury.
B Markree Castle, Collooney, T071-9167800, www.markreecastle.ie. A seriously grand, oak-panelled, 17th-century castle with a 3-star rating from the tourist board and lots of family heirlooms lying about the place. Horse riding on the estate, lots of walks and a good restaurant where a reservation is a

For an explanation of the sleeping and eating price codes used in this guide, see inside the front cover. Other relevant information is found in Essentials pages 39-45.

good idea and dinner in very grand surroundings will cost around €39.

D Castle Arms Hotel, Enniscrone, T096-36516, www.castlearmshotel.com. A reasonably priced 2-star hotel with a family atmosphere.

D Glebe House, Collooney, T071-9167787, www.glebe-house.com. Set in an old rectory with only 6 rooms so it has a homely atmosphere.

D-E Cawley's, Emmet St, Tobercurry, T071-9185025, cawleysguesthouse@eircom.net. 10 rooms in a restaurant/guest house in the centre of the village. Nice gardens and comfortable rooms.

Camping

Atlantic Caravan Park, Enniscrone, T096-36980 atlanticcaravanpk@eircom.net. Despite its name, takes tents also, but is very small with few facilities.

Eating

Sligo town *p435, map p436*

The big hotels all have sound restaurants with traditional potato-based evening meals.

TTT Montmartre, Market Yard, T071-9169901. This is the poshest place to eat in Sligo but make a reservation because it's quite small and very popular. Run by French staff and serving unstuffy French dishes it has a spacious, calm feel to it.

TT Bistro Bianconi, O'Connell St, T071-9141744. Open 7 days from 1730 till the customers stop, a cheery tiled place with the chefs making the pizzas in the window. Lots of vegetarian options and Italian dishes.

TT The Embassy, Kennedy Parade, T071-9161250. Looks like a big old hotel, which is what it used to be, but now it's a restaurant and snooker hall. Traditional potato-orientated food. Try the early-bird menu from 1800-1930.

TT The Loft, Lord Edward St, T071-9146770. In town, open 1200-1430 for a carvery lunch, 1800-2300 for dinner. It has an interesting menu, which includes Mexican dishes, a railway theme with seating in compartments, live music most nights and a good atmosphere. Worth making a reservation.

TT Sligo Park Hotel, the restaurant here is very popular, set in a conservatory area. There is also pub food in the bars.

TT Tower, restaurant here has a darker atmosphere with lots of deep brown panelled wood. Set dinner is fairly traditional and has some interesting sauces.

TT Fiddler's Creek, Rockwood Parade, T071-91418666. Serves lunch till 1600 and evening meals till 2200. Its menu is vaguely ethnic with Portuguese, Moroccan and Mexican dishes. Vegetarians will be impressed by the 4 choices. It has live music on special occasions.

TT Pepper Alley, Rockwood Parade. Serves Mexican food till late, closed Mon evenings. At lunchtime it's a sandwich bar.

TT Gurns City Bar, Stephen St, close to *Garavogue*, T071-9144134. Open 7 days for lunch and dinner till 2200. It serves challenging good quality food in a an atmosphere of white linen and posh table settings, although a little cramped. Vegetarians will be safe here.

TT Garavogue, 15-16 Stephen's St, T071-9140100. Named after the river, it is the smoothest place in Sligo with clever lighting, raised balconies and a long bar. Downstairs is bar food redolent with grilled parmesan and guacamole and upstairs are more substantial meals in the same vein. It shuts however by 2000 at weekends and earlier during the week.

T Galaxy Internet Café, Riverside, T071-9140441. Open 0800-midnight, serving food all day, chiefly filled jacket potatoes, salads, breakfast, all at less than €5.

T Roof Top Restaurant, Wine St Car Park, T071-9144421. Try here for basic potato based meals, closes at 1800.

Pubs that do reasonable food include:

T Ark, High St;

T Donaghy's, Lord Edward St;

T The Harp Tavern, Lower Quay St;

T McGarrigles, O'Connell St;

T Murray's, Connolly St.

Drumcliff to Mullaghmore *p437*

TTT Eithna's Seafood restaurant, Mullaghmore, T071-9166407. Serves locally caught seafood to an enthusiastic clientele some of whom drive a long way to eat there. Closed Tue, weekends only in winter. Dinner could cost as much as €50.

TTT La Vecchia Posta, on the main road at Cliffoney, T071-9176777. About the strangest place you'll ever find serving Tuscan food!

Closed Mon, dinner could cost around €45.
¶¶ **Yeats Tavern Restaurant**, Drumcliff, T071-9163117. Serving a fairly standard Irish menu in an olde-worlde setting and has music at weekends and traditional sessions in summer.
¶¶-¶ **Beach Hotel**, Mullaghmore. Good restaurant inside which serves seafood, and a bar serving food.
¶¶-¶ **Pier Head House**, Mullaghmore. Has a good restaurant serving seafood, and a bar with food.

Rosses Point *p437*
¶¶ **Moorings**, T071-9177112. Mainly seafood.
¶¶ **Yeats**. Serves mainly seafood.
¶¶-¶ **Waterfront**, T071-9177122. An excellent pub which overlooks the sea with outside seating and a pretty interior. It does pub lunches but rather superior Irish continental dinners till 2200.

West of Sligo *p440*
¶¶ **Rollers**, Ocean View hotel, Strandhill. A good option.
¶¶-¶ **The Venue**, Strandhill, T071-9168167. Another good option.
¶ **Shell's café**, Strandhill. Right on the beach. Good home cooked cakes and snacks.
¶ **Strand**, Strandhill, T071-9168149. Serves bar food in the pub all day.

South and southwest of Sligo *p441*
Easky's pubs are good for music in summer and there is food in several of them.
¶¶¶ **Cromleach Lodge**, Castlebaldwin (see 'Sleeping'). Serves nouvelle Irish cuisine, seating is in a series of small rooms, better suited to small groups than couples, with a 5-course gourmet-tasting menu as well as à a carte and others.
¶¶ **Castle Arms Hotel**, Enniscrone. This is your best bet for food.
¶¶-¶ **Cawley's**, Tobercurry (see 'Sleeping'). There is a restaurant here.
¶¶-¶ **The Gable End**, T096-36110. Open daily in summer but ring in advance in winter for the evening meal. Seafood menu. Pub food all year.
¶¶-¶ **Killoran's**, T071-9185111. A pub with a great reputation for both traditional music and dancing and traditional Irish cooking and where you can try boxty, colcannon, and stampy. They also do a good line in tourist information about the area.

Pubs and music

Sligo town *p435, map p436*
Places to look out for music in are manifold.
The Ark, bar at the Innisfree Hotel. Karaoke and nightclub.
MJ Carr's, downstairs from the Loft, has traditional sessions on Sat and other forms of live music on Mon.
Donaghy's, traditional sessions on Sun nights.
Foleys, Castle St. There are traditional sessions on Sat.
Fureys, Bridge St. You will easily spot this place because of the gigantic and rather tasteless Sheela-na-gig over the door, has traditional sessions on Mon, Tue, Thu and Sun.
Hargadan's, O'Connell St. Doesn't have music, but it's a genuinely traditional Irish pub, still with the groceries on the shelves from the days when it was a grocer's-cum-bar. Quiet during the day but can get crowded at weekends. Nice snugs and pub lunches.
The Harp, Quay St. Has traditional sessions on Mon and jazz at lunchtime on Sun.
McGarrigles, traditional sessions on Wed and Sun.
Schooner's Nightclub, above The Ark at the Innisfree Hotel, T071-9142014. Karaoke and nightclub music.
Shoot the Crows, Market St. A very trendy scruffy sort of place with unusual ladies' toilets and music most nights.
Toffs Nite Club, the Embassy, has disco music most nights of the week.

West of Sligo *p440*
Strand, has music of some sort every night.
The Venue, Strandhill. Has folk and traditional music several nights a week.

Entertainment

Sligo town *p435, map p436*
Cinema Gaiety cinema complex, Wine St, T071-9174004. Has 12 screens.

Theatre The Factory Theatre, Lower Quay St, T071-9170431. Home to the Blue Raincoat Theatre company, who perform there and at the Hawk's Well.
Hawk's Well Theatre, Temple St, T071-9161526. Hosts travelling theatre groups as well as local efforts.

Festivals and events

Sligo town *p435, map p436*
The WB Yeats Summer School happens in **late Jul to early Aug** and is worth attending, even if you don't approve of Yeats, for the music and dancing sessions, T071-9142693. At Ballintogher, 13 km south of Sligo the annual Ballintogher Traditional Music Festival is held, usually in early **Nov**. There is a feis, concerts, ceilidh dancing and master classes as well as lots of spontaneous sessions in the pubs at night.

Shopping

Sligo town *p435, map p436*
Sligo has the usual slew of outlets, but there are 3 places worth seeking out.
The Cat and the Moon, 4 Castle St. Mon-Sat 0930-1800, sells exclusive designer jewellery by Martina Gillan as well as lots of other really great, functional stuff by other Irish designers.
Michael Kennedy Ceramics, Church St. Sells pottery, and very attractive and useful it is too.
Michael Quirke's, Wine St. A butcher-turned-sculptor who carves figures from pieces of wood that he finds.

Activities and tours

Drumcliff to Mullaghmore *p437*
Horse riding Horse Holiday Farm, Grange, T071-9166152, hhf@eircom.net. Easter-Nov. For experienced riders.

Transport

County Sligo *p435*
Air Sligo Airport, T071-9168280, www.sligo airport.com, is 8 km west of town at Strandhill. Aer Arann, T0818-210210, www.aerarann.com, provides twice daily flights to **Dublin** with connections to **Europe**. Taxis can be hired at the airport and there is a car hire service at the terminal, Avis, T071-9168386. A bus service connects the airport with Sligo town.

Bus There are 4 Bus Éireann buses a day connecting Sligo with **Derry** via **Bundoran**, **Donegal**, **Ballybofey** and **Letterkenny**. Sligo to Dublin buses leave Sligo 3 times a day calling at **Ballysadare**, **Boyle**, **Carrick-on-Shannon** and **Longford**. To **Belfast**, buses leave 3 times a day calling at **Enniskillen**. For **Athlone** there are 2 buses a day. 5 buses a day connect Sligo with **Galway**. To **Rosses Point** there are 4 buses a day (none on Sun), and for **Strandhill** there are 4 buses a day (none on Sun). A bus to **Ballina** leaves 5 times a day (once on Sun), connecting from Ballina with **Castlebar**, **Westport** and **Newport**. The bus station is in Lord Edward St, T071-9160066. A private bus company, Feda O'Donnell Coaches, T074-9548114, 091-761656, www.fedaodonell.com, runs a twice-daily service between Donegal and Galway calling at Sligo and lots of smaller towns en route. There are 3 buses on Fri and Sun. At Sligo the bus stops outside Matt Lyon's shop in Stephen St. Innisfree Coaches, T071- 9168138, another private company does coaches to Dublin. Pick up is at Quay St car park.

Car hire Dooley Car Rental, Sligo Airport, T062-53103. Hertz, T071-9144068. Murray's Europcar, Sligo Airport, T071-9142091.

Taxi Joe's Cabs, T071-9168900.

Train There are 4 trains a day to **Dublin** calling at **Collooney**, **Ballymote**, **Boyle**, **Carrick-on-Shannon**, **Dromod**, **Longford**, **Edgeworthstown**, **Mullingar**, **Enfield** and **Maynooth**.

County Leitrim

Here you are definitely off the main tourist circuit, and for understandable reasons. Leitrim is tiny, 80 km wide with only 3 km of coastline, but it has some mountain scenery to nod at and the large Lough Allen with its water sports and fishing. It shares its biggest attractions with County Sligo around Lough Gill and these have been covered as part of the tour of Lough Gill on page 441. ▸▸ *For Sleeping, Eating and other listings, see pages 448-448.*

Water, water everywhere

"Leitrim, like Cavan, is a watery country, but Cavan collects the water into a thousand little lakes and Leitrim, being hilly, indeed a maze of mountains and hills, pours it all over the place. It is a boggy, soggy rushy land, full of burrowing streams, tiniest crevices of water everywhere and this I found very affecting like a tearful woman."
Sean O'Faolain, *An Irish Journey*, (Longman/Green, 1940)

★ Carrick-on-Shannon → *Phone code: 071. Colour map 1, grid C1.*

A good place to base yourself for any length of time in Leitrim, Carrick-on-Shannon sits prettily on the shores of the Shannon, with lots of very expensive motor launches bobbing about as they do the long trip from Belleek in County Fermanagh to the Shannon, or even travel further on to Dublin. Carrick's one sight is **Costello Chapel**, an 1877 tomb to the wife of one Edward Costello, a local shopkeeper. He bought a Methodist chapel and knocked it down to build this place, where he joined her in 1891. This wacky little oratory is stuck incongruously between two high-street shops. Their coffins lie either side of the tiny aisle, right in the middle of town, a little essay in self-importance. The **tourist office** is at the Old Barrel Store, The Marina, T071-9620170, www.leitrimtourism.com. Open May-Oct Mon-Fri 0900-1300.

Jamestown → *Colour map 1, grid C2.*

If you are travelling through this part of Leitrim, Jamestown is a good place to pause for a while. It was named after James I by Sir Charles Coote, who organized the plantation of the area in 1625. The old town gate is all that remains of the original planter town. You will go through it as you pass by on the Dublin to Sligo road. The arch of the gate was removed in the 1970s. It is a peaceful Georgian village full of people swapping fish stories and a couple of good pubs, especially the Arch Bar.

Mohill → *Colour map1, grid C2.*

Mohill is serious fisherman territory, with five loughs in the immediate area, and its chief claim to fame is its association with Turlough O'Carolan, the last of the travelling bards. He was born in 1670, the son of a blacksmith who worked in an iron foundry in County Roscommon. The wife of the foundry-owner took a fancy to the child, had him educated, and when he went blind at age 18 had him taught the harp. He travelled the countryside playing at the big houses, with a guide and horse supplied by his benefactress Mrs MacDermott Roe. He met and married May Maguire and settled in Mohill. After her death he took to the road again. He was welcome in the wealthiest of houses, and played to Jonathan Swift, and his music has been revived in modern times by the Chieftains. His portrait hangs in the National Gallery. Close by Mohill is another literary association: Anthony Trollope worked for the post office in Ireland for some years, and on a walk in Drumsna discovered the ruin of a house that inspired him to plan the novel *The Macdermots of Ballycloran*. If you stop in Mohill, look out for the art nouveau Bank of Ireland building.

North of Carrick → *Colour map 1, grid C2.*

Travelling north from Carrick, you come to the place that gave the county its name and **Leitrim village** is the start of the 382-km long Shannon-Erne Waterway. The two companies listed above under Carrick-on-Shannon rent boats for three nights, a week or more. Beyond Leitrim village, is **Drumshanbo**, another fishing centre on the southern shore of Lough Allen. For many years this was a small-scale coalmining area, and the **Sliabh an Iarrain Visitor Centre** ⓘ *Apr-Sep Mon-Sat 1000-1800, Sun*

1400-1800, €2, gives lots of information about the traditions of the area, from the methods of coal and iron extraction to the unusual tradition in this area of the sweat house: a kind of Celtic sauna.

Another good reason to come to Drumshanbo is the **Joe Mooney Summer School** held in one week in July, where there are classes in traditional music for serious learners but also lots of sessions in the bars at night and lots of set dancing to join in with.

Sleeping

Carrick-on-Shannon *p447*

C Bush Hotel, T071-9620014, www.bushhotel.com. An old-town hotel, now renovated, where some of the old-world charm has survived the construction of theme bars and cafés.

C Hollywell Country House, Liberty Hill, T071-9621124. Guest house beyond the bridge in town, with river frontage and fishing in the garden. Comfortable lounge area with open fire, good breakfast, no evening meals.

E Aisleigh Guest House, Dublin Rd, T071-9620313. Small, amenable guest house with games room, sauna, nice big rooms.

F An Oíche Hostel, The Bridge, T071-9621848. Dorm beds only and the rate, around €20 per person, seems overpriced.

Eating

Carrick-on-Shannon *p447*

ŸŸ-Ÿ Oarsman, Bridge St. Above-average pub food during lunch hours and, Thu-Sat, dinner in an upstairs restaurant.

Ÿ Cryan's, Bridge St. Another pub serving filling food.

Ÿ Shamrat, Bridge St, T071-9650934. An Indian restaurant open for lunch and a dinner menu around €16.

Pubs and music

Carrick-on-Shannon *p447*

Carrick-on-Shannon is awash with pubs, the best of which do good music sessions, try: **Cryan's** or **Burke's**, both on Bridge St.

Shopping

Carrick-on-Shannon *p447*

Leitrim Design House, Market Yard, T071-9650550. Brings together the arts and crafts of studios throughout the county: furniture, glass, jewellery and textiles.

Transport

Carrick-on-Shannon *p447*

Bike hire Geraghty's, Main St, T071-9621316.

Bus The **Dublin** to **Sligo** bus passes through 3 times a day in both directions (stopping outside *Coffey's Pastry Case* close to the tourist office). 2 buses a day connect with **Athlone** and Sligo in both directions, T071-60066 for information.

Ferry River trips set off daily from the Marina, organized by Moon River, T071-9621777. Companies that hire out cabin cruisers in town include Emerald Star, T071-9620234, www.emeraldstar.ie, and Riversdale Barge Holidays, T071-9644122, www.riversdalebargeholidays.com.

Taxi Joe Brock, T071-9620707; Colm Spellman, T086-8232424.

Train The train station, T071-9620036, is on the Roscommon side of the river. Trains link the town with **Dublin** and **Sligo** 3 times a day in both directions.

For an explanation of the sleeping and eating price codes used in this guide, see inside the front cover. Other relevant information is found in Essentials pages 39-45.

Counties Donegal and Derry

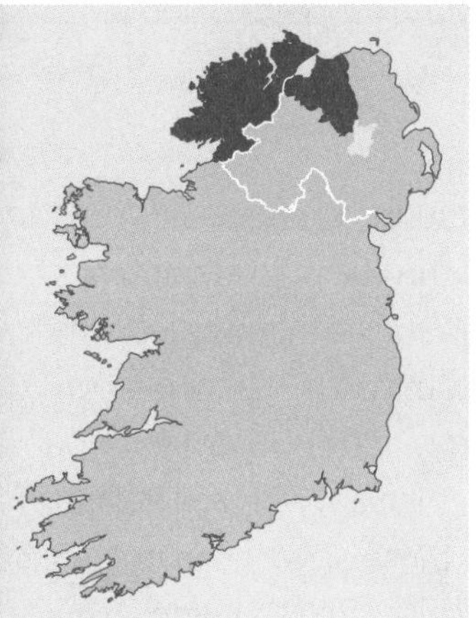

Footprint features

Introduction

All the superlatives that the Irish tourist board spreads out like jam for Ireland would still apply if the rest of the country floated off and sank in the Atlantic and all that was left was the county of Donegal. It's a big county: a place for hiking boots and binoculars during the day and cosy corners in pubs at night. It stretches further north than anywhere in Ireland and by any reasoning, other than those of sectarian politics, it belongs historically and culturally with neighbouring Derry.

Donegal town has limited appeal because the wild beauty of the county around. Try the surf at Rossnowlagh, or the melancholy of the seaside town of Bundoran in the off season, and drive along Fintra Bay with the coast on one side and the mountains inland on the other. Walk along the coast from Kilcar to Teelin or enjoy the real Gaelic Ireland of Glencolmcille. Even in July and August, unless you are stuck in Donegal town or Buncrana, the county is never overcrowded and out of season you will have the place to yourself.

The town that should not be missed is Derry. Energetic, creative and confident, this is one of Ireland's most dynamic urban centres and it naturally complements its neighbouring county. The currency difference – the euro in Donegal and sterling in Derry – may be irksome but it is easily managed and many places close to the virtually unnoticeable border accept both.

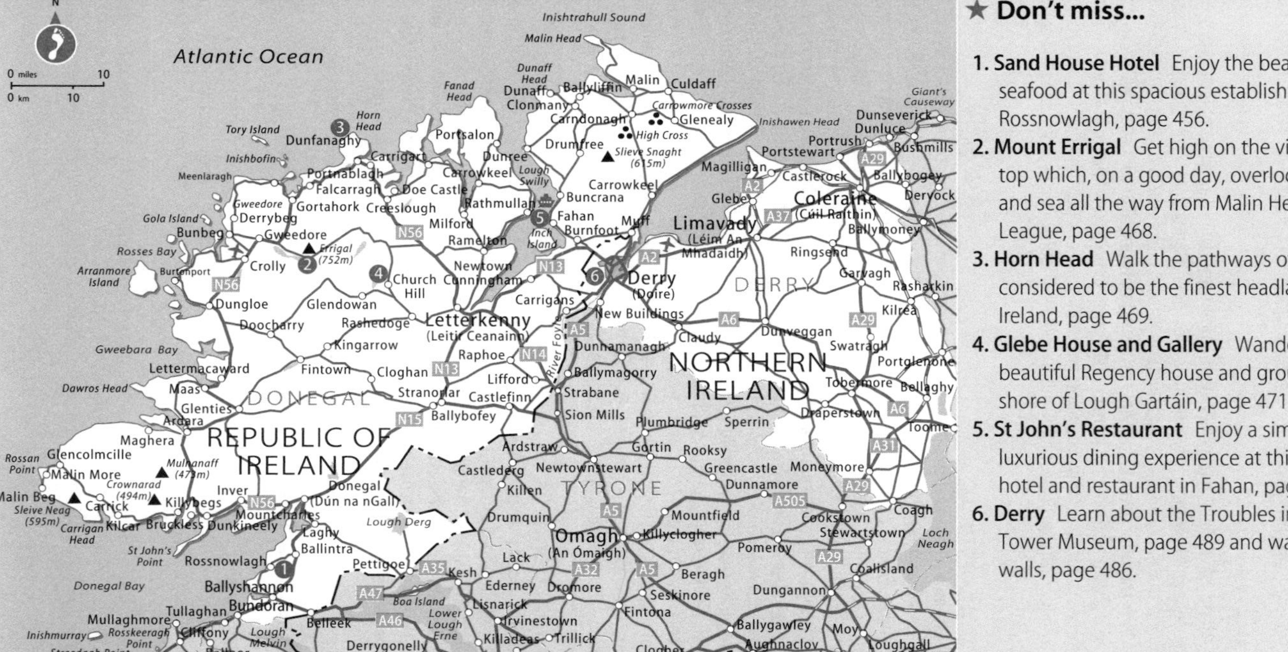

★ Don't miss...

1. **Sand House Hotel** Enjoy the beach and seafood at this spacious establishment at Rossnowlagh, page 456.
2. **Mount Errigal** Get high on the views from the top which, on a good day, overlook the land and sea all the way from Malin Head to Slieve League, page 468.
3. **Horn Head** Walk the pathways of what is considered to be the finest headland in all of Ireland, page 469.
4. **Glebe House and Gallery** Wander round this beautiful Regency house and grounds on the shore of Lough Gartáin, page 471.
5. **St John's Restaurant** Enjoy a simple and luxurious dining experience at this 18th-century hotel and restaurant in Fahan, page 482.
6. **Derry** Learn about the Troubles in the first-class Tower Museum, page 489 and walk the city walls, page 486.

County Donegal

Ins and outs

Getting there

Aer Arann have daily flights between Dublin and Donegal airport, T074-9548284, www.donegalairport.ie. The airport is not near Donegal town but in the Rosses between Dungloe and Crolly and, with no airport bus service, a taxi (T087-2618885) between the airport and Donegal town costs around €60. Most travellers in cars arrive via Sligo on the N15 of from Enniskillen in County Fermanagh, but if your heart is set on wild Donegal, only when you get to Killybegs or Glenties does the adventure really begin. Alternatively, hit the Inishowen Peninsula directly by entering the county from Derry.

Getting around

Bus Éireann, T074-9131008/9721101, does not provide comprehensive travel to all corners of Donegal but private bus companies fill most of the gaps. **McGeehan Coaches**, T074-9546150, www.mcgeehancoaches.com, is one of the biggest companies: their daily Dublin to Glencolmcille bus serving Donegal, Ardara, Killybegs, Kilcar and Carrick is very useful. Another company (timetables online) is **Feda O'Donnell Coaches**, T074-9548114, 091-761656, www.fedaodonnell.com. Other companies are: **Lough Swilly Bus**, T074-9122863 (Letterkenny), T048-7126 2017 (Derry); **John McGinley**, T074-9135201, www.johnmcginley.com, with a twice-daily Donegal to Dublin service via Gweedore, Falcarragh, Dunfanaghy and Letterkenny; **North West Busways**, T074-9382619, www.foylecoaches.com, which links Derry, Letterkenny and the Inishowen Peninsula; and **Patrick Gallagher**, T074-9531107, running a daily Belfast to Donegal bus via Letterkenny and Derry. As an example of fares, Feda O'Donnell charges €15-22 for a single/return between Donegal and Galway, McGinley charges €16-22 for a single/return between Dublin and Donegal.

Information

Walking books and maps For Donegal these don't come any better than *Hill Walkers' Donegal* by David Herman: over 30 walks with maps and directions and usually available in bookshops around Donegal. Other books worth considering include Alan Warner's *Walking the Ulster Way* and Patrick Campbell's *Rambles around Donegal*, both available in paperback. The Ordnance Survey Discovery series maps are essential for any long walks in the county.

South Donegal

A very different kettle of fish from the rest of this county this area is dominated by the seaside town of Bundoran, a strange mixture of huge sandy beaches and sub-Blackpool amusement arcades, pubs and clubs and cafés. The other main draw here is Donegal town, with its restored Jacobean fortified house and quiet air of a working town. In August Ballyshannon comes alive with buskers, music and more at its annual folk festival. Add in good surfing beaches, Lough Derg and its ancient island retreat, and Lough Eske and the Blue Stack mountains and there is much to do in this region.

▸▸ *For Sleeping, Eating and other listings, see pages 456-459.*

Tennyson...

Tennyson: Couldn't they blow up that horrible island with dynamite and carry it off in pieces – a long way off?
Allingham: Why did the English go there?
Tennyson: Why did the Normans come to England? The Normans came over here and seized the country, and in a hundred years the English had forgotten all about it, and they were living together on good terms...The Irish with damned unreasonableness are raging and foaming to this hour.

From a conversation between Tennyson and William Allingham, as recorded by Allingham.

Bundoran → *Phone code: 071. Colour map 1, grid B1.*

Bundoran has two superb stretches of beach, but this has helped turn the place into a fairly conventional seaside resort packed with families in July and August. It is still a favourite destination for Catholic families from across the border seeking a respite from the marching season and there are some lively pubs at night, like the Allingham Arms on Main Street (see also 457). **Waterworld**, an indoor complex with exciting-sounding gimmicks like a tidal wave, aqua volcano and tornado slide is also a big draw. Surfers also like Bundoran, while out of season it is a real gem for deserted seaside town lovers. On holiday weekends, there are often big names in Irish big bands and country music and the many hotels fill up. The **tourist office** is at Bundoran bridge, T071-9841350. Apr-Oct daily 1000-1700.

A few miles further along the N15, before reaching Ballyshannon, the **Donegal Parian China Centre** ⓘ *T071-9851826, all year Mon-Fri 0900-1800, May-Sep Mon-Sat 0900-1800, Sun 1300-1800, bureau de change, free*, is easy to spot on the right side of the road. There are free guided tours of the factory, purchases can be mailed home from the shop and there is an adjoining tearoom.

Ballyshannon → *Phone code: 071. Colour map 1, grid B2.*

The scruffy but rather charming town of Ballyshannon bursts into life over the holiday weekend at the beginning of August. This is the time of the **Folk and Traditional Music Festival** ⓘ *for advance information, T071-9851088, www.ballyshannonfolkfestival.com*, which has been going for over 20 years, with a programme of street entertainment, workshops and a busking competition through the day, and pubs and a marquee overflowing with revellers at night. Big names like Christy Moore, Mary Black, Dervish and Sean Keane have appeared in past years so expect a full line-up of talented performers and book accommodation in advance.

Tony Blair, the British prime minister, has a family connection with Ballyshannon, and the poet William Allingham (1824-1889) was born and educated in the town. Known to the Brownings and Pre-Raphaelites, Allingham became a good friend of Tennyson (see box) and worked in London before moving to Surrey near where Tennyson was living. His ashes are buried in the Church of Ireland, easily reached by walking up Main Street and taking the left turning after passing Dorrian's Imperial Hotel (see page 456) on the other side of the road. Go to the left after entering the churchyard and look for the word 'poet' on a tombstone.

Continue walking further up Main Street and take the left onto Bridge Street, which leads to the R231 road signposted for Rossnowlagh. A short way along, a sign

From the Republic, to phone Derry, or anywhere in Northern Ireland, dial 048 and then the number. To phone the Republic from Northern Ireland, dial 00-353 and then the number dropping the 0 of the area code.

points left for **Abbey Assaroe Mills and Waterwheels.** Only one wall by the graveyard stands as testimony to a Cistercian abbey founded here in the 12th century, but their water-powered mill inspired the interpretive centre and its displays on the legacy of the medieval monks in Ireland. There is a small coffee shop, and a signpost nearby points the way to **St Patrick's Well** ⓘ *T071-9851580*, overlooking the bay, where the saint himself is said to have once trod.

Rossnowlagh → *Phone code: 071. Colour map 1, grid B2.*

If time allows, the R231 road is a more attractive way of reaching Donegal Town than the main N15, not least because it accesses the splendid 4-km sweep of sandy beach at Rossnowlagh. This is Robinson Crusoe land compared to the beach at Bundoran, surfers often have it all to themselves and walks can be enjoyed across the hinterland of dunes and fields. Overlooking the beach from the road is a **Franciscan friary** ⓘ *T071-9851342, daily 1000-1800*, open to the public for walks in the garden or taking tea in the tearoom. It houses a small museum run by the Donegal Historical Society.

Donegal Town → *Phone code: 074. Colour map 1, grid B2.*

A harmless little place, Donegal attracts far more visitors each year than the town warrants, possibly attracting them with its name, which makes it seem like the hub of the county. It's good for a short visit – with its lively bars (see page 458), one or two places to visit, and a lovely walk along the river – but longer than that and the traffic will start to irritate you. The **tourist office** is at The Quay, T074-9721148. Open Mon-Fri 0900-1600.

The name, Donegal (*Dún na nGall*) means 'fort of the foreigners', and it was probably originally established by Vikings. Later, the O'Donnell clan built a tower here overlooking the river Eske. They held it for a 100 years or more before burning it to prevent it falling into English hands, when the town itself fell to Sir Basil Brooke after the flight of the Earls in 1607. Brooke planted the town with English settlers and laid out the modern streets, including the Diamond. The town has passed into modern times little changed from the days when Brooke planned it.

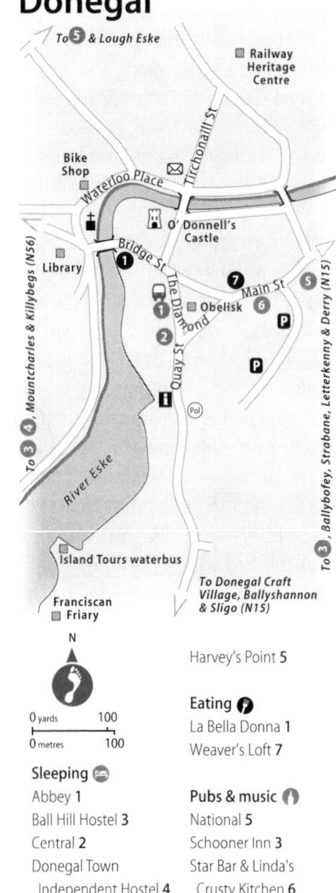

O'Donnell's Castle ⓘ *T074-972405. Mid-Mar to Oct daily 1000-1800, Nov-Jan Fri-Sun 0930-1630. €3.50.* O'Donnell's Castle, in the centre of town, is a largely Jacobean building, erected by Brooke with the 15th-century tower rebuilt and extended and a 17th-century three-storey house added. It was abandoned in the 18th century and adopted by the Office of Public works in the late 19th century. The tower has been restored and holds displays about the history of the castle and the O'Donnell's, one of whom was St

The Annals of the Four Masters

Annála Ríoghacta Eireann, The Annals of the Kingdom of Ireland, are a compilation of all the ancient histories of Ireland put together by Míchéal Ó Cléirigh and three colleagues in the years following the English conquest of the area in 1607. These four friars left the church in Donegal town after it was granted to Sir Basil Brooke: as Franciscans they were not considered Catholic priests and were able to move freely. They travelled post-Reformation Ireland gathering older manuscripts and making copies, in an attempt to collect all the history and culture of Ireland in the face of the encroaching Anglicization. There are two memorials to the Four Masters in Donegal town – the obelisk in the Diamond and the new Catholic Church – but in fact the annals weren't written in the Friary here, but in Drowes, County Donegal between 1632 and 1636. They cover Irish history from the years before the flood to 1616 and several of their sources, older manuscripts held in other monasteries, are now lost, making the Annals an important source for early Irish history. Early copies of the Annals are in the National Library in Dublin.

Colmcille. The grand fireplace in the main room in the tower shows Brooke's coat of arms and that of his wife's family. It's a grand place to visit, at once a cosy house and a defensive tower, and the exhibitions inside are well worth studying. Visit before this place gets turned over to banquets as Bunratty has.

Franciscan friary Another O'Donnell construction is the very ruined but picturesque Franciscan friary, on the town side of the river Eske. It was built in 1474 by Red Hugh O'Donnell and his wife Nuala O'Brien and, like most other defensible buildings in Ireland, was taken and taken again in the assorted wars between the clans and the English. At one stage there were gunpowder stores in the friary which exploded and destroyed most of the buildings. In 1607 under Sir Basil Brooke the building became the Protestant church, and it serves as a graveyard now. On the opposite bank a quiet pathway leads behind bungalows along the river bank in a 1½-hour walk to **Revlin Point**, a route that has been popular since the turn of the century. There is an accompanying leaflet that tells you about the plant life you can see, which can be picked up at the tourist office.

Railway Heritage Centre ⓘ *Old Station House, Tirconaill St, T074-9722655. Jun-Sep Mon-Sat 1000-1700, Oct-May Mon-Fri 1000-1700. €1.50.* Donegal town has a collection of steam-train fanatics who are renovating old carriages, and the hope is that they will eventually resurrect a bit of the line and run trains. For now, however, you can visit the Donegal Railway Heritage Centre with lots of information, old posters and restored carriages and engines.

Lough Derg → *Phone code: 071. Colour map 1, grid B2.*

Getting there Special buses run to Lough Derg during the pilgrim season. Bookings and transport information are available from **The Priory** ⓘ *T071-9861550, www.loughderg.org*. Lough Derg can also be reached on the remote R233 road from Pettigo.

Ireland's most historic penitential pilgrimage site lies to the west of Donegal Town, and its lineage is indeed impressive. An 1184 text, the *Tractatus de Purgatorio Sancti Patricii*, referred to an island where St Patrick fasted to expel demons, and the earliest maps of Europe marked Lough Derg as the destination for medieval pilgrims in search

A pilgrim's progress

In 1397 a courtier of King John of Aragon set off from France for Lough Derg in the hope that he could redeem the soul of his master, who had died too suddenly to confess his sins. When he reached Dublin from England he was warned of the dangers of "savage, ungoverned people" but an armed escort took him as far as Ulster from where he continued alone. The courtier met King O'Neill who took him to Lough Derg where monks rowed him across to the island where he meditated and suffered visions of lost souls. On his return he spent Christmas with the O'Neills where "his table was of rushes spread out on the ground while nearby they placed delicate grass for him to wipe his mouth".

of Patrick's island. A pope tried to forbid the practice in 1497, and Cromwell vandalized the place, but all to no effect, and an increasing popularity in the 19th century established the practice that is still followed every year between June and August, when thousands visit the small Station Island in the lough. They take part in retreats which last three days, walking barefoot and living off black tea and toast (plus smuggled supplies of chocolate bars) without proper sleep.

Lough Eske and the **Blue Stack Mountains** that lie to the north make for a superb day trip by bicycle or car from Donegal town. Take the N56 heading north out of Donegal town, and look for the sign pointing to a road on the right for the Lough Eske Drive. A small road loops around the lough and it is possible to join up with the N15 road on the east side of the lough and return to Donegal that way. Walks in the Blue Stack Mountains now form a way marked trail and a guide is available from the Donegal tourist office for €10.20.

Sleeping

Bundoran *p453*

A-B **Great Northern Hotel**, T071-9841204, greatnorthernhotel.com. The most stylish place around, with huge rooms, amazing views over the beaches and well away from the gadding about that goes on in town at weekends. Pool and leisure centre, nice old dining room, and a golf course in the garden.

E **Gillaroo Lodge**, T071-9842357, www.gillaroo.net. At the west end of the town, on the main road, near to all the facilities. It has lots of information on fishing and hires tackle and boats. Drying room.

F **Homefield House**, Bayview Av, T071-9841288, www.donegalequestrian holidays. com. Hostel with 10 private rooms and room rate includes breakfast. Bike hire.

Ballyshannon and Rossnowlagh *p453*

★ B **Sand House Hotel**, Rossnowlagh, T071-9851777, www.sandhouse-hotel.ie. You are guaranteed to appreciate the hotel's name when you arrive at this superbly spacious establishment. Be sure to check out the lift.

C **Dorrian's Imperial Hotel**, Main St, Ballyshannon, T071-9851147, www.dorians imperialhotel.com. Right in the town centre and dating back to 1781, this cleverly modernized place has a small leisure centre with a gym and steam room.

E **Rockville House**, Belleek Rd, Ballyshannon, T071-9851106. A gracious dwelling that overlooks the river.

Camping

Lakeside Centre Caravan and Camping Park, Belleek Rd, Ballyshannon, T071-9852822. Overlooks Assaroe Lake, 5-min walk from Ballyshannon.

Donegal Town *p454, map p454*

A **Harvey's Point Country Hotel**, Lough Eske, T074-9722208, www.harveys point.com. Only 6 km from town but its alpine location on the lonely shores of Lough

Eske takes you a million miles away from the bustle of Donegal. Famous restaurant and inspiring opportunities for country walking.

C **Abbey Hotel**, The Diamond, T074-9721014. A very busy place with lots of night- time entertainment. Restaurant and bar food.

C **Central Hotel**, The Diamond, T074-9721027, www.whites-hotels.com. Very busy but comfortable hotel in the heart of the town. Big rooms, nice views of the river from the back, leisure centre with a big swimming pool available to guests.

E **Ardeevin**, Lough Eske, Barnesmore, T074-9721790, seanmcginty@eircom.net. Scenically located on the shores of the Lough.

E **Island View House**, T074-9722411, www.eircybyte.com/islandview. 10 mins out of town at Tullacullion, modern B&B overlooking the bay.

F **Ball Hill Hostel**, turn left at the Texaco garage 5 km out of town on the Killybegs Rd, T074-9721174. Superb location overlooking the bay, a former coastguard station. Bring your food and drink. Taxi from town costs €7.

F **Donegal Town Independent Hostel**, Killybegs Rd, T074-9722805, lincunn8@eircom.net. Dorm beds and €28 for a double room in this well-provisioned hostel with attractive murals on the walls and garden space for tents. It is about 1 km from town and a free pick-up can be arranged.

Eating

Bundoran *p453*

Chateaubrianne, Sligo Rd, T071-9842160. A really posh place to eat, French and nouvelle Irish in a seaside setting. Lots of seafood, like prawn and crab profiteroles for starters, but meat-eaters and vegetarians do well here too. Dinner menus under €40. Open Tue-Sat and Sun lunch (€25).

Great Northern Hotel, the restaurant has lots of nostalgic charm about it. It is huge with enormous bay windows shrouded in 1990s over-the-top curtaining. Good quality, down-to-earth food.

La Sabbia, Bayfield Ave. A good Italian-style place where dishes average around €15.

Ballyshannon and Rossnowlagh *p453*

The Sand House Hotel Restaurant, Rossnowlagh, T071-9851777. Has all the usual suspects – beef, lamb, veal, duck – enhanced by sauces like Madeira and shallot or port and berries.

Smuggler's Creek, Rossnowlagh, T071-9852366. The clifftop location is hard to beat, serves pub food.

Abbey Assaroe Mills and Waterwheels, just outside Ballyshannon. Coffee shop.

Kitchen Bake, Main St, Ballyshannon

Shannon's Corner, Bishop St, Ballyshannon.

Donegal Town *p454, map p454*

The two hotels in town have busy lunchtime and evening restaurants. Along and off Main St there are pubs doing food, Indian take-aways and fish-and-chip shops.

Harvey's Point Country Hotel Restaurant, Lough Eske, T074-9722208. Noted for its French and Swiss gourmet cooking and opens daily for lunch and dinner. Weekends only Nov-Mar. Evening set dinner starts at around €50 and the calming views are thrown in for free.

La Bella Donna, just before the bridge on Bridge St, T074-9712 5790. Italian-style, does pasta and pizza dishes around €12 and meat dishes around €20.

Central. Has a Thai-style restaurant, dinner only and closed Thu.

Weaver's Loft, in the Diamond above the Magee store, T074-9722660. For lunch or a very early evening meal, serves wraps, open sandwiches and the like.

Lough Derg *p455*

Pettigo Inn and Milers Restaurant, Main St, Pettigo, T074-9861720. Food served all day.

Pubs and music

Bundoran *p453*

Bundoran is very partial to that curiously Irish version of American country music – not so much "my wife has left me and my dog is dead" but "how sad I am to be leaving Ireland" type stuff. Expect to find 1960s-style showbands and party people from Dublin and further afield. For traditional Irish music try: **The Ould Bridge Bar**, while **Brennans**, Main

For an explanation of the sleeping and eating price codes used in this guide, see inside the front cover. Other relevant information is found in Essentials pages 39-45.

St, and **The Railway Bar**, are good places for a quiet drink in traditional surroundings.

Clubs

In the summer there are nightclubs: **Planet Earth**, **Pepés**, **Jumping Jack's**, and more. Just stroll along and pick one.

Ballyshannon and Rossnowlagh *p453*

Live music, traditional and modern, can be found in some of Ballyshannon's pubs throughout the summer.

Dicey Reilly's, on the other side of the road to Sean Ógs. Worth checking out.

Sean Ógs, Market St, T071-58964. One of the best pubs.

The Smugglers' Creek, Rossnowlagh. Timber beams everywhere, has traditional music every Sat and Sun and has been recommended by travellers.

Thatch Pub, Bishop St. Tiny, has character as well as live music most nights.

Donegal Town *p454, map p454*

Abbey Hotel. Has a disco on Sun aimed at the over-21s, and at weekends and when a tour bus calls in, as they regularly do, there is an organized Irish session, featuring the Londonderry Air and suchlike.

National Bar. Irish music at weekends all year in an unreconstructed '50s sort of place.

The Schooner Inn, Upper Main St. Traditional music, Mon-Fri, during the summer.

Star Bar. Live music but a younger trendier, Irish crowd. Inside is **Linda's Crusty Kitchen**, which does good cheap breakfasts and sandwiches and some hot meals.

Shopping

Donegal Town *p454, map p454*

Craft and gift shops are dotted about the town square.

Donegal Craft Village, Ballyshannon to Sligo Rd, 800 m south of the tourist office. Part shopping centre, part tourist attraction, is a purpose-built village where craftworkers have their workshops and sell their produce. You can observe a jeweller making traditional designs, admire the stonemasonry of Brendan McGloin and the blacksmithing of Jack Voss and of course you can buy what you like. Open all year, Mon-Sat 0900-1800; Summer Mon-Sat 0900-1800, Sun 1100-1800. Coffee shop, picnic area.

Magee, www.mageeshop.com. This is the most famous, with weaving demonstrations in the store, a range of nice but pricy handwoven garments and a shipping service if required. Check prices with **John Molloy**, also in The Diamond, www.johnmolloy.com.

Activities and tours

Bundoran *p453*

Surfing **Donegal Adventure Centre**, T071-9842418, www.donegal-holidays.com. Teaches surfing at all levels. Book in advance They also hire out equipment.

Fitzgerald's Surfworld, T071-9841223. Try this place to purchase equipment.

Walking There are lots of good cliff top walks around the town. Try the Roguey walk which goes from Bundoran Bridge to Tullan Strand along the cliffs, passing fairy bridges and the wishing chair. The West End walk starts at Sheen Av and goes along the coast to Tullaghan, County Leitrim.

Donegal Town *p454, map p454*

Fishing **Doherty's**, Main St, T074-9721119. Permits and licences for salmon and trout.

Transport

South Donegal *p453*

Bike hire Hire and Sell Centre, West End, Bundoran, T071-9841526. Will deliver. The Bike Shop, Waterloo Pl, Donegal, T074-9722515.

Bus Bus Éireann run daily buses connecting **Bundoran** with **Sligo**, **Derry**, **Letterkenny**, **Glenveagh National Park**, **Ballyshannon** (for connections to Dublin), and **Galway**. Call Ballyshannon Bus Station, T071-9821101, for times.

Bus Éireann run daily buses connecting **Ballyshannon** with **Donegal**, **Derry**, **Sligo**, **Galway** and **Dublin**, T074-21309. Feda O'Donnell, T074-9548114, runs its private buses connecting Ballyshannon with **Crolly**, **Donegal**, **Dunfanaghy**, **Gweedore** and **Letterkenny** as well as another service heading west for **Galway** and **Sligo**.

From **Donegal Town**, Bus Éireann, T074-9131008/9721101, has services to **Dublin**, **Cork** and **Limerick** in the south, **Galway** and **Sligo** to the west and **Belfast**, **Derry** and

Enniskillen in Northern Ireland. McGeehan Coaches, T074-9546150, have a daily service between **Dungloe** and **Dublin**, which calls at Donegal, and a **Glencolmcille** to **Dublin** service, calling at Donegal twice daily. **Feda O'Donnell**, T074-9548114, www.fedaodonnell.com, has a twice-daily service between Donegal Town and **Galway** and, daily in Jul-Aug, Donegal to **Glasgow** via **Derry** and **Belfast** airport. Patrick Gallagher, T074-9531107, has a daily Donegal to **Belfast** via **Derry** and **Letterkenny** service.
Ferry Island Tours Waterbus, T074-9723666. Organizes twice daily tours of Donegal Bay during the summer months. Departure times are determined by the tide. The guided tour includes a sighting of Seal Island, where 200 harbour and Atlantic seals breed.

Taxi Mulherns, Bundoran, T071-9842222. Daly's, Bundoran, T071-9841111. In Donegal Town there's a taxi rank opposite the Abbey Hotel.

Southwest Donegal

The southwest of Donegal characterises all that remains of the old Ireland. Scattered coastal villages, narrow twisting roads with sudden outbreaks of searing seascapes, quiet village pubs with local musicians playing beside smouldering peat fires, ancient ruins, Gaelic speakers, deserted country walks, craft workers whose skills have been handed down for generations. It's enough to make you go all teary. OK, there's also the fish factory at Killybegs, heritage centres and organised tour groups, but this area is still the genuine article. ▸▸ *For Sleeping, Eating and other listings, see pages 462-464.*

Donegal to Killybegs → *Phone code: 074. Colour map 1, grid B2.*

The N56 road leaves Donegal for the route west to Killybegs and Glencolmcille and it is not long before Donegal Bay comes into view with Benbulben and the mountains of Sligo providing an impressive backdrop. In the first village, **Mountcharles**, off the N56, the attractive water pump that might catch your eye is dedicated to Seamus MacManus, a local storyteller and author.

At the next village, **Dunkineely**, there is a detour worth taking to **St John's Point** if a quiet picnic spot or scenic views seem in order. After leaving the village, a signposted road goes south for 8 km and ends in a limestone enclave, where there is a splendid, little-visited sandy beach and a lighthouse. Here too you will find the hand-weaver **Cyndi Graham** ⓣ *T074-9737072*.

The last village before Killybegs is **Bruckless**, home to a holy well that has some early Christian cross-slabs nearby. There is a good B&B and a hostel here (see page 462), so the village is worth considering as a possible stopping point if you want something quieter than Killybegs.

Killybegs → *Phone code: 074. Colour map 1, grid B1.*

Killybegs, as your nostrils will soon inform you, is a major fishing port, and the large fish processing plant is what blocks the view of the bay when arriving from the east. The piscine theme is hard to escape in Killybegs; it accounts for the best dishes on restaurant menus, and there are various sea-angling events during the summer that culminate in a major festival in late July. **Tourist information** is available from a local community-run office, T074-9732346, and there is a town map and noticeboard in front of the Harbour Store.

For something non-fishy in nature, take a stroll up the hill from the main road to **St Catherine's church** to admire the Celtic-inspired carvings of gallowglasses on the tomb of Niall Mór MacSweeney.

Without being facetious, you get the best of Killybegs when you leave the place, for as the road swings west out of town the seascape begins to take on some of the

Gaelic place names

The Irish language is alive and well in parts of southwest Donegal and place names on signs often appear in Irish as well as, or instead of, English.

An Charraig	Carrick
An Caiseal	Cashel
An Port	Port
Ard a'Ratha	Ardara
An Bhroclais	Bruckless
An Tráigh Bhán	Silver Strand
Cill Chartha	Kilcar
Dún Chionn Fhaola	Dunkineely
Gleann Cholm Cille	Glencolmcille
Gleann Locha	Glenlough
Málainn Mhóir	Malinmore
Málainn Bhig	Malinbeg
Na Gleanntaí	Glenties
Na Cealla Beaga	Killybegs
Tamhnach an Salainn	Mountcharles
Port Nua	Portnoo
Ros Beag	Rosbeg

characteristics that make Donegal so special. **Fintra Bay** comes into view, with the expanse of sea beyond it, while the mountains of **Crownarad** and **Mulnanaff** loom up inland. Look for the sign pointing left for a spectacularly scenic coastal route to Kilcar, and consider following the signs that appear along the route to **White Strand** or **Muckross Head** for a picnic spot and viewing point.

Kilcar to Glencolmcille → *Phone code: 074. Colour map 1, grid B1.*

As the road from Killybegs approaches Kilcar the N56 bears to the right and goes over the mountains to Carrick, while a smaller road bears left into Kilcar and continues to Carrick along the coast. **Kilcar**, a small village and a centre for the Donegal hand-woven tweed industry, is pleasantly low-key compared to Killybegs, or at least it is outside of the sea-angling festival and accompanying street festival that raises the jollity level in the five pubs. Good food, pubs with music and accommodation are all available (see page 462) and **Studio Donegal** ⓘ *The Glebe Mill, T074-9738194, www.studiodonegal.ie*, is one of the community's small spinning and hand weaving factory shops that you can visit. **Tourist information** is available from the community centre in Main Street, T074-9738376.

There are also opportunities to arrange guided walks and fishing trips or attendance at a weekend writing workshop. The tourist office can supply a map and brochure of the local **Kilcar Way** walk.

Further along the main road at **Carrick**, a road is signposted to the left for Bunglas and Slieve League and walking along this stretch of coast is one of the highlights of a trip to Donegal. From the main road it is a few miles to the tiny Irish-speaking village of **Teelin** and its pub, and just beyond it the road divides: left for Bunglas and right for a signposted Slieve League walking trail.

Walking Going left, vehicles can be taken up the steep and winding road around the southern slopes of Slieve League to a rough parking area and from here, **Bunglas**, there are awesome views of the cliffs and their shifting colours, while hundreds of feet below the silent sea churns up foam against coloured rocks (bunglas means 'green bottom').

Walkers have a choice of routes. From the first signpost for the Slieve League Walk the lengthier but less precipitous route leads on to **One Man's Pass** and the summit of **Slieve League** (595 m). Alternatively, you can start from the parking area up a well trodden route to **Scregeighter** (308 m) and **Eagle's Nest** (323 m; see box page 461) and then a very precipitous 1.5 m wide path to One Man's Path (this section is not as scary as the 1.5 m wide steep stretch). While due warning needs to be given about proper footwear and avoiding windy or misty days (there have been fatal accidents), reaching the summit of Slieve League is more than ample reward. On a clear day it

Eagle's Nest

David Marshall in his excellent *Best Walks in Ireland* retells a story first recorded in 1867 about the point on the walk from Bunglas known as Eagle's Nest. An 80-year-old woman, Nanny O'Byrne of Malinbeg, remembered her great-grandmother who, when only nine months old, was carried off by an eagle from the nest on the cliff. The bird was pursued and the child was dropped near Carrigan Head; although seriously injured she survived to a ripe old age bearing the scars from her abduction. The nest was apparently destroyed in the early 19th century after 'human limbs' (more probably sheep bones) were discovered inside it. Eagles from Scotland have been spotted between Slieve League and Glencolmcille, and there is a chance they will nest here again.

should be possible to make out the distinctive shapes of Croagh Patrick in County Mayo and Ben Bulbin in County Sligo.

From the summit, you can continue to Malinbeg along the edge of the cliff (from Teelin this walk takes about six hours). It will take another hour or more to reach accommodation at Malinmore, or on a little further still to Glencolmcille.

Glencolmcille → *Phone code: 074. Colour map 1, grid B1.*

After leaving Carrick, instead of staying on the main road all the way, a more leisurely approach to Glencolmcille can be enjoyed by taking the signposted road to the left for Malinbeg. Along the way you will see a signpost for **portal tombs**, a line of six that make up the largest group of portal stones in Ireland. After passing them take another signposted left turn which ends in Malinbeg and its secluded, little-visited sandy beach of Silver Strand. The island you can see from here, **Rathlin O'Birne Island**, marks the northern entrance to Donegal Bay, and ruins of an early Christian hermitage are crumbling away on it. Retrace your route to the junction, where a left turn leads to the Glencolmcille Hotel, and carry on to Glencolmcille this way. There is another sandy beach at Glencolmcille but, unlike Silver Strand, it is not safe for swimming.

Folk Village Museum ⓘ *T074-9730017. Easter-Sep Mon-Sat 1000-1800, Sun 1200-1800. €3.* Glencolmcille is a culturally vibrant, Irish-speaking area – the village itself is called Cashel and is basically one main street – well tuned to tourism but thankfully on its own terms. There is a spirit of independence here that was nurtured by that most rare breed in Ireland, a priest with a socialist conscience, who came here in 1951 to a community impoverished by emigration and government indifference. Father James McDyer spent 30 years encouraging community-based industries and a video about him can be seen in the Folk Village Museum that he established. Informative displays on history and geology make this a useful first call when visiting the area and there are guided tours around a series of cottages devoted to aspects of local cultural life, including a shebeen and a schoolhouse. A shop sells local wines and some crafts, and there is a tearoom. Local guidebooks and brochures are available from the museum shop and from the combined **tourist information** (T074-9730116, open Jun-Aug daily 1000-1800) and **craft shop** in the main street; look for the lovely *Gleann Cholm Cille* guide (€7.50), illustrated in colour and including some of Rockwell Kent's paintings inspired by his stay here.

Local walk An enjoyable walk, which is highly recommended, leads out of the village, past the Church of Ireland church and across a bridge, to the cliff top at **Glen Head** (234 m) and an old watch tower built in the early 19th century when a French invasion was expected (another one can be seen at Malinbeg). There are superb views from here of the jagged **Sturral promontory**, and the walk can be continued by following the coastline to **Port** and then over Port Hill to the deserted and hauntingly lonely **valley of Glenlough**. This is where the American landscape painter Rockwell Kent (1882-1971) stayed, and where he was prevented from returning to live in the early 1950s because his government refused him a passport, on account of his left-wing sympathies and a visit to the Soviet Union. Some years later Dylan Thomas stayed in the same house, but he was not enamoured of the place and took off, leaving unpaid bills. The walk from Glencolmcille to Glenlough will take about four hours, but you could also cycle or drive to Port and walk from there to Glenlough. Ordnance Survey Map No 10 in the Discovery series covers the walk.

Sleeping

Donegal to Killybegs *p459*

D **Bruckless House**, Bruckless, T074-9737071, bruc@bruckless.com. An attractive, 18th-century house overlooking the bay, furnished with artefacts and art from the Orient. You can practise your French or Chinese here. There are 4 rooms, (2 have their own bathroom).

F-G **Blue Moon Hostel**, Main St, Dunkineely, T074-9737264, bluemoonhostel@eircom.net. Apleasant hostel with private rooms, camping space and good facilities.

Camping

Gallagher's Farm Hostel and Camping Park, Darney, Bruckless, T074-9737057. Signposted off the N56 before the village. An attractively converted stone-built barn with 2 kitchens, maps for walking, but no private rooms. Campers have their own facilities in a converted hay barn.

Killybegs *p459*

B&Bs line the roads going in and out of Killybegs, especially the road to Kilcar, and it is difficult to differentiate between them, for they are all variations on the bungalow theme, and most charge a fixed rate of €30 per person. A new hotel, the **Tara**, about to open opposite the Harbour Store, is likely to be the best place to stay.

C **Bay View Hotel**, Main St, T074-9731950, www.bayviewhotel.ie. Benefits from a smart leisure centre and indoor pool.

E **Bannagh House**, Fintra Rd, T074-9731108, bannaghhouse@eircom.net. The archetypal bungalow, but with an elevated site overlooking the harbour.

Kilcar to Glencolmcille *p460*

E **Cairnsmore**, Glen Rd, Carrick, T074-9739137, dl8@familyhomes.ie. B&B in a quiet little bungalow with Slieve League in the background. Single and double rooms, tea and coffee, and the option of an evening meal. Warmly recommended by a reader.

E-F **Dun Ulun Hostel**, Kilbeg, Kilcar, T074-9738137, closer to the village. More of a guest house with hostel accommodation and camping space included.

F **Derrylahan Independent Hostel**, Derrylahan, Kilcar, T074-9738079, derrylahan@eircom.net. Popular hostel with terrific views of the bay and good facilities. Includes 3 private rooms, and camping space. Will pick up from Kilcar or Carrick.

G **Cara's Hostel**, Kilbeg, Kilcar, T074-9738368. An 8-room thatched cottage with lovely traditional features. There are 13 beds and one room has just 2 beds, all at a flat rate of €7.

Glencolmcille *p461*

D **Glencolmcille Hotel (Ostan Ghleann Cholm Cílle)**, Malinmore, T074-9730003, www.glenhotel.com. The only hotel in the area, with B&B.

E **Atlantic Scene**, Dooey, T074-9730186. Outside the village, family-run, close to the hostel and shares with it breathtaking views of the Atlantic. €50 per person.

E **Corner House**, Cashel, T074-9730021. On the road to Ardara, 5 mins from the Folk Museum. Open Jun-Sep.

F **Dooey Hostel**, T074-9730130, www.dooey hostel.com. This establishment was a founding member of the IHO, and is 1.5 km from the

For an explanation of the sleeping and eating price codes used in this guide, see inside the front cover. Other relevant information is found in Essentials pages 39-45.

village. Superb location overlooking the bay, part of the building built onto the rockface, includes 6 private rooms and camping.

F **Malinbeg Hostel**, T074-9730006, malinbeg hostel@oceanfree.net. A new hostel with a range of rooms, good facilities, open all year.

Eating

Donegal to Killybegs *p459*

Not a lot of choice, and it is better to bring a picnic or eat in Killybegs.

TTT **Castle Murray House Hotel Restaurant**, St John's Point, Dunkineely, T074-9737022, www.castlemurray.com, At night this award-winning place is noted for its French-style cuisine, with dinner at around €40.

T **The Village Tavern**, Mountcharles, T073-9735622. Bar meals are an option here.

Killybegs *p459*

Cope House, Main St, T074-9731834. A nautical themed pub serving bar food and a restaurant serving Chinese-style dishes.

TT **The Fleet Inn**, Main St, T074-9731518. Has a restaurant with a small menu featuring dishes like baked seabass for under €25. Dinner only daily in summer. Closed Mon and Tue in winter.

T **Kitty Kelly's**, Largy, T074-9731925. A little way outside Killybegs on the road to Kilcar, this was an old farmhouse which has been converted, serves a good menu of seafood and pastas in the €10-15 range, from 1800.

Kilcar to Glencolmcille *p460*

TT **Restaurant Teach Barnaí**, on the other side of the road from Piper's Rest, T074-9738160. Specializes in seafood and international dishes in the €12-30 range.

TT-T **Blue Haven**, before reaching Kilcar on the road from Killybegs, T074-9738090. Open for lunch and dinner, has amazing views, serves modern Irish food at very reasonable prices.

TT-T **The Piper's Rest**, Kilcar, T074-9738205. Has a well-deserved reputation for its seafood chowder, and Guinness and oysters are a favourite combination here.

T **Gate House**, 1 km from Carrick on the road to Glencolmcille, T074-9739366. Stone-built tearoom, has indoor and outdoor seating for home-baked goodies, open 1000-1800, May-Sep. There is an attached craft shop selling handloomed knitwear.

The following all serve basic pub grub:

T **An Sliabh a'Liag**, Kilcar, T074-9739041;

T **John Joe Byrne**, (known to everyone as John Joe's) Kilcar;

T **Kilcar House**, Kilcar.

Glencolmcille *p461*

TT-T **An Chistin Restaurant**, above *Foras Cultúir Uladh* (Ulster Cultural Institute) on the same road as the Folk Museum, T074-9730213. Appropriately devoted to traditional Irish cooking and has fresh seafood on a daily basis. Open 0930-2130, with prices from €7 to over €25.

T **The Folk Museum**, tearoom serves home-made scones and light meals from 1000-1800.

T **Óstán Ghleann Cholm Cille**, Main St, T074-9730003. Has bar food and a small restaurant.

TT **Silver Strand House**, out at Malinbeg overlooking Donegal Bay, T074-9730220. A seafood restaurant worth checking out.

TT-T **Teach an Lása**, main street. A restaurant and teashop above the **Lace House**, seafood is the speciality here at night.

Pubs and music

Killybegs *p459*

In summer there is usually live music in at least one of the pubs at night.

Harbour Bar, Main St. A good place to try.

Fleet Inn, Main St. Usually has music at weekends and midweek.

Kilcar to Glencolmcille *p460*

Kilcar's 5 pubs are all within staggering distance of each other and between them there is music most nights in the summer.

An Sliabh a'Liag, Carrick, T074-9739041.

Cellar Bar (Doc's), Carrick, T074-9739067.

Enright's, Carrick, T074-9739070.

Piper's Rest, thatched, and has loads of atmosphere and really traditional music.

Tigh Mhic Fhionnlaoich, Carrick, T074-9739120.

Glencolmcille *p461*

Glencolmcille is not Killarney, which means traditional music is not on tap, but when it is played in the pubs or at the Feile Gleann Cholm Cille (Festival) in early Aug, T074-9730111, you can be sure you are hearing the real thing.

Roarty's Bar, T074-9730273, and **Glen Head Tavern**, T074-9730008, both in Cashel. Have fairly regular sessions.

Shopping

Glencolmcille p461

The Folk Museum, the craft shop has a range of knitwear, pottery and other handicrafts. **Glencolmcille Woollen Mill**, T074-9730070, a little south of the village on the R263 in Malinmore Valley. Shop open daily during the summer, Mon-Fri 0930-2100, and at weekends 1000-1900. Quality knitwear is produced here in a small factory open to the public for demonstrations of knitting, spinning and hand-weaving of Donegal tweeds. As well as clothes, the shop stocks Donegal china, ceramics and jewellery. **Lace House**, handmade garments for sale. **Taipeis Gael**, at Malinbeg near Silver Strand, T074-9730325. Makes art tapestries and holds tapestry-making courses. Mon-Fri.

Activities and tours

Killybegs p459

Diving There is a local diving school, T074-9731169.

Fishing **Harbour Store** has a good selection of fishing and nautical gear as well as wet gear, camping equipment and a selection of gifts.

Kilcar to Glencolmcille p460

Fishing **Mc Breaty's**, Main St, Kilcar, T074-9738492. Tackle and info on where to fish. **SWD Angling Service**, T074-9738211.

Horse riding **Little Acorn Farm**, Carrick, T074-9739386.

Glencolmcille p461

Malinmore Outdoor Pursuits Centre, T074-9730123. Diving, canoeing, hill walking, boat trips, archaeological trails, among others.

Transport

Southwest Donegal p459

Bus Bus Éireann, T074-9721101, runs a Mon-Sat service between **Killybegs** and **Donegal**, stopping at **Mountcharles**, **Inver** and **Dunkineely**. There's also a service between **Killybegs** and **Glencolmcille** (via **Carrick**) between **Killybegs** and **Portnoo** (via **Ardara** and **Glenties**), and between Killybegs and **Donegal**. McGeehan's Coaches, T074-9546150, also stops in Killybegs on its daily services between **Glencolmcille** and **Dublin**, via **Carrick**, **Kilca**, **Killybegs**, **Ardara**, **Donegal** and **Cavan** on 1 route and with **Killybegs**, **Fintown** and **Letterkenny** on their 2nd route.

Directory

Glencolmcille p461

Irish language and culture courses Between Apr and Oct a rich variety of courses is held around Glencolmcille and Glenfin. Irish language courses cater for complete novices as well as those wishing to improve their fluency, and the bilingual cultural activity programmes are open to all. For details of all the courses – Irish, hill-walking, archaeology, landscape and culture, marine painting, Donegal dances, celtic pottery, flute playing and bodhrán playing. **Oideas Gael**, Gleann Cholm Cille, Co. Dhún na nGall, Éire (Oideas Gael, Glencolmcille, Co. Donegal), T074-9730248, www.oideas- gael.com. Accommodation can be arranged.

Northern Donegal

Northern Donegal is a grand place for driving, or better still cycling through turn after turn of coastal views, the Rosses, around Glenties, Horn Head and the Dunfanaghy and Rossguill peninsulas. Quiet settlements are few and far between. For those with the time and sense of adventure there are islands to visit and heritage buffs can visit Glebe House and Glenveagh Castle, both close to Letterkenny, a good place for stocking up on supplies. In between are unassuming villages like Glenties, Ardra and Dungloe or the inland Ballyboffey and Dunlewey where the scenery has all the beauty you'd ever want and none of the disadvantages of more well-trodden areas. ▸▸ For Sleeping, Eating and other listings, see pages 472-478.

Glencolmcille to Gweebarra Bay → *Phone code: 074. Colour map 1, grid B2.*

The road to Ardara from Glencolmcille travels through the Glengesh Pass with its intoxicating views of Loughros Beg Bay, framed by mountains and luring you to take the road that is signposted on the left for Maghera and its caves. This road cuts its way through the rock, as does the magnificent Assarancagh Waterfall, which you pass en route. A signposted way takes you to the beach in 15 minutes but don't explore the caves without checking the state of the tide. Also from Ardara there is another equally scenic 8-km route leading out along the north side of the bay to the sparkling white stones at Loughros Point.

If you have a bike consider cycling the minor road from Maghera to Port (17 km) through lonely, unspoilt scenery.

Ardara Ardara is a centre for the manufacture of handwoven tweed and handknit garments, and the **Heritage Centre** ⓘ *T074-9541473, Easter-Sep, Mon-Sat 1000-1800, Sun 1400-1800, €2.50, café*, in the centre of town has an interesting exhibition on the history of the industry, with a weaver busy at work on the premises. **Tourist information** is available at the entrance to the Heritage Centre, T074-9541262.

The Romanesque-style Catholic **church** in town has a startling wheel window at the west end: *Christ Among the Doctors*, designed by the Irish artist Evie Hone in 1953.

Dawros Head Dawros Head to the north of Ardara might look suitably remote on a map, but a vast sandy and safe beach at Narin and Portnoo and nearby camp and caravan sites combine to make this corner of Donegal very popular with families on holiday from other parts of Ulster. Come here outside of summer, however, and it's another proposition altogether. A picnic spot worth seeking out whatever the season is **Doon Fort**, on a tiny island in the middle of Lough Doon. To reach it, take the road signposted to Rosbeg on the road for Ardara outside Narin, and then a right turn just past a school on to a narrow lane. Look for a sign advertising boats for hire on Doon Lake, and here a rowing boat can be hired to reach the fort.

Glenties and around → *Phone code: 074. Colour map 1, grid B1.*

Glenties is as neat and pristine as you would expect for a five-times winner of the national Tidy Towns Award, and the town is a comfortable place to stop off for refreshments or even a night's stay to enjoy some traditional music in one of the many pubs. For quiet walks or cycle trips away from tourist attractions, there are scenic diversions to Dooey Point to the north and Fintown inland to the east, and the latter also provides an interesting route to Letterkenny and Derry, if there is not enough time to take in the northern coastline.

St Conal's Museum and Heritage Centre ⓘ *Apr-Sep Mon-Fri 1100-1300 and 1400-1700. €2.50.* There is no tourist office in Glenties, but information is available from the hostel (see page 473) or St Conal's Museum and Heritage Centre, at the Ardara end of town which houses a miscellany of local memorabilia relating to the Famine era, a railway line which once serviced the town and other assorted bits and pieces.

Dooey Point From Glenties the N56 goes north to Maas before crossing a bridge on the River Gweebarra and then, at Lettermacaward, a coast road is signposted to the left for Dooey Point at the end of the peninsula. The scenic road, with picnic tables along the way, ends in a cul-de-sac, but walking over the dunes from here leads to a long beach with fine views of the two bays.

Brian Friel's play, 'Dancing at Lughnasa', is set in a house in Glenties.

The Navvy Poet

Patrick MacGill (1889-1963) was 12 when he became a bonded servant at Strabane's hiring fair, a slave market by any other name, and two years later he was in Scotland as a 'tatie-hoker' (potato digger). Later a labourer on the railways, MacGill wrote two novels – *Children of the Dead End* and *The Rat-Pit* – that shock the reader with their desolate tales of poverty and emigration. However, they only came back into print in the 1980s. Perhaps no other writer has so successfully captured the Third World lifestyle of Ulster's poor and their stoical resistance, but his *Glenmornan* is also worth reading for its anti-clerical blast. Glenties, where the writer grew up as the eldest of 11 children, is home to an annual MacGill summer school, run by his niece Mary Clare O'Donnell. T074-9551103.

Inland to Ballybofey The R250 from Glenties heads inland through bleak moorland and valley to Fintown, with poetic glimpses of the River Finn rushing into a lake surrounded by heather-coloured hills. A little way past the lake the R252 can be picked up for Ballybofey, where there is a very interesting hostel with horse riding facilities and information on local walks in the hills (see page 473). If you want a couple of days away from tourist Ireland, this is the place to stay.

The Rosses and Arranmore Island → *Phone code: 074. Colour map 1, grid A1.*

The Rosses is a rocky stretch of land, a stalwart Gaeltacht area, that takes in Dungloe in the south, Burtonport on the coast from where boats leave for Arranmore Island, and Crolly in the north. If not visiting Arranmore, the chances are you will skip the Rosses by travelling directly between Dungloe and Crolly, but the coastal road via Burtonport and Annagry has mixed diversions along the way, including a signposted road that leads to **Cruit Island** across a small bridge. There are beaches and scenic views of the bay that on a sunny day make a quiet destination for a picnic.

Dungloe and Burtonport Dungloe (An Clochán Liath) is not a particularly attractive place and, apart from having a meal here, there is little reason to stay. There is a small **tourist office** in Main Street, T074-9521297. Open Jun-Sep Mon-Sat 1000-1400 and 1500-1800. At the end of July and beginning of August the annual **Mary from Dungloe Festival**, www.maryfromdungloe.info, livens up the town, but the festival itself is an utterly synthetic event dating from the 1960s, which serves mainly as an excuse for late-night drinking. **Burtonport** (Ailt an Chorráin) is the departure point for Arranmore Island, which is the main attraction of the Rosses. The small town is also a centre for sea angling and fishing trips (see page 477).

Arranmore Island The boat trip (see page 478) to the little Island of Arranmore, 9 km by 5 km, takes 25 minutes, and while there are places to stay overnight (see page 473), a day trip with picnic provisions is feasible because the island can be walked around in a day if you catch the first and last ferries. Most of the 900 inhabitants live on the eastern side of the island, around where the ferry lands at **Leabgarrow**, and to the south at **Aphort**, but to enjoy a spot of ornithology and

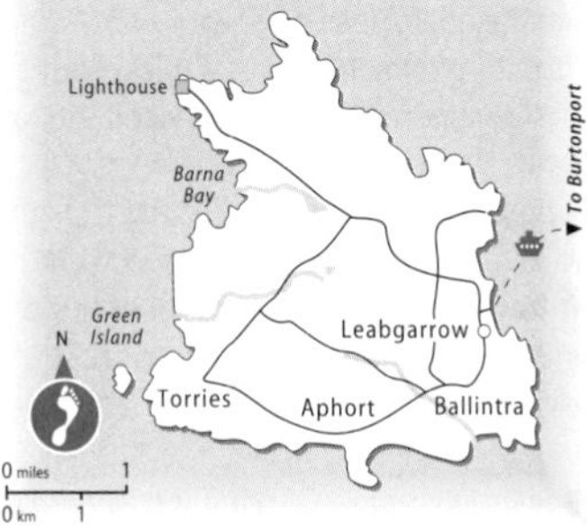

The Gaeltacht → *www.gaelsaoire.ie.*

The Gaeltacht means areas where Irish is still spoken. Yet despite sustained government encouragement and vigorous support from concerned groups, some people claim that the term is becoming more and more notional because spoken Irish is in terminal decline. Supporters, however, can point to the burgeoning applications for places on language summer schools, the Irish language television and radio stations, and places such as Glencolmcille and the Rosses where spoken Irish seems alive and well. Donegal has the largest Gaeltacht areas in the country but pockets can also be found in Connemara, Dingle, the Ring area west of Waterford, Ballingeary in Cork, west Mayo near Belmullet and a vigorous community in County Meath where Gaeltacht families were resettled in the 1930s.

views from high ground, head inland from Leabgarrow on the road that ends at the lighthouse in the northwest. Another enjoyable walk goes to **Torries** in the southwest, looking across to uninhabited **Green Island**. It is also to possible to follow the little known **Arranmore Way**, which is signposted on the island with colour-coded routes, but unfortunately the Way is not regularly waymarked and is not indicated on the relevant Ordnance Survey map, No 1. Call in at the shop next to Phil Ban's Bar for an island map that does show the route.

Burtonport to Crolly Back on the road to Annagry the village of **Kincasslagh** has local fame for its hotel, the Viking House (see page 473) owned by the inordinately popular Irish singer, Daniel O'Donnell, who hails from here. Beyond the village are the reedy waters of **Mullaghderg Lough**, near where a sign points to tiny **Donegal airport**. The road continues on to a T-junction, where it meets the N56 just outside the village of Crolly (Croithlí), which marks the boundary with the Gweedore area. Just before the village a sign points the way to Leo's Tavern, Menalck, home to both the group Clannad and the singer Enya, with gold and platinum discs lining the pub's walls and regular singsongs in the evening.

Gweedore to Gortahork → *Phone code: 074. Colour map 1, grid A2.*

There are two routes between Gweedore and Gortahork: the coastal R257 road that runs west of Gweedore to Bunbeg, Derrybeg and Magheroarty before rejoining the N56 just before Gortahork, and the main N56 itself that travels inland.

Coastal route This accesses the departure point for ferries to Tory Island from Bunbeg and Magheroarty, but as it passes on through Bunbeg and neighbouring Derrybeg there is little reason to stop until reaching a viewing point off the road at **Bloody Foreland**. The name suggests the site of another ungodly massacre from a chapter of Ireland's relations with the English, so it comes as a pleasant surprise to discover that the term refers to the startling red hue that the setting sun casts on the rocks. As the R257 continues eastwards the unmistakable outline of Tory Island stays in view and Horn Head rears up in the east.

Inland route The N56 has its own unforgettable charisma as it takes you through empty countryside so shockingly beautiful that you will wonder what everyone is doing in Killarney when places like this exist. About 15 km south of Falcarragh look for a sign pointing down a road to the right off the N56, the R251, to the Errigal youth hostel (see page 473) and the **Dunlewy Lakeside Centre** (*Ionad Cois Locha*) ⓘ *3 km* *away by the side of Lough Dunlewy (also spelt Dunlewey), T074-9531699, www.dunleweycentre.com. Easter-Oct Mon-Sat 1030-1800, Sun 1100-1800. €5.50 for house and grounds, €5.50 boat trips, €9 combined ticket.* Here, in the shadow of the distinctively shaped Errigal, there is a tiny village where a famed weaver, Manus Ferry, lived and worked until his death in the mid-1970s. His home is now the centre for weaving and spinning displays and a craft shop selling Donegal tweeds, paintings, pottery and other crafts. There are story-telling trips on a 50-seater boat on the lough, activities for children, a reasonably priced restaurant and tearoom, and traditional music on Tuesday nights in July and August.

From Dunlewy, signs point the way to **Poisoned Glen**, which most probably got its name from local spurges with a distinctive milky sap (*Euphorbia peplus* and *Euphorbia amygdaloides*), a perfectly benign and beautiful place that is wonderful for walks.

★ **Mount Errigal** A climb up the quartzite cone of Mount Errigal (752 m) is highly recommended because there are unsurpassed views of the county from the summit and, as long as you choose a suitable day when winds or visibility are not a problem, it is a reasonably manageable hike that takes less than four hours. There are various well trodden paths up the mountain, and a good place to start is from the R251, a little way past the Errigal youth hostel: it may be worth calling in here or at the Lakeside Centre (see above) for suggested routes. Whatever route is taken, the walk begins by walking across boggy grass and up the slope to the ridge of the summit, where a series of cairns mark the way. From here you should be able to see from Malin Head on the Inishowen Peninsula to Slieve League in the south. Map No 1 in the Ordnance Survey Discovery series covers the walk.

Tory Island → *Colour map 1, grid A2.*

Wind-swept Tory Island, under 6 km long and less than 2 km wide, was infamously difficult to reach or leave, until a new 40-minute ferry-boat service was introduced a few years back (see page 478). It lies 11 km off the mainland and the boat ride there is an excursion in itself as it churns its way along the rocky northwest coast and then out to sea to the island. St Colmcille founded a monastery on Tory in the sixth century, and there are scanty monastic remains and the ruins of a round tower made, uniquely, from rounded beach stones. A day trip allows time for invigorating walks around the island and some birdwatching (the rare corncrake is often heard because land here is farmed in the traditional way), but there are a couple of places to stay (see page 474) and two pubs to while away an evening (page 476). The island's hotel has one of these pubs, The People's Bar, and any entertainment, like evening sessions of music, will be advertised here. What might inspire a longer stay is a visit beforehand to Glebe Gallery (page 471), where there are some excellent examples of paintings by Tory Island painters who were inspired to paint by Derek Hill when he visited Tory. Three of those he inspired, Patsy Dan Rodgers, Anton Meenan and Ruari Rodgers, are still painting and their work is on show and for sale on the island. For walking, head for East Town and climb the stile near the *Beannaí dainsíreach (Dangerous Cliffs)* sign. Keep climbing for stupendous views of the west side of the island and, with binoculars, there are guillemots, puffins and terns to appreciate.

> *Tales of life on Tory, from childbirth to wakes and a bit of poitin-making along the way, are collected in 'Stories from Tory Island' (see page 626).*

Gortahork to Dunfanaghy → *Colour map 1, grid A2.*

Gortahork and Falcarragh are two small villages strung out along the coastal N56 road that leads to Dunfanaghy. During the day nothing much happens, but at night the pubs are lively enough and sessions of traditional music occur on an irregular and impromptu basis. From Falcarragh there are small roads at both ends of the long main street that lead down to a stupendous stretch of wild and lonely beach; beware of swimming here, an unpredictable undercurrent has caused accidents. There is also the **Falcarragh Visitor Centre** ⓘ *T074-9180888, www.falcarraghvisitorcentre.com, Apr-Oct Mon-Fri 0900- 1700, Sat-Sun 1200-1700*, devoted to local history, and with a coffee shop.

Dunfanaghy → *Phone code: 074. Colour map 1, grid A2.*

Dunfanaghy, tucked on the edge of a long inlet of Sheephaven Bay with majestic Horn Head to the north and flat-topped Muckish Mountain to the south, has a more rounded appeal than Falcarragh. There are better amenities and Horn Head offers irresistible clifftop walks or a scenic tour by bicycle or car, *tour de force* scenery and a safe beach for swimming. In the village itself there is an interesting museum devoted to local history, good places to eat, craft shops and a small art gallery.

The workhouse ⓘ *Main St, T074-9136540. Easter-Sep Mon-Fri 1000-1700, Sat and Sun 1200-1700. €3, no charge for art exhibition, shop, café or study room.* The workhouse was built in 1844 for 300 'paupers', but that figure swelled to over 5,000 during the Famine; it evolved into a hospital and home, which closed in 1922. The place reopened recently as a museum and study centre with sensitively presented material. A nine-minute audio-visual show sets the scene for the exhibition area that tells its tale through the true story of a workhouse resident who died in 1926. A study room has books on the Famine to consult and an audio-visual display on the local ecology; a craft shop and a coffee shop complete an admirable centre. Ask about the occasional sessions of traditional music and storytelling that take place in the evening.

Around Dunfanaghy → *Phone code: 074. Colour map 1, grid A2.*

★ **Horn Head** In his book *The Way That I Went* (see page 626) RL Preger was not exaggerating when he labelled Horn Head the "finest headland on the Irish coastline". The signposted Horn Head Drive circles its eastern side and, if only cars were banned from driving around it, a trip around the headland on a bicycle would be a highlight of any visit to Ireland. Modern farming methods have destroyed the haunts of the now-endangered corncrake, but the area around Dunfanaghy is one of the few places where it can still, occasionally, be heard. Horn Head is alive with birds: gannets dive-bombing vertically into the ocean, puffed-up puffins, the not-so-common chough (like a blackbird but with red legs), guillemots and storm petrels. It takes a good six hours to walk the 18 km around the perimeter of Horn Head, and in places there are mildly scary stretches along the clifftop. A lot of walkers prefer to stick to the west and north sides by walking across the Horn Head bridge for an easy-going jaunt across the dunes and along Tramore Strand and, further north, Pollaguill Bay and its smaller beach. From here follow a ruined stone wall to **Marble Arch**, a tremendous arch in the rock formed by nature over the millennia. If you are driving, go clockwise; the road is very narrow.

Cresslough and beaches The N56 road passes through the village of Cresslough, and here what will surely catch your eye is the flowing white curvature of **St Michael's Church**, designed to reflect the formidably solid outline of Muckish (*An Mhucais* being 'the pig's back'). The church, built in 1970 and influenced by Le Corbusier's ecclesiastical work at Ronchamp, adds a delightful touch of modernism perfectly at ease with rugged north Donegal. Inside, etched in glass, are the names of the architects, builders and artists who brought this elegant building into existence.

For a scenic detour follow the signposted road on the left, coming into the village from Port Na Blagh, for a Capuchin friary established here in the 1960s. A half-mile walk from the friary leads down to tiny **Monk's Beach**, usually only visited by locals, while another half-hour walk leads on to the lovely **Silver Strand**. One quarter of all Ireland's beaches are in Donegal, and these are two of the lesser-known ones. **Marble Hill Strand**, a more populous beach safe for swimming and windsurfing, is reached by turning off at Port Na Blagh, and there are canoes and boogie boards for hire. The beach you can see on the other side of Sheephaven Bay is Rosapenna. **Ards Forest Park**, signposted off the N56 and free to enter, offers a quieter and more rural destination, with nature trails winding their way through the former estate of the Scottish landlord who once owned this land and Horn Head.

Doe Castle ⓘ *About 5 km from Cresslough, signposted off the road, N56, to Carrigart. Free.* The sturdy, romantically sited fortress of Doe – built in the early 16th century by the MacSweeneys, and said to have provided refuge to some shipwrecked Spanish Armada sailors in 1588 – was constantly fought over throughout the 17th century. An English assault on the castle early in the century, headed by Sir Oliver Lambert, led him to exclaim that it was "the strongest hold in all the province which endured 100 blows of the demi-cannon before it yielded". A Captain George Vaughan Hart (his initials are over the door) converted the castle into a home in the early 1800s and the last occupant, by one account, was a Victorian rector from Cresslough who had nowhere else to live.

Carrigart and the Rosguill Peninsula → *Phone code: 074. Colour map 1, grid A2.*

Carrigart is a little village between Sheephaven Bay and the Fanad Peninsula: it opens the door for the gratifying Rosguill Peninsula with its signposted 12-km **Atlantic Drive** that takes you past the resort of **Downings**, known for its popular caravan ground. During summer weekends, and particularly the August bank holiday, the Atlantic Drive has its share of vehicles but otherwise the road provides an enjoyable route for cycling and walking, with photogenic views of Horn Head and Tory Island. The extremity at **Melmore Head** (Meall Mor) is worth visiting, passing on your way a hostel occupying a **hunting lodge** designed by Lutyens and a signpost pointing the way to the ruined **Meagh Church** with its ancient Latin cross and Ogham stone.

There are no bus services serving the Peninsula or Carrigart and so you will need your own transport.

Fanad Peninsula → *Phone code: 074. Colour map 1, grid A2/3.*

Travelling south from Carrigart and reaching nondescript Milford, the R246 can be taken for an approach up the west side of the Fanad Peninsula but it's hard to think of a good reason for making this journey because the scenery is unspectacular and there is nothing that compels a stop. The west coast has far more to recommend it, but if time is limited and a choice has to be made, the Inishowen Peninsula further east (see page 478) wins hands down in terms of stirring scenery.

Rathmelton Rathmelton is the first town on the west coast and though its slightly rickety appearance is not instantly endearing, the place can grow on you and a picnic could be enjoyed on the quayside overlooking the River Leannan (also spelled Lennon), as it flows past towards Lough Swilly. Behind you stand some ramshackle but attractively gaunt warehouses that date back to the second half of the 19th century when Rathmelton prospered from corn mills, linen works and a brewery. The **Meeting House** *T074-9151266*, in the village, now restored as a genealogical centre, dates back to the 17th century when Rathmelton was laid out by William Stewart, a Scottish planter.

You'll see signs to **Killydonnell Friary**, 6 km away, and though only the ruins remain, the tranquil setting is another inviting picnic spot. The River Leannan is a favourite cast for salmon and, though the nearest place for gear and tackle is Letterkenny (see page 477), fishing packages can be arranged through the Bridge Bar, T074-9151119.

Rathmullan There are satisfying views of Lough Swilly from Rathmelton to Rathmullan, and as you approach the village the ruins of **Rathmullan Priory** are on your right. From just outside this Carmelite friary, founded in the 15th century, an event took place in September 1607, when "leaving their horses on the shore with no one to hold their bridles, they went aboard a ship". The "they" in question included the earls of Tyrone and Tyrconnell, and their departure, with other members of the cream of Irish aristocracy, signalled the end of a millennium of Gaelic rule in Ireland, and the *Annals of the Four Masters* (see box on page 455) recorded the significance of the event known to history as the Flight of the Earls: "Woe to the heart that meditated, woe to the mind that conceived, woe to the council that decided on, the project of their setting out on this voyage."

In the centre of Rathmullan village the **Heritage Centre** ⓘ *T074-9158178, Easter to mid-Sep Mon-Sat 1000-1800, Sun 1200-1800, €2.50,* unfolds the historical background and consequences of the event through a series of text-based displays. If the lovely safe beach at Rathmullan tempts you to stay in the area the Heritage Centre also doubles as an unofficial tourist information office.

Fanad Head The journey to the northern tip of the Peninsula is signposted as the Fanad Drive and includes, a little way before the village of Portsalon, a viewing point that looks down on Ballymastocker Bay and its triple array of beaches. A left turn in the village of Portsalon, where nothing need detain you other than a couple of places to eat, leads on along the coast to Fanad Head and a lighthouse. The nearby Lighthouse Tavern, T074-9159212, serves a quiet pint.

Letterkenny → *Phone code: 074. Colour map 1, grid A2.*

Letterkenny is County Donegal's largest town, a thriving commercial centre with good transport links and supermarkets but with little of intrinsic interest. A number of main roads converge on the town, from Donegal in the west and Derry in the east, while the N56 heads up to the northern coast accessing Glenveagh National Park and the must-see Glebe House (see below) along the way. Letterkenny is a good place to stop over for a meal or collect provisions for a picnic on the Fanad or Inishowen Peninsula. The town also has some indoor activities, including the local history **Donegal County Museum** ⓘ *High St, T074-9124613. Mon-Fri 1000-1630 (closed 1230-1300), Sat 1300-1630. Free.*

On the R250 Churchill Rd the **Newmills Corn and Flax Mills** ⓘ *T074-9125115, mid-Jun to mid-Sep, daily 1000-1830, OPW site, 5 km from Letterkenny, €2.50*, is a complex of machinery powered by one of the largest watermills in Ireland, using the power of the River Swilly.

The **tourist office** is a couple of kilometres out of town on the Derry road, T074-9121160. Open Jun-Aug Mon-Fri 0900-1800, Sat 1000-1600, Sun 1200-1500; Sep-May Mon-Fri 0900-1700.

Around Letterkenny

★ Glebe House and Gallery ⓘ *T074-9137071. Easter week and mid-May to 27 Sep Sat-Thu 1100-1830. €2.75. 18 km west of Letterkenny on R251. For good value it is hard to beat the €2.75 cost of admission to Glebe House and Gallery.* Everything about this house is a wonderful surprise. Inside you will find paintings by Picasso, Kokoschka, Jack Yeats, Passmore and Bonnard, not to mention some work by the Tory Island painters that Derek Hill, the man who made Glebe House so special, inspired to take up a brush and easel. Hill decorated his Regency house with William Morris textiles alongside superb touches of Islamic and other oriental art. To cap it all there are beautiful gardens that sweep down to the lake shore.

Colmcille Heritage Centre ⓘ *Gartan, Churchill, 24 km north of Letterkenny, T074-9137306. Easter week and from 1st Sun in May to last Sun in Sep, Mon-Sat 1030-1830, Sun 1300-1830. €2.* The life story of St Colmcille, an important Irish saint, up there with St Patrick and St Brigid, is told through illustrated panels and a wax model and there are other displays on the era that gave rise to Ireland's epithet as the "land of saints and scholars". Perhaps the most engrossing displays are those that cover the craft of ancient manuscript-making.

Glenveagh Castle ⓘ *Churchill, T074-9137090. Daily 1000-1830. €2.75 for park, €2.75 for castle, tearoom and restaurant.* John George Adair was a 19th-century landlord who lorded it over 25,000 acres of land and was regarded as a tyrant even by his own class. When his steward was murdered in 1860 he felt sure that his tenants were behind the deed and so, over a period of three days in winter, he had all 244 of them evicted and their homes unroofed, so that "the police officers themselves could not refrain from weeping" it was said. A fund raised money for the former tenants to emigrate to Australia and many of the families left as a group to start a new life. Adair went on to build Glenveagh Castle in 1870. The property passed into the hands of the American Henry McIlhenny, who later donated the house and gardens to the state and it is now part of Glenveagh National Park. Self-guided walking trails meander through the park.

A visit to the park begins at the Visitors' Centre, where there are informative displays on the local ecology and the perfidious Adair. Glenveagh Castle is well worth a visit, for it is a particularly successful example of a mock castle, partly due to its setting on a promontory with the battlements set against a backdrop of mountains, and partly because this is a castle really built to defend its occupants against attack. Glenveagh Castle was built, as Williams in his definitive *Architecture in Ireland* puts it, "to ensure a sybaritic existence to inmates holding out against the vagaries of Irish politics or climate". Everything worth admiring inside, the fireplace and the wall-hangings for example, was put there by McIlhenny, while the lovely garden outside was a combined effort of McIlhenny and his wife Cornelia.

Sleeping

Glencolmcille to Gweebarra Bay *p465*

D **Nesbitt Arms Hotel**, T074-9541103, nesbitta@indigo.ie. Small 19th-century hotel in the centre of Ardara with restaurant.

D **Woodhill House**, T074-9541112, www.woodhillhouse.com. Under 3 km from Ardara taking Woodhill Rd from the Diamond. A 17th-century country house, the

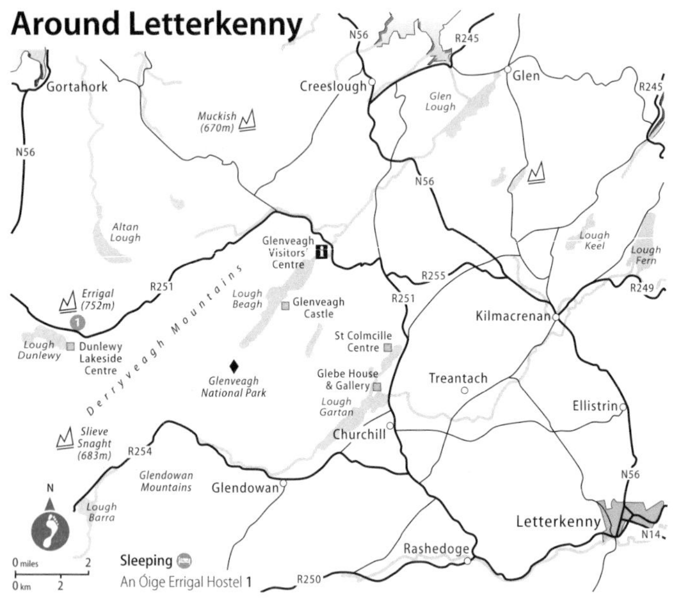

ıome of Ireland's last commercial whaling ·amily, offering quality accommodation, with estaurant and bar.

E **The Green Gate**, Ardvally, T074-9541546. A 1.5-km climb up a steep road from Ardara brings you to a traditional and tranquil cottage B&B.

E **Greenhaven**, Portnoo Rd, Ardara, T074-9541129. Named after a shipwreck, from which the ship's wheel and mast-head lamp now decorate the breakfast room. A comfy place within walking distance of town.

E **Whinecrest**, Loughros Point, T074-9541254. Away from it all with miles of beach, a turf fire, and a piano in the guest room. Open May-Sep.

F **Drumbaron Hostel**, The Diamond, Ardara, T074-9541200. Over a dozen beds and 1 private room; basic but comfortable.

Camping

Dunmore Caravan and Camping Park, Dawros Head, T074-9545121.

Tramore Beach Caravan and Camping Park, Dawros Head, T074-9551491.

Glenties and around *p465*

C **Highlands Hotel**, Main St, Glenties, T074-9551111, www.thehighlandshotel.com. The only hotel in the area. Smallish, family-run, good restaurant.

E **Avalon**, Glen Rd, Glenties, T074-9551292. B&B in a bungalow.

F **Marguerite's**, Lower Main St, Glenties, T074-9551699. Townhouse B&B.

F **Campbell's Holiday Hostel**, Glenties, T074-9551491, www.campbellireland.com. A welcoming place, on the left side of the road as you enter Glenties from Ardara.

F **Finn Farm Hostel**, Cappry, Ballybofey, T074-9132261. Look for the 'Hostel' sign after a mile or so out of Ballybofey on the N15 road to Donegal. There is also camping space at this interesting hostel and information on local walks.

The Rosses *p466*

C **Viking House**, about 13 km outside Crolly, T074-9543295. Hotel owned by Daniel O'Donnell.

E **Atlantic House**, Main St, Dungloe, T074-9521061, www.atlantichouse dungloe.com. Centrally located and welcoming B&B.

E **Inismil House**, Leckenagh, Burtonport, T074-9542087. Less than 1 mile from Burtonport, a double room sharing facilities is €52, en suite bathroom is €56.

E **Sea View**, Mill Rd, Dungloe, T074-9521353. B&B, which overlooks Dungloe Bay and is walkable from the town.

F **Crohy Head Hostel**, T074-9521950. *An Óige* hostel, 8 km from Dungloe and 2 km from Maghery, is positioned on a cliff overlooking Boylagh Bay. Beaches nearby but bring provisions with you. A taxi from Dungloe costs about €12.

F **Greene's Hostel**, Cornmare Rd, Dungloe, T074-9521943, greensholidayhostel@ eircom.net. Has 12 beds and 5 private rooms. Bike hire, open all year.

F **Screag An Iolair Mountain Centre**, Tor, Crolly, T074-9548593. A hostel that receives rave reviews from travellers who enjoy the physical and metaphysical comfort of a laid-back retreat some 250 m up in the mountains. Open Mar-Sep, with 12 beds and including 3 private rooms. This is the place to stay if you desire rural bliss with sociable evenings thrown in.

Arranmore Island *p466*

E **Bonner's Bed and Breakfast**, T074-9520532. Conveniently close to where the ferry lands.

F **Arranmore Hostel**, Leabgarrow, T074-9520737. Near the pier, open all year, dorms and 2 private rooms, bikes for hire.

Gweedore to Gortahork *p467*

B-C **Ostán Gweedore Hotel**, Bunbeg, T074-9531177, www.ostangweedore.com. Good views and its own pool and leisure centre, which attracts families during holidays.

D **Ostán Radharc Na Mara** (Sea View Hotel), Bunbeg, T074-9531159, www.ostanradharcnamaranet. Nearly 40 rooms and a good seafood restaurant.

E **Foreland Heights Guesthouse**, Bloody Foreland, T074-9531785. Rooms with en suite bathrooms overlooking the Atlantic. Restaurant and a bar with live music at weekends.

F **An Óige Errigal Hostel**, Dunlewy, T074-9531180. In a perfect position if you're going to climb Mt Errigal: 3 km to the northwest of the village and stays open all year. The **Lough Swilly Bus**, T074-9122863 (Letterkenny), T048-7126 2017 (Derry), connecting Dungloe with Letterkenny and Derry will stop at Dunlewy Cross and the hostel is a 3-km walk away.

Tory Island *p468*

D-E Ostán Thóraigh, West Town, T074-9135920. Modest but comfortable, 14 beds, closes Jan-Mar. A double is around €80.

E Ms Grace Duffy, East Town, T074-9135136, graceduffytoryisland@eircom.net. Opens Apr-Oct for B&B, 3 bedrooms and a friendly atmosphere.

F Teach Bhilie, Seaview, T074-9165145. A short walk from the pier, open all year, double rooms with tea- and coffee-making facilities and a continental breakfast thrown in for around €20 per person.

Gortahork to Dunfanaghy *p468*

E Ferndale, Main St, Falcarragh, T074-9165506. At the Gortahork end of the village, a large bungalow with 4 bedrooms, one of which has its own shower, open Jun-Sep for B&B.

F Shamrock Lodge Hostel, Main St, Falcarragh, T074-9135859. Above a busy pub (traditional music on Sat, non-trad on Fri) and, depending on your tastes, this will be either a bonus or a blight. Rooms with 4 and 5 beds, one room with two beds and one family room.

Dunfanaghy *p469*

B Arnold's Hotel, T074-9136208, www.arnoldshotel.com. Has been in the same family for 3 generations and travellers have recommended it for comfort and friendliness.

E Carrigan House, Kill, T074-9136276. B&B 5 mins from the village on foot, 4 rooms with en suite bathroooms. Open Mar-Oct.

E Rockhaven, Kill, T074-9136159. A good-value B&B overlooking Sheephaven Bay. Open Apr-Sep.

E Rosman House, T074-9136273. B&B in a large bungalow with above-average room amenities and open all year.

F Corcreggan Mill, T074-9136409, www.corcreggan.com. Hostel on the N56 3 km west of Dunfanaghy. Has some character and lots of dorm beds. Some of the private rooms, admittedly special because you sleep in a wheel-less railway carriage, are tipping into the next price category; a small camping space outside.

Carrigart and Rosguill Peninsula *p470*

C Hotel Carrigart, Carrigart, T074-9155114, www.carrigarthotel.com. Built in 1882, with its mansard-style façade, plus one of Ireland's first hotel swimming pools and a challenging links golf course, this hotel is in the middle of the village and the friendly owner is a mine of local information.

D Beach Hotel, Downings, T074-9155303. Can get busy, but it's the only hotel on the Rosguill Peninsula.

E Mevagh House, Carrigart, T074-9155693. Just outside the village and close to beaches. Apr-Sep.

F Trá na Rosann, Downings, T074-9155374. *An Óige*'s most northerly hostel in Ireland, open Easter-Sep, is 6 km from Downings.

Fanad Peninsula *p470*

Rathmelton

C Frewin, T074-9151246. This restored Victorian rectory has been recommended by a reader for its comfort, good breakfasts, dinner and caring attitude.

E Crammond House, Market Sq, T074-9151055. B&B in an 18th-century house near the old grain miller's building.

E Lennon Lodge, T074-9151227/8. Round the corner from Crammond House, with some private rooms with bathroom. A good modern kitchen and a lounge for guests and a flat rate that just nudges the place into the bottom end of this price category.

Rathmullan *p470*

B Fort Royal Hotel, T074-9158100, www.fortroyalhotel.com. Good reputation for comfort and for food, set in private grounds with its own beach and tennis courts.

B Rathmullan House, Lough Swilly, T074-9158188, www.rathmullanhouse.com. 19th century hotel with award-winning gardens, indoor pool and top-notch breakfasts.

E Pier Hotel, T074-9158178. Gregarious place in the centre of the village.

Letterkenny *p471*

A-B Radisson SAS Hotel, T074-9194444, www.radissonsas.ie. This is a shiny new branch of the stylish hotel chain and easily the best place to stay.

B Castle Grove Country House Hotel, Ballymaleel, T074-9151118, www.castlegrove.com. 17th-century country house-turned-hotel. Overlooks Lough Swilly with lots of grounds, drawing room, library, classy dining room.

E Glencairn, T074-9124393. A large house with television and tea in the bedrooms, fairly typical of the B&Bs in town.

E Oaklands, 8 Oaklands Park, T074-9125529. Within walking distance of town centre and benefiting from a quiet location.

F Port Hostel, 24 Port Rd, T074-9126288. This hostel, near the cinema, is open all year but if no one answers the door, enquire at the small shop next door.

Eating

Glencolmcille to Gweebarra Bay *p465*

ŸŸ Woodhill House Restaurant, T074-9541112, Ardara. Has a licensed bar and occasional music and well-deserved reputation for good food; expect to pay around €40 in the restaurant, with bar food from 1300-1500. There are 13 pubs in Ardara and some of them serve food in between their efforts at slaking the mighty thirst of the town.

Charlie's West End Bar, Main St. Serves standard pub grub. Look out especially for the Beehive Bar.

Nancy's Bar, T074-9541187, from the Diamond, cross the bridge for the road to Glenties, serves chowder, toasties and meals from 1200 to 2100, Easter to Sep.

Nesbitt Arms, Ardara. Does good basic meals with lots of fresh seafood. There is a tearoom in the Heritage Centre serving sandwiches and cakes.

Glenties and around *p465*

-Ÿ Highlands Hotel, in the middle of Glenties. A hostelry with a comfortable and spacious eating area for bar food and meals, as well as a separate restaurant. A pasta dish or a vegetarian salad with brown bread and tea is under €10 in the bar and in the hotel's **Owenea Restaurant**, T074-9551111, for grills, chicken, duck and fish dishes.

The Rosses *p466*

Ÿ Doherty's, Main St, Dungloe. Open for breakfast, lunch and dinner.

Ÿ Lobster Pot Restaurant, Main St, Burtonport, T074-9542012. An affordable pub serving fresh seafood dishes.

ŸŸ-Ÿ Ostan na Rossan, Dungloe, T074-9522444. A hotel with a pleasant dining room doing fairly traditional food.

Arranmore Island *p466*

Some of the 6 pubs here serve light meals.

Ÿ Ferryboat Restaurant, by the pier, serves standard standard meals.

Ÿ O'Donnell's, Aphort.

Ÿ Phil Ban's Bar, near the pier in Leabgarrow.

Gweedore to Gortahork *p467*

There are a few pubs, cafés and fast-food-type places scattered along the road between Dunbeg and Derrybeg and while none is worth singling out, they will suffice for a quick bite.

ŸŸ Ostán Gweedore Hotel, Bunbeg. A good restaurant, overlooking the Atlantic from where the seafood on the menu has been caught, with an evening meal around €35.

Ÿ Lakeside Centre Restaurant, at the Dunlewy Lakeside Centre. Good value for lunch but closes early in the evening.

Ÿ Ostán Radharc Na Mara (Sea View Hotel), Bunbeg. The restaurant is less expensive, and bar food is available at both hotels.

Tory Island *p468*

ŸŸ Ostán Thóraigh, the best place for a meal; expect to pay around €10-15 for a main dish.

Ÿ Ms Grace Duffy's B&B can do an evening meal for around €15.

Gortahork to Dunfanaghy *p468*

ŸŸ Maggie Dan's, Gortahork, T074-9165022. In the centre of the village and with open fires and a pizza/wine bar this is a grand place to stop for a drink and a meal.

Dunfanaghy *p469*

ŸŸ The Mill, T074-9136985. On the shore of New Lake in a converted old building. Using local produce, a fine meal can be enjoyed in the evening for under €40; closed Mon.

Ÿ McGilloway's Oyster Bar, T074-9136438. A welcoming pub with turf fires and music.

¥ **Muck 'n' Muffins**, in the village square. Has a café above its craft shop dishing out soup, sandwiches, home-bakes and take-aways. Internet access too.

¥ **The Workhouse**, modern, airy café with flagged floor, open fire and art-work for sale, is fine for cakes.

Carrigart and Rosguill Peninsula *p470*

¥¥¥ **Hotel Carrigart**, the old-fashioned and spacious dining room here has a 5-course dinner for around €40.

¥¥-¥ **Old Glen Bar**, in the village of Glen. Has a restaurant with good seafood and meat dishes.

¥¥-¥ **Weavers Restaurant**, across the road from Hotel Carrigart. Serves dishes for around €15 and the bars do pub grub.

The Fanad Peninsula *p470*

Rathmelton

¥¥-¥ **The Bridge Bar**, signposted after crossing the bridge coming into town from the south has a fish restaurant upstairs with reasonably priced dishes.

¥ **Lennon Lodge**, T074-9151055. Has a pub that has bar food all day, with traditional music on Fri and Sat nights.

¥¥ **Mirabeau Restaurant**, The Mall, T074-9151138. Does steaks and seafood, with dishes around €12-20.

Rathmullan

¥¥¥ For good food in the €40+ bracket, the **Fort Royal Hotel** and **Rathmullan House** are equal contenders.

¥¥ **An Bonnan Bui**, close to the Pier Hotel, T074-9158453. More affordable meals, with dishes around €12-20.

¥¥ **The Water's Edge**, T074-9158182, www.theblaneygroup.com. New olde-worlde restaurant with huge windows and views over Lough Swilly. Bar food served all day and dinner should come into the mid-range. If you like the place they also do B&B.

Letterkenny *p471*

¥¥ **Yellow Pepper**, 36 Lower Main St, T074-9124133. A bistro-style café with a wine bar, open for breakfast, lunch and dinner 1030- 2200 Mon-Sat, and 1600-2000 on Sun. A catholic menu of chicken, fish, pasta and vegetarian meals ranging from €10-20.

¥ **Galfee's**, across the road from The Quiet Moment (below). Advertises itself as a gourmet takeaway, and light meals are available inside.

¥ **The Quiet Moment**, a tea-shop and sandwich bar on Upper Main St.

Pubs and music

Glenties and around *p465*

The Glen Tavern, halfway between Glenties and Fintown. Famous for its musical entertainment on a Sat night.

Keavney's, Main St, T074-9551333. Always worth a visit when sessions of traditional music are on.

Paddy's Bar, Main St, T074-9551158. Usually has a session or 2 during the week.

Tory Island *p468*

Ostán Thóraigh, worth checking out for a drink and one of the regular musical sessions during the summer.

Tory Social Club, T074-9165121. Serves drink and has regular sessions of traditional music and ceilidh dancing.

Carrigart and Rosguill Peninsula *p470*

Fleet Inn, Downings. Attracts youngsters from the caravan site, and they set the tone at the discos that take place here in summer.

Harbour Bar, is quiet during the day but a younger crowd livens it up at night.

Old Glen Bar, if the Downings pubs don't appeal to you then take the road from Carrigart to the minuscule village of Glen, where locals and knowledgeable visitors escape for a quiet drink. The television over the bar comes only on for a sports fixture (though Manchester United fans will find no comrades here) and there is the occasional burst of live music.

The Singing Pub, on the Atlantic Drive road. A heartwarming, traditional bar which has good music and good food.

Fanad Peninsula *p470*

Rathmelton

Beachcomber Bar, the first pub you see when coming into the village. Pleasant, does not do food, but a quiet drink can be enjoyed here with views of the water and outdoor tables by the beach.

Letterkenny *p471*
An Grianan Theatre, Port Rd, T074-9124950. Host to both local and international music, theatre and dance performances.
Brewery Bar, Market St, T074-9127330. Worth taking a look.
Central Bar, 58 Upper Main St, T074-9124088. Worth checking out.
McGinleys, 25 Lower Main St, T074-9121106. Can be relied on for traditional sessions on Mon nights.

Shopping

Glencolmcille to Gweebarra Bay *p465*
There are many factory shops in Ardara and they are all worth sampling for their share of shirts, hats, caps, ties, socks, grandfather shirts, table linen, scarves, rugs and throws. Their tweeds and knitwear, which find their way into Bloomingdales and Liberty's, include items that are sold only in their own stores.
Stephen Bennet, a couple of miles out of town on the Portno Rd, T074-9541652, www.stephenbennet.net. Landscapes and figurative paintings for sale in his studio.
Bonner, Front St, T074-9541303.
Kennedy, Front St, T074-9541106.
McGills, at the west end of Main St, T074-9541262.
John Molloy, outside of town on the Killybegs Rd, T074-9541133. You can buy tweeds and knitwear and in the summer there are free tours of the factory.

Dunfanaghy *p469*
The Gallery, next door to the workhouse, T074-9136224. Has a vast collection of pottery, clothes, handbags, prints and jewellery, besides its main gallery of paintings for sale. In the coffee shop at the Workhouse, shifting art exhibitions of work that is also for sale.
McAuliffe's, in the village centre, T074-9136135. Craft shop with knitwear and handcrafts and a overseas mailing service.

Activities and tours

The Rosses *p466*
Fishing Trips can be organized with the **Burtonport Sea Angling and Boating Centre**, T074-9542077, on their 36-ft (11-m) boat.

Dunfanaghy *p469*
Golf **Dunfanaghy**, T074-9136335. 18-hole.

Horse riding **Dunfanaghy Stables**, Arnold's Hotel, Dunfanaghy, T074-9136208.

Fishing **Dunfanaghy Angling Association**, T074-9136208.
Pat Robinson, Kill, Dunfanaghy, T074-9136290. Dessie McGilloway.

Carrigart and Rosguill Peninsula *p470*
Diving **Mevagh Dive Centre**, T074-9154708, www.mevaghdiving.com. Courses for beginners.

Fishing 3-hr trips for mackerel off a boat, T074-9155386, depart from Downings at 1300 and 1800, Mon-Fri, gear provided and cost depends on number of people.

Horse riding **Carrigart Riding Course**, T074-9153583.

Letterkenny *p471*
Fishing **McCormick's**, 56 Upper Main St, T074-9127833. Fishing gear.
West Donegal Sea Angling Charters, Annagry east, T074-9548403, 95484035, mosh@indigo.ie.

Transport

Northern Donegal *p465*
Bike hire Don Byrne Bikes, West End, Ardara, T074-9541658. Bike hire is available on Tory Island, T074-9565614.

Bus Bus Éireann has 2 buses a day in Jul and Aug connecting **Ardara** with **Killybegs** and the rest of the year the service operates on Tue, Thu and Fri. T074-9121309. McGeehans Coaches, T074-9546150, also run through Ardara on routes to **Dublin**, **Glencolmcille** and **Letterkenny**.

McGeehan Coaches, also stop in **Glenties** and **Fintown** and so does Bus Éireann's **Dublin-Donegal-Killybegs** bus and the local **Killybegs** to **Glenties** service, T074-9121309. Feda O'Donnell's, T074-9748114, **Galway** to **Croilly** bus goes via **Ballybofey**, **Falcarragh** and **Dunfanaghy**.

McGeehan Coaches also have a daily service in the summer between **Dublin** and

Burtonport via **Dungloe**, **Donegal** and **Enniskillen**. Feda O'Donnell runs a limited service between **Annagry** and **Killybegs**, which stops in **Dungloe**, but check which days the bus operates. O'Donnell Buses, T074-9548356, run a daily service that leaves **Donegal** early in the morning to reach **Belfast** at noon via **Derry**, stopping at **Dungloe**, **Burtonport**, **Dunfanaghy**, **Cresslough** and **Letterkenny**.

Lough Swilly Bus, T074-9122863 (Letterkenny), T048-7126 2017 (Derry), runs a **Derry-Dungloe** service, Mon-Sat, via **Burtonport**, **Crolly**, **Falcarragh**, **Dunfanaghy** and **Letterkenny**.

John McGinley's, T074-9135201, twice-daily **Donegal** to **Dublin** bus stops in **Falcarragh** and **Dunfanaghy** (0735, 1555).

From Bus Éireann's large bus station in **Letterkenny**, T074-9121309, daily buses run to and from **Dublin**, **Galway**, **Westport**, **Sligo**, **Derry**, **Enniskillen** and **Belfast**. Private bus companies also stop near here, including John McGinley's daily service, T074-9135201, between **Cresslough** and **Dublin** via Letterkenny, McGeehan's, T074-9546150, daily route between **Glencolmcille** and Letterkenny. North West Busway's, T074-9382619, daily services to **Inishowen**, **Derry** and **Dublin**.

Ferry **Arranmore Island**: Arranmore Island Ferries Service, T074-9520532, www.arainnmhor.com/ferry, runs a all-year service from **Burtonport**. In Jul and Aug there are 8 boats departing daily (7 on Sun) from 0830-2000 and returning 0900-2030. Between Apr and Jun, and in Sep, there are 6-7 journeys a day, and around 5 a day the rest of the year. €9 return for passengers, €26 return for a car and driver.

Tory Island: Donegal Coastal Cruises, T074-9531320/9531340, from **Bunbeg**, Apr, May, Jun and Sep, daily at 0900, or from **Magheraroarty** at 1130 1700, returning to Bunbeg at 1030 and to Magheraroarty at 1600 and 1800. In Jul and Aug there is also a 1330 departure from Magheraroarty but no 1800 return. In Oct there is 1 daily sailing from Bunbeg and more from Magheraroarty at weekends. Nov-May there are 7 sailings a week from Bunbeg. Always check departure times as the schedule is subject to the weather. €20 return.

Taxi Letterkenny Cabs, T1800-272000. Swilly Cabs, T1800-216666.

The Inishowen Peninsula

The Inishowen Peninsula reaches out into the north Atlantic and a more extreme and isolated spot is hard to find in the British Isles. At its furthermost point it becomes Malin Head, Ireland's most northerly point while to its east and west it is bounded by huge loughs. There is something enticing and irresistible about simply reaching this extremity of land and the pleasure which accompanies this achievement lies in the lyrical desolation of the Peninsula's landscapes. Driving around here conveys more about what life must have been like for the peasant farmers of Ireland than any heritage centre can. The mountain scenery, and ancient sites, are good for the soul. Better for the children stuck in the back of your car are the lovely, sandy deserted beaches where they can run amok and no one will hear them scream. The area is often visited on speedy four-wheeled trips but as a place where people linger it is probably one of Ireland's least-known peninsulas and worth a few nights' stay to do it justice.

▸▸ *For Sleeping, Eating and other listings, see pages 481-483.*

Ins and outs

Getting there The route that follows works its way up the Lough Swilly west side through Fahan and Buncrana and along to Carndonagh then north to Malin Head. The route then returns down the east side to Inishowen Head before moving down the coast along Lough Foyle and into Derry. Much of the way is signposted as the

Inishowen 100 (*Inis Eoghain 100*), from the approximate distance in miles it takes to complete a circuit of the peninsula. ▸▸ *See Transport, page 483, for further details.*

Grianán of Aileach → *Phone code: 074. Colour map 1, grid A3.*

Grianán of Aileach is a stone fort strategically placed overlooking the flat land that separates the Inishowen Peninsula from the rest of the county. Built during the early Christian period, it was the headquarters of the O'Neill clan who ruled from here for centuries until a revengeful king of Munster attacked in 1101 and, so the story goes, ordered his men each to take away a stone from the walls. What you see today is largely a 19th-century reconstruction but managed more sensitively than many similar sites in the Republic.

There is no charge to visit the stone fort, unlike the nearby Grianán of Aileach Visitor Centre, on the main road where you turn off for the fort, which offers a fairly uninspiring exhibition on the top floor devoted to the fort's history.

Burt Church, the modern functioning church that stands on the corner before turning uphill for the stone fort, was designed in the mid-1960s by the same team of architects that produced St Michael's church at Cresslough. Like much of the best of modern Irish church architecture, St Michael's comes from the practise of Liam McCormick and partners. Cresslough is a curved shape which fits into the mountain backdrop, using ideas thought up by Le Corbusier in the 1950s such as spouting gargoyles and irregular coloured glass windows. This church, with its curving copper roof and sharp spire, echoes these ideas as well as looking towards the shapes of the stone fort.

★ Fahan and Buncrana → *Phone code: 074. Colour map 1, grid A3.*

There are three reasons to stop in the village of Fahan: a modest but good beach, superb food for an evening meal that outclasses anything Buncrana can offer and a cross-slab near the modern church that dates from around the eighth century, decorated with elegant Latin crosses and carrying a barely decipherable but unique Greek inscription from early Christian Ireland.

There is very little reason to stop in Buncrana, even though this is the main town and resort on the peninsula. The beach (5 km long) attracts crowds of Irish holidaymakers during the summer but you can escape the hustle and bustle by seeking out the small beach that is reached by a path from the pier at the north end of the long main street.

Buncrana to Ballyliffin

An alternative to the direct inland route to Carndonagh from Buncrana involves taking the R238 road north and following signs for **Dunree Fort** ⓘ *T074-9361817, Jun-Sep Mon-Sat 1000-1800, Sun 1300-1800, €4,* where there is a small military museum with displays on the fort's history, assorted weaponry and a tea-room. It is not very interesting, but the small sheltered beach has its charm and there are fabulous views of Lough Swilly across to Fanad Head.

The Rusty Nail, T074-9376116, is a fine old country pub that serves food in the evenings during the summer and a popular Sunday lunch.

Back on the main road the journey continues north up through the dramatic Mamore Gap before descending 243 m and bringing **Dunaff Head** and the bay into view. Shortly after the Rusty Nail pub a signposted turning off to the left leads to sandy Tullagh Bay, while the R238 continues on to the village of Clonmany where an angling festival takes place annually in August. A little way before entering the next village of Ballyliffin, on the main road, bicycles can be hired from **McEleney's Cycles**, T074-9376541, and day trips made to nearby **Pollan Bay**, which is sandy but not safe for swimming, or you could visit to **Doagh Famine Village** ⓘ *T074-9378078, Easter-Sep, 1000-1730, €5,* which focuses on the impact of the Famine.

Self-catering in Donegal

Ramelton: Regina Gibson, T074-9151246, www.zaccommodation donegal.net. Sleeps 2-3 in a cottage from €450 to €525 per week.
Fanad: Sheila Mailey, T74-9121646. Sleeps up to 4 in 2-bedroomed little house with sea view. From €150 midweek to €280 in summer.
Donegal Town: Eileen McElhinney, T074-9722354. Sleeps up to 8 in stone-built house at Mountcharles, from €200 midweek to €650 in Jul and Aug.
Malin: Marian Doherty, T074-9379294. 4-bedroom bungalow, 6 km from Main and 4 km from beach.From €60 nightly to €400 in Jul and Aug, available all year.
Moville: River House, T074-9382052, hknorris@hotmail.com. Sleeps from 7 to 10 from €375 to €550 in 3 houses set in private woodlands.
Dunfanaghy: Lafferty's Holiday Homes, T074-9136247, james lafferty@eircom.net. 3-bedroom cottages sleep 6, Apr-Sep, from €300 to €730 in pretty countryside.

Carndonagh → *Phone code: 074. Colour map 1, grid A3.*

The alternative inland route to Carndonagh is by way of the R238 to Drumfree and then the R244. It is the quickest way to reach Malin Head from Buncrana and takes you across flat and lonely countryside where turf is still cut. Carndonagh is an undistinguished small town but a useful watering hole and home to the last supermarket south before Malin Head.

One reason to stay hereabouts for a night or two might be the surprising number of early Christian sites in the vicinity (ask at the helpful tourist office for more details). Entering the village from Ballyliffin you will have already have passed **Donagh Church,** where there is a group of early Christian monuments made up of a cross and two carved stones from around the ninth century, while to the east of town there are the **Carrowmore high crosses** and the **Clonca Church cross**. They are not visually arresting and will prove disappointing if you are expecting something along the lines of Clonmacnoise; but some archaeologists think they may be the result of some independent missionary movement from Scotland.

Malin and Malin Head → *Phone code: 074. Colour map 1, grid A3.*

The R238 presses on to the village of Malin, situated where a charming 10-arch stone bridge crosses Trawbreaga Bay. The neat triangular village green bears testimony to its origins as a 17th- century planter's creation and the sparse tidiness of the place evokes a suitable sense of the terminal. North of the village a signposted detour leads to **Five Fingers Strand** and the oldest church (1784) still functioning on the peninsula. The beach is exhilarating to walk along but swimming is dangerous here.

Malin Head, marked by the remains of a 19th-century signal tower, lacks visual drama, so your imagination must get to work on the flat vista of surrounding grass that faces out to uninhabited Inishtrahull Island. You are standing on the most northerly piece of Irish mainland and the next stop north is Greenland. Weather reports, first recorded here in 1870, still feature in the Shipping Forecast and the buildings of the meteorological station can be seen at the head. Just east of the head, **The Cottage** has some photographs of historical interest and a path leads east past the Seaview Tavern to the **Wee House of Malin**, a hermit's rock cell in the cliff. Birdwatchers can listen for the elusive corncrake and in autumn time migrating gannets, shearwaters and skuas pass overhead.

Culdaff → *Colour map 1, grid A3.*

The route south that avoids going back through Malin takes you through the small village of Culdaff before carrying on through fairly deserted countryside as far as Moville or by way of a narrow winding road to Stroove. But there is more to Culdaff than meets the eye. In late June every year the **Culdaff Sea Angling Festival** (T074-9379141) attracts anglers from all over the country and overseas for cash prizes, cups and trophies.

In early October the **Charles Macklin Autumn School** is an arts festival (T074-9379104, 074-9397427, www.charlesmacklin.com) based around the life of the actor and playwright Charles Macklin (1697-1797). The festival lasts over three days of a weekend and includes drama, storytelling, the ancient Irish tradition of recitation, music sessions, creative writing workshops, art exhibitions and visiting writers.

While both these occasions bring seasonal life and laughter to Culdaff, there is also entertainment most of the time at the remarkable McGrory's pub (see page 482).

Bocan stone circle lies to the south of Culdaff near Bocan church, but many of the stones have collapsed.

Stroove to Muff

The lough-facing east side of the Inishowen Peninsula stretches from Stroove and Inishowen Head to the blink-and-it's-gone village of Muff barely inside the border with Northern Ireland. At Stroove there is a signposted walk, with fine views of Inishowen Head along the way, to picnic tables near a lighthouse, and you could walk from here to Kinnagoe Bay and return by the same route.

Greencastle is a fishing port at the mouth of Lough Foyle with the ruins of a castle that are crumbling away on the coast and an early 19th-century fort, which is now a bar and restaurant (see page 482). There is a fair choice of places to enjoy a meal, and infinitely better than what is available further down the coast in listless **Moville**.

The R238 hugs the coast all the way from Moville to the tiny village of **Muff**, where there is more going on than meets the eye. The place comes alive when the annual festival (T074-9384024, 074-9384982, www.mcdco-op.com) is unleashed over the holiday weekend at the end of July. This is a family festival aimed chiefly at local people with activities for children during the daytime and music sessions in the evening. If you want to experience rural Ireland at its best this would be a good place to aim for during the long weekend.

Sleeping

Fahan and Buncrana *p479*

L-C **St John's Country House and Restaurant**, at the Buncrana end of Fahan, T074-9360289. By the shores of Lough Swilly; offers comfortable accommodation (with an exemplary breakfast) and a delightful dinner experience (see below).

Carndonagh *p480*

Ashdale Farmhouse, Malin Rd, T074-9374017, www.ashdalehouse@eircom.net. A 2-storey farmhouse on the road to Malin.

Malin and Malin Head *p480*

C-D **Malin Hotel**, Malin, T074-9370645, malinhotel@eircom.net. Faces the green and is distinctively coloured both inside and out.

F **Malin Head Hostel**, Malin Head, 2 miles (3 km) from the headland, on the left side of the road, T074-9370309. Open Mar-Oct. Tidy, clean and efficient and bike hire available.

G **Sandrock Holiday Hostel**, Port Ronan Pier, Malin Head, T074-9370289, sandrockhostel@eircom.net. Open all year, cheaper than the other hostel, has a laundry, bikes for hire and suggested walking routes. No private rooms.

For an explanation of the sleeping and eating price codes used in this guide, see inside the front cover. Other relevant information is found in Essentials pages 39-45.

Culdaff *p481*
D **McGrory's**, T074-9379104. 10 bedrooms with their own bathroom facilities.
E **Ceecliff House**, T074-9379159. B&B in a modern house for around €30 per person.

Stroove to Muff *p481*
E **Admiralty House**, Moville, T074-9382529. Overlooking Lough Foyle and a 5-min walk from Moville but only open Jun-Aug.
E **Bruach An Domhain**, T074-9367359. A restored coastguard station overlooking Tremone Bay. Open Apr-Oct for B&B.
E **Dunroman**, Carrownaffe, Moville, T074-9382234. Also overlooking Lough Foyle but open all year and set in a quiet cul-de-sac.

Eating

Fahan and Buncrana *p479*
TTT **St John's Country House and Restaurant**, T074-9360289. Dinner begins with drinks in a late 18th-century room with a turf fire burning. The understated menu disguises exquisitely simple dishes and the fair-priced wine list makes the €40-dinner money well spent.
TT **Railway Tavern**, Fahan, T074-9360137. Bar and restaurant, food cooked on an open wood-burning firebox. Open for dinner Tue-Sun 1800-2200 and for lunch on Sun.
T **The Town Clock Restaurant**, 6 Main St, Buncrana, T074-9363279. More of a café and opens for breakfast, lunch and dinner.

Carndonagh *p480*
TTT **Corncrake Restaurant**, Malin St, on your right leaving the village for Malin, T074-9374534. A good meal is available here, starters like mussels in cream sauce or crab soufflé to Donegal lamb. Home-cooking at its best. Does vegetarian dishes if book in advance. Open Tue-Sat, Jun-Sep, but only weekends at other times; main dishes €18-24.
TT **Túl Na Rí** (Simpson's Bar), outside town on the Culdaff road, T074-9374499. An olde-worlde pub serving good food 1230-2200, booking ahead is often necessary to secure an evening table.
T **The Arch Inn Bar**, in the Diamond, T074-9373029. Serves good bar food and has live music at weekends.
T **Boston Burger**, Bridge St. Does what its says over the door – burgers.
T **Bridge Street Café**. Soups and sandwiches and a take-away menu.
T **Quiet Lady**, Malin Rd, T074-9374777.
T **Sportsman Inn**, in the Diamond, T074-9374817. Does pub food.
T **Trawbreaga Bay House**, in the Diamond, T074-9374352. Serves pub food.

Malin and Malin Head *p480*
TT **Malin Hotel**, Malin. Bar food and an elegant little restaurant in the evening that has a fish, poultry and grill menu, and a dish like monkfish with coconut and curry sauce is under €20.
T **The Cottage**, Malin Head, T074-9370257. Soup and sandwiches and light meals. Open Jun-Sep 1100-1830 (from 1330 on Sun), and Mar-May Sun only.
T **Seaview Tavern**, Malin Head, T074-9370117. Ireland's most northerly pub and is open daily 0900-2100 for meals.

Culdaff *p481*
TT **McGrory's**, T074-9379104. Has a restaurant serving seafood as well as meat dishes, open Tue-Sun from 1800.

Stroove to Muff *p481*
Greencastle has a few places close to each other along the seafront.
TT **Greencastle Fort**, a little further on from Kealy's Seafood Bar, T074-9381044. An atmospheric interior in the old fort. Serves up seafood as well as steaks and duck, and the menu is chalked up on blackboards in the spacious bar area.
TT **Kealy's Seafood Bar**, T074-9381010. A seafood restaurant with a dinner menu for €35, and bar food that includes a delicious chowder. Closed Mon.

Pubs and music

Carndonagh *p480*
Bradly's, Bridge St, T074-9374526.
The Persian Bar, the Diamond, T074-9374823. Try this for pub music.
Sportsman Inn, the Diamond, T074-9374817. Has pub music.

Festivals and events

Carndonagh *p480*
In the **mid-Jul** each year the **Inishowen Agricultural Show** has competitions with

udging of sheep, cattle and horses in the morning and family activities during the afternoon. A street festival that takes place later in the month is not as much fun.

Transport

Inishowen Peninsula *p478*

Bike hire Bikes can be rented from McCallion's Bikes & Toys, Carndonagh, T074-9374084, 3 miles (5 km) from Carndonagh on the Ballyliffin Rd, usefully with delivery and collection anywhere on the peninsula.

Bus Busways, T074-9382619, run Mon-Sat buses connecting **Culdaff** and **Derry** via **Malin** and **Carndonagh**. Mon-Sat buses also connect **Greencastle** and **Derry** via **Moville** and a third service connects **Moville** and **Buncrana** via **Culdaff**, **Malin** and **Ballyliffin** (Mon-Fri, departing at 0730, 0905, 1145, and on Sat at 0905 and 1145). Lough Swilly, T074-9122863, T048-7126 2017 (office in Derry), has daily buses between **Derry** and **Moville** and, on Mon, Wed, Fri and Sat, a **Derry-Malin Head** bus via **Carndonagh**.

Ferry Lough Swilly and Lough Foyle Ferry, T074-9381901. The Lough Foyle service connects **Greencastle** with **Magilligan** in County Derry and operates a continuous shuttle service all year, Apr-Sep 0720-2150 (0900 Sun), Oct-Mar 0720-1950 (0900 Sun), costing €2 (£1.40) single, for foot passengers/cars and €3.50 (£2.40) return. Pay in euro or sterling.

County Derry

Derry

→ *Colour map 1, grid A3.*

Derry is a lovely, compact, vibrant little city, full of business and bustle, where life has moved on from the Troubles but without turning its back on the suffering and sacrifices endured by its citizens in the past. Highlights of a visit include the intact 17th-century walls and the equally ancient cathedral. The modern Tower Museum is a model of well-balanced and fascinating storytelling and the well-run tourist office does excellent tours of the Bogside which give you an idea of the city's turbulent history, as well as the more traditional tours of the city walls and architecture. Derry's a place you won't want to leave, so if you have time plan for at least an overnight stay. There is music in the bars at night, some good restaurants offer exciting food and the number of quality hotels grows every year. ▸▸ *For Sleeping, Eating and other listings, see pages 490-492.*

Ins and outs

Getting there Derry is a very accessible city. The airport, T7181 784, www.cityofderryairport.com, is 7 miles (11 km) northeast of the city on the A2, and access to the city is by **Ulsterbus** service 143 or taxi. Derry's Waterside railway station, T7134 228, is on the eastern side of the River Foyle, and there is a free bus service to and from the Ulsterbus depot in Foyle Street. **Express Ulsterbus**, T7126 2261, Foyle St, buses, connect Derry with the Republic and towns in Northern Ireland. ▸▸ *See Transport, page 492, for further details.*

Phone code: 048 if phoning from the Republic but within Northern Ireland only phone the 8-digit number. Use 00+353 + the area code without the '0' to phone the Republic from Derry.

Getting around Local buses begin their journeys at the Ulsterbus depot: they are indicated by the letter 'D' in front of the service number. Black taxis wait at Foyle Street and collect a full load of passengers before setting off. Regular cabs operate around the city in the usual manner; ask the price before you set off, since few have meters.

Information Derry tourist office, 44 Foyle St, T7126 7284, www.derryvisitor.com. Open Jul-Sep Mon-Fri 0900-1900, Sat 1000-1800, Sun 1000-1700; mid-Mar to Jun and Oct Mon-Fri 0900-1700, Sat 1000-1700; rest of year Mon-Fri 0900-1700.

History → *See also page 592.*

Early history The earliest settlement here was in an oak grove on an island in the River Foyle. Archaeological sites reveal that people lived hereabouts and revered the wooded hill long before St Colmcille (Columba) built a monastery on it in the sixth century. During medieval times, it expanded into a flourishing town with prestigious buildings, a school and the patronage of the MacLochlains, a local clan who claimed the kingship of all Ireland.

English settlement In 1566, an unsuccessful English garrison was established in the town. Then, at the turn of the 17th century, a more concerted attempt at settlement was made when another garrison was established and the town was given the status of city, but the settlement lasted only until 1608, when the O'Dohertys attacked it and erased the English presence.

Under James I a new settlement was established in 1613 using Protestant settlers from Scotland and England, who were more likely to be loyal to the crown. The project was financed by the wealthy London guilds, which is why the city spent the next 38 years under the name 'Londonderry'. Great walls were erected around the city, while within them stone buildings were constructed, including St Columb's Cathedral. Despite this, the population grew slowly, perhaps deterred by the continuing unrest in the province. In 1649 England's internal divisions came to Derry when the city fathers declared themselves in support of the English Republic. The Catholic Irish and the Scottish Presbyterian settlers, all of whom were condemned to live outside the city walls, besieged the town in support of King Charles I. Strangely, this is one act of loyalty to the crown that the Apprenticeboys don't celebrate each year.

The siege of Derry The big event in Derry's history started on the day in 1688 when some apprentices shut the city gates against Catholic troops loyal to James II because the town had declared its allegiance to William of Orange. As a result, Protestants fled to the city, increasing its population from around 2,000 to 30,000. A siege began later that same year and lasted 105 days. After a third of the people inside had died, of mortar attack or starvation, the siege was finally broken by a fleet of ships that broke through the barriers across the river. The siege held up the Catholic forces long enough for William of Orange to gather strength and win the Battle of the Boyne and the event is celebrated every year with bonfires and the ritual burning of an effigy of Protestant governor Robert Lundy, who escaped from the siege, went to London and was forever known in the city as a traitor.

The 20th century Over the next few centuries Derry developed as a major textile centre and more sadly a major emigration point for the poor, both Catholic and Protestant, who left Ireland for America. In the 20th century Derry suddenly found itself a border town when six of the counties of Ulster became 'Northern Ireland'. Like the other cities of Northern Ireland, sectarianism had become a major problem in Derry with streetfighting between Catholics and Protestants in 1920 and the withdrawal of the police force, the Royal Ulster Constabulary, from rural areas. Organizations like the IRA and UVF operated within their own communities and the struggle, as in Belfast, was over scarce jobs, housing and land.

The Second World War brought prosperity and activity to Derry, as it became a base for refuelling and rearming destroyers and other escort ships for the transatlantic convoys. In early 1941 technicians from the US arrived in Derry and began building a new quay, a ship repair base, a radio station and personnel camps

Derry's part in the Troubles

In October 1968 civil rights marchers in Derry including John Hume, Gerry Fitt (both leaders of the moderate SDLP) and three Westminster Labour MPs were trapped by police and bludgeoned till they fled. The event was filmed by an Irish film crew and broadcast worldwide – Ulster policemen were seen randomly hitting out at demonstrators and bystanders alike. This event was the trigger that sent Northern Ireland spiralling into the Troubles. Prior to this, the RUC had commanded the respect of the minority communities in Northern Ireland.

By 1969 the civil rights movement had grown, become largely Catholic and contained Socialist and Republican elements, who had their own goals – a socialist Republic of Ireland. A march planned from Belfast to Derry turned into utter chaos as Loyalists attacked the participants, who got no protection from the police – on the contrary, they were seen and filmed joining in the with attacks. In Derry, policemen smashed their way into a supermarket and attacked shoppers; in the Bogside policemen rioted in the streets smashing windows and attacking anyone foolish enough to be out. All of this fuelled the Free Derry movement: its slogan appeared on the gable end of a block of houses; moderates left the movement and it became dominated by Republicans. Support for the IRA, which had been practically defunct, increased.

The Battle of the Bogside began in August 1969, when fighting broke out between the Loyalist Apprentice Boy marchers and Catholics from the Bogside. The battle raged for two days, and CS gas was fired into the Bogside. The Taoiseach, Jack Lynch, called for the UN to enter what was effectively an out-of-control situation. Finally British troops entered the city, replacing the RUC. But three years later worse was to come: in January 1972 a civil rights march was fired on by paratroopers, killing 13, many of whom were shot in the back. Another person died later of his wounds. The event came to be known as Bloody Sunday.

During this time parts of the city had become no-go areas for the army. After a series of IRA bombs in Belfast and Derry the British Prime Minister, James Callaghan, gave the order to clear the no-go areas, and Operation Motorman began. Tanks and armoured cars were brought into the city as the biggest British military operation since Suez began in the Bogside and in Protestant no-go areas.

By May 1942 there were 149 vessels and 20,000 American sailors based in Derry. A massive underground bunker and the most important radio station in the Western Approaches made Derry a vital link in the war in the Atlantic.

After the war Derry found itself a manufacturing city on the extreme west of the United Kingdom. It attracted few big businesses, and unemployment rose to about 10 times that of the rest of Northern Ireland. Housing became a big issue, as the Unionist-run city council was afraid to extend the city's boundaries with housing estates since it might affect their electoral chances. Moderate organizations such as the Derry Housing Associations raised money to build houses while the protests against Unionist policy grew ever more vocal and physical.

To the present day Over the years new housing developments went up on the east bank and were allocated to Protestants, while Catholics moved into the untenanted houses they left behind. The river became a peace line with only the Fountains area on the west bank remaining Protestant. Gradually, the old slums of the Bogside were cleared and wide boulevards were created. In the early 1990s a major programme of investment began, clearing bombed-out buildings within the city walls, rebuilding the courthouse, creating the craft village, the museum and the genealogy centre. For many years there has been genuine power-sharing in this city which could teach some of the big names in Belfast quite a lot about compromise.

Sights

The city centre of Derry can easily be experienced in a day's wander around the walls, dropping down into the city to visit the various sights. The sights of Derry, as set out below, take in a clockwise walk of the city walls beginning at Shipquay Gate.

★ **The city walls** Considering Derry's history, it is amazing the walls are intact: two-storey ramparts of earth and stone a mile long with a wide protected walkway along their top. Starting the walk at Shipquay Gate, one can imagine the 17th-century walled town. The gate had a drawbridge that could be closed against attackers and the river lapped against the walls themselves.

Inside Shipquay Gate there are steps up on to the wall, which you can follow in a clockwise direction. At regular intervals bastions project out beyond the walls; they were used as defensive positions when the city was under attack. Beyond the third gate, **New Gate**, the Church of Ireland cathedral comes into view with its tower projecting above the walls. During the siege of Derry the tower was given wooden platforms for the defenders to use. The walls around the church are built higher than usual, again as a defensive measure during the siege. Beyond the church and outside the walls is the Fountains area, distinguished by its red, white and blue decorations.

Approaching **Bishop's Gate** you can see the one remaining tower of the old Derry jail which has a long list of famous inmates including Wolf Tone, the leader of the United Irishmen, and Eamon de Valera, later president of Ireland. Descending by the Bishop's Gate, notice the carved ornamentation on the gate, which is built like a triumphal arch, rebuilt in 1789 to honour William of Orange. After its construction a united procession of church leaders passed through the gate (in those days William of Orange represented order, not sectarianism). Passing along Bishop's Gate Within you pass the pink, columned **Bishop's Palace** on the left where Cecil Frances Alexander, the wife of a later bishop lived, famous for writing a collection of hymns for children including those old favourites There is a Green Hill and All Things Bright and Beautiful. On the right is the **courthouse**, which suffered three car bomb attacks and was restored in 1994. Turning right brings you past the Irish Society (The Honourable) houses where the clergy live and into the grounds of the Cathedral.

St Columb's Cathedral ⓘ *T7126 7313, www.stcolumbscathedral.org. Mar-Oct Mon-Sat 0900-1700, Nov-Feb Mon-Sat 0900-1300, 1400-1600. £1.50.* The cathedral was built by the Irish Society between 1628 and 1633 and is one of the few churches in Ireland that is in a single style – late Gothic. The spire is the church's third – the first was wooden and was pulled down in preparation for the siege (see page 484), the lead being used to make bullets; another spire went up in 1778 but was taken down again in 1801 because it was about to fall down, and the spire you see before you was put in its place. The interior is impressive, and has great wooden pews, those at the back very usefully allowing people to rest their heads while listening to interminable sermons. The regular pew ends are all individually carved, and the Gothic roof arches rest on the carved heads of past bishops.

The church also houses some crumbling flags, one of which is a pre-St Patrick's cross Union Jack. The yellow flags are replacements for Bastille flags taken from the

St Columb's Cathedral is the first post-Reformation church to have been built in the British Isles.

besieging French troops of 1689; they ought to be white, but when the replacements were made, the originals had turned yellow with age and that yellow was taken for the correct colour. The other flags were donated by American battalions stationed in Derry during the war. There is a silver cross made of roof nails from the ruins of Coventry cathedral. The Chapter House is a treasure of junk – a chair said to be made from the pear tree that Robert Lundy climbed when he escaped from the besieged city, huge padlocks used to lock the gates of the city, gold pieces given by William to his loyal supporters and a doctored photo of Cecil Frances Alexander (see above) – if you look

Derry city

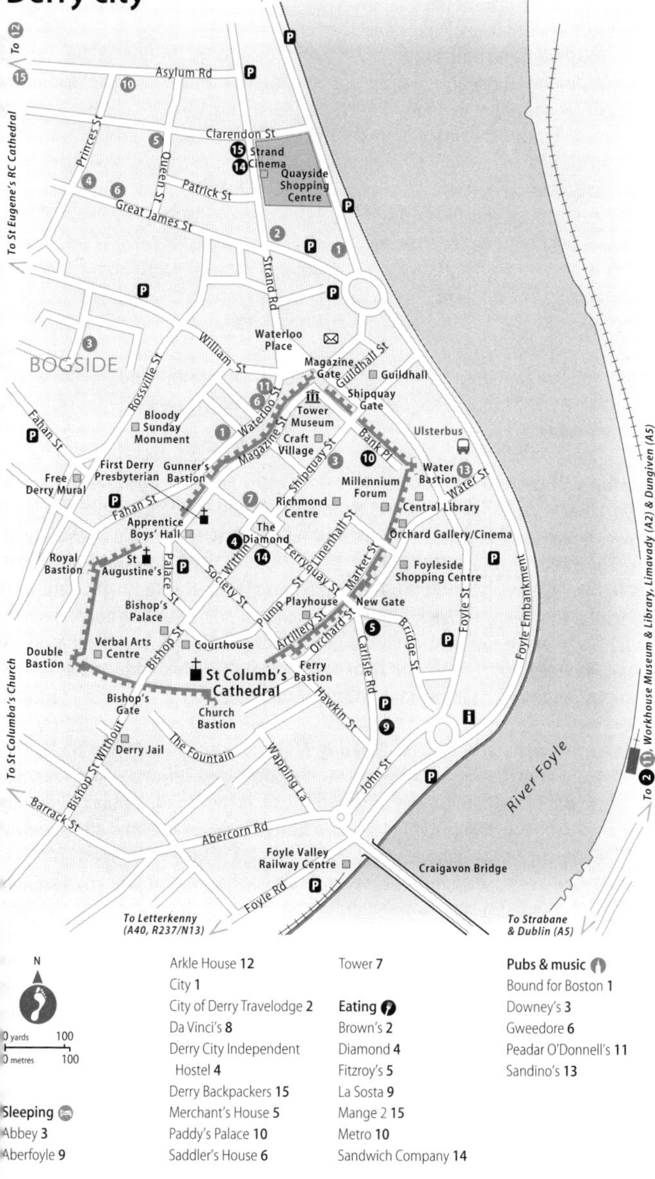

The Bogside Murals

The murals on the walls around the Free Derry mural depict key moments in the Troubles and they are the work of three local artists – Tom Kelly, Kevin Hasson and William Kelly – who lived through the conflict. 'The story of the Bogside is our story and vice versa. Our murals stand therefore as the not-too-silent witnesses to the colossal price paid in suffering and brutalization by hopelessly innocent people in their struggle for basic human rights. Our fervent wish is that the peace process will give us time to put right what has been so drastically put wrong.'

The mural of a young girl is that of 14-year-old Annette McGavigan, the 100th victim and the first child to die in the conflict. The mural of Bernadette Devlin, a leader of the civil rights movement who was elected to the British parliament, pays homage to the many women who took part in the struggle for civil rights. The banging of dustbin lids, in the background, was a familiar tactic used to alert Bogsiders to the fact that the British army were in the neighbourhood. The grey-and-white mural of a petrol bomber was painted in 1994 to mark the 25th anniversary of the Battle of the Bogside.

A book of the murals, *Murals*, is available from the Bookworm bookshop in Bishop St, T7128 2727, the Eason bookstore in the Foyleside Shopping Centre, or through www.bogsideartists.com.

closely you will see that only the face and shoulders are a photo and the body has been painted in. In the lobby is the cannonball that carried the message telling those inside to surrender.

St Columba's Church ⓘ *Off Bishop St, T7126 2301. Summer 0900-2100, winter 0900-2030.* Back up on the walls, the double-bastioned west side looks out over some waste ground and beyond to St Columba's Church, which stands on the site of Tempull Mor (the medieval cathedral). It is possible to walk down to the church through Bishop's Gate, passing the barricaded Fountains Estate on the left, and turning right at the lights at Barrack Street. The church now standing dates back to 1784, very early in the Catholic church-building era. Inside are vast quantities of Connemara marble, and banks upon banks of fluorescent lights and candles, more reminiscent of a Buddhist temple than a Catholic church.

Bogside As the walls go on, past **'Roaring Meg'**, the cannon dedicated by the London Fishmongers, the view becomes the Bogside, and beyond it the Creggan estate. Below, out of sight, tucked in behind the wall, is the monument to those who died on Bloody Sunday. To the right is the **Free Derry mural** and beyond all the newly erected and already crumbling council houses is **St Eugene's** Roman Catholic Cathedral (T7126 2894) designed by several hands, the last of which was Liam McCormack, creator of the altar in Armagh.

Behind you, inside the city walls, is the **Apprentice Boys' Hall**, built in 1937. On the walls overlooking the Bogside once stood a 27-m tall monument to George Walker, successor to Lundy and governor of Derry at the time of the siege. It was blown up in 1973, and the head changed hands several times. It was beside this statue that the effigy of Lundy was traditionally burned in December, but in recent times, out of respect for their Bogside neighbours, the Apprentice Boys now burn it outside the walls on the south side in the Fountains area.

Continuing along the city wall, you pass the **First Derry Presbyterian Church**, originally built in 1690, rebuilt during the Georgian period and added to in 1863. What you see is almost entirely of Victorian construction with sandstone Corinthian pillars. This was one of the first places of worship not affiliated to the Church of Ireland that was allowed within the city walls.

★ **Tower Museum** ⓘ *Union Hall Pl, T7137 2411. Sep-Jun Tue-Sat and Bank Holiday Mon 1000-1700, last admission 1630, Jul-Aug Mon-Sat 1000-1700, last admission 1630. £4.* At Magazine Gate in the north corner of the walled city, this is a modern recreation of an ancient tower house that once stood here. The museum has won many awards, and deservedly so: it's the only museum in Ireland that makes any effort at all to confront the events of the last 30 years with anything near objectivity. What's more, it's interesting, relaxing and provides an excellent balance between information and artefacts. Towards the end of the trip around the museum you enter a mock-up street with orange, white and green kerbstones on one side, and red, white and blue stripes on the other. Above the kerbstones, display cases give two versions of the events of the last century. A permanent Armada in Ireland exhibition is about to open and this should make a visit here even more irresistible.

The exit from the museum brings you into the Craft Village. In summer the cafés, shops and open areas, where there is often live music and set dancing, are well worth a visit.

Guildhall ⓘ *T7137 7335. Mon-Fri 0830-1700, enquire at the tourist office regarding its reopening to the public.* Leaving the walled city by Magazine Gate brings you to this Gothic extravaganza built in 1887 and burned down three times, once in 1908 by accident when only the main outer walls were left standing and the second and third times in 1972 by design, when the entire interior was wrecked. One of those convicted of the bombings in 1972 later sat as a council member in the same building. The interior is Victorian bombast, with vast stained glass windows representing the London liveries and the stories associated with Derry. Upstairs in the little kitchen alongside the great hall, look at the feet of George V in the stained glass window portraying his coronation: he has his shoes on the wrong feet. In the Great Hall most of Brian Friel's plays were premiered. In the lobby is a stained-glass panel representing those who lost their lives on Bloody Sunday with, intriguingly, a sled with 'Rosebud' written on it. The statue of Queen Victoria has several fingers missing from the time when she was toppled over in one of the 1972 blasts.

Workhouse Museum and Library ⓘ *23 Glendermott Rd, Waterside, T7131 8328. Oct-Jun Mon-Thu 1000-1630, Sat 1000-1630, Jul-Sep Mon-Sat 1000-1630. Free.* This museum is on the other side of the river from the walled city and represents an excellent piece of reconstruction and renovation. Downstairs in the old workhouse building is a public library, while the upper floors are the unaltered sleeping quarters of the women's section of the poor house. Not much to look at here, but a fascinating insight into the conditions that these poor women must have lived in. There is also a permanent exhibition about Derry's part in the Battle of the Atlantic during the Second World War. There are often other temporary exhibitions and performances here. Those who died in the Workhouse during the Famine were buried in the yard, now a housing estate. When the estate was built hundreds of remains were exhumed and reburied in local graveyards.

Amelia Earhart Centre ⓘ *Ballyarnett, T7135 4040. Mon-Thu 0900-1600, Fri 0900-1300. Free. Bus number D17 from the bus station.* About 8 miles (5 km) northwest of Derry is the Amelia Earhart Centre, commemorating the spot where she accidentally landed in 1932 having just made the first female solo crossing of the Atlantic. She mistook the village of Ballyarnett for Paris and landed there instead. Includes photos and memorabilia.

Sleeping

Derry city *p483, map p487*
The hotels are modern and well-equipped, though disappointing in terms of style, and there is a fair range of accommodation – most of which should booked in advance. The tourist office will book accommodation.

C-D City Hotel, Queen's Quay, T7136 5800, www.gshotels.com. Plush in a commercial, forgettable kind of way.

C-D Tower Hotel, The Diamond, T7137 1000, www.towerhotelderry.com. The style is international/contemporary but given its significant location, the only hotel inside the city walls, this is a rather charmless place.

D-E Da Vinci's Hotel, 15 Culmore Rd, T7127 9111, www.davincishotel.com. Inconveniently located, 1 mile (1.6 km) north of the city centre, but good eating and drinking options and inexpensively-priced rooms are available. There are also Da Vinci apartments, advertised from £67, in College Place, Strand Rd.

E Abbey, 4 Abbey St, T7127 9000, www.abbey accommodation.com. 5 rooms, mostly with en suite bathroom, in the Bogside. A 5-min walk to the centre. A friendly B&B in a historic location.

E Aberfoyle, 33 Aberfoyle Terr, Strand Rd, T7128 3333, aberfoyle@ntlworld.com. A B&B 5 mins from the centre. Good tourist advice.

E Arkle House, 2, Coshquin Rd, T7127 1156, www.derryhotel.co.uk. A Victorian house offering B&B, 1½ miles (2.5 km) northwest of the centre of Derry.

E City of Derry Travelodge, T1800-709709/ T0870-1911733, www.travelodge.ie. From £40 a room sleeping up to 2 adults and 2 children, or 3 adults. Functional but affordable accommodation in a rather noisy spot, ask for a room at the back.

E Derry City Independent Hostel, 44 Great James St, T7137 7989, derryhostel@ hotmail.com and **F Derry Backpackers**, 4 Asylum Rd, T7137 7989, derryhostel@ hotmail.com. Both hostels under same ownership and both charge £10 for a single and £14 in a private room, including breakfast and internet access. The Great James St one has the larger rooms but no private doubles whereas there are some private rooms in Asylum Rd. Newly acquired houses in Princess St will increase the number of beds and more double rooms will be available.

E The Inn at the Cross, 171 Glenshane Rd, T7130 1480, innatthecross@virgin.net.uk. Out-of-town guest house, 3 miles (5 km) away, with popular restaurant and bar.

E The Merchant's House, 16 Queen St, T7126 9691, www.thesaddlershouse.com. Lovingly restored Georgian house. Great breakfasts, lots of good information, sitting area and library. 1 room with en suite bathroom. The most central B&B in town and best value place for single rooms.

E The Saddler's House, 36 Great James St, T7126 9691, www.thesaddlershouse.com. Equally lovingly restored Victorian townhouse. All rooms with en suite bath, lots of information, informal breakfasts. The other most centrally located B&B in town.

F Paddy's Palace, 1 Woodleigh Terr, Asylum Rd, T7130 9051, www.paddyspalace.com. This hostel is linked with the company that runs group tours (www.paddywagon tours.com), so expect gaggles of travellers but it also functions as a walk-in hostel. All beds are in dorms, £10 per person including breakfast, and there is a kitchen.

Eating

Derry city *p483, map p487*

Brown's Restaurant, 2 Bond's Hill, T7134 5180. Excellent, small menu of innovative dishes in a little converted shop opposite the train station. Popular at lunch when less than £9 will buy you something you'll remember for days.

Fitzroy's, 3 Carlisle Rd, T7126 6211. Big, popular, does inexpensive lunches and very modern dinner menu – lots of drizzles and pestos. Early dinner menu as well as post- theatre one. Open till late daily.

Mange 2, 2 Clarendon St, T7136 1222. Starters like mussels and garlic for under £4 and main meat and fish dishes around £13. Open for lunch and dinner.

For an explanation of the sleeping and eating price codes used in this guide, see inside the front cover. Other relevant information is found in Essentials pages 39-45.

La Sosta, 45a Carlisle Rd, T7137 4817. ·n authentic, family-run Italian restaurant erving fillet steak, cannelloni, ravioli, and lesserts like lime tart with papaya sauce. 'egetarians could eat here and the itmosphere is friendly. Tue-Sat, 1830-2200.

At lunchtime the range of options is much vider with most of the pubs in town doing ood of some kind. The pubs along Waterloo it will be busy but they have atmosphere nd most do bar grub.

The Diamond, the Diamond. Easy to find, Wetherspoon pub doing cheap food and he cheapest drinks in the city.

Café Mezzo, the Diamond. Tiny place in ustin's department store, has a large menu, vith take-away service, and vegetarians could at here. All the food is under £5. Views over he square on the top floor of Austin's help ompensate for the predictable meals.

Metro, in Bank Pl, T7126 7401. A little ouristy but satisfactory food.

The Sandwich Company, 61 Strand Rd, 7126 6771. Popular with lunchtime eaters. here is another branch of this popular shop t the Diamond, T7137 2500.

Pubs and music

erry city *p483, map p487*

he tourist office dispenses a useful directory f what's on in the pubs.

weedore, Waterloo St, T7126 3513, close y Peadar O'Donnell's. Plays traditional nusic. Recommended.

eadar O'Donnell's, Waterloo St, T7137 318. Traditional Irish music. Recommended. he other pubs along Waterloo St will have otices up advertising their music nights.

ound for Boston, T7127 1315. Usually has ve bands Thu-Sat and its Club Q has pool ables for £3 an hr.

andino's, Water St. An easy-going, velcome-all pub with music.

iver Inn, **Downey's** and **Metro**, inside the ity walls, have live music.

Entertainment

erry city *p483, map p487*

inema

he Orchard Cinema, T7126 2845. The own's film club, housed in St Columb's heatre (see below).

Strand Multiplex, Strand Rd, T7137 3900. Has 7 screens.

Theatre

Guildhall, now the Bloody Sunday enquiry is over, hosts orchestral concerts etc.

Millennium Forum, Newmarket St, T7216 0516, www.milleniumforum.co.uk. A regular schedule of local productions and touring theatre groups.

Nerve centre, 7-8 Magazine St, T7126 6946, www.nerve-centre.org.uk. A performance venue, café, cinema and other arty stuff.

Playhouse, 5-7 Artillery St, T7126 8027, www.derryplayhouse.co.uk. Another multimedia venue, where you can catch art exhibitions, theatre, dance and concerts.

Verbal Arts Centre, near Bishop's Gate, T7126 6946, www.verbartscentre.co.uk. Worth a visit just to see the beautifully renovated former Blue Coat School (1894) and the glass sculpture by Killian Schuman which contains manuscripts donated by Ireland's many writers. The place is an archive of stories and poetry collected from around Ireland and there is a lively programme of events well worth checking out. Mon-Thu 0900-1700, Fri 0900-1600.

Festivals and events

Derry city *p483, map p487*

The **Foyle Film Festival** takes place in **Nov** and the **City of Derry Jazz Festival** is in late **Apr**. The largest and noisiest festivals in Derry take place in **Oct** with the **Two Cathedrals** festival followed by a week or so of fireworks and fun at Hallowe'en. Look out for the Hallowe'en tours – great fun.

Activities and tours

Derry city *p483, map p487*

Bowling **Brunswick Superbowl**, Brunswick Lane, T7137 1999. 0900-late.

Fishing **Enagh Trout Lake**, 12, Judges Rd, T7186 0916.

The Loughs Agency, 22 Victoria Rd, T7134 2100. Information and licences.

Greyhound racing **Brandywell Greyhound Racing Co**, Brandywell Football ground, T7126 5461.

Brooke Park Leisure Centre, Rosemont Av, T7126 2637. Squash, fitness training, sauna, tennis, bowls.
Lisnagelvin Leisure Centre, the Waterside, T7134 7695. Pool, wave-making machine.
Templemore Sports Complex, Buncrana Rd, T7126 5521. Pools, sauna, squash; major sporting events in the main sports hall.

Tours **Free Derry Tours**, T0779-3285972, www.freederry.net. There are numerous city tours but this is the most interesting and educational one. The cost is £3.50, departing at 1200 and 1400, and the focus is on the city's political history. Departing from the tourist office, in Jul-Aug at 1115 and 1515, and Sep-Jun at 1430, cost £4. Bus tours also depart from the tourist office for £6.

Transport

Derry city *p483, map p487*
Air From Derry Airport, Longfield Rd, Eglinton, T7181 0784, there are flights to **Dublin** and **Glasgow** with British Airways, **London Stansted** with Ryanair, and **Manchester** and **Birmingham** with Aer Arann. From Dublin and Stansted there are connections to most British and European cities. The airport is 11 km from the city centre on the A2, facilities include a free car park, information desk, bureau de change, ATMs, shop, bar and café.

Bus All buses depart from the Ulsterbus Depot in Foyle St, T7126 2261, www.translink.co.uk. Express services go to **Belfast** (half-hourly Mon-Fri, hourly Sat, and 1130, 1430 and 1730 Sun; £8.60-11 single/return), **Dublin**, and all major towns in Northern Ireland, while Bus Éireann, T074-9131008 (in Donegal), connects Derry with **Cork** via **Longford**, and **Galway** via **Letterkenny**, **Donegal** and **Sligo**. Airporter Quayside Shopping Centre, Strand Rd, T712 9996, www.airporter.co.uk, directly connect Derry with **Belfast City** and international airports. Coaches run Mon-Sat, 0600-2230 (2000 on Sat), and Sun, 1030-2200. £15-20 single/return. A private bus company, the Lough Swilly Company, T7126 2017, connects with **Buncrana**, **Moville**, **Carndonagh**, **Letterkenny**, **Dungloe** and **Fanad**. North West Busways, T074-938261 (in the Republic) has a Derry-**Culdaff** service via **Carndonagh** and a Derry-**Greencastle** service via **Moville**.

Car Dooley Budget Car Rental, Derry Airport, T028-7181 0784. Ford Rent-a-car, Desmond Motors Ltd, 173 Strand Rd, T7136 7137; City of Derry Airport, T7181 2220.

Taxi A1 Taxis, 7 Chapel Rd, T7134 2626. Auto Cabs, 85 Spencer Rd, T7134 3030. Derry Taxi Association, Foyle St, T7126 024

Train From the station in Waterside, T7134 2228, trains go to **Belfast** via **Coleraine**, **Portrush**, **Ballymena**, **Antrim** and **Lisburn**. There are around 7 trains a day

Around Derry

The countryside around Derry city lacks the breathtaking scope of coastal Donegal bu there are good things to discover if you choose to travel this area. Portstewart doesn have the chutzpah of Bundoran but it's a tidy little seaside town with places to eat an surf while Downhill offers an 18th-century folly and close by the long empty sand Benone strand. Inland are plantation towns such as Moneymore and the worthwhil Roe Valley Country park. »» *For Sleeping, Eating and other listings, see page 494.*

Derry to Coleraine

To Downhill The A2 follows the south side of Lough Foyle, moves inland a wee bit t Limavady, then heads north to Magilligan, now connected to Greencastle in count Donegal by a ferry (see page 483) where the B202 is a spur off to **Magilligan Point** an the incredible 7-mile (11-km) stretch of sandy **Benone Strand**. The A2 continues t Downhill where, on top of a 55-m cliff, a Bishop of Derry in the 1780s commissione he building of an extravagant palace and a Greek-style temple. The whole project vas manifestly absurd, cost a small fortune to build and decorate with paintings by ?ubens, Dürer and Tintoretto, and the whole lot burnt to the ground in 1851. The ›ishop had taken off in the 1790s for a tour of the continent where, thought to be a py, he was arrested by Napoleon and found in possession of more valuable works of ırt. "Oh, what a lovely thing it is to be an Anglican bishop or minister," exclaimed a 'rench visitor to Ireland at the time. The ruins of **Downhill Palace** and the intact **Aussenden Temple** ⓘ *Mussenden Rd, Castlerock, on the A2, T7084 8728, www.ntni. ›rg.uk, grounds always open; temple mid-Mar to May Sat-Sun 1100-1800, Jun daily 110-1800, Jul and Aug daily 1100-1930; Sep, Sat and Sun 1100-1800m, Oct Sat-Sun 110-1700, £3.60 for car park*, are National Trust properties and can be visited.

Iezlett House ⓘ *T7084 8728. Mid-Mar to May Sat-Sun 1300-1800, Jun-Aug Ved-Mon 1300-1800, Sep Sat-Sun 1300-1800, early Oct Sat-Sun 1300-1700. House our £3.60.* Also on the A2, 4 miles (6.5 km) northwest of Coleraine, Hezlett House is ınother National Trust property, a thatched 17th-century former rectory noted for its 'ruck truss roof.

'ortstewart The A2 takes you through **Coleraine** but there is little good reason to top in this depressing urban centre when the seaside towns of the north are so close ıt hand. The main coastal town is Portstewart, a bustling place popular with families ınd surfers, and a good stopping off point (either for a meal or a walk along the eafront) between Derry and Portrush. Start at the Crescent area in the west end of own where the Dominican convent, now a school, is perched on the hilltop and ollow the surfaced path along the cliff until the glorious vista of the **Portstewart itrand** opens up. Descend to the beach here: access by car costs £5. In places, signs varn of dangerous currents but this is a prime surfing beach. The **tourist office** is in he Town Hall, T7083 2286. Open Jul and Aug Mon-Sat 1000-1630, closed 1300-1400.

nland Derry

'he appeal of inland Derry is limited, but there are some interesting alternatives if easide resorts such as Portstewart and Portrush are not to your liking.

?oe Valley Country Park ⓘ *T7772 2074. Centre open Easter-Sep daily ›900-1700. Free. Open access. Once in the park, a sheet outlining short walks is ıvailable, the park is off the B192, 1 mile (1.6 km) south of Limvady, from where the ?us No 146 runs.* The Roe Valley Country Park stretches for 3 miles (5 km) along both ides of the Roe River near Limvady; the best of the walks pass industrial relics from he time when clattering water wheels powered machinery here for the manufacture f linen (see page 541). Head south, upstream, to see the bleaching greens where he cloth was spread out and guarded from the watch towers that still stand stealing linen was a capital offence), cross by the first or second footbridge and eturn on the other side for a hour's walk. A second walk, downstream, passes a ;reater variety of industrial buildings, and returning via the second footbridge this vay is also an hour' walk. The Centre provides a slide-show on the linen industry nd there is a separate Weaving Shed Museum. If industrial machinery really hooks ou, request a visit to the Power House, Ulster's first domestic hydro-electric power tation that opened in 1896.

Come dusk on a summer's day otters can be spotted in the river and buzzards ccasionally fly overhead, while in springtime the woodland floor is dotted with wood nemones and lesser celandine.

'lantation towns South Derry detains few travellers, but you could make a pit stop t one of the Plantation towns whilst journeying between Derry and Belfast on the A6.

The town of **Moneymore**, and close to Cookstown and County Tyrone, is a veritable museum in itself, so well preserved and decorous are the Georgian houses. Close by, **Springhill** ⓘ *T8674 8210, Jul-Aug daily 1200-1800, mid-Mar to Jun and Sep Sat and Sun 1200-1800, £3.90, on the B18 1 mile (1.6 km) southeast of Moneymore*, is a 17th-century manor house characteristic of the type built by the planters and, true to its spirit, saw the UVF training in the grounds in 1913 in preparation for armed resistance to Home Rule.

Sleeping

Derry to Coleraine *p492*
D **Cromore Halt Inn**, 158 Station Rd, on the left entering town from Coleraine on the B185, Portstewart, T7083 6888, www.cromore.com. This smart guest house has hotel-standard facilities and a restaurant.
E **Craigmore House**, 26 The Promenade, Portstewart, T7083 2120. Facing the ocean and in the thick of the seaside scene.
F **Causeway Coast Hostel**, 4 Victoria Terr, Atlantic Circle, Portstewart, T7083 3789. Open all year, its 30 beds include 3 private rooms at £20-24 each. Bus No 218 from Coleraine stops close by.

Inland Derry *p493*
C **Radisson Roe Park Hotel**, Roe Park, Limavady, T7772 2222, www.radissonroepark.com. Big bedrooms, indoor pool, gym and its own 18-hole golf course.
C **Streeve Hill**, Dowland Rd, Limavady, T7776 6563. The same price as the Radisson, but with a better breakfast and a country house atmosphere. Also does a fine dinner.
E **Alexander Arms**, 34 Main St, Limavady, T7776 3443. A town-centre pub with rooms and serves inexpensive food.
E **Keady View Farm**, 47 Seacoast Rd, Limavady, T7776 4518. 3 rooms at £20-36 for single/double room. There are quite a few more B&Bs along this road.

Eating

Derry to Coleraine *p492*
🍴 **Morelli's**, The Promenade, Portstewart. An authentic seaside feel, this is the place for a quick meal, a coffee or ice-cream.
🍴 **Shenanigans**, 78 The Promenade, Portstewart. Has a varied menu of standard meals and lively bars at night.
🍴🍴-🍴 **Smyths**, 2 Lever Rd, Portstewart, T7083 3564. Lunch and dinner menus, Tue-Sun, to suit a variety of tastes, including mildly innovative vegetarian dishes. The bar sometimes has music.

Inland Derry *p493*
🍴 **Crumpet**, Market St, Limavady. Try this place if it's a quick fix you're after, serves potato dinners till 1730.
🍴🍴-🍴 **The Lime Tree**, 60 Catherine St, Limavady, T7776 4300, www.limetreerest.com. A little gem of a place in one of the town's main streets. Innovative food that is something to talk about at the table. This is one of those menus where you feel that the words 'balsamic', 'peppercorn', 'terrine' and 'goujons' are used purposefully rather than as dressing. The dinner menu is £20 but bear in mind the early evening dinner at £10 and the £7 lunch menu which are good value.
🍴 **Shanvey**, Aghanloo Rd, Limavady. Bar and restaurant.

Activities and tours

Derry to Coleraine *p492*
Aquaholics, T7083 6909. Scuba-diving and PADI courses.
Ocean Warriors, opposite the Anchorage Inn, on The Promenade, Portstewart. Has surfing gear and information.

For an explanation of the sleeping and eating price codes used in this guide, see inside the front cover. Other relevant information is found in Essentials pages 39-45.

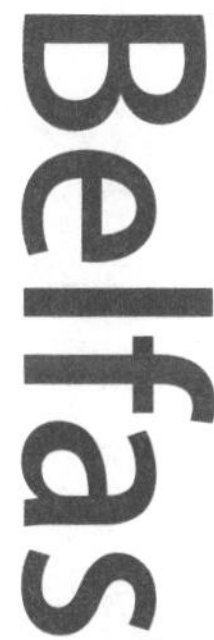

Footprint features

Introduction

A name long synonymous with bombs and sectarianism, Belfast has undergone a miraculous renaissance. Since the Good Friday Agreement big money has poured in from governments, business interests and corporations. The refreshing consequence is restaurants, leisure facilities and mushrooming housing where derelict factories and burned-out buildings once reigned. Despite the setbacks caused by the recent failure to compromise over creating a fairly representative Northern Ireland Assembly and the problems seized on by Sinn Féin's opponents regarding the 2004 bank robbery in Belfast and other issues, it seems fairly certain that the people of Belfast's will to live a normal life outweighs the very small minority that still need to cling to the violent conflicts of the past. The Falls Road, the Divis Flats, Shankill, Andersonstown, the Ardoyne – names that still carry echoes of mayhem – were, once upon a time, places where first-time visitors to Belfast saw armoured cars, gates used to close down the city at night, the fortress-like police posts and the grim murals. A visitor's instinct was to move on quickly and find somewhere else to go but now visitors have good reason to stay. This city has a life: its tourist infrastructure is sorted, hotels are bursting out of the pavement and restaurants have Michelin ratings. Belfast's 19th-century architecture may seem pompous, though it remains a worthy monument to the people who helped build this city, and it serves as a solid counterpoint to the flimsy steel and glass of the city's more modern developments.

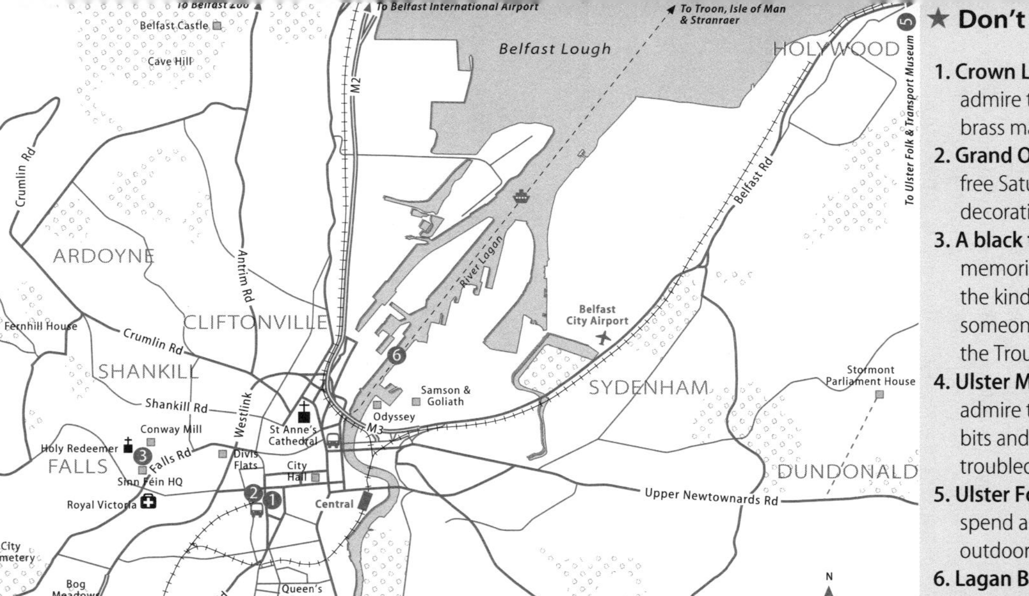

★ Don't miss...

1. **Crown Liquor Saloon** Have a pub lunch and admire the beautiful old fittings, especially the brass match plates, page 506.
2. **Grand Opera House** Watch a musical or take the free Saturday morning tour to admire the lavish decorations, page 506.
3. **A black taxi tour** Take a trip around the memorials, murals and sights of west Belfast with the kind of background information that only someone who drove a taxi through the worst of the Troubles can give you, page 507.
4. **Ulster Museum** Gawp at the giant machines, admire the jewellery, fiddle with the interactive bits and watch some old footage of Belfast's troubled history, page 509.
5. **Ulster Folk and Transport Museum** You could spend a day in this fascinating and authentic outdoor museum, page 511.
6. **Lagan Boat Tours** Take a trip along the river to see the huge cranes, Samson and Goliath and the dry dock where the Titanic was built, page 521.

Ins and outs

Getting there

→ *See also page 28 for more details on getting to Belfast.*

Air Belfast is served by two airports. **Belfast International Airport**, T9448 484 www.belfastairport.com, handles most international flights, and **Belfast City Airpo** T9093 9093, www.belfastcityairport.com, has a smaller number of flights, largely fro regional airports in Britain. Belfast International Airport, at Aldergrove, is 19 miles (km) north of the city on the M2. From outside the airport, Airbus number 300 runs to th Europa and Laganside bus stations every 30 minutes, hourly on Sunday. Taxis go fro beside the bus stop and cost around £24. The city airport is 3 miles (5 km) northeast the city. A direct bus service travels from the airport to the Europa Bus Centre every minutes between 0600 and 2150 Mon-Sat, hourly on Sundays. **Citybus** 21 runs fro Sydenham, near the airport, to City Hall. Sydenham Halt rail station is nearby and w connect with Central Station. Taxis from the city airport cost around £7.

Boat Ferries arrive at several locations along the river. The **Seacat** ferries from Troc in Scotland and the Isle of Man (both summer only) arrive at Donegall Quay, fro where it is a 5-minute walk to Laganside bus terminal, or a 15-minute walk to the ci centre. From Ballast Quay, where the **Stena** ferry from Stranraer docks, the be option is again a taxi, while an **Ulsterbus** number 256 connects Belfast's Laganside bus station with Larne, 20 miles (30 km) to the north, and from where the **P&O** ferri from Cairnryan, Troon and Fleetwood dock.

Bus Long-distance buses from the Republic or within Northern Ireland arrive at eith Laganside bus station or the Europa bus station, both of which are very central.

Train Trains arrive at Central Station and a free bus service goes into the centr Alternatively, get another train into Botanic Station for the university area.

Getting around

Bus A series of buses radiate out from the city centre in Donegall Square, Upp Queen Street, Wellington Place and Castle Street.

Taxi There are taxi stands outside the Europa bus station, and in Donegall Squar Smithfield market and North Street. See also tours, page 521, below for information c taxi tours of west Belfast. The Smithfield market taxis travel into Catholic west Belfas taking several passengers at a time for about £1 per passenger, while the North Stre taxis travel to Protestant west Belfast. The Donegall Square and Europa bus statio taxis have a starting price of £1.50 and do not wait to load up with passengers first.

Car Note that while the severe parking restrictions of yore are more relaxed, there a still no parking areas around sensitive buildings such as the courthouse. There is r shortage of secure car parks and most streets have pay and display systems.

Information

Belfast Welcome Centre, 47 Donegall Pl, T9024 6609, www.gotobelfast.com, has lo of useful information, a left luggage office and will book accommodation and travel f you. Open Jun-Sep, Mon-Fri 0900-1900, Sat 0900-1715, Sun 1000-1600, Oct-M Mon-Sat 0930-1730. There is also tourist information at the City Airport, T9045 778 daily 0530-2200, and at Belfast International Airport, T9442 2888, 24 hours. **Fáil Ireland**, 53 Castle St, T9032 7888, Mon-Fri 0900-1700, Sat 0900-1230, Mar to end-Se only, provides information for your onward journey to the Republic. **Usit Now**, Founta Centre, College St, BT1 6ET, T9032 4073. Open Mon-Fri 0930-1700, Sat 0930-1230.

History

→ *See also history of Northern Ireland on page 603.*

Belfast sits in a valley created by two rivers, the Lagan and the Farsett (now piped below the streets) which once necessitated a series of forts to guard their crossings. If you had wandered this way in the 12th century, you would have seen little more than a Norman castle, built in 1177. The land was under the control of the Gaelic lords, the O'Neills, until the Plantation (see page 592) began under James I. By the middle of the 17th century a small town had blossomed. Carrickfergus, in Antrim, dominated trade in the area until Belfast's population rose to a critical mass with the immigration in the late 17th century of Huguenots fleeing persecution in France. They brought their traditional industry, linen production, with them and the burgeoning city now had a reason to expand. The Plantation continued with rope-making, shipping, and export of beef, corn and butter to Britain and France, making the city the fourth largest town in Ireland by the end of the century.

The 18th century The 18th century saw a fourfold increase in population, and the further development of the shipbuilding and linen industries. Catholics and Protestants lived harmoniously in the city throughout the century, culminating in the formation in 1791 of the United Irishmen, a cross-denominational nationalist organization. It was, of course, stamped out and many Protestant and Catholic men, who would be national heroes in other circumstances today, lost their lives.

Beginnings of sectarianism From an initial apathy following the eradication of the United Irishmen, northern Protestants began to see the increasing militancy of the Catholics throughout Ireland as a threat. In the 1820s Protestant clubs were set up all over Ulster; their members made great parades, bore arms and formed bands to play anti-Catholic songs. After Catholic Emancipation in 1829 an Orange Order parade on 12 July was banned which led to riots all over the city.

As agricultural prices declined and Industrial Revolution came to Belfast, thousands of the rural poor of both denominations flocked to the city to compete for scarce work. But Protestants now held all the power in the city and were increasingly reluctant to give it up in the light of the Irish Catholic militancy that threatened their power base. The Famine (see pages 406 and 595) drove more people into the city where the fight for work and housing forced the two groups ever further apart.

In 1857 riots hit the streets of Belfast as huge Catholic and Protestant mobs met in open battle. This happened again in 1864, forcing the closure of factories. The Catholic minority suffered the worst of the attacks, the Catholic Pound district being sandwiched between Sandy Row and the Shankill Road. Reform of Parliament and changes in the property qualification to vote in 1867 gave Catholics more rights, but every move in favour of equality was met with an Orange, unionist reaction, and ever-increasing displays of affection for William of Orange each 12 July. Further reforms, the disestablishment of the Church of Ireland and the introduction of the secret ballot, disturbed the control of the Protestants, but were met with the repeal of the act banning sectarian marches. Home Rule gained power in the rest of Ireland, but in Belfast it became the bogey that kept the riots coming each year. The Home Rule Bill of 1886 polarised even liberal Protestants' feelings with Monster Meetings of Conservatives and Orangemen opposed to it. Its eventual defeat was accompanied by the worst riots so far. Catholics drove Protestants out of their workplaces and were in their turn driven out of work and beaten; Catholic pubs were attacked and burned out. The police, largely Catholic but commanded by Protestant officers, became a third party in the fighting, battling both sides. The riots lasted from June to the end of September; between 31 and 50 people died.

Into the 20th century In 1891 Belfast officially outstripped Dublin in terms of population (around 26% was Catholic). It had an opera house and many grand commercial buildings. Besides shipbuilding and linen there was a flourishing engineering industry and this was Ireland's centre for building steam engines. In the early 20th century, the Gaelic Revival came to Belfast, and committed intellectuals on both sides of the sectarian divide found a common interest in Irish culture and tradition. But in 1911, the issue of Home Rule reared its head yet again, bringing to an end the period of relative peace. Unionists began to talk of taking power in Ulster rather than accepting Home Rule for Ireland. The Ulster Volunteer Force was established in order to fight for independence and by 1912 there were 90,000 volunteers, and the old town hall in Belfast was their headquarters.

The First World War brought a certain amount of prosperity to the region. In 1914 Harland and Wolff, the Belfast-based shipbuilders, were producing eight percent of the world output of ships. At first orders declined as workers were called up and materials became scarce but then the war orders came flooding in. Farmers knew a wealth previously unimagined as imports died away under U-boat attacks. The linen industry also boomed with orders for uniforms, tents and aeroplane fabric.

After 1918 hundreds of men inured to the horror of war returned to Belfast ready to take up the old quarrels. In the south, the Black and Tan war was a particularly bloody interlude, while in Belfast sectarian violence reached new heights. In 1920 Loyalist mobs drove all Catholics and socialists out of Harland and Wolff, Sirocco, Mackie's, McLaughlin and Harveys: all the big employers in Belfast. About 11,000 Catholic people lost their jobs in this way while Catholic houses and businesses were attacked and the convent of St Matthew's Church in Belfast was burned down. Belfast Catholics, now a quarter of the population, fought back just as violently but were greatly outnumbered. The violence continued unabated for two years. Because of the fear of the increasingly powerful IRA the Ulster Special Forces were created, made up entirely of Protestants; the B Specials in Belfast were part-time, uniformed and armed.

In 1921 the Protestants, who had fought for so long against it, got Home Rule while the 32 southern counties received dominion status. In 1922 more riots and deaths occurred: 61 people were killed in March in Belfast alone. Outside the city the IRA was burning and looting, while inside Catholics suffered reprisals from Loyalists and B Specials alike: the Special Powers Act allowed suspects to be detained indefinitely without charge or trial. After the murder of an MP internment was introduced, as well as a curfew. In May 1922, 66 people died, two-thirds of them Catholic.

After the assassination of Michael Collins (see page 599) in that year, things calmed down a little, the southern government encouraging the IRA to join the mainstream Irish army. While the civil war and its aftermath raged in the south, those who might have caused disruption in the north were occupied and so peace broke out for a time in Belfast.

By the 1930s Belfast had settled to become an anti-Catholic, sectarian city with annual displays of Orange power attended by cabinet ministers who abused their southern Catholic neighbours, who, in retaliation, abused them. The economic war between Dublin and London polarised attitudes even more, and employers were encouraged by the Belfast government to employ Protestants who would be loyal to the state. In 1935 there were more riots as the Orange parades were first banned and then allowed. In 1937 the new constitution for the south set out a claim on the sovereignty of the north, as well as establishing the special position of the Catholic Church in the south; these claims made matters considerably worse.

Second World War Belfast had suffered during the Great Depression, but things began to boom again as war began to seem likely. An airport was built, and the industries that had benefited from the First World War came into their own again. Harland and Wolff received commissions to convert passenger ships for war use and two huge warships were built. In 1941, however, Belfast became a target for the Luftwaffe. The first waves of bombers missed the industrial targets, and hit instead the impoverished housing estates of the north city centre. Fires raged throughout the city, and fire engines from the south were sent up to help deal with them. Hundreds of people died and their corpses were laid out in the swimming baths and St George's Market. After the first night of bombing tens of thousands of people left the city. The second wave of attacks in May the same year saw Belfast become one huge conflagration across the harbour, with small firestorms breaking out in the industrial sites: half of the houses and most of the industry in the city were destroyed. The glow was visible 50 miles away. Middle-class ladies living outside the city took in refugees, and were appalled at the condition of the slum children, whereas wealthier Belfast citizens retired to the hotels of Donegal for the duration of the war. Catholic churches opened their crypts to one and all as air raid shelters, and Protestant and Catholic stood shoulder to shoulder putting out the flames, uniting the two sides of the religious divide. That, fortunately, was the last of the air raids over Belfast.

In 1942 American soldiers came to the city, completing a circle that began during the Famine years when thousands of Belfast Protestants left for the US. The arrival of foreign troops on Irish soil sparked a protest from De Valera, and increased activity on the part of the IRA. After a gunfight in west Belfast six men were arrested and sentenced to death for the murder of an RUC man. Only one was executed but it brought back all the old antagonisms in the city. In 1943 an IRA man held up the audience of the Broadway cinema in the Falls Road and insisted that they take part in a commemoration for the dead of the Easter Rising. But suppression and arrest in both north and south ensured that by the end of the war the IRA was defunct.

To the present From 1945 to the mid-1960s the city experienced not so much sectarian harmony but at least a degree of peace. The modern trouble in the North began in the civil rights demonstrations in Derry but Belfast communities enthusiastically joined in (see page 603).

The present situation is one where an entire generation of people in their 20s want nothing to do with the old disputes; Belfast clubs resound to the enjoyment of young people who don't know or care what sect their dancing partners belong to, restaurant owners are glad of the custom from whomever walks into their place, the mural painters have become far more conscious of an international audience for their work and only the sadder parts of the city still paint their kerbstones red, white and blue.

Sights

City centre

City Hall

ⓘ *T9027 0456. Tours Jun-Sep Mon-Fri 1100, 1400, 1500, Sat 1430; Oct-May Mon-Fri 1100, 1430, Sat 1430. Free.*

Dominating the centre of town in Donegall Square is the massive City Hall, a pompous Victorian testament to what money can build. Completed in 1906, the Portland stone edifice, designed by Brumwell Thomas and covering 1½ acres, is topped by a copper dome 173 ft high. You can't wander around inside at will but there are guided tours all year. Inside is an extravaganza of imported marble, stained glass dedicated to various moneymen and soldiers, and paintings of mayors in their regalia. Very few women feature in this place at all, except those who lead the guided tours. The tour takes in the council chamber, the Great Hall, the banqueting hall and robing rooms.

In 1988 an IRA bomb did what German air raids had failed to do, and destroyed the stained-glass windows of the Great Hall.

Belfast centre

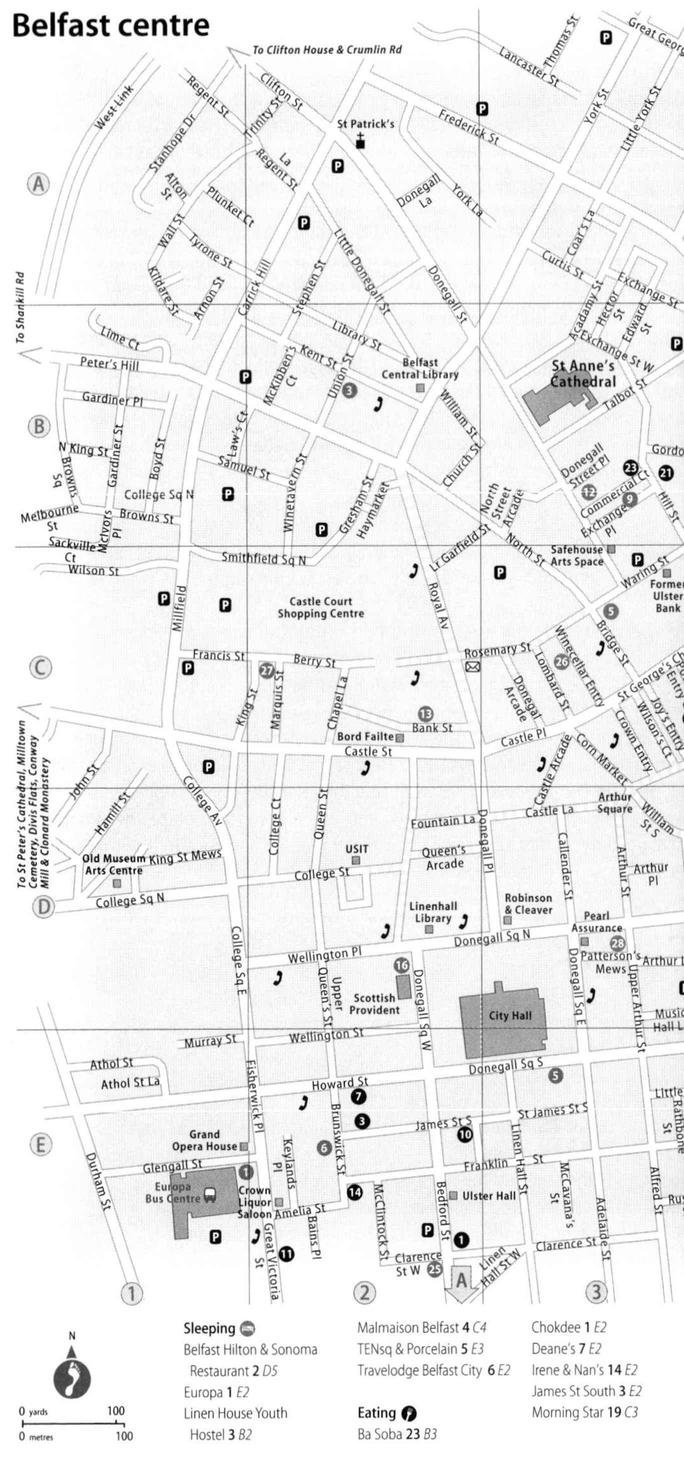

Sleeping
Belfast Hilton & Sonoma Restaurant **2** *D5*
Europa **1** *E2*
Linen House Youth Hostel **3** *B2*
Malmaison Belfast **4** *C4*
TENsq & Porcelain **5** *E3*
Travelodge Belfast City **6** *E2*

Eating
Ba Soba **23** *B3*
Chokdee **1** *E2*
Deane's **7** *E2*
Irene & Nan's **14** *E2*
James St South **3** *E2*
Morning Star **19** *C3*

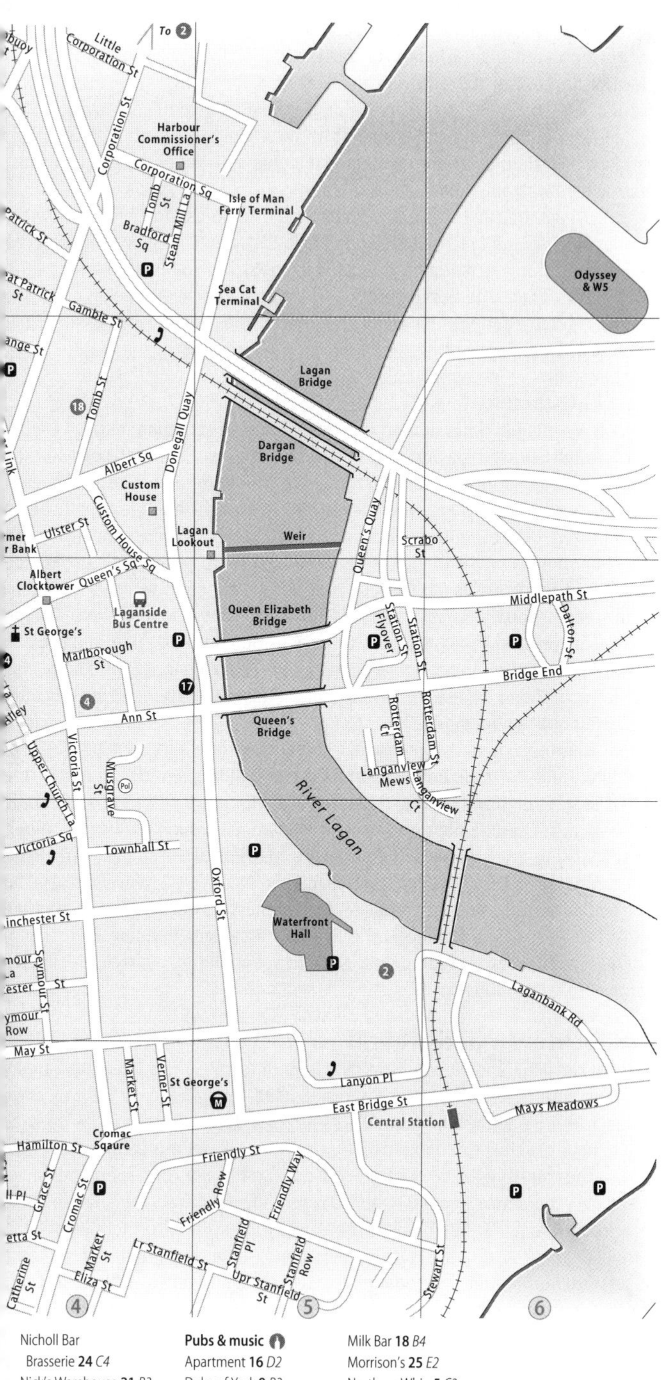

Nicholl Bar Brasserie **24** *C4*
Nick's Warehouse **21** *B3*
Red Panda **11** *E2*
Roscoff Brasserie **10** *E2*
Tedford's **17** *C4*

Pubs & music
Apartment **16** *D2*
Duke of York **9** *B3*
John Hewitt **12** *B3*
Kelly's Cellars **13** *C2*
Madden's **27** *C2*
Milk Bar **18** *B4*
Morrison's **25** *E2*
Northern Whig **5** *C3*
Rotterdam **2** *A4*
Thompsons **28** *D3*
White's Tavern **26** *C3*

The grounds contain more testimony to the doings of men. Statues of Edward Harland, of shipbuilding fame, James Haslett, the Rt. Hon Daniel Dixon, Lord Dufferin and RJ McMordie, several of the movers and shakers of the 19th century, all pay court to the quite lissom figure of Queen Victoria, flanked by representatives of the spinning and shipbuilding industries and, as an afterthought, education. A cenotaph also stands in the grounds, as does a memorial to one of Belfast's biggest mistakes, the *Titanic*, which was built here.

For many years the city council was dominated by unionist politicians who were partly responsible for the failure of the 1985 Anglo-Irish agreement, in large part the same agreement that was made on Good Friday 1998. They refused to take part in council business while the Agreement was in place, effectively making the city unrunnable. A huge banner hung along the front of the building expressing their opposition to any dealings with the Republic.

Donegall Square

There are a few other buildings around Donegall Square of some interest. At number 17 is the **Linenhall Library**ⓘ *17 Donegall Sq, T9032 1707, www.linenhall.com, Mon-Fri 0930-1730, Sat 0930-1600, free, ring in advance to join tours*, which has been a lending library for over 200 years. Not much to look at from the outside despite being designed in 1864 by the big guns of Victorian Belfast, Lanyon, Lynn & Lanyon, it has a vast collection of early Irish material and is used by research students studying the recent history of the Troubles. It is not a public library, although you can wander in and use the reading room and café on the first floor, and browse around the collection of prints that are on sale. The library holds regular exhibitions and talks, and you can join one of the many free tours of the building and its collections. The library was established in 1788 and its first librarian, Thomas Russell, was hanged in 1803 after an abortive Republican uprising.

A wander around the Square reveals some more late Victorian bulwarks of respectability. The 1884-1885 **Robinson and Cleaver building** stands out among the solidity: six storeys high with rounded corners rising to ornate turrets, its exterior is highly carved with cherubs, fruit and contemporary figures such as Victoria, Albert and, for some reason, George Washington. At the east side of the square is the **Pearl Assurance building**, originally called the Ocean building, erected between 1899 and 1902 in a Gothic revival style, with oddly-shaped pinnacle towers creating a startling skyline. At the west of the Square is the **Scottish Provident building** (1897-1899) covered in wild carvings of dolphins, sphinxes and lions as well as figures representing Belfast's industry.

Albert Clocktower and around

Northwest of City Hall and close to the river is another cluster of late 19th-century constructions. Now beautifully restored and stabilised, for many years the 1865-1869 Albert Clocktower leaned a little more with every year that passed and as early as 1879 had to have several bits chopped off that looked as if they might bring the whole thing down. The clock tower had been erected on land that was once part of the river Farsett and over the years its wooden foundations had rotted away until nothing held the thing up but gravity. Beside it the AIB bank was formerly the Northern Bank head office. Built in 1852 by Charles Lanyon in Portland stone and granite, it makes a grandiose statement about the permanence of Protestant values, with giant Doric columns and a great carved frieze above the entrance. In High Street is **St George's Church**, one of the few churches in the city that you can wander into. Built in 1811 it has a tacked-on portico salvaged from an earlier building, and pre-Raphaelite decorations. Along Waring Street, a block to the north of the clock tower, is the now unoccupied but soon to be a boutique hotel, **Ulster Bank**, another magnificent temple to Mammon. Its architect won the commission in 1857 in a competition where

Organized crime

On Sunday 19 December 2004 at around 2200 three masked men entered a house on the western outskirts of Belfast and took four people hostage. A fifth person, an employee of the Northern Bank in Donegall Square West was taken away. He and his supervisor from Downpatrick, whose family were also being held, were given instructions which led to the biggest bank heist in the history of the UK or Ireland. At 1800 on the following day, one of the men carried £l million out of the bank in a holdall. No one checked what was in it. Outside he handed the bag to another man. Later that night a white van parked outside the bank and crates of cash were brought out by the men whose families were being held hostage. At 2000 the van made a second collection. More than £26 million left the bank this way, without a single bank robber setting foot inside. Most of the notes were in relatively unusable Ulster Bank sterling notes (the bank called in all its notes) but lots of it was in used regular notes. The families were released unharmed.

As with much crime in Belfast, what happened has had huge political repercussions which threaten the peace process. The IRA has been accused of the crime, though at the time of writing no evidence to back this up has been produced. Early in 2005, accusations of Sinn Fein involvement were made by political parties in both the North and the Republic – parties whose objectivity is questionable given that they stand to gain electorally by such accusations. The political fall out continues.

other architects proposed designs. It is based on St Mark's Library in Venice, and s just about every architectural idiosyncrasy known at the time: Doric and rinthian columns, allegorical sculptures, ornate railings and Victorian lamps.

Back down Victoria Street a little way, take time out to admire the façade of the 66-1867 Lytle's and McCausland's, now the **Malmaison Belfast Hotel**, but once two eat warehouses whose fronts were preserved with their marble relief figures of the e continents and animals, and arcaded windows.

Back at the Albert Tower the road sweeps round through some ugly modern road ilding past McHugh's, the oldest pub in Belfast, to the **Custom House**, where once e commercial life of the city bustled. Built in 1854-1857, it still functions as the city's stoms building. Its two fronts, one facing the river and the other the city, are ghlighted by ornate Corinthian columns, but the river side is the more elaborate, th the traditional riverine heads as the keystones of arches, and figures of angels, itannia and Roman gods decorating the pediment.

Also on the waterfront is the **Harbour Commissioner's Office**, its exhibition of aritime history (including the captain's table intended for the Titanic) occasionally en to the public. Enquire at the tourist office.

agan Lookout

1, Donegall Quay, T9031 5444. Apr-Sep Mon- Fri 1100-1700, Sat 1200-1700, Sun 00-1700; Oct-Mar Tue-Fri 1100-1530, Sat 1300-1630, Sun 1400-1630. £1.50. Self-ided tours are available price £2.50 with a £10 deposit. The tour covers the artwork tted around the river, the new Gasworks centre and the Cathedral Quarter.

e modern Lagan Lookout is a little exhibition centre built on the weir. Part of a scheme renovate the rundown waterfront, the £14 million weir holds back the tidal flow of the er, which in the past made the area very unsavoury when great banks of fetid mud ere exposed twice a day. With the water held back, regeneration of the area beyond was possible and the place now has a state-of-the-art concert hall, bijou apartmer whose prices are rising at a rate of knots and the jewel in the crown that is the Hilt hotel, one of the first companies to venture huge capital in the newly peaceful city.

The Lookout sits right on the weir and has displays of history and audio-visu material. You can watch the water rising and falling over the bollards which preve the river bed becoming exposed during low tide. A walk across the weir revea Samson and Goliath, the two massive cranes of the shipyards reflected in th glass-walled buildings on the other bank. It is possible to take a boat ride upstrea and around the old docks area (see Tours page 521).

W5

ⓘ Odyssey, 2 Queen's Quay, BT39QQ, T9046 7700, www.w5online.co.uk. Mon-F 1000-1800, Sat and Sun 1200-1800, last admission 1700. £5.50.

Part of the squillion-pound Odyssey redevelopment area beside the river, this is a ve hands-on science and engineering centre aimed at families and schools, with lots things to do and build, handles to pull, things to swing on, throw and bash and puzzl to solve. The complex includes a food court, cineplex and omniplex cinema and th 10,000 seat sports arena where the Belfast ice hockey team, the Belfast Giants, pla

★ Grand Opera House and Crown Liquor Saloon

ⓘ 2-4 Great Victoria St, www.goh.uk, free guided tours of the building start from th booking office, Sat, Wed 1100, booking not necessary.

Great Victoria Street is dominated by the Europa hotel, an ugly place that looks li some brutalist piece of architecture from the era of the Iron Curtain and which w targeted by IRA bombs several times during the Troubles. But also in this street a two Belfast institutions. The Grand Opera House was designed by British theat architect Frank Matcham and opened in 1895 as a popular variety hall. In 1899 visiting American show required that the theatre be flooded with 50,000 gallons water! Much later in 1963 it unwittingly became the venue of the United Kingdo debut of Pavarotti who was understudying in Dublin and travelled up to replace a si performer. The theatre is mostly restoration work nowadays after two IRA bom reduced it to rubble in 1991 and 1993. The best way to see it is when it is in operation and it is in constant use for concerts, operas and plays.

On the other side of the road is the **Crown Liquor Saloon**, which looks like over-the-top 1990s theme pub but is in fact the genuine Victorian article. It was built Patrick Flanagan, a publican, in 1839 and later encased in th glorious exterior tiles you see today. Inside are carved wood snugs, each with its own motto and brass match striker, gas lamp the original carved wooden bar and beautiful lighting through th stained glass windows. If you are in Belfast on one of its somnolent Sundays, go around lunchtime when it's quite empty; otherwise you'll have to fight your way in.

! The pub was damaged by the bomb in the Opera House in 1993.

The Cathedral Quarter

Long marked up as the city's answer to Temple Bar in Dublin, the Cathedral Quart the streets around St Anne's Cathedral, hasn't really become the bohemian hub of that is alternative as the city's developers had hoped. But things are moving and nc there are some good pubs, restaurants and clubs here as well as a couple of galleri worth poking around in. As for sights, **St Anne's Cathedral** is the main attractic commissioned in 1896, following Belfast's elevation to city status, and built in eclectic style (the design changed several times while it was being built) the buildi wasn't completed until 1981. The nave is the work of the original architect, Thom Drew and features Irish marble floors marking out the path to salvation and t corbelled pillars bearing carvings of religious figures. In the baptistery, designed Drew's successor, W H Lynn, the ceiling is covered in a mosaic representing Creatior

★ West Belfast

West Belfast was a working-class area which developed around the linen industry – an area where sectarian violence created two entirely separate communities: the Catholic Falls and the Protestant Shankill. When the Troubles started in 1969, West Belfast, separated from the city centre by the Westlink motorway, became a battleground. The Falls Road, Crumlin Road, Divis Street, the Shankill are names that ring of riot, burning, assassination and mayhem. However, walk down any of them today and you see streets that could be any suburb – dull, suburban maisonettes, corner shops, kids on bikes, Victorian terraces. True, there are intermittent police posts looking like something from the Berlin Wall, the occasional armoured car, and places with security devices than you would normally expect but, apart from the gable ends of houses which tell the story in a series of graphic images – red hands, shamrock leaves, silhouettes of gunmen, you have to look quite carefully to spot evidence of the sectarian war waged here for over 25 years.

The Falls

If a stroll along some of the most battle-hardened streets in Belfast to a cemetery where many of the Troubles' victims lie buried is your cup of tea, then walk along the now-quiet suburban streets of the Falls to **Milltown Cemetery**, where the republican graves commemorate some of the many lives lost. The walk begins at the Smithfield Market where, if you choose, you can negotiate with a taxi driver for a personal tour of the area. Alternatively, head westwards along Divis Street towards Divis Tower, the last remaining building of the notorious **Divis Flats**. The roof was occupied for a time by a Republican group, but is now part of an army post, along with the top two storeys (access by helicopter only). As you walk away from the centre you can see the 'peace line' between the houses on your right, the iron wall built to keep apart the residents of the Falls and Shankill roads. What strikes home as you walk is the small size of the war zone – a few blocks east and west and only one block between the two groups.

In Conway Street is **Conway Mill**, a former flax spinning mill which now houses lots of local projects, artists' studios and a craft shop which also has displays about the history of the mill and some mementoes of the Republican prisoners' time in the H Block. From the outside the place looks like a ruin, with pigeons flying through the open windows but funding is on its way and it should look a lot livelier soon. In Clonard Street is the **Church of the Holy Redeemer**, or **Clonard Monastery**, which has now entered the history books as the place where the initial, very secret, meetings leading to the 1994 IRA cease-fire took place. The church was built in 1908-11 in the Gothic style and is worth a look for its rose window over the entrance way and mosaic depictions of the story of the Redemption on the ceiling and floors. Next stop along the Falls Road is the **headquarters of Sinn Féin**, its walls paying tribute to Bobby Sands, the IRA hunger striker, and three party workers who were shot down by a deranged off-duty policeman who then killed himself. On the left as you continue is **Dunville Park**, given to the people of the Falls Road in 1889 by Robert Dunville, a distiller. Its centrepiece is a huge ceramic fountain built by Doultons in London.

Continuing on along the road on the left you will pass on the right the **Royal Victoria Hospital**, which dealt with many of the victims of the Troubles. Note its railings which are designed to copy the pattern of a DNA molecule with x's and y's along the top. Beyond the hospital look out for **An Culturlánn** ⓘ *216 Falls Road, T9096 4188*, a cultural centre and **tourist information** point housed in an old Presbyterian church.

Further west and on the north side of the Falls Road appears the **City Cemetery**, the city's first municipal burial place, laid out 1866-1869. It contains many of Belfast's Victorian worthies and huge expensive testimonials to their own greatness. Look for Lord Pirrie, who built the Titanic, WH Lynn the architect who designed his own tomb

The writing on the wall

Painting murals has a long history in Belfast. The earliest date back to the beginning of the 20th century, before Northern Ireland came into existence, and were all Unionist in nature. The first one in Belfast depicted the victory of Protestantism over Catholicism at the Battle of the Boyne on 12th July 1690 and featured Prince William of Orange, or 'King Billy', on horseback. These early murals were always associated with the celebrations surrounding 12th July and were part of the street decorations, along with bunting, flags, painted kerbstones and the huge parade. Other paintings included celebrations of the victory at the Battle of the Somme, the sinking of the Titanic, Scottish and United Kingdom flags and the red hand of Ulster. They became part of a two-week national celebration when factories closed and everyone took their holidays. Painting the murals was a civic duty and a party in itself. The whole street would turn out to watch the artist at work, making new murals or repainting the old ones. Catholics were of course merely spectators in this celebratory, sectarian, triumphalist parade. Catholic culture was private, ignored by the state, and allowed no public statements in the form of murals.

Matters changed when the civil rights campaign took hold. The first nationalist public statement came in 1981 during the Republican prisoners' hunger strike. For five years they had taken part in a protest demanding political status and their supporters had taken to graffiti to express their support of them. By the time the hunger strikers began to die the graffiti had become murals. They depicted the 'H Block' prison, the prisoners, bearded, rake-thin and wearing blankets, their coffins, and the tricolour flag of the Republic. The themes began to extend beyond the deaths of the hunger strikers to what had become an armed struggle for a united Ireland. It was in these murals that the images of hooded gunmen first appeared. As Sinn Féin candidates began to stand in local elections the muralists had more incentive for their work and the murals began to reflect various political and social demands.

The Unionist murals have always been permanent displays – some have been repainted every year for decades – but the nationalist ones are more like graffiti – a mural painted one week may be wiped out the next as some new political issue emerges. None of the muralists considers their work to be art and whole communities turn out with their DIY ladders to do the colouring in with paint left over from redecorating their front rooms.

In contemporary Belfast the murals are still as important as ever but they have changed their nature in many ways. While many of the murals are still romantic idealisations of the past – the Titanic, the Queen Mother, King Billy, the 1916 Uprising in the Republic – they have also begun to make political statements of contemporary and urgent intent, looking to what might come as their leaders negotiate a shared future.

and Lord Edward Carson, the Unionist leader. The Carson plot includes a beautiful 1905 Art Nouveau memorial.

Opposite, on the south side of the Falls Road **Milltown cemetery** is a quiet place watched over by an army post. In 1988 the war invaded when a grenade was thrown at mourners at the funeral of Séan Savage, one of the IRA members killed in Gibraltar by the British army. To find the Republican graves, head south to the end of the graves and turn right. Bobby Sands is buried here. The cemetery was created in 1869 and its entrance gate is a typical Victorian over-the-top piece of masonry designed by Timothy Hevey, as is the cross just inside the entrance, but most of the headstones are a much more modest set of memorials than those across the road. One large green space marks a mass grave brought about by the flu pandemic of 1918. Beyond the cemetery the Falls Road continues into **Andersonstown**, another Republican estate where there are more murals. Beyond that is **Twinbrook**, where Bobby Sands lived, and where a gable end has been turned into a permanent memorial.

Bog Meadows

ⓘ *Ulster Wildlife Trust, 438 Falls Rd, T9031 4772. Open 24 hrs. Free. Guided tours.*
Squashed between the motorway and the cemetery are the 53 acres of the Ulster Wildlife Trust's Bog Meadows. Filled with footpaths and ponds and areas of scrub the meadows are a haven in the middle of the city for a disappearing wildlife. Twitchers will love the place and for others it's a relief from the stress of the Falls Road.

Shankill Road

A walk along the Shankill Road begins further north from the city centre. The murals are more in evidence here and are slightly more threatening: silhouettes of gunmen and slogans such as "We know who you are" adorn the walls. Typical symbols are the red hand of Ulster, maps of the six counties detached from the rest of the island, William of Orange on horseback, flags (usually the Union Jack and St George's Cross but also the Scottish flag and, both disconcerting and revealing, the Star of David), and generally lots of red, white and blue posts, kerbstones, fences, and so on. Trips along the Shankill can be arranged with the taxi drivers at North Street. They should ask for about £10 for an hour. One possibility is to negotiate a trip out to **Fernhill House** ⓘ *Glencairn Park, Mon-Sat, 1000-1600, Sun, 1000-1600, £2, buses 39, 73, 63 travel along the Shankill Rd but not as far as Fernhill*, a museum that explores the history of the Shankill area.

South of the city centre

★ Ulster Museum and the Botanic Gardens

ⓘ *Ulster Museum: Mon-Fri 1000-1700, Sat 1300-1700, Sun 1400-1700. Free. Botanic Gardens: Apr-Sep Mon-Fri 1000-1700, Sat, Sun, bank holidays 1400-1600; Oct-Mar Mon-Fri 1000-1600, closed 1300-1400, free, buses 69, 70, 71 from Donegall Sq east.*
This is probably the least stressful place to visit in Belfast. The museum is laid out as a kind of walk around the interesting features of Ulster with some dinosaurs, an art collection and a bit of geology thrown in. The ground floor is occupied by some massive machinery connected with linen production and steam power. The size of it all is admirable – huge boards set apart from the machines give a description of the process of linen manufacture – but it is difficult to connect the two. Heading onwards on this floor, you find a children's dinosaur exhibition. On the second floor are some interesting exhibits on early Ireland, this time much more hands-on, with video clips, reconstructed huts and other bits and pieces. A display of Spanish artefacts, taken from the *Girona*, a sunken Armada vessel excavated near the Giant's Causeway in 1968, gives a nice insight into life on board, and some odds and ends of ancient Egyptian and native American artefacts complete this level. Finally, on this floor, in **The Irish at War**, the museum gets around to confronting the history of the last century in Northern Ireland. Exhibits are a bit limp but perhaps there's no point in stirring up trouble unnecessarily. What is interesting, though, is the vast archive of radio and TV footage which you can access and which gives a stirring picture of what life must have been like in the worst of the Troubles.

Level three is taken up with jewellery, glassware and a wildlife exhibition, while the top floor displays some of the museum's collection of art.

The museum is in the grounds of the **Botanic Gardens**, more of a park than a collection of rare plants but the two long herbaceous borders are beautifully kept and there are some lovely mature trees. The highlight of the park, though, lies in the two beautiful glasshouses. The gardens were begun in 1827, during the 19th-century craze for plant hunting. The 14 acres were open to the public for a fee, but they never really became self-supporting financially and were eventually sold to the Belfast City Corporation, which made them a public park in 1895.

The best section of the gardens is the reconstruction of a **tropical ravine**, begun in 1889 and extended in 1900 and again in 1902 to include the heated pond where you can see giant water lilies growing. It was renovated once more in 1980. Look out for pitcher plants, tree ferns, bananas, cinnamon trees, papyrus at the water's edge and a great mass of water hyacinth, an invasive weed all over the Far East.

The **Palm House**, completed in 1852, is more beautiful but less interesting inside, being filled with the sort of plants that you can buy in department stores. The designer, Lanyon, used the new invention of curved glass to create the central elliptical dome with two wings. The building was renovated in 1975 when whole sections of glazing were replaced and a new heating system installed.

North of the city

Cave Hill

ⓘ *Entrances to the country park are Belfast Castle, Belfast Zoo, Upper Cave Rd; Cave Hill Heritage Centre is in Belfast Castle.*

The north of the city is defined by the high backdrop of mountains, which make up the country park of Cave Hill. Bought up by the city at various times from 1911, the park consists of about 750 acres of parkland, escarpments and woodland. It is grand wandering territory, criss-crossed with numerous footpaths, and is dotted with Bronze Age sites, including the caves themselves (which are man-made Iron Age mines). The best walk of all is to the top of the hill from where there are wonderful views of the city and lough, and even beyond them to the Scottish coast.

Belfast Castle

ⓘ *Antrim Rd, T9077 6925, daily, 0900-1800, free, if the heritage centre is closed, ask for the key at reception, Citybus 45, 46, 47, 48, 49, 50, 51 from Donegall Sq west.*

Set in the grounds of the country park is Belfast Castle, a Scottish baronial pile built in 1870 for the Marquis of Donegall. From a distance it looks imposing enough set against the mountains, but close up it is twee, with too many turrets and curlicues, rather in the style of Balmoral. It almost bankrupted the family, who fortunately married well and were able to complete it. It was given to the city in 1934 and refurbished in the 1970s at a cost of a couple of million pounds. It is run now as a series of businesses – a classy restaurant, a bistro, shop and pub all done up in Victorian street style – and is available for hire for weddings and functions.

Belfast Zoo

ⓘ *Apr-Sep 1000-1800 daily, Oct-Mar 1000-1530. Summer £6.70. Winter £5.70.* The zoo is a pleasant day out, as long as you enjoy looking at captive animals. It is a vibrant place, and so it should be. It has had around £10 million invested into the creation of new enclosures and general renovation, meaning the animals are well kept and there are some unusual creatures. The zoo has a respectable breeding programme with several endangered species producing offspring. Some, such as the golden lion tamarin, are even put into programmes to return them to the wild.

East of Belfast

Stormont

ⓘ *Bus 16 or 17 from Donegall Sq in Belfast.*

When Stormont was opened in 1932 it was accompanied by a triumphalist Protestant pageant, but when the post-Good Friday Assembly was inaugurated (see page 606), the political balance became a wee bit more level. Perhaps one day a public gallery will open, but the grounds are always open and the shining neo-classical Parliament building stands at the end of a mile-long drive before a statue of Edward Carson (1854-1935). He was a Unionist leader who brought Ulster perilously close to civil war by using the threat of military action to scupper attempts at Irish independence in the years leading up to the establishment of Northern Ireland.

★ Ulster Folk and Transport Museum

ⓘ *Cultra, T9042 8428, www.uftm.org.uk. Jul and Aug Mon-Sat 1000-1800, Sun 1100-1800; Apr-Jun Mon-Fri 1000-1700, Sat 1000-1800, Sun 1100-1800; Oct-Mar Mon-Fri 1000-1600, Sat 1000-1700, Sun 1100-1700, last admission 1 hr before closing time. £5, combined ticket to Folk Museum and Transport Museum £6.50. Trains and buses to Bangor stop at Cultra, 7 miles (11 km) east of Belfast.*

This is justly praised as one of Ireland's best museums. Dozens of buildings have been transplanted here to form a vibrant recreation of life in Ulster around 1900, complete with staff in period costume. Do not forget to pop into the corner sweet shop, which actually sells sweets and marbles and yo-yos. Also worthy of particular attention is the beautiful row of thatched houses rebuilt entirely from an Antrim townland, dating back to the 1600s and lived in until the 1950s. Both entertaining and educational, a visit is highly recommended. A bridge leads across the road to the transport museum where the largest locomotive built in Ireland is just one of the myriad forms of transport represented. The *Titanic* exhibition pulls in the crowds but there is a lot more to see. Miniature train rides, exhibitions on the history of food and farming, displays of lace making, spinning and weaving and blacksmithing.

Sleeping

In Dublin, hotel prices go up in summer and at weekends; here for many years the opposite has happened. During the summer restaurants, guest houses and shops closed down for the marching season, and at weekends the city centre emptied, a throwback to the old days of car bombs and assassinations. Accommodation prices still reflect those days with prices dropping at weekends although with the advent of cheap flights from Britain things are beginning to change. There are no great bargains in the city centre, but the hotels are classy enough. There are more modest places to the south of the city around Queen's University, while B&Bs and hostels provide cheaper accommodation. Eglantine Av has several good value places.

City centre *p501, map p502*

L Belfast Hilton, 4 Lanyon Pl, T9027 7000, www.hilton.co.uk/belfast. Don't be put off by the dull reception and uniformed staff – if you can possibly afford it stay here. It is a masterpiece of modernity in a sea of pompous Victoriana. Great views over the river, wonderful rooms, fluffy bathtowels, fitness centre and tiny pool, great *Sonoma* Restaurant with glass walls overlooking a hundred years of industry. Amazing discounts at weekends and a good breakfast.

L-A Malmaison Belfast, 34-38 Victoria St, T9022 0200, Belfast@malmaison.com. This is the third incarnation of these beautiful old buildings that were once warehouses. In their new Malmaison style they hold a classy

For an explanation of the sleeping and eating price codes used in this guide, see inside the front cover. Other relevant information is found in Essentials pages 39-45.

boutique hotel with 64 bespoke rooms, all black, cream and burgundy, with broadband, cable TV and DVD players.

L-A **TENsq**, 10 Donegall Sq East, T9024 1001, www.tensquare.co.uk. Very classy boutique hotel in beautiful old bank buildings beside the City Hall. Weekend break bargains.

A-B **Europa Hotel**, Great Victoria St, BT2 7AP, T9027 1066, www. Hastingshotels.com. The best you can say about this rather ugly building is that it's central and comfortable and that it stood here for years when the big hotel chains were nowhere to be seen.

D **Days Hotel**, 40 Hope St, T9024 2494, T0800-0280400, www.dayshotelbelfast.com. A great bargain for families. Room rate of £69.99, lower at weekends with children staying free in parents' room.

D **Travelodge Belfast City**, 15 Brunswick St, T0870-7522235. The best value for the centre, at £59.00 per room, which can sleep up to 4, without breakfast. Newly renovated but slightly cramped rooms, this would suit non-breakfast-eaters. Also has restaurant.

F **Linen House Youth Hostel**, 18-29 Kent St, T9058 6400, www.belfasthostel.com. Close to the main bus and train terminals, the main shopping area and City Hall, this is one of the largest of Belfast's hostels, in a renovated linen factory. Lots of room, large, well-equipped kitchen, good security. Mixed and single-sex dormitories. Double rooms. Left luggage room, bike storage, laundry, internet. Book in advance in the high season.

South of the city centre *p509, map p514*

L-A **Holiday Inn**, 22 Ormeau Av, T0870-4009005, www.belfast.holiday-inn.com. Very central, comfortable rooms, leisure centre, close to the Golden Mile.

B-C **Crescent Townhouse**, 13 Lower Cres, T9032 3349, www.crescenttownhouse.com. A small hotel with large, attractively appointed rooms. Set in the centre of the Golden Mile, its restaurant and bar are popular with office workers on their way home from work. The hotel itself is quiet, with the lobby upstairs, away from the activity of the bar and restaurant.

C-D **Duke's Hotel**, 65-67 University St, T9023 6666, www.dukeshotelbelfast.com. Well located at the end of the Golden Mile, interesting restaurant, big rooms, gym, good weekend rates.

D **Benedicts of Belfast**, 7-21 Bradbury Pl, Shaftesbury Sq, T9059 1999, www.benedictshotel.co.uk. Hotel with vaguely Gothic decor using reclaimed features from older buildings. Big rooms, excellent value, especially at weekends if you don't mind late nights and a bit of noise. Restaurant and breakfast to the sound of local music stations. Check in time 1400. 'Beat the clock' menu in the restaurant means the earlier you eat the less you pay.

D **Ivanhoe Hotel**, 556 Saintfield Rd, T9081 2240, www.ivanhoeinn.co.uk. Small, family-run hotel in pleasant rural surroundings. Well appointed big rooms, comfortable bar that doubles as a bistro in the evenings, more formal restaurant for dinner. Bus or taxi ride back into city. Open for Sun lunch.

D **Madison's**, 59-63 Botanic Av, T9033 0040, wwwmadisonshotel.com. Very trendy, modern hotel, popular with local swingers.

D **Ravenhill House**, 690 Ravenhill Rd, T9020 7444, www.ravenhillhouse.com. Pretty, child-friendly Victorian house in quiet location off the Ormeau Rd. Open fires, library, lots of maps and information. Vegetarian breakfast an option.

D **Tara Lodge**, 36 Cromwell Rd, T9059 0900, www.taralodge.com. Close to Botanic Av with all the bars and restaurants, walking distance of the city centre, good transport links, nice breakfasts, private car park. Lots of noise from the train station right behind the building. Ask for a room at the front.

E **All Seasons B&B**, 356 Lisburn Rd, T9068 2814, allseasons@fsmail.net. Another small well placed house, albeit set on the main Lisburn Rd, with off-street parking and friendly service.

E **Helga Lodge**, 7-13 Cromwell Rd, T9032 4820. Right in the heart of the Golden Mile on the corner of Botanic Av, this large rambling B&B is particularly good value but most rooms don't have en suite bathroom.

E **Marine Guest House**, 30 Eglantine Av, T9066 2828, www.marineguesthouse 3star.com. Another well located, good value place, close to the restaurants of Lisburn Rd and walking distance of town with good buses into the centre too. Off-street parking.

Halls of residence and hostels

E **Elms Village**, 78 Malone Rd, T9038 1608, qehor@qub.ac.uk. Single and twin rooms vailable during vacation periods, 24 Dec-Jan, 7-21 Apr, 19 Jun-10 Sep. Kitchen, TV oom, laundry. Public phones.

Farsett International Hostel, 466 pringfield Rd, T9089 9833, www.farset nternational.com. Set in scenic countryside, his is an upmarket place with restaurant as vell as self-catering facilities.

The Ark, 18 University St, T9032 9626, www.arkhostel.com. Hostel comprising 2 eorgian townhouses, 2 kitchens, double nd single rooms.

Belfast International Hostel, 22 Donegall d, T9032 4733, www.hini.org.uk. This is a ery central hostel, right beside the heart of he best nightlife in the city. Double and amily rooms as well as dorm beds. Secure arking and internet access.

Paddy's Palace, 68 Lisburn Rd, T9033 367, www.paddyspalace.com. Big new ddition to the hostel scene in Belfast, this is ne of a chain of hostels which aim to give ou the Irish experience. Loads of offers for ng term stays, reductions for staying at ther Paddy's Palaces, breakfast included in ate, free internet.

-G **Arnie's Backpackers**, 63 Fitzwilliam St, 9024 2867, www.arniesbackpackers. co.uk. elf-catering hostel in a small Victorian ouse off the Golden Mile. Dorm beds only.

ast of the city *p511*

Rayanne House, 60 Demesne Rd, olywood, T9042 5859, rayannehouse@ ol.com. Holywood is a middle-class eighbourhood a short way east of Belfast ity Airport, with its own cluster of restaurants nd this decidedly superior guesthouse in a rge detached house in a quiet location. The ecor and style of the place, a cross between e Victorian and Edwardian, is something ou tend to either love or loathe, but the hole house exudes comfort and calm. An vening meal can be arranged in advance but ere are lots of local eateries.

Eating

ity centre *p501, map p502*

James Street South, 21 James St Sth, 9043 4310. Elegantly designed and serving ccessible haute cuisine. Another place for a ecial night out. If you can't afford the vening menu, lunch is a bit cheaper.

Porcelain, 10 Donegall Sq Sth, T9024 1001, in the TenSquare Hotel. Much more than the typical hotel restaurant. It has an excellent reputation, is small and cosy and is often booked up at weekends long in advance. The cuisine is a kind of nouvelle Irish French with kedgeree, lamb Provençale, and some imaginative desserts.

Restaurant Michael Deane's, 38 Howard St, T9056 0000. The place to be seen in the city centre, upstairs is a restaurant where reservations well in advance are necessary as well as a well endowed charge card. Interestingly decorated with a kind of *fin de siècle* mood to the dining room. Great for a special occasion.

Roscoff Brasserie, 7-11 Linenhall St , T9031 1150. Telly chef Paul Rankin's newest effort. French brasserie cuisine, white tablecloths, sophisticated and efficient atmosphere, masterly food. Set dinner won't put you too far into debt while a 2-course set lunch is moderately priced.

Sonoma, Hilton, T9027 7000. Best of all in this area for the food and the views, has a glorious window with views of river and excellent modern Irish cuisine with lots of careful service. Pre-theatre menu comes into a lower price range.

Chokdee, 44 Bedford St, T9024 8800. Open for lunch and dinner Mon-Sat. A Michael Deane offshoot serving a very original blend of southeast Asian, spicy stir-fries and Italian home cooking. A spur of the moment kind of place. Lively and right at the bottom of this price range.

Deane's, 34-40 Howard St, T9056 0000. Downstairs is a brasserie which is enormously popular, focusing on modern Irish cooking where dinner will cost £18 plus.

Nick's Warehouse, 35-39 Hill St, T9043 9690. A long-established place, serving thoughtful modern Irish cuisine in a vast old warehouse with an open kitchen and lots of bustle. Avoid weekends when it gets very busy and noisy. Lunch is very popular too. Closed Sun, Mon.

Oxford Exchange, St George's Market, T9024 0014. Developing a good reputation as a hearty, meaty grill room with some curious versions of bangers and mash, fish and chips as well as boar. All served with posh chips and grilled veg. Closed Sun.

South Belfast

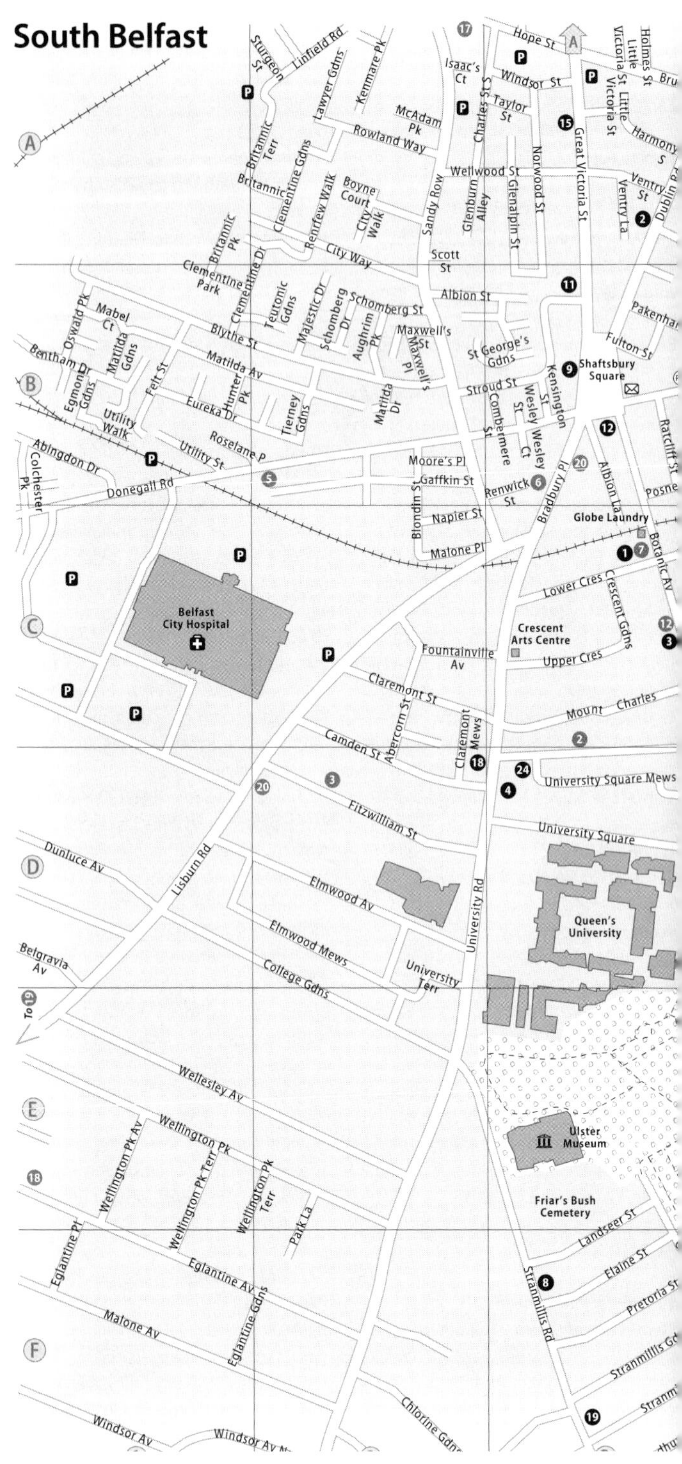

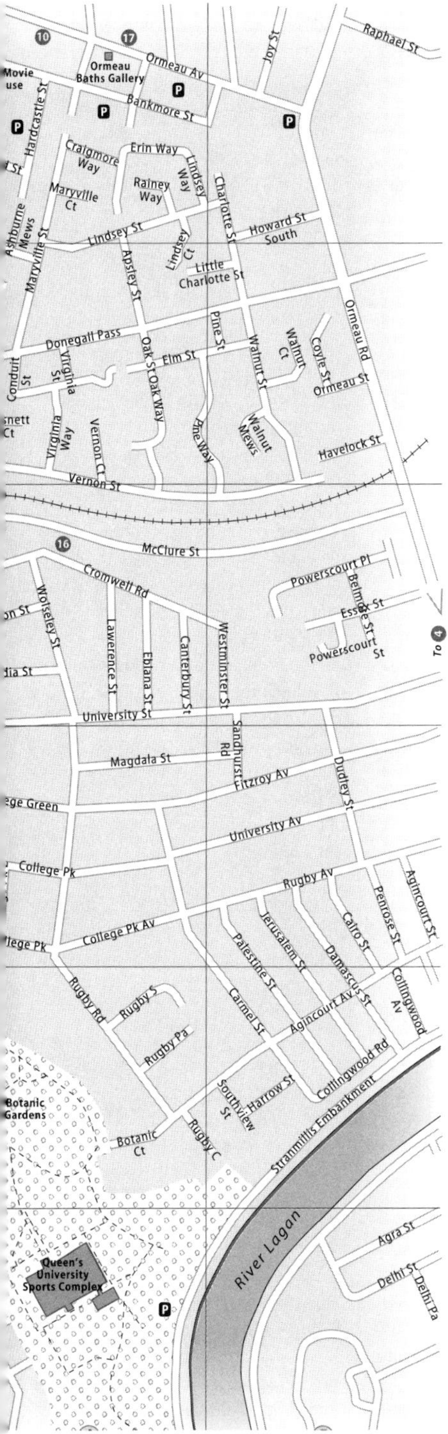

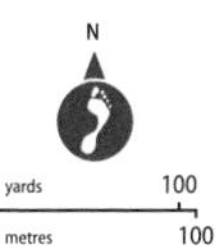

Sleeping

All Seasons B&B **19** *E1*
Ark **2** *C3*
Arnie's Backpackers **3** *D2*
Belfast International Hostel **5** *B2*
Benedicts of Belfast & Restaurant **6** *B3*
Crescent Townhouse **7** *C3*
Day's **17** *A2*
Duke's **8** *D3*
Helga Lodge **9** *C3*
Holiday Inn **10** *A4*
Madison's & Restaurant **12** *C3*
Marine Guest House **18** *E1*
Paddy's Palace **20** *D2*
Ravenhill House **4** *C5*
Tara Lodge **16** *C4*

Eating

Archana **2** *A3*
Beatrice Kennedy's **4** *D3*
Café Vincent **7** *C3*
Café Zinc **8** *F3*
Cayenne **9** *B3*
Gingeroot **15** *A3*
Giraffe **19** *F3*
Indie Spice **29** *F3*
Istana Malaysian **11** *B3*
Lemongrass **24** *D3*
Madison's **3** *C3*
Maharajah **22** *C3*
Metro **1** *C3*
Sun Kee **12** *B3*
Villa Italia **18** *D2*

Pubs & music

Katy Daly's & Limelight **17** *A4*
Lavery's Gin Palace **20** *B3*

Red Panda, 60 Gt Victoria St, T9046 6644. A good, Belfast-influenced, brightly-lit Chinese place serving hot spicy Szechuan dishes alongside Belfast gravy and chips and more experimental offerings.

Tedford's, 5 Donegall Quay, T9043 4000. A well established fish restaurant with the regulation Asian overtones in what was once an old ship's chandler shop. Good pre-theatre menu Tue-Sat makes for an affordable meal close to the Waterfront.

The Waterfront Brasserie, in the Waterfront Hall, T9024 4966. Worth visiting for its views alone, does breakfasts and lunches, and dinner between 1800-1930 when there is a show on. Book in advance.

Bar Seven, Odyssey Pavilion, T9046 7070. One of the city's many trendy designer bars but its food stands out among the rest with a set dinner menu under £20 and some good offers on combined cinema tickets and dinner. Style is modern Irish and the place gets booked up well in advance.

Ba Soba, 38 Hill St, T9058 6868. Belfast's first noodle bar with lots of south east Asian stir-fries, Thai curries, noodle dishes and the atmosphere of a posh Bangkok bar. Lots of combination lunch and dinner options keeps prices low and there are early evening offers of less than £8 for a main course.

Irene and Nan's, 12 Brunswick St, T9023 9123. A very trendy café bar at night but during the day and early evening has some great food. Try the evening 2- or 3- course set menus which barely get up into double figures plus laughably inexpensive wine.

Morning Star, 17-19 Pottinger's Entry, T9023 5986. No-nonsense cuisine here – giant steaks, gravy dinners, and the occasional shark, kangaroo or crocodile for bushmeat lovers, followed by lashings of dessert.

Nichol Bar Brasserie, T9027 9595, caught between the city centre and the Cathedral Quarter. A tiny place serving Mediterranean style food upstairs, lunch Mon-Sat, dinner Thu-Sat. Nicer in summer when the tables go out on the street and a Mediterranean atmosphere infuses more than the menu.

South of the city centre *p509, map p514*

Cayenne, 7 Ascot House, Shaftsbury Sq, T9033 1532. Starting at the 'haute' end of the market is telly-chef Paul Rankin's well established endeavour. Not a place for a romantic candlelight dinner, it bustles from 1800 onwards, while the menu is about as eclectic as it can get. Sushi, Moroccan spiced lamb, chorizo and borlotti beans, Italian penne, chicken with guacamole. Pleasant surroundings in a warm brown kind of way, service is just at the right pace. Open lunch and dinner. Closed Sun. Reservations essential.

Beatrice Kennedy's, 44 University Rd, T9020 2290. Offers a choice of early evening and dinner menus, serves modern Irish cuisine. Early evening menu is around £12 for 2 courses, while dinner works out around £26 plus. Open for lunch on Sun.

Benedicts, 7-21 Bradbury Pl, T9059 1999. Has a heavily designed restaurant and a dizzying range of menus. Dinner in this Californian-influenced but fairly traditional restaurant will be around £20 plus. Several vegetarian options. Lunch around £8.50 for 2 courses. Prices for main courses are determined by the time you choose to eat: at 1900 any main course is £7, at 2000 it's £8 and so on. Carvery lunch on Sun.

Café Vincent, 78 Botanic Av. Open daily. Does pasta dishes and is good for lunch.

Indie Spice, 159 Stranmillis Rd, T9066 8100. A stylish modern place, no pictures of the Taj Mahal here. Lots of dishes, good for vegetarians and a takeout menu too.

Lemongrass, 1 University St, T9032 4000. A branch of a popular chain of Asian fusion restaurants. Stylish modern interior, good lunch boxes to take out. Extra brownie points for being open 7 days, 1230-2300.

Madison's, 59-63 Botanic Av, T9050 9800. A popular restaurant, open daily, serving modern Irish/European cuisine and a more casual lunch menu.

Metro, on the corner of Botanic Av and Lower Cres, T9032 3349. A very stylish place with an inexpensive early evening menu (1800-1900), modern with Californian overtones. Very popular as a starting out point for Fri and Sat night partyers.

Archana, 53 Dublin Rd, T9032 3719. Winner of lots of awards for its Indian food. Very respectable vegetarian lunch thalis for around £4. Dinner upstairs at around £15. Open Sun evenings.

Gingeroot, 73-5 Gt Victoria St, T9031 3124. Less authentic and much more trendy, a north Indian place with modern overtones and a huge plate glass window to sit beside.

Lots of tandoor-cooked things and good breads. Try some of the north Indian sweets.

🍴 **Istana Malaysian Restaurant**, 127 Gt Victoria St, T9032 2311. Brightly lit canteen-like atmosphere and a mixture of Malay, Chinese and Thai food. The Penang Laksa is particularly good. Open late Fri and Sat.

🍴 **Sun Kee**, Donegall Pass, T9031 2016. Excellent, authentic Chinese restaurant. Reservations are essential at weekends and you still may have to queue. While the majority of the dishes are Cantonese there are lots of hotter Szechuan dishes and a few concessions to the blander western version of Chinese cooking.

🍴 **Villa Italia**, 37-41 University Rd, T9032 8356. Long established, all chequered tablecloths, plastic grapevines and chianti bottles where long queues form for a table at weekends. Italian home cooking – pizzas, pasta and more. Open Sun evenings.

🍴🍴 **The Maharajah**, 62 Botanic Av. Serves western versions of Indian cuisine, but good nonetheless.

🍴 **Café Zinc**, 12 Stranmillis Rd, T9068 2266. A little way beyond the Ulster Museum. In the evening the food is put away and it becomes a student café bar but through the day it serves an excellent menu of modern Irish cuisine, lots of fine cheeses and salads and more substantial dishes.

🍴 **Giraffe**, 54 Stranmillis Rd, T9050 9820. A slightly more interesting Clements clone with good inexpensive food, sofas and newspapers to read. Open Mon-Sat till 2200 and on Sun mornings.

Pubs and music

There are very few pubs in the city that don't have music of some kind or a late-night club attached somewhere. The last few years have seen a burgeoning of ultra cool, minimalist, steel and glass-style bars where cash rich, time poor Belfast white collar workers eat, drink and chill out but there are still etched glass, mahogany panelled, folksy sorts of places as well as the regulation vast screen sports bars. For up to date listings of events consult the free *The Big List* newspaper, available from the tourist office, rail and bus stations and newsagents.

City centre *p501, map p502*

Apartment, 2 Donegall Sq West, T9050 9777. Another style bar with a confusing vocabulary but very hip clientele.

The Crown Liquor Saloon (see page 506). This takes pride of place in the city centre with its authentic decorations and cosy snugs, but you must get there early if you want a seat.

Duke of York, 11 Commercial Court, T9024 1062. Another of the city's cherished ancient pubs, hidden away down one of the little alleys. Once the hang-out of newspaper types it has a more varied clientele nowadays with lots of live music sessions.

Irene and Nan's (see page 516). One of the new-style bars in the city, its design based, apparently, on photographs of Prague airport in the 1960s. Happy hour Thu and Fri 1700-1900.

John Hewitt, 53 Donegall St, T9023 3768. A recently-built traditional bar which has no TV so people just have to talk to each other. It serves good food and has regular traditional music, storytelling and jazz.

Kelly's Cellars, 30 Bank St. For good Irish music this is one of the city's oldest pubs, is worth a look in. Legend has it that the United Irishmen met here to plan the uprising in 1798.

Madden's, Berry St, T9024 4114. An old-fashioned kind of place, full of locals, good for a quiet drink and some live music.

McHugh's, 29-31 Queen St, T9050 9990. Belfast's oldest surviving building or at least the white part of the building is, the rest being fairly recent additions. The basement bar holds live music sessions of all kinds with traditional music on Thu in the main bar.

Morning Star (see page 516). A listed building and winner of awards for its food. It is quiet at night and a good place for music, TV and a casual drink.

Northern Whig, 2 Bridge St, T9050 9888. Here the city's young and restless sip their cocktails beneath statues of men who once held power over swathes of eastern Europe. Retro brown and café au lait sofas, DJs start early on Fri.

White's Tavern, in Winecellar Entry, T9024 3080. Another ancient pub, has music upstairs and good pub food downstairs.

Rotterdam Bar, 54 Pilot St, T9074 6021. This is the kind of place where beat poets, if they still existed, would hang. Dim, smoky (for now at least) and filled with live music: sing-song on Sun, folk and traditional music Mon, Thu, jazz and blues on Tue, a quiz night Wed, and assorted live bands at weekends.

Clubs

Limelight, 17 Ormeau Av, T9032 5942. Beside *Katy Daly's* pub, this is a serious dance club and also holds some major live performances. Tue is *Shag* – students' night.
Milk Bar, Tomb St, T9027 8876. Ferociously fashionable and was voted Northern Ireland's Best Small Club in 2003. Something on every night and Wed is free entrance and 2 free drinks for women.
Thompsons, 3 Patterson Pl, off Arthur St, T9032 3762, www.clubthompsons.com. Thu-Sat 2100 till late. A variety of DJ sounds with Sat being the most popular followed by Fri. Lots of regulars and a wide age range.

South of the city centre *p509, map p514*

Lavery's Gin Palace, 16 Bradbury Pl, T9087 1106. A vast warren of bars dedicated to alcohol consumption with a clientele that covers the entire spectrum. Just choose the bar that suits you. Upstairs is **Heaven** and there's live music in the Back Bar.
Morrison's, 21 Bedford St, T9032 0030. Has music at weekends and a good atmosphere as well as big screen football matches. Lots of pub food and cool cocktail bar upstairs.

Clubs

The Empire Music Hall, 42 Botanic Av, T9024 9276. A converted church has something to attract every night but really gets going at the weekends.
Hell @ Lavery's, above Lavery's Gin Palace. Popular on Sat nights.
M Club, 23-5 Bradbury Pl, T9023 3131. Heaves with revellers Mon, Thu and Sat while Tue is student night. Admission prices rise at weekends.

Entertainment

Art galleries

Belfast is home to several innovative art galleries displaying regular exhibitions of local artists' work.
Belfast Exposed, 23 Donegall Pl, T9023 0965. A gallery dedicated to photography by local and international photographers whose work focuses on social themes. Besides the exhibitions is a huge collection of archive material recording the social and political history of the city.
The Fenderevsky Gallery, 2-4 University Rd, T9024 2338, at the The Crescent Arts Centre. Has a changing exhibition of local painters.
Old Museum Arts Centre, 7 College Sq North, T9023 5053. Also has varying exhibitions of local artists in what was once the first museum on the island of Ireland. Again, very innovative exhibitions. The corridors of the W5 exhibition at the Odyssey Pavilion are also often filled with some beautiful travelling exhibitions.
Ormeau Baths Gallery, 18 Ormeau Av, T9032 1402. Presenting the more experimental work of local artists and work in multi-media from all over Europe in what was once a public bath house.

Smaller private galleries can be visited at: **Safehouse Arts Space**, 25 Donegall St, T9031 4499; **Lawrence St Workshops**, 1a Lawrence St, off Botanic Av, T9023 4993; **Eakin Gallery**, 237 Lisburn Rd, T9066 8522; and **Mullan Gallery**, 239 Lisburn Rd, T9020 2434.
Raymond Watson, in the Conway Mill, west Belfast, T9077 3264. A sculptor whose work is exhibited in the craft shop.

Cinemas

The Movie House, 14 Dublin Rd. Multi-screen cineplex showing all the big releases.
Queen's Film Theatre, 7 University Sq Mews, T0800 328 2811, www.qub.ac.uk/qft. The city's arty cinema, good value.
Village Cinemas International, Odyssey Pavilion, T0870 240 6020. Really big complex.
Yorkgate Centre, 100 York St, T9075 3300. Multi-screen cineplex showing the latest Hollywood stuff.

Gay and lesbian

There has been a disturbing rise in the number of attacks on gay men in Belfast, although it is unlikely that being gay in Belfast is any more dangerous than in any other major city. Lots of gay people travel to Dublin for the weekend but the gay scene in Belfast changed a few years ago with the opening of Kremlin. Check out www.gaybelfast.net.

Custom House, 22-8 Skipper St, T9024 5558.
Kremlin, 96 Donegall St, T9080 9700, www.kremlin-belfast.com. A vastly extravagant place with a huge statue of Lenin outside. The largest gay venue in Ireland and attracts people from all over the island.
The Kube 2-16 Dunbar St, T9023 4520, www.kubeonline.com. Has some basic food and a nightclub called Club Heat.
Union St Bar, Union St, www.unionstreet pub.com. Gay orientated and has an all night-long Sat club, Event Horizon.
Some pubs/clubs have dedicated gay nights: **Apartment**; **John Hewitt**; **Milk** (see all page 517). Mon is *Forbidden Fruit* with Titti Von Tramp at Milk.
Mono Café, 100 Ann St. Bar that dedicates its Thu nights to a gay evening called *Attitude*.
Opium, Skipper St. Gay-friendly bar.
The Pavilion, 296 Ormeau Rd, T9064 0914. Has a gay night on the 1st Fri of each month called *Howl*.
Queen's Bar, 4 Queen's Arcade. Gay friendly.

Music venues

King's Hall, at Balmoral, T9066 5225, www.kingshall.co.uk. Stages the really big rock shows. Lisburn Rd buses.
Odyssey Arena, T9073 9074, www.Odysseyarena.com. The city's latest addition to the big concert scene, more commonly home to the Belfast Giants ice hockey team but stepping out for the big names that come to the city.
Ulster Hall, Bedford St, T9032 3900. Hosts classical performances by the Ulster Orchestra as well as some rock concerts.
Waterfront Hall, Lanyon Pl, Laganside, T9033 4455. Hosts a whole range of events from classical music to school parents' evenings, stand-up gigs by ageing comics, ballet, jazz, and big-name pop stars.

Other places which occasionally play host to classical music are **St Anne's Cathedral** (see page 506), the **Linenhall Library** (see page 504), **Clonard Monastery** (see page 507) and the **Mandela Hall**, Queen's University Students' Union, T9023 6057.

Theatres

Grand Opera House, Great Victoria St, T9024 1919. Worth a visit just for the decorations, but it regularly has big-name shows transferred from Dublin or London's West End.
Lyric Theatre, off Ridgeway St, which is off Stranmillis Rd south of the city, T9038 1081. The city's serious theatre. It regularly has important modern productions. There is a student standby scheme where remaining tickets will be sold off at reduced prices to students after 1930 on the night.
Old Museum Arts Centre, College Sq North, T9023 3332. Has a small theatre where the avant garde can be found.

Festivals and events

Cathedral Quarter Arts festival, in early **May**, T9023 2403, www.cqaf.com. 10 days of music, theatre, comedy, circus, art exhibitions and street events. Belfast Summer in the City, T9027 0222, late **May-Sep** includes all kinds of events from local stuff to major concerts, including the Lord Mayor's Show. Orange Marches, basically the city goes pretty quiet for 2 weeks around the height of the marching season, the 1st 2 weeks in **Jul**. A week-long gay pride festival takes place in the city in late **Jul**-early **Aug**, www.2005@belfast pride.com, and includes a parade, pub quizzes, parties and the like. Ardoyne Fleadh, T9075 1056, is 3 days of open-air concerts and community events in north Belfast, in early **Aug**. Féile an Phobail, T9031 3440, www.feile-belfast.com, takes place during the 1st 2 weeks in **Aug** and includes street parties, concerts, Irish-language events and a carnival parade. Originally a Republican-inspired event, it is now huge and includes contributions from Unionists. Also look out for the Belfast Film festival in late **Sep**. Belfast Festival at Queens, T9066 7687 for information, T9066 5577 for bookings, www.belfast festival.com. An arts festival with 400-plus shows during 3 weeks around **Nov**, based around Queen's University. Belfast's answer to the Edinburgh Festival.

Shopping

Antiques **Donegall Pass** is the best place for looking for curios and more expensive items. Shops include **Alexander the Grate** which has an antiques market on Sat, **Bernard's Fine Art**, **Archives**, **Past and Present** and **Oakland Antiques**. Particular mementoes of the area might be the many pottery representations of King Billy on his white horse.

Arts and crafts **Conway Mill**, the craft shop in the ground floor is open from about 1000-1500 also has the work of local craftspeople, most of them with workshops in the mill buildings.
Craftworks, Bedford House, Bedford St. Has beautiful handmade clothes and craft objects from all over Ireland.
Global Creations, in the Fountain Centre. Sells craft objects from a round the world selling at fair trade prices.
Ogham Gallery, 497 Antrim Rd, T9077 2580. Sells locally-made crafts such as bodhrans, carved bog oak and hand-crafted slate items.
The Steensons, Bedford House, next door to Craftworks. Makers of exquisite, reasonably priced silver jewellery, they sell their own creations plus the work of many others.
The Wicker Man, Donegall Arcade. Belfast's biggest craft shop with the work of craftspeople from all over the island in stock.

Books **An Leathrá Póilí**, 513 Falls Rd. Has books on Irish issues from a Republican perspective. It also has a café.
Emerald Isle Books, 539 Antrim Rd, T9037 0798, F9077 7288. Private dealer. It is necessary to make an appointment.
Ex Libris, Unit 28, Victoria Centre. Has a large stock of second-hand material and sells graphic novels.
Familia Bookshop, 64 Wellington Pl. Has books on Irish issues.
P&B Rowan, Carleton House, 92 Malone Rd, T9066 6448. Private dealer. Appointments are necessary.
Roma Ryan's, 73 Dublin Rd. Sells prints and rare antique books.

The regular bookshops can be found in the city centre: **Dillons**, 42 Fountain St; **Eason's**, 16 Ann St; **Waterstones**, at 8 Royal Av.

Markets **St George's Market**, May St. Has existed for many years and has undergone major renovations recently. It is still a fruit and vegetable market, but also has stalls selling bric-à-brac, second-hand and new clothes, and on Fri has more than 200 stallholders. It is also home to a twice monthly Sat farmers' market.
Smithfield Retail Market, behind Castlecourt Shopping Centre. Sells new and second-hand furniture and clothes.

Sporting goods **Beaten Track**, Arthur St.
Millets, Cornmarket. Branch with its usual collection of sportswear and camping equipment.
Surf Mountain, 12 Brunswick St. Specializes in surfing gear but also has an excellent collection of camping gear.

Activities and tours

Football There are regular matches at **Seaview**, off Shore Rd, home ground of the Crusaders; the **Oval**, Redcliffe Pde, in the Newtownards Rd, home ground of Glentoran; and **Solitude**, Cliftonville, the home ground of Cliftonville. International matches are held at Windsor park near the Lisburn Rd, the home of Linfield Park football club, T9024 4198. For details of matches check the weekend papers or ring the Irish Football League on T9024 2888, or check out www.irishfa.com.

Gaelic football Matches at weekends at **Roger Casement Park**, Andersonstown Rd, T01232-613661, 01232-213490.

Hurling Weekends at **Roger Casement Park**, Andersonstown Rd, T01232-613661, 01232-213490. Hurling final is in early Jul.

Ice skating **Ice Bowl**, 111 Old Dundonald Rd, T9048 2611. Olympic-sized rink.
Ice hockey, The Belfast Giants play at the Odyssey Arena, www.belfastgiants.co.uk.

Leisure centres **Maysfield Leisure Centre**, East Bridge St, T9024 1633.
Olympia Leisure Centre, Boucher Rd, T9023 3369.
Shankill Leisure Centre, 100 Shankill Rd, T9024 1434. Includes 'Water Wonderland' a leisure pool.

Running **The Belfast Marathon** is in early May.

Rugby **Collegians**, Deramore Park, Malone Rd. For details try the Irish Rugby Football Union at T9064 9141 or www.ulsterrugby.com, for details of the

Jlster team's fixtures. At Ravenhill Grounds, 35 Ravenhill Park, T9049 3222.
Malone Rugby Club, Malone Park, off Woodstock Rd.

Ten-pin bowling Euphoria Bowling Alley, Odyssey Pavilion, T9046 7030.
Ice Bowl, 11 Old Dundonald Rd, 5 miles out of city centre. 30 lanes.
Superbowl, Bedford St.

Tennis Belfast Tennis Arena, Ormeau Embankment, T9045 8024.

Tours

Bailey's Historical Pub Tour of Ireland, T9268 3665, www.belfastpubtours.com. May-Sep Thu 1900 and Sat 1600. £6 including a glass of Baileys. Departs from the Crown Dining Room, upstairs in the crown, Great Victoria St. A 2-hr walk around some of the city's oldest pubs, hidden away in some of the entries and back streets.
Belfast Castle, free tour. 1 hr. Advance booking necessary, T9077 6925.
Belfast City Hall (see page 501), T9027 0456. Has free tours of the building.
Belfast Safaris, T9022 2925, www.belfastsafaris.com. Just started in 2004 these are walking tours through the suburbs of the city, covering the Cathedral Quarter, Clifton House, Clifton St graveyard, Crumlin Rd and on to Belfast Castle. They offer guided tours or self-guided tours. Phone to arrange a tour.
City sightseeing Belfast, T9062 6888, www.city-sightseeing.com. An open top bus tour of the city, that takes in Laganside, the Odyssey Complex, the old dockyards, the Crumlin Rd and the Falls and Shankill wall murals. Departs from Castle Pl. hourly, more often in summer. £8. Tickets can be booked in advance or bought on the bus.
Historic Belfast Walking Tour, T9023 8437. May-Oct, 1400 Wed, Fri, Sat Sun. From Welcome Centre 47 Donegall Pl. Covers the old town; 1½ hrs. £5.
Irish Political Tours, 10 Beechmount Av, T9020 0770, www.coiste.ie. The national network for Republican ex-prisoners organizes these tours to suit individual need. Ring to arrange a tour.
Lagan Tours, T9033 0844, www.laganboatcompany.com. A trip along the river on *The Joyce*, Mon-Thu, 1230, 1400, 1530. £5. The same company does **Titanic Tours**. Another boat ride which takes in the docks area and the locations connected with the building of the Titanic. Fri, Sat, Sun 1230, 1400, 1530. Collect a flyer from the Welcome Centre for a £1 reduction.
Life Cycle Tours, 36-7 Smithfield Market, T9043 9959, www.lifecycles.co.uk. 3-hr guided cycle tour of the city. Book at least 1 day in advance. £12 (includes bike hire).
Mini Coach, 22 Donegall Rd, T9031 5333, www.minicoachni.co.uk. Organizes a city tour and a tour to the Giant's Causeway and Causeway coast, taking in Bushmills Distillery and the Carrick-a-rede rope bridge. Giant's Causeway tour departs daily from Belfast International Hostel at 0930, returns approx. 1745. £16, city tour Mon-Fri 1030, 1230, Sat Sun 1030, 1400, £8. All tours stop for photo opportunities.
Pedal Power, 10 Joanmount Park, T9071 5000, www.pedalpowercycleireland.co.uk. 23-day cycle tour of Ireland, 17-day tour to Kinsale, 10-day tour to Galway.
West Belfast Taxi Tours, 5-7 Conway St, T9031 5777, www.jadepro.com/wbta. 1-4 people £17 per hr and £12 per hr thereafter. A tour of the Republican sites of west and north Belfast.

Transport

Air

See the Getting there section of the Essentials chapter (page 28) for flight connections to Britain, Europe and the US, and the Getting there section of this chapter (page 498) for information on how to get to Belfast from its two airports.

Bus

Europa Bus Centre, Glengall St, T9033 3000, has services to **Enniskillen**, **Tyrone**, **Derry**, **Armagh**, **Downpatrick**, **Kilkeel**, **Newcastle**, **Newry**, **Limavady**, **Portadown** via **Lurgan**, **Dungannon**, **Bundoran**, **Ballycastle**, the **ferry terminals**, and destinations in the Republic, including **Achill**, **Sligo**, **Ballina**, **Westport**, **Galway**, **Athlone**, **Cork**, **Dublin**. The Laganside bus station has services to **Cookstown**, **Portrush**, **Ballymena**, **Antrim**, **Larne**, **Coleraine**, **Portstewart**, **Ballycastle** and **Carrickfergus**. There is also a service to **Dumfries**, **Carlisle**, **Preston**, **Manchester**,

Birmingham and **London** via **Stranraer**, run by **Eurolines** which has a booking office in the Europa Bus Centre, T9033 7002. There are no left-luggage facilities at either bus station. A private company, **Patrick Gallagher**, T00353-74-9531107, operates a daily service between **Donegal**, **Letterkenny**, **Derry** and Belfast, leaving from Jury's Hotel at 1730 Mon-Sat, 2115 Sun, price £10. An express bus service operates between **Belfast International Airport**, **Derry** and **Donegal**, daily in Jul and Aug, Mon, Wed, Fri, Sun Sep-Jun, T00353-74-9548114, www.fedaodonnel.com.

Car hire

There are Budget, Europcar Rental, Hertz and McCausland desks in the arrivals hall at Belfast International Airport and Budget and Avis desks at the City Airport. Desks are manned as incoming flights arrive. Rental is per day or per week. **Avis**, 69 Great Victoria St, T9024 0404, Belfast International Airport T9442 2333, City Airport, T9045 2017, www.avis.co.uk. **Budget**, 96-102 Great Victoria St, T9023 0700, Belfast International Airport, T9442 3332, City Airport T9045 1111,www.budget-Ireland.co.uk. **Dan Dooley**, Belfast International Airport, 175 Airport Rd, Crumlin, Co Antrim, T9445 2522, T0800-282189, www.dan-dooley.ie. Also operate a meet and greet service in Belfast City Airport. **Europcar**, Belfast International Airport, T9442 3444, City Airport, T9045 0904, www.europcar.com. **Hertz**, Belfast International Airport, T9442 2533, www.hertz.co.uk.

Ferry

Ferries arrive at several locations along the river. The **Seacat** ferries, T08705 523523, www.seacat.co.uk, from **Troon** in Scotland (2 hrs 30 mins) and the **Isle of Man** (2 hrs 45 mins) (both summer only) arrive at **Donegall Quay**. The **Stena Line** ferry, T9074 7747, from **Stranraer** docks at **Ballast Quay** (105 mins on the Stena HSS and 3 hrs 15 min on the Superferry). **Larne**, 20 miles (30 km) north, is where the **P&O** ferries, T0870-2424777, www.poirishsea.com, from **Cairnryan**, **Troon** and **Fleetwood** dock. It is also possible to get to Belfast's Victoria terminal, from **Birkenhead** (8-9 hrs). For information on all crossings contact **Direct Ferries**, T0870-458 5120, www.directferries.co.uk.

Train

Except for the excellent Belfast to Dublin route, trains are an expensive option when moving on from Belfast. There are 3 train routes out of Belfast: 1 travels north and then west along the lovely coastline scenery to **Derry**, another west and then south through **Portadown** towards **Dublin**, and a 3rd, smaller line, travels east to **Bangor**. Trains leave from 2 stations, **Great Victoria St**, T9023 0671, and **Belfast Central**, T9089 9411. From Belfast Central trains go to **Larne**, **Derry**, **Bangor**, **Portadown**, **Newry** and **Dublin**, while Great Victoria St serves **Portadown**, **Lisburn**, **Bangor**, **Larne Harbour** and **Derry**. A free citylink bus serves Belfast Central from Donegall Sq. The Belfast to Dublin route is very fast and comfortable and costs £23 one way, £33 return stopping at **Portadown**, **Newry**, **Lisburn** and **Dundalk**. There are no left-luggage facilities at the stations.

Directory

Banks Bank of Ireland, 54 Donegall Pl, T9023 4334 (linked with Barclays). **Northern Bank**, Donegall Sq West, T9024 5277. **Ulster Bank**, 47 Donegall Pl, T9024 4112 (linked with Natwest). **Consulates** Denmark and Sweden: **G Heyn & Sons Ltd**, Head Line Buildings, 10 Victoria St, T9023 0581. **Greece, Norway, Portugal: M F Ewings, (Shipping) Ltd**, Hurst House, 15-19 Corporation Sq, T902 2242. **Italy**: 7 Richmond Park, T9066 8854. **USA**: Consulate General, Queen's House, 14 Queen St. **Libraries** Belfast Central Library, Royal Av, Mon and Thu 0930-2000, Tue, Wed, Fri 0930-1730, Sat 0930-1300. **Medical services** Hospitals: Accident and Emergency services are at **Belfast City Hospital**, Lisburn Rd, T9032 9241, **Mater Hospital**, Crumlin Rd, T9074 1211, **Royal Victoria Hospital**, Grosvenor Rd, T9024 0503 and **Ulster Hospital**, Dundonald, T9048 4511.

Counties Antrim and Down

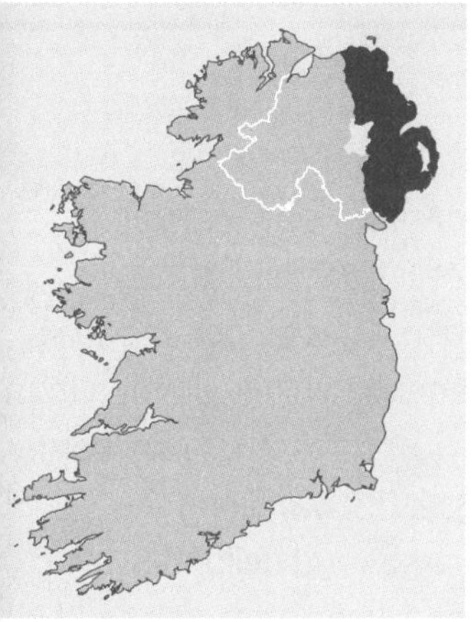

Footprint features

Introduction

Travelling the coastline of County Antrim is a memorable experience, and coming up the coast from Belfast the departure from cityscapes to sudden vistas of rock and sea is an instant therapy for any lingering urban blues. Starting from the other end, in seaside Portrush just across the Derry border, the dazzling Antrim coast road works its way along the northern coast to the Giant's Causeway and delightful Ballycastle, gateway to Rathlin Island, before heading south past the wild hillsides of the Glens of Antrim and a string of settlements that dot the highly scenic journey down to Belfast. This is the province's most tourist-orientated area but those who fear the heritage centre/tour bus brigade need not worry. It is easy at the hot spots of Bushmills and the Giant's Causeway to get away from the crowds and do your own thing. The Ulster Way runs through the county if you like to really be alone and there are many more activities to nourish and delight the soul.

South of Belfast, County Down is a series of surprises: reminders of sectarianism in towns like Kilkeel one moment; tolerant places like Downpatrick the next; and then, in the blink of an eye, shifting shades of green and purple where, in the words of the familiar song, "the Mountains of Mourne sweep down to the sea".

★ Don't miss...

1. **Giant's Causeway** Tread in the steps of Finn McCool, page 527.
2. **Walking** Try the North Antrim Cliff Path between Portballintrae and Ballintoy, page 528.
3. **Thrills** Scare the life out of yourself on the Carrick-a-rede rope bridge, page 530.
4. **Carnlough** Enjoy the pleasant olde-worlde charms and fine lunches at the Londonderry Arms Hotel, page 539.
5. **Downpatrick** Look out for 18th-century graffiti in the old gaol in Down County Museum, and try and time your visit for the St Patrick's Day celebrations, page 548.
6. **Mountains of Mourne** Take a walk in the majestic granite of these well-known but little visited hills, 552.

County Antrim

North Antrim Coast

The north Antrim Coast is one of the most visited parts of Northern Ireland since it is home to the curious Giant's Causeway, the province's most well known attraction. But beyond the attractions of this and the almost equally famous Bushmills Distillery are other places worth seeking out: Ballycastle, Portrush and Portstewart are unassuming little seaside towns, Rathlin Island is a quick day trip out of Ballycastle and if you only want to go a few yards offshore there's the Carrick-a-rede rope bridge to wobble across. The Ulster Way threads through the area and there are beaches and a castle to explore. ▸▸ *For Sleeping, Eating and other listings, see pages 531-534.*

Ins and outs

Getting there **Ulsterbus** services connect Portrush with Antrim, Armagh, Ballymena, and Cookstown. Portrush is accessible by train from Derry, Belfast and Dublin via Coleraine (8 trains a day). Ulsterbus runs to Ballycastle from Belfast and Coleraine, Mon-Sat. **McGinn,** T2076 3451, a private company, runs a Ballycastle to Belfast return bus, departing from the Diamond at 1600 on Fri, 2000 on Sun, and outside the Europa Hotel in Belfast at 1815 on Fri, 2145 on Sun. ▸▸ *See also Transport, page 533, for further details.*

Getting around See page 533 for details of the Antrim Coaster service.

Information The **Portrush tourist office** is in the Dunluce Centre, Sandhill Rd, T7082 3333. Open Apr to mid-Jun Mon-Fri 0900-1700, Sat and Sun 1200-1700; Mid-Jun to Sep daily 0900-1900; Mar and Oct Sat and Sun 1200-1700. **Giant's Causeway Visitors Centre**, Giant's Causeway, T2073 1855 (see page 527). **Ballycastle tourist office,** 7 Mary St, T2076 2024. Open Mon-Fri 0930-1700, Sat 1000-1800 and Sun 1400-1800.

Portrush → *Colour map 1, grid A4.*

Portrush is a busy seaside resort packed with activities for families and while the downside may be the usual tackiness and the excess of buckets and spades dangling from shop doorways there are upbeat surprises in store as well: Portrush is a superb centre for surfing.

Sights **Curran Strand** is the sandy beach that stretches eastwards for over a mile, past the famous golf course to the **White Rocks**. Erosion has weathered and sculpted arches and caves into weird shapes. Surfing is good here: try the East Strand, which can be reached by car, although the West Strand is just as good.

The **Ulster Way** path, rising up to clifftop level, follows the coast from Portrush to Portstewart. From Portrush Harbour **boat trips** head out to tour **The Skerries**, a chain of small islands off the coast. Horse riding is also available, see page 533.

The **Dunluce Centre** ⓘ *Sandhill Dr, T7082 4444, open weekends only in Sep-May, daily in Jun, Jul and Aug*, has computer-age attractions for children.

Waterworld ⓘ *T7082 2001, daily, £4.50 but family tickets are available*, by the harbour, is a water playground with all the works as well as a bowling alley and sauna

Portrush to the Giant's Causeway → *Colour map 1, grid A4.*

Between Portrush and the Giant's Causeway there are two points of interest. Dunluce Castle, beside the A2 and not to be missed on a fine day, is just west of the smal

“” It really does seem as though some bad tempered giant hand set the rocks down here in an ugly fit of pique...

harbour at Portballintrae, while Bushmills and its famous distillery are just off the A2 a little further to the east. Bushmills makes a convenient watering hole for lunch, before or after a visit to the Causeway.

Dunluce Castle ⓘ *T2073 1938, open Apr-May and Sep, Mon-Sat, 1000-1800, Sun, 1400-1800; Jun-Aug, Mon-Sat, 1000-1830, Sun, 1200-1600; Oct-Mar, Tue-Sat, 1000-1600, Sun, 1400-1600, £1.50, Visitor Centre, guided tours.* The castle at Dunluce, one of the most enjoyable to visit anywhere in Ireland, is not one of those brutal Norman impositions, for there is something whimsical as well as dramatic about its spectacular location on a rock stack. A fortification of some kind here goes back two millennia perhaps, but the earliest of the castle walls were built for the MacQuillans, originally Scottish mercenaries, in the 14th century and completed later by the MacDonnells. The English under Sir John Perrott, determined to clear the Scots from Antrim, took the castle with artillery in 1584, but the following year Sorley Boy MacDonnell (see box on page 537) and his men scaled the cliffs on ropes and hung the constable (his Scots mistress is said to have played an invaluable part in this). Perrott was philosophical: “I do not weigh the loss but can hardly endure the discredit”. The MacDonnells made a deal and remained the residents and their subsequent repair work lasted 60 years until the kitchen and servants' quarters collapsed into the sea and ruined a perfectly good night's dinner. There is plenty of the castle left standing and a visit is recommended.

Bushmills Distillery ⓘ *T2073 1521, http://irish-whiskey-trail.com, Apr-Oct, Mon-Sat 0930-1730, Sun 1200-1730, last tour at 1600; Nov-Mar, Mon-Fri, tours on the hour between 1030 and 1530 (but not 1230), £3.95.* Bushmills developed with the rise of water-powered industry in the early 17th century – the first hydro-electric tramway in the world came through here on its way from Portrush to the Causeway – and whiskey was first legitimately distilled here in 1608. A guided tour of **The Old Bushmills Distillery** covers history and technology and finishes with the customary taster of the famous single malt, triple distilled, whiskey.

★ Giant's Causeway → *Colour map 1, grid A5.*

ⓘ *Giant's Causeway Centre, T2073 1582, Jul-Aug, daily 1000-1900, shorter hours rest of the year, audio-visual show £1, car park £5. Tea-room open mid-Mar to Nov. There is no charge to visit the Giant's Causeway unless arriving by car or wishing to hop in the minibus, £20 return, from the Causeway Centre to the shore.*

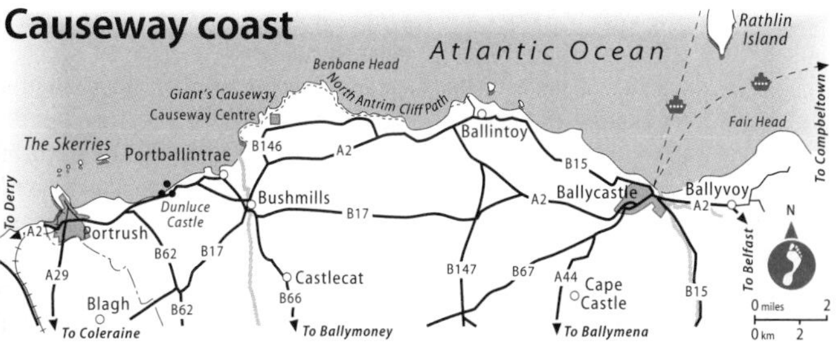

"And her hands were bound behind her back"

When Deirdre was born, a druid named her as a source of misfortune, but Conchobar had her brought up in secret with the intention of marrying her. It was not to be, for Deirdre knew in her heart that her lover would have black hair, a white body and red cheeks. She met such a man at Emain Macha (Navan Fort) and together with his two brothers they fled, pursued by the revengeful Conchobar, until they found refuge in Scotland and then on a remote island. Lured back with a false message they landed at Ballycastle, but the brothers were murdered and Deirdre brought to Conchobar – "and her hands were bound behind her back" and later forced to marry one of his accomplices. At Emain Macha, on the day of her wedding, Deirdre commited suicide.

So runs a tale, first written down in the eighth century, that inspired Lady Gregory and, through her, Yeats and Synge and other 20th-century writers.

Formed by the cooking and cooling of vast quantities of basalt, the giant crystals of the Giant's Causeway have been attracting countless visitors since they were first 'discovered' by the Victorians. The novelist Walter Scott selected four of the basalt columns to take home with him but changed his mind, the poet Keats set out to walk here from Donaghadee but found it too long a journey, while Thackeray in his 1842 tour was led to exclaim that when God fashioned the world out of chaos "this must have been *the bit over* – a remnant of chaos".

One version has it that the polygonal columns were spewed forth as the result of a cataclysmic convulsion in the crust of oceanic tectonic plates, but the Causeway Centre is not bound by modern dogma and the exhibition allows visitors to choose between this prosaic account and the rather more fanciful story about lusty Finn McCool (Fionn MacCumhaill), who wanted a passageway across the water to reach a giantess on the island of Staffa, off the coast of Scotland. (This is backed up by science, for similar rock formations are indeed to be found there as well.)

Once you leave behind the rather tasteless interpretive centre and actually see the rocks you can understand what has been bringing so many people here over the years to see them. It really does seem as though some bad tempered giant hand set the rocks down here in an ugly fit of pique.

From the Causeway Centre it is a short walk to the shore and Finn's stepping stones, but in summer you will have to dodge minibuses and hordes of visitors. Follow instead the path up behind the Centre and take the **North Antrim Cliff Path**; a few hundred steps bring you down to the shore.

The **Causeway School Museum** ⓘ *T2073 1777, Jul-Aug, daily 1100-1700, 75p*, an original 1920s classroom next to the Centre, is worth a visit with children, or on a wet day.

The tourist office in Portrush has a leaflet describing a walk following the tracks of the Causeway Tram that ran between Portrush and the Causeway between 1883 and 1949. There is talk of relaying part of the line.

★ **Walking the Causeway coast** Having ticked off the Giant's Causeway on the 'been there, done that' list, it seems a pity to leave the majestic North Antrim coast too quickly, and luckily the **Causeway Coast Way** (North Antrim Cliff Path) provides an exhilarating way of extending one's stay. It takes about five hours to walk the 17 km (10 miles) between Portballintrae and Ballintoy, and with the aid of a bus timetable it should be possible to catch a bus (see page 533) back to your vehicle or accommodation. While the path (marked on the Ordnance Survey map 5 in the Discoverer series) can be walked in either direction, the best fun can be had if you start from Ballintoy and cross White Park beach to the little harbour of Portbraddan, where St Gobhan's claims to be the smallest church in Ireland, and on to Dunserverick and up to the clifftop for a spectacular couple of miles to the Giant's Causeway. Walking in Northern Ireland doesn't come much better than this.

Giant's Causeway to Ballycastle

Dunserverick ⓘ *Jun-Aug, Mon-Sat 1000-1600.* As well as the main A2 coast road there is also the B146 road, running parallel to it but closer to the coast, and this leads past the fragmentary ruins of **Dunserverick Castle** and, by the harbour, the small **Dunserverick Museum**. There is a meagre collection related to disasters at sea – parts from the doomed Spanish Armada and coal from the *Titanic* – but the location makes an attractive spot for a picnic. Emigrants used to be rowed out from here to hitch a ride on a passing schooner for Derry or Glasgow, thence to America or Australia, never to return.

Ballintoy From the village of Ballintoy a winding road leads down to the shore, passing the white-towered Ballintoy **church**: if you're thinking the tower looks a little incongruous you're quite right, for there used to be a steeple before a hurricane demolished it in 1894. The rocky but quaint limestone **harbour**, sheltered by basalt rock formations such as Sheep Island, was built to ship out paving sett stones from a nearby quarry that employed over 100 men in the 19th century. The village landlord was one Downing Fullerton, his name giving us Downing St in London and the Cambridge college that he endowed. From the harbour it takes half an hour to walk around the headland leading to the mile-long sandy **White Park Bay**, and if you want to continue walking follow the Causeway Coast Way (North Antrim Cliff Path) signs (see above) for a most dramatic approach to the Giant's Causeway.

Carrick-a-rede ⓘ *T2073 1582, (weather permitting) mid Mar-Jun and Sep, daily 1000-1800; Jul-Aug, daily 1000-1900, £2, centre and tea-room: Jun-Aug and*

Ballycastle

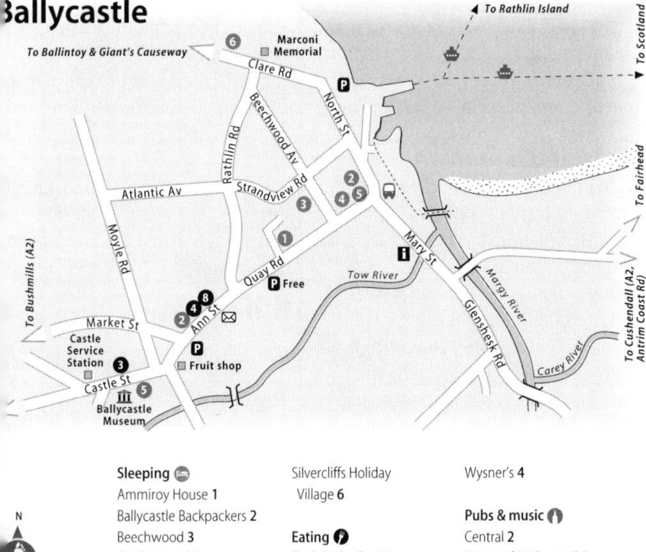

Sleeping
Ammiroy House 1
Ballycastle Backpackers 2
Beechwood 3
Castle Hostel 4
Marine 5
Silvercliffs Holiday Village 6

Eating
Flash in the Pan 3
Herald's 8
Wysner's 4

Pubs & music
Central 2
House of McDonnell 5

weekends in May, daily 1200-1800. Every year some 100,000 visitors cross the rop bridge at Carrick-a-rede but that may prove scant comfort when you are half wa across and you realize that turning back means going as far as carrying on to the othe side. It's only 80 ft (24 m) above the sea, but when the rope bridge starts to sway an your nerves wither, try to remember you're really just on holiday – having fun. Th bridge is erected annually by fishermen throwing across a string with a lead weight t access a salmon fishery on the small island. The centre by the car park ha information panels on the geology and the quarrying in the 1930s-50s that remove the entirety of Larrybane Head and the remains of a promontory fort.

Kinbane Castle A couple of miles before Ballycastle the remaining walls and mai tower of the 16th-century Kinbane Castle are worth visiting just for the locatior perched on a limestone headland amidst basalt cliffs with Rathlin Island directl across the water and the towering majesty of Fair Head in the distance. Primroses an orchids in Spring, and perfect for a picnic any time.

Ballycastle → *Colour map 2, grid A5.*

Ballycastle is a modestly vivacious little place with some history and a characte reminiscent of the Republic. There are pubs with traditional music, fair restaurant and an infrastructure that recommends it both as a base for exploring the Nort Antrim coast and as a place to pause before or after seeing the Glens of Antrim on th east coast. Northern Ireland's only inhabited island (Rathlin Island) lies off the coas Scotland is a short ferry ride away, and every year three festivals light up the plac with song, dance and live music on a stage in the Diamond. The **tourist office** (se page 526) hands out the useful **Ballycastle Heritage Trail** leaflet that covers a variet of places of historical interest around town, including the little **Ballycastle Museur** ⓘ *59 Castle St, T2076 2942, Jul-Aug, daily, 1200-1800, free.*

Walking around Ballycastle The Ulster Way passes through Ballycastle but th route west of town is not recommended until Ballintoy is reached (see Walking th Causeway coast on page 528). While the route east is a tough hike of 20 miles (32 km to Cushendall, a more manageable trek could end in Cushenden and would take in glorious clifftop walk around Fair Head and the ascent of Caranmore (1,243 ft). Yo need Ordnance Survey maps 5 and 9 in the Discoverer series.

For gentle strolls collect the *Forest Walks* leaflet from the tourist office which map out the circular 2-mile Glentaisie Trail and the 3-mile Glenshank Trail, both waymarked

Rathlin Island → *Colour map 1, grid A5.*

Just 9.6 km from Ballycastle and 22.5 km from the Mull of Kintyre in Scotland, Rathli has an inverted L-shape (6.5 x 4.8 km) and is never wider than 1.6 km. Collect brochure with map from the tourist office in Ballycastle (see page 526) and jump o the ferry for a day out in the fresh air.

Famous people come to Rathlin. The Vikings started their tour of Ireland here in 795. Half a century later, Robert the Bruce, in hiding after a whipping by the English at Perth, was inspired by a spider to never give in, and left to fight the English again at Bannockburn. Sir Francis Drake commanded a ship sent here in 1575 to hunt down the family and friends of Sorley Boy MacDonnell (see box on page 537) and massacre them. Marconi, or at least his assistant, sent

Rathlin Island

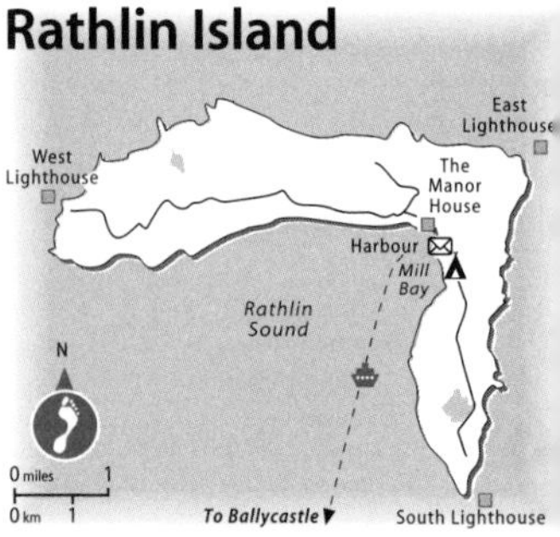

East Lighthouse
West Lighthouse
The Manor House
Harbour
Mill Bay
Rathlin Sound
N
0 miles 1
0 km 1
To Ballycastle
South Lighthouse

ne world's first wireless message here from Ballycastle in 1891, and around a century ater the capitalist Richard Branson came down in a balloon near here. See also ctivities page 533.

Sleeping

'ortrush *p526*
&B rates peak in July and August to £25 per erson, dropping to around £15+ at other mes for rooms sharing bathroom facilities. 1ost of the caravan parks will take only a oken number of tents, but a couple are sted that will take more.

Magherabuoy House Hotel, 1 Magherabuoy Rd, T7082 3507, ww.magherabuoy.co.uk. Outside town vith unrivalled views over the Atlantic.

Maddybenny Farm, 18 Maddybenny Park, 7082 3394, www.maddybenny.freeserve. ɔ.uk. This may be out of town, but a more regarious guest house would be hard to find nd your enjoyment of a visit will be roportional to your appetite for a gargantuan reakfast (porridge with Drambuie and cream s an appetizer) that makes the usual B&B fering seem like child's play.

Windsor Guest House, 67 Main St, T7082 793. A family-run period townhouse in the eart of town.

-**F Atlantis**, 10 Ramore Av, T7082 4583. B&B not in a quiet part of town but with the dvantage of a kitchen available for snacks.

Macool's Hostel, 35 Causeway St, T7082 345, www.portrush-hostel.com. Close to ne bus and train station, even closer to the each, comfortable and well-provisioned – nd that includes a dog called Guinness!

amping

allymacrea Caravan & Camping Park, 20 Ballybogy Rd, T7082 4507, on the B62 allymoney to Portrush road, less than 3 km om Portrush. Caravan park. Will take only tents at £7-11 per night.

arrick Dhu Caravan Park, 12 Ballyreagh Rd, 7082 3712, just west of Portrush on the A2 oast road to Portstewart. This caravan park ill take up to 20 tents at £11-14 per night.

Portrush to Giant's Causeway *p526*

A-B Bushmills Inn, 25 Main St, Bushmills, T2073 2339, www.bushmillsinn.com. One of the best hotels in Ulster and a place you will remember; saying it has nooks and crannies hardly does justice to its geography (check out the hidden room); complete with turf fires and gas lamps.

D Craig Park, 24, Carnbore Rd, T2073 2496, www.craigpark.co.uk. Big country house set in 20 acres with lovely views over the mountains of Donegal and the hills of Antrim.

E Ahimsa, 243 Whitepark Rd, T2073 1383. A traditional cottage specializing in vegetarian meals and using produce from its organic garden.

F Mill Rest Hostel, T2073 1222, www.hini.org.uk. A new Hostelling International place with a range of smart rooms, bicycle store and walled garden.

Camping

Ballyness Caravan Park, 40 Castlecatt Rd, T2073 2393, on the B66 towards Dervock from Bushmills. Has 15 tent pitches for £9.

Giant's Causeway *p527*

D Whitepark House, Whitepark Rd, T2073 1482, www.whiteparkhouse.com. With 3 rooms sharing bathroom facilities, this has been warmly recommended by readers. B&B is £60 for a double and the odd-looking place is hard to miss on the road between the Causeway and Ballintoy.

D-E Causeway Hotel, Causeway Rd, T2073 1226, www.giants-causeway-hotel.com. Should prove more satisfying than it did to Thackeray in 1842: "It was impossible to feel comfortable in the place, and when the car wheels were heard, I jumped up with joy to take my departure and forget this awful shore, that wild, dismal, genteel inn."

For an explanation of the sleeping and eating price codes used in this guide, see inside the front cover. Other relevant information is found in Essentials pages 39-45.

Giant's Causeway to Ballycastle *p529*
F **Ballintoy House**, Main St, Ballintoy, T2076 2317. The house carries the 1737 date of its building on its front wall and the B&B single/double rate is £20-34.
F **Sheep Island View**, Main St, Ballintoy, T2076 9391, www.sheepislandview.com. In the centre of the village by the bus stop, has a terrific kitchen, includes one double, camping space, meals available, guided walks can be arranged, and musical entertainment in the pub most nights.
F **Whitepark Bay Hostel**, 10 km west of Ballycastle on the A2, T2073 1745, www.hini.org.uk. It's hard to beat this place. A top-notch YHANI hostel overlooking White Park Bay with 6-bed and 4-bed rooms, and 4 superb double rooms with TV and tea- and coffee-making facilities, foreign exchange, a restaurant and bike hire. Buses stop 200 m away.

Ballycastle *p530, map p529*
D **Marine Hotel**, North St, T2076 2222, www.marinehotel.net. Fairly standard hotel with restaurant and fitness centre.
E **Ammiroy House**, 24 Quay Rd, T2076 2621. Two rooms in a family house, is typical of the B&Bs along this road.
E **Beechwood**, 9 Beechwood Av, T2076 3631, stay@beechwoods.f9.co.uk. Can be recommended for its quiet location and friendly welcome. The house has 2 double rooms sharing a bathroom, but best value has to be the 2 chalet-type rooms at the back with their own facilities including a fridge and sink. No avoiding the Ulster fry-up though.
F **Ballycastle Backpackers**, 4 North St, T2076 3612. A small hostel, but with 4 private rooms from £20.
F **Castle Hostel**, 62 Quay Rd, T2076 2337. Has 40 beds including 3 private rooms for £20. The preferred hostel for some travellers.

Camping
Silvercliffs Holiday Village, 21 Clare Rd, T2076 2550, www.haganleisure.co.uk. Popular campsite with an indoor pool, sauna and bar. Some 50 tent pitches at £11-14 per night.
Watertop Open Farm, 188 Cushendall Rd, 10 km southeast of town on the A2, T2076 2576. Charges £7-11 for each of its 4 pitches around a working farm.

Rathlin Island *p530, map p530*
E **The Manor House**, T2076 3964. A large Georgian house by the harbour, open all yea and run by the National Trust as a B&B establishment. A single is £24 (£28 with en suite bathroom), a double is £50 (£54 including en suite bathroom).
E **Rathlin Guest House**, The Quay, T2076 3917. Open Apr-Sep and evening meals are available.
F **Soerneog View Hostel**, T2076 3954. Overlooks Mill Bay and is a short walk from the harbour. Open all year but only 3 beds – 1 double and 2 twin rooms – so book ahead in the summer. £8 per person.

Eating

Portrush *p526*
D'Arcy's, 92-4 Main St, T7082 2063. Open for lunch, around £7, and dinner around £12-15, with contemporary-style food and lots of fish dishes.
Don Giovanni's, 9 Causeway St, T70825516. Fine for pizzas and pasta and also does some veal and fish dishes.
Ramone Wine Bar, The Harbour, T7082 4313. Has a menu to suit holiday folk and most dishes are around £10.

There are some truly dreadful places in the centre of town serving fish-and- chips-type meals; don't be misled by nautical themes and seemingly reasonable prices.

Portrush to Giant's Causeway *p526*
Bushmills Inn, 25 Main St, Bushmills, T2073 2339. Good food like steak flambéed in a drop of the local hard stuff served at tables privately snuggled around rough, whitewashed stone walls under a low ceiling. Expensive but worth it.
Copper Kettle, by the roundabout, T2073 2560. Serves tea and scones and standard meals around £5-7, 0830-2000 in summer, and is fine if you are on the move.
Sweeney's, Seaport Av, Portballintrae, T2073 2405. A pleasant stone-built pub with conservatory, and popular sessions of live and loud music on weekend evenings; decent food is served daily from 1200 to 2130.

For picnics, there is a supermarket next to Bushmills Inn and take-away food is available from the **Village Bistro**.

Giant's Causeway to Ballycastle *p529*
Carrick-a-rede pub, Ballintoy, T2076 2241. Has pub food all day in the summer.
Fullerton Arms, Ballintoy, T2076 9613. Has a restaurant open 1730-2030, between Wed and Sun in summer; weekends only in winter.
National Trust tearoom, Carrick-a-Rede. Serves dismal fried food redeemed by some local breads.
Roark's Kitchen, perched on the rocks at Ballintoy, T2076 3632. Open daily between Jun and Aug from 1100 to 1900, and at weekends in May and Sep, for lovely light meals such as buttered mackerel or baked potato with filling for around £3 and lunches listed on a blackboard outside.

Ballycastle *p530, map p529*
If seeking out a local edible seaweed, dulse, go to the Fruit Shop in the Diamond. The shop also stocks yellowman, a chewy toffee eaten hereabouts.
Flash in the Pan, Castle St. An excellent, sit-in or take-out, traditional fish and chip outlet.
Glass Island Restaurant, in the Marine Hotel, 1-3 North St. Has a typical hotel potato-based menu, is open daily until 2200, while the bar serves snacks.
Herald's Restaurant, next to Wysner's on Ann St at No 22. Competing for quick meals and coffee breaks, comes up with beef, potato and vegetables for £4.
Wysner's, 16 Ann St, T2076 2372. Has won awards for its meat-based dishes and a separate day menu downstairs in the café features bangers and champ (pork sausages and potato and shallots), pasta, and chicken dishes for around £6. Closed Sun.

Rathlin Island *p530, map p530*
Bruce's Kitchen, at the harbour, opens daily between 1030 and 2330 for quick fish meals. Dinner is an option at both the **Rathlin Guest House** and **The Manor House**, but needs booking in advance.
For a picnic on the island stock up with provisions at **Brady's** supermarket in Castle St or the **Co-Op** at the Diamond, Ballycastle.

Entertainment

Portrush *p526*
On summer nights pubs and hotels are blasting out music, but not of the traditional Irish kind.
Kelly's, Bushmills Rd, T7082 6611, www.kellysportrush.com. This is the top club by a mile and its nightclub **Lush!** wins particular acclaim.

Ballycastle *p530, map p529*
The tourist board (see page 526) issues a useful directory of what's on, where and when in all the Ballycastle pubs.
The Central Bar, Ann St. Has a regular Wed night session of traditional music that goes al fresco in the summer with the occasional barbecue thrown in for good measure.
The House of McDonnell A pub that's been in the same family for over 200 years. Grand for a quiet chat and a drink, and on a Fri night musicians are welcomed.

Festivals and events

Ballycastle *p530, map p529*
On the last Mon and Tue of **August** the **Oul' Lammas Fair**, with a good claim to be Ireland's oldest traditional fair, is a very lively event.

Activities and tours

Portrush *p526*
Horseriding Maddybenny Riding Centre, 18 Maddybenny Park, T7082 3394.

Surfing Troggs, 88 Main St, T7082 5476, www.troggs.com. Has all the gear and advice.

Rathlin Island *p530, map p530*
Land The main attractions of a visit to Rathlin Island are walking and bird watching, T2076 3948, Apr-Aug. There is a viewing platform at the West Lighthouse. In late spring and early summer the rocks are crowded with fulmars, guillemots, kittiwakes, Manx shearwaters, razorbills and puffins.
Water Diving trips can be arranged, T2076 3922 and T2076 3154. Fishing off the rocks is possible and boats can also be hired. Colonies of grey and common seals can be seen at Mill Bay, just south of the harbour, near the hostel and camping ground, and at Rue Point near the South Lighthouse (T2076 3948).

Transport

North Antrim coast *p526*
Between 31 May and 25 Sep the **Ulsterbus 252 Antrim Coaster** service, T9066 6630,

www.translink.co.uk, runs daily between Belfast and Coleraine, stopping at all the main towns of interest around the coast. Buses leave **Belfast** at 0900 (leaving Coleraine at 0955) and stop at **Portrush**, **Portballintrae**, **Bushmills**, **Giant's Causeway**, **Ballintoy**, **Ballycastle**, **Cushendon**, **Cushendall**, **Carnlough**, **Glenarm**, **Larne**, **Carrickfergus** and Belfast.

A 2nd **Larne-Coleraine** service departs at 1500 (from Coleraine at 1540) and does all the coast except the Larne to Belfast sector. This service operates all year, as does the Larne-Coleraine morning sector of the Antrim Coaster route.

In Jul and Aug the Bushmills Open Topper runs 5 times a day between **Coleraine** and the **Causeway**, via **Portstewart**, **Portrush**, **Portballintrae** and **Bushmills**, but flaggable anywhere along its route.

The Ulsterbus 152 service, T9066 6630, www.translink.co.uk, runs throughout the year between **Ballycastle** and **Portrush** on the B146, via **Carrick-a-Rede**, **Ballintoy** and the **Giant's Causeway**.

The Causeway Rambler, service number 402, operates daily, 7 times a day from **Bushmills Distillery** (from 1015 to 1700, and from 1045 to 1730 from Carrick-a-Rede) to **Carrick-a-Rede** between early Jun and early Sep, calling at the **Giant's Causeway**, **Dunserverick Castle**, **White Park Bay**, **Ballintoy** and **Carrick-a-rede**. An all-day, hop on and hop off ticket costs £3.50.

Ballycastle *p530, map p529*
Bike hire Castle Service Station, T2076 2355, Castle St. **Taxi** Connors, T2076 8611; Castle Cabs, T2076 8884.

Rathlin Island *p530, map p530*
Bike hire From the hostel, T2076 3954. **Bus** **Minibus tour** McCurdy's, T2076 3909. **Ferry** Caledonian MacBrayne, T2076 9299, run the M.V. Canna on its 45-min journey to Rathlin 4 times a day between Jun and Sep (1000, 1200, 1630, and 1830-1900 on Fri), and twice a day the rest of the year. Day return £8.60, bicycles £2, and best booked ahead in the summer.

Ballycastle to Carrickfergus

The journey south from Ballycastle to Carrickfergus is best done clinging to the smaller coastal roads which skirt between the Glens of Antrim and the sea. Travelling along this junction between sea and sky and mountain has many rewards and the quiet Antrim towns of Cushendall, Cushenden, Carnlough and Glenarm each have their modest charms. » *For Sleeping, Eating and other listings, see pages 538-540.*

Ins and outs

Getting there and around See Transport section page 533.

Information **Cushendun information office**, Main St, T2176 1506. **Cushendall tourist office**, Mill St, T2177 1180. Jul-Sep Mon-Sat 1000-1300 and 1500-1930 but has varied, shorter hours rest of the year. **Carnlough tourist office**, in McKillop's shop on Harbour Rd, T2888 5236. Open Easter-Sep. **Glanarm tourist office**, T2884 1705, open in the summer. **Larne tourist office**, Narrow Gauge Rd, T2826 0088. Open Jul and Aug Mon-Fri 0900-1800, Sat 0900-1700. Easter to Jun and Sep Mon-Fri 0900-1700, Sat 1000-1600; Oct-Easter Mon-Fri 0900-1700. **Carrickfergus tourist office**, in the Museum & Civic Centre on Antrim St, T9335 8049. Open Apr-Sep Mon-Sat 1000-1800 Sun (Jul and Aug only) 1200-1800. Closes an hour earlier the rest of the year.

Ballycastle to Cushendun

Unless you're in a hurry to be somewhere else, the inland route between Ballycastle and Cushendun on the A2 is best passed over for the sake of the coastal road via **Torr Head** and **Murlough Bay**. Other than walking parts of the Ulster Way, this route offers the best coastal scenery in Northern Ireland. At Murlough Bay there is a series of three car parks with noticeboards detailing short walks in the area, and near the middle car park a commemorative stone to British diplomat and Irish nationalist Roger Casement (see page 325). After being hanged in London in 1916 for treason, his remains were finally returned in 1965 to this corner of Ireland.

Cushendun → *Colour map 1, grid A5.*

The distinctive buildings of Cushendun were designed by the architect Clough Williams Ellis, who also designed Portmeirion in north Wales, where the cult 1960s television series *The Prisoner* was filmed. In 1912 Ronald and Maud MacNeil, later Lord and Lady Cushendun, commissioned William Ellis for the Square with its dormer windows and slate roofs, and so pleased were they that more building followed in the same style. Most of Cushendun, the nearest port in Ireland to Britain, is now owned by the National Trust and it is a strange place, which manages to be attractive and alienating at the same time. A leaflet describing three local walks of 2, 4 and 6 miles in length should be available from the tourist office (see Ins and outs above).

Cushendall → *Colour map 1, grid A5.*

Cushendall is an engaging village, the name of which had been changed to Newtown Glens until a certain Francis Turnley turned up in the early 19th century, having made his fortune trading in China, bought the whole village, restored its original name and generally injected life and commerce into what was a very sleepy backwater. A predominately Catholic village, Cushendall was frequently visited by the Belfast poet John Hewitt (an annual summer school on Hewitt is held further down the coast at Garron Point) who was led to reflect on the religious divisions of Ulster:

> *"This is our fate: 800 years' disaster*
> *crazily tangled as the Book of Kells;*
> *the dream's distortions and the land's division,*
> *the midnight raiders and the prison cells.*
> *Yet like Lir's children banished to the waters*
> *our hearts still listen for the landward bells."*

The village is gratifyingly free of tourists but there is not a great deal to see other than the **Curfew Tower** that Turnley had built in 1817 to house those who failed to share his ultra-industrious attitude to life. McCollam's Bar on Mill Street is definitely worth calling into, because the sessions of traditional music will give a fillip to any Friday night, and often a Saturday and a Tuesday in the summer as well. The second week in August, when the **Heart of the Glens Festival** arrives in Cushendall, sees all the pubs full to overflowing. Take either Layde Road from the village past the hostel and a campsite or a cliff-top path from the north end of the beach to reach **Layde Old Church**, its miscellany of MacDonnells tombs and a church with a Michael Healy window, *The Light of the World*.

Glenariff Forest Park

ⓘ *On the A43 Ballymena/Waterfoot road, T2955 6000, from 0900- dusk, car-park £3, pedestrian £1.50.*

The trails are rich in flowers: liverworts, mosses and ferns abound; in spring, bluebells and wild garlic and in summer woodruff, pink herb Robert and bugle.

The Glenariff River flows down to Waterfoot, south of Cushendall, and its glen is the most accessible of the famed Glens of Antrim, due mainly to the Forest Park and its waymarked trails. The Park's visitor centre is fairly useless so consult the map on the board near the car park for a brief explanation of the four available walks. The longest is a 8 km Scenic Trail through forest and across the Inver River for views down the glen, and the most popular is a 5 km Waterfall Trail.

 These walks can also be reached from a separate entrance at the back of the Manor Lodge restaurant and its car park. The catwalk from the restaurant was originally built in the late 19th century to encourage day-trippers to use the Ballymena train to Parkmore station at the top of the glen.

Walking from Cushendall

Apart from walks in the Glenariff Forest Park, the tourist office has a *Heart of the Glens Guide* that describes a variety of short walks from Cushendall and Cushendun into the glens. A section of the **Ulster Way**, from Cushendall or Waterfoot (also called Glenariff) to Carnlough is an exciting day's walk of around 18 km. Although the Way signs peter out as you near Carnlough this will not present a problem if you have Ordnance Survey maps 9 and 5.

The **Moyle Way** is a 32-km route between Glenariff Forest Park (the starting point is opposite the Park entrance on the A43) and Ballycastle. The entire walk needs completing on one day and it no longer goes over Knocklayd, which was one of the highlights, but the tourist office in Cushendall (see page 534) sells a £2 leaflet covering the walk.

★ Carnlough and Glenarm → *Colour map 1, grid A5.*

The splendid coast road that continues south to Carnlough was being completed when Thackeray reached this part of the country on his grand tour of 1842, and he was quick to perceive its importance: "one of the most noble and gallant works of art that is to be seen in any country ... torn sheer through the rock here and there; and immense work of levelling, shovelling, picking, blasting, filling, is going on along the whole line". The local limestone, which gives Carnlough its characteristic colour, had already been blasted and picked for the coffers of the Marquis and Marchioness of Londonderry, and you can still see the fine stone bridge that carried a rail line down to the harbour for export of the stone. Part of the railway line has now been turned into a walkway. The town's political sympathies are displayed in the flying of the Republic's flag and – making a pointed contrast with the flying of the Israel flag in Kilkeel in County Down (see page 553) – the Palestinian flag.

Glenarm If coming up from Belfast the picturesque village of Glenarm, a couple of miles south of Carnlough on the other side of the bay, not only has attractive patterning in sections of pavement but also lies at the foot of the first of the nine glens of Antrim and may be the first place that tempts you to linger. There are also some walking possibilities around Glenarm including a historical trail through the village itself, and the **Layde Walk**, which leads to a scenic viewing point and places for a picnic. Leaflets with maps are available from the tourist office here or in Larne (see page 534).

Glenarm to Larne

Travelling south, the sharply defined topography of the Antrim coast is coming to an end as you leave Glenarm for the final stretch of road that continues to command the sea until you reach Larne. If you've just arrived off the ferry at Larne or travelled up from Belfast, this is where the coastal scenery makes an immediate impact but in either direction a place that might suggest a quick stop is **Ballygally**, mainly due to the eye-catching Ballygally Castle Hotel. Sweeping sea views can be enjoyed from the bar while a remnant of the original 17th-century castle has a ghost room, which can be visited by non-residents.

Larne → *Colour map 1, grid B6.*

Chances are you will only spend time in Larne if delayed by the ferry, but there are ways to while away time: the well organized **tourist office** (see page 534) has local information, including an Ulster American Heritage Trail, with maps describing

Sorley Boy and the MacDonnells

The MacDonnells were a branch of the Scottish MacDonalds who took over most of Antrim in the 16th century, a process completed by Sorley Boy MacDonnell who then had to deal with an early English attempt to colonize Ulster. His family were massacred on Rathlin Island by the English in 1575 but Sorely Boy fought back with grit. His son, Randy MacDonnell, accepted the English Crown in return for a grant of 300,000 acres and the earldom of Antrim. His great-great-grandson was the grandfather of Francis Anne Vane Tempest, Marchioness of Londonderry, who built the coaching inn that is now the Londonderry Arms at Carnlough.

laques and graveyards associated with emigration and merican forces stationed here in the Second World War. **arnfunnock Country park** ⓘ *T2827 0541, 5.6 km north of Larne n the coast road, visitor centre, café, gift shop, car park £4*, is a eat place for whiling away a sunny afternoon. Once the home of ord and Lady Dixon it retains their walled garden, the old ice ouse and the family's private church. It has a caravan park, iniature railway, a wildlife garden and a maze. The **Carnegie rts Centre** ⓘ *2 Victoria Rd, T2827 9482, Tue-Sat 1400-1700, ee*, has old photographs and artefacts, and tells the story of the uilding of the Antrim coast road.

The recent history of Larne is little to boast about: in 1974, to destroy the Sunningdale Agreement, masked UDA men closed the ferry, built a barricade of vehicles around the town and forced shops to close down.

slandmagee → *Colour map 1, grid B6.*

landmagee, a teetotal, conservative retreat where few foreign travellers venture, has s own little surprises. Little known outside the North of Ireland, this island-like eninsula points north between Whitehead and Larne, with basalt cliffs facing Scotland ut a more welcoming west side and a sandy and safe beach, Brown's Bay, on the north nd, which receives a smattering of families on sunny summer days. On the road etween Mill Bay and Ballylumford, look out for the astonishing **Ballylumford Dolmen**.

ns and outs Islandmagee can be reached on the B90 from Whitehead or by foot on passenger ferry, T2827 3785, between Larne and Ballylumford, that departs eekdays at 0745, 0800, 0830, 0900, 1500, 1600, 1630 and 1700; Sat-Sun at 0800, 900, 1600 and 1630. The scheduled fare £1 each way, twice that if you phone and ook an unscheduled trip. ▸▸ *See Transport, page 540, for further details.*

ights **The Gobbins**, a clifftop walk on the east side, is still under repair and only a hort part of it can be safely traversed. For information on walks and birdwatching call to **Ford Farm Museum** ⓘ *Low Rd, T9335 3264, Mar-Oct, daily 1400-1800, £2*, where e main attraction is butter-making and spinning demonstrations.

Halfway along on the west side, at Mill Bay facing Larne Lough, there is an **oyster nd mussel farm** ⓘ *at the harbour, T9338 2246*, where produce can be purchased, cluding lobster and crab. See also Activities, page 540.

arrickfergus and around → *Colour map 1, grid B6.*

assing the town on the A2 heading on along the north side of the Belfast Lough, it is npossible to miss Carrickfergus Castle, but don't be misled by its dramatic posture to thinking that the town itself is an exciting place. It is an unastonishing place that eed hardly detain the visitor, especially if travelling north where more interesting

The good old days

"The inhabitants of all sexes and classes [of Islandmagee] are perhaps a more immoral race than is to be found in any other rural district in Antrim ... What makes their immorality the more disgusting is the openness and want of shame with which it is exhibited. The women whenever from home, or indeed whenever they can procure the means, drink raw spirits in such quantities as would astonish any but a native ... several have lost their reason, and many still remain as examples and warnings, in their paralysed bodies and shattered intellects, to those who are treading in their footsteps."

After Lord Dungannon broke up all 14 pubs on Islandmagee in the early 19th century a born-again temperance set in, the legacy of which can be seen today when you look for somewhere to have a drink on the peninsula. The same report also noted that Islandmagee had not "the slightest tinge of party or sectarian feeling."

destinations await. But if the weather is inclement there are sufficient diversions i and around Carrickfergus to pass a day. The small **museum** in the tourist office (se page 534), which is free, provides an interesting history of the town. The poet Loui MacNeice (1907-1963) grew up in Carrickfergus, for his father was the rector c **St Nicholas' church** ⓘ *in the Market Pl, T93360061, mornings only*. The interior is nc dull, there is a fine memorial to the Chichester family, and the adjoining cemetery i where the poet could "hear the voice of the minister tucking people into the ground".

Carrickfergus Castle ⓘ *T9335 1273, Apr-Sep, Mon-Sat 1000-1800, Sun 1400-180 (from 1200 on Sun, Jun-Aug) Oct-Mar, Mon-Sat, 1000-1600, Sun, 1400-1600, £3*. Th castle is a formidable-looking Anglo-Norman edifice with a long history. A famou siege by Edward Bruce in 1315 was resisted for longer than it could otherwise hav been with the help of the capture of some Scots, eight of whom provided an edibl repast for the beleaguered forces. Sorley Boy MacDonnell ran amuck here in reveng for the massacre on Rathlin (see box on page 537).

Carrickfergus Gasworks ⓘ *T9336 9575, www.gasworksflame.com, May-Sep Sun-Fri, 1400-1700; Apr and Oct, Sun, 1400-1700, £1.50*. The industrial history her will make a welcome relief for anyone suffering from castle fatigue. The only Victoria coal-fired gasworks in Ireland, built in 1855 to light street lamps, they were sti producing gas here in the early 1960s.

Andrew Jackson Centre ⓘ *Boneybefore, 2 miles north of Carrickfergus on the Larn Rd, T9336 6455, Apr-Oct, Mon-Fri, 1000-1300 and 1400-1800, Sat and Sun 1400-180c £1.20*. The parents of the seventh US president emigrated from Carrickfergus in 176 and a recreated dwelling of that period makes up the Andrew Jackson Centre an houses exhibitions on the president and the USA connection. Quite a dull plac enlivened a little by the adjoining **US Rangers' Centre** which is devoted to the Fir Battalion US Rangers who trained in Carrickfergus before leaving for Europe.

Sleeping

Cushendun *p535*

E Cushendun Guesthouse, Strandview Park, T2176 1266. Overlooking the harbour, only opens in Jul and Aug. B&B is £20 per persor sharing bathroom facilities, credit cards not accepted and 'room reservations at

eekends for overseas visitors only'. Meals e available in the evening and its ›peworks Bar opens at 1700 each day.
Villa Farmhouse, 185 Torr Rd, T2176 1252, aggiescally@amserve.net. A more orthodox ɹest house with a reputation for good eakfasts and evening meals available if ooked in advance.

amping

ushendun Caravan Park, Glendun Rd, 2176 1254. Next to the safe beach, with) pitches for tents at £7-11 a night.

ushendall *p535*

The Glens Hotel, 6 Coast Rd, T21771223. ne only hotel in town, has 11 rooms and narges up to £60 for a double.
Cullentra House, 16 Cloughs Rd, T2177 1762, ıllentra@hotmail.com. A welcoming B&B here guests are made to feel comfortable and ith the option of an evening meal.
The Meadows, 81 Coast Rd, T2177 2020. n award-winning B&B establishment on the ain A2 road.
Riverside, 14 Mill St, T21771655. As central s you can get, next to the tourist office.

amping

ushendall, 62 Coast Rd, T2177 1699. council-run site with room for 4 tents at 7-11 per night.

arnlough and Glenarm *p536*

Londonderry Arms Hotel, Carnlough, 2888 5255, www.glensofantrim.com. nis ivy-clad building is the most mfortable and historic place for a night's dging, but ask for one of the older-style edrooms. Packed lunches can be provided nd suggested walk sheets are available.
Bethany House, Bay Rd, Carnlough, T2888 567. Outside the village on the coast road verlooking the bay.
Bridge Inn, 2 Bridge St, Carnlough, T2888 569. Has rooms sharing bathroom facilities r £18 per person and there is a popular ıb below the bedrooms.
Riverside House, 13 Toberwine St, enarm, T2884 1474. In the centre of the llage with its rear overlooking the river.

Glenarm to Larne *p536*

C **Ballygally Castle Hotel**, T2858 3212, www.hastingshotel.com. Terrific sea views and some rooms in the original 17th-century castle.

Larne *p536*

B-D **Curran Court Hotel**, 84 Curran Rd, T2827 5505. On the continuation of Main St and close to the ferry.
D **Highways Hotel**, Ballyloran, T2827 2272. Just off the A8 road a mile outside Larne on the road to Belfast.
E **Cairnview**, 13 Croft Heights, Ballygarry, T/F2858 3269. A B&B 4 miles north of Larne on the Antrim Coast Rd. 3 rooms, 2 with en suite bathrooms, at £18 per person.
E **Manor Guest House**, 23 Olderfleet Rd, T2827 3305, www.themanorguesthouse.com. B&B in a smart Victorian terrace house, virtually next door to the ferry, open all year and good facilities.

Islandmagee *p537*

E **Millbay Inn**, 77 Millbay Rd, T9338 2436. Has 4 rooms and has the benefit of food on the premises (see below).
F **The Farm**, 69 Portmuck Rd, T9338 2252. Enjoys sea views and sandy beach close by.

Carrickfergus *p537*

D **Dobbins Inn Hotel**, High St, T9335 1905, www.dobbinsinnhotel.com. Ancient lineage but modern facilities in town centre hotel.
E **Langsgarden**, 72 Scotch Quarter, T/F9336 6369. Overlooks Belfast Lough. Most rooms, at £20 per person, share bathroom facilities.

Eating

Cushendun *p535*

Cushendun Village Tea Room, Main St, T2176 1281. Looks the ideal place for a homely cup of tea and apple pie, but fails to live up to expectations. Sandwiches and toasties and grilled food with chips from £4-£8 are served and on Sat evenings an à la carte menu beckons.
McBride's, just across the road, has a tiny bar that needs squeezing into, with hardly the elbow space needed to lift a pint to your mouth. Pub food is served daily in the summer.

For an explanation of the sleeping and eating price codes used in this guide, see inside the front cover. Other relevant information is found in Essentials pages 39-45.

Cushendall *p535*
Arthur's, Shore St. Opens daily 1000-1700 for coffee, toasted sandwiches, panini and salads.
Harry's Restaurant, 10 Mill St, T2177 2022. With a bar menu from 1230 to 2130 of dishes such as chicken curry and prawn sandwich, and a more formal menu from 1800 featuring steak and fish dishes around £12.

Glenariff Forest Park *p535*
Manor Lodge, Glen Rd, T2175 8221, reached before the Park if travelling up from Cushendall. Serves burgers, cod and chips, and salads for £7 as well as grills and fish dishes from £12 to £17. There is also a bar and picnic tables.
Tea House, T2175 8769. Serves quiche.

Carnlough and Glenarm *p536*
Londonderry Arms, Carnlough. The lunch menu has excellent choices such as Caesar-style salads or mussels for around £4, pasta and salmon dishes for a little more. High tea from 1700 to 1830 and formal dinner from 1900.
The Schooner Castle St, Glenarm. Bar, serves pub grub from 1100 until 2300.

There are also 2 bars in Carnlough serving reliable pub food: the **Glencloy Inn** and the **Bridge Inn**, near each other on Bridge St and High St respectively.

Larne *p536*
The 2 hotels serve bar food and have restaurants see Sleeping, above.
Kiln, out of town on the Old Glenarm Rd that runs north parallel to the coast road, T2826 0924. A pub restaurant with a good local reputation.
Robert Brown's, 21 Lower Cross St, T2826 0293. Comes recommended by locals.
The Bailie, 111 Main St. A cheerful pub serving inexpensive meals daily at lunchtime and from 1700 until 2000.
The Meeting House, 120 Brustin Brae Rd, about a mile inland from Larne in the village of Cairncastle. A long-established pub which has good pub food, a restaurant serving fairly traditional food and traditional music on Saturday and Wedneday evenings.

Islandmagee *p537*
Millbay Inn, 77 Millbay Rd, T9338 2436. The best place for food and the only place for a drink. It opens daily for lunch and, except on Sun, from 1900 for dinner. Traditional dishes such as champ and sausages, plus à la carte, around £16 for a meal.

Carrickfergus *p537*
Dobbin's Inn Hotel, High St, T9335 1905. Meals throughout the day in comfortable, olde-worlde setting.
The Courtyard Coffee House, 38 Scotch Quarter, for lunch or afternoon tea, plus a take away menu until closing time at 1645, Mon-Sa
Northgate, 59 North St, T9336 4136. Larg portions for lunch.

Activities and tours

Larne *p536*
Diving **North Irish Lodge**, Islandmagee, T9338 2246. **Leisure centre** Tower Rd, T2826 0478. Closes 2200 Mon-Fri and 1700 at weekend.

Islandmagee *p537*
Horse riding **Islandmagee Riding Centr** T2838 2108. **Rainbow Equestrian Centre**, 24 Hollow Rd, Islandmagee, T9338 2929.

Transport

Ballycastle to Carrickfergus *p534*
Bike hire Ardclinis Activity Centre, High St, Cushendun, T2177 1340.

Bus See Transport, page 533. Buses serve Cushendall and Cushendun from **Belfast** and **Ballymena**, Mon-Sat. No 162 travels daily between Cushendun and **Larne** via Cushenda and the 162A travels Mon-Fri between Cushendall and **Ballycastle** via Cushendun. Se also the Antrim Coaster service on page 534.

Car hire Avis, Terminal Building, Larne Harbour, T2826 0799.

Ferry P&O, T0990-980777, operate 2 rout out of Larne: to **Cairnryan** in Scotland, with 1-hr service on the **Superstar Express** and 2¼ hrs on the **European Causeway**; and to **Fleetwood** in England. Larne Harbour, T2827 9221, is at the end of Olderfleet Rd.

Taxi AA, T2827 7888. **Cas Cabs**, T2827 498

Train Station, Circular Rd, T2826 0604. Trains to **Belfast**, **Coleraine** and **Derry**.

nland Antrim

land Antrim has some pleasant countryside but it is of limited appeal to the traveller, specially when the scenic coast road beckons. But if you are travelling between Belfast nd the north coast on the A26, the town of Ballymena makes for a far more diverting top than nondescript Antrim town itself. ▸▸ *For Sleeping, Eating and other listings, see page 542.*

allymena and around → *Colour map 1, grid A5.*

resbyterian and ultra-loyal Ballymena was founded in the 17th century, for Lowland cottish settlers, by William Adair from Kinhilt and developed into a thriving ommercial town on the back of the linen industry from the middle of the 18th century nwards. Ballymena is where Loyalist leader the Reverend Ian Paisley comes from, nd the actor Liam Neeson also grew up here. While there is not a lot to see in the own itself, Ballymena is a classic Protestant town and an essential part of the omplex whole that makes up Northern Ireland. Adjoining the **tourist office** ⓘ *Church t, T2563 8494, Mon-Fri 0900-1700, Sat – Easter-October – 1000-1600)*, there is a ny **museum** filled with old photographs, radios and shaving mugs and every Vednesday between June and August a **town tour** takes place from the town hall. ontact the tourist office for confirmation of time and place. Try to find time for a short ip west of town to the Moravian church at Gracehill (see box).

rthur Cottage ⓘ *Dreen, Cullybackey: from Cullybackey, northwest of Ballymena, ake the B96 to Portglenone and it is signposted on the right, T2563 8494, Easter-Sep, 1on-Fri, 1030-1700 (1600 on Sat), closed 12 Jul, £2, craft demonstrations Jun-Aug, ue, Fri and Sat at 1330.* The area's American connection is kept alive at Arthur ottage, the ancestral home of long-forgotten 21st US president, Chester Alan Arthur. Vorth a visit for the occasional summer evenings of song and storytelling or the fternoon craft demonstrations.

lemish Mountain

o the east of town the A42 goes to the floral village of **Broughshane,** best visited in arly summer or at the end of August when bulbs from the stock of the famous daffodil rower Guy L Wilson can be purchased. From Broughshane the B94 to the distinctively ontoured Slemish Mountain is signposted, and the way up the mountain is clearly narked from the car park. People flock here on St Patrick's Day because of the nountain's association with the saint – he tended pigs here for six years as a young lave – but it is a quiet enough spot the rest of the year and outside of weekends the limb to the top and its views can be enjoyed in splendid isolation. The mountain is ,437 ft (438 m) high but it is only a 700-ft (213-m) climb from the car park.

isburn → *Colour map 1, grid B5.*

o the southwest of Belfast, and easily visited from the city by bus from the Europa uscentre, the best reason for coming to Lisburn is the **Irish Linen Centre & Lisburn luseum** ⓘ *Market Sq, T9266 3377, Mon-Sat 0930-1700, free, restaurant and linen nd craft shop.* The growing of flax and making of linen was a part of Irish farm life om earliest times but the plantations brought artisans from Britain, and before the nd of the 17th century Ulster linen had acquired a particular renown. This did not onflict with any commercial interests in England and was allowed to develop nhindered. In 1698 a group of Huguenot weavers were paid to settle in Lisburn and neir special skills were rapidly assimilated. By the end of the following century echanization had been introduced into the bleaching process, and this set the tage for the development of Ireland's only major industry in the 19th century, with

Belfast the world centre for linen manufacturing. Not until the 1920s and 30s di demand begin to drop and a terminal decline set in. The Centre and Museum tell th story and weaving workshops bring the craft to life.

Sleeping

Ballymena and around *p541*

B **Galgorm Manor**, 136 Fenaghy Rd, Ballymena, T2588 1001, www.galgorm.com. This 19th-century house was previously the home of a textile magnate, and can deliver comfort and recreation by way of river views, fishing rights, riding stables and clay pigeon shooting.

E **Ben Vista**, 79 Galgorm Rd, Ballymena, T2564 6091, michael.joyce@btinternet.com. A large Victorian house conveniently close to the bus and train stations, charging £22 per person for B&B.

E **Tullymore House**, 2 Carnlough Rd, Broughshane, T2568 1233. Has a good reputation and a lovely setting.

Eating

Ballymena and around *p541*

Fern Room, 80 Church St, Ballymena. Is a self-service restaurant inside **McKillen's** department store and closes at 1700, but it is the best place for a quick meal and value for money: peppered meat balls with rice, or chicken goulash are under £7.

Galgorm Manor, Fenaghy Rd, Ballymena, T2588 1001. Good food, lunch or dinner, in a classical-style restaurant.

Pantry, Jubilee Mews off Main St. Opens until 1700 Mon-Sat and serves soup, stews and home-baked goodies.

Solomon Grundy's, Tower Centre, Ballymena. Is a long-established coffee shop which does soups, fresh bread and more substantial things with chicken.

Thatch Inn, 57 Main St, Broughshane. The best place for pub food at lunchtime during the week.

Transport

Ballymena and around *p541*

Car hire Ballymena Car Hire, 205 Cullybackey Rd, T2563 0077. **Taxi** Regent Taxis, 1 Hill St, T2564 4777.

County Down

Bangor to Downpatrick

To the south and east of Belfast the countryside surrounding Strangford Lough has it own strange character. Almost a suburb of the city Bangor still has a little of the peculiar character of a Victorian seaside town. The coastal drive around the Ard Peninsula brings, if not the stunning views and seascapes of the Antrim coast, some pretty beaches and walks. East of Strangford Lough, Mount Stewart house and gardens will thrill lovers of the formerly filthy rich while the quiet town of Portaferry can offer some good music and a day out at the aquarium and seal sanctuary. The western shore of the lough is characterised by castles and tower houses, left over from the days when there were enemies to protect things from and finally at its southwest corner is the lively little town of Downpatrick with its pubs, music, lovely old church and wacky railway museum. *» For Sleeping, Eating and other listings, see pages 549-552.*

Ins and outs

Getting there By the A2 road, Bangor is 22 km east of Belfast. Trains from Belfast's Great Victoria Street station reach Bangor via Belfast Central in half an hour and a peak times there is a train every 30 minutes, at other times about one an hour. Ulsterbus, T9181 2391, run regular daily services between Belfast and Bangor, Portaferry (via Newtownards), Mount Stewart, Greyabbey and Downpatrick. There is also a Downpatrick-Newry service that stops at Dundrum and Newcastle. ➜ *See Transport, page 552, for futher details.*

Information **Bangor tourist office** Quay St between the Marine Court and Bangor Bay Inn hotels, T9127 0069, www.northdowntourism.com. Jan-Feb and May-Oct Mon and Wed-Fri 0900-1700, Tue and Sat 1000-1700; Jun and Sep same hours plus Sun 1300-1600; Jul-Aug Tue 1000-1800, Wed-Fri 0900-1800, Sat 1000-1700, Sun 1300-1700. **Newtownards tourist office** on the Ards Peninsula at 31 Regent St, T9182 6846. Jul and Aug Mon-Sat 0900-1730; Sep-Jun Mon-Sat 0930-1700. Not the prettiest town in Ireland but a useful information centre. **Portaferry tourist office** Castle St, T4272 9882. Easter and Jul-Aug Mon-Sat 1000-1730, Sun 1300-1800. **Downpatrick tourist office** 53A Market St, T44612 233. Sep-Jul Mon-Fri 0900-1700, Sat 0930-1700; Jul and Aug Mon-Sat 0900-1900, Sun 1400-1800. A useful series of free leaflets with maps outlining short walks in the Kilclief/Killyleagh/Downpatrick/ Castlewellan and districts is available from most tourist offices. Ordnance Survey Map No 21 in the *Discovery* series is useful if staying in the Strangford Lough area.

Bangor ➜ *Colour map 1, grid B6.*

The railway link from Belfast put Bangor on the map as a late Victorian seaside resort. But these days the marina has put paid to the beach, and while a lingering seaside feel is still faintly in the air, the town is basically a commuter-fuelled, overwhelmingly Protestant, suburb of Belfast. Several places of interest in the area (see below) mean that you may find yourself here looking for a meal or even an overnight stay (see listings page 549). The town's only official 'sight' is the **North Down Heritage Centre** ⓘ *Castle Park Av (cross the road from the train and bus station and walk down to the rear of the town hall, T9127 1200. Jul and Aug Tue-Sat 1030-1730, Sun 1400-1730, Sep-Jun Tue-Sat 1030-1630 and Sun 1400-1630. Free.* It's a mixed collection including a fifth-century BC set of swords, a ninth-century handbell, the Jordan Room with its engrossing set of Far Eastern art, and an observation beehive (in the summer). The tourist office (see above) is in one of Bangor's few surviving buildings of historical note and was the **Old Custom House and Tower**.

Around Bangor

Crawfordsburn Country Park ⓘ *Helen's Bay, off the B20, T9185 3621. Park open to dusk. Gun site 1400-1700, Apr-Sep, closed Tue. Oct-Mar, Sun only. Free.* On the coast, this place makes a pleasant change from museums. **Grey Point Fort**, with its restored gun site, is a popular destination and the Park Centre provides an excellent introduction to the local flora and ecology, the chief delight in coming here.

Somme Heritage Centre ⓘ *233 Bangor Rd, Newtownlands, T9182 3202, www.irishsoldier.org. Jul and Aug Mon-Fri 1000-1700, Sat and Sun 1200-1700; Apr-Jun and Sep Mon-Thu 1000-1600, Sat 1200-1600; Oct-Mar Mon-Thu 1000-1600 and first Sat of each month 1200-1700. £3.75. Situated north of Newtownlands on the A21.* When the First World War broke out, the parliamentary leaders of nationalists and unionists, John Redmond and Edward Carson, urged their supporters to enlist and many thousands did so. The 16th and the 10th Divisions were Catholic and nationalist respectively, while the 36th Ulster was a new division, created by 30,000 UVF men volunteering virtually as one body. In total some 200,000 Irishmen saw active service, and around 30,000 paid with their lives. The Ulster 36th Division were at the battle of the Somme from the beginning, in July 1916, suffering 5,000 casualties in the first 48 hours; they were joined by the 16th Division in September of that year.

 The Centre also has a static wall display reflecting the 10th Division's participation in the Gallipoli campaign.

Guided tours through the various displays and a reconstructed trench take from 45 minutes to an hour and, while interesting, rarely manage to convey the visceral horror of the war. A static exhibition on the role of Irish women during the war is just as enlightening. A good selection of books, posters and educational material is available.

Ark Open Farm ⓘ *T928 20445. Mon-Sat 1000-1800, Sun 1400-1800. £3.10, children £2.50.* On the other side of the A21 from the Somme Heritage Centre, the Ark Open Farm has over 80 rare species of pigs, goats and poultry. There are also a tea room and picnic sites.

Scrabo Country Park ⓘ *T9181 1491. Tower open Easter-Sep, 1030-1800, closed Fri. Free. Just over a mile southwest of Newtownlands and signposted from there.* The park itself is dominated by Scrabo Tower (122 steps to the top) built in 1857 as a memorial to the third Marquis of Londonderry. However, come here not for the tower, but for the panoramic views of Strangford Lough (see box page 547) and walks in the surrounding country park.

Ards Peninsula

The Ards Peninsula is the narrow slot of land between Strangford Lough and the Irish Sea. Of the two roads that run down either side of it, the windier A2, trailing its way through legions of caravan parks, takes a lot longer than the A20, which also passes Greyabbey and Mount Stewart along the way. Without your own transport, relying on scheduled bus services (see Portaferry below) could prove time-consuming, but Ulsterbus conduct various day tours – general, historic homes, gardens, heritage, and wildlife – starting in Newtownards. Contact Ulsterbus or the tourist office in Newtownards, see page 543.

For a flavour of Presbyterian life on the peninsula in the early 20th century, there is no better novel than 'December Bride', by Sam Hanna Bell (1951), later made into a film.

Coastal route As you head east from Bangor on the A2 you will come to the village of **Donaghadee** where ferries plied to and from Scotland until Larne took over the service in 1849. Daniel O'Connell left from here six years earlier, after a failed attempt to gain the support of Ulster for the repeal of sectarian laws barring Catholics from sitting in parliament. After having a cup of tea thrown at him by a woman he remarked to a fisherman, "You have very pretty girls here." "Yes," the man replied, "but none of them are Repealers". The only boat journey now possible is a day trip to the uninhabited **Copeland Islands** ⓘ *Nelson's Boats, Donaghadee, T9188 3403, www.nelsonboats.co.uk*, off the coast for bird-watching and this too may be coming to an end.

Continuing south, near caravan-infested Millisle, **Ballycopeland Windmill** ⓘ *B172, 1.6 km west of Millisle, T9054 6552, Jul-Aug Fri-Sun 1400-1800, Wed-Thu 1000-1300, free*, is a late 18th-century tower mill in use until 1915 and still in working order. **Portavogie**, further down the coast, is a fishing port of local renown and a drink and good food is available here (see page 551). At **Cloughey** there is a sandy beach safe for swimming, and at **Kearney** a fine beach walk before the main road heads inland for Portaferry.

East Strangford Lough route The chief attractions of travelling the A20 route, apart from access to the east side of Strangford Lough where there are parking spaces and points to observe bird life, are Mount Stewart House and Greyabbey.

Mount Stewart House ⓘ *T4278 8387. House: May-Sep 1300-1800, daily except Tue; daily over Easter; Apr and Oct Sat and Sun 1300-1800. Last tour 1700. Garden: Apr-Sep daily 1100-1800; Mar Sun only 1400-1700; Oct Sat and Sun*

1100-1800. House and garden £5.20. Garden only £4.20. Tearoom. Mount Stewart was home to the powerful Marquess of Londonderry, who also owned large tracts of County Durham in England from where coal from family mines was shipped in by the boatload to Strangford Lough. The tour of the house is for the most part an oleaginous animated page from a Sotheby's catalogue as it relates the date of this, the value of that, the spot where Castlereagh penned a letter and whether the eyes in one portrait show a family resemblance to some other aristocratic has-been. The tour pauses to take in the most famous piece of art in the house, a painting of a racehorse by George Stubbs. Like so many of these tours, this one improves enormously when it comes to the servants' quarters and what is known of their dealings. The English class structure was nothing if not precise and at Mount Stewart House even the visiting ladies' maids could pull some clout, having meals with the housekeeper in a special room and waited on by a lowly footman. One large bedroom was divided into cubicles for their sleeping arrangements, supervised by the head housekeeper who "wore grey alpaca in the morning and black silk in the evening" according to a maid who went home to her own lady to boast of the lavish wealth.

The **gardens** are also a little disappointing, but best in the early morning when peacocks stroll, hares and rabbits sport and serene swans glide by on the lake. There are some fine specimens of mature trees and a map guides you through the various set pieces laid out by Lady Londonderry in the 1920s. It is enlivened by the occasional jazz band on Sundays between April and September.

If you've ever endured a ferry journey to Ireland in a winter storm you will believe the story that Affreca, wife-to-be of John de Courcy, made a vow on her voyage to build an abbey if she arrived safely. The result in 1193 was **Greyabbey** ⓘ *East side of Greyabbey village, about 3 km south of Mount Stewart House on the A20, T9054 3033, Apr-Sep Tue-Sat 1000-1900, Sun 1400-1900, free*, one of the earliest Gothic churches in Ireland, peopled by Cistercian monks from Cumberland in England. The Gothic style has survived best in the superb west door, while inside there are stone figures, a Norman knight and a female figure taken to represent Affreca. The **herb garden** containing examples of medicinal plants that medieval monks nurtured is fascinating.

Portaferry, the visitor-friendly village from where ferries ply their way across the lough to Strangford, is an interesting place on the Ards Peninsula for an overnight rest (see page 549) and some good traditional music at the weekends (see page 551). Once an important little port with a herring industry, the village saw some action in the 1798 uprising and might have been captured by the rebels but for the timely presence of a government ship that fired on them from the quay. A more peaceful pursuit is offered nowadays at **Exploris** ⓘ *Castle St, T4272 8062, www.exploris.org.uk, Easter-Sep Mon-Fri 1000-1800, Sat 1100-1800, Sun 1300-1800, Sep-Easter, closes 1 hr earlier, £6 and £3.50 for children*, an aquarium that attracts families but is of interest to all. There is a seal sanctuary as well as sting rays, starfish and sea urchins to stroke in the touch tank. Collect a map of the village from the tourist office (see page 543) and walk up **Windmill Hill** for fine views of the choppy Narrows.

Western shore of Strangford Lough → *Colour map 1, grid B6.*

Another way of getting to the Ards Peninsula is on the A22 road by the western shore of Strangford Lough, and there are a couple of diversions worth taking along the way. **Castle Espie** ⓘ *Ballydrain Rd, Comber, T9187 4146, Mar-Oct Mon-Sat 1030-1700, Sun 1130-1730, Nov-Feb Mon-Fri 1100-1600, Sat-Sun 1100-1630, £4.40, 5 km south of Comber*, run by the Wildfowl and Wetlands Trust, is home to a large collection of ducks, geese and swans, and provides access to bird-watching hides over the lough.

A little further south the **Nendrum Monastic Site** ⓘ *T9054 3037, Mahee Island, museum open Apr-Oct Mon-Sat 0900-1800, Sun 1300-1800, shorter hours in winter, free access to site*, makes up for its scattered and scant remains by an informative visitor centre and a peaceful setting – very appropriate for the site of a monastic settlement. Founded in 445 by St Mochaoi, a pupil of St Patrick, it was rediscovered in 1844.

Comber has a few places to eat (see page 551), including Old Schoolhouse Inn, and The Cooperage Bistro.

Near the bottom of the lough, **Killyleagh Castle** (closed to the public) looks like a film set but is actually one of Ireland's oldest inhabited castles, going back to the 12th century but given its schmaltzy appearance by the Victorians. In 1913, when unionists resolved to use "all means which may be found necessary" to scupper Home Rule, the newly founded Ulster Volunteer Force trained in the grounds here.

Strangford to Newcastle

The winding road from Strangford (via Clough) to Newcastle has fine views of the sea before the Mourne mountains open up at Newcastle.

Strangford If it wasn't for the ferry crossing to Portaferry, Strangford might be a place to miss. **Strangford Castle**, one of the many tower houses you'll see dotted around Strangford Lough, dates from the late 16th century (key-keeper lives opposite at 39 Castle Street), but that's all there is to see. There are good places to eat though (see page 551).

Castle Ward ⓘ *T4488 1204. House: May-Aug 1300-1800 daily (except Tue in May); Apr, Sep, Oct, Sat and Sun 1300-1800. £3.50. Last guided tour 1700. On A25, under 2 miles west of Strangford.* Outside the village of Strangford, on the Downpatrick Road, Castle Ward is a distinctly odd 18th-century manor house now managed by the National Trust but formerly the property of Bernard and Ann Ward. The couple eventually parted but, before they did, the divorce of their minds was reflected permanently in the design of their house. The front of Castle Ward is classical in style (his taste), while the rear is Gothic (her preference), and the dichotomy is also apparent in the interior. The extensive grounds include a tower house and landscaped gardens.

Kilclief Castle ⓘ *Open Jul and Aug Tue-Sat 1000-1900, Sun 1400-1900.* Another quick stop could be made here, a couple of miles south of Strangford on the A2, where another fortified tower house stands in good condition and the interior gives some idea of just how well provided they could be.

Ardglass If you've taken a fancy to comparing tower houses, there are no

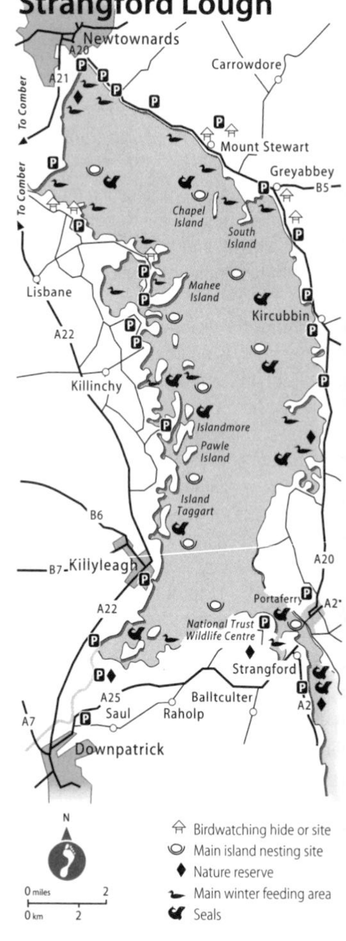

Strangford Lough

Strangford Lough would be a lake but for a narrow 8-km gap at the southern end between Portaferry and Strangford that is as little as 500 m wide at its narrowest point. It whips up some treacherous tides and probably explains the Viking appellation *Strangfjörthr* (the strong fjord). The lough is rich in wildlife: in the northern half in winter wildfowl, waders, gulls and auks feed in the soft mud and sands; in autumn up to 15,000 pale-bellied Brent geese fly in from Arctic Canada for rest and recreation on their way south; common and grey seals cling to rocks close to the shore and the occasional orca also slips through the narrows.

Now managed by the National Trust, based at Castle Ward near Strangford, T4488 1411, the Wildlife Centre has a wealth of ecological information and is open May-Aug 1300-1800 daily (except Tue in May); mid-Mar to Apr and Sep Sat and Sun 1400-1800. Grounds open May-Sep, daily, 1000-2000; Oct-Apr, daily 1000-1600. Grounds, centre and house tour £5, grounds only £3.50.

less than seven of them at Ardglass, 13 km south of Strangford, one of which is now in the grounds of a golf club. In its late 19th-century heyday Ardglass was a profitable little fishing port cashing in on seasonal shoals of herring and mackerel, which were salted and exported to the West Indies. It is still a good place to purchase fresh fish and there is a restaurant worth visiting (see page 551) as well as the only accessible tower house, **Jordan's Castle** ⓘ *T9181 1491, Jul and Aug Tue-Sat 1000-1900, and Sun 1400-1900.*

Killough The A2 follows the coast around an inlet, through the village of Killough, and from the coastguard station just south of the village there is an enjoyable 6.4-km circular **coastal path** that follows the shore across stiles until reaching Point Road near St John's Point Lighthouse. Turn right on to Point Road to head back to the village.

Tyrella beach ⓘ *£2 to park a car.* The A2 between Killough and Clough passes this beach, ideal for families because it has shallow sands, warden service and amenities, but consequently busy on a fine summer's day. When it is quieter, enjoy a longish walk on the dunes or the beach to the east.

Clough Before reaching Newcastle the road passes Clough, at the junction with the A25 from Downpatrick, and its eponymous **motte castle** with free access and fine views from the top of the mound. The original occupant of the castle living in his fortification on top of this artificial mound needed a good view to espy hostile movements, and the Clough motte also had defensive wooden palisades around the perimeter.

Dundrum This village is the last stop, with a particularly fine castle: "one of the strongyst holtes that ever I sawe in Ireland", reported a henchman for the Tudor monarchy in 1538. The Norman John de Courcy first established a castle here known as Rath. When he fell out of favour with King John and the land passed to Hugh de Lacy, de Courcy found himself unsuccessfully besieging his own **Dundrum Castle** ⓘ *Apr-Sep Tue-Sat 1000-1900, Sun 1400-1900, 75p*, in 1205. Hugh de Lacy added a sturdy keep and later a gatehouse to the castle and what you see today is still a very impressive sight. There are picnic tables in the car park, but more appealing is one of the many grassy areas under the shade of trees inside the castle grounds.

★ Downpatrick → *Colour map 1, grid B6.*

This is a thriving, tolerant little town with several cracking sites to visit, and it is well worth an overnight stay to do so. If you can make your visit on St Patrick's Day (17th March), all the better: you will see genuine cross-cultural celebrations.

History In the 12th century, Down was the capital of Dál Fiatach; the real trouble started when the Norman John de Courcy turned up here in 1177 from Dublin with 22 horsemen and 300 foot soldiers. Down's Gaelic ruler, Rory MacDonleavy, was routed from the town; several major battles followed, with hand-to-hand fighting along the banks of the Quoile River, but the small Norman force held fast.

So Down became the first Norman foothold in Ulster. De Courcy gave the ancient site of Dún-da-lethglas, which had been an Augustinian Priory before the Norman takeover, to the Church, and renamed it Downpatrick. By the 13th century it was the second most important Norman settlement in Ulster, after Armagh, with defensive walls and a Benedictine monastery.

Downpatrick gaol saw its share of executions during the 1798 rebellion, when the area was second only to Wexford in the strength of the rebels and the ferocity with which they fought. After this the town went into a decline, which in a way is lucky for visitors, who can see the 18th-century structure of the town almost unencumbered by modernity.

Sights A church stood on the site of what is now **Down Cathedral** ⓘ *The Mall, T4461 4922, Mon-Sat 1000-1700, Sun 1400-1700, free, choral evensong third Sun of the month at 1530*, long before de Courcy generously gave back a little of what he had taken in the 12th century. The site is associated with Patrick, who built his first church, and is reputed to have died at Saul, a few miles to the north. Before de Courcy, there was an Augustinian settlement on the hill. Nothing remains of it, or of the building that replaced it, which was destroyed in the 14th century. In 1609 James I made Down a cathedral, despite the fact that it was a set of ruins and the bishop was enthroned here beneath a gaping roof. Rebuilding got underway in the 18th century. Inside, it's a cosy little place with 18th-century box pews labelled with the names of their owners on little brass plaques. The organ is built on to a pulpitum, which you walk through to enter the church. The two thrones that face each other across the nave are the bishop's throne and the judge's seat, dating back to a time when trials were held in the church. In the graveyard the remains of St Patrick, St Colmcille and St Brigid are said to be buried. The stone that supposedly marks the site was put there in 1900. In the grounds are several other antiquities which have largely been removed to here from other places.

In the town's gaol is the really excellent **Down County Museum** ⓘ *The Mall, T4461 5218, www.downcountymuseum.com, Mon-Fri 1000-1700, Sat-Sun 1300-1700, free, shop*. There are exhibitions on St Patrick, the history of County Down – with lots of fascinating material on the 1798 rebellion, a changing series of exhibitions of art and artefacts, and the barely changed prison cells complete with 18th-century graffiti and some unrealistic models. Sensors along the passages set off recorded prison noises, which can be quite startling if you are not expecting them.

The **Saint Patrick Centre** is a very interactive kind of place detailing the life of the saint and the early church in Ireland. Aimed more at local children perhaps than the tourist market, this is good for a wander round on a rainy day and may genuinely interest those of a historical bent. ⓘ *T4461 9000, www.saintpatrickcentre.com. Jun-Aug Mon-Sat 0930-1800, Sun 1000-1800; Apr, May and Sep Mon-Sat 0930-1730, Sun 1300-1730; Oct-Mar Mon-Sat 1000-1700. £4.75.*

If nothing else convinces you that you are not in the Republic of Ireland, the wacky **Downpatrick Railway Museum** ⓘ *Market St, T44615779, www.downpatricksteamrailway.co.uk, trains run from Jul to mid-Sep, 1400-1700, Sat* and Sun only, also St Patrick's Day, Easter Sun and Mon, Hallowe'en weekend, Dec weekends 1400-1700, workshop and Station House open Jun-Sep Mon-Sat 1100-1400: only the British are this barmy. This museum is run entirely by volunteers and is populated by every crumbling railway carriage that farmers could take off their fields and dump here. One of the trains actually works, and you can take a short train ride to **King Magnus Halt** on a restored but creaky steam engine whose provenance will be lovingly described by the volunteer guides. You can also visit the worksheds where skeleton carriages are being worked on, the signal box (carried brick by brick from Ballyclare) and the station house itself (actually the old gasworks building, also shifted block by block). The volunteers have great plans for expanding the line and adding more carriages, and their enthusiasm alone is worth the visit.

There are a good few other things to peer at in this city. **St Patrick's Roman Catholic church** ⓘ *daily*, is quite an impressive building: much more modern than the cathedral, set on another hill. It was built in the late 19th century and replaces an earlier church of around 1787. Most of what you see, though, is a modern extension added to hold the increasing congregations in this predominantly Catholic town. Stained glass and mosaic panels detail the life of St Patrick.

In Mount Crescent is a pathway leading to the **Mound of Down**, the remains of de Courcy's fortifications. It is a motte and bailey fortification, said to be the finest example of such in Ulster, probably built around 1200. Within sight of the Mound, and reached from the Belfast road, is **Inch Abbey** ⓘ *free access, turn left off the Belfast Rd at the Abbey Lodge Hotel*, another de Courcy job. Built around 1180, it was a Cistercian monastery, and is on the site of a much older place, called Inis Cumhscraigh, which dates back to at least 800. In its 12th-century state, this was a church, with a cloister and several community buildings, including a bakehouse, whose oven was found nearby. There are a good few walls remaining, even though the abbey was burned in 1404 and completely suppressed by 1541.

Around Downpatrick At **Saul** (Sabhal Pádraic), 3 km northeast of town, is the reputed site of Patrick's first church in Ireland which was said to be in a barn given to him by the local lord. An Augustinian monastery was built here some time after 1130, but today the site is occupied by a Church of Ireland building, erected in the 1930s in the style of a medieval church. There are a few ancient relics in the graveyard, including two mortuary houses of unknown date, cross pillars and a medieval gravestone. Inside the church, the font is 13th century. If you are feeling a bit under the weather, go to **Struel Wells** ⓘ *Ardglass Rd, free, 2 km east of Downpatrick*: here there are four ancient wells reputed to have the power to heal internal organs, eyes, body and limbs.

Sleeping

Bangor *p543*

C Bangor Bay Inn, 10 Seacliff Rd, T912 0696. A small hotel in a former doctor's residence where American officers were billeted in the 1940s and with large rooms overlooking the sea. Cheaper at weekends.

D Cairn Bay Lodge, 278 Seacliff Rd, T9146 7636, www.cairnbaylodge.com. A detached house that is an award-winning B&B.

D Marine Court Hotel, 18-20 Quay St, T9145 1100, www.marinecourthotel.net. Has a gym, pool and comfortable rooms.

E Number 108, 108 Seacliff Rd, T9146 1077, seacliff108@aol.com. More typical of the other B&Bs also found lined up in Seacliff Rd and facing the sea.

Ards Peninsula *p544*

E Lakeview, 92A Windmill Rd, Donaghadee, T9188 3900. With 2 rooms and single/double at £20-30 it is typical of the many B&Bs around this part of the county.

Portaferry *p545*

C The Narrows, Shore Rd, T4272 8148, www.narrows.co.uk. Not cheap at £42-50 per person sharing in the high season but this is Portaferry's smartest accommodation, with a sauna and views of the ferry drifting by through the windows of uncluttered bedrooms (no alternative to the fried breakfast in the morning, however).

E **Adair's**, 22 The Square, T4272 8412. In the centre of the village, 3 rooms, 1with en suite bathroom, for £18 per person.

E **Lough Cowey Lodge**, 9 Lough Cowey Rd, T4272 8263. Just outside the village.

F **Barholm**, 11 The Strand, T4272 9598, www.barholmportaferry.co.uk. A detached Edwardian house overlooking the lough with hostel beds and double rooms, from £13, a fully-equipped kitchen but meals also available.

Strangford to Newcastle *p546*

E **Burford Lodge**, Quay St, Ardglass, T4484 1141. Does B&B and evening meals for residents.

E **Margaret's Cottage**, Castle Pl, Ardglass, T4484 1080. Has some charm and is a very nice place for an overnight stay.

Camping

Castle Ward Caravan Park, just over a mile west of Strangford on the A25, T4488 1680, has tent pitches for £5.50 per night.

Downpatrick *p548*

C **Tyrella House**, 100 Clanmaghery Rd, T4485 1422, www.hiddenireland.com/tyrella. A good choice for an out-of-town, country house sort of stay, has its own beechwoods, private beach and stables. Also has a self-catering cottage.

D **Denvir's**, 14-16 English St, T4461 2012. An ancient building recently renovated to a Spartan prettiness. The dining room has the most enormous fireplace with the old hooks that were used for smoking meat still in place. Huge rooms, very central but quiet. The best place to stay in Downpatrick. Single/double rooms: £32.50-55.

E **Arolsen**, 47 Roughal Park, T4461 2656 bryancoburn@compuserve.com. Fairly central B&B. Evening meals by arrangement. Single/double rooms: £20-36.

E **Dunnleath House**, 33 St Patrick's Dr, T4461 3221. B&B with 2 big triple rooms.

E-F **Hillside**, 62 Scotch St, T4461 3134. A B&B in a listed Georgian house with 3 double rooms, 1 with en suite bathroom. Residents' lounge. Single/double rooms: £18-35.

Eating

Bangor *p543*

TTT **Restaurant 1614**, The Old Inn, Main St, Crawfordsburn (9.5 km after Holywood, off the A2), T9185 3255, www.theoldinn.com. A tad less expensive, and less sassy, than Shanks (see below) but the hotel as a whole exudes charm. A good meal can also be enjoyed at affordable prices in the characterful bar or the Churn Bistro.

TTT **Shanks**, Blackwood Golf Centre, 150 Crawfordsburn Rd, Bangor, T9185 3313, www.shanksrestaurant.com. One of Ireland's best restaurants and don't be put off by knowing it's designed by Conran. The food is broadly European, using local produce with imaginative, contemporary touches and in summer, lobster salad niçoise is a typical creation from the kitchen of Robbie Millar. Open Tue-Fri for lunch, around £20, and Tue-Sat for dinner for approaching twice that amount. The vegetarian dinner menu is under £35.

TT **First Port**, T9146 7699, next to the tourist office. Has a large lunch menu around £7, a 2-course early dinner menu (in Bangor it has to be called high tea) from 1700-1900 for £9, and a fish and meat evening menu that will work out around £20 or more for 3 courses.

T **Bangor Bay Inn**, Seacliff Rd, Bangor. A cosy little restaurant offering a relaxing evening meal for £15 and a good value bistro menu.

T **Café Brazilia**, facing the clock tower on the marina, T9127 2763. Has outdoor tables and is the place to enjoy a decent cup of coffee and one of their dozen toasties, potato bakes or sandwiches; all around £4.

T **Castle Garden**, at the North Down Heritage Centre, T9127 0371. Restaurant, a peaceful place for a coffee or lunch (closed Mon).

T **Coyle's**, directly opposite Jenny Watts, T9127 0362. Award-winning bar food for around £6 and a restaurant offering home-made beef burgers, Thai steamed mussels, salads all under £7.

For an explanation of the sleeping and eating price codes used in this guide, see inside the front cover. Other relevant information is found in Essentials pages 39-45.

¥ **Donegan's**, up the hill of High St, T9146 3928. An old-style Irish pub and restaurant with a 2-course lunch for £7 and an early dinner around £8.

¥ **Jenny Watts**, T9127 0401, next door to Donegan's. Does food and has live music on Tue, Thu and Sun afternoons and evenings.

Ards Peninsula *p544*

¥ **Grace Neill's**, 33 High St, Donaghadee, T9188 2553, www.graceneills.co.uk. A good bet for food, daily except Mon and Sun evenings, and serves a delicious dish of homemade pork and leek sausage with red onion marmalade and champ. The front bar is one of the oldest in Ireland and dates back to the early 17th century. Sunday brunch, with live music, is a big draw with locals.

¥ **Pier 36**, The Parade, T9188 4466, www.pier36.co.uk. It is attractive and friendly and food is available daily until 2130 from an imaginative menu that includes lunch specials, pork and stilton sausages for £7, and fish dishes around £10-12. Recommended.

¥ **The Quay's Pub & Restaurant**, New Harbour Rd, Portavogie, T4277 2225, www.quayrestaurant.co.uk. The restaurant is open Wed-Sun but pub food all week.

¥ **Wong's Royale Restaurant**, also in New Harbour Rd, T4277 2511. The place to go for something Chinese at lunch or dinner time.

Portaferry *p545*

¥¥ **The Narrows**, Shore Rd. Serves fresh fish and meat dishes daily, with all the tell-tale touches of the modern and trendy – expect puy lentils, shiitake mushrooms, Parmesan shavings – in a plain, pine-furnished room looking out at the lough. Expect to pay about £12-18 for a main course, rising to £23 for grilled lobster, during evening, £8-12 for a lunch like spicy pasta or a lobster salad.

¥¥ **Portaferry Hotel**, The Strand. Does a good lunch, plus a basic set evening dinner for around £20. Not a puy lentil in sight.

¥ **The Quarterdeck**, at the Fiddler's Green pub. The best alternative for a meal (see also Bars and music below).

Western shore of Strangford Lough *p545, map p546*

¥ **Old Schoolhouse Inn**, Comber, next to Castle Espie, T9754 1182. Maintains its reputation for serving the best dishes, especially seafood, in the area. Open Mon-Sat, 1900-2200, and lunch on Sun.

¥ **The Cooperage Bistro**, Killinchy St, Comber, T9187 1818. The last remaining part of the an old distillery and retains an old-world atmosphere. Good for lunch or dinner on Fri and Sat.

Strangford to Newcastle *p546*

¥¥-¥ **The Cuan**, Strangford, T4488 1222, www.thecuan.com. Does tasty bar food like smoked brie, homemade paté, seafood chowder and chicken curry. As well as a more formal, restaurant menu there is also a fish and chips takeaway that proclaims itself 'the best in county Down'.

¥¥-¥ **The Lobster Pot**, Strangford, T4488 1288. Has tables outside for drinks and food that varies from the mundane to a grand lobster menu.

¥¥-¥ **Aldo's**, in Castle Pl, Ardglass, next to the post office, T4484 1315. Opens daily in Jun-Aug, irregularly at other times, and is also known as 'Downs'. Italian-style food with main courses costing around £10-12. Fish and chips are available down by the harbour in Ardglass.

Downpatrick *p548*

¥ **Denvir's**, 14-16 English St, T4461 2012. Enormously popular with locals and visitors alike. Nothing special, but good hearty food and very reasonable prices.

¥ **Harry Afrika's**, inside Supervalu shopping centre. Does grills and the like, and opens on Sun too.

Pubs and music

Portaferry *p545*

Fiddler's Green, facing The Square, T4272 8393, www.fiddlersgreenportaferry.com. Well known for its traditional music at weekends.

Downpatrick *p548*

The Cabin at the bottom of Church St is a bright airy bar with live music on Sat nights.

Denvir's, 14-16 English St, T4461 2012. Has music at weekends, usually country-style folk music or something louder.

The other pubs have music, occasionally live.

Festivals and events

Downpatrick *p548*
The big event of the year is **17 Mar**, St Patrick's Day, which is extended into a week of cross-cultural activities that attracts large crowds.

Activities and tours

Bangor *p543*
Diving **David Vincent**, T9146 4671, www.dvdiving.co.uk.
Fishing T07779-600607, www.bangorboat.com. Deep sea fishing aboard the **MV Purple Heather** from the North Pier, twice daily in Jul-Aug for £8, and herring fishing at 1900 on Fri-Sat for 10. Rods and tackle are provided.

Transport

Bangor to Newcastle *p543*
Bus Bangor bus station, T9127 1143. Ulsterbus runs Mon-Fri from **Belfast** at 0810, via **Newtownards** and **Greyabbey**, arriving in Portaferry at 0950. For local services check with the local tourist office (see page 543).
Ferry Ferries to **Portaferry** depart from **Strangford**, T4488 1637, on the hour and half-hour, 0730-2230 weekdays, 0800-2300 Sat, and 0930-2230 Sun. From Portaferry, departures are at quarter past and quarter to the hour 0745-2245 weekdays, 0815-2315 Sat, and 0945-2245 Sun. Single fare for passengers is £1, for cars £4.80-£7.70.
Train Bangor train station, T9066 6630. Frequent trains from Belfast.

Around the Mourne Mountains

South Down, between Newcastle and Newry, has a schizophrenic quality. On the one hand there are the majestic Mourne Mountains imposing their granite beauty on the surrounding wilderness, while down on the coast there are unimpressive towns like Newcastle and scruffy villages like Kilkeel. Seen in terms of nature and nurture there is no question about who wins out in this part of the world. » *For Sleeping, Eating and other listings, see pages 556-558.*

Ins and outs

Information **Newcastle tourist office** Central Promenade on the way out of town on the A2 to Kilkeel, T4372 2222. Open Mon-Sat 1000-1700, Sun 1400-1800. **Kilkeel tourist office** Bridge St, T4176 2525. Open all year, Mon-Sat 0900-1730 (closed Sat in Jan and Feb. **Warrenpoint tourist office** in the town hall on Church St, T4175 2256. Open Jun-Aug daily 0900-1700; Sep-May Mon-Fri 0900-1700. **Newry tourist office** in the town hall, T3026 8877. Open Apr-Jun Mon-Fri 0900-1700, Sat 1000-1600; Jul-Sep Mon 0900-1700, Tue-Fri 0900-1900, Sat 1000-1600; Oct-Mar Mon-Fri 0900-1700. **Banbridge Gateway Tourist Information Centre** 200 Newry Rd, T4062 3322. Open Jul and Aug Mon-Sat 0900-1900, Sun 1400-1800; Sep-Jun Mon-Sat 1000-1700; Easter-Oct Sun 1400-1800.

Newcastle → *Colour map 1, grid C5.*

The excellent tourist office is a good place to collect information and pick up a colour town map that lists useful amenities such as banks and chemists but once your business here is done there is little reason to linger in Newcastle.

Walking around Newcastle For short walks, take Bryansford Road out of Newcastle to **Tollymore Forest Park** ⓘ *T4372 2428, daily, 1000-dusk, car £4, pedestrian £2, tea room*, covering some 500 acres at the foot of the Mourne Mountains and with four way-marked trails. Once a private estate, the mansion house fell into disrepair after the Second World War and was demolished in the early 1950s What remains is a stupendous avenue of cedar trees leading up to where the house

Walking and cycling in the Mourne Mountains

Newcastle, with its shops and amenities, suggests itself as a quartermastering base for walking in the Mourne Mountains and the **Mourne Heritage Trust**, 87 Central Promenade, T4372 4059, has information and literature on suggested walks. The villages of Annalong, Kilkeel, Warrenpoint, and even Newry, are also possible bases for a few days spent walking the Mourne mountains and all have tourist offices where maps and information are available.

Newry and Mourne Council dispense free booklets, *Walking in Newry & Mourne* and *Cycling in Newry & Mourne*, that give lots of ideas for trips. They could be used in conjunction with the Ordnance Survey 1:25000 map, *The Mournes*, printed on water resistant paper and showing all the walking tracks. It's also worth getting hold of the Newcastle local bus timetable, useful when planning a walk between Newcastle and either Kilkeel or Annalong and using a bus to return to your accommodation. Experienced walkers will want to ascend to Slieve Donard, using Ordnance Survey Map No 29 in the Discovery series, while a gentler introduction is provided by Donard Park to the south of Newcastle. From here the mountain can be climbed, or you can try a shorter walk by just following the path up the slopes for a hour or so.

From Annalong, the inland roads lead up to the Carrick Little car park from where day-walks into the mountains or just along the Mourne Wall (see page 554) are possible. From this car park it takes under 4 hours to complete a circular walk up Slieve Binnian, starting by following the Mourne Wall, and returning along the side of the Annalong River. A great day out.

stood which forms a magnificent entrance to the park. The most interesting short walk is the **Rivers Trail** that follows the Shimna River through swathes of violets in early summer before crossing by Parnell's Bridge and returning through forest on the other side. A longer 13-km trail heads into the forest and offers excellent views of the countryside and Mourne Mountains.

Further inland, the **Castlewellan Forest Park** ⓘ *Castlewellan, T4377 8664, daily 1000-dusk, car £4, pedestrian £2*, is famous for its arboretum that dates back to 1740, but walking is restricted to a 5-km trail around a lake with sculptures created from local materials. Enjoy tea in the Queen Anne-style courtyard or bring food to eat in the picnic and barbecue areas.

Annalong → *Colour map 1, grid C5.*

Annalong is a small fishing village 12 km south of Newcastle and is worth considering for an overnight stay. The beach is too shingly to attract hordes of visitors and near the harbour the 1830 **Annalong Corn Mill** ⓘ *T4376 8736, Apr-Oct Wed-Mon 1400-1600, £1.90, guided tours*, makes for a mildly interesting visit when a flour-making demonstration is taking place. A coastal path can be followed northwards from here for about half an hour.

Kilkeel → *Colour map 1, grid C5.*

The small fishing town of Kilkeel seems an unlikely setting for an unattractive display of sectarianism but there is no mistaking the curious blend of in-your-face triumphalism and aggressively defensive posturing revealed in the choice of flags that dominate the centre of town. The flag of Israel flutters alongside those of

 Scotland and the paramilitary UVF (at Carnlough further up the coast you will see the Palestinian flag flying) and the mural reading '9 in a row' refers to the 9 years of standoff at Drumcree. Notwithstanding this visual blather, Kilkeel is a friendly place and an access point for the Mourne mountains.

The **Mourne Grange Craft Shop** ⓘ *169 Newry Rd, T4176 0103*, is worth a visit with heaps of craft goods and a tea room. For a general introduction to the role of fishing in Kilkeel's history, the **Nautilus Centre** ⓘ *Rooney Rd, T4176 5555, Easter-Sep Mon-Sat 1000-2100, Sun 1200-1800, same hours the rest of the year but closed Mon*, by the harbour has displays and exhibits and a shop selling fresh fish. The tourist office (see page 552) is an excellent source of local information for walking and cycling maps covering the Mourne mountains.

The Silent Valley → *Colour map 1, grid C5.*

A huge reservoir supplying Belfast from the valley of the River Kilkeel was completed in 1933 and its story is told in the Information Centre near the car park in the reservoir grounds. The most incredible aspect of the whole project was the building of the **Mourne Wall** ⓘ *Easter-Sep 1000-1830, Oct-Apr 1000-1600, £3 per car, in May, Jun and Sep at weekends, and daily in Jul and Aug, a bus service operates between the car park and the top of Ben Crom, £2 return, coffee shop and craft shop, see the Newcastle section for the Mourne Rambler service between Newcastle and the Silent Valley*, around the catchment area – Ireland's Great Wall – up to 2.5 m high, 35 km long and connecting the summits of 15 mountains. Why it was built, apart from being a massive job creation scheme, is not entirely clear, but it took from 1904-1923 to complete. A 5-km **walk** by the side of the reservoir is well worth it for the fine views.

Kilkeel to Newry → *Colour map 1, grid C5.*

A detour southwest from Kilkeel leads to the tip of a promontory where you'll find **Greencastle Fort** ⓘ *Jul-Aug, Tue-Sat, 1000-1900, Sun, 1400-1900, 75p*. It was built by the rapacious Hugh de Lacy to stand sentinel over Carlingford Lough and the views from the castle are a better reason for making the journey here than the remains themselves.

The A2 road gradually creeps closer to the north coast of the lough, looking across to the Cooley Peninsula in Louth, and passing a signpost to the **Kilfeagham dolmen** with its 35-tonne capstone, a few miles out from Kilkeel.

Rostrevor The village of Rostrevor has more charm than most of the coastal towns in south Down and nearby **Kilbroney Park**, ⓘ *T4173 8134, Jun-Aug daily 0900-2220, shorter hours the rest of the year*, has plenty of open space, riverside walks and an energetic path up to the 40-tonne, pink granite Cloughmore boulder stone, from where there are scenic views across to the Republic, as well as tennis courts, picnic areas and a café.

Warrenpoint On the road between Rostrevor and Warrenpoint is the **Narrow Water Castle** ⓘ *T4175 2256, guided tours normally available in Jul and Aug Tue-Fri 1100-1630, but check with the tourist office in Warrenpoint (see page 552)*, where de Lacy built a fortress in the 13th century to guard access to the river up to Newry. Narrow Water Castle was where, in 1979, the Provisionals hid a bomb in a haystack and detonated it from the shore of the Cooley Peninsula when a platoon of the 2nd Parachute Regiment passed by. Survivors took refuge in the gateway to the castle where another bomb had been planted. A total of 18 soldiers died and an Englishman on holiday was accidentally shot dead by an army helicopter returning fire on the Cooley Peninsula.

Warrenpoint is not as interesting a town as its picturesque appearance and location might suggest. The pubs cater to Irish holidaymakers in the summer and the

Newry Canal

The River Clanrye and the Newry Canal make an unusual sight, running cheek by jowl through the centre of town. Surveying work for the canal started in 1703, prompted by the notion of transporting newly discovered coal in east Tyrone from Lough Neagh and out to sea through Newry and the Carlingford Lough. The canal's completion in 1741 was a remarkable achievement. It pre-dated the first canals in Lancashire, England, was built without machinery and remained in operation for almost 200 years. The whole canal is now in public ownership and you can walk or cycle along the towpath using the brochure map available from the tourist office (see page 552) or maps 20 and 29 in the OS Discoverer series.

pubs are heaving at night. Many of the pubs have live music but it's more likely to be in the Country and Western vein than traditional Irish.

Newry → *Colour map 1, grid C5.*

Newry has suffered from a bad press for years and guide books have tended to write the place off; don't believe a word of it. It's not postcard pretty, but it has history and attitude, and in the coming years could see quite a few changes as the importance of the border further diminishes.

The flourishing activity of the 18th century associated with the Newry canal petered out with the coming of the railways and economic decline set in. At the time of partition in 1922, it was so widely accepted that the Boundary Commission would allocate the town to the Republic that two businessmen, one Catholic and one Protestant and living respectively in Newry and Warrenpoint, exchanged their houses so they could live in the state of their choice. It was not to be, but the legacy surfaced in 1969, with the Civil Rights Association calling for pressure to be taken off the Bogside, when Newry was quick to rise in revolt. Finally, 30 years later, the appearance of two new hotels and the expansive Buttercrane Shopping Centre point to a new and more equitable future for the town.

A guide to the Newry Canal Way is also available from the tourist office.

Nowadays Newry is at peace, and while there are no special attractions it is a most interesting place to wander around (free town map from the tourist office, see page 552) because the lack of developments over the last 30 years has helped preserve examples of industrial architecture that will soon no doubt succumb to the bulldozer. It is well worth using the **Newry Heritage Trail**, available from the tourist office, for a self-guided tour. There is also the waymarked **Newry Canal Way**, a 20-mile cycling and walking route connecting Newry with Portadown that follows the towpath of the now non-navigable Newry Canal.

Sights Right next to the tourist office stands the magisterial **town hall**. It dates from 1893 and was built on a bridge near where the road from Armagh becomes Canal Street and meets Merchants Quay by the side of the canal. Tucked away behind it is a more interesting example of late Victorian building, a five-storey brick-built structure with three arched doorways built in 1879. An even better example of Victorian industrial architecture can be admired by leaving the town hall and walking away from the town centre and across the junction with Canal Street to **Sand's Mill** in New Street: seven floors of red and yellow bricks, arcaded, and still in use since it first opened for business in 1873.

The **Newry Museum** ⓘ *Arts Centre, next to the town hall, Bank Parade, T3026 6232, Mon-Fri 1030-1300 and 1400-1630, free,* is a history-based museum with assorted exhibits and a restored early 18th-century room, using original panelling taken from a local house of that period. Not rivetingly interesting but fine for a rainy afternoon.

The Brontë Homeland

The tourist board has made the best out of the least interesting part of Down by dubbing an area to the south of Banbridge, about half-way between Newry and Belfast, the 'Brontë Homeland', as it was here that Patrick Brontë, father of the famous literary family, lived and worked before moving to Haworth in Yorkshire. If travelling south to Banbridge from Belfast, the Georgian-style town of **Hillsborough** offers a touch of genteel elegance: break here for tea and cakes. Alternatively, push on for Banbridge and stop outside town, on the A1 Belfast to Newry road, at the **Banbridge Gateway Tourist Information Centre** (see page 552). There is a café serving lunches and light meals and the centre sells a useful little collection of eight route cards with directions and maps for suggested local walks (including a Brontë walk) averaging 8 km each.

The first stop on a Brontë tour should be the **Brontë Homeland Interpretative Centre** ⓘ *Church Hill Rd, T4063 1152, Mar-Sep Tue-Fri 1100-1700, same hours Oct-Feb but closed Mon, £2,* at Drumballyroney Church and School House near Rathfriland, 13 km from Banbridge off the B10. Patrick Brontë and the novelist sisters' brother, Bramwell, taught and preached here. The importance of Ireland in gaining an understanding of Emily and her brother is not a tenuous one, as Terry Eagleton brings to light in his book, *Heathcliff and the Great Hunger*. A free leaflet with a map outlines a tour that takes in four other sites associated with the Brontës' father and provides a good a reason as any for threading one's way through a little-visited part of Down.

Sleeping

Newcastle *p552*

C **Enniskeen House Hotel**, 98 Bryansford Rd, T4372 2392. Has bedrooms with views and the benefit of being a mile out of town, giving it the edge on other similarly-priced hotels. Closed mid-Nov to Feb.

E **Harbour House Inn**, 4-8 South Promenade, T4372 3445. Nearer town, and a reasonably priced restaurant is part of the establishment.

F **Newcastle Hostel**, 30 Downs Rd, 60 m from the bus station, T4372 2133. This YHANI hostel has almost 40 beds and is open all year.

Camping

Tollymore Forest Park, Tullybrannigan Rd, T4372 2428, on the B180, 5 km from town. There are loads of caravan parks around town but this is the only one accepting campers; charges between £8-12 a night.

Annalong *p553*

B **Glassdrumman Lodge**, 85 Mill Rd, signposted off the main road at the Newcastle end of the village, T4376 8451, www.glassdrummanlodge.co.uk. Reassuringly peaceful atmosphere, quality accommodation and good food help make this a congenial place to stay.

E **The Sycamores**, 52 Majors Hill, T4376 8279. Old farmhouse building with parts dating back to the 18th century and views out to sea.

Self-catering

Manx View, 257 Kilkeel Rd, Annalong, T4176 3222, margaret_ bingham@hotmail.com. Sleeps 3, close to beach, £170-225 per week depending on time of year.

Kilkeel *p553*

E **Heath Hall**, 160 Moyadd Rd, T4176 2612. A friendly and comfy farmhouse B&B, about

For an explanation of the sleeping and eating price codes used in this guide, see inside the front cover. Other relevant information is found in Essentials pages 39-45.

a mile inland, fine for a one-night stopover.
E **Mourne Abbey**, 16 Greencastle Rd, T4176 2426. Just south of town, opens from Easter-Sep and an evening meal is an option.

Self-catering

Mountain View House, 20 Head Rd, Moyadd, Kilkeel, T4172 3120, sjlavery@fsadvice.co.uk. Rural self-catering from £170-£250 a week.
Mountains of Mourne Cottages, Hanna's Close, Kilkeel, T4176 5999, www.travel-Ireland.com/hannas. Restored traditional Irish cottages sleeping from 2-6 people and a 4-person cottage in low/high season is £275-£375 per week.

Kilkeel to Newry *p554*

E **Fir Trees**, 16 Killowen Old Rd, Rostrevor, T4173 8602, www.firtrees-bedbreakfast.co.uk. A bungalow B&B overlooking the lough.
E **The Mournes**, 16 Seaview, Warrenpoint, T4177 2610, is on the sea front overlooking Carlingford Lough but may not be the quietest place at the height of summer. Some en suite rooms.
E **Ryan B&B**, 19 Milltown St, Burren, Warrenpoint, T4177 2506, dryanbb@hotmail.com. Open all year.

Camping

Kilbroney Caravan Park, T4173 8134, Kilbroney Park. With 30 tent pitches for around £7 per night.

Self-catering

Lecale Cottages, 125 Kilbroney Rd, Rostrevor, T4173 8727, www.rostrevorholidays.com. 3 self-catering, traditional-style cottages, overlooking the lough and costing £220-£270 a week. It is often possible to book a self-catering place for less than a week.

Newry *p555*

B **Canal Court Hotel**, Merchant's Quay, T3025 1234, www.canalcourthotel.com. Alex Ferguson stayed here and, while that might deter the anti-Man U league, he knew, as usual, what he was doing and chose the best on offer. Smart bedrooms, leisure centre with pool.
D **Mourne Country Hotel**, 52 Belfast Rd, T3026 7922, www.mournecountryhotel.com. A little way out of town at the roundabout on the Belfast Rd, with weekend and midweek deals.
E **Millvale House**, 8 Millvale Rd, T3026 3789. B&B with 4 rooms, serves high tea for £5, dinner for £7 and stays open all year.
F **Carrow House**, 22 Newtown Rd, Belleek, T3087 8182. This B&B is not in town, but a double there is only £24, open Apr-Sep. Numerous other keenly-priced B&Bs in and around town: enquire at the tourist office.

Eating

Newcastle *p552*

ΨΨ **Buck's Head**, restaurant further out of town at 77 Main St, Dundrum, T4375 1868. Regarded as the most upmarket place in the area, and the innovative menu has featured oysters and ostrich, though thankfully not in the same dish. Expect to pay around £25.
ΨΨ **Enniskeen House**, 98 Bryansford Rd, T4372 2392. Oak-panelled restaurant offering home-style dishes like stuffed pork and apple sauce, steak and scampi.
ΨΨ **Seasalt**, Central Promenade, Newcastle, T4372 5027. Has a large menu at lunch and dinner time and reservations are needed in the evening because it's very popular.

Annalong *p553*

ΨΨΨ **Glassdrumman Lodge**, 85 Mill Rd, signposted off the main road at the Newcastle end of the village, T4376 8451, www.glassdrummanlodge.co.uk. Features traditional country food at its best, including local lamb and shellfish. Dinner around £35.
Ψ **Harbour Inn**, 6 Harbour Dr. Serves more conventional food.

Kilkeel *p553*

Ψ **Jacob Halls**, Greencastle St, in the middle of town. Try this for one of the most substantial pub lunches in Ireland.

Kilkeel to Newry *p554*

ΨΨ-Ψ **Celtic Fjord** 8 Mary St, Rostrevor, T4173 8005. Opening times and hours may vary – Wed or Thu to Sat at the moment – but worth a visit for the innovative food and the congenial atmosphere. Dinner menus for £18 and £21 and a good value early dinner for around £9.
ΨΨ-Ψ **Kilbroney**, in the spacious pub of the same name in Bridge St, Rostrevor, T4173 8236. Does meals from £9 for fish

and chips to £15 for a steak. Traditional music on Wed nights.

Boathouse Inn, 3 Marine Pde, Warrenpoint, T4175 3743, www.boathouseinn.com. Has a good restaurant, the Vecchia Roma, with an evening meal for under £20.

The Whistledown Inn, facing the sea in aptly named Seaview, Warrenpoint, T4175 2697. Has a large menu of snacks and salads plus fish, meat and grills.

Newry *p555*

The Bank, 2 Trevor Hill, by the bridge at the tourist office end of town, T3083 5501, www.thebanknewry.com. The new kid on the block. Burgers and salads for lunch around £6 and an evening menu with dishes like tempura monkfish, Cajun pork or grilled aubergine for £8-10. It's a stylish kind of place and brings a bit of glamour to the town as you sit sipping a cocktail at the bar. A nightclub jumps into action here every Fri and Sat night.

Brass Monkey, 1 Sandy St, T3026 3176. Could be your first choice for a quick meal, serving seafood, steaks and salads daily till 2200.

Deli Lites, 12 Monaghan St. Serves up better-than-average sandwiches.

Pubs and music

Annalong *p553*

The Halfway House at the Newcastle end of the village, on the main road. Good for a drink and a game of snooker.

Newry *p555*

There are a number of pubs where sessions of traditional Irish music take place throughout the year. These include: **Crossan's Bar**, Hilltown Rd, T3026 7193, on Tue nights, **The Forkhill**, Forkhill, T3088 8273, on Thu, **O'Hanlon's**, Mullaghbawn, T3088 8759, Fri-Sat.

Festivals and events

Kilkeel to Newry *p554*

The **Maiden of the Mournes Festival** in Warrenpoint is a week-long festival at the beginning of **Aug**, established in 1990 along the lines of the Rose of Tralee festival.

The last week in **Jul** is the setting for Rostrevor's **Fiddler's Green Festival**, a celebration of Irish culture with a ceilidh band on an open-air stage, nightly folk sessions in the pubs and classes for traditional instruments such as the fiddle, flute and pipes. T4173 9819, www.fiddlersgreenfestival.com.

Activities and tours

Kilkeel to Newry *p554*

The East Coast Adventure Centre, Warrenpoint, T4177 4006. Covers windsurfing, canoeing, archery and other activities.

Transport

Around the Mourne Mountains *p552*

Bike hire Wiki Wiki Wheels, 10b Donard St, T4372 3973.

Bus Ulsterbus runs frequent daily buses between **Kilkeel** and **Belfast** via **Newcastle**. There are also daily services between **Downpatrick** and **Newry**, also via **Newcastle**, and connecting with the daily Newry to **Dublin** service. In Jul and Aug, service 34A, known as the **Mourne Rambler**, runs between Newcastle and the **Silent Valley**. From **Newcastle** it departs Mon-Fri at 1010, 1135, 1405 and 1530, Sat at 1010, 1135 and 1430, and Sun 1010 and 1430. It departs Silent Valley Mon-Fri at 1200, 1430 and 1600, Sat 1200 and 1450, and Sun only 1450. From Newry buses go to **Warrenpoint**, **Rostrevor** and **Kilkeel**. The daily **Belfast** to **Dublin** express bus also stops in Newry as do the **Belfast-Galway** and **Belfast-Cork** services.

Train Newry station: T3026 9271, a local bus ride out of town. The **Belfast** to **Dublin** trains stop here every day.

Tyrone, Fermanagh, Armagh and Monaghan

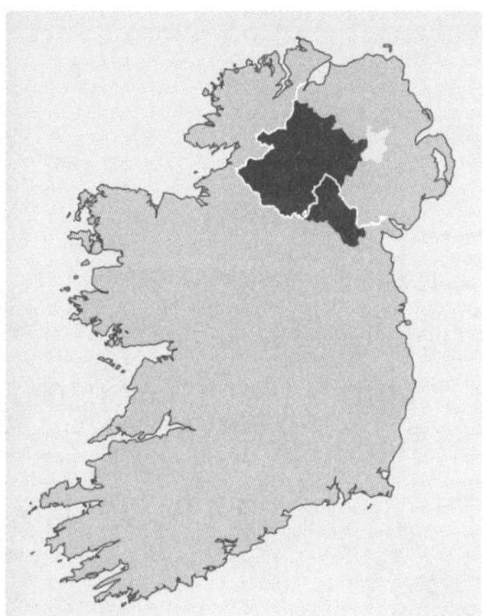

Footprint features

Introduction

County Tyrone generally lacks a readily identifiable pre-packaged image but of course this is precisely what makes it so appealing. For anyone contemplating a few days in an unhyped part of Ireland, taking in country walks in the Sperrin Mountains and quiet villages where nothing much happens and where population is thin on the ground, County Tyrone definitely fits the bill.

Fermanagh is defined by its central lake, Lough Erne, which is 50 miles (80 km) long. The lake is now joined to the River Shannon by the Shannon to Erne Waterway, making it the longest navigable inland waterway in Europe. The lakeland setting invites water-based activities and this undoubtedly is Fermanagh's main attraction, but in Boa Island and Killadeas Churchyard, the county also has cultural sites that rank among the most significant and intriguing to be found anywhere in Ireland.

Armagh has always been border country, forming with Monaghan and Louth the southern edge of the Drumlin belt that formed Ulster as a place apart when the Ice Age retreated, leaving massive boulders in its wake. St Patrick still found his way here and Cromwell confiscated over a third of the county. Armagh is a beautiful place and even a fleeting visit will whet the appetite for a longer stay. The historic city of Armagh should not be missed while the secret delights in the south of the county are waiting to be discovered by a new generation of visitors.

When it comes to appreciating County Monaghan in the Republic, the political border is best forgotten, for in terms of history, culture and geography the county should be explored and enjoyed along with its Ulster neighbours.

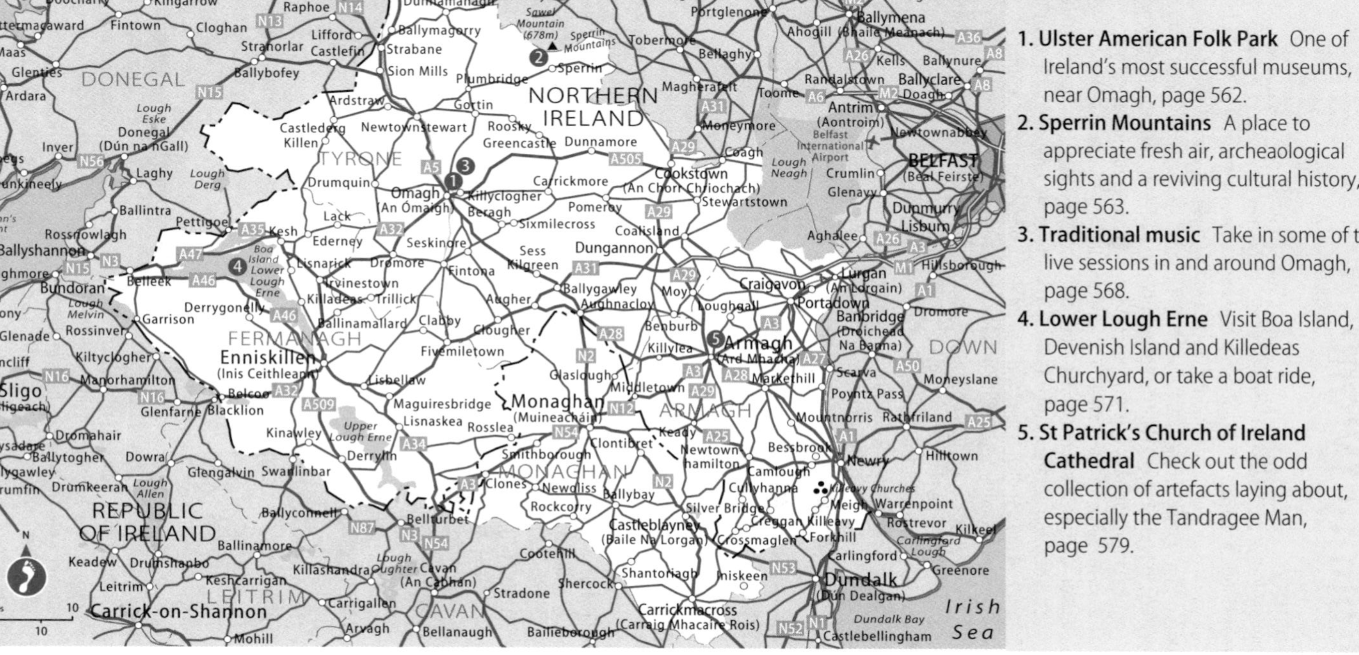

★ Don't miss...

1. **Ulster American Folk Park** One of Ireland's most successful museums, near Omagh, page 562.
2. **Sperrin Mountains** A place to appreciate fresh air, archeaological sights and a reviving cultural history, page 563.
3. **Traditional music** Take in some of the live sessions in and around Omagh, page 568.
4. **Lower Lough Erne** Visit Boa Island, Devenish Island and Killedeas Churchyard, or take a boat ride, page 571.
5. **St Patrick's Church of Ireland Cathedral** Check out the odd collection of artefacts laying about, especially the Tandragee Man, page 579.

County Tyrone

History

History lies at the heart of Tyrone, for the Elizabethan conquest of this county, the most intractable part of an intractable province, sealed the fate of Gaelic Ireland. Surrounded by wood, bog and the Sperrin Mountains to the south, the O'Neills held out in their Tyrone homelands against the English in the second half of the 16th century. In 1562 Shane O'Neill came to London to parley with Elizabeth's government and the clash of cultures was evident to all: the doublets and hose and fancy ruffs of the English confronted the Gaelic entourage with their shoulder-length hair, cloaks and shirts of linen dyed yellow with urine. Shane only managed to buy some time and it was left to his nephew, Hugh O'Neill, to witness the final subjugation of Gaelic Ireland and the door left open for the plantations of the early 17th century.

In 1641 a rebellion started in Tyrone and spread across the country, and the same year the massacres of settlers by hungry and dispossessed Catholics – an event that still haunts the loyalist subconscious – was Cromwell's justification for his own massacres, "the righteous judgement of God", which reasserted foreign rule over Ireland. The killing and counter-killing continued intermittently over the following centuries, the most recent outrage being the horrific bombing that killed 29 people out shopping on a sunny Saturday afternoon in Omagh in August 1998.

Omagh → *Colour map 1, grid B3.*

Church and State are represented in Omagh by the two overbearing monuments to the claims on people's lives in this part of the world: the Catholic church and the courthouse – an example of monstrous Victorian architecture, built in 1863 some 30 years before the church. They loom over the top half of the town, calling everyone to obedience – to Crown or God. The dissident Republican group responsible (allegedly the Real IRA, although no one has actually been prosecuted), for the 1998 slaughter was probably intending to destroy the courthouse at the western end of the town's main street. The bomb went off, probably because they panicked and left it in the wrong place, at the east end of the street. A memorial garden for those who lost their lives now marks the place where they died.

The well-resourced and very helpful **tourist office** is at 1 Market Street, T8224 7831. Open Mon-Sat 0900-1700 (1730 in Jul and Aug, Mon-Fri in Oct-Mar). Collect the town trail map that takes in the various places of historic interest. » *For Sleeping, Eating and other listings, see pages 566-568.*

★ **Ulster American Folk Park** ⓘ *on A5, 3 miles north of Omagh, T8224 3292, www.folkpark.com. Easter-Sep Mon-Fri 1000-1800, Sat 1030-1830, Sun 1100-1830, Oct-Easter Mon-Fri 1030-1700, last admission 90 mins before closing. £4.* Emigration from Ireland has become so entwined with the Famine and with post-Famine history that it often comes as a surprise to learn that an exodus of impoverished Protestants began in the early 18th century from Ulster, which alarmed the government, for "the humour has spread like a contagious distemper, and the people will hardly hear any body that tries to cure them of their madness". By the 1770s, some 10,000 were leaving annually and Benjamin Franklin estimated that one-third of Pennsylvania's population were Ulster Scots-Irish emigrants. The Ulster American Folk Park, which can claim that half of all US presidents to date are of Ulster descent, celebrates and records emigration to North America with a wealth of reconstructed buildings and entire streets that make up one of Ireland's most successful museums.

★ Sperrin Mountains → *Colour map 1, grid B3/4.*

The Sperrin Mountains, rolling areas of blanket bog with summits over 500 m, stretch across north Tyrone from the border with Derry for some 56 km and encapsulate the appeal of this county: fresh air, uncluttered space, country and hill walks from the casual to the demanding, archaeological sites and a cultural history that is only now emerging from a long period of repression. Omagh is the nearest town of any size and with a fair choice of accommodation; though Gortin (see page 566) is more convenient for the area, accommodation and places to eat are scarce so plan and book ahead. **Sperrin Tourism** ⓘ *T8674 7700, www.sperrintourism.com*, dispenses a free visitor guide and a useful cycling guide that details routes and contact information. ▸▸ *For Sleeping, Eating and other listings, see pages 566-568.*

Getting there and around The 182 bus service is called the **Sperrin Rambler**, T9066 6630, www.translink.co.uk, and it stops at the Sperrin Heritage Centre at Cranagh and then Gortin on its twice-daily route between Castledawson and Omagh. It departs from Castledawson at 1012 and 1341 and from Omagh at 1010 and 1345. ▸▸ *See Transport, page 568, for further details.*

The Sperrin Heritage Centre ⓘ *Glenelly Rd, Cranagh, Gortin, T8164 8142, www.strabanedc.com. On B47, 9 miles (14.4 km) east of Plumbridge. Easter-Oct Mon-Fri 1130-1730, Sat 1130-1800, Sun 1400-1800. £2.50.* This Heritage Centre provides introductory information on the ecology and culture of the Sperrins, including the history of gold mining in the area and the chance to pan in a stream nearby.

An Creagán Visitor Centre ⓘ *Creggan, T8076 1112, www.an-creagan.com. A505 between Omagh and Cookstown. Apr-Sep daily 1100-1830, Oct-Mar daily 1100-1630. £2.* Another information centre, but with more activities, in the foothills of the Sperrins. It is spearheading an attempt to resuscitate the culture of the area, and details of local festivals dedicated to this purpose are available here. There is a restaurant, a bar with live music at weekends, sessions of storytelling and song throughout the year, self-catering cottages (see page 566), and an 'interpretative exhibition' with an overview of the cultural, archaeological and environmental landscape of the area. Bikes can also be hired (see page 568) and there are good walking possibilities nearby.

Walking in the Sperrins

Little is gleaned by just travelling through the Sperrins, but there are some waymarked trails and walking routes and one of the easiest to organize is a 6-mile (10-km) section of the **Ulster Way** between Gortin and Glengawna. Both places are on the B48 road along which Bus No 92 (Mon-Sat) travels between Omagh and Gortin, so, with the help of a bus timetable, it is possible to catch a bus to the start and/or from the end of the walk. The Way is marked on Ordnance Survey map 13, although there is a small change from the map just south of Gortin where it crosses the B48. Along the Way the route passes the the **Gortin Glen Forest Park** ⓘ *T8167 0666, on B48, 7 miles (11.2 km) north of Omagh, daily 1000-dusk, £3 for car*, which has its own waymarked trails and from here one could also walk 10 miles (16 km) of the Ulster Way as far as the Ulster American Folk Park, from where Bus No 97 travels to Omagh. Gortin Glen Forest Park also has a vehicular drive through the forest and there is a café and picnic area.

Short walks of between 6 and 10 miles (9.6-16 km) are also possible from the An Creagán Visitor Centre, which provides walk sheets, and most of these take in archaeological sites along the way.

The two highest points in the Sperrins, **Sawel Mountain** and **Dart Mountain**, can be climbed in one day and a good starting point is just to the east of Sperrin village on

“”...Castlederg used to have separate Protestant and Catholic Christmas trees... One can only wonder what the frontiersman Davy Crockett, whose family came from here, would have made of that...

the B47 in the Glenelly valley. However, there have been problems with some landowners in the area and walking west of Dart Mountain is definitely not on. Ordnance Survey map No 13 is essential for this walk, and it might be worthwhile calling in at the Sperrin Heritage Centre to check your proposed route with them.

Castlederg and around → *Colour map 1, grid B3.*

This is one of the least visited parts of Ireland and the **Castlederg Visitor Centre** ⓘ *26 Lower Strabane Rd, T8167 0795, Easter-Oct, Tue-Fri, 1100-1600, Sat, 1130-1600, Sun, 1400-1700, £1.20*, is worth calling in at to learn something about the area and get information on how to reach local archaeological sites. Such were the sectarian divisions of Castlederg, that the town used to have separate Protestant and Catholic Christmas trees erected annually. One can only wonder what the frontiersman Davy Crockett, whose family came from here, would have made of that.

Sion Mills

If travelling the road between Newtownstewart and Strabane, **Sion Mills** is worth a look if only to peer in at the still-functioning linen factory that gave rise to this purpose-built mill village created by the Herdmans in 1835. It was praised by the myopic 19th-century travel writers Samuel and Anna Hall in their 1843 tour of the country, for giving work to 700 workers, mostly women, conveniently forgetting the 15-hour days and the horrific accidents that led Dickens to call the linen employers' union the Association for the Mangling of Operatives.

Strabane

A beleaguered Catholic enclave that has seen its share of rioting during the last 30 years, Strabane has the rather sad distinction of being noted for the people that left the place. The novelist, Flann O'Brien, deserted at the age of 12 in 1923, and two centuries earlier John Dunlap, having learnt his trade as a printer, went off to America and printed the American Declaration of Independence. This, and other stories, can be found at the fairly uninspiring **Gray's Printer's Museum** ⓘ *49 Main St, Strabane, T7188 4094, Tue-Sat, 1100-1700, guided tours Apr-Sep, 1400-1700, £2.70.*

Less significant was the emigration of one James Wilson in 1807, even though his grandson managed to end up in the White House. Hence the **Wilson Ancestral Home** ⓘ *Dergalt, 2 miles (3.2 km) from Strabane off the Plumbridge Rd, T7138 2204, Jul-Aug, Tue-Sun, 1400-1700, free.*

Cookstown and around → *Colour map 1, grid B4.*

The east of Tyrone is home to a scattered set of archaeological sites with Cookstown being the main town in the area. Cookstown has had a troubled past ever since a Scottish landlord established a small town and market here in the 1620s. In the 1641 uprising the town was taken by the native Irish and burnt to the ground after its recapture by the army, and it lay derelict for a century until 1736. In that year the grandson of the original settler, inspired by the streets of Dublin and Edinburgh, laid out a new town with a main street stretching for well over a mile. During the Troubles a major army camp was established in the centre and driving into the town involved having a rifle pointed at your head until clearance was given.

There's a **tourist office** at the Burnavon, Burn Rd, T8676 6727, www.cookstown.gov.uk. Open Oct-May Mon-Fri 0900-1700, Sat 1000-1600, Jun and Sep Mon-Sat 0900-1700, Jul and Aug Mon-Sat 0900-1700, Sun 1400-1600.

Wellbrook Beetling Mill ⓘ *T8675 1735, Jul and Aug daily 1300-1800, Mar-Jun and Sep Sat and Sun 1400-1800. £2.80. 4 miles west of Cookstown off A505.* Beetling was a stage of linen production, consisting of pounding the fabric with wooden hammers, the 'beetles', until the weave was tightened, giving the cloth its characteristic texture. Beetling started at this mill in the 1760s, and Wellbrook was the last mill still in operation when it finally closed down two centuries later. Working demonstrations are given in this National Trust property and exhibits explain the process.

Beaghmore Stone Circle and Tullaghoge Fort ⓘ *Free access, between Cookstown and Gortin, signposted off A505.* Beaghmore Stone Circle is the most interesting of the ancient sites in the area and a more worthwhile journey than the flat and boring B73 road that leads to the largely illegible **Ardboe High Cross** ⓘ *off B162 2.5 miles (4 km) southeast of Cookstown on the shore of Lough Neagh.* At Beaghmore, on the southern foothills of the Sperrins, archaeologists in 1945 discovered under the peat a strange series of stone circles and stone alignments as well as cairns. The run-of- the-mill stone circle is relatively easy to explain but the complex arrangement of stones at Beaghmore, especially the presence of many hundreds of small stones inside one of the seven circles has so far eluded interpretation.

The enjoyment of a visit to **Tullaghoge Fort** will be in proportion to the degree of historical imagination brought to bear on the place, because all that remains today is a hillock, albeit with fine views. Between the 11th and 16th centuries the chieftain of the O'Neills was inaugurated here as ruler of Tyrone, an area which then extended beyond the present county confines, until Mountjoy arrived in the wake of Kinsale and symbolically destroyed the ancient coronation stone seat. More to the point, he also burnt the corn in the fields, which led to cannibalism in the ensuing famine that brought O'Neill to his knees.

Dungannon → *Colour map 1, grid B4*

Dungannon is a dreadfully dreary town, which sparked into life in 1968 when it became a focus of demonstration for the early civil rights movement in Northern Ireland. It was well known that Dungannon, like Derry, was gerrymandered to produce a permanent Unionist council even though the population was split evenly between Catholics and Protestants, and the first civil rights march in August 1968 planned to end in Dungannon but was stopped by the RUC on the outskirts with dogs and 400 men. The only reason to pause here today is for a visit to the cross-community-inspired **Tyrone Crystal** ⓘ *T8772 5335, www.tyronecrystal.com, Mon-Sat 0900-1700, and also Sun, 1300-1700 in the summer, £2,* where guided tours of the factory workshop make it hard to resist purchasing something afterwards from the shop.

Killymaddy Tourist Information, is on Ballygawley Road, 7 miles (10 km) southwest of Dungannon, on the A4. T8776 7259. Open all year.

Benburb → *Colour map 1, grid B4*

To the south of Dungannon, the graceful village of Benburb, with a population under 300, has a quiet charm, and a scenic riverside walk along the Blackwater in **Benburb Valley Park** has the rich and surprising bonus of the ruins of **Benburb Castle** towering over the river. Shane O'Neill fortified the cliff-top location in the 16th century but it was a planter, Sir Richard Wingfield, who built the castle at the beginning of the following century and it was another 100 years before a house was actually built inside its walls. In 1646 an overwhelming victory by the Irish under Owen Roe O'Neill took place by the River Blackwater and resulted in the death of over 3,000 Scottish soldiers, an event which did a great deal to convince Cromwell of the need to subdue the Irish thoroughly once and for all. The Ulster historian Jonathan Barden (see page 626) has described this Battle of Benburb as "the greatest and most annihilating victory in arms the Irish ever won over the British." A model layout of the battle can be seen, just south of the village, in the **Benburb Valley Heritage Centre** ⓘ *79 Milltown Rd, T3754 9885. Easter-Sep daily 1000-1700. £2*. The centre is set in a 19th-century weaving factory and if you have missed the other places in Tyrone devoted to the Ulster linen industry then this is a place to catch up on the subject, and enjoy a cup of tea.

Clogher Valley

ⓘ *off A4, 13 miles (21 km) west of Dungannon, T8555 7133. Apr-Sep Mon-Sat 1200-1800, Sun 1400-1800. £1.50.*

The Blackwater River forms the Clogher Valley to the west of Benburb and the A4 travels west to Enniskillen. Along the way the **Grant Ancestral House** is yet another reminder of Ulster's connection with the US, this time through John Simpson, who was born here in 1738 and whose great-grandson distinguished himself in the American Civil War and became the 18th President, Ulysses Simpson Grant. The two rooms of Grant's small cottage have been restored in the style of the 19th century and there is also an outdoor display of Victorian farm equipment.

The Carleton Trail

The novelist William Carleton (1794-1869) was born into a family of Irish-speaking peasants near Clogher, and his connection gives its name to this series of three walking and cycling routes, from 6-30 miles (10-48 km), that all start and finish in Clogher and follow minor roads and forest paths. Details and a map are available from the tourist office in Dungannon and the cottage where Carleton lived for a while before leaving for Dublin can be seen in **Clogher**, a village on the A4 half-way between Dungannon and Enniskillen. Food and accommodation is available here or a little further west at **Fivemiletown** (5 miles from Clogher) on the border with Fermanagh.

Sleeping

Omagh *p562*

C **Silverbirch**, 5 Gortin Rd, T8224 2520, www.silverbirch.com. Omagh's only hotel: one of those large modern places where the corridors are interchangeable and there are always big wedding parties at weekends. But the rooms are comfortable and there is a popular restaurant.

D **Hawthorn House**, 72 Old Mountfield Rd, T8225 2005, www.hawthornhouse.co.uk. Out of town off the Gortin Rd. A comfortable guest house with an excellent restaurant.

E **Golden Hill**, 32 Tattykeel Rd, T8225 1257, www.goldenhillguesthouse.com. Friendly B&B, 5 rooms with en suite bathroom. £25-39 for single/double. Option of evening meal.

F **Omagh Independent Hostel**, 9a Waterworks Rd, T8224 1973, www.omaghhostel.co.uk. Family-run hostel with rooms ranging in size from singles to dormitory and lots of room to relax. Free pickup from bus station as 4 km out of town; by road take the B48 to Gortin and look for sign pointing right onto the Killybrack road before the Spar shop.

Sperrin Mountains *p563*

F **Gortin Accommodation Suite and Activity Centre**, 62 Main St, Gortin, T8164 8346, www.gortin.net. A complex of accommodation and an activity centre which will suit most needs. It has a 40 bed hostel, family rooms and self-catering units which sleep 4. An ideal base for the Sperrins.

An Clachan, Creggan, T8076 1112. Self-catering cottages managed by the An Creagán Visitor Centre.

Castlederg and around *p564*

E **Beau Vista**, 9 Barron Rd, Artigarvan, Strabane, T7139 8380. A large farmhouse with rooms (en suite) at reasonable rates.
F **Ardmourne House**, 36 Congary Rd, Castlederg, T8167 0291, www.hiking-n-biking.com. A modern house with kitchen facilities and pony trekking.

Cookstown and around *p564*

B-C **Glenavon House Hotel**, 52 Drum Rd, Cookstown, T8676 4949, www.glenavonhotel.co.uk. Fifty rooms, a pool and gym.
D **Tullylagan Country House**, Tullylagan Rd, Cookstown, T8676 5100, www.tullylagan.co.uk. Quite good value, a wine bar and a decent restaurant Check the special offers for B&B and dinner.
E **Killycolp House**, 21 Killycolp Rd, Cookstown, T8676 3577. Does single/double B&B for £26-40 in a Georgian house with original features that help make this friendly place a worthwhile night's lodging. On the A29 towards Dungannon from Cookstown.

Camping

Dungannon Park, Moy Rd, T8772 7327, www.dungannon.gov.uk. Caravan and camping park off the A29 less than 2 km from Dungannon. Eight pitches at £7 each.
Killymaddy Tourist Amenity Centre, 190 Ballygawley Rd, west of Dungannon on the A4, T8776 7259, www.dungannon.gov.uk. Has a dozen tent pitches for £6 each.
Clogher Valley County Caravan Park, Fardross Forest, T8554 8932. Signposted a mile or so west of Clogher on the A4 and accepts tents from £12 per night.

Eating

Omagh *p562*

ΨΨ **Coach Inn**, Railway Terr, T8224 3330, on the right just after the railway bridge on the road out to Enniskillen from the town centre. It is worth a walk to this comfortable inn. Bar food, including an excellent vegetarian salad, is served until 1800 when a separate dining area opens up with a menu of standard main courses between £10 and £15 and a small wine list.
ΨΨ **Grant's**, 29 George's St, T8225 0900. In town, opposite the Catholic church, a bistro-cum-pub open for lunch and dinner till 2200. It has lively dishes, which include chilli prawns, priced around £10-15.
ΨΨΨ **Hawthorn House** (see page 566). The classiest place to eat – fresh local food, traditional Irish dishes, mixed with a welcome Californian touch – and usually needs booking in advance. Good lunches all week but Sun is particularly fine. Main courses average £15.
Ψ Along the High St/Market St are lots of conventional lunchtime places like: **Bogan's Bar**, and the **Shopper's Restaurant**, which does things with chips and filled potatoes.
Sperrin Restaurant, T8225 0200, www.sperrinrestaurant.com. If heading out to the Folk Park, consider dropping by for lunch – it's on the main road.

Sperrin Mountains *p563*

ΨΨ-Ψ **Badoney Tavern**, 16 Main St, Gortin, T8164 8157. Serves pub meals in the evening from 1800 to 2100.
ΨΨ-Ψ **Pinkertons Café**, 25 Main St, Plumbridge, T8164 8327. Open daily for steaks, curry and chicken meals.
Ψ **An Creagán Restaurant**, at Creggan on the A505, at the Visitor Centre, T8076 1112. Open daily for cheap lunches, and evening meals from £9, Thu-Sun.
Ψ **Sperrin Heritage Centre**, east of Plumbridge on the B47, T8164 8142. Serves very light meals until 1800 Mon-Sat and 1400-1900 on Sun.

Castlederg and around *p564*

There are a few pubs in Castlederg serving pub grub, including:
ΨΨ **Fir Trees Hotel**, Dublin Rd, T7138 2382; serves meals such as duck in sweet and sour sauce, and grills;
Ψ **Castle Inn**, 48 Main St, T8167 1501;
Ψ **Crescent Inn**, Ferguson Cres, T8167 1161, also has live music in the evening;
Ψ **County Inn**, 43 Main St, Newtownstewart, T8166 2105;

For an explanation of the sleeping and eating price codes used in this guide, see inside the front cover. Other relevant information is found in Essentials pages 39-45.

ᛘ **Flann O'Brien**, 3 Derry Rd, Strabane, T7188 4427, food every lunchtime except Sun;
ᛘ **Harry Avery Lounge**, 19 Dublin Rd, Newtownstewart, T8166 1431;
ᛘ **Market Bar**, 59 Main St, T8167 1247.

Cookstown and around *p564*
ᛘᛘ-ᛘ **Tullylagan Country House Restaurant**, a few miles south of Cookstown. Serves an evening meal in a pleasant dining room for around £25 every night and lunch every day except Sat.
ᛘ **Cornmill Tea Room**, 89 Milltown Rd, Benburb, T3754 9885. In the Benburb Valley Heritage Centre and opens from 1000 to 1700, Tue-Sun, in the summer and Mon-Fri between Oct and Easter.
ᛘ **Corrick House**, 20 Corrick Rd, Clogher, T8554 8216. Opens in the evening from 1730, Wed-Sun, for dinner under £25.
ᛘ **Courtyard**, 56 William St, Cookstown, T8676 5070. Good value and tasty lunches. Closes at 1700 Mon-Sat.
ᛘ **Four Ways Hotel**, Fivemiletown. Pub food.
ᛘ **McSorley's Tavern**, 39 Main St, Clogher, T8554 8673. Pub food available.
ᛘ **Trident Inn**, 97 Main St, Clogher, T8554 8924. Serves pub food.
ᛘ **White Pheasant**, Burn Rd, Cookstown, opposite the cinema. Quick meals.

Pubs and music

★ Omagh *p562*
Dún Uladh Cultural Heritage Centre, on the Carrickmore Rd, T8224 2777. Often has concerts, ballroom and Irish dancing sessions, and traditional music on Sat.
Sally O'Brien's, John St, just behind the Town Hall. The trendiest place is town, with its wonderful window display. Open till past midnight on the nights it has live music.
Teach Ceoil, north of town near Gortin. This is worth confirming with the tourist office but during the summer there should be good music sessions.

Cookstown and around *p564*
Burnavon Arts and Cultural Centre, Burn Rd, Cookstown, T8676 9949, www.burnavon.co.uk. A purpose-built arts centre hosting regular mixed programmes.

Festivals and events

Omagh *p562*
An **arts festival** takes place in early **Oct**, see www.omagh.gov.uk.

Sperrin Mountains *p563*
In **mid-Oct** there is a **festival of traditional Irish music** at the An Creagán Visitor Centre.

Transport

County Tyrone *p562*
Bike hire An Creagán Visitor Centre, T8076 1112. Bicycle hire, also cycling route information for 10- to 14-mile trips.

Bus From **Omagh**, T8224 2711,daily buses to and from **Belfast**, (2 hrs), **Derry** (over 1 hr), **Enniskillen**, **Dublin** (over 3 hrs), and 1 a day (not Sun) to **Cork** (over 9 hrs) departing 1010. The Mon-Sat **Sperrin Rambler** service departs Omagh at 1010 and 1345. **Cookstown**, T8676 6440, has services to **Belfast** and **Dungannon** every 30 mins or so during the day and there are also services between Dungannon and **Armagh**, **Monaghan** and **Dublin**.

County Fermanagh

History

Fermanagh's natural isolation is part and parcel of the county's stubborn resistance to early Norman intrusions in the 13th century, so imagine how prolonged and complex must have been the process of transition from the pagan world of the Celts to Christianity. This may help explain the exceptional nature of the ancient stone monuments found north of Enniskillen.

The Maguires came to rule Fermanagh from the early 14th century and before their land passed (after two centuries) to the O'Donnells, one of their bards praised the family to high heaven: "Towards Ulster he [Brian Maguire] is the ocean's surface; towards Connacht a rampart of stone. Fermanagh of the fortunate ramparts is the Adam's paradise of Inisfáil."

After the defeat of Gaelic Ireland at Kinsale and the Flight of the Earls, Fermanagh eventually went the way of the rest of the island: planters took over Adam's paradise and built the castles still standing around Lough Erne. Enniskillen became a major military fortress and in the early 1920s the town and county were embroiled in conflict over Partition. The nationalist voice in this part of Ireland reached a climax in 1981 when the democratically elected Member of Parliament for Fermanagh and South Tyrone, Bobby Sands, was left to die in prison on a hunger strike.

Enniskillen and around

Enniskillen → *Colour map 1, grid B3.*

Another predominantly Catholic border town, Enniskillen doesn't have the old-world charm of Derry, but it's a lively enough place, with lots of development going on and a blossoming nightlife. The main reason to spend any time here, though, is as a base for exploring the area or taking off on a boat trip around Lough Erne. There's a **tourist office** on Wellington Road, T6632 3110. Open Jul-Aug Mon-Fri 0900-1900, Sat 1000-1800, Sun 1100-1700; Sep-Jun Mon-Fri 0900-1730. ›› *For Sleeping, Eating and other listings see pages 574-576.*

Enniskillen Castle ① *Castle Barracks, T6632 5000, www.enniskillencastle.co.uk. May, Jun and Sep Tue-Fri 1000-1700, Mon and Sat 1400-1700; Jul-Aug Tue-Fri 1000-1700, Mon, Sat-Sun 1400-1700; Oct-Apr Tue-Fri 1000-1700, Mon 1400-1700. £2.50.* This is the chief tourist attraction of the town: a beautiful old building not used particularly effectively but worth a wander around. The castle has certainly seen some bloodshed over the years; the 16th century was probably its worst time:

Hunger strike

The origins of the hunger strike in Ireland are not clear and, while the suffragettes certainly offered an example to follow, the tactic has also been traced back to an early Irish tradition of fasting before an enemy in order to shame him for his misdeeds. Thomas Ashe was the first hunger striker to die, in 1917, protesting at conditions in Dublin's Mountjoy gaol and in 1920 Terence MacSwiney, the mayor of Cork, and two others died in London prisons. In Northern Ireland the tactic developed out of the withdrawal of 'special category' status in 1976 which denied political status to Republican prisoners. A 'dirty protest' campaign began, with prisoners refusing to clean out their cells, and in May 1981, a hunger strike. The first hunger striker was Bobby Sands, the Member of Parliament for Tyrone and Fermanagh, but that cut little ice with Thatcher's government and he died in due course followed by 10 others before the strike was called off in October 1981.

it changed hands from its original builders, the Maguires, to the O'Neill's (*not* by a negotiated sale), then later the same century the English took it off the O'Neills – poetic justice you might say. The only original 15th-century part of the building is the lower storey of the keep – now the regimental museum full of polished brass and pride. On the river side of the complex is the Watergate, a 17th-century addition with no gate in it. The heritage centre is housed in buildings from around the 18th century and holds assorted rural paraphernalia, two pretty naff videos about the area, and changing exhibitions.

Buttermarket ⓘ *Mon-Sat 1000-1730. Coffee shop, craft workshops, gallery, yoga studio.* The other place for a good wander around, is this craft village full of interesting things to buy, especially the hand-painted furniture and copies of the White Island stone figures, although you'd need a big rucksack to carry one of those away.

Around Enniskillen

Castle Coole ⓘ *T6632 2690, www.ntni.org.uk. On A4, 1 mile (1.6 km) east of Enniskillen. Grounds open Apr-Sep daily 1000-2000, Oct-Mar 1000-1600; house open for guided tours Jul-Aug daily 1200-1800, Jun Wed-Mon, Mar-mid May Sat-Sun and Easter 1200-1800. £4.* Built in the late 18th century at massive expense by the first Earl of Belmore, who ruined himself in the process, this is said to be the finest neoclassical mansion in Ireland. It certainly created lots of employment in the area for the many stonemasons, plasterers, carpenters and other craftsmen brought to the place to build it over two decades from 1789. Levelling the site took 18 months, while shipping the Portland stone for its exterior involved building a quay at Ballyshannon, chartering the brig *Martha*, and 10 miles of bullock carting. By 1791 there were 25 stone cutters, 26 masons, 10 stone sawyers, 17 carpenters and 83 labourers on the site.

The house is a great day out, especially on a rainy day when its chilly interior matches its name perfectly. It is difficult to imagine the Belmore children having a good romp round this place. It was designed by James Wyatt, a contemporary of Gandon who designed many of the big houses of the Irish countryside. The main rooms are all pomp and austerity, the later 19th-century furniture adding a lumpiness to the fine lines of the 18th-century building, but that's what happens when Dad blows everything he has on the building and you have to wait a generation to put the furniture in.

Florence Court ⓘ *T6634 8249, www.ntni.org.uk. Southwest of Enniskillen on A4, then A32, 8 miles (13 km). House open for guided tours, mid-Mar to mid-May Sat-Sun 1200-1800, Jun Mon-Fri 1300-1800 and Sat-Sun 1200-1800, Jul-Aug daily 1200-1800, Sep Sat-Sun 1200-1800, Oct Sat-Sun 1300-1700. £4.* What would the landed gentry of Northern Ireland do without the National Trust? They bought this pile in 1950 from the Coles, Earls of Enniskillen. The original building predates Castle Coole by 30 years; the wings are later additions by later generations of Coles. The place was damaged by fire in 1955 but has been partly restored. It is smaller and homelier, if such a word can be applied to these huge places, than Castle Coole. There is a walled garden and walks around the 200-year old oakwoods.

Marble Arch Caves ⓘ *T6634 8963, www.marblearchcaves.net, off A4, then A32, 12 miles (19.2 km) southwest of Enniskillen, mid-Mar-Sep, 1000-1630 (last tour), £6, café, exhibition, shop.* This is a very busy commercial enterprise and is best booked well in advance; you should be prepared for the one-hour guided tour to be spent in a large company. The tour starts off with a boat trip underground and then on foot past stalactites and stalagmites and underground waterfalls. A good rainy day activity and great fun for children.

★ Around Lower Lough Erne → *Colour map 1, grid B2.*

A tour around Lower Lough Erne is a journey through cultural history from the prehistoric, Celtic, Iron Age, which began roughly around 500 BC, through the transition to Christianity a millennium later, and down the ensuing centuries to the Plantation of Ulster and the 1641 uprising. The journey is recorded through a series of remarkable stone monuments – pagan and semi-pagan deities, early Christian images, round towers and castles – relieved by a healthy small dose of 21st-century consumerism at the Belleek pottery works.

The following circular route follows the A32 north of Enniskillen and proceeds along the east shore of Lower Lough Erne on the B82 to the village of Kesh and Boa Island. The A47 then goes along the northern shore to Belleek, where the A46 can be picked up for the return to Enniskillen back down the west side of the lough. ▸ *For Sleeping, Eating and other listings, see pages 575-576.*

Devenish Island

ⓘ *Apr-Sep Tue-Sat 1000-1800, Sun 1400-1900, Easter-Sep. Ferry, £2.25, departs at 1000, 1300, 1300, 1500, 1700 from Trory Point, 4 miles (7 km) from Enniskillen and signposted off the A32.*

Sometimes it seems that round towers are two a penny in Ireland, but the one on Devenish Island (a 10-minute ferry ride from the mainland) is a particularly fine example. The doorway is the customary 3 m above ground level, and this common feature led to the conjecture that round towers were built as defensive structures. The old Irish name for the towers (*cloig theach*) means simply 'bell house' and the height of the doorway may have had more to do with preserving the physical integrity of the building, research having shown the foundations to be often quite shallow for a structure typically five storeys high. The mystery of the round towers is why builders chose to erect such tall structures beside typically small churches. Whatever the reason, they were built across Ireland between the late 10th and 13th centuries, and the example on Devenish can be partly dated to the 12th century because of the Romanesque sculptural decorations near its top.

Other sites and sights on the island are the ruins of the church and abbey, a High Cross, old gravestones and a small museum.

Cruising through Ireland

With the restoration of the Ballinamore-Ballyconnell Canal in Leitrim, a 19th-century disaster which operated for nine years and was used in all that time by eight boats, a waterway route has opened up from Belleek at the far end of Lough Erne to the mouth of the River Shannon in Counties Kerry and Clare in the south, and to Dublin via the Grand Canal. The route can encompass weeks of pottering about Lough Erne and the islands, side routes and jetties along its banks, or it can steam straight through to the Woodford River which is the start of the Shannon-Erne waterway. The river is navigable to Ballyconnell, where it joins the 62.5 km canal and lough stretches with their 34 stone bridges and 16 smart card-operated locks. From there the route passes by river, canal and lough to Leitrim, where it joins the Shannon. At Shannon Harbour the river links up with the Grand Canal, and it is possible to motor all the way to Dublin along the canal.

There are cruiser and canal boat hire companies all along the waterways. Many of them will arrange one-way hires, so that you do not have to return to your starting point, and all of them have fairly luxurious bases with restaurants, pools and other facilities. The following list covers the Shannon-Erne, section but boats from some of these operators can be taken on to the Grand Canal.

Upper Lough Erne, T3834 4993, www.carrickcraft.com. One way and return hires.
Emerald Star Line, The Marina, Carrick-on-Shannon, T049-9522933, www.emeraldstar.ie. One way hire.
Manor House Marine, Lough Erne, Killadeas, Co. Fermanagh, T6862 8100, www.manormarine.com. Huge marina with lots of resort facilities and up to 8-berth boats for hire.
Erincurragh Cruising, Blaney, Lower Lough Erne, T6864 1737, www.boatingireland.com.

Killadeas Churchyard

ⓘ *Take the B82 road along the eastern side of the lough and the church is on the left, a short way after the turn-off for the Manor House Country Hotel.*

The establishment of Christianity in the northwest of Ireland is marked with a series of carved crosses and slabs thought by some to be associated with a particular outside impetus, perhaps from Scotland. Whatever the explanation, one of the most curious is the stone carving that lies in the graveyard of a church a few miles outside Enniskillen. One side of the rectangular slab bears the traditional image of a bishop with a bell and crozier, but the other side bears a startling face that is anything but conventional and its positively pagan appearance contrasts dramatically with the ecclesiastical form. It looks as though the face was carved before the bishop, but both are impossible to date with any certainty. Showing clear signs of having been trimmed at probably a later date, the stone is thought to have been carved some time between 800 and 1000, when Christianity was still having to come to terms with pagan Ireland.

Castle Archdale Country Park

ⓘ *T6862 1333, 10 miles (16 km) from Enniskillen on the B82 Kesh Rd, Jul and Aug Tue-Sun, 1100-1900; Easter-Jun, Sun, 1200-1800, free.* This park, containing a marina from which ferries depart, was a military base during the Second World War. There is a Centre with a tea room, nature trail, activities that include pony trekking and bicycle hire, and an exhibition on the Battle of the Atlantic.

White Island

ⓘ *T6862 1333. The 15-min ferry journey to White Island departs from Castle Archdale marina (see above) departing every hour on the hour, except 1300, for £3. Jul and Aug, daily, 1100-1800; Apr, May, Jun and Sep, Sat and Sun, 1100-1800.*

The earliest references to a stone church in Ireland dates from 788, and while the remains of the church on White Island are from the 12th century, there is archaeological evidence of an earlier wooden structure, which may well be contemporaneous with the curious stone figures built into the interior north wall. They are thought to date from the 9th or 8th century, compelling evidence that White Island is one of Ireland's earliest Christian sites and lending support to one theory that the sculptured figures represent pilgrims and/or clerics. When you see the figures you may feel this is too prosaic an explanation, for there is something mysterious and even haunting about these large, grimacing faces, and presumably there was some iconographic significance to their belongings: bell, staff, sword, shield, pouch, and small griffin-like animals. One of the figures is also a *sheela-na-gig*.

Boa Island

ⓘ *Caldragh cemetery at the west end of Boa Island connected by a bridge and signposted off the A47.*

One of the two stone figures found on Boa Island at the northern tip of the lough is quite extraordinary. It is a **Janus idol** comprising two figures joined by their backs, with interwoven hair and sharing a belt; they have a stiff posture with arms crossed, bearded triangular faces and strange penetrating eyes that evoke Celtic magic in a very startling manner. It has been controversially compared with the Tandragee Idol, now resting in Armagh Cathedral (see page 579), because of a supposedly shared sense of pagan inhumanity. The Tandragee figure is undoubtedly menacing, and if you come to Boa thinking of pagan gods as fearsome and a little barbaric then this Janus figure may seem similar in spirit; shake off these associations, however, and the face of the Boa idol can be read as genial and even a little mischievous. The mystery of interpretation is deepened when the context is taken into account: the idol is situated in an early Christian burial ground, as is the other two-sided figure in Killadeas Church, which also shows sign of being trimmed from a larger piece of stone. Virtually nothing is known about how the transition from paganism to Christianity was experienced in Ireland but these stone figures provide a fascinating and tantalizing glimpse of the interface between the two belief systems.

The other figure on Boa is known as the **Lustymore** or Lusty Man idol since it was brought here from nearby Lusty Beg Island. It is not as intriguing, and while the squatting posture has been likened to *sheela-na-gig* figures, this is mostly conjecture.

Castle Caldwell Forest Park

ⓘ *T6863 1253. On A47, 4 miles (7 km) east of Belleek. Free access 24 hrs.*

Within two decades of the defeat of the Irish at Kinsale even wild Fermanagh was ripe for plantations, and Castle Caldwell was one of the early castles built on the shores of the lough. The crumbling ruins that stand today give little indication of how impressive it once looked, and when Arthur Young toured Ireland in 1776 the castle was already over 150 years old and enhanced by the natural beauty of the setting: "the promontories of thick wood, which shoot into Lough Earne, under the shade of a great ridge of mountains" led him to exclaim that "nothing can be more beautiful than the approach to Castle Caldwell". The grounds are now a wildlife reserve with shore walks, and leaflets on trails can be picked up at the small centre during the summer.

Belleek

A quiet little village on the shores of Lough Erne, bleak Belleek is home to the **Belleek Pottery Works** ⓘ *T6865 9300, www.belleek.ie. Apr-Sep Mon-Fri 0900-1800, Sat*

1000-1800, Sun 1400-1800 (1100-1800 in Jul-Aug); Oct Mon-Fri 0900-1730, Sat 1000-1730, Sun 1400-1800; Nov-Mar Mon-Fri 0900-1730; Jul and Aug Mon-Fri 0900-2000, Sat 1000-1800, Sun 1100-2000. There is a good tour of the factory where you can see the parian china being made, a video about the history of the place and lots of display cabinets showing the evolution of the style of the china. The pottery is highly burnished, hand-made and delicate: not much use for anything except admiring but it sells well, particularly the clover-leaf design. This is the best place to buy some if you want a piece. All seconds are smashed rather than allowed to lower the standard of the work.

Also in Belleek is the engaging and informative **Explore Erne** ⓘ *T6865 8866, May-Sep daily, £1,* exhibition in the little tourist office, just outside the village. It has information on the waterway and its history.

Belleek picnic site ⓘ *Daily 1000-dusk. Car £2.50. Signposted off A46 between Belleek and Tully Castle.* The views over the lough are tremendous, and a car is needed to complete the 7-mile (11-km) route through **Lough Navar Forest** to the viewpoint, but bring provisions for a picnic with a panorama.

Tully Castle

ⓘ *T9054 6552. Jun-Aug Wed-Sun 1000-1800, Apr, May, Sep Sat-Sun 1000-1800. Free.*

Built in the early 17th century for Sir John Hume, a Scottish planter, Tully Castle had a short life as a residence: in the 1641 uprising the Maguires laid siege to it. Hume surrendered upon a promise of being spared, but this proved of little worth to all the others who had fled here for safekeeping for they were slaughtered and the castle set alight. The castle and its formal garden have now been restored and there is a small visitors' centre, but if you only have time for one castle visit then consider instead a visit to the ruins of Monea Castle.

Monea Castle

ⓘ *On B81 7 miles (11 km) northwest of Enniskillen. Free access 24 hrs.*

This castle was built around the same time as Tully and for another Scottish planter, Malcolm Hamilton, and although it has not been restored the ruins and the setting are more successful in evoking the past, and a Scottish past at that, than Tully. Four storeys high and with imposing towers there is little doubt that this castle was built with defence in mind. In 1641 it did fall for a short while to the insurgents but remained a home until well into the 18th century. The ruins slumber on.

Sleeping

Enniskillen *p569, map p569*

L-B Killyhevlin Hotel, Dublin Rd, T6632 3481, www.killyhevlin.com. This is probably the best place to stay in Enniskillen. Beside Lough Erne with truly stunning views (ask for a room at the back but be aware there's a £15 supplement for the view), lovely gardens to walk in and spacious rooms it's a little holiday all on its own. You can tie your boat up at the jetty or rent one of the self-catering bungalows for a week for £395 (less in the off-peak season).

L-B Manor House Country Hotel, Killadeas, T6862 2211, www.manor-house-hotel.com. A lovely old manor house 7 miles outside of town with fourposter beds, chandeliers and 19th-century charm combined with modern luxuries including pool, sauna etc.

C Belmore Court Motel, Tempo Rd, T6632 6633, www.motel.co.uk. Self-catering rooms prices based on room size, not the number of people staying, so this could turn out to be a good deal.

D Fort Lodge Hotel, 72 Forthill St, T6632 3275, hotel@fortlodge.freeserve.co.uk A little way out of town, this hotel is beside Forthill park and done out in a kind of baronial hall style. It's a traditional pub with lunchtime carvery, comfortable bar and lots of travelling salespeople. Entertainment and special offers at weekends.

D **Railway Hotel**, 34 Forthill St, T6632 2084, www.railwayhotelenniskillen.com. Busy, small hotel, which has been here for 150 years. Music at weekends.
E **Dromard House**, Tamlaght, T6638 7250, www.dromardhouse.com. B&B 2 miles out of town in converted stable loft in a farmhouse. Close to some scenic walks. Good value.
E **Mountview**, 61 Irvinestown Rd, T6632 3147, www.mountviewguests.com. Pretty house and gardens close to town. Has a snooker room and an evening meal option. Will collect from town.
F **The Bridges**, Belmore St, T6634 0110, www.hini.org.uk. A range of rooms, good kitchen, restaurant, laundry.

Around Lower Lough Erne *p571*

C **The Courtyard**, Lusty Beg Island, T6863 2032, www.lustybegisland.com. Has its own car ferry from the pier on Boa Island, for transport to this private island. B&B single/ doubles for £55-£85, restaurant and bar, indoor pool, sauna, tennis, cycling and canoeing.
D **Hotel Carlton**, 2 Main St, Belleek, T6865 8282, www.hotelcarlton.co.uk. Modern hotel beside the lough with pleasant big rooms and friendly attentive staff. Nice grounds, good breakfasts but don't expect an early start.
E **The Fiddlestone**, 15-17 Main St, Belleek, T6865 8008. Rooms above a traditional and atmospheric Irish pub, so the bar is close at hand.
F **Castle Archdale Hostel**, Irvinestown, T6862 8118, www.hini.org.uk. Only 2 dorms and 2 family rooms.

Camping

Blaney Caravan and Camping Park, T6864 1634, on the A46 at Blaney and adjacent to the service station. Open all year but has only 5 pitches for tents, at £8-12.
Castle Archdale Caravan Park, T6862 1333, www.castlearchdale.com. Charges £10-15 for one of its 50 tent pitches.
Lakeland Caravan Park, Boa Island Rd, Drumrush, T6863 1578, www.drumrush.co.uk. Tent pitch £12-14.
Lough Melvin Holiday Centre, Main St, Garrison, T6865 8142, www.loughmelvinholidaycentre.com. Run by Fermanagh District Council and has plenty of tent pitches for £9.

Eating

Enniskillen *p569, map p569*

While there are any number of places open for lunch in town, breakfast and dinner can be a little more tricky. The hotels are all worth considering if you want classy food. Beyond these your evening options are to eat early, try pub food or eat Chinese or Indian food.
¥¥¥-¥¥ **Oscar's**, Belmore St, T6632 7037. Bookish, with lots of recommendations to its name, some interesting items on the menu and attractive surroundings. Dinner will cost around £20 plus and there are vegetarian choices.
¥¥-¥ **Scoff's**, 17 Belmore St, T6634 2622. Has a large evening menu with some nice but not always cheap dishes to consider.
¥ **Café Merlot**, 6 Church St, T6632 0918, downstairs at *Blake's of the Hollow* pub. Attractive and roomy, has a dinner menu between 1700 and 1900 for around £12.
¥ **Crow's Nest**, High St, T6632 5252. If you eat earlier this is a pub that has seriously gone into pub food with a huge menu of snacks and much more substantial dishes and serves food 6 days till 2100, 1430 Sun.
¥ **Franco's**, Queen Elizabeth Rd, T6632 4183. Very popular, opens daily till 2300 for very tasty pizza, pasta and seafood at reasonable prices.
¥ **Kamal Mahal's**, 1 Water St, T6632 5045. Open till midnight Wed-Mon and serves good Indian food in attractive surroundings.
¥ **Pat's Bar**, Townhall St, T6632 2040. Does grilled things with chips.
¥ **Saddlers**, 66 Belmore St, T6632 7432. Does pub food, mostly seafood with some vegetarian choices.

At lunchtime there are so many places to choose from that it's difficult to know where to start. All the pubs already mentioned do pub food and in addition there is a string of good lunchtime stops along Townhall and East Bridge St all doing filled potatoes, chips and things, sandwiches and more substantial fare. There are picnic tables by the water's edge near the castle. You could also try:
¥ **Bistro**, in the shopping centre; or
¥ **Rebecca's**, in the Buttermarket.

For an explanation of the sleeping and eating price codes used in this guide, see inside the front cover. Other relevant information is found in Essentials pages 39-45.

Around Lower Lough Erne *p571*
₩-₩ **Hotel Carlton**, Belleek. Has a restaurant and does pub food.
₩-₩ **Drumrush Lodge**, Boa Island Rd, Kesh, T6863 1578. Opens daily in the summer for affordable lunches and dinners.
₩-₩ **Lusty Beg Island Restaurant**, Lusty Beg Island, T6863 1342. Opens daily in the evening from 1830 to 2130 and there is also a tea room open from 0900 in the summer.
₩ **Fiddlestone**, Belleek. Does bar food.
₩ **McMorrow's**, Belleek. The usual bar food.
₩ **Thatch Coffee Shop**, Belleek. Rather special vintage place, serves home-made soups, sandwiches, light meals, delicious bakes and a range of coffees. Open Mon-Sat, 0900-1700.
₩ **May Fly**, 14 Main St. Serves pub food.

Pubs and music

Enniskillen *p569, map p569*
There are some good pubs in Enniskillen and some have occasional music sessions – check for notices.
Ardhowen Theatre, Dublin Rd, T6632 5440. In addition to pubs and music there are performances of music and theatre and a good daytime café.
Blake's of the Hollow, Church St. Very old and is divided up into little private rooms. At the back is a pool table and there are live music sessions on Fri.
The Bush, Townhall St. Has regular traditional music sessions in summer.
Crow's Nest (see above). A very trendy place at night with live music most nights and weekend afternoons in summer.

Activities and tours

Enniskillen *p569, map p569*
Boat hire **Belleek Angling Centre**, T6865 8181. Hires rowing boats, £10 per day, and ones with outboard motors for £30 a day.
George Boyd, Enniskillen, T6634 0270. Also has motorboats for half a day at £25 per day.

Fishing Licenses from the tourist office in Wellington Rd.
Home, Field and Stream, 18 Church St, T6632 2114.

Leisure centre **Lakeland Forum**, Enniskillen, T6632 4121.

Tours
Erne Tours, Round 'O' Jetty, Brook Park, A46 Belleek Rd, T6632 2882. The *MV Kestral* departs from the jetty for a cruise of Lough Erne, stopping off at Devinish Island, at 1030, 1415 and 1615 in Jul-Aug; 1430 on Sun in May and Jun, and Tue, Sat and Sun in Sep at 1430 (£6-7). Special trips at Easter and from evening dinner trips from mid-May to early Sep.

Around Lower Lough Erne *p571*
Bicycle hire, canoeing and ponytrekking **Castle Archdale Country Park**, T6862 1892.

Watersports **Boa Island Activity Centre**, Tudor Farm, Boa Island Rd, T6863 1943.
Drumrush Watersports Centre, Lakeland Caravan Park, Boa Island Rd, T6863 1943.

Transport

County Fermanagh *p568*
Air There is talk of reopening **St Angelo Airport**, Trory, 4 miles (6.4 km) north of Enniskillen, T6632 5050, but nothing definite at the time of writing.

Bike hire The nearest places to hire bicycles is Castle Archdale, T6862 1892.

Bus Enniskillen bus station is Wellington Rd, T6632 2633, opposite the tourist office. It handles local buses to small villages in the area as well as regular services to **Belfast**, **Derry**, **Omagh**, **Dungannon**, **Cork**, **Sligo**, and the Bus Éireann **Dublin** to **Donegal** bus stops here.

Ulsterbus, No 194 goes from **Enniskillen** to **Pettigo** via **Irvinestown** and **Kesh**, daily. Nos 59 and 59A from **Enniskillen** to **Derrygonnelly** via **Monea** and **Blaney**, Mon-Sat. No 64 from **Enniskillen** to **Belleek** via **Garrison**, Mon-Fri and Sun; on Thu travels on to **Bundoran**. No 261 from **Belfast** to **Bundoran** via **Enniskillen** and **Belleek**, daily. No 99 **Enniskillen** to **Bundoran** via **Blaney** and **Belleek**, daily.

Car hire Lochside Garages, Tempo Rd, T6632 4366, charges £20-30 a day or £165-200 a week.

Taxi Speedie Cabs, T6632 7327. County Cabs, T66328888.

County Armagh

Armagh City → *Colour map 1, grid B4.*

Once the religious and cultural heart of Ireland, Armagh has slumbered fairly peacefully through the economic regeneration of the last few years and beyond. The result is that the city stands almost exactly as it was when it was first laid out with the mall in the centre of town and the courthouse and gaol facing one another across from it. » *For Sleeping, Eating and other listings, see pages 582-584.*

Ins and outs

Getting there Armagh is easily accessible by bus from Belast, Dublin, Galway and Enniskillen as well as local towns. The nearest train station is at Portadown, T3835 1422, which connects with the Dublin to Belfast line.

Getting around Everything in this little city is packed into three parallel streets and their side roads, with a couple of sights outside the town yet easily accessible by bus or car. The **tourist office** is at 40 English St, T3752 1800, www.armagh-visit.com. It has a bureau de change and B&B booking servics. Open Sep-Jun Mon-Sat 0900-1700, Sun 1400-1700; Jul and Aug Mon-Sat 0900-1730, Sun 1300-1730. » *See Transport, page 584, for further details.*

History

In the ninth century Armagh was the largest and most important settlement in Ireland, but the place was settled long before that. A neolithic circular enclosure, filled with pot shards, was revealed by a bomb in Scotch Street in 1979 and, outside of town, the Navan hill fort was the capital of the kings of Ulster from around 600 BC. St Patrick established a church here in the fifth century and a large monastic community developed, supporting schools, poor houses, and a lay community. Armagh became a beacon of learning while the rest of Europe fell into the Dark Ages.

At the height of its power Armagh bore the brunt of the Viking raids of Ulster. The Annals of Ulster record three raids; in 832 and again in 840 and 852, this time by Vikings who had settled in Dublin and came overland. After 866 there was a respite from the attacks as the Viking threat passed on to the southern provinces, until 921 when a fresh series of plunderings began. The next to set his sights on Armagh was Brian Ború, the 10-11th century High King of Munster, who came relatively peacefully, paid a tribute to the church of Armagh and declared it the primacy of Ireland.

For the next 300 years the city remained an important centre of learning, while all around the Irish clans fought first one another and then the Normans for supremacy. In the middle of the 16th century the Reformation came to Armagh, more powerfully than in other parts of Ireland because of the city's position within the Roman Catholic Church. The monasteries were disbanded, church property confiscated and all forms of religion except Anglicanism banned from the churches. Armagh ceased to be a city.

Armagh entered a new golden age in the 18th century with a massive wave of building projects that created most of the modern city. Archbishop Richard Robinson and his friend the architect Thomas Cooley built the Bishop's Palace, the Public Library, the Gaol and the Royal School. A second wave by Francis Johnson built the Courthouse, the Bank of Ireland (now part of St Patrick's Trian) and the (presently closed for renovation) Observatory.

In the late 19th century the efforts of the Land Leaguers to get a fairer deal for small tenant farmers were met with Protestant riots in the city, the first real example of sectarian differences in Armagh, and in the 20th century the Depression brought more of the same. Never the flashpoint for disturbance that Derry or Belfast were during the Troubles, Armagh nevertheless saw some unpleasant scenes, notably the night in November 1968 when a convoy of Protestant cars led by Ian Paisley was stopped and 220 weapons, including two revolvers, were seized by police. The Loyalists held Armagh, refusing to leave while a civil rights march approached the city. Fortunately the civil rights marchers were persuaded to divert, thus avoiding serious bloodshed. Riots followed the introduction of internment in August 1971 and as the IRA gathered strength and support, Armagh saw its share of bombs.

These days peace reigns in the city, the courthouse has been rebuilt after its destruction and the Arts Centre is encouraging nightlife back to the city. Nonetheless, there is a closed-down atmosphere at night due mainly to the metal grilles and shutters that descend over the shop fronts, a legacy of the Troubles that with luck will soon disappear.

Sights

St Patrick's Trian ⓘ *40 English St, T3752 1801. Sep-Jul Mon-Sat 1000-1730, Jul and Aug, additional opening Sun 1300-1800. £4.25.* Trading on the association of Swift with the town the best thing here is the story of Gulliver, told in one room by an extremely realistic giant, in others by a series of models in glass cases. There is also the story of Armagh, which is vaguely interesting but a bit too dependent on gadgetry, and the story of St Patrick.

Armagh County Museum ⓘ *The Mall, T3752 3070. Mon-Fri 1000-1700, Sat 1000-1300, 1400-1700, closed bank holidays. Free.* Set in an old 1833 schoolhouse this is a

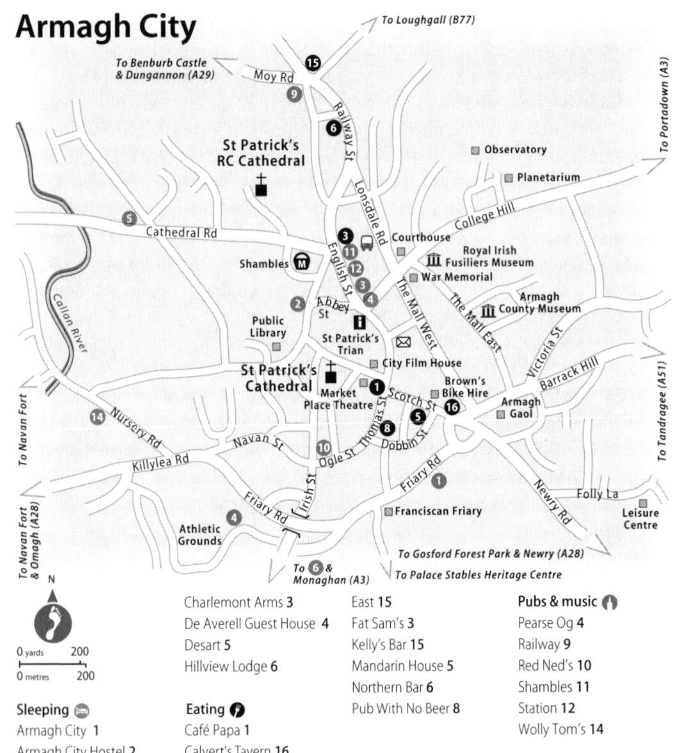

leasant hour's meander through the detritus of Armagh's past. Collected here are ssorted bits and pieces – bog butter, leather shoes, an ox yoke discovered in the ogs, assorted carved stone heads found while renovations were taking place, old lothes, examples of the city's past as a lacemaking centre, Orange memorabilia, and n interesting display about the railway and its great disaster of 1889 when a day trip vent horribly wrong and 89 people died. There is also a little display of stuffed nimals, an art gallery and an exhibition on the museum itself and its work.

oyal Irish Fusiliers Museum ⓘ *The Mall, T3752 2911. Mon-Fri 1000-1230, 1330-600. Free.* This is a vast collection of First World War medals, a dugout, uniforms, ilver cups, banners and, more interestingly, an exhibit on the terrible damage done y the IRA bomb aimed at the nearby courthouse in 1993. The whole building more or ess folded in on itself, but the museum was closed at the time and so there were no njuries. Most of the material on display was picked out of the rubble.

St Patrick's Church of Ireland Cathedral ⓘ *Cathedral Close, T3752 3142. pr-Oct daily 0930-1700, Nov-Mar 0930-1600. Photographic permit £1 from verger or t the shop.* This building has been knocked down 17 times in eight centuries – in nother city, one might think it was time to find somewhere else, but not in Armagh. A hurch has stood on this site since Patrick's time, and from the eighth century the hill vas covered in monastic buildings. The present design is an enlarged version of a hurch of 1268, restored in 1834. Thackeray visited the renovated building and said it ad as much religious feeling to it as a drawing room. It certainly lacks the wesomeness of Dublin's cathedrals or even Belfast's, but it has a cosy sort of arochial austerity to it.

Just as the Victorians' efforts to Gothicize Christ Church Cathedral in Dublin (see age 77) didn't go down too well, so the efforts here lack power. There are lots of ccumulated bits and pieces around the church, the most fascinating of which is the rutal-looking Tandragee Man, an ancient granite idol, thus named because of the heory that he came from Tandragee in County Down. This and several other human igures in the church are thought to have been discovered when the church was enovated in the 19th century. Another of the figures shows a crudely carved man with ays radiating from his head, perhaps a sun god from pagan times or a representation f early Irish men, who wore their hair in stiffened dreadlocks pulled back from their eads. There is also an amalgam of two high crosses, possibly 11th-century, thought o have been brought to the cathedral in 1441. Brian Ború is supposedly buried here; a lab on the exterior wall claims to be his burial place.

rmagh Public Library ⓘ *Cathedral Close, T3752 3142. 1000-1300 and 1400-600. Free.* Close to the church in Cathedral Close is the public library (1771, Cooley), till very much in its original condition. You must ring to be let in. In the lobby is a eries of displays about the *Book of Armagh*, currently in Dublin, while upstairs in the brary itself is a pretty impressive collection of old books including an annotated copy f *Gulliver's Travels*, a 1611 Breeches Bible, a case of tiny books, a Roman missal from 587 and a 13th-century Dutch missal.

t Patrick's Roman Catholic Cathedral ⓘ *Cathedral Rd, T3752 2802.* Begun in 840 in a neoclassical style, the design and building of this Cathedral were bandoned during the Famine. When work began again, it was in a different vein ltogether. A third architect designed the interior of mosaic, fresco and stained glass, vhile the last person to have a hand in the design of this place was Liam McCormack 1 1977-1982. The result is, as many have pointed out, a little schizophrenic, but it ertainly grips the imagination. The altar, like many other efforts of the 1970s, looks ke it's used for pagan sacrifices rather than Catholic worship.

Armagh Gaol ⓘ *The Mall.* Although only open to groups, the gaol still stands as i was when it became notorious for its strip-searches of women political prisoner during the 1980s. Thomas Cooley is responsible for its design, and its façade i certainly beautiful enough. Inside the yard was the treadwheel (no longer i existence) where, as a punishment for bad behaviour, prisoners were set to turn th wheel, stepping on to 8-inch high steps and making 48 steps per minute.

Palace Stables Heritage Centre ⓘ *Palace Demesne, Friary Rd, T3752 9629 or ask a the tourist office about what remains open to the public.* When Archbishop Robinso decided to make Armagh his headquarters in the 1760s, he couldn't be expected to liv in any old shack and so this complex of buildings, restored in the late 1980s, is hi personal statement of authority. The palace itself is now council offices and only som parts are open to the public. The chief tourist attraction is the stables, which have bee converted into an exhibition about life in the late 18th century but this is likely to clos in the near future. By the entrance gates are the remains of a 13th-century Francisca friary founded in 1264. The grounds have walking trails and an ornamental garden.

Navan Fort ⓘ *Killylea Rd, T3752 5550, access to the fort 24 hrs and free, it is nearly miles from town but bus No 73 takes you close, a new interpretative centre is about t open and there will be an entrance charge; enquire at the tourist office.* A unremarkable-looking mound on a hilltop 2 miles (3.2 km) out of Armagh, this i Ireland's most significant ancient site. There is evidence of habitation here going bac 7,000 years, but the most significant activity took place during the Bronze Age when th place was built and rebuilt about seven times, and finally, inexplicably, a huge woode building was created, filled with limestone blocks and burned to the ground. In 1993 acquired the obligatory heritage centre, which is quite attractively designed and does pretty good job of explaining what is basically a big grassy mound at the momen Excavations are planned for the future, which may open up the site a little more.

South Armagh → *Colour map 1, grid C5.*

Steeped in ancient culture, this is the most beautiful part of the county despite th assorted remnants of military paraphernalia that blight the green and grey hills. Even o a wet and doleful day the allure of Slieve Gullion is palpable and this tour starts i Newtownhamilton: reached to the south of Armagh city or the northwest of Dundalk o the A29, or from Newry by going due west on the A25. The tour finishes in Crossmagle
▸▸ *For Sleeping, Eating and other listings, see pages 583-584.*

Camlough and Bessbrook

From Newtownhamilton, take the A25 road east to Newry, and consider stopping i tricoloured Camlough for a drink before passing on to Bessbrook, a purpose-built, tim capsule of a mill town laid out in the 1840s by the Quaker Richardsons. This gem of place, characterized by the generous use of local granite, was known as 'the villag without three Ps' because there were no pubs and thus no need for pawnshop or polic station. Five soldiers were killed by a landmine near here at the height of the violenc unleashed by the deaths of hunger strikers in May 1981.

Derrymore House

ⓘ *T3083 0353. May-Aug Thu-Sat 1400-1730. £2.50.* On the Newry side of the A2 Derrymore House is a National Trust thatched 18th-century cottage where the Act Union was drafted. The park and woodlands that surround it are always freely ope

Killeavy churches

Hop back to Camlough and turn left to take the road south passing a lake setting that can match Killarney's for sheer breathtaking beauty. Continue south to the Killeavy churches on the gentle slopes of Slieve Gullion, where St Monenna's nunnery lasted for a millennium after her death in the early sixth century. The western, 12th-century church is joined by a shared wall to a later 15th-century one. St Monenna's likely burial place is marked by a large slab near the churchyard wall to the north and a holy well associated with her is a little way up the mountain to the west.

Forest Park

ⓘ *T3755 1277. Easter-Aug 1000-dusk. £2.50 for a car, visitor centre, self-catering apartments and coffee shop.* On the other side of Killeavy village, on the B113, you will find the entrance to the Slieve Gullion Forest Park where an 8-mile (13-km) drive and a walking trail lead up to the summit. Weather permitting, there are unrivalled views of the random set of volcanic hills known as the Ring of Gullion.

A short detour to the east goes to **Jonesborough**, famous for its Sunday market which draws in a fair crowd. A couple of miles south of here a path to the handsome **Kilnasaggart Stone** (*Cill na Sagart*, church of the priests) is signposted across fields. This eighth-century pillar is clearly and elegantly inscribed and marks an early Christian burial place. Jonesborough is also a good place to stop for a meal (see page 583).

Crossmaglen and around

From Mullach Ban continue north to the junction with the B30 and turn left for Crossmaglen. In the 1880s over 150 young women were employed here in lace schools. Less than a century later the town's proximity to the border had made it infamous as the epicentre of militant republicanism; by the beginning of 1976 over 30 soldiers had been killed, over half in the town square where a tourist office now stands as a refreshing sign of changing times. On the first and last Friday of every month a fair is held in the square. The **tourist office** is at O'Fiaich House, T3086 8900. Mon-Fri 0900-1700.

In the village of **Creggan**, 4 km northeast of Crossmaglen, the parish churchyard has interesting tombstones of local 18th-century Gaelic poets and other curiosities; pick up the useful leaflet on the churchyard from the tourist office in Crossmaglen.

North Armagh → *Colour map 1, grid B5.*

A greater contrast with south Armagh is hard to find for in place of attractive countryside and progressive culture there is an unsightly industrial landscape and reminders of the kind of sectarianism that led to the Troubles in the first place.

Portadown

The town of Portadown, where loyalist mobs rioted against the Anglo-Irish Agreement in 1985, is not the most attractive place to visit in Ireland. It does, however, boast a Paul Rankin café, in the High Street Mall, serving tasty food.

To visit **Garvaghy Road** (see box next page) leave your car in the Dunnes store car park or, closer still, the Wilson Street car park opposite the *Laser* electronics store. Garvaghy Road begins where the Haldane Fisher & Ulster Carpet Mills Factory sign can be seen and the Union Jacks soon give way to the tricolours of the Catholic enclave. To reach **Drumcree Church**, walk up the road for 1 mile and take the second turning on the right after the Mayfair Centre. Continue along this road for about a mile and it is on the left by the Y-junction.

On a more upbeat note, there are also two National Trust houses in the area. The 17th-century **Ardress House** ⓘ *T3885 1236, on B26 7 miles (11.2 km) west of Portadown, Easter and Jun-Aug Wed-Mon 1400-1800, Apr-May and Sep, Sat and Sun only, same*

Drumcree and Garvaghy Road

The issue of whether the Orange Order has the right to march from Drumcree Church down Catholic Garvaghy Road on its route back to Portadown each July was a major issue in the evolving politics of Ulster until very recently. With David Trimble's rise to the leadership of the Unionist Party they received vital support from diehard loyalists after he joined the march and championed their cause. In 1998, after the Parades Commission banned the march, the ensuing violence resulted in the death of three children in a Catholic house firebombed by loyalist extremists. The Orange Order is adamant about its right to march down the road, and the residents of Garvaghy Road are equally adamant that the days of triumphalist and provocative marches through Catholic areas are over. Since 1999 the stand-off has been relatively peaceful, but some loyalists continue to insist on their 'constitutional right' to march down the road.

hours, guided tour, £3, has a renowned neoclassical interior and a working farmyard outside. The tour takes you around beautifully furnished rooms filled with Adam fireplaces and family portraits. Outside is a fine park and children's playground.

Close by on Derrycaw Rd in Moy, is **The Argory** ⓘ *T8778 4753, same hours as Ardress House, grounds and house tour £4.30*, with what was a state-of-the-art gas lighting system in the early 19th century still illuminating some of the original furniture. All the paraphernalia of the 19th century nob is still there – carriages, the laundry, musical instruments and there are long walks in the 130 ha of gardens.

Loughall

This is a pretty little village which nestles quietly in its surroundings and has a huge country park with lots of good walks and a lake where there is coarse fishing. It is also famous for being the place where the Orange Order was founded in 1795 after the battle of the Diamond between Catholic and Protestant militias.

The inn where the order was inaugurated is now the **Dan Winter Ancestral Home** ⓘ *9 The Diamond, Derryloughan Rd, Loughall, T3885 1344, Mon-Sat 1030-2030, Sun 1400-2030, voluntary donation, call at the house next door for the key*, and contains memorabilia from the Battle of the Diamond.

In 1986 the Provisionals mounted an attack on the RUC station at Loughall but a tip-off led to an ambush by SAS soldiers, who fired 1,200 rounds killing eight of the Provisionals as well as an innocent civilian driving past in his car.

Loughall has some quality **antique shops** along its main street, including **Heritage Antiques** *T3889 1314*, and **Meredith Antiques** *T3852 8739*, and a noted restaurant, **The Famous Grouse** *T3889 1778*, a couple of miles out on Ballyhagan Road.

Sleeping

Armagh City *p577, map p578*

B-C Armagh City Hotel Friary Rd, T3751 8888, www.armaghcityhotel.com. A newish hotel that has everything you could wish for including leisure centre and pool, grounds where you can pretend to be lord of the manor, and a good restaurant.

D Charlemont Arms Hotel, 63-5 English St, T3752 2028, www.charlemontarmshotel.com. Very central, good basic restaurant, closed over Christmas.

D De Averell Guest House, 3 Seven Houses English St, T3751 1213, www.deaverell house.com. Nicely renovated, centrally located Georgian house with pretty sitting room for guests. Has a well regarded restaurant and comfortable rooms.

E **Desart**, The Desart, Desart Lane, off Cathedral Rd, T3752 2387. Small, no rooms with bathroom, but affordable.

E **Hillview Lodge**, 33 Newtownhamilton Rd, T3752 2000, www.hillviewlodge.com. Outside town, on the B31, a turning off the A29 going south to Keady. A friendly place with a lounge and single/doubles for £30-50.

E **Ni Eoghain Lodge**, 32 Ennislare Rd, T3752 5633. All rooms with en suite bathroom, breakfast choices, inexpensive evening meals (a godsend on Sun nights).

F **Armagh City Hostel**, 39 Abbey St, T3751 1800, www.hini.org.uk. A grand, positively lavish, hostel with dormitories and twin rooms, all with en suite bathroom, kitchen and a restaurant. Reception is closed between 1100 and 1700 but open access all the time once you're booked in. Book well in advance.

South Armagh *p580*

E **Greenvale**, 141 Longfield Rd, Forkhill, T3088 8314. A farmhouse with views of Slieve Gullion. One double and one single, £17.50 per person, and horse riding available.

E **Murtaghs**, 13 North St, Crossmaglen, T3086 1378, aidanmurtagh@hotmail.com. A family-run bar and B&B in the centre of town. Two doubles, one with bathroom, and a single.

Self catering

Cranny Farm, 16 Cranny Rd, Mullach Ban, T9020 7041. £225-£250 in low/high season a week, sleeping up to 4.

Slieve Gullion Courtyard, Slieve Gullion Forest Park, 89 Dromintee Rd, T3084 8084, www.slievegullioncourtyard.com.

Eating

Armagh City *p577, map p578*

Eating out in Armagh needs planning beforehand. Many places shut by 1730 and those that don't often require a booking.

¥-¥ **De Averell Guest House**, serves a mixture of meat-based continental and local dishes, from sausages and champ (£5) to steak (£14).

¥ **Charlemont Arms Hotel**, has a fairly unexciting evening menu with dishes around £7 – burgers, fish and chips, chicken tikka masala – available until 2030.

¥ **Café Papa**, 15 Thomas St, T3751 1205. Filled rolls, sandwiches and pastries at lunchtime but turns into a little bistro on Fri and Sat nights.

¥ **East**, a Chinese place above Kelly's bar deserves a medal for being open 7 nights till late and comes recommended by local people. Dinner for around £12.

¥ **Mandarin House**, 30 Scotch St, T3752 228. Deserves another, smaller medal – open 6 days, closed Mon. Western and Chinese.

¥ **Pub With No Beer**, 30 Thomas St, T3752 3586. Open Mon-Sat till 2130 and serves pub food – burgers, champ, salads, chicken pie.

¥ **Fat Sam's**, 7 English St, T3752 5559. Filled potato, sandwiches or pastries. Mon-Fri lunch.

¥ **Pilgrim's Table**, 38 English St, T3752 1801, inside the St Patrick's Trian complex. Lunch only. The best place in town, does homely dishes like filled potatoes, soups and hotpot.

¥ **Calvert's Tavern**, 3 Scotch St. Pub food.

¥ **Northern Bar**, 100 Railway St, T3752 7315. A little out of town, but the best place, has a large menu ranging from sandwiches to a 3-course meal 1230-1500 (1700 weekends). The 3-course option will set you back £8. Also open for Sun lunch. Vegetarian options.

South Armagh *p580*

¥¥-¥ **Flurrybridge Inn**, Jonesborough, T3084 8181. Serves the best choice of food – European, Chinese and Indian – for miles around and opens in the evening Thu-Sun and at lunchtime on Sun, 1230-1530, for the open-air market.

¥¥-¥ **Lima Country House**, 16 Drumalt Rd, Silverbridge, T3086 1944. Evening meals between Mon and Sat, but telephone first.

¥¥-¥ **Ma Kearney's**, Newry St, Crossmaglen, T3086 8944. Good for bar food and a restaurant, Mon-Sat, and lunch on Sun.

¥¥-¥ **Slieve Gullion Courtyard Restaurant**, 89 Dromintee Rd, Killeavey, Slieve Gullion Forest Park, T3084 8084. Does meals on Sat and Sun 1400-2200. Dishes from £6-15. If you phone ahead you can book a meal during the week.

¥ **Cartwheel**, The Square, Crossmaglen. Pub food, Mon-Sat, in the evening.

¥ **Murtagh's** (see 'Sleeping' above). Another pub where bar food is available.

For an explanation of the sleeping and eating price codes used in this guide, see inside the front cover. Other relevant information is found in Essentials pages 39-45.

Pubs and music

Armagh City *p577, map p578*
There's a lively nightlife among the pubs here. Other pubs not listed have music at weekends, but it's likely to be tribute bands or a disco.
Pearse Og, in Dalton Rd, T3751 1004 (Pat Prunty). Set-dancing classes are held in this club on Mon and visitors are welcome. There are no classes during the summer months.
Railway Bar, plays traditional Irish music.
Red Ned's, Ogle St. Has music at weekends.
Shambles Bar, live music at weekends.
Station Bar, try here for traditional music.
Wolly Tom's, Nursery Rd. Live music Fri-Sun.

South Armagh *p580*
Keenan's, Crossmaglen. Traditional music.
O'Hanlon's Pub, Mullaghbawn, T3088 8759. A favourite for improvized music eruptions. Regular sessions on Fri and Sat in summer.
The Welcome Inn, 35 Main St, Forkhill, T3088 8273. Music session every Tue.

Entertainment

Armagh City *p577, map p578*
Armagh City Film House, Market St, T3751 1033, at the bottom of the Arts Centre.
Market Place Theatre and Arts Centre, T3752 1821, www.marketplacearmagh.com. The city's major venue for theatre and concert performances. But besides visiting theatre and concerts it has a regular jazz night on the last Sat of each month and a stand-up comedy on the last Thu of the month.

Activities and tours

South Armagh *p580*
Horse riding **Greenvale Trekking Centre**, Forkhill, T3088 8314.

Transport

County Armagh *p577*
Bike hire McCumiskey Cycles, Dromintee, T3088 8593.

Bus Armagh bus station, 14 Londsale Rd, T3752 2266, has direct express buses to **Belfast**, **Dublin**, **Cork**, **Galway** and **Enniskillen**, stopping at major towns along the route. Local buses connect with smaller local towns and a change at **Dungannon** brings connections to the **northern coast** and **Derry**.

There is a bus service Mon-Sat between **Newry** and **Crossmaglen** via **Camlough**, T3026 3531. Other services run Mon-Sat between **Forkhill** and **Newry** and between **Bessbrook** and **Newry**.

Taxi Euro Cabs, Armagh City, T3751 1900. Cross Cabs, Crossmaglen, T3086 8550. M.T. Taxis, Crossmaglen, T3086 8300.

County Monaghan

Monaghan's characteristic drumlins, hills formed by the retreating Ice Age, stretch from Donegal to Strangford Lough and formed a natural barrier that helped define Ulster from prehistoric times onwards. Monaghan town is where most visitors pause and it makes an obvious base for sampling the surrounding countryside. ▸▸ *For Sleeping and Eating, see page 586.*

Ins and outs

Information For general visitor information and on-line booking of accommodation in the county: www.momaghantourism.com.

Monaghan town and around

→ *Phone code: 047. Colour map 1, grid C4.*

Monaghan is a town to walk around, admiring the Victorian civic edifices that range from an elaborate drinking fountain to a distinguished and very churchified bank building built on a curve in Church Square. Monaghan needs to be appreciated as a splinter of Ulster divorced from its natural context. "Men not prone to emotion shed tears", relates a historian, when it was learnt that Monaghan, Cavan and Donegal would be severed from the six counties making up Northern Ireland.

The **Monaghan County Museum** ⓘ *Tue-Sat, 1100-1300 and 1400-1700, free*, has an excellent collection of finds and a visit here is worth the time. Look for the riveted Bronze Age cauldron, stone mounds for bronze spears, the Cross of Clogher, a Viking sword, 13th-century leather shoes with stitches intact, medieval combs, hairpins and a thumbscrew.

The **tourist office** on Castlemeadow Street, T047-81122, is open May-Oct Mon-Fri 0900-1700, Sat 1000-1700.

County Monaghan is in the Republic and to phone Northern Ireland dial 048 before the 8 digit number. To phone a Monaghan number from Northern Ireland, dial 00+353+ and the area code minus the 0.

Around Monaghan

Places of interest are scattered about the county like drumlins and your own transport is pretty essential. Glaslough is 6 miles (9 km) northeast of Monaghan town, Clones is 12 miles (19 km) to the southwest, while Carrickmacross and Iniskeen are tucked away in the east near Dundalk.

Glaslough → *Phone code: 047. Colour map 1 grid B4.*

The pre-plantation ruling family in Monaghan were the MacMahons, and after the death of Ross MacMahon in 1589 the English partitioned the land amongst members of his family in a classic divide-and-rule ploy designed to extend England's control. Plantation properly got under way the following century and there is no better expression of Protestant hegemony, in what is now the Republic, than in the earnest, saturnine soberness of Glaslough's stone cottages.

Clones → *Phone code: 047. Colour map 1, grid C3.*

The railway station at Clones was the scene of a shoot-out between constables and Republicans early in 1922, just after the Treaty was signed, and sparked sectarian attacks by loyalists in Belfast that saw 44 dead. Convivial Clones (pronounced *clo-nez*) today carries no trace of such discord and a rich Protestant legacy can still be seen in the centrally located **St Tiernach's Church**. What remains of St Tiernach's monastery is in Abbey Street near a damaged round tower. More satisfaction may be gained by deciphering the fine **high cross**, which stands in the Diamond.

Some 3 miles (5 km) south of Clones on the Ballyhaise road, **Hilton Park** ⓘ *T047-56007, May-Sep daily 1400-1800, €3*, has been replanted to reflect the original 18th-century formal garden.

Carrickmacross → *Phone code: 042. Colour map 1, grid C4.*

A one-street town famous for its hand-made lace industry, established in the early 19th century, is still surviving and with items for sale in the town centre. The Catholic church has two Harry Clarke windows and for country walks the **Dún a Rí Forest Park** is a couple of miles away on the R179 Kingscourt Road.

Iniskeen → *Colour map 1, grid C4.*

To the east, the village of Iniskeen celebrates being the birthplace of Patrick Kavanagh (1904-1967), Ireland's best poet after Yeats and Heaney, and author of the great *Tarry Flynn*, but hardly known outside the country. The **Patrick Kavanagh Centre** ⓘ *T042-9378560, www.patrickkavanaghcountry.com, all year Mon-Fri 1100-1700;*

Nine people were killed in Monaghan in 1974 when a car bomb exploded, planted by a loyalist group from Northern Ireland.

 mid-Mar to Nov also Sun, 1400-1800; Jun-Sep also Sat, 1400-1800, €4, Patrick Kavanagh Weekend, annually, last weekend in Nov, which has a set of paintings illustrating the poet's greatest epic, *The Great Hunger*, dispenses an inexpensive Kavanagh Trail Guide which usefully locates sites associated with the poet.

Sleeping

Monaghan town *p584*
E **Ashleigh House**, 37 Dublin St, T047-81227. Centrally located, close to the museum, and all the rooms have their own bathrooms.
E **Hilldene House**, Canal St, T047-83297. Same rate as Ashleigh House, €60 for a double, but has shared bathroom facilities.

Glaslough *p585*
A **Castle Leslie**, Glaslough, T047-88109, www.castle-leslie.ie. Come here for a 2-night package, no television, no children, bedrooms worth photographing, and let the baroque eccentricity of the place work its magic (try not to be put off by the fact that Paul McCartney chose to have his wedding reception here). Excellent, candle-lit dinner just under €50.

Clones *p585*
A **Hilton Park**, T047-56007, www.hiltonpark.ie. A country house with a reputation for hospitality and organic produce.
D-E **Creighton Hotel**, Fermanagh St, T047-51055. A few euro more.
E **Lennard Arms Hotel**, The Diamond, T047-51075. A modest but very comfortable hotel and proud to portray photographs of the town's most famous son, Barry McGuigan, world featherweight boxing champion.

Carrickmacross *p585*
L-A **Nuremore Hotel and Country Club**, Carrickmacross, T042-9661438, www.nuremore-hotel.ie. Outstanding hotel in terms of facilities, comfort and service. See below for its restaurant.

Eating

Monaghan town *p584*
YY **Andy's Bar and Restaurant**, Market St, T047-82277. The finest place for a meal in town, Victorian-style, pub food at lunchtime and 1800-2200, and a restaurant upstairs with a good-value dinner for around €35.
YY-Y **The Squealing Pig Bar**, the Diamond. Has a restaurant serving American-style food.
Y **Vesuvio**, close to Andy's Bar. An affordable pizzeria, closed Mon, while.

Glaslough *p585*
YYY **Castle Leslie**, see above for a meal.

Clones
Y While both hotels serve food, it is worth first checking out **Cúil Darrach** at The Diamond or **The Round Tower Bar** on Cara St.

Carrickmacross *p585*
YYY-YY **Nuremore Hotel and Country Club**, Carrickmacross, T042-9661438. Exceptionally good restaurant. Expect to find beef, lamb, maybe duck, or even plain old chicken – enlivened by foie gras tortellini – and vegetables cooked to perfection. Dinner menu for €45 and a vegetarian one for €25.

Transport

County Monaghan
Bus Éireann, T047-82377, run daily buses between **Dublin** and **Monaghan** via **Slane**. The routes to **Letterkenny** and **Derry** from Monaghan also stop in **Slane**, **Carrickmacross** and **Omagh**. 3 buses daily, and 2 on Sun, the **Dublin – Dungannon – Coleraine – Portrush** service stops in Slane and Monaghan. The daily **Belfast** to **Galway** service connects Monaghan with these towns as well as **Armagh**, **Athlone**, **Cavan**, **Clones**, **Enniskillen**, **Longford**, **Roscommon** and **Sligo**. The **Sligo – Dundalk** and **Dundalk – Cavan** routes both come through Monaghan. There is no bus link with **Glaslough**, but for **Iniskeen** a local service between Dundalk and Cavan, 4 daily buses Mon-Sat, stop here before going on to **Carrickmacross**.

McConnon's, T047-9282020, also run a frequent service to Dublin, Mon-Fri at 0645 and 0900, Sat 0900 and on Sun at 1800. €8 single and €12 return.

Background

Footprint features

History

Prehistory

Between nine and eleven thousand years ago, nomadic Mesolithic people fror Europe came to the northwest fringes of the continent bearing flint instruments. B 5500 BC, the east coast of Ireland had submerged and Ireland became an island Around 4000 BC people arrived with farming skills, and the first settled communitie arose, as revealed in north Mayo at Céide Fields, giving rise in the due course c centuries to megalithic stone tombs which survive to this day. Court-tombs ar probably the earliest, dating as far back as 3500BC and characterized by an ope space or court in front of the tomb, flanked by standing stones.

Passage-tombs are similar in that they are also covered by a stone mound but ar more interesting to visit, not least because of the geometrical motifs inscribed on th stones, and the best places to see them are at Carrowkeel, Newgrange and Knowth Equally dramatic are the portal-tombs or dolmens (from a Breton word meaning 'stone table'), popularly known as Druids' altars, composed of three or more massiv standing stones supporting one large capstone which can weigh up to 100 tons. The were built somewhere around 3000-2000 BC.

Newgrange, dating from around 2500 BC, stands as testimony to the astonishin engineering skills possessed by these people, and the National Museum in Dubli has dazzling displays of their working with gold and silver and, later, bronze.

The Bronze Age, 2000-500 BC, gets its name from the main material used durin a period which also made use of copper and gold, and a major site from this period i the stone circle at Lough Gur. Other stone circles belong to the ensuing Iron Age, bui by a people who never developed an alphabet beyond the characters known a Ogham (see box page 243).

The Celts

Much of what we know about pagan Celtic society in Ireland is due – ironically – to th earnest chronicling efforts of early Christian monks. The Iron Age Celts are bes viewed as a linguistic group, an offshoot of the Indo-European family, which emerge around 2000 BC and spread from Turkey in the east to Ireland in the west. From wher exactly they came is open to interpretation and there is a theory that an Atlanti culture arrived in Ireland via the Mediterranean, through Spain and possibly nort Africa. Berber jewellery and north African music and dance have a striking kinshi with 'Celtic' art forms.

In the late 1990s Simon James, a scholar at the British Museum (see page 627) attacked the notion that the Celts as a uniform people ever existed, and he claime that the idea they were somehow the first nation to emerge north of the Alps is a myth His debunking thesis is a useful corrective to the excessive claims of born-agai Celtomaniacs, who would have us believe they are part of a long-repressed culture Nevertheless, 'Celtic Ireland' remains a useful shorthand term for the pre-Christia period, and there are intriguing cultural overlaps between the Celts and those wh followed them.

The Celtic calendar was based on the duality of dark and light – they counte nights rather than days – and great significance was attached to those pivot moments when the two came together. Sunrise and sunset were such moments while the two annual equinoxes – when day and night were momentarily balanced b the sun crossing the celestial equator – were profoundly magical in their import. Th

"A land of fog and gloom ... Beyond it lies the Sea of Death, where Hell begins." Homer's 'Iliad' describes the far northwest of Europe.

supernatural was most alive at these critical times and paganism was in awe of this cosmic balancing act.

The summer and winter solstices, when the sun is furthest away from the equator, were also powerful and dangerous moments in time. There were four great pagan festivals when Celts celebrated the turning points between the seasons. Most is known about Lughnasa, celebrated at the beginning of August and dedicated to the god Lug.

Monasticism

The Romans never settled in Ireland but they traded with the island, men from Ireland served with Roman legions, and it was through the Romans that Christianity arrived on the island. The first bishop was appointed in 431 (the first bona fide date in Irish history), but it was the missionary Patrick who is now best associated with early Christian Ireland. Notwithstanding his iconic Irishness, Patrick first arrived as a captured slave from Britain and returned years later as a proselytizing missionary, establishing his main church in Armagh.

Christianity brought with it a world of learning and literacy as well as technological innovations like the mouldboard plough and the horizontal mill. Monasteries also allowed for organized farming, and the overall effect of these influences from 'across the water' was an increase in population which is associated with the 45,000 ringforts that were built across Ireland during this era.

From the sixth to eighth centuries, when the rest of Europe was in the doldrums after the collapse of the Roman empire, Ireland's monasteries continued to burn the light of culture and learning. Irish monks travelled throughout Europe, rekindling some of the intellectual embers endangered by barbarism, and the survival of wonderful illuminated manuscripts provides eloquent testimony to their achievement.

Irish monasticism, associated above all with the great figure of Columcille, gave the Irish Church a unique idiom through its ability to fuse the sacred with the profane, recording pagan myths and soothing the revolutionary transition from a pagan world of magic and mysticism with a degree of sympathy that seems difficult to comprehend today. What explanation, other than a sensibility capable of being excited by paganism, accounts for Irish monks recording and preserving the pagan vernacular literature of their island? The stories and chronicles that they recorded are the primary source materials for the contemporary study of early Irish history, and it is thanks to them that we know the tales of Cuchulainn and the other Irish heroes and heroines.

Irish monasticism was also enriched by an ascetic Coptic strain, more akin to the eastern church than Rome, which incorporated a tradition of holy people seeking out secluded and remote hermitages – a *fuga mundi* or 'flight from the world' – which were often the seedbeds of monastic communities. This is the origin of Glendalough and the fastness of Skellig Michael – an 800-ft rock 8 miles off the remote Kerry coast – two holy sites which now attract tourist pilgrims in greater numbers than they ever did in their own austere times.

The Vikings

Norse Viking invaders first raided the monasteries of Ireland in the late 10th century, and in the following century Irish annals report sightings of vast fleets of ships appearing on the Boyne and the Liffey. The Danes came in their wake, and fierce fighting developed between the invaders and between them and the Irish. Settlements and intermarriage with the Irish gave rise to coastal communities that would evolve into the towns of Dublin, Wexford, Waterford, Cork and Limerick. In 917 the king of Leinster was defeated by the Norse, commanded by Sitric, who went on to

"The wind is fierce tonight Ploughing the wild white ocean; I need not dread fierce Vikings Crossing the Irish Sea." Words of an anonymous monk scribbled in the margin of a 10th-century manuscript.

establish a strong kingdom in Dublin. Raiding parties by the Norse into the Irish interior is one plausible explanation for the building of defensive round towers near monasteries, for this is when many of them were built.

The Vikings kept paganism alive and healthy in Ireland until around the 11th century, a period which saw their defeat by the Irish under Brian Bóruma (Brian Ború) at the momentous battle of Clontarf in 1014. Brian Bóruma was killed at Clontarf and his body carried in state to Armagh, then the ecclesiastical capital of Ireland, the significance of this epic battle being recorded in both Irish annals and Icelandic sagas.

The coming of the Normans

After the death of Brian Bóruma, Ireland was torn apart by internecine dynastic wars that petered out when Rory O'Connor was accepted as king of all Ireland in the middle of the 12th century. Then in August 1167 one of his erstwhile rivals, Dermot MacMurrough, arrived home from exile, and with the help of Welsh soldiers set about reclaiming his kingdom. MacMurrough had earlier sought out the Norman King Henry II of England, and with promises of land had procured his support for an invasion of Ireland. The event proved to be traumatically momentous, for MacMurrough's support included the Earl of Pembroke, better known as Strongbow. When the Earl arrived in 1170, the stage was set for 800 years of foreign rule and conflict which still bedevils politics and peace in Northern Ireland. With the arrival of these French-speaking Normans, mostly from South Wales, Irish history would never be the same again.

Strongbow brought a professional army of 1000 men and their menacing longbows, and he first captured Waterford and then Dublin. Henry II, alarmed that this rich new conquest might slip from his personal grasp, began assembling his own fleet for an invasion. He landed in 1171 near Waterford with a fleet of 400 ships and as many as 4000 men. In the course of the 13th century the Normans began to build their great stone castles, and those at Kilkenny, Carrickfergus and Trim give some idea of the awe they must have instilled in the minds of the wood-building Gaels.

The Normans brought to Ireland the idea of the absolute ownership of land, as opposed to the Irish idea that land was only given in trust to individuals. Under Brehon Law, the ancient legal code of pre-Norman Ireland, woodlands were common land.

Conquered, not colonized

Henry II secured Waterford, Wexford and Dublin, and the Irish nobility submitted to his rule. Ireland had been conquered, and after a visit to Lismore the acquiescence of the Irish bishops was obtained, but the country was not yet colonized in any systematic way. Before leaving Ireland, Henry gave the central swathe of the country from the Shannon to the Boyne to the English family of Hugh de Lacy who, together with Strongbow, established a permanent English presence on the island. They soon intermarried with the Irish, and by the time Henry's son John, who became king in 1199, strengthened royal rule over Ireland, the first Anglo-Irish families had become established. A trickle of new English settlers came, lured by the promise of good land and families like the Desmonds and the Butlers began to emerge as powerful Anglo-Irish political forces.

The mass of Irish peasants struggled and toiled as before, while their Irish lords brooded in the background ever ready to take advantage of internal power squabbles amongst the Anglo-Normans. English rule was confined to an area around Dublin known as the Pale (hence the expression 'beyond the pale') while Gaelic custom and Brehon law – with communal property, secular marriage and divorce – operated for the majority of the population. The most powerful Norman-Irish families, known as the 'Old English', were the loyal Butlers and their earldom of Ormond, and the Fitzgeralds, whose earldoms of Kildare and Desmond became a thorn in the side of the English crown. Kilkenny became the political and cultural centre of medieval Anglo-Norman Ireland, and in 1366 a set of 36 clauses, the Statutes of Kilkenny (se box page 184), were passed as law in an attempt to preserve the English culture from the encroachments of Gaelic life. "Now many English of the said land, forsaking the English language, fashion, mode of riding, laws and usages, live and govern themselves according to the manners, fashion and language of the Irish enemies, and also have made divers marriages and alliances between themselves and the Irish." (The Statutes of Kilkenny.)

During the 16th century Henry VIII of England had trouble keeping some of these Anglo-Irish magnates under his control, and after his breach with Rome over his marriage to Anne Boleyn in 1533 this became a serious problem, because of the danger of European Catholic plots being hatched in Ireland. England became more serious about combating dissent in Ireland and suppressing Brehon law, but there were still five Anglo-Irish rebellions between 1568 and 1574. In 1580 Spanish and Italian Catholics landed at Smerwick in Kerry where, trapped by Lord Grey, 500 were slaughtered after they had surrendered. It was a sign of things to come.

After the failure of rebellions by the Desmonds in 1569-1573 and 1579-1583, and consequent confiscations of land, the first plantations, planned in London, began in Munster. By 1592 there were over 3000 settlers, but some were killed after the Nine Years War broke out and their land was taken over by former owners. The colonists who were still around in 1598 fled to Irish towns and to England for safety. The colony was successfully re-established after 1601, spreading around Youghal, Kinsale and Baltimore and exporting wool and cattle. By 1641 there were over 20,000 settlers and the remnants of these families can still be traced in parts of West Cork.

The end of Gaelic Ireland

The ruthless conquest of Ireland under Elizabeth I extended English control far beyond Dublin, but it met with strong resistance in Ulster, where the queen thought she had a willing ally in Hugh O'Neill. Instead, joining forces with Red Hugh O'Donnell, he rose in rebellion in what became known as the Nine Years War (1593-1603). Lacking artillery but employing successful guerrilla tactics, the rebels spread across Ireland, attempting unsuccessfully to enlist the support of the Anglo-Irish. Support came from the Spanish who landed a storm-weakened army at Kinsale in 1601, but they were trapped there. The English forces, who by now had been strengthened by the new military leadership of Lord Mountjoy, pursued a scorched earth policy as they hounded the rebels. At the same time the rebellion which had broken out in Munster was effectively met by Sir George Carew. The rebel leaders, O'Neill and O'Donnell, had no choice but to move their armies south in an attempt to join forces with the beleaguered Spanish. A tactical blunder by O'Neill handed victory to Mountjoy, the Spanish secured terms and sailed home, and the greatest challenge yet to English rule – one that would not be repeated until the War of Independence in the early 20th century – was over. It cost the English a massive £2 million but English control over Ireland was now complete.

An emotive and emblematic postscript to the end of Gaelic Ireland came in 1607 when the pardoned and humbled O'Neill left Ireland for ever, in the company of other chieftains. Known as the 'flight of the earls' it concluded with the death of Hugh O'Neill in Rome in 1616. It was the legacy of the flight of the earls and its aftermath that erupted on the streets of Derry and Belfast in 1968.

"They looked like anatomies of death; they spake like ghosts crying out of their graves ... And if they found a plot of watercress or shamrocks, they flocked there as if to a feast." Edmund Spenser, author of 'The Faerie Queen', describing the aftermath of the Desmond rebellion in Munster, where he was stationed.

Oliver Cromwell

Oliver Cromwell, with God on his side, meted out divine revenge for the 1641 rising to the "barbarous and bloodthirsty Irish". The massacre at Drogheda, where possibly 1,000 citizens were slaughtered, has ensured Cromwell's infamy as Ireland's most ruthless public enemy, though a remarkable book by Tom Reilly, published in 1999, paints a different picture (see page 136).

Cromwell went on to capture Cork, Kinsale and Bandon from the rebels, Catholicism was driven underground and his soldiers, as well as fresh waves of settlers, were rewarded with extensive grants of confiscated land.

Plantation and rebellion

The seeds of the present discord in Northern Ireland were laid within two weeks of Hugh O'Neill's departure, for this is how long it took to submit proposals for the plantation of the lands left behind in the flight of the earls. Ulster was surveyed, mapped and divided as thousands of Protestants took root, especially Scots in Down and Antrim, as both landlords and tenants. Such was the influx that by 1636 the government prohibited further emigration from Scotland without licence.

Settlers, known officially as undertakers, also moved into other parts of Ireland, and a radical and far-reaching change in the ownership of land took place. Nearly all of Gaelic Ireland was owned by about 2,000 Catholic gentry, but by 1660 they held only a little over 20%, and by the beginning of the 18th century the figure was below 15%.

Old English families grew alarmed at anti-Catholic measures and the threats to their property rights, and rebellion broke out in Ulster in 1641. Many of the leaders considered themselves loyal to the Crown, while others like Sir Phelim O'Neill were probably more keen to recover their lost land. The real revolutionaries were the native dispossessed Irish who rebelled against the injustice of plantation and the consequent shortage of land. The 1641 rising has gone down in loyalist mythology as a savage sectarian bloodletting, and violent outrages were indeed inflicted on Protestant settlers. Many were stripped naked in cruel mockery of having arrived in Ireland with nothing, and driven from their homes to perish in the winter cold. As many as 8,000 may have died, but propaganda multiplied this number out of all proportion and fuelled anti-Catholic hatred with lurid and exaggerated tales of torture and rape, and a premeditated plot to ethnically cleanse Ireland of Protestants. The rising was used as justification for the confiscation of two million acres of Irish land, while in England the rebellion became entwined with the emerging civil war as Charles I was accused of supporting the rebels. In 1649, after the execution of Charles, an army of 12,000 men landed in Ireland under Oliver Cromwell. When he left nine months later the ground was prepared for the final chapter in the colonization of Ireland, and the only refuge left for Catholics was across the Shannon in land-poor Connacht – thus the saying 'to hell or to Connacht'.

Siege of Derry and the Battle of the Boyne

An estimated 150,000 emigrants arrived in Ireland in the 20 years after 1652, and it was the 17th century that saw large-scale deforestation as a direct result of the felling of trees for charcoal to sustain English industry. The second half of the century also witnessed a European power struggle that was to involve Ireland in a highly momentous manner. James II, who had been deposed from the English throne landed in Kinsale in 1689 with French troops. The new king of England, William of Orange, was allied with Spain, the Dutch and the Pope, and together they were determined to oppose any increase in French power. "If Ireland should be lost

England will follow" was the fear in the English Houses of Parliament when they voted funds of over £1 million for another army to land in Ireland and oppose James. European politics became entwined with the Catholic and Protestant struggle in Ireland, and the stage was set for another dramatic confrontation.

The defeat of James was played out in two events that were to shape Ireland in fact and in myth: the resistance of Derry to James' army, and the Battle of the Boyne, north of Dublin. The military commander in Derry, Robert Lundy, with the support of the Protestant bishop, was prepared to recognize James as the legitimate king before he arrived in Ireland, but many townspeople, alarmed at the thought of another 1641 massacre, thought otherwise. In December 1688, 13 apprentice boys slammed the gates of Derry shut and Lundy, whose name and image is still reviled in loyalist wall art in Northern Ireland, was forced to flee the city in disguise. In April 1689 James laid siege to a defiant Derry – 'No surrender' was the clarion call – until, in July, a Williamite fleet managed to break through with supplies and save the city from starvation.

In May 1689, the last Irish parliament to include Catholics until 1922 took place in Dublin and in July William's army defeated James at the Battle of the Boyne, with cathedrals across Catholic Europe offering prayers in thanksgiving. King James fled the battlefield, earning for himself the epitaph *Séamus a chaca* (James the Shit), though Irish resistance lasted another year. The end truly came with Sarsfield surrendering at Limerick in October 1691 after securing an honourable peace and exile to France, where he died two years later fighting William of Orange: "Oh, that this were for Ireland" were his reported last words. Pockets of Irish soldiers fighting in Europe became known as the 'Wild Geese'; one became a general in the Russian army, another a governor of Spanish Louisiana.

The 18th century

The treaty negotiated at Limerick in 1691 promised religious tolerance, but this was reneged on with the passing of laws like one in 1695 that made it illegal for a Catholic to own a horse worth more than £5. By this time only about five percent of useful land in Ireland was owned by Catholics. The Protestant ruling class ruled the roost, Dublin flourished as their commercial and cultural capital, and the Protestant Ascendancy seemed too secure to ever feel threatened again. It was not to be.

The decade which began in 1790 is one of the most important in Irish history, not just for the tumultuous events of the 1798 uprising but also for the fact that it saw the birth of Republicanism, Unionism and Orangeism.

The Irish Parliament can be traced back to medieval times, but it met very irregularly and even in the 18th century only once a year. Like its parent British institution, it was riddled with patronage and, quite apart from bizarre franchises that led to the election of MPs for 'rotten boroughs' where no one actually voted, only Protestants and Presbyterians were allowed to vote in elections. There were few Presbyterian MPs, mainly due to the property criteria for those eligible to vote, and in Ulster this led to Presbyterian interest in parliamentary reform. For most of the 18th century, the Parliament sitting in Dublin was completely subordinate to Westminster, but with the emergence of the Volunteers, and the pressure they were able to apply, there were constitutional changes in 1792 that came to be known under the term 'legislative independence'.

The Volunteers were a part-time military force originally created in 1778-1779 for the purpose of protecting Ireland against a French invasion and generally maintaining law and order at a time when regular troops were needed to deal with the American Revolution. Predominantly based in Ulster and rising to 60,000 in number, the force consisted of urban, middle-class men, and as such emerged as a powerful expression of that class's aspirations for a greater say in the running of their country.

The 1792 reforms did not actually make the Irish Parliament autonomous, but they did help create a political climate which nurtured the idea that further constitutional change was both desirable and possible. There were demands for more regular sittings of Parliament, an extension of the Protestant electorate and other reforms, but they all came to nothing. English aristocratic rule, operating through Dublin Castle, remained firmly entrenched. The major reason for the failure of the post-1792 movement, led by Dublin radicals like James Napper Tandy (c.1737-1803) and the Belfast Presbyterian William Drennan (1754-1820), was the Catholic question. This revolved around the repeal of the Penal Laws, an issue that aroused deep-rooted fears amongst Protestants whose worst nightmares imagined a return to sectarian massacres and Catholic supremacy. They therefore argued for further political reforms, but these were clearly not to include equal rights for Catholics. Yet without the involvement of Catholics it was impossible for any reform movement to move up a gear and mount an effective challenge to British hegemony. As Wolfe Tone put it, it was foolish to plan "an edifice of freedom on a foundation of monopoly".

Wolfe Tone and 1798

Wolfe Tone changed everything by confronting the Catholic question and successfully arguing that Catholics be brought into the political equation. Tone was by no means the first to propound the idea that Irish people should unite behind a non-denominational front, but he did crystallize the notion and made it common currency. Towards the end of 1791 he was invited to Belfast to help establish a new political association being formed there by Presbyterian radicals. It was Tone who suggested the name 'United Irishmen' for this new political club, and on his return to Dublin he quickly set up a branch there consisting of both Protestants and Catholics. Events moved quickly within the next couple of years: the Volunteers were outlawed, and in 1794 the Dublin Society of United Irishmen was too. This pushed the movement underground, closer to outright republicanism and the contemplation of armed insurrection. When war broke out between Britain and France, Tone saw the opportunity to recruit some foreign help.

The first French invasion force was defeated by winter storms in 1796, but it gave the British a jolt – "England has not had such an escape since the Spanish Armada", declared Tone at the time – and the Irish such a fillip that within the next 18 months the United Irishmen claimed to have well over 250,000 members. The British authorities too were not idle, and developed counter-insurgency policies that seriously weakened the effectiveness of the general insurrection that came in 1798. Many of the leaders were arrested, and the revolutionary movement suffered from a lack of co-ordination and the prevarications of the French in mounting another invasion fleet. Napoleon became more interested in a campaign in Egypt than in Europe's northern fringes, and his ships were in the Mediterranean when the uprising broke out.

The 1798 insurrection broke out across the country, starting in counties Dublin, Kildare and Meath in May, when mail coaches leaving the capital were stopped and set on fire. Government forces subdued the rebels, as they also did in eastern Ulster, but the uprising in County Wexford was more problematic. It cost around 30,000 lives, and was easily the most bloody event in Irish history since the 17th century.

Union and Daniel O'Connell

The events of 1798 convinced Britain that only the abolition of the Irish Parliament and a union of the English and Irish kingdoms could guarantee security. "Ireland is like a ship on fire, it must be extinguished or cut adrift", observed the British prime minister, Pitt, who set about securing the Act of Union which came into effect in 1801. The Catholic clergy was won over by a promise of Catholic emancipation that would allow Catholics to sit in the new parliament and hold other important positions, and existing members of the Irish Parliament were bought off with pensions and bribes.

The year 1803 marked the short-lived and abortive rebellion planned by 25-year-old Robert Emmet, who paid for his daring by being sentenced to be hanged, drawn and quartered. "Let no man write my epitaph. When my country takes her place

Theobold Wolfe Tone

Wolfe Tone was born in 1763 into a Protestant middle-class family in Dublin. His father was a coachmaker and his mother the daughter of a sea captain. He more or less drifted into Dublin politics, and the height of his early political ambitions was a hoped-for seat in the Irish Parliament. The French Revolution and Thomas Paine's *Rights of Man* helped radicalize his thinking and in 1791 he published *An Argument on Behalf of the Catholics of Ireland*. Calling for a united front of Catholics and Protestants, Tone's pamphlet was enormously popular and influential. In 1792 a further 10,000 copies were printed and Dublin Castle sent a copy to London to warn of this dangerous new polemic. By 1796 Tone was in France promoting a French invasion of Ireland, and before the year was out he was sailing into Bantry Bay with over 14,000 French troops, only to be defeated by adverse weather that saw the remnants of the fleet returning to France in January 1797. In 1798 Tone was once again on board a French ship as part of a third invasion force (the second invasion had landed earlier in north Mayo). Bad weather again thwarted the expedition, but it was anyway too late to effect the outcome of the general uprising of 1798. Even the few ships that made it to Donegal were intercepted by the British. The ship Tone was on decided to make a fight of it, and Tone himself refused the offer of escaping on a French frigate. Tone was captured and sentenced to death, but took his own life before he could be hanged.

among the nations of the earth, then, and not till then, let my epitaph be written. I have done." Emmet's last words from the dock in 1803.

The promised Catholic emancipation did not happen until a new leader arrived on the scene, Daniel O'Connell (1775-1847). The man who has given his name to countless streets in Irish towns was a prosperous middle-class radical of liberal instincts who captured the minds and hearts of ordinary Irish people. He created a political mass movement for Catholic emancipation through a Catholic Association with a membership of one penny a month. It was a revolutionary act and one that would reverberate through Europe, for never before had a popular reform movement been organized in this manner. Membership climbed to 500,000, and with 100,000 Catholic 40-shilling freeholders with a vote the time was ripe for change. Public rallies were held throughout the country, and O'Connell stood as a candidate in a Clare by-election. He gained nearly 70% of the vote, and the British knew that a concession had to be made. Catholic emancipation became a reality in 1829, and a new mood of confidence spread like wildfire across Ireland.

Buoyed by success, O'Connell set about securing home rule – a repeal of the Act of Union and the return of an Irish Parliament. It was a far cry from Wolfe Tone's republicanism, and although it was meant to be achieved without physical force it had a very physical dimension. Giant public meetings, dubbed 'monster meetings' by *The Times*, attracted hundreds of thousands of people and, although he tried to keep within the law, legal grounds were found for him to be tried for sedition and he was sentenced to jail. Now aged 70, he was released after six months. A younger wing of the movement was now calling for more radical opposition to British rule.

Nationalism and Famine

Thomas Davis (1814-1845) split with O'Connell and articulated a new and more exciting idea by calling for a brake on Anglicization, a revival of the Irish language and a "nationalism which may embrace Protestant, Catholic and Dissenter ... the Irishman of a hundred generations and the stranger who is within our gate." Davis died suddenly of scarlet fever, but an Ulster Presbyterian, John Mitchel (1815-1875), took the movement further forward by agitating for an independent Irish republic. He was sentenced to transportation for 14 years in 1848, and a small rebellion broke out the same year but achieved little.

The failure of the 1848 rebellion was due not least to the awful Famine that was traumatizing Ireland (see box page 406). A potato blight was first noticed in 1845 when the population of Ireland was over 8 million and by 1851, when the Famine was over, the population had dropped to 6½ million; by 1901 the figure was 4½ million. Death through starvation and disease accounted for a million deaths, and accelerated the process of emigration from Ireland as peasants desperately sought a new and better life in North America and Australia. The Famine has been seen by some historians as an act of genocide, with ships leaving some of the worse-affected areas carrying profitable grain for export to Europe while peasants died for want of a meal. Others point out that the prevailing philosophy of free trade made it impossible for people to think otherwise, and indeed for some the haemorrhaging of people was seen as a positive economic gain.

Fenians and Home Rule

Irish tenants had no security of tenure on the land they rented, and if they could not afford the rent most landlords had them evicted so that the land could be rented to someone else. In 1850 a Tenant League was formed for land reform, but in 1858 an organization of more consequence was formed, the Irish Republican Brotherhood (IRB), more popularly known as the Fenians. In 1867 they mounted an abortive uprising: some of the participants were hanged, and a failed Fenian rescue of prisoners in London led to an explosion which killed 30. For his part in this botched rescue a Fenian was executed in the last public hanging in England.

Fenianism focused the minds of English liberal politicians like Gladstone on the problem of Ireland. In 1870 he introduced the first in what would become a series of land reforms that the Tenant League had called for. At the same time a new Home Rule movement arose in Ireland, its leader, Charles Stewart Parnell, taking up where Daniel O'Connell had foundered. Parnell, a Protestant landlord with an American mother, was quite prepared to use the threat of direct action alongside conventional political action, and joined forces with the newly formed Land League. The Land League was founded by the Fenian Michael Davitt in 1879 with Parnell as president, and together they led a formidable campaign. Davitt used official statistics to show that fewer than 20,000 men owned the whole of Ireland; in fact fewer than 2,000 owned 70% of the land, while 3 million tenants and labourers owned nothing. Radical mass action, which became known as the Land War, demanded redistribution of land with compensation to landlords, and backed it up with a vigorous campaign that became famous for ostracizing anyone who dared take over the land of an evicted tenant. One of the first to suffer was a Captain Boycott – hence the new synonym for ostracism – and when Parnell was imprisoned in 1881 he became even more of a hero, and a policy of withholding rents altogether was put into action. He was released with a promise by Gladstone to introduce further, more far-reaching land reforms.

Even before the divorce issue destroyed Parnell (see box) he had started to lose some of his political clout in Ireland when he failed to back campaigns for more vigorous action for land reform. His sister Anna (see box page 164) never lost her drive in organizing the Ladies' Land League, and struggled tirelessly across America for the cause, suffering disillusionment only when she realized that the Land League tended to benefit larger tenants and was not prepared to see through the need for a radical redistribution of land.

Parnell's downfall

After the 1885 general election, Parnell's Home Rule party wiped the board in southern Ireland and the following year Gladstone announced his conversion to the need for a dissolution of the union. Aged 76, he introduced the first Home Rule Bill to Parliament and then a bombshell came out of the sky in the form of one Captain O'Shea who, when filing for divorce on the grounds of his wife's adultery, named Parnell as the third party. It gave opponents of Home Rule a moral excuse for denouncing Parnell and when the Irish Catholic Church jumped up on the moral bandwagon, the Irish parliamentary party was split. Parnell married Katherine O'Shea in 1891 but died the following year, a broken and tired man.

Gladstone's land reforms were carried even further by later Liberal and Conservative administrations which sought quite consciously to "kill Home Rule by kindness". The Ashbourne Act in 1885 allowed landlords to sell land to their tenants at fixed prices, and this was encouraged by the Wyndham Act of 1903 which saw landlords gaining a 12% payment, the Bonus, on top of the sale price. George Wyndham is said to have encountered an Irish peer in Monte Carlo brandishing his stack of chips and exclaiming to the Chief Secretary, "George! George! The Bonus." These reforms saw the end of the Protestant Ascendancy, because without the regular income from rents their economic base was terminally fractured. Leaking roofs went unrepaired, and as many of the 'big houses' entered the final chapters of their existence, so too did the memorable lifestyle of those who lived in them. To many observers, like Louis MacNeice, the end was long overdue: "In most cases these houses maintain no culture worth speaking of – nothing but absolute bravado, an insidious bonhomie, and a way with horses."

The land reforms introduced a whole new class of peasant proprietors, but the problem of Ireland – or rather, Ireland's problem with England – did not go away. A new struggle for national independence was under way.

Cultural revolution

"Damn Home Rule! What we're out for is the land. The land matters. All the rest is talk." This remark by a nationalist was recorded during the Land War, but the speaker was wrong, for all the rest was not just talk. In the closing decades of the 19th century, an emerging sense of national consciousness gave rise to a cultural revolution that allied itself with and radicalized the political movement in preparation for a break with Britain. The cultural renaissance started with events like the 1884 founding of the Gaelic Athletic Association (GAA) and its call for Irish sports to replace English ones.

In 1893 the Gaelic League was established in the wake of a seminal lecture by the Protestant Douglas Hyde on "The necessity of de-Anglicising the Irish people." "We are daily importing from England ... her music, her dances and her manifold mannerisms, her games and her pastimes, to the utter discredit of our own grand national sports... as though we were ashamed of them," Hyde declared. In response there followed a dramatic literary revolution that began with Anglo-Irish writers: Lady Gregory, WB Yeats and others founded the Irish Literary Theatre, later the Abbey Theatre, in 1898, and the following year Arthur Griffith started the *United Irishmen* newspaper. Griffith knew Yeats, but he also knew the socialist James Connolly, and out of such a matrix evolved the movement for complete separation from Britain and not just Home Rule. Sinn Féin ('Ourselves Alone') was formed in 1903, and the idea of withdrawing elected Irish MPs from the British Parliament at Westminster began to take shape.

At this stage Irish MPs were still committed to Home Rule rather than complete independence, and when elections in 1910 left the nationalists holding the balance of power it seemed certain that the Liberal party would have no choice but to push through a Home Rule Bill. The ability of the House of Lords to veto legislation was limited by the Liberals to two years, and when Home Rule legislation was blocked by the House of Lords in 1912, it was only a matter of waiting. In September 1914 the bill became an act. By that time, however, events outside Parliament's control were shaping Ireland's future.

Easter 1916

Armed opposition by Protestants to Home Rule in Ulster and the obvious willingness of groups in Ulster and Britain to subvert Home Rule quickly led to the formation of parallel nationalist forces. The Irish Volunteers were founded in 1913, and in March of the following year the Irish Citizen Army was re-formed from a nucleus force that had emerged in response to the lockout in a great Dublin strike of the year before. Militants like Hanna Sheehy Skeffington formed *Cumann na mBan* (Association of Women) to make sure women were not left out of the struggle. Erskine Childers, with his wife Molly and Mary Spring Rice, imported guns on his yacht *Asgard*, and soon Volunteers were marching openly on the streets of Dublin.

The outbreak of the First World War in August 1914 led to the suspension of the Home Rule Act, and when Redmond, the leader of the Irish MPs, declared support for the war and a willingness for nationalists to volunteer, this led to a decisive break with Sinn Féin. Redmond and the bulk of the Volunteers formed their own group and the radicals who were left, members of the IRB, began planning for an armed uprising in conjunction with James Connolly and the Irish Citizen Army.

On Easter Monday, 24 April 1916 strategic areas around Dublin were occupied, and an Irish Republic was declared from outside the occupied General Post Office on O'Connell Street.

While middle-class Dubliners were quick to condemn the rising as British troops moved in and the city centre became a war zone, the rebels gained some support in working-class areas. The insurgents surrendered on 29 April with the loss of around 64 Republicans, 132 British troops and 250 civilians. Military trials and the shooting dead of 15 rebels, the first execution of rebels since Robert Emmet in 1803, led to a dramatic shift in public opinion and a surge in support for Sinn Féin. In July 1917 Eamon de Valera, the only commander of the rising to survive, won a by-election in Clare and became president of Sinn Féin. By the following year, after the death of Redmond, the Irish parliamentary party withdrew from Westminster and in the 1918 general election Sinn Féin swept the board. At the beginning of 1919, an alternative Irish government was formed in Dublin, with the minutes recorded in Irish and French, and the Republic, first declared in 1916, was ratified. In the same month the first shots were fired in what became known as the War of Independence.

War of Independence

By January 1919 the Volunteers, who had shot dead two Royal Irish Constabulary men in Tipperary that month, were becoming known as the Irish Republican Army (IRA). Britain faced the problem that, much as they wanted to ignore the illegally constituted Irish government, it was fast becoming the de facto ruling body for the people of Ireland. Homeowners were paying taxes, in the form of rates, to the new Dáil Éireann (Irish Parliament) and alternative Sinn Féin courts were operating across the country.

In Clare two men were left on an island for three weeks as a punishment by a Sinn Féin court and when the RIC tried to rescue them by boat the two men hurled stones at them and waved them away because they were 'prisoners of the Republic'.

The ranks of the IRA were being filled by professional soldiers returning from the First World War, and Michael Collins emerged as the charismatic and intelligent director of organization for the new rebel army. Collins had taken part in the 1916 rising and was subsequently elected to the first Dáil for South Cork, becoming minister for finance, but he achieved popular and lasting fame as a guerrilla Republican fighting the British. There were by now around 3,000 IRA men on active duty, and the British were forced into recruiting thousands of ex-servicemen to help the RIC defeat them. Known as the Black and Tans (a famous pack of hounds in Limerick) because they wore khaki and police caps and belts (there was no immediate supply of police uniforms available), they were responsible for retaliating against Collins' most daringly planned deed in 1920 when 10 government intelligence officers were assassinated one Sunday morning. The Black and Tans retaliated by executing three prisoners in jail, and driving lorries into Croke Park where a Gaelic Athletic Association (GAA) game was taking place. They fired into the crowd, killing 14 and shooting a Tipperary player. The next month, December 1920, a large part of Cork City was burned in retaliation for a guerrilla attack that killed 18 Black and Tans at Kilmichael in County Cork.

Attempts by British intelligence to infiltrate the guerrilla Republican movement failed because its officers could not understand the Irish accent; surveillance equipment, according to a secret report written in 1921 by the head of Dublin Castle (the headquarters of Britain's counter-insurgency group), failed because "microphones of English manufacture seem ill-adapted to the Irish brogue." The report made an observation that could easily have been from 1970s or 80s Belfast: "It has been said that no European can fathom the mind of an Oriental, and it might equally be said that no Englishman can fully grasp the inner psychology of the Irish rebel character."

Partition and civil war

By May 1920, when the IRA were able to launch an attack on the Custom House in the heart of the capital, the British were ready to start talking. A truce was signed in July and peace talks scheduled in London. The perceived difficulty for the British in recognizing an Irish republic was the impact it might have in other parts of the Empire, especially India, so they bargained for an independent Ireland owing allegiance to King and Commonwealth. The Ulster problem was dealt with by the partition of Ireland, and the notion of a boundary commission that, the Irish delegates were told, would later recommend the transfer to Ireland of counties with a nationalist majority and thus render impractical the continued partition of Northern Ireland.

The sticking point was not partition but the required oath to the King and the British Commonwealth, the latter term being used here for the first time by Britain, and the denial of republican status to an independent Ireland. The delegates should have consulted with de Valera and others who were back in Dublin before signing any treaty, but Michael Collins, who was in London, knew that his guerrilla army was running out of ammunition; so, on the morning of 10 December, the treaty was signed in London pending ratification in the Dáil in Dublin.

The treaty was ratified but it was a very close call – a majority of only seven secured its passage – and de Valera and his anti-Treaty supporters walked out of the Dáil in protest.

The split vote in the Treaty debate in the Dáil also led to a split in the IRA, and those opposed to the deal signed in London became known as the Irregulars. In April 1922 the Four Courts in Dublin were occupied by Irregulars, and following the assassination of a British army officer in London demands were made by Britain for action against the rebels. In June the Four Courts were shelled under orders from Collins, and a civil war began that divided families, occasioned terrible atrocities on both sides, and led to a trauma in Irish politics that was felt well into the 1970s. It also killed far more people – over 800 government soldiers and around 5,000 anti-Treaty men – than the War of Independence, even though it lasted only a year.

Anti-revolution, 1920s-1950s

When the Irish finally took charge of their own country – or at least most of it – they inherited a sorry state of affairs. The British had confined industrial activity to the north, and the rural economy of the new state was stagnant after years of neglect. The political and social conservatism of the Catholic Church helped institutionalize a national malaise that was to last nearly half a century. In 1927 de Valera left Sinn Féin and founded a new party, Fianna Fáil ('Soldiers of Destiny'), which became the main opposition in the Dáil.

Disagreement with Britain over the payment of land annuities – de Valera refused to pay – led to Britain imposing high tariffs on Irish imports. Ireland retaliated in like manner, and life was hard for many. After the turmoil of revolutionary struggle and a bitter civil war, Ireland's leaders embarked on a social and political programme decidedly unrevolutionary in nature. In 1926 a Committee of Inquiry into Evil Literature led to the creation of a censorship board that kept most 20th-century classics out of the country. Freud, Sartre, Steinbeck, Salinger, Orwell, Gide, Mailer, Tennessee Williams, Dylan Thomas were all banned, not to mention every Irish writer then winning recognition elsewhere: Shaw, O'Casey, Joyce (for *Stephen Hero*, not *Ulysses*), Beckett, Behan, Kate O'Brien. Under successive de Valera governments the country went into a near-terminal state of moribund conservatism: Sean O'Casey summed up the malaise by declaring "We're standing on our knees now." The country closed in on itself, and the legacy of resentment saw Ireland refuse to take sides in World War II, withdraw from the Commonwealth and decline to join NATO.

In 1937 de Valera produced a new constitution that enshrined church ideology: blasphemy was made a crime, divorce made impossible and, until the 1998 referendum allowed for their change, Articles 2 and 3 claimed the right to unite the whole of Ireland and oppose partition. In a radio broadcast in 1943 de Valera evoked a vision of Ireland as a rural paradise filled "with the contests of athletic youths and the laughter of comely maidens".

1960s – the awakening

In 1959 de Valera finally moved aside to become President of Ireland, a non-executive and largely ceremonial role, and his successor, Sean Lemass, started to breath new life into the country. The emigration rate halved as new jobs were created, and the ebullience of this era was enshrined in John F Kennedy's presidential visit in 1963. The great-grandson of an Irish emigrant, Kennedy's visit gave a much-needed boost to the national psyche. Three years later saw the 50th anniversary of the Easter Rising, and the event was marked by the blowing up of the 36m-high Nelson's Pillar in O'Connell Street in Dublin by unknown nationalists. The event, causing no injuries or damage to property, was received with glee, much humour being directed at the military experts who managed to damage surrounding properties while demolishing what remained of the statue's column. In 1962 the Republic's own television channel was established.

The Haughey era

Charles Haughey attracted a few nicknames during his long reign as Taoiseach between 1979 and 1992; while respected by many, his political machinations and dubious accumulation of wealth and privilege led to him also being labelled 'The Great National Bastard'. An acronym, GUBU ('Grotesque, Unprecedented, Bizarre and Unbelievable') was coined to define the era, based on Haughey's response to events surrounding a suspected serial killer staying in the apartment of the Attorney General and the latter's decision to go on holiday before discussing it with him.

Ireland was officially neutral during the Second World War. Conscription was never extended to Northern Ireland. Yet 68,000 men enlisted from Southern Ireland and 52,900 from Northern Ireland. Southern Irishmen won eight Victoria Crosses, one went to a Belfast sailor.

Ulster Says No

The British Conservative Party's attitude to Ireland and the nature of present-day opposition to the Good Friday Agreement can be directly traced back to events in the early decades of the 20th century. Opposition to Home Rule in Ulster led to calls for retaining the union with Britain and Edward Carson, the lawyer who destroyed Oscar Wilde in court, emerged as the unionist leader. The Ulster Volunteer Force was formed in 1913, arms were imported from Germany, and calls for violent opposition to Home Rule became strident. There was no doubting the willingness of the 'law and order' Conservative Party led by Bonar Law to support such extra-parliamentary measures, and the façade of parliamentary politics was further weakened in 1914 when 58 British army officers stationed at the Curragh made it clear that they would refuse to take action against an armed uprising in Ulster. The Orange Order, resurrecting the 1641 rising and the Siege of Derry, was able to point to the Catholic Church's ruling that mixed marriages between Catholics and Protestants take place only in Catholic churches and that children of such marriages be brought up as Catholics. The fear that Home Rule meant Rome Rule was not paranoia; it was a fear fully justified in the light of the later Catholic-inspired legislation that characterized post-independence Ireland, but unionists acted as if the whole of Ulster was Protestant when they only constituted 56% of the population and held a majority in only four counties. This did not prevent Bonar Law from pledging active support for resistance to Home Rule: "We intend, with the help of the Almighty, to keep the pledge, and the keeping of it involves more than the making of speeches."

GUBU sums up fairly well the life of a politician who in 1970 was on trial for gun running to the besieged nationalists in the north, before going on to manage successfully the economy by winning the confidence of both business and trade unions. He bought Inishvickillane, a small island off the Dingle Peninsula, and a mansion set in 200 acres of land, at the same time as owing a bank nearly IR£1 million. Largesse from important businessmen, most spectacularly IR£1 million from Ben Dunne (of Dunne's stores) which had not been declared to the income tax authorities, have been the subject of government tribunals, and there is no shortage of other scandals associated with Haughey's reign as Taoiseach. He finally came to political grief in 1992 over the phone tapping of journalists, but the Houdini of his age has still somehow managed to survive imprisonment over his financial shenanigans.

Contemporary Ireland

After Haughey's resignation in 1992 Albert Reynolds was elected Taoiseach of a Fianna Fáil-Progressive Democrat (PD) government, but this fell apart when Reynolds accused a PD of dishonest testimony to an inquiry into fraud in beef exports. It was a deliberate attempt to force an election and gain an outright majority for Fianna Fáil, but it failed miserably, and this time a coalition government with Labour was formed. Another election followed in 1994 and a Fine Gael-Labour government took its turn until June 1997, when Fianna Fáil and the Progressive Democrats came to power under Bertie Ahern. This remains the ruling coalition of government, although in Ireland general elections and new governments are formed with what seems startling frequency.

Travelling through the countryside in the west of Ireland one is struck by what appears to be a cow-based economy. Indeed, over 70% of farm output comes from

Fianna Fáil and Fine Gael – Spot the Difference?

Sometimes, it seems, the historical difference between the two main political parties in Ireland is the only one worth mentioning. Fine Gael (pronounced 'Feen Gale') was formed in 1933 from an older pro-Treaty party whereas Fianna Fáil (pronounced 'Feena Foil') was founded by de Valera from the anti-Treaty faction of nationalists. Fianna Fáil still carries the mantle of republicanism, and because they were in power at the time of the 1998 negotiations over the North they were able to sell the Agreement to nationalists in the Republic in a way that Fine Gael could never have done. Apart from this ideological difference, it is difficult to tell the two apart. Fine Gael portrays itself as more middle class, gaining more support from farmers, professionals and business people than Fianna Fáil, which likes to present itself as the party of ordinary working people and small farmers. Their economic policies are basically the same, and what makes contemporary politics in Ireland so boring is the fact that the other main parties, the Progressive Democrats and Labour, offer few alternatives to the electorate. Coalition governments come and go, and much of the electorate seems content to have it continue in this way. Change might be in the air, though, for Sinn Féin has moved onto the political stage south of the border and is promising to shake the complacency of Fianna Fáil by challenging its stale claims to the nationalist legacy. The next general election, due in 2006, could, just possibly, see Sinn Féin holding the balance of power in the Republic. Now that would be interesting…

cattle and milk. In the eastern counties the land supports more cereals and giant fields of barley and beet thrive alongside the ubiquitous herds of black and white Friesian cows. What is surprising, however, is that less than 15% of the working population is engaged with the land. The prosperity that is so evident in contemporary Ireland is based on new light industries like electronics and computer components. Ireland's GDP per head now exceeds the European national average, and Eurokids flock to the capital for work and language learning. The 1916 rising is no longer celebrated, problems in the North are being argued over in constitutional non-violent terms, and Irish people at long last feel confident about themselves because, as more than one commentator has noted, Ireland may have lost the leprechaun but has most definitely found the pot of gold.

There are signs, however, that the pot of gold is too dependent on foreign investment for its own good. Every now and again redundancies are announced when an American company closes down one of its factories and decamps for better profit margins elsewhere. Ireland is dependent on American economic power and this affects the country's political autonomy. Claiming to be neutral, the Irish government allowed American warplanes to land and refuel at Shannon airport for its invasion of Iraq in 2003. In March 2005 Sinn Féin leaders, used to being feted at the White House as peacemakers were badly snubbed by the Bush administration following the accusations of their prior knowledge of the December 2004 bank robbery in Belfast and their reaction to the murder of Robert McCartney in a pub brawl by people known to be members of the IRA. It was this treatment that probably gave Gerry Adams enough power over the IRA to announce in April 2005 that the only future in Northern Ireland lay in democratic and legal means.

Northern Ireland

Origins of the province

Northern Ireland came into existence with the Government of Ireland Act of 1920 and remained within the United Kingdom after the rest of the island achieved dominion status following the treaty of 1921. The story starts with the plantation of Ulster in the 17th century (see page 592), but the more pressing background to the partition of Ireland lay with the successful resistance of Ulster unionists in the 1911-1914 period to the increasing likelihood of Home Rule for Ireland (see page 596). They originally wanted to be ruled directly from London, but grew to cherish their devolved parliament, where they enjoyed an overall majority of seats, once it became clear the British would let them get on with what was in effect a one-party state. In 1925 the boundary commission recommended no significant changes in the border between the Free State and Northern Ireland, and an issue that was not paramount in the causes or course of the civil war was left to fester.

From inequality to direct rule

From its inception in 1920 until the Good Friday Agreement of 1998, Northern Ireland was an artificial construct designed to secure unionist control. Three counties of Ulster – Cavan, Donegal and Monaghan – were excluded from its creation because their majority Catholic populations would have weakened the ability of unionists to control the state and form every government, until direct rule from Westminster was established in 1972. The Northern Ireland Parliament began life in Belfast City Hall in June 1921, moving to the grandiloquent, purpose-built building at Stormont, in the eastern suburbs of Belfast, in 1932. By this time, gerrymandering of the constituencies ensured unionist majorities and the Special Powers Act of 1922 gave the government the right to prohibit meetings or processions without cause. The 12th July, marking the defeat of Catholics at the Battle of the Boyne (see page 592), became a national holiday and Easter processions by Catholics were attacked. The Royal Ulster Constabulary (RUC) was formed in 1922 and its Catholic element rapidly declined from a peak of around 20% in 1923 to half that.

The civil and political strife that erupted in 1968, and which led four years later to direct rule, was the result of decades of misrule which saw Catholics become second-class citizens, discriminated against in housing and employment and their cultural identity as Irish people vigorously suppressed.

The Northern Ireland Civil Rights Movement, modelling itself on the movement for racial equality in the USA, was formed in 1967. The following year saw their marches attacked by loyalist gangs. In 1969 an Apprentice Boys' march notched up the level of violence. The event was an annual march, triumphantly celebrating the siege of 1689 (see page 592) that paraded through Catholic residential areas in Derry, but this time the march provoked rioting. The Protestant backlash saw Catholics fleeing as refugees across the border in trains that were stoned by mobs as they passed through Protestant areas. British troops were called in to restore order, the IRA re-emerged, direct rule was introduced and 30 years of bombing and bloodshed followed. Unionist control of the Stormont government between 1920 and 1972 allowed its permanent majority to vote down every nationalist proposal, bar one solitary measure – the 1930 Wild Birds Act.

It is easy to blame sectarian unionism for the inequalities and iniquities that led to the explosive events of the late 1960s and their aftermath, but it is equally clear that the sectarian Catholicism of the southern Ireland state gave Protestants in the North good reason to fear for their cultural survival in a united Ireland.

The British Army arrived in Northern Ireland in August 1969, intended as a short-term measure to deal with the escalating violence that was developing

Glossary of political terms

Alliance Party Formed in 1970, a non-sectarian mix of middle-class members of both communities, with seats in the Assembly but none at Westminster

Black and Tans British recruits, so-called from the colours of their uniform, recruited to combat republicans fighting for independence after 1918; infamous for their brutality

Civil War War that broke out in Ireland, after the signing of the 1921 Treaty, between those who accepted the Treaty and those who opposed it

Continuity IRA Also known as Irish Continuity Army Council, came to public notice in 1996 after claiming responsibility for a number of attacks

Dáil Eireann The Irish parliament, often referred to as simply the Dáil (pronounced *doil*)

DUP The Democratic Unionist Party; led by Ian Paisley, vehemently anti-Republican and until very recently vigorously opposed to the Good Friday Agreement. Now the main non-nationalist party in Northern Ireland

Fenian Member of the 19th-century Irish Republican Brotherhood

Fianna Fáil Political party (Soldiers of Destiny), founded in 1927 by de Valera in terms of opposition to partition and while still perceived by some to be more republican than Fine Gael, it is every bit as right wing

Fine Gael Right-wing political party, with origins in the pro-Treaty group after 1922, barely distinguishable from Fianna Fáil

IRA Irish Republican Army; between 1916 and 1921 the IRA was the army of the Provisional Government fighting the British and relatively dormant until trouble erupted in Northern Ireland at the end of the 1960s. Between 1970 and the still-existing ceasefire called in 1998 the IRA was actively engaged in a guerrilla war against the British

Loyalist People in Northern Ireland, staunch Protestants mostly, who are strongly in favour of remaining part of Britain

LVF Loyalist Volunteer Force; banned sectarian paramilitary group

Nationalists People who wish to see an united Ireland

Orange Order Protestant society dedicated to preserving the memory

between Catholic street action and the loyalist backlash. At first, beleaguered Catholic residents welcomed the presence of troops but this soon changed as the army was seen to be not acting impartially. At this stage, the IRA was virtually non-existent but it quickly re-emerged as Catholic communities looked for support. The violence began to spiral upwards, with events like Bloody Sunday (see page 485) and the Provisional IRA soon eclipsing the less militant official wing of the movement. The Provisionals launched a campaign of terrorist warfare against the security forces and commercial targets, and the introduction of internment, imprisonment without trial, caused the violence to escalate even more. In 1970, 25 people died and by 1972 this number had reached 467 and all but 30 of these fatalities occurred after internment.

In March 1972, the British government suspended the Northern Ireland government at Stormont and direct rule was introduced. A new government post was created at Westminster, a secretary of state for Northern Ireland.

The collapse of politics

In 1973, the Sunningdale agreement was an attempt to find a political settlement. Although its power-sharing executive was established for a brief while, it was destroyed by the Ulster Workers' Council, a loyalist grouping with paramilitary of William's victory at the Battle of the Boyne. Founded in 1795 and formerly represented within the Ulster Unionist Party

Progressive Democrats Political party founded in 1985 by a group of Fianna Fáil politicians opposed to the rule of Charles Haughey

PSNI See RUC

PUP Progressive Unionist Party; the political wing of the UVF, and crucial to the success of the Good Friday Agreement. Led by David Ervine, and a moderating force compared to the DUP

Real IRA Formed in 1997 by dissident IRA members who opposed the peace process and the political leadership of Sinn Féin

Republicans People committed to a united Ireland as a republic; sometimes used interchangeably with the term nationalist

RUC Royal Ulster Constabulary; Northern Ireland's armed police force, predominantly Protestant. Very much a sectarian force until reformed and renamed the Police Service of Northern Ireland (PSNI)

Sinn Fein (Ourselves Alone) Nationalist organization founded in 1903 and nowadays a political party in Ireland, particularly strong in the North, where it represents the political wing of the IRA. Led by Gerry Adams

SDLP Social Democratic and Labour Party; led by John Hume for many years, nationalist but not as republican as Sinn Fein

Treaty The treaty of 1921 that divided Ireland into the Republic and Northern Ireland

Taoiseach (Pronounced *tee-shock*) The prime minister of the Republic

UDA Ulster Defence Association; largest Protestant paramilitary organization, formed in 1971

UDF Ulster Defence Force; an illegal paramilitary Protestant organization

UDP Ulster Defence Regiment; political wing of the LVF

UFF Ulster Freedom Fighters; officially non-existant, a Protestant paramilitary force used by the UDA to carry out attacks against republicans

UUP Ulster Unionist Party; the largest and most important party opposed to republicanism, led by David Trimble

UVF Ulster Volunteer Force; an illegal Protestant paramilitary force formed in 1966 and supported by several thousand hardliners

support. The inability or unwillingness – it depends on your point of view – of the British government to stand up to the Council heralded a new and bloodier chapter in the province's history.

What followed was an intense period of open warfare between the IRA and the security forces. The IRA campaign was extended to the British mainland, hoping to force the hand of the government into making a political deal. In 1974, a bomb in a pub in Birmingham killed 21 people and more pub bombings followed in Woolwich and Guildford. The Prevention of Terrorism Act was introduced to allow lengthy detention without trial and although people were found guilty and imprisoned for the Birmingham and Guildford bombings they were released after 15 years behind bars and admitted to be innocent (one died in prison).

Up until 1976, prisoners in Northern Ireland jails who were there by dint of their involvement in the ongoing conflict had a special status that gave them the right not to wear prison uniforms. Republican protests at the denial of this right led to hunger strikes, and in 1981 this led to the death of Bobby Sands (see box page 570), who by the time of his death had been elected Member of Parliament for Fermanagh and South Tyrone. Nine more hunger strikers died over the following months.

The road to peace

The mid-1980s saw a fresh start with the signing at Hillsborough in County Down of the Anglo-Irish Agreement, the signatories being the British and Irish prime ministers. It was a significant step forward, recognizing the failure of attempts to bring peace to Northern Ireland by a purely internal settlement, and was motivated to some extent by alarm at the growing electoral success of Sinn Féin, the political wing of the IRA.

Even more significant was the Downing Street Declaration in 1993 which pointedly invited dialogue with Sinn Féin and the IRA. In August 1994 the IRA dramatically announced "a complete cessation of military operations", and loyalist paramilitary groups followed likewise. It seemed that everyone, including the gunmen, was tired of the endless violence, and Sinn Féin under Gerry Adams emerged with a new voice that recognized continual violence was not going to solve the problems. Unionists, also aware that some kind of compromise was necessary, would later elect David Trimble as a leader willing to negotiate with the traditional enemy.

Enter President Clinton, stage right, who now brought a powerful American influence to bear on the various talks and discussions that were going on in every camp. United States Senator George Mitchell headed an international commission that pushed matters forward with the enunciation of six ground rules for future discussions between the various parties. These included a commitment to peaceful means, but the astonishing progress that seemed to be in the making was shattered by a bomb at Canary Wharf in London in 1996, announcing the end of the IRA ceasefire. The fragile alliance between moderate and diehard members of the IRA had come to an end over the perceived willingness of the British government to bow to Unionist intransigence by insisting on the decommissioning of IRA weapons before talks could get under way.

The electoral defeat of Britain's Tory government in mid-1997, and its replacement by a Labour government not dependent on the Unionist votes at Westminster, heralded another fresh start. The IRA declared a restoration of their ceasefire and new talks got under way. Despite some outbreaks of violence at the end of 1997, including the assassination of Billy Wright, the leader of a loyalist paramilitary group, by a republican paramilitary group known as the Irish National Liberation Army (INLA), a breakthrough emerged and the Good Friday Agreement was signed in April 1998.

Good Friday Agreement

The Good Friday Agreement provided for a new Assembly of 108 members and an executive of 12 from the various communities. The new Assembly would bring direct rule from Westminster to an end and return to a devolved government responsible for the affairs of Northern Ireland. The essential difference is that the new Assembly cannot be gerrymandered to ensure unionist control.

The Good Friday Agreement in 1998 reached as fine a political balance as could ever be achieved in Ireland and the terms of the agreement were resoundingly endorsed by referendums held both sides of the border: 71% in the North and 94% in the Republic voted yes to peace and a political settlement. Elections for the new assembly that would govern the six counties gave the Social and Democratic Party (SDLP), representing the moderate middle-class nationalist vote, 24 seats and 21.99% of the vote, the Ulster Unionist Party (UUP) 28 seats with 21.28% of the vote, the Democratic Unionist Party (DUP), hardline unionists opposed to the Good Friday Agreement, 18% and 20 seats, and Sinn Féin 18 seats with 17.65% of the vote.

Opposition to the Good Friday Agreement continued to threaten the chances of a lasting peace. The summer of 1998 saw the continuation of conflict over the Orange

"We are committed to making conflict a thing of the past. There is a shared responsibility to removing the causes and to achieving an end to all conflict. Sinn Féin believe the violence we have seen [at Omagh] must be for all of us now a thing of the past, over, done with and gone." Sinn Féin statement, 1 September 1998.

Order's traditional march through the Catholic Garvaghy Road area of Portadown (see page 582). On the morning of 12 July, a loyalist firebombing of a Catholic house in a mainly Protestant estate resulted in the death of three children. Breakaway IRA dissidents formed the Real IRA and in August 1998 their bombing campaign led to horrific atrocity in Omagh, the worst in 30 years, a bomb which saw the slaughter of 29 people. Sinn Féin came off the fence with an unequivocal statement, followed by IRA visits to the homes of 60 members of the Real IRA within a 90-minute period making them an offer they could not refuse: on 7 September the Real IRA declared a total ceasefire.

Opposition to the Good Friday Agreement from hardline unionists continued to bedevil progress. As much as Trimble and his supporters wanted to move forward, there was sufficient unwillingness within his own party to bite the bullet of compromise, never mind the pressure from Ian Paisley to insist on IRA decommissioning as a pre-condition for any further movement.

Post-Good Friday

The impasse over the implementation of the Good Friday Agreement was finally overcome in November 1999 when, after 300 hours of face-to-face talks between David Trimble and Gerry Adams, agreement was reached. In a remarkable switch of the language codes that characterise political talk in the six counties, Trimble spoke of the need to recognise different cultural traditions (acknowledging that both nationalists and republicans have rights) while Adams spoke of the need for decommissioning (a possible end to the IRA).

On 29 November 1999 a new date entered the annals of Irish history when a coalition government was formed in Northern Ireland and direct rule from London was finally ended. The local government that had been dissolved in 1972 was replaced by one with David Trimble as First Minister but which for the first time included three Sinn Féin ministers, including as minister for education, Martin McGuinness, who could easily have been shot dead by security forces when he was the most wanted republican in Derry in the 1970s.

Then, just when everything seemed to be going smoothly, grassroots Unionists began to get cold feet and turned to Ian Paisley's DUP party. Paisley stood opposed to the Good Friday Agreement and claimed that Unionism was being betrayed by Trimble and his party. New elections saw the DUP replace Trimble's UUP as the main Protestant party and the British decided to suspend the power-sharing Stormont government. A state of limbo prevailed for a time and then talks resumed between all the players and the DUP. By the end of 2004 it seemed as if another historic, and truly astonishing, deal had been secured which would see Sinn Féin and the DUP sharing power at Stormont. This became possible because the IRA made a breathtaking statement that it would put its entire armoury beyond use by the end of 2004. It even agreed to allow a member of the clergy, chosen by the DUP, to witness the destruction of its weapons. Then Paisley made a speech calling for the humiliation of the IRA and insisted on there being photographic evidence of the destruction of arms. This was too much for the IRA and deadlock prevailed.

It seems – unless this proves to be wishful thinking – that it is only a matter of time before this final hurdle is overcome. It may, though, have to wait until the British general election in May 2005. The DUP wants to see off Trimble and the UUP in these elections and then, with Sinn Féin confirmed once more as the largest nationalist party, a deal will be brokered. The incredible but likely outcome is Ian Paisley as first minister and Martin McGuinness as his deputy. It will be a strange combination given that the DUP refuse to talk to Sinn Féin and especially in the light of the 2004 Northern Bank robbery and the offer by the IRA to shoot the men responsible for the murder of Robert McCartney (see page 602). Such a deal stands little chance of uniting a divided Northern Ireland but this is probably an impossible aspiration anyway. At the time of writing a statement by the IRA seems likely which may alter any future negotiations.

Culture

Art and architecture

Pre-Christian art and architecture

At Carrowmore in County Sligo, Swedish archaeologists have recently discovered the world's oldest building. The site (see page 440) has always been considered a Neolithic graveyard, built by people who had acquired farming skills and led fairly settled lives; then in summer 1999 a new site was discovered containing the cremated bones of about 50 people which carbon-dated to about 7,400 years ago, making its construction 700 years earlier than the oldest previously known free-standing building, a neolithic tomb near Poitiers in France. This indicates that in Ireland a mesolithic culture, a hunter-gatherer society, had all the skills required to erect substantial buildings.

Most of our knowledge of the architecture of early Ireland comes from funeral buildings. The earliest are the dolmens, tripod-like structures with upright megaliths supporting one or two massive capstones and covered by a cairn. Newgrange represents the next stage of Irish art and architecture, adding the sophistication of corbelling for the roof and several chambers, many of them decorated with the earliest examples of Irish art – triple spirals, double spirals and lozenge patterns. The Bronze Age in Ireland has left us a legacy of quite stunning complex designs in gold torcs, collars and pins, decorated bronze shields where the design is both functional and decorative. Like the weaponry, the architecture of this time reflected the need for defence with hill forts and promontory forts being simple stone boundaries which possibly had wooden structures inside.

The Iron Age/early Christian period still saw defensive buildings in the raths and stone cashels, but usually no longer on high ground, and often with a souterrain for escape or hiding. Stonework had become decorative as well as functional, and we have several items in the Armagh cathedral and county museum reflecting this primitive but distinctly creative form, particularly the stone heads like the Tandragee Man with his brutalist appearance, and the figure with what seems rays emanating from its head. Other decorative effects are consistent with the La Tène style of decoration – swirling loops and whorls both on stonework and weapons.

The early Christian period

This was a peaceful and productive time for Irish art and architecture before the Normans arrived, bringing their European sensibilities with them. Many people still lived in raths and crannógs, essentially settlements with an eye to defence, while church architecture was largely in the medium of wood, only a few stone buildings – such as the beehive huts of Skellig Michael or the ruins on Inismurray in County Sligo – still surviving. Where church buildings are of stone and have survived they are simple in design with arched doors, a simple nave added to the basic cell structure, and perhaps sculpture around the doors and windows. Some round towers such as the one at the monastery at Kells, County Meath, were built in the latter part of this period. The arts on the other hand were flourishing in the monasteries around the coast, demonstrated by the production of illuminated manuscripts such as the Book of Kells, the gold and metalwork of the beautiful Ardagh chalice in the National Museum, and the work of the stonemasons building the high crosses and tombs.

High crosses

Many of Ireland's Celtic crosses date back to this period before the Norman invasion. Sometimes as tall as 5 m/16 ft, they are carved from whatever stone was available,

Newgrange

The monuments at Newgrange were constructed around 2500 BC, following a sweeping bend of the River Boyne and utilizing an area of some 12 sq km. There are three huge similarly sized hilltop mounds, Newgrange, Knowth and Dowth, with one tomb in the Newgrange cairn and two in each of the other two. A score of smaller passage tombs, known as satellite tombs, have been found and excavated in the area around the main monuments. Fragments of bones belonging to a few people, some cremated, were found by archaeologists working at Newgrange in the 1960s, but the site has been open for 300 years so this find is not conclusive.

Excavations at other passage tombs in Ireland have revealed evidence of mass burials, up to 24 people being buried together. The nearest equivalent groupings of megalithic tombs outside Ireland are in Brittany and Orkney, and one theory is that the people who built these tombs at Newgrange came from Brittany, and before that the Iberian Peninsula. However, the artwork of Newgrange has few parallels outside Ireland, and it has been argued that the Boyne Valley represents a unique Irish development.

The artwork inscribed on the stones at Newgrange are geometrical in design, and their non-representational nature suggests symbolic meanings. Whether they were conceived as ornamental in nature or whether they signify spiritual or magical ideas remains a mystery. In the case of some of the stones, like the huge entrance boulder, it is clear that the artist or artists regarded the whole stone as a canvas which was to be filled with an intricate and integrated pattern of spirals, concentric arcs and other designs that strove to utilize even the curving surface of the material. Tools – flint stones and wooden hammers – would have been fairly basic, and the carved motifs may be divided into curvilinear ones, like triple spirals, circles, arcs and serpent shapes, and rectilinear chevron zigzags, parallel lines, lozenge and triangular shapes. What is odd is that other types of megalithic tombs in Ireland show little evidence of any wish to inscribe patterns on stone in this way. Considering the unwieldy nature and the sheer size of these giant stones, the artwork that has survived represents one of the finest achievements of prehistoric art in Western Europe.

often sandstone or limestone which has not subsequently worn well. Their east side is often decorated in scenes from the Old Testament while the west side conveys stories from the New Testament. Usually in the centre of the west face is the crucifixion surrounded by the typical carved and decorated ring of stone which may have stood for the cosmos, with Christ and his sacrifice at its centre. The stories chosen often illustrate a theme, and their purpose was practical – to teach and inspire the congregation. The base and side panels are covered in complex geometric designs like those in the illuminated manuscripts of the period, and when first erected they were probably painted so that the designs and stories stood out much more clearly. The best examples of high crosses from this period are at Glendalough, County Wicklow, Durrow and Clonmacnoise in County Offaly and Monasterboice in County Louth, a particularly beautiful example.

Round towers

The earliest of the Irish round towers are pre-Norman, although they continued to be built into the 12th century. They are the medieval equivalent of the muezzin's minaret, and once held a bell to call the monks in from the fields. Usually five storeys high, they have one window at each level, and their defensive nature is seen in the fact that the doorway is about 10 ft off the ground so that the steps could be drawn up to protect the church property in time of attack. Inside would have been a series of wooden storeys and steps.

Irish Romanesque

The Irish Romanesque style is most clearly seen in Cormac's Chapel at the Rock of Cashel in County Tipperary, and the 12th-century doorway to Clonfert Cathedral in County Galway. A typical arched doorway at Clonfert is surrounded by highly decorated columns which shelve inward in a style typical of this period, with ever more complicated swirls and patterns on the arches above the doorspace. The steeply arched pediment is again ornately carved with primitive human heads set in triangular recesses and surrounded by more ornate carvings.

Norman Gothic

The Normans brought European sophistication to the architecture of Ireland with complex gothic-style church buildings such as Christ Church Cathedral in Dublin and many monasteries, such as Sligo Abbey, which included a quadrangle with the church on the north side, the sacristy and meeting rooms on the east, refectory and dormitories on the south and storerooms on the west. Buildings were bigger and arches pointed, not for aesthetic reasons but because they were more efficient at loadbearing. Churches became larger with ornate triple-arched windows where the main characteristic of the Romanesque church had been a bulk of stone wall. Stained glass made an appearance, and later in the period the lancets between the windows become narrowed to thin stone pillars or mullions.

Secular architecture has been preserved in the form of castles, reflecting the period of warfare which filled the power vacuum after the death of Brian Ború. The first Normans built motte and bailey castles consisting of a huge mound of earth with a wooden tower on top and a semicircular fenced area at the bottom where the cattle were kept. Later, more settled Normans built square stone castles such as King John's Castle in Limerick, with towers at the corners.

Artistic expression in Norman times found its outlet in religious paraphernalia such as the shrines built to hold holy relics. Examples of these are in the Hunt Collection in Limerick and the National Gallery in Dublin.

The 15th and 16th centuries

This period was marked by the struggle between the Norman lords and the Gaelic chieftains, and as you might expect architecture was dominated by the need to build fortified houses and towns with protective walls around them. This is the age of the tower houses, a high square building capable of being defended but essentially a home. Artwork of the time is very practical – the misericords of St Mary's Cathedral in Limerick date from this period, for example, and while they are beautifully carved with the figures of mythical animals they are also eminently useful pieces of furniture.

The 17th and 18th centuries

The end of the 17th century saw the first completely domestic and non-defensive Irish architecture. The castles and fortified houses of the Plantation years began to give way to grand mansions without any fortifications. An example of 17th-century architecture at its most creative is the 1680 Royal Hospital at Kilmainham, Dublin's oldest existing public building. Here style is as important as the purpose of the building, and great attention to detail has gone into both its exterior and interior. The Georgian period saw a flowering of architecture in both public buildings and private houses in all of Ireland's cities, and in the countryside in the grand houses; a proud statement of ownership of the land on the part of the Protestant Ascendancy. Georgian architecture is modelled on the work of the 16th century architect Palladio, who left books of his designs for later architects to admire. Buildings are highly symmetrical with fake doors mirroring real doors so as to keep the symmetry. There is very little exterior ornamentation and much emphasis on proportion. The most famous and prolific of the Irish Georgian architects was Richard Castle, who designed much of Georgian Dublin as well as Powerscourt in County Wicklow.

The enormous creativity of the time was also expressing itself in the paintings of Nathaniel Hone and George Barret, and in the craft skills of the men such as Michael Stapleton, who created the plasterwork and woodcarvings of public buildings. In many cases the names of these artists are lost, but the men who made the intricate plasterwork of Newman House which still survives were called the Francini brothers. Georgian silverware is also very distinctive, as is cut glass.

Victorian Ireland

With the Act of Union the great Georgian building spree came to an end, and apart from some public buildings architecture went into a decline. Gothic Revival style emerged, characterized by decoration such as flying buttresses, pointed arches and ribbed vaults. The middle years of the century saw a massive number of churches being built as Catholic emancipation gained momentum, but the Famine brought most building to a full stop. Railway station buildings in particular provided an outlet for the eclectic style of the time. Portrait painting was popular and sentimental, as were allegorical historical and biblical paintings such as those of Francis Danby. James Arthur O'Connor was another important painter of the time, concentrating on landscapes.

The 20th century

After a brief Arts-and-Crafts-influenced Celtic Revival (Limerick Art Gallery contains some excellent examples) the modernist movement was the next big influence on Irish architecture, characterized by *Busáras* in Dublin and Dublin airport. Big blocks of concrete and glass followed, many of them borrowing ideas from ancient Irish structures – the public library in Bantry, for example, looks a little like a concrete dolmen if you squint sideways at it. In church architecture this pre-Celtic look has influenced the work of Liam McCormick in his additions to cathedrals such as the Catholic Cathedral in Armagh or the Church of St Aonghas at Burt, County Donegal. In the field of pure art Jack Yeats and Paul Henry are well known figures, focusing on ordinary events in the lives of their Irish subjects. In more modern times the most visually obviously aspect of art is in the many sculptures which decorate the cities and towns. With typical irreverence Dubliners have given these sometimes peculiar objects their own names, so Dublin now has 'the floozy in the jacuzzi', 'the hags with the bags' and 'the tart with the cart' among others.

Literature

→ *See also Books, page 625.*

When it comes to Irish literature it is hard to know where to start. Take Irish playwrights, poets and novelists out of university English Literature syllabuses and there wouldn't be a lot left to teach. The Irish took the language that the English imposed on them and made their own inspired use of it, superimposing their own patterns and making it a musical language rather than one of shopkeepers and factory owners. But Irish literature flourished long before English ever drove out the native language, and is the oldest written literature in Europe.

Just as in ancient Greece, an oral tradition existed in pre-Christian Ireland for centuries before the monks arrived around the fifth century AD with their writing skills. It wasn't long before the monks began to write these epic stories down, and many of them have survived. The earliest is the Mythological Cycle which tells stories in prose of the Tuatha Dé Danaan, the deities of the pagan Irish. When the monks came to write down these stories the characters changed from deities (not allowed in Christianity with its single omnipotent god) to the heroes of the earlier culture. The main characters are Lug, the leader of the gods, the sea god Manannán and their families, and the chief story is that of their battle with the Formori, giants who first oppress them and then are defeated by them, calling up parallels with the Greek stories of the Olympians and Titans, and perhaps also reflecting an earlier struggle between belief systems.

The best known of the early Irish stories is the Ulster Cycle, a group of tales which features people called the Ulaid and the Connachta, the children of the gods, and the conflicts between them. The stories involve gods and heroes, magic and lots of fighting, death and blood, and feature Cú Chulain (or Cúchulainn), the son of the god Lug, and Medb, a queen with magical powers associated with the goddess of sovereignty, often called Macha. The *Taín Bó Cuailnge* (*The Book of the Dun Cow*), so called because part of it was written on vellum made from cowhide, contains many of these stories.

A third cycle of stories concerns the early rulers of Ireland, people such as Cormac McAirt, Conaire King of Tara, and others. They were composed between the ninth and 12th centuries and deal with real figures from the sixth to eighth centuries. These stories would have been memorized by the *ollam*, professional story tellers and poets who would have brought them out on public occasions to recite.

The last cycle of stories is known as the Ossianic Cycle and deals with the exploits of Fionn mac Cumhaill and his sons and grandsons. The source of the stories is a 12th century text, featuring St Patrick, who meets Oisín, Fionn's son, and hears his stories and orders that they be written down. The cycle is seen as a reaction of the Gaels to the dominance of Cistercian monasticism in Ireland. Fionn and his band or Fianna are outlaws in the stories. Although the first written versions are medieval in origin, they are probably as old in oral tradition as the Ulster Cycle.

In the Middle Ages a tradition of bardic poets developed. These were a combination of praise-singers and *filí*, professional poets who memorized and told the stories of Celtic warriors and gods. Their function was to legitimize the chieftain who showed them patronage. As the centuries progressed the bards took up the political and social changes of the time, writing songs about the history of Ireland, the many battles fought, and the gradual decline of Gaelic Ireland in the face of Anglo-Irish control. By the 19th century the bardic tradition was almost extinct; some of the poems had been translated and printed but many were lost. Gaelic as a language was fast disappearing from Ireland. The Gaelic Revival in the late 19th century stirred things up a little, but the old style of epic writing had finished and the Irish-language poets of the 20th century wrote in a modern vernacular idiom about things that were real to them. In modern times there is a large output of writing in Irish, but a very small reading public.

As Gaelic went into terminal decline Anglo-Irish writing, as if to rub salt in the wounds of the conquered, flourished. The 17th century saw the terrible wit of Jonathan Swift (1667-1745), the son of an Englishman, born in Dublin and educated in Ireland. Deeply committed to Anglicanism, opposed to religious toleration or equality, he nonetheless used his writing to accuse the government in England of misgovernment and short-sightedness in relation to Ireland. A contemporary of Swift was William Congreve, genetically English but educated in Kilkenny and Dublin, and a lawyer at the Middle Temple in Dublin. He wrote comedies of manners and is considered one of the English Restoration dramatists. George Farquhar (1677-1707), another contemporary of Swift's, was the son of an Anglican clergyman from Derry,

Wittgenstein's Dublin

The philosopher Wittgenstein visited Ireland on five occasions, spending almost two years there in total, appreciating the atmosphere of peace and the tranquillity of the landscape. His longest visit was in 1947, after he had given up his professorship in Cambridge. After staying first in a house in Redcross in County Wicklow and then in a remote location in Connemara, he returned to Dublin for the winter of 1948. He stayed at Ross's Hotel in Parkgate (now the Ashling) working on his final draft of what was posthumously published as *Philosophical Investigations*. Wittgenstein dabbled with the idea of settling in Dublin and becoming a psychiatrist and felt he could live in the city, though he had little time for Dublin's Georgian architecture: "The people who built these houses had the good taste to know that they had nothing very important to say: and therefore they didn't attempt to express anything." Far more to his liking was Bewley's Café (which closed down in 2004) in Grafton Street where, after repeated visits, he was delighted to be recognized by a waitress who brought him his customary lunch of an omelette and coffee without being asked. Unlike Yeats, who reluctantly visited a pub on one occasion in his life, there is no record of Wittgenstein ever ordering a pint of Guinness in a bar. He did enjoy walking in Phoenix Park though, and in the Botanic Gardens he used to sit and think in one of the heated greenhouses and make jottings in his notebook.

and may well have lived through some of the siege of that city. His stage comedies featured some of the first sympathetic stage Irishmen who, unlike those of previous writers, had a higher moral sense than the Englishmen they dealt with, and often, like Roebuck in *Love and a Bottle*, were the hero of the play. From Clonmel, County Tipperary, the son of an Englishman and Irishwoman, Laurence Sterne (1713-1768) is famous for his novel *Tristram Shandy*. The novel is innovative and stands in the Anglo-Irish tradition despite his only half-Irishness. It self-consciously refers to Swift, and its influence can be seen in the work of James Joyce. Sheridan (1751-1816), Wilde (1854-1900) and Shaw (1856-1950) are more widely read authors, all in the Anglo-Irish tradition but all living their adult lives in London.

An innovative novelist of the early 19th century is Maria Edgeworth (1767-1849) whose novels are among the earliest to be set in a specific region of the country; she inspired Sir Walter Scott in his writings. Much of the work of her middle years is heavy and moralistic, influenced by her father who actually wrote the worst of the sermonizing contained within them, but *Castle Rackrent*, *Belinda* and *Ormonde* are good reads and provide great insight into the Irish landlord classes of the 19th century. In her later years she spent much time trying to alleviate the sufferings of the people on her estate during the Famine.

Later writers from the same class are Edith Somerville (1858-1949) and Violet Martin (1862-1915), who wrote as Somerville and Ross. They examine the foolishness and pathos of the declining years of the big houses and their occupants. After Martin's death Somerville wrote several more successful novels, which she continued to publish under the joint names in the belief that she had an understanding with her partner which went beyond death.

At the end of the 19th century the Irish literary revival began with writing both in Irish and English. William Butler Yeats (1856-1939) was a member of the movement. The son of Irish Church of Ireland parents, he grew up in England and Ireland. He read

Field Day

At a time when no one wanted to know about Ireland and its culture, a relatively unknown writer, Brian Friel, and a very unknown actor, Stephen Rea, formed a theatre group called the Field Day Theatre company in Derry. They attracted the co-operation of other writers and people in the arts – Tom Paulin, Seamus Deane (a poet who later became the director of Field Day), David Hammond the film maker, and Seamus Heaney. Situated on the border of the two states, with the benefit of two cultural traditions, Catholic and Protestant, Field Day offered writers and audiences a 'Fifth Province', a place where it was safe to look at what Ireland was without breaking cultural taboos. One of its first successes was Friel's *Translations*, which was performed in the Guildhall in Derry and then went on tour around Ireland with Stephen Rea and Liam Neeson in its cast, playing in school halls to audiences of farmers who recognized its cultural significance. Throughout the 1980s Field Day grew in reputation, putting on productions by Friel, Tom Kilroy, Stewart Parker and Terry Eagleton, and producing pamphlets on all aspects of Irish culture, culminating in 1991 in the *Field Day Anthology of Irish Writing*, which sadly left out most women writers (redressed in 2002 with two new volumes).

translations of the Irish myths and became determined to revive the cultural heritage of Ireland, and his early poetry reflects that determination. In 1894 he met and became close friends with Lady Gregory, and the two planned the Irish Literary Theatre, to be realized as the Abbey Theatre in Dublin. His poetry is full of a sense of the mystical nature of the Irish countryside and sadness for the loss of the Celtic culture. In his last years he became disillusioned with Irish politics and took to spiritualism.

James Joyce (1882-1941) died just two years after Yeats, but was a very different kettle of fish. He scoffed at the mysticism of the Gaelic Revival, but his work is in many ways more recognizably Irish than anything Yeats wrote. He was the son of a Catholic chancer, who put his money into this and that and lost all of it. Extremely intelligent, Joyce was educated free of charge by the Jesuits, but then turned his back on his religion and Ireland and never lived there again. His works – *Dubliners*, a series of short stories; *A Portrait of the Artist as a Young Man*; *Ulysses*; and *Finnegans Wake* – make great reading for anyone interested in the workings of the Irish mind, and since the Irish state started to acknowledged his existence – some time after his death – he has gained the recognition in his own country that he deserves. You used to be able to see him artificially smiling at you from the now-defunct 10 pound note, or you can join the hundreds of people who celebrate his novel *Ulysses* on June 16th every year in Dublin.

A good friend of Joyce was Samuel Beckett (1909-1989), Nobel Prize winner and author of the play *Waiting for Godot*. Beckett's biography reads like an adventure story – stalked by Joyce's daughter Lucia, stabbed by a pimp in the backstreets of Paris, a member of the Resistance during the war, betrayed but escaped to Free France, holder of the Croix de Guerre. His works are painfully funny though full of suffering, and he was notorious for refusing permission for his material to be produced for fear that it wouldn't be done exactly right. His shortest play is *Breath*, which lasts about a minute. He too despised the Celtic Revival, and in his novel *Murphy* the protagonist attempts to kill himself by repeatedly headbutting the buttocks of the statue of Cú Chulain in the GPO in O'Connell Street, which was erected in memory of those who died in the Easter Rising.

Kate O'Brien (1897-1974) was born in Limerick, the daughter of a horse dealer who made lots of money and then lost it. Her novels are about the complexities of being female and living up to the demands of the church. Several of them were, as you might expect, banned in Ireland. Her most famous novel is *The Ante-Room*. Although she lived most of her adult life in England, her novels are centred very much on the Irish middle classes.

Brendan Behan (1923-1964) is another writer whose life story would fit neatly into one of his plays. Born into a working-class Dublin family, he was arrested and imprisoned in Britain at the age of 16 for taking part in an IRA bombing campaign. He spent three years in English borstals, where he began to practise his craft of writing. Back in Ireland he was arrested again for the attempted murder of a detective, and spent five more years in prison in Ireland. While in prison he wrote poetry in Irish and his autobiographical novel *Borstal Boy*. He died of drink at the height of his popularity. His best works are *The Quare Fellow* and *The Hostage*, both plays.

Like Behan, Sean O'Casey (1880-1964) was working-class, but this time born into a Protestant family. Like Behan he did manual work to make ends meet and in his early years was a great joiner... He 'joined' both the fledgling IRA and the Orange Order, but it was James Larkin's trade union which finally claimed his allegiance. His first play, *Shadow of a Gunman*, was produced by the Abbey Theatre in 1923, and was followed by *Juno and the Paycock* and *The Plough and the Stars*. His plays are written in the Dublin vernacular, and shocked and horrified middle-class Irish audiences with their language and honesty. Like other writers of his generation he was disgusted by the new Irish government and moved permanently to England.

In modern times the names come thick and fast. Christy Brown, Roddy Doyle, JP Donleavy, Liam O'Flaherty, John McGahern, John Banville, Mary Lavin, Edna O'Brien, Frank McCourt, Iris Murdoch, Clare Boylan, Molly Keane, Maeve Binchy are all highly successful and revered novelists.

Playwrights include Brian Friel, whose brilliant play *Translations* changed the way that people looked at Irish history, John B Keane whose play *The Field* is an essential read for anyone who wants to understand the Irish attitude to the land. Sebastian Barry, a novelist, short story writer and playwright, has had considerable critical success in London and New York with his plays *The Steward of Christendom* and *Our Lady of Sligo*, which are concerned with the sense of Irish identity and fitting in.

In poetry there is the Nobel Prize winner Seamus Heaney (1939-) from County Derry, Louis MacNeice (1907-1963) whose poetry, like Heaney's, is influenced by his Northern Ireland childhood, Patrick Kavanagh whose poetry reflects the harsh lives of a farming community in the North and Tom Paulin (1949-) from Belfast, whose poetry is full of the state of mind created by the political situation in the North. Other poets who write about Ireland include Thomas Kinsella, John Montague, Eavan Boland and Brendan Kennelly.

Film

→ *See page 159 for more information on Irish cinema.*

Ireland has always provided an excellent source of actors and locations for movies, although the recent cash injections of the last decade haven't always been available. In recent years both Dublin and Belfast have rarely had a day without a film crew blocking the streets, and in little pubs all over Ireland you can see black and white stills of the locals dressed up as mariners, Scottish warriors and 19th-century peasants amongst other things. In the 1950s the village of Cong came to the screens of the world in the movie *The Quiet Man* directed by John Ford, and has never really recovered. Then *Ryan's Daughter* was filmed on the Dingle Peninsula in 1970, and you can now take guided tours of the spots where Robert Mitchum nearly drowned and the set was built for the village, although most of it blew down in 1997. The next big star movie made with chiefly American actors was *Far and Away* in 1991, a Cruise and Kidman vehicle which left everyone wincing at the Irish accents and which actually used some of the backstreets of Dublin to represent Boston. These were all movies with an Irish theme, but Ireland has provided some other strange locations. *Moby Dick* was filmed by John Huston around Youghal in County Cork in 1956, while *Educating Rita*, a movie about an English Open University student and her tutor, was filmed in Trinity College. In 1994 a piece of Irish mountainside became Scotland for a few weeks while Mel Gibson filmed *Braveheart*, and lots of Irish students as well as the Territorial Army filled in the crowd scenes. If you look very carefully you might see some of the same faces in *Saving Private Ryan* directed by Stephen Spielberg. The biggest surprise hit movie made in Ireland has to be *The Commitments*, directed by Alan Parker in 1990, filmed with an entirely Irish cast around north Dublin and displaying the grim reality of urban life as opposed to the quaint beauty of the Irish countryside in the earlier big movies. It, and the previous year's *My Left Foot*, the story of a paralysed young boy's life directed by Jim Sheridan, set a high standard and created interest in the real Ireland which has spawned several good films since. In 1990 Jim Sheridan made *The Field*, from the play by John B Keane, about the desperate fight for one small field in western Ireland. Filmed around Leenane in County Galway, it is harsh and unsentimental in its portrayal of rural Ireland. The 1992 movie *The Crying Game* directed by Neil Jordan tells the bleak story of an IRA man who strikes up a relationship with the lover of the man he helped to kill. Jim Sheridan took up the theme of the Troubles in 1993 to make *In the Name of the Father* with Daniel Day-Lewis and Emma Thompson about the injustice meted out to the Conolly family, better known as the Guildford Four, in the early 1970s. In 1995 *Nothing Personal* took up the theme of the North again, this time looking at the chaos created in the lives of bystanders caught up in the Troubles and the terrible waste of young lives which the last 25 years has brought about. *Michael Collins* was a big blockbuster in 1996, which set the whole of Ireland arguing about the treatment of de Valera and displayed Julia Roberts' feeble efforts at an Irish accent. By this time the Troubles had become a moneyspinner, and 1996 also saw the release of *Some Mother's Son*, another innocent person caught up in the troubles as her son takes part in the hunger strike which killed Bobby Sands. Helen Mirren does an excellent job as the respectable mother. By this time the North and the IRA were almost a cliché: witness Harrison Ford inadvertently twice getting caught up in the Troubles, once with Brad Pitt in *The Devil's Own* (1996).

Back in the world of intelligent movie-making, the best film to come from Ireland in 1998 was *The General*, by John Boorman, about a comical Dublin thug who gets caught up with the UVF and suffers the consequences. In the same year the first Irish road movie was released, *I Went Down* directed by Paddy Breathnach, a funny story about innocents mixed up with gangsters and refreshingly free of hooded gunmen.

Neil Jordan stands out in particular as an excellent Irish film-maker. Before he got big money and made *Michael Collins* his films included *Angel* (1982), set in Northern Ireland long before it became chic, *Mona Lisa*, *The Crying Game*, *The Company of Wolves*, and his most recent movie, set in small town Ireland, *The Butcher Boy*.

Music

The earliest form that Irish music is known to have taken is in the songs sung by the bards to the music of the metal-stringed harp. None of it was written down until the 17th century, and the earliest music to survive is the work of the harpist Turlough O'Carolan. Later collections date back to the Belfast harp festival of 1792. These were Gaelic and Scottish jigs and reels which took on an Irish character. In the 18th century the Irish traditional music that we recognize emerged. The harp, the instrument of the

Step we gaily on we go

For some of the best traditional music currently being produced in Ireland, check out Ossian Publications (www.ossian.ie). They produce **John Feeley's** *Celtic Classics*, excellent recordings of traditional songs on the classical guitar, and **Hammy Hamilton, Séamus Creagh, Con Ó Drisceoil's** *It's No Secret*, great songs by three musicians who came to the fore in the famous Phoenix Bar on Union Quay in Cork city in the 1970s.

Van Morrison and The Chieftains *Irish Heartbeat*, is a delightful collection of classics like *Carrickfergus*, *Star of the County Down* and *Marie's Wedding*. **John McCormack** *Popular Songs and Irish Ballads*, produced by EMI, is a collection worth listening to, as is *Joyce's Parlour Music*, by Magini Enterprises, and on sale at the James Joyce Cultural Centre in Dublin.

Tim O'Riordan's *The Langer*, a hit release in 2004, opens a window on West Cork wit and wisdom and is recommended listening for the visitor to Ireland.

bards, was in decline, and the playing of reels and hornpipes on fiddle, flute and uillean pipes emerged. Each county had its own style of music, and some of the distinctions can still be heard. Early in the century the flute was introduced via Dublin.

The most commonly available printed source of music was the ballad sheets which emerged after every national event, telling the story in song; these sheets were bought and copied, thus making their way around the country. Murders, rebellions, hangings – the news travelled via the songsheets. Some of these songs outlived their immediate interest and survived; other disappeared. Dance masters travelled around the country, staying in each village for a few weeks and teaching the latest dances and tunes to the locals. They were eagerly awaited and received a royal welcome when they arrived. If two masters met on their journey the village would have a contest between them. This powerful social custom attracted even the Ascendancy class, busy listening to Handel in Dublin, and traditional music concerts took place in the houses of the rich.

In the 19th century traditional music continued as an unschooled family event, celebrated at wakes and weddings and at the crossroads on holidays. Songs were traditional or made up for the moment, about friends and relatives or events in history. Instruments were the tin whistle, the fiddle and the bodhrán, a modern instrument made of goatskin stretched over a frame and played with the hand or both ends of a wooden stick. Less common but much older are the uilleann pipes, a complicated version of the bagpipes with a much more complex range of sounds. You'll be lucky to see anyone play this instrument in Ireland – it takes a good few years to master.

The Famine almost destroyed Irish music altogether as those who practised it died or emigrated. The music that survived did so because the emigrants in America, Australia, London, Liverpool and Glasgow kept their culture alive and, thankfully, had the sense to record the tunes, far away from the music's origins. In the USA piping clubs emerged and Irish performers joined the Variety Club circuits, adapting their music to American tastes. The Taylor Brothers, an emigrant family from Drogheda, developed the uillean pipes, bringing them to concert pitch and making them more suitable for performance. Then in 1890 the Gaelic League regenerated interest in music in Ireland itself, inventing the *ceilidh*, a showcase for Irish music and dancing. Traditional music went into a bit of a decline in the middle years of this century with the advent of radio, but it emerged again in the 1960s, first with Seán O Riada and traditional band Ceoltóririí Chualann, but especially with The Chieftains who took the combination of traditional instruments and orchestral arrangements of Irish music all over the world.

The bent note and the twisted word

Our understanding of pre-Christian attitudes to music depends on surviving Gaelic myths which suggest that the songs and music of the bards were much more than a bit of light entertainment while they feasted. Rhyme and music formed a powerful magical weapon in the war against one's enemies as a story from *Lébor Gabadla*, the Book of Invasions tells. Daghda, one of the three leaders of the Tuatha de Danaan, the triumvirate of deities of pagan Ireland, has the power of music and one day slips into his enemies' camp to rescue a friend. He uses music to put three spells on the enemies, making them weep with sad music, dance with happy music and finally fall asleep to soothing music, allowing the captive to escape. Another story, of Oengus son of Daghda, tells how he and his lover Caer Iborméith, in the form of swans, make such beautiful music as they fly together that all who hear it fall asleep.

Much later, in early Christian Ireland the bards were highly valued intellectuals who could make or break a reputation with their poetry and the idea of the power of rhyme and music lingered a long time in Irish culture. In the 1959 play by John B Keane, *Sive*, a travelling tinker poses real threats to the local people with his chanted curses.

There are several branches of the traditional music scene. One is the rebel song, sung late at night in bars in Donegal and made almost respectable by bands such as the Wolfe Tones. Another is the Dublin-based bawdy strain, epitomized by the Dubliners and their song *Seven Drunken Nights*, the last two verses of which were too bawdy to record. The most inward-looking and sentimental is the ballad, often involving dead wives and abandoned homes, sung by Daniel O'Donnell and a host of clones and closely linked to the American country music scene. In pubs all around the country what you are most likely to hear is a mixture of Irish dance tunes, *Fonn Mall* or slow airs and rebel songs. If you are lucky you might come across *sean nós*, a strange nasal unaccompanied singing in Irish which takes a great deal of effort both to sing and to listen to. To the untrained ear it sounds like a monotone but the trick is to listen for the subtle nuances of the song.

As traditional music has lost its sweater-and-corduroys image it has changed and fused with other musical traditions as new generations of talented players have taken it up. Christy Moore is probably Ireland's favourite traditional musician. He has been in the business since the early days of the 1960s and early on formed the band Planxty with Liam O'Flynn, Donal Lunny and Andy Irvine. Planxty mixed traditional music with acoustic guitar folk music and ballads, but above all it was their skill with instruments which marked them out. All of them have moved on to other things, Moore forming the band Moving Hearts which fused his traditional style with his own compositions, jazz and rock music. Many of Moore's songs have political overtones and comment on the Troubles and Irish politics. Since 1998 he has retired to West Cork. Other musicians who have influenced the traditional music scene are Moore's brother, Luka Bloom, and Paul Brady, both of whom have played with Moore in different bands.

Most dynamic of all were the band Pogue Mahone (Irish for Kiss my Arse), Londoners led by the musical icon Shane McGowan. They were a wild mix of punk, rebel song, traditional ballad and just plain rock music. McGowan and the Pogues split as a result of McGowan's chaotic personal life, and he formed a new band, The Popes. If you listen to nothing else in Ireland, listen to some of McGowan's songs, some of the finest music to emerge from the rock scene in the last decade.

Francis O'Neill

Born near Bantry, County Cork, in 1849, the youngest of seven children, Francis O'Neill was a typical child of his time, speaking both Irish and English, attending the school in Bantry, and learning by ear to play the wooden flute. He was good at remembering the tunes – an advantage since no one he knew was literate in musical notation. He spent his first adult years on board ships and was shipwrecked on Baker Island, a little atoll 1,650 miles southwest of Honolulu, for some time before a passing American ship rescued him. Landing in San Francisco he settled in America and eventually became chief of police in Chicago, arresting the anarchist Emma Goldman in 1901. His hobby remained traditional Irish music, and with the help of a musically literate fellow officer he began collecting and transcribing Irish tunes from the many Irish immigrants he encountered. Between 1903 and 1924 he published nine volumes of Irish tunes which would otherwise have been lost. While the collections became essential material for traditional musicians, his work as a collector and biographer of American Irish musicians was never recognized in Ireland, until in 1999 when he got a hotel named after him in Smithfield, Dublin.

Another icon of the Irish music scene is Van Morrison, who came to the fore via a very different route. In the 1960s he led the band Them with pop hits in Britain. He spent many years in the USA and made his mark with albums such as *Astral Weeks* and *Moondance*. As a solo singer he has recorded with The Chieftains and has figured prominently in the efforts to reach peace in the North, where his home town is Belfast.

There are many other names to mention in a description of the vibrant Irish music scene. You can't go far in Dublin without tripping over U2, who own the Clarence Hotel and the Kitchen nightclub, two of the coolest places to be seen in. Clannad belong to the traditional music scene and have been around for what seems like a very long time. Rory Gallagher, who died in 1996, achieved world fame with his music in the 60s and 70s, selling 30 million records and touring all over the world first with his band Taste and then pursuing a solo career. There are also the Boomtown Rats and Bob Geldof, who have produced some good pop music. The early 90s witnessed Sinead O'Connor's tempestuous appearance on the world music scene, while other women such as Mary Black, Dolores Keane and Maura O'Connell have had quieter but equally successful careers. Sharon Shannon is based firmly in the traditional music scene and plays vigorous accordion and fiddle music.

Irish sports

In Ireland you will encounter all the regular sports, and Irish people tune in to the Sky Sports stations just like the rest of Europe, but Ireland also has some sports which are purely Irish in origin, even if that origin wasn't too long ago. The Gaelic Athletic Association was established in 1884, around the time of the Gaelic Revival, and established rules for games which had more or less existed before but had never been organized. Gaelic football is the Irish version of the game played in America and is a cross between English rugby and English football. There are 15 players and the round ball is played with both the hands and feet. Goals, as in football, and scores, as in rugby, are possible, with one goal equal to three scores. It is a very physical, fast game with few rules.

More popular is hurling, a kind of hockey which is played on the same pitch as Gaelic. It is a very old game. Brehon Law, the law which operated in pre-Christian Ireland, allowed for compensation for the families of those injured in hurling matches, and tradition says that the battle of Moytura, fought in 200BC, began as a hurling match. Between the 14th and 17th centuries hurling was banned three times. Nowadays it's a little less rough than the days when whole clans became professional hurling players and fought for the various clan chiefs. As in Gaelic there are 15 players to a team, and the object is to get the soft ball between the opponent's goal posts. The stick is wide at one end, and good players can carry the ball for several paces balanced on the stick. It is recognized as one of the fastest team sports in the world. Both games are just as popular as regular football, and each year the whole country bedecks itself with its county's colours as the two sets of teams play towards the All Ireland finals at Croke Park in September.

Lifestyle

The last 10 years have seen such changes that make it almost difficult to believe that the Ireland of the past ever existed. Ireland was an amazing little country, stuck out on the very western edge of Europe, poor, underdeveloped, underpopulated and with a history that just wouldn't go away and let it move on. Dominated by the Catholic Church physically, politically and emotionally, it was seriously in danger of becoming a banana republic, taking handouts from the EU, sending its brightest and best off to other countries to find work, forever in the shadow of its bullying big brother, Britain. It seemed unable to move decisively into the future.

Take women for example. Half the population, well educated, women have contributed to every aspect of Irish life from politics and war to science, medicine, art and literature. But try naming 10 famous Irish women. At the turn of the century Irish women were pretty much the social equals of their sisters in Britain – no vote, none in parliament, none at universities, no doctors. Irish suffragettes fought and suffered for their demands just as British ones did. Under the Free State Irish women got the vote stood for the Dáil, attended universities, practised medicine, did very nearly everything that Irish men did. But within 20 years most of that had disappeared – under the Irish constitution and the laws passed in the 1930s women had no access to contraception, no right to terminate a pregnancy under any circumstances whatsoever, no right to divorce, no right to own the family home or take authority over the children, no senior civil service jobs, no place in industrial management and certainly no equality of pay. It was as if Irish women voluntarily gave up all the rights and freedoms they had won in the early years of the century. And, weirdly, this continued more or less well into the 1980s. The first women sat on juries in the 1970s the first condoms became available outside a prescription from a chemist shop in 1993, it was EU laws that forced equal pay and opportunities into Irish law (if not into practice). Finally, in the late 1990s, contraception and abortion advice became available in Ireland, and a referendum narrowly put divorce in a very limited number of cases on to the statute books.

In the last decade Ireland has undergone seismic changes that no one would have believed possible. The Catholic Church has lost its place in politics forever, with terrible stories emerging about child abuse by priests and nuns (and covered up by the church), the treatment of unmarried mothers in the Magdalen laundries (laundry workshops run by nuns), the scandal – hilarious though it was – of Bishop Eamo

When the city authorities tried to prevent an Ann Summers sex shop opening in O'Connell St in Dublin, a 10,000-strong petition was part of the campaign directed against the attempted ban.

Riverdancing

Dancing has always been a tricky thing in Ireland. Traditionally Irish people have always loved to dance, and in the days before the radio and TV a good night out would have been spent at the crossroads where there was enough space and where people knew to meet each other, dancing set dances – a little bit like a hoedown with someone calling out the moves as partners moved about in fixed patterns of jigs and reels to the tune of a tin whistle, violin or accordion. In the 1940s and 50s, when dance halls opened up, it offered the possibility of all kinds of shenanigans between unmarried men and women, and the church frowned heavily on it with the parish priest often turning up late at night to check on the souls of the young.

Then there is Irish dancing, the name given to the peculiar rigid dancing performed mostly by young girls in heavily embroidered dresses. All over Ireland – and England too – little girls compete for medals which they collect and sew on to a harp-shaped frame. Rooted in the dancing of sailors on shipboard (hornpipe) and probably a hangover from the military past, this quite frigid kind of dancing with the arms held firmly at the sides somehow produced *Riverdance*, the modern version with very short skirts and bare-chested leading men stamping about the stage. Unlike traditional music which is green and cool, *Riverdance*, which was a breath of fresh air when it first hit the stage, must surely now have a limited lifespan.

Casey and his teenage son. There have been corruption charges against once invulnerable men; the Good Friday Agreement saw the end to Ireland's claim to sovereignty over the North; the 1995 divorce laws brought about after a very narrow referendum finally liberated thousands of people from dead marriages; and most amazingly of all the emergence of high-wattage economic growth which has led to Ireland becoming dubbed 'The Celtic Tiger'.

For two centuries Irish people had to leave their homes in order to prosper or even survive. There are millions of Irish-descended people living in Britain, something like 43 million Americans claim Irish descent, and the diaspora spreads to Australia and beyond. When American visas became hard to get in the 80s, the Irish government set up emigration agencies to arrange for young people to go to Europe for work. Suddenly the reverse is true, and not only are Irish people returning home to take up work but for the first time since the Plantation English people are emigrating to Ireland in large numbers. Europeans have been settling in Ireland for the past 30 years, but it was always the oddballs who discovered the real Ireland and gave up money, possessions and city life to live as blow-ins and hippies in little cottages in the west of Ireland, setting up hostels, potteries, small engineering businesses or cafés, or just signing on for unemployment benefit each week. But in the last few years companies like Microsoft and Dell, Fruit of the Loom and others have taken advantage of government subsidies and moved into the cities, providing employment and spending power that never existed before on such a scale. A few miles west of Dublin, in Leixlip, County Kildare, Intel has set up a $2.5 billion plant employing 4,000 people, the biggest building project in the history of Ireland. FÁS, the employment agency, had 10,000 unfilled skilled vacancies in 1999. Forty-four thousand people moved to Ireland in 1998 to take up work, 21,000 of them from Britain. Dublin, Limerick, Galway, Belfast even, have become young vibrant, cosmopolitan places where there are opportunities, a great social life, lots of beautiful countryside, and lots to spend your euros on, whether it be an extremely expensive apartment (Dublin prices now match London's), beautifully designed Irish clothes or a theme café bar serving post-modern bacon and cabbage.

If Dublin belongs to the young and mobile, the west still belongs to the culchies. In the villages of the west of Ireland scant attention is paid to *Microsoft* or *Intel*, although mobile phones have their uses when you're bringing the cows in. In Dublin not locking your front door is asking for trouble – in the west anyone with a door locked too often has something to hide. In Dublin the man walking towards you is a potential danger – in the west he's someone to chat to for a few minutes. No one locks up their car or even bothers parking it properly, pub closing time depends on how close the police are, while shops, banks and any other useful place you could visit in your lunch hour are firmly closed so that everyone can enjoy their lunch.

The Ireland that you visit in the 21st century is not the Ireland of the 1980s. It has undergone changes that the leaders of the 1916 Rebellion, de Valera, Michael Collins or even Gay Byrne, the radical TV chat show host of the 60s, could not have imagined or even wanted. It has moved into the 21st century with skill and panache, but whether Ireland's wealth of culture will survive the culture of wealth remains to be seen.

Land and environment

Ireland's physical landscape was shaped millions of years ago when mountains formed in the wake of cooling lava, and a mere 200,000 years ago the famous valleys of Killarney were created by shifting blocks of ice. Ice caps melted, sea levels rose and Ireland detached itself from Britain, but it took a longer time for the land joining Britain with Europe to be submerged. This is why snakes that had reached Britain on land could not travel further west to the island of Ireland, though the idea that St Patrick banished them is part of the Irish ABC. The post-glacial period brought a rise in sea level and these river valleys of the southwest flooded to form Dingle Bay, Bantry Bay and Killary Harbour. Around this time, too, the Aran Islands separated from the Burren and the wide Clew Bay flooded and its drumlins submerged, leaving their island crests.

Geography

Ireland is an old country. Its oldest rock, near Rosslare in County Wexford, is 2,400 million years old. Geologists suggest that 4,000 million years ago Ireland was two separate halves, one attached to early America and one to early Europe. When the two continents collided Ireland was squashed together and raised above sea level; huge rivers appeared which dumped red sand into the south, making the old red sandstone of the Cork and Kerry peninsulas. Three hundred and seventy five million years ago, Ireland found itself under a shallow warm sea where millions of tiny sea creatures lived and died, their remains forming great limestone swathes filled with fossil remains. On top of the limestone, shale and clay collected and supported primeval trees which in their turn decayed to form coal. Then, 300 million years ago, the European and African tectonic plates collided, and the old red sandstone with its covering of limestone and shale burst upwards and sideways to make the mountains of West Cork and Kerry, the Ballyhouras, the Galtees, the mountains of Limerick, and finally the Clare hills. If you compare these today you will see how the Kerry mountains took the worst of the upheaval, folding alarmingly into almost vertical sandstone sheets, while the Clare hills are almost flat, demonstrating how the power of the movement declined.

The next big burst of activity occurred 65 million years ago as the American and European continents drifted apart, creating the Atlantic Ocean. The west of Ireland sank as its support fell away, while to the north and east great lava flows and molten rock poured upwards creating the Giant's Causeway, the Mourne Mountains, and Doon Hill in Connemara. About 35 million years ago a depression formed in the middle of Ireland, creating a central low lying plain drained by the Shannon and surrounded by mountains. The basic structure of the country was now in place, only requiring erosion by rivers, glaciers and icesheets, and a few late tectonic shifts. These relatively recent landforms include the Wicklow hills, Lough Hyne in West Cork, thousands of drumlins and many U-shaped glacier-carved valleys.

Forests

A thousand years ago Ireland was covered in dense broadleaved forests with cleared patches on the tops of hills. Its main arteries were the rivers and coasts. Communities depended utterly on woodland products and, before the Normans arrived, the Danes in Dublin exported wood to treeless Iceland and elsewhere. As various waves of invaders encroached on the land, roads were built for their armies and the forests were cleared for settlements, to fuel mineworkings or to build English ships, so that today almost none of the aboriginal forests of Ireland remain. The best examples are in the southwest, at Muckross in Killarney, Glengarriff and Knockomagh Woods near Skibbereen, West Cork, and Shillelagh in south Wicklow. Visiting these places, especially in autumn, is one of the delights of the southwest of Ireland. Despite Ireland's limited range of plants the woods are pollution free, and you can see this in the enormous range of lichens that cover the trees. Holly, ferns, honeysuckle, wood sorrel, anemones, bluebells and celandines flourish in the spring before the trees grow leaves to shade out the light. By contrast, if you look into the understorey of the fast-profit conifer plantations which now seem to cover so much of the upland areas of Ireland, very little thrives at all.

Raised bogs

Thanks to hundreds of years of decline and neglect, much of rural Ireland is today a paradise of undamaged environments, worked on in the past only by farmers using small-scale technology. As a result, ecological niches such as raised peat bogs which were lost years ago in other countries are still thriving here. When the ice retreated from Ireland 9,000 years ago, it left great dammed lakes which gradually filled with water plants. As they decayed and formed a subsoil, a habitat was created for plants such as reeds and sedges which could tolerate partly wet conditions. The decay process continued until the debris rose above the water level and became fenland. Meanwhile, in the middle of the bog, oxygen depletion was taking place and plants which could tolerate low levels of oxygen moved in, notably sphagnum moss. This plant can capture and store rainwater, and needs very little else as nutrient. It quickly builds great domes which stand above the water level and hold large quantities of water, raising the water table as they do so. Other plants are starved out and the sphagnum takes over the area. Over thousands of years these plants flourished, creating ever higher mounds as the plants underneath died and formed a new base.

The bogs of Ireland are most abundant along the west coast and almost non-existent in the east. They are an important habitat for thousands of plant and animal species, and in addition have covered and protected thousands of years of human habitation, so that any little museum in Ireland will contain artefacts found in the bogs, ranging from fossilized bog butter to jewellery, from weapons to whole bodies which have hardly deteriorated at all. Roadways, villages, field systems have all emerged from the bogs as they have been excavated. But there lies the problem. The bog is an intact entity, its structure holding the water which keeps it growing and surviving. If the bog is cut, even by a hand tool, the water drains away and the bog dies, becoming dry enough to support first heathers and then other moorland plants and trees. With the wholesale peat cutting taking place in modern times in the biggest bogs in Ireland, the entire bog habitat, even those parts protected by the government, is ultimately doomed.

The fields

The Irish landscape, even nowadays, is a network of small fields bounded by stone ditches or hedgerows of whitethorn and blackthorn. The east of the country is largely fertile arable land, growing vegetables and sugar beet, while the north has small orchards and the west is given over to bog, cattle, sheep and grass. Most farms once had both pasture land and cultivated fields for oats and rye, but in modern times this is rare. Animal feed is bought in, there are few horses to grow oats for, and barley is produced on a large scale or not at all. Many of the fields systems you see are ancient, having been marked out long before any recorded history took place. Traditionally field boundaries were made of earth and stone ditches, each year's cleared sods of grass being added to the ditch along with anything else the plough turned up. The ditches were planted with hawthorn slips, and over the years the seeds of oak, ash, elder, wild rose and honeysuckle were brought by birds and small creatures. The hedgerows have become highways for animal life, providing home and food for hundreds of species of animals. In the west of Ireland fuchsia, an introduced plant, has become the dominant hedgerow plant – not a good choice for the native bees which cannot feed on the narrow flowers. Rhododendron has become another useful plant, providing windbreak all year round, though its invasive nature threatens the few remaining oakwoods.

The seashore

Ireland has more than 2000 miles of coastline, the eastern coasts being more heavily populated and sheltered. The major ports of Waterford, Wexford, Dublin and Belfast, being heavily industrialized, have taken over much of the coastal habitat, but the west and southern coasts are exposed and have high cliffs and so provide an unspoiled habitat for plant and animal life. From the cliffs all over the west coast seals, dolphins and migrant birds can be spotted, while in the mouth of the Shannon colonies of dolphins thrive. Although golf courses are breeding like rabbits all over the west, there are still some undamaged sand dunes which make up a complex ecosystem of their own. The marram grasses bind the dunes together and provide a solid base for other plants such as sea holly, heartsease, sea sandwort, burnet rose and the rare ladies' tresses orchid to find a niche. These plants are a food source and shelter for snails, sand hoppers and butterflies, which in their turn provide a food source for birds such as skylarks and meadow pipits. Many of Ireland's dune systems have revealed evidence of neolithic culture, shell middens and cooking places, and even traces of iron smelting. In the shallow seas in front of the dunes systems wading birds feed, and the summer sees migrants from northern climates which come to the west of Ireland to breed. High cliffs and the offshore islands provide a breeding ground for other sea birds. Here too there is evidence of early cultures in the many promontory forts and other antiquities.

A planned golf course at Doonbeg, County Clare, was put on hold in December 1999 after it was found to be the habitat of the rare narrow-mouth whorl snail (Vertigo angustior).

Flora and fauna

After the end of the last Ice Age both Ireland and Britain were connected to Europe by land bridges, and plants and animals from the mainland quickly recolonized both soon-to-be islands. But Ireland was cut off sooner by the rising sea levels and consequently has a much smaller range of both plants (around 70% of Britain's species) and animals (65% of Britain's insect species, for example), even in today's polluted times. There are no snakes in Ireland, only two amphibians as compared with Britain's six, 354 bird species compared with Britain's 456, and so on. Not that you'd notice when walking around the countryside in Ireland where plants that only survive in tiny niches in Britain peek out of every hedgerow. The plants and animals that Ireland is home to are less endangered here than in most of the rest of Europe. Interestingly, Ireland has 15 native species that are missing in the British flora and fauna. If you imagine a post-Ice-Age land link from Europe to Britain and then to Ireland you have to ask how the plants could have hopped over Britain, missing it completely and landing in Ireland. The theory is that at some point a land link existed between Ireland and southern Europe, and that these plant and animal species travelled to Ireland this way, bypassing Britain. Three heathers, St Daboc's heath, Mediterranean heath and Mackay's heath, are found in tiny colonies in Connemara and Donegal and southern France, while the greater butterwort, an insectivorous plant, is found only in the southwest of Ireland. The strawberry tree is found only in the southwest of Ireland, Brittany and the Mediterranean, and the spotted slug is again restricted to the southwest of Ireland.

Fauna is a little less easy to spot – you're more likely to see a dolphin than a stoat, for example. Neither are they as safe in the Irish environment as you would think. Woodpeckers disappeared when the last of the primeval forests were cut down, the very common corncrake almost disappeared because improved artificial fertilizers have made two harvests of grass possible each year. The birds, which nested in the long grass, had no time to rear their young before the first grass was cut – consequently very few young Irish people have heard the call which was so familiar to their parents. With the commercial cutting of the peat bogs, hundreds of species could disappear. In contrast minks, not a native species, are a common roadkill. They were introduced in farms, from which they of course escaped, and have found a niche in the woodlands and hedgerows. In 1999 the varroa mite, which infests bee colonies and eventually destroys them, was found in County Sligo, so it is merely a matter of time before the wild bee population in Ireland is wiped out. That would change the entire face of the Irish countryside, since so many of its wild flowers depend on pollination by bees.

Books

→ *All books are paperback unless stated as hardback (HB).*

Art, architecture and gardens

Hill, Judith *Irish Public Sculpture.* (Four Courts Press, 1998) HB. The stories and history behind the best of the many sculptures found across Ireland.

McAfee, Patrick *Irish Stone Walls.* (O'Brien Press, 2004) HB. For enthusiasts, builders, landscape gardeners and anyone with an interest in this remarkable landscape feature.

Rothery, Sean *The Buildings of Ireland.* (Lilliput Press, 1997). Delicate ink drawings accompany each of the 194 buildings selected by the author as fine examples of buildings dotted around towns and dating from early Christian times to the 20th century.

Williams, Jeremy *Architecture in Ireland 1837-1921.* (Irish Academic Press, 1994) HB.

Comprehensive gazetteer detailing the architecture of post-Georgian Ireland county by county and building by building; opinionated and knowledgeable.

Cookery

Allen, Darina *Ballymaloe Cookery Course.* (Kyle Cathie Ltd, 2001) HB. A doorstep of a book with over 1,000 recipes from the famous Ballymaloe Cookery School in Ireland. Footprint readers can purchase it without paying any hefty postage charges if they call T020-7692 7221 or from the publisher at 122 Arlington Rd, London, NW1 7HP, quoting ref Foot1.

Johnson, Margaret *The Irish Heritage Cookbook.* (Wolfhound Press, 1999). Onion and Murphy's stout soup followed by chicken with cabbage and bacon, plus another 200 recipes of traditional and not-so-traditional meals.

O'Neill, Molly *A Feast of Irish Cooking.* (Colin Smythe Ltd, 2000). An inexpensive book of Irish recipes.

Culture

Brennan, Helen *The Story of Irish Dance.* (Brandon, 1999). From medieval times to contemporary set dancing; far too sympathetic to *Riverdance* but a useful study nonetheless.

Eagleton, Terry *The Truth About The Irish.* (New Island Books, 1999). A laugh a minute, literally, in this alphabet of Irish mores. Worth reading for the entry on B&Bs alone.

Harrison Therman, Dorothy *Stories from Tory Island* (Town House & Country House, 1989). Transcriptions of conversations with the Antrim islanders; foreword by Derek Hill.

Levy, Pat *Culture Shock! Ireland* (Graphic Arts Center Publishing, 2000). Full of insights (well, we would say that wouldn't we?) into the lifestyle and mentality of contemporary Ireland.

Synge, J M *The Aran Islands.* (Oxford). The 1907 travelogue sparkles with the writer's affection for the place, though tales told around turf fires about children taken by the fairies are now ancient history.

Culture and autobiography

Carberry, Mary *West Cork Journals, 1898-1901.* (Lilliput Press, 1998) HB. Encounters with local life and customs and the writer's winning indifference to the grander aspects of an Anglo-Irish Ascendancy makes this a fascinating read.

Countess of Fingall, Elizabeth *Seventy Years Young.* (Lilliput Press, 1991). Anglo-Irish memoirs of Countess who married at the age of 17 into the Ascendancy and ended up working for the United Irishwomen.

McCafferty, Nell *Nell.* (Penguin Ireland, 2004) HB. autobiography of the Derry-born journalist, charting her gay life and her political experiences with a refreshing frankness.

Thomson, David *Woodbrook.* (Vintage, 1991). A memoir of Anglo-Irish life in Sligo in the 1930s and a moving love-story. Lyrical and hauntingly sad.

Ecology and natural history

Cabot, David *Ireland.* (HarperCollins, 1999) HB. Expensive but comprehensive and well nigh indispensable account of the natural history of Ireland, focusing on the diverse habitats and with over 200 illustrations.

Cabot, David *Irish Birds.* (Collins, 2004). Colour photographs grouped around where the birds are most likely to be seen.

Lloyd Praeger, Robert *The Way That I Went.* (Collins Press, 1998). One of Ireland's greatest naturalists (1865-1953) and of all his works (*The Botanist in Ireland* (1934), *Natural History of Ireland* (1950), *Irish Landscape* (1953) and others), this topographical classic is his most memorable.

Michael Viney *Ireland.* (Blackstaff, 2004) HB. Engaging and informative descriptions of the country's ecosystem through time.

Nelson, Charles *Wild Plants of the Burren and the Aran Islands.* (The Collins Press 1999). Useful little, all-colour field guide for nature walks in the places it covers.

History

General

Barden, Jonathan *A History of Ulster.* (Belfast, 1992). Easily the best history of the northern province, even-handed throughout and in

style that makes it a pleasure to read.
onnolly, S J, editor *The Oxford ompanion to Irish History.* (Oxford, 1998). omprehensive and indispensable reference uide for Irish history.
oulter, Colin and Coleman, Steve *The nd of Irish History?* (Manchester University ress, 2003). More timely reflections of a ritical kind on the Celtic Tiger syndrome.
uffy, Sean, editor *Atlas of Irish History.* Gill & Macmillan, 1997). A visual and highly atisfying summary of the sweep of Irish istory and politics up to modern times.
erriter, Diarmaid *The Transformation f Ireland 1900-2000.* (Profile, 2004). gripping account of the making of nodern Ireland, rooted in social history nd full of insights. Recommended.
oster, R F *The Irish Story.* (Allen Lane, 2001) IB. Examines how key moments in Irish istory have been transformed into arratives. An excellent introduction to one trand of current thinking on Irish history.
irby, Peaddar, Gibbons, Luke and Cronin, lichael *Reinventing Ireland.* (Pluto Press, 004). A much-needed challenge to the ommon idea that contemporary Ireland is ltogether a wonderful economic miracle.
ydon, James *The Making of Ireland.* Routledge, 1998). One of the best eneral histories of the country from ncient times onwards.
tewart, ATQ *The Shape of Irish History.* Blackstaff Press, 2001) HB. Not for the ewcomer to Irish history, a series of anny reflections on Irish history through he centuries.
ownshend, Charles *Ireland: The 20th entury.* (Arnold, 1998). Detailed but eadable account of modern Ireland from he origins of Sinn Féin onwards.
he Penguin Atlas of British & Irish History. Penguin, 2001). A multi-faceted approach o the entangled histories of the 2 countries, vith maps galore.

re-history

arbison, Peter *Pre-Christian Ireland.* Thames & Hudson, 1998). Comprehensive nd readable synthesis of early Ireland and s archaeology.
ames, Simon *The Atlantic Celts.* (British Museum Press, 1999). Controversial but onvincing thesis, delivering a big blow to New Age Celtists, that the false idea of an insular Celtic identity was engendered by the rise of nationalism in the 18th century.
James, Simon *Exploring the World of the Celts.* (Thames & Hudson, 1993) HB. Well illustrated survey of Celtic history and culture.
O'Kelly, Michael J *Early Ireland.* (Cambridge University Press, 1989). Covering much the same ground as Harbison's book but with a more scholarly tone.
Twist, Clint *Atlas of the Celts.* (George Philip Limited, 2001). Less an atlas and more a very visual general history of the Celts, their culture and impact.

Topics

Barry, Tom *Guerilla Days in Ireland.* (Anvil 1981). First published in 1949, a participant's extraordinary account of the war against the British in west Cork.
Breen, Dan *My Fight For Irish Freedom.* (Anvil 1981). First published in 1924, the story of the guerrilla war in Tipperary by a man who the wanted posters described as having as looking 'rather like a blacksmith coming from a walk'.
Furlong, Dáire and Nicholas, editor *The Women of 1798.* (Four Courts Press, 1998). Long overdue account of the role of women in the tumultuous events of 1798.
Gonne McBride, Maud *A Servant of the Queen.* (Colin Smythe Ltd, 2000). The woman who told WB Yeats where to get off, matrimonially speaking, because fighting the British was a more urgent task.
Hopkinson, Michael *The Irish War of Independence* and *Green Against Green.* (Gill & Macmillan 2004). Thoroughly researched and dispassionate accounts of the war for independence and the civil war that followed.
McDonald, Henry and Cusack, Jim *UDA.* (Penguin Ireland 2004). History of the sectarian slaughter, feuding and gangsterism that made the Ulster Defence Association infamous.
McKay, Susan *Northern Protestants.* (Blackstaff Press 2000). A journalist offers an uncompromising, in-depth examination of her own people; prepare to be shocked.
Marreco, Anne *The Rebel Countess.* (Phoenix Press 1967). Good biography of the rebel Anglo-Irish countess who played her

part in the 1916 Rising.

Morgan, Hiram, editor *The Battle of Kinsale.* (Wordwell, 2004). Some 20 authors from Europe and America deal with the momentous battle that marked the beginning of the end of Gaelic Ireland.

Reilly, Tom *Cromwell An Honourable Enemy.* (Brandon, 1999). Who said Cromwell was the scourge of the Irish? A daring reassessment of the most reviled figure in Irish history.

Somerville-Large, Peter *The Coast of West Cork.* (Appletree 1991). A worthwhile companion if travelling at length in west Cork between Clonakility and Ardgroom; full of history, impressions and anecdotes.

Taylor, Peter *Provos.* (Bloomsbury, 1997). The most informative and balanced account of the IRA to be published.

Ward, Margaret *Hanna Sheehy Skeffington: A Life.* (Attic Press, 1997). Valuable biography of the feminist socialist who became an important figure in Sinn Féin at the turn of the century.

Journals

Film Ireland, FilmBase, Irish Film Centre, 6 Eustace St, Dublin 2. F01-6796717, www.iftn.ie. Film reviews, interviews, research articles.

History Ireland, P.O. Box 69, Bray, Co Wicklow, T01-2765207, carol@wordwellbooks.com. A refreshing range of articles from the obvious to the marginal.

Irish Studies Review, Carfax Publishing, PO Box 25, Abingdon, Oxfordshire OX14 3UE, F01235-401550. A scholarly but broad-based journal covering history and the arts.

Literary studies

The individual books listed here make up a very partial and subjective selection of mostly modern writers.

Arnold, Bruce *The Scandal of Ulysses.* (Liffey Press, 2004). The story of the book, as dramatic as any piece of fiction, up to and including the battles with the current holder of the Joyce copyright.

Brady, Eoin (ed) *The Quiet Quarter.* (New Ireland, 2004). An anthology of new Irish writing from the likes of Dermot Bolger, Rita Ann Higgins, Carlo Gebler, Donall O'Kelly, Iggy McGovern and Mary Wilkinson. Just the thing to carry round for those sleepless nights in B&Bs.

Ellmann, Maud *Elizabeth Bowen: The Shadow Across the Page.* (Edinburgh University Press, 2003). We all know about Joyce and Beckett but this is an illuminating study of one of Ireland's finest writers of fiction (*The Last September* is one of best novels).

Gunn, Ian and Hart, Clive *A Topographical Guide to the Dublin of Ulysses.* (Thames & Hudson, 2004). A hardback volume, one for your reference shelf, with over 80 maps and an account of the characters' movements episode by episode.

Healy, Elizabeth *Literary Tour of Ireland.* (Wolfhound, 2001). A hefty paperback and a little bland but worth packing if you want the literary background to different towns and areas of Ireland.

Kavanagh, P J *Voices in Ireland.* (John Murray, London, 1994). This traveller's literary companion, divided into geographical regions, has more soul than the Elizabeth Healy guide.

Montague, John *Company.* (Duckworth, 2001). Masterly account of literary life in Dublin in the 1950s.

Nicholson, Robert *The Ulysses Guide.* (New Island, 2002). The best pocket-sized *Ulysses* guide, it follows the 18 episodes on their original locations accompanied by clea maps, detailed directions and summaries of each episode. Suitable for the newcomer or the seasoned Joycean.

Welch, Robert, editor *The Oxford Companion to Irish Literature.* (Oxford, 1996). Perfect general purpose reference guide to Ireland's literary heritage.

Novels and plays

Banin, John *The Nowlans.* (Appletree, 1992) HB. First published in 1826, this powerful novel confronts the strains of clerical celibacy.

Craig, Patricia, editor *The Belfast Anthology* (Blackstaff, 1999) HB. Where else would Gerry Adams, Graham Greene, Philip Larkin and Van Morrison rub shoulders? Material from the 17th century to the present: memoirs, poetry, fiction, travel writing, history and letters.

Deane, Seamus *Reading in the Dark,*

Vintage, 1997. Set in Derry in the 1950s and 60s and reaching into a personal and political heart of darkness.
Joyce, James *Ulysses*. (Houyhnhnm Press, First published 1922 and best read in a new edition edited by Danis Rose). The first couple of chapters put most would-be readers off ever finishing the novel. Persevere, make use of a recorded reading (see CDs above) and listen to the voices of Dublin that have never been so astonishingly recreated in written form before or since. *Finnegans Wake* is another kettle of fish but recorded readings will open a window on this extraordinary work.
Keane, John B *Three Plays*. (Mercier Press, 1990). *Text of Sive*, *The Field* and *Big Maggie* by the Kerry playwright who is finally being recognized.
Ledwidge, Francis *Selected Poems*. (New Island Books, 2001). Born in 1887, a worker and trade unionist who died in Flanders in 1917; the introduction to this collection by Seamus Heaney helps explain why he should be better known.
Lever, Charles *Lord Kilgoblin*. (Appletree, 1992) HB. First published in 1872, a gripping tale of Irish politics in the age of imperial misrule.
MacGill, Patrick *Children of the Dead End* and *The Rat-Pack*. (New Island Books, 2001). Two books, originally published in 1914 and 1915, that tell you more about colonial Ireland than many a history book.
McGahern, John *Amongst Women*. (Faber, 1990). Perhaps the most resonant of McGahern's works, blending the personal and the political in a masterful and disturbing way.
McLaverty, Michael *Call My Brother Back*. (Blackstaff, 2003). First published in 1939, this has been acclaimed the best novel out of the North of Ireland.
Ní Dhuibhne, Éilís *The Dancers Dancing*. (Blackstaff Press, 1999). A group of girls attending a summer school in county Donegal provide a setting for this exploration of sex, politics, and Irishness.
O'Brien, Flann *The Third Policeman*. (Grafton). Written in 1940, this brilliantly subversive and enormously comic novel deconstructs the deadening conventionality of Irish life under de Valera.
O'Reilly, Sean *Curfew and Other Stories*. (Faber & Faber). Derry-born author's collection of eight, bleakly lyrical stories.
Park, David *Swallowing the Sun*. (Bloomsbury, 2004) HB. Gripping contemporary fiction by a Northern Ireland writer.
Somerville and Ross *The Real Charlotte*. (Quartet Books, 1977). The female cousins' most accomplished work, a haunting microcosm of the Anglo-Irish world.
Tóibín, Bairbre *The Rising*. (New Island Books, 2001). A terrific first novel, both a love story and a dramatization of events leading up to and including the 1916 Rising.

Poetry

Heaney, Seamus *North*. (Faber, 1975). Heaney's most engaging set of poems as he sets about confronting brute facts regarding colonialism and the social divisions of his country. His mythologizing instinct comes face to face with violence and the poetry reaches new heights.
Heaney, Seamus *Opened Ground*. (Faber, 1998). To date, this is the closest Heaney comes to presenting his *oeuvre*, containing selections from *Wintering Out* (1972), *Stations* and *North* (1975), *Field Work* (1979), *Station Island* (1983), *The Haw Lantern* (1987), *Seeing Things* (1990) and *The Spirit Level* (1996). Enough here to last a lifetime.
Kavanagh, Patrick *Collected Poems*. (Penguin Ireland, 2004). The son of a cobbler and a none-acre farm who redefined Irish poetry and transcended the preoccupation with history, politics and national identity by writing of rural and urban life in a vernacular style.
Murphy, Richard *Collected Poems*. (Gallery Books, 2000). Anglo-Irish poet from Mayo who explores the past with a rare sensibility and a deep sense of history.
O'Brien, Eugene *Seamus Heaney*. (Pluto Press, 2003). Exploration of Heaney's ethical and political project with respect to issues of Irish identity as outlined in his writings.

Walking and cycling guides

Corcoran, Kevin *West of Ireland Walks/West Cork Walks/Kerry Walks*. (O'Brien Press, Dublin). Superb little books with maps and ecological anecdotes of the politically correct kind along the way.

Dillon, Paddy *The Ulster Way.* (O'Brien Press, 1999). The complete Ulster Way written by a noted author of many walking guides.

Fewer, Michael *The Way-Marked Trails of Ireland.* (Gill & Macmillan, 1996). A reliable guide to the best waymarked trails in the Republic, with maps and practical information on where to stay and eat.

Lynam, Joss *Dublin.* (Gill & Macmillan, 2004). 35 walks in the Dublin region.

Malone, J B *The Complete Wicklow Way.* (O'Brien Press, 1999). An updated edition of a guide to this long-distance walk.

Marshall, David *Best Walks in Ireland.* (Constable, London, 1996). Five in the North and 15 in the Republic, graded in difficulty from an easy day's stroll to an ambitious and demanding climb up a mountain. Good maps, clear instructions and anecdotes along the way.

Walsh, Brendan *Cycle Touring Ireland.* (Gill & Macmillan, 2004). Covers the coastal parts of the island in a series of tours with some tributary inland routes.

Footnotes

Glossary

→ *See page 604 for a glossary of political terms.*

An Óige (lit. 'the youth') Irish youth hostel association
Bailey enclosure beside a castle
Bally a town; hence the hundreds of places beginning with the prefix
Bartizan defensive turret overhanging a wall
Bawn walled enclosure, part of a tower-house or castle
Beag and béal Irish for small
Bodhrán hand-held, goatskin drum (pronounced *boor-run)*
Boreen small lane
Bog decomposed vegetable matter, peat, used as fuel
Bronze Age approximately between 2000 BC and 500 BC; between the Stone Age and Iron Age
Caher a fort build of stone without cement or concrete
Cairn a mound of stones
Capstone a massive stone, weighing as much as 100 tons, covering a megalithic tomb
Ceilí session of traditional Irish music and dancing
Celt Iron Age culture arriving in Ireland around 300 BC
Chevaux-de-frise projecting sharp stones placed in the ground outside an Iron Age fort to deter an enemy
Claddagh ring traditional ring from Connaught characterized by a crowned heart between two hands
Clochán beehive-shaped, stone-built hut from early Christian times
Cloister covered square-shaped passage accessing monastery
Corbel a projecting stone; and the name of a building technique where stones are built out, one above the other, forming a kind of vault
Court-tomb earliest kind of megalithic burial site
Craic common expression for a good time (pronounced *crack)*
Crannog ancient lake dwelling
Culchies Irish expression for country people, rarely used affectionately
Currach/curragh a small boat covered with a waterproof material, originally stretched hides and later tarred canvas
Demesne landed property of country house or castle (pronounced *domain)*
Diamond town square, most common the North
Dolmen megalithic tomb consisting of a flat stone laid on upright ones
Dubh Irish for black
Dun/Doo Irish for a fort
Éire Irish for Ireland
Fáilte Ireland Irish Tourist Board
Fir Irish for men
Fulacht fiadh ancient method of outdoor cooking, using heated stones to bring water to the boil
Gaeltacht an Irish-speaking district
Garda policeman (plural: *gardaí*, pronounced *gar-dee*)
Inis Irish for island
Iron Age From c 500 BC to the arrival of Christianity
Jarvey driver of the traditional jaunting cars, most commonly found in Killarney
Kill/cill Irish for chapel or church
Langer West Cork slang for a good-for-nothing, unreliable individual
Lough a lake
Martello Tower round, squat tower built on coasts for protection against an expected French invasion by sea
Megalithic literally 'big stones', used to describe Stone Age burial tombs using large stones
Mná Irish for women
Neolithic late Stone Age, 4000-2000 BC
North shorthand for Northern Ireland
NTIB Northern Ireland Tourist Board
Ogham a form of writing from around the 4th-9th centuries BC, inscribed on standing-stones
OPW Office of Public Works, formerly *Dúchas*, the Government department responsible for various historical sites in the Republic
Passage grave Megalithic tomb consisting of a corridor of stones leading to a burial chamber
Pishogue something that relates to the world of magic and Irish fairies
Piscina perforated stone basin for carrying away the water used in rinsing chalices
Plantation term referring to the settlement of the English and Scottish, beginning in the late 16th century in southwest Cork and in the early 17th century in Ulster
Poteen/poitín illicitly distilled spirit, made from potatoes or molasses, and still available in parts of Ireland (pronounced *putcheen)*
PSNI Police Service of Northern Ireland, the new name for the police force in the North that aims to be – unlike the Royal Ulster Constabulary (RUC) it is replacing – non-sectarian in its make-up and behaviour.
Ráth Irish for ring fort; ancient dwelling place surrounded by a rampart
Republic shorthand for the 26 counties of the Republic of Ireland
Round Tower tall, circular, stone-built towers built from 9th century onwards and usually associated with monasteries
Sheila-na-gig a carved medieval female figure with exaggerated genitalia, most commonly found on exterior stonework. Thought to be an off-beat symbol from Romanesque and Gothic iconography representing the sin of lust, though Gaelic culture came to regard them as protective
Shillelagh The village of this name in County Wicklow once produced oak walking sticks, sometimes used for fighting, but the blackthorn cudgel sold in tourist shops is pure blarney.
Souterrain an underground passage in a ringfort (archaeological)
TD elected members of the Dáil *(Teachta Dala), the Republic's parliament*
Tinkers politically incorrect term for travellers
Trá Irish for beach
YHANI Youth Hostel Association of Northern Ireland

Place names, townlands and name translations

A townland, a division of land which defies its name by very often being non-urban, can vary in size from 1 acre to 7,000 acres. Their origins can sometimes be traced back to plantation divisions and old clan divisions while the etymologies of many of the 60,000 townlands in Ireland suggest ancient Gaelic origins rooted in a reverence for natural features. In Brian Friel's seminal play *Translations* (1980) the compulsory translation of Gaelic place-names into English by soldiers working on the Ordnance Survey becomes a powerful cultural metaphor for the invasion and expropriation of Ireland by the English.

The following glossary offers some help in recovering the original meaning behind the evocative names of places and townlands across Ireland. They are nearly all Gaelic in origin, although some reveal the impact of Christianity, like kill/cill from the Latin cella.

agh, augh, achadh	field
aglish	church
ah, atha, áth	ford, crossing
aill, anna, canna	cliff
árd, ar	marshland
as, ess, eas	high ground
aw, ow, atha	waterfall
bal, bel, béal	river
bal, bally, baile	town
bán	white
beann (ben)	peak
bearna	gap
beg, beag	small
binn	peak
buí	yellow
bun	bottom, base
caher, cahir	rock
caol	narrow
carraig	rock
cashel, caisel, caisleán	castle
céibh	quay
cloich, cloch	stone
cnoc	rocky hill
cuainín	small harbour
derg, dearg	red
doire	oakwood
doo, dubh	black
dumhaig	of the sandy shore
dúna	of the fort
dun, dún	fort
dysert	hermitage
fada	long
fóin	small cove
géar	sharp
glas, gleann	valley, green
inbhear (inver)	river mouth
inis	island
kill, cill	church
kin	headland
knock, cnoc	hill
leac	flat rock
léith	grey
lis, lios	fort
lough, loch	lake
mainistir	monastery
moy, magh	lake
maol	bare hilllock
mona, móna	bog, turf
mór	big
oileán	island
owen	river
poll	hole, hollow
rath	ring-fort
rinn, reen	headland, point
rón	seal
ross	wood
sceilig (skellig)	rock
sidh	a hill of the fairies
slieve, sliabh	mountain
staca	pinnacle/stack (of rock)
tir	country
tubber, tobar	well
trá, tráigh	beach

Index

D

I

J

K

L

M

Maps

Acknowledgements

Seán Sheehan and Pat Levy would like to thank John Lahiffe at Fáilte Ireland in London and Fiona Ure in the Belfast Visitor and Convention Bureau for the help and consideration they have given to the Footprint Ireland guide. Special thanks to Alan Murphy, Sarah Thorowgood, Emma Bryers, Sarah Sorensen and everyone else at Footprint who has worked so hard to get this third edition out on time.

Many other people have helped in the research for this third edition and our apologies to those whose names we have forgotten to add here:

Alice in Lismore, Alison in Enniskillen, Roy Bolton in Bushmills, George Bradshaw in Omagh. Sharon Brennan in Galway, Margaret Brooks in the US, Lorraine Burns in Westport, Stephen Corrigan in Achill, Liam Duffy in Cahir, Alan Dunlop in Bushmills, Eileen in Ballycastle, Susan Farrell in Trim, Mary Gaunt in Killorglin, Graham Hall in Annalong, Claire Harkin in Donegal, Ross Lewis in Dublin, Eamon & Mireille Jordan in Crolly, Karen in Cashel, Vince Keaney in Cobh, Maria Kelly in Galway, Margaret Kelly in Wexford, Maureen in Derry, Michelle McCauley in Bundoran, Mary McGreal in Westport, Andrea McLoughlin in Oughterard, Alice Maguire in Waterford, Paul Madden in Ennis, Michael Martin in Cobh, Maireed in Clonmel, Gráine Ní Chonchúr in Dingle, Martina O'Dwyer in Dundalk, Mary O'Sheen in Tralee, Pauline in Kilkenny, Ruarí Ó'Heára in Derry, Eileen O'Rourke in Carlow, Daphne D.C. Pochin Mould in Cork, Stan Power in Waterford, Liam Reilly in Drogheda, John Ryan in Galway, Sandra in Kilkeel, Olive Roberts in Cork, Sarah Rodgers in Bangor, Tom Shanahan in Limerick, Jenny Hooder in Stuttgart, Annette Turner in Wicklow, Eileen Vickers in Bray, Mary Whelan in Wexford.

About the authors

Pat Levy visited West Cork one Easter when she was 19 and the memory of the spring flowers and heather on the hills has continued to draw her back like a narcotic. Pat is now hooked for life and looks forward to the time when she can tend full time to her garden in the southwest of Ireland.

Seán Sheehan was born and brought up in London and was a teacher in England and southeast Asia before becoming a full-time writer. He has written travel guides to Thailand, Malaysia, Hong Kong, Beijing and other places and his most recent book is *Anarchism* (Reaktion 2003). Seán Sheehan spends most of his time on a farm in southwest Ireland, looking after a small number of bullocks but many thousands of bees.

Seán and Pat are also the authors of Footprint guides to Dublin and Belfast.

Credits

Footprint credits

Editor: Sarah Thorowgood
Assistant editor: Emma Bryers
Map editor: Sarah Sorensen
Picture editor: Claire Benison
Proofreader: Stephanie Egerton
Publisher: Patrick Dawson
Editorial: Alan Murphy, Sophie Blacksell, Claire Boobbyer, Felicity Laughton, Laura Dixon, Nicola Jones
Cartography: Robert Lunn, Claire Benison, Kevin Feeney, Angus Dawson, Esher Monzón García, Thom Wickes
Series development: Rachel Fielding
Design: Mytton Williams and Rosemary Dawson (brand)
Advertising: Debbie Wylde
Finance and administration: Sharon Hughes, Elizabeth Taylor, Lindsay Dytham

Photography credits

Front cover: Connemara Ponies Irish Image collection
Back cover: Irish Image collection
Inside colour section: Irish Image collection

Print

Manufactured in Italy by LegoPrint
Pulp from sustainable forests

Footprint feedback

We try as hard as we can to make each Footprint guide as up to date as possible but, of course, things always change. If you want to let us know about your experiences – good, bad or ugly – then don't delay, go to **www.footprintbooks.com** and send in your comments.

Every effort has been made to ensure that the facts in this guidebook are accurate. However, travellers should still obtain advice from consulates, airlines etc about travel and visa requirements before travelling. The authors and publishers cannot accept responsibility for any loss, injury or inconvenience however caused.

Publishing information

Footprint Ireland
3rd edition

May 2005

ISBN 1 904 77736 8
CIP DATA: A catalogue record for this book is available from the British Library

Published by Footprint

6 Riverside Court
Lower Bristol Road
Bath BA2 3DZ, UK
T +44 (0)1225 469141
F +44 (0)1225 469461
discover@footprintbooks.com
www.footprintbooks.com

Distributed in the USA by

Publishers Group West

Neither the black and white nor coloured maps are intended to have any political significance.

Advertisers' index

Ireland

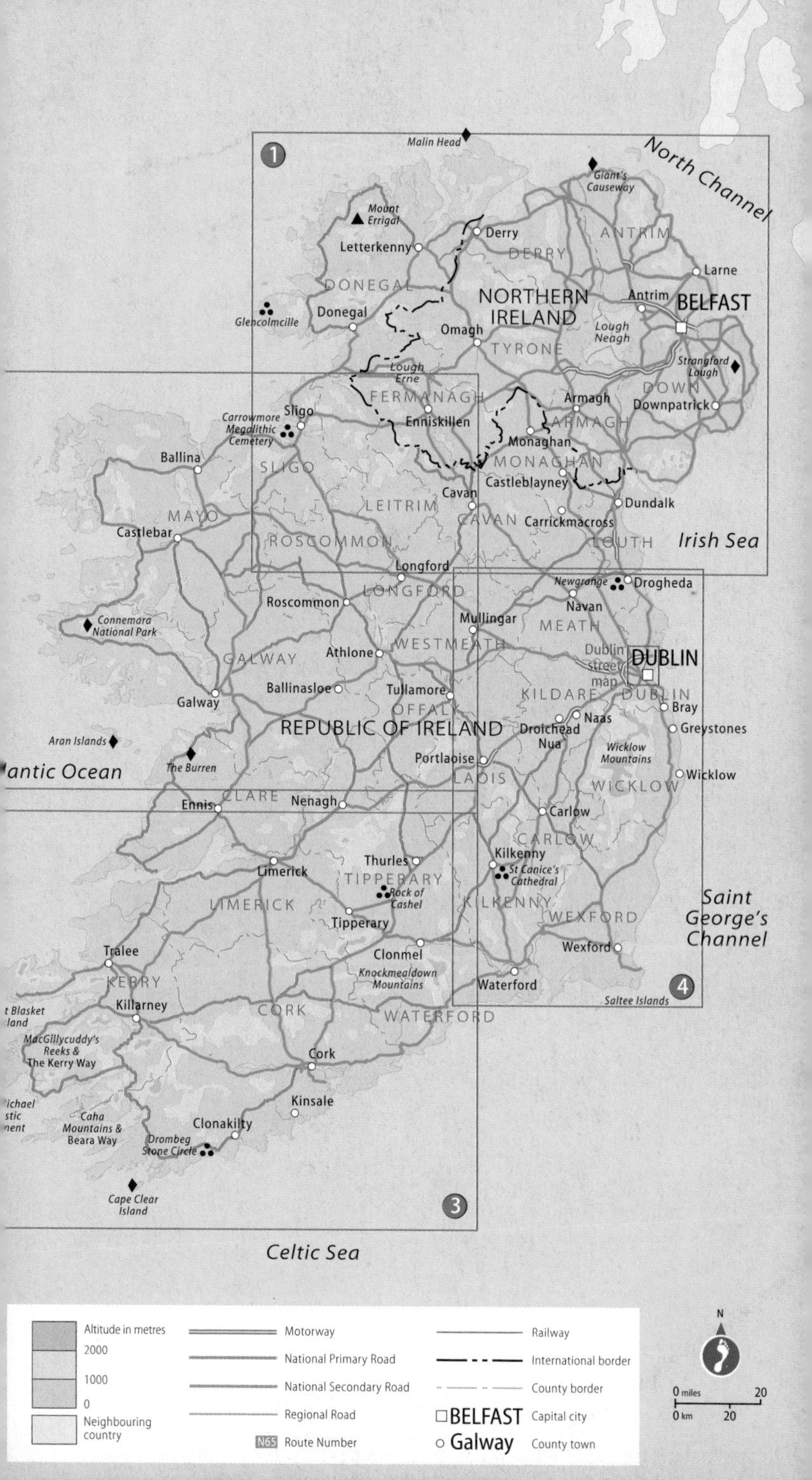

North Channel
Irish Sea
Saint George's Channel
Celtic Sea
Atlantic Ocean
NORTHERN IRELAND
REPUBLIC OF IRELAND
BELFAST
DUBLIN
Dublin street map
Malin Head
Giant's Causeway
Mount Errigal
Derry
Letterkenny
Larne
Antrim
Donegal
Glencolmcille
Omagh
Lough Neagh
Strangford Lough
Lough Erne
Sligo
Carrowmore Megalithic Cemetery
Enniskillen
Armagh
Downpatrick
Monaghan
Castleblayney
Ballina
Cavan
Dundalk
Carrickmacross
Castlebar
Longford
Newgrange
Drogheda
Navan
Roscommon
Mullingar
Connemara National Park
Athlone
Ballinasloe
Tullamore
Galway
Naas
Droichead Nua
Bray
Greystones
Aran Islands
The Burren
Portlaoise
Wicklow Mountains
Wicklow
Ennis
Nenagh
Carlow
Kilkenny
St Canice's Cathedral
Thurles
Limerick
Rock of Cashel
Tipperary
Wexford
Tralee
Clonmel
Knockmealdown Mountains
Waterford
Saltee Islands
Killarney
Blasket Island
MacGillycuddy's Reeks & The Kerry Way
Cork
Kinsale
Caha Mountains & Beara Way
Clonakilty
Drombeg Stone Circle
Cape Clear Island
DONEGAL
DERRY
ANTRIM
TYRONE
FERMANAGH
ARMAGH
DOWN
MONAGHAN
SLIGO
LEITRIM
CAVAN
MAYO
ROSCOMMON
LOUTH
LONGFORD
MEATH
WESTMEATH
GALWAY
KILDARE
DUBLIN
OFFALY
LAOIS
WICKLOW
CLARE
CARLOW
TIPPERARY
LIMERICK
KILKENNY
WEXFORD
KERRY
CORK
WATERFORD
1
3
4

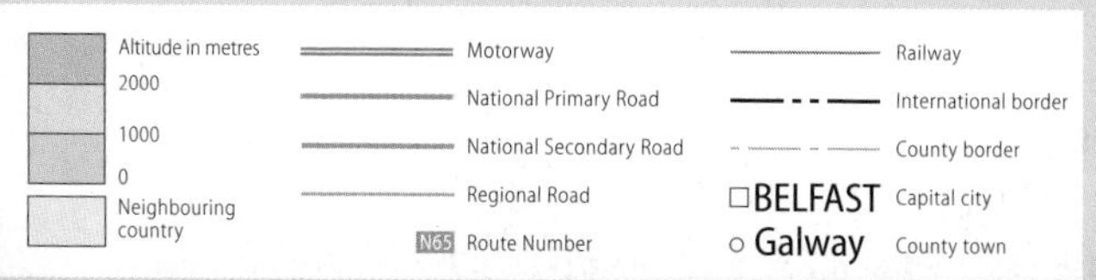

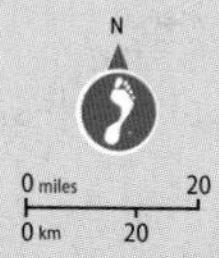

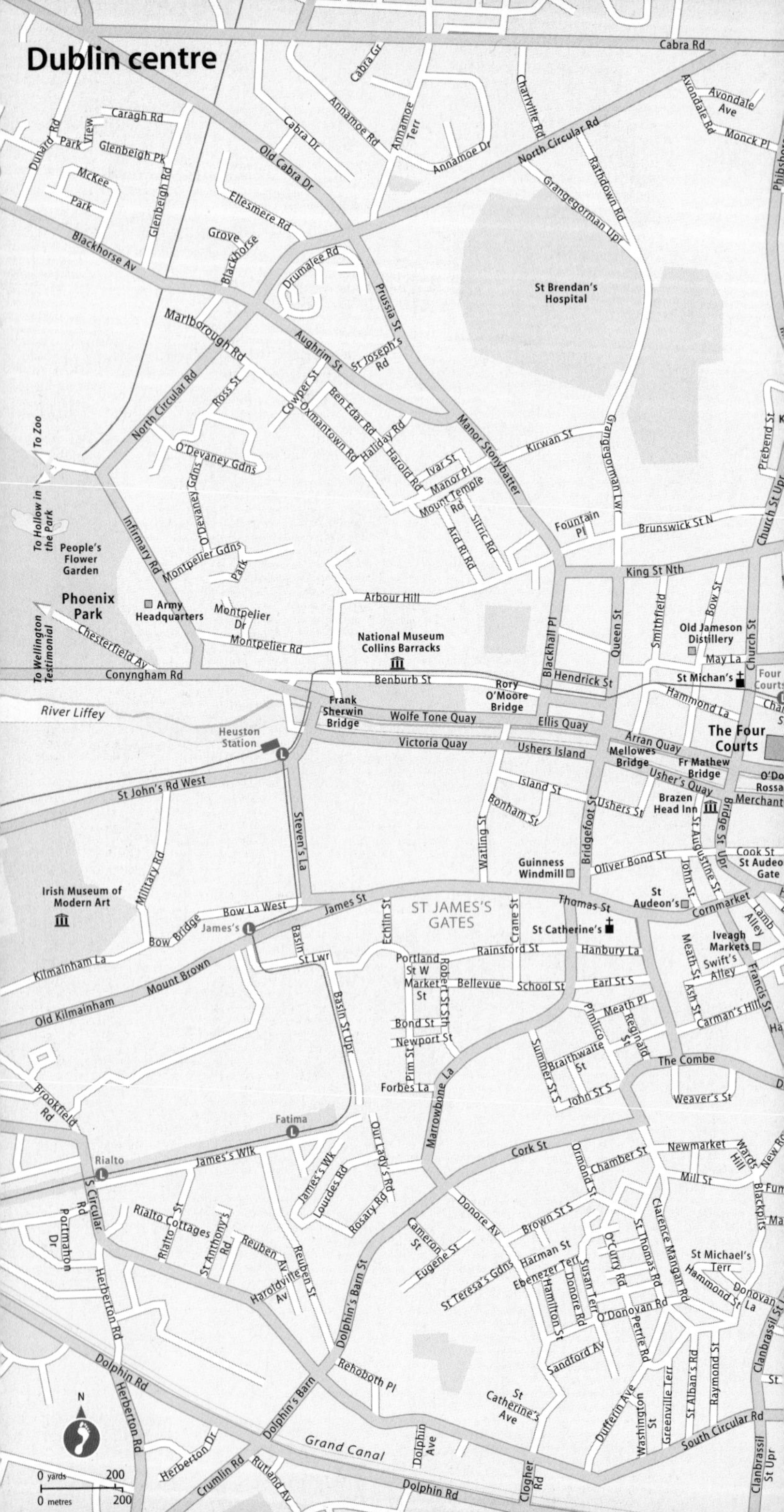
Dublin centre
Cabra Rd
Cabra Gr
Annamoe Rd
Annamoe Terr
Annamoe Dr
Charleville Rd
Avondale Rd
Avondale Ave
Monck Pl
North Circular Rd
Rathdown Rd
Grangegorman Upr
Caragh Rd
Dunard Rd
Park View
Glenbeigh Pk
Glenbeigh Rd
McKee Park
Old Cabra Rd
Cabra Dr
Ellesmere Rd
Blackhorse Av
Grove
Blackhorse
Drumalee Rd
Prussia St
St Brendan's Hospital
Marlborough Rd
Aughrim St
St Joseph's Rd
North Circular Rd
Ross St
Cowper St
Ben Edar Rd
Oxmantown Rd
Haliday Rd
Harold Rd
Manor St
Stonybatter
Kirwan St
Grangegorman Lwr
Prebend St
To Zoo
O'Devaney Gdns
O'Devaney Gdns
Ivar St
Manor Pl
Mount Temple Rd
Sitric Rd
Ard Ri Rd
Fountain Pl
Brunswick St N
Church St Upr
To Hollow in the Park
People's Flower Garden
Infirmary Rd
Montpelier Gdns
Park
King St Nth
Phoenix Park
Army Headquarters
Montpelier Dr
Arbour Hill
Blackhall Pl
Queen St
Smithfield
Bow St
Old Jameson Distillery
May La
Church St
To Wellington Testimonial
Chesterfield Av
Montpelier Rd
National Museum Collins Barracks
Conyngham Rd
Benburb St
Rory O'Moore Bridge
Hendrick St
St Michan's
Four Courts
Hammond La
River Liffey
Frank Sherwin Bridge
Wolfe Tone Quay
Ellis Quay
Heuston Station
Victoria Quay
Ushers Island
Arran Quay
Mellowes Bridge
The Four Courts
Fr Mathew Bridge
Usher's Quay
Merchant
St John's Rd West
Island St
Ushers St
Brazen Head Inn
Bonham St
Bridgefoot St
Steven's La
Watling St
Military Rd
Guinness Windmill
Oliver Bond St
John St
St Augustine St
Bridge St Upr
Cook St
St Audeon Gate
Irish Museum of Modern Art
James St
ST JAMES'S GATES
Thomas St
St Audeon's
Cornmarket
Lamb Alley
Bow La West
James's
Bow Bridge
Basin St Lwr
Echlin St
Crane St
St Catherine's
Iveagh Markets
Kilmainham La
Portland St W
Rainsford St
Hanbury La
Meath St
Swift's Alley
Market St
Robert St Sth
Bellevue
School St
Earl St S
Ash St
Francis St
Mount Brown
Old Kilmainham
Basin St Upr
Meath Pl
Carman's Hill
Bond St
Pimlico
Reginald St
Newport St
Summer St S
Braithwaite St
Pim St
The Combe
Forbes La
Marrowbone La
John St S
Weaver's St
Brookfield Rd
Fatima
Our Lady's Rd
Cork St
Ormond St
Newmarket
Wards Hill
New Row
Rialto
James's Wlk
James's Wlk
Chamber St
Mill St
Fumbally La
Lourdes Rd
Rosary Rd
S Circular Rd
Rialto Cottages
Rialto St
Donore Av
Brown St S
Blackpitts
Portmahon Dr
St Anthony's Rd
Reuben Av
Cameron St
O'Curry Rd
St Thomas Rd
Clarence Mangan Rd
St Michael's Terr
Reuben St
Eugene St
Harman St
Haroldville Av
St Teresa's Gdns
Ebenezer Terr
Hamilton St
Donore Rd
Susan Terr
Hammond St
Donovan La
Herberton Rd
Dolphin's Barn St
O'Donovan Rd
Petrie Rd
Clanbrassil St
Sandford Av
Rehoboth Pl
Dolphin Rd
St Catherine's Ave
Dolphin's Barn
Dufferin Ave
Washington St
Greenville Terr
St Alban's Rd
Raymond St
South Circular Rd
N
Grand Canal
Dolphin Ave
Clanbrassil St Upr
Herberton Dr
0 yards 200
0 metres 200
Crumlin Rd
Rutland Av
Dolphin Rd
Clogher Rd

North Circular Rd
Belvedere Rd
Sherrard St Lwr
Portland St N
Russell St
Royal Canal
Spring Gdn St
Foster Terr
Sackville Av
Ballybough Rd
King's Av
Bayview Ave
Charleville Av
Clonmore Rd
Newcomen Av
Leo St
Dorset La
Sherrard St
Belvedere Pl
Fitzgibbon La
Emmet St
Richmond St N
Summerhill Pde
William St N
Charleville Mall
Ossory Rd
Eccles St
Eccles Pl
Berkeley St
Nelson St
St Josephs Rd
Dorset St Lwr
Gardiner St Upr
North
Charles La
East
Charles St Gt
Summer St N
Blessington St
Hardwicke St
Temple St N
Mountjoy Sq
West
South
Pig La
Portland Row
Dunne St
Wellington St
Gardiner Pl
Hill St
Grenville St
Gardiner La
Summerhill
Rutland St Lwr
Buckingham St Upr
Empress Pl
Frederick St N
Denmark St Gt
North Gt George's St
Dublin Writers' Museum
National Wax Museum
Hugh Lane Gallery
Parnell Sq N
Rutland Pl
James Joyce Centre
Cumberland St N
Sean Mac Dermott St Lwr
Buckingham St Lwr
Frankfort Cot
Dorset St Upr
Paradise Pl
Parnell Sq E
Parnell St
Railway St
Beaver St
Seville Pl
Oriel St Lwr
Dominick Pl
Parnell Sq W
Granby Pl
Parnell Monument
Sean Mac Dermott St Upr
Corporation St
Connolly Station
Dominick St Lwr
Brugha St
Foley St
Sherriff St
Oriel St Upr
Kings Inn St
O'Connell St
Pro-Cathedral
Gardiner St Lwr
Amiens St
Lwr
Bolton St
Lotus La
Moore St
Parnell St
Marlborough St
Cathedral St
Talbot St
Talbot Pl
Store St
Commons St
Earl St N
Busárás
Mayor St Lwr
Capel St
Jervis St
Henry St
General Post Office
Abbey Street
Beresford Pl
Memorial Rd
Custom House
Liffey St Upr
Abbey St Lwr
Abbey Theatre
Mary St
The O'Connell Monument
Docklands Visitor Centre
Custom House Quay
Jervis
Abbey St Mid
Lotts
Eden Quay
Butt Bridge
Talbot Memorial Bridge
Abbey St Upr
Liffey St Lwr
Lwr Batchelor Wlk
O'Connell Bridge
George's Quay
River Liffey
Mary's Abbey
Strand St Gt
Burgh Quay
Tara
City Quay
Ha'penny Bridge
Hawkins St
Poolbeg St
Tara St
Moss St
Gloucester St
Windmill La
Upr Ormond Quay
Millennium Bridge
Aston Quay
Westmorland St
D'Olier St
Creighton St
Lime St
Grattan Bridge
Wellington Quay
Townsend St
Lombard St East
Essex Quay
Anglesea St
Fleet St
Temple Bar
Fire Station Tower
Hanover St E
Parliament St
Essex St E
Eustace St
Bank of Ireland Arts Centre
West Front
Pearse St
Sandwith St Lwr
Irish Film Centre
College Gn
Campanile
Erne St Lwr
Lord Edward St
Dame St
Provost's House
Oscar Wilde No 21
Dublin Local Studies Library
City Hall
St Andrew St
Book of Kells
Pearse
Pearse St
Dublin Castle
Sth Gt Georges St
Exchequer St
Suffolk St
Trinity College
Westland Row
Werburgh St
Wicklow St
Nassau St
Sandwith St Upr
Erne St Upr
Ship St Lt
Chester Beatty Library
Drury St
Leinster St S
Lincoln Pl
Ship St Gt
William St S
Clarendon St
Duke St
Heraldic Museum & Genealogical Office
Clare St
Fenian St
Chancery La
Stephen St Lwr
Grafton St
Anne St S
National Library
National Gallery
Denzille La
Hollies St
Golden La
Whitefriar Street Carmelite
Chatham St
Molesworth St
Kildare St
Dawson St
Leinster House
North
Bride St
Peter Row
Aungier St
King St S
National Museum of Archaeology & History
Merrion Sq
Rutland Fountain
Grattan St
Mercer St Lwr
Stephen's Green Shopping Centre
St Stephen's Green
Natural History Museum
Merrion St Upr
Mount St Lwr
Peter St
York St
Huguenot Cemetery
Govt Buildings
Duke of Wellington No 24
South
East
Marsh's Library
National Archives
Mercer St Upr
Merrion Row
Bishop St
Digges St Upr
Cuffe La
Hume St
Ely Pl
Fitzwilliam La
Mount St Upr
Kevin St Lwr
Cuffe St
St Stephen's Green
Fitzwilliam St Lwr
James St East
St Stephen's
REDMOND HILL
Wexford St
South
Baggot St
Pembroke St Lwr
James Pl East
University Church
Newman House & The Commons
Pembroke La
Herbert St
New Bride St
Camden Row
Montague St
University College
Quinn's La
Fitzwilliam St Upr
Herbert Pl
Camden Pl
Fitzwilliam Sq
Lad La
Peasants St
Camden St Lwr
Iveagh Gardens
Earlsfort Terr
Pembroke St Upr
Arnott St
Heytesbury St
Harcourt St
Harcourt
Hatch St Upr
Hatch St Lwr
Fitzwilliam Pl
Cumberland Rd
Wilton Pl
Baggot St Upr
Curzon St
The Shaw Birthplace
Charlotte Way
Leeson St Lwr
Wilton Terr
Grand Canal
Synge St
Grantham Pl
Camden St Upr
The Findlater Museum
Mespil Rd
Flemings Pl
Emor St
Harcourt Rd
Adelaide Rd
Harrington St
Stamer St
Richmond St S
Charlemont St
Harcourt Terr
Burlington Rd
Waterloo La
Waterloo Rd
Victoria St
Lennox St
Charlemont
Charlemont Pl
Grand Parade
Leeson St Upr
Irish Jewish Museum
Lennox Pl
Portobello College
Charlemont Mall
Dartmouth Sq
Sussex Rd

Map 1

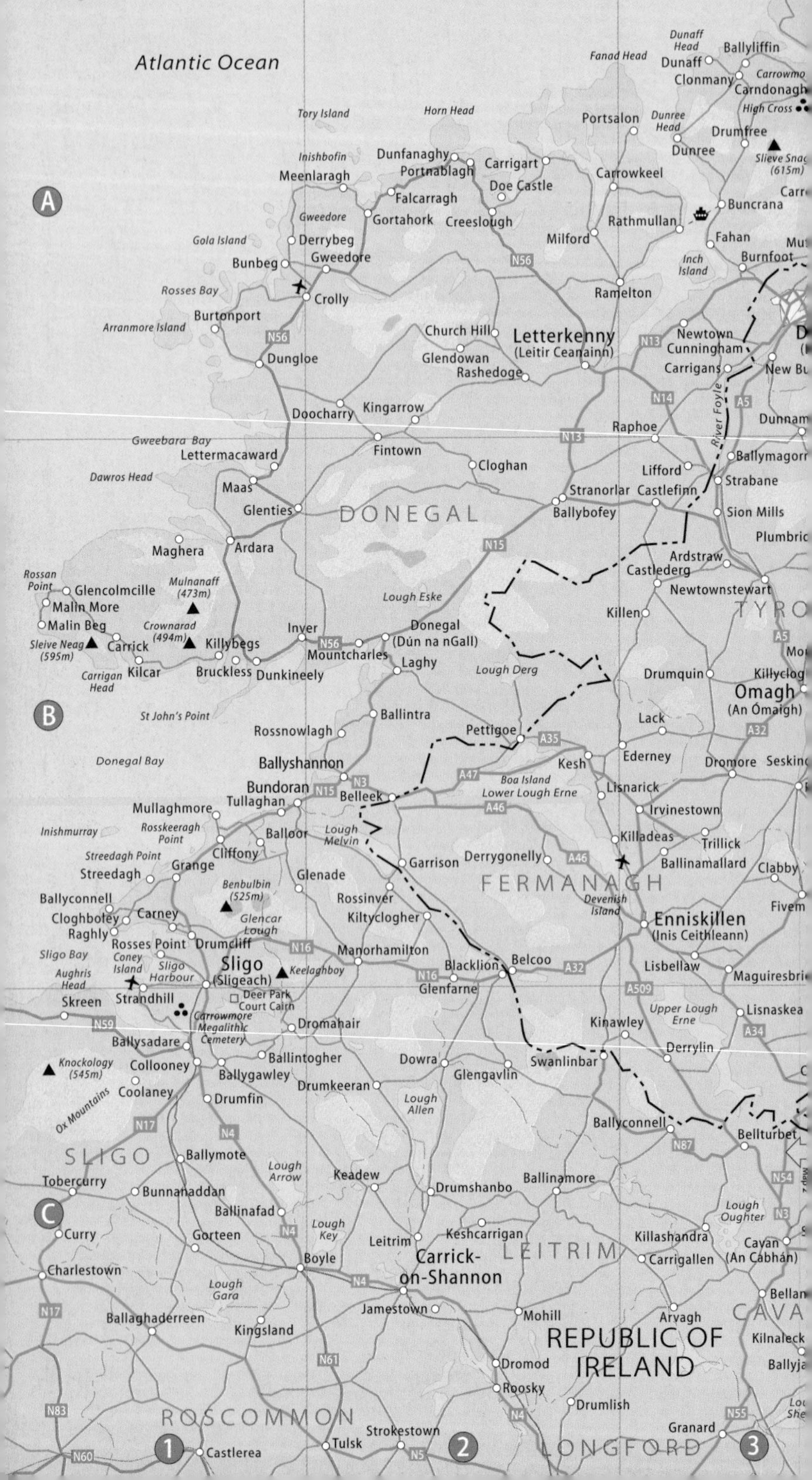
Atlantic Ocean
Inishtrahull Sound
Malin Head
Dunaff Head
Dunaff
Ballyliffin
Fanad Head
Clonmany
Carndonagh
High Cross
Tory Island
Horn Head
Portsalon
Dunree Head
Dunree
Drumfree
Slieve Snag (615m)
Inishbofin
Dunfanaghy
Portnablagh
Carrigart
Meenlaragh
Doe Castle
Carrowkeel
Falcarragh
Buncrana
Gweedore
Gortahork
Creeslough
Rathmullan
Gola Island
Derrybeg
Milford
Fahan
Gweedore
Inch Island
Burnfoot
Bunbeg
Rosses Bay
Crolly
Ramelton
Burtonport
Arranmore Island
Church Hill
Letterkenny
(Leitir Ceanainn)
Newtown Cunningham
Dungloe
Glendowan
Rashedoge
Carrigans
New Bu
River Foyle
Doocharry
Kingarrow
Raphoe
Gweebara Bay
Fintown
Lettermacaward
Cloghan
Lifford
Ballymagorr
Dawros Head
Maas
Stranorlar
Castlefinn
Strabane
Glenties
DONEGAL
Ballybofey
Sion Mills
Maghera
Ardara
Plumbric
Ardstraw
Castlederg
Rossan Point
Glencolmcille
Mulnanaff (473m)
Newtownstewart
Malin More
Lough Eske
Killen
TYRO
Malin Beg
Crownarad (494m)
Inver
Donegal
(Dún na nGall)
Sleive Neag (595m)
Carrick
Killybegs
Mountcharles
Carrigan Head
Kilcar
Bruckless
Dunkineely
Laghy
Lough Derg
Drumquin
Omagh
(An Ómaigh)
St John's Point
Ballintra
Lack
Rossnowlagh
Pettigoe
Ederney
Donegal Bay
Ballyshannon
Kesh
Dromore
Seskin
Bundoran
Belleek
Boa Island
Lower Lough Erne
Lisnarick
Mullaghmore
Tullaghan
Irvinestown
Inishmurray
Rosskeeragh Point
Balloor
Lough Melvin
Killadeas
Trillick
Streedagh Point
Cliffony
Garrison
Derrygonelly
Ballinamallard
Clabby
Streedagh
Grange
Glenade
FERMANAGH
Ballyconnell
Benbulbin (525m)
Rossinver
Devenish Island
Cloghboley
Carney
Kiltyclogher
Enniskillen
(Inis Ceithleann)
Raghly
Glencar Lough
Sligo Bay
Rosses Point
Drumcliff
Manorhamilton
Coney Island
Sligo Harbour
Sligo
(Sligeach)
Keelaghboy
Blacklion
Belcoo
Lisbellaw
Aughris Head
Strandhill
Deer Park Court Cairn
Glenfarne
Maguiresbri
Skreen
Carrowmore Megalithic Cemetery
Dromahair
Kinawley
Upper Lough Erne
Lisnaskea
Ballysadare
Derrylin
Knockology (545m)
Collooney
Ballintogher
Dowra
Swanlinbar
Glengavlin
Coolaney
Ballygawley
Drumkeeran
Ox Mountains
Drumfin
Lough Allen
Ballyconnell
Belturbet
SLIGO
Ballymote
Lough Arrow
Keadew
Ballinamore
Tobercurry
Bunnanaddan
Drumshanbo
Lough Oughter
Ballinafad
Lough Key
Curry
Gorteen
Keshcarrigan
Killashandra
Leitrim
Carrick-on-Shannon
LEITRIM
Cavan
(An Cabhán)
Boyle
Carrigallen
Charlestown
Lough Gara
Bellan
Jamestown
Ballaghaderreen
Mohill
Arvagh
CAVA
Kingsland
REPUBLIC OF IRELAND
Kilnaleck
Dromod
Ballyja
Roosky
Drumlish
ROSCOMMON
Strokestown
Granard
Castlerea
Tulsk
LONGFORD
A
B
C
1
2
3

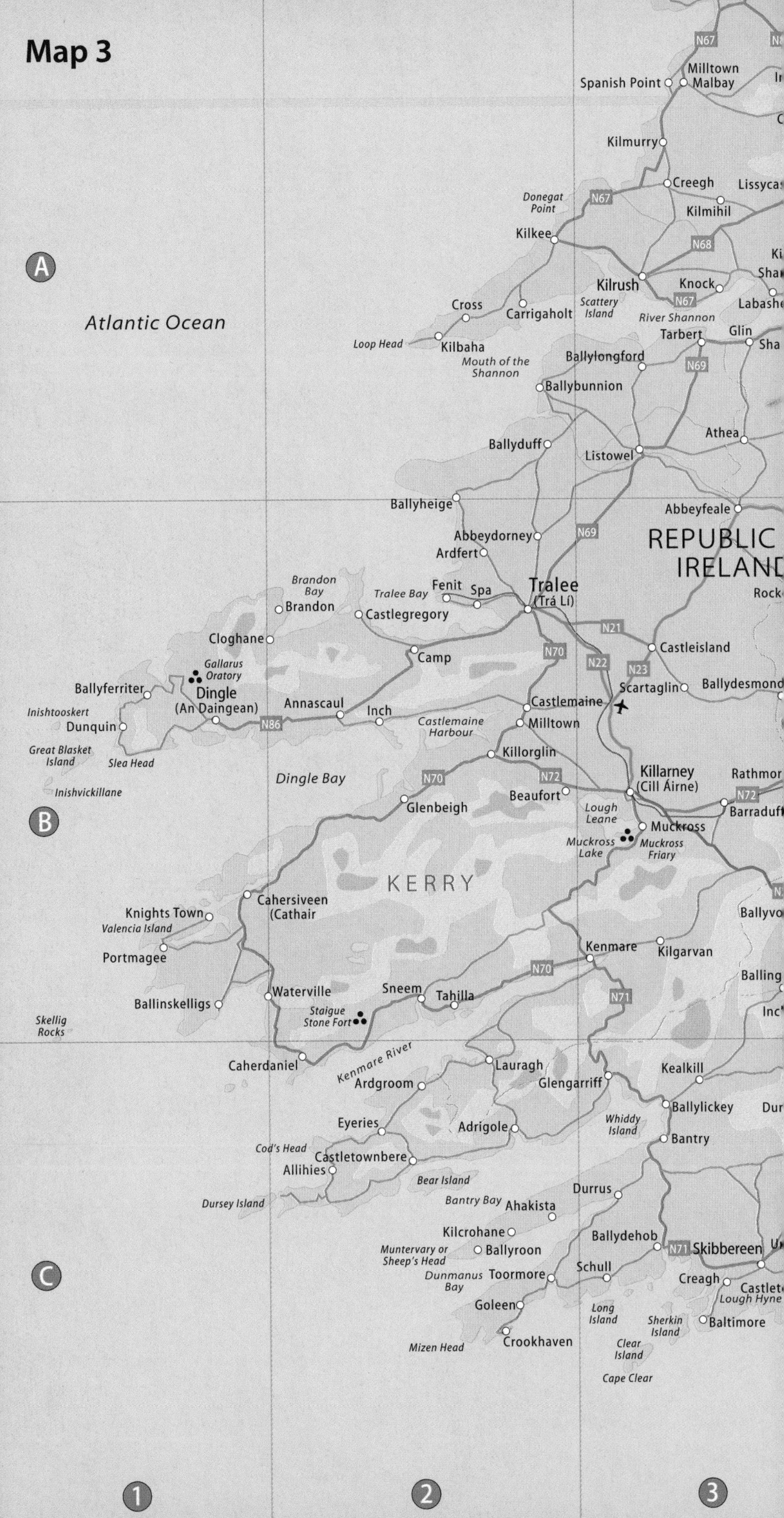

Map 3
Atlantic Ocean
A
B
C
1
2
3
Spanish Point
Milltown Malbay
Kilmurry
Creegh
Lissycas
Donegat Point
Kilmihil
Kilkee
Kilrush
Knock
Labashe
Scattery Island
River Shannon
Cross
Carrigaholt
Loop Head
Kilbaha
Mouth of the Shannon
Tarbert
Glin
Ballylongford
Ballybunnion
Athea
Ballyduff
Listowel
Ballyheige
Abbeyfeale
REPUBLIC
IRELAND
Abbeydorney
Ardfert
Brandon Bay
Brandon
Tralee Bay
Fenit
Spa
Tralee
(Trá Lí)
Castlegregory
Cloghane
Camp
Castleisland
Gallarus Oratory
Ballyferriter
Dingle
(An Daingean)
Annascaul
Inch
Scartaglin
Ballydesmond
Inishtooskert
Dunquin
Castlemaine
Milltown
Castlemaine Harbour
Great Blasket Island
Slea Head
Killorglin
Dingle Bay
Inishvickillane
Killarney
(Cill Áirne)
Rathmor
Beaufort
Glenbeigh
Lough Leane
Muckross
Barraduff
Muckross Lake
Muckross Friary
KERRY
Cahersiveen
(Cathair
Knights Town
Valencia Island
Portmagee
Kenmare
Kilgarvan
Waterville
Sneem
Tahilla
Ballinskelligs
Staigue Stone Fort
Skellig Rocks
Caherdaniel
Kenmare River
Lauragh
Ardgroom
Glengarriff
Kealkill
Ballylickey
Eyeries
Adrigole
Whiddy Island
Bantry
Cod's Head
Castletownbere
Allihies
Bear Island
Dursey Island
Bantry Bay
Ahakista
Durrus
Kilcrohane
Ballydehob
Muntervary or Sheep's Head
Ballyroon
Skibbereen
Schull
Dunmanus Bay
Toormore
Creagh
Lough Hyne
Goleen
Long Island
Sherkin Island
Baltimore
Crookhaven
Mizen Head
Clear Island
Cape Clear
N67
N68
N69
N21
N22
N23
N70
N72
N86
N71

Mullaghmore
Inishmurray
Rosskeeragh Point
Streedagh Point
Streedagh
Grange
Cliffony
Bundoran
Balloor
Lough Melvin
Belleek
Garrison
Derrygonelly
Lower Lough Erne
Irvinestown
Killadeas
Trillick
Ballinamallard
Clabby
FERMANAGH
Fivemiletown
Ballyconnell
Cloghboley
Carney
Benbulbin (525m)
Glenade
Rossinver
Kiltyclogher
NORTHERN IRELAND
Enniskillen (Inis Ceithlean)
Lisbellaw
Raghly
Drumcliff
Glencar Lough
Rosses Point
Coney Island
Sligo Harbour
Sligo (Sligeach)
Sligo Bay
Aughris Head
Keelaghboy
Deer Park Court Cairn
Manorhamilton
Blacklion
Belcoo
Glenfarne
Maguiresbridge
Skreen
Strandhill
Carrowmore Megalithic Cemetery
Dromahair
Kinawley
Lisnaskea
Upper Lough Erne
Ballysadare
Collooney
Ballintogher
Ballygawley
Knocknaree (545m)
Coolaney
Drumfin
Ox Mountains
Drumkeeran
Dowra
Glengavlin
Swanlinbar
Derrylin
Lough Allen
Ballyconnell
Belturbet
SLIGO
Ballymote
Bunnanaddan
Lough Arrow
Keadew
Drumshanbo
Ballinamore
Ballinafad
Lough Key
Leitrim
Keshcarrigan
Lough Oughter
Killashandra
Cavan (An Cabhán)
Curry
Charlestown
Gorteen
Boyle
LEITRIM
Carrigallen
Carrick-on-Shannon
Lough Gara
Jamestown
Arvagh
Bellanagh
Ballaghaderreen
Kingsland
Mohill
CAVAN
Kilnaleck
REPUBLIC OF IRELAND
ROSCOMMON
Dromod
Roosky
Drumlish
Lough Sheelin
Ballyhaunis
Castlerea
Tulsk
Strokestown
Granard
Longford (An Longfort)
Edgeworthstown
Coole
Tullynally Castle
Lough Derravaragh
Ballymoe
LONGFORD
Roscommon
Fuerty
Keenagh
Carrickboy
Dunmore
Glennamaddy
Ballynacarrigy
Taghshinny
Ballymahon
Lough Owel
Athleague
Moyvore
Mullingar (An Muillean gCearr)
Tang
Lough Ree
Ballymore
Moylough
Curraghboy
Glassan
Loughanavally
Lough Ennell
WESTMEATH
Athlone (Baile Átha Luain)
Kilbeggan
Monivea
Clonmacnois Monastery
Durrow
Ballinasloe (Béal Átha na Sluighe)
Athenry
Tullamore (Tulach Mhór)
Ferbane
OFFALY
Laurencetown
Cloghan
Killeigh
Loughrea
Banagher
Kilcormac
Clonaslee
Killimor
Abbey
Portumna
Kinnitty
Birr
Map 4
Derrybrien
Powers Cross
Portumna Forest Park
Gorteeny
TIPPERARY
Mountrath
Borrisokane
Coolrain
LAOIS
Roscrea
Mountshannon
Cloghjordan
Feakle
Scarriff
Loch Derg
Map 3
Borris-in-Ossory
Tuamgraney
Portroe
Nenagh (An tAonach)
Tulla
Bodyke
Moneygall
Errill
Rathdowney
Toomyvara
Durrow
N15
A46
N16
A32
A509
A34
N59
N17
N4
N87
N54
N3
N61
N83
N55
N60
N5
N52
N6
N80
N62
N66
N65
N7
A
B
C
4
5
6

Map 2

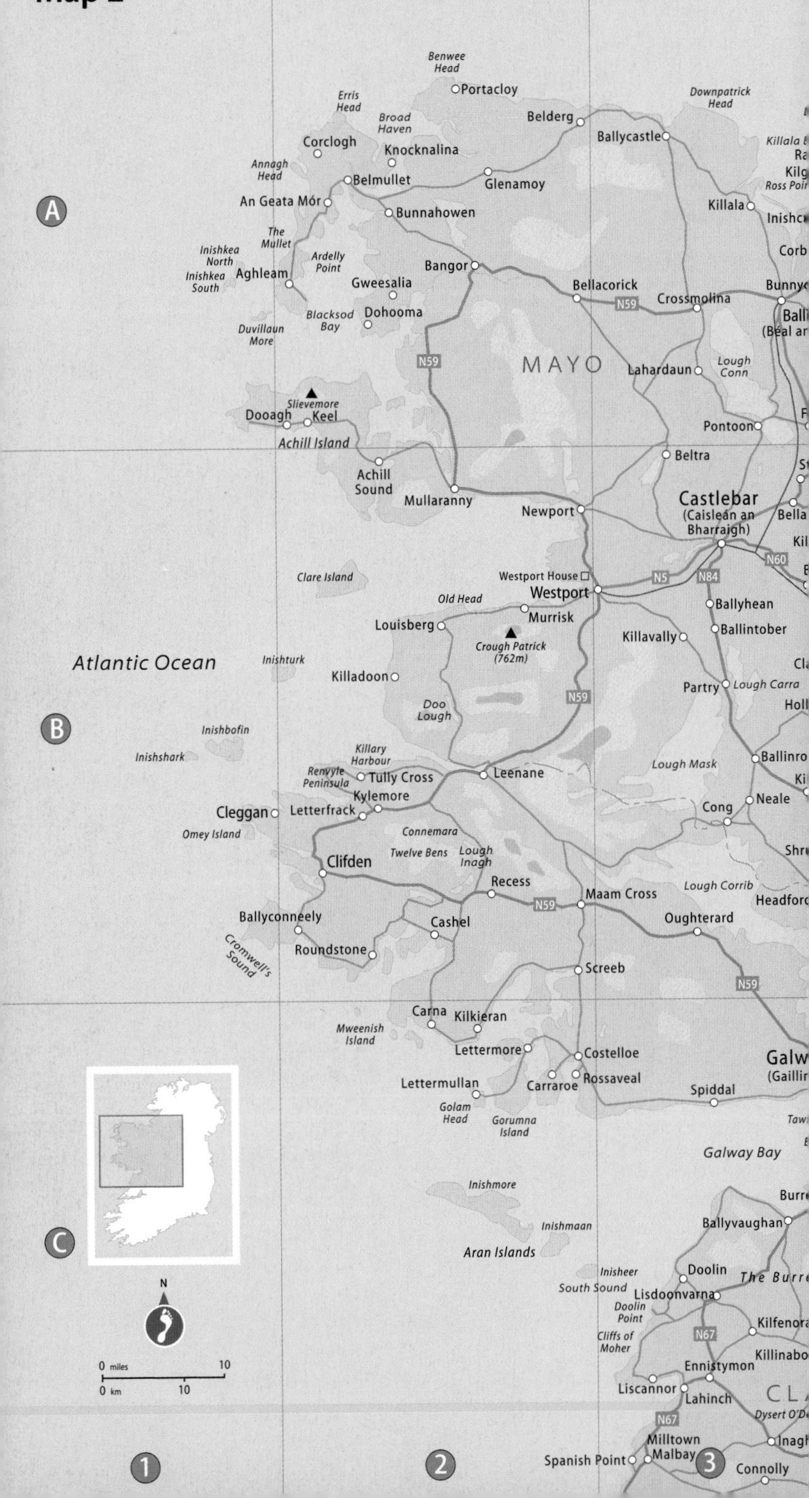

Benwee Head
Portacloy
Erris Head
Broad Haven
Belderg
Downpatrick Head
Corclogh
Knocknalina
Ballycastle
Annagh Head
Belmullet
Glenamoy
An Geata Mór
Bunnahowen
Killala
The Mullet
Inishkea North
Inishkea South
Aghleam
Ardelly Point
Bangor
Gweesalia
Bellacorick
Crossmolina
Blacksod Bay
Dohooma
Duvillaun More
MAYO
Lahardaun
Lough Conn
Slievemore
Dooagh
Keel
Pontoon
Achill Island
Beltra
Achill Sound
Mullaranny
Castlebar
(Caisleán an Bharraigh)
Newport
Clare Island
Westport House
Westport
Ballyhean
Old Head
Murrisk
Louisberg
Crough Patrick (762m)
Killavally
Ballintober
Atlantic Ocean
Inishturk
Killadoon
Partry
Lough Carra
Doo Lough
Inishbofin
Inishshark
Killary Harbour
Lough Mask
Renvyle Peninsula
Tully Cross
Leenane
Kylemore
Cleggan
Letterfrack
Neale
Cong
Omey Island
Connemara
Twelve Bens
Lough Inagh
Clifden
Recess
Lough Corrib
Maam Cross
Ballyconneely
Cashel
Oughterard
Roundstone
Cromwell's Sound
Screeb
Carna
Kilkieran
Mweenish Island
Lettermore
Costelloe
Lettermullan
Carraroe
Rossaveal
Spiddal
Golam Head
Gorumna Island
Galway Bay
Inishmore
Inishmaan
Ballyvaughan
Aran Islands
Inisheer
Doolin
South Sound
Lisdoonvarna
Doolin Point
Cliffs of Moher
Ennistymon
Liscannor
Lahinch
Milltown Malbay
Spanish Point
Connolly
N59
N5
N84
N60
N67
A
B
C
1
2
3
N
0 miles 10
0 km 10

North Channel
Irish Sea
NORTHERN IRELAND
ANTRIM
DERRY
ARMAGH
DOWN
LOUTH
MEATH
BELFAST
(Béal Feirste)
Rathlin Island
Mull of Kintyre
Giant's Causeway
Carrick-a-rede
Ballintoy
Dunseverick
Bushmills
Dunluce
Portrush
Portstewart
Coleraine
(Cúil Raithin)
Ballycastle
Ballyvoy
Torr Point
Cushendun
Cushendall
Ballymoney
Larne
(Latharna)
Ballymena
(Bhaile Meánach)
Antrim
(Aontroim)
Lough Neagh
Belfast International Airport
Newtownabbey
Carrickfergus
Bangor
Donaghadee
Newtownards
(Baile Nua Na hArda)
Lisburn
Dunmurry
Cookstown
(An Chorr Chríochach)
Dungannon
Craigavon
Lurgan
(An Lorgain)
Portadown
Banbridge
(Droichead Na Banna)
Armagh
(Ard Mhacha)
Newry
Downpatrick
(Dún Pádraig)
Newcastle
Dundrum Bay
Strangford Lough
Warrenpoint
Carlingford Lough
Dundalk
(Dún Dealgan)
Dundalk Bay
Carrickmacross
(Carraig Mhacaire Rois)
Castleblayney
(Baile Na Lorgan)
Ardee
Slieve Gullion (575m)
Camlough (421m)
Killeavy Churches
Map 4
0 miles 10
0 km 10
A
B
C
4
5
6

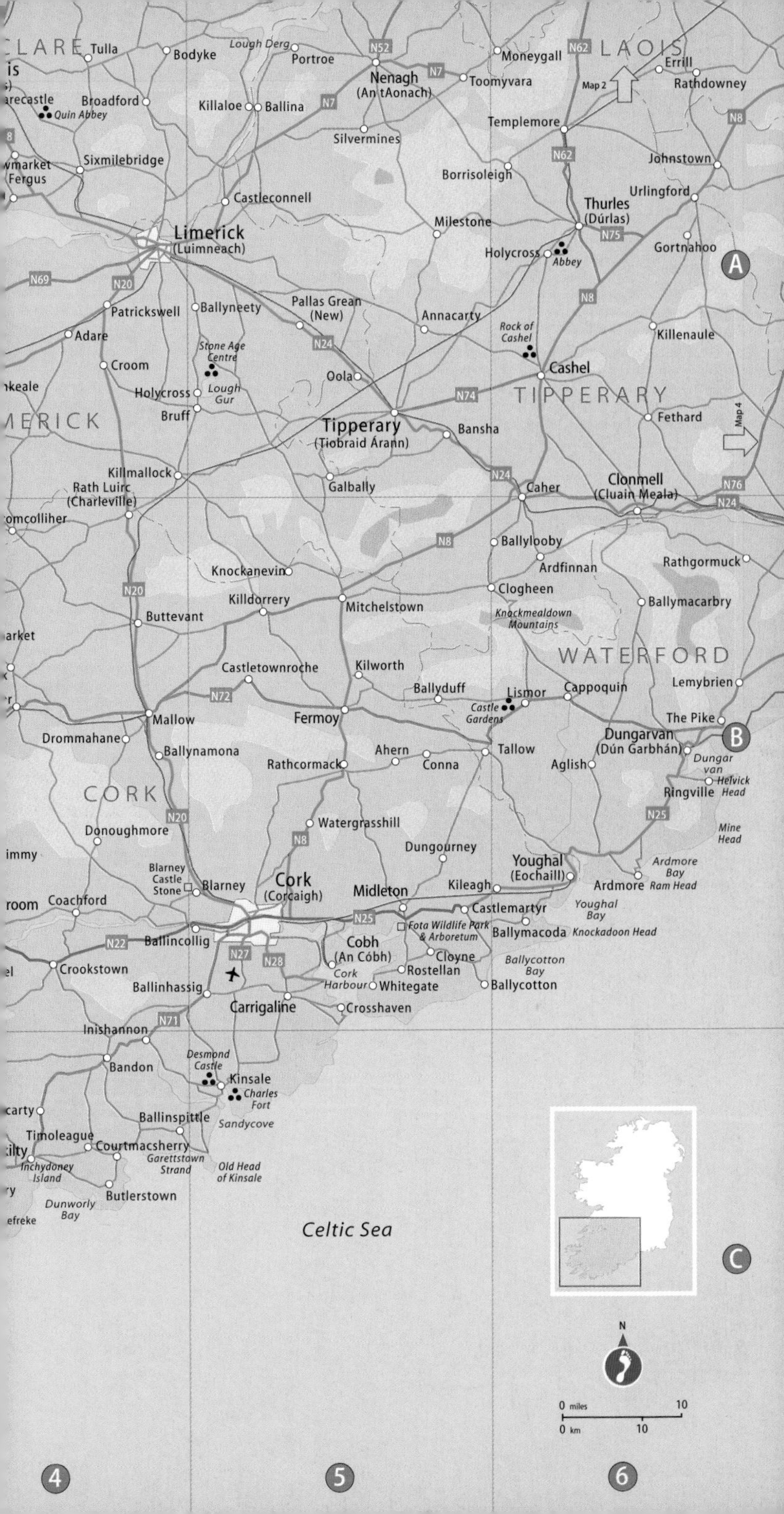
CLARE
Tulla
Bodyke
Lough Derg
Portroe
Nenagh
(An tAonach)
Moneygall
LAOIS
Errill
Rathdowney
Toomyvara
Map 2
Broadford
Quin Abbey
Killaloe
Ballina
Templemore
Silvermines
Sixmilebridge
Fergus
Johnstown
Borrisoleigh
Urlingford
Castleconnell
Thurles
(Dúrlas)
Milestone
Limerick
(Luimneach)
Holycross
Abbey
Gortnahoo
A
Patrickswell
Ballyneety
Pallas Grean
(New)
Annacarty
Rock of Cashel
Killenaule
Adare
Stone Age Centre
Croom
Oola
Cashel
Holycross
Lough Gur
TIPPERARY
Bruff
Fethard
MERICK
Tipperary
(Tiobraid Árann)
Bansha
Map 4
Killmallock
Rath Luirc
(Charleville)
Galbally
Caher
Clonmell
(Cluain Meala)
Ballylooby
Ardfinnan
Rathgormuck
Knockanevin
Clogheen
Ballymacarbry
Killdorrery
Mitchelstown
Buttevant
Knockmealdown Mountains
WATERFORD
Castletownroche
Kilworth
Ballyduff
Lismor
Cappoquin
Lemybrien
Castle Gardens
Mallow
Fermoy
The Pike
Dungarvan
(Dún Garbhán)
B
Drommahane
Ballynamona
Ahern
Tallow
Conna
Aglish
Rathcormack
Dungarvan
Helvick Head
Ringville
CORK
Watergrasshill
Mine Head
Donoughmore
Dungourney
Youghal
(Eochaill)
Ardmore Bay
Blarney Castle Stone
Blarney
Cork
(Corcaigh)
Kileagh
Midleton
Ardmore
Ram Head
Coachford
Castlemartyr
Youghal Bay
Fota Wildlife Park & Arboretum
Ballymacoda
Knockadoon Head
Ballincollig
Cobh
(An Cóbh)
Cloyne
Crookstown
Rostellan
Ballycotton Bay
Cork Harbour
Whitegate
Ballycotton
Ballinhassig
Carrigaline
Crosshaven
Inishannon
Desmond Castle
Bandon
Kinsale
Charles Fort
Ballinspittle
Sandycove
Timoleague
Courtmacsherry
Inchydoney Island
Garettstown Strand
Old Head of Kinsale
Butlerstown
Dunworly Bay
Celtic Sea
C
N
0 miles 10
0 km 10
4
5
6

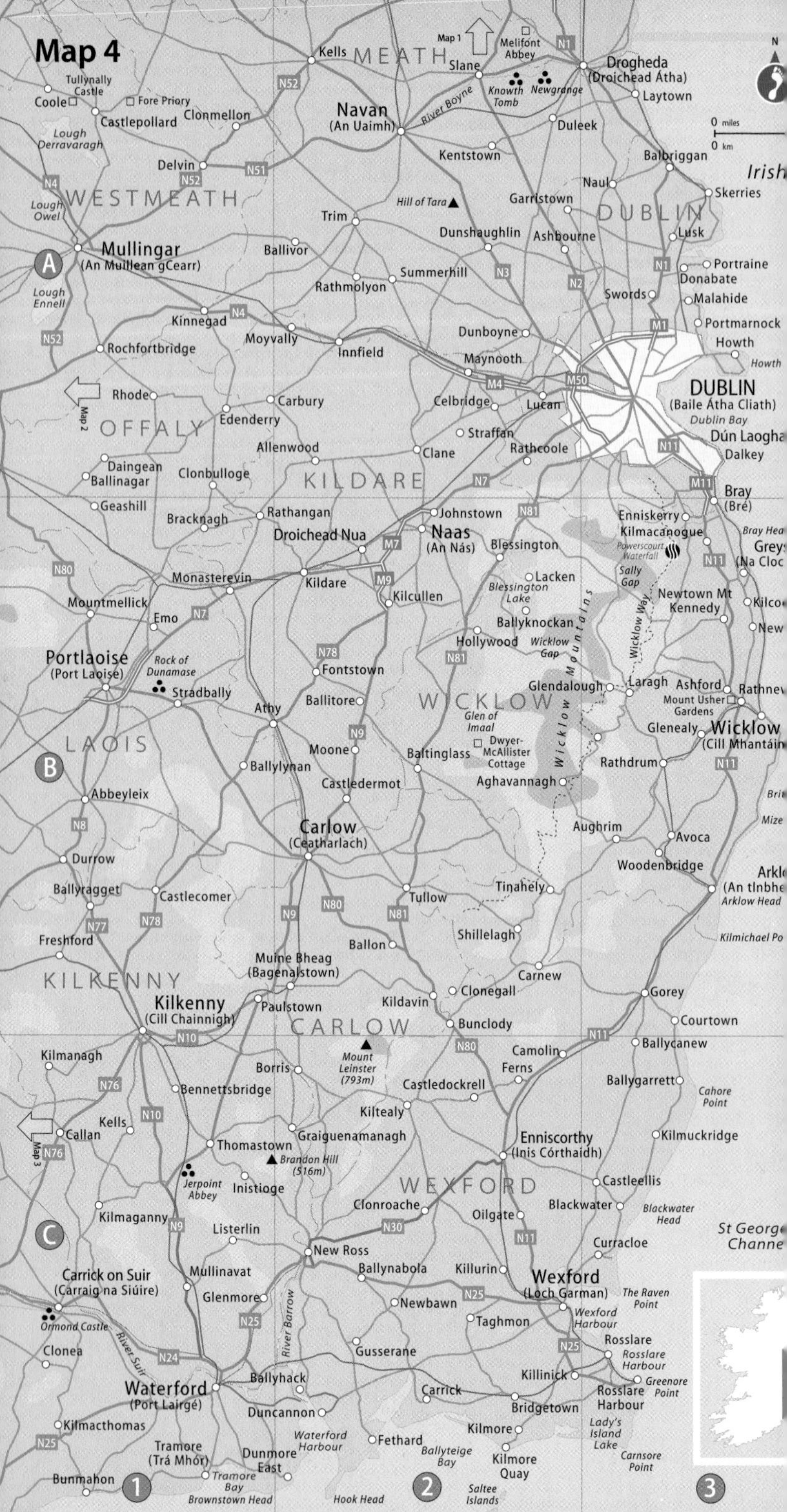
Map 4
Map 1
Map 2
Map 3
N
0 miles
0 km
MEATH
WESTMEATH
OFFALY
KILDARE
DUBLIN
LAOIS
WICKLOW
KILKENNY
CARLOW
WEXFORD
A
B
C
1
2
3
Kells
Melifont Abbey
Slane
Drogheda
(Droichead Átha)
Laytown
Knowth Tomb
Newgrange
River Boyne
Tullynally Castle
Coole
Fore Priory
Castlepollard
Clonmellon
Navan
(An Uaimh)
Duleek
Kentstown
Balbriggan
Lough Derravaragh
Delvin
Lough Owel
Hill of Tara
Garristown
Naul
Skerries
Irish
Trim
Dunshaughlin
Ashbourne
Lusk
Mullingar
(An Mullean gCearr)
Ballivor
Portraine
Donabate
Lough Ennell
Summerhill
Rathmolyon
Swords
Malahide
Kinnegad
Portmarnock
Moyvally
Dunboyne
Howth
Rochfortbridge
Innfield
Maynooth
Rhode
Carbury
Celbridge
Lucan
DUBLIN
(Baile Átha Cliath)
Dublin Bay
Edenderry
Straffan
Dún Laogha
Allenwood
Clane
Rathcoole
Dalkey
Daingean
Ballinagar
Clonbullogue
Bray
(Bré)
Geashill
Rathangan
Johnstown
Enniskerry
Bray Hea
Bracknagh
Droichead Nua
Naas
(An Nás)
Kilmacanogue
Blessington
Powerscourt Waterfall
Greys
(Na Cloc
Monasterevin
Kildare
Lacken
Sally Gap
Kilcullen
Blessington Lake
Newtown Mt Kennedy
Mountmellick
Emo
Ballyknockan
Hollywood
Wicklow Gap
Wicklow Way
Wicklow Mountains
Portlaoise
(Port Laoise)
Rock of Dunamase
Fontstown
Glendalough
Laragh
Ashford
Stradbally
Athy
Ballitore
Mount Usher Gardens
Glen of Imaal
Glenealy
Wicklow
(Cill Mhantáin
Moone
Dwyer-McAllister Cottage
Baltinglass
Ballylynan
Rathdrum
Castledermot
Aghavannagh
Abbeyleix
Carlow
(Ceatharlach)
Aughrim
Avoca
Durrow
Woodenbridge
Arklo
(An tInbhe
Arklow Head
Ballyragget
Castlecomer
Tullow
Tinahely
Freshford
Shillelagh
Kilmichael Po
Ballon
Muine Bheag
(Bagenalstown)
Carnew
Kilkenny
(Cill Chainnigh)
Paulstown
Kildavin
Clonegall
Gorey
Courtown
Bunclody
Ballycanew
Mount Leinster
(793m)
Camolin
Kilmanagh
Borris
Ferns
Ballygarrett
Bennettsbridge
Castledockrell
Cahore Point
Kells
Callan
Kiltealy
Graiguenamanagh
Kilmuckridge
Thomastown
Brandon Hill
(516m)
Enniscorthy
(Inis Córthaidh)
Jerpoint Abbey
Inistioge
Castleellis
Clonroache
Oilgate
Blackwater
Blackwater Head
Kilmaganny
Listerlin
St George
Channe
New Ross
Curracloe
Carrick on Suir
(Carraig na Siúire)
Mullinavat
Ballynabola
Killurin
Wexford
(Loch Garman)
Glenmore
The Raven Point
Ormond Castle
River Suir
River Barrow
Newbawn
Wexford Harbour
Taghmon
Clonea
Gusserane
Rosslare
Rosslare Harbour
Waterford
(Port Lairgé)
Ballyhack
Killinick
Greenore Point
Carrick
Bridgetown
Rosslare Harbour
Kilmacthomas
Duncannon
Lady's Island Lake
Waterford Harbour
Fethard
Kilmore
Tramore
(Trá Mhór)
Dunmore East
Ballyteige Bay
Kilmore Quay
Carnsore Point
Tramore Bay
Bunmahon
Brownstown Head
Hook Head
Saltee Islands
N1
N2
N3
N4
N7
N8
N9
N10
N11
N24
N25
N30
N51
N52
N76
N77
N78
N80
N81
M1
M4
M7
M9
M11
M50

Map symbols

Administration

- Capital city
- Other city/town
- International border
- Regional border
- Disputed border

Roads and travel

- Motorway
- Main road (National highway)
- Minor road
- Track
- Footpath
- Railway with station
- Airport
- Bus station
- DART station
- Luas stop
- Cable car
- Funicular
- Ferry

Water features

- River, canal
- Lake, ocean
- Seasonal marshland
- Beach, sandbank
- Waterfall

Topographical features

- Contours (approx)
- Mountain
- Volcano
- Mountain pass
- Escarpment
- Gorge
- Glacier
- Salt flat
- Rocks

Cities and towns

- Main through route
- Main street
- Minor street
- Pedestrianized street
- Tunnel
- One-way street
- Steps
- Bridge
- Fortified wall
- Park, garden, stadium
- Sleeping
- Eating
- Bars & clubs
- Building
- Sight
- Cathedral, church
- Chinese temple
- Hindu temple
- Meru
- Mosque
- Stupa
- Synagogue
- Tourist office
- Museum
- Post office
- Police
- Bank
- Internet
- Telephone
- Market
- Hospital
- Parking
- Petrol
- Golf
- Detail map
- Related map

Other symbols

- Archaeological site
- National park, wildlife reserve
- Viewing point
- Campsite
- Refuge, lodge
- Castle
- Diving
- Deciduous/coniferous/palm trees
- Hide
- Vineyard
- Distillery
- Shipwreck
- Historic battlefield

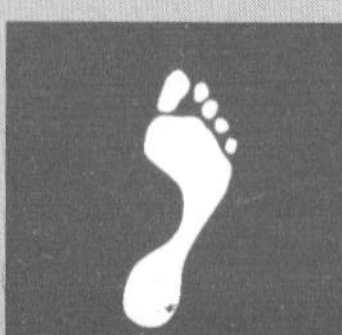